W9-CND-126

Generalized Anxiety Disorder

Anxiety Disorder Due to General Medical Condition

Substance-Induced Anxiety Disorder

Somatoform Disorders

Somatization Disorder

Undifferentiated Somatoform Disorder

Pain Disorder

Conversion Disorder

Hypochondriasis

Body Dysmorphic Disorder

Factitious Disorders

Dissociative Disorders

Dissociative Amnesia

Dissociative Fugue

Dissociative Identity Disorder

Depersonalization Disorder

Sexual and Gender Identity Disorders

Sexual Dysfunctions Sexual Desire Disorders; Sexual
Arousal Disorders; Orgasmic Disorders; Sexual Pain Disorders;
Sexual Dysfunction Due to a General Medical Condition

Paraphilias Exhibitionism, Fetishism, Frotteurism, Pedophilia,
Sexual Masochism, Sexual Sadism, Transvestic Fetishism,
Voyeurism

Gender Identity Disorders

Eating Disorders

Eating Disorders Anorexia Nervosa; Bulimia Nervosa

Sleep Disorders

Primary Sleep Disorders Dyssomnias; Parasomnias;

**Sleep Disorders Related to Another Mental
Disorder Other Sleep Disorders**

**Impulse-Control Disorders not Elsewhere
Classified**

Intermittent Explosive Disorder; Kleptomania; Pyromania;
Pathological Gambling; Trichotillomania

Adjustment Disorders

**Other Conditions That May Be
a Focus of Clinical Attention**

Psychological Factors Affecting Medical Condition

Medication-Induced Movement Disorders

Other Medication-Induced Disorder

Relational Problems

Problems Related to Abuse or Neglect

Additional Conditions That May Be a
Focus of Clinical Attention

Axis II

Personality Disorders

Paranoid Personality Disorder

Schizoid Personality Disorder

Schizotypal Personality Disorder

Antisocial Personality Disorder

Borderline Personality Disorder

Histrionic Personality Disorder

Narcissistic Personality Disorder

Avoidant Personality Disorder

Dependent Personality Disorder

Obsessive-Compulsive Personality Disorder

Mental Retardation (Specified as to Severity)

Mild Mental Retardation

Moderate Mental Retardation

Severe Mental Retardation

Profound Mental Retardation

Mental Retardation, Severity Unspecified

Axis III General Medical Conditions

A listing of general medical conditions that might be
related to mental disorders

Axis IV Psychosocial and Environmental Problems

Problems that might affect the diagnosis, treatment, and
prognosis of mental disorders. These include problems
with the primary support group, problems related to
the social environment, educational or occupational
problems, housing problems, economic problems,
problems of access to health care services, and
problems related to the person's difficulties with the
legal system or with being a victim of a crime.

Axis V Global Assessment of Functioning

A rating scale of 1 to 100 to reflect the overall social,
psychological, and occupational functioning of the
individual. Useful for tracking the progress of the
person over the course of treatment.

Abnormal Psychology

Abnormal Psychology
The Problem of Maladaptive Behavior

Tenth Edition

Irwin G. Sarason
University of Washington

Barbara R. Sarason
University of Washington

Upper Saddle River, New Jersey 07458

Library of Congress Cataloging-in-Publication Data
Sarason, Irwin G.
     Abnormal psychology: the problem of maladaptive behavior / Irwin
G. Sarason, Barbara R. Sarason.—10th ed.
        p. cm.
     Includes bibliographical references and index.
     ISBN 0-13-091849-0
     1. Psychology, Pathological. I. Sarason, Barbara R. II. Title.
RC454.S28 2001
616.89—dc21   2001031165

VP, Editorial Director: *Laura Pearson*
Executive Editor: *Stephanie Johnson*
Editorial Assistant: *Carmen Garcia-Prieto*
Development Editor in Chief: *Susanna Lesan*
Development Editors: *Stephanie Carpenter, Carolyn Smith*
VP, Director of Production and Manufacturing: *Barbara Kittle*
Senior Managing Editor: *Mary Rottino*
Production Editor: *Randy Pettit*
Prepress and Manufacturing Manager: *Nick Sklitsis*
Prepress and Manufacturing Buyer: *Tricia Kenny*
Director of Marketing: *Beth Gillett Mejia*
Senior Marketing Manager: *Sharon Cosgrove*
Marketing Assistant: *Ron Fox*
Creative Design Director: *Leslie Osher*
Art Director: *Anne Bonanno Nieglos*
Cover and Interior Design: *Anne Bonanno Nieglos*
Cover Art: *Jose Ortega/Stock Illustration Source, Inc.*
Director, Image Resources: *Melinda Lee Reo*
Image Specialist: *Beth Boyd-Benzel*
Photo Researcher: *Melinda Alexander*
Manager, Rights and Permissions: *Kay Dellosa*
Electronic Art Creation: *Mirella Signoretti*
Art Coordinator: *Guy Ruggiero*

For permission to use copyrighted material, grateful acknowledgment is
made to the copyright holders listed on pages 663-664, which is
considered an extension of this copyright page.

This book was set in 10/12 Garamond by Carlisle Communications, Ltd.
and printed and bound by R.R. Donnelley & Sons Company.
The cover was printed by Phoenix Color Corp.

© 1999, 2002 by Pearson Education, Inc.
Upper Saddle River, New Jersey 07458

Printed in the United States of America
10 9 8 7 6 5 4 3 2 1

ISBN 0-13-0918490

Prentice Hall International (UK) Limited, *London*
Prentice Hall of Australia Pty. Limited, *Sydney*
Prentice Hall Canada Inc., *Toronto*
Prentice Hall Hispanoamericana, S.A., *Mexico*
Prentice Hall of India Private Limited, *New Delhi*
Prentice Hall of Japan, Inc., *Tokyo*
Pearson Education Asia Pte. Ltd., *Singapore*
Editora Prentice Hall do Brasil, Ltda., *Rio de Janeiro*

To three individuals whose ability to adapt we admire
(in order of their appearance)

Sue, Jane, and Don

Brief Contents

Contents

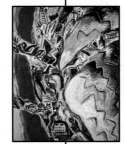

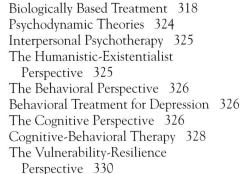

Special Features

First Person

Research Close-up

(continued)

Q&A

Resilience and Vulnerability

Case Study

Preface

*A*s in previous editions, one of our major goals is to introduce students of abnormal psychology to (1) the nature of psychopathology, (2) how clinicians diagnose and treat it, and (3) the research that contributes to understanding maladaptive behavior, its prevention and treatment. Another goal is to explain the growing complexity of psychopathology in a clear and engaging way. Complexity does not have to be confusing. With a few organizing principles, it can lead to an appreciation of richness. This is exactly what occurs in a fine Persian carpet that may have several complex designs integrated by means of a few organizing esthetic principles. In this edition, we have made a special effort to introduce the student to complexity so that it becomes rich and nuanced rather than just potentially confusing information.

Changes and New Pedagogical Features

Each time we produce an edition, we are always amazed at how much new and exciting knowledge has been uncovered since the previous edition. The tenth edition is no exception. Following are some of the most outstanding improvements.

Vulnerability-resilience theme: The importance of person-situation interactions is a theme running through every chapter of the book. We emphasize this theme because of the growing evidence that personal vulnerabilities reduce the ability to cope effectively with stress-arousing, problematic situations and, as a consequence, increase the likelihood of maladaptation.

Integration of biological and experiential factors: We now know that, in addition to interactions that involve persons and the situations they confront, other types of interactions involving mind, body, and experiences are also important. Individual's experiential histories can exert impacts, not only on how they behave but also on their bodily processes (for example, how their brains work). These bodily processes, in turn, can influence how people respond to future situational challenges. For instance, in Chapter 16 we present recent evidence suggesting that the brain processes traumatic memories different from the way ordinary memories are recorded and stored.

Two related issues that are receiving attention today are (1) the variables (for example, age and experiential history) that play roles in brain plasticity and (2) how changes in brain structure and function influence vulnerability and resilience with regard to life's challenges. For example, Chapter 7 examines the increasingly evident role of the hippocampus in anxiety disorders, and Chapter 12 discusses new evidence concerning brain-experience interactions and their implications for understanding cognitive impairment disorders.

Another frontier biological issue relates to gene interactions. Not too many years ago, clinicians and researchers harbored the hope that specification of the human genome would reveal the single genes associated with particular disorders such as schizophrenia. However, the more we know about the human genome, the less likely it seems that this hope will be realized. Rather, complex gene combinations and interactions are the likely route to understanding genetic influences over maladaptive behavior. Chapter 2's expanded discussion of biological processes helps us illustrate this complexity. Likewise, Chapter 11's new material on the neurodevelopmental model of schizophrenia clarifies the roles of genetic and prenatal environmental factors in this disorder.

Expanded discussion of sociocultural factors: The broadened interactional perspective in this edition extends to new evidence in the sociocultural domain. Ethnic, racial, cultural variables interact with a host of other variables in shaping personality, including individuals' attributions, expectations, and coping styles which, in turn, influence how they respond to life circumstances. Many chapters now discuss the relationship among these variables. For instance, Chapter 9 includes a new discussion of cultural variables and personality disorders; Chapter 4 shows how racism can be a pervasive stressor for many members of minority groups; and by presenting new data on racial and ethnic differences in suicide rate, Chapter 10 emphasizes the importance of taking these factors into account in all aspects of clinical work.

Another sociocultural factor, public policy, plays a key role in a given community's level of functioning. Chapter 17, taking account of recent court decisions and research, presents additional material on the legal and public policy aspects of mental illness. Public policy, in so far as it affects the availability (or unavailability) of mental health services, certainly concerns those who work in mental health.

Therapeutic advances: There have been a number of therapeutic advances, one of the most important being the growing evidence that drug therapies and psychological processes interact. In Chapter 16 we discuss how clinician-patient relationships influence the ways individuals respond to both medications and psychological therapies. We also give examples of the role cultural factors play in patient's receptivity to medications. The many new applications of

Special Features

Resilience and Vulnerability series explores the roles of resilience and vulnerability in maladaptive behavior.

Resilience and Vulnerability   Box 15-2

The Resilient Budding Scientist

Seventeen-year-old Jamel Oser-Sweat is a member of a fatherless family who lives in an apartment in a New York City housing project. Jamel's mother had been a foster child, has a chronic psychological disorder, and has been hospitalized for this condition (necessitating that Jamel be placed in a group home). When Jamel comes home at the end of the day, he passes drug dealers who ask "What do you want?" and young ladies who make eyes at him. At his housing project he sometimes has to stand on his toes in the elevator to avoid the urine puddles. His family only recently acquired a telephone.

What makes Jamel remarkable is his resilience. In 1994, he was named one of 40 finalists in the nationwide Westinghouse Science Talent Search scholarship competition. The project that led to this

recognition was an experiment he conducted at Mount Sinai Medical Center on bacteria showing that certain materials could cause skin lesions and other diseases if not decontaminated regularly. In 1993, he received a top award in the New York City Science Expo and an invitation to have dinner with the mayor.

Because life in the projects held little for Jamel Oser-Sweat, he plunged himself into a range of activities, finding people along the way who cared for him and advised him. Although his grades were not exceptionally high, one teacher noticed how quickly Jamel was able to synthesize difficult information and arranged for him to participate in a special Mount Sinai program. On his own, Jamel decided to tutor children in a Harlem elementary school (see Figure 1-1).

There is a certain sadness to Jamel (he has been told he rarely smiles). But he is highly intelligent, has a strong desire to help others, and is able to establish rewarding supportive relationships—for example, with the teacher who noticed his exceptional ability to process information. In the face of overwhelmingly negative life experiences, he is a case study not of pathology but of resilience.

Figure 1-1 Jamel Oser-Sweat tutoring a student in English at an elementary school in Harlem.

Source: *New York Times*, January 30, p. 7. Photo by Suzanne De Chillo.

First Person series presents accounts of mental illness told by people who have experienced it.

First Person   Box 15-1

Four People: Sources and Expressions of Distress

Most people who have emotional problems refer to the distress they are experiencing. Sources of distress and how they are expressed range widely. Sometimes distress is caused by an easily identifiable life event (for example, losing a job), while in other cases the source seems to be as much within the individual as coming from the environment. In addition to diversity of sources, there is also diversity in how distress is expressed. The source of Bob Cates's distress is unclear. It might be attributable either to something going on in his life over which he doesn't have control (pressure from his parents to achieve), or to being too hard on himself (blaming himself unrealistically), or to some combination of environmental and personality factors. Regardless of the source, Bob experiences his distress internally; for example, he

side himself (Professor Harris's exam) and directs his anger outward (wanting to hit Professor Harris). As a result of psychotherapy, Jerry is beginning to see that his anger is part of him and not just a normal reaction to provocation.

Nancy Raine has experienced a lot of personal distress stemming from a rape experience. While the source of her distress was external (being raped), she continues to react internally, to suffer in silence.

I know how to mark my birthday, my wedding anniversary, even the anniversary of my brother's death. But the day I was raped? How should I observe the passing of another year? . . . I can never again be that woman who locked her door and felt safe. My husband, my mother, my friends still suffer their own brand of helplessness when they try to imagine the

afraid she might gather up her black briefcase and suddenly remember a dentist's appointment. (Raine, 1994, p. 34)

Billy Henderson is different from Bob Cates, Jerry Calabrese, and Nancy Raine in that what is going on within him is so confused that one can only guess the sources of his distress. The big challenge in any effort to treat Billy would be to break through his psychotic way of expressing himself and achieve some meaningful discussion of his situation in life.

Billy, who is currently living in the community but had been in mental hospital on three occasions, responded to the question "Tell me about yourself" in a way that can only leave us puzzled and worried about his ability to function:

My hands feel paralyzed and I feel under unbearable stress. I'm going to do something.

I believe in free elections of the Pro-

Research Close-Up series reviews in depth, particular techniques, methods, and findings.

Research Close-Up   Box 15-3

The Clinical Trial

Most people who have emotional problems refer to the distress they are experiencing. Sources of distress and how they are expressed range widely. Sometimes distress is caused by an easily identifiable life event (for example, losing a job), while in other cases the source seems to be as much within the individual as coming from the environment. In addition to diversity of sources, there is also diversity in how distress is expressed. The source of Bob Cates's distress is unclear. It might be attributable either to something going on in his life over which he doesn't have control (pressure from his parents to achieve), or to being too hard on himself (blaming himself unrealistically), or to some combination of environmental and personality factors. Regardless of the source, Bob experiences

side himself (Professor Harris's exam) and directs his anger outward (wanting to hit Professor Harris). As a result of psychotherapy, Jerry is beginning to see that his anger is part of him and not just a normal reaction to provocation.

Nancy Raine has experienced a lot of personal distress stemming from a rape experience. While the source of her distress was external (being raped), she continues to react internally, to suffer in silence.

I know how to mark my birthday, my wedding anniversary, even the anniversary of my brother's death. But the day I was raped? How should I observe the passing of another year? . . . I can never again be that woman who locked her door and felt safe. My husband, my mother, my friends still suffer their own brand of

afraid she might gather up her black briefcase and suddenly remember a dentist's appointment. (Raine, 1994, p. 34)

Billy Henderson is different from Bob Cates, Jerry Calabrese, and Nancy Raine in that what is going on within him is so confused that one can only guess the sources of his distress. The big challenge in any effort to treat Billy would be to break through his psychotic way of expressing himself and achieve some meaningful discussion of his situation in life.

Billy, who is currently living in the community but had been in mental hospital on three occasions, responded to the question "Tell me about yourself" in a way that can only leave us puzzled and worried about his ability to function:

Billy Henderson is different from Bob Cates, Jerry Calabrese, and Nancy Raine in that what is going on within him is so confused that one can only guess the

Case Study series presents clinical material that brings to life key ideas related to particular clinical disorders.

Q & A series presents clinical material that brings to life key ideas related to particular clinical disorders.

cognitive-behavioral therapies are reviewed in several chapters.

New chapters on Bodily Dysfunction and Bodily Pre-occupation: This edition includes two new health-related chapters. Chapter 5 deals with the growing body of evidence showing that psychosocial variables are implicated in a number of major diseases (for example, coronary heart disease and cancer). This chapter also includes greatly expanded coverage of eating and sleeping disorders, both of which can have negative effects on bodily functioning and even lead to death. Chapter 6 is devoted primarily to excessive bodily preoccupation as a type of maladaptive behavior. This chapter also deals with pain disorders and disorders involving an unrealistic, devalued sense of bodily identity.

Q&A boxes: In order to deal directly with questions students frequently ask, we have included a Q&A box in each chapter. Each box presents a question that students have asked enough times for us to be very aware of it. We answer each question in a direct, conversational manner. We have informally tested our Q&A boxes on our students and they have liked them. The Q&A's seem to be effective at stimulating students' thinking and eliciting their comments and further questions.

Chapter-by-chapter keyword lists: Another new pedagogical feature is a list of Keywords at the end of each chapter. This list will help motivate students as they study and serve as a guide in identifying the main concepts.

More first-person accounts: We have increased the number of first-person accounts of mental illness because students tell us that they make generalizations about clinical work come alive. These also help students feel empathy towards those with maladaptive behavior.

New material in each chapter:

The changes mentioned above are but a small fraction of the updated, expanded, and new discussions of important topics throughout the book. Additional ones include:
Chapter 1. Epidemiological evidence concerning risk factors and the effects of stigmatization.
Chapter 2. Biological processes related to maladaptive behavior.
Chapter 3. Ethnic and cultural factors in maladaptive behavior; DSM-IV-TR (published in 2000).
Chapter 4. Racism as a stressor; the grieving process; antecedents of dissociative identity disorder.
Chapter 5. Diagnostic dilemmas posed by chronic fatigue syndrome, headaches, and irritable bowel syndrome; role of cultural factors in health practices; eating disorders; sleep disorders.
Chapter 6. Body dysmorphic disorder; male dysmorphia (excessive preoccupation with achieving a high degree of muscularity); techniques useful in coping with pain.
Chapter 7. The role of avoidance in anxiety disorder; similarities and differences between generalized anxiety disorder and panic disorder; mass hysteria.
Chapter 8. Criteria for diagnosing sexual dysfunction; treatment of the dysfunctions; sex education; cognitive-behavioral treatment of sexual victimizers; dangerousness, expert testimony.
Chapter 9. Cultural factors in personality disorders.
Chapter 10. Psychological changes produced by electroconvulsive therapy (ECT) and ECT's effectiveness; racial and ethnic differences in suicide rate.
Chapter 11. Neurodevelopmental model of schizophrenia; relationship between genetic factors and the prenatal environment.
Chapter 12. Brain-experience interactions; use of brain imaging techniques in Alzheimer's disease.
Chapter 13. Use of incentives to discontinue use of cocaine; pathological gambling; use of the nicotine patch.
Chapter 14. Attention deficit hyperactivity disorder in adults.
Chapter 15. Early identification of autism; the spectrum of autistic disorders.
Chapter 16. Three extensive therapy case studies; similarities and differences between cognitive and social-cognitive therapeutic approaches.
Chapter 17. The rights of patients and duty to warn; public policy issues.

Retained Pedagogical Features

We continue to use the successful pedagogical features of previous editions. All the tables and figures have been designed for ease of understanding and attractiveness. Boxes throughout the book highlight concepts, illustrate phenomena, and present information in detail. These boxes present case studies, research close-ups, and reinforce concepts such as vulnerability and resilience that run through the book.

A Focus on the Student:

We see the Abnormal Psychology course as having enormous applicability to students' lives. Virtually every time we have taught the course, several students have told us about family members and friends who are struggling with serious psychological problems. Each of these struggles involves other people who care about the suffering individual. As a consequence, each instance of maladaptive behavior affects several, often many, people. We have borne this multiplier effect in mind in writing this book. We have also borne in mind the science of abnormal psychology and its treatment. Whether students are psychology majors or students in other areas who want to know what psychological abnormality is about, we believe it is important for them to appreciate abnormal psychology as a scholarly, research-oriented discipline and to become familiar with the theories, methods, and findings that make the field so vibrant. We hope our book helps students personally, as well as, intellectually.

Teaching and Learning Package

For the Instructor

The Instructor's Resource Manual Barbara Mitchell, St. Edwards University, has prepared this comprehensive teaching tool. Each chapter of the Instructor's Resource Manual contains a Chapter Outline which highlights the main topics of the chapter, a list of Learning Objectives describing the key concepts students should master, Lecture Suggestions including supplemental topics for generating class discussions, Student Activities including suggestions for out of class exercises and projects, and Video and Media Resources listing the multimedia products available to accompany the text.

The Test Item File Joseph J. Palladino, a test construction specialist at the University of Southern Indiana, has reviewed, revised, and written new test questions to create a Test Item File of over 1,800 test questions, including multiple choice and essay. To facilitate the creation of tests, each question is identified as conceptual/applied or factual/definitional and is page referenced to the textbook.

Prentice Hall Custom Test Manager (available for Windows and Macintosh platforms) The test item file is also available in electronic format, allowing instructors to create multiple tests, add their own questions, or edit existing questions.

Prentice Hall Color Transparencies for Abnormal and Clinical Psychology Add visual impact to the study of abnormal and clinical psychology with these color illustrations. Designed for large classroom settings, the set includes many illustrations in addition to the ones found in the text, offering a wealth of additional resources to enhance lectures and reinforce student learning.

ABCNEWS **ABC News/PH Video Library for Abnormal Psychology** Segments from award-winning ABC News programs, including 20/20, Primetime Live, and Nightline cover issues such as drugs and alcoholism, psychotherapy, autism, crime motivation, depression, and a variety of additional topics. These three- to eighteen-minute segments are used by many instructors as platforms from which to launch class lectures or classroom discussion.

Patients as Educators: Video Cases in Abnormal Psychology by James H. Scully, Jr., MD and Alan M. Dahms, Ph.D., Colorado State University. This exclusive video contains a series of ten patient interviews illustrating a range of disorders. Each interview is preceeded by a brief history of the patient and a synopsis of some major symptoms of the disorder, and ends with a summary and a brief analysis.

For the Student

The Study Guide Elaine Cassel, Marymount University, has prepared this study guide to aid students in learning, studying, and understanding the concepts. Every chapter has a brief chapter overview, a brief outline with space for note-taking, a list of learning objectives, a key-terms exercise, and two practice tests; one testing concept recollection, and the other testing concept understanding and application.

The Companion Website. www.prenhall.com/sarason A free electronic study guide is available to help your students review the major points of each chapter. Each chapter contains an outline, a list of learning objectives, a series of objective quizzes to test comprehension and retention, and hot links to a variety of website destinations relevant to the subject matter of the chapter. Students receive immediate feedback on the quizzes and have the ability to e-mail their results to their instructors and/or teaching assistants.

Asking the Right Questions in Abnormal Psychology This book by Stuart M. Keeley, Bowling Green State University, presents a basic critical-thinking methodology, then asks students to apply this method to a variety of classic research studies in psychopathology.

Acknowledgments

Our debt to researchers who have studied aspects of abnormal psychology is enormous. We are also indebted to our colleagues who have discussed various clinical and research issues with us. We appreciate their interest, patience, and lucid explanations. Many individuals, most of whom we did not know, have told us about their personal problems and shared their experiences with us. Finally, we thank our many students who, over the years, have raised probing questions and sometimes suggested answers to difficult conceptual and research questions. Our indebtedness to all the individuals we have mentioned is deep. We wish we could thank all of them individually. Because there are hundreds of them, we cannot list their names here. We hope they all accept the heartfelt thanks we offer here.

We have also benefited from the insightful comments and suggestions provided by these reviewers:

Pamela Balls Organista
University of San Francisco

Lawrence G. Calhoun
University of North Carolina, Charlotte

James W. Selby
University of North Carolina, Charlotte

William A. Montgomery
Angelo State University

Howard Markowitz
Hawaii Pacific University

David G. Weight
Brigham Young University.

We want to express our appreciation to the Prentice-Hall team for all they have contributed to the publication of this book. We especially thank Stephanie Johnson, Jayme Heffler, Randy Pettit, Stephanie Carpenter, and Sharon Cosgrove. As usual, Betty Johnson made a major contribution. Myrna Torrie did a fine job when we needed her help.

—*Irwin Sarason, Barbara Sarason*

About the Authors

Irwin and Barbara Sarason are deeply interested in the multiple causes of maladaptive behavior and how it can be effectively treated. They are perhaps best known for their work on the role of social support as a modifier of stress and a promoter of mental health and adaptive coping. The questions of individual vulnerability and resilience and how adaptation can be encouraged have been of particular interest to them. A current focus of their research is how relationships with family and friends can be protective and aid individuals in coping with daily stresses and strains as well as helping to promote overall psychological adjustment. The topic of social support in general, and as a function of specific relationships, has implications for understanding individual development, abnormal behavior, health status, and the factors within the psychotherapeutic relationship that contribute to positive clinical outcomes. The Sarasons believe that a major ingredient of psychotherapy is the therapist's communication of acceptance and positive evaluation of the patient. Beyond the psychotherapeutic relationship, their work suggests that even vulnerable people who feel that they are accepted and valued by others are more likely to cope well with stress and are less likely to develop maladaptive symptoms. In addition, their work focuses attention on prevention and ways in which communities can become more supportive places to live.

The effects of ethnic and cultural differences on expectations of oneself and others have been an important recent research focus of the Sarasons. They see the need for mental health professionals to develop increased understanding and respect for cultural differences. The stresses of the immigrant experience, the impact of being a member of a minority in our society, and the intergenerational conflicts associated with such status may enhance vulnerability but also allow a focus on individual resilience and moderator effects.

Irwin Sarason received his B.A. degree from Rutgers University and Barbara Sarason received her B.A. degree from Depauw University. They first met while graduate students at the University of Iowa. Each has a Ph.D. degree with a specialization in clinical psychology from Indiana University. After completing their clinical internships in West Haven, Connecticut, they moved to Seattle. Irwin Sarason is currently professor and Barbara Sarason is research professor in the Psychology Department at the University of Washington.

The Sarasons have published over 300 articles and many books on such topics as anxiety, stress and coping, personality research, social support, and techniques for facilitating behavioral change. They have each lectured extensively in the United States, Japan, and throughout Europe.

Abnormal Psychology

Marc Chagall "I and the Village" 1911, oil on canvas, 6' 3⅝" × 59' ⅝". The Museum of Modern Art, NY. Mrs. Simon Gugenheim Fund. Photograph © 2002 The Museum of Modern Art, NY. © 2002 Artists Rights Society (ARS), New York/ADAGP, Paris.

1

Introduction

*B*ob Cates had felt tense, anxious, and worried a lot of the time during his entire stay at the large university he attended. There seemed to be so much to do. However, in his senior year, despite the fact that he was usually an energetic person, even small things seemed to require a major effort. He felt particularly overwhelmed at pressure points like taking exams, writing papers, and having to say things in class.

For reasons that were not clear, Bob became increasingly depressed and began to feel that he couldn't go on much longer. His classes, and life in general, seemed less and less worth the effort they required. He couldn't concentrate on his schoolwork and spent several hours each day sitting in his dormitory room—sometimes just staring into space.

Bob's friends noticed the changes in his behavior and mood and were concerned. As a result of their encouragement, Bob went to the university counseling service and had a series of sessions with a counselor. The questions that passed through the counselor's mind included the following:

- What is Bob experiencing at the present time—what is he feeling and thinking about?
- How serious is the problem that he is experiencing, and to what degree is he aware of its seriousness?
- What are the causes of Bob's problem—is it due to something that has arisen in his current situation, or is it a continuation of a long-term, perhaps lifelong, pattern?
- What can be done to help Bob overcome his unhappy state? ■

What is going on in a particular person's life that results in unhappiness and disordered behavior? What can be done to alleviate the problem? These questions are the focus of abnormal psychology. In the case of Bob Cates, the problem was part of a long-term pattern, but it was also related to things going on in his current life situation. His parents had always emphasized the importance of hard work and achievement. His excellent high school record showed to what degree he had learned to strive for success. What seemed to have happened at the university (many of the facts were far from clear) was that for the first time he began to question the values on which his need to achieve was based.

As Bob's counseling proceeded, he came to see that in many subtle ways his parents had shaped him to be a "producer." During his junior year, Bob began to feel that he could never achieve as much as his parents wanted him to. This thought had a nagging, depressing effect on him. The future seemed hopeless, and he felt helpless to do anything about it. After several counseling sessions Bob admitted that he had had suicidal thoughts, although he had never seriously considered taking his own life.

Most of Bob's counseling sessions were devoted to discussing his parents' pressure on him to be a high achiever and how he felt about that pressure. Bob showed clinical improvement after a few months (he felt less depressed, had more energy, and seemed to get more enjoyment out of life). The series of counseling sessions ended because the school year was over and Bob had gotten a summer job in another city, but also because the counseling service's limited budget permitted only short-term therapy for its clients. Although gratified at her client's improvement, Bob's therapist thought that his depressed mood might have been related to an interplay of multiple factors rather than simply to parental pressure. When asked to comment on the sort of interplay she had in mind, this is what she said:

> I hope Bob is over his depression and that it never returns. But I know that depression often does recur, perhaps because of a genetically driven tendency in that direction. I also worry that Bob might be vulnerable to other types of pressures, for example, from a boss or a spouse. Vulnerability could also come from unresolved unconscious conflicts, incorrect perceptions about how the world works, bad habits, and various pressures coming from the culture (not just parental pressure to achieve a lot). I know it sounds a little vague, but I wish Bob were more in touch with himself and knew what he wanted out of life. Based on my clinical experience, I know that the problems that people have in living their lives are a lot more complicated than what happens when a bothersome rash develops after you have been exposed to poison ivy or poison oak. In our personal lives we are exposed to a lot of things—some help us, some create problems. I don't know if I will ever see Bob again. I hope I do—I would like to see how his life develops.

What Is Abnormal Behavior?

How abnormal is Bob Cates? While there is no basis for concluding that Bob is "crazy," he definitely has had serious difficulties in adjusting to college. Just how much pressure his parents actually placed on him is not answered by the available information. His suicidal thoughts, together with the fact that he spent hours just sitting in his room, suggest that he was experiencing adjustment difficulties that were much greater than those that are typical for college students.

Bob Cates's difficulties were quite different from those of Buford Furrow, whose story follows. Whereas Cates harmed no one, Furrow violently attacked others and reacted negatively to certain racial and ethnic groups. Whereas Cates clearly wanted to change important aspects of his life and fervently wanted help, Furrow seemed ambivalent about obtaining and using professional help. Yet they did share one characteristic: feelings of depression.

On August 10, 1999, 37-year-old Buford O. Furrow Jr. walked into a Los Angeles Jewish community center and shot five people, including three young boys at a day camp. He fled the scene and shortly thereafter fatally shot a letter carrier. Eluding a police dragnet, Furrow took a taxi 275 miles across the desert and paid an $800 fare. The next day he walked unarmed into the Las Vegas FBI office and admitted that he was the man who did the shootings. He stated that he fired at the day-care center because he was concerned about the decline of the White race and wanted to send a message to America by killing Jews. He apparently came upon the letter carrier, a Filipino American, by chance on a street a few miles from the community center, asked him if he would mail a letter for him (the letter carrier agreed to do so), pulled a pistol from his back pocket, and shot him at close range nine times. He later said that he shot the letter carrier because he was a non-White "target of opportunity." Furrow, who lived in Washington State, had come to Los Angeles with a daunting arsenal that included a machine gun, high-powered rifle, and hand grenades.

How can these seemingly senseless acts of violence be explained? They probably will never be accounted for in a totally satisfactory manner, but a number of pertinent facts emerged as the investigation of them unfolded. Furrow had belonged to White supremacist groups in the Pacific Northwest for several years. He told officials that he had had thoughts of both committing a mass killing and killing himself: "Sometimes I feel like I could lose it and kill people. I also feel like I could kill myself."

People who knew him described Furrow as being involved in a religious sect that holds that Jews are subhuman and the offspring of the devil. He once taught a course in hand-to-hand combat at the Aryan Nation (a White supremacist organization) compound in Idaho (Figure 1-1). One informant described him as having a violent

Figure 1-1 Buford Furrow at an Aryan Nation compound.

temper and wanting to control everything. Yet some people who had had contact with Furrow made favorable comments about him. A former employer said: "He showed up to work every day, did his job, and never got involved with any trouble that I knew of."

A year before the Los Angeles shootings, Furrow had tried to stab a woman at a psychiatric center outside Seattle. He had come to the center, Fairfax Hospital in Kirkland, Washington, appearing drunk and seeking admission. When hospital officials tried to take his car keys away from him, he threatened to stab one of them. He served 165 days in jail for attempted assault. Jail personnel evaluated his mental status many times during this period. In hindsight, it is easy to conclude that experts had let a plainly dangerous man slip through their fingers. Furrow's father believes that his son should have been under closer supervision by the state mental health care system. The family could not hospitalize Furrow themselves because Washington State law prohibits a family from committing a member who is older than the age of 13 to a mental facility against that person's will. Furrow had come to Fairfax Hospital because of feelings of depression and suicidal impulses. Records show that at certain points he had been given antidepressant medications and that he seemed much improved, even normal, when he took them. However, he did not always take the prescribed medications. There is evidence that twice Furrow slashed his arm deeply enough to require stitches, occasionally drank alcohol until he blacked out, and espoused hatred for anyone who is not White.

The tragic story of Buford Furrow raises many questions. Were his violent acts due to a disturbed mental condition or did they grow out of beliefs and attitudes that most of us would regard as hateful and bigoted? What does, and what should, society do with people like him? Should he have been held in a mental institution in Washington State instead of serving a few months in jail for assault? It surely appears that a strong case can be made that he posed a threat to himself and others. Yet Ron Sims, the King County Executive stated: "The problem I have is that people are trying to build a case that this killing (in Los Angeles) was done because the man was insane. What he did was cowardly, repulsive and a very unrational act. But mental illness was not the cause. Hatred was. This guy came out of a culture of hatred" (*New York Times*, August 14, 1999, p. A8). Alvin F. Poussaint, a psychiatrist at Harvard University took a different view of Buford Furrow's violent acts. He believes that individuals who commit racial bigotry and hate crimes are mentally disordered and that those who believe non-Whites and Jews are responsible for the world's troubles and must be eliminated are delusional (*New York Times*, August 26, 1999, p. A21).

This difference of opinion is provocative because it relates to several questions that are at the heart of abnormal psychology. If there is a border between normality and abnormality, how do we decide when it has been crossed? Many people who have serious mental health problems function in at least a minimally adequate manner in certain aspects of their lives. Many people who seem normal have annoying or troubling idiosyncrasies. What are the responsibilities of providers of mental health services to those who seek their help? This question cannot always be answered easily. For example, Buford Furrow sought help at Fairfax Hospital but also created roadblocks to clinical workers by threatening them with physical harm. While some psychological problems are clearly not in the ballpark of normality (e.g., inability to maintain even minimal relationships with other people or having hallucinations and delusions), normal–abnormal judgments are often not made so easily. Identifying mentally troubled individuals and helping them involves judgment calls by many people and community agencies. Research bearing on these judgment calls, the prevention of and treatment of clinical conditions, and the causes of personal and social maladjustment is extremely important. Most of the advances in the conceptualization and treatment of mental disorders have come from the domain of research. Current research is likely to set the directions of the future of abnormal psychology.

Buford Furrow and Bob Cates are two very different, troubled individuals. Yet their tendencies to become depressed raise questions about the causes of their problems and what might constitute effective treatment for them. Are their depressions biologically caused, attributable to their histories of experience, or due to some combination of biological and experiential factors?

Terms like *abnormal behavior* and *mental illness* encompass a wide variety of problems ranging from those that are private, in the sense that others might not guess that someone is experiencing distress, to a public tragedy such as the one inflicted by Buford Furrow. Some symptoms that might seem relatively mild could, nevertheless, have important consequences. For example, mild depression experienced over an extended period of time could be related to physical disorders, poor school performance, inability to hold jobs, difficulty making and sustaining friendships, marital discord, inappropriate behavior as a parent, and general failure to fit into society. Box 1-1 conveys the wide range of experiences that people have in response to either identifiable external stimuli or unknown processes within themselves. The likelihood of a return to normal functioning and a relatively distress-free life is greater when the cause of the problem can be identified than when it is a mystery.

As we explore various types of abnormal behavior, we will be trying to identify the relevant factors whose interplay produces problems requiring clinical attention. Because our goal is not simply to describe abnormal behavior, but to understand its causes, we will review theoretical frameworks within which instances of human failure, inadequacy, and unhappiness have been conceptualized. At the same time we will also review basic research pertinent to theories of abnormal behavior. This review of existing theory and research will give us a general framework within which to interpret the wide variety of human problems that find expression in abnormal behaviors. This framework emphasizes the roles played by stress, personal vulnerabilities, and resilience. How we cope depends on the amount of stress we undergo, together with our limitations and our ability to bounce back under pressure.

Mental disorders, like anything unusual, may make us uncomfortable and even a little frightened. A mentally ill person should not be seen as evil, however—merely as different. Abnormal psychology is the area within psychology that is focused on maladaptive behavior—its causes, consequences, and treatment. **Abnormal psychology** deals with how it feels to be different, the meanings that get attached to being different, and how society deals with people whom it considers to be different. The spectrum of differentness is wide, ranging from reality-defying delusions and severe debilitation to worries and behavioral quirks that we would be better off not having but that do not interfere significantly with our daily lives.

An example of this milder end of the spectrum is a man who was an eminently successful district attorney, was elected governor of New York on three occasions, and was almost elected president of the United States in 1948. This man, Thomas E. Dewey, reached the pinnacle of success, displaying such qualities as rectitude, efficiency, precision, and a nearly limitless capacity for hard work. Yet it was just this combination of traits that made Dewey seem too good to be true. For instance, he was never late or absent in his first 12 years of schooling. He lacked a sense of humor and seemed to enjoy life only when he was achieving some goal. He also had personal rigidities that restricted the spontaneity so important in public figures. For instance, he had a phobia about germs. When he toured prisons, he would not touch a doorknob without first wiping it off with a folded handkerchief concealed in his palm. He also drank three quarts of water a day because of its presumed healthful effects. Dewey achieved much, but had he been less rigid he might have achieved even more; perhaps more important, he might have been a happier person (R. N. Smith, 1982).

Governor Dewey's differentness was quite mild in comparison to problems like those experienced by Joan Houghton. Houghton's break with reality required intensive treatment during a 5-week period of hospitalization. After her recovery she wrote an account of her experiences.

> My mother and I sat next to each other in the waiting room while my father investigated admission procedures. A young man was seated near us. Perspiration dripped across his brow and down his cheeks. In silence I took a tissue from my purse, moved close to him and gently wiped the moisture from his face. I reassured him that everything would be fine.
>
> Then my father rejoined us. We went together to a small room where I met Kay, the psychiatric social worker assigned to my case, and a psychiatrist (whose name I don't recall). We talked a few minutes. I was presented with a piece of paper and instructed to sign my name. Obediently, I wrote "Saint Joan" on the paper, not realizing that I was voluntarily admitting myself to a state mental hospital. . . . At the time of my hospitalization I had both a sense of death and of rebirth about me. My first psychotic episode appeared as a private mental exorcism, ending with the honor of sainthood and the gifts of hope and faith. (Houghton, 1982, pp. 548–549)

Governor Dewey and Joan Houghton might be described as showing differentness in mental health in distinctive ways. Mental health refers to the capacities to (1) think rationally and logically, (2) cope effectively with stress and the challenges that arise in situations and throughout the life course, and (3) demonstrate emotional stability and growth. When mental health deteriorates, problems can arise in a wide variety of areas, including the following:

- Low self-regard ("I'm no good")
- Distortion of reality ("Everybody plots against me")
- Reduced competence (e.g., socially and occupationally)
- Anxiety ("I feel tense all the time")
- Depression ("Life isn't worth living")
- Anger ("I feel mad twenty times a day")
- Heightened physiological reactivity (e.g., fast heart rate and high blood pressure)

First Person

Box 1–1

Sources and Expressions of Distress

Most people who have emotional problems refer to the distress they are experiencing. Sources of distress and how they are expressed range widely. Sometimes distress is caused by an easily identifiable life event (for example, losing a job), whereas in other cases the source seems to be as much within the individual as coming from the environment. In addition to diversity of sources, there also is diversity in how distress is expressed. The source of Bob Cates's distress is unclear. Regardless of the source, Bob experiences his distress internally; for example, he gets depressed and has difficulty concentrating. The source of Buford Furrow's distress is also unclear, but, unlike Bob Cates, its expression was outward rather than inward.

Three other individuals, Jerry Calabrese, Nancy Raine, and Billy Henderson also have experienced stressful events. Each of them reacts somewhat differently.

Jerry Calabrese seems, like Buford Furrow, to be an angry externalizer but one whose anger does not reach catastrophic proportions. Like Bob Cates, he sought help at a student counseling center. As Jerry Calabrese's personal account indicates, his difficulties are quite different from those of Bob Cates.

I've been going to the student counseling center once a week for the past two months. The reason I went there was that I just couldn't stand getting "burned up" so often. Just before my first visit to the center, I got so angry at the stupid questions on Professor Harris's psychology exam that I actually thought of hitting him. And that's not new—for as long as I can remember, I've had a short fuse. I see now that I'm not very tolerant of other people's mistakes and what I assume is lack of thoughtfulness. My anger has gotten me

into fights and breakups of relationships. I've had enough.

Jerry typically sees his sources of distress as being outside himself (Professor Harris's exam) and directs his anger outward (wanting to hit Professor Harris). But as a result of psychotherapy, Jerry is beginning to see that his anger is part of him and not just a normal reaction to provocation.

Nancy Raine also sees her distress as coming from an external source. Nancy was raped a few years ago, and although time has passed she continues to react internally, to suffer in silence.

I know how to mark my birthday, my wedding anniversary, even the anniversary of my brother's death. But the day I was raped? How should I observe the passing of another year? . . . I can never again be that woman who locked her door and felt safe. My husband, my mother, my friends still suffer their own brand of helplessness when they try to imagine the content of my memory. My father, who spent his life in law enforcement, leaves the room if the subject of rape in general, or my rape in particular, creeps into the conversation. Why remind them? And dare they remind me, when they secretly hope I might be "over it" at last?

On this anniversary, more or less safe in the cradle of the day's routine, I began to think back. To the first anniversary, when I realized that I had to stop talking about what happened to me because the people who loved me could not bear to hear it. The second, when I pretended to myself I was "over it." The third, when I realized I wasn't. The fourth, when I was in treatment for posttraumatic stress syndrome. The fifth, when I was convinced my treatment wasn't helping and secretly

wondered if I had the guts to kill myself. The sixth, during a lunch date, when I told a woman I barely knew that our meeting was occurring on the anniversary of my rape. I spoke matter-of-factly, afraid she might gather up her black briefcase and suddenly remember a dentist's appointment. (Raine, 1994, p. 34)

Billy Henderson is different from Bob Cates, Buford Furrow, Jerry Calabrese, and Nancy Raine in that what is going on within him is so confused that one can only guess the sources of his distress. Billy is currently living in the community but had been in mental hospitals on three occasions. He responded to the question "Tell me about yourself" in a way that can only leave us puzzled and worried about his ability to function:

My hands feel paralyzed and I feel under unbearable stress. I'm going to do something. I believe in free elections of the Protection and Advocacy for Military Intelligence Officers (PAMIO). The Secretary of the Department of Insubordinate Criminals (DIC) is confused about the Genetic Research Committee (GRC) and needs to be briefed and redirected. In addition, the oat-bran fiasco needs to be analyzed and publicized. I feel strongly about these issues as well as some even more basic ones, including:

- Mental institutions function by "denying the self" in their victims.
- Love should be withdrawn from evil so that it takes its deserved fall.
- People suffer as public martyrs for the existence of loves that threaten power (power is the ability to mistreat people with impunity).
- A new support group is needed for people who have in common things that were but aren't (for example, victims of electric shock "therapy").

The Stigma of Abnormal Behavior

Although Joan Houghton's recovery enabled her to obtain and hold a job at the National Institute of Mental Health and to write sensitively about her experience, she faced many barriers that made the recovery process more difficult than it had to be. Her ordeal continued after discharge from the hospital.

My recovery from mental illness and its aftermath involved a struggle—against my own body, which seemed to be without energy and stamina, and against a society that seemed reluctant to embrace me. It seemed that my greatest needs—to be wanted, needed, valued—were the very needs which others could not fulfill. At times, it felt as though I were trying to swim against a tidal wave. (Houghton, 1980, p. 8)

The following incident illustrates what swimming against that tidal wave was like:

One Sunday I went to church alone after being absent for several weeks. The minister (who knew of my history, faith, and strong belief in God) began his sermon with reference to the devil. He said, "If you ever want to be convinced of the existence of the devil, you should visit a mental institution." To illustrate his point, he described people who had lost control of their bodily functions, who screamed out obscenities. I left church after the sermon, drove home vowing never to return to that church as long as that minister preached from the pulpit. At home, however, I began to replace my anger with doubt. Maybe I misunderstood.

At my invitation the minister visited our home to discuss his philosophy about mental illness and the mentally ill. His visit was our last encounter. Not only did he see evil in mental illness but he conveyed an unforgiving attitude to those who have the misfortune of residing in mental hospitals. (Houghton, 1980, p. 10)

As Houghton's account makes clear, people who are noticeably deviant may experience prejudice and discrimination. The stigma associated with mental illness may express itself directly, as when people reject outright individuals who behave in abnormal ways, or indirectly, as when former mental patients anticipate rejection even though they have not been rebuffed by anyone. In the course of socialization we all develop ideas about how mental patients are viewed and treated. If we are not mental patients ourselves, these beliefs may be relatively unimportant to us, applicable only to people on the margins of our lives. For those who do become patients, however, the beliefs become personally relevant. If they think that people devalue and discriminate against mental patients, they feel threatened. They may keep their personal worries and preoccupations a secret, or they may remove themselves from any social situation where they might be rejected. The resulting social withdrawal, uncertainty, and tentativeness affect their job performance, their relationships with others, and their opinion of themselves.

A challenge to the field of abnormal psychology is to correct the public's misperceptions about the nature of abnormal behavior. Many people erroneously attribute abnormal behavior to emotional weakness or bad parenting. While these types of attributions may be appropriate in certain instances, they are by no means accurate universally. As Box 1-2 shows, troubled individuals are in need of compassion, not bias or blame. The stigma that en-

velops the psychologically troubled often deters them from seeking help.

An example of an effective program that reduces the stigma often associated with psychological problems is one instituted by the U.S. Air Force. It has more than halved the number of suicides among Air Force personnel. The program involves encouraging officers, enlisted members, and their families to get help at the first sign of a problem and teaching health-related personnel about risk factors and intervention resources. The net effect of this effort has been to reduce stigma and debunk the idea that seeking help will hurt career development (Rabasca, 1999).

Adaptive and Maladaptive Behavior

Most of the behaviors studied by abnormal psychology are related to human failures and inadequacies. These failures in living are due mainly to failures in adaptation. **Adaptation** involves the balance between what people do and want to do, on the one hand, and what the environment (the community) requires, on the other.

Adaptation is a dynamic process. Each of us responds to our environment and to the changes that occur within it. How well we adapt depends on two factors: our personal characteristics (skills, attitudes, physical condition) and the nature of the situations that confront us (e.g., family conflict or natural disaster). These two factors jointly determine whether we survive, are content, and prosper, or whether we fall by the wayside. Because nothing—not ourselves, not the environment—stays the same for very long, adaptation must take place all the time. The extremely rapid rate of change in the modern world puts a particular strain on our ability to adapt. Moreover, successful adaptation to one set of conditions is not a guarantee of successful adaptation to others.

Unlike those of animals, the adaptive successes and failures of human beings cannot be measured simply in terms of the survival and reproduction of the species. For most people in the modern world, concerns about quality of life and level of contentment far overshadow the need to satisfy biological requirements. Human beings have developed subtle language forms, a refined level of thinking, superior problem-solving skills, intricate social relationships, and complex communication processes, all of which affect behavior and its interpretation. The notion that a failure to adapt may affect survival of the species has some credibility—individuals' feelings of failure may damage their social relationships, and the human gene pool might be significantly affected by the failure of such people to marry and have children. On the other hand, many individuals with certain types of inadequacies, who would probably be unable to hold their own in a subsistence economy, can survive and reproduce in the modern world because of social institutions such as welfare programs, Social Security, and health insurance. How we live

Research Close-up   Box 1–2

The Mentally Ill Need Understanding

Dear Abby: I am the director of a rehabilitation program for the chronically mentally ill. From time to time, I notice that you print letters that deal with stereotypes and negative attitudes society often holds toward certain groups. I wonder if you might print a similar letter on behalf of people who have a mental illness. One of the foremost issues facing this group is the negative prejudice that society holds against them.

I asked our group of patients to provide suggestions on how to treat a person who has a mental illness. Some of their ideas:

1. Don't be afraid of us. Despite what you see on TV and in the movies, studies have shown that the mentally ill population does not have a greater propensity toward violence than anyone else.
2. Please avoid negative stereotypical words such as "psycho," "nuts," "schizo," "loonies," etc. The emotional pain these dehumanizing words inflict upon us hurts worse than our illness does.
3. Give us job opportunity. Abraham Lincoln and Winston Churchill, both of whom experienced mental illness, held two of the most important jobs in history. Many of us are intelligent and long for the chance to be productive members of society.
4. Please don't tell us that if we just tried harder we could "snap out of it." This insults our intelligence and implies that we are lazy. There is nothing fun or positive about having a mental illness and none of us chooses to have it.
5. Be patient when you notice we are having a difficult time. It is OK to ask us if we need help.
6. Don't ask if we have taken our medication when we are angry, sad, or irritable. These questions make us feel like we don't have the right to experience normal human emotions without being viewed as having an "episode."
7. Treat us as you would treat anyone else. We have a need for acceptance, just as you do. Most of us lead quite normal lives complete with families, children, employment, and financial responsibilities.

Abby, with the help of recent medications and psychotherapy interventions, the treatment of mental illness has made tremendous strides in the last 10 years. Unfortunately, the prejudice against this group remains one of the most painful aspects of the disease.

Mike Ashworth, Ph.D.,
Arlington, Texas

Dear Dr. Ashworth: You have written a very important letter. There is a lot of ignorance and misunderstanding about mental illness. Some mental illnesses can be managed effectively with therapy and medication. Others can be cured entirely. People coping with mental illness have enough complicated challenges to overcome without having to deal with the irrational fears of the supposedly "normal."

Let's face it—there are few among us who don't have a few "kinks" here or there.

SOURCE: *Seattle Times*, September 19, 1999, p. L5.

and how we feel about the way we live are important factors in human adaptation. For the authors of this book, adaptation refers to people's ability or inability to modify their behavior in response to changing environmental requirements. This book, therefore, focuses primarily on people's personal and social adaptations.

Maladaptive Versus Deviant Behavior All maladaptive behavior is deviant behavior. However, deviant or unusual behavior is not necessarily maladaptive. This can be seen in the case of Albert Einstein. At the age of 12, Einstein decided to devote his life to solving the "riddle of the huge world." Early in his career, while working as a patent office examiner, he wrote five papers that eventually changed our view of the universe. Although public recognition of the importance of Einstein's theory was many years away, his ability to think about the properties of matter in a completely new way began almost at once to influence the thought of physicists. While other kinds of deviant behaviors, such as wearing very bright ties, refusing to travel by airplane, drinking 10 cups of coffee a day, and needing to read in bed for 2 hours before falling asleep, are not as productive as Einstein's behavior and may seem odd or annoying, people who act in these ways do not need major rehabilitative efforts to live happy, productive lives.

Describing behavior as **maladaptive** implies that a problem exists; it also suggests that vulnerability in the individual, inability to cope, or exceptional stress in the environment has led to problems in living. Students of maladaptive behavior are especially interested in behavior that is not merely different or deviant but that also represents a source of concern to the individual, to his or her family and friends, or to society. This means, for example, that students of maladaptive behavior direct more of their attention toward those with very low IQs than toward those with high IQs, and toward those who are not happy rather than toward those who are extremely content.

There are many causes of maladaptation. In some instances—for example, in certain forms of brain damage—organic cause is uncovered. In other cases, undesirable present or past social relationships—for example, an incestuous relationship—may be implicated. In still other cases, a combination of these factors, along with a stressful event, such as the death of a loved one or the birth of a child, plays a decisive role.

Maladaptations range from chronic fears that are troubling but not disabling to severe distortion of reality and inability to function independently. A person may simply be unhappy about his or her maladaptive behavior, or the community may be worried about what might happen if the person is not removed from society. Throughout this book many different kinds of maladaptive behavior—some linked primarily to biological defects, others to life history problems—will be described, along with the social reactions they evoke.

Many people who do not receive a formal diagnosis of mental disorder may nevertheless have personal problems that interfere with optimal schoolwork or job performance, making and sustaining friendships, and fitting into society. Relatively mild conditions may merit treatment if clinical attention helps people to live happier lives and prevents the development of more serious problems later in life.

Historical Background of Modern Abnormal Psychology

Today the idea that abnormal psychology is concerned with the scientifically established causes and treatment of thinking, mood, and behavior disorders does not evoke controversy. Someone might observe that modern techniques are surely much more effective, enlightened, and sophisticated than those used in earlier times, and ask: Why not concentrate on them instead of getting bogged down in accounts of the past? The trouble with this approach is that it misses important links between the past and the present. Much of what seems modern is an outgrowth of the past, not a rejection of it. In abnormal psychology, as in other fields of study, there are fewer completely new ideas than one might think. A review of the history of abnormal psychology provides a context within which the best of the modern discipline can be understood.

People have always been concerned about their physical well-being, their social relationships, and their place in the universe. They have posed many questions about these issues, have evolved theories about them. Some of those theories seem almost universal. They can be observed in many parts of the world and in many periods of human history. Many of the past ideas offered to explain and treat maladaptation have been shown to be incorrect when exposed to scientific investigation. For example, while we now know that certain bodily processes are critically important in causing disordered behavior, early writers often were quite incorrect in how they tried to link mind and body. Perhaps the greatest benefit of studying the history

of abnormal psychology is the discovery that certain theories of maladaptive behavior have occurred over and over again and, whether correct or incorrect, reflect the interest over time in what constitutes "differentness."

One ancient theory that is still encountered today holds that abnormal behavior can be explained by the operation of supernatural and magical forces such as evil spirits or the devil. In societies that believe in this theory, therapy generally involves **exorcism,** that is, removing the evil that resides in the individual through countermagic and prayer. Although this view is most prevalent in nonliterate cultures, it is still found in industrialized societies and often exists side by side with more modern approaches. For example, many people who use folk healers also seek assistance from health care professionals. Professionals can improve the effectiveness of the help they provide by understanding what folk healers do and why their patients seek them out.

In many societies the **shaman,** or medicine man, a magician who is believed to have contact with supernatural forces, is the medium through which spirits communicate with human beings (see Figure 1-2). Through the shaman, an afflicted person can learn which spirits are responsible for his or her problem and what needs to be done to appease them. To accomplish this, the shaman conducts a seance in which he displays intense excitement and often mimics the abnormal behavior he seeks to cure. Through mystical utterances and violent movements, and by acting out his dreams, the shaman reveals messages from spirits. Often the liberation of an evil spirit from the patient's body is expressed by what appears, through sleight of hand, to be the actual expulsion of an object, such as a stone, from the patient's ear or mouth. These rituals are based on specific theories about supernatural forces or evil powers as the cause of abnormal behavior and as the basis of therapeutic change.

It is tempting to view seemingly primitive beliefs about mental illness as part of the dead past. Yet the fact is that even in a relatively advanced and enlightened society like the United States there is a wide range of views about the causes of personal problems. The following case concerned a 33-year-old man from a rural area near Little Rock, Arkansas:

The patient had been having seizures recently and had become increasingly irritable and withdrawn from his family. He was hospitalized, and when he could no longer be detained safely on the neurology service, he was transferred to the psychiatric ward, where he became increasingly more agitated, confused, and almost delirious. He became very fearful whenever people approached him, and he began to hallucinate. He finally slowed down after being given 1000 mg of chlorpromazine (a tranquilizer), but the necessity for bed restraint remained. All neurological findings, including a brain scan, proved normal. After two weeks of hospitalization the patient suffered a car-

Figure 1-2 A shaman anoints a man with holy water to protect him from evil spirits as the latter embarks on a pilgrimage.

diac arrest. All efforts to revive him failed. An autopsy provided no reason for the death. After he died, the patient's wife told staff members that her husband had been seeing a "two-headed," an older woman considered by the community to be a witch who cast spells and healed people. The widow stated that her husband had angered the two-headed and that she had caused his death. (Golden, 1977, p. 1425)

A recurring theme in the history of abnormal behavior is the belief that individuals behave strangely because their bodies are not working right. Such people have been thought to have an organic defect. The source of the presumed defect might vary according to the nature of the abnormality, the society's cultural beliefs, and—particularly in the modern era—scientific knowledge. One of the achievements of the modern era is solid evidence not only that bodily processes can be linked to many types of maladaptive behavior, but also that, for certain types of disorders, correcting defective biological processes results in improved behavioral functioning. Whereas in the past an organic component of maladaptive behavior was often mainly a matter of belief, scientific evidence today is decisive.

The finding of ancient skulls with holes in them that were not caused by battle wounds has led some anthropologists to conjecture that abnormal behavior was sometimes treated by means of a procedure called **trephination.** In this technique a sharp tool such as a stone was used to make a hole in the skull about 2 centimeters in diameter (see Figure 1-3). Evidence that trephination was performed as early as 3000 to 2000 B.C. has been uncovered in eastern Mediterranean and North African countries. Studies of trephined skulls suggest that the operation often was not fatal, a remarkable achievement given the diffi-

culty of the procedure. Trephination may have been done to permit demonic spirits to escape. However, because of the absence of written records and the fact that our only data are the trephined skulls themselves, we need to be cautious in speculating about their significance.

Another general approach to the causes of abnormal behavior reflects what might be called the psychological perspective. According to this point of view, behavioral disturbances are caused by inadequacies in the way an individual thinks, feels, or perceives the world. According to the psychological perspective, people are at least potentially capable of examining their own thinking and modifying their behavior in light of that examination. Many modern psychotherapists see their task as helping people

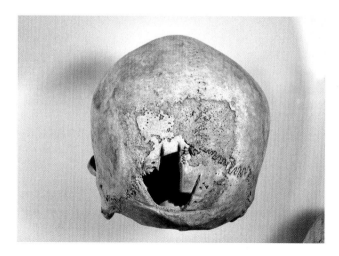

Figure 1-3 The technique of trephining involved chipping a hole in the person's skull.

learn to think more rationally about themselves and their social relationships.

All three of these perspectives—supernatural, organic, and psychological—have recurred throughout the history of Western civilization.

The Ancient Western World

The philosophers of ancient Greece were the earliest to write about psychological and organic approaches to deviance. At the height of their civilization, the Greeks emphasized the rational analysis of the natural world. The concepts of motivation and intelligence were among those that they developed in their efforts to explain the behavior they observed in everyday life. Although we tend to see the modern era as the period in which human beings have sought to extend the boundaries of human understanding through the application of reason, the foundations for this period were laid by the writings of the ancient Greek philosophers. The main difference between us and the Greeks of antiquity is that we have access to all the knowledge that has accumulated in the past two thousand years, as well as the tools of the scientific method.

Even in ancient Greece, knowledge evolved over a period of several centuries. At the time the *Iliad* and the *Odyssey* were written (about the ninth century B.C.), disturbed or psychotic behavior was interpreted as a form of punishment for offenses against the gods. ("Those whom the gods would destroy, they first make mad.") Therapy took place in a group of temples dedicated to Asclepius, the god of healing. Each temple was a mazelike structure in which mental patients walked and slept and ultimately reached the center. In the process it was believed that Asclepius attended to their dreams and healed them.

In the centuries that followed, the idea that a person's life is in the hands of the gods gradually declined, at least among educated citizens. The Greek philosophers became increasingly curious about aspects of the individual that might explain normal as well as abnormal behavior. Extreme mental deviations and disorders came to be viewed as natural phenomena for which rational treatments might be developed.

The ancient Egyptians, as well as the Mesopotamians and Hebrews, believed the seat of the mind to be in the heart. When the Pharaohs were embalmed, the heart was venerated, but the brain was removed and thrown away. For the Greeks, however, the brain was the seat of the mind. (Shakespeare referred to the lingering heart-mind controversy in act III of *The Merchant of Venice* when he wrote: "Tell me where is fancie bred,/Or in the heart or in the head?") Despite his lack of anatomical knowledge, the Greek physician Hippocrates (460–377 B.C.) looked to the brain in his efforts to explain why people behave as they do. He described the brain as the interpreter of consciousness and as the body's most important organ.

Hippocrates described epileptic seizures and concluded that they were caused by a diseased brain. He also wrote about depression, states of delirium, psychosis, irrational fears (what we now call phobias), and hysteria (organic symptoms in the absence of an organic disturbance). He and his followers became known for their ability to recognize and treat mental illness. Their therapeutic techniques consisted of rest, bathing, and dieting. There is even a record of Hippocrates appearing as an expert witness at the trial of an insane person. Today physicians continue to pay their debt to Hippocrates by taking the Hippocratic oath when they graduate from medical school.

Three other Greek philosophers—Socrates (470–399 B.C.), Plato (427–347 B.C.), and Aristotle (384–322 B.C.)—also deserve mention for their contributions to abnormal psychology. Socrates was interested in self-exploration and considered reasoning to be the cornerstone of the good life and personal happiness. He believed in using inquiry to further knowledge; his goal was to teach by asking questions instead of giving answers. Today this procedure—called the Socratic method—is a valuable teaching tool as well as a component of the scientific method.

Socrates' most famous student, Plato, developed the **organismic approach.** He saw behavior as a product of the totality of psychological processes. Like many modern writers, Plato believed that disturbed behavior grew out of conflicts between emotion and reason. In contrast to those who saw abnormal behavior as having a physical cause, he stressed the power of ideas, going so far as to say that the mind is the only true reality of human existence. According to Plato, the ideal individual is, above all, guided by reason. In his *Laws*, he expressed the belief that people who have lost their reason should be separated from society: "No lunatic shall be allowed to be at large in the community; the relatives of such persons shall keep them in safe custody at home by such methods as they contrive, on penalty of fine."

Plato's belief is similar to those held by many societies in the past. However, as time went on, separation of the mentally ill from others in the community became the responsibility of the government rather than of the family. The large institutions created to care for the mentally ill are described later in this chapter. Since the middle of the 1960s, an emphasis on the civil rights of those who are mentally ill has resulted in the closure of many of these institutions and the return of many patients to the community and, for those that have them, to the care of family members.

Aristotle, a pupil of Plato and the teacher of Alexander the Great, wrote extensively on the nature of reasoning and consciousness and also sought to analyze human emotions. He described and speculated about a number of emotional and motivational states, including anger, fear, envy, courage, hatred, and pity. Like most of the Greek philosophers, Aristotle placed the highest value on reason and application. He also believed that the various forces in the body need to be in balance in order for reason to prevail.

Galen (A.D. 130–200), the great Greek physician, consolidated and augmented the Greek theories of mind and body. He elaborated on ancient theories about the role of the **four humors** in personal character and temperament. According to these theories, the material world was made up of four elements—earth, air, fire, and water—which combined to form four essential bodily fluids, or humors, whose balance shaped each individual's temperament. Imbalances among the humors—blood, black bile, yellow bile, and phlegm—were believed to cause various disorders. Humoral theories were popular throughout the medieval period (see Figure 1-4).

The rational approach of the ancient philosophers laid the groundwork for modern science. It led to attempts to classify abnormal behavior according to some consistent scheme. It temporarily replaced magical and religious explanations of abnormal behavior with a quest, through observation and reason, for natural causes. Except for a break during the Middle Ages, that quest has continued up to the present time.

Figure 1-4 These medieval paintings reflect the view that certain temperamental qualities are the result of an excess of one of the four humors. Top left and right show, respectively, the sluggish man who has too much phlegm and the changeable man who has an excess of blood. The lower left and right paintings illustrate the hot-tempered man who has an excess of yellow bile and the melancholic man affected by too much black bile.

The Middle Ages

A host of changes accompanied the decline of ancient Greek culture and the rise and fall of the Roman Empire. Perhaps the two most obvious causes of these changes were the invasions of western Europe by barbarian tribes and the growth of the Christian religion. The invaders, whose ideas were primitive compared to those of the Greeks and Romans, caused great social unrest. The Christian religion served to comfort people in those troubled times. In addition, the Christian church acted as a unifying force when the civil government of Rome finally fell.

The unrest of the Middle Ages was intensified by nearly constant warfare as well as by the Black Death and other epidemics that came without warning and wiped out hundreds of thousands of people. During this period fear and terror spread like brushfires, causing many outbreaks of group hysteria. The nature of these outbreaks varied. Some groups of people behaved like packs of wolves; others danced in the streets, making spiderlike movements.

During the early Middle Ages, the importance of the Christian spirit of charity, particularly toward stigmatized groups such as the severely mentally disturbed, cannot be overestimated. Also during this period, music and dance were thought to cure insanity by restoring the chemical balance within the body (see Figure 1-5).

One figure in the early Christian era, the theologian and philosopher Saint Augustine (A.D. 354–430), stands out because he helped lay the groundwork for modern psychodynamic theories of abnormal behavior. He wrote extensively about feelings, mental anguish, and human conflict. It was not so much the topics he dealt with as his method of approaching them that most resembles the psychoanalytic method of today. Saint Augustine used introspection, or examination of his own thoughts, feelings, and motives, to discuss mental processes like the conflict between pleasure and discipline. In his *Confessions* he revealed his innermost thoughts, temptations, and fears. By demonstrating that introspection and exploration of the individual's emotional life could be valuable sources of psychological knowledge, Saint Augustine made an important contribution to modern abnormal psychology.

Unfortunately, these efforts were not continued during the Middle Ages. As the church's control and influence increased, so did its role in governmental affairs, and it was religious dogma, not civil law, that became the supreme voice of authority. The church came to control the practice of medicine, defining its goals and prescribing treatments for various conditions. To the degree that this control reflected a feeling of charity toward people suffering hardships of various kinds, the church played a positive role. To the extent that it was intolerant, authoritarian, and repressive, however, its role was decidedly negative.

Figure 1-5   In this medieval engraving, the insane are shown being led through a dance in an effort to improve their mental condition.

The legacy of rationality that the Middle Ages had inherited from the Greek philosophers was quickly abandoned in the late medieval period. Demonology and superstition gained renewed importance in the explanation of abnormal behavior. Although many people continued to take a benign, naturalistic view of mental illness, in the late Middle Ages anti-intellectualism and belief in magic and witchcraft increased. Many people believed strongly in exorcism, the casting out of evil spirits from the body of an afflicted person (see Figure 1-6).

History does not move in a simple, uncomplicated way. Even while demonology and exorcism were popular ideas, there were some relatively enlightened governments that made serious efforts to care for mentally troubled individuals. In England, for example, the Crown had the right and duty to protect the mentally impaired, who were divided into two categories: natural fools and persons *non compos mentis*. A **natural fool** was a mentally retarded person whose intellectual capacities had never progressed beyond those of a child. **Persons *non compos mentis*** (Latin for "not of sound mind") did not show mental disability at birth. Their deviant behavior was not continuous, and they might show long periods of recovery. (For reasons that are not clear, by the fifteenth century the term *lunatic* had replaced the phrase *non compos mentis* and *idiot* had replaced *natural fool*.

There is also evidence that hearings to judge a person's mental status and legal competency were held as early as the thirteenth century (Neugebauer, 1979). Such examinations were designed to assess a person's orientation, memory, and intellect. The following description of a woman named Emma de Beston, which dates from 1383, is typical of the reports that were based on such examinations:

The said Emma, being caused to appear before them, was asked whence she came and said that she did not know. Being asked in what town she was, she said that she was at Ely. Being asked how many days there were in the week, she said seven but could not name them. Being asked how many husbands she had had in her time she said three, giving the name of one only and not knowing the names of the others. Being asked whether she had ever had issue by them, she said that she had had a husband with a son, but did not know his name. Being asked how many shillings were in forty pence, she said she did not know. Being asked whether she would rather have twenty silver goats than forty pence, she said they were of the same value. They examined her in all other ways which they thought best and found that she was not of sound mind, having neither sense nor memory nor sufficient intelligence to manage herself, her lands or her goods. As appeared by inspection she had the face and countenance of an idiot. (as cited in O'Donoghue, 1914, pp. 127–128)

The Renaissance

Although ideas like demonology and exorcism persisted during the Renaissance (roughly the fourteenth through the sixteenth centuries), this period was marked by increased humanism, curiosity about nature, and interest in scholarship. For example, Johann Weyer (1515–1576), a physician, emphasized psychological conflict and disturbed interpersonal relationships as causes of mental disorder. Weyer had the courage to insist that witches were mentally disturbed individuals rather than creatures of Satan. He vigorously asserted the need to treat such people medically rather than theologically. His enlightened humanism undoubtedly saved countless mentally ill people from death at the stake.

Figure 1-6 This late-fifteenth-century painting by Girolamo Di Benvenuto, *St. Catherine Exorcising a Possessed Woman,* shows Saint Catherine of Siena casting the devil out of a possessed woman. The devil is seen fleeing from the woman's head.

SOURCE: Girolamo Di Benvenuto "St. Catherine Exorcising a Possessed Woman." Samuel H. Kress Foundation Collection. ©Denver Art Museum.

On the basis of careful psychological examination of mental patients, Weyer described a wide range of abnormal behavior, including the disorders known today as paranoia, epilepsy, psychosis, depression, and persistent nightmares. He argued that clinical treatment must be oriented toward meeting the needs of disturbed people rather than merely following rules of religious institutions. He spent much time talking with and observing his patients because he felt that he could not treat psychopathology without firsthand knowledge of it. The knowledge led him to the conclusion that inner experiences (such as psychological conflict) and disturbed relationships with others were significant causes of mental illness. Weyer's writings represent a major step toward the separation of abnormal psychology from theology.

The Age of Reason and the Enlightenment

The seventeenth century, known as the Age of Reason, and the eighteenth century, known as the Enlightenment, have been so labeled because during these two centuries reason and the scientific method came to replace faith and dogma as ways of understanding the natural world. During these two centuries major advances were made in such diverse fields as astronomy, biology, and chemistry.

Scientists and philosophers alike emphasized the need to support assertions with observations of natural phenomena. The English physician William Harvey (1578–1657), best known for his work on the human circulatory system, also wrote about the relationships between the psychological and physiological aspects of life.

Although human emotions and motivations are less accessible to direct observation than the moon, the human circulatory system, or molecular structures, a number of philosophers and scientists focused on the subjective experiences of human beings. Baruch Spinoza (1632–1677) anticipated modern approaches to psychology and physiology with his argument that mind and body are inseparable. He discussed psychological causation and the roles of emotions, ideas, and desires in human life. Spinoza even referred to unconscious mechanisms that influence behavior. His main contribution to abnormal psychology was his argument that psychological processes, though not directly observable, are equal in importance to the material processes of the natural world.

Among the perceptive observers of the human experience in every age have been playwrights, novelists, and poets. During the Age of Reason, a number of authors probed especially deeply into the problems of human motivation and emotions. The clearest examples can be found in many plays of William Shakespeare (1564–1616), particularly *Hamlet*. Hamlet wants to take revenge on his uncle for the murder of Hamlet's father but continually hesitates to act. Psychoanalysts have interpreted this hesitation as a reflection of Hamlet's neurotic conflicts concerning his mother, who had married the uncle after the death of Hamlet's father. Another literary work that dealt with human emotions was *The Anatomy of Melancholy* by Robert Burton (1577–1640). In this book Burton focused on the emotional core of depression and observed that depressed people tend to be very angry, not only with themselves, but with others as well. Burton, a professor of divinity at Oxford, based his description and analysis of depression on his own experience.

These literary developments mirror the long-standing conflict between psychological and physical explanations of abnormal behavior. However, during the seventeenth and eighteenth centuries, both groups—those who analyzed subjective experience and those who sought to identify physical defects—finally rejected the idea that demons and supernatural forces were the causes of abnormal behavior. As a consequence, by the end of the eighteenth century, superstition had been almost totally replaced by a commitment to rationality, scientific observation, and humane treatment of the mentally ill.

In England the movement toward humane treatment gained impetus as a result of the psychotic breakdown suffered by King George III in 1765. This event precipitated a constitutional crisis and made many people aware that even prominent individuals were not immune to mental derangement. Madhouses had existed in England for many years, but only in 1774 did Britain pass its first parliamentary act licensing such institutions and regulating the admission of patients to them.

From the late seventeenth to the nineteenth century, interest rose in **physiognomy,** the art of judging character, personality, and feelings from the form of the body, particularly the face. In the early nineteenth century, another new approach to abnormal psychology emerged. Franz Joseph Gall (1758–1828), a physician, studied the brains of different kinds of people (young, old, deranged) and gathered evidence suggesting that brain size and mental development were related. On the basis of this evidence he formulated the theory of **phrenology.** Gall believed that bumps and indentations on the surface of the skull were accurate reflections of the underlying parts of the brain. Figure 1-7 shows a device that was used to measure these irregularities. Interest in this now-discredited theory lasted a long time: the journal of the Ohio State Phrenological Society was published until 1938, and the British Phrenological Society was in existence until 1967.

Two additional examples that illustrate the growing interest in physical approaches to mental illness are the ideas of Cullen and Mesmer. The Scottish physician William Cullen (1712–1790) believed that neurotic behavior was

Figure 1-7 The Lavery electric phrenometer, invented in 1907, was designed to measure bumps on the head. Such bumps were thought to indicate the location of different psychological faculties.

caused by physical defects of the nervous system. Cullen's therapeutic efforts seem naive, but they were a logical outgrowth of his organic orientation. He treated his patients with cold dousings, bloodletting, inducing of vomiting, special diets, exercise programs, and physiotherapy. Like most of his contemporaries, Cullen used severe restraints and straitjackets to control violently disturbed individuals.

An even more famous example of the quest for organic explanations of abnormal behavior is the career of a Viennese physician, Franz Anton Mesmer (1734–1815). In 1774 Mesmer heard about the work of some English physicians who were treating certain diseases with magnets. He then treated a patient by making her swallow a preparation containing iron and attaching three magnets to her body, one on her stomach and two on her legs. Following her dramatic recovery, Mesmer speculated about the mechanisms that had brought about the cure. We would all agree with his first conclusion: the favorable result could not reasonably be explained by the action of the magnets alone. But Mesmer, a flamboyant and ambitious man, went on to assert that the magnets had simply reinforced or

Figure 1-8 Mesmer treated his patients by using a *baquet*, a round tub in which he placed magnetized water. This eighteenth-century engraving shows patients using rods and ropes connected to the tub to touch the afflicted areas on their bodies.

strengthened the primary cause of the cure: his own personal or animal magnetism. Mesmer contended that all human beings were endowed with a special magnetic fluid, a kind of sixth sense that, when liberated, could cure and prevent all illnesses (see Figure 1-8). Furthermore, he was convinced that he possessed an unusual abundance of the fluid. Mesmer believed that gesturing with his hands was enough to make his patients feel the transmission of his magnetic force.

Mesmer's patients entered a thickly carpeted, dimly lit room amid soft music and perfumed air. They held hands, forming a circle around the *baquet,* a tub filled with magnetized water. Mesmer entered, dressed in an elegant cloak and carrying a sword. These dramatics were deliberately contrived to accomplish the emotional crisis needed for the cure.

Many testimonials claimed that Mesmer's treatment had been helpful. However, the mechanism of his therapy had more to do with the power of suggestion than with human magnetic fluids. His animal magnetism was a forerunner, not of an organic cure, but rather of a complex psychological means of influencing attitudes and behavior. Mesmer thus was an important figure in the history of hypnosis, a clinical technique that, while far removed from Mesmer's *baquet,* still relies on suggestion as a means of influencing the patient's state of awareness.

The Reform Movement

The growth of a scientific attitude toward mental disorders in the eighteenth century contributed to an increase in compassion for people who suffered from them. This new compassion became the basis for the reform movement of the nineteenth century. Philippe Pinel (1745–1826), a leader in the reform of French mental hospitals, had expressed great sympathy for the plight of the deranged. He firmly believed that they required humane care and treatment. Although this orientation is widely accepted by both professional workers and the public today, Pinel's ideas were far from commonplace in his time. Pinel had to fight against the view that institutions for the insane were needed more to protect society than to help the deranged.

An important step toward humane treatment of the mentally ill occurred on May 25, 1815, when the British House of Commons ordered a "Parliamentary Inquiry into the Madhouses of England." One of these, the Hospital of St. Mary of Bethlehem in London, had become known for the noise and chaos prevailing within it. The activities in this "madhouse" were of such great interest to the public that visitors often came to observe the antics of the patients at Bethlehem (from which the word *bedlam* is derived). Tickets were even sold to this popular tourist attraction (see Figure 1-9). A full-scale investigation was initiated after incidents of physical abuse at the hospital were revealed by a citizen's committee, which rallied public support for enlightened legislation on behalf of the mentally ill.

By the middle of the nineteenth century, the growing acceptance of humanitarian ideas had led to a broad recognition of the need to reform social institutions. Vigorous movements were begun to establish protective and benign asylums for the mentally ill. The sometimes huge asylums for the insane that were built in the nineteenth century came into existence because it was felt that the only way to treat mentally disturbed people was to isolate them from the damaging influences of family, friends, and community. Accompanying this view was the belief in **moral treatment.** This

Figure 1-9   This drawing by William Hogarth, for his series *The Rake's Progress,* shows two women visitors who have purchased admission tickets to view the antics of the patients at an insane asylum. Although it is hard for us to believe today, tickets for such viewings were sold at Bethlehem Hospital in London until the late eighteenth century, and people enjoyed the novelty of these sights much as they would enjoy attending a circus.

approach sought to control and rehabilitate the patient through a fixed schedule that encouraged regular habits; kind treatment with a minimum of restraint; a daily visit from the hospital superintendent, who assumed the role of persuader and inspirational leader; calm, pleasant surroundings; accommodations that separated patients with different degrees of disturbance; proper diet; some medication; and organized physical and mental activities (see Figure 1-10).

The Reform Movement in America   The eighteenth century was not a good time to be insane in the fledgling British colonies; often the mentally ill simply languished in jail. In early colonial days the mentally ill generally were ignored unless they were thought to be a nuisance or a menace to the community. In this way, the insane became identified with criminals and paupers. In some communities a group of these people would be loaded into a stagecoach in the middle of the night and dumped in the town square of some distant locale. The Philadelphia Almshouse, erected in 1732, illustrates the type of public institution in which the mentally ill were placed. The Almshouse served the poor, the infirm, and the psychologically disturbed. In 1750, Benjamin Franklin wrote that the Almshouse was "by no means fitted" to treat the mentally ill and that they needed treatment in a separate hospital.

Benjamin Rush (1745–1813), a signer of the Declaration of Independence, is often credited with the founding of American psychiatry. He believed that "madness" was caused by engorgement of the blood vessels of the brain. Although the treatment methods that Rush advocated (bleeding, purging, and water cures) today seem more like punishment than therapy, his work took place in a hospital rather than in a

custodial institution, and his methods were intended to reduce pressure on the brain's blood vessels and thus alleviate mental illness. The Pennsylvania Hospital, where Rush introduced his new treatment methods, was the first hospital in America to admit mentally ill patients. Rush's *Medical Inquiries and Observations Upon the Diseases of the Mind,* published in 1812, was the first American textbook on psychiatry and was used as a basic reference for more than 50 years. Figure 1-11 shows a reproduction of a "tranquilizer" chair designed by Rush. It was intended to calm patients by restraining them and depriving them of the use of their senses (Gamwell & Tomes, 1995).

The lack of humane treatment and decent facilities for the insane in America appalled Dorothea Dix (1802–1887), a Boston schoolteacher. By 1847 she had visited 18 penitentiaries, 300 county jails and houses of correction, and 500 almshouses where the mentally ill were kept. Through her personal efforts, 32 mental hospitals were constructed. Another important force in improving care and treatment of the mentally ill was an American businessman named Clifford Beers. In 1908 Beers recorded his own experiences as a mental patient in his book A *Mind That Found Itself.*

No incidents of my life have ever impressed themselves more indelibly on my memory than those of my first night in a straitjacket. Within one hour of the time I was placed in it I was suffering pain as intense as any I ever endured, and before the night had passed it had become almost unbearable. My right hand was so held that the tip of one of my fingers was all but cut by the nail of another, and soon knifelike pains began to shoot through my right arm as far as the shoulder. After four or five hours the excess of pain rendered me partially

Figure 1-10 As a result of the reform movement, mental hospitals made special efforts to provide patients with cheerful surroundings and enjoyable entertainment. For example, the Middlesex County Lunatic Asylum in England held elaborate parties for its patients on New Year's Day.

insensible to it. But for fifteen consecutive hours I remained in that instrument of torture; and not until the twelfth hour, about breakfast time the next morning, did the attendant so much as loosen a cord. (Beers, 1908/1981, p. 107)

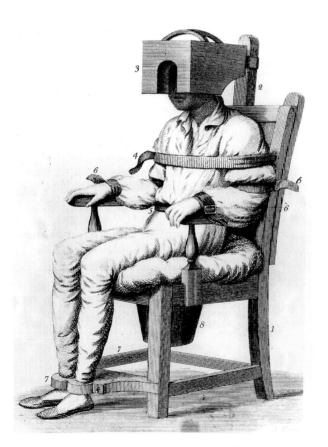

Figure 1-11 This engraving shows the tranquilizing chair developed by Benjamin Rush. Although it may appear more humane than some of the methods used earlier, today such restraints would be viewed as nontherapeutic.

After his recovery Beers became determined to make changes in the conditions in mental hospitals, and his book helped him gather support for a citizens' reform group, the National Committee for Mental Hygiene (now called the National Association for Mental Health), which was founded in 1909. The group promoted social programs aimed at preventing mental illness as well as ensuring humane treatment of the mentally ill.

Despite the progress toward more humane treatment of mental patients in the nineteenth century, the mentally ill in the United States continued to be persecuted well into the twentieth century. An example of this inhumane treatment was the experience of Perry Baird. Baird was a graduate of the University of Texas and Harvard Medical School and a successful Boston dermatologist. In 1945, at the age of 34, he was hospitalized because of a manic-depressive condition that today would probably be described as a bipolar disorder. Between 1944 and 1948 he wrote a manuscript titled *Echoes From a Dungeon Cell*. Baird's daughter later published excerpts from his manuscript that made his experience sound very much like that of Clifford Beers, many years before (Baird & Baird, 1996). Like Clifford Beers, Baird also was forced to contend with straitjacket experiences.

After reaching my room, a type of treatment known as "constraint treatment" is put into effect. . . . The procedure consists of maintaining constant restraints, alternating between straight jackets and cold packs. After three or six hours in either of these, one is allowed to go to the bathroom and then one is returned to jacket or pack, regardless of how exhausted one may be. Never in my life can I remember suffering greater physical pain.

A straight jacket was brought forward and I was instructed to put my arms in the sleeves built into a solid rectangular pattern. . . . I was then told to lie on the bed which stood at one end of an otherwise empty room next to the window. I followed orders without making any comment but with a mounting sense of indignation and deep despair. The straight jacket was made of canvas and from its edges dangled strong canvas ribbons in pairs. These were tied securely to each side and to the foot of the bed. The sixteen or eighteen pairs formed powerful anchors to the bed, allowing slight motion. . . .

I pray to God that in the future I shall be able to remember that once one has crossed the line from normal walks of life into a psychopathic hospital, one is separated from friends and relatives by walls thicker than stone—walls of prejudices and superstition.

Unfortunately, straitjackets and cold packs (being tightly wrapped in cold sheets) were not the worst of Baird's "treatments." In 1949 he underwent a prefrontal lobotomy, a surgical procedure in which a hole is drilled through the skull and nerve fibers connecting the frontal lobe with the thalamus are cut. He was never able to resume his medical practice and in 1959 was found dead in a bathtub, where he had suffered one of the seizures that had plagued him ever since the lobotomy.

Today conditions such as those that Beers and Baird described are unlikely to exist. However, although the quality of care in many mental hospitals has improved over time, the deinstitutionalization movement begun over 25 years ago has resulted in a lower standard of care for many people afflicted with mental illness and an increase in suffering for some. For instance, the situation of homeless mentally ill persons in many ways parallels the less humane treatment of the mentally ill in earlier periods of history.

Our review of the history of abnormal psychology has emphasized two themes: (1) the changing beliefs about what abnormal behavior is and what it should be about, and (2) the need for humane approaches to the mentally disturbed. The history of abnormal psychology has not been all progress; there have been advances and retreats. However, as Figure 1-12 shows, steps forward have predominated.

Recent Concepts of Abnormal Behavior

How maladaptive behavior is conceptualized influences how it is studied and how individuals with various types of thinking, mood, and behavioral problems are treated. An important focus of the twentieth century was recognition of research as a path to identifying the causes of maladaptation and developing effective therapies. Until recently, most research was based on two ideas that usually were viewed as competitive. One group of theorists and researchers saw maladaptive behavior as a product of psychological and social difficulties, whereas another saw it as organically caused. This dichotomy between psy-

chosocial and organic causation is becoming less and less tenable because psychological and organic variables are often intimately related. It is a safe prediction that research in the twenty-first century will take combinations of psychological, social, and organic variables into account. We will describe the two conceptual approaches that dominated the twentieth century and then describe the more recent integrative approach.

The Psychological Approach

Eighteenth-century theories emphasized **rational thinking** as the way to achieve personal and social adjustment. During the first half of the nineteenth century, however, the important role of **irrational thought** in both normal and abnormal behavior attracted much more attention. This shift in emphasis took place as a reaction against the views of philosophers and scientists who gave little weight to the role of emotions, motivations, and internal conflicts in human behavior. Many clinical workers and researchers began to view internal conflicts as a major cause of personal unhappiness and failure to adapt socially. This focus on emotion and irrational feelings laid the groundwork for Sigmund Freud's early twentieth-century writings about mental processes and their relationship to disturbed behavior (see Chapter 2).

The Organic Approach

Influenced by progress in physiology and anatomy, many writers interested in abnormal psychology during the nineteenth century argued that most mental disorders are caused by the direct or indirect influence of disturbances in brain function. The slogan "Mental diseases are brain diseases" became popular. Behind this perspective was the assumption that the material (brain cells) almost invariably causes the mental manifestation (personal unhappiness). The major implication of this viewpoint was that it is necessary to find out more about how the body (particularly the nervous system) works. One way of doing so was to dissect the brains of mentally disturbed individuals after their deaths. Researchers reasoned that the unusual behaviors exhibited by those individuals had been caused by structural abnormalities in the brain. Through direct examination of the brains of such people, they hoped to discover relationships between the brain and behavior. From this point of view, introspection as a path to understanding psychological disturbance held little appeal. Nor was there much interest in how thoughts direct observable behavior.

The Approaches Converge

An **interactional** or **biopsychosocial approach** currently directs the work of most researchers and clinicians. From this perspective, instances of maladaptive behavior need

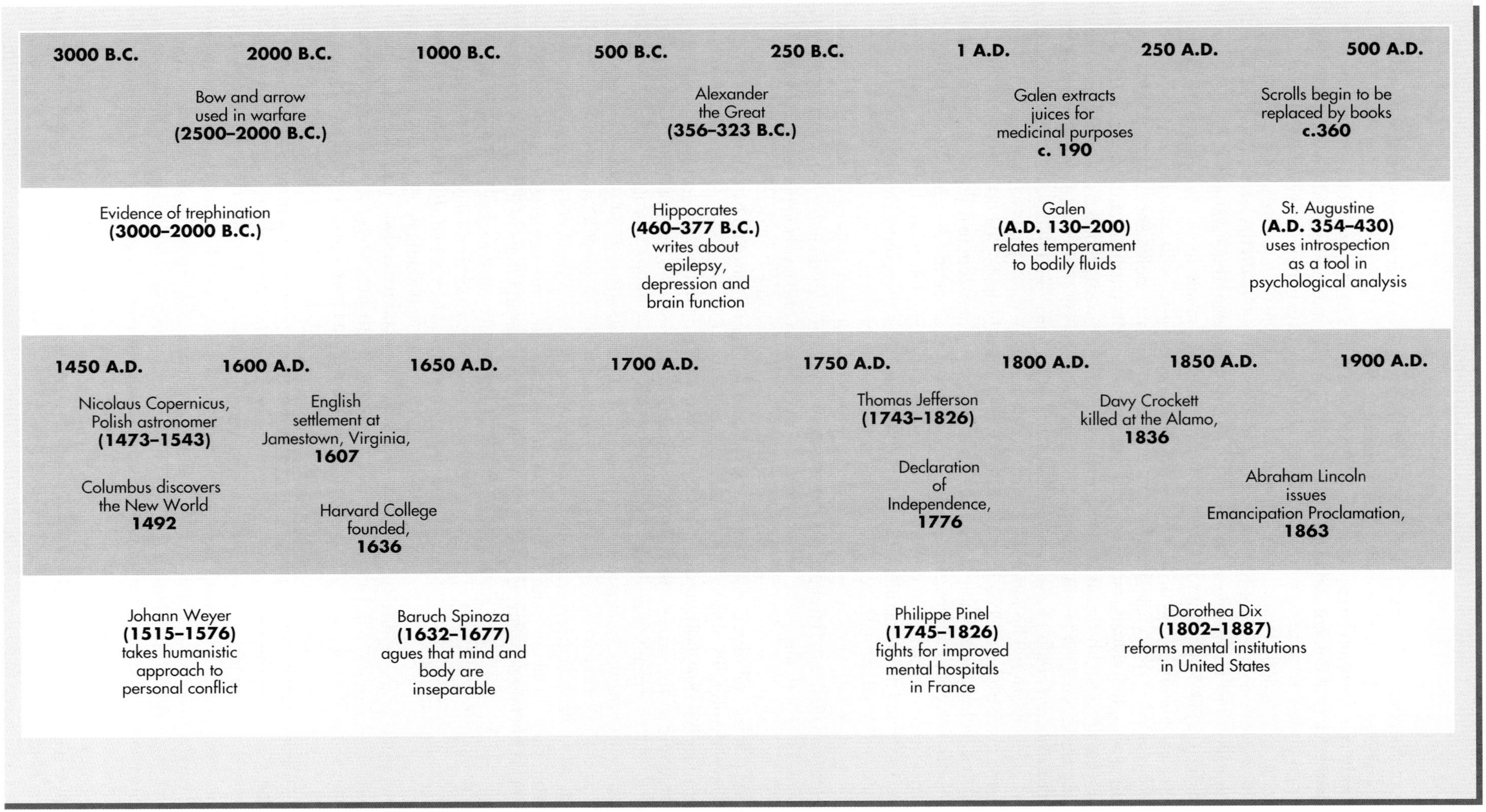

Figure 1-12 An abnormal psychology timeline: some highlights.

to be considered in terms of the operation of biological, psychological, and social variables. The relative importance or role of these factors in causation can be expected to vary depending on the particular problem. For instance, schizophrenia seems strongly linked to genetic factors. However, this does not mean that genetic factors alone determine the nature of the disorder and that psychological and social factors are unimportant. There is good reason to believe that all three factors play important roles in influencing the expression and outcome of many disorders. The relative roles of biological, psychological, and social factors vary not only among individuals, but also across stages of the life span. For example, the occurrence of certain types of depression increases in later life. In some people, depression arises primarily as a result of exposure to stressful life events, whereas in others the foremost cause of depression is genetic predisposition. The interactional perspective holds that biological, psychological, and social factors may be causes, correlates, and/or consequences in relation to various types of maladaptive behavior. Their contributions, singly and in interaction with each other, need to be evaluated and dealt with in helping people cope with problems that arise in their lives.

Research shows that there is much that is "physical" in "mental" disorders and vice versa. For example, the brain chemistry of a person with major depression is different from that of a nondepressed person, and medication can be used, often in combination with psychotherapy, to bring the brain chemistry back to normal. Similarly, a person who is suffering from hardening of the arteries in the brain—which reduces the flow of blood and thus oxygen in the brain—may experience such "mental" symptoms as confusion and forgetfulness. We will discuss the interactional approach in more detail in Chapter 2 and see that the inner lives of individuals, their social environments, and the ways in which their bodies function interact and influence each other.

Vulnerability, Resilience, and Coping

The interactional approach leads to questions that play roles in clinicians' work as they try to understand what is causing a particular problem and as they devise effective therapies. The questions include: What made this person vulnerable to the disorder? What set of circumstances activated it? What needs to be done to help him or her cope with problems in a more effective manner?

When we talk about how well people adapt, it is important to consider the conditions under which the adaptations are made. The same person may handle a frightening or difficult situation well at one time and maladaptively at others. Some people may behave adaptively in the same situation that others handle poorly. This diversity suggests that it is insufficient to argue that maladaptive behavior occurs simply because of the nature of the situation or stress associated with a particular event.

Stress, our reaction to a situation that poses demands, constraints, or opportunities, is usually not a pleasant state. People are likely to experience psychological stress when they have to deal with an unexpected or unusual change, such as a natural disaster. They are likely to experience even greater stress than usual when the change occurs at the same time as a severe life crisis (such as the death of a loved one) or at the beginning of a critical developmental period (such as adolescence). The average number of stressful life events (such as family disturbances or the serious illness of a parent, brother, or sister) is greater for clinical cases than for comparable control persons. Although cause and effect are not clear, this added stress may lead to poorer adaptation. However some people—even those with clinically diagnosed disorders—are not sidetracked by stress. They seem to roll with the punches and function well in the face of adversity. We might think of some *risk* and *protective factors* as characterizing each person's life. The risk factors contribute to vulnerability and the protective factors to resilience.

Vulnerability refers to how likely we are to respond maladaptively to certain situations. An individual can be an effective coper in one situation but not in another. Vulnerability may be increased through heredity, such as having a schizophrenic parent; by certain personality characteristics, such as a tendency to worry or feel anxious; by the lack of certain skills, such as the inability to make decisions calmly; or by a buildup of unexpected negative experiences. Some people are more vulnerable in all situations because they deal less effectively with what happens to them in daily life. Others are more vulnerable simply because of a combination of recent stressful events. Certainly people are more vulnerable in particular kinds of situations that remind them of former problems or difficulties. For example, upon seeing a child swept away in a river, a person who had seen one of her younger brothers killed in an accident when she was 5 might freeze, while someone who had not had such an experience might be able to act in time to save the child.

Certain life conditions in and of themselves increase people's vulnerability and increase their risk of maladaptive behavior. People who share these conditions become a part of a high-risk group that is more likely than the rest of the population to experience the negative effects of stress. Population groups that may be at high risk for certain conditions include children and adolescents, the aged and the disabled, and disadvantaged minority groups.

Protective factors may compensate for high-risk elements in someone's life and contribute to **resilience,** the ability to function effectively in the face of adversity and to "bounce back" following significant stress. There are people who, despite their exposure to multiple risk factors, do not show the dire consequences one might expect under the circumstances. These resilient people can behave adaptively despite undesirable living conditions or personally threatening experiences.

Several protective factors have emerged as recurrent themes in the lives of children who behave with resilience despite growing up in difficult circumstances (Werner, 1995). These resilient children are engaging to other people (both adults and peers); they have good communication and problem-solving skills, including the ability to recruit substitute caregivers; they often have a talent or hobby that is valued by their elders or peers; and they have faith that their own actions can make a positive difference in their lives. In general, resilience is enhanced when children have warm ties with others who encourage trust, personal autonomy, and initiative. The following account describes two resilient individuals: a mother and her daughter, who is a high school student. Each of them must deal daily with the challenges of economic insecurity and family difficulties.

It's 10 o'clock, time to wake up Mama. Frustration washes over me because I'm sitting on my bed, covered with books. One by one, I push them aside.

I open my bedroom door into a wall of darkness. I look back into my lighted room with regret and creep into the living room. All the lights are off and the shades are drawn.

On the couch lies Mama. Her hair is standing on all ends and her face is a perfect mask of peace. I give her shoulder a shake, telling her that it's 10 o'clock. Instantly, her eyes pop open and she starts to get up. I turn to go back to my bright room, when she asks me to make her a cup of coffee. I swivel around, and a spark of anger flicks through my eyes. The guilt quickly replaces it. How can I be angry? Every day she gets up and goes to work on four or five, sometimes only two hours of sleep. She even works overtime every chance she gets. I tell her not to push herself, but she says we need the money. And all she's asking me for is a cup of coffee.

So I go to the kitchen. I leave the lights off, as if light would be an intrusion on Mama's dark world. I pour a cup of coffee and add milk and sugar just the way Mama likes it. I take it back to her. She's already dressed and sitting up on the couch.

I hand her the cup of coffee and she thanks me. I tell her Dad called and said he wasn't coming to do the work on the porch on Saturday. She simply nods her head as she drinks her coffee.

All too quickly, she has to leave. She hands me my $3.60 for school and kisses me on the cheek. As always, she tells me she loves me. Then she walks out the door and drives off to her job.

I watch from the door in wonder. How does she do it? How does she always remember to give me $3.60 for school? How does she always remember to tell me that she loves me? How does she work all night and do errands all day? How does she raise me and my sisters on her own? She never gives up or says, "I can't go today." She never, ever, doesn't get up, no matter how little sleep she's gotten.

I shut and lock the door. I walk silently through Mama's dark world and go back to my bright room. I replace the books on my lap. Before I begin again, I turn my eyes toward God and silently thank the Lord for Mama. (*New York Times,* March 25, 1995, p. 15) ■

Resilient people are often described as being good copers. **Coping** refers to how people deal with difficulties and attempt to overcome them. **Coping skills** are the techniques available to an individual in making such attempts. A number of general skills are useful in handling stressful situations. These include thinking constructively, dealing with problems as they arise, behaving flexibly, and providing feedback to oneself about which tactics work in a given situation and which ones do not. How useful any particular skill will be depends upon the nature of the situation and the individual's vulnerabilities and assets. Having an effective repertory of coping skills strengthens a person's sense of self-control and self-direction. By gaining greater control over our behavior, we may be able to alter environmental conditions that influence us.

Clinical interventions are ways of helping people deal with their vulnerabilities and improve their resilience. The intervention selected for someone who is experiencing a short-term crisis, such as the serious illness of a loved one, might be a tranquilizing drug. In this case, the tranquilizer reduces vulnerability to intense anxiety experienced over a specific period of time. In other cases, insight into the person's desires, motivations, and conflicts is needed in order to help the individual cope more effectively with stress and become less vulnerable to the crises that are the inevitable ingredients of every human life. Sometimes the person needs to learn new skills or behaviors that are effective in dealing with difficult situations. For some people, the way they think about a situation needs to be changed. If a low test grade makes you think, "I'm dumb; it's no use trying to finish this course," later academic performance might be very different than it would be if you thought, "I didn't study very effectively; I'd better organize my work better and check with the professor before the next test to ask about the points that aren't clear." Clinicians thus will vary their approaches depending on their assessment of the factors in a given case and the psychological perspective or viewpoints they favor.

One of the guiding principles of this book is that each person has a particular set of vulnerability and resilience factors that influence how well he or she adapts to life's circumstances.

In addition, people differ in how supportive their environment is in helping them adjust to adversity. Seven-year-old Denton may adapt well when he has a sympathetic teacher, when his parents are getting along well, and when he is healthy. However, if he has a teacher whom he hates, if his parents bicker half the night and are on the edge of divorce, and if he is constipated, he may become much more upset about not being a starting player on his soccer team than he might otherwise. Or if Mrs. Block has just lost an important client for her firm and comes home to find that someone has smashed into her car as it sat parked in the driveway, and then her 12-year-old son tells her he has just left his violin on the school bus, she may not respond as constructively as she might under other circumstances.

The concepts of vulnerability and resilience have implications not only for treatment and prevention, but also for improving our understanding of the determinants of maladaptive behavior. Three dimensions of resilience seem especially important: (1) *temperamental factors*, such as activity level and responsiveness to others; (2) *family factors*, such as warmth, cohesion, and caring; and (3) *external support*, such as neighbors, parents of friends, and members of the clergy who are supportive and actively want to help. The following anecdote illustrates this last factor:

> In the foyer of a walk-up apartment building in Harlem there was a large frame on the wall within the entrance way. The photographs of children who lived in the apartment building were pasted on the frame with a written request that if anyone saw any of these children endangered on the street to bring them back to the apartment house. My thoughts focus on those who conceived the idea, put up the sign, and joined in providing photographs of their children. Can there be a better example of adult competence and concern for the safety of children? Is this effort not a dramatic reflection of what we mean when we seek to describe "protective" factors on behalf of the well-being of children under stress? (Garmezy, 1993, pp. 134–135) ∎

In this book we will present a number of different perspectives on why maladaptive behavior occurs and how adaptive behavior can be substituted for it. Running through our discussion of abnormal psychology will be a consideration of the effects of vulnerability and resilience on the outcome of any particular situation. The more we understand what causes an individual to feel stressed, and the more we can identify the factors that produce vulnerability, the clearer the sources of the maladaptive behavior will be and the more likely we will be to come up with effective treatment procedures. This search for understanding is what the study of abnormal psychology is all about.

The Epidemiology of Maladaptive Behavior

While the primary task of a clinician is to diagnose and treat illness in individual patients, the epidemiologist investigates the occurrence of illness in populations and identifies factors (e.g., heredity and family history) that influence their occurrence. Psychologists use findings from **epidemiological research** to help them understand patterns and possible relationships between maladaptive behaviors of certain populations or groups and a variety of environmental and behavioral factors. Information for epidemiological research may come from analyses of various types of data, such as hospital and clinic records, the geographical distribution of mental disorders, and the types of community facilities available for the treatment of the mentally disturbed. For example, a study of institutional records has shown that the northeastern and Pacific Coast regions of the United States have had consistently higher rates of schizophrenia over an 83-year period than have other regions of the country (Torrey & Bowler, 1990). Research is needed to identify the reasons for these geographical differences.

Another example of the role of epidemiological research emerges from the finding that a number of basic personal factors, such as age and sex, are correlated with types of disorders and use of clinical facilities. Table 1-1 shows the rates per 100,000 population for different age groups admitted to outpatient facilities for the treatment of mental and behavioral problems. It is noteworthy that children and youth are admitted at a higher rate relative to their number in the population than are both the elderly and those aged 45 to 64. In contrast, the admission rates for the elderly are low relative to their number in the population. Table 1-2 lists a number of examples of recent epidemiological evidence.

Table 1-1	
Admission to Outpatient Mental Health Services in the Civilian Population	
Age Group	Rate per 100,000
Under 18	872.3
18–24	1098.9
25–44	1276.2
45–64	567.4
65 and over	229.6
All ages	888.6

Source: Based on National Institute of Mental Health (1990), p. 164.

Table 1-2
Some Epidemiological Facts

1. During the course of any given year, 22% to 23% of the adult population are affected by one or more mental disorders.
2. Six percent have addictive disorders.
3. Approximately one-sixth of people with mental disorders are severely disabled by their problems.
4. Most have disorders that persist for at least 1 year.
5. Approximately 5% to 9% of children ages 9 to 17 have serious emotional problems.

Source: Based on *Mental Health: A Report of the Surgeon General* (1999) and Redmond (1998).

Table 1-3
Epidemiological Concepts

Incidence. The rate of new cases during a defined period of time (for example, one year).
Prevalence. The rate of both new and old (existing) cases for a defined period of time (for example, 6-month prevalence).
Lifetime prevalence. The proportion of people in the general population who have ever had a particular disorder.
Risk factor. A specific characteristic or condition whose presence is associated with an increased likelihood that a specific disorder is present or will develop at a later time.

Incidence, Prevalence, and Risk Factors

Epidemiologists conduct surveys to estimate the extent of a health problem. Although their primary focus is on the occurrence of various types of abnormality, epidemiologists also gather information about the frequency of behavior in the normal population. This information often provides a valuable context for interpreting statistics about conditions that are clearly pathological. Epidemiological research has identified a number of factors that must be attended to in order to ensure the accuracy of survey results. These include representative sampling of the population, clearly worded questions, and careful training of interviewers.

One survey has shown that almost half of all Americans—48%—have experienced a mental disorder at some point in their lives (Kessler et al., 1994). The results of this survey are important because it included face-to-face interviews with more than 8,000 people between the ages of 15 and 54 in 34 states. The survey found that the most common disorder was major depression, with 10% of Americans experiencing the problem in a given year and 17% having had major depression at some point in life. The second most common disorder was alcohol dependence, with 7% having the problem during a given year and 14% at some point in life. The most severe psychiatric disorders were concentrated among a small number of people who tend to suffer from several disorders at once.

Table 1-3 gives the definitions of a number of concepts used in epidemiological research. **Incidence** data relate to the number of new cases of a specific condition that arise during a particular period of time. For example, if 10 out of 1,000 people studied developed new cases of depression, the incidence rate would be 1%. **Prevalence** data describe the frequency of occurrence of a given condition among a certain population at a particular point in time. For example, if, on a given date, 100 cases of depression were counted in a community of 1,000 people, the prevalence rate would be 10%.

In addition to incidence and prevalence, another important epidemiological concept is **risk factor.** This concept is based on the finding of a statistically significant association between a disorder and some other factor (e.g., lung cancer and smoking; cardiovascular disease and high cholesterol level). Risk factors are those characteristics, variables, or hazards that, if present for a given individual, make it more likely that this individual, rather than someone selected at random from the general population, will develop a disorder. Risk factors can change in relation to a developmental phase or a new stressor in one's life, and they can reside within the individual, family, community, or social institutions. Much current research is focusing on the interplay between biological risk factors and psychosocial risk factors and how they can be modified. While a particular disorder might have some unique risk factors (e.g., a particular gene defect), many risk factors are common to many disorders—for example, below-average intelligence, social disadvantage, maternal mental disorder, paternal criminality, and living in an area with a high rate of community disorganization or inadequate schools.

Risk factors can serve as early warning signs of the need for intervention regarding particular conditions. When risk factors are identified, they may also be useful in suggesting prevention efforts. For example, children who have been abused or neglected might be given the opportunity to have positive experiences with caring adults as a step toward preventing long-term frustration and anger. The following are risk factors that have been identified for violent behavior (Reid & Balis, 1987):

- History of aggressive, destructive behavior
- History of repeated traffic violations (reckless driving, etc.)
- History of abuse and neglect in childhood
- Childhood history of severe hyperactivity and restlessness

- Habitual alcohol use and dependence
- Suicidal attempts and gestures
- Hypersexuality
- Low frustration tolerance
- Low self-esteem and failure to achieve
- Inability to examine one's own behavior
- Impulsivity
- Self-centeredness

The value of identifying risk factors is reflected in studies of the relationship between diagnosis of abnormal behavior and the likelihood of committing violent acts. Contrary to what many people believe, only a small minority of all people who commit violent acts have a psyological disorder. For instance, epidemiological research on a large representative sample of residents in several cities has shown that persons diagnosed with anxiety disorders have low rates of violence (Swanson et al., 1990). However, some disorders are associated with a higher than average risk of violent behavior. For example, there is a statistical connection between psychosis (particularly schizophrenia) and violence and between drug- and alcohol-related disorders and violence (Hodgins et al., 1996; Torrey, 1994). Psychotic delusions and hallucinations may provide the individual with a rationale for violence because of the need to counterattack. If substance abuse were reduced through some combination of education and treatment and if more effective long-term treatment of patients with psychotic disorders were provided, violence in these groups might be substantially reduced.

Socioeconomic status as well as diagnosis affects the likelihood of violence. Young males of lower socioeconomic status are found to be at substantially higher than average risk levels for violence. There is also a relationship between the number of diagnostic categories used in describing individuals and the risk of violent behavior. As Figure 1-13 shows, the rate of reported violent behavior increases sharply with the number of diagnostic categories assigned to an individual by clinical workers. A greater number of diagnostic categories might be taken as an indicator of the complexity of a case and the gross amount and variety of psychopatho-logy present. Thus, the more symptoms and problems someone has, the more likely that violent behavior will be among them. We should bear in mind the limitations of this epidemiological survey, however. The reports of violent behavior came from the survey respondents themselves. The results might have been different if reports from independent observers had been available.

In addition to establishing connections between various factors and disorders, epidemiological surveys are valuable in correcting false assumptions (Robins & Regier, 1991). It had been thought that minority groups must have high rates of antisocial personality and substance abuse disorders because they have high rates of arrest and in-

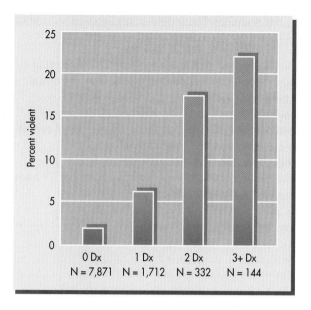

Figure 1-13 Percentage of respondents reporting violent behavior by the number of diagnoses (*Dx*).

Source: Swanson et al., 1990, p. 767.

carceration. However, recent evidence suggests that the high arrest and incarceration rates among minority groups cannot be explained simply by diagnoses of antisocial personality and substance abuse disorders. Also, until recently it had been generally assumed that women are particularly liable to develop psychological problems. However, recent surveys have shown that psychological disorders in men are at least as common as they are in women. Women are more likely to have depressive and anxiety disorders, but men are more apt to have substance abuse and antisocial personality disorders (Robins & Regier, 1991).

Table 1-4 lists several factors that are significantly related to the presence of mental illness although cause and effect cannot be definitely determined. However, it seems clear that interpersonal, economic, and educational factors play important roles in the frequency of abnormal behaviors. There is also evidence that people who have good coping skills and supportive friends and relatives are less likely to suffer psychological distress than those who do not.

Mental illness has an effect not only on diagnosed individuals, but also on their family members. An estimated 30 to 40 million people experience some direct consequences because of their close personal ties to someone who has a mental illness. In this book, we will focus not only on the effect of maladaptive behavior on the person whose problems are described but also on the impact of the behavior on family members—parents, husbands, wives, and children.

Table 1-4

Factors Associated With Rates of Diagnosed Mental Disorder

1. *Age.* Younger people have higher rates than older people.
2. *Marital status.* Separated, divorced, and single people have higher rates than the married and widowed.
3. *Education.* Less educated people have higher rates than people who have more education.
4. *Personal income.* The lower the income, the higher the rates.
5. *Employment status.* Unemployed people have higher rates than employed people.
6. *Contact with friends.* Lack of social contacts is associated with relatively high rates.
7. *Satisfaction with relationships with friends and relatives.* The greater the satisfaction, the lower the rates.
8. *Marital happiness.* The greater the degree of marital happiness, the lower the rates.

Classifying Abnormal Behavior

Epidemiological studies reflect the modern emphasis on objectivity. One question epidemiologists frequently ask is: How many people have particular types of disorders? This question presupposes the existence of a scheme for classifying various types of problems. For many years much effort has been expended in devising reliable classification systems. Typically, classification takes note of the symptoms that characterize various types of problems. Some disorders are marked especially by anxiety (e.g., feelings of fear or dread, rapid heart rate, and muscle tension); others involve disturbances of perception and thought and significant distortions of reality (these symptoms characterize many psychotic conditions); and still others involve unusual mood states (such as extreme sadness or happiness). Because the classification of disorders plays a key role in understanding and treating maladaptive behavior and in conducting clinical research, Chapter 3 will be devoted to this topic.

Seeking Help for Abnormal Behavior

Treatment of problems related to abnormal behavior requires that individuals in need of help seek it or that others seek it for them. We need some idea of why people seek help. Although people seek help for a variety of reasons and from a variety of clinical facilities, almost half of the five-and-a-half million Americans over the age of 9 who suffer from severe mental illness are not receiving any kind of professional treatment (Torrey, 1997). Many people in need of help are not receiving it for economic reasons or because of the lack of clinical facilities where they live (Mental Health, United States, 1996; *Mental Health: A Report of the Surgeon General,* 1999).

Reasons for Clinical Contacts

Some people seek professional help because they are dissatisfied with themselves and certain aspects of their lives; others do so because of concerns expressed by family members, friends, or co-workers; still others are forced to see clinicians because they have gotten into trouble in the community.

Personal Unhappiness In the following case, personal unhappiness seems to have been the factor that led this person to seek help:

> Jack Farmer was a 40-year-old executive in a large multinational corporation. From all outward appearances, any differences he might have had from other people were positive. Whatever weaknesses he had were minor. For example, his athletic ability was probably below average. The opinion of his company and community was that Jack Farmer was a very well-functioning individual. While he and his wife and two children got along reasonably well, Jack had some concerns that shaped his family role, particularly as his children approached high school age. These concerns had to do with the burdens of family responsibility, especially the need he felt to ensure his family's happiness should anything happen to him. He occasionally commented to his wife that television commercials about the need to have plenty of life insurance seem to have been written specifically with him in mind. However, Jack was concerned about more than money. He felt that he should be a closer friend to his children and less distant from his wife than he often was. He was also very concerned about the issues of pollution and destruction of the natural environment. His concerns often led to his feeling depressed and hopeless about the future.
>
> One Sunday Jack read a newspaper article about a local mental health center that had opened recently. The article pointed out that the center's services were not restricted to severely disturbed individuals, that perfectly normal people who had hit a rough spot in their lives might find it valuable to talk with an expert about their personal problems. After several weeks of internal debate ("Could I be a little crazy?"; "I'd be ashamed if my friends ever found out that I went to a shrink"), Jack decided to go to the mental health center.

By conventional standards, Jack Farmer's case is not serious. He sought help because of personal dissatisfactions and concerns. Wrestling further with his personal tensions seemed worse to him than his fear of being stigmatized if he sought professional help.

The Concerns of Others Sometimes it is difficult even for professionals to decide what the dividing line should be between maladaptive and merely unusual behavior. In the following case, there was no agreement about whether the woman concerned was psychotic (out of touch with reality) and needed institutionalization, or whether her behavior was simply unusual and presented no hazard to her or her family:

Mary Waverly was in her late twenties. A university graduate, she had run a successful boutique in a large western city until shortly before the birth of her daughter, Alice, two years earlier. During the year before Alice was born, Mary's mother had been treated for cancer. She died when Alice was fourteen months old. During Alice's first year and a half, the baby had surgery several times to correct a birth defect.

Recently, Mary's husband had attempted to have her committed to a psychiatric hospital. He said he was concerned about their daughter's welfare. Mary had become preoccupied with rather unusual religious ideas. Although she came from a very religious family, until recently—when she joined a cult group—her behavior had not seemed out of the ordinary. Since joining the group she refused to have sexual relations with her husband because he was not a "believer." Although she seemed to take good care of her child, she made all decisions only after listening to the "voice of the Lord."

When Mary Waverly was examined, her judgment did not seem impaired, her intelligence was found to be above average, and her religious thoughts, although they took up a great deal of her time, did not seem to differ from those of other enthusiastic converts to cult groups. A pediatrician examined her daughter and reported that she was well cared for. A question was raised about what Mary Waverly might do if she thought God told her to harm her child or someone else. Neither of the clinicians who examined her was willing to give a definite answer to this question.

Mary Waverly didn't think she had a mental disorder and didn't think she needed treatment. One of the clinicians agreed. He believed that her behavior was unusual but that she was not mentally ill. Another clinician thought she had paranoid schizophrenia and should be hospitalized for drug therapy. What should be done when professionals disagree? In this case, after hearing the conflicting views, Mr. Waverly decided not to press for hospitalization.

Legal and Community Problems Mild personal maladaptations like Jack Farmer's affect the lives of the individual who suffers from them and possibly a small number of other people. Mary Waverly's behavior was a matter of concern to her husband because he was worried that she might harm their daughter. In the case of Charles Clay, a legal problem arose over something he had done.

Charles Clay, aged 45, owned what had been a successful 24-hour-a-day grocery store. Now, however, he was having increasing difficulty containing his anger toward his customers. Until 5 years ago he had been a cheerful, friendly merchant. Then his wife died, and his personality seemed to change. Increasingly he worried that people were trying to shoplift his merchandise. (There was a problem with a few high school students who frequented his store right after school.) As time went on, he began to confront customers with his suspicions and even to demand that some of them submit to being searched.

Not surprisingly, Charles's business began to decline. When this happened, he got very angry and even more suspicious. The culminating event occurred when a woman entered the store, walked around for a few minutes, and then bought a newspaper. When he tried to search her (at the same time yelling, "Don't tell me you were just looking around!"), she ran from the store and summoned the police. The ensuing police investigation led him to seek advice from his lawyer, who had been a friend since high school. Although Charles insisted that "there is nothing the matter with me," his anger and suspiciousness bothered his lawyer. Using tact and persuasion, the lawyer got him to agree to visit a psychiatrist. Unfortunately, the visit did not work out well. He was reluctant to talk about his concerns with the psychiatrist and was angered by what he viewed as the psychiatrist's inquisitiveness. He refused to return for a second visit. Nevertheless, the lawyer was able to get Charles out of trouble with the police. Unfortunately, several months later he was arrested and convicted of physically attacking another customer.

Many people saw Charles Clay as having problems that he refused to recognize. In spite of the social consensus about the maladaptive quality of his behavior, Charles gave himself a clean bill of health. In part because of his failure to perceive his own behavior accurately, he eventually got into trouble with the law. His first contact with the police did not result in formal charges; the community's agents recognized his psychological difficulties, and the focus of their attention was on helping a citizen with his personal problems. The second contact, however, resulted in punishment for a crime. Society had decided that he was not going to help himself and moved to protect itself.

Gross failure to see oneself accurately, as illustrated by the case of Charles Clay, is characteristic of several of the most serious forms of maladaptive behavior. In such cases, it is a highly positive development if the person begins to suspect that his or her behavior is contributing to difficulties in getting along with others.

Sources of Help

People whose behavior is maladaptive can receive help in various types of facilities staffed by several types of mental health specialists.

Types of Treatment Facilities Despite the decrease in recent years in number of beds in state mental hospitals, these institutions continue to play an important role in caring for the most disturbed and troublesome patients in the U.S. mental health system. State hospitals serve as 24-hour emergency backups, the institutions of last resort and ultimate responsibility. Nevertheless, most experts agree about the desirability of treating people in the community as early as possible so as to avoid institutionalization.

Since the 1960s there has been a movement to **deinstitutionalize,** or return to the community, mental patients whose problems can be expected to continue for long periods. Under the banner of deinstitutionalization, many former hospital patients now live in community-based group homes, boarding houses, residential hotels (often in undesirable neighborhoods), and subsidized apartments (see Figure 1-14). This change, based partly on concern for the civil rights of the individual, is also a result of scientific advances like the use of antipsychotic drugs. Such drugs make it possible for many people to function adaptively enough so that they don't need to be institutionalized, although many of these individuals still behave in a marginal, ineffective fashion.

The development of community support programs in conjunction with established therapeutic programs for chronically mentally ill individuals offers promise of better lives for many people. At the present time, however, a comprehensive range of residential, therapeutic, and social services is not available in many communities. As a result, many people who might be able to function in a protected environment or with psychological support or supervision of antipsychotic medication instead end up as part of the homeless population in large urban areas. Chapter 17 will look at this problem in more detail.

Figure 1-14 Group homes provide for living arrangements with opportunities for independent living, self-care, and contact with others.

Types of Mental Health Specialists Most of the behavior patterns with which this book deals are of special interest to four groups of mental health specialists: clinical and counseling psychologists, psychiatrists, psychiatric social workers, and psychiatric nurses. A **clinical psychologist** holds a graduate degree, usually a Ph.D. or Psy.D., and specializes in abnormal behavior. Clinical psychologists are trained to diagnose and treat personality problems that are not medical or organic in nature. They also plan and conduct research investigations. **Counseling psychologists** may hold a Ph.D. or an Ed.D. degree and typically work with clients experiencing current life stress rather than ongoing problems. They also work with people who are trying to clarify their vocational goals. A **psychiatrist** is a physician (an M.D.) with postgraduate training and experience in treating emotional disorders. Psychiatrists have legal responsibilities in commitment proceedings and in the supervision of mental hospitals. Somatic therapies, such as drugs and electroconvulsive therapy, are supervised by psychiatrists.

A **psychiatric social worker,** holder of a graduate degree in social work, is most often concerned with the link between a person who displays problematic behavior and his or her home environment. Psychiatric social workers are trained in mental health care and how to work with families and help them utilize social agencies and other community resources to get practical help with such things as finances. A **psychiatric nurse** has special training in the care of mentally ill patients. Psychiatric nurses play a variety of roles. They are skilled in working closely with patients and understanding their needs so that all contacts the patient has with others during a hospitalization have as much of a therapeutic focus as possible. Within hospital settings, psychiatric nurses often supervise ward personnel and train them in the approach they should take with each patient.

The activities of these mental health workers—especially of psychiatrists, clinical psychologists, and social workers—often overlap. For example, all three are trained to conduct psychotherapy and counseling. Table 1-5 shows the numbers of men and women in each of these mental health specialties.

A survey conducted by the American Psychological Association (1996) revealed that clinical practitioners on average spend 44% of their time doing psychotherapy. Other activities include intellectual and personality assessment (14%), teaching and supervision (11%), and administration (9%).

The following account by a clinical psychologist accurately reflects the diversity of activities in which some clinicians engage:

I wish the time passed more slowly because there is just so much to do. From talking to my clinician friends I know I'm

Table 1-5			
Number of Clinically Trained Mental Health Personnel			
Professional Group	Total Number	Number of Men	Number of Women
Psychology	69,817	39,098	30,719
Psychiatry	28,970	21,651	7,319
Social Work	92,841	21,497	71,344
Source: *Mental Health, United States, 1996*			

not alone in feeling that way. Part of the problem is that most of us don't just do one thing. Sure, some do mainly therapy and others are primarily diagnosticians. But most of us do many things.

Take me, for example. I work in a big-city general hospital that has two wards for psychiatric cases and a large outpatient clinic. Many of these patients are not in very good contact with reality. In some cases police officers picked them up because they were wandering aimlessly around town in the middle of winter, in the dead of night. In other cases, they are people who have had some recent situational stress and are just not able to come to terms with it.

In still other cases, physicians who have patients on other wards in the hospital ask us for help. Yesterday, for example, a surgeon referred a case to me because the patient, who is supposed to undergo abdominal surgery tomorrow, has been in such a psychological panic that the doctor felt something had to be done—and he didn't know what to do. So far, I've talked with the patient twice. Really, all I did was listen and let her ventilate her feelings. You'd be amazed how much just listening in a sympathetic and supportive manner does to help a person who is going through a stressful situation. When I told the surgeon that this patient was very worried about getting too strong a dose of anesthetic and dying, he was amazed. He said the patient had never mentioned that worry to him.

About twenty percent of my time is spent dealing with problems nonpsychiatric physicians need help with. Perhaps thirty percent is spent doing therapy either on the wards or in the outpatient clinic. Another twenty percent involves administering psychological tests to patients with particular problems. The rest of the time I do research. That's what usually gets squeezed out when a number of pressing clinical problems arise. That's when I most need a time-stretcher. But all the pressure is nothing compared to how much I like what I'm doing. I wouldn't trade with anybody.

Types of Treatment Although some stereotypes of clinical psychologists and psychiatrists portray them as all-knowing dispensers of advice, the work of professionals in the mental health field is challenging because it requires the ability to think on one's feet correctly and quickly size up a problem ("Is this person depressed enough to be

thinking about suicide?") and to devise appropriate and sometimes unusual treatment plans for clients. This means that while clinicians strive for complete objectivity in their work and try to use proven techniques, they often must devise on-the-spot tactics to deal with the particular problem confronting them. Various professional groups concerned with diagnosis and treatment of maladaptive behavior often have different theoretical perspectives. For example, psychologists tend to emphasize the link between patients' psychological states and their social ties (e.g., their relationships with family and friends), whereas psychiatrists often take a much more biological approach to treatment, for example, by prescribing medications.

There are many therapeutic approaches applicable to mental health problems. Some are specific to particular disorders; others seem to have wide applicability. As we review the various types of maladaptive behavior, we will describe the therapeutic approaches that seem to be especially relevant. Chapter 16 compares different forms of therapy and raises several general questions about how to evaluate different approaches. One question of particular importance is, What are the active therapeutic ingredients in a given approach? Another is, How can the value of a therapeutic approach be determined objectively? Research has provided clues to the answers to these questions.

Research in Abnormal Psychology

Scientific investigation, or the use of the scientific method, has greatly increased our understanding of abnormal behavior, how to treat it, and how to prevent it. As a consequence, observation and fact have replaced beliefs and hope in the effort to help people suffering from behavior disorders. Most of the scientific information on which contemporary abnormal psychology is based comes from in-depth studies of deviant people. Although researchers may differ on their interpretation of data, they agree that careful observation is essential for scientific progress.

Observing Behavior

Observation and description are important first steps in the scientific process; eventually they lead to the formulation of hypotheses that can be tested experimentally and applied in clinical situations. As the following passage illustrates, observation plays an important role in psychological treatment:

I noticed that Mr. R. never looked directly at me. He answered my questions but always looked the other way. He seemed terribly shy and afraid. I was tempted to ask him what he was afraid of, but decided not to because he might take my comment as a criticism.

Some clinicians might have decided to ask Mr. R. about his apparent fearfulness. However, all would agree on the importance of carefully observing and noting his anxious behavior.

The scientific process always begins with some kind of noteworthy observation. Researchers often stumble onto important discoveries quite by accident. When this happens, a good researcher heeds the advice of B. F. Skinner, one of the outstanding psychological theorists of the twentieth century. "When you run into something interesting, drop everything and study it" (Skinner, 1959).

One problem in psychological research is that people cannot be completely disinterested observers of themselves. Personal values, goals, and interests, together with cultural norms, influence our judgments about the success or failure of human adaptation. Maladaptation is neither a universal nor a timeless concept. Behavior that may be quite adaptive in one society may be a failure in another.

With this in mind, how do scientists study human behavior objectively? They record responses, describe events and the conditions surrounding them, and then draw inferences about causes. In order to overcome the effects of personal bias, several observers make reports on each of the individuals or events under study. Reliability increases when these observers have a common frame of reference, agree on which particular aspects of behavior to emphasize (and which not to emphasize), and do not have to draw too many inferences from their observations. Observational methods are used in specially created laboratory conditions as well as in naturally occurring situations.

Observation is more than simply using one's eyes in a seemingly straightforward way. Certain questions must be asked first: What types of responses should be selected for observation? How capable is the observer of making reliable and unbiased observations? Will the observer's presence influence the behavior that he or she wants to study? Is it preferable to observe behavior within naturally occurring settings or under controlled laboratory conditions? Should observations be limited to motor responses (walking, running), verbal responses (phone conversations, requests for help), or expressive behavior (smiling, crying)? How long a period of time is needed for reliable observation? Is time sampling needed—that is, should observations be gathered during several different time intervals? Even mental patients who hallucinate frequently do not engage in this kind of cognitive behavior all the time; time sampling can provide data on the conditions under which certain types of responses are most likely to occur. Reliable observations can provide useful records of both the incidence of a certain kind of behavior in a given environment and the events that elicit and maintain it.

Types of Observational Methods Various types of observational data are gathered in most research dealing with abnormal behavior. The types of observations made and the observational methods employed depend on a number of factors, including the hypothesis being investigated and the situations in which the observations must be made. Observations might be made by means of hidden videotaping equipment, by visible observers who do not interact with the people they are studying, or by participant observers who become actively involved in the behavior they are observing. Each of these methods has advantages and disadvantages. For example, secret videotaping allows us to observe behavior without the knowledge of the individual who is being observed, but this technique is often questionable for ethical reasons. Participant and nonparticipant observations have been used by anthropologists and sociologists as well as by psychologists. However, any observer may affect people's behavior simply by being present. Participant observers may damage their objectivity by becoming overinvolved with the people they are studying. Nonparticipant observers may come to superficial conclusions because they are not involved enough. Each of these techniques can be valuable, and each has both supporters and critics.

Types of Observational Data The value of observations is greatest when what is to be observed is defined explicitly. Four types of data are of special interest in observational research:

1. *The stimuli that elicit particular types of responses*—for example, the influence of family members' behavior (such as criticism or hostility) on a person who is prone to become depressed.
2. *The subjective response to the stimuli*—for example, the person's feelings when he or she is criticized.
3. *The behavioral response to the stimuli*—for example, the person's level of social activity after receiving criticism.
4. *The consequences of the behavior*—for example, the way the hospital environment responds when the person behaves in a depressed manner.

Although they are subjective and therefore are susceptible to personal bias, **self-observations** can be useful in clinical research. For example, a patient who had been admitted to a mental hospital because of depression was asked to keep track of her mood (level of sadness) and activity (number of social exchanges with hospital staff or other patients). Figure 1-15 shows a progressively less depressed mood and increased social activity during her first 15 days of hospitalization. In this case, there was good agreement between the patient's self-observations and the observations made by the hospital staff. This concordance will not always be the case. As we all know, the people

Figure 1-15 The mood and activity changes in a patient treated for depression. The patient's mood ratings are based on her self-observations.

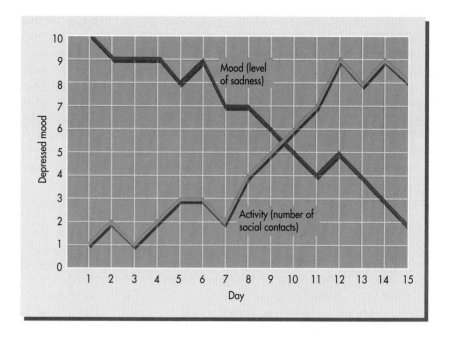

with whom we come into contact in our daily lives may not see us as we see ourselves (see Figure 1-16).

Self-observations are useful in keeping records of responses to clinical treatment. In the case of the patient whose self-observations are recorded in Figure 1-15 the treatment was complex, consisting of a benign hospital environment, daily individual and group psychotherapy, and medication. It would be interesting to compare the self-observation records of groups of comparable patients whose treatment consisted of only one of these elements— the hospital environment, psychotherapy, or medication alone—as well as all the possible combinations of these treatments.

The Role of Theory

While bird-watchers, museumgoers, and children in the back seat of a car may observe—often very precisely— what is going on around them, scientists seek to make observations that not only describe what is going on but also explain it. Scientific study involves a continuous interplay between observations and attempts to explain and understand what was observed. Typically, the path of scientific understanding involves these steps:

1. Initial, often informal, observations
2. Tentative hypotheses to explain the meaning of the observations
3. Further observations (if possible, under controlled conditions) to test the hypotheses
4. Theory building

Scientists like to proceed from observation to theory because they want to figure out why or how a particular

phenomenon occurs. Behaving just as lay people would, they use reason, logic, and sometimes simple guesswork to arrive at an initial tentative explanation. However, whereas casual observers may be satisfied with such a tentative answer, scientists recognize it as only tentative and go on to test their understanding by "if *a* then *b*" hypotheses that can be evaluated (e.g., "If patients are con-

"You are fair, compassionate, and intelligent, but you are perceived as biased, callous, and dumb."

Figure 1-16

SOURCE: Drawing by Mankoff; © 1985 *The New Yorker Magazine, Inc.*

cerned about rejection by the therapist, then they will be uncomfortable in therapy," or "If children are frustrated, then they are likely to behave aggressively"). They then proceed to collect the observations needed either to support or refute the hypothesis. If the hypothesis is supported by their observations, they return to their original "Why?" question and attempt to formulate increasingly broad concepts and principles that go beyond initial observations. This is the way that theories are developed.

Good theories have a number of functions. First, they are able to incorporate many existing facts, observations, and relationships within a single, broad explanatory framework. Second, additional hypotheses may be derived from the theory and tested, and may lead to new observations. In this way theories provide a foundation on which to build knowledge. If new observations do not support the theory, it may be modified or discarded. However, it will still have served a valuable function by leading to the discovery of new knowledge and to the development of an even better and more inclusive theory.

In order for a theory to be useful, it must be capable of being tested and refuted. It should be able to specify the types of relationships that are not possible as well as those that are. If it seems able to account for everything and anything, even contradictory facts, it is not a good scientific theory. The essence of the scientific method is systematic observation and the use of objective procedures to identify cause-and-effect relationships. Because theory plays important roles in how maladaptive behavior is defined and conceptualized, how it is treated, and how pertinent research studies are planned and carried out, we are devoting Chapter 2 to a review of theoretical perspectives that are currently influential.

The Research Journey

The path of research from observation to theory is a little like going on an automobile trip. There is a lot more to the journey than knowing where one is and where one wants to go. What route should be followed? Will there be detours? Would bad weather make a difference? How should one prepare for the trip? Following are some of the important steps in the scientist's research journey:

1. *Specifying the topic as clearly as possible.* Suppose you are intrigued by psychotherapy. Why are you drawn to that topic? Is it because you think verbal interchanges are crucial to achieving therapeutic change? Or are you more interested in the interpersonal relationship between client and therapist?

2. *Reviewing the relevant literature.* Some library work can save a researcher a lot of time and frustration. Studying the pertinent books and journals can answer many questions: How have other people dealt with this idea? What were the outcomes of their research?

3. *Defining the variables.* A variable is any aspect of a person, group, or setting that is measured for the purposes of the study in question. **Independent variables** are conditions manipulated by the researcher in order to investigate their effects on particular outcomes (e.g., behavioral changes) that are called **dependent variables.**

4. *Developing a specific hypothesis.* A **hypothesis** is a statement to be proved, an idea that has been formulated so that it may be evaluated using scientific methods. A hypothesis is a kind of educated guess that states a predicted relationship between events or variables. It is typically stated in the form "If A exists, then B will occur."

5. *Selecting a research strategy.* What plan of action will permit the hypothesis to be tested? Does the researcher plan to see each subject on one occasion (e.g., at the beginning or end of psychotherapy), or will several observations be necessary in order to test the hypothesis? Should an experiment be conducted? Conducting an experiment means systematically varying one or more conditions for some groups but not for others. Is experimental research possible in a particular clinical setting?

6. *Conducting the study.* The research should be carried out objectively enough to permit others to replicate it. Therefore, all the steps in the research process must be specified. For example, how was the sample of subjects selected? Were the subjects chosen on the basis of age, sex, or intelligence? If so, the selection variables must be specified.

7. *Analyzing the results.* How did the group or groups perform? What is the likelihood that the results are simply due to chance? An analysis of research results usually includes making a distribution of the scores obtained by subjects; calculating relevant **descriptive statistics,** the numerical measures (scores) that enable a researcher to describe certain aspects of subjects' performance (e.g., the mean or average); and calculating **inferential statistics,** the statistics that are used for judgments about the probability that the results are due to chance.

8. *Reporting research findings.* Writing up a piece of research not only permits communication of ideas and findings to others but also forces researchers to think through all that they have done and the meaning that might be attached to it. Going public serves an important communication function. The scientific journey would be much less valuable if research results were not written up and published.

Types of Research

Researchers use a variety of methods to better understand maladaptive behavior. We will focus on clinical observations here because of the valuable insights they provide about individual cases. Clinical studies also suggest profitable directions for projects involving various samples of subjects and methods. The following sections will discuss the most common types of clinical observations.

Case Studies Case studies involve detailed observations of a single patient's behavior. The clinician tries to organize many observations conceptually. In most case studies, explanations of the events occur after the fact and there is little, if any, opportunity to rule out other possible explanations by controlling for them. Even the most intensive study of an individual case cannot assure us that we have isolated the true causes of the behavior. Nevertheless, such studies can provide important leads for more controlled research. Clinicians recognize that each case is different because of the particular circumstances surrounding it, and cases may become more complicated because of clients' verbal reports. Troubled people more often than not leave out important information in telling their stories to clinicians. They frequently fail to remember significant experiences and the feelings and thoughts related to them. Each case study thus is unique, although with experience clinicians become sensitive to commonalities that aid them in understanding and helping people.

Correlational Studies In discussing the causes of abnormal behavior and the reasons why therapies work or don't work it is necessary to distinguish two key terms: *correlation* and *causation*. A correlation is an association or linkage of two (or more) events. A correlation simply means that the events are linked in some way. Establishing causation is often difficult because people are complex and it frequently isn't possible to be sure about which biological, psychological, or social factors have caused a particular type of behavior. Experimental studies are stronger than correlational studies in permitting inferences about causation. However, experimental research with humans may be logistically, ethically, or financially impossible.

In **correlational studies,** researchers investigate relationships between events. These studies show us that two things are associated (see Figure 1-17), but they do not explain which factor causes what. For example, a correlational study may identify a significant relationship between socioeconomic or marital status and severity of psychopathology. Although we do not know which is the key factor, a potentially important association has been singled out.

Both case studies and correlational studies provide bases for hypotheses. In evaluating a hypothesis it is important to decide on the observations that are relevant to it and the conditions under which those observations should be made. The conditions might be the same for all subjects or different for designated groups. In assessment studies (discussed next), the conditions are the same, the aim being to gather information under standard conditions for

"WHICH IS IT— DO PEOPLE HATE US BECAUSE WE DRESS THIS WAY, OR DO WE DRESS THIS WAY BECAUSE PEOPLE HATE US?"

Figure 1-17 It is dangerous to infer causality from correlational data. These witches are trying to infer causality on the basis of an association they have observed.

SOURCE: By permission of Sidney Harris and *Saturday Review World;* © 1987 by Sidney Harris.

purposes of description and prediction. In experimental studies (discussed later), the conditions are varied so as to test hypotheses about the effects of the conditions.

Assessment Studies The purpose of **assessment studies** is to provide an objective account of behavior at any given time. Assessment methods range from recording how often certain responses occur in natural situations to noting the types of behavior displayed in specially created settings such as interviews. Assessment is not simply a measuring device; it is a general approach to observing and interpreting behavior. As such, it extends beyond traditional procedures such as interviews and tests in much the same way that the concept of intelligence and the judgments based on it extend beyond the tests used to measure it.

Assessment data can be used in a number of ways. They might be employed to predict future behavior, to identify correlates of present behavior, or to measure the likelihood of a positive reaction to therapeutic procedures. For example, a study of junior high school students might indicate the type of person who is most likely to engage in antisocial behavior in the future; a comparison of the assessed characteristics of depressed individuals might point out those who are most likely to commit suicide; and a comparison of the personality traits of people who respond positively to psychotherapy and those who respond negatively might help in screening candidates for therapy. Assessment research ranges from in-depth studies of one or a few people to surveys of large populations.

When people are assessed, several kinds of data are usually gathered, including age, sex, personal history, and number of previous hospitalizations. This information can be intercorrelated and the degree of relationship among the various items determined. Assessment studies, which often involve large samples of subjects and sophisticated assessment techniques, are limited by their correlational nature, but despite this limitation they have much to contribute to the study of abnormal behavior. This is particularly true when, for practical or ethical reasons, it is not possible to manipulate conditions experimentally. Suppose, for example, that we wanted to study the possibility that having been abused as a child increases the likelihood that one will abuse one's own children. It would be highly unethical as well as impractical to subject an experimental group of children to severe abuse and then wait 20 years to see whether or not they beat their own children. However, information obtained through assessment about such a correlation could be of great value in understanding the causes of abuse, and could perhaps be used in selecting high-risk parents for programs designed to prevent abuse.

As an alternative, we might find ways to measure the amount of abuse parents received when they were children as well as the extent to which they now abuse their own children. For each of a large group of parents, we could obtain a score for each of the two abuse variables—each parent's reports of being abused as a child and some measure of his or her abusiveness as a parent—and then determine what kind of relationship, if any, exists between the two sets of measures. If being abusive and having been abused are correlated, that would provide a potentially useful clue to how child abuse could be prevented. For instance, perhaps parental counseling and training for people who were abused as children would be of preventive value.

If we find a positive correlation, we might be tempted to conclude from the data that child abuse is caused by parents having been abused as children. This is certainly a possibility, but it is important to remember that correlation is not the same as cause. There are other possible explanations for the positive correlation. It may be, for example, that guilt about abusing their children causes parents to exaggerate the extent to which they were abused by their own parents. Another possibility is that some other variable not measured in the study (such as some form of psychological disturbance) actually caused the parent to become the target of abuse as a child and causes him or her to become a child abuser as an adult. We simply cannot be certain which of these and other possible causal relationships may account for the positive correlation between recalled childhood experiences and present adult behavior.

Longitudinal Studies One way to deal with limitations inherent in assessment studies is the **longitudinal study,** whose goal is to observe and record the behavior of people over long periods—perhaps 20 or 30 years. This type of study is costly, time-consuming, and often frustrating to the investigator, who may not live to see the study completed. There are other problems as well. The nature of the group under study may change greatly as people move away or die. The methods chosen at the beginning of the study may become outdated. The importance of new variables that were ignored in the study may become recognized by the scientific community. For these reasons, few longitudinal studies are done. Nevertheless, because they deal so directly with the developmental process, the value of such studies is widely recognized.

Figure 1-18 illustrates the predictive value of longitudinal studies. Researchers were able to identify a group of men who at ages 8 to 10 had been socially withdrawn and inhibited (Caspi & Elder, 1988). Because they had been studied over a period of more than 20 years, it was possible to relate social withdrawal in childhood to these men's experiences at three adult life transitions: getting married, becoming a father, and beginning a work career. As Figure 1-18 shows, men with a childhood history of social withdrawal marry at a significantly older age than men with no such behavioral history—the difference between the groups is 3 years. Not surprisingly, delayed age at marriage corresponds with delayed parenthood. Finally, withdrawn behavior in childhood seems to hinder men's transition into an occupational career. Men with a childhood history of withdrawn behavior assumed a work career

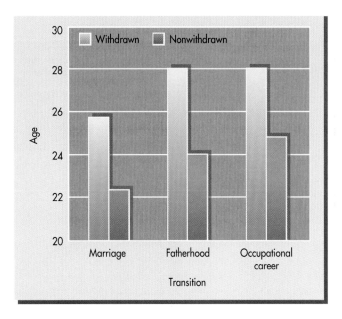

Figure 1-18 Timing of life transitions by withdrawn behavior in childhood.

SOURCE: Based on Caspi & Elder (1988).

3 years after the majority of their peers were already established in an occupation.

The delays in life transitions revealed by this study can generate conflicting obligations and options that may enhance stress and the risk of maladaptation. Evidence about the connection between withdrawn behavior in childhood and disorganization later in life could be of value in developing programs to improve the social adjustment of withdrawn children. Another group that could benefit from intervention efforts are children who are prone to be impulsive. Longitudinal studies have shown that preschool children's ability to inhibit socially inappropriate behavior is predictive of delinquency and antisocial behavior in adolescence (Kagan & Zentner, 1996).

Follow-up Studies One type of research that avoids some of the logistical problems of longitudinal studies, but still has longitudinal features, is the **follow-up study.** In such studies, people are given an initial assessment and then are contacted again months or years later to see whether there have been any changes in their behavior during that time. Follow-up studies are used to assess the effects of different therapeutic approaches as well as to observe the development of particular conditions.

Cross-Sectional Studies The **cross-sectional study** is a useful way to assess the views or status of one or more groups of people at any given point in time. Cross-sectional studies are the most common assessment method used by social scientists. Because no follow-up is required, these studies are less time-consuming and expensive than longitudinal studies. A public opinion poll is an example of a cross-sectional study that is carried out in the field. The epidemiological surveys described earlier in the chapter were cross-sectional studies.

Experimental Studies Experimental research involves the observation and assessment of behavior, but with an important additional ingredient. In experimental studies, or **experiments,** variables can be manipulated. This degree of control is impossible in many real-life situations. Because experimenters can control the variables in the laboratory, they can more easily isolate and record the causes of the behavior they observe.

The variables that are manipulated by researchers in experiments are *independent variables; dependent variables* are any observed changes in behavior due to the manipulation. Psychological experiments are designed to discover relationships between environmental conditions and behavior. Figure 1-19 illustrates a conventional experimental design. For example, an experiment might be done to discover the relationship between the temperature in a room and people's performance on a test. In this experiment the independent variable would be the temperature. The experimenter would use a different temperature for each experimental room. The dependent variable would be the test scores. If the average test scores for the individuals in the rooms were significantly different, the experimenter would conclude that this result was related to the different temperatures in the rooms in which the groups of individuals worked. Asking people how they felt under both conditions would be simpler, but the results would not be nearly as accurate or objective.

Types of Experiments There are two general types of experiments. The first type is the **hypothesis-testing experiment,** in which the researcher makes a prediction based on a theory and then conducts an experiment to see whether the prediction is correct. In the following excerpt, a psychologist outlines her plan for such a study:

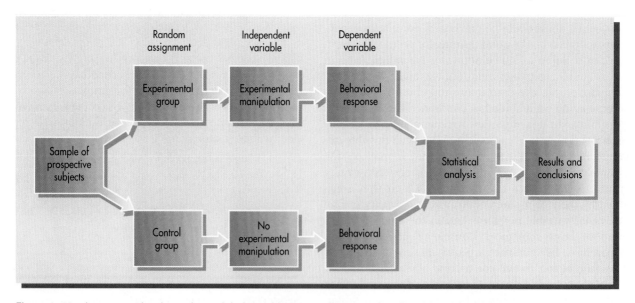

Figure 1-19 In a conventional experimental design, subjects are randomly assigned to an experimental or control group for manipulation of the independent variable. Their dependent-variable behaviors are then measured; differences between the two groups of subjects are assessed through statistical analysis to determine the effects of the independent variable.

I'm interested in determining whether, if children have an early close, secure relationship with an adult—what psychologists call attachment—they will have fewer problems getting along with other children when they enter school. My hypothesis is that if children are securely attached when they are very young, their social skills will be better and they will be less likely to be described as having behavior problems.

I have some records of nursery school children's behavior in a situation designed to measure attachment. In that research setup, a young child and his or her mother sit together in an attractive room with some playthings. Then a "stranger" (a research worker) comes into the room and sits down. After a while the mother leaves; she comes back a short time later. The way the child behaves, both while the mother is gone and when she returns, is a measure of attachment. If the child does not cling to the mother when the stranger enters, and if the child continues to play with the toys, is not distressed when she leaves, and greets her warmly but does not cling to her when she returns, the child is said to be securely attached.

Now those children are in the first grade, and I want to determine whether those who were securely attached in nursery school behave differently from the other children in either stressful or nonstressful situations. For half of each of the attachment groups, I am observing the children in a frustrating situation where they are given an impossible task to solve. For the other half of each group, I will give the children another task that is not difficult but takes a fairly long time to do. My hypothesis is that children who are securely attached will work longer at the impossible task than the other attachment group. For the other task, I expect no difference between the two groups. I base these predictions on the idea that children who are securely attached in their early years develop feelings of competence and tolerance of frustration superior to those of children who did not have a positive attachment experience. ■

I'm trying to devise procedures that will help patients with schizophrenia return to the community more quickly and be more effective when they make their return. My approach is to start with one obvious deficiency of the patients: inadequate social skills. They just don't do a very good job of relating to other people. What I've been doing is finding out, by asking them questions and observing them, what social skills the patients lack; for example, they have a lot of trouble introducing themselves to strangers and making small talk. I'm modeling—that is, demonstrating—for them various ways of being effective in social situations. I also have a control group that doesn't get the social skills training, as well as a group that participates in discussions about how to handle social situations but gets no modeling. If I'm on the right track, follow-ups should show that the modeling group is better able to adjust back into the community than the control group and maybe also better than the discussion group. ■

The second type of experiment, the **behavior-change experiment,** is concerned primarily with the development of therapeutic techniques. It is also designed to test hypotheses, but in this case the goal is to make an immediate contribution to the development of practical rehabilitative techniques. For example, a behavior-change experiment might test the hypothesis that supervised work experiences are significantly more effective than group psychotherapy in changing the attitudes and behavior of convicted criminals. The researcher who wrote the following account is studying schizophrenia. However, the researcher's goal is a very practical one: improving the social skills of those with schizophrenia.

An increasingly important type of behavior-change experiment is the clinical trial. A **clinical trial** is a planned experiment designed to determine the effectiveness of a treatment by comparing the outcomes in a group of patients given the test treatment with those in a comparable group of patients receiving a control treatment. Thus, both groups are treated and followed over the same period of time. There might also be an untreated control group. Clinical trials are costly because they usually require a large number of subjects who are studied at several clinical centers over a considerable period of time. Box 1-3 gives an in-depth look at the clinical trial.

Experiments With Animals For obvious reasons, certain types of experimentation cannot be carried out using human subjects. For example, it would be impossible—and unethical, even if it were possible—to try to observe and control the course of a person's life. However, the telescoped life span of nonhuman primates like monkeys makes it possible to study the long-term consequences of early experiences. Under controlled conditions these experiences can be observed either as they unfold or after experimental manipulations. Animal studies permit levels of control and ways of carrying out experimental manipulations that are not possible with humans. As a consequence, animal experimentation plays an important role in the study of abnormal behavior.

Animal studies can be used to investigate both biological and social factors in behavior. One example of research with a biological focus is the investigation of the effects of drugs. A group of drugs called amphetamines, which function as stimulants, can produce psychotic symptoms in people. Once the effects of amphetamines on animals are shown to be similar, animals that had been injected with amphetamines can then be given antipsychotic drugs to

Research Close-up   Box 1-3

The Clinical Trial

Because of the lack of effective treatments, for a long time the study of abnormal behavior was primarily descriptive. Now the situation is different. Today a major goal of clinical researchers is evaluation of the effectiveness of specific forms of therapy for specific types of patients. Potentially practical treatments for a number of conditions are now available and require careful evaluation. This type of evaluation requires methodological rigor and the ability of researchers to draw conclusions about the target intervention that are applicable, not just to a particular clinician, clinic, or hospital, but to entire regions and populations.

Clinical trials are studies of patients that systematically test the safety and effectiveness of new therapies and compare the results with standard treatment. Whether the condition in question is cancer, heart attack, or depression, clinical trials are the only sure way to determine whether one approach is better—or worse—than another. Clinical trials offer the potential benefits of promising new treatments to the trial participants and to all patients who will come after them.

The most scientifically sound method of determining which therapies are effective and which are not is the randomized controlled clinical trial. Eligible participants are given either the experimental treatment, in addition to standard therapy, or if they are in the control group, they receive standard therapy or the usual clinical care. Participants cannot choose which group or condition of the study they will be in, and in trials that test new medications, neither the patients nor the evaluating doctors know which medication is being given to whom until the study is complete.

The clinical trial is illustrated by a study comparing brief psychotherapy and medications in the treatment of nonhospitalized depressed people (Elkin, 1994). This clinical trial involved four treatment approaches including combinations of psychotherapy and antidepressant drugs, as well as a control. The project was designed to determine the effectiveness of psychotherapy and drugs singly and in combination. In order to increase the generalizability of the results, the project was carried out at three clinical centers in the United States. The treatments at these centers were provided by experienced therapists who had been carefully selected to take part in the program and received further training in their respective treatment approaches. The patients were followed for 18 months after the end of treatment. This experiment showed that, in comparison with the control condition, both the psychotherapy and medication groups improved. However, the control group also showed some improvement, thus demonstrating the need for appropriate groups with which treatment interventions can be compared. Other evidence suggests that combinations of psychotherapy and antidepressant medications may be especially effective.

Clinical trials are costly because they require seven major steps, summarized in Table 1-6. The research design of each clinical trial must be planned, the procedures in the treatment(s) specified, patients recruited into the study, the treatment(s) given, one or more posttrial follow-ups carried out to assess long-term effects, data analyzed, and a report of results written (usually in the form of journal articles or a book). The complexity of a clinical trial is demonstrated by the need for research subjects to complete all phases of the treatment and participate in the follow-up (for example, by filling out questionnaires at specified intervals). Each trial must make a concerted effort to maintain patient interest and participation by assuring that each clinical center in which the trial is carried out is easily accessible (public transportation and parking must be available), has pleasant physical surroundings, and treats patients with courtesy and dignity.

In a sense, complex clinical trials in abnormal psychology are indications of the field's success. There would be no need for clinical trials if there were no interventions that seemed likely to help people overcome their difficulties. Clinical trials have limitations because what works well in a special study employing highly trained personnel might not work well in everyday clinical practice settings. The frequently diminished level of treatment effectiveness in real-world settings has a name, the **efficacy-effectiveness gap**. *Efficacy* is the term for what works in the clinical trial setting, and *effectiveness* is the term for what works in typical clinical practice settings. Efficacy studies test whether a treatment works under ideal circumstances. They typically exclude patients with other mental or somatic disorders. The efficacy-effectiveness gap applies to both drug therapies and to psychotherapy. The gap is not unique to mental health; it is found with somatic disorders too.

Table 1-6

Steps in Clinical Trials

1. Research design
2. Specification of all intervention procedures
3. Patient recruitment
4. Implementation of the intervention(s)
5. Long-term follow-up of treatment effects
6. Data analysis
7. Report writing

---

determine whether they are able to counteract the amphetamines' psychosis-inducing action. This provides a way to identify promising antipsychotic drugs for later use with people with psychotic disorders.

Another example of animal studies with a biological focus can be seen in the work of Harry Harlow and his co-workers. They were interested in the effects of early experience on the later development of monkeys. Infant monkeys show a number of innate behaviors, such as clinging and sucking. When the infants are separated from their mothers and reared with other young monkeys, their clinging behavior lasts much longer than it does for mother-reared monkeys (see Figure 1-20a). Young monkeys also begin to show innate fear behavior when they are about 2 months old. When they are reared with other monkeys, the fear behaviors do not disappear but last into adulthood (Suomi & Harlow, 1978).

(a) (b)

Figure 1-20 (a) All monkeys go through a clinging stage, but monkeys reared without their mothers show a greatly prolonged period of clinging. (b) A young monkey, still in the clinging stage, can be an effective therapist for an older monkey reared in isolation.

When infant monkeys are not only separated from their mothers but also reared in isolation for 6 months, they show several disturbed behaviors. They suck their fingers or toes, constantly rock back and forth, and are very timid. When their isolation ends, they behave very aggressively toward other monkeys. The research showed, however, that monkeys that are reared in isolation for 6 months can later develop normally if they are "treated" by "therapist monkeys." The most successful therapist monkeys were 3-month-olds who still showed a great deal of clinging behavior. They clung to the isolates affectionately (see Figure 1-20b). The isolates soon responded, and within 6 months their behavior was hard to distinguish from that of their therapists (Suomi & Harlow, 1972).

Young monkeys separated from their mothers often show symptoms similar to depression in humans. Depression in young monkeys may be preceded by a protest phase characterized by immediate frantic activity that appears to reflect attempts to communicate with and locate the missing mother. The depression is often followed by a detachment phase in which the young monkey shows an emotional detachment or aloofness from its mother upon reunion. This phase has been observed in human children when in the presence of mothers from whom they have been separated (Rosenblum & Paully, 1987).

Experiments With Humans In this book we are particularly interested in (1) the problems people experience as they move through life and (2) what can be done to help them solve these problems. Consequently, many of the experiments we will discuss involve efforts to effect behavior change in humans. Clinical trials, described earlier in Box 1-3, are human experiments on a grand scale. There are, of course, many experiments carried out on a more modest scale aimed at developing useful approaches to treating particular types of disorders. This behavior change research is illustrated by studies that have been conducted on the difficulties (ranging from annoying to serious) many people have in getting a good night's sleep.

Insomnia is one of the most frequent health complaints dealt with by clinicians. Epidemiological surveys have shown that between 9% and 15% of the adult population complain of chronic insomnia whose symptoms include difficulty in falling asleep, trouble staying asleep, and early morning awakening. Two approaches that are used in treating insomnia are psychological therapy and medication. These are two questions researchers ask: are these two approaches equally effective, and does it make a difference whether a patient with insomnia is treated with psychotherapy or medication? Behavior change experiments with insomnia patients have shown that both psychological treatment and medication are effective in the short term (e.g., during the first 3 months of treatment) (Morin & Wooten, 1996). However, while medications for sleep problems may yield quicker results, psychological treatments often produce more durable sleep improvements. When medications are discontinued, problems of insomnia tend to return, whereas the positive effects of psychological therapy often continue after termination of treatment. Combining psychological therapy with medication yields results only slightly superior to either clinical approach alone. The experiments dealing with treatment for insomnia are thus especially useful because, while many patients and physicians focus their attention on sleeping pills as the best treatment, the results of these experiments have shown that psychological treatment may lead to longer-lasting positive outcomes.

Studies that include groups receiving medications usually include a placebo condition. A **placebo** is an inactive substance whose effect on a person's behavior depends on his or her expectations. When placebos are used, a double-blind manipulation is also usually included in the study. With the **double-blind method,** neither the patients nor the clinicians know whether any particular patient is receiving pills with active or inactive ingredients (Figure 1-21).

The placebo effect has been recognized since antiquity (the word *placebo* is derived from a Latin word that means "I shall please"). Placebo effects have been found in many patients (often 50%) in studies of medical treatments. The

"It was more of a 'triple-blind' test. The patients didn't know which ones were getting the real drug, the doctors didn't know, and, I'm afraid, nobody knew."

Figure 1-21 Imagine how you would feel if you carried out a study and then could not find out which subjects were in which group. This "research nightmare" is, fortunately, purely a function of the cartoonist's imagination.

SOURCE: © 1993 by Sidney Harris.

placebo effect is so frequent that the Food and Drug Administration requires a placebo or other control group in clinical trials of a new medication to establish its efficacy prior to marketing. If it is not found to be statistically superior to the control, efficacy cannot be established. The basis of the placebo response is not fully known, but the attributes of the disorder, the treatment setting, personality characteristics, expectations, and attitudes seem to be relevant factors.

Research Design, Statistical Analyses, and Inference

Planning is a key feature of scientific research. Researchers must identify their goals and figure out how to reach them. Is the goal to describe some phenomenon (such as the social behavior of depressed individuals), establish a correlation between events (such as the association between viewing violent television programs and committing crimes), or demonstrate a cause-and-effect relationship between independent and dependent variables (such as the effects of psychotherapy and medication on depressed mood)? Some types of behavior can be studied only in their natural settings, where little or no control is possible; others can be studied under controlled laboratory conditions. Where they are appropriate, controlled experiments

have the advantage of exposing subjects to conditions that permit a good test of the researcher's hypothesis. A well-controlled experiment has high **internal validity** because the results can be attributed to manipulation of the independent variable rather than to some extraneous or confounding variable. The independent variable could be a condition far removed from the subject's life. However, if the condition mirrors what happens in the "real world," the experiment also has **external validity.**

Scientific observation results in data that are usually numerical in nature. Statistical procedures allow the researcher to summarize and bring order to data, as well as to measure relationships among variables.

Descriptive Statistics **Descriptive statistics** are used to summarize observations. The summaries might be of patients' responses to psychological tests, the ages at which various types of patients develop their conditions, and clinicians' ratings of patients' progress. **Measures of central tendency** provide descriptive numerical summaries of a group's behavior. The three most commonly used measures of central tendency are the **mean,** or arithmetic average; the **median,** the point that cuts the distribution of scores in half, so that half of the rank-ordered scores fall above it and half below it; and the **mode,** the score that the largest number of subjects obtained. Because of its desirable mathematical properties, the mean is typically favored in statistical analyses.

Measures of central tendency, such as the mean, provide information about the average score in a distribution. However, knowing the average score in a distribution does not provide all of the information required to describe a group of scores. In addition, **measures of variability** are required. The simplest idea of variability is the **range,** which is merely the difference between the highest and lowest scores. The most commonly used measure of variability is the **standard deviation,** which takes into account all of the scores in the distribution rather than only the highest and lowest. The standard deviation reflects the size of the deviation of the scores in the distribution from the group mean.

Inferential Statistics Whereas descriptive statistics help us characterize a group of subjects, it is often important to make comparisons among two or more groups (e.g., the mean IQs of students at two high schools). **Inferential statistics** help us determine whether any observed differences between groups should be attributed to chance or to some systematic difference between the groups (for example, the socioeconomic status of students at the two schools). Statistical tests, such as the *t* test, evaluate the null hypothesis, the theory that the groups really do not differ. If the null hypothesis is rejected, it is unlikely that the observed differences could have arisen by chance. Statistical tests yield what is known as a **level of significance,** which is determined by comparing the results of the statistical tests with a set of probability tables.

Correlation Coefficients Quite commonly, clinicians or researchers are interested not so much in how groups might differ, but in how variables that represent characteristics of some particular sample or population are related to each other. The **correlation coefficient** provides this information. Correlation coefficients can range from -1.00 to $+1.00$. A coefficient of $+1.00$ means that there is a perfect positive association between two variables. A correlation of -1.00 signifies a perfect negative, or inverse, relationship, and a correlation of .00 means that there is no relationship between the variables. Figure 1-22 illustrates three kinds of correlation results.

Interpreting Results of Research There are many types of statistical tests, some of which are complex. For example, some procedures involve evaluating the relationships among combinations of three or more variables. But regardless of the procedures employed, interpretation of the results obtained is required. The experiment is a powerful scientific tool, but it is not infallible. Certain factors can seriously undermine the validity of research results. Four of the most serious issues that researchers must consider in conducting studies and interpreting results are confounding of variables, reactivity, demand characteristics, and expectancy effects. How we interpret the results of research depends not only on the outcomes of the statistical tests employed but also on how well the research was conducted; that is, how successful the researcher has been in eliminating these biasing factors.

Confounding occurs when uncontrolled variables affect the dependent variable in a way that is mistakenly attributed to the independent variable. For example, some depressed individuals might be given psychotherapy while others serve as control group. Comparing the two groups might show a statistically significant difference in depressed mood, with the group that received psychotherapy showing less depression after psychotherapy than the control group. This result would suggest that psychotherapy is a useful treatment for depression. But what if the experimental and control groups differed in age, sex, or initial

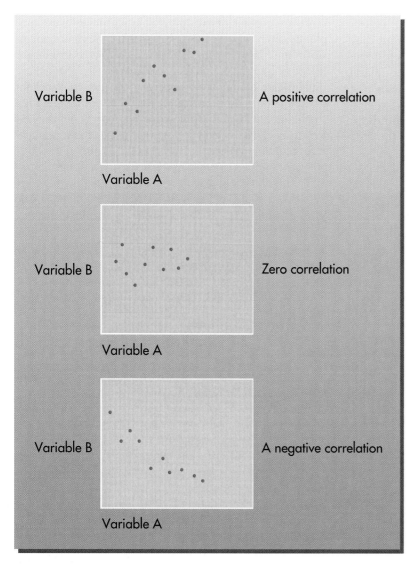

Figure 1-22 Correlation coefficients can be computed between pairs of variables, A and B, in which we might be interested—for example, between intelligence and performance in school; between socioeconomic level and anxiety; or between self-rated stress and social skills.

level of depression? These possibly confounding variables would lead us to be very cautious about any statistically significant results we might obtain.

Reactivity refers to changes in behavior that occur when subjects know they are being observed or studied. If subjects in a laboratory experiment react to being observed by behaving differently from the way they would outside the laboratory, we might easily draw false conclusions from the experimental results.

Demand characteristics are features of research situations that give subjects information about how they are expected to behave. Subjects may pick up these clues about the nature of a study and how they are "supposed" to behave. Some patients in psychoanalysis might report more dreams than patients in other forms of psychotherapy because their analysts may give the impression that reporting and analyzing dreams is what they want their patients to do. Because demand characteristics can be a threat to valid results, researchers often feel a need to hide the true intent of their experiments.

Expectancy effects can be a source of bias in experiments if they lead to systematic errors in observations. Researchers' expectancies about what will happen in a given situation might actually influence the observations they make. In a study involving tranquilizers, for example, some experimenters might rate patients who have been taking tranquilizing drugs as being less anxious because in past research such drugs were found to reduce anxiety. In such cases, scientists making the evaluations should not have information about which patients are receiving the drug and which are receiving the placebo.

An additional factor that influences the results of research is **sampling.** A researcher virtually can never study every member of the larger group to which experimental results are expected to apply. We are almost always restricted to a segment, or sample, of that larger group, which is called the population. If valid conclusions are to be drawn, the sample must reflect the important characteristics of that larger population. For this reason, public opinion pollsters use samples that possess the important characteristics (age, gender, political party, geographical location, and so on) in the same proportion as contained in the general population. The responses of such a representative sample are more likely to mirror those of the larger population. Clearly, interpretation of research investigations depends on the nature of the samples studied—if the sample does not adequately reflect the general public, results will have a limited application.

When confronted with all the factors that need to be considered in any particular research project, it would be understandable to feel a bit overwhelmed by the complexity of it all. Students might ask: Is all this complexity necessary? Why don't we get simple, straight answers? These are reasonable questions. Researchers don't want to create complexity unless it is really necessary. Complexity often is necessary to be sure that the right conclusions are drawn from a research study. Fortunately, identifying the factors that might influence a phenomenon usually leads to discovering a practical way to take account of them—either by controlling for them or manipulating them. Identifying relevant factors and figuring out the best way to deal with them are among the most exciting features of doing research (see Box 1-4).

Q&A Box 1-4

Over the years, students in our Abnormal Psychology classes have asked many questions. In this edition, from time to time, we paraphrase some of those frequently asked questions and try to answer them.

Q. Alzheimer's disease is a chronic brain disorder that usually occurs late in life and results in intellectual deterioration, growing lapses of memory, and in its later stages, may require round-the-clock care of the affected person. Although there is, as yet, no treatment for the disorder, research has shown that brain atrophy (a wasting away of bodily tissues) is its cause. Once, when one of us stated in class that there were many complexities involved in the onset and progression of Alzheimer's disease, a student said something like this: "I'm sure

almost everything is complex, but isn't the problem of Alzheimer's disease simply a matter of the brain atrophy that causes it?"

A. *A very good question, and to a certain extent the student was correct. However, because of the many studies that have been conducted on the disease, a number of potentially valuable and nonobvious, clues have been exposed that may be applicable to reducing the problem that Alzheimer's poses. For example, epidemiological studies carried out in many countries have all shown a robust negative correlation between the amount of schooling received when people are young and the prevalence of Alzheimer's disease in old age (Eisenberg, 1998). Where does education fit into the puzzle of Alzheimer's disease? Three hypotheses need to be considered. Do individuals who will develop the disease in later life have*

reduced cognitive resources early in life that lead them to poor performance and becoming a school dropout? Or, is poor education simply a product of poverty, malnutrition, and poor health care that progressively damages the brain? Or, does the intellectual stimulation provided by schools lead to better functioning of the synapses (points at which nerve impulses are passed to other nerve cells) that are affected by Alzheimer's disease? We do not yet have answers to these questions, but they certainly provide stimulation to curious researchers. Additionally, identification of the inverse relationship between education and brain deterioration leads to another provocative question: What would be lost by promoting enhanced public education as a policy for preventing brain deterioration? At the least, we would have a population that is intellectually more competent before its members become senile.

Ethical Aspects of Research

Regardless of the scholarly merits of doing research, investigators should never place people in either physical or psychological jeopardy. Subjects should be informed regarding what the experiment is about and any hazards associated with participation in it. They also must be clearly told that they are free to withdraw from the experiment at any time. If deception must be used to investigate the questions asked in the research, the subjects must be completely debriefed after the experiment, and the entire procedure explained to them. Special measures must be taken to provide confidentiality regarding the subject's behavior and responses.

As a result of the increasing emphasis on the protection and welfare of both human and animal subjects used in psychological research, psychologists now must restrict their experimentation with certain groups of people who are not in a position to give their consent, such as children, individuals who are mentally retarded, and seriously disturbed mental patients. When such people, or others who are not able to give consent, are involved, consent must be obtained from their parents or guardians. Strict guidelines are also being developed for research in prisons. No prisoner can be forced to participate in research or penalized for refusal to do so, and in the case of rehabilitative programs, prisoners must be permitted to share in decisions concerning program goals. Researchers must adhere to the ethics of research or risk serious legal and professional consequences. We discuss several ethical issues in Chapter 17.

Chapter Summary

WHAT IS ABNORMAL BEHAVIOR?

Abnormal psychology deals with how it feels to be different, how others interpret these differences, and how society deals with those it considers different. An understanding of the roles of **stress,** personal **vulnerabilities,** and **resilience** is important in interpreting abnormal behavior.

The Stigma of Abnormal Behavior Beliefs and assumptions about mental illness affect the way people respond to someone who shows abnormal behavior. Those who behave in unusual ways or have been diagnosed as having a mental illness may be rejected by others, either directly or indirectly. Many false beliefs exist about the causes and the outcome of mental illness.

Adaptive and Maladaptive Behavior **Adaptation,** as the term is used in this book, refers to people's ability or inability to modify their behavior in response to changes in their environment. Deviant or unusual behavior is often not maladaptive. **Maladaptive** behavior refers to behavior that causes problems in living. Maladaptive behavior ranges from relatively minor but troubling fears to severe distortion of reality and inability to function independently.

HISTORICAL BACKGROUND OF MODERN ABNORMAL PSYCHOLOGY

It is important to know about the history of abnormal psychology because certain perspectives about deviance—supernatural, organic, and psychological—have recurred throughout history. Some early mystical beliefs concerning the role of supernatural or magical forces in the origin of abnormal behavior are still found in many cultures. From this point of view, therapy often involves **exorcism,** or the removal of the evil through counter-magic or prayer. This practice is often performed by a **shaman,** or folk healer. Another perspective links abnormal behavior with organic defect. Early evidence of this view is found in skulls from prehistoric times that show evidence of **trephination,** chipping holes in the skull. The psychological perspective suggests that abnormal behavior is related to disturbances in the way a person thinks, feels, or perceives the world and that these disturbances are potentially modifiable.

The Ancient Western World In ancient Greece disturbed behavior was originally interpreted as punishment for offenses against the gods. Later, several Greek philosophers, beginning with Socrates, held a more psychological view, considering reasoning to be basic to adaptive behavior. Plato developed the **organismic approach,** which explained behavior as an overall expression of a person's psychological process. He thought of disturbed behavior as arising from internal conflicts between reason and emotion. Galen, a Greek physician, taught that psychological characteristics were expressions of bodily process influenced by a balance of the **four humors.**

The Middle Ages During the Middle Ages, contrasting views of mental illness existed. Saint Augustine helped lay the groundwork for modern psychodynamic theory through his use of introspection to discuss mental processes. During the late Middle Ages, the church played both important positive and negative roles in the treatment of the mentally ill. Some governments, such as that in England, took responsibility for the protection of those who were mentally ill.

The Renaissance During the late fifteenth and the sixteenth centuries, despite an increase in learning, demonology and exorcism persisted. However, Johann Weyer, argued for clinical treatment for the mentally ill rather than religious persecution. Weyer emphasized disturbed interpersonal relationships and psychological conflict as causes of mental disorder.

The Age of Reason and the Enlightenment In the seventeenth and eighteenth centuries, scientific knowledge increased greatly. Scientists such as William Harvey wrote about the relationship between the physiological and psychological aspects of life. Philosophers such as Spinoza wrote about the roles of emotions, ideas, and desires in life and made reference to unconscious mechanisms that influence behavior. Literature also dealt with emotion and motivation. Many of Shakespeare's plays focus on the effects of emotion on behavior. Robert Burton, in his *Anatomy of Melancholy,* described and analyzed depression from a psychological viewpoint. New ideas appeared, such as **physiognomy,** the art of judging personality from physical appearance, and **phrenology,** the view that mental faculties could be "read" by feeling the bumps on a person's head. Franz Anton Mesmer developed the idea of animal magnetism, which led to the use of hypnotism as a treatment for mental disorder.

The Reform Movement The movement toward more humane treatment of the mentally ill began with the development of **moral treatment** by Philippe Pinel in France. In the nineteenth century, special institutions were developed to care for and treat children who were mentally ill or retarded. The reform movement in the United States was led first by Benjamin Rush, later by Dorothea Dix, and then by Clifford Beers, who used his experiences as a patient to improve conditions in mental hospitals and to establish community clinics.

RECENT CONCEPTS OF ABNORMAL BEHAVIOR

Because much is yet to be learned about the causes of abnormal behavior, the debate over the role of psychological factors and bodily functioning is ongoing.

The Psychological Approach The emphasis on irrational thought arose in the early nineteenth century as a reaction to the focus on rational thinking that characterized the Age of Reason and the Enlightenment. Sigmund Freud emphasized the roles of emotion and irrational feelings in maladaptive behavior.

The Organic Approach Another group of writers saw mental disorders as the result of disturbances in brain function. They stressed the need to uncover evidence concerning how the body (particularly the nervous system) works.

The Approaches Converge The contemporary view of maladaptive behavior is that biological, psychological, and social factors combine in influencing maladaptive behavior. The relative roles of these factors vary among individuals and across the life span; and their contributions, singly and together, need to be evaluated in helping people cope.

Vulnerability, Resilience, and Coping Stress refers to people's reactions to situations that pose demands, constraints, or opportunities. **Vulnerability** refers to the likelihood of maladaptive response. Vulnerability is affected by heredity, personality factors, lack of certain skills, a history of negative life events, and certain environmental conditions. **Resilience** is the ability to function effectively in the face of adversity and to recover from the effects of stress. Resilient people are often good copers. **Coping skills** are the techniques—such as constructive thinking and flexibility—that people use to deal with stress. A person's level of coping varies from time to time because of differences in vulnerability and resilience in various types of situations.

THE EPIDEMIOLOGY OF MALADAPTIVE BEHAVIOR

Epidemiologists look for clues about the causes of disorders by investigating environmental, personal, and behavioral characteristics that are associated with different rates of various disorders.

Incidence, Prevalence, and Risk Factors **Incidence** data are the number of new cases of a condition occurring during a given period. **Prevalence** data describe the frequency of occurrence of a condition at a given point in time. **Risk factors** are personal or situational characteristics that have been found to have a significant association with a disorder.

CLASSIFYING ABNORMAL BEHAVIOR

Because the clinical treatment of troubled individuals depends on the nature of their problems, the classification of types of maladaptive behavior is an important topic.

SEEKING HELP FOR ABNORMAL BEHAVIOR

Many people who suffer from mental illness do not receive any professional treatment because of the cost of treatment, the lack of clinical facilities nearby, or because they do not seek help for a variety of reasons.

Reasons for Clinical Contacts People, even those whom others might not believe are behaving maladaptively, may seek help for themselves because of personal unhappiness. Others may seek help for someone because of their concern for the person's well-being or the safety of others around them. Sometimes problems caused by the person's behavior cause legal or community agencies to become involved in seeking help.

Sources of Help Facilities for the treatment of mental disorders range from inpatient treatment in psychiatric hospitals and in psychiatric wards of general hospitals to outpatient resources in the community. The outpatient facilities include hospital emergency rooms, mental health clinics, and the services of mental health workers. Because of the movement toward **deinstitutionalization** of mental patients, many people were discharged from mental hospitals and returned to the community. In many cases adequate community facilities for their treatment and support were not available. Currently, relatively few people, even those with the most severely maladaptive behaviors, are treated for long, if at all, in inpatient facilities. A variety of mental health specialists including **clinical psychologists, counseling psychologists, psychiatrists, psychiatric social workers,** and **psychiatric nurses** may be involved in treatment of mental disorders. Although the responsibilities of these groups ordinarily differ, many of the therapeutic activities they carry out are similar.

RESEARCH IN ABNORMAL PSYCHOLOGY

Observing Behavior Observation is the beginning stage in the scientific process. It is important to recognize that observations are susceptible to cultural and personal bias. To make observation useful it is necessary to determine such things as the types of responses to be observed, how the observer's presence will affect the behavior, and the period of time necessary for reliable observation. In addition to observation by others, **self-observation** by the client can provide useful research data. The data obtained from observation can include the stimuli that elicit particular responses, the subjective and behavioral responses to particular stimuli, and the environmental consequences of certain behaviors.

The Role of Theory Theories in abnormal psychology often begin with informal observations in clinical settings. Researchers then make hypotheses based on their observations and test these through further observations, preferably under controlled conditions. As these studies show whether or not each hypothesis is supported by research findings, a theory can be built. Theories are used to relate many facts into a single framework and also to provide new questions for researchers to test in a systematic manner. For this reason it is very important that theories are constructed to be testable and refutable.

The Research Journey The vital steps in scientific research are specifying the topic, reviewing the literature, defining the variables to be measured, developing the hypothesis, selecting a research strategy, conducting the study, analyzing the results, and reporting the research findings. Both **independent variables,** or those that are manipulated by the researcher, and **dependent variables,** or outcomes, must be specified.

Types of Research Case studies provide descriptions of single individuals who are usually studied through many observations. Correlational studies provide information about how much variables are related or associated, but like case studies they do not show cause and effect. **Assessment studies** describe behavior at any given time. They can be used for prediction of future behavior or to identify correlates of present behavior, but like case and correlational studies they cannot be used to show causality. **Experimental studies** can be used to infer causality.

Two major types of experimental studies are the **hypothesis-testing experiment** and the **behavior-change experiment.**

Research Design, Statistical Analyses, and Inference Researchers need to identify their goals and plan their studies so as to attain them. Statistical procedures enable a researcher to summarize data and measure relationships among variables. The results are calculated in terms of both **descriptive statistics,** or numerical measures, and **inferential statistics,** which are used to provide information about whether the results might be due to chance. Included among descriptive statistics are measures of **central tendency,** which include the **mean, median,** and **mode.** The **range** of scores is a simple measure of variability. The most commonly used variability measure is the **standard deviation.** Inferential statistics are used to evaluate the null hypothesis (to determine whether the groups in an experimental study differ). These statistics can be used to determine the level of significance, or the probability that the results occurred by chance. When the results of an experiment are interpreted, several factors that can negatively affect the validity of the results must be kept in mind. The factors include **confounding of variables, reactivity** of subject behavior, **demand characteristics** of the experiment, and **expectancy effects.**

Ethical Aspects of Research Research in the field of abnormal psychology is governed by many ethical considerations and by regulations for the protection of the research participants. Researchers must not treat people without their informed consent, and must never treat them in a way that might possibly cause them either physical or psychological harm. Potential subjects must be informed about the nature of the experiment and any risks it might involve, and their written consent must be obtained. They must be given a chance to withdraw and, if any deception is used, they must be debriefed afterward by having the procedures explained. All data from research must be kept confidential so that no one except the researchers will know the subjects' responses.

Key Terms

The Elements of Maladaptive Behavior

Theory, Treatment, and Research

Fred Price, aged 38, has been experiencing occasional pain in his chest for two months. He is a high school vice-principal in a large city. His job is a high-pressured one requiring many daily contacts with teachers and students. The teachers often have complaints, and the students are almost always having problems or causing them. Fred's task is to handle the problems effectively and quickly. He has put off seeing a doctor, attributing his chest pain to indigestion associated with stress at work. In fact, Alka-Seltzer seemed to help somewhat. Recently he and his wife have been arguing a lot, often about money to pay for braces for one child's teeth, tuition and living expenses for his oldest child who wants to go to college away from home, and nursing home expenses for his wife's mother. Last night, during an especially fierce argument with his wife, he had another bout of chest pains that took several hours to subside, even after he took Alka-Seltzer. Afterward Fred began thinking about the fact that his father had had his first heart attack at the age of 47. Like Fred, Fred's father had had a demanding job that took a lot out of him, leaving him exhausted at night. In the morning Fred called his doctor for an appointment. ■

It would be difficult to summarize Fred Price's problems in a neat, straightforward manner. Is he a man who is about to have a heart attack? If so, is it because he has "bad" genes that make him prone to have one? Or might his somatic problems simply be expressions of a high anxiety level engendered by a stressful job? Are his physical resources or stress-coping skills inadequate to handle the demands of being a vice-principal of an inner-city high school? What role do family pressures and marital discord play in his symptoms? Like most of us, Fred Price is a complex person. His thoughts, behavior, and physical status probably have multiple determinants. From the information provided, it is not possible to determine the likely cause or causes of his symptoms and apparent unhappiness.

Clinicians and researchers have developed theories they hope will be helpful in identifying the causes of behavioral maladaptation and physical illness. These theories guide clinicians as they inquire into the determinants of maladaptation.

The Role of Theory in Abnormal Psychology

Everyone wants to know why things happen. Scientific theories are created to organize what we know and explain what it means. Theories are never complete, because there are different ways of looking at what we do know and because there are always some pieces missing from our knowledge. Even an incomplete theory is useful, however, if it provides a perspective for examining the information we have. A good theory can help us not only to explain why clinical disorders occur, but also to decide how they might be treated effectively.

Clinical workers and researchers operate on the basis of formal theories, but they also use informal theories or hunches based on past experience. A psychiatrist, clinical psychologist, or social worker who is assigned a case will use a particular theoretical perspective to analyze the available information. We all use theoretical perspectives in our lives; these perspectives serve as lenses that reflect and shape our conceptions of human nature. Thus, according to one theoretical perspective a bad cold may be thought of as a viral infection; according to another it may simply be "God's will"; and according to your mother it may be "your own fault for getting your feet wet."

The diversity of theories in abnormal psychology is wide. We will review six theoretical perspectives that are particularly influential today: (1) the *biological perspective*, which emphasizes the role of bodily processes; (2) the *psychodynamic perspective*, which emphasizes the role of anxiety and inner conflict; (3) the *behavioral perspective*, which examines how the environment influences behavior; (4) the *cognitive perspective*, which looks to defective thinking and problem solving as causes of abnormal behavior; (5) the *humanistic-existential perspective*, which emphasizes

our uniqueness as individuals and our freedom to make our own decisions; and (6) the *community-cultural perspective*, which is concerned with the roles of social relationships and the impact of socioeconomic conditions on maladaptive behavior.

Which of these theoretical perspectives is right? In Jewish lore there is a story about a couple who came to their rabbi for marriage counseling. The rabbi interviewed each partner separately about the problems in their relationship and then met with them together. They asked him who was right and who was wrong. The rabbi told the puzzled couple, "You are both right." The rabbi's observation also applies to these theoretical perspectives. Each one deals with pieces of reality, but the pieces are often quite different. Some theories are more pertinent to an understanding of the causes of stress, others to the ways in which we cope, and still others to the nature of human vulnerabilities. Consequently, there is no reason why we should commit ourselves to a particular theoretical position and feel called upon to explain all abnormal behavior in terms of its concepts. With a topic as complex as abnormal behavior, it is a good idea to remember that even a respected theory may be too simple an explanation.

It is important to note that theories are not static. In Chapter 1 we saw that, through the centuries, explanations of deviance have undergone wide swings. New facts exerted an influence on existing theories, but so did people's beliefs, which may or may not have scientific validity. Besides accommodating new facts or changes in public attitudes, a new theory may be developed as a reaction to weaknesses in a currently popular theory or conventional approach to a problem. For example, Sigmund Freud was a successful neurologist who found himself devoting more and more time to patients with "nervous disorders" for whom neurology had little to offer. As a result, his interest turned to possible psychological causes of these patients' problems. Psychoanalysis as a theory of and treatment for psychological disorders grew out of this new direction in Freud's thought.

Although the theoretical viewpoints discussed in this chapter are important and are actively used and researched today, it is worthwhile to keep in mind that each was a reaction to the situation prevailing at the time it was initially proposed. We might think of the content of theories as having *elements* that probably need to be combined in order to achieve their maximal explanatory value. When to combine them and how to do so are major challenges in the study of abnormal psychology.

The Orientation of This Book

We believe that the six theoretical perspectives described in this chapter merit attention because each deals with a significant piece of the puzzle of maladaptive behavior. What should the various theories be telling us? As we stated in Chapter 1, we think of maladaptive behavior in terms of personal vulnerabilities and resilience. What is it that we bring to situations that pushes us in the direction of functioning effectively or ineffectively? Although the words *vulnerability* and *resilience* may not occupy prominent places in all of the theories we will review, the theories do in fact deal with issues related to these characteristics. For example, each of us has biological assets and liabilities, as well as assets and liabilities in the way we think, perceive ourselves and others, and cope with various types of stress.

Because each of us is probably both vulnerable and resilient in particular ways, a profile of assets and liabilities is needed for each person. In addition to this profile, methods are needed for reducing vulnerabilities and increasing resilience. The six theoretical perspectives we will review approach this need in several ways. For example, biological theories focus attention on somatic interventions, such as tranquilizing or antipsychotic drugs; psychoanalysis seeks to help people cope more effectively with disturbing thoughts and emotions; behavioral theories are concerned with modifying specific types of undesirable behavior; and cognitive theories have led to therapeutic techniques for changing unrealistic ideas.

As each individual is a complex product of biology and experience, ultimately we will need ways of integrating the variables, mechanisms, and treatments—the elements inherent in each theoretical position. The field of abnormal psychology is not yet at this point. By understanding the six theoretical perspectives and their elements described in this chapter, we may be able to combine or integrate some aspects of them so as to provide a better picture of the individual. In a sense, this chapter is about the building blocks for the integrative theories that we hope will emerge in the years ahead rather than about each perspective alone.

The Biological Perspective

In our review of the history of abnormal psychology in Chapter 1, we saw that the idea that bodily disturbances cause disordered behavior has been around for a long time. It is not surprising that the **biological perspective** gained renewed popularity in the eighteenth and nineteenth centuries, when great leaps forward in anatomy, physiology, and genetics made it seem reasonable that a biological cause might eventually be found for every disorder, be it physical or behavioral. Major impetus for the biological point of view came from findings about the relationship between bodily infections and defects, on the one hand, and disordered behavior on the other.

Recent information about the role of biological factors supports the argument that such factors are important to some, but certainly not all, mental conditions. Modern advances in several areas of biology and medicine have continued to motivate researchers. For example, equip-

ment and techniques like the positron emission tomography (PT) scan and the computerized tomography (CT) scan, which make it possible to see how the brain works without the use of surgical or other invasive procedures, are beginning to permit previously unthought-of studies of the relationships between behavior and the brain. And research on heredity and genetics has shown that certain chromosomal defects are responsible for metabolic disorders, such as phenylketonuria, that in turn may lead to specific forms of mental retardation. The list of behavioral problems in which biological processes play at least some role is lengthening, as is the list of biologically based therapies.

Most people distinguish between the body and the mind, although the meanings attached to these words vary widely. *Body* refers to organs, muscles, bones, and brain; *mind* usually refers to attitudes, feelings, and thoughts. Although we generally speak as if the worlds of body and mind were totally separate, the separation between body and mind is actually an intellectual invention rather than a reality. Cognitive and bodily processes are closely intertwined, though how much weight one assigns to each process in accounting for maladaptive behavior depends on one's view. And new evidence may alter prevailing views from time to time.

At its most extreme, the biological viewpoint assumes that all maladaptive behavior is due to a disordered body structure or function. Such a disorder can be explained by an inherited defect that may cause permanent damage, by a defect acquired through injury or infection before or after birth, or by a more or less temporary physiological malfunction caused by some condition that is present at a particular time, such as a high fever caused by a temporary infection. A less extreme view, which still emphasizes the importance of biological functioning, recognizes that maladaptive behavior is a joint product of three types of disordered processes: in the body (e.g., a hormonal deficiency), in psychological functioning (e.g., a tendency toward shyness), and in the social environment (e.g., a high unemployment rate in the community). This interactional view is discussed later in the chapter.

A number of biological factors influence the behavior of organisms. How we behave and think depends not only on the action of each factor by itself but also on the interrelationships among them. Genetic factors, the brain and nervous system, and the endocrine glands all play important roles in psychological processes and in abnormal behavior.

Genetic Factors

The field of genetics has expanded dramatically in recent years. Evidence that genetic abnormalities account for a significant number of medical problems has led researchers to seek hereditary roots for maladaptive behavior as well. Available evidence suggests that genetic factors may contribute to such diverse disorders as schizophrenia, depression, criminality, and mental retardation. The idea that people can inherit certain behavioral tendencies arouses skepticism among some people who feel it conflicts with egalitarian ideals and conjures up the specter of "biological determinism." Yet research, particularly within the past two decades, has shown that few dimensions of behavior seem to be immune to the effects of genetic factors.

A major factor in some genetic abnormalities is irregularities in the structure or number of an individual's chromosomes. **Chromosomes** are threadlike bodies that are present in pairs in all body cells. Humans have 46 chromosomes in each cell. **Chromosomal anomalies** are likely to produce abnormalities in the brain. For instance, persons with Down syndrome, a type of mental retardation, typically have three no. 21 chromosomes instead of two.

Arranged linearly along the chromosomes are the **genes,** each of which occupies its own characteristic position, or **locus.** In contrast to the 46 chromosomes that are contained in a cell, thousands of genes function as the elements of human heredity. About 60% of these genes are related to specific brain functions. More than 4,000 diseases are known to result from failure or abnormality of a gene, but in most cases the actual genes have not been identified or assigned to any particular chromosome. While maps of chromosomes, called **karyotypes,** have assisted geneticists in identifying chromosomal anomalies for some time, recent work on mapping the human **genome**—the complete set of a person's genes—is likely to have a revolutionary effect on biology. It is no exaggeration to say that current maps of human chromosomes compare in accuracy to the navigational charts that guided the explorers to the New World. Mapping the human genome could yield maps comparable to today's most detailed geographical surveys (see Table 2-1).

Scientists know that faulty genes, or genes that are defective in some way, can exist in the absence of obvious chromosomal deviations and may cause metabolic or biochemical abnormalities. Particular genes influence behavior through a long series of steps. Their influence may be modified by events that happen before and after birth, as well as by the actions of other genes. Thus, genes are not islands; a host of other genes, as well as factors in the outside world, can affect their activities. One recent study showed that a particular alteration of genes in mice resulted in an increase in intelligence and ability to solve problems arising in the environment (Tang, 1999). The DNA sequence manipulated in this experiment is 98% identical to that in humans and suggests that altering it by drugs or gene therapy might also make people smarter. Thousands of patients in almost three dozen countries are currently undergoing gene therapy for various diseases (for example, cancer and AIDS). However, gene therapy might

---

Table 2-1

The Human Genome Project

The primary goal of the Human Genome Project was locating each of the thousands of genes in human DNA. These are some of the consequences and questions that will flow from the ability to do this gene mapping:

1. Genetic testing will permit the identification of individuals with genes that pose risks for the development at some point in their lives of illnesses or disorders.
2. The potential for obtaining information about genetic vulnerability will raise several psychological questions. For example, how will receiving the information affect psychosocial development, family interactions, and sense of self?
3. Psychologists will be able to provide support to individuals and families who are confronted with stress-arousing information about their genetic vulnerability or who are considering genetic testing.
4. How can individuals with known risk factors effect behavior changes to reduce those risks?
5. Should parents be able to gain genetic testing information about their children with or without the child's consent?

---

also be used for nontherapeutic purposes, including attempts at genetic "enhancement" to increase physical or mental capacities above those currently deemed normal.

The basis for gene action is a complex substance, **deoxyribonucleic acid (DNA),** that is found in the chromosomes. The discovery of DNA as the means by which genetic information is transferred led to the discovery of how genes work. The structure of DNA consists of two strands shaped like a double helix. The strands of particular DNA molecules determine what specific genetic information they encode and permit the reproduction of any living thing, be it a bacterium or an astronaut.

Sometimes a specific gene is present that has been identified as causing a certain characteristic or disease, yet the person may show no sign of the problem, or perhaps only mild symptoms. The term **penetrance** has been used to refer to the percentage of cases in which, if a specific gene is present, a particular trait, characteristic, or disease will actually manifest itself in the fully developed organism. For example, the molecules of DNA you receive from your parents may carry the blueprint for a strong, sturdy body. But this will not automatically make you an athlete. Your nutrition, the amount of exercise and training you get, and your motivation, as well as any illnesses or injuries you experience before or after your birth, will all influence how your genetic predisposition toward physical strength is expressed. **Heritability** refers to the degree to which a particular characteristic is affected by genetic influences. However, heritability also depends on environmental influences. For example, identical twins have the same genes but they might differ somewhat with regard to certain behavioral characteristics because of differences in their environments (for example, they might have been treated differently by their parents). Both genes and environmental factors combine in shaping development (Turkheimer, 1998).

Behavior Genetics A young but rapidly developing field is **population genetics,** the study of the distribution of genes in groups of people who mate with each other. Such information is used in predicting the incidence of certain genetically carried disorders. For example, Tay-Sachs disease is a form of retardation that is caused by genes carried by some Jews whose ancestors came from a particular area of Europe.

Behavior genetics studies the effects of genetic inheritance on behavior. Behavioral genetic research with humans usually takes one of two forms: analysis of family histories or twin studies. **Pedigree studies** begin with an individual who manifests a particular trait. His or her relatives are then assessed to see whether they have the same trait. When such an analysis is carried out over at least two generations, some inferences about family genetics can be drawn. Twin studies are a more direct way of studying the effects of heredity on behavior. **Monozygotic** (identical) twins have been compared with **dizygotic** (fraternal) twins with respect to a variety of behaviors. Because monozygotic twins develop from the same fertilized egg, they have identical genes and hence identical heredities. Dizygotic twins, on the other hand, are the products of two entirely different eggs. If monozygotic twins exhibit a particular behavior disorder more often than dizygotic twins do, the identical heredity of the monozygotic pair may be the important factor.

The degree of **concordance** in twin studies refers to the relationship between twins or other family members with respect to a given characteristic or trait. If both twins show the trait, the pair is described as concordant (see Figure 2-1). If they do not, the pair is described as discordant. For example, studies have shown that the concordance rate for schizophrenia is high for monozygotic twins and drops precipitously for dizygotic twins of the same sex. The drop is even greater for dizygotic twins of opposite sexes. However, the fact that the concordance rate is not 100% for monozygotic twins suggests that environmental influences play a role. Figure 2-2 presents concordance rates for monozygotic and dizygotic twins for several types of maladaptive behavior. Although there is a very strong suggestion of a genetic component in these disorders, we must not forget that experience can lessen or augment the effects of any hereditary tendency.

The latter point is illustrated by a study of a set of identical triplets, all of whom suffered from serious chronic disorders (McGuffin et al., 1982). Two of the brothers had periods of auditory hallucinations and other clear schizophrenic symptoms. Between these periods they functioned at a low level and were unable to work. The third brother also had psychotic periods (although not as clearly schizophrenic), but he was able to function at a relatively high level and could hold a job between his psychotic episodes. His IQ was higher than that of his brothers, and his relationship with his father was much less stormy than theirs. This case demonstrates that even when people have identical heredities, their levels of functioning may vary in important ways.

The extent to which genes affect behavior has been a subject of debate for at least the last two centuries. In the nineteenth century, fierce battles were fought in what has come to be known as the nature–nurture controversy. Heredity (nature) and environment (nurture) were seen as separate and distinct forces that worked in an either/or

Figure 2-1 These identical twins were reunited at age 31 for the first time since they were adopted by two different families shortly after birth. They found that, despite different upbringings, they were very similar in many of their habits and interests—and even in their choice of occupation, firefighting.

Figure 2-2   Identical twin (monozygotic, MZ) and fraternal twin (dizygotic, DZ) concordances for behavioral disorders. Genetic influence is substantial for schizophrenia, Alzheimer's disease, autism, major affective disorder, and reading disability. The concordance for diagnosed alcoholism is much more modest, particularly for females. Interestingly, autism—characterized by severe impairment in social relationships, communication, and activity—was assumed until the 1970s to be primarily environmental in origin.

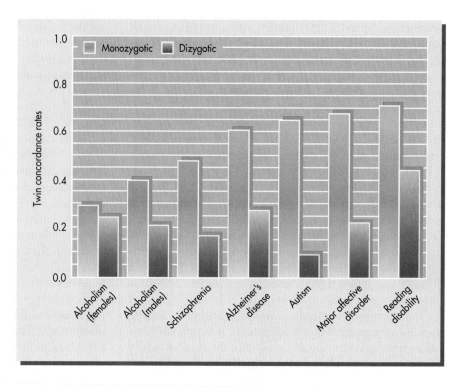

fashion. Either nature determined a certain behavior, or nurture did; you couldn't have it both ways. Today, however, it is recognized that the interplay of many forces—in particular the interaction between the information carried by genes and the experience provided by the environment—determines behavioral patterns.

Research has shifted from simply demonstrating the existence of genetic influence to exploring its details and interactions with other factors. The focus of attention is now on "nature *and* nurture" rather than "nature *versus* nurture." For example, studies of the developing visual systems of mammals have shown that the visual cortex is, to a large extent, ready to be used at birth. Yet if animals are deprived of early visual experience, dramatic changes in the structure of the visual cortex will occur. There is a critical period early in visual development in which both innate neural wiring and visual experience must interact in order to ensure proper development of the visual system. Similarly, the genes that predispose one toward schizophrenia may not be expressed except under special environmental circumstances; for instance, conditions of great stress. Throughout life, experience continues to modulate the fine pattern of cortical connections, allowing us to acquire new skills and knowledge. The operations of the brain result from a balance between inputs from heredity and environment—nature and nurture—and this balance should also be reflected in research into the biological basis of behavior.

As the case of the triplets and other studies suggest, even the family environment, close and constant as it may

seem, affects children differently. Children growing up in the same household have different experiences. They may be at different ages when the family's income and social status rise and fall. They are treated differently by parents and their brothers and sisters. Birth order, age spacing, and sex differences are important. Furthermore, children have different experiences outside the family, with schoolmates, teachers, and friends. Random events of all kinds may also have effects that are compounded over time and make children in the same family different in unpredictable ways. Current work by behavioral geneticists suggests that differences in personality among family members are accounted for by a combination of genetic differences among the children and the effects of the **nonshared environment** (the unique relationships and life experiences of each child).

The Nervous System and the Brain

The nervous system is the body's master control center. It consists of increasingly complex structures that appear as one moves up the evolutionary scale. The 3-pound grapefruit-sized brain that you carry around inside your skull is the most complex structure in the known universe. It can even wonder about itself.

The Nervous System   The nervous system has two major divisions: the **central nervous system (CNS),** which includes all the nerve cells (neurons) of the brain and spinal cord, and the **peripheral nervous system (PNS),** which includes all the neurons connecting the central

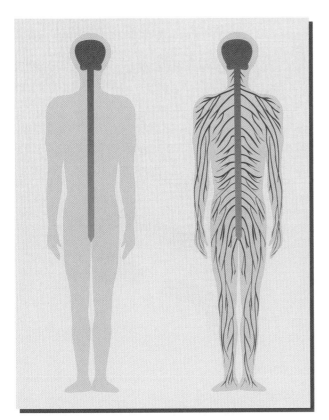

Figure 2-3 The central nervous system and the peripheral nervous system. The central nervous system (CNS) (left) consists of the brain, brain stem, and spinal cord; the peripheral nervous system (PNS) (right) includes all nerve fibers extending to and from the rest of the body. The CNS acts on the world through the PNS (a brain without a mouth cannot speak); it also learns about the world through the PNS (a brain without eyes cannot see).

nervous system with the glands, muscles, and sensory receptors (see Figure 2-3). The peripheral nervous system also has two divisions: the **somatic system,** which transmits information from sense organs to the muscles responsible for voluntary movement, and the **autonomic system,** which directs the activity of the glands and internal organs.

The fundamental unit of the entire nervous system is the **neuron,** or nerve cell, which has a long extension called the **axon** and several shorter extensions called **dendrites.** The function of nerve cells is to transmit electrical impulses to other nerve cells and to structures outside the nervous system (such as muscles and glands). A typical nerve cell receives a messenger chemical, or **neurotransmitter,** from other nerve cells through specific receptor sites on its dendrites. It changes the chemical signal to an electrical one and sends it through the axon. When the electrical signal reaches the tip of the axon, the nerve cell releases molecules of neurotransmitters that pass through a tiny region called the **synapse** and are taken up by specific receptors on the dendrites of adja-

cent nerve cells. This process can be repeated many times to transmit signals throughout the nervous system (see Figure 2-4).

How the neurotransmitters, which cross the minute space (synapse) between the sending cell and the receiving cell, function is becoming clearer. Axons reabsorb some transmitters, and enzymes in the synapse neutralize others. Neuroreceptors in the brain proteins in and on brain cells, which receive chemical messages dictating what a brain cell does, control functions as different as mood, the coordination of movements, sexual interest, and digestion. Until recently it had been thought that there were just one or two variations of each type of receptor. Now researchers realize that there may be as many as a hundred or more variations of a given receptor protein. Fifteen different receptors have been found for serotonin, a neurotransmitter involved in depression; five for dopamine, which plays a role in schizophrenia; and six for norepinephrine, which is important in both anxiety disorders and depression. Various types of medications are being developed that target the specific receptor controlling a particular type of symptom. New automated methods allow identification of an array of molecules in the brain that influence neurotransmission.

The Brain

In 1848 Phineas Gage, a foreman for the Rutland and Burlington Railroad Company, suffered a horrifying accident. He and his men were clearing away boulders for a new rail line by setting off explosive charges. Gage's job was to "tamp," or compress, the explosive compound into a bored hole with an iron rod. While he was tamping, a charge prematurely exploded, sending the iron rod up, like a harpoon, through Gage's left eye socket up into his frontal lobes, and out through the top of his skull. The rod landed 30 meters behind him. Eyewitnesses reported that Gage never lost consciousness and, after a few minutes, rose to his feet and told bystanders that they did not need to carry him. The fact that a person could sustain such a horrendous brain trauma and appear to experience rather minimal aftereffects intrigued people, as indicated by the amount of popular press given to the incident.

Phineas Gage survived his accident and lived for another 13 years. However, the injury to his frontal lobes produced a distinct psychological impairment that was reflected primarily in emotional instability. Prior to the accident, Gage had been known to be a calm and respectable individual. After his accident, he was rude, irreverent, and profane. Although the accident did not appear to have disrupted severely Gage's intellectual, language, or memory capacities, he could not hold his position as foreman because he was unable to suppress or control his emotional outbursts.

The remarkable case of Phineas Gage offers important insights into the workings of the brain. The fact that the control of emotional responses could be affected without affecting

Figure 2-4   The relationship between a pair of typical neurons. A neuron consists of a cell body and two types of extensions—dendrites and an axon. Specific receptors, or dendrites, receive neurotransmitter molecules from the axons of adjacent neurons. This transfer sets up an electrical impulse in the receiving neuron by the nerve terminal at the tip of its axon. The arrival of the impulse at the nerve terminal causes the release of neurotransmitter molecules (shown by dots), which diffuse across a small gap (the synapse) to receptors on the dendrites of the next neuron. The process can be repeated many times to send signals throughout the brain and the rest of the nervous system.

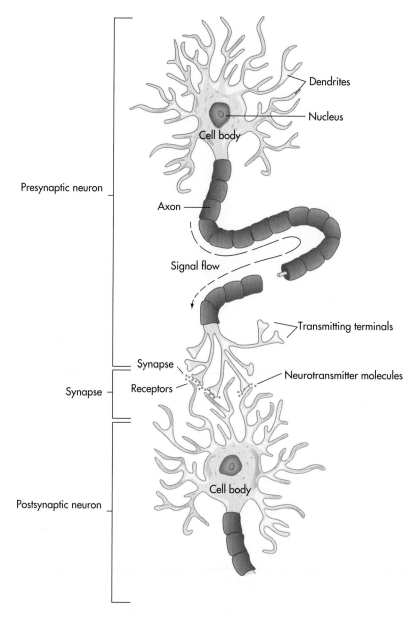

other mental capacities suggests that mental functions are to some extent encapsulated in specific brain regions or brain pathways.

The brain is easily the most complex part of the nervous system (see Figure 2-5). Its two cerebral hemispheres are highly developed centers for processing sensory information. The **cerebral cortex,** the convoluted layer of gray matter that covers each hemisphere, controls our distinctively human behavior. The cortex has areas that monitor hearing, vision, body sensations, and other processes. Disturbances in specific parts of the brain (caused, for example, by tumors) will result in specific behavioral deficits (e.g., loss of speech). Electrical stimulation of certain areas of the cerebral cortex also produces specific motor responses or sensory effects.

The brain and its neurons are active continuously. This activity occurs spontaneously as well as in response to external stimulation. The activity of nerve cells generates electrical energy, and the voltage differences between cells or regions can be amplified and measured as brain potentials. A record of these brain potentials, called an **electroencephalogram (EEG),** shows a pattern of brain waves. Researchers have found that most behavioral states have distinct brain wave patterns. For example, the patterns designated as beta waves dominate during wakefulness, whereas theta and delta waves characterize deep sleep. Researchers have also been able to correlate brain wave pat-

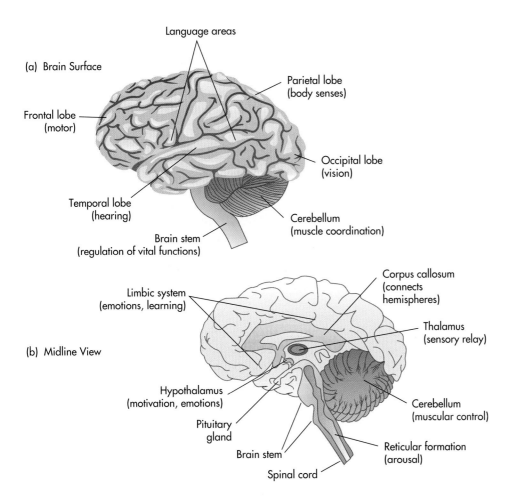

(a) Brain Surface

Language areas

Frontal lobe
(motor)

Parietal lobe
(body senses)

Occipital lobe
(vision)

Temporal lobe
(hearing)

Cerebellum
(muscle coordination)

Brain stem
(regulation of vital functions)

(b) Midline View

Limbic system
(emotions, learning)

Corpus callosum
(connects
hemispheres)

Thalamus
(sensory relay)

Hypothalamus
(motivation, emotions)

Pituitary
gland

Brain stem

Spinal cord

Cerebellum
(muscular control)

Reticular formation
(arousal)

Figure 2–5   The human brain.
(a) The surface of the left
hemisphere, with major areas and
their functions labeled. (b) A
midline view of the right
hemisphere, with major areas and
structures and their functions
labeled.

terns with psychological functions such as dreaming and attention, and with abnormalities caused by tumors or by the unusual electrical activity found in epilepsy (see Figure 2-6).

The Brain and Behavior Abundant evidence exists that various behavioral deficits result from defects in the central nervous system, but many questions remain unanswered. Frequently, neither the particular type of deficit nor the available information about possible organic damage is sufficiently clear-cut to permit a high degree of certainty about the causes of behavior. A person who experiences memory losses and thought disturbances may have fallen on his or her head, but the actual effects of the fall on brain tissue may not be obvious.

Researchers are now pretty sure that memories are made by forging new connections between brain neurons. A healthy brain responds to new experiences by creating more of these links (synapses) or by strengthening the ones that are already there. The rose we just put in the vase on the living room table is mirrored in the brain by a newly forged cluster of neurons. Damage to brain cells can interfere with this forging process.

An important part of current brain research concerns recently identified systems within the brain. For example, work on the basic psychology and biology of motivation has resulted in the discovery of the brain reward system in higher animals. The brain reward system involves the hypothalamus and structures of the limbic system. The **limbic system** is part of the primitive lower part of the cortex and is associated with emotional and motivational functions; the **hypothalamus,** located above the roof of the mouth, plays a role in motivation and emotions but also has connections with many other areas of the brain. Activation of the brain reward system by electrical stimulation produces an intense feeling of pleasure that is much more powerful than ordinary reinforcers, such as food and sex. In experimental work with rats it has been found that if an electrode is implanted so that an animal can deliver a weak shock to its own brain reward system by pressing a lever, it will do so at a very fast rate. If the animal is starved and then given a choice between food and electrical self-stimulation, it will self-stimulate until it starves to death.

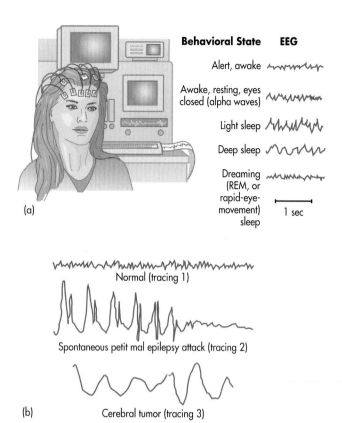

Behavioral State	EEG
Alert, awake	
Awake, resting, eyes closed (alpha waves)	
Light sleep	
Deep sleep	
Dreaming (REM, or rapid-eye-movement) sleep	1 sec

(a)

Normal (tracing 1)

Spontaneous petit mal epilepsy attack (tracing 2)

(b)   Cerebral tumor (tracing 3)

Figure 2-6 An EEG and three EEG tracings. (a) An electroencephalogram (EEG) uses scalp electrodes to measure the activity of specific types of neurons. Particular EEG patterns are associated with certain behavioral states, as illustrated here. (b) EEG tracings from patients who have different disorders are often visually distinguishable from one another and from those of normal subjects. Tracing 1 shows a normal EEG. Tracing 2 shows the onset of wave and spike discharges that are characteristic of petit mal epilepsy, a disorder in which sudden transitory disturbances of brain function may cause brief periods of loss of consciousness. Tracing 3 demonstrates the slow wave activity that is often associated with a cerebral tumor.

Early researchers who studied the brain reward system had no idea that their work might be related to addiction to substances like opium, but recent evidence is rapidly changing the situation. Researchers have discovered that there are chemical receptors on neurons in certain regions of the brain that respond to opiates. In fact, the greatest concentration of these opiate receptors is in the brain reward system. Moreover, the brain produces substances called **endorphins** that activate these receptors; they are even more powerful analgesics (pain relievers) than opium and, when administered directly, are addictive.

The endorphins work like keys in a lock. They fit only into sites, or receptors, that are specifically designed to accept them. Because the endorphins are similar to opium and related chemicals, knowledge of how they work may lead to a better understanding of drug addiction and its treatment. If scientists can create nonaddictive chemicals

that function like the opiates, they may be able to ease pain of all kinds, including the pain connected with stopping a heroin habit. Before this can happen, however, much more information about the brain reward system and endorphins is needed. There are, of course, equally important environmental, psychosocial, and personality factors that influence the actual addictive behaviors.

Brain Plasticity New discoveries are changing old concepts of how the brain develops and works. Researchers now believe that genes, the chemical blueprints of life, establish the framework of the brain, but that the external environment provides the customized finishing touches. The new discoveries are overturning the old concept of a static brain—a self-contained unit that slowly begins the process of learning from a preset, unchangeable set of rules, like a tape recorder that stores whatever words it happens to hear. Now, thanks to advances in molecular biology and genetics, new imaging techniques, and a better understanding of the role of environmental influences, it is clear that the brain adapts to many types of experiences.

In the past it had been thought that the brain develops according to a fixed biological process and that environmental events determine only the content of memories, attitudes, and particular habits. Recent developments concerning developmental plasticity demonstrate the mutual influences of biology and environment in shaping the development of brain and behavior. **Neural plasticity** is defined as the ability of the nervous system to change in response to stimulation and the degree to which it can do so (Hann et al., 1998). Plasticity research shows that brain development is malleable and at times dependent on stimulation available in the environment. Enriched or deprived environments influence intellectual and social development and the brain processes associated with them (Bruer, 1999). Linked to the concept of plasticity is the idea of **sensitive periods,** times during which a particular brain circuit change or a particular kind of learning is possible. The end of a sensitive period occurs when such changes are no longer possible. Environmental influences may be especially potent during sensitive periods.

The brain learns and remembers throughout life by using the same processes it uses to shape itself in the first place: constantly changing its network of trillions of connections between cells as a result of stimuli from its environment. Although we cannot say for sure exactly what the implications of further advances in our understanding of how the brain works will be for abnormal psychology, it is safe to guess that they will be considerable and, perhaps, surprising.

Until recently, it was thought that the adult brain cannot form new neurons. It was assumed that people are born with a fixed allotment of these cells, which then die off one by one over time. Recent research has shown thousands of new neurons a day are formed in the brains of monkeys (E. Gould et al., 1999). (The production of new brain cells is called **neurogenesis**). These neurons migrate to various areas including the prefrontal cortex, the seat of intelligence and decision making. There is also evidence that to some extent, brains can recover from injuries, especially early in life. Lost functions, like language, can be transferred to other undamaged regions. Thus, the brain may be capable of changing its own architecture.

The Endocrines

Your body contains a marvelous system of glands and nerves that quickly organizes your heart, lungs, liver, kidneys, blood vessels, and bowels, causing them to work at top efficiency in an emergency. And when the threat ends, that same glandular system calms everything down.

Several glands, including the pituitary, thyroid, adrenal, and gonadal (sex) glands, as well as the part of the pancreas that produces insulin, make up the **endocrine system** (see Figure 2-7). These glands are ductless: the endocrines, unlike the salivary glands or tear glands, have no ducts for delivery of the substances they produce. Instead, they discharge those substances directly into the bloodstream, which carries them to all parts of the body. Hormones secreted by the endocrine glands act as chemical messengers (the word *hormone* is derived from a Greek word meaning "messenger"). They correlate our reactions to external events and coordinate bodily growth and development.

Hormones are very potent, so it takes very little of them to exert an influence over their specific target cells. Cells that respond to hormones are genetically endowed with special surface molecules, or receptors, that detect even very low hormone concentrations. Once these cells receive a hormone, they initiate a series of adjustments within the cell that are dictated by the hormone. Hormones will usually increase the cell's activity temporarily.

In the study of abnormal psychology there is particular interest in the role played by the endocrine glands in dealing with stress. The word **stressor** is often used to refer to a condition that makes it harder to achieve or maintain biological and psychological adaptation. Examples of stressors to which the endocrine glands respond are biological factors such as disease germs and psychological experiences such as receiving an insult or engaging in combat. The hormones secreted by the glands help us mobilize our physical resources to deal with stressors by fighting or escaping.

The stress response involves the pituitary gland and the part of the adrenal gland called the **adrenal cortex.** In times of stress the brain is activated and sends messages to one of its structures, the hypothalamus, which is close to the pituitary gland. The hypothalamus releases a substance called **corticotrophin-releasing factor (CRF),** which goes to the pituitary to form and release another chemical, **adrenocorticotrophic hormone (ACTH).** ACTH is released into the bloodstream and can go directly to the adrenal cortex, where it causes the adrenal

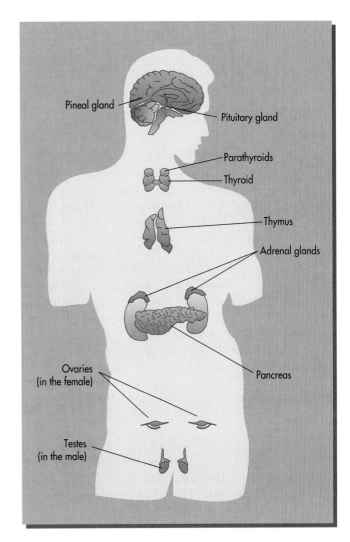

Figure 2-7 The endocrine glands and their location in the body.

cortex to form and release **adrenal corticosteroids,** which affect the brain's and the body's response to mental and physical stress. Some researchers have used the levels of these steroids as an indicator of the degree of stress experienced by the individual.

The Neuroscience Revolution

Exciting as developments in the fields of genetics, neurology, and endocrinology have been, equally impressive are recent advances in our understanding of their interrelationships. A new interdisciplinary field called **neuroscience** has emerged. Researchers in the neurosciences aim to understand the relationship between the structure and function of the brain and human thoughts, feelings, and behavior. The neuroscience disciplines include the following specialties:

- Neuroanatomy—the study of brain structure
- Neuropathology—the study of disease processes caused by disorders of brain structure

- Neurochemistry—the study of the chemical processes that control brain function
- Neuropharmacology—the study of the effects of drugs on the brain
- Neuropsychology—the study of the relationship between various psychological or mental functions and brain structure

Considering the brain from all these perspectives, one can say that it has three major aspects. First, it is a complex *physical and chemical system* in which numerous enzymes, receptors, and other active molecules operate under subtle gene regulatory mechanisms. Neuroscientists seek to clarify how the brain functions as a molecular-cellular machine. This may pave the way for describing the basis for a number of problems, for example, what happens within the brain as people age. Second, the brain is a highly complex and flexible *information system* comprising billions of cells with capabilities far surpassing those of modern computers. Finally, the human brain, the pinnacle of evolution, developed its functional capacity to such an extent that it eventually became the *center of complex processes* tied to thought, emotion, and behavior. With recent progress in cognitive neuroscience, it is possible to foresee a time when we may be able to understand who we are.

The neurosciences seek to protect the brain when it is healthy and to heal it when it is ill. As more and more neuroscience research has been undertaken, it has become increasingly clear that a multitude of factors may cause mental illness. At present, we can only partially understand these causes. We do know, however, that several forms of mental illness are due to different types of brain abnormalities, including the loss of nerve cells and excesses or deficits in chemical transmissions between neurons. We can also attribute some maladaptive behaviors to defects in the wiring or circuitry pattern within the nervous system, to deficiencies in the command centers of the brain, or to the way messages move through the nervous system. The tendency to develop such abnormalities may run in families and therefore be partially hereditary. A broad range of environmental factors (e.g., infections, nutrition, head injuries, or even the shocks and stresses of everyday life) may also play important roles in causing some mental illnesses.

The value of the neurosciences' multidisciplinary approach can be illustrated with the disorder of Parkinson's disease. Parkinson's disease was described by James Parkinson in 1817. It has been called the "shaking palsy" because its victims suffer from a tendency to shake, most noticeably in their hands, as well as a tendency to become stiff and rigid, sometimes to such a degree that they are nearly paralyzed. A significant percentage of people with Parkinson's disease, particularly the elderly, develop lapses of memory, disorientation, and poor judgment. As techniques to study brain structures were developed, it was found that victims of this disease had a loss of nerve cells in a particular and quite small part of their brains called the *substantia nigra*. Neurochemists have shown that certain neurochemical abnormalities contribute to this loss. Spurred on by this clue, neuropharmacologists have found that giving Parkinson's patients the substance L-dopa could correct this neurochemical deficiency. The use of L-dopa has revolutionized the treatment of Parkinson's disease. Patients who receive it often have a marked decrease in their symptoms, particularly rigidity. Many patients who were nearly incapacitated are now able to live normal lives.

The case of Parkinson's disease illustrates how the neuroscience disciplines interrelate closely, with discoveries in one branch often put to use by researchers and clinicians in another branch. Neuroscientists have shown that behavior, perception, and cognition are results of integrated actions of networks of nerve cells. Understanding the complex activities of the nervous system requires identifying the relevant anatomical connections and chemical factors. Sensitive techniques now permit study of the discrete molecular events that take place at the synapses, the junctions between nerve cells where clinically useful treatments are known to exert their actions. Great strides have been made in identifying transmitter substances and the process of neural transmission pertinent to a number of types of maladaptive behavior.

Brain Imaging In the 1970s, advances in applied physics and computer science laid the basis for the later development of instruments that permit the study of both brain anatomy and brain function in living individuals. The development of neuroimaging has provided a window through which the brain can be viewed.

Prior to this development, researchers' conclusions were based mainly on autopsies of the brains of cadavers, or on observations of how brain injuries and lesions affected living patients. **Computerized tomography (CT,** also known as computerized axial tomography, or CAT), in which images are collected on X-ray film, was the first neuroimaging technique applied to the study of abnormal behavior. It requires processing by a computer of 51,200 pieces of data to generate visually and physically meaningful images. More recent imaging technology has produced several even more sophisticated types of equipment. **Magnetic resonance imaging (MRI)** now provides the capacity to examine brain anatomy visually and to measure it quantitatively with a fine resolution of approximately 1 millimeter or less in a routine, rapid, and efficient manner.

An MRI machine has a 1.5-ton magnet that helps in the detection of subtle changes in blood flow within the brain. Figure 2-8 shows someone undergoing an MRI evaluation. The individual must lie still for about 50 minutes in an enclosure that somewhat resembles a telephone booth. MRI machines divide the brain into 185,000 units

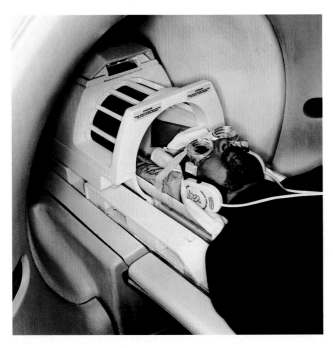

Figure 2-8   A person undergoing an MRI evaluation.

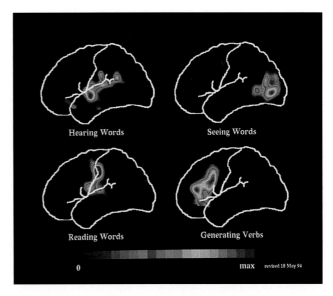

Figure 2-9   PT scans of normal subjects give researchers clues as to which areas of the brain are involved in everyday activities and how the metabolism in the brain is affected.

and measure each activity occurring in every 4-second interval. Increases in activity in particular parts of the brain have significance; for example, increased activity in the hippocampus may indicate the involvement of memory and increased activity in the thalamus is often associated with sensory processing.

The MRI image is derived from signals generated by changes in the levels of electromagnetic radiation from tissues under observation. MRI can make out details one-tenth the size of those detected with CT, and it discriminates much better between different types of brain tissue. **Magnetic resonance spectroscopy (MRS)** extends the capacity of magnetic resonance to permit the study of tissue chemistry and metabolic function. **Single photon emission computed tomography (SPECT)** is an imaging technique that provides direct measurement of cerebral blood flow and several specific physiological and neurochemical features of the brain. SPECT is being used to study brain function while subjects perform various kinds of cognitive tasks. Thus, it is now possible to compare the SPECTs of anxious, depressed, or schizophrenic individuals. Although more precise and flexible than SPECT, **positron emission tomography (PT)** is much more costly and complex (Figure 2-9). Consequently, SPECT can be more widely available and more suitable for general use than PT. Scanning techniques have provided greater understanding of the role of neurotransmitters in brain function and mental disorders. Prior to their development, researchers had been hampered by the lack of techniques for directly assessing the way these substances function in the living human brain.

These various imaging techniques are now being used in the search for clues to evaluate and measure the functions and dysfunctions of the brain. However, research will have to deal with a number of methodological issues before these techniques are maximally useful. Although many different imaging techniques may be helpful for studying disease processes and assessing and understanding brain function in individual patients, none of the imaging techniques has as yet yielded a clear and definitive diagnostic laboratory test that differentiates different types of DSM-IV disorders.

Neuropharmacology Neuropharmacology is a field concerned with the development of drugs for disorders that involve defects or deficiencies in brain chemistry and neural transmission. Many medications for disorders involving behavior, thought, and emotion are designed to either increase or decrease the amount of a neurotransmitter. Neurotransmitters generally are concentrated in separate brain regions and circuits. Within the cells that form a circuit, each neurotransmitter has its own biochemical pathway as well as its own specialized molecules known as receptors. The mechanism of action of a pharmacological agent, such as an antidepressant medication, refers to how the agent interacts with its target in the body to produce therapeutic effects. At the time of transmission a traveling signal reaches the tip (terminal) of one cell and migrates across the synapse to the next one in the circuit. Depression is thought to be reflected in the decreased transmission of a substance called serotonin, and antidepressant medications boost the level of serotonin.

One reason why many drugs have been created to influence behavior disorders is that there is a diversity of neural receptors. A drug typically interacts with a receptor in either of two ways—as an agonist or as an antagonist. When a drug acts as an **agonist,** it inhibits or blocks a neurotransmitter's action, often by binding to the receptor and preventing the natural transmitter from binding there. An **antagonist** disrupts the action of the neurotransmitter. The more selective a drug's action, the more targeted it is to one receptor rather than another, the narrower its spectrum of action, and the fewer the side effects. The broader its action, the less targeted it is to a receptor type or site, the broader the effects, and the broader the side effects.

Psychoneuroimmunology Psychoneuroimmunology simultaneously studies three bodily systems—the nervous, endocrine, and immune systems—that can communicate with one another through complex chemical signals. It is possible that some people who exhibit severe emotional and behavioral abnormalities show psychoneuroimmunological abnormalities as well.

The immune system has two major tasks: recognition of foreign materials (called **antigens**), and inactivation and/or removal of these materials. The immune system influences a person's susceptibility to the course of a disease. It consists of several distinct groups of cells called **lymphocytes.** Research has provided a preliminary understanding of how stress and emotional factors lead to hormonal changes that can sometimes decrease the efficiency of the immune system and thus increase susceptibility to disease. Studies of immune system changes in persons taking academic exams have illustrated these changes (Kiecolt-Glaser & Glaser, 1992).

The immune system is affected by stress from major losses and separations. Many physicians have noted associations between significant losses, like a death, and subsequent illness. The association often seems greatest when the person experiencing the loss is unable to express strong emotions, for example, the grief that normally accompanies personal tragedies. Cases like Larry Jackson's illustrate the stress-illness connection.

> *Larry Jackson, a 50-year-old high school teacher, was divorced five years ago, and four years ago his high school–age daughter died unexpectedly. Since then he has had a series of infections and fevers, swollen lymph nodes, and a nagging cough. Recently he had experienced severe respiratory difficulties, as a result of which he had been hospitalized. The three months prior to the hospitalization had been particularly stressful because of his disagreements with the school principal, who seemed always to be annoyed with him. While he was in the hospital, treatment with antibiotics resulted in some symptomatic improvement, but he continued to feel weak and the lymph node swelling persisted. A lymph node biopsy showed the existence of some cancerous cells. His physician was not sure how Jackson's physical symptoms were related or caused,*

> *but the doctor concluded, after several conversations with his patient, that Jackson had not yet gotten over his daughter's death. Jackson seemed to work very hard at denying his grief. He never expressed the feelings that the doctor felt would be normal under the circumstances.*

The first demonstration of a relationship between bereavement and alterations in the functioning of the immune system was a study of 26 surviving spouses of patients who either had been fatally injured or had died after a prolonged illness (Bartrop et al., 1977). Although the effects were not large, the evidence suggested diminished immune system functioning among the survivors. Subsequent research has shown that bereavement caused by the death of a spouse is associated with a suppression of immunity and that the absence of a supportive social network also contributes to suppression of the immune system (M. Stein et al., 1987). Furthermore, certain psychological states, such as loneliness, depression, and feelings of helplessness, have a negative impact on the immune system. In this connection it is noteworthy that Larry Jackson's divorce had occurred a year before his daughter's death. The divorce had greatly restricted his social network. He had fewer contacts with other people and lacked social relationships that made it easy for him to express his grief, loneliness, and anger at the terrible things that had happened to him.

Integration of Biological and Psychological Systems

For many years chemicals have been known to influence behavior—for example, to reduce pain and induce sleep. Chemicals are used extensively in treating maladaptive behavior. Several kinds of psychoactive drugs (antipsychotic, antianxiety, and antidepressant) are often highly effective in reducing particular types of maladaptive behavior. The introduction of antipsychotic drugs resulted in a sharp decline in the number of patients in mental hospitals. Prior to the introduction of these drugs, there had been a steady increase in the number of hospitalized mental patients. Their use has greatly reduced and even eliminated hospital stays for many individuals.

The biological perspective has proven fruitful because of the therapies, such as drugs, that it has produced, and also because of the questions it has raised. If the abnormal behavior of schizophrenics can be muted or eliminated by certain chemical compounds, can schizophrenia be regarded merely as a sign of a specific chemical disorder in the nervous system? Unfortunately, this sort of question can almost never be answered in a true-or-false fashion. For example, there are instances in which purely psychological treatment of schizophrenic disorder has led to marked reductions in bizarre behavior.

To what degree can maladaptive behavior be viewed as a disease? The boundaries between health and disease are far from clear, partly because of the roles played by psychological, social, and cultural factors as well as biological ones. Given the multiple factors that affect people, an extreme organic perspective is likely to be overly simplified. More likely to stand the test of time is a model that views maladaptive behavior as a product of these interacting factors. Although it does not provide a final answer, the biological perspective has enhanced our understanding of one of these sets of factors.

From the standpoint of abnormal psychology, it is important to relate biological processes to maladaptive behavior. Theories about these relationships range from those that reject the importance of the relationship for most disorders, to those that see value in exploring them but do not draw many firm conclusions, to those that argue that mental illnesses are diseases in the same sense as cancer or high blood pressure. However, there is growing evidence that cancer and high blood pressure are not pure illustrations of physically caused conditions. Most diseases are probably caused by multiple determinants, including physical, environmental, psychological, and hereditary factors. Disentangling these various kinds of causes from one another can be a difficult scientific problem.

It is clear that the multiple causes of mental illness, like those of cancer and high blood pressure, are only partially understood. The biological perspective implies that many types of abnormal behavior are due largely to factors beyond people's control—primarily to the type of brain and body people are born with and the environment in which they live. While this point of view may seem extremely deterministic, it is not totally so. Most theorists recognize that, to varying degrees, biological systems have plasticity. For example, the brain has built into it the ability to adapt and change in response to injury or changes in the environment. The limits that biological processes place on behavior and the degree to which those processes can be influenced represent topics of current research and theory.

The Psychodynamic Perspective

Old notions of the dichotomy between mind and brain and between nature and nurture have been supplanted by an increasingly rich web of mutual influences between mind and brain, nature and nurture. From a biological perspective, the brain provides the elements of both adaptation and maladaptation. While most biologically -oriented clinicians and researchers conceptualize mental phenomena as products of the activity of neuronal circuits in the brain, there is growing recognition that the environment and personal experiences play roles in how the brain functions. Traditionally, the psychodynamic perspective has looked to the mind for the major elements—the causes—of how well or how poorly people

function. Although a merger of the biological and psychodynamic points of view has certainly not yet happened, there is a growing recognition by psychodynamic theorists of the desirability of conceptualizing the biological and the mental as being mutually influencing contributors to human life (Pally, 1997).

The **psychodynamic perspective** is based on the idea that thoughts and emotions are important causes of behavior. Psychodynamic approaches to behavior assume that, to varying degrees, observable behavior (overt responses) is a function of intrapsychic processes (covert events). Not all psychodynamic theorists emphasize the same inner events and the same sources of environmental stimulation, but they do agree that personality is shaped by a combination of inner and outer events, with emphasis on the inner ones. Sigmund Freud, the originator of the psychodynamic perspective, believed that eventually all behavior could be explained by bodily changes; however, because so little was known in his time about the relationships between the body and the personality, he actually gave biological factors little emphasis. Impressed by Charles Darwin's theory concerning the importance of emotions, Freud directed his attention to their influences over thought. Freud believed that to understand behavior it is necessary to analyze the thoughts preceding and associated with it, and that to understand those thoughts, a person's deepest emotions and feelings must be explored.

Because thoughts and feelings are not directly observable, psychodynamic theorists must infer them. They relate their inferences about inner processes to important features of overt behavior. The following account by a psychotherapist illustrates how this is done:

By the fourth session I realized that he had never mentioned his father. It seemed as if there wasn't and never had been a father. I asked myself: How could it be that this man who is so unhappy and has so many problems fails to even mention his father? I guessed that he was either so ashamed of his father that he couldn't talk about him or he harbored so much anger toward him that consciously or unconsciously he couldn't deal with it. I decided to wait and see what would happen rather than push the client in the direction of talking about something that was very sensitive for him.

During the ninth session he told me about a dream he had had the night before. A large dark man sat at a table and a small child watched from a corner as the man ate great quantities of food and ordered a small, frightened woman to bring him more and more. After he ate each helping he would raise a gun and shoot down a few people who were standing in a row against the wall.

The client reported how frightened he had felt during the dream. As we discussed his associations to the dream, it became clear to me that the man in the dream represented his father. After several more sessions he told me he felt very angry with me because I constantly told him what to do and verbally cut him down. After pointing out that in reality I had said almost nothing, I asked him if I seemed like the man in the dream. Finally the dike burst. For the rest of the session and the next one all of his seething hatred toward his father came out. He blurted out that when he was a child he had seen his father strike his mother several times. When he saw this happen, he had wanted to kill his father.

This example shows the complex information-processing task confronting therapists. This therapist not only attended carefully to what the patient said and how he behaved but also drew pertinent inferences (e.g., that the patient's failure to mention his father might be significant) and made important decisions (e.g., to wait and see what happened rather than ask questions about his patient's father).

Apart from the contribution that psychodynamic theories have made to our understanding of human behavior, they seem especially influential because they are the systems out of which all types of psychotherapy developed. While clinical psychoanalysis as originated by Freud is infrequently used today, its basic elements and the theory of mental events underlying it have greatly influenced the development of the entire field of psychotherapy.

Psychodynamic therapies, even though they often differ in their theories and approaches, all emphasize certain key elements. One is the idea that significant past experiences play roles in present functioning—the past shapes the present. Another common element is the belief in the unconscious—there is much that influences our behavior of which we are not aware. We often act for reasons we cannot state, and these reasons are linked to previous experiences. An important part of psychodynamic psychotherapy is to make the unconscious conscious and to help the patient understand the origin of actions that are troubling so that they can be corrected. For some psychodynamic approaches, such as classical Freudian psychoanalysis, the focus is on experiences in the early years of life that give shape to current behavior, even beyond the awareness of the patient. In other approaches the focus is primarily on the relationship between the person and others.

Freud and Psychoanalysis

Sigmund Freud, a Viennese neurologist (1856–1939), is clearly one of the most influential writers of the twentieth century, admired for his wit, intellect, and willingness to revise and improve his theories as his clinical experience grew. Freud began his practice at a time when there were few effective forms of treatment in most fields of medicine. Effective treatment generally depends on an understanding of the causes of a disorder, and at that time, although accurate diagnoses could sometimes be made, little was known about the causes of disease, whether physical or mental. A disorder that was particularly common during the late 1800s was hysteria, the presence of physical problems in the absence of any physical causes. Like other well-trained neurologists of his time, Freud originally used hypnosis to help his hysterical patients lose their symptoms. Then a friend, Joseph Breuer, told Freud that while under hypnosis one of his patients had recalled and understood the emotional experience that had led to the development of her symptoms, and that her symptoms had then disappeared. For a time Freud and Breuer used this method of recapturing memories with some success. However, because some patients were not easy to hypnotize and sometimes the positive effects did not last long, Freud began to develop his method of **psychoanalysis,** in which the patient recaptures forgotten memories without the use of hypnosis. Freud's psychoanalytical method made him enormously influential among European clinicians. By the time he visited the United States in 1909, his reputation had already spread across the Atlantic (see Figure 2-10).

Freud's Theories of Personality Freud's theories of personality may seem complicated because they incorporate many interlocking factors, but two basic assumptions underlie them all: psychic determinism and the conscious–unconscious dimension.

The principle of **psychic determinism** states that all behavior, whether overt (e.g., a muscle movement) or covert (e.g., a thought), is caused or determined by prior mental events. The outside world and the private psychic life of the individual combine to determine all aspects of behavior. As a clinical practitioner, Freud sought to modify unwanted behavior by identifying and eliminating its psychic determinants.

Freud assumed that mental events such as thoughts and fantasies varied in the ease with which they come to the individual's awareness. For example, aspects of mental life that are currently in awareness are **conscious.** Mental contents that are not currently at the level of awareness but can reach that level fairly easily are **preconscious.** Mental contents that can be brought to awareness only with great difficulty are **unconscious.** Freud was interested mainly in how these unconscious mental contents could influence overt behavior (see Figure 2-11).

Freud was especially intrigued by thoughts and fantasies that seem to go underground but then reappear at the conscious level. He asserted that the level of intrapsychic conflict was a major factor in determining our awareness of particular mental events. According to Freud, the classic example of intrapsychic conflict is when a young boy desires to take his father's place in relation to his mother but at the same time feels love and affection for his father. Freud believed that the greater the degree of intrapsychic conflict, the greater the likelihood that the mental events connected with it would remain unconscious. The more massive the unconscious conflict, the greater the person's

Figure 2-10 Sigmund Freud's visit to the United States in 1909 was important in extending his influence in North America. He is shown here at Clark University in Worcester, Massachusetts, with some of the pioneers of psychoanalysis and psychology. From left to right in the front row are Freud, G. Stanley Hall, and Carl Jung. Standing behind them are A. A. Brill, Ernest Jones, and Sandor Ferenczi. Hall, who had been a president of the American Psychological Association, was the president of Clark University. At the time of the Clark University visit, Jung was Freud's principal follower. Soon after the visit, Jung broke with Freud and developed his own psychodynamic theory. Brill, Jones, and Ferenczi remained loyal adherents to Freud's theory.

vulnerability to stress. Freud believed that behavior disorders that occur after childhood are caused by a combination of early traumatic experiences and later experiences that trigger the emotions and unresolved conflicts associated with the early events.

Freud contended that hidden emotions or drives are involved in human conflict. He referred to these drives as

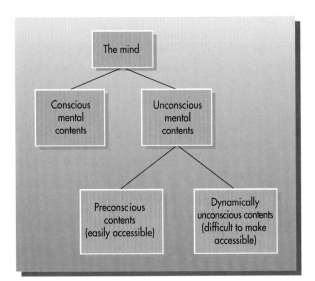

Figure 2-11 Freud's model of the mind. Freud viewed the mind as having conscious and unconscious levels. Material in the unconscious level varies in the ease with which it can be brought to consciousness. The more intense the emotions linked with unconscious thoughts, the greater the difficulty in bringing these thoughts to the level of awareness.

libido and believed that they were a form of psychic energy analogous to the individual's supply of physical energy. Just as some people are more athletic, some have stronger libidos. Freud also believed that the psychic energy or drive level of the individual sets up an inner state of tension that must somehow be reduced. In general, libido can be seen as desire for pleasure, particularly sexual gratification.

One novel feature of Freud's theory was his emphasis on sexuality. This emphasis was no doubt related to the often prudish, repressive atmosphere of Vienna at that time. The concept of sexuality within psychoanalytic theory is very broad and, rather than referring only to sexual intimacy, can be equated with the individual's total quest for pleasure and gratification. Freud also saw the process of development as being expressed in sexual terms.

Stages of Psychosexual Development Freud's theory of personality development placed tremendous emphasis on the effects of experiences that occur during the first 5 years of life. During this period children pass through a number of stages during which their libido is focused on a series of pleasure-giving or erogenous zones in the body. Those zones are the mouth, the anus, and the genitals, resulting in the **oral, anal,** and **phallic psychosexual stages.** In the phallic period, which occurs at about age 3, the child's pleasure in touching his or her genitals is accompanied by fantasies related to the sexual and aggressive impulses the child feels towards his or her parents. The child then enters a more or less sexually inactive latency period, which lasts until adolescence, when the sexual impulses are once again activated. If all has gone well to this point, the individual reaches the **genital stage,** in which pleasure comes from a mature heterosexual relationship. In well-socialized adults, the self-centered sexuality of earlier psychosexual stages blossoms into mature love and the individual becomes capable of genuine caring and adult sexual satisfaction.

What happens to children during these psychosexual stages helps mold their adult personalities. If they are unsuccessful in resolving the psychosexual conflicts that accompany a given stage or are severely deprived or overindulged, they may become fixated at one stage or another. **Fixation** is an arrest in personal development caused by the unresolved difficulties experienced at a given stage. Moreover, even if people resolve their conflicts successfully, severe difficulties later in life may cause them to go into **regression**—to adopt some of the feelings or behavior of earlier, more satisfying stages.

Freud's ideas about psychosexual development are undoubtedly the most controversial aspect of his theory. Although many theorists agree that childhood experiences are very important in personality development, many of them reject Freud's assertions about childhood sexuality.

The Psychic Apparatus For Freud, the mental world of the individual is divided into three structures: the id, the ego, and the superego. A basic distinction is made between the ego and the id. The **id** is a completely unorganized

reservoir of psychic energy. The **ego,** on the other hand, is a problem-solving agent. Whereas the id is concerned simply with maximizing pleasure, the ego's efforts are directed toward maximizing pleasure within the constraints of reality. The id says, "I want it now." The ego says, "Okay, but first we have to do our homework" or "No, that's illegal." The ego performs the valuable functions of avoiding danger or coping with it when avoidance is not possible. There are three major sources of danger for the individual: the environment, id impulses, and guilt. Guilt comes from the third structure of the psychic apparatus, the **superego,** which represents the person's moral code and reflects social values as imposed by parents, schools, and so on. The superego uses guilt to keep the id in line. The superego might say, "Work is more important than pleasure" or "You know that's wrong" (see Figure 2-12).

In early infancy, the id is in control of all phases of behavior. Freud described the thought processes of the infant as **primary process thinking,** or thinking characterized by inability to discriminate between the real and the unreal, between the "me" and the "non-me," as well as by inability to inhibit impulses. Primary process thinking reflects uninhibited adherence to the **pleasure principle**—the immediate satisfaction of needs and desires without regard for the requirements of reality. The

Figure 2-12   The id, ego, and superego can give very different messages. See if you can identify which one is the source of each message in this cartoon. (Answers, left to right: ego, superego, ego, id.)

SOURCE: Drawing by R. Chast; © 1983 by *The New Yorker Magazine, Inc.*

desire for immediate gratification that characterizes primary process thinking is dominant in childhood. Thus, most children, when given a piece of candy, eat it immediately, whereas an adult might wait until after lunch. A child who can't get immediate gratification often shifts a goal in order to achieve gratification in some other way. Thus, a baby crying for its bottle may gratify itself at least temporarily by sucking vigorously on its thumb.

Secondary process thinking, which is reality-oriented, is characteristic of older children and adults and is dependent on the development of the ego. The adult has learned to wait for gratification. Saving money for a goal—a new stereo system, a nest egg for old age—rather than going out for an expensive dinner on payday would be an example. The adult is also less likely than the child to substitute another object for gratification. An adult will generally keep working for the originally desired object even if setbacks occur.

Primary process thinking is still found in adults. It can be seen in humor, in dreams, in the parent who feels better after coming home and yelling at the children because her boss criticized her on the job, and in the person who eats a pint of ice cream out of the container while standing right in front of the refrigerator. However, maladaptation is considered to exist only when the primary process plays an overriding role in the adult's behavior.

Anxiety Freud defined **anxiety** as a response to perceived danger or stress. He distinguished between two kinds of anxiety-provoking situations. In one, of which birth might be the best example, anxiety is caused by stimulation that exceeds the organism's capacity to handle it. In the other, Freud assumed that psychic energy (libido) accumulates if inhibitions and taboos keep it from being expressed. This accumulated energy may build up to the point where it may overwhelm the controls of the ego. When this happens, a panic or traumatic state results. Psychoanalysts believe that these traumatic states are likely to occur in infants and children who do not know how to cope with much of their environment.

Anxiety often arises in anticipation of danger rather than after a dangerous situation has actually occurred. Anxiety, like physical pain, thus serves a protective function by signaling the approach of danger and warning us to prepare our defenses. Anxiety can also indicate inability to cope with danger. The meaning of anxiety is a central problem of psychoanalysis.

Defense Mechanisms Freud believed that the ego was not helpless in the face of the demands of the id, the outside world, and the superego. Anxiety alerts the individual to danger, such as the presence of an intense unconscious conflict or unacceptable wish. If this anxiety cannot be managed by direct action, so that the wish can be gratified, the ego initiates unconscious defenses in order to ward off awareness of the conflict. A variety of defensive responses to perceived danger are possible. Since everyone experiences danger, the use of these responses, called **defense mechanisms,** clearly is not a special characteristic of maladaptive behavior. Defense mechanisms are used, either singly or in combination, by all people at one time or another. The level of adaptive behavior depends on the repertory of defenses available to the individual.

The most important and basic of the defense mechanisms is **repression.** Freud called it the cornerstone on which psychoanalysis rests. Repression, like other defenses, is directed at both external dangers, such as fear-arousing events, and internal dangers, such as wishes, impulses, and emotions that cry out for gratification but arouse guilt. Repression reduces anxiety by keeping anxiety-laden thoughts and impulses out of the person's consciousness.

Repression is often described as motivated forgetting. It is necessary to distinguish between two kinds of forgetting: forgetting neutral mental content such as an unimportant telephone number is not the same as forgetting a traumatic childhood experience. Psychoanalysts are not nearly as interested in neutral material as they are in personally significant events. For instance, a recent college graduate may forget to go for a job interview if she is afraid that she will fail and not be hired, or a man may forget to attend the wedding of his brother to a woman to whom he himself was attracted. In each case, the forgetting is real. The person is not making an excuse but actually is unaware of the engagement at the time. The effort required to achieve such repression sometimes makes other behavior less effective. The person is, in a sense, preoccupied with the effort to maintain the repression. Sometimes repressed thoughts and wishes leak out and are expressed indirectly. Table 2-2 lists some other defense mechanisms.

Clinical Psychoanalysis Psychoanalysis is both a theoretical perspective and a clinical technique. As a clinical technique, it takes time. One of its conditions usually is that both patient and analyst make a commitment to the process for an indefinite period. Freud believed that much unhappiness and ineffectiveness are caused by forgotten conflicts that occurred long ago. Many a psychoanalyst has commented that a lifetime of difficulty cannot be straightened out in a few months.

Today most psychoanalysts are physicians who receive special training in the field of psychiatry and even more specialized analytic training. Some people without medical training, including psychologists, are also qualified to do psychoanalysis. All psychoanalysts believe that the roots of maladaptive behavior may be found in early childhood experiences and in infantile thoughts and feelings that persist into later life. They believe that insight into what went on in childhood enables the individual to adopt more mature and effective ways of living a happier, more productive adult life.

Many of Freud's ideas emerged from his studies of the dreams, fantasies, and memories of his patients. He

---

Table 2-2

Some Defense Mechanisms Used in Addition to Repression

Freud mentioned a number of defense mechanisms, but he devoted most of his attention to repression as an all-inclusive defense. His daughter, Anna Freud, defined most of the concepts we refer to today as defense mechanisms.

- **Displacement:** A shift of feelings and attitudes from one object to another, more acceptable substitute. *Example: A man is criticized by his boss and then feels angry. He comes home and yells at his wife (yelling at the boss might be too dangerous).*

- **Intellectualization:** Dealing with problems as interesting events that can be explained rationally and that have no anxiety or emotional content attached to them. *Example: A woman whose husband has just died discusses the inadequacy of America's mourning rituals rather than her anger at her husband for leaving her.*

- **Reaction formation:** Expressing an unacceptable impulse by transforming it into its opposite. *Example: A mother who feels angry and rejecting toward her child checks many times to see if the child is all right during the night and worries excessively about the child's safety on the way to and from school.*

- **Denial:** Refusal to acknowledge the anxiety-arousing aspects of the environment. The denial may be related only to the emotions connected to an idea or event, or it may involve failure to acknowledge the event itself. Denial is often seen in adults who are under very severe stress often related to loss or failure. *Example: A student who has to take a final exam on material she doesn't understand tells herself the exam is really not important and goes to a movie instead of studying the material with which she is having trouble.*

- **Identification with the aggressor:** Adopting the traits or mannerisms of a feared person. *Example: A child who is afraid of his father takes on certain of his characteristics.*

- **Projection:** Externalizing characteristics or impulses that arouse anxiety by attributing them to others. Psychotics are particularly likely to use projection. *Example: A man who has a strong desire to have extramarital affairs but feels guilty about it constantly accuses his wife of being unfaithful to him even though he has no evidence.*

- **Regression:** Going back to earlier ways of behaving that were characteristic of a previous development level. Typical of people who go to pieces under stress. *Example: A student consoles himself, whenever things get rough, with several hot fudge sundaes, repeating behavior learned when his mother gave him ice cream to make him feel better after a scraped elbow or a disappointment.*

- **Sublimation:** A socially useful course of action developed when more direct forms of gratification are blocked. *Example: A teenager with strong aggressive feelings expresses them without danger by becoming a football player.*

- **Undoing:** Engaging in behavior designed to symbolically make amends for or negate previous thoughts, feelings, or actions; expressing a wish and then denying it. *Example: Knocking on wood after saying "Our house has never been robbed." (Knocking on wood serves as a ritual to undo or atone for what appears too assertive or confident a statement).*

- **Rationalization:** A self-serving explanation and justification of behavior, serving as an excuse for doing something the person believes to be socially unacceptable. *Example: A student caught cheating on an exam justifies the act by observing that the professor's exam is unfair and that other students are also cheating.*

---

developed the technique of **free association,** which calls for patients to express their thoughts and feelings as freely as possible during analysis. With censorship (defense) reduced in this way, Freud hoped to gain a clearer picture of the conflicts underlying maladaptive behavior. As his work proceeded, it occurred to him that dreams might provide evidence about the workings of unconscious impulses. Clinical psychoanalysis places great weight on the interpretation of dreams and other types of fantasy and their relationship to thought and behavior (see Figure 2-13).

Psychotherapists agree that not all cases of maladaptive behavior are suitable for psychoanalysis. There are several situations in which psychoanalysis might not be recommended. For example, a person might not have adequate financial resources to pay for the many sessions needed, or might lack the necessary intellectual resources,

particularly the verbal skill to engage in the required level of communication. Freud believed that the most severe mental disorders, psychoses, could not be treated successfully with psychoanalysis.

Today, while most psychoanalysts believe in the fundamentals of Freud's "talking cure"—the power of unconscious images and fantasies to influence behavior, the importance of childhood experiences in shaping development, and the central role of the patient–therapist relationship, in which early patterns of relating to others are displayed in therapy sessions—there seems to be a growing flexibility in doctrine and practice. For example, some barriers between traditional psychoanalytic practice and the approaches of other psychodynamic points of view appear to be diminishing and intersections between psychoanalytic and other therapeutic approaches are being taken into account.

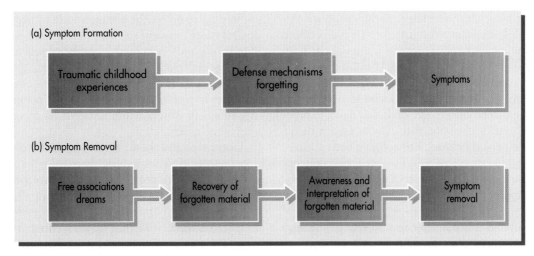

Figure 2-13 Process hypothesized by Freud to be involved in symptom formation and removal. Symptoms (abnormal behavior, worries, unhappiness) result from traumatic, emotion-laden childhood experiences that, while defended against and forgotten, continue to exert unconscious influence that distorts behavior, thought, and emotions. In the accepting, benign atmosphere of the psychoanalytic session, clues to the forgotten material come to the fore and are interpreted. Realization of the infantile quality of the forgotten material permits the individual to give up the symptoms.

More Recent Approaches to Psychoanalysis

Several psychoanalysts have disagreed with aspects of psychoanalytic theory as created by Freud. Among the early revisionists were Carl Jung (1875–1961) and Alfred Adler (1870–1937), both originally members of Freud's inner circle of supporters. Both men had much more optimistic conceptions of human nature than Freud did. Jung did not think that all behavior was determined by earlier events. A controversial feature of his theory is the belief that each of us has a genetic inheritance, a **collective unconscious,** that contributes to our unconscious life. Jung's emphasis on the need to emphasize spiritual qualities as well as rational ideas, and his interest in Eastern religious thought, have made him popular with many people today.

Adler believed that people could be changed for the better through the creation of social conditions designed to develop realistic and adaptive lifestyles. For example, children have to be helped to overcome the inferiority that they naturally feel in comparison to adults. Consequently, Adler attached great importance to training parents in effective child-rearing techniques and to the early education of children. He was a strong believer in the need to prevent psychological disorders rather than simply treat them after they occur.

Erik Erikson (1902–1994) is a central figure in contemporary psychoanalytic theory. His theory is a psychosocial one that emphasizes the "mutual fit between the individual and environment, that is, of the individual's capacity to relate to an ever-changing life space of people and institutions, on the one hand, and, on the other, the readiness of these people and institutions to make him

part of an ongoing cultural concern" (Erikson, 1975, p. 102). Erikson stressed the role Freud assigned to the ego, but he gave it additional qualities such as the needs for trust and hope, industry, intimacy and love, and integrity. He thought of the ego as a strong creative force that can deal effectively with problems.

Of special interest to psychologists is Erikson's idea of stages of development. Unlike Freud, who believed that development was essentially completed early in life, Erikson saw development as a lifelong process. Erikson's view reflects his interest in the interpersonal and cultural needs of the developing individual. He described a life cycle of stages, each of which presents the individual with tasks to be achieved. Whereas Freud centered development around psychosexual stages of the infant and child, Erikson directed attention to psychosocial stages throughout the life cycle. Failure to resolve the conflicts of a particular stage makes coping at succeeding stages more difficult. Erikson's stages range from the acquisition of a sense of trust in others—developed particularly in relation to the mother during the first year of life—to a satisfaction with oneself and one's accomplishments and a sense of order and meaning in life developed in later years. In between these stages, and at particular periods of life, individuals who successfully meet life cycle challenges develop a sense of autonomy and self-control, initiative and purpose, industriousness, a fulfilling self-concept and sense of identity, the ability to form satisfying intimate ties with others, and the ability to lose themselves in work and significant interpersonal relationships.

One of the most noticeable differences between the traditional Freudian approach to the person and the one with which Erikson felt comfortable was his optimism. Although he recognized the often intense struggle between the id and the superego, Erikson was more upbeat than Freud in his belief that the ego could master both instinctual urges and environmental challenges, resulting in a life of relative satisfaction. While Freud focused his attention on the compromises a person has to make in order to adjust to the stresses of life, Erikson was especially interested in the person's capacity to achieve both mastery and creativity (Friedman, 1999). His expanded conception of the ego represents a further development of a psychoanalytic approach called **ego psychology,** which sees the executive functions of the ego as less an outgrowth of the id and more an independent agency. Ego psychology focuses more attention than Freud did on the processes of perception, memory, learning, and thinking, and the development of rationality and the individual's ability to plan for the future.

Object relations theorists offer another approach to psychoanalytic theory. While working within a psychoanalytic framework, these practitioners emphasize the view that the mind is made up of internal representations of significant others, who are referred to as objects. Object relations proponents focus attention on the emotional bonds between one person and another. Melanie Klein (1882–1960), a controversial British pioneer in the psychoanalysis of children, gave great emphasis to complex, presumably "prewired" object fantasies that she believed occurred in very young infants. Other object relations theorists, including those who differ with Klein, give central importance to the concept of **splitting,** the capacity of an infant to divide a single object (e.g., the mother) into separate good and bad mothers, depending on the infant's experience of gratification or frustration. They believe that splitting is common in several types of maladaptive behavior in which an individual has developed a poor capacity for loving and reacting appropriately to others.

Self psychology is a relatively recent theory put forth by Heinz Kohut (1913–1981), an Austrian psychoanalyst who spent much of his professional life in the United States. Kohut held that a person's self-concept is the central organizer of psychological development. His approach to personal development focuses on the maturation of the sense of self from its infantile state of fragility and fragmentation into the cohesive and stable structure of adulthood. The sexual and aggressive drives so emphasized by Freud are not the forces of psychological development for Kohut. That role is played instead by the self. Kohut believed that psychological disorder results when there are major deficits in the structure of the self. Undesirable early experiences—for example, inadequate mothering and attention—can interfere with development of the self. Therapists who adhere to self psychology see their task

as helping to repair the damage done by previous unloving relationships and environments. They seek to facilitate in the patient a healthy sense of self, a satisfactory and reasonably stable level of self-esteem, and the ability to take pride in accomplishments. These practitioners also aim to instill an awareness of and responsiveness to the needs of others while patients learn to respond to their own needs.

Contemporary theorists have helped broaden the perspectives of psychoanalysis, particularly through their emphasis on the role of distorted interpersonal relationships in maladaptive behavior. They have insisted that disordered behavior and thought must be viewed as outgrowths of the individual's efforts to cope with personal crises in a world peopled by others. In presenting their views, these theorists have deemphasized the role of biology in personality and instead have looked to the social environment for explanations of maladaptive behavior.

Evaluating Psychoanalytic Theory

Psychoanalytic theory contains many ideas about human development, psychopathology, and treatment. However, its formulations are difficult to study scientifically because the events they hypothesize are not directly observable. Because psychoanalytic theory contains many general and somewhat unclearly defined concepts, it is hard to evaluate objectively. It seems to be better at explaining what has already happened than at predicting future events.

Because psychoanalytic concepts are difficult to prove experimentally, some researchers have tended to reject them out of hand. Others recognize that certain psychoanalytic concepts are vaguely stated and in fact untestable, but nevertheless feel that scientific investigations should be conducted whenever possible.

Is psychoanalysis a theoretical framework within which human behavior can be studied scientifically, or is it a therapeutic method? These two possibilities are not inconsistent, as Freud pointed out on several occasions. A full evaluation of psychoanalytic theory will be possible only when the effectiveness of psychoanalysis as a therapy for maladaptive behavior has been objectively assessed and its links with the scientific method have been strengthened.

Although several of Freud's basic concepts (such as the id and its powerful drives) seem problematic, some aspects of his ambitious theory have stimulated a number of productive lines of research (Westen, 1998). These include the nature of unconscious thought and memory; the effects of strong, but unexpressed emotions and motivations; assessment of psychological defenses; dissociated or compartmentalized aspects of personality; the nature of childhood experiences and their long-term consequences; and the relationship of concepts of self and others to various types of psychopathology. While some aspects of psycho-analytic theory seem scientifically untestable, its concepts of unconscious thought and motivation, the importance of early experience, and complexity of psychodynamic processes have been fruitful.

The Behavioral Perspective

Give me a dozen healthy infants, well-formed, and my own specified world to bring them up in and I'll guarantee to take any one at random and train him to become any type of specialist I might select, doctor, lawyer, artist, merchant-chief, and yes, even beggarman and thief, regardless of his talents, penchants, tendencies, abilities, vocations, and race of his ancestors. (Watson, 1925, p. 82)

For John B. Watson (1878–1958), an American psychologist who was the founder of behaviorism, development was a thoroughly mechanical affair. The complete personality—by which Watson meant the whole system of overt behavior—was built up out of the conditioning process. Although many contemporary learning theorists are not as confident as Watson about the simplicity of the processes of behavior acquisition and behavior change, the behavioristic approach continues to exert a powerful influence.

Just as dissatisfaction with a narrow biological orientation was one factor in the development of the psychodynamic perspective, the **behavioral perspective** developed in part because psychologists found many of Freud's ideas about the mind vague, complicated, and untestable. These theorists thought that the same behaviors examined by Freud could be explained in a simpler fashion and in a way that would make it possible to study them experimentally. The behavioral perspective asserts that human beings behave according to the dictates of their environment.

Both the psychoanalytic and behavioral approaches are deterministic, but each finds the source of behavior in a different place. (**Determinism** means that every event or act is caused by what has happened before, not by the overt decisions of the individual.) Psychologists using the behavioral perspective focus on learning. They view behavior as a product of stimulus–response (S–R) relationships, not of intrapsychic events. They do not delve into the past or try to get people to figure out why they are the way they are. To change behavior, they concentrate on altering the relevant aspects of the environment, particularly sources of **reinforcement** (reward).

Whereas early behavioral approaches employed relatively few elements (such as the roles of conditioning and reinforcement in learning), this perspective now encompasses such complex processes as the interrelationships among learning and cognitive processes. We begin our study of the behavioral perspectives with two of its most important and widely studied pillars, classical and operant conditioning.

Classical Conditioning

In **classical conditioning,** the response that an organism automatically makes to a certain stimulus is transferred to a new stimulus through an association between the two stimuli. The most famous classical conditioning experiment was the Russian physiologist Ivan Pavlov's (1849–1936) investigation of salivation in dogs. Pavlov placed a hungry dog in a harness and turned on a light at certain intervals. The dog did not salivate in response to the light, which was the **conditioned stimulus (CS).** After a few such trials, meat powder was delivered immediately after the CS had been turned on. Since the dog was hungry, it salivated—an **unconditioned response (UCR)**—upon presentation of the **unconditioned stimulus (UCS),** the meat powder. After a number of trials in which turning on the light was followed by delivery of meat powder, Pavlov found that the dog salivated when the light was turned on even if food did not follow. A **conditioned response (CR)** to the light had been established. Pavlov also carried out experiments with sounds, such as the ringing of bells, as the conditioned stimulus.

In some classical conditioning situations, the UCS is painful. Unpleasant UCSs are used when the goal is to strengthen **avoidance** or **escape responses.** For instance, an electric fence gives pets or cattle a mild but uncomfortable shock when they touch it. The sight of the fence alone then becomes enough to cause them to stay within a certain limited area. Conditioned responses that are not reinforced periodically through the presence of the UCS become weaker and ultimately disappear from the organism's repertory of responses. This disappearance of a previously learned response is called **extinction.**

Students of maladaptive behavior have been intrigued by the process of classical conditioning because it seems to explain fear, anxiety, and other types of emotional reactions. Some of these reactions may come about because of accidental classical conditioning. A child who has been bitten by a dog may fear all dogs and, through generalization, other types of animals as well. Classical conditioning is also the basis for some therapies. An example is **systematic desensitization,** a therapeutic procedure whose goal is to extinguish a conditioned response. For example, this procedure might be used to help a woman who has been afraid of cars ever since being injured in a serious auto crash—at first merely uncomfortable in a car, but eventually so fearful that she cannot even look at a picture of a car. A diagram of the classical conditioning situation would look like this:

Unconditioned stimulus	→	Unconditioned response
Car crash and injury		*Fear*
Conditioned stimulus	→	Conditioned response
Car		*Fear*

Through a series of steps that break down the bond between the conditioned stimulus and the conditioned response and substitute another conditioned response, the woman's fear could be removed. First she would be taught to relax, then to imagine she was looking at an automobile ad in a magazine. Her relaxed state would counteract the anxiety response. Once she could do this successfully, she might be asked to look at a real ad, then to look at a real car, to touch a car, to imagine herself in a car, and so on. At each step she would relax first and then experience the conditioned stimulus. In this way a new conditioning bond would be built up between a car and a relaxed state.

Operant Conditioning

In **operant conditioning,** also called *instrumental conditioning,* the organism must make a particular response before the reinforcement occurs. The organism "operates" on its environment and produces an effect. The American psychologist B. F. Skinner (1904–1990) is famous for demonstrating the effectiveness of operant conditioning. Skinner devised an experimental "Skinner box," in which a rat will press a bar repeatedly if this activity is reinforced by pellets of food falling into a dish (see Figure 2-14). Whereas classical conditioning makes use of natural as well as contrived responses, operant conditioning deals with responses that occur relatively infrequently prior to being reinforced.

The concepts of *reinforcement, punishment,* and *extinction* play important roles in operant conditioning. A **reinforcer** is an event whose occurrence increases the probability that a certain stimulus will evoke a certain response. Reinforcers reward the individual for doing the right thing or not doing the wrong thing. If the reward is desirable enough, the individual is likely to keep on performing properly as long as the response is reinforced. The response can be either an approach response (asking for another glass of milk) or an escape or avoidance response (running from a pursuer or refusing to go out at night). A **positive reinforcer** increases the probability that the proper response will be made by giving the individual something pleasant. A **negative reinforcer,** on the other hand, increases the probability that the proper response will be made by taking away something unpleasant as soon as that desired response occurs.

Figure 2-14   B. F. Skinner was one of the most influential psychologists of the twentieth century. Because we tend to see famous individuals such as Skinner as being somewhat larger than life, the following account by his daughter on one of the last days of his life is both touching and enlightening: *I set up a cot in his study and brought my guitar. For an hour I played for him—all of the classical pieces I could play reasonably well. It pleased him.... Later, ... we talked. I sat on the edge [of his bed], holding his hand, as so many times, dewy-eyed, he had held mine when putting me to bed as a child. Only this time there were tears in both of our eyes.* (Vargas, 1990, p. 410)

Punishment, another way of changing behavior, is an unpleasant consequence for a wrong response. For example, a wife may positively reinforce her husband for not drinking by having sex with him only when he is sober; she may negatively reinforce his drinking by stopping her nagging when he stops drinking; and she may punish him for drunkenness by locking him out of the house. Table 2-3 illustrates the differences between reinforcement and punishment and contrasts them with extinction, still another way of changing behavior.

Positive and negative reinforcers and punishment have been applied to a variety of situations. Smiles, gold stars, and hugs are often highly effective in stimulating productive behavior in schoolchildren; and frowns or scolding may be used to discourage undesirable behavior. However, punishment, a negative consequence of behavior that is intended to discourage its repetition, is not very effective when used alone. It may cut down on undesired behavior, but it does not necessarily stimulate productive activity, since the person does not learn an acceptable substitute behavior.

Table 2-3		
Some Mechanisms of Behavior Change		
Mechanism	Definition	Examples
Positive reinforcement	Encouraging any behavior by using a desired reinforcer as a reward.	Giving a child candy when he brings in a homework assignment. Saying "good girl" when a baby swallows a spoonful of cereal.
Negative reinforcement	Encouraging any behavior by removing an aversive stimulus when the behavior occurs.	Ceasing to scold a child when he hangs up his coat after throwing it on the floor. Giving in to a roommate or spouse in order to bring an unpleasant argument to an end.
Punishment	Aversive stimulus given as a result of an undesired behavior in an attempt to suppress that behavior in the future.	Slapping a child for swearing at you. Sending a child to her room because she broke her brother's toy.
Extinction	Suppressing behavior by removing the reinforcers for it.	Ignoring a child when he has a temper tantrum. Removing all rock records from the record collection of your roommate, who likes only rock music and plays the stereo too often for your comfort.

A diagram of operant conditioning looks like this:

Response

↓

Reinforcement

↓

Increased probability
of repetition of response

For example, in teaching a child to talk, parents reward the child with smiles and hugs whenever she says a desired word. These parental behaviors are positive reinforcements; they increase the chance that the child will repeat the word.

We hear over and over again how complex human behavior is. We point to our lofty thoughts, fine feelings, and obscure motives. But those who use the behavioral perspective see human behavior as complex for other reasons. Even the simplest act can be seen as a chain of responses, each of which needs to be learned. Few of us get things right the first time. Children are particularly likely to become discouraged and give up if reinforcement is withheld until they do something perfectly. Thus, **shaping**—obtaining the desired response by reinforcing successfully better approximations of it—is one of the basic processes in operant conditioning.

Considerable thought and planning are needed to decide what sorts of reinforcers are best for achieving particular behavior-shaping goals. In some situations an effective reinforcer may be rejected for purely practical reasons. A teacher who wanted to control disruptive behavior in the classroom probably could not use candy as a reinforcer, because it might have an undesirable effect on the pupils' appetites.

In addition to deciding which reinforcers would be most effective and practical, it is necessary to decide on a *schedule* for reinforcing particular types of responses. A **schedule of reinforcement** refers to the pattern in which reinforcements are administered. Sometimes we receive reinforcement after every response of a given type, but more typically only a proportion of our responses are reinforced. These are some of the reinforcement schedules used in research on learning:

- *Continuous reinforcement schedule*—every response of a particular type is reinforced.
- *Partial or intermittent reinforcement schedule*—only some of the responses are reinforced.
- *Fixed-ratio schedule*—reinforcement is given after a fixed number of responses.
- *Variable-ratio schedule*—reinforcement varies around an average number of responses (e.g., it might be required that on average 10 responses must be made before a reinforcement is given).
- *Fixed-interval schedule*—reinforcement follows the first response that occurs after a certain time interval.
- *Variable-interval schedule*—reinforcement occurs after a variable interval of time.

Clinical Use of Reinforcement The following case, which involves shaping verbal behavior in a 13-year-old boy with a suspected hearing problem, illustrates the clinical use of reinforcement:

Benjie, who wore a hearing aid, had never been observed to make verbal responses (except for occasional grunts). He did not smile, cry, or interact meaningfully with others in any way. A reinforcement program was instituted in which candy was used as both a positive and a negative reinforcer. In addition to negative reinforcement (removal of a previously earned piece of candy), mild punishment (a slap on the hand) was used. This was how the operant treatment of Benjie began:

    a. *The experimenter sat across from Benjie and said, "Do you hear me, Benjie? If you do, nod your head." The experimenter nodded his head in the hope that Benjie would imitate him and gave Benjie some candy. Initially, Benjie made no head-nodding response.*

    b. *Next, the basic procedure remained the same; however, candy was made contingent on the head-nodding response. Soon, Benjie was making 100 percent imitative head-nodding responses.*

    c. *In the next procedure, the experimenter stood behind Benjie when giving the verbal cue. Benjie responded by nodding his head. This was the first indication to the experimenters that Benjie did, in fact, have the ability to hear verbalizations given at a normal conversational volume. From that point on Benjie did not wear his hearing aid in the laboratory or at home.*

This reinforcement procedure was not effective in inducing Benjie to make sounds. Because he seemed unresponsive to rewards, the experimenters decided to try a food deprivation schedule as a means of modifying Benjie's behavior. At breakfast, as soon as he made a sound he received a bite of food. This procedure proved to be effective. When he was hungry, he would make sounds at the command, "Benjie, tell me something." Eventually he came to respond to the command even when he was not hungry. After several months Benjie responded with a vocal sound every time a verbal command was directed toward him. (Knowles & Prutsman, 1968, p. 2)

Although the ethical guidelines for working with subjects would generally prohibit the use of food deprivation as a way of motivating behavior, this kind of approach may be used in very special situations such as this one. Here the acquisition of a new behavior is important for treatment, and less intrusive ways of promoting the needed change are not effective. Another example of this controversial approach to behavior change is the use of mild electric shock or other painful stimuli to treat disturbed and retarded children who are self-mutilating; that is, they constantly inflict injury on themselves by knocking their heads against the wall, pulling out their own hair, and so on. The use of this technique has been debated by both professionals and the courts, but because of the lack of any effective alternative it is often considered to cause less damage to the patient than the self-inflicted behavior.

Social–Cognitive Theories

A major development in analyses of the role learning plays in maladaptive behavior is the increasing attention being given to social and cognitive factors. While in no way denying the importance of conditioning and reinforcement, many researchers and clinicians now see social and cognitive processes as also being pertinent to all aspects of human behavior. According to **social-cognitive theory,** internalized beliefs, perceptions, and goals influence the impact that experiences associated with conditioning and reinforcement have on behavior and thoughts. Similarly, our interpersonal relationships play significant roles. It appears that there is a two-way street between learning variables, on the one hand, and cognitions and social ties, on the other.

Research on modeling illustrates work growing out of the social-cognitive perspective. Reinforcement is not always necessary for learning to occur. **Modeling** can be used to change behavior because people are able to learn by watching how other people do things. Opportunities for observational learning arise when another person—a model—performs some response or group of responses. One of the first learning theorists to point this out was Albert Bandura (b. 1925). He emphasized that the observer does not need to have had practice in making the observed response and does not necessarily have to be reinforced in order to learn it. Exposure to models whose behavior and skills we admire plays an important role in our personal development and contributes to our self-esteem (see Figure 2-15). Models may have desirable or undesirable effects on those who observe their behavior.

Clinical studies support the conclusion that observational learning plays a part in the acquisition of maladaptive behavior. Anxiety in patients can often be traced to modeling experiences. A severe phobia, for example, may represent an exaggeration of a major or minor fear observed in a parent. Watching television is basically a symbolic modeling experience, especially for children. Noticeable and sometimes dramatic changes in behavior can result from modeling experiences.

Modeling exposes the observer to the specific responses displayed by the model. Even more important, it provides the observer with food for thought. A child who observes continual arguing between parents forms a concept of what marriage is like. Poor people who observe the parade of commercials on television come to believe

Figure 2-15 While modeling behavior can occur at all ages, it is seen most clearly in children. This girl's perception of her father as a loving, caring person probably plays an important role in her imitative behavior.

that most other people are free from financial worries. Modeling, then, not only illustrates possible overt behavior but also contributes to the formation of concepts, attitudes, and needs. **Role playing,** or practicing behavior shown by a model, is another important learning technique.

Clinical Use of Modeling The way in which modeling and role playing can strengthen adaptive behavior is illustrated by the case of John R., an unemployed 18-year-old who had been placed in a juvenile correction facility for stealing a car. Therapists noted that his problem was not simply a failure to adhere to social norms but a weak behavioral repertory.

A particularly serious deficiency was his fear about and inadequacy in job interview situations. He had never had an opportunity to observe the effective behavior of others in situations that required putting one's best foot forward. In the institution he was given the opportunity to observe job interview behavior as modeled by persons (noninmates) who were effective in this area. On several occasions John observed simulated job interviews and then practiced being interviewed himself. After leaving the institution, he found that the modeling experience had helped him. He reported that while waiting for an actual job interview he had remembered and thought about the behavior he had observed. He then mentally rehearsed how he might handle himself when confronted by the personnel manager. He was hired, he felt, because of the new skill and security he brought to the previously traumatic job interview situation. His increased skill and security seemed to result from his having a better idea of what to expect in a job interview.

A strength of social-cognitive theory is its recognition of two developmental aspects of behavior. One is the individual's history of experiences, including various types of events and associated conditioning and modeling. The other aspect, less well understood but no less important, is how the individual analyzes and interprets past experiences. Much of what is learned, especially after the early years of childhood, occurs implicitly—that is, without being a direct consequence of external environmental effects. **Implicit learning** takes place when an individual arranges memories of experiences (such as his father's need to read the newspaper right after dinner) into new patterns of thought (such as the role of the reading as a barrier to family interaction). As the child develops an extensive symbolic repertory of words and images, he is no longer dependent on actual environmental experience to learn. Instead, children can manipulate their growing storehouses of symbols and images, imagine new attainments, and thus develop new strategies for dealing with the environment. Similarly, by reorganizing their internal symbolic world, adults supplement the external world with novel thoughts that in turn provide new opportunities for learning and self-administered reinforcements.

While the behavioral perspective focuses attention on the role of the external environment in shaping and governing our actions, social-cognitive theorists believe that the environment often exerts its influence on behavior indirectly through the individual's thought processes. Our behavior is affected by our memories of the past and anticipations of the future as well as by the impact of stimulus configurations.

In addition to his emphasis on social-cognitive theory, Albert Bandura (Figure 2-16) has more recently emphasized the symbolic and cognitive aspects of learning as opposed to the stimulus–response aspects. Bandura (1978) is interested in studying self-regulation, or learning by internal reinforcement, as opposed to modifying behavior by external reinforcement alone. According to Bandura (1981, 1986), we can solve problems symbolically without having to resort to trial-and-error behavior because we can foresee the consequences of our behavior and act accordingly. For example, we buy fire insurance because we think about what might happen if our house burned down. Similarly, in preparing for our first winter camping trip, we assemble protective gear because we can anticipate the effects of a blizzard. The ability to anticipate consequences operates in more routine behaviors as well as in special instances like these.

Learning is a change in behavior or in potential that occurs as a result of experience. The three major examples of learning we have discussed are classical conditioning, operant conditioning, and modeling or observational learning. As the cases of Benjie and John R. show, opportunities

Figure 2–16   Albert Bandura's work on modeling, as well as his more recent work on self-regulation, has been important not only theoretically but also in the development of new therapeutic approaches.

to experience certain types of learning can be valuable in modifying maladaptive behavior.

The Cognitive Perspective

People are disturbed not by things, but by the views which they take of them. (Epictetus, first century A.D.)

If the Greek philosopher Epictetus were alive today, he would likely be a cognitive psychologist. The word *cognitive* comes from the Latin word *cognitare*, meaning "to have known." Cognitive psychology addresses human beings as information processors and problem solvers. The cognitive view seeks to account for behavior by studying the ways in which the person attends to, interprets, and uses available information.

Like the psychodynamic perspective, the **cognitive perspective** is concerned with internal processes. Rather than stressing urges, needs, and motivations, however, it emphasizes how people acquire and interpret information and use it in solving problems. Unlike psychoanalysis, it places great emphasis on mental processes that we are aware of or can rather easily be made aware of, as opposed to hidden motivations, feelings, and conflicts. Its approach has been contrasted with the learning theories' emphasis on the external environment as a prime cause of behavior. Typically, the cognitive perspective pays more attention to our present thoughts and problem-solving strategies than

to our personal histories. However, histories of cognitions also receive some attention (I. G. Sarason, 1979). The relationships among emotions, motivations, and cognitive processes and thus the overlap between the cognitive perspective and other approaches is becoming more evident.

In its view of the individual as information processor, the cognitive perspective holds that people are continually collecting, storing, modifying, interpreting, and understanding both internally generated information and environmental stimuli. Humans are seen as active, selective seekers, creators, and users of information, and behavior is viewed as both a product and an initiator of mental acts and environmental changes. The mental life of the individual is conceived of as consisting of **schemata** (plural of *schema*) that contain information in particular domains such as parents, work, and pets. Through their influence on cognitive processes, schemata enable people to identify stimuli quickly, cluster them into manageable units, fill in missing information, and select a strategy for obtaining further information, solving a problem, or reaching a goal.

From a clinical standpoint, self-schemata are especially important. They organize and guide not only our social experiences but any experiences that are personally relevant. Personally relevant experiences are often laden with emotions and are likely to reflect an individual's prior learning history. Self-schemata are capable of distorting a person's perceptions of reality. Schemata that concern our self-evaluations influence not only how we feel about ourselves but also how we relate to others. For example, **self-efficacy** refers to the strength of our convictions about our personal effectiveness (Bandura, 1997). People may imagine potential difficulties as more formidable than they are in reality if they perceive themselves as ineffective in important types of situations. Inappropriate or maladaptive behavior in those situations may confirm the individual's self-perception as inadequate, helpless, or cowardly. This confirmation may cause the person to avoid problematic situations or reduce his or her task-relevant efforts. A vicious cycle is thereby created and perpetuated.

Many cognitive psychologists are developing techniques by which people who lack behavioral self-control can be helped to acquire it. The following examples illustrate techniques for strengthening self-control that make use of cognitive mechanisms:

1. A student studies every night even though no test has been announced.
2. A heavy smoker teaches herself nonsmoking behavior.

In the first example, the student may motivate himself by means of cognitive representation of future consequences. That is, he may think about how bad he would feel if he scored poorly on the next test or how stressful it would be to try to learn all the information the night before the test. Another motivation may be his own goal-setting behavior.

He wants to receive a high grade for the course. Whenever he feels like turning on the television set or stopping for a snack, he visualizes how he will feel if he attains his goal. When people evaluate their own behavior in this way, they tend to persist until they achieve their goals.

In the second example, each time the former smoker has the impulse to smoke, she may imagine an X-ray of lungs afflicted by cancer, or she may see herself coughing and unable to breathe. Such self-generated cognitive mechanisms would provide negative reinforcement for her thoughts about smoking.

Maladaptive Behavior and Cognition

Many psychological disorders involve serious cognitive disturbances. These disturbances may not be just symptoms but actual causes of the disorders. Several cognitive theorists have suggested some of the causal pathways. For example, Dollard and Miller (1950), in their effort to integrate psychoanalysis with mainstream psychology, focused attention on the cognitive process involved in resolving conflicts. Kelly (1955) emphasized the importance of personal constructs in problem solving. By *personal constructs*, Kelly was referring to how people interpret or develop ideas about themselves, the world, and future events. He saw personal constructs as causes of emotional reactions.

More recently, Aaron Beck (b. 1921) (Figure 2-17) has directed attention to the concept of the schema as an enduring cognitive structure that represents an individual's organized knowledge in a particular domain.

Schemata exert important influences over (1) affect and feelings and (2) behavioral responses. For Beck, maladaptive behavior results from dysfunctions of the cognitive system, for example, highly idiosyncratic schemata that are not consistent with reality. Dysfunctional schemata concerning the self (for example, "I am a selfish person") often develop early in life in response to certain situations and are reactivated later in life. This can result in distortions, such as catastrophizing about the consequences of being less than perfect (Beck & Emery, 1985; Beck et al. 1979).

The content of these idiosyncratic schemata influences the type of maladaptive behavior a person displays. For example, a depressed person might attend unduly to failure, rejection, and their consequences. Beck's cognitive therapy is intended to help patients restructure their thinking and gather evidence to refute the validity of the illogical beliefs that are maintaining their abnormal behaviors. This restructuring often involves revising negative interpretations of events, viewing the future less pessimistically, and thinking more positively about oneself. For Beck, psychological difficulties are due to automatic thoughts, faulty assumptions about the motivations and reactions of others, and negative self-statements. These

Figure 2-17 Aaron Beck has applied his cognitive theory to the understanding and treatment of several types of maladaptive behavior, including depression, anxiety, and personality disorders.

are examples of the cognitive distortions with which Beck's theory and therapy deal:

- "My life is wasted unless I am a success."
- "It is awful to be disapproved of by people important to you."
- "A person should do well at everything she or he undertakes."

Cognitive Therapies

The idea that maladaptive thoughts are the cause of maladaptive behavior and that people must be taught new ways of thinking has been used as a basic approach by many therapists. Several forms of **cognitive therapy** are based on the cognitive perspective.

Aaron Beck thinks that the job of the therapist is to help clients restructure their thinking and replace maladaptive thoughts with thoughts that are more helpful in coping with stressful situations. Beck's work was originally focused on the cognitions of depressed individuals, but his approach has been extended to several other types of disorders and problems, such as proneness to anger easily (Beck, 1999; Beck & Emery, 1985; Beck et al., 1990). Beck thinks that people's emotions and behavior are based largely on the way they view the world. In his view, many people exaggerate their difficulties and minimize the possibility that anything can be done about them. Applying this idea in therapy, it becomes important to identify those beliefs (e.g., "People don't like me") that shape personal interpretations of events and facilitate or inhibit action. Beck believes that people generally have broad goals that are very important to them but that may not be completely in their awareness. The therapist's job is to help translate the client's stated aspirations and inhibitions into these underlying goals.

Patients in cognitive therapy are encouraged to test their perceptions of themselves and others, as if they were testing hypotheses. They receive homework assignments from their therapists and learn to express and view more objectively their assumptions and schemata about how they and the world work. For example, with patients convinced that they must always be perfect, Beck suggests that the therapist gently ask questions like "Would you agree that it is against your best interests to have this belief?" "What are the disadvantages of thinking this way?" "Do you think it is possible to ignore these thoughts?" Table 2-4 summarizes four questions cognitive therapists consider in working with patients (Needleman, 1999).

In addition to Beck, Albert Ellis (b. 1913) has pioneered the development of cognitive approaches to the treatment of psychological problems. His **rational-emotive therapy** is based on the belief that behavior depends more on individual belief systems and ways of interpreting situations than on objective conditions. Ellis contends that all effective psychotherapists, whether or not they realize it, function as teachers for their clients. They help their clients to review, reperceive, and rethink their lives; to question their irrational beliefs; and to modify their unrealistic and illogical thoughts, emotions, and behaviors. Ellis regards both intense emotions and maladaptive behavior as the modifiable consequences of thoughts. He admits that faulty beliefs are probably formed in childhood. However, he feels that finding out how people got to be the way they are is less important than helping them respond more constructively to their present situation.

In rational-emotive therapy the clinician explains and demonstrates productive thinking, persuades the client to think and behave in more effective ways, and discusses homework assignments. Through such assignments the client might practice ways of behaving more assertively

with co-workers or family members without alienating them (Ellis, 1970).

The cognitive perspective seeks to understand how dysfunctional and irrational thought patterns create emotional problems. Clinicians who take the cognitive perspective analyze distress and maladaptive behavior in terms of what we tell ourselves about situations rather than the external situations themselves. Box 2-1 discusses a frequently asked question about the cognitive and social-cognitive perspectives.

The Humanistic–Existential Perspective

The **humanistic-existential perspective** presents a sharp contrast to the theoretical approaches described so far. Its roots are found in a number of philosophical and religious systems that have stressed the dignity, inherent goodness, and freedom of human nature. The growth of this perspective within psychology was partly a product of this tradition and partly a reaction to the less flattering conceptions of human nature that are characteristic of psychoanalysis and radical behaviorism.

Clinicians with humanistic and existential orientations have their differences, perhaps the main one being that humanists tend to be more optimistic about the human condition than the existentialists. Humanistic clinicians see undesirable environmental influences as disruptors of self-actualization, whereas existentialists emphasize the responsibility of the individual to deal realistically with environmental givens. However, both believe that scientific psychology is missing the mark when it dwells only on observable behavior and neglects the person's inner life. They believe that inner experiences and the search for the meaning of existence are the core of the individual and hence should be the focus of psychology. They therefore regard introspection as a valid and indeed indispensable source of psychological information. From the standpoint of therapy, these orientations emphasize the role the therapist plays in expanding the patient's awareness of his or her worth, potential, and need to assume responsibility for directing one's life course.

The Humanistic View

One of the central assumptions of the humanistic view is that in every person there is an active force striving toward **self-actualization,** a desire to be "all that you can be." When the human personality unfolds in a benign environment that gives these creative forces free rein, the positive inner nature of the human being emerges. Human misery and pathology, on the other hand, are fostered by

---

Table 2-4

Four Questions Asked in Cognitive Therapy

1. What situations trigger maladaptive cognitions?
2. What are these cognitions and how do they intrude on the patient's life?
3. How does the patient interpret or make sense of the cognitions?
4. What are the consequences of the cognitions with regard to behavior and experiencing strong emotions?

Q&A   **Box 2-1**

Q. There seems to be a lot of overlap between the cognitive and social-cognitive approaches. Is that correct? If it is correct, why are the two approaches described in different parts of the chapter?

[The social-cognitive approach is presented as part of the behavioral perspective; the cognitive approach as a perspective in its own right.]

A. *Good questions. There is considerable overlap between these two approaches. Their placements in the chapter reflect differences in their historical roots and certain differences in their approaches to problems of living. The social-cognitive approach developed originally as part of the psychology of learning and came about because a number of psychologists interested in the learning process felt that the field needed broadening beyond the influences of conditioning and reinforcement to include important social influences exemplified by the child's mimicking of parent's behavior. Because the nature of the social relationship between the imitator (child) and the person imitated (parent) plays such an important role in what is learned and how much learning takes place, a* **social learning** *approach developed within the psychology of learning. It has become increasingly clear that relationships between people are not just*

a matter of the behavior they observe. People in relationships—especially close relationships—have thoughts and feelings about each other that are products of the circumstances that surround the relationships. These social relationships influence how individuals respond in situations and the social initiatives they take. Adding cognitions to the recipe led to the social-cognitive approach we have described.

The cognitive perspective developed as part of what is often referred to as the cognitive revolution, the idea that each person is an information processor. How might the information processing system best be characterized? While there continues to be controversy over how this question should be answered, adherents to the cognitive perspective agree that people form representations of themselves and the world about them and these representations (what Beck called schemata) are important influences over our behavior, feelings, and how we live our lives. Another dimension of this perspective can be seen as a reaction against the psychoanalytic idea that overcoming maladaptive thought and behavior requires a lengthy, intensive exploration of the history of a person's unconscious mental life. Therapists such as Beck and Ellis argued that what is on a person's mind now is the critical issue, not what he or she might have thought about in kinder-

garten. Further, they feel that, with the help of a therapist, people can develop needed insights about themselves and their behavior and change their behavior in positive ways.

Despite the different paths that led to the cognitive and social-cognitive points of view, they seem to be converging. Cognitive therapists give their patients homework assignments and ask them to use insights gained about their cognitions in day-to-day practice. Someone who is often unpleasant because of anger over beliefs about the untrustworthiness of other people can be helped to consider the possibility that most people are trustworthy and to do everyday life "experiments" in which positive thoughts about others are acted upon. When these "experiments" are carried out, the person can observe that the people with whom he or she interacts are usually pleasant, trustworthy, and nice to be with. In this way, the person is reinforced for thinking and acting positively (trustingly) in social situations. Today, cognitive-behavioral therapies are being developed that make use of concepts related to both learning experiences and the person as an information processor.

So, if it occurred to you that there is overlap between the cognitive and social-cognitive viewpoints you were right. It will be interesting to see where the increasing convergences of recent years will lead in the future.

---

environments that frustrate the individual's natural tendencies toward self-actualization.

Carl Rogers (1902–1987) (Figure 2-18), one of the leaders of humanistic psychology, used the self-image as the centerpiece of his perspective on personality (Rogers, 1951, 1959, 1980). Rogers related the ability to achieve self-understanding and self-actualization to the individual's self-regard and perception of acceptance by others. An adult who felt wanted and highly valued as a child is likely to have a positive self-image, to be thought well of by others, and to have the capacity for self-actualization. Optimal adjustment results in what Rogers calls the fully functioning person and is characterized by a low level of anxiety. Anxiety is due to uneasiness or tension resulting from inconsistencies between people's self-perceptions and their ideas of what they would like to be.

Although the ways in which they conceptualized behavior contrast sharply, both Rogers and Freud developed their theoretical positions on the basis of similar observational data: the behavior of clients and therapists in psychotherapy. However, Rogers rejected the psychoanalytic notion that people are irrational and unsocial by nature. He asserted, on the contrary, that each person is basically rational, socialized, and constructive.

For Rogers, psychotherapy is a situation in which anxious, troubled people with low self-regard and distorted perceptions of themselves and the world seek help. Rogers thinks that healthy people are those who move away from roles created by the expectations of others, that is, they do not pretend to be something they are not. Instead, they learn to trust themselves and reject the false selves that others have created for them. Neurotic and psychotic people, on the other hand, have self-concepts that do not

Figure 2-18   Carl Rogers. "My experience in therapy and in groups makes it impossible for me to deny the reality and significance of human choice. To me it is not an illusion that man is to some degree architect of himself." (C. R. Rogers, 1980, p. 57)

match their experiences. They are afraid to accept their own experiences as valid, so they distort them, either to protect themselves or to win approval from others. A therapist can help them give up these false selves.

The task for Rogerian therapists is neither to provide interpretations nor to give advice. Rather, the therapist must accept clients as having worth and dignity in their own right despite their problems. This acceptance means that the therapist must understand the client's feelings, no matter how positive or negative they are or how much they contradict the therapist's own attitudes.

Rogers (1959) believed that "there is no such thing as scientific knowledge; there are only individual perceptions of what appears to each person to be such knowledge." This statement expresses the humanistic-existentialist view that inner experience and a search for individual meaning should be the focus of psychology.

The Existential View

The existential perspective became popular in Europe after World War II as psychologists and philosophers sought to understand how the horrors of the war could have occurred and how certain people were able to rise above them and find meaning in life. While the humanistic theories focus on the process of self-actualization, existential theorists emphasize self-determination, choice, and the responsibility of the individual to rise above environmental forces. "We are our choices," maintains the existentialist. "Our existence and its meaning are squarely in our own hands, for we alone can decide what our attitudes and behaviors will be."

The question of the meaning of life is very significant from the standpoint of existentialism. Viktor Frankl's (1905–1997) book *Man's Search for Meaning* (1959) described his experiences as a prisoner in German concentration camps in World War II and how it stimulated his existential approach to psychotherapy. Although he lost virtually his entire family in the war, Frankl always kept in the forefront of his mind his freedom within certain limits to choose how he lived his life. He observed how every day in the camps prisoners had moral choices to make about whether to submit internally to those in power who threatened to rob them of their inner life and their freedom. Prisoners who focused on positive meanings and tasks tended to survive. Often this occurred within the context of helping one another and discovering that they had the will and strength to endure. In his book, Frankl argued that behavior is driven by the meanings, values, and purposes that characterize a person's life. He believed that life ultimately means taking responsibility to find the right answers to its problems and to complete the tasks that it constantly sets for each individual. Frankl used the term **logotherapy** (after the Greek term *logos* or "meaning") to describe his existential, humanistic approach to treatment.

Existentialists believe that people are free to choose among alternative courses of action. Of course there are many aspects of our lives over which we do not have control (e.g., our genetic dispositions and our families). However, we do have the freedom and responsibility to respond to our life circumstances within the constraints of reality. Rather than focusing on the past, existential therapists direct attention to the choices involved in an individual's present situation and how they can be made effectively and responsibly.

A person can choose to act either authentically or inauthentically. **Authentic behavior** is freely establishing one's own goals. **Inauthentic behavior** is letting other people dictate those goals. For each person there are also certain givens that place definite limits on what he or she may become. These may be characteristics that are present at birth, such as learning ability, physical appearance, or the presence of a disabling disease, or they may be environmental, including the influence of parents and later of school and peers. These expand or contract the individual's chances for fulfillment based on the qualities present at birth. The primary task of the therapist, according to this view, is to help empty, lonely people expand their experiences and fulfill their own uniqueness, that is, to help them make constructive choices.

The humanistic-existential perspective is more a philosophical position than a formal scientific theory. However, it does address crucial aspects of human existence. Humanistic-existential writers believe that scientific psychology misses the mark if it dwells on observable behavior and neglects the individual's inner life, particularly motivations and personality styles.

The Community-Cultural Perspective

Many people see mental illness as a personal health problem or as a character defect. In contrast, from the **community-cultural perspective** maladaptive behavior results from inability to cope effectively with stress. It is not viewed as a disease or problem that exists only within the individual; instead, it is seen as at least partly a failure of the individual's social support system. This system includes the person's spouse, parents, siblings, relatives, friends, teachers, employer, religious adviser, and others, as well as community organizations and government agencies. Cultural factors might play a role in the failure of someone's support network to be helpful, not because the network members desire to play a negative role, but rather because the values, beliefs, and habits prevalent in a particular culture may apply to certain situations. Cultural variations can play a role either in the maladaptive behavior for which clinical help is sought or in the therapy situation, for example, when the therapist is unfamiliar with the cultural realities of the client's life.

Proponents of **community psychology** do not deny the role of life history or genetic makeup in causing maladaptive behavior, but these are not seen as necessarily sufficient to produce such behavior. For example, a person vulnerable to schizophrenia may develop hallucinations for many reasons: biochemical factors, traumatic early experiences, or unusual social relationships are all possibilities. However, the presence of an especially strong stressor or the breakdown of the person's social support system may be equally important in producing the schizophrenic behavior.

The community approach attempts to reduce maladaptive behavior through preventive measures, by intervening in people's lives before catastrophes occur. Such measures include a variety of special programs: discussion or mutual support programs for recently separated, divorced, or widowed people; preschool enrichment programs for children from low-income single-parent homes; combined school programs and child-care facilities for teenage single parents; day-care centers for elderly people who may not be able to live self-sufficiently. Implicit in community psychology is the belief that the effects of social disorganization (slums, bad schools, and high unemployment rates) are a major cause of many personal problems. For this reason, mental health professionals with a community orientation tend to become involved in efforts to change society by lobbying for legislation and becoming actively involved in community affairs.

Community psychologists study the social environment and factors related to it, such as socioeconomic status. When the living places of people who are identified as psychologically and socially impaired are plotted on a map, it can be shown that the frequency of such problems is much higher in certain areas than in others. The **social causation theory** argues that the poor schools, crime, inadequate housing, and prejudice often found in deteriorating, low-income neighborhoods may increase the stress experienced by already vulnerable people. The **social selection theory,** on the other hand, argues that lower socioeconomic groups show a greater incidence of maladaptive behavior because people who do not function well tend to experience downward social mobility.

Those who believe in the community-cultural perspective are more likely to support the social causation theory. They point out that, while social selection may be a factor, the theory does not rule out the stress-producing situations—related to cultural disparities or encountered by low-income people—that may aggravate existing disorders. Such people may have not only less power to control their environment but also fewer resources for dealing with stress. For a variety of reasons, including the difficulty of carrying out controlled research in community settings, one cannot completely rule out either the social selection or the social causation theory. Each theory might apply to certain types of disorders. In either case, psychologists with a community-cultural perspective see a need to develop special programs aimed at reducing cultural disparities and counteracting undesirable aspects of urban life such as poverty and overcrowding. Such programs would improve the lives of the general population as well as those of people with specific psychological problems (Reppucci, Woolard, & Freud, 1999).

Social Roles and Labeling

All individuals belong to cultural and social groups. These groups shape people's behavior by providing the distinctive reinforcements, punishments, and models that are part of life in a particular cultural setting. The members of a cultural or social group share a set of meanings or symbols, experience a feeling of unity, and participate in a network of mutual obligations. The group or groups to which a person belongs influence nearly every aspect of his or her life.

Social roles are particular functions that a person plays as a member of a social group. Some theorists have maintained that we always attempt to project an image and that, in fact, we have no true self. This position is presented by Erving Goffman (1959), who argues that in all of our encounters with other people we adopt particular roles. Each role is accompanied by a script that includes different actions and signals. In effect, we vary our behaviors continuously as the situation requires. This viewpoint implies that there is no such thing as a fixed personality.

Less extreme than this position, and more widely accepted, is the composite position: There is a basic personality that is overlaid with situational role-playing. Research has shown that a number of factors influence the roles people play in social relationships. These factors are often important because they serve to label an individual in a particular way. **Labeling** occurs whenever people are categorized on some basis, whether that basis is relevant and fair or not. Labels can be destructive because they draw attention to one aspect of the person while ignoring other aspects that make him or her unique. (Would you like to be labeled as a slob simply because you don't like to put your shoes away at night?) Some labels, such as "good student" and "loyal friend," are desirable, but many others carry negative social connotations. For example, the role of mental patient is widely viewed as socially unacceptable, and the label "mentally ill" often causes permanent damage. The damage takes many forms, including discrimination by others and feelings of self-doubt and inadequacy. Negative labels lead to branding and shame. Everyone knows why it is wrong to discriminate against people because of their race, religion, culture, or appearance. They are less aware of how people with mental illnesses are discriminated against. Although such discrimination may not always be obvious, it exists—and hurts. When people feel stigmatized, they may become reluctant to seek help because they don't want to be labeled as "mentally ill" or "crazy."

Contributions of the Community-Cultural Perspective

What we know at present suggests that cultural, social, and economic factors play roles in emotional expression and maladaptive behavior. For example, children's levels of distress and depression increase sharply when they live in an environment in which adults express high levels of anger and behave aggressively. There is some evidence that this responsiveness to family discord is greater for boys than it is for girls (Cummings & Davies, 1994).

The community-cultural perspective has been influential in producing new approaches to maladaptive behavior and in reaching segments of the population whose psychological needs hitherto have been ignored. It has been effective both in changing the perspective of academic thinking and in altering social policy. As important, it has raised questions for future research whose answers will contribute to our understanding of both the cultural and social causes of maladaptive behavior and ways the social environment can enhance the lives of children and adults. Included among these questions are: How does stress in personal lives and in the community influence whether maladaptive behavior occurs? Can the community provide social support that either prevents maladaptive behavior or limits its undesirable effects? How can communities best meet the needs of special groups such as chronically mentally ill people, recent immigrants, and the homeless?

An Interactional Approach

We have reviewed six widely varying perspectives on the causes and treatment of maladaptive behavior. You may be wondering how these perspectives relate to the rest of the book. Which one is emphasized most? We think you should know our biases and how our views will affect what you learn in this book. We look upon these theoretical perspectives as elements that individually or in combination help us explain how maladaptive behavior arises and how it can be treated effectively. We have attempted to use the most valuable contributions of each viewpoint in our discussions of abnormal behavior. Abnormal behavior can result from any or all of a large number of factors. One perspective may contribute more than another under one set of conditions; under a different set, another viewpoint may be more useful. Our approach, which is shared by many other psychologists, is interactional. That is, what we think about and how we behave usually depends on interactions among several factors. These factors combine in giving direction to our lives. For example, the state of our health, concerns about parental expectations, self-doubts, our past experiences and present values, and our cultural background interact in influencing our approach to an upcoming final exam. We might feel perfectly healthy, have had rewarding experiences with taking exams in the past, and not feel strong cultural pressures to attain a certain level of performance on exams; but if we feel a lot of pressure from our parents to get perfect grades, have troubling self-doubts, and feel a responsibility to society to be very successful, anticipating and taking the exam might be an unpleasant experience. It would be even more unpleasant if, in addition, we had a bad cold.

The factors emphasized by the six theoretical perspectives can be thought of as contributing to our vulnerability and resilience. We might be vulnerable to poor performance because of our worries and those of our parents regarding the consequences of not being successful. At the same time, being intelligent, resourceful, and hardworking helps us be resilient under academic stress. The way a situation influences behavior depends on our particular mix of vulnerability and resilience and the conditions we are confronting. These conditions, together with personal characteristics, can be thought of as interacting or combining to produce a special product, the individual's behavior. Why maladaptive behavior occurs in some people and not in others can be understood in this way.

In addition to influencing behavior, personal and environmental factors also can influence each other. For example, someone who is aggressive and always gets into fights is likely to alienate other people and thereby reduce social support. At the same time, someone who experiences a succession of stressful life events may become discouraged and feel pessimistic about a positive outcome.

This interactional approach not only provides a general framework for thinking about maladaptive behavior but also allows for specification of the factors that are especially pertinent to particular disorders. For example, whereas in the past schizophrenia may have been thought of as being caused by demonic possession, we now know that certain personal and environmental factors, as well as specific biological conditions, play roles in the incidence of this serious disorder. Researchers today are investigating the possible relevance to schizophrenia of a large variety of these factors, including the following personal variables:

1. A reduced capacity for information processing in situations requiring attention to complex stimuli
2. Hyperactivity of the autonomic nervous system to aversive stimuli in the environment
3. Poor social and coping skills

There is also evidence that stressful life events and a nonsupportive social network contribute to the incidence and recurrence of schizophrenia and other types of mental disorder. Research has shown that it is particular combinations of these personal vulnerabilities and environmental handicaps, not their individual existence, that pose special risks for people with tendencies toward various types of maladaptive behavior.

Another example of the application of the interactional approach can be seen in the study of depression. For instance, there is evidence that many people do not become depressed for either purely mental or purely environmental reasons. A full understanding of depression requires information about both the person's internal state and the state of his or her social and community ties. Depression can be viewed as despair over a severe loss or disappointment from which, for a longer or shorter time, there seems to be no escape. Recovery from this crisis depends on whether the situation changes and/or how the person's cognitions about the situation change.

Each of us has expectations and goals that color our thoughts. A stamp collector probably has different thoughts when going to the post office than a noncollector does. Our thoughts serve as **mediators:** they provide links between informational inputs and behavioral outputs, just as an intermediary in the business world links a manufacturer and a retailer. Several theories of abnormal behavior deal with the mediating process, though there are differences of opinion about which ones are most important. The various theoretical perspectives reflect these differences by focusing on such different mediators as chemical processes in the body, drives and emotions, thinking styles, values and needs, or the social milieu.

How these mediators interact is a major question yet to be answered fully. In the past, some writers believed in an essentially one-way influence process in which behavior was viewed as a product of bodily events. While this type of influence can certainly be very important, an approach that recognizes the possibility of multiple pathways is more likely to provide a more comprehensive understanding of body-behavior relationships. There now is evidence that synaptic circuits in the brain can be shaped by experience. For example, a monkey's childhood environment can have dramatic effects on its level of serotonin, a chemical that implements neural transmission across the synapse and plays a role in depression. We believe that an integrative approach to personal problems needs to study the multiple processes that may be involved in maladaptive behavior (see Box 2-2).

Each of us confronts diverse situations each day. They provide us with information (pleasant, unpleasant, frightening, reassuring) and often call forth certain reactions. The information available to us influences our way of looking at things. At the same time, our personal characteristics—our skills and vulnerabilities—help determine how we handle the situations to which we must respond. As psychologists and authors, we are interested in what makes an individual vulnerable to particular situations, what kind of stressors cause maladaptive behavior to appear, and how people can be helped to deal better with stressors and compensate for their vulnerabilities.

After reviewing six traditional theories, we have concluded that it is most likely that, rather than adhering to any one theory of maladaptive behavior, we need to consider combinations of them in an effort to identify the causes of problems that arise in people's lives. How these combinations come together and integrate as complex causes can be expected to vary from case to case. This chapter began with an account of Fred Price's bodily symptoms and some general questions about their possible causes. We conclude the chapter by mentioning factors each theory would direct attention to that might help us conceptualize this particular case.

- *Biological perspective:* Fred's heredity may be a major determinant of his somatic complaints.
- *Psychodynamic perspective:* Fred's conflicts with his wife compound the effects of his stressful job.
- *Behavioral perspective:* Strengthening his behavioral skills (e.g., improving his ability to negotiate disputes with his wife) would help Fred cope better at home and at work.
- *Cognitive perspective:* Fred may have unrealistic expectations about the extent to which he can meet his responsibilities at home and at work.
- *Humanistic-existential perspective:* Fred needs to think more about what he wants to accomplish in his life and how he wants to live it.
- *Community-cultural perspective:* A large urban multicultural high school will almost inevitably create a complex social system and prove challenging to a vice-principal, particularly for someone like Fred who feels he must solve all the problems that come to his attention.

As researchers explore the interactions among the multiple factors in people's lives, we believe this contemporary *interactional approach* may result in a more integrative and all-encompassing seventh theory of maladaptive behavior.

Research Close-up

Box 2–2

Interactional Aspects of Research on Maladaptive Behavior

Interactions among factors (elements) that contribute to maladaptive behavior often provide the basis for research studies in abnormal psychology. A research investigation might deal with one or two relevant factors. Sometimes after the research has been completed, the potential roles of additional factors also seem to be important. When this happens, the original investigation might be done again incorporating additional factors. Let us look at three examples of research that illustrate interactions among elements and the potential interaction of elements not included in the original research but which might be pertinent.

Fast Track

An example of the community-cultural perspective in action is the Fast Track Prevention Trial (Conduct Problems Prevention Research Group, 1999). This multisite, multicomponent intervention has many of the attributes of clinical trials described in Chapter 1, except that its focus is on the prevention of rather than treatment for conduct problems in children. It is a long-term project based on a comprehensive model of child development and includes, in addition to traditional classroom activities, social skills training, academic tutoring, parent training, and home visiting to improve compe-

tencies and reduce conduct problems. The children in the Fast Track program live in communities with undesirable levels of crime and poverty. Schools in these areas were divided into comparable experimental and control groups. When these groups were compared at the end of the first grade, the experimental was superior to the control group in the students' ability to attend to the feelings of others, to be effective in coping with strong emotions, and to handle social problems. In addition, they had better relationships with other children and were less likely to display aggressive disruptive behavior. The parents of children in the experimental group improved in their parenting behavior, for example, by feeling less of a need to use physical punishment.

Although this intervention is only in its beginning stages, the results available suggest that changes in child, family, and school-based risk factors can be achieved with a multifaceted community intervention. The Fast Track Prevention Trial is complex because it takes into account the roles of learning experiences, cognitions, and the community environment. Another factor that might also be valuable to study is each child's temperament. **Temperament** refers to biologically based aspects of personality present at very early ages. Children who are temperamentally shy and reserved might need help in being

more assertive in certain situations, whereas active, aggressive children might need help in controlling their impulses. Awareness of the potential role of temperament in no way diminishes the significance of the ambitious Fast Track project. Rather, it shows how research studies lead not only to conclusions about the effects exerted by variables, but often also to further studies that go beyond what is currently known.

Does Being Religious Prolong Life?

Elsewhere in this book we will review what is known about the role psychological factors play in physical illness. There is increasing reason to believe that mind-body relationships often are two-way streets with bodily processes influencing psychological functioning in certain types of situations and psychological processes influencing bodily functioning in others. One recent longitudinal study of the relevance of religious interests and activities to survival in older adults has provided some food for thought about this relationship (Koenig et al., 1999). Prior research had often produced mixed or conflicting findings. Because the sample sizes and the characteristics of the groups compared often varied widely, Koenig and his colleagues decided to study a large group (N=3,968) of adults between the ages of 64 and 101 who were still living in communities in North Carolina. They assessed attendance at religious services at the beginning of the study and 6 years later determined

Chapter Summary

THE ROLE OF THEORY IN ABNORMAL PSYCHOLOGY

Theories play an important role in guiding research on the causes of behavioral maladaptations and physical illness. The six currently influential theoretical perspectives are: (1) the **biological perspective,** (2) the **psychodynamic perspective,** (3) the **behavioral perspective,** (4) the **cognitive perspective,** (5) the **humanistic-existential** perspective, and (6) the **community-cultural** perspective. Each of these theories has something to contribute to the understanding of maladaptive

behavior, personal vulnerabilities, and resilience in coping with challenging situations.

THE BIOLOGICAL PERSPECTIVE

The **biological perspective** concerns the role bodily disturbances play in disordered behavior. The bodily disturbance may be due to a genetic defect, an injury or infection before or after birth, or a more or less temporary physiological malfunction caused by some condition present at a particular time.

Box 2-2

which participants were still alive and which had died. Of the participants who attended religious services at least once a week at the beginning of the study, 22.9% had died at the 6-year point, compared to 37.4% for people who attended services less than once a week.

If religious practices did have an impact on health, how might this have occurred? Koenig and his fellow researchers found that frequent attenders at religious services had larger social networks and had stronger feelings of being socially supported than did infrequent attenders. Because frequent attenders have more contact with others, they may have more people who check on their health status and help them get medical attention when needed. In addition to the social activity side of religious attendance, religious people might have more meaning in their lives than do nonattenders. Thus, existential factors might also be pertinent regarding survival. Another possible factor is that frequent religious attendance may foster attitudes of compliance and care for the physical body, as well as adherence to their doctors' suggestions and prescriptions for medications. One of the study's interesting results was an inverse relationship between religious attendance and rates of anxiety, depression, and stress. A strong religious faith reinforced by active religious participation may help people to cope better with stressors, such as the inevitable health problems of later life. Intriguing as this study's finding are, more information is needed concerning interrelationships among the variables of so-cial activity, strength of religious beliefs, type of community in which a person lives (e.g., rural town or urban city), and biological factors. The elements of longevity might combine in complex ways.

Somatization Disorders

While we will examine the topic of somatization and hypochondriasis later in the book, touching on the topic now illustrates one of the main points of this chapter: the need to consider the multiple elements or contributors to maladaptive behavior. The maladaptive behavior in somatization disorders and hypochondriasis (preoccupation with contracting a disease) is the presence of physical complaints that persist for years and lead to often extensive medical treatment and changes in lifestyle. The medical treatment can be extensive because of the absence of reliable evidence regarding a physical basis of the complaint. When a patient reports persistent pain and discomfort, many medical tests may be needed to explore all the possibilities. To be considered a somatization disorder, a patient must have multiple bodily complaints in the absence of evidence of their physical cause. Actually, one biological aspect of somatization disorders is that they tend to run in families. Studies of individuals with this problem, some reared by their birth parents and some by adoptive parents, suggest that genetic factors contribute to the problem. Among the questions asked concerning preoccupation with physical complaints is the relative contributions of various pertinent factors.

We have just mentioned the factor of heredity. Learning might also play a role because children may acquire a tendency to have bodily complaints because of their observations of a parent's complaining style. Also in some cultures it is more socially acceptable to report having physical complaints than psychological problems, such as anxiety and depression.

Cognitive processes may also be relevant in trying to understand why some people are preoccupied with bodily symptoms and complaints. In one recent study, it was found that somatic complaints and preoccupations in the absence of a diagnosed physical condition are associated with a set of distinctive cognitive concerns and assumptions (Rief, Hiller, & Margraf, 1998). Somatizers tend to see themselves as being weak and unable to tolerate stress and they catastrophize about minor bodily complaints. They often believe that good health means being completely symptom-free. As a consequence, undangerous physical symptoms come to be seen as signs of a serious disease. It appears that a core cognitive aspect of frequent somatizing in the absence of physical indicators of disease is misinterpretation of bodily sensations as somatic symptoms. The interpretation of being physically ill can lead to avoidance behavior that is accompanied by a lower rate of physical activity. The consequent reduction of physical fitness may enhance the probability of bodily misperceptions. Thus, cognitive, as well as learning, cultural, and physical factors need to be considered in cases of maladaptive bodily preoccupations.

Genetic Factors Genes, the elements of human heredity, are transmitted from parent to child in the form of **deoxyribonucleic acid (DNA).** DNA is found in the **chromosomes,** present in pairs in all body cells. Behavior genetics emphasizes the interaction of heredity and environment. Research in behavior genetics is carried out either through the study of family histories or through studies of twins.

The Nervous System and the Brain The two major divisions of the nervous system are the **central nervous system (CNS),** the nerve cells in the brain and spinal cord, and the **peripheral nervous system (PNS),** the neurons connecting the CNS with the glands, muscles, and sensory receptors. Research has shown that brain development is malleable and at times dependent on environmental stimulation.

The Endocrines The endocrine system is made up of several glands including the pituitary, thyroid, adrenal, and gonadal (sex) glands. The glands are ductless, which means they discharge hormones directly into the bloodstream. The endocrine system plays an important role in reactions to stress.

The Neuroscience Revolution Neuroscience is an interdisciplinary field aimed at understanding the relationship between thinking, feeling, and behavior and the structure and function of the brain. The use of new techniques to study molecular-level events at the synapse and the use of imaging techniques that make possible the study of the living brain are contributing to the understanding of relationships between the brain and behavior. **Psychoneuroimmunology** is an area of research focused on the effects of psychological and neural events on immunological processes.

Integration of Biological and Psychological Systems

One major contribution of the biological perspective is drug therapy. A variety of drugs are used in treating maladaptive behavior. However, it is important to recognize the multiple determinants of abnormal behavior, which include interactions among the physical environment, psychological factors, and biological functioning.

THE PSYCHODYNAMIC PERSPECTIVE

The **psychodynamic perspective** is based on the idea that thoughts and emotions are important causes of behavior.

Freud and Psychoanalysis

Freud developed **psychoanalysis,** a method in which the patient recaptures forgotten memories without the use of hypnosis. The two most basic assumptions of Freud's theories of personality are **psychic determinism** and the conscious–unconscious dimension. The latter includes three levels of consciousness: the **conscious, preconscious,** and **unconscious.** Freud's theory placed great emphasis on the first 5 years of life. During this period he thought that the **libido,** or basic human drives, was focused on a series of specific erogenous zones or sources of pleasure. His theory divided the mental world into three structures—the **id,** the **ego,** and the **superego.** Freud also placed great emphasis on the concept of **anxiety** and on the use of **defense mechanisms** to ward off anxiety. He believed the most important of the defense mechanisms was **repression.**

More Recent Approaches to Psychoanalysis

Psychoanalytic theory has been modified by many later theorists. Erikson developed a psychosocial theory. He described a series of **psychosocial stages** of development over the entire life cycle. **Object relations** theory was developed by psychoanalysts such as Klein. Kohut developed a theory of **self-psychology.**

Evaluating Psychoanalytic Theory

Psychoanalysis is both a theoretical framework and a therapeutic method. Its full evaluation will be possible only when its therapeutic effectiveness can be objectively assessed and its concepts explored using scientific methods, such as the experiment.

THE BEHAVIORAL PERSPECTIVE

The **behavioral perspective** focuses on behavior as a response to stimuli in the environment.

Classical Conditioning

In **classical conditioning,** the response that occurs automatically to one stimulus is transferred to a new stimulus by pairing the two stimuli.

Operant Conditioning

In **operant conditioning** the response precedes the **reinforcement.** Behaviors that receive reinforcement, or reward, have an increased probability of occurring again. **Negative reinforcers** take away something unpleasant after the behavior occurs. **Punishment** provides a negative consequence for the behavior.

Social-Cognitive Theories

Social learning theories do not claim that direct reinforcement is always necessary for learning. They stress the use of **modeling,** or observational learning, as the way a great deal of behavior, especially social behavior, is learned. **Role-playing,** or practice of the modeled behavior, is also an important learning technique. Bandura is especially interested in self-regulation through the use of internal rather than external reinforcement. **Social-cognitive theorists** believe that the environment influences behavior indirectly through the individual's thought processes.

THE COGNITIVE PERSPECTIVE

The **cognitive perspective** focuses on how people acquire and interpret information and use it in problem solving. Each person develops **schemata** that contain information about different domains in a person's life and assist in information processing and strategy development. In the study of maladaptive behavior, **self-schemata** are particularly important.

Maladaptive Behavior and Cognition

Cognitive disturbances can cause unhappiness and personal maladjustment. If our ideas about ourselves and what we should expect of ourselves and others are unrealistic, we may live our lives in such a way that undesirable outcomes are inevitable. For Beck, maladaptive behavior results from dysfunctional cognitions, highly idiosyncratic schemata that are not consistent with reality.

Cognitive Therapies

Beck focuses on helping clients replace maladaptive thoughts with more effective coping techniques. His work initially focused on depression but now also includes problems with anxiety as the major symptom. **Rational-emotive therapy,** developed by Ellis, is based on the idea that behavior is more a function of belief systems than of actual conditions. The therapist's role is to explain, demonstrate, and assist the client in practicing more productive ways of thinking.

THE HUMANISTIC-EXISTENTIAL PERSPECTIVE

The Humanistic View

The **humanistic perspective** assumes that in every person there is an active striving toward **self-actualization.** Rogers emphasized the importance of the self-image. He believed a primary role of the therapist was the total acceptance of the client as a person of worth.

The Existential View

Existentialists focus on the need to help people to establish their own goals and then to make constructive choices to reach these.

THE COMMUNITY-CULTURAL PERSPECTIVE

The **community-cultural perspective** directs attention to the roles played by community-wide factors (for example, poverty) and cultural diversity in maladaptive behavior. **Community psychologists** focus on the failure of social support systems as the cause of maladaptations. They emphasize preventive intervention—such as special programs in schools—and programs for specific groups that are at high risk because they need help in solving problems of living.

Social Roles and Labeling

Social roles are defined by the person's group and the functions of the person in that group. Each role has a script that determines how the person is expected to act in different situations. **Labeling** is the result of categorizing people on some basis, such as the social group to which they belong, without attention to their individual characteristics.

Contributions of the Community–Cultural Perspective

Social, economic, and cultural factors play roles in emotional expression and maladaptive behavior. Community psychology has been influential in reaching people whose needs have been ignored by the other perspectives that focus more on treating the individual instead of changing the environment. How best to provide support in the community setting is still a question that needs extensive research.

AN INTERACTIONAL APPROACH

All of the perspectives make contributions to identifying personal vulnerabilities and factors in resilience that relate to maladaptive behavior, its prevention, and its treatment. In an interactional approach an important issue is how these factors combine with stressful life experiences to produce the various types of maladaptive behavior.

Key Terms

Biological perspective, p. 49
Psychodynamic perspective, p. 61
Behavioral perspective, p. 69
Cognitive perspective, p. 74
Humanistic-existential perspective, p. 76
Community-cultural perspective, p. 79
Chromosomes, p. 50
Chromosomal anomalies, p. 50
Genes, p. 50
Genome, p. 50
Deoxyribonucleic acid (DNA), p. 50
Penetrance, p. 50
Heritability, p. 51
Population genetics, p. 51
Behavior genetics, p. 51
Neurotransmitter, p. 53
Hypothalamus, p. 55
Endorphins, p. 56
Brain plasticity, p. 56

Endocrine system, p. 57
Neuroscience, p. 57
Brain imaging, p. 58
Neuropharmacology, p. 59
Psychoneuroimmunology, p. 60
Lymphocytes, p. 60
Psychic determinism, p. 62
Psychosexual development, p. 63
Psychic apparatus, p. 64
Id, p. 64
Ego, p. 64
Superego, p. 64
Primary process thinking, p. 64
Secondary process thinking, p. 65
Anxiety, p. 65
Defense mechanisms, p. 65
Repression, p. 65
Psychoanalysis, p. 65

Free association, p. 66
Ego psychology, p. 68
Object relations, p. 68
Self psychology, p. 68
Classical conditioning, p. 69
Operant conditioning, p. 70
Social-cognitive theory, p. 72
Modeling, p. 72
Implicit learning, p. 73
Self-efficacy, p. 74
Cognitive therapy, p. 75
Rational-emotive therapy, p. 76
Self-actualization, p. 76
Authentic behavior, p. 78
Community psychology, p. 79
Social roles, p. 79
Labeling, p. 79
Interactional approach, p. 80

3

Classification and Assessment

"*I* know about stigma and psychiatric labeling from a personal and professional perspective. At age 14 I was misdiagnosed with schizophrenia. I spent the next two years with this diagnostic label, which indeed took on a life of its own, following me to numerous hospitals and psychiatrists and influencing treatment plans.

"Before being correctly diagnosed with bipolar affective disorder at age 16, I was captive within the medical model. The label 'schizophrenic' stereotyped me and biased the way clinicians regarded me. For those two years, I was treated solely as a schizophrenic patient and relegated to a dim and hopeless status. The label had matured and took over my adolescent identity. . . .

"The label, shadowing me at all times, radically dehumanized and devalued me. This process transformed me from being a person to being an illness; from being Robert Bjorklund to being 'a schizophrenic,' lost in a shuffle of myopic treatment plans.

". . . Psychiatric diagnosis has a profound effect on the way a person is assessed and treated within the mental health system and elsewhere. The labels that clinicians use to set individuals apart must be more than merely matters of medical convenience." (Bjorklund, 1996, pp. 1329–1330)

For a month, Pete Harnisch, a pitcher for the New York Mets, had been battling a mystery ailment that had disrupted his sleep, eating patterns and game: "I felt very withdrawn. I felt very much to myself. The sleeping problem was back from the previous week, and there was a lot of anxiety. . . . I wasn't eating anything. I had a lot of things going together."

When Harnisch gave up three back-to-back home runs in one game after having pitched five scoreless innings, he linked his abrupt exhaustion to nicotine withdrawal; he had just quit chewing tobacco. But resuming the tobacco chewing didn't stop his symptoms, which were variously attributed to a thyroid condition and Lyme disease. Finally, a psychological examination cleared up the mystery, and Harnisch went public at a press conference: "I'd just like to let everybody know I've been diagnosed with depression." He added: "I never really thought I'm a different person than normal. I never considered that. . . . It's hard to pinpoint exactly why it happened." (New York Times, May 1, 1997, p. A21) ■

Diagnosis is an important step in the process of identifying, and classifying a clinical condition. A correct diagnosis is useful, not only as a way of classifying a condition, but also as a basis for effective treatment. Robert Bjorklund's misdiagnosis led to stigmatization and inappropriate therapy. The correct diagnosis, bipolar affective disorder, led to treatment that enabled Bjorklund to participate fully in community life and to further his education. When treated appropriately, Harnisch's depression improved. The correct diagnosis also did wonders for his pitching.

The fact that misdiagnoses occasionally are made does not negate the value of the diagnostic process. In making a diagnosis, the clinician seeks to answer the question, What is this patient's problem? We all can appreciate the per-sonal significance of this question because we have all had the experience of going to a doctor in order to find what is causing a set of symptoms we are experiencing. When the doctor tells us what the problem is and confidently prescribes medicine to eliminate it, we breathe a sigh of relief.

This chapter is about the diagnostic process as it applies to behavioral, cognitive, and emotional problems. The chapter has two parts: (1) a review of the current psychiatric diagnostic system and (2) a review of the types of information and procedures used in making a diagnosis.

We start with the diagnostic system used to classify clinical conditions. Diagnostic systems are particularly valuable because they represent attempts to organize what a great many clinical workers know about the various types of problems they deal with. The classification of personal problems is based on assessments of what clients say and how they behave. Both current life conditions and past experiences are taken into account. Classification is not simply an intellectual exercise, however. It has far-reaching effects on the lives of people who exhibit maladaptive behavior, as well as on the activities of clinical workers.

Classification: Categories of Maladaptive Behavior

The need to classify various types of personalities and personal problems has long been recognized. Since the time of Hippocrates, classification systems have continually been revised to incorporate new knowledge and changing viewpoints. Nevertheless, the **classification** of abnormal behavior is still in an early stage of evolution, partly because of the arbitrary nature of the process of attaching labels to people. For example, there is no precise point at which an excessive drinker becomes a full-blown alcoholic, or when

the tension you feel when you are alone in a strange room becomes the intense dread known as claustrophobia.

A classification statement, or **diagnosis,** places a disorder within a system of conventional groupings based on important similarities in symptoms. Most classification systems in psychology are organized in hierarchical fashion, just as they are in the natural sciences. Thus, in the system that is used to classify animal life, human beings are members of the species *Homo sapiens*, genus *Homo*, which is a subdivision of the family Hominidae, of the order Primates, of the class Mammalia, of the phylum Chordata, of the kingdom Animalia. Similarly, a manic episode is a subdivision of bipolar disorders, which in turn is a subgroup in the family of mood disorders.

While classification is generally regarded as a scientific and clinical tool, we should remember that all people continually use some form of classification in their daily lives. The people we meet, the day's weather, and other everyday experiences are all put into groups on the basis of similarities to past experiences or of other ways of classifying events. Classification is a way of trying to understand and to learn from experience. Without a classification system, everything that happens to us would be unique. We could not prepare for the future in any way.

Advantages and Disadvantages of Classification

General use of a widely recognized classification system is very important. If every clinical worker created his or her own system, communication problems would be enormous. For example, it would be difficult to make use of research data on effective treatment. In addition, classification systems are useful for statistical purposes. Government and other planning agencies need records of how often various types of maladaptation occur. Without such records, it would be impossible to say whether the incidence of certain forms of maladaptation was increasing or decreasing. Moreover, to the extent that the categories used in established classification systems are distinctive and can be rated reliably, they contribute to the planning of treatment programs and facilities.

Still, the usefulness of classification for understanding the causes of some disorders and treating them remains controversial, as shown by the following comments by an experienced clinician:

> You would think that after working with troubled people for twenty years I'd know what their major problems are and what I should be diagnosing. Yet I'm not really sure what diagnosis is, what it should be, or how it can do more than just name and pigeonhole. I classify cases because it helps me keep records and communicate with other clinicians. At the same time, my major job is to treat people, to decide what I can do that will help them figure out what

they should do to make their lives happier and more worthwhile. People are different more than they are similar. Two people may come in with a similar symptom, such as delusions of grandeur, but the mechanisms that produce the symptom may be different. I wish diagnosis helped me better understand the basis for the conditions I diagnose.

The idea of classifying maladaptive behaviors has been criticized on several counts. Most important to many people is the fact that a diagnosis puts a label on a person. Labeling might make it difficult for a former patient to get a job, gain admission to a professional program, or obtain custody of a child. Another argument is that many diagnoses are not useful because the diagnostic categories are imperfect and the same label may be assigned to behaviors that appear similar but have different causes and require different treatment.

Yet, on balance, the case for classification is a strong one. It is easy to defend the idea that each patient is unique, yet nothing can be done to help an individual without referring to general principles. What is known about an individual case, however detailed, can be utilized only if the case is viewed within the context of existing knowledge. At the same time, general principles will have validity only if they are based on observation of individuals.

There are two major sources of unreliability in diagnoses. One concerns clinical judgment: differences in therapists' clinical training and theoretical orientation may lead to different diagnoses. The other major source of unreliability is that diagnostic labels are attached to people, and no two people (or their problems) are alike. The same person might also describe his or her problem differently on two separate occasions, depending on how he or she was feeling at the time and on what events relating to the problem had occurred recently. Diagnosticians might change their original assessment of a case, or two people with similar problems might describe their conditions differently and therefore be classified differently.

Ambiguities and inconsistencies also arise because most clinics and hospitals are burdened with more cases than they can handle. Leisurely and protracted study aimed at accurate classification is often impossible. Another difficulty in classification is the range of problems treated by a particular clinical facility. The staff of a facility that treats a narrow range of disorders may tend to describe and interpret its cases differently than would the staff of a more broadly based institution. Diagnostic methods will achieve a firmer scientific basis as assessment becomes more standardized and less susceptible to distortion by such factors. Table 3-1 lists some of the important features of a good classification system. Currently, for most types of maladaptive behavior, the characteristics listed in Table 3-1 remain goals—they are not yet achievements. For example, the causes of most psychiatric disorders have not yet been identified.

Table 3-1
Characteristics of a Good Clinical Classification System

1. Provides information about the cause or causes of a condition
2. Provides a common language for communication among clinicians and researchers
3. Enables clinicians to give patients and their families a short- and long-term outlook
4. Indicates possible treatment
5. Suggests paths to prevention

Vulnerability, Resilience, and Coping

Our own interactional approach to abnormal psychology has definite implications for the process of classification. This approach argues that abnormal behavior must be understood in the context of several factors: the recent stressful events in a person's life, such as a bereavement or loss of a job; the person's general vulnerabilities, such as a tendency toward low self-esteem possibly engendered by early childhood experiences or a highly reactive nervous system; and what the individual has going for him or her, such as coping skills, intellectual ability, and family and friends who are willing and able to help. An especially important asset in coping with stress is resilience, the ability to think clearly and function well despite adverse circumstances.

Classifying abnormal behavior should be a matter of creating a complete portrait of a person rather than simply marking a point on a graph. In classifying a person who is experiencing a problem, we want to know not only what the problem is, but also the context of the problem. The context includes (1) recent experiences that may have created stress and led to a worsening of the patient's condition, (2) the patient's vulnerabilities and weaknesses, and (3) his or her assets and strengths. The fact that a person who is quite disturbed and maladjusted at the present time has had long periods of good adjustment (e.g., being able to hold a job) in the past is encouraging and should not be ignored. Optimally, the way we classify people's problems tells us something about their future prospects and likely responses to therapeutic efforts.

The Multiaxial Approach

Over the years, classification and diagnosis have meant many things: the simple assignment of a name or label, as well as a statement providing information about several aspects of a particular case. (The root of *diagnostic* means "thorough knowledge.") Official classifications of mental disorders first came into use in the United States in 1840 with the adoption of a one-item classification scheme. In the census that year, "idiocy" was the single label used to categorize mental illness. By the 1880 census, there were eight categories for mental disorder.

An important contribution to psychiatric classification was made by Emil Kraepelin (1856–1926) who noted two symptom patterns that seemed to hang together and recur. He described one condition, *dementia praecox*, in which there appears to be mental deterioration early in life. Today this would be called schizophrenia. He also described a condition marked by wide mood swings, which he called *manic-depressive insanity*. Today this would be described as bipolar disorder. Kraepelin regarded both of these disorders as being caused by brain pathology. We now know much more about both organic and environmental factors involved in these disorders. Beyond this additional information about the diagnostic system, modern approaches to classification encompass a great variety of problems of living with multiple causes and varying likelihoods of recovery.

Today, practitioners make use of **a multiaxial classification system** designed to summarize the diverse information relevant to an individual case rather than to provide a single label. Instead of merely assigning a case to a category (such as schizophrenia), clinicians using a multiaxial system can describe an individual in terms of a set of clinically important factors, or *axes*. The American Psychiatric Association's multiaxial classification system is currently so widely accepted that it is easy to lose sight of the fact that the multiaxial feature is a relatively new development in the classification of mental disorders. The first multiaxial system, the **Diagnostic and Statistical Manual of Mental Disorders** (referred to as DSM-III), was presented in 1980. A revision of DSM-III, referred to as DSM-III-R, was published in 1987, and a further revision, called DSM-IV, was published in 1994. Like its predecessors, DSM-IV is a multiaxial system with five axes.

A multiaxial system is primarily concerned with the description of clinical problems. Its categories take note of the etiology, or cause, of the disorder when it can be identified (although some critics of DSM maintain that this system does not pay sufficient attention to etiology), as well as the subjective experiences of clients (e.g., how worried or angry they seem to be) and their assets and liabilities. DSM-IV provides information about the context in which abnormal behavior occurs as well as a description of the behavior. In 2000, a number of textual revisions were made in DSM-IV-TR by adding information that has resulted from recent research. Despite these additions, the diagnostic categories and their criteria presented in the 1994 manual remain unchanged.

DSM-IV

The axes of **DSM-IV** provide information about the biological, psychological, and social aspects of a person's condition.

- *Axis I* reports most of the disorders or conditions in the classification system except personality disorders and mental retardation. When necessary to accurately describe a given individual, more than one disorder can be listed on Axis I. In such a case, the principal diagnosis is listed first.
- *Axis II* deals with personality disorders and mental retardation, both of which begin in childhood or adolescence and usually persist into adult life. An example would be the personality disorder in which there is an unwarranted tendency to interpret the actions of other people as threatening. Axis II may also be used for noting maladaptive personality features and defense mechanisms that do not meet all the criteria for a personality disorder.
- *Axis III* describes general medical conditions that seem relevant to a case (e.g., the client's history of heart attacks).
- *Axis IV* describes psychosocial and environmental problems (e.g., housing problems, a negative life event, or family stress). In some cases, these problems may stem from adjustment difficulties created by the disorder.
- *Axis V* is a global assessment of the individual's psychological, social, and occupational functioning. The clinician makes a **global assessment of functioning (GAF)** rating on a scale from 1 to 100. Low ratings indicate that individuals pose dangers to themselves or others. High ratings indicate good or superior functioning (e.g., being involved in a variety of activities and showing effectiveness in interpersonal relationships).

Let's use DSM-IV in characterizing a particular case.

Robert Frank, a 37-year-old married man, has come to a community mental health center because some of his thoughts have been bothering him.

For as long as he can recall, he has been introverted and somewhat fearful of people. He has wanted social contact but, because of his fearfulness, has usually been unsuccessful in forming relationships. At the time he has come to the center, he has been keeping certain disturbing thoughts to himself. In the past he had discussed these thoughts with his wife and with clinicians at a mental hospital. He thinks he is being spied upon by some unknown group, which he believes to be a government intelligence agency. He also feels that his television set is providing him with special messages and that an attempt is being made to control his will and thoughts. He has a job in a large corporation. In the judgment of his supervisor, he has performed well in the past but recently his work has deteriorated somewhat.

Frank has been hospitalized twice, after which he seemed to make a good adjustment back into the community. His mother's death six months ago had upset him greatly. During the past few months he has increasingly restricted his social activities to members of his family, and even with them has been somewhat withdrawn. He has come to the community mental health center because the thoughts are becoming more persistent. His discomfort level is increasing, and he realizes that he is becoming more incoherent; he wants to avoid another hospitalization if at all possible.

The clinical worker who talked with Frank wanted to assess the seriousness of his problem and evaluate vulnerability and resilience factors in his life. The fact that he has been hospitalized twice reflects his vulnerability to becoming preoccupied with paranoid thoughts. But he also seems to be resilient in important ways: he has a job that until recently he performed well and has had good recoveries from his two hospitalizations. The clinician hoped to use all the information at her disposal in order to recommend the most practical and effective therapeutic program. She went through a series of steps gathering and interpreting information about Frank and arrived at these DSM-IV classifications:

Axis I: Paranoid schizophrenia
Axis II: Avoidant personality disorder
Axis III: No apparent medical conditions
Axis IV: Several severe problems
Axis V: GAF = 55 (moderate to severe symptoms)

An innovation of the DSM-IV system is that it provides criteria for coding the relatively subjective factors of Axes IV and V. Axis IV provides guidelines for rating the overall severity of recent events (e.g., death of a child, retirement) and long-lasting circumstances (e.g., unemployment, serious chronic illness). Guidelines for Axis V pertain to level of functioning (e.g., violence to self or others, conflict with co-workers). The behavior of two severely disturbed people would probably be interpreted differently and even treated differently if one had a history of good relationships with others and an excellent

work record whereas the other had a history of social inadequacy and inability to hold a job.

The more complete the available information about a given case, the more reliable the classification and ratings will be. Often, particularly in acute or emergency cases, a classification is made even though there are major informational gaps. In such cases, the classification is considered to be tentative and may be revised as more information is acquired.

The Major Diagnostic Categories

Beginning with DSM-III in 1980, a special effort has been made to be as specific as possible in describing major diagnostic categories and in listing the symptoms and factors relevant to particular disorders. These include the typical features of the disorder, the age at which it usually develops, its likely progression or outcome, the amount of social and occupational impairment involved, possible complications (e.g., suicide attempts by depressed individuals), aspects of a person's life that increase the risk of a severe disorder, sex differences, and relevant family patterns. Table 3-2 lists indicators such as these, which the clinician observes in making classifications.

Axis I Categories As stated earlier, Axis I includes all the clinical disorders except personality disorders and mental retardation.

- **Disorders Usually First Diagnosed in Infancy, Childhood, or Adolescence.** (Excludes mental retardation, which is diagnosed on Axis II). These include disruptive behavior, autistic disorder, and learning disorders.
- **Delirium, Dementia, and Amnestic and Other Cognitive Disorders.** Impairments in cognition (e.g., memory deficit, failure to recognize or identify objects, or a perceptual disturbance) that appear to be caused by one or more substances and/or general medical conditions.
- **Mental Disorders Due to a General Medical Condition Not Elsewhere Classified.** Mental disorder in association with a general medical condition that is judged to be its cause.

Table 3-2
Clinical Observations and Symptoms Used in DSM-IV Classification

While a given symptom may be part of several different clinical pictures (e.g., headaches may be present in cases marked by high anxiety, hypochondriasis, or somatic complaints), this list suggests the kinds of data clinicians attend to and that go into a psychiatric diagnosis. The presence of groups of symptoms characteristic of a particular disorder increases the likelihood of accurate classification.

Anxiety	Mood	Personality traits
Behavior	Motor activity	Physical symptoms
Cognitive functioning (attention, memory)	Occupational and social impairment	Sleep disturbance
Eating disturbance	Perceptual disturbance	Speaking manner
Energy level	Personal appearance	Thought content

- **Substance-Related Disorders.** Conditions marked by adverse social, behavioral, psychological, and physiological effects caused by seeking or using one or more substances (for example, alcohol, cocaine, and amphetamines).
- **Schizophrenia and Other Psychotic Disorders.** Significant distortion in the perception of reality; impaired capacity to reason, speak, and behave rationally or spontaneously; impaired capacity to respond with appropriate affect and motivation (e.g., delusions, hallucinations, incoherence, and social isolation).
- **Mood Disorders.** Abnormal mood characterized by depression, mania, or both symptoms in alternating fashion. Depression is indicated by sadness, gloominess, and dejection; mania is indicated by excitement, irritability, and expansiveness.
- **Anxiety Disorders.** High levels of anxiety, tension, and worry over extended periods of time that may be accompanied by avoidance of feared situations, ritual acts, or repetitive thoughts.
- **Somatoform Disorders.** Physical symptoms for which no medical causes can be found; persistent worry about having a physical illness; exaggerated concern about minor or imagined physical defects in an otherwise normal-appearing person.
- **Factitious Disorders.** Physical or behavioral symptoms that are voluntarily produced by the individual, apparently in order to play the role of patient. These often involve chronic blatant lying.
- **Dissociative Disorders.** Temporary, often sudden disruptions in the normal functions of consciousness (e.g., loss of memory, consciousness, or identity).
- **Sexual and Gender Identity Disorders.** Difficulty in the expression of normal sexuality (e.g., confusion about gender identity, decreased sexual desire or arousal, sexual acts and fantasies involving the production of suffering or humiliation for either sexual partner, and sexual activity with children or nonconsenting adults).
- **Eating Disorders.** Significant disturbances in eating (e.g., anorexia, binge eating).
- **Sleep Disorders.** Disturbances in the sleep process (e.g., difficulty in going to sleep or staying asleep, excessive daytime sleepiness, disturbances of the sleep-wake cycle).
- **Impulse-Control Disorders Not Elsewhere Classified.** Repeated expression of impulsive acts that lead to physical or financial damage to the individual or another person and often result in a sense of relief or release of tension (e.g., assaultive acts, stealing objects that are not needed, setting fires, and recurrent maladaptive gambling).
- **Adjustment Disorders.** Persistent emotional or behavioral reactions in response to an identifiable stressor (such as a negative life event). The reactions may be dominated by depressed mood, anxiety, or withdrawal.
- **Other Conditions That May Be a Focus of Clinical Attention.** Presence of one or more psychological or behavioral factors that adversely affect a general medical condition; medication-induced movement disorders; family relationship problems; problems related to abuse or neglect; extended bereavement reactions.

Axis II Categories Personality disorders and mental retardation are coded on Axis II. These conditions begin in childhood or adolescence and continue into adult life without much change. Axes I and II are separated so that when individuals are evaluated, these continuing characteristics, which may affect cognitive, social, or motor functioning or the ability to adapt, will be taken into consideration. Axis II may also be used to indicate prominent maladaptive personality features that do not meet the threshold for a personality disorder. Axis II may not distinguish clearly enough between commonly seen personality styles or traits that appear to cause few problems for the individual and the rigid, clearly maladaptive personality styles that lead to personal unhappiness or ineffectiveness. Imperfect as it may be, however, this attempt to include personality factors in psychiatric classification is a step forward.

- **Personality Disorders.** Pervasive and enduring patterns of maladaptive behavior and thought that begin by early adulthood, often interfere with normal interpersonal relationships, and reduce personal effectiveness. Subjective distress may or may not be present. Personality disorders specified in DSM-IV include paranoid personality disorder; schizoid personality disorder; schizotypal personality disorder; antisocial personality disorder; borderline personality disorder; histrionic personality disorder; narcissistic personality disorder; avoidant personality disorder; dependent personality disorder; obsessive-compulsive personality disorder; and personality disorder not otherwise specified.
- **Mental Retardation.** Disorders marked by delays in development in many areas. These disorders are predominantly characterized by pervasive impaired intellectual functioning as well as specific learning problems. Retardation levels range from mild (IQ ranging from 50 to 70) to profound (IQ below 20 or 25).

Evaluation of the DSM Multiaxial Approach

DSM-I and DSM-II were published in 1952 and 1968, respectively. They were not multiaxial in character. Both the revision of DSM-III published in 1987 and the 1994 DSM-IV provided improvements in DSM-III's multiaxial approach that enhanced its comprehensiveness and usefulness. DSM-IV, like DSM-III and DSM-III-R before it, seeks to describe clinical problems rather than interpret them; it lists specific descriptive criteria for each diagnostic category.

Emphasis on the accurate description of clinical conditions came about as a result of widespread concern that psychiatric diagnoses were often unreliable because they were based on guesses about the underlying causes of problems. The language of both DSM-I and DSM-II was heavily influenced by psychoanalytic theory, and the manuals focused on internal nonobservable processes. As a result, clinicians' diagnoses often varied greatly. In contrast, the recent DSMs have used much more precise language. Another reason for the superiority of the most recent DSMs is that extensive field trials were carried out in their development. These trials, involving thousands of patients and hundreds of clinicians, made it possible to check for ease of usage and reliability and to correct deficiencies before publication.

Although the most recent DSMs represent advances in clinical classification, no one believes that these manuals are the final word on the subject of diagnosis. Among their limitations are continued reliance on impressionistic clinical judgments (e.g., in estimating the severity of a disorder). DSM-IV might best be viewed as a set of guidelines for characterizing clinical problems. It is concerned primarily with the description of these problems.

Whereas the first multiaxial DSM (DSM-III) represented a major innovation in the concept of classification, DSM-IV reflects the need to fine-tune the diagnostic system. Another important reason for producing DSM-IV such a short time after DSM-III-R was the desirability of an internationally standardized system. Extensive international research on mental disorders requires that worldwide diagnostic systems be as similar as possible if researchers in all countries are to be able to take advantage of new information. The latest edition of the World Health Organization's International Classification of Diseases (ICD-10) includes maladaptive behavior and is widely used throughout much of the world. Those who developed ICD-10 and DSM-IV have cooperated and shared information in an effort to make the systems similar. However, the two systems are not identical. For example, in addition to descriptions of disorders and diagnostic guidelines for clinical work, ICD-10 also has a set of research diagnostic criteria for use in research projects that allow for the selection of very homogeneous groups of individuals whose symptoms and other characteristics resemble each other in clearly stated ways. Perhaps future revisions of DSM-IV and ICD-10 will be able to incorporate the best features of both systems.

DSM-III and its successors have sought to be quite specific about the criteria for using each diagnostic category. It appears that these manuals have successfully achieved that objective. By emphasizing descriptions of behavior rather than theoretical ideas about its cause, the DSM approach has reduced the amount of inference needed to make a particular diagnosis and has increased reliability. Not only have recent manuals increased the dimensions for describing particular disorders, they have also greatly increased coverage

of the range of disorders. This increase is especially evident in the extensive coverage of childhood disorders.

Although much more research is needed in order to make a definitive evaluation of the DSM multiaxial approach, practitioners agree that it has been successful in facilitating communication among clinicians and contributing to more reliable classification. For example, prior to DSM-III, clinicians often complained about the difficulty, using available classification criteria, of distinguishing between certain affective disorders and schizophrenia. Furthermore, as a consequence of criteria that were too vague, diagnoses of schizophrenia were made more often than this disorder actually occurs in the population. Evidence since the introduction of DSM-III suggests that this overrepresentation of schizophrenia diagnoses has been much reduced (Adamson, 1989).

It is possible that the comprehensiveness of the multiaxial approach is a mixed blessing. Clinicians show a high level of agreement in classifying patients on broad general diagnostic categories, such as depression and juvenile delinquency, and less consistency in classifying finer subdivisions within these general categories. Much research will be required in order to determine the breadth and specificity needed to maximize the value of current multiaxial approaches.

Critics have argued that recent DSMs have paid too much attention to how a person appears at a particular point in time (e.g., upon admission to a clinic or hospital) and not enough to his or her prior history and developmental crises. The DSM system has also been criticized for providing little information about the causes of abnormal behavior. Several writers argue that since the publication of DSM-III, etiology has not been given sufficient attention in classification, and that both description of and inferences about the processes involved in maladaptive behavior are needed.

Despite these criticisms, most practitioners recognize the unique value of the multiaxial approach. By including axes that pertain to severity of stress and previous level of adjustment, as well as to long-lasting personality patterns, DSM-IV reflects the need for integrating what is known about people's vulnerabilities, assets, and stressful life events with what is observed in their behavior. Efforts are continuing to improve the existing axes in the light both of the research findings and of the needs of practicing clinicians.

In Chapter 2 we presented an interactional approach to maladaptive behavior that builds on the major current theories in abnormal psychology. We pointed out that, although these theories differ in the determinants of behavior they emphasize, all the determinants have potential value. For example, whereas biological factors might be especially important in certain disorders, community and cultural factors might be particularly important in others. We pointed out that, for most conditions, combinations of factors need to be taken into account. A noteworthy feature of DSM-IV is its attempt to pay attention to the multiple aspects of a person's life that play roles in clinical conditions. In addition to describing each clinical condition (Axis I and Axis II), DSM-IV also deals with the relevance to the condition of the medical status of the individual (Axis III); pertinent psychological and environmental problems (Axis IV); and how well the individual is functioning in important domains of life (Axis V). Thus DSM-IV provides for each case five pieces of information concerning the biological, psychological, and social determinants of human problems. While there may be differences of opinion about which determinants are especially pertinent in particular cases, the important point is that, beginning with DSM-III, classification has become a task of recognizing and integrating several pieces of information rather than simply attaching a label to a condition.

Despite its shortcomings there seems little doubt that DSM-IV is an improvement over previous diagnostic systems. Many of its limitations grow out of deficiencies in our understanding of what mental health and mental disorder are. Any classification system can be no better than available knowledge and attitudes about what is being classified. As we will see later, experts who have devoted their entire careers to studying a specific topic such as schizophrenia have strong differences of opinion about which types of behavior should be examined. The greatest contributions of DSM-III, DSM-III-R, and DSM-IV

may turn out to be the new knowledge that results from the arguments they have stimulated (see Box 3-1).

Research on Classification

Research on the classification of abnormal behavior has focused on the role of clinical judgment in classification and on the effects of the labeling process. Information is also needed on how complex a classification system should be. How many categories should it have? Which variables must be assessed in making a diagnosis? Which variables should be optional? In what way should an individual's life story be taken into account in assessing his or her present behavior? The psychoanalytic perspective might lead to the conclusion that information about early childhood is essential to assessment, whereas a behavioristic viewpoint might emphasize a detailed description of present-day behavior. A diagnosis is not simply a label that is attached to a client by a clinician; it is a complex product of present knowledge and opinion about maladaptive behavior. As such, diagnosis is not an immutable process. Rather, it changes with advances in knowledge and alterations in what society defines as a problem (D. Goldberg, 1996).

Earlier we mentioned the importance of achieving agreement among clinicians in classifying cases. Until about 20 years ago, diagnosis was handicapped by the low reliability of diagnostic agreement. **Reliability** is concerned with whether a classification decision is reproducible, either by the same clinician at a different time or

---

 Q&A

Box 3–1

Q. You said that, while DSM-IV has been widely adopted as a reliable standard for psychiatric classification, its biggest contribution might turn out to be the issues and questions it poses for researchers and clinicians. Could you explain that further and give an example of what you mean?

A. *The fact that DSM-IV has been successful in becoming widely adopted is not inconsistent with the belief that it is an imperfect instrument. It is probably better than what preceded it and not as good as future generations of classification systems are likely to be. Axis II provides an illustration of what we are talking about. Since DSM-III, when it first appeared as part of the classification system, Axis II has been seen as contributing to a more well-rounded way of describing people and*

their maladaptations. The traditional problem categories of Axis I are embedded in personality patterns, and Axis II tells us something about that larger picture. So, Axis II is part of the effort to capture the whole person rather than simply to pin a label on someone.

Having recognized the importance of the whole person in DSM-III, DSM-III-R, and DSM-IV, the question arises: Can the picture of the whole person be brought into sharper focus so as to bring out details—personality features—that can improve our understanding of the causes and correlates of maladaptive behavior? There have been many definitions of personality but in all likelihood it is not one thing. Rather, personality has a number of dimensions. One of these concerns the cognitive side of life: what people tend to think about and their personal theories of themselves

and others. Another concerns their emotional reactions—how easily they become anxious, angry, or bored. Yet another are their motivations—their goals and what they want in life. Perhaps what is needed is not so much a unitary diagnosis of their personality (their personality type) as a personality profile that provides information about not only their cognitive styles, emotions, and motivations, but perhaps also their coping styles (how they approach various types of situations) and characteristic defense mechanisms. In other words, maybe we need a more elaborate, multidimensional Axis II than currently exists in order to capture the whole person.

The current Axis II might be regarded as a first step. What additional steps should DSM-V take in describing personality so as to place clinical problems within their proper contexts?

by different clinicians. In order to have high reliability, the defining characteristics of a class and the criteria that must be met in order to establish class membership must be clearly defined. For example, it must be clearly specified which specific symptoms all patients in this class would have in common and which symptoms would cause their exclusion from the class. Reliability can be assessed with several specific statistical tools. Often, reliability is simply assessed by the degree of agreement when the same patient is diagnosed by several different clinicians. However, simply using the percentage of agreement overlooks the possibility that some clinical agreement might occur by chance. A clinician who sees schizophrenia in a high percentage of his or her cases will show a fair amount of chance agreement with other clinicians in using the label of schizophrenia. A reliability index, the **kappa statistic,** corrects the amount of observed agreement for the amount of chance agreement. This correction is based on information about the overall frequency with which clinicians use particular classifications. By correcting for chance agreement, use of the kappa statistic provides a truer estimate of diagnostic reliability and has become the standard method for indexing agreement in studies relating to classification.

Validity is concerned with the appropriateness of the classification system—whether or not the classification puts together people whose symptoms arise from the same causes and respond to similar treatments. An ideal demonstration of the validity of a diagnosis requires similar causes and mechanisms underlying the symptoms of all those with the same diagnosis. A more usual way to view validity is the predictability of clinical course and outcome and the most effective treatment approach. The highly specific descriptions of most DSM categories have greatly increased the reliability of the diagnoses made using the system, but the validity of many DSM classifications has yet to be fully established. One of the reasons for this is that not enough is known about the causes of many disorders. It is likely, for instance, that some DSM-IV categories may contain disorders with very different causes despite the similar symptoms that are the basis for the classification. Another problem is that the DSM system allows a diagnosis if the person has only a certain number of symptoms from a much larger list. This means that two people who have the same diagnosis may have just a few symptoms in common. Determining more about the similarity of causation within the same diagnostic group is currently a major focus of research.

Clinical Judgment A variety of data go into classification statements. In arriving at a diagnosis, the clinician goes through a series of problem-solving and decision-making steps. The more complete and standardized the data and the more explicit the intervening cognitive steps, the greater the reliability of the diagnosis. This holds true

whether we are talking about a clinician making a diagnosis on two different occasions using the same data or about two clinicians making independent diagnoses on the basis of the same information.

Studies of clinical judgment have been carried out in order to determine just how the clinician's role affects the reliability of classification. When diagnostic criteria are described clearly and intensive training is given in their use, and when the clinicians using them employ comparable methods, the reliability of diagnoses increases significantly. Additional factors also affect clinical judgments. One such factor is that certain disorders are more easily classified than others (e.g., the reliability of diagnoses for organic brain disorders is higher than that of diagnoses for schizophrenia). Irrelevant or tangential information, such as labels, may throw a clinician off course. In addition, the attitudes and characteristics of diagnosticians often influence the judgments they make. A study using the 10th edition of the International Classification of Diseases (ICD-10) showed that explicit diagnostic criteria similar to those provided by DSM-IV contributed to agreement among clinicians in patient classification (Sartorius et al., 1993). However, there was less agreement regarding personality disorders than most other conditions because the participating clinicians found the categories of these disorders somewhat difficult to use.

Research on clinical judgment suggests that even though they may not carry out formal research projects, clinicians use a research process in making their diagnoses. Like more research-oriented scientists, clinicians make observations, integrate them, and draw conclusions on the basis of the evidence they have gathered.

Evidence gathered in formal research on clinical judgment has helped identify factors that contribute to disagreement and error in day-to-day clinical research. Among them are the following:

1. *Client factors.* The client is not a constant. In fact, he or she may contribute to differences in clinical opinion by behaving in different ways at different times. If one clinician assesses an individual who is in the midst of an alcoholic delirium and another clinician's assessment is carried out several days after the delirium has lifted, differences in classification would not be surprising.
2. *Method factors.* Clinicians who use different assessment techniques might describe people who are actually similar as being different.
3. *Criteria factors.* Clinicians who have different standards for classifying cases might differ in their diagnoses.
4. *Clinician factors.* Clinicians differ in how they assess data. Personality differences among clinicians, along with differences in training and theoretical orientation, influence the clinician's information processing.

Since clinicians differ in how they process information and in how much they can keep track of, computers may prove to be valuable aids to clinical assessment because they are capable of scanning and retaining larger amounts of information than a human diagnostician can. Whether or not clinicians are aided by computers, the process by which they form judgments and make decisions is an important part of research on classification and the clinical process.

Classification is a necessary first step toward introducing order into discussions of the nature, causes, and treatment of maladaptive behavior. It is essential to determine and to increase the reliability and validity of the labels attached by clinicians to patterns of maladaptive behavior and to people.

Cultural Context The classification of problematic behavior cannot be done in isolation. The cultural context in which the behavior occurs can be a crucial factor in judging whether or not the behavior poses a problem. Racial and ethnic populations may differ significantly from one another and from the larger society with respect to beliefs, values, norms, and behavioral styles. Language, country of origin, gender, age, social class, religious/spiritual beliefs, sexual orientation, and physical disabilities play roles in a person's cultural identity. Many people have multiple ethnic or cultural identities. Cultural identity imparts distinct patterns of beliefs and practices that have implications for the willingness to seek and the ability to respond to mental health services. These patterns include coping styles and ties to family and community (see Figure 3-1). Table 3-3 shows the four major racial or ethnic

Table 3-3	
Four Major Racial or Ethnic Groups in the United States as a Percentage of the Country's Population.	
Group	Percentage (%)
African American	12.8
Hispanic	11.4
Asian/Pacific Islanders	4.0
Native Americans	0.9

Source: *Mental Health: A Report of the Surgeon General, 1999.*

minority groups in the United States designated by the Federal government. Hispanic Americans are among the fastest-growing groups. Because their population growth outpaces that of African Americans, they are projected to be the predominant minority group (24.5% of the U.S. population) by the year 2050.

The need for a more culturally sensitive classification system, one that acknowledges the role cultural factors play in mental disorders and clinical judgments about them, is a topic of much debate. It has been noted that while religious and spiritual dimensions of culture are among the most important factors in human experience, psychiatric classification systems have tended to ignore them (Lukoff et al., 1992). However, DSM-IV does deal with cultural variations in the expression of maladaptive behavior by noting culture-related features of particular disorders.

Figure 3-1 African Americans are underrepresented in some outpatient treatment populations, but overrepresented in public inpatient psychiatric care in relation to Whites. Asian Americans have low levels of seeking help for mental health problems, often because of the stigma they perceive in seeking this type of help. One of the distinctive relationships in mental health problems of Hispanic Americans is a poorly understood much higher prevalence of depression among Hispanic women than men. Depression and alcohol abuse seem to be especially prevalent problems among Native Americans. Therapists need to take into account the ethnic identities, cultural viewpoints, and special problems of their patients.

Ethnic identity is a significant cultural variable that influences a person's self-concept and sense of belonging with other members of an ethnic group, based on shared characteristics. It can influence both a person's willingness to seek help concerning a mental health problem and the way in which the problem is described to a professional worker. As the following case demonstrates, ethnic identity can also play a role in the nature of the problem. The case involves a 7-year-old fourth-generation Japanese American who negatively evaluates physical characteristics of her ethnic group.

The girl frequently did not want to go to school and was withdrawn at home and at school. When she was at school, she avoided playing with the other children, did not participate in class, and sought to go home early. Her family sent her to therapy. During play therapy, she would select a doll with dark hair and another with blond hair. The two dolls would battle. The blond doll would always be victorious and the dark-haired doll would be knocked to the ground. When the girl picked stuffed animals, the light-colored animals always won. She "eventually revealed that children at school made fun of her 'tiny eyes' and black hair and did not pick her for sports teams. [Her play in therapy] sessions indicated that she wished she were not Japanese and felt anger toward her parents, blaming them for the differences in her eyes. [She reasoned that] if her parents were not Japanese, she would not be experiencing the ostracism she now faced." (Nagata, 1989, p. 103)

This case shows the need for clinicians to be sensitive to cultural differences and to see the world the way the patient does. The following comments by a psychologist who works in a culturally diverse urban setting exemplify clinicians' growing recognition of the role of ethnic identity in clinical interactions:

People with different ethnic backgrounds often pose special challenges for me. They may have had unusual or harmful experiences. For example, the environments that African American children encounter are less likely than those of White children to promote the skills needed to do well on IQ tests. People from certain ethnic or cultural groups may come for psychological testing or therapy with certain assumptions, concerns, and beliefs that I need to be aware of. Otherwise, I might end up making assumptions about them and the nature of their problems that are unwarranted. I've had some African American and Asian American patients, some of whose personality characteristics seemed unusual. When I got to know these people well, I realized that what seemed unusualness to me was as much or more a reflection of their cultural backgrounds as of their psychological problems.

The following comments by a psychiatrist working for the first time in a rural Appalachian setting reinforce the need for clinicians to question assumptions that they might make about regional differences:

Religious and folk beliefs—which some call superstitions—of Appalachian people are fascinating but do not seem to be as strong a guiding force as I had originally assumed. I have come to appreciate how much rural people take care of their own. Many mentally disturbed patients have help from family and people in the community to make sure they take their medications, eat properly, and are living comfortably. Working with the people of Appalachia offers many rewards: a rich and diverse culture; a refreshing, interconnected life; and patients who, to me, are surprisingly hopeful, optimistic, and flexible.

There has not been enough research on the roles played by ethnic and cultural differences in diagnosis and treatment of abnormal behavior. In some respects, members of minority groups may view and react to the world just like all other people; in other respects, they may see it differently (e.g., as a result of exposure to racism). In recent years, research on personality and maladaptive behavior has increased concerning these similarities and differences and the impact of feeling different from most people in one's community (Jackson, 1991; Uba, 1994). Research on cross-cultural comparisons of emotional disturbance and its expression is also increasing. For example, it has been shown that depression often has very different meanings and forms of expression in different societies. Most cases of depression worldwide are experienced and expressed in bodily terms of aching backs, headaches, fatigue, and a wide assortment of other somatic symptoms that lead patients to regard this condition as a physical problem. Only in contemporary Western societies is depression seen principally as an intrapsychic experience ("I feel depressed"), and even in these societies, many cases of depression are still lived and coped with as physical conditions (Jenkins et al., 1991).

Comparisons of Asian American groups with other groups in the population have yielded valuable information. The preponderance of research has indicated that many Asian Americans tend to somaticize their mental health problems (Uba, 1994). That is, it seems that they manifest their worries, guilt feelings, and strong negative emotions (such as depression) as physical complaints. The tendency to somaticize mental health problems may be a reflection of Asian American cultural values that emphasize avoiding shame and maintaining the honor of the family. Somatic problems do not carry the stigma or negative social consequences that psychological problems do. Perhaps Asian Americans present their problems as somatic rather than emotional problems because they are more comfortable talking about physical problems than psychological ones. Clinicians need to take account of the meanings people in various groups attach to expressing emotion-laden thoughts and having certain kinds of difficulties.

DSM-IV recognizes that certain unusual forms of behavior are restricted to specific cultures and areas. Documentation of the existence of **culture-bound syndromes** dates back to the early explorers. For example, in 1770, Captain Cook noted the Malaysian syndrome amok, a condition of homicidal frenzy preceded by a state of brooding and ending in sleepiness and amnesia. What is being recognized increasingly today is that cultural factors are important, not only with regard to exotic disturbances like amok, but also with regard to cultural variations in emotional expression, body language, and religious beliefs and rituals within particular societies such as the United States and Canada. These subtleties need to be attended to in order to give proper weight to the cultural context in which a set of symptoms is presented (Rogler, 1996).

Several roadblocks to seeking diagnosis and receiving appropriate treatment for mental health problems in racial and ethnic minority groups are: (1) resistance to seeking help because of perceived stigma and language, (2) mistrust and fear of mental health personnel, (3) lack of insurance or funds to pay for mental health services, and (4) overdiagnosis or misdiagnosis of the problems presented by minority group members because of clinicians' failure to take into account sufficiently the role of cultural factors. Additional problems may arise in treating with medications the mental health problems of members of different racial groups. For example, there may be genetic variations in drug metabolism among the groups, cultural differences in willingness to use prescribed medications, and simultaneous use of traditional and alternative healing methods.

Despite the attention given to cultural factors in the DSM-IV, some clinicians make the error of implicitly assuming that the various diagnostic categories and measures are universally applicable (Thakker & Ward, 1998). To some extent, this error is understandable in view of the fact that so little is known currently about how the cultural context operates in clinical situations and its effects. Much more research on this topic, ranging from biological sensitivities to culturally related meanings and values, is needed (Rogler, 1999).

Assessment: The Basis of Classification

While efforts are made to improve classification systems, clinical workers must employ currently available methods in their work. The major methods used to assess behavior in clinical settings include interviews, intelligence tests, neuropsychological tests, and personality and behavioral assessment. Assessment methods of other aspects of individual behavior have also been developed and are discussed later in the chapter.

Structured interviews are used primarily in two settings in which information obtained in a standard way is particularly important. One of these settings is in large institutions where a client will be assigned to treatment only after initial information is collected and a group of health professionals have discussed a diagnosis and agreed on an initial treatment plan. In this type of setting it is especially important that information on all clients be obtained in a uniform manner so that the conference concerning the treatment plan is minimally affected by the particular person who gathered the data and also so that all needed information is likely to be obtained. The other major setting for structured interviews is one in which research is being carried out. Again, the ability to obtain client data that can be meaningfully compared with data on many other individuals is of crucial importance.

In contrast to these situations, clinicians who will carry out the treatment program themselves often develop individual approaches to gathering data. They may find that a standardized interview makes it more difficult to begin forming a relationship with the client. In addition, they may fit their interview approach to their own personalities and to information they have personally found important in treating other clients.

Although there is agreement about the need to develop valid ways of characterizing individuals, clinicians disagree on how this can best be accomplished. Because no single assessment tool is considered foolproof, assessment is commonly approached in more than one way in order to yield a more complete and accurate description of the individual.

The Interview

The interview continues to be the most widely used assessment tool. Clinical interviews are of two types: assessment and therapeutic. The purpose of the **diagnostic** (or **assessment**) **interview** is to gather information and assess behavior. On the basis of the client's verbal and nonverbal behavior during the interview, the interviewer tries to understand why the client is seeking help and what, from a therapeutic standpoint, might be done. The **therapeutic interview** (or therapy session) occurs after a preliminary assessment has been made. Its aim is to modify maladaptive behavior and attitudes.

Interviews usually involve two individuals, the interviewer and the client, although other people, such as family members, are sometimes included. Family members may also be interviewed separately. Treatment decisions are often based largely on the data gathered in a diagnostic interview, which may begin as a telephone call and then be followed up in a face-to-face setting. Table 3-4 lists four important components of the clinical interview.

Table 3–4

Four Components of the Clinical Review

While the following components are found in virtually all types of clinical interviews, they are especially pertinent to the diagnostic interview.

1. *Rapport.* Rapport refers to how the interviewer and client relate to each other. To achieve rapport, the interviewer seeks to put the client at ease and show interest in the problem being discussed.

2. *Technique.* Depending on the client and the problem, the interviewer selects techniques to build rapport and to obtain information. Techniques range from open-ended questions to a tactful challenge of something the client has said.

3. *Mental status.* To determine the mental level at which the client is functioning, the interviewer will evaluate his or her answers to questions. Are they clear or fuzzy, pleasant or angry, reality-oriented or full of strange and bizarre ideas?

4. *Diagnosis.* The interviewer is continually revising his or her formulation of the client's problems and personality. This process includes a diagnosis.

Content of the Interview Assessment interviewers seek to identify problems and determine the nature and extent of maladaptive behavior. Typically, interviewers begin by trying to find out how the client describes, understands, and interprets his or her problem. In some cases, the complaint is nonspecific, such as "I feel tense and worried all the time." In other cases, it may seem deceptively clear, as in "My child is hyperactive—I can't control him." Then the interviewer may inquire into the history of the problem. In the course of obtaining this information, the interviewer may get a better understanding of the stressors or difficulties present in the client's life as the problem was developing.

Initial interviews often are relatively unstructured. Depending on the problem and how it is described, the interviewer may have to move back and forth among a number of topics. However, an attempt is made to answer the following questions:

1. *Who is the client?* That is, what is his or her name, age, ethnic and cultural background, marital status, and occupation? What led to his or her decision to obtain professional help?

2. *How does the client think and feel about life at this time?* What are the client's preoccupations and feelings?

3. *What is the history of the problem and the client's developmental background?* Depending on the particular problem, an inquiry might be made into the physical and emotional climate of the client's home during infancy and childhood, as well as the client's sleep patterns, physical and motor development, and sexual and social development.

4. *What is the client's present psychological state?* What is noteworthy about the client's speech, thought, judgment, cooperativeness, and social skills?

5. *How vulnerable and how resilient is the client?* What are the client's assets and liabilities?

During an assessment interview, many aspects of behavior must be observed and noted. These include the client's general appearance and grooming, voice and speech patterns, and the kinds of thoughts described, as well as facial expression, posture, and style of movement.

People with serious problems state facts, opinions, attitudes, and, in some cases, distortions and lies. They behave in a variety of ways: they may sigh, gesture, avert their eyes, tap their feet, smile, or grimace at the interviewer. As a consequence of this flood of responses, the interviewer usually can extract and use only a small percentage of the data presented during the interview. On the other hand, some clients hesitate to discuss their problems openly and provide very little information. Answers to questions such as "How does your wife get on your nerves?" can differ widely in honesty, clarity, and feeling. Unanticipated reactions by the client and indications that he or she is not in contact with reality must be noted. In the following case, a woman is talking about a physician she had wished to consult:

> Patient: *I wanted to see him desperately, and called once and then again. I got him the third time. But did he come? No, he didn't. But he should have, shouldn't he?*
>
> Interviewer: *I don't know. Can you tell me more about . . .*
>
> Patient: *You're interested in part of my story, aren't you?*
>
> Interviewer: *Yes.*
>
> Patient: *Would you like me to write it down for you?*
>
> *The interviewer gives the patient paper and pencil and the patient proceeds to write the following: "Alpha, beta, gamma, delta, epsilon, epsilon, Bactrim, bacterium, back." The patient concludes by writing her signature.*

There is no apparent connection between the failure to make contact with the physician, the Greek alphabet, and the antibiotic Bactrim. During the interview, the interviewer noted several indicators of incoherence and delusions as the patient talked about her life.

Interviewers need to observe the relationship between their clients' verbal and nonverbal behaviors. Often what interviewers hear contradicts what they see. The client's verbal manner may be calm and dispassionate even though tension is evident from nonverbal signs such as sweating and hand-wringing. In some cases, gestures, movements, and facial expressions yield clues to the sources of a client's anxiety. Experienced clinicians are adept at observing nuances of behavior that clients are unaware of or believe they are suppressing successfully, as can be seen in the following interview:

During the interview she held her small son on her lap. The child began to play with his genitals. The mother, without looking directly at the child, moved his hand away and held it securely for a while. Later in the interview the mother was asked what she ordinarily did when the child played with himself. She replied that he never did this—he was a very "good" boy. She was evidently entirely unconscious of what had transpired in the very presence of the interviewer. (Maccoby & Maccoby, 1954, p. 484)

Another interviewer recorded the frequency of a client's blouse-clutching behavior during an assessment interview (see Figure 3-2), and noted a particularly high frequency of this behavior during one portion of the interview (Mahl, 1968). The client had at that time been describing how, at the age of 8, she and her twin sister had been told that they had "killed their mother" during their birth.

The Role of the Interviewer Every type of assessment involves taking a behavior sample for the purpose of predicting future behavior. Much of the behavior sampled in an interview is self-description. To facilitate the planning of treatment, the interviewer must establish valid relationships between the responses made during the interview and the client's behavior in current or future life situations. If the interview behavior is not representative of the client's characteristic response tendencies, inappropriate treatment decisions may be made. The interviewer attempts to construct a situation that, within a short period, provides reflections of complex lifelong patterns.

In most applied settings, assessment interviewers make mental and written notes, subjectively interpreting the behavior sample as it unfolds. A truly objective evaluation of an interview, however, cannot focus on the client alone. Because each interview involves a developing and distinctive relationship between the interviewer and the client, their characteristics jointly influence what takes place during the interview. Research supports clinical impressions that interviewers are a major factor in the interview. Are they accurate observers of the client's behavior? Do they unduly influence the behavior of the person being interviewed? These questions arise frequently in discussions of interviewing. Interviewers don't always note or interpret correctly much of what goes on. In both diagnostic and therapeutic interviews, the interviewer's behavior may influence the data obtained, as well as how those data are analyzed. The following are some characteristics of interviewers that might influence the course of an interview and its content:

- Age
- Gender
- Ethnicity
- Professional background
- Interviewing style
- Personality pattern
- Attitudes and values
- Expectations

As the following case suggests, the unique characteristics and styles that both client and interviewer bring to the clinical situation make it difficult to perfectly standardize clinical interviews:

The interviewer knew nothing about Robert Hatton except that he was 19 years old, had just begun his studies at a large university, and had a skin condition of apparently recent origin. The skin condition included redness, the breaking out of large welts, and itchiness. Hatton had come to the student

Figure 3-2 Frequency of one nonverbal response (blouse clutching) during an interview.

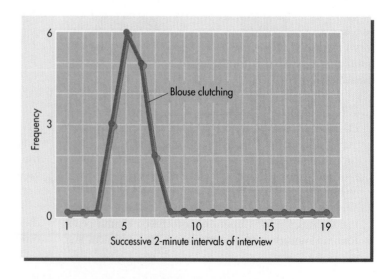

health service for the skin condition, but the ointment prescribed gave only minor, temporary relief. Because the physician who treated him suspected that the problem might be a result—at least in part—of psychological factors, she recommended that he talk with a clinical psychologist who was a consultant on the staff of the student health service in order to investigate whether any psychological factors were playing a role in his symptoms.

The first thing Hatton mentioned to the psychologist was the skin condition: how annoying and disruptive it was because of the incessant itching, and his puzzlement at being referred to a psychologist. During the initial interview he sweated a lot, occasionally had to catch his breath, and tapped his foot continually. Noting the shame Hatton seemed to feel about talking with what he called "a mental specialist," the psychologist made the following internal analysis of the situation: "If Robert's skin condition does have a psychological component, he has to learn that it is okay to talk to me. My main job right now is to listen and not to ask a lot of questions that make Robert think he's crazy."

The psychologist did ask some questions ("Have you had skin problems in the past? Under what circumstances? How do you like it at the university?"), but mainly she listened patiently, avoiding making quick judgments about what the client had to say and carefully observing what the client said and did, as well as which topics seemed to be upsetting to him. While avoiding aloofness, the psychologist maintained a detached but friendly attitude. When Hatton expressed concern about his ability to succeed at the university, the clinician did not say, "You're obviously intelligent enough to be very successful at this university," even though Hatton's vocabulary and manner of expressing himself were obviously outstanding. (She mused to herself, "What good would it do if I told Robert what all his friends and relatives tell him? What he is saying is that he's scared and really is worried about flunking out. I've got to let him know I realize what he is going through. The flip reassurance of other people hasn't done him one bit of good.")

The interview was uncomfortable for both Hatton and the psychologist. Hatton was tense, and there were long pauses during which he seemed unable to think of anything to say. Each of these pauses posed a conflict for the interviewer. ("If the pause is too long and too uncomfortable, he might decide not to come to see me again. On the other hand, what clients say after pauses is often very significant. I've got to steer along just the right path with Robert.") The interviewer noted when the client was experiencing a lot of anxiety or felt that he needed a show of interest and support.

The clinical psychologist had seen many cases in which physical problems (such as skin conditions) were related to the stress of university life. But she did not want to pigeonhole Hatton. Her main goal in the initial interview was to establish a relationship of mutual trust with him. She liked him, wanted to help him, and thought she could. But the first task was to accept him as a likable, unique person and hope that he would want to come back. Apparently her approach worked, because Hatton came back four times, as a result of which much in-

formation was brought out and the clinical picture became clearer. What emerged was a person of exceptional potential for whom the university created an intense stress because of the need he felt to be worthy of all the sacrifices his family was making for him. While he wanted to reward his parents for their help, he was also deeply angered at the way in which they blithely assumed he would make Phi Beta Kappa if he avoided being lazy.

On the basis of the series of interviews, the psychologist pieced together a picture of an intense stress reaction because of all the pressures to which Hatton felt he was being subjected. The psychologist did not know for sure what had caused the skin condition, but she felt that it might have been an accompaniment of the anxious thoughts connected with going to the university. Her recommendation to Hatton and to the referring physician was that psychotherapy might be helpful. Because the student health service did not provide psychotherapy sessions, the psychologist recommended to Hatton that he see a psychotherapist who might help him decide on his own goals in life, rather than uncritically accept his parents' goals for him. After a series of twenty therapy sessions, Hatton was much less anxious, his skin condition was gone, and he felt more accepting of both himself and his parents.

The clinical psychologist who talked with Hatton was not following a standard interview format, nor did she feel pressured to uncover a lot of factual material. Rather, she quickly saw the need to establish an accepting working relationship with someone who came to the interview with hesitancy and reservations. Such a relationship-building orientation is valuable in most clinical interviews.

One important interviewing skill is the ability to size up a situation quickly and to devise an appropriate clinical strategy in light of the assessment. In the following case, the interviewer quickly picked up on the patient's denial of having a problem and turned the focus to how others might have perceived it. The 25-year-old patient was a man diagnosed as experiencing a manic episode, a condition marked by a euphoric, hyperactive state and impaired judgment.

Patient: By the way, before we start, I just wanted to tell you that everything I say, there's no bullshit. It's the truth.

Interviewer: Why don't we begin by your telling me exactly what it was that got you into the hospital?

Patient: I was transferred from City Hospital.

Interviewer: Okay, what got you into that hospital?

Patient: I was pretending to be an undercover cop.

Interviewer: You were pretending to be an undercover cop? How come?

Patient: How come? I had just seen the movie Serpico. And I knew I could do a better job.

Interviewer: Was it recently that you saw the film?

Patient: About two months ago.

Interviewer: This had been going on for some time then?

Patient: Yeah.

Interviewer: So, how long has it been since you were last feeling well?

Patient: Last feeling well? Right now!

Interviewer: You've been feeling well, then?

Patient: Oh, yeah. I've been feeling well for the past . . . I've been feeling well for a long time.

Interviewer: However, going into the hospital means that other people are not certain that you're well.

Patient: Of course! That's what I've been dealing with.

Interviewer: Well, then, let's rephrase the question. How long has it been since others have felt that there was something the matter with you?

Patient: That began about three months ago. I was telling my sister that I could take any amount of cyanide or mescaline, or any other drug, and that it wouldn't have any effect on me at all. She didn't believe me.

Mental Status Examination Especially with new patients, it is important to evaluate current mental status. How well is this person functioning at the present time? Are there noticeable strengths, weaknesses, and dysfunctions? If these questions can be answered, the possibility of achieving diagnostic accuracy increases.

The **mental status examination** usually takes place in an interview setting and does not employ a structured format in which the individual is tested formally. In the mental status examination, the clinician carefully observes the behavior of the individual, engages him or her in casual conversation, and explores pertinent areas such as thought content, mood, perception, judgment, and the patient's insight into his or her personal problems. The clinician observes the patient's appearance, hygiene, dress, ability to maintain eye contact, and psychomotor behavior (e.g., abnormal movements). An important reason for engaging the patient in conversation is to assess the patient's attention and concentration (Is the patient able to understand what is being discussed and respond appropriately?), speech and thought patterns, and orientation to place. The clinician pursues carefully difficulties that might fall into these domains. For example, to check orientation to place, new patients might be asked how they found the clinician's office. The clinician tries to determine the probable accuracy of the information provided by the patient, watching for distortions of memory and judging the patient's insight (e.g., is the patient aware of delusions or hallucinations?).

Table 3–5
The Mental Status Examination: Key Features of the Patient's Behavior
▪ Appearance
▪ Consciousness or alertness
▪ Psychomotor behavior
▪ Attention and concentration
▪ Speech
▪ Thought patterns
▪ Orientation
▪ Memory
▪ Affect and mood
▪ Energy
▪ Perception
▪ Judgment and insight

In the course of the mental status examination, the clinician might ask the patient to perform certain tasks that reflect particular psychological functions. Immediate memory might be tested by asking the patient to repeat letters, numbers, or unrelated words 5 or 10 seconds after hearing them. Visual memory might be tested by asking the patient to copy a figure, either with the figure still visible or a few minutes after it has been withdrawn from view. Long-term memory might be evaluated by asking the patient to reconstruct the interview or to recall something said at the beginning of the interview. Table 3-5 summarizes the components of the mental status examination.

The Structured Interview We noted earlier that standardized procedures increase the reliability of classifications of abnormal behavior. This makes a lot of sense, since standardization guarantees that clinicians will at least ask the same questions of each person they interview. An argument against standardized interviews is that they do not give the clinician the flexibility needed to form a productive relationship with a client. However, there is no reason for a clinical worker not to use a standardized format in one interview and a more flexible one in another.

Structured, or **standardized, interviews** use a standard series of questions to determine whether specific symptoms are present. Standardization is achieved by providing the interviewer with a glossary of symptom definitions, a series of questions pertinent to symptoms, a set of topics requiring information, and cutoff points that indicate when to stop probing on a particular topic. The clinician also is given instructions for rating, in numerical terms, the presence and severity of symptoms. Most structured interviews permit the interviewer to depart from the standardized format under specified circumstances. The interviewer also has the option of pursuing lines of inquiry (including a return to a former line of questioning or a jump to a completely different section of the interview) that are suggested by the client's responses.

The Diagnostic Interview Schedule The **Diagnostic Interview Schedule (DIS)** illustrates the potential of the structured interview (Malgady et al., 1992; Robins et al., 1981). The DIS is designed to permit diagnosis of selected disorders, such as panic disorder. A person who has a panic disorder has recurrent anxiety attacks that often occur unpredictably, although certain situations—such as riding on a bus—may become associated with them. Panic attacks are noted for their frequency, severity, and symptoms, which include sweating, trembling, faintness, and heart palpitations. The section of the DIS that pertains to panic disorder provides the following questions and offers procedures for interpreting the answers and deriving the appropriate classification:

- Did a panic attack occur?
- How many attacks have occurred?
- What are the symptoms?
- Are the attacks repetitive rather than isolated?
- Are the attacks characteristic of the person's life rather than confined to a brief, atypical period?
- At what age did the attacks begin?
- Are the attacks explainable as symptoms of another disorder?
- Is the person tense, nervous, or high-strung between attacks?

The DIS has continued to evolve and now includes procedures, probes, and criteria appropriate for use with specific clusters of symptoms. New clusters are added periodically. Questions are asked not only about symptoms, but also about recent and past experiences associated with their onset. For example, in the case of bulimia, a disorder whose main symptom is binge eating, questions are asked about the types of food eaten, the respondent's mood during and after the binge, the environment in which the eating is done, how the binges are terminated, any associated weight gain, and the respondent's efforts to prevent weight gain. The onset and most recent occurrence of the disorder are determined from the dates of the first and the most recent binges.

The DIS can be employed by both professional and nonprofessional interviewers who have been trained in its use. Table 3-6 lists examples of some of the types of interview questions used. Training (a week-long course), supervision, quality control in the use of the interview, and periodic retraining sessions are recommended with the use of the DIS. Programs for computer scoring of interview data are available. Studies are being carried out to determine the feasibility of using computers either to directly administer the DIS or to aid the interviewer in administering it.

Table 3-6
Examples of Questions Used in Structured Interviews
How old were you the first time you were bothered by these particular fears?
Has there ever been a period of 2 weeks or more when you felt worthless, sinful, or guilty?
Have you ever gotten into physical fights while drinking?
For how many weeks, months, or years did you continue to have no interest in an activity that had meant a lot to you before?
Has there ever been a period of 2 weeks or more when you had a lot more trouble concentrating than is normal for you?
Has there ever been a period of 2 weeks or more when you wanted to die?

Research has shown that lay interviewers (i.e., non-professionals) are able to use the DIS in a reliable fashion and that their judgments tend to agree with those of professionals and with the impressions gained by clinicians in non-DIS psychiatric interviews (Helzer et al., 1987; Helzer, et al., 1985). Although the goal of an instrument like the DIS is to assess the occurrence of specific symptoms, determining whether that goal has been achieved is not a simple matter, as there is no objective and absolute standard against which to measure results. Nevertheless, clear specification of diagnostic definitions is a major achievement because it makes possible uniform diagnostic methods for diverse populations and places.

Instruments like the DIS, based on specific clinical criteria, have the potential to make comparability across studies a reality. However, much more research will be needed to determine whether this potential can be fully realized.

Structured diagnostic interviews vary in the degree to which the interview is structured. The **Structured Clinical Interview for DSM (SCID)** is less structured than the DIS and encourages the interviewer to ask follow-up questions based on clinical judgment. Its reliability in making diagnoses appears to be satisfactory (Spitzer et al., 1992; Williams et al., 1992).

Intelligence Tests

The value of assessing abilities has been recognized for a long time. The Chinese developed a standardized civil service testing program that was in operation for about 4,000 years. The United States and England adopted civil service ability testing during the latter portion of the nineteenth century as people came to believe that appointments should be based on talent. By the beginning of the twentieth century, psychology had become more and more concerned with quantifying personal characteristics pertinent to various types of situations. **Intelligence tests** became the first widely used psychological assessment tool in schools and clinical situations.

As the study of intelligence has evolved, it has come to be thought of as having two components: **general intelligence,** demonstrated by a global capacity to solve problems, and **specific abilities,** such as spatial perception. In examining intelligence, psychologists have focused on two main areas. One area is theoretical and is broken down into three general categories: what intelligence is, where it comes from, and how it works. The second area is practical—the goal of constructing tests to measure characteristics that can be used to predict future achievements.

The Binet Tests In the late nineteenth and early twentieth centuries, the French psychologist Alfred Binet developed a series of tests that differed noticeably from those that had previously been used to measure intelligence. Binet viewed intelligence as something that grows with age; older children are, on average, more intelligent than younger ones. The **Binet tests** sought to measure reasoning, ability to understand and follow directions, and the exercise of judgment or good sense.

The child's score on the original Binet test was expressed as a mental level corresponding to the age of normal children whose performance reached the same level. Later the term *mental age* was substituted for *mental level* and an **intelligence quotient (IQ)** age was computed by dividing the person's test score, or mental age (MA), by his or her chronological age (CA) and multiplying the result by 100. In equation form,

$$IQ = \frac{MA}{CA} \times 100$$

Although this method is no longer used, the term *IQ* has remained in use. The current test, called the Stanford-Binet scales, has undergone periodic revisions. Stanford-Binet scores are now derived from norms based on how much the individual's score deviates from the mean score for a particular age.

In its first three editions the Binet test yielded one overall intelligence score, but use of the Binet-type tests declined beginning in the 1960s, partly because the Binet scale tasks did not lend themselves to separate, reliable quantitative analyses. In addition, they were designed primarily for work with children. As a result of criticism of the shortcomings, the test was revised to include several different scores, and many of the items have been rewritten to apply to adults as well as children (Thorndike et al., 1986). The current edition (*Fourth Edition Stanford-Binet*) resembles the widely used Wechsler tests, discussed next, more than did the earlier editions.

The Wechsler Tests David Wechsler (1955, 1958) believed that intelligence is an aggregate of different abilities and should be measured as such. He regarded the Binet tests as deficient because they produced only a single score. The **Wechsler tests** include subtests on various abilities. The current version of the Wechsler test for those 16 years and older, the **Wechsler Adult Intelligence Scale (WAIS-III)** (1997), consists of 6 verbal subtests and 5 nonverbal. An important advantage of a test like the WAIS is that in addition to yielding an aggregate score, each of its subtests can be scored separately.

Three IQs are obtained on the Wechsler scales. **Verbal IQ** reflects level of attainment on subtests dealing with general information, comprehension, ability to think in abstract terms, and arithmetic. **Performance IQ** reflects level of attainment on tasks requiring solution of puzzles, substitution of symbols for digits, and reproduction of designs. Finally, the **Full Scale IQ** represents the total score on the test.

The success of Wechsler's Adult Intelligence Scale led to the development of the **Wechsler Intelligence Scale for Children (WISC)** (now in its third edition, WISC-III; see Figure 3-3). The WISC was developed as a downward extension of the adult level WAIS. It uses the same categories of subtests and many of the same items as the WAIS, with some easier items added. Like the WAIS, it also provides a Verbal IQ, a Performance IQ, and a Full Scale IQ.

For use with even younger children, the **Wechsler Preschool and Primary Scale of Intelligence (WPPSI)**

Figure 3-3 This child is completing one of the puzzlelike tasks that make up the Object Assembly subtest of the WISC.

was developed. This test's revision in 1989 (WPPSI-R) improved the instrument's content, broadened its scope, and updated norms. Just as most subtests on the WISC are downward extensions and adaptations of the WAIS, the majority of the subtests on the WPPSI are downward extensions of the WISC subtests. The additional subtests cover the same general skills as subtests on the WAIS and WISC, but the material is presented differently because of the age of the children to be tested. For example, instead of being asked to use blocks to reproduce a series of designs, the child is asked to copy simple designs using a colored pencil. Like the WAIS and the WISC, the WPPSI provides verbal, performance, and full-scale scores that then can be converted into IQ scores.

Kaufman Assessment Battery for Children The **Kaufman Assessment Battery for Children (K-ABC)** has come into frequent use because of concern about the effects of a child's cultural experiences on test results. The K-ABC is designed to incorporate ideas from cognitive psychology and neuropsychology into the assessment of intelligence (Kaufman & Kaufman, 1983). The K-ABC consists of 16 subtests, some for older and some for younger children. The tests fall into several categories: sequential processing, such as remembering a series of digits or hand movements; simultaneous processing, such as arranging a series of related pictures in the correct order; and tests that measure school experience more directly, such as naming pictures of well-known places and objects (see Figure 3-4).

(a)

(b)

(c)

(d)

Figure 3-4 Some of the tasks from the Kaufman-ABC. In the Face Recognition subtest, the child is shown a picture of a face, such as (a), for 5 seconds and is then asked to select that same individual from a group picture such as (b). In the Hand Movements subtest, the examiner tells the child, "Watch my hand," and after making a series of hand movements, says, "Now you try it." Two series of movements appropriate for children who are aged two and one-half are illustrated (c). In the Gestalt Closure subtest, the child is shown a series of partially completed drawings such as (d). The task is to name the object pictured, in this case a bird.

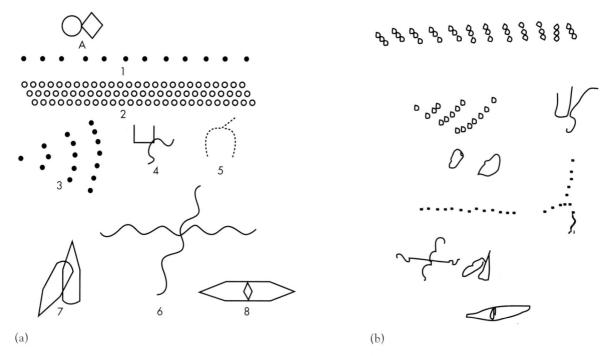

(a)   (b)

Figure 3-5   Perceptual performance in a case of organic brain damage. (a) The Bender Visual-Motor Gestalt Test (1938) is a deceptively simple test in which the subject is asked to copy geometric forms like these. (b) The Bender-Gestalt protocol of a patient suffering from organic brain damage.

Source: (a) From Bender Visual-Motor Gestalt Test, published by American Orthopsychiatric Association, 1938. (b) From Lacks (1984), p. 34. © 1984 by John Wiley & Sons. Reprinted by permission.

Many of the tests do not require a verbal response, and those that do require a few words at most. In most cases, the child can respond by pointing or in other nonverbal ways. The test has been described as a way to learn more about the child's approach to problem solving and learning tasks. The test's emphasis on short-term memory has been questioned by some critics, but the test authors argue that what is being measured is not memory as such but the sequential and simultaneous processing abilities that are defined as intelligence by cognitive psychologists.

Although the K-ABC tests have been described as being particularly fair to minority children, scores on these tests show the same Black–White differences that are seen on other intelligence tests. However, the K-ABC tests do demonstrate that if parental education is taken into account, there is little racial or ethnic difference on many nonverbal reasoning tasks. The similarities in performance are due primarily to the test's emphasis on short-term memory.

Neuropsychological Tests

Many of the tests that psychologists construct are related to theories concerning brain functioning. A variety of **neuropsychological tests** have been constructed to measure the cognitive, sensorimotor, and perceptual consequences of brain abnormality, such as a tumor or brain

deterioration. Some of the simpler tests are used for screening purposes, and if the suggestion of a brain abnormality arises, a more intensive neuropsychological assessment battery might then be recommended. One screening test, the Bender Visual-Motor Gestalt Test, asks the person tested to copy a series of figures (Figure 3-5). The accuracy of the copied figures is then compared to the performances of comparable persons in a reference group. In addition, the individual's behavior is observed carefully to detect any unusual approaches to the task or expressions of concern about the adequacy of the copied figures.

The tests we have described, as well as ones that we will describe shortly, differ from interviews in that they restrict the client's freedom of expression. Just as it is easier to quantify and compare scores on a multiple-choice test than on an essay test, the responses obtained on psychological tests can be more readily quantified and compared than the more open-ended and unstructured responses obtained in interviews. A tester's observation of how individuals approach particular test items often provides valuable insights into significant aspects of their everyday lives. To achieve a well-rounded picture of the individual, most clinicians interpret assessment results in light of behavioral observations made in less restricted situations. Box 3-2 provides information about two key features of assessment situations, the behavior observed while an individual is in the situation and the psychometric

Research Close-up   Box 3–2

Formal and Informal Features
of Assessment Situations

Any psychological test should have certain psychometric properties and meet generally accepted standards of what a satisfactory assessment instrument should be. However, the scores individuals receive on these instruments also depend on such factors as whether they are upset or unsure about what is expected in the situation. Formal features of assessment situations include the psychometric properties of the instrument(s) employed. The informal features are the observations of the person being assessed that may have more to do with the characteristics the person brings to the situation than the standardized instrument per se.

Some Important Psychometric Properties of Tests

1. *Reliability.* An assessment instrument should show consistency, that is, barring a change such as in the person's state of health or life circumstances, the scores obtained on a retest should be similar to those on the original test. A reliable test is consistent even though different clinicians are involved and the assessment situations take place at different times and even under somewhat different conditions.

2. *Validity.* Is the test doing what it was designed to do? The validity of an assessment instrument refers to the degree to which it is fulfilling its function. Validity is established when there is a strong relationship between a test and appropriate independent criteria, for example, the correlation between scores obtained on intelligence tests and success in academic pursuits.

3. *Norms.* Psychological tests often have no predetermined standards of passing or failing performance. Rather, an individual's test score is interpreted by comparing it with the scores obtained by others on the same test. Norms are established by the availability of scores for a group of typical people. Norms do not necessarily refer to the most desirable or ideal performance. They refer to how the scores are distributed in the norm group.

4. *Norm sampling.* Norms are as good as the groups from which they are derived. A distinction is made between a *sample* and the *population* from which the sample was drawn. The sample on which norms are based should be large enough to provide stable values and be representative of the population under consideration. A test designed for universal use, for example, throughout the United States, should optimally have norms based on a normative group that includes the major segments of the country's population.

Information That May Be Contributed by a Tester's Behavioral Observations

What do testers notice? In addition to the test responses themselves, testers are attentive to how clients approach tasks, how they react emotionally, and how they relate to the tester. These are some of the behavioral observations the tester may note and use in writing a case report.

1. How persistent is the client? Does the client keep trying or give up easily?
2. Is the client able to concentrate on the task at hand?
3. What is the client's attitude toward the test? Is it casual or serious? Is it competitive?
4. What is the client's problem-solving style? Methodical? Reasoned? Impulsive? Fragmented?
5. What emotions does the client exhibit? Is he or she anxious about being tested? Angry? Depressed?
6. How does the client react to failure or possible failure? Does the client get upset at failures or expect to fail?
7. How does the client react to the tester? As an authority figure? As an adversary?
8. How verbally expressive is the client? How articulate?

---

properties of the assessment instrument employed, for example, an intelligence or personality test.

Personality Assessment

Think how long it takes you to get to know a person; in many situations psychologists do not have that kind of time. Research on personality has stimulated the development of a variety of tests, rating scales, and questionnaires aimed at **personality assessment,** that is, measuring personality differences. These devices have predictive value and can be useful shortcuts to understanding behavior (Krueger et al., 1996). Personality tests and other assessment methods are used in clinical settings in making diagnoses, estimating the client's strengths and weaknesses, deciding whether treatment is required, and planning the treatment to be used.

For example, special assessment aids have been developed to diagnose the types of personality disorders classified on DSM-IV's Axis II. Table 3-7 gives examples of items used to classify particular personality disorders.

Personality Inventories The success of intelligence tests in predicting future achievement led researchers to try to develop similar ways to measure personality. But personality isn't something that can be measured by a total score that is high, medium, or low. The testlike measures used in personality assessment are meant to indicate the types of characteristics that combine to make up an individual's personality.

Rather than testing general knowledge or specific skills, **personality inventories** ask people questions about themselves. These questions may take a variety of forms. When

Table 3-7	
Assessing Axis II Personality Disorders: Examples of Items	
Axis II Classification	Sample Item
Paranoid personality disorder	"Certain people will take unfair advantage of me if they get the slightest chance."
Antisocial personality disorder	"Before I was 15 years old, people were already giving me a hard time for breaking the rules at home or school."
Avoidant personality disorder	"When people look at me, I am afraid that they will criticize or make fun of me for being strange or weird."
Obsessive-compulsive personality disorder	"I often get so involved in making each detail of a project absolutely perfect that I never finish."
Schizoid personality disorder	"Other people's feelings just don't move me one way or the other."

taking such a test, you might have to decide whether each of a series of statements is accurate as a self-description, or you might be asked to respond to a series of true-false questions about yourself and the world. Several inventories require the respondent to rate a set of statements on a scale based on how well they reflect his or her characteristics. Modern personality inventories yield several scores, each of which is intended to represent a distinct aspect of the personality.

Since its introduction in 1943, the **Minnesota Multiphasic Personality Inventory (MMPI)** has been one of the most widely used psychological tests. A revision, entitled MMPI-2, was published in 1989; it consists of 567 items. In developing MMPI-2, the wording of many of the original MMPI items was updated and a number of items were dropped, changed, or added. The standardization of MMPI-2 was superior to that of the original MMPI because of the new normative sample's greater size, geographic representativeness, and racial balance. Although there is still much work to be done in analyzing the MMPI-2, it appears to be a successful revision and should be used as widely as the original MMPI (Butcher, 1999; Graham, 1993).

The MMPI-2 includes 10 scales related to different groups of clinical disorders (the scales are usually referred to by the abbreviations in parentheses): hypochondriasis (Hs), depression (D), hysteria (Hy), psychopathic deviate (Pd), masculinity-femininity (Mf), paranoia (Pa), psychasthenia (Pt), schizophrenia (Sc), hypomania (Ma), and social introversion (Si). In addition to these standard clinical scales, there are numerous special scales—for example, the 16-item anger scale reflects irritability, impatience, grouchiness, and hot-headedness. People who sometimes feel like swearing or smashing things may get high scores on this scale. Scores on MMPI-2 scales can be compared with those of the normal standardization group and samples of reliably diagnosed clinical cases.

Besides the clinical scales, the MMPI-2 also includes several validity or control scales. These were designed to assess test-taking attitudes and response biases that might distort the picture presented by the clinical scale scores alone. High scores on these scales may indicate invalid clinical scale profiles. The validity scales consider the tendency of people to create a favorable impression, and consist of items dealing with minor flaws and weaknesses to which most people are willing to admit. People with high L (or lie) scores appear impossibly good and virtuous. The F scale (or validity score) was designed to detect deviant or atypical ways of responding to test items. High scores on this scale indicate those people who describe themselves as having a number of rare and improbable characteristics. While the F scale was included to reflect people's carelessness and confusion in taking the MMPI, it has also come to be seen as a good indicator of psychopathology.

The K scale (or defensiveness score) is more subtle than the L and F scales and covers several different content areas in which a person can deny problems (e.g., suspiciousness or worry). Its construction was based on the observation that some open and frank people may obtain high scores on the clinical scales, while others who are very defensive may obtain low scores. The K scale was devised to reduce these biasing factors. People who get high K scores are defensive; they tend to answer "False" to items like "I feel bad when others criticize me." K corrections are made on a number of clinical scales in order to compare the scores of people who differ in these tendencies.

In addition to the L, F, and K scales that were part of the original MMPI, MMPI-2 has three new validity scales. The Fb scale is intended to reflect a subject's tendency to answer later items in the test booklet differently than those that occur earlier. The VRIN scale provides an indication of subjects' tendencies to respond inconsistently to MMPI-2 items. Inconsistencies can result when subjects do not read the content of the items and respond instead in a random or near-random way. The TRIN scale was developed to identify subjects who respond indiscriminately by giving either mainly true responses (acquiescence) or mainly false responses (nonacquiescence) without taking into account the meaning of the item statement.

Table 3-8

The MMPI-2: Clinical and Validity Scales

The name, abbreviation, and number of each scale is given. (Clinical workers typically refer to the scales by number rather than by name or abbreviation.) Interpretations are given for high scores on the scales.

Name and Abbreviation	Scale Number	Interpretation of High Scores
Clinical Scales		
Hypochondriasis (Hs)	1	Bodily preoccupation; pessimistic
Depression (D)	2	Depressed; lacks self-confidence
Hysteria (Hy)	3	Psychologically motivated physical symptoms; lacks insight
Psychopathic deviate (Pd)	4	Antisocial tendencies; impulsive
Masculinity-femininity (Mf)	5	Sex-role conflict
Paranoia (Pa)	6	Suspiciousness; resentful
Psychasthenia (Pt)	7	Anxiety; insecure
Schizophrenia (Sc)	8	Bizarre thinking; withdrawn
Hypomania (Ma)	9	Excessive psychomotor activity; unrealistic goals
Social introversion (Si)	0	Social anxiety; shy
Validity Scales		
L scale	—	Need to present unrealistically favorable impression
F scale	—	Severe psychological disturbance
K scale	—	Defensiveness; inhibited
Fb scale	—	Inattention to some items
VRIN scale	—	Inconsistent responses
TRIN scale	—	Acquiescence or nonacquiescence biases

Table 3-8 describes the MMPI-2's clinical and validity scales. The principal application of the MMPI-2 is in deciding how to classify a given case. In general, the greater the number and magnitude of deviant scores on the MMPI-2, the more likely it is that the individual is severely disturbed. In making diagnostic decisions, the MMPI-2 user must be adept at interpreting not only the scores on the individual scales, but also the pattern of those scores in a particular person's profile. For example, the assessor cannot assume that a high score on the schizophrenia scale indicates the presence of schizophrenia. Other psychotic groups may show high elevation on this scale, and persons with schizophrenia often score higher on other scales than on the Sc scale.

The **Millon Clinical Multiaxial Inventory (MCMI)** is used to screen individuals with serious psychological difficulties (Millon, Millon, & Davis, 1994). It consists of 24 clinical scales, as well as three scales intended to assess tendencies to distort responses. A feature of the MCMI is the fact that its scales assess all the major personality disorders of DSM-IV's Axis II, as well as several Axis I disorders. The MCMI scales were specifically designed to correspond to DSM-IV classifications.

Personality inventories are aids in describing and understanding individuals, identifying their problems, and making appropriate clinical decisions. The construction of new inventories grows out of methodological advances and changes in how personality is conceptualized. An example of a recent approach that seems promising is the **five-factor model,** which reflects growing discussion among personality researchers about the basic elements of individuality. The five factors are: emotional stability, extroversion, agreeableness, openness to experience, and conscientiousness. Table 3-9 lists some features of each of these factors. Research is being conducted with regard to the relationship of combinations of the five factors to particular disorders and the prediction of how most effectively to treat them.

Rating Scales There are many other personality assessment techniques. The rating scale is one of the most venerable and versatile of these. **Rating scales** present respondents with a question that focuses on a concept, person, or situation and asks them to select from a number of choices. The rating scale is similar in some respects to a multiple-choice test, but its options represent degrees of a particular characteristic.

Table 3-9
The Five-Factor Model: Features of the Factors

Emotional Stability
Nervousness, anxiety, moodiness, anger.
Extroversion
Gregariousness, warmth, assertiveness, talkativeness.
Agreeableness
Kindness, trust in others, cooperativeness, modesty.
Openness to Experience
Interest in new experiences, curiosity, imaginativeness.
Conscientiousness
Thoroughness, reliability, competence, self-discipline.

An example of a rating scale item is "To what degree are you shy?" People might be asked to place this item on a scale ranging from "Not at all" to "Extremely." They can do this simply by placing a check mark at an appropriate point on a continuum. Rating scales can be used to rate other people's behavior as well as one's own. For instance, a teacher might use rating scales to rate students. In this case, the earlier item might read, "To what degree is this student shy?" An example of this use of rating scales in clinical work is the assessment of children's ability to pay attention to what is going on around them and to exercise self-control. The degree to which children possess these abilities is an indicator of their personal development.

Many clinical problems in children are related to their inability to delay responding until a suitable time, to plan activities, and to engage in socially appropriate behavior. Kendall and Wilcox (1978) devised a convenient series of rating scales to assess children's self-control. Their measure, the **Behavior Rating Scale for Children,** has proven reliable and can be used in a variety of settings and by untrained observers such as parents. The Behav-

ior Rating Scale for Children presents the rater with 33 questions, each of which is responded to on a 7-point rating scale (1 = always, 7 = never). The following are some representative items from the scale:

- Does the child sit still?
- Does the child disrupt games?
- Does the child think before he or she acts?
- Does the child grab for the belongings of others?
- Is the child easily distracted from his or her work or chores?

Another type of rating scale, the **visual analogue scale (VAS),** has been used in clinical and research settings to measure a variety of subjective phenomena, such as pain, anxiety, and craving for substances like cigarettes. One or several visual analogue scales might be used in a given study. The VAS provides a convenient, easy, and rapidly administered measurement strategy. However, the applicability of these scales is limited by subjects' ability to conceptualize and understand the method itself, that is, to translate a personal perception of an abstract concept into a linear unit. Figure 3-6 shows examples of different types of visual analogue scales that measure pain and anxiety.

Rating scales, like self-report questionnaires, are not immune to inaccuracy. One possible biasing factor, the **halo effect,** results when an individual rates a person more favorably than is realistic on a specific characteristic because the rater has a generally favorable reaction to the person. Other methodological problems include the tendency to want to say only nice things about oneself or someone else and the tendency to overuse the midrange of the scales. Research has shown that many of these problems can be reduced through careful wording of items, instructions to the rater, use of minimally ambiguous concepts and scales, and in some cases actual training in making ratings.

Figure 3-6 Various forms of visual analogue scales: (a) and (b) measure perception of pain, while (c) and (d) assess degrees of anxiety.

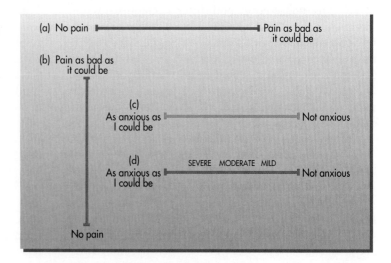

(a)

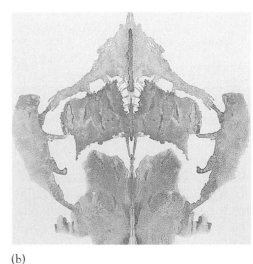

(b)

Figure 3-7 (a) As the client responds to the Rorschach card, the clinician records both verbal responses and behavior. (b) This Rorschach inkblot produced a variety of responses, including (1) "Looks like a long tunnel or channel in the center."; (2) "On its side, I see a crabby old man frowning, with a long nose. I don't like him"; (3) "There is a head of a camel in the middle there—no body, just the head."

Projective Techniques Some assessment specialists believe that the more freedom people have in picking their responses, the more meaningful the description and classification that can be obtained. Because personality inventories do not permit much freedom of choice, some clinical psychologists prefer to use **projective techniques,** in which a person is shown ambiguous stimuli and asked what he or she thinks they are about. Some clinicians believe that projective techniques are very sensitive to unconscious dimensions of personality. Defense mechanisms, latent impulses, and anxieties have all been inferred from data gathered in projective situations.

The **Rorschach inkblot test** developed by the Swiss psychiatrist Hermann Rorschach (1884–1922), consists of 10 cards, half colored and half black-and-white (see Figure 3-7). The test is administered by showing the cards, one at a time, and asking the person to describe what he or she sees in them. There are no right or wrong answers. After the person has responded to the inkblots in a free-association manner, the examiner asks questions about particular responses ("What gave you that impression?" "What made it seem like a _____?"). Besides recording what is said in response to the inkblots, the examiner also notes the person's mannerisms, gestures, and attitudes. Figure 3-8 offers a lighter view of the Rorschach test and its origins.

Rorschach developed the inkblot test as part of an experimental effort to relate perception to personality. He believed that people's responses to inkblots could serve as clues to their basic personality traits. There are

some striking examples of the ability of the Rorschach to assess important aspects of personality. For example, Sirhan Sirhan, a 24-year-old Palestinian immigrant, assassinated presidential aspirant Robert F. Kennedy on June 5, 1968. Sirhan fostered his identity as an Arab and hated Zionists, whom he equated with Nazis. His hatred of Zionists generalized to all Jews. Sirhan gave the following response to the inkblot shown in Figure 3-7b (Meloy, 1992):

Figure 3-8

SOURCE: Drawing by R. Chast; © 1989 by *The New Yorker Magazine, Inc.*

I don't know, it's a desert plant. Grows very tall—not a cactus. I don't know the name. The colors shock me—no—I don't know—I feel very jittery—I can't hold still—it stirs me. I read this magazine article on the 20th anniversary of the State of Israel. It was in color—that color—I hate the Jews. There was jubilation—I felt that they were saying in the article, we beat the Arabs—it burns the shit out of me, there was happiness and jubilation. ■

Because of a large number of negative findings in research studies using the Rorschach, many users of projective techniques became dubious about the validity of the Rorschach inkblots as perceptual indicators of personality. However, the test can still be used in analyzing people's social behavior and the content of their responses. Attempts to elicit assistance from the examiner and the use of stereotyped verbal responses are examples of observable types of behavior in the Rorschach situation. There have also been a number of attempts to develop a Rorschach scoring system that is more psychometrically sound; however, their validity in diagnosing complex clinical conditions has yet to be established (Hunsley & Bailey, 1999).

Like the Rorschach test, the **Thematic Apperception Test (TAT)** employs ambiguous stimuli to which people can respond in a free manner. The TAT uses pictures that show people engaging in a variety of activities; hence, it is less ambiguous than the Rorschach inkblots. The total test consists of 30 picture cards and one blank card, although in most test situations not all of the cards are used. The cards are presented one at a time, and the client is asked to make up a story describing the scene in each picture, the events that led up to the scene, and the situations that will grow from it. The client is also asked to describe the thoughts and feelings of the people in the story. As the client looks at the card and tells the story, the clinician not only records the story itself but also notes behavior such as pauses, facial expressions, and changes in tone of voice.

Henry A. Murray (1893–1988), the author of the TAT (Murray, 1943), described the picture in Figure 3-9 (Card 12-F) as a portrait of a young woman, with a weird old woman grimacing in the background. Following is a story about that picture related by a 37-year-old woman who was diagnosed with paranoid schizophrenia and was also depressed. How might her story be interpreted? Note the perceptual distortion that changed the usual mother-daughter relationship into a father-son relationship. (The examiner's questions are indicated in parentheses.)

It's an old man standing behind a young man thinking, or knows what this young man should do, what he has ahead of him. He is very tired [old man] and the young man has a lot more—I can't explain it. The young man hasn't had the expe-

Figure 3-9   Cards from the Thematic Apperception Test are more structured than the Rorschach stimuli, yet they also produce many different responses. This card produced the two very different stories.

Source: Murray, H. A. (1943); From THEMATIC APPERCEPTION TEST by Henry A. Murray, Cambridge, Mass: Harvard University Press; © 1943 by the President and Fellows of Harvard College; © by Henry A. Murray. Reprinted by permission of the publisher.

rience and gone through as much as the old man. That's all I think of now. (Relationship?) There is no relationship. I said father and son though didn't I? (Related?) No. (Happening?) They're both concentrating on life. (Explain?) Well, the old man, as I said, is concentrating on what the young man has ahead of him. (?) Whatever he chooses. (What did old man go through?) He looked like he had gone through suffering. (Explain?) Suffering from living. (?) Working hard. (Else?) No. (?) Well, I thought of other things. The trouble he'd had. (?) Family troubles. (Story!) They lived way out in a lonely place, worked and existed. Nothing much to do, and they became very tired, and that's all. (Schafer, 1948, pp. 188–189)

Here is the response to the same card that was given by a 27-year-old married woman who would probably be diagnosed as having an anxiety disorder. How does it compare with the first response?

[Shakes head, swallows.] The old woman must be either the mother or the grandmother of the young woman. The young woman has a strong face. She has lots of character. The old woman has a sly expression on her face or around her mouth. If it wasn't for that expression on her face, I might try to interpret it. I can't imagine why she looks that way. The old woman looks like she worked hard all her life. (?) I don't

know, just can't imagine. If this old lady had a different expression on her face, say, one of worry. . . . (?) Then I'd say she must be cherishing a lot of ambitions for the girl. Maybe she would be hoping that the girl would do things she always wanted to do. Maybe her ambitions would be realized in this woman. (Schafer, 1948, p. 258)

These two stories ascribed to the same picture differ in several ways, in addition to the unusual perceptual distortion of the 37-year-old woman. While her story reveals little concerning the relationship between the two people in the picture, the 27-year-old woman is very much involved in their feelings, motives, and personalities. The 27-year-old woman seems much more absorbed in the storytelling task than is the 37-year-old woman.

Clinical interpretation of a TAT story usually begins with an effort to determine the character with whom the person seems to have identified. Attention is paid to such variables as the person's behavior in the testing situation, characteristics of his or her utterances, the way the stories are told, the stories' emotional tone, and the conscious and unconscious needs that are revealed by the story content.

Whereas Rorschach viewed his test as an experimental perceptual task, Murray conceived of the TAT as a probe of the unconscious. Most contemporary users of projective techniques such as these consider them to be methods of tapping unconscious processes, an emphasis that is derived largely from the influence of psychoanalytic theory. Some psychotherapists use TAT responses as clues to hidden problem areas that require in-depth exploration.

In addition to the Rorschach and the TAT, many types of tasks are used as projective stimuli. In a **word-association test,** for example, a list of words is presented one at a time and the client is asked to respond with the first word or idea that comes to mind. Clinicians are most interested in how long it takes a person to respond and how unusual the associations are. The **sentence-completion test** is a logical extension of word associations. Here the subject is presented with a series of incomplete sentences and asked to complete them. Sentence-completion methods are typically analyzed in terms of the attitudes, conflicts, and motives reflected in them. The following are typical sentence stems:

- I worry about _____
- My mother _____
- What makes me mad is _____
- My greatest regret is _____

Other widely used projective methods include asking people to draw pictures of themselves and others, to finger-paint, or to tell stories. These approaches have been used as means of increasing knowledge about fantasy, its determinants, and its behavioral correlates. At times the clinical application of these methods has been based more on theoretical usefulness than on objectively demonstrated

validity. Researchers who are concerned with the evaluation of clinical tools continue to study these techniques.

Behavioral Assessment

Behavioral assessment has grown out of the behavioral therapy movement. It is frequently used to identify response deficits, which are then treated through the use of behavioral methods such as reinforcement schedules and modeling. Clinicians often use behavioral observations to get information that cannot be obtained by other means. Examples of such observations include the frequency of a particular type of response, such as physical attacks on others on the school playground, and observations by teachers of certain behaviors such as a schoolchild's frequent interruptions in the classroom. In both cases, observational data must meet the same standards of reliability as data obtained by more formal measures.

Consider the case of a 10-year-old boy who, according to his teacher, is doing poorly in his schoolwork and, according to his parents, is difficult to manage at home and doesn't get along with other children. A measure of the boy's general intelligence, which might help to explain his poor schoolwork; personality tests, which might reveal trends related to his inadequate social relationships; an interview with him to provide insights into his view of the problem; and an interview with his parents, since the boy's poor behavior in school may be symptomatic of problems at home—all could be supplemented by behavioral assessments to gain valuable information. Appropriate types of behavioral observations might include observations of the boy's activities and response patterns in school; observations of his behavior in a specially created situation, such as a playroom with many interesting toys and games; and observations of his behavior at home—while he is interacting with one or both of his parents as well as while he is playing alone or with friends.

Making all of these assessments would be a major undertaking and not practical under most circumstances. Because of the variety of data that are potentially available, the assessor must decide which types of information are most obtainable and desirable under a given set of circumstances. In most cases, the clinician is interested in both subjective and objective information. Subjective information includes clients' thoughts, their emotions, and their worries and preoccupations. Interviews, personality inventories, and projective techniques provide indications of subjective experience, although considerable clinical judgment is needed to infer what is going on within the client from the way he or she responds to a test. In contrast, objective information includes the person's observable behavior and usually does not require the assessor to draw complex inferences about such topics as attitudes toward parents, unconscious wishes, or deep-seated conflicts. Behavioral assessment is directed toward this latter type of observation (see Figure 3-10).

(a)

(b)

Figure 3-10   (a) This child's aggressive behavior in a playroom situation is being rated by observers through a one-way mirror. Behavioral observations made in a controlled environment are helpful to clinicians because they make comparisons among children more meaningful. (b) Children's behavior can also be observed in a natural setting. For example, aggressive behavior on a playground can be rated by observers. Because the situation is less standardized and other children are involved, these naturalistic ratings may be less easily compared. At the same time, the observed behavior may give important information about the child's everyday behaviors.

The following are some of the questions likely to be covered in behavioral assessments. Notice the absence of references to unconscious motivations or intrapsychic tensions.

1. What is the problem as described by the clinician?
2. Who are the people involved in the problem (e.g., parents or spouse)?
3. Under what circumstances is the problem most in evidence?
4. What reinforcers contribute to maintenance of the problematic behavior?
5. What is the developmental history of the problem?
6. What are the assets and liabilities of the client's behavioral repertoire?
7. How modifiable are aspects of the client's situation that bear on the problem, and how can modification be made?

Baseline, or **operant, observations** are a type of behavioral observation that is becoming increasingly popular. These observations are recordings of response frequencies in particular situations before any treatment intervention

has been made. They can be used in several ways. Observations might be made simply to describe a person's response repertoire at a given time. For example, the number of aggressive responses made by children of different ages might be recorded. Such observations also provide a baseline for judging the effectiveness of behavior modification techniques. A similar set of observations, made after behavior modification procedures have been used, could be compared with the baseline measurement as a way of determining how well the therapy has worked. For example, here are some questions that behavioral observations of schoolchildren can answer concerning the effectiveness of a special program to train teachers in the handling of children with particular types of behavioral problems:

1. Is the student engaged in an activity other than schoolwork?
2. Is the student looking around and not engaged in any other activity?
3. Is the student interacting with one or more other students?
4. Is the student interacting with the classroom teacher?

Cognitive Assessment

Just as it is important to know what a person does and how his or her behavior affects other people, it is also necessary to assess the thoughts that may lie behind the behavior. **Cognitive assessment** provides information about thoughts that precede, accompany, and follow maladaptive behavior. It also provides information about the effects of procedures whose goal is to modify both how someone thinks about a problem and how he or she behaves.

Cognitive assessment can be carried out in a variety of ways. For example, questionnaires can sample people's thoughts after an upsetting event. Electronic beepers have been used to signal subjects to record their thoughts at certain times of the day. There are also questionnaires to assess the directions people give themselves while working on a task and their theories about why things happen as they do.

Cognitions play an important role when a person is trying to concentrate on an intellectual task (see Figure 3-11). Anyone who has taken exams knows that worrying about one's ability, the possibility of failure, and what other students might be doing interferes with effective performance. But while thoughts that reflect worry have undesirable effects, thoughts that are directed toward the task at hand are helpful. The Cognitive Interference Questionnaire (Sarason & Stoops, 1978) was developed to assess the degree to which people working on important tasks have thoughts that interfere with their concentration. Subjects respond to the questionnaire by indicating how often thoughts like the following ones enter their minds while they are working on an assigned task:

- I thought about how others have done on this task.
- I thought about things completely unrelated to this task.
- I thought about how poorly I was doing.
- I thought about something that made me angry.
- I thought about something that happened earlier in the day.

The assessment of thoughts and ideas is a relatively new development. It has received impetus from the growing evidence that thought processes and the content of thoughts are related to emotions and behavior. Cognitive assessment provides information about adaptive and maladaptive aspects of people's thoughts and about the role thoughts play in the processes of planning, making decisions, and interpreting reality.

Relational Assessment

Maladaptive behavior always occurs in some environmental context. One person might hallucinate only when other people are not present. Another person might become angry, and even violent, only when in the presence of certain other individuals. Because of the importance of an individual's social context, this book emphasizes an interactional approach to abnormal psychology that directs attention to the interrelationships among personal and situational variables. Our relationships with other people are important types of contextual variables; clinicians thus recognize the importance of making **relational assessments,** or evaluating key relationships, such as those within a family. Families are complex units of people who, while they may be alike in some ways, are unique individuals each with a particular set of needs, behavioral styles, emotions, and beliefs about themselves and the world in which they live (see Figure 3-12).

Clinicians try to develop ways of characterizing a person's social relationships, both with the outside environment and with other individuals. Are the relationships assets or liabilities? Information is needed about specific features of a person's key close relationships. Each person can be viewed as one component of the numerous two-or-more-person interactions that fill daily activity. How does the person function in these interactions? What are his or her relational or interpersonal skills?

The family is one of the most powerful interactional systems affecting all people. To conceptualize patients without considering the dynamics of their family is to see half a picture at best. To plan treatment without considering the needs and opinions of the patient's family might represent an invitation to treatment failure. Moreover,

Figure 3-11 People have different kinds of thoughts while taking an exam. Worries or thoughts that are unrelated to the exam interfere with good performance.

Figure 3-12

Source: Drawing by R. Chast; © 1987 by *The New Yorker Magazine, Inc.*

whether clinicians admit it or not, the patient's family is often psychologically present, representing a powerful determining force in the patient's behavior. For this reason, interviewers need to make some type of assessment that gathers information about both individual family members and the family as a system. The following topics about the family might be brought up in a clinical interview:

- What were holidays like at your house?
- Who makes the decisions in your family?
- What kinds of things did your brothers and sisters like to do?
- What sorts of things did your parents argue about?

Because of the important role the family plays in shaping personality and the development of maladaptive behavior, researchers are beginning to develop ways of objectively measuring close relationships, such as those within a family. For example, Pierce and his colleagues (1991) developed the Quality of Relationships Inventory to assess various aspects of close relationships with specific people (e.g., family members, romantic partners, or friends). This inventory obtains subjects' quantified responses to such questions as the following:

- To what extent could you turn to your mother for advice about problems?
- How much does your father like you?
- How much does your mother want you to change?
- How critical of you is your brother?
- How often does your sister make you angry?

Another relational assessment tool, the Family Environment Scale (Moos, 1974), asks subjects to describe the overall social climate within their families by responding to items like these:

- There are a lot of spontaneous discussions in our family.
- In our family, each person has different ideas about what is right and wrong.
- In our family, we are strongly encouraged to be independent.

Clinicians can use the results of these assessments to understand more about the client's social network. If several family or network members complete these measures, the clinician has a better idea of how representative the client's views are of the quality of the relationships and the general atmosphere in the immediate social environment. If the client is being treated in a family setting, with other family members present at therapy sessions, the measures give the clinician valuable clues about family relationships.

Bodily Assessment

Insights into clients' feelings and motivations are provided by their expressive behavior and how their bodies function. **Bodily assessment** can be accomplished with sophisticated devices developed to measure such physiological changes as pupil dilation, blood pressure, and electrical skin responses under specific conditions.

Technological advances are making it possible to monitor an individual's physiological state on a continuous basis. Sweat, heart rate, blood volume, blood pressure, and the amounts of different substances in the bloodstream can all be recorded and correlated with the presence or absence of certain psychological conditions such as stress. This approach seems promising.

An example of the use of automated assessment can be seen in the measurement of blood pressure. It is now possible to measure blood pressure while a person is engaged in everyday activities. Such measurements are a considerable medical advance, since resting blood pressure readings may not give a full picture of changes in pressure or provide an accurate 24-hour average. Ambulatory monitors can show changes in a patient's blood pressure throughout the day and during sleep (Figure 3-13). Such data are useful in diagnosing cases of high blood pressure in which cognitive and behavioral factors play important roles. These data may also be important in the selection and evaluation of treatment programs.

Figure 3-13 also shows the pattern of blood pressure changes for a 45-year-old woman during a typical day. The patient had been diagnosed as having chronically elevated blood pressure, but as the figure shows, the readings actually covered a wide range. Other studies of patients who

(a)

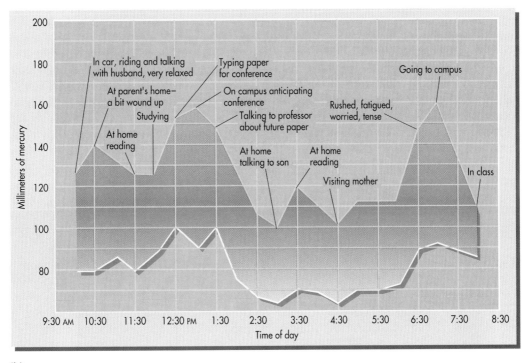

(b)

Figure 3-13   (a) The portable blood pressure monitor allows a person's blood pressure to be recorded automatically at predetermined times without interfering with his or her normal daily activities. Here we see a physician instructing a patient in the use of a monitor. While engaging in normal daily activities, the patient can place the monitor on the belt or in a coat pocket. (b) An ambulatory blood pressure monitor was used to record the changes in a 45-year-old woman's blood pressure during a one-day period. The chart is annotated with descriptions of the subject's daily activities. The top line charts systolic blood pressure; the bottom line, diastolic blood pressure. Systolic pressure represents the higher point in the blood pressure cycle as the heart contracts and sends the blood through the circulatory system. Diastolic pressure represents the low point in the cycle, which occurs as the heart fills with blood.

Source: Chart from Werdegar et al., 1967, p. 103.

had been diagnosed as having high blood pressure have shown that blood pressure readings taken in the doctor's office may be significantly higher than readings taken during normal activity, even though the office readings are usually taken after a period of rest.

On the technological horizon is equipment that hooks up wearable sensors to a small portable computer that can be easily carried around throughout the day. It will make possible gathering many bits of data about bodily functioning (such as sweat gland secretions, heart rate, muscle activity, and breathing) in various types of situations.

Another measure of emotional response is the **polygraph,** or lie detector. It records physiological reactions (heart rate, blood pressure, respiration rate, and galvanic skin response). Use of the polygraph in the criminal justice system has been criticized because it violates the right of privacy and the right to avoid self-incrimination. Even more important, questions have been raised about its reliability and validity. Criminal cases suggest that the accuracy of the polygraph in judging guilt can be made with 75% to 97% accuracy, but the rate of false positives (people who are innocent but whose polygraph records suggest guilt) is too high for the polygraph to be used as the sole basis of determining guilt or innocence (Council on Scientific Affairs, 1986).

Research may suggest novel applications for the polygraph in the field of mental health. For example, it may be possible to use the polygraph to determine what situations or topics caused a particular emotional reaction on the part of a client. This knowledge might provide some clues about areas that should be explored during therapy. In one study (S. Abrams, 1973), the polygraph was used in much the same way that a word-association test would be used. Stimulus words—some neutral, some thought to

be especially relevant—were read to each of 20 psychiatric patients while they were attached to a polygraph. Figure 3-14 shows a typical set of polygraph tracings from this study. Respiration is at the top, galvanic skin response in the center, and a combination of heart rate and blood pressure at the bottom. (The **galvanic skin response [GSR]** is an increase in the electrical conductivity of the skin that occurs when sweat glands increase their activity.) Stimulus word 23, *window,* was included as a neutral control word. However, instead of the expected lack of response, the patient showed a definite reaction to it. On the other hand, while there is a response to *sex,* it does not compare with the GSR to *window.* The patient later disclosed that he had considered committing suicide by jumping out a window. Word 26, the therapist's name, resulted in a large GSR, a slight rise in blood pressure, and suppression of breathing. In contrast, the patient reacted relatively little to neutral word 27, *pen.*

Biofeedback is being used increasingly in the treatment of certain bodily complaints. The patient receives continuous reports of a particular index of bodily functions, such as blood pressure, and is helped to find ways of bringing the index within normal limits. Thus, the opportunity to monitor one's own behavior and bodily functioning can have a therapeutic effect.

Techniques of bodily assessment are becoming more and more sophisticated and play increasingly important roles in diagnosis. At several points in this book we will describe a variety of **brain imaging techniques,** such as those mentioned in Chapter 2, that enable clinicians to study in great detail the brain anatomy of patients, to observe shifts in metabolic activity as the brain responds to cognitive and perceptual tasks, and to measure quantitatively the neurochemical activity of

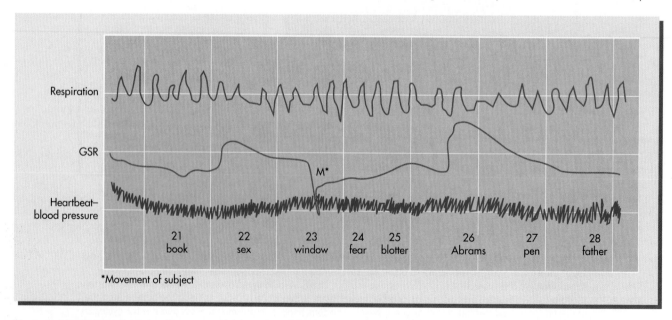

Figure 3-14   Polygraph tracing for one psychiatric patient. Stimulus words are numbered.

Source: S. Abrams, 1973, p. 95.

neurotransmitter circuits in the brain. These brain imaging techniques may make it possible to identify the anatomical, metabolic, and neurochemical bases of mental illnesses.

Assessment techniques help in defining the nature and scope of clinical problems, selecting appropriate treatments, and evaluating the results of treatment. The use of multiple techniques (e.g., interview, projective techniques, and bodily assessment) may provide a particularly firm basis for valid clinical judgments.

As theories of maladaptive behavior become more comprehensive and more firmly based on scientific findings, approaches to classification can be expected to change. Assessment and classification methods help clinicians describe disordered behavior and plan therapeutic interventions to change it. What is assessed and how people are classified and treated depend on what we know about the factors involved in abnormal behavior.

Chapter Summary

CLASSIFICATION: CATEGORIES OF MALADAPTIVE BEHAVIOR

Classification is necessary in all branches of knowledge. In the area of personality and abnormal behavior, classification is based on assessment of what clients say and how they behave; it also takes account of events they have experienced in the present as well as their past histories. In abnormal psychology, the classification of a person's disorder is referred to as a **diagnosis.** The diagnosis places the disorder within an existing system or grouping of disorders.

Advantages and Disadvantages of Classification An ideal classification system for abnormal behavior would group together behaviors with similar causes. However, in the field of abnormal psychology not enough is known about the causes of many disorders to do this. Therefore, the classification is a descriptive one in which different types of disorders are described in detail. On the one hand, even a descriptive classification system is valuable for communication concerning treatment, in research, and for statistical purposes. On the other hand, classification may result in labeling that creates stigmatization. If the groupings in the system are incorrect because of incomplete knowledge, they make it harder for researchers to see true relationships between disorders.

Vulnerability, Resilience, and Coping In classifying individuals, it is important to characterize their problems within the context of their stresses as well as of their vulnerabilities, resilience, and coping abilities.

The Multiaxial Approach A **multiaxial classification system** is designed, not to provide a simple label, but to summarize information about several aspects of the person's history and behavior. Since 1980, the diagnostic system used for most purposes in the United States, the **Diagnostic and Statistical Manual of Mental Disorders (DSM),** has used a multiaxial system. This system began with DSM-III in 1980 and has continued with DSM-III-R and DSM-IV.

DSM-IV DSM-IV has five axes: Axis I, the primary disorder(s), except those in Axis II; Axis II, personality disorders and mental retardation; Axis III, relevant medical conditions; Axis IV, psychosocial and environmental problems; and Axis V, a global assessment of psychological, social, and occupational functioning, currently and in the past year.

The Major Diagnostic Categories Axis I includes groupings for developmental disorders, serious cognitive disorders, mental disorders due to a medical condition, substance-related disorders, schizophrenia and other psychotic disorders, mood disorders, anxiety disorders, somatoform disorders, factitious disorders, dissociative disorders, sexual disorders, eating disorders, sleeping disorders, impulse-control disorders not classified elsewhere, adjustment disorders, and psychological factors that affect a physical condition. Axis II includes personality disorders and mental retardation.

Evaluation of the DSM Multiaxial Approach The DSM-IV approach is to use highly specific descriptive diagnostic criteria for each category. This approach increases the reliability of diagnoses among clinicians. DSM-IV is more comprehensive than previous editions and includes many more disorders and subdivisions of different disorders. But more research is needed to know whether these additional classifications are justified. Overall, the changes in DSM-III, DSM-III-R, and DSM-IV have added clarity to the diagnostic process.

Research on Classification Unreliability in diagnosis or classification made by the clinician is based on the characteristics of the diagnostic system and a variety of other factors. These include client factors, the way the client is behaving at a particular time; method factors, such as the different assessment techniques used by clinicians; criteria factors that are a function of baselines the clinician develops as a result of the types of patients seen; and clinician factors related to the clinician's own personality and theoretical orientation. The cultural context in which behavior occurs is an especially important factor in clinical work. Research on classification must take into account all of these factors and how they interact with the characteristics of the diagnostic system.

ASSESSMENT: THE BASIS OF CLASSIFICATION

Because no single assessment tool is perfect, a variety of different ways of characterizing individuals have been developed. The major methods include interviews, intelligence tests, neuropsychological tests, and personality and behavioral assessment as well as more specialized approaches.

The Interview The interview can be used for both diagnosis and therapy. Initial interviews are often relatively unstructured, but during the intake interview the clinician tries to determine why the client came for help, the current state of the client's mood and view of life, the history of the problem, and how the client is currently functioning. Interviewers typically note both the verbal and the nonverbal behavior of the client. In the **mental status examination,** the clinician assesses the patient's thought content, mood, perception, judgment, and insight. Personal characteristics of the interviewer as well as the client determine how the interview will proceed. It is important for the clinician to be culturally sensitive, for example, with regard to the client's ethnic identity. The clinician needs to have the ability to size up the situation quickly and adopt the appropriate clinical strategies to assess the problem clearly. In some circumstances, a structured interview format such as the **Diagnostic Interview Schedule** is useful to increase comparability across interviews and help to ensure that the same types of information are gathered about each client.

Intelligence Tests The first **standardized intelligence tests** were developed by Alfred Binet. These yielded an **intelligence quotient (IQ)** score based on dividing the child's mental age by his or her actual or chronological age and multiplying by 100. Although this method is no longer used, the term *IQ* has remained in use. Currently, the scores on the Binet test as well as other intelligence tests are determined by deviation from a predetermined norm based on test results of a large and representative sample of people. At present, the Wechsler tests are the most frequently used intelligence tests. These tests report three different IQ scores: a **Verbal IQ,** a **Performance IQ,** and a **Full Scale IQ** that represents the total score on the test. There is a series of Wechsler tests, each suitable for a different age group. These include the **Weschler Adult Intelligence Scale (WAIS-III),** the **Wechsler Intelligence Scale for Children (WISC),** and the **Wechsler Preschool and Primary Scale of Intelligence (WPPSI).** Currently, the **Kaufman Assessment Battery for Children (K-ABC),** a test based on ideas from cognitive psychology and neuropsychology and designed to reduce cultural bias in intelligence testing, is used extensively for testing children.

Neuropsychological Tests Cognitive, sensorimotor, and perceptual results of some brain abnormality caused by physical trauma or disease can be assessed for screening purposes by such tests as the Bender Visual-Motor Gestalt Test that measures ability to copy a series of figures. If results of the screening test indicate some abnormalities in these functions, more complex test batteries can be used.

Personality Assessment Personality assessment encompasses many different approaches. These include personality inventories, rating scales, and projective techniques. **Personality inventories** ask people questions about themselves. Because personality is not conceptualized as a single construct, most personality tests yield several scores. The **Minnesota Multiphasic Personality Inventory (MMPI)** is a widely used personality inventory. **Rating scales** present a series of items and allow the respondent to select from a number of choices, often concerning the degree to which the item is descriptive of him or her. A variation of the rating scale is the **visual analogue scale (VAS).** This approach is often used to measure the degree of some sensation experienced by the client. **Projective techniques** use ambiguous stimuli to which the client is asked to respond. These are most often used by clinicians with a psychodynamic orientation. Two well-known projective techniques are the **Rorschach inkblot** test and the **Thematic Apperception Test (TAT).**

Behavioral Assessment **Behavioral assessment** focuses on observations of the frequency of particular types or categories of response. It is often used to identify response deficits. **Baseline,** or **operant, observations** are used to describe a person's response repertory at a particular time. Behavioral observations may be made either in a controlled setting or in the person's natural environment.

Cognitive Assessment **Cognitive assessment** provides information about thoughts that precede, accompany, and follow maladaptive behavior. Questionnaires and beepers are often used. Cognitive assessment has been used most extensively in studying the factors that affect concentration on important tasks.

Relational Assessment Because people's behavior is affected by their interpersonal relationships, it is important to assess both general and specific social relationships. One important area of relationship for many people is the family. Relationships can be assessed either as general categories such as family or at the level of specific relationships such as mother, brother, or best friend.

Bodily Assessment A person's inner state can be assessed by measuring bodily functions such as blood pressure, heartbeat, respiration, and galvanic skin response. Biofeedback techniques have been developed that allow a person to monitor and learn to control his or her own bodily responses.

Key Terms

Classification, p. 88
Diagnosis, p. 88
Vulnerability, p. 89
Resilience, p. 89
Coping, p. 89
Multiaxial classification
    system, p. 90
DSM-IV, p. 90
Reliability, p. 94
Kappa statistic, p. 95

Validity, p. 95
Clinical judgment, p. 95
Culture-bound syndromes, p. 98
Assessment, p. 98
Diagnostic interview, p. 98
Therapeutic interview, p. 98
Mental status examination, p. 102
Structured interview, p. 102
Intelligence tests, p. 103

Binet tests, p. 104
Wechsler tests, p. 104
Neuropsychological tests, p. 106
Personality assessment, p. 107
Personality inventories, p. 107
Minnesota Multiphasic Personality
    Inventory (MMPI), p. 108
Five-factor model, p. 109
Rating scales, p. 109

Stress, Coping, and Maladaptive Behavior

One morning, while brushing her teeth, Sheila Mason noticed a small lump on her gum. It didn't hurt, but she was sure that it had not been there before. She wondered whether it might be related to an upset stomach or a cold, but there had been no recent changes in her diet and she felt fine. She was worried about the lump, but at the same time she didn't want to bring a trivial symptom to the attention of her physician or dentist. After three days the lump was still there. It was no bigger than it had been when she had first noticed it, and it still didn't hurt. Sheila concluded that it was not her responsibility to decide whether or not the lump was a trivial symptom. That was a professional's job. Having decided to get an expert to look at the lump, Sheila was left with only one question: Should she call her physician or her dentist?

Grace Dolby, married and the mother of two children, felt a small but noticeable lump in her right breast. Her first reaction was one of alarm bordering on panic, but then she told herself it was really nothing. She must have been mistaken. Then she simply tried to stop thinking about the lump. She put it out of her mind whenever her thoughts strayed to the topic. She also said nothing to anyone else about it for over two months and made a tremendous effort to wish it away. Grace was usually outgoing and cheerful, but during those months her husband, Jack, noticed that she had become moody, tense, and depressed. At times she also seemed distant and preoccupied. Toward the end of the two-month period, Grace's moodiness and distance from others (including her children) increased. Her sleep became fitful, and she had frequent headaches, even though previously she had almost never had them. If her husband insisted that she tell him what the matter was, her reply was always, nothing's the matter. I'm perfectly normal. Finally, one evening during lovemaking, Jack felt the lump in Grace's breast, and despite her protests that it was "nothing," he insisted that she see the family physician. ■

Just about the only thing that Sheila Mason and Grace Dolby have in common is that they discovered lumps that worried them. The two women dealt with their worries in quite different ways. After some doubt about whether she should undergo a clinical examination, Sheila made a rational decision to seek help. She realized that there was a chance the lump could be serious but that she could not evaluate the possibility herself. She knew that the longer she waited, the worse it would be.

In contrast, Grace Dolby seemed unable to act realistically and decisively. She first attempted to cope with the discovery of the lump in her breast by unsuccessfully trying to deny that it was really there. She then tried to tell herself that it "wasn't anything." The stress aroused by her discovery could only temporarily be reduced by denial and secrecy. She was still unable to deal with the reality of the lump.

Finding a lump in one's body would be stressful for anyone, but most people who find themselves in such a situation go to a doctor immediately. Grace Dolby's response is considered maladaptive mainly because it did not work; the lump (or reality) did not go away. In fact, Grace's behavior simply increased the amount of stress she experienced. A clinician working with Grace would want to understand the personal needs, motivations, and dispositions that combined with the situation (discovery of the lump) to produce her decision to be secretive and not to act. What made Grace Dolby so much more vulnerable to stress than Sheila Mason?

In this chapter we describe ways in which people react to stress. We primarily present examples of maladaptive behavior in response to two types of situations: those that arise suddenly (an earthquake, a sudden illness, becoming a crime victim), and those that develop more gradually or represent life transitions, such as marriage (see Figure 4-1). Most of the research on the relationship between stress and maladaptation has involved the effects of acute conditions or life transitions. However, there are other types of stress that, unfortunately, have not received enough study. One of these, the stress of caregiving, is now receiving attention and information is accruing concerning the psychological and physical wear and tear caused by the need to take care of the daily needs of individuals with severe incurable illnesses, such as Alzheimer's disease. We now know that this chronic wear and tear is significant.

Another type of stress, one that has also received inadequate attention, is lifelong racial stigmatization. There is every reason to believe that being a member of a minority group and exposure to racism can be a continuous stressor. *Racism* refers to beliefs, attitudes, and living conditions that tend to demean and denigrate members of particular racial groups (Clark et al., 1999). What is it like to grow up African American? What is it like to grow up African American under undesirable social and economic conditions? What is it like to grow up feeling despised and discriminated against? These are important questions with regard to which there is surprisingly little

Figure 4-1 Everyone has times when they must deal with stress. Stress may build up gradually, as the consequence of an ongoing unsatisfactory work or life situation or as the result of an upcoming life transition such as college graduation, marriage, or becoming a parent. Stress may also result from sudden catastrophes—for example, unexpected illness and other serious traumatic life events caused by outside forces. Here we see a postal worker who is reacting to a stressful event that occurred suddenly: a shoot-out that took place in a post office in Dearborn, Michigan. For unknown reasons, but possibly as a result of accumulated job stress, an average of about 500 violent acts involving postal workers take place in the United States each year. While this postal worker is dealing with a completely unanticipated stress, the person responsible for the shoot-out was probably reacting to a stressful life situation that developed over a long period of time.

information. In Chapter 1 we noted that the mentally ill often feel stigmatized because of their condition and, as a consequence, do not move to recovery as fast as they might. Because of the stress associated with it, stigmatization in the form of racism might play an important role in the development of certain types of psychological problems.

In this chapter, we will examine the concept of stress, explore the different ways in which people handle it, and review clinical conditions in which stress plays a major role. Even though the behavioral reactions observed in these conditions seem quite different, stress plays a crucial role in each, and its removal is often followed by improvement.

Because this is the first chapter in which we study particular disorders in some depth, it is worthwhile to anticipate an observation that has been made many times by both experienced clinicians and students: the discussion of various disorders cannot be conveniently arranged so that the disorders have mutually exclusive features. Although stress is the main topic of this chapter, we will also refer to stress as we discuss other forms of maladaptation. What is distinctive about the disorders discussed here is that the sources of stress are often more evident than they usually are in other forms of abnormal behavior.

Stress and Coping

The term **stress** refers to negative emotional experiences with associated behavioral, biochemical, and physiological changes that are related to perceived acute or chronic challenges. **Stressors** are the events that stimulate these changes. However, a stress-arousing situation for one person might be a neutral event for another. Whether a certain situation is stressful for us or not depends on how we appraise a life event and how we rate our ability to deal with it.

People differ not only in the life events they experience but also in their vulnerability to them. A person's vulnerability to stress is influenced by his or her temperament, resilience, coping skills, and available social support. Vulnerability increases the likelihood of a maladaptive response to stress.

Psychosocial, genetic, or biological vulnerabilities might be especially relevant to particular types of stressors. Figure 4-2 shows the general relationship between vulnerability and stress. This relationship applies, both to serious maladaptation requiring professional help (such as a major depression) and to many lesser problems that lower the quality of life but usually do not lead a person to go to a psychiatrist or clinical psychologist. An example of the latter kind of problem is difficulty falling or staying asleep. Stress is the leading cause of insomnia, and 40% of the people who claim they do not get enough sleep attribute the deficit to stress (Rosch, 1996). As one would expect from Figure 4-2, people who generally tend to be tense (high in vulnerability) and who are confronted with an unexpected challenge (stressor) are most likely to develop sleep difficulties.

The study of abnormal psychology would be easier if we could classify disorders into two groups, those that are stress-related and those that are not. However, such a distinction would be artificial. While stress plays a particularly significant role in the problems with which this chapter is concerned, a degree of stress is also present in most other conditions. For example, people suffering from lifelong tendencies toward anxiety and depression often experience intensifications of their conditions when they must confront stress-arousing challenges or reversals. We will use the concepts of stress and vulnerability throughout this book and will observe many instances of maladaptive behavior that reflect the relationship schematized in Figure 4-2.

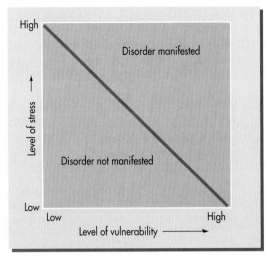

Figure 4-2 Stress and vulnerability influence whether or not maladaptive behavior will occur. When there are both a high level of stress and high vulnerability, maladaptive behavior is most likely. A highly vulnerable person, such as someone with schizophrenia, might show significant behavioral deterioration with only a mild increase in challenge. A relatively resilient person might show deterioration only if confronted with an extraordinary life reversal or challenge.

Coping Skills

Coping skills—characteristic ways of dealing with difficulties—influence how we identify and try to solve problems. People who cope successfully not only know how to do things, they also know how to approach situations for which they do not have a readily available response. As a consequence, they are less vulnerable.

The coping skills that people bring with them to life experiences (their expectations, fears, skills, and hopes) influence how much stress they feel and how well they cope with it. Experience and success in coping with similar situations, well-founded self-confidence, and the ability to remain composed and "think on one's feet" instead of falling to pieces when faced with a problem all contribute to realistic appraisals of and responses to situations. These characteristics are products of personality development, which, in turn, is influenced by social relationships.

A task-oriented, matter-of-fact response to a tough situation is usually more effective than becoming anxious, angry, or defensive. Failure to be task-oriented can happen for a variety of reasons. A person may simply lack the coping resources needed to take a matter-of-fact approach. In that case, the situation is beyond his or her capabilities. It could also be that certain elements of the situation may prevent an individual from taking a constructive approach to it. For example, a man might have the coping resources needed to be assertive with other men but not with women. His vulnerability with regard to women might keep him from complaining about being shortchanged by a waitress, whereas he would be quick to complain if he were shortchanged by a waiter.

Resilience and Vulnerability

Box 4–1

Adaptive and Maladaptive Coping

Harvey Weinstein

Harvey Weinstein, 68 years old and in the clothing business, was kidnapped in a matter of 20 seconds after he had finished breakfast and emerged from a New York diner near his office. A man held a knife to his throat and pushed him into a car. He was taken to a scraggly urban woodland near a highway and a city park. For 13 days, Mr. Weinstein was forced to remain hunched in a 4-foot-wide pit as his family and police detectives frantically sought his freedom and conducted fruitless, nightmarish negotiations over ransoms demanded by his captors. Mr. Weinstein never knew where he was or what precisely he was trapped in. When the police located him, Mr. Weinstein had lost over 15 pounds and was, not surprisingly, a bit shaky. (His captors had lowered water and some fruit into his pit during the ordeal.) As soon as he was found by the police, while still in the pit, he asked for a cellular phone and called his

family. The police quoted him as saying, "Sorry I'm putting you through what I'm putting you through. I'm in a hole." When he was helped out of the pit, he said, "I'm going to hug and kiss all my beautiful people."

Julienne Schultz

Thirty-seven-year-old Julienne Schultz, her throat viciously slashed by a violent stranger, fought to keep her senses as her life flowed from her. Bleeding profusely, she played dead until she was sure the assailant was gone. Fearing she might die, she took a small note pad and scratched tender "I love you"s and last thoughts to her three daughters aged 8 to 17, and to her parents. She also found the strength to scratch out a rough description of the assailant (and the van driven by him) who tried to kill her at a remote North Dakota rest stop. Schultz's cool head is credited for allowing the police to find the assailant, a convicted rapist who had killed a woman in Washington State a few days before. Afterward she observed: "I remember writing notes, but I can't remember what I wrote . . . I was so glad someone kept them and showed them to me . . . I don't think I'll ever be normal, but I think I'm a better person . . . mostly I wanted to live for my kids and my parents. I thought 'I'm not that bad of a person that God would allow this to happen'" (Seattle Post-Intelligencer, September 17, 1999, pp. C1, C9).

Figure 4–3 Harvey Weinstein, who was kidnapped and incarcerated in an underground pit, embraces his sons Mark and Dan as he talks with reporters about his ordeal. His thoughts about his family helped him endure the captivity.

In trying to identify the basis for a particular behavioral coping response, it is necessary to analyze carefully what is going on in the situation, along with the person's assets and liabilities (coping resources and vulnerabilities). In addition, attention must be paid to how the person sizes up the situation and his or her coping resources. Grace Dolby, the subject of the second case at the beginning of the chapter, had in the past experienced many physical symptoms that required action, such as high temperature and skin rash. The lump in her breast, however, was different because of its life-threatening implications. Grace's mother had died when Grace was 4 years old, and Grace was concerned about depriving her children of the maternal love and attention that she had missed as a result of her mother's early death. Her intense concern about

abandoning her own children may have made Grace particularly vulnerable to worry about her symptom and resulted in her denial of its significance.

Like Grace, many people with bodily symptoms cope with them by denying them. They may intentionally ignore them and try to keep thoughts of them out of awareness or they may misinterpret them. A common response to the chest pain of a heart attack is denial of its significance. It has been estimated that 80% to 90% of people who experience such pain attribute it to other causes, usually indigestion (Hackett & Cassem, 1975). Once the possibility that it might be a heart attack strikes them, they think "It couldn't be happening to me." This thought alone seems to be enough to keep them from seeking medical help. Even some physicians, who should know better,

Box 4–1

Although the assault left scars on her neck and other parts of her body and her vocal cords were damaged, she generally tries to be upbeat about life.

Herbert Greenberg

Now 70, blind since he was 10, Herbert Greenberg is the founder and owner of Caliper Management in Princeton, New Jersey. This human resources consulting company with 195 employees has grown into a $14 million business. "As a 10-year-old, I thought I'd be stuck off in a school for the blind, and I'd weave baskets and maybe run a newspaper stand" (New York Times, April 19, 2000, p. C10). Greenberg's parents rejected that sort of outcome. Public schools turned him away for a year until his parents found one that offered Braille classes. Greenberg was also motivated by adversity. He fought to get into the Boy Scouts and go to summer camp, graduated from high school with honors, and went on to earn a Ph.D. from New York University. After getting his doctorate, Greenberg fired off 600 applications for jobs, but was continually turned down because of his disability. These setbacks taught him the valuable lesson of not overpersonalizing failure. He went on to get a teaching position at Rutgers University. Later, he started Caliper Management, which became successful (its clients include Federal Express and Avis). Recently, Mr. Greenberg, who loves basketball, bought a minor league professional basketball team. Before that he bought an African American radio station in Trenton, New Jersey, even though he knew nothing about broadcasting.

Mrs. A

Mrs. A, a woman in her early 40s, has come to a psychiatrist's office to talk about a traumatic experience she had had almost two years previously. She came to the office appearing angry and suspicious, although her behavior was polite and socially correct. She chose the chair farthest from the psychiatrist and closest to the door. Nearly two years before, she had been shot and critically wounded in an incident with an acquaintance in her own home. After a long hospitalization and convalescence, her physical recovery is complete, but her life has totally changed. She has moved to another area. She stays in her house. In a market, she scans the surroundings, expecting to be shot. Seeing a man with a hat like that of her assailant is enough to produce a marked physiological arousal response. She avoids contact with family and former friends. She has not been able to return to work. Her sleep is poor. She dreams of the shooting and its aftermath. After such dreams, fear can leave her feeling weak for days.

All of us would agree that these four people had extremely traumatic experiences. Why did Mr. Weinstein get over his awful experience quickly (a few days after regaining his freedom, he said "I feel great!"), whereas Mrs. A continued to relive hers? Among Mr. Weinstein's outstanding characteristics is his resilience, reflected in his ability to be task-oriented when faced with challenges, and his good, warm relationships with other people. While he was trapped in the pit, Mr. Weinstein thought of his foxhole experiences as a Marine decades earlier. As an 18-year-old Marine corporal in World War II, he had seen some fierce fighting. Sitting in the armored cavelike interior of an amphibious tank, he had survived shelling and smoke. He told detectives: "I survived this kind of thing once. I knew I could survive it again. I closed my eyes and I was back there. That's what got me through this. I kept thinking, 'I am a Marine. I can survive this.' "

Julienne Schultz lives today with physical and psychological scars. Despite these, she clearly continues to be a resilient coper with a positive outlook on life. Unlike the other individuals we have described, Herbert Greenberg was not the victim of a physical assault (his blindness resulted from a mutant strain of a tubercular germ). His challenge was to cope with a sudden change in his physical abilities. In all likelihood, his resiliency grew out of the adaptive modeling his parents displayed for him every day. His parents refused to accept the common consequences of adversity—and so did he.

have gone jogging when they experienced chest pains in order to "prove it's nothing." Clearly, there is a common tendency to deny the true significance of pain despite its severity, intensity, or duration.

This kind of denial is typical with psychological pain as well. Many people deny the reality of an unhappy or unsatisfying marriage rather than seek counseling or even a divorce. People who have lost their jobs may blame their employers instead of recognizing their own inadequacies as employees. They may put off looking for work because they "deserve a rest," denying even to themselves that they are afraid of being fired again. As Table 4-1 shows, denial can play a reality-distorting role at various stages of a stressful experience.

Heightened stress levels have detectable, though perhaps not immediately noticeable, psychological consequences. For example, a significantly higher percentage of depressed and suicidal people have had undesirable recent experiences than people with other disorders have had. The undesirable events that contribute most to depression include the departure or loss of significant people in one's life during the previous year.

The psychological disorders discussed in this chapter usually begin with a specific event that has definable characteristics and special meaning for the person involved. This event is then appraised or processed, and as a result of the appraisal, the person's emotions or thoughts (fears, plans) are affected and coping strategies are considered. The end product is some response that reflects the level of stress as well as the person's resources and vulnerabilities. Box 4-1 describes the experiences of four people, each of whom lived through a terrible experience. Three coped in an exemplary fashion; the fourth was less successful.

Table 4-1	
Types of Denial of Stress	
Type of Denial	**Example**
Denial of provided information	"No one ever told me about it."
Denial of information about a threat	"No one ever told me there was anything to worry about."
Denial of personal relevance	"It doesn't apply to me."
Denial of urgency	"No need to hurry."
Denial of vulnerability	"No matter what happens, it can't happen to me."
Denial of emotion	"I'm not scared."
Denial of the emotion's relevance	"I'm scared, but there is no reason to feel that way."

The Coping Process

In coping, people use their personal resources to master a problem, overcome or sidestep an obstacle, answer a question, or resolve a dilemma. Different coping strategies are effective in different types of situations. People who generally cope successfully have a varied array of personal resources, which include the following abilities:

- The ability to seek pertinent information
- The ability to share concerns and find consolation when needed
- The ability to redefine a situation so as to make it more solvable
- The ability to consider alternatives and examine consequences
- The ability to use humor to defuse a situation

A growing body of research is devoted to the question of how people can be helped to cope more effectively with stress. One finding of this research is that what you don't know can hurt you. People who know what to expect beforehand are better able to cope with stress than people who do not know what lies ahead. Many surgical patients, for example, suffer unnecessarily because they have not been warned that they will have considerable pain after the operation. It has been shown that patients are less anxious and recover faster when the surgery and recovery process are explained to them before the operation takes place.

In one study (E. A. Anderson, 1987), 60 men undergoing coronary bypass operations were divided into three groups. One group received the hospital's standard preparation: a brochure on the procedure and a short visit from a nurse to answer questions. The other groups watched a videotape that followed a patient through the operation

and recovery. In addition, one of these groups received advance instructions in the postoperative physical therapy exercises—such as deep breathing to expand their lung capacity—that they would be doing to help the recovery process.

While 75% of those with the standard preparation suffered after the surgery from acute hypertension—a condition that can endanger coronary bypass patients in the first 12 hours after surgery—less than 45% of those who saw the tape had the problem. The patients who viewed the tape also had less anxiety in the hospital before the surgery and reported less stress and seemed more relaxed to nurses in the week after the surgery. The group that received extra instruction in the physical therapy went into surgery feeling even less anxious than the other groups.

Learning the specific skills needed in stressful situations helps individuals cope more effectively. Many people enter dangerous situations without proper training. For example, many hiking and mountain climbing accidents are a result of poor training and preparation. Besides learning specific skills, individuals can be trained for stressful situations by being put through a series of experiences that are graded from relatively low to relatively high in stress. In addition, observing a model who copes with stress in an effective way can help people about to enter a strange or dangerous situation.

Sometimes people fail to cope with stress because a high level of arousal interferes with their ability to concentrate on adaptive thoughts. Because such people do not observe their own thoughts, feelings, and behaviors in challenging situations, they fail to engage in constructive problem solving. Learning general skills for coping with stress involves learning how to think constructively, solve problems, behave flexibly, and provide feedback to oneself about the tactics that work and those that do not (see Table 4-2).

People who cope effectively with stressful situations have learned to direct their thoughts along productive lines and to avoid being distracted by fear and worry. Actors, quarterbacks, and other people who are often in the limelight soon learn that attention to the task at hand is more constructive than self-preoccupied thoughts ("There are 100,000 people out there waiting for me to fumble that ball"). They also learn to anticipate problems that might complicate a stressful situation and think about the way to deal with them. (The woman in Figure 4-4a is admirably resourceful in this regard, as is the studious canine in Figure 4-4b.) Actors come to accept that they will occasionally get their lines mixed up and that de-emphasizing their mistakes and moving on to the next line reduces the impact of their errors. On the other hand, the thoughts of some people who are prone to stress disorders are saturated with self-blame and catastrophizing ("The worst will surely happen").

Table 4-2

Aids to Behavioral Coping

1. *Be task-oriented.* Focus only on the task confronting you. It is not productive to spend time with thoughts or feelings that are unrelated to accomplishing the task. Being task-oriented means that you are concentrating completely on the job at hand. Negative or disruptive thoughts and emotions are the enemies of task orientation.
2. *Be yourself.* Don't role play. You will be more effective acting naturally than trying to fit a role. Place your confidence in *yourself,* not in the role.
3. *Self-monitor.* Pay attention to the way you are thinking and feeling in a given situation. It is important to learn about what causes stress for you and about your personal reactions to stress. Effective self-monitoring is your early warning system. It can alert you to the necessity of using the other coping skills to prevent a blowup.
4. *Be realistic about what you can achieve.* Know your own limits as well as your strengths.
5. *Use your sense of humor.* At times, laughter is the best medicine—don't lose your sense of humor.
6. *Have a constructive outlook.* Try to look for the positives in the people around you. Don't be too quick to conclude that people are behaving the way they are just to upset you. Put yourself in the other person's shoes—from that point of view, his or her behavior may make perfect sense.
7. *Use supportive relationships.* Compare notes, blow off steam, and get support from your friends. Don't draw into yourself when you are feeling stressed. Remember that we all "get by with a little help from our friends."
8. *Be patient with yourself.* Don't punish yourself for not achieving perfection. Your mistakes should become learning experiences, not times for heavy self-criticism. Keep your expectations of yourself at a reasonable level.

Social Support

Our social network includes people on whom we can rely, people who let us know that they care about, value, and love us. Someone who believes that he or she belongs to a social network experiences **social support.** Evidence is increasing that maladaptive ways of thinking and behaving occur disproportionately among people with little social support. The amount and adequacy of social support available to a person play a part in both vulnerability and coping. Vulnerability to physical and psychological breakdown increases as social support decreases. That is, social

(a)

(b)

Figure 4-4 Two examples of task-oriented coping.

SOURCES: (a) *The Wall Street Journal,* 1994, p. A15. Reprinted by permission of Cartoon Features Syndicate, Inc. (b) *The Wall Street Journal,* 1997. Reprinted by permission of Mark J. Cohen.

Figure 4-5   The coping process. How a person actually copes with a stressful situation depends on the person's skills and coping resources, vulnerabilities, and the availability of a supportive social network.

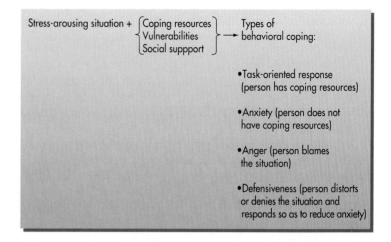

support serves as a buffer against the upsets of living in a complex world. Not only is social support very helpful during a period of stress (it is nice to know that there are people pulling for us in a tough situation), but it is also helpful in times of relative calm. It gives us the security and self-confidence to try out new approaches and gain additional coping skills. With an expanded repertory of coping skills, we are in a better position to handle demands, frustrations, and challenges when they do arise.

Maladaptive ways of thinking and behaving are more common among people who have little social support particularly within their families. Strong family ties seem to encourage self-reliance. Self-reliance and reliance on others are not only compatible but complementary. Social support facilitates coping with crisis and adapting to change.

Why do some people have many rewarding ties that help them smooth out the rough spots in their lives, whereas others are lonely and socially isolated? Are the number and quality of social ties simply a matter of luck? There is evidence that people with high and low levels of social support differ in the social skills needed to attract the interest of others (Pierce et al., 1997; I. G. Sarason et al., 1985). When engaging in conversations with strangers, people who are high in social support feel more competent, comfortable, and assured than people who report having little support. In addition, people who are low in social support tend to be perceived by others as being less interesting, dependable, friendly, and considerate than people who are high in social support. They are also less wanted as friends and co-workers and report feeling more lonely. There appears to be a strong link between social skills and social support. People with low levels of support may not believe that other people could be interested in them. This belief would tend to increase their vulnerability to stress, especially in situations that called for interactions with other people. Training in social skills might not only increase their interpersonal effectiveness but also help reduce their perception of social isolation.

As we have seen, the coping process involves a number of interacting factors. Figure 4-5 summarizes the role of three especially important factors in this process: coping resources, vulnerabilities, and perceptions of available social support. These perceptions are products of the individual's personality (e.g., how trusting of others they are) and prior experiences (Figure 4-6).

Stressful Situations and Life Transitions

The interacting factors in Figure 4-5 come into play in a variety of stress-arousing contexts that require the individual to make some type of adjustment. Since stress has undesirable effects on behavior, thought, and bodily functioning, it is important to build up resources for behavioral coping. The experience of stress involves uncomfortable psychological feelings. Physical functions—blood pressure, hormone levels, and brain waves—are also affected by stress. Very high levels of stress can result in trembling, stuttering, and a decline in the effectiveness with which tasks are carried out.

There is often little consistency in different people's reactions to stress. That is, one person might react to stress primarily in a bodily way, another might develop psychological symptoms, and yet another might show a profound deterioration in performance. Responses to stress involve bodily, psychological, and behavioral systems, but the correlation among these systems is often low. Table 4-3 on page 132 lists ways in which the three systems may react to stress.

There seems to be some truth to the commonly held belief that everyone has a breaking point. The more stress people experience, the more likely they are to break down either physically or psychologically. Dealing with several stressful situations at the same time obviously places great demands on a person's resources, and stress can have cumulative effects (Dougall et al., 2000).

Figure 4-6 How people respond to what usually appears to be a friendly overture depends on how wary they are of other people and their prior experiences. Social relationships can serve as a buffer against stress or a source of it.
© Ted Rall. Reprinted with permission of Universal Press Syndicate. All rights reserved.

People who have experienced multiple stressors in the recent past are especially susceptible to depression, anxiety, and overreactivity of physiological systems.

Jan Carroll, a 60-year-old widow, was seen by a clinical psychologist because of feelings of depression. When her husband had died a year-and-a-half earlier she became depressed with poor sleep, poor appetite (she lost 15 pounds in six weeks), low energy, and poor concentration. After about three months, the depression lifted quite a bit and she decided to begin a business venture (a franchise restaurant) with the money her husband had left her. Her expectation was that she would become financially successful on her own and as a result be better able to assure the security and well-being of her family. Unfortunately, she became a victim of fraud in acquiring the franchise ("They robbed me of everything") and had to give up the business. During this particularly stressful and upsetting period, Mrs. Carroll's problems were compounded when her apartment was broken into and many of her most valuable and cherished possessions were stolen, including a pearl necklace that her husband had given to her. She became depressed again. At this point, an antidepressant was prescribed for her by her doctor and she showed some improvement. Because her

finances had been decimated by the failed business venture she decided to return to her hometown where most of her family still resided. Despite her desire to be financially independent, she was forced to accept money from them ("I was living off my family's charity"). Her confidence was shattered and she felt unable to care for herself, much less provide for others.

Fortunately, Mrs. Carroll was accepted as a patient at a community mental health center. She was given antidepressant medications and was seen by a clinical psychologist for 24 sessions. The psychotherapy focused her attention on the grief she experienced over her husband's death, making the momentous decision to use all her money in order to go into the restaurant business while she was still upset over her husband's death (and was not thinking clearly), being the victim of fraud, returning to her hometown, and having to be financially dependent on her family. The therapist observed that she had experienced multiple reverses and blows, any one of which would pose a serious challenge. He and Mrs. Carroll discussed the inability she had had to accept her husband's death and her painful feelings of victimization and dependency. Discussing these issues seemed helpful. With the clinical psychologist's help she decided to seek employment and found a job at a department store that, while not providing all the money she felt she

Table 4-3

Some Psychological, Bodily, and Behavioral Reactions to Stress

Psychological Responses

- Feeling upset
- Inability to concentrate
- Irritability
- Loss of self-confidence
- Worry
- Difficulty in making decisions
- Racing thoughts
- Absent-mindedness

Bodily Responses

- Rapid pulse
- Pounding heart
- Increased perspiration
- Tensing of arm and leg muscles
- Shortness of breath
- Gritting of teeth

Behavioral Responses

- Deterioration in performance effectiveness
- Smoking and use of alcohol or other "recreational" drugs
- Accident proneness
- Nervous mannerisms (foot tapping, nail biting)
- Increased or decreased eating
- Increased or decreased sleeping

needed, enabled her and her two teenaged children to move into a modest apartment. Her depressed mood lifted, she found that she enjoyed her work, and discontinued the antidepressant medication. Although she still faced many challenges, Mrs. Carroll became less and less preoccupied with worries about more disasters, like the ones she had suffered through, that might befall her. Her life seemed to be more manageable.

There is growing reason to believe that mental and physical breakdowns could be predicted if there were a way to quantify how stressful certain life experiences are. For this reason, researchers have sought ways of assessing those experiences. Because recent experiences often exert a more powerful influence and are more easily recalled than those that occurred many years before, efforts have been made to quantify stressful life changes for specific time periods, such as the past year. Questionnaires have been constructed to assess not only whether certain events have occurred in the recent past, but also how the individual perceived the event and felt its impact (Cohen et al., 1995; I. G. Sarason et al., 1978). These questionnaires deal with such events as being fired from a job, getting a new job, breaking up with a boyfriend or girlfriend, and ex-

periencing financial difficulties. While the occurrence of any one particular event might not put a person at a greater risk for an adverse outcome (such as getting sick), the occurrence of several different kinds of events close together in a brief period of time would create significant added risk.

Stress-Arousing Situations

Two broad types of stress-arousing conditions that require adjustment are situations that arise in life, often unexpectedly, and developmental transitions. The death of a close friend illustrates the need for a situational adjustment; going to kindergarten or college is an example of a transitional adjustment (see Figure 4-7). Stress-arousing conditions have varying characteristics. Here are some of the ways in which challenging situations and circumstances vary.

1. *Duration.* Stressful situations differ in duration. A job interview lasts for a short time, whereas a marital quarrel might last for hours or days.
2. *Severity.* Situations vary in the severity of the circumstances confronting the individual. In general, a minor injury is easier to cope with than a major injury.
3. *Predictability.* In some cases predictability is high (we know what is going to happen), whereas in others predictability is low. The amount of stress caused by a request to give an oral presentation in class would depend on whether the request was made on the spot or was a previously given assignment.
4. *Degree of loss of control.* One of the most upsetting aspects of a situation is the feeling that one is unable to exert any influence on the circumstances. For example, earthquake victims can do nothing to prevent or control the quake's initial impact and aftershocks.
5. *The individual's level of self-confidence.* Lack of self-confidence often results in reduced personal effectiveness, even though the person may really know how to handle the situation. For example, a recently divorced woman may feel ill at ease in social situations that she was able to handle very well during her marriage.
6. *Suddenness of onset.* Suddenness of onset influences how prepared we are to cope with a particular situation. An accident is usually completely unexpected, whereas the crises of adolescence build up gradually.

Accidents, natural disasters, and military combat are examples of situations that typically evoke high levels of stress and may result in emotions so intense they interfere with normal functioning. Their psychological impact comes both from actual physical injury and from threat of injury or the possibility of loss of life. Prior experiences and personality also influence whether or not a stressor evokes a strong stress response. For example, people with

Pepper...and Salt

THE WALL STREET JOURNAL

(a)

"Don't ask. Wait till I wind down."

B. Smaller

*"Don't cry, Mom. Lots of parents have children who didn't get into their
first-choice college, and they went on to live happy, fulfilled lives."*

(b)

Figure 4-7 It is easy to think of educational transitions as wonderful opportunities. They
are, but stress is often associated with them. (a) This boy seems to have had a hard day at
elementary school, just as his father may have had a hard day at work. (b) The stress of
applying for college admission is not limited only to the applicants.

SOURCE: (a) *The Wall Street Journal*, permission, Cartoon Features Syndicate (b) © *The New Yorker*. Collection,
Barbara Smaller from CartoonBank.com. All rights reserved.

histories of depression and intense reactions to prior unexpected and unwanted events are at greater risk for stress-related disorders following automobile accidents than are others (Harvey & Bryant, 1999).

Extreme stressors set in motion a cycle of reactions aimed at restoring an equilibrium between the person's self-concept and the new realities of his or her life. Pre-existing personality characteristics may interfere with an adaptive response after a disaster. People who see themselves as incompetent, who tend to respond defensively to challenges (e.g., by using denial or projection), who have conflicts involving themes similar to some aspect of the disaster, or who believe that their past thoughts might somehow have influenced what happened—such people are likely to have long-lasting maladaptive reactions to traumatic situations. These prolonged reactions usually include feeling dazed and having intrusive thoughts and images about the traumatic event. Such thoughts and images may interfere with the ability to sleep.

Personal Crises Stressors can be widespread events that affect many people, such as an airplane crash, or they can be highly **personal crises.** The death of a loved one, the loss of a job, and the need to care for a parent who has an incurable illness are all examples of personal crises. Rape is another type of personal crisis whose frequency of occurrence and seriousness are now receiving increased attention (Marx, et al., 1996). Rape affects men as well as women, married persons as well as single ones. Date rape is a particularly serious problem among adolescent and college-age persons (see Box 4-2).

The fears that persist after the experience of rape tend to restrict and control the victim's life (Ruch et al., 1991). The most prevalent fears are of being alone, of strangers, of going out, and of darkness. Women who have been victims of sudden and violent assaults by strangers are especially likely to remain fearful and depressed for a long time, and they are also more likely to avoid dating for a long period.

From the behavioral perspective, a rape is part of a real-life, classical conditioning situation in which the threat of death or physical damage elicits a strong autonomic arousal response—fear. Any stimulus that is present during the rape—darkness, a man with a particular appearance, being alone—becomes associated with the fear response. These cues then become conditioned stimuli that independently evoke fear and anxiety. Because some of these stimuli are often encountered by the victim in daily life, she may begin to use avoidance behavior to escape them. This decreases the likelihood that the conditioned fear response will dissipate over time. Behavior therapy offers a way of overcoming these problems. By using both cognitive and behavioral techniques, victims can learn to overcome their avoidance behavior and thus extinguish their anxiety.

Since an estimated 10% to 20% of rape victims have continuing problems of sexual dysfunction several years after the rape, they may also be helped by sex therapy that takes into account anger and resentment toward men, guilt and self-blame, and attitudes toward their partners that may be a residue of the rape. Victims of uncontrollable events, such as rape, blame themselves for what has happened beyond what an objective assessment suggests is realistic. Such self-blame is illustrated in this account of a rape victim's experience:

> *The young woman who was raped after the fraternity party berated herself initially for not picking out some flaw in her assailant's character. She recalls wondering whether her blouse was too low-cut, or whether she had said or done anything to provoke the assault. "It took me a long time," she says ruefully, "to realize that it wasn't my fault." (Sherman, 1985, p. 19)*

Rape victims need to know what to do and where to go after the rape in order to obtain medical, mental health, social, and legal services. They also need immediate and follow-up medical care for physical trauma, collection of medicolegal evidence, prevention of venereal disease, and protection against unwanted pregnancy. Rape victims need to be listened to and helped to talk about their experiences, as well as to be given basic information and assistance in making decisions about further steps to be taken. An important source of help for rape victims is rape-relief centers, where information and psychological support are available (see Figure 4-9 on page 136).

Bereavement and Grief While we now know that rape is much more prevalent than had previously been thought to be the case, the near universality of experiencing the death of a loved one has been obvious for a long time. More than 2 million people can be expected to die in a single year in the United States alone. Of these, more than 16,000 are children between the ages of 1 and 14, and as many as 38,000 are young people between the ages of 15 and 24. More than 40,000 babies die each year before reaching the age of 1. For each of these deaths, bereaved persons at increased risk of harm to their mental and physical health are left behind (Stroebe et al., 1993).

Bereavement refers to the loss of someone significant through that person's death. The normal course of recovery from bereavement often extends to a year or more, and such a pattern of recovery is not considered to be an adjustment disorder. It is only when a person's response differs from this normal pattern and when coping difficulties and emotional distress continue without gradual improvement that the diagnosis of adjustment disorder would

Research Close-up   Box 4-2

Date Rape

College women are a high-risk group for sexual assault. Nationally, the age group with the highest rape victimization rate is 16- to 19-year-olds, with the age-20-to-24 group having the second-highest rate (Ward et al., 1991). About 15% of women college students in two different surveys reported that they had been raped by someone they knew or were dating (Koss, 1998). In another survey of a representative sample of university students, 6% of the women replied "Yes" to the question "Have you ever been raped?" However, when the definition was broadened somewhat, percentages went up substantially; 21% of the women said that they had had sexual intercourse with a man when they didn't really want to because they had felt pressured by his continual arguments (Koss & Oros, 1982). Eleven percent of the college men in the surveys said they had forced a woman to have intercourse. A typical story was something like what happened to a 20-year-old college student in Pittsburgh:

> She met him two years ago at a fraternity party on a neighboring campus. His dashing good looks, she recalls now, coupled with his shy grin and friendly manner made him appear "sweet, but not macho." They talked and danced for hours, and later that evening, he took her in his arms and they kissed.
>
> When he asked if she would like to get something to eat, she agreed. But instead of heading toward a nearby restaurant, he swerved onto a side street, pulled over to the curb, and stopped the car. Then he raped her. (Sherman, 1985, p. 17)

Sexual activity that goes farther than one of the participants would like is not new among college students, nor are the forces behind it. But the term *date rape* is recent, and this label itself may have given such activity a new identity, defining nonconsensual sex between dates or acquaintances as a form of male assault rather than a form of female fault.

Research with both high school and college students shows that a sizable minority of students do not believe that date rape is definitely unacceptable behavior.

Men who have been charged with rape by women they have known or dated are often befuddled by the situation. Many of them have been conditioned to believe that initial refusals are an essential part of a "mating game" ritual, one that dictates that women must resist somewhat to make themselves more attractive to men.

Several studies have examined the attitudes of college students toward date rape. In one such study, based on questionnaire responses of several college students, those students who were more accepting of date rape were less sure that forcible date rape was really rape, were more traditional in their attitudes toward women, were more self-permissive about premarital sex with friends or acquaintances, and had less knowledge about sex than other students (G. J. Fischer, 1986). A measure of acceptance of force in sexual intercourse was found to be correlated with how often college men admitted using force to have intercourse, with how much force was used, and with a lower degree of social responsibility and social conscience (K. Rapaport & Burkart, 1984). Research also has shown that alcohol and drugs play important roles in date or acquaintance rape. Approximately 75% of the men and 55% of the women involved in date rape had been drinking or taking drugs prior to the incident (Abbey, 1991; Ullman et al., 1999; Ward et al., 1991). The role of alcohol was especially important when combined with participation in party-related activities.

Because research findings show that perceptions of what is sexually appropriate have an important influence on behavior, many schools have begun to educate students about the role that attitudes play in sexual intimacy and about the relationship between behaviors that impair judgment, such as heavy drinking, and the occurrence of date rape. This type of educational program not only heightens students' awareness of the problem, but also provides them with information about how to cope in situations that might likely result in unwanted sexual intercourse (see Figure 4-8).

Figure 4-8 These students are watching a video used in school-sponsored programs designed to combat date rape by increasing awareness about the rights of individuals and factors that increase vulnerability. The programs also illustrate coping strategies.

Figure 4-9   Rape-relief centers provide information about medical and legal services for rape victims as well as offering immediate supportive interactions. Such centers attempt to reduce the feelings of shame experienced by many rape victims.

Table 4-4
Behavioral and Physiological Aspects of Bereavement in Adults

Behavioral Changes

- Crying
- Agitation, restlessness
- Preoccupation with the image of the deceased
- Social withdrawal
- Decreased concentration and attention
- Depressed mood
- Anxiety

Physiological Changes

- Muscular weakness
- Sighing
- Sleep disturbance
- Immunological changes
- Endocrine changes
- Cardiovascular changes
- Decreased body weight

be given. Table 4-4 lists behavioral and physiological changes frequently observed in the period following the loss of a loved one.

Grief is the emotional or affective response to the loss. The symptoms of grief are part of a normal recovery process and not a sign of pathology. Nevertheless, grief takes more prolonged, pervasive, and complicated forms than many people realize. These forms vary greatly; there is no uniform and orderly succession of stages through which all bereaved people must pass. However, certain phases are observed often enough to be recognized as, if not typical, at least common after the death of a husband, wife, or child. The first reactions are often shock, numbness, bewilderment, and a sense of disbelief—even denial of the reality for a time. This reaction is common even when the death was anticipated. After a few days, numbness turns to intense suffering. Grieving people feel empty. They are repeatedly reminded of the person who has died. Waves of crying sweep over them with each reminder; they may have dreams and even hallucinations in which the dead person is still alive (Clayton, 1990).

After this comes a period of despair as the grieving person slowly accepts the loss. The dominant feelings are sadness and inability to feel pleasure. Tense, restless anxiety may alternate with lethargy and fatigue. Physical symptoms are common—weakness, sleep disturbances, loss of appetite, headaches, back pain, indigestion, shortness of breath, heart palpitations, and even occasional dizziness and nausea.

Grieving persons may alternate between avoiding reminders of the deceased and reliving memories (see Figure 4-10). Some desperately seek company, and others withdraw. Sadness is mixed with anger—at doctors who failed, at friends and relatives thought to be unappreciative, even at the dead person for abandoning the living. The motives of people who try to help are sometimes suspect, and grieving persons may alienate their friends by irritability and quarrelsomeness. Most painful of all is self-reproach for having treated the deceased person badly or having done too little to prevent the death. For example, there is evidence that a spouse's recovery from grief is quicker and more complete when the marriage was happy (Stroebe et al., 1993). When the grieving process becomes abnormal, the bereaved person may suffer persistent anxiety or depression produced by morbid or unresolved grief. In such a case psychotherapy may be helpful (Raphael & Minkov, 1999).

Research on grief, and the failure of some bereaved people to resume a normal life in a reasonable period of time, is needed because bereavement is so common and because popular ideas about how people do or should respond to loss may not be correct. One focus of this research concerns high-risk factors for poor outcome of bereavement. Table 4-5 summarizes evidence on this topic. Studies are also being conducted on the role of counseling or psychotherapy in overcoming intense grief reactions. Enabling bereaved persons to explore their loss and express

Figure 4-10   While he was a Cleveland Indians pitcher, Bob Ojeda was injured in a boating accident that caused the deaths of two of his teammates. Ojeda recovered from his physical injuries, but the psychological impact of his teammates' deaths persisted. For a while after the accident, he wanted to run away from the world and from himself. He went to Stockholm for two days—just getting on a plane and leaving without telling anyone. He shut out his wife, Ellen, and he tried to suppress the event, hoping it might just go away. It was terrible for his wife, too, since she wanted to help and didn't understand his reaction. When Ojeda returned to the Indians, he felt estranged, as if he were a reminder to them of the accident—a ghost, a burden—and he seemed to distance himself. When he walked to the mound for the first time after the boating accident, the roar of the crowd was deafening and there were tears in many eyes. Nevertheless, Ojeda's feelings of estrangement persisted.

Table 4-5
Factors That Heighten Risk for Poor Outcome of Bereavement

- Sudden, unexpected death, such as suicide, murder, and stigmatized deaths (e.g., death due to AIDS)
- Ambivalence toward and dependency on the deceased
- Death of a parent
- Perceived lack of social support
- Concurrent crises (e.g., illness in other family members)
- Reduced material resources
- Gender of a surviving spouse (widowers are often at higher risk than widows)

4. Major educational transitions, such as going to college
5. Entry into the world of work
6. Marriage
7. Bearing and rearing children
8. Moving to a new place of residence
9. Children's milestones
10. Retirement

The period of adolescence illustrates the role stress plays in a life transition.

Adolescence   The role of cultural factors in adolescence cannot be overestimated. As a reasonably distinct period of life, adolescence might be described as a byproduct of the Industrial Revolution. Prior to that event, there had been no need to provide a special niche for people who were biologically no longer children but to whom society did not find it convenient to assign adult roles. Since the Industrial Revolution, the age at which individuals are admitted to adult occupational roles has repeatedly been raised, with the result that the period of adolescence has been lengthened. The stress experienced by adolescents has been increased by the lack of agreement about when adolescence ends as well as by the greater number of life choices young people have to make.

Adolescence can be divided into early, middle, and late periods. The dominant theme of early adolescence, approximately ages 12 to 14, is the individual's response to changes in sex hormone levels and a general growth spurt. For girls, the onset of puberty comes at an increasingly early age—the average age at first menstruation has declined from 16.5 years in 1860 to 12.5 years today. The comparable events of puberty for boys lag approximately 2 years behind those for girls.

By the end of this early period, the young teenager has acquired a body that is quite different from the one he or she had as a child. Changes in body image have a significant

their feelings about it and encouraging them to focus on the present and future can be helpful (see Box 4-3).

Life Transitions

Whereas disasters and many personal crises are imposed on people from outside, other crises involve **life transitions** that grow out of the individual's own path of personal development. Some of the transitions in the life cycle that can cause stress are the following:

1. Birth and development of a mother-child relationship
2. Initial steps toward independence and transition to an out-of-home facility (e.g., school, day-care center)
3. The biological and social changes that mark puberty and adolescence

Q. A couple of months ago, the mother of a friend of mine died. The first time I saw him at school after his loss I was tongue-tied. I felt uncomfortable, didn't know what to say, and worried that I might blurt out something stupid. Do you have any suggestions?

A. *Your experience occurs often. You want to help, but you aren't sure what might be helpful. Here are some "Dos" and "Don'ts" you might consider. Let's start with the "Don'ts."*

"Don'ts"

- *Don't judge the way people grieve. Someone who doesn't cry can be just as* devastated as someone who can't stop crying.
- *Don't say, "I know how you feel." There is no knowing how a newly bereaved person feels.*
- *Don't say things you really don't believe (e.g., "His death is for the best," "He won't suffer anymore," "It is God's will").*

Dos

- *If you feel comfortable doing so, give the person a hug and simply say, "I'm sorry."*
- *If you have an especially warm or humorous recollection concerning the person who died, tell the bereaved person about it.*
- *If there is some task you can perform—such as, fixing a broken doorknob or doing some weeding in the garden—do it.*
- *After the funeral, there will be fewer visitors and phone calls. Keep in touch, drop by, or extend an invitation for lunch or dinner (although it is always important to bear in mind that the bereaved person might not yet be ready for extended social encounters).*
- *Be patient with your friend, provide a shoulder for the tears and respect the times he or she wants to be alone.*

---

effect on an adolescent's self-concept. How well an adolescent likes his or her body often depends on how other people respond to it. For example, late-maturing boys generally show more personal and social maladjustment at all stages of adolescence than those who mature early. They tend to be characterized by negative self-concepts, prolonged dependency, and feelings of rejection by important peer groups. The picture is different for girls. Early-maturing girls often lack poise and are submissive in their social relationships. Late-maturing girls, on the other hand, seem more outgoing and self-assured.

The extent to which the unpredictable moodiness, depression, anger, and emotionality often seen in early adolescence are related to changes in sex hormone levels is unclear. It has been shown, however, that adolescence does not necessarily have to be a stormy and stressful time. Parental interest, reasonable guidelines, and support, particularly from the same-sex parent, play important roles in helping the younger teenager make the necessary developmental transitions.

During middle adolescence (roughly 15 to 17 years of age), the teenager receives increasing responsibility and more privileges (e.g., holding down a part-time job or driving a car). There are also increases in stress created by the fact that the adolescent is in many ways a marginal character: too old to be treated as a child but too young to have the rights of an adult. Perhaps the most noteworthy developmental occurrence in middle adolescence is the gradual shift from a here-and-now perspective to a point of view that is oriented toward the future. In addition, the individual be-

comes less self-absorbed and grows increasingly concerned with values and ideals.

In late adolescence, teenagers begin to relinquish their parents as primary attachment figures. Living with the family, which is seen as protection by some adolescents and as restraint by others, can now come to an end. Some individuals move directly into the adult roles of marriage and full-time work, whereas others enter a more or less extended adolescence through college or job-training experience. Major tasks of this period include development of a personal identity, renegotiation of the relationship to the family, and the development of stable and enduring ties to others. Late adolescence can be difficult for a variety of reasons, including high unemployment rates among teenagers and young adults, the problems posed by alcoholism and drug abuse in this age group and high crime rates among some peers.

During late adolescence, teenagers often feel isolated and in limbo. Various factors contribute to this adolescent loneliness. The adolescent experiences new desires and expectations that may not be readily satisfied but that disrupt existing personal relationships. A predisposition to loneliness may originate in such personality characteristics as shyness and low self-esteem and may be intensified by cultural factors such as the existing social network.

We have noted that everyone has a breaking point and that breakdowns can occur either as a result of sudden personal crises or gradually developing life transitions. In either case, an effective repertory of coping skills and the availability of supportive friends and family keep the individual from feeling overwhelmed by stressors.

Table 4–6	
Normal and Abnormal Responses to Stress	
Normal Responses	Abnormal Responses
Feeling strong emotions subsequent to the event (e.g., fear, sadness, rage)	Being overwhelmed by intense emotions; experiencing panic or exhaustion
Resistance to thinking about the event; some use of denial	Extreme resistance to thinking about the event (e.g., through use of drugs); massive denial
Having unwanted, intrusive thoughts about the event	Having disturbing, persistent images and thoughts that interfere with usual functioning
Temporary physical symptoms (headaches, stomach distress)	Strong, persistent bodily reactions (e.g., continuing headaches, chronic stomach pains)
Resuming one's normal pattern of life	Long-term problems in ability to love and work

Clinical Reactions to Stress

Stress plays a role in most of the conditions that make up abnormal psychology. Stress disorders that require clinical attention are pathological because they go beyond expected, normal emotional and cognitive reactions to severe personal challenges. Table 4-6 lists some of the normal and abnormal responses to stress. As the table makes clear, many normal responses become abnormal reactions when symptoms persist and are excessive. Successful coping often involves the individual's somehow coming to terms with overwhelming feelings such as sadness or anger. For example, one researcher (Bohmfalk, 1991) documented the case of a physician who, while delivering terrible news to families of patients with dismal or hopeless prognoses, would develop an irrational urge to laugh. The doctor had to learn to face the overwhelming distress he felt in delivering such news. The physician described how conveying bad news to a particular patient's family had helped him face his own distress and free himself of his urge to laugh:

The patient and her family were perfectly typical. The girl was neither beautiful nor brilliant, her family neither overbearing nor solicitous. Their deep concern for her fate was overblown by neither guilt nor persecution. Her severe injuries were ordinary, her operation went smoothly, and there was no problem over several days with any aspect of her care. She just wasn't going to survive. This time, however, after bracing myself for the ultimate family conference and hoping I would be able to suppress an involuntary smile or chuckle, something wonderfully different happened. As the parents, grandparents, and siblings accepted my report and began to cry quietly, tears began flowing down my face. I had no guilt, I had nothing for which to apologize; I hadn't even come to know this

family very well. But there I was, crying right along with them. I didn't want to cry, it just happened. I didn't feel stupid or self-conscious. I simply felt really sad.

. . . Since those initial belated tears, I never had to fight an inappropriate smile. Misery is no longer a laughing matter. (Bohmfalk, 1991, p. 1245)

Although he experienced stress, this physician managed by himself to come to terms with the challenge of conveying bad news to family members of patients. As we pointed out at the beginning of the chapter, knowing only that a stressor (such as the need to convey bad news) exists does not tell us how an individual will respond to it. There are important individual differences in how people appraise events, in their coping skills and the social support available to them. We also noted that stress plays a role in many types of maladaptive behavior. Now we review three conditions which, though different in their clinical presentations and dealt with by DSM-IV in different ways, are marked by stressors that serve as powerful triggers for behavior that requires clinical attention. The triggers lead to strong emotional reactions—which may be denied—and clinical symptoms. In *adjustment disorders*, a recent increase in life stress precedes what is usually a temporary maladaptive reaction. In *acute stress disorder*, changes in behavior, thought, and emotion are linked to an extremely traumatic stressor. *Dissociative disorders* are among the most dramatic and puzzling forms of abnormal behavior and are usually preceded by an upsurge of stress that the individual cannot handle.

Adjustment disorders and acute stress disorders are considered to be more straightforward than dissociative disorders because of the ease of identifying the trigger and the relatively good prospects for recovery. Varying interpretations of dissociative disorders depend upon the weight given to a number of factors, including the stressors that immediately precede clinical flare-ups, stressors that may have occurred early in the person's life, and biological causes. A major challenge in the real world of maladaptive behavior is the multiplicity of factors involved in most cases.

Adjustment Disorder

A person with an **adjustment disorder** is someone who has not adapted as well as the average person to one or more stressors that have occurred in the previous 3 months. The stressors might involve a developmental transition (such as marriage, divorce, childbirth, or menopause), or they might be situational (such as changing schools, getting a new supervisor at work, or having been socially rejected), or they might be multiple stressors that have recently accumulated. (DSM-IV deals with bereavement reactions as a special condition and does not categorize them—despite several similarities—as adjustment disorders.) Most of the time a person's maladaptive reactions to these stressors tend to disappear when the stressful circumstances dissipate or when the person learns how to live with new conditions. In the following case, the stressful transition to marriage resulted in an adjustment disorder:

Mark Catton, aged 23, had recently married. He and his wife, Dorothy, had known each other for two years at college and were deeply in love. Their getting married seemed a perfectly logical consequence of their affection for each other. The first several weeks after the wedding were wonderful for the couple. They looked forward to their evenings together and often took short trips on the weekend.

One evening at dinner Dorothy talked about a new salesman at her office. She described him as intelligent, handsome, and charming. When Dorothy used the word "charming," something seemed to click inside Mark. He wondered why she had chosen that particular word to describe the new salesman, and why she talked so much about someone she had known for only a day. During the next few weeks, Dorothy made several additional references to the salesman. Her liking for him was more obvious with each reference. Each time it came up, Mark became increasingly suspicious and depressed. When Dorothy worked until late in the evening twice in one week, his suspiciousness and depression increased. When he confronted her with his suspicion that she was dating the salesman, Dorothy displayed shock and outrage.

During the next few weeks, Mark became increasingly depressed. His depression was interrupted by occasional outbursts of venom directed toward Dorothy. Their sex life soon ceased to exist, and their evenings were filled with silence. The problem reached clinical proportions when Mark began to stay in bed all day. It took great effort for Dorothy to get him to see a psychotherapist, although by this time even Mark knew that something was very wrong.

During his sessions with the psychotherapist, Mark came to see how unrealistic his expectations about marriage were.

He also was able for the first time to bring all of his thoughts and feelings out into the open. One recollection about his parents seemed particularly important. He remembered that when he was about 6 or 7 his parents had quarreled a great deal, apparently over his father's suspicion about his mother's activities at home while he was at work. His father had accused his mother of infidelity and had been very nasty. Mark couldn't remember exactly how the situation had been resolved. Although he had not thought about the incident for years, it became very meaningful to him, and discussing it in psychotherapy seemed to help him.

Mark Catton's case is interesting because it shows so clearly the interaction between past and present experiences. His own marital problems, created by his irrational suspicions about his wife's activities, seemed to be linked to things his wife had told him about the salesman and to his unrecognized dread that what his father had feared was actually being inflicted on him. One additional point about this case is that Mark had no history of suspiciousness and depression. Both reaction patterns had apparently been ignited simply by getting married. His psychological functioning had deteriorated primarily because of the expectations and concerns he had brought to the marital situation, not because of a traumatic development within the marriage. His psychotherapeutic experience, which consisted of 11 sessions, enabled Mark to resume a normal, gratifying marital relationship.

Depression, anxiety, disturbances in conduct (truancy, fighting, reckless driving), disrupted sleep patterns, deterioration in performance at work or school, and social withdrawal are typical behaviors of individuals who have adjustment disorders. Table 4-7 lists information pertinent to making a DSM-IV diagnosis of adjustment disorder. The severity of the disorder is not directly proportional to the severity of the stressor, because personality characteristics and cultural or group norms both contribute to how well an individual copes with a given set of circumstances. However, one characteristic of adjustment disorders is that the behavior displayed is in excess of what would normally be expected under the circumstances. A return to pre-stressor functioning within 6 months can be expected, and the chances of complete recovery when the stress level comes down are good. An adjustment disorder usually does

Table 4–7
Information Needed in Making an Adjustment Disorder Diagnosis
■ Time of onset and duration of the stressor (symptoms must develop within 3 months after onset)
■ Duration of symptoms (usually less than 6 months)
■ Depressed mood, and/or anxiety, and/or inappropriate or antisocial conduct

not involve extremely bizarre behavior and is not part of a lifelong pattern of maladaptation.

Acute Stress Disorder

While experiencing an extremely traumatic stressor (such as physical assault or witnessing an event that involves death or injury), or soon afterwards, a person might show major changes in behavior, thought, and emotions. These changes stem from the intense fear, helplessness, or horror associated with the event. **Acute stress disorder** is marked by symptoms of dissociation that include a subjective sense of numbness, detachment, and absence of emotional responsiveness; feeling as if one were in a daze; a feeling of unreality about oneself or about what is happening in one's life; and inability to recall important aspects of the trauma. These symptoms indicate a disruption in the usually integrated functions of consciousness, memory, identity, and perception of the environment and are referred to as *dissociative symptoms*. In *dissociation* there is a breakdown or fragmentation in the coherence of mental life; one group of mental processes seems to become separated from the rest.

A 19-year-old college student was attacked and robbed at gunpoint while walking across the campus one evening. The attack involved being pushed to the ground and told, "Do as I tell you—or suffer the consequences!" Afterward, the student could not get images of the assault out of her mind. She felt dazed and had a feeling of unreality about what had happened. In addition to her frightening recurrent thoughts, she was constantly surveying the paths on which she walked in order to check whether an assailant might be lurking in the bushes. Every little noise seemed to startle her, and she avoided walking in any but the most public places. After several weeks, her dazed feeling, recurrent thoughts, and watchfulness decreased considerably.

While other symptoms might also be present in acute stress disorder, what is clinically clearest is the linkage between a traumatic experience and dissociative symptoms. To make the diagnosis of acute stress disorder, DSM-IV requires that the disturbance last for at least 2 days and at most 4 weeks after the traumatic event. As with adjustment disorder, people diagnosed as having an acute stress disorder are expected to recover in a relatively short period of time. (Posttraumatic disorders in which the symptoms are observable for longer than 1 month are discussed in Chapter 7.) Persons suffering from acute stress disorder show high levels of anxiety and arousal, and they are often unable to keep from thinking with intense emotion about the traumatic event. As a consequence, they persistently reexperience the trauma. Table 4-8 lists the major diagnostic criteria for acute stress disorder. Clinical interviews with persons who may have an acute stress disorder usually include the following types of questions that are intended to determine whether the DSM-IV criteria have been met (Bryant & Harvey, 2000):

Table 4-8

Diagnostic Criteria for Acute Stress Disorder

- Exposure to an extreme event that evokes fear, helplessness, or horror
- Dissociative symptoms (numbing, detachment, feelings of unreality, depersonalization, amnesia)
- Persistent reexperiencing of the event
- Marked avoidance of stimuli associated with the traumatic event
- Marked anxiety and arousal
- Clinically significant symptoms that last for a minimum of 2 days and a maximum of 4 weeks, emerge within 4 weeks of the traumatic event, and are not due to the effects of a substance (such as a medication or abused drug) or a general medical condition

1. *During or since [the traumatic event] have you felt numb or distant from your own emotions?*
2. *During or since [the traumatic event] have things around you seemed unreal?*
3. *Have you had bad dreams or nightmares about [the traumatic event]?*
4. *Have you avoided people or places or activities that may remind you of [the traumatic event]?*
5. *Since [the traumatic event] have you had difficulty concentrating?*
6. *Since [the traumatic event] have you felt unusually irritable or have you lost your temper a lot more than usual?*

Dissociative Disorders

In this section we discuss the dramatic behavioral patterns seen in dissociative disorders that extend far beyond those seen in acute stress disorders. However, before turning to these patterns, we need to note a growing interest on the part of researchers in the possibility that dissociative processes fall along a continuum ranging from normal to pathological. Examples of pathological processes are the bizarre behavior seen in multiple personality and fugue states, both of which we will describe.

The Dissociation Continuum Most of us have had some dissociative experiences that fall within the normal range. The following account describes a type of dissociation that is not uncommonly seen in recently bereaved individuals:

The phone rang at 1:45 A.M. She was dead. When I arrived at her hospital room, I stood in the doorway. I could not cross the threshold into the room and face her lifeless body. For moments I was paralyzed at the door, with unbearable tenderness and fear welling up. God knows what I felt. I know it was a moment of the deepest truth of my existence and my identity.

I forced myself into the room; parts of myself seemed to have been vacated as I stood in awe and love and sadness and fear and disbelief. Time and mourning have come to pass, yet a part of me still stands at the doorway, a part of me is still vacated, a part of me is still at each crossroads of acceptance/ denial that I have walked through. The fact of my mother's death was and is perfectly well known to me, yet simultaneously not fully realized. (Kauffman, 1993, p. 34)

As a process, **dissociation** can be viewed as a severing of the connections between ideas and emotion. This happens to all of us when we divide our attention between two or more simultaneous tasks. From this perspective, dissociation might be regarded as an attribute that facilitates dividing one's attention. It might also play a role in fantasy, imagination, and acting. A good actor is able to become immersed in various types of roles. Could it be that dissociation becomes pathological only when a significant trauma occurs and the individual loses control of dissociative processes? Might a person high in dissociative ability who suffers a trauma use dissociation as a defense that normally might be adaptive? Researchers have only recently begun to study these questions. A first step in this effort is the assessment of individual differences in dissociation. Table 4-9 contains examples of items currently being used in making this assessment. By studying how these items relate to various types of behavior, it may be possible to determine the degree to which the tendency to dissociate is a basic personality trait. A dissociation trait might have multiple components that influence the extent to which people can compartmentalize their experiences, identity, memory, perception, and motor function.

Dissociation should not be considered inherently pathological, and it might not lead to significant distress, impairment, or the need to seek help. Furthermore, cross-cultural studies have found that dissociative states are a common and accepted expression of cultural activity or religious experience in many societies (Spiegel, 1994). It

---

Table 4–9

Examples of Questionnaire Items Intended to Place Individuals on the Dissociation Continuum

- I like to fantasize about doing interesting and exciting things.
- Sometimes the things around me do not seem quite real.
- Sometimes, while driving a car, I suddenly realize that I don't remember what has happened during all or part of the trip.
- I have such a vivid imagination that I really could "become" someone else for a few minutes.
- Sometimes I feel as if there is someone inside me directing my actions.

---

seems reasonable that individuals who in the past learned to dissociate when under stress are likely to do so again when confronted with new trauma. They might forget some or all of the traumatic experience when they feel threatened and be prone to seek or find new identities.

Dissociation often involves feelings of unreality, estrangement, and depersonalization, and sometimes a loss or shift of self-identity. Less dramatic but somewhat similar examples of dissociation are commonly observed in normal adults and children. When the first impact of bad news or a catastrophe hits us, we may feel as if everything is suddenly strange, unnatural, and different (estrangement), or as if we are unreal and cannot actually be witnessing or feeling what is going on (depersonalization). These feelings are not classified as dissociative disorders but are useful in understanding what the much more severe dissociative disorder is like.

Types of Dissociative Disorders DSM-IV classifies four conditions as **dissociative disorders:**

1. Dissociative amnesia
2. Dissociative fugue
3. Dissociative identity disorder
4. Depersonalization

All of these disorders involve large memory gaps and drastic changes in social roles. They are disturbances or alterations in the functions of identity, memory, and consciousness. The disturbances may come about suddenly or gradually and may last only a brief period or be long-lasting and chronic. The person's identity may be temporarily forgotten, or a new identity assumed, or there may be a feeling that one's sense of reality is lost. The maladaptive behaviors that arise from dissociative disorders provide a striking contrast to those that arise from adjustment and acute stress disorders. Stress plays a major role in all three, yet the reactions involved appear to be poles apart. Once again we see that similar situations can elicit drastically different responses in people with different dispositions and vulnerabilities.

People with dissociative disorders seem to use a variety of dramatic maneuvers to escape from the anxieties and conflicts aroused by stress. Their behavior involves sudden, temporary alterations of consciousness that serve to blot out painful experiences. In contrast, individuals with acute stress disorders cannot get the distressing experiences that they have undergone out of their minds, whereas those with adjustment disorders show milder disturbances and decreased ability to cope but their behavior clears up when they learn to adapt to the stressor or when the stressor is removed.

Many dissociative disorders appear to begin and end abruptly and are precipitated by stressful experiences. Although these disorders usually emerge after childhood, in most cases there is a history of serious family turmoil. Separation from parents in early childhood and abuse by parents have frequently been reported (Putnam, 1991). Thus, both recent traumas and traumas that have occurred in the distant past seem to combine to produce the seriously maladaptive and bizarre behavior seen in dissociative disorders.

Dissociative Amnesia **Dissociative amnesia** involves extensive but selective memory loss in the absence of indications of organic change (e.g., head injury). The memory losses characteristic of amnesia are too extensive to be explained by ordinary forgetfulness. Some people cannot remember anything about their past. Others can no longer recall specific events, people, places, or objects, while their memory for other, simultaneously experienced events remains intact.

Amnesia is usually precipitated by a physical accident or an emotionally traumatic event such as an intensely painful disappointment. Cases of amnesia demonstrate that the unity of consciousness is illusory. Our conscious representation of our actions is incomplete; our attention is usually divided among two or more streams of thought or courses of action. Unconscious systems of ideas may come to be split off from the major personality and exist as subordinate personalities, capable of becoming represented in consciousness under certain conditions. The following account illustrates the power of such unconscious forces:

A young man who was dressed in work clothes came to the emergency room of a hospital in the city in which he lived with the complaint that he did not know who he was. He seemed dazed, was not intoxicated, and carried no identification. After being kept in the hospital a few days, he woke up one morning in great distress, demanding to know why he was being kept in the hospital and announcing that he had to leave immediately to attend to urgent business.

With the recovery of his memory, the facts related to his amnesia emerged. The day his amnesia began, he had been the driver in an automobile accident that resulted in the death of a pedestrian. Police officers on the scene were convinced that the driver had not been in the wrong: the accident had been the pedestrian's fault. The police told the driver to fill out a routine form and to plan to appear at the coroner's inquest. The man filled out the form at the home of a friend and accidentally left his wallet there. Later, after mailing the form, he became dazed and amnesic. He was led to the hospital by a stranger. This amnesia was probably related to the stress of the fatal accident, fear of the inquest, and worry that he might actually have been responsible for the accident. (Based on Cameron, 1963, pp. 355–356)

While amnesia is probably the most common dissociative disorder, there are no accurate statistics on the incidence of any of the dissociative disorders. Dissociative amnesias are seen more often in adolescents and young adults than in children and older people, and they occur more often among females than males.

There are several types of dissociative amnesia:

- *Localized amnesia,* in which the individual fails to recall events that occurred during a particular period of time (e.g., the first few hours after a profoundly disturbing event).
- *Selective amnesia,* in which the person can recall some, but not all, of the events during a particular period of time.
- *Generalized amnesia,* which involves a recall failure that encompasses the person's entire life. This type occurs rarely.
- *Continuous amnesia,* the inability to recall events subsequent to a specific time, up to and including the present.
- *Systematized amnesia,* the loss of memory for certain categories of information, such as memories relating to a particular person.

Dissociative Fugue **Dissociative fugue** has as its essential feature unexpected travel away from home and customary workplace, the assumption of a new identity, and the inability to recall the previous identity. The travel and behavior seen in a person experiencing a fugue are more purposeful than any wandering that may take place in dissociative amnesia. Such a person sets up a new life in some distant place as a seemingly different person. The fugue state, or amnesic flight, usually ends when he or she abruptly wakes up, mystified and distressed at being in a strange place under strange circumstances (see Figure 4-11).

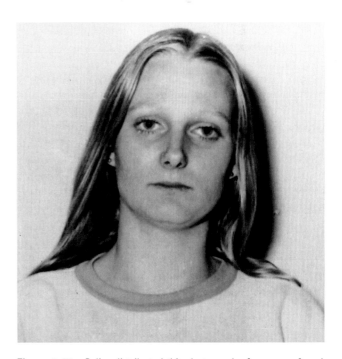

Figure 4–11 Police distributed this photograph of a woman found wandering on a New Jersey highway in the hope that someone would recognize her. When she was found, she was unable to remember her name, where she lived, or how she came to be walking along the highway.

Fugues, like amnesia, are often precipitated by intolerable stresses, such as marital quarrels, personal rejection, military conflict, and natural disasters. Fugues are usually of brief duration, with complete recovery and little likelihood of recurrence. After "waking up," the person frequently has no recollection of the events that took place during the fugue. The following case illustrates a fugue state with massive amnesia:

Samuel O., a graduate student, impoverished and far from home, was invited to dinner at the home of an instructor whom he had known when they were socioeconomic equals in another town. He accepted the invitation because he was lonely and hungry, but he regretted it almost at once because his clothes were shabby. He thought, in retrospect, that the instructor had seemed condescending. That evening he left his rooming house in plenty of time for the dinner, but he failed to show up at the instructor's home. Two days later he was picked up by the police in a neighboring state. He could vaguely remember riding a freight train, talking with strangers, and sharing their food, but he had no idea who he was, where he had come from, or where he was going.

Later on, the young man was able to remember the events leading up to the fugue and something of what went on during it. When he started out for the instructor's house, he was still experiencing strong conflict about going there. He was ashamed of his appearance, resentful over the condescension, and afraid to express what he felt and call the dinner off. On his way, he was delayed at a grade crossing by a slowly moving freight train. He had a sudden impulse to board the train and get away. When he acted on this impulse, he apparently became amnesic. (Based on Easton, 1959, pp. 505–513)

People experiencing a fugue generally appear to be without psychopathology and do not attract attention. Most fugues do not involve the formation of a new identity. However, the person might assume a new name or take up a new residence.

Dissociative Identity Disorder **Dissociative identity disorder,** often referred to as multiple personality, is the most dramatic of the dissociative disorders. In this disorder, an individual assumes alternate personalities, like Dr. Jekyll and Mr. Hyde. Each personality has its own set of memories and typical behaviors. Frequently, none of the personalities has any awareness of the others. In other cases, there is a one-way amnesia in which personality A is aware of the experiences of personality B while B remains unaware of A.

Although multiple personality is a rare disorder, it is of increasing interest because of the marked increase in the number of cases described in recent clinical literature and the linkage that has been made in many of these cases between multiple personality and traumatic childhood experiences. The improved diagnostic criteria for the disorder that first appeared in DSM-III are thought to have contributed to the increased number of reported cases

(Kluft, 1991). Many more female than male dissociative identity disorders have been reported, the ratio being about 4 to 1 (Kluft, 1988).

Clinically, the multiple personalities' behavioral differences and disparate self-concepts seem striking and puzzling. The personalities may experience themselves as being of different genders, ages, and sexual orientations. They may have separate wardrobes, possessions, interests, and interpersonal styles. Their values, beliefs, and problems may diverge. They may even have different handwritings, handedness, speech patterns, and accents.

In the following case, a 38-year-old woman named Margaret B. was admitted to a hospital with paralysis of her legs following a minor car accident that had occurred 6 months earlier:

She reported that until three years before her admission to the hospital she had enjoyed smoking, drinking, visiting nightclubs, and otherwise indulging in parties and social activities. At that point, however, she and her husband, who was an alcoholic, were converted to a small, evangelical religious sect. Her husband achieved control of his drinking, she gave up her prior social indulgences, and the two of them became completely immersed in the activities of the church.

[The] history revealed that she often "heard a voice telling her to say things and do things." It was, she said, "a terrible voice—that sometimes threatened to take over completely." When it was finally suggested to the patient that she let the voice "take over," she closed her eyes, clenched her fists, and grimaced for a few moments during which she was out of contact with those around her. Suddenly she opened her eyes and one was in the presence of another person. Her name, she said, was "Harriet." Whereas Margaret had been paralyzed, and complained of fatigue, headache and backache, Harriet felt well, and she at once proceeded to walk unaided around the interviewing room. She spoke scornfully of Margaret's religiousness, her invalidism and her puritanical life, professing that herself liked to drink and "go partying" but that Margaret was always going to church and reading the Bible. "But," she said impishly and proudly, "I make her miserable—I make her say and do things she doesn't want to." At length, at the interviewer's suggestion, Harriet reluctantly agreed to "bring Margaret back," and after more grimacing and fist clenching, Margaret reappeared, paralyzed, complaining of her headache and backache, and completely amnesic for the brief period of Harriet's release from her prison. (Nemiah, 1988, 247–248)

The clash between Margaret's religiousness, on the one hand, and her inclinations to indulge in pleasure, on the other, is a frequent theme in cases of multiple personality. It is noteworthy that as a child Margaret had had a playmate, Harriet, to whom she had been very devoted. When they were both 6 years old, Harriet had died of an acute infectious disease. Margaret had been deeply upset at her friend's death and wished that she had died in Harriet's place. Perhaps internalizing the image of her dead friend had in some way protected Margaret from prolonged despair and sorrow at her loss. As Margaret grew older, that internalization became the depository for all of her unacceptable impulses and feelings.

Many clinicians think of dissociative identity disorder as a psychological adaptation to traumatic experiences in early childhood. These experiences are severe and dramatic; examples include being dangled out of a window or being the victim of sexual sadism. In addition to having experienced harsh trauma in childhood, people with dissociative identity disorder seem prone to go into spontaneous hypnotic trances. Such a temporary defense may become stabilized into this disorder when the child faces repeated, overwhelming trauma (Draijer & Langeland, 1999). Dissociation can be an effective way to continue functioning while the trauma is going on, but if it continues to be used after the acute trauma has passed, it comes to interfere with everyday functioning. It is possible that elements of the traumatic experience linger as a separate state of mind that may only come into play when those elements are activated.

Some researchers question whether dissociative identity disorder represents anything more than an extreme form of the normal ability to present a variety of distinctive "selves." An important reason for such disagreements about dissociative identity disorder is that cases of this disorder are rare, making it difficult to do good research and to compare cases seen at different times under different circumstances. Despite methodological difficulties, studies of dissociative identity disorder are proceeding on a number of fronts. One provocative lead in dissociative identity disorder research relates to the possible role of brain abnormalities. Some studies have found that people with multiple personalities have an elevated risk of epileptic seizures (D. F. Benson et al., 1986). It is possible that there is a connection between seizures and the switch between personalities. However, although some cases of epilepsy may involve a neurological condition associated with dissociative identity disorder, the strength and basis of the association are not yet established. Future work is needed to explore the possibility of a biological basis to the capacity to dissociate, the ways in which stress early in life and later on interact with biological factors, and the development of effective therapies. Clinicians believe that establishing a secure, trusting relationship with the therapist is essential for therapeutic progress (Kluft, 1988). When such a relationship is achieved, it becomes possible to deal with conflicts between the personalities and help the patient move toward cooperation among them and, optimally, integration of the various personalities (Gleaves, 1996).

In most cases of dissociative identity disorder, the emergence of new personalities begins in early childhood, frequently in response to severe physical and sexual abuse. The emerging personalities, which appear to be a means of self-protection, often create another self to handle the stressor. Over time, the protective functions served by the new personality remain separate in the form of an alternate personality. In the majority of cases of dissociative identity disorder, the individual tries to hide the alternate personalities. This tendency may contribute to a large number of erroneous diagnoses.

Depersonalization While depersonalization is usually included among the dissociative disorders, some clinicians question its inclusion because it does not entail memory disturbances. In **depersonalization** there is a change in self-perception, and the person's sense of reality is temporarily lost or changed. Someone who is experiencing a state of depersonalization might say, "I feel as though I'm in a dream" or "I feel that I'm doing this mechanically." Frequently the individual has a feeling of not being in complete control of his or her actions, including speech. The onset of depersonalization is usually rapid and causes social or occupational impairment. The state of estrangement from oneself gradually disappears.

The following case illustrates several features of depersonalization:

A 24-year-old graduate student sought treatment because he felt he was losing his mind. He had begun to doubt his own reality. He felt he was living in a dream in which he saw himself from without, and did not feel connected to his body or his thoughts. When he saw himself through his own eyes, he perceived his body parts as distorted—his hands and feet seemed quite large. As he walked across campus, he often felt the people he saw might be robots; he began to ruminate about his dizzy spells—did this mean that he had a brain tumor?

. . . He often noted that he spent so much time thinking about his situation that he lost contact with all feelings except a pervasive discomfort about his own predicament.

. . . He was preoccupied with his perception that his feet had grown too large for his shoes, and fretted over whether to break up with his girlfriend because he doubted the reality of his feelings for her, and had begun to perceive her in a distorted manner. (Kluft, 1988, p. 580)

As is true with most clinical cases, explanations for several aspects of this case are by no means obvious. Why does the student often see people as robots? What might account for the distortions in his bodily perceptions? Nevertheless, the case provides several examples of the experience of depersonalization. These include doubts about one's own reality, feeling as though one is living in a dream, and losing contact with one's feelings.

People with depersonalization disorders may either have a persistent sense of depersonalization or suffer recurrent episodes. In either case, they perceive themselves as having lost their usual sense of reality, or as having had it changed. They feel as if they are in a dream and fear losing their sanity. A number of cases have been reported in which depersonalization seemed to be a response to extreme stress (Kluft, 1988).

Table 4-10 summarizes the major features of the dissociative disorders.

Interpreting Dissociative Disorders Dissociation seems to represent a process whereby certain mental functions that are ordinarily integrated with other functions presumably operate in a more compartmentalized or automatic way, usually outside the sphere of conscious awareness or memory recall. It might be described as a condition in which information—incoming, stored, or outgoing—is actively deflected from its usual or expected associations. This phenomenon results in alteration of the person's thoughts, feelings, or actions so that information is not associated or integrated with other information as it normally or logically would be.

The dissociative disorders are difficult to explain for several reasons. Often it is unclear whether a given case involves dissociation or is some sort of psychotic manifestation. Also, it is often difficult to obtain the information needed to draw reasonable conclusions. In the dissociative identity disorder case of Margaret B., for example, one wonders about the stressors that led to Harriet's emergence. How important were the loss of the 6-year-old playmate and the recent changes in Margaret's adult life? To what extent did Margaret forget or distort events that occurred when she was a child? Whereas the source of stress is easy to identify in adjustment and acute stress disorders, in the dissociative disorders the source might not be obvious. Dissociative disorders may be related to combinations of vulnerability factors (e.g., certain aspects of biological makeup) and stresses that occurred many years before maladaptation reached clinical proportions. Because human beings are able to distort their memories, considerable probing is often needed to determine the true nature of the stress.

Dissociative disorders are often discussed in psychodynamic (seeing dissociation as a defense mechanism) and cognitive (seeing dissociation as a memory failure) terms. These disorders help the individual escape from reality and seem to facilitate the expression of a variety of pent-up emotions. They have been interpreted as attempts to escape from excessive tension, anxiety, and stimulation by separating some parts of the personality from the rest. When there are no indications of a recent experience that might have functioned as a stressor, these perspectives raise questions about earlier stressors that might still have symbolic meaning for the individual. (The child Margaret's loss of her friend Harriet illustrates this possibility.) In treating dissociative disorders, many clinicians seek to uncover the dissociated memories and to help the individual face them and deal with them more directly. Psychoanalysis, behavior therapy, hypnosis, and videotaped interviews combined with sedative drugs have all been useful for this purpose.

Reactions to stress can lead to clinical problems. Adjustment disorders involve behavioral deterioration following a stressful experience. However, as the stress level lowers, the individual usually returns to normal. Acute stress disorders are set in motion by unusual stressful experiences and persist for a relatively short period of time. Although dissociative disorders also often follow stressful experiences, these disorders occur in people who have psychological vulnerabilities, including a tendency to sever the connection between ideas and emotions and a strong need to escape from unpleasant realities.

Treating Stress-Related Problems

People often overcome their maladaptive reactions to stress in the course of time, but help from an expert may speed up the process. The clinician has two broad functions: (1) to provide support for troubled people, and (2) to strengthen their coping skills. Several procedures are used in treating stress-related problems.

Supportive Therapy

It is hard to recover from a stress-related disorder if one is or feels socially isolated. Because most stress reactions

Table 4–10	
Major Features of Dissociative Disorders	
Disorder	**Characteristics**
Dissociative amnesia	Usually follows severe stress. Involves an inability to remember significant events: either everything that occurred during a particular time period or things that lasted only for certain periods (such as the birth of a child).
Dissociative fugue	Often follows severe stress. Involves suddenly leaving home and going on a journey that is purposeful (i.e., the journey does not involve aimless wandering).
Dissociative identity disorder	Involves the possession of at least two distinct personalities or personality states. The transition from one personality to another is usually sudden, often precipitated by stress.
Depersonalization	Involves a sense of being cut off or detached from one's self; often precipitated by stress.

involve feelings of inadequacy and isolation, many people can be helped by **supportive therapy,** in which the therapist listens sympathetically and provides encouragement. Although they use different terms, both psychodynamically and humanistically oriented clinicians emphasize the client-therapist relationship as a means of facilitating adaptive coping. Freudians describe their efforts in this regard as strengthening the client's ego. When the ego is able to manipulate reality more effectively, it can handle the id's incessant demands with less stress. The Rogerian therapist's acceptance of clients as they are, coupled with recognition of their strengths and de-emphasis of their failings, helps clients feel more positive about themselves and creates a supportive climate.

Clients who receive supportive therapy often comment with relief that the therapist did not criticize them either directly or indirectly for their handling of difficult situations. Within a supportive environment, clients can relax enough to engage in problem solving and the careful consideration of alternatives that had previously seemed impossible.

Being supportive may not be easy for the therapist. Working with dissociative disorders can be arduous and demanding. Many therapists, sensitive to their patients' isolation, find it difficult to be both accessible and able to set reasonable and nonpunitive limits. In dissociative identity disorders, it is particularly difficult to follow the threads of the separate personalities.

Medications

A variety of antianxiety and antidepressant drugs are available to help people who have experienced trauma. While drugs are not a cure, they can be of value in helping the patient overcome panic states and other maladaptive reactions to intense short-term stress. Tranquilizers are often used along with psychological approaches, such as, supportive therapy.

Relaxation Training

It is possible for people to learn ways of helping themselves deal with stress. It is well known that people can learn to regulate voluntarily certain effects of the autonomic nervous system. This, in turn, can affect their emotional state. For example, anxiety can be caused by the sensation of tension experienced when muscle fibers are shortened or contracted, as they are during stress. Conversely, tension cannot be present when muscle fibers are lengthened or relaxed. **Relaxation training** involves the following steps:

1. Focusing attention on a series of specific muscle groups
2. Tensing each group
3. Maintaining tension for 5 to 7 seconds
4. Telling oneself to relax and immediately releasing tension
5. Focusing attention on each muscle group as it relaxes

Relaxation training is used not only as a technique in its own right but also as a basis for other therapies. It is applicable to a wide variety of stress-related problems and can be readily taught both individually and in groups.

Systematic Desensitization

Systematic desensitization consists of combining relaxation training and a hierarchy of anxiety-producing stimuli to gradually eliminate the fear of a specific situation. The person learns to maintain the relaxed state while imagining anxiety-associated stimuli from various stages of the hierarchy. The result is often a significant reduction in fear.

Cognitive Modification

Behavioral problems can arise in part because an individual persists in a particular maladaptive line of thought. If someone can be guided to think about a situation in a different, more productive way, adaptive coping may become possible. **Cognitive modification** involves learning new internal dialogues and new ways of thinking about situations and about oneself. In this sense, cognitive modification is a step toward productive problem solving.

Social Intervention

Some therapists prefer to treat troubled individuals alone, whereas other therapists feel that treatment can be more helpful if people are treated within a social context. **Social intervention** is an approach to treatment that not only involves interacting with the client, but also attempts to modify the client's home or work environment. Family therapy, in which all members of the family go into treatment together, is based on the latter idea. In some instances, the clinical worker might even decide to make one or more home visits to observe the family's interactions in more natural surroundings.

Challenges in Treating Stress–Related Problems

Stress-related problems stem from a wide variety of stressors. The selection of an appropriate treatment depends on a number of factors associated with the individual experiencing the difficulties. Does the person want to talk about what happened? What is his or her interpersonal sittuation (e.g., are there family members and friends who can help)? What is the mix of strong emotions and troubling thoughts that is creating difficulties? What are the person's strengths and vulnerabilities? All of these questions pose problems in planning a therapeutic approach and for researchers who want to evaluate therapeutic effectiveness.

From time to time, new therapeutic approaches are developed that might be helpful but lack empirical verification. For example, **eye movement desensitization and reprocessing (EMDR)** is a type of imaginal exposure in which an individual focuses attention on a traumatic memory while simultaneously visually tracking the therapist's finger as it is moved across the patient's visual field (Shapiro, 1995). Originally proposed as a specific treatment for posttraumatic stress disorder, it has since been applied to many other conditions. Some reports suggest that some people improve rapidly when asked to recall images of a traumatic event while systematically moving their eyes rapidly. At the heart of EMDR is the idea that accelerated processing of disturbing material can be directly facilitated at a neurophysiological level using certain dual attention tasks (such as imagining a traumatic experience while following the therapist's finger). The EMDR procedure grew out of Shapiro's observation that after recalling disturbing thoughts while deliberately moving her eyes the thoughts seemed to be less upsetting. The opinions of researchers and clinicians are divided about the effectiveness of EMDR. What is needed is a well-developed theoretical rationale for the treatment and well-controlled research.

In addition to recognizing the need for more research on all treatments for stress-related disorders, most clinicians see the need to treat stress-related disorders with combinations of acceptance of what the individual is going through, education and training regarding useful coping responses to stressors, overcoming fear of trauma-related memories, and cognitive restructuring (e.g., questioning and revising trauma-related schemas.)

The trouble with stress is that it is so very personal. Stress-related disorders cannot be explained simply on the basis of the terrible things that happen to people. They depend a lot on how the person experiencing a stressor is put together—psychologically and physically. Not only that, the same person may deal effectively with certain stressors, but not others. A given stressor can have a multitude of consequences including feelings of abject misery, loss of hope, dissociative experiences, breakdown of bodily processes, anger over reversals and disappointments, *and* personal triumph. The topic of stress is not restricted to the bad things that happen to people. We can learn much from studying how people use their personal resources in overcoming the challenges of life. Learning more about human resilience and resourcefulness may ultimately contribute a better understanding of and treatment for stress-related disorders.

Chapter Summary

STRESS AND COPING

How people cope with stress depends on their vulnerability and resilience. *Vulnerability* increases the likelihood of a maladaptive response to stress, *resilience* decreases it. Having a positive self-concept, enjoying new experiences, and having good interpersonal relationships all contribute to resilience.

Coping Skills Coping skills refer to a person's ability to deal with different types of situations. People who are effective copers usually have a variety of techniques available and are able to choose those most appropriate for the situation. Effective copers also learn to direct their thoughts toward problem solving and are able to avoid distraction caused by fear and worry.

The Coping Process Coping is a process that includes the acquisition of pertinent information, consideration of alternatives, deciding on a course of action, and behavior. High levels of emotional arousal often interfere with the effectiveness of the coping process.

Social Support Social support, the feeling of being cared about, valued, and loved by others, can help make people less vulnerable to stress. The belief that social support is available also encourages people to develop new ways of coping during periods that are not highly stressful. Researchers have shown a relationship between the availability of social support and both psychological and physical health.

STRESSFUL SITUATIONS AND LIFE TRANSITIONS

Stress can have undesirable effects on behavior, thought, and bodily functioning. Because different people react to stressors in different ways, the correlation between particular stressors and their effects on different bodily functions is often low. It is particularly hard for people to deal with several stressors that occur at nearly the same time. However, the cumulative effects of stressors over a long period of time can also have a negative effect on a person's mental and physical health. Questionnaires are often used to assess which events a person has experienced in the recent past as well as how he or she perceived the events and reacted to them.

Stress-Arousing Situations Stress can arise either from specific situations or from developmental transitions. Stressful events can vary in a number of ways: duration, severity, predictability, degree of loss of control, self-confidence of the person experiencing the stress, and suddenness of onset. Accidents, natural disasters, and military combat all can bring about high levels of stress and may result in a stress disorder. Stress may also be the result of a personal crisis such as being raped or bereaved.

Life Transitions Life transitions, such as going to college, getting a job, having a baby, and moving, may also be stressful. Adolescence is a time of particular stress because of physical changes, role changes, and changes in parent-child relationships.

CLINICAL REACTIONS TO STRESS

Among the disorders that seem most related to stress are adjustment disorders, acute stress disorders, and dissociative disorders.

Adjustment Disorder An **adjustment disorder** is a reaction to recent stress and usually disappears when the stress level decreases. Common symptoms of adjustment disorder are depression, anxiety, disruptive or reckless behavior, sleep problems, deterioration in performance, and social withdrawal.

Acute Stress Disorder An **acute stress disorder** occurs in response to a traumatic stressor and is marked by fear, horror, or helplessness, together with symptoms of dissociation such as numbness, feelings of detachment, diminished awareness of surroundings (as in a daze), depersonalization, and often amnesia. The symptoms begin within 4 weeks of the trauma and last from 2 days to 4 weeks.

Dissociative Disorders Sudden temporary alterations of consciousness that blot out painful experiences are characteristic of **dissociative disorders.** Four conditions are included in this group: dissociative amnesia, dissociative fugue, dissociative identity disorder, and depersonalization. **Dissociative amnesia** involves extensive but selective memory loss that has no known organic cause. This disorder is often associated with overwhelming stress. In **dissociative fugue,** the person loses identity, leaves home, and sets up a new life in a distant place. The fugue usually ends when the person suddenly "wakes up" with no memory of events that occurred during the fugue. **Dissociative identity disorder** often seems to be associated with traumatic experiences in childhood. In this disorder, the person assumes alternate personalities that may or may not be aware of each other. **Depersonalization** involves a dreamlike state in which the person has a sense of being separated both from self and from reality. This state may be persistent or recurrent, and it is often difficult to identify the source of the stress.

TREATING STRESS-RELATED PROBLEMS

A variety of approaches are used, either alone or in combination, to treat stress-related disorders.

Supportive Therapy In **supportive therapy** the therapist provides acceptance and adopts a noncritical attitude in order to give the client an opportunity to relax enough to engage in problem solving.

Medications Drugs and sedatives act on the nervous system to allow the person to feel a temporary decrease in stress. This treatment is often combined with a psychological therapeutic approach.

Relaxation Training **Relaxation training** is a structured approach to tension reduction that also helps to decrease feelings of stress so that the person can focus on working out problems.

Systematic Desensitization **Systematic desensitization** is a process designed to eliminate fear in specific types of situations by pairing relaxation techniques with imagining the presence of the anxiety-associated stimuli.

Cognitive Modification **Cognitive modification** is the process of learning to think about or construe anxiety-producing situations in a different way.

Social Intervention **Social intervention** involves treating not just the individual with the problem, but also involving other people, usually family members, in the individual's social context in the treatment process.

Challenges in Treating Stress-Related Problems Appropriate treatment of stress-related problems requires careful planning by clinicians that is based on objective evaluations of therapeutic methods. Often combinations of treatment approaches are useful (e.g., psychotherapy and medications).

Stress is very personal, and reactions to it depend on an individual's psychological and physical makeup. Studying people's resilience and their resourcefulness in overcoming challenges may improve understanding of and treatment for stress-related disorders.

Key Terms

Stress, p. 125
Coping skills, p. 125
Coping process, p. 128
Social support, p. 129
Personal crises, p. 134
Bereavement, p. 134
Grief, p. 136

Life transitions, p. 137
Adjustment disorder, p. 140
Acute stress disorder, p. 141
Dissociative disorders, p. 141
Dissociative amnesia, p. 143
Dissociative fugue, p. 143
Dissociative identity disorder, p. 144

Depersonalization, p. 145
Supportive therapy, p. 147
Relaxation training, p. 147
Systematic desensitization, p. 147
Cognitive modification, p. 147
Social intervention, p. 147

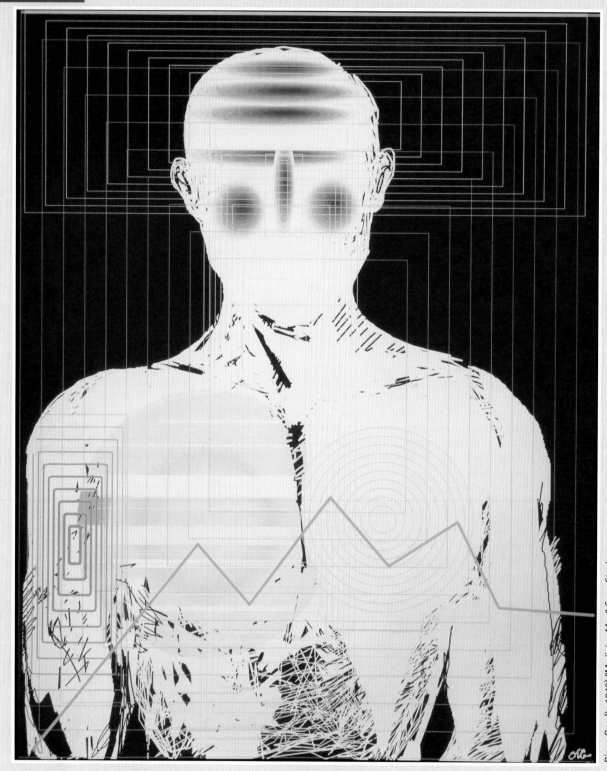

Bodily Dysfunction

Eating and Sleeping Problems and Psychophysiological Disorders

Twelve-year-old Valerie Harris, the only child of worried, devoted parents, had for several years been diagnosed as having bronchial asthma, a chronic respiratory disease often arising from allergies and marked by attacks of labored breathing, chest constriction, and coughing. Because they thought that too much physical activity would bring on an asthmatic attack, Valerie's parents had significantly reduced her activity level (they were secretly worried that she might collapse and die). Valerie had all of the usual asthmatic symptoms, but medications had reduced their severity somewhat. Her father's behavior when he came home from work typified Valerie's parents' anxiety. Every evening he devoted himself entirely to the task of diverting and amusing his daughter so as to minimize her attacks. Actually, her attacks tended to increase in frequency and severity following his arrival home. Unfortunately, neither Valerie nor her parents suspected a possible connection between the parents' behavior and the occurrence of Valerie's asthmatic attacks. Because Valerie's physician had noticed and been concerned about the parents' anxiety and their overprotection of Valerie, she had recommended that the family consult a psychiatrist. A series of sessions, some involving the entire family and some just the parents, helped everyone see that to a significant extent, Valerie noticed that her parents were working very hard—too hard—to observe and help her and that this increased her tension. She thought: "There must be something serious that they are worried about." As the parents gained insight into their anxiety and overprotective behavior, they were able to become somewhat more relaxed about Valerie and her condition. As a result, Valerie's wheezing diminished, and her severe attacks decreased in frequency. ■

Valerie Harris's condition involves a set of observable physical symptoms that are reduced somewhat by medication. Stress and vulnerability seem to contribute to her bronchial asthma. The reactions of her parents (especially, of her father) seem to be stress-arousing and increase her symptoms. The symptoms, in turn, make her especially vulnerable to parental overprotection.

It makes sense intuitively that the strains of intense and/or prolonged stress might reactively affect how the body functions. Added burdens usually lead to more wear and tear. This chapter inquires into the roles played by stress, personal vulnerabilities, and resilience in physical illness. While the focus of attention in this chapter is on bodily dysfunction, the next one deals with often intense bodily concerns in the *absence* of a diagnosable medical condition. In Chapter 6 we shall describe these concerns and how clinicians deal with them and also consider hypotheses about the factors that contribute to concerns about bodily dysfunction in the absence of physical symptoms.

The previous chapter showed that a combination of stress and vulnerability can lead to maladaptive psychological outcomes. Under certain conditions, it can also lead either to physical symptoms or to a preoccupation with the body even when there is no discernible malfunction. While the popular press and television often leave the impression of an almost automatic stress-illness relationship (Figure 5-1), physical symptoms are not necessarily a result of stress. In the case of Valerie Harris, her asthma is an allergic condition that leads to respiratory difficulties, but it is made worse when there is stress.

Rewarding interpersonal relationships and social support contribute to resilience when individuals confront threats to health and well-being. An example of this is Supreme Court Justice Sandra Day O'Connor, who several years ago had breast cancer that necessitated a mastec-

tomy. Her husband accompanied her to doctors' appointments to provide support and to ensure that she didn't miss any important information. While the availability of caring others contributed to her resilience and speedy recovery, recognition of her responsibilities to loved ones also played a positive role. She said to herself: "You'd better shape up and make a go of this because you're causing a lot of distress for other people" (*Seattle Times*, November 4, 1994, p. A4).

Research has shown that psychological and social factors may play important roles in health and fitness—an idea that has intrigued clinical workers and patients alike for a long time. There is evidence that (1) acute and chronic stressors play a role in certain types of physical conditions, (2) vulnerability and resilience influence bodily functioning and recovery from illness, and (3) for some people, bodily complaints seem to be a way of coping with stress. In this chapter we will review present-day knowledge about the relationships among personality, environment, and illness, and examine how psychological and social variables operate in health and illness. The first part of the chapter deals primarily with two basic biological processes, eating and sleeping, that can result in increased risk of medical problems, accidents, or even death when they are affected by abnormal thoughts and behavior.

Many of the disorders covered in this chapter are thought to result from frequent, intense, and prolonged physiological arousal. Whereas some people respond to stress primarily with bizarre thoughts and behavior, others respond primarily with physical illnesses ranging from cancer to migraine headaches. But while it is known that there are wide differences in individual patterns of physiological, cognitive, and behavioral reactions to stress, the mechanisms behind those patterns remain unclear. Whatever the mechanisms turn out to be, it is now certain that they involve interactions between personal variables (e.g.,

Figure 5-1   While stress can have important physical and psychological consequences, the cause-effect relationships are not quite as straightforward as this cartoon seems to suggest.

SOURCE: © by Jim Borgman. Reprinted by permission of the Cincinnati Enquirer/King Features Syndicate.

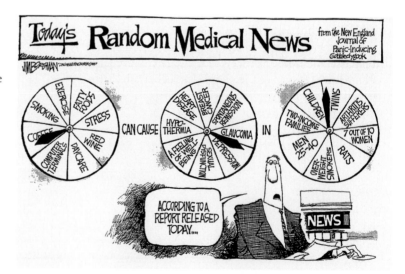

attitudes and physiological patterns) and situational variables (such as past and recent life experiences and social support). Illness clearly results from multiple factors.

Psychological, Social, and Bodily Interactions

Awareness that one's state of mind can influence one's body has a long history (see Chapter 1). In the eighteenth century, Franz Anton Mesmer claimed that he could modify the course of physical symptoms by using his "personal magnetism." In the nineteenth century, Jean Martin Charcot pioneered the use of hypnosis in the treatment of bodily complaints; and early in this century, Sigmund Freud applied psychoanalytic concepts to physical symptoms. Freud believed that somatic symptoms had symbolic significance; they represented compromises among forbidden impulses, intrapsychic conflicts, and the need to defend oneself from anxiety. In the 1930s and 1940s a number of clinicians attempted to integrate Freudian ideas into a growing body of knowledge concerning the bodily aspects of emotional experiences. During this period the **psychosomatic hypothesis** became popular. According to this theory, bodily symptoms can be caused by a blocking of emotional expression.

Recent research has focused on how bodily reactions change when people are exposed to various emotion-arousing stimuli. For example, emotional tension has been shown to influence the autonomic nervous system and the endocrine glands. One of the endocrine glands, the adrenal medulla, releases its hormones when the situation calls for "fight or flight." As a result, the rates of breathing, heartbeat, and muscle tension increase. These and other bodily changes caused by emotional responses to stress prepare the organism to meet challenges (Selye, 1976). For example, pituitary and adrenal hormones are influenced by events that occur in the course of conflicts, as between husbands and wives. Marital researchers typically ask couples to discuss a topic on which they are known to disagree and, while this discussion is taking place, measure the levels of several hormones and blood pressure. Anger-prone people frequently show the largest increases in levels of stress-sensitive hormones and blood pressure. The health consequences of these exaggerated bodily responses to conflict are now being evaluated by researchers.

The Biopsychosocial Model

Today most researchers look at physical symptoms from an interactional viewpoint: bodily defects may cause psychological problems, and psychological problems may in turn cause bodily defects. When psychological factors are involved in illness, their role is usually indirect. For example, personality characteristics by themselves may not cause an illness like asthma, but in combination with hypersensitive lungs and certain situational stresses, they may play an important role.

In the past 2 decades, emphasis has been placed on the interaction between psychological states and social and biological variables. According to the **biopsychosocial model,** a person can be regarded as a system with interacting biological, psychological, and social subsystems (Engel, 1977). Sources of vulnerability and resilience exist throughout this system. The model can be illustrated by some of the complex activities involved in brain function. The brain processes both physical and nonphysical inputs (environmental events, ideas); it generates thoughts and behavior; and it regulates bodily functions. At any given moment the brain's circuitry permits simultaneous "programming" of data pertaining to the biological, psychological, and social spheres. The challenge facing researchers is to identify the factors and conditions that play roles in this complex type of information processing.

Biopsychosocial problems often arise when people's lives are disrupted by environmental changes, challenges, and constraints. The word **homeostasis** refers to the mechanism by which an organism mobilizes itself to restore a dynamic equilibrium in the face of these disruptions. At present most researchers and clinicians believe that, for any given individual, a host of variables—physical, psychological, and social—contribute to the phenomenon that we call "getting sick." The idea that illness is due simply to the influence of external agents seems outmoded. While it is true that there are individual differences in the vulnerability of bodily organs to disease, these differences must be considered in light of personality characteristics, environmental factors, and the general condition of the body. The biopsychosocial point of view is not limited to the causes of illness. It is also relevant to prevention and treatment, major fields of concern to the specialty areas of behavioral medicine and health psychology (see Box 5-1).

Stress and Illness

There is growing evidence that stress plays an important role in illness and health. We have observed that stress leads to diverse bodily reactions. The heart, the lungs, and the digestive, endocrine, and nervous systems, among others, work overtime when people experience stress. When these systems are consistently overloaded throughout long periods of a person's life, the likelihood increases that some sort of physical weakness or disturbance will occur. It makes good medical sense, therefore, to study the personal characteristics and aspects of life that go along with strong and persistent stress reactions or that might predispose a person

Research Close-up

Behavioral Medicine and Health Psychology

The biopsychosocial model's emphasis on interrelating factors has contributed to the development of two new fields: behavioral medicine and health psychology. These fields are based on the idea that combinations of biological, psychological, and social factors influence an individual's health, vulnerability to disease, and reactions to disease. Studies in these fields strongly indicate that virtually every ill that can befall the body—from the common cold to cancer and heart disease—can be influenced, positively or negatively, by a person's mental state, life-style, and social relationships. By unveiling the mechanisms behind these effects, research may point to new ways of preventing and treating disease (Shumaker et al., 1998).

Behavioral medicine is concerned with ways of improving diagnosis, treatment, and rehabilitation by using psychological techniques that help people adopt healthier ways of living. An important goal of behavioral medicine is the improvement of service delivery by providers of health care. Researchers in behavioral medicine are particularly concerned with direct patient evaluation and treatment.

The related field of **health psychology** is directed toward the prevention of disease. Health psychologists seek to reduce health risks by changing people's thinking and living habits. Researchers in health psychology tend to be concerned with broader topics, including the acquisition and modification of behavior that influences health or is guided by concerns about health. Since as much as 50% of mortality from the leading causes of death

can be traced to such behaviors as inactivity, poor nutrition, and smoking, health psychologists seek to strengthen those behaviors that contribute to good health.

Both behavioral medicine and health psychology are concerned with reducing the stressfulness of illness and, wherever possible, preventing such stress. Prevention often involves helping people to make healthful life-style changes. Examples of targets of prevention efforts are smoking, a form of voluntary behavior clearly harmful to health and a major cause of cancer; alcohol abuse, which contributes to cirrhosis of the liver; injuries from accidents and violence; and overeating and underexercising, which contribute to obesity, high blood pressure, and diabetes. The great need for effective health promotion techniques is suggested by the facts presented in Table 5-1.

One example of this need is the fact that eating more calories than is desirable over decades results in an overflow of fatty acids that spill out of fat cells and get taken up and trapped by nonfat cells. When this happens the nonfat cells are likely to become damaged. For some people this leads to diabetes, because the fatty acids crowd into cells responsible for making insulin. Over time, the excess of fat undermines the capacity of the cells to make insulin, thus compromising the body's ability to metabolize sugar. The fatty acids also may contribute to clogging arteries and destroying heart muscle cells.

Behavioral medicine and health psychology are interdisciplinary fields that integrate the behavioral and biomedical

sciences. Common to both of these fields is a philosophy that emphasizes individual responsibility as a means of maximizing health. According to this view, health is a personal achievement, and people's behavior influences whether they attain it or not. Physical, mental, social, and economic factors all influence health and recovery from illness. We will examine three areas—the doctor-patient relationship, the relationship of gender to longevity, and a biopsychosocial approach to the common cold—areas in which these factors play roles.

The Doctor-Patient Relationship

The character of the relationship between doctor and patient influences patients' perceptions of their problems and clinical outcomes as well. A good relationship contributes to the patient's morale and perception of the doctor as truly interested in his or her welfare. This patient's perception of his doctor contributed to strong negative emotions:

I guess in becoming a great surgeon you forgot those early courses in doctor-patient relations: that patients tend to panic and imagine the worst; that they need reassurance. You said outright that I had two malignant tumors that must be removed at once. That meant cancer. The word scared the hell out of me. I broke out in a sweat. But you didn't seem to notice. You frowned your usual frown and said that radiation or chemotherapy were not options. You gave no explanation and I was too clobbered to ask.

In contrast, it is highly likely that this doctor plays a positive and important role in his patients' lives:

I have practiced medicine long enough to sense intuitively that even when a person with significant medical problems has a presenting complaint, more than half the time the complaint is related to stress. On a daily basis, therefore, I assess the disease process and adjust the medical management as needed, but my joy comes from listening carefully, helping people to identify their stressors, providing my best advice when I think it is appropriate, but always offering my caring and understanding—especially when I see that the problem, as presented, is insoluble. I am both rewarded and

Table 5-1

Facts About Health in the United States

- About one-fourth of the adult population are 20% or more above desirable body weight.
- About one-half of adults experience at least a moderate amount of stress in a 2-week period.
- Some 40% of the population say they exercise or play sports, but only 28% are very physically active.
- About 30% of persons 18 years of age and older smoke cigarettes.
- One-half of young mothers 18 to 24 years of age with less than 12 years of education have smoked in the year preceding the birth of their last child.

Box 5-1

fascinated to observe that people feel better just by recognizing that I care.

Gender and Longevity

Gender is a significant factor in longevity. While women live longer than men, the cause of this difference is unclear. Probably both genetic and life-style factors play roles. Sex differences in longevity are smaller in nonindustrial than in industrial societies. To a large extent this distinction reflects smaller sex differences in mortality for coronary heart disease in nonindustrial societies. In industrial societies like the United States, higher male mortality rates seem to be related to society's expectations that men be more aggressive, adventurous, ambitious, and hard-driving than women. If these expectations were changed, would male mortality rates become lower as a result? As more and more women hold jobs and support families, will their mortality rates go up? We do not have definite answers to these questions. Research that compares mortality among men who differ in their need to adopt traditional male roles and among women who differ in their conceptions of female roles may clarify this issue.

Gender is only one of several factors that seem to be related to longevity. Social relationships, the feeling of being supported by others, and the ability to experience difficulties without feeling overwhelmed by them all seem to contribute to living a long satisfying life (Avlund et al., 1998) (see Figure 5-2). There is also evidence that high levels of trust in other people and positive interpersonal attitudes are correlated with life satisfaction and longevity (Barefoot et al., 1998).

Stress and Colds

Both observation and experiments suggest that stress increases susceptibility to colds and other respiratory infections. In a 1-year study of 100 subjects, throat cultures were taken every 3 weeks for bacteria, and blood was drawn every 4 months for antibodies to cold viruses. Events that caused stress, as indicated by diaries, were four times more likely to precede than to follow new infections. People who developed a cold or bacterial infection had often been feeling more angry and tense than usual, and these feelings were not early signs of illness, since they appeared an average of 4 days before the physical symptoms. The effect persisted even with controls for sex, family history of respiratory infections, family size, and allergies (S. Cohen & Williamson, 1991).

Another experiment provides even more persuasive evidence for a connection between stress and colds. Here 420 subjects (154 men and 266 women) were exposed to one of five cold viruses after answering questionnaires on psychological stress, personality, health practices, and behavior. The following three measures of stress were used: occurrence of certain events (job loss, death in the family, moving, divorce, and so on) in the previous year; feeling frightened, upset, nervous, sad, angry, or irritated; and feeling unable to cope with current demands (S. Cohen et al., 1991).

Before exposure and also 1 month later, the researchers asked about cold symptoms and tested for antibodies to the cold viruses. They found that the more stress a person was under, the greater the chance of infection (as indicated by the presence of antibodies). Among the 25%

Figure 5-2   This photograph of Jeanne Calment was taken two years before her death in 1997 at the age of 122. At the time, she was believed to be the world's oldest person. During her long life, she took up swimming, bicycling, roller skating, played the piano and enjoyed opera. She was described as being unflappable and able to handle stress easily. She once said, "If you can't do anything about it, don't worry about it." (*New York Times*, August 5, 1997, p. C21).

Research Close-up   Box 5-1

of subjects under greatest stress, 90% became infected; among the 25% under least stress, 74% became infected. But once they became infected, people under stress were no more likely to develop cold symptoms. In other words, stress increased the danger of infection itself, not the resulting discomfort (which is produced by the immune system's defenses against the virus).

While stress decreases resistance to infection, social support seems to increase it. People with diverse social networks are less likely to develop upper respiratory illness after viral exposure than those with relatively restricted support networks. This difference in response to infection applies both to subjective reports of illness and objective measures of mucus production

(S. Cohen et al., 1999; S. Cohen et al., 1997). Might clinicians, like physicians, be able to help patients resist infections or recover from them? This is one of the possibilities suggested by the findings we have reviewed concerning the doctor-patient relationship and susceptibility to infection. It merits thoughtful consideration and study (see Figure 5-3).

Figure 5-3   Listening supportively, with empathy and understanding, to patients' spoken concerns might have considerable therapeutic value.

to psychological or physical breakdown. Stress is created when individuals face difficult situations and have to ask themselves, "How am I going to handle this one?" or "Can I do it?" (Figure 5-4). These factors increase stress and the risk of illness:

1. Inability to adapt to changes in environmental demands
2. Inability to handle strong feelings and emotions, and to express them realistically
3. Inability to interpret demands, constraints, and opportunities correctly
4. Inability to form rewarding, lasting interpersonal ties, particularly love relationships

Only some of the people who are biologically predisposed to a particular condition actually fall ill. Others

who are equally biologically vulnerable are able to cope effectively and thus reduce the negative effects of stress on health. The chance of onset of illness may vary with a number of factors, including age, the particular form of the illness, and what is going on in the person's life. These interacting factors provide a clue as to why it is practically impossible to make statements like "John Jones got pneumonia because he had been working overtime for 2 months" or "Mary Smith developed ulcers because she is such a nervous person." Many people develop pneumonia without working overtime, and most people can work overtime without becoming sick. Similarly, many people who develop ulcers do not appear to be especially nervous, and most nervous people do not develop ulcers.

As noted earlier, stress causes a variety of physical changes. Among other things, it stimulates hormonal

Figure 5-4 Being well-prepared for challenges reduces the risk of illness due to stress. For example, research on police officers assigned to dangerous tactical and negotiation units has demonstrated that those who have received intensive training and supervision do not show an unusually high level of psychological or physical stress-related symptoms.

Source: Messer, 1994.

secretions (particularly those of the pituitary and adrenal glands), activates the autonomic system, brings about biochemical changes, and alters the brain's electrical level. Although all people have these reactions to stress, the strength and pattern of the reactions depend not only on the nature of the stressful stimulus but also on the individual's biological characteristics, personality, and life experiences. Recent and past life experiences play important roles in influencing our appraisal of situations and the coping mechanisms we use to deal with stress.

Eating Disorders

Health problems, the focus of this chapter, can (1) be major or minor, (2) be short-term or long-term conditions, and (3) have easily identifiable causes or ones that are vague and diffuse. In some cases, there is tissue damage to which stress, coping, and resilience seem to contribute. We will review these disorders later in the chapter. However, in other cases, the problem is—or, at least, starts out being—primarily behavioral in the sense that the individual behaves in a way that, while not causing impairment at the outset, can become serious or even fatal down the road. Eating disorders and sleep disorders (discussed next) fall into this group. Both of these disorders have in common that they are often not well understood and the relative contributions of psychosocial and biological factors are not well delineated. They are relatively recent additions to psychiatric classification systems. Extensive research on them has existed for only about 30 years. Nevertheless, there is sufficient evidence implicating psychological and social variables in their development and treatment to justify their inclusion in a survey of abnormal psychology.

The three most studied **eating disorders** are:

- *Anorexia nervosa,* in which individuals have a distorted body image that causes them to see themselves as overweight even when they are dangerously thin. Often refusing to eat, exercising compulsively, and developing unusual habits such as refusing to eat in front of others, anorexics lose large amounts of weight and may even starve to death.
- *Bulimia nervosa,* in which individuals eat excessive quantities of food, then purge their bodies of the food and calories they fear by using laxatives, enemas, or diuretics; vomiting; and/or exercising. Often acting in secrecy, bulimics feel disgusted and ashamed as they binge, yet relieved of tension and negative emotions once their stomachs are empty again.
- *Binge eating,* in which, like bulimia, there are frequent episodes of out-of-control eating. The difference is that binge eaters don't purge their bodies of excess calories.

Eating is one of life's great pleasures. In this chapter we are concerned with the difficulties that people have controlling their food intake. Each year millions of people are affected by serious eating disorders. The vast majority—more than 90%—of those afflicted with eating disorders are adolescents and young adult women. One reason that women in this age group are particularly vulnerable to eating disorders is their tendency to go on strict diets to achieve an "ideal" figure. Stringent dieting plays a key role in triggering many eating disorders. The damaging effects of eating disorders represent personal problems for those who have them, but preoccupation with thinness is also, to some extent, a social problem because of the widespread positive value attached to avoiding being fat and having an "ideal" figure. A manifestation of this social problem is the advertising of food, clothes, and life-style products by commercial enterprises (Sobal & Maurer, 1999). The prevailing thinness-centered approach in our society may in certain respects be somewhat short-sighted. Body weights above the "ideal" level are not equally hazardous to health (while extreme rates of obesity may be dangerous, there is less evidence that moderate degrees of overweight are harmful) (Ernsberger & Koletsky, 1999).

Anorexia Nervosa

In order to be diagnosed with **anorexia nervosa,** an individual must refuse to allow his or her body weight to be more than 85% of the weight considered to be normal on height and weight charts. Table 5-2 lists the diagnostic criteria for this disorder. The main characteristic of those with anorexia nervosa, besides their excessive thinness, is an exaggerated desire to be thin and a conviction that, however thin they may appear to others, their bodies are too large. The primary feature is this obsessive preoccupation with body image and with losing weight. People with anorexia nervosa are morbidly afraid of becoming fat.

Early in the course of the condition, a patient begins to restrict many food items, as is typical of most dieters. As the disorder progresses, though, the anorexic's menu becomes grossly constricted and rigid. Minor variation in meal content can produce tremendous anxiety. Unlike the average dieter, the anorexic continues the pursuit of thinness to an extreme and becomes dependent on the daily registration of weight loss. This fuels even more restrictive dieting. Extreme dieting is often complicated by other weight-reducing behaviors. Exercise is frequently compulsive and hyperactivity in underweight patients is a cu-

---

Table 5-2

Diagnostic Criteria for Anorexia Nervosa

1. Refusal to keep body weight at or above 85% of the generally recognized normal level for age and height
2. Intense fear of gaining weight or becoming fat, even when underweight
3. Disturbance in experience of body weight or shape, undue influence of these factors on self-esteem, or denial of the seriousness of the health risks of the current low body weight
4. If menstruation has begun, the absence of three consecutive menstrual cycles

Two types of anorexia are recognized: (1) the restricting type in which the main focus is on restricting food intake, and (2) the binge-eating/purging type in which there is regular binge eating followed by purging by vomiting, laxatives, etc.

Source: Adapted from DSM-IV

---

rious but often-encountered concomitant. Weakness, muscle aches, sleep disturbances, and gastrointestinal complaints, including constipation and bloating after meals, are common physical findings. Disruption of menstruation, reflecting endocrine dysfunction, is present in females, and lack of sexual interest is frequently observed in both males and females.

As mentioned earlier, a distinguishing psychological feature is the irrational fear of becoming fat, frequently in concert with a grossly distorted view of oneself as overweight. This persists even in the presence of severe emaciation and in the face of life-threatening medical sequelae. The patient often exhibits a phobic response to food, particularly fatty and other calorically dense items. Anorexics develop an obsessive preoccupation with food, eating, dieting, weight, and body shape, and they frequently exhibit ritualistic behaviors involving choosing, preparing, and ingesting meals. An example of ritualistic behavior is cutting food into very small pieces or chewing each bite a specific number of times.

Unlike the true reduction of appetite in depression, in anorexia there is a conscious and deliberate refusal of food. Those with this disorder are not only preoccupied with weight regulation, they also take pride in their ability to control the urge to eat. They do not seem to perceive the consequences of anorexia—weight loss, cessation of menstruation, and other symptoms—as important, or they are very defensive about the subject. Despite this apparent lack of concern about the consequences of their behavior, anorexia disturbs the body's functioning in many ways. It may result in retarded bone growth, anemia, dry skin, low body temperature and basal metabolism rate, and slow heart rate. If there is vomiting, a number of other serious health effects are likely. One of these, low level of serum potassium, may cause cardiac arrhythmia, a tendency toward an irregular heart rhythm that can result in death. Vomiting can also damage the esophagus and tooth enamel. Anorexia nervosa is a serious disorder: up to 20% of anorexia patients who do not respond to therapy are likely to die as a result of the disorder.

Anorexia nervosa rarely begins before puberty. Its first appearance seems to occur in two peak periods, around age 14 and around age 18, although the mean age when it is first diagnosed is 17. The outcome tends to be poorer for those who develop anorexia in the earlier age period. Anorexia is much more common in girls than boys; about 90% of those diagnosed with the disorder are female.

Wendy's case is typical of anorexia:

Wendy was 16 years old when her parents insisted that she be seen by the family pediatrician because of severe weight loss. Wendy was 5 feet, 3 inches tall and weighed 78 pounds. She had been dieting for the past two years because she had decided, at a weight of 110 pounds, that she was too fat. Wendy had begun menstruating at age 13, but she had not had a menstrual period for the past 1 1/2 years. She indicated that she was not concerned that her periods had stopped, but she was extremely concerned that she was still too fat.

Over the course of the past two years' dieting efforts, Wendy had become increasingly strict about how much she would eat, and each mealtime ended in a battle with her parents over her food intake. . . . Typically, her daily food consumption consisted of an egg, a small portion of bread, a carrot stick, and some water or diet soda. . . . As Wendy grew thinner, she became increasingly preoccupied with planning how much she was going to eat each day, and with how to avoid situations in which she would be pressured to eat more than she had planned to. Wendy had begun an exercise program at the time she started dieting and her daily exercises, carried out in a strictly ordered routine, became lengthier and more strenuous each day. Wendy always swam a given number of laps four times a day. During the summer, she swam these laps outdoors even in lightning or thunder. Over time, even though feeling exhausted, she added an extra swimming session at night without her parents' knowledge, [climbing] out of her second-story bedroom window to go outside to swim. Wendy felt extremely hungry, tired, and irritable almost all of the time. She was also preoccupied with thoughts of food and how she looked. Her weight continued to drop, and her schoolwork suffered. She stopped interacting with the few girls she had talked to at school and became quite isolated from others.

Despite the efforts of her parents and her pediatrician, Wendy refused to stop dieting. She indicated that she felt extremely good about herself, knowing that she could control her bodily urges to the extent that she would not eat when hungry, and that she could exercise strenuously even though she felt exhausted. Eventually, Wendy was hospitalized for treatment, despite her strong objections that there was nothing wrong with her. Her weight at the time of hospitalization was 68 pounds. (Leon & Dinklage, 1989, p. 206)

Although Wendy's behavior of combining low-calorie intake and a great deal of exercise is typical for girls and women with anorexia, the relatively small number of men with this diagnosis seem to rely mainly on excessive exercise as a weight-loss or weight-control strategy (Touyz et al., 1993). In recent years, there has been an increased recognition that, while the figures for men are much less than for women, the problem of eating disorders in men is sufficiently large to merit increased clinical and research attention.

Epidemiology and Risk Factors Available evidence suggests that the prevalence of eating disorders has increased over the past 50 years (Steiner & Lock, 1998). The increase may be as high as threefold, with perhaps as many as 1 case per 100 girls 16 to 18 years of age (Goldstein, 1999). This persistent and willful restriction of food in-

take can lead to death in 5% to 7% of patients within 10 years of the onset of the disorder.

Causes Although the specific causes of anorexia nervosa are not known, both personality factors and aspects of the environment are believed to play a role.

Personality Factors There is a high frequency of perfectionism and obsessive-compulsive behavior in anorexia that seems to remain stable over time and is not a function of the weight problems. In one group of adolescents studied over a 6-year period, almost one-third of those who were anorexic also met the criteria for obsessive-compulsive disorder at some time during the study as compared to 8% of those in the control group (Rastam et al., 1996). Obsessive-compulsive symptoms were associated with a more negative outcome and predicted the eventual outcome much better than the eating disorder symptoms alone. Although people with anorexia are also likely to be depressed, the depression does not seem to precede the eating disorder or to continue after the eating disorder improves.

Family Factors Eating disorders tend to run in families, with female relatives most often affected (Strober et al., 2000). This raises the possibility that genetic factors may predispose some people to develop the disorders. However, behavioral and environmental influences may also play a role. For example, mothers who are overly concerned about their daughters' weight and physical attractiveness may put the girls at increased risk of developing an eating disorder. In addition, girls with eating disorders may have fathers and brothers who are overly critical of their weight. Although there are many unanswered questions, the available evidence suggests that abnormal family relationships play a role in anorexia nervosa and other eating disorders (Ward et al., 2000).

Cultural Factors Eating disorders are found most often among Caucasians, but they also affect African Americans and other racial and ethnic groups. People pursuing professions or activities that emphasize thinness—like modeling, gymnastics, wrestling, and long-distance running—are more susceptible to them (see Figure 5-5). Elite female athletes, particularly those in sports emphasizing leanness, are at especially high risk (Otis et al., 1997). Special populations, such as ballet dancers, are also at high risk for the development of anorexia (S. Abraham, 1996). In a study of more than 600 elite female athletes in Norway, for example, 15% met the criteria for an eating disorder. In a study of female collegiate gymnasts, only 22% of the group reported eating behaviors that could be classified as normal or not disordered (Sundgot, 1994).

Thinness bias is pervasive in the United States and many other countries. This bias is manifested in everyday interactions between teachers and students and coaches and athletes, on television screens, and in the pages of

Figure 5–5   Several groups at special risk for anorexia because of pressure for thinness include female gymnasts, ballet dancers, and entertainers. Outstanding gymnast Christy Heinrich, shown here 5 years before her death and before anorexia became a problem, ultimately died from the effects of the disorder. At the time of her death at 22 from multiple organ system failure, she weighed only 60 pounds.

SOURCE: *New York Times*, July 28, 1994, p. C19. Article by Eric Pace.

Figure 5-6 A photograph illustrating fashion trends.
SOURCE: *New York Times Magazine,* January 10, 1999.

magazines. The photograph in Figure 5–6 appeared not in an article about eating disorders, but in the "Style" section of *The New York Times Magazine.* Esthetic biases favoring slender figures are deeply ingrained in our society (Austin, 1999).

Treatment A wide variety of treatments, influenced by most of the theoretical perspectives covered in this book, have been used with anorexia. Treatments used have ranged from biologically based approaches involving antidepressants, antianxiety drugs, and appetite stimulants to psychotherapy and family therapy based on psychodynamic principles, behavioral and cognitive-behavioral therapies, and educational therapies such as nutritional education. Most of the treatment approaches use a combination of medication and behavior modification or psychotherapy in a hospital setting.

Thus far, the usefulness of medication in reliably changing eating behavior, assisting in weight gain, or altering distortions in body image or fear of weight gain has not been demonstrated in controlled studies. Behavior therapy was originally used as a contingency management or operant technique of rewarding eating in order to normalize eating behavior and promote weight gain. As understanding of the cognitive distortions in anorexia has grown, the use of cognitive interventions has increased. These seek to replace the thoughts that exacerbate anorexic behavior with thoughts that promote healthful eating and activity patterns. The cognitive studies available are mainly single-subject designs. Thus far, there is no strong evidence that behavioral treatments produce more than small gains, and the evidence for the usefulness of cognitive interventions has been disappointing. A study that compared the effects of family therapy with those of individual therapy, each combined with dietary and medical treatment, showed that they were comparable in reducing dissatisfaction with body shape and eating-related family conflict (Robin et al., 1995). However, of the two approaches, the family therapy approach produced greater weight gain. When the researchers reassessed the status of these subjects and their families a year later, they found that the improvements were still evident.

Anorexia nervosa, like all eating disorders, is most successfully treated when diagnosed early. Nutritional rehabilitation is important and includes restoring weight, normalizing eating patterns, achieving normal perceptions of hunger and satiety, and correcting any consequences of malnutrition. Psychological treatment is used to help patients understand and cooperate with their nutritional and physical rehabilitation, change dysfunctional behaviors and attitudes, improve interpersonal and social functioning, and deal with psychological conflicts that may reinforce or maintain eating disorder behaviors. Once malnutrition has been corrected and weight gain started, psychotherapy can be useful in helping patients understand what they have been through, the family and cultural antecedants of their condition, and how to cope more effectively with stress (*Practice Guidelines for the Treatment of Patients With Eating Disorders*, 2000). There is evidence that women with eating disorders often cope less effectively with stress than women without eating disorders. Negative moods and mild stressors may increase maladaptive behavior associated with eating disorders (Troop, 1998). A recent study showed that both patients with anorexia nervosa and bulimia nervosa differ significantly from people who do not have eating disorders with regard to core beliefs and attitudes that do not appear to have anything directly to do with eating and nutrition (Leung et al., 1999).

A major challenge to clinicians who treat eating disorders is the patient's tendency to deny that they have a problem. Because of this denial, people with anorexia may not receive clinical help until they already have become dangerously thin and malnourished. The longer abnormal eating behavior persists, the more difficult it is to overcome the disorder and its effects on the body. Families and friends offering support and encouragement can play a valuable role in the success of a treatment program. Another treatment challenge concerns metabolic changes associated with the disorder. Just to maintain a stable weight, individuals with anorexia may actually have to consume more calories than someone of similar weight and age without an eating disorder.

Because little is known about the causes of anorexia nervosa, treatment targeted at etiological factors is often not possible. In some cases, inpatient treatment is needed for very emaciated patients, those weighing less than 75% of average weight. Psychotherapy is usually directed at dysfunctional thoughts about eating and interpersonal relationships, the therapeutic task being aimed at helping the patient to balance self-acceptance with perceptions of acceptance by others. Anxiety and depression are frequent in anorexia and, thus, are topics with which therapists deal. Effective strategies to prevent relapse are also dealt with after the patient appears to be on the road to recovery.

Bulimia Nervosa

The two most essential characteristics of the eating disorder **bulimia nervosa** are binge eating and attempts to

Table 5-3
Diagnostic Criteria for Bulimia Nervosa

1. Frequently occurring episodes of binge eating that are characterized by both (a) eating an amount of food that is definitely larger than most people would eat within a similar specific period of time and in similar circumstances and (b) a sense of lack of control over eating during the overeating episode
2. Recurrent behavior to compensate for the overeating and prevent weight gain, including vomiting, laxatives, fasting, or excessive exercise
3. The occurrence of both the binge eating and the compensatory behaviors at least twice a week for at least a 3-month period
4. Self-evaluation that is overinfluenced by weight and body shape
5. Bulimic behavior that does not occur only during episodes of anorexia nervosa

Two types of bulimia nervosa are recognized; (1) the purging type, in which vomiting or doses of laxatives are used during the current episode, and (2) the nonpurging type, in which fasting or excessive exercise, but not purging, is used to prevent weight gain.

Source: Adapted from DSM-IV

compensate for the weight gain that this might cause through inappropriate methods. *Binge eating* means eating much more food in a relatively short period of time (less than 2 hours) than is considered normal. Binge eaters don't seem to crave one specific type of food such as chocolate or peanuts; instead, they simply consume an abnormally large amount of food while feeling a loss of control over their eating behavior. This feeling is especially likely to occur during the beginning stages of the disorder. During the binge, those with the disorder may feel as if they are in a frenzied state. The loss of control is not total, however. For example, if the person is "caught" during the bingeing—as, for example, when another person unexpectedly enters the room—the eating behavior may stop immediately. Table 5-3 lists the criteria for the diagnosis of bulimia nervosa. Although those with this disorder feel ashamed of their behavior, they also feel unable to resist binge eating. Like anorexia, bulimia is much more common in women than in men. However, bulimia usually begins somewhat later than anorexia nervosa, typically between late adolescence and early adulthood. It seems to occur at about the same rate in most industrialized countries and has been reported in various ethnic groups. Table 5-4 contrasts the cognitive and behavioral features of anorexia nervosa and bulimia nervosa.

People with bulimia nervosa generally take in a very large number of calories in the binge period. Their intake

Table 5–4				
Cognitive and Behavioral Features of Anorexia Nervosa and Bulimia Nervosa				
	Anorexia Nervosa		Bulimia Nervosa	
Cognitive and Behavioral Features	Restricting Type	Bulimic Type	Purging Type	Nonpurging Type
Fear of obesity	Strong	Strong	Strong	Strong
Dietary/eating-habit control	Strong	Variable	Variable	Weak
Compensatory Behavior				
Exercise	Strong	Strong	Variable	Strong
Self-induced vomiting	Slight	Strong	Strong	Weak
Laxative abuse	Slight	Strong	Strong	Weak
Body image distortion	Strong	Variable	Slight	Slight

of 2,000 to 5,000 calories during a typical binge is up to twice what the average person consumes in a day. One way caloric intake is increased is that binge eaters tend to consume high-calorie items such as fast foods and rich desserts during the binge periods. They then try to control any weight gain that might result from their high caloric intake in one of two ways: either by removing the food quickly from their systems by vomiting or the inappropriate use of laxatives, or by excessive exercise to compensate for the additional calories. Of these two weight control strategies, the use of purging (or ridding the system of the excess calories through forced vomiting or laxative use) is the most common. This is referred to as the **binge-purge cycle.**

Most of those diagnosed with this disorder maintain a roughly average weight. Lisa's case is characteristic of bulimia:

Lisa became bulimic at the age of 18. Her strange eating behavior began when she started to diet. Although she dieted and exercised in order to lose weight, periodically she ate huge amounts of food and attempted to counter the effects of the extra calories and to maintain her normal weight by forcing herself to vomit.

Lisa often felt like an emotional powder keg, by turns angry, frightened, and depressed. Sometimes she stole things on impulse; sometimes she drank too much. Sometimes she couldn't stop eating for hours. Unable to understand her own behavior, she thought no one else would either. She felt isolated and lonely. Typically, when things were not going well, she would be overcome with an uncontrollable desire for sweets. She literally ate pounds of candy and cake at a time, and often didn't stop until she was exhausted or in severe pain. Then, overwhelmed with guilt and disgust, she would force herself to vomit.

Her eating habits so embarrassed her that she kept them secret until, depressed by her mounting problems, she attempted

suicide. Luckily, she didn't succeed. While recuperating in the hospital, she was referred to an eating disorder clinic where she became involved in group therapy. There she received the understanding and help she so desperately needed from others who had bulimia.

Family and friends may have difficulty detecting bulimia in someone they know. Many with the disorder remain at normal body weight or above because of their frequent purges following binges, which can range from once or twice a week to several times a day. Dieting heavily after episodes of bingeing and purging is common. Many anorexic individuals later develop bulimia.

Clinicians have noted certain differences between anorexia and bulimia that seem related to underlying personality characteristics. Anorexia nervosa patients frequently are described as being inflexible, rigid, and stubborn, whereas the bingeing and purging behavior of bulimia nervosa patients are suggestive of problems stemming from poor impulse control and inadequate regulation of diet.

Epidemiology and Risk Factors   Since bulimia nervosa was first described in the clinical literature in the late 1970s, it is not surprising that there have been few epidemiological studies. However, there is some reason to believe that approximately 4% to 9% of high school and college aged students show some symptoms of bulimia and that vomiting is a very widely used response to bingeing (Romano, 1999). Table 5-5 lists major methods of weight control identified in one sample of bulimic women.

As with anorexia nervosa, there is a high incidence of family discord and negative mood states (e.g., depression) in the families of bulimic individuals. In contrast to anorexia, many patients with bulimia do not seek clinical help until their 20s and 30s, often having suffered with the condition for a number of years. Males appear to be

Table 5-5	
Methods of Weight Control and Their Frequency of Use in Bulimic Women	
Method	Percentage Using Method
1. Vomiting	100
2. Dieting	95
3. Excessive exercise	83
4. Laxative use	58
5. Diet pills	40
Source: Cavanaugh & Lemberg, 1999	

affected more frequently by bulimia nervosa than by anorexia nervosa, representing 10% to 15% of cases. For both men and women, anxiety, impulsivity, and especially depression are frequently observed in cases of bulimia, as are problems related to substance use (Romano, 1999).

As we have seen, there are some similarities among individuals with anorexia and bulimic problems. However, in bulimia the individual is likely to have a more accurate perception of body image than in anorexia and is more likely to acknowledge abnormal eating patterns. Bulimics also are more likely to be in a relationship or to be married than persons suffering from anorexia nervosa. In some respects, the pattern of seeking comfort and escape in binge eating can be compared with seeking relief from anxiety through the use of alcohol or drugs.

While binge eating is quite common among college women, clinically significant bulimic behavior is not. And even when the criteria for bulimic behavior are met, the condition may not be long lasting. Although bulimia is sometimes described as an epidemic on college campuses, that is not true unless one is referring to self-reported overeating with or without occasional purging. Although two-thirds of college women report eating binges, these are not as severe or as frequent as those of bulimics, and they are not usually accompanied by self-induced vomiting or the use of laxatives. Only 1.3% of college women can be classified as bulimic (Schotte & Stunkard, 1987).

The frequent self-induced vomiting used as a method of weight control in bulimia can have serious long-term health effects. For instance, it may eventually lead to permanent loss of tooth enamel. The frequent use of certain methods to induce vomiting—such as taking syrup of ipecac—can also result in serious cardiac problems, especially related to heart rhythm, and can contribute to loss of bone density. The chronic use of laxatives can result in changes in the electrolyte balance in body fluid, which may also contribute to serious and sometimes fatal medical problems such as cardiac arrhythmia.

Causes A number of personal variables have been identified as risk factors for eating disorders. These include low self-esteem, distorted body image, and general psychopathology. In addition, stress seems to play a role in the development of symptoms of eating disorder in those who may already be vulnerable because of personal factors. More negative life events in the past year, especially those involving disruption of family or social relationships, have been found in young females who develop bulimia nervosa than are present in a comparable control group (Welch et al., 1997). Some researchers have also suggested that childhood sexual abuse can be a nonspecific vulnerability factor that may be related to eating disorders, particularly bulimia, although this link has been disputed by others. In those who already have the disorder, stress seems to play a role in precipitating binges. Pressures at work or school or problems with personal relationships often precede the onset of a binge.

Binge eating that characterizes bulimia is likely to begin during or after an episode of dieting. This means that many people are at risk. Dieting among adolescents is very common, although researchers have concluded that most young people who diet already fall within the normal weight range. One survey of a representative sample of young people in Australia found that almost half of the girls and over 10% of the boys could be classified as dieters (Patton et al., 1997). Within this group, about 1 in 6 of the girls and 1 in 10 of the boys were classified as extreme dieters who were very concerned about weight gain. The extreme dieters were very likely to report high levels of depression and anxiety in addition to their dieting behavior.

Concerns about body image are characteristic of those with both anorexia and bulimia. In the United States, concern about body image is more common among White adolescents than among the African American adolescent group. Adolescent White girls are more than twice as likely as Black girls to see themselves as overweight (Neff et al., 1997). White female high school students were more than six times as likely as Black female students to use pills and vomiting as a way to control their weight. Although eating disorders have typically been defined as an adolescent problem, evidence suggests that concerns about body image appear before puberty and may precede the onset of some eating disorders (Sands et al., 1997). Boys and girls seem to respond to these concerns somewhat differently—boys by increased physical activity and girls by dieting or the control of eating.

Some genetic factors may also enhance risk for bulimia. There is a higher frequency of pathology in the families of those diagnosed with bulimia than in comparable groups (Patano et al., 1997). Other researchers have found a higher incidence of both mood disorders and alcoholism in relatives of bulimic individuals. This has led to a theory that dysfunction of serotonin, a neurotransmitter associated with depression, may be a vulnerability factor.

Treatment Antidepressant drugs, together with a variety of cognitive and behavioral techniques, have been used to treat bulimia. The cognitive and behaviorally based treatments focus on breaking the binge-purge cycle, either by preventing binges or by preventing purges. The treatments often involve self-monitoring (keeping records of antecedents and consequences related to binge eating and purging), relaxation training, identifying and modifying cognitive distortions and developing enhanced feelings of self-efficacy, and altering the environment as necessary.

Among psychological treatments, both individual and group cognitive-behavioral therapy seems to be the most effective in the treatment of bulimia nervosa (Leung et al., 1999; Walsh et al., 1997). For example, in one randomized trial (a trial where patients were randomly assigned to treatment conditions), cognitive-behavioral therapy was found to be superior to supportive psychotherapy in reducing both binge eating and frequency of vomiting in the bulimia patients. Cognitive-behavioral therapy also produced better results than the antidepressant medication fluoxetine alone. The combination of cognitive-behavioral therapy and fluoxetine was only slightly more effective than the use of cognitive-behavioral therapy without the medication.

Another study that compared different periods of treatment with antidepressants alone or in combination with cognitive-behavioral therapy found that if the medication was continued for 24 weeks, the results a year later showed that the combination of medication and cognitive-behavioral therapy had been the most effective treatment, producing a 95% decrease in binge eating (Agras et al., 1994). Figure 5-7 shows the results of the study. These findings also made clear that antidepressants alone were not an effective treatment if used only for 16 weeks, although if the medication was continued for 24 weeks, a decrease in binge eating of more than 60% was still seen a year later. This decrease is similar to the result found a year later for cognitive-behavioral therapy alone.

An important question in the treatment of all disorders is how well the former patients do over time. A review of 88 studies of female patients treated for bulimia found that 5 to 10 years following treatment, about half the women had recovered, 30% had relapsed at least once,

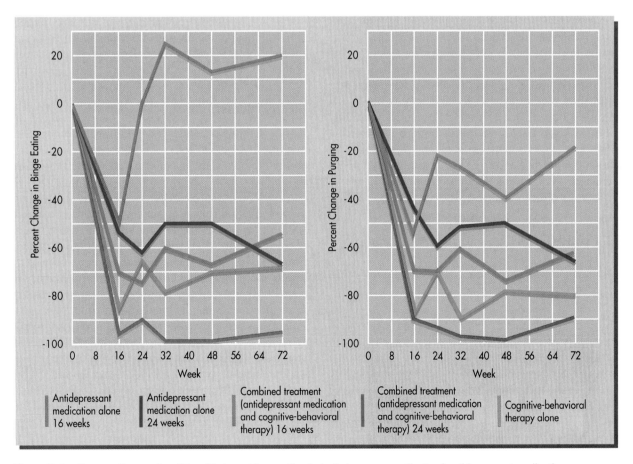

Figure 5-7   Comparative results of the effects on binge eating in bulimia nervosa patients of antidepressant medication, cognitive-behavioral therapy, and treatment combining both therapies.

Source: Agras et al., 1994, pp. 179–183.

and about 20% had improved so little that they still met the diagnostic criteria for bulimia (Keel & Mitchell, 1997). The overall risk of having a relapse seemed to decline after 4 years, but a history of substance abuse, certain personality traits (such as impulsivity), and a lack of commitment to achieving therapeutic change contributed to a poorer long-term outcome (Keel et al., 1999; Mussell et al., 2000).

Binge Eating

Binge eating is a relatively recently described problem characterized by episodes of bingeing described earlier *without* the use of compensatory behaviors, such as purging, that are seen in bulimia nervosa. Two common patterns characterize binge eating: compulsively snacking over long intervals (such as all day at work or all evening in front of the computer or television) and/or a consumption of large amounts of food at one time, significantly beyond the requirements to satisfy normal hunger. Binge eating disorder often leads to problems with weight regulation and sometimes obesity.

In clinical practice it may be difficult to distinguish between a binge eating disorder and nonpurging bulimia nervosa. While there is not much hard data concerning the epidemiology and risk factors related to binge eating, it may be fairly common, affecting perhaps 1% of the population. One recent study found that binge eating women experienced more negative affect (depression and anxiety) than non–binge eating women (Greeno et al., 2000). This might suggest that treatment approaches should focus especially on helping binge eaters learn to cope more adaptively with poor mood. In addition to mood, situational and cognitive factors often play important roles in binge eating. Table 5-6 summarizes several factors that have been identified (Stickney et al., 1999).

Sleep Disorders

> *O Sleep, O gentle Sleep!*
> *Nature's soft nurse, how have I*
> *Frightened thee,*
> *That thou no more wilt weigh mine eyelids down*
> *And steep my senses in forgetfulness?*
>
> Shakespeare: *Henry IV III.i.*

Like eating disorders, **sleep disorders** involve very basic processes of life. Sleep is as essential for well-being as food and water. The scientific and clinical aspects of sleep and problems associated with it have been studied intensively only during the last 50 years or so. Until the 1950s most people thought of sleep as a passive, dormant part of our daily lives. Many misperceptions persist about what sleep is, needs regarding sleep, and the criteria by which

Table 5-6
Triggers of Binge Eating

1. Particular stressful situations
2. Particular upsetting thoughts
3. Feeling guilt about something one has done
4. Feeling socially isolated or excluded
5. Worries about responsibilities, problems, or the future
6. Boredom

people decide whether they have a sleep problem. For example, while the average adult needs 8 or 9 hours of sleep a night, most only get 7 or fewer hours. (A person's sleep needs are biologically determined; some people need only 6 hours a night, others need 10, but for most adults, at least 8 hours a night is required to function optimally.) Many people report being so sleepy during the day that it interferes with their daily activities. Falling asleep at the wheel of an automobile is a common cause of automobile accidents. Drowsy drivers can fall asleep with little or no warning. Drowsiness can also result in industrial accidents, decreased productivity, and interpersonal problems. While many problems related to sleep are minor, the number of major clinical problems is greater than most people might expect. Table 5-7 offers suggestions for people with sleep problems.

Sleep Processes

Nerve-signaling chemicals called *neurotransmitters* control whether we are asleep or awake by acting on different groups of nerve cells, or neurons, in the brain. Neurons in the brainstem, which connects the brain with the spinal cord, produce neurotransmitters such as serotonin and norepinephrine that keep some parts of the brain active while we are awake. Other neurons at the base of the brain begin signaling when we fall asleep. These neurons appear to "switch off" the signals that keep us awake. Research also suggests that a chemical called *adenosine* builds up in our blood while we are awake and causes drowsiness. This chemical gradually breaks down while we sleep.

During sleep, we usually pass through five phases: Stages 1, 2, 3, 4 and REM (rapid eye movement). These stages progress in a cycle from Stage 1 to REM sleep, then the cycle starts over again with Stage 1. We spend almost 50% of our total sleep time in Stage 2 sleep, about 20% in REM sleep, and the remaining 30% in the other stages. Infants, by contrast, spend about half of their sleep time in REM sleep.

During Stage 1, which is light sleep, we drift in and out of sleep and can be awakened easily. Our eyes move very slowly and muscle activity slows. People awakened from Stage 1 sleep often remember fragmented visual images. When we enter Stage 2 sleep, our eye movements stop

Table 5–7

Suggestions for Avoiding Sleep Problems

Many people have sleep problems that may be minor, but are troubling to them. Here are some tips for the sleep deprived:

1. Avoid caffeine, nicotine, and alcohol in the late afternoon and evening.
2. Exercise regularly, but do it at least 3 hours before bedtime.
3. Establish a relaxing bedtime routine like taking a hot bath or meditating.
4. Use your bed only for sleep and sex, not for reading or watching television.
5. Get out of bed if you don't fall asleep within half an hour.
6. Go to sleep and wake up at the same time every day, even on weekends.
7. Avoid daytime naps if you have trouble falling asleep at night.

and our brain waves (fluctuations of electrical activity that can be measured by electrodes) become slower, with occasional bursts of rapid waves called *sleep spindles*. In Stage 3, extremely slow brain waves called *delta waves* begin to appear, interspersed with smaller, faster waves. By Stage 4, the brain produces delta waves almost exclusively. It is very difficult to wake someone during Stages 3 and 4, which together are called *deep sleep*. There is no eye movement or muscle activity. People awakened during deep sleep do not adjust immediately and often feel groggy and disoriented for several minutes after they wake up. Some children experience bedwetting, night terrors, or sleepwalking during deep sleep.

When we switch into **REM sleep,** our breathing becomes more rapid, irregular, and shallow, our eyes jerk rapidly in various directions, and our limb muscles become temporarily paralyzed. Our heart rate increases, our blood pressure rises, and males develop penile erections. When people awaken during REM sleep, they often describe bizarre and illogical tales—dreams (see Box 5-2).

The first REM sleep period usually occurs about 70 to 90 minutes after we fall asleep. A complete sleep cycle takes 90 to 110 minutes on average. The first sleep cycles each night contain relatively short REM periods and long periods of deep sleep. As the night progresses, REM sleep periods increase in length while deep sleep decreases. By morning, people spend nearly all their sleep time in Stages 1, 2, and REM.

People awakened after sleeping more than a few minutes are usually unable to recall the last minutes before they fell asleep. This sleep-related form of amnesia is the reason people often forget telephone calls or conversations they've had in the middle of the night. It also explains why we often do not remember our alarms ringing in the morning if we go right back to sleep after turning them off.

Sleep and sleep-related problems play a role in a large number of human disorders. For example, problems like stroke and asthma attacks tend to occur more frequently during the night and early morning, perhaps due to changes in hormones, heart rate, and other characteris-

tics associated with sleep. Sleep also affects some kinds of epilepsy in complex ways. Neurons that control sleep interact closely with the immune system. As anyone who has had the flu knows, infectious diseases tend to make us feel sleepy.

Sleeping problems occur in almost all people with mental disorders, including those with depression and schizophrenia. People with depression, for example, often awaken in the early hours of the morning and find themselves unable to get back to sleep. The amount of sleep a person gets also strongly influences the symptoms of mental disorders.

Neuroscientists are interested in sleep because it is a process influenced by multiple bodily systems, as well as by our life-styles and anxieties. Disturbances in brain function (e.g., its electrical activity), hormonal secretions (e.g., *melatonin,* a hormone produced by the pineal gland in the center of the brain), and genetic factors (e.g., whether other family members have had certain problems in sleeping) all are potentially relevant to the treatment of sleep disorders.

Today, sleep researchers are studying many aspects of what takes place when we sleep, including circadian rhythm, the daily cycle of changes in bodily characteristics such as temperature, blood pressure, and hormonal secretions; stages of sleep, as reflected in brain wave patterns; brain processes correlated with dreaming; and genetic factors. Figure 2-6 showed brain wave patterns characteristic of different sleep stages. Valuable information about what goes on when we sleep is coming from neuroscience research conducted in sleep laboratories (see Figure 5-10), in which a number of biological processes are monitored while subjects sleep, a process called **polysomnography.** Through such sleep studies, researchers in the neurosciences have significantly contributed to an understanding of the complex processes involved in sleep.

Dyssomnias

Whether it is the sole problem or part of a more complex clinical picture, a sleep disorder can increase vulnerability to other difficulties (e.g., doing poorly in school).

Resilience and Vulnerability

Box 5–2

REM Sleep and Dreams

REM sleep was discovered in the sleep laboratory of Nathaniel Kleitman (1895–1999) at the University of Chicago in 1953 (Figure 5-8). Kleitman and his students noticed that there were regular periods of jerky eye movements during sleep. If awakened during these periods, people usually reported dreams. This did not happen during non-REM. Kleitman estimated that the average person dreamed a total of about 2 hours every night. This, and other evidence, suggested that sleep was an active process rather than a passive one. Kleitman not only recorded events correlated with the stages of sleep, he also stud- ied the effects of experimental variables on sleeping. For example, in an effort to see if human beings could adapt to a 28-hour day (he and his students were the first subjects studied), adults lived in Mammoth Cave, Kentucky, for over a month in 1938. Since the temperature in the cave was a constant 54 degrees and there was no natural light, there were no environmental cues for the time of day (see Figure 5-9). Kleitman found that while some subjects seemed to adapt satisfactorily to a 28-hour day, others could not. He also found that there was a slight but regular fluctuation in body temperature throughout the day. Peak efficiency on tasks occurred while body temperature was highest. Later in his career, Kleitman studied the effects of sleep deprivation. (He once stayed awake for over a week to see how he reacted to sleep deprivation). He found that forcing someone to stay awake is an effective form of torture and that individuals were very susceptible to confessing anything just to be allowed to sleep.

Figure 5-8   A photograph of Nathaniel Kleitman taken in 1961 when he was making some of his greatest contributions to sleep research and the development of scientific laboratories. Kleitman died in 1999 at the age of 104.

Source: *New York Times*, August 19, 1999, p. C26.

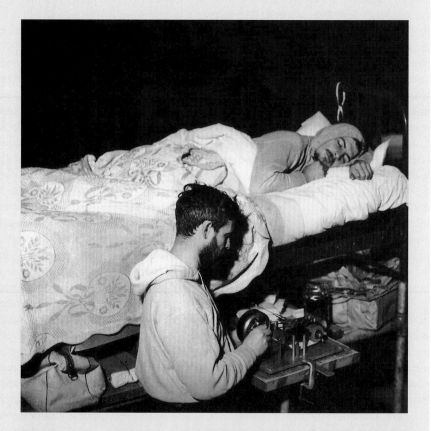

Figure 5-9   In a 1938 sleep experiment in Mammoth Cave, Kentucky, Dr. Nathaniel Kleitman checked on the restiveness of Bruce Richardson, an assistant.

Source: *New York Times*, August 16, 1999, p. C26.

Sleep disturbances affect about one-third of the U.S. population. Patients with sleep problems are concerned not only about the immediate distress and discomfort caused by inability to sleep, but also about the effects of their sleep deficit on family life, employment status, and general social adjustment. Sleep disorders accompany a number of forms of maladaptive behavior.

Dyssomnias and parasomnias are the two most widely studied types of sleep disorder. **Dyssomnias** involve abnormalities in the amount, quality, or timing of sleep, and

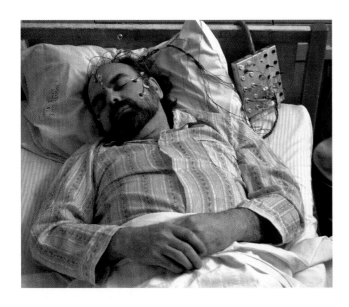

Figure 5-10 Electrodes attached to the face and head of this sleep laboratory study participant make it possible for researchers to monitor his brain and muscle activity during an entire night's sleep.

parasomnias are characterized by abnormal behavioral or physiological events occurring in association with sleep, specific sleep stages, or sleep-wake transitions.

DSM-IV describes these two sets of conditions as **primary sleep disorders** because they are not attributable to other mental or medical conditions or to substance abuse. There are many types of dyssomnias ranging from the related common insomnia to the less common **hypersomnia** in which there is excessive sleepiness marked by prolonged sleep at night (e.g., 12 hours) and/or long daytime periods of sleep.

Insomnia Almost everyone occasionally suffers from short-term insomnia. However, perhaps a third of the population has difficulty initiating or maintaining sleep and/or complains of not feeling restored or rested upon awakening (Culebras, 1996). These people have **insomnia** as defined by DSM-IV if the condition persists for at least a month. Irritability, anxiety, depression, difficulty in concentration, and preoccupation with their sleeping difficulties are common correlates of the condition. Insomnia often has a sudden onset related to a set of stressful circumstances. However, it persists after the upsetting experience has ended. It tends to be more prevalent with increasing age and among women. The course of insomnia is variable ranging from a month or two to a lifelong pattern and often occurs in the context of other problems such as anxiety and depression. When this happens, it is difficult to differentiate cause and effect. Individuals who complain of insomnia usually report being distressed by the inability to function properly during waking hours.

As a symptom, insomnia reflects the perception of inadequate sleep duration, continuity, or quality, or of difficulty of sleep initiation. The specific complaints are often quite idiosyncratic, some people emphasizing the inability to get to sleep in a reasonable period of time (e.g.,

30 minutes), while others have difficulty maintaining sleep (e.g., getting up in the middle of the night). Because it has only relatively recently been diagnosed as a psychiatric problem, there is insufficient information about its prevalence, course, and effective treatments. It is often difficult for a clinician to decide when complaints of sleep difficulties becomes a diagnosable disorder. The reason DSM-IV uses the criterion of the sleep difficulty lasting for a month or more is that a number of temporary occurrences can cause short-term sleep problems, for example, jet lag, recent stress, conflict, or environmental changes that lead to emotional arousal. However, some individuals seem to be especially susceptible to persistent sleep difficulties even if stress is not present. These people have a tendency to operate generally at a high level of emotional arousal. For example, this happens among people who are generally tense and anxious. A hallmark of the insomnia syndrome is the focused absorption of the individual with the sleep problem. While anxiety-prone individuals comprise a large group of insomniacs, another large group does not report the family and work problems seen in cases of anxiety and does not show the pervasive maladaptive behavior seen in many psychiatric patients. In varying degrees, emotional arousal, mood, sleep habits, circadian rhythm, and physiological processes can play roles in sleep disorders. For this reason, careful history taking is important in making a diagnosis.

Insomnia is only the most common type of sleep disorder. **Narcolepsy** is a condition of marked daytime sleepiness that seems to involve the sudden onset of REM for reasons that are poorly understood. When they fall asleep at night, people with narcolepsy go almost directly to REM sleep without going through all the stages of sleep that normally precede it. They may experience vivid, terrifying dreamlike states often referred to as **hypnogogic hallucinations.** They also may often experience **sleep paralysis** in which they cannot move or speak for a period of time. Narcolepsy seems to have a strong genetic component, especially with regard to a cluster of genes on chromosome number 6. In the following case, the narcolepsy involved daytime periods of sudden onset of sleep, but no hypnogogic experiences or paralysis:

Sidney is a 16-year-old high school student who recently developed a problem with excessive daytime sleepiness. Periodically during the day she suddenly falls asleep for several seconds to a minute. Often this occurs in the middle of a class. Sometimes she awakes to find the teacher standing over her calling her name and some of the other students laughing.

Several of the teachers have spoken to Sidney and her parents about her sleeping in class. She explains that she can't control the sleeping, but her teachers are reluctant to believe her. The sleep episodes have made it difficult for Sidney to keep up with her studies because she misses important information during class. Several of her friends are sympathetic and help by loaning her class notes. One friend says, "I can always tell when you're asleep. Your mouth drops open or your head falls on your chest."

Several other conditions are also related to physical dysfunction. For example, in **breathing-related sleep disorders,** individuals experience brief disruptions in breathing that may interrupt their sleeping several times a night. In **sleep apnea,** the breathing disruptions can last for 10 to 30 seconds. Sleep apnea tends to occur in overweight and older individuals.

Neuroscience research is contributing to the understanding of sleep, sleep disorders, and other clinical conditions by directing attention to the complexity of their determinants. Instead of simply looking for the biological cause of a clinical condition in a particular region of the brain, we now know that intricate brain circuits involving more than one area often require investigation in order to explain behavioral disturbances.

Treatment Given how recently sleep difficulties and their causes have received research attention, it is not surprising that much less is known about their treatment than is desirable. Medications are probably the most widely used treatment. While they can be helpful in the short term, they have drawbacks long term. Antianxiety drugs, such as *benzodiazepine*, can cause excessive sleepiness and lead to drug dependency. Longer-term cognitive and behavioral treatments are likely to be more effective. These range from exposing the person with insomnia to very bright light that might help readjust sleep patterns affected by a circadian rhythm disruption to changing bedtime to psychological treatments. Cognitive treatment for sleep problems is often helpful if the problems are related to the individual's unrealistic beliefs and expectations regarding sleep. For example, individuals who believe that

they should be asleep 10 minutes after going to bed and who do not meet this expectation might become unduly alarmed. Relaxation training (e.g., thinking about relaxing images or meditation) is also helpful. In some cases, short-term medication combined with psychological treatment is the clinical approach of choice.

Parasomnias

The **parasomnias** are marked by unusual behavioral or psychological events occurring during sleep. These conditions involve abnormal activation of bodily systems and processes (e.g., the automonic nervous system and sleep-wake transitions). Different parasomnias occur at different times during sleep and specific parasomnias often occur during specific sleep stages. People with parasomnia complain of unusual, disturbing experiences during sleep, rather than insomnia or sleepiness. In **nightmare disorder,** frightening dreams awaken the individual; the nightmares often involve lengthy, elaborate dream sequences that are terrifying and leave the individual fully awake and very anxious. Nightmares are common in children but are usually outgrown. The prevalence of persistent nightmares is not known, but when nightmares are persistent, the individual experiencing them is often motivated to seek help.

Another parasomnia is **sleep terror disorder.** Whereas nightmares tend to occur later in the night during REM sleep and produce vivid dream imagery and awakening, sleep terrors typically occur earlier in the sleep cycle and produce no dream recall or only single images that are not embedded in a dream narrative. Sleep terrors lead to partial awakening, confusion, disorientation, and a high level of autonomic activation. During typical episodes individuals abruptly sit up in bed screaming and crying, but are unresponsive to the efforts of others to awaken or comfort them.

Jeremy is a 25-year-old man who has been working long hours to finish an important project in his company. He often comes home late, feeling exhausted; eats a small dinner with his wife; and goes to bed.

In the last few weeks he has had several strange and disturbing experiences during the night. They usually occur 1 to 2 hours after he goes to sleep. His wife describes the episodes as follows: "Jeremy suddenly sits bolt upright in the bed, screams, and looks panicky." The first time it happened, Jeremy's wife was so startled that she woke up and jumped out of bed. She continues with her description: "I looked at Jeremy. His eyes were wide open, he was sweating and breathing fast. When I sat next to him I could feel his heart racing. I tried to find out what was wrong, but he wouldn't respond." A minute or two later Jeremy awoke and looked at his wife. When she asked him what was wrong he replied, "I feel terrified but I don't know why." She held him for a few minutes until he fell asleep again. In the morning Jeremy did not remember anything about the episode. The succeeding episodes were similar, but his wife became accustomed to them and was less startled.

In **sleepwalking disorder** there are repeated episodes of complex motor behavior initiated during sleep and the individual rises from his or her bed and walks about. This is most likely to happen in the first third of the sleep cycle. Sleepwalking is diagnosed in DSM-IV when it results in disruptions of important areas of life, such as interpersonal relationships, and when they are very upsetting. The activities performed during sleepwalking are usually routine and the individual may have no recollection of them in the morning.

Surveys of the prevalence of the parasomnias are rare. However, one recent study found that they are much more common in younger (aged 15–64) than older (65 and over) people and that 2.2% of the general population report having night terrors, 2% report sleepwalking and 4.2% report awakening in a confused state (Ohayan et al., 1999). It is important to note that these figures are based on interviews conducted in the community and not with groups of clinically diagnosed patients. An interesting finding is that depression is a frequent characteristic among people who report symptoms suggestive of parasomnia. Another study has found that people who have nightmares tend to be generally more anxious than those who do not (Zadra & Donderi, 2000). These findings and clinical observations suggest that sleep disorders are often not "pure," but rather result from complex interactions among psychological, physical, and situational factors. Their effective treatment will require determining the relevant factors and their interactions.

Psychophysiological Disorders

We have seen that both eating disorders and sleep disorders can be approached from a biopsychosocial perspective. These conditions usually do not involve worn out or damaged body parts (organs). In this section, we review a group of disorders in which problems involving specific bodily defects play important roles. Psychological difficulties can be important either in contributing to organ breakdown or adjusting to illness, even though psychological factors might not have played a role in causing the illness.

The body is made up of many millions of cells that, grouped together, form organs whose functions overlap to produce the body's systems. In this section, we review a number of bodily systems that have been approached from a biopsychosocial point of view and that are believed to be related to psychological processes.

Several groups of physical disorders in which personality and social factors may play a part have been studied over the years. There is no evidence that these conditions are directly attributable to the mental state of the individual or that a person suffering from one of these disorders has a completely different personality from a person suffering from another disorder or none at all. What is becoming increasingly clear, however, is that people—not just cells or organs—have diseases and that diseases must be studied in the context of physical, psychological, social, and cultural environments.

The term **psychophysiological disorder** has traditionally been applied to physical conditions in which psychologically meaningful events are closely related to bodily symptoms. Psychophysiological disorders might be thought of as end products of biopsychosocial processes. A large number of physical problems have been studied from a psychophysiological standpoint. These include disorders of the cardiovascular, respiratory, gastrointestinal, musculoskeletal, and genitourinary systems, as well as of the skin. Both clinical data and informal observations suggest the importance of psychological factors in many of these disorders. Consider the following case:

A 38-year-old mother of four children had a 5-year history of attacks of hives, a skin condition characterized by itching, burning, and stinging. During these attacks, areas of her face, trunk, waist, thighs, and arms would swell. There would be swelling even on her tongue and inside her respiratory passages. The attacks initially occurred about once a month, but at the time that she sought help, their frequency was closer to once every 4 or 5 days. Each attack was accompanied by depression and nausea.

An examination in an allergy clinic yielded negative results. After a psychiatrist placed the patient on tranquilizing drugs, the incidence of hives declined markedly. Further study indicated that her attacks usually occurred when she was having marital difficulties. When she was forced to face the possibility that her husband might leave her, she had an especially severe series of attacks. At one point she felt so overwhelmed by situational stresses that she was hospitalized. During this period she was protected from family tensions, and her hives disappeared completely. After leaving the hospital, the patient entered psychotherapy on a twice-weekly basis. In these sessions she was able to express her frustrations at leading a very restricted life because of her small children's demands and her husband's inability to see why she might need time away from home. Another point that emerged in therapy was the patient's inability to express to her husband how much she needed to have him acknowledge her value as a person, not just as the mother of his children. After several months of therapy, she felt able to tell her husband about her unfulfilled psychological needs as well as her resentment and frustration. At the time that therapy ended, she had been completely free from hives for 4 months.

In this case, it seems clear that this particular woman's skin condition was linked to events and conditions in her personal life. A major hurdle for the researcher is figuring out how to proceed from relationships that may be at work in a given case to generalizations that could apply to whole groups of people. Another major hurdle is finding out which aspects of people's lives (e.g., their personalities and experiences) contribute to health and illness. These are topics of particular importance in health psychology and behavioral medicine (see Box 5-1). While there are many unanswered questions, there is growing evidence that optimism, a sense of personal control, and feeling that there is meaning in one's life help people stay mentally and physically healthy. They seem to function as resources or buffers when stress arises (as, of course, it inevitably does) and when it becomes necessary to cope with serious illness (Taylor et al., 2000). Positive emotions and good health outcomes seem to be linked, though as yet the pathways are not well understood (Salovey et al., 2000). In general, negative emotional states are associated with unhealthy habits and patterns of physiological functioning, whereas positive emotional states are associated with healthier patterns of responding both in regard to cardiovascular activity and the immune system.

Two findings related to stress and the immune system illustrate the complexity of mind-body relationships involved in psychophysiological disorders. One is that there is considerable individual variability in the immune system response to stress. The other is that acute and chronic stress may have different impacts on the immune system. **Chronic stress** (such as marital problems, work-related stress, and bereavement) generally suppress important aspects of immune function, whereas **acute stress** (such as the stress of taking a final exam) can, for some people, have an activating effect on the functioning of the immune system (Olff, 1999). Complex interactions between the central nervous system and the endocrine glands seem to play roles in these relationships.

Cardiovascular Disorders

It is not the delicate, neurotic person who is prone to angina, but the robust, the vigorous in mind and body, the keen and ambitious man . . . whose engine is always at full speed ahead. (Sir William Osler, 1910)

This observation by an internist almost a hundred years ago concerning behavioral attributes that might predispose some people to develop angina pectoris, one type of coronary heart disease, illustrates the belief held by many clinicians of a link between behavioral patterns and coronary heart disease. The heart is a highly specialized muscle that pumps blood to the body. The blood flows through the body in an unending loop of blood vessels called the *circulatory system*. Each day the human heart beats approximately 100,000 times, delivering the equivalent of 4,300 gallons of blood to all parts of the body. The

arteries provide food and oxygen to the cells, while the veins remove carbon dioxide and waste products. The term **cardiovascular disorder** refers to a pathological condition that is related to the functioning of the heart and blood vessels. There is growing evidence that psychological and social factors play a role in two major cardiovascular disorders: coronary heart disease and hypertension. These conditions have caused over half of all deaths in the United States for more than 40 years.

Coronary Heart Disease The leading cause of death and disability in the United States is **coronary heart disease (CHD),** accounting for 40% of all deaths. A million new cases are identified annually. CHD is produced by lesions of the coronary arteries, the arteries that circulate blood within the heart itself. In CHD one or more of the three coronary arteries are partially or totally obstructed by deposits, called **plaques,** that thicken the arterial wall. When the coronary arteries become rigid and narrow as a result of these plaque deposits (referred to as **atherosclerosis**) the supply of blood to various portions of the heart muscle is temporarily or permanently cut off.

CHD takes a variety of forms. In **angina pectoris,** people suffer from periodic chest pains caused by an insufficient supply of oxygen-rich blood to the heart. A **myocardial infarction,** also caused by an insufficient blood supply to the heart, is more serious than angina pectoris because it involves a more complete curtailment of the heart's blood supply. When people speak of a heart attack, they are usually referring to a myocardial infarction.

A significant factor in heart attacks is stress. From the Stone Age to the present day, human beings have responded to environmental challenges and threats by releasing larger amounts of adrenal and other stress hormones followed by increases in heart rate and respiration and dilation of the vessels that transport blood to the muscles. Although these responses are adaptive and even lifesaving when the threat is a wolf pack, you would do better without them if you are stuck in a traffic jam. In fact, not only are these primitive physiological responses of little help in dealing with most modern-day problems, they may actually be related to the development of disease.

Stress seems to contribute to coronary disease through the body's general reactions to aversive stimulation. Under arousing conditions, hormonal substances called **catecholamines** are secreted. Two of the catecholamines, **epinephrine** and **norepinephrine,** accelerate the rate of arterial damage and ultimately can lead to heart attacks. Identifying which people are most likely to have heart attacks under high levels of stress and learning what steps lead from psychological stress to cardiac damage are both topics of current research. It is now recognized that this research needs to be sufficiently complex to incorporate the several factors that often interact in producing coronary symptoms. Table 5-8 lists factors that individually and in

Table 5-8	
Four Types of Coronary Heart Disease (CHD) Risk Factors	
Risk Factors	Examples
Bodily characteristics	Age, hypertension, cholesterol, obesity, heredity
Health habits	Smoking, alcohol use
Community, life-style, and cultural factors	Socioeconomic status, education
Personality	Anxiety, hostility, life goals

combination contribute to CHD risk, particularly in the context of stress. What is striking about these factors is the degree to which they pertain to several of the six theoretical perspectives described in Chapter 2. While all theoretical perspectives might not be helpful in a particular case of CHD, several of them, individually and in interaction, are likely to be helpful interpretatively in many individual cases.

One of the challenges confronting research on health outcomes is how to evaluate the particular contributions that several possibly pertinent factors make in bringing about illness. For example, people who have suffered major bouts of depression may be up to four times more likely than others to have a heart attack (Pratt et al., 1996). However, it is not clear why this is the case. One possibility is that depression is a severe reaction to stress and stress raises the risk of a heart attack. If depression plays a key role in bringing about heart attacks, treatment for depression might lower the likelihood of their occurrence (Musselman et al., 1998). The study by Pratt and his colleagues is especially valuable because, unlike previous studies of depression and CHD, it assessed depression prior to and independent of the occurrence of heart attacks. Its results are consistent with growing evidence that *both* biological and psychological risk factors need to be taken into account in predicting CHD. Established biological predictors include metabolic factors, high blood pressure, blood clotting factors, obesity, gender, and family history. Psychological factors that are increasingly turning up as predictors are depression, hostility, impulsivity, emotional instability, and cynicism. Important behavioral factors are smoking, self-care regarding health, and working habits (Marusic et al., 1999).

Sex Differences   There are important differences between coronary heart disease in men and women. While most middle-aged heart attack victims are men, heart attacks that occur in later life are a principal cause of death for both men and women. Heart disease is the leading cause of death in women after the age of 66; in men it is the leading killer beginning at age 39. Women often have

chest pains for a long time before a heart attack; in men, such pains more often mean a heart attack has already begun. Researchers are currently examining the reasons for these differences. There may be important biological differences between the sexes in the functioning and development of the heart and cardiovascular system. In addition, men and women differ in their temperaments and how they react to stress. For example, they may differ with regard to *cardiovascular activity*, the change from a resting baseline to an active cardiovascular condition. The active condition could involve a task that requires mental processes or physical exertion. One study found that while both men and women show about the same level of increased cardiovascular activity when harassed, women show more reactivity when confronted with a task that they must perform (Fichera & Andreassi, 1998). Within each sex, racial and ethnic differences may be significant, for example, more African American women die from heart disease than any other racial group.

Personal Life-Styles and CHD   Death due to CHD has decreased more than 35% in the last 40 years, and recently this decrease has accelerated. Factors that may be contributing to the decline in mortality are improved medical services, the development of coronary care units in hospitals, advances in surgical and medical treatment of CHD, and improved control of blood pressure. Life-style changes, such as less smoking, better eating habits, and increased physical fitness also seem to play an important preventive role.

Personal life-style patterns may be significant in development of CHD. Studies of twins living in the same community may play a valuable role in answering this question. A study conducted in Sweden (Liljefors & Rahe, 1970) provided a unique set of data about the relationships among CHD, personality, and life-style. The sample consisted of 32 pairs of identical male twins, 42 to 67 years of age, who were discordant for CHD—that is, only one member of each pair had a heart condition. Virtually all the twins had been raised together, at least until their early teens.

The twins' characteristic behavior patterns in four areas—devotion to work, lack of leisure, home problems, and life dissatisfactions—were assessed through interviews. The overall results are illustrated by a comparison of one of the pairs of twins. Although the twins were at the same hereditary risk, the twin with CHD had a high-pressure job during parts of the year and, because he was self-employed, may have experienced more stress because of concerns about the success of his business. He reported continually feeling that he lacked sufficient time for his tasks, and perhaps for this reason had fewer periods of relaxation than his twin. In addition, he seemed dissatisfied with his achievements and his ability to carry out his business dealings effectively, while his twin was relatively satisfied with his own progress. Since the twins examined were discordant for CHD, the researchers concluded that life-style as well as heredity is an important factor in the disease. Another study provided further support for this hypothesis (Kringlen, 1981).

On the basis of their clinical observations as cardiologists, Meyer Friedman and Ray Rosenman (1974) developed a theory about the existence of a heart attack–prone personality pattern. They thought that people who were habitually hurried, competitive, and hostile would tend to be prone to heart attacks. They labeled these people **Type A personalities.** People who lived less pressured and hard-driving lives they called **Type B personalities.**

Specially designed interviews and questionnaires have been used to assess Type A tendencies. One study showed that during 8 1/2 years of follow-up, Type A men had more than twice as much heart disease as Type B men (Rosenman et al., 1975). This difference could not be explained simply in terms of traditional risk factors, such as cigarette smoking, because those factors had been equalized for the two groups.

One type of investigation that may help chart the relationship between personality and CHD and also clarify the way that known risk factors combine to bring about physical illness is the longitudinal or prospective study. Most clinical problems have been studied retrospectively, that is, after the fact. After someone gets sick, the doctor inquires about past illnesses and experiences that might explain the current problem. More powerful—but also more time-consuming and costly—is the prospective, or before-the-fact, investigation. Such a study gathers infor-

mation over a relatively long period. Because prospective studies are longitudinal, they can provide a picture of how a person's thinking, behavior, and bodily reactions unfold over time. Depending on the data gathered, this approach permits the researcher to identify interactions between particular personality variables and important life events and the effects of those interactions on the person's health.

The Framingham study is an example of a prospective investigation (Haynes et al., 1980). A group of 5,127 adult residents of Framingham, Massachusetts, volunteered to participate in a study on coronary heart disease for the rest of their lives. They have been monitored for the incidence of illness, hospitalization, and death since 1948. Every 2 years, each surviving participant is given a physical examination that includes blood tests, electrocardiograms, X-rays, and blood pressure readings. Several physical risk factors have been identified by the Framingham study, including elevated blood pressure, cholesterol level, and cigarette smoking. The study has confirmed that weight gains result in elevated blood pressure, and thus indirectly increase the risk of coronary heart disease.

Between 1967 and 1969, a subgroup of more than 1,600 male and female Framingham participants was assessed for Type A tendencies and then monitored for CHD during the next 8 years (Haynes et al., 1980). The study examined the relationship of employment status to the incidence of CHD. The results showed the importance of an interactional view of both personal and environmental influences when studying CHD. Figure 5-11 shows that for women

Figure 5-11   Eight-year incidence of coronary heart disease among Framingham working women and housewives with Type A and Type B behavior patterns.

<small>SOURCE: Findings from the Framingham study; adapted from Haynes, Feinleib, & Kannel, 1980.</small>

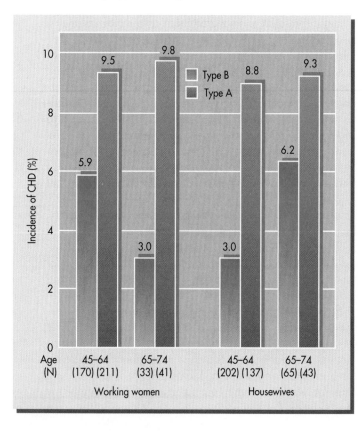

under 65, Type A women were much more likely to develop CHD than Type B women whether or not they worked outside the home. For women over 65, this difference was found for working women but it was less strong for housewives. However, working women who had clerical jobs and women who had raised three or more children were at added risk, suggesting that additional stress may play a role in CHD. For men, Figure 5-12 shows a different pattern. Type A characteristics were an added risk for men of all ages who had white-collar jobs. However, the difference in risk from Type A for men who held blue-collar jobs was not statistically significant. The results of this Framingham study show that although Type A is an important risk factor for cardiac disease, other factors such as job stress and stress from family responsibilities are also important.

Despite many positive results concerning this relationship there have also been some contradictory findings. For example, one study found that Type A men who had had heart attacks were less likely than Type Bs to have recurrences (Ragland & Brand, 1988). This unexpected result, as well as other findings not consistent with the Type A formulation, might have been due to methodological aspects of the particular investigations or to some factor that has not yet been identified. In any case, there is good reason to believe that the original Type A–CHD relationship proposed by Friedman and Rosenman needs some revision.

According to one hypothesis, hostility may be the most active Type A ingredient, and there is evidence that people who are hostile, angry, cynical, and suspicious of others have an especially high risk of fatal coronary disease (Barefoot et al., 1987). The results found for women in the Framingham study who were classified as Type A were consistent with this hypothesis. They showed that suppressed hostility was an important predictor of CHD for this group. It may be that the impatience, ambition, and work drive seen in so many Type A people is not nearly as important from a cardiovascular standpoint as their hostility (suppressed or expressed anger) and cynical view of other people's motivations. Table 5-9 presents sample questionnaire items designed to measure such cynical hostility. In one study, husbands and wives rated each other's hostility levels. As Figure 5-13 shows, the higher the spouse-rated hostility, the greater the likelihood of CHD (Kneip et al., 1993). Hostility has been found to be generally associated with declines in physical health (T. Q. Miller et al., 1996).

Because hostility has a number of aspects, it will be necessary to isolate its components and relate these to clinically significant events, such as whether people have heart attacks. Three components that merit study are (1) distrust of others (expecting someone to cheat or take advantage of you), (2) feeling very angry when you find someone cheating (the person in the 10-item supermarket express line who has 12 items), and (3) showing anger

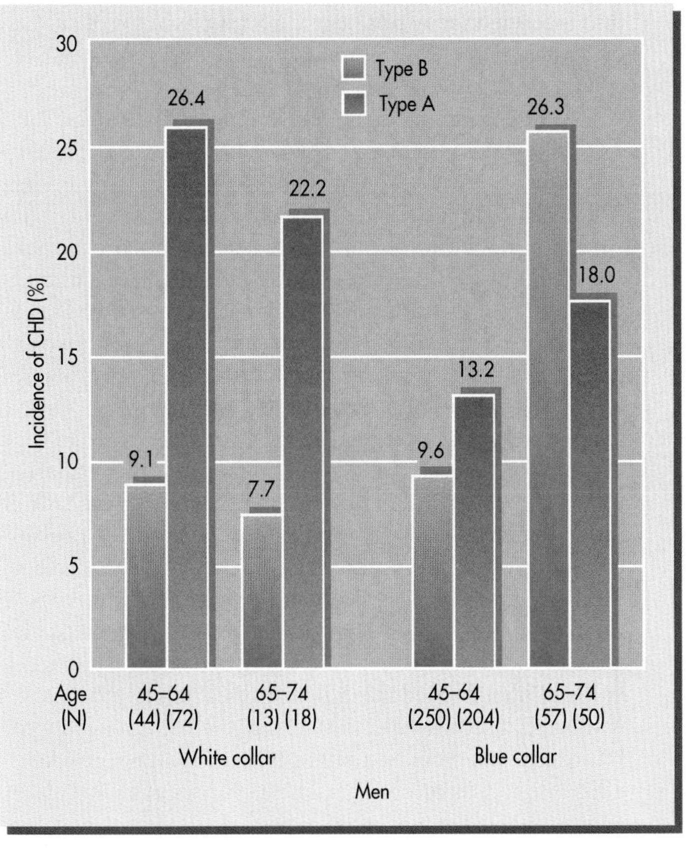

Figure 5-12   Eight-year incidence of coronary heart disease among white-collar and blue-collar Type A and Type B men in the Framingham study.

SOURCE: Adapted from Haynes, Feinleib, & Kannel, 1980.

Table 5-9
Questionnaire Items Used to Assess Cynical Hostility

Subjects are asked to circle the word "Never," "Sometimes," "Often," or "Always" as it best describes their behavior in these situations. It is believed that people who circle "Often" or "Always" in answers to these items are in a high-risk heart disease group.

1. When anybody slows down or stops what I want to do, I think they are selfish, mean, and inconsiderate.
2. When anybody does something that seems incompetent, messy, selfish, or inconsiderate to me, I quickly feel angry or enraged. At the same time, my heart races, my breath comes quickly, and my palms sweat.
3. When I have such thoughts or feelings (no. 2), I let fly with words, gestures, a raised voice, and frowns.

Source: MacDougall et al., 1981

(telling the person with 12 items that he or she is a cheater). Because the Type A pattern has many elements, researchers are exploring facets of the pattern that might be of special importance (M. Friedman, 1996). Work on two topics currently being investigated—hostility and physiological reactivity—may help clarify relationships among personality, behavior, and CHD. Interestingly, one study found that among Type A men, those with the lowest anger as well as depression levels had the best chances of achieving at least a normal lifespan (Carmelli & Swan, 1996). If cynical attitudes and hostile emotions cause biological responses that lead to coronary disease, clinicians may be able to devise ways of changing disease-producing thoughts and feelings. Further research on hostility and CHD is needed to assess this relationship and possible responses to it (Barefoot et al., 1991).

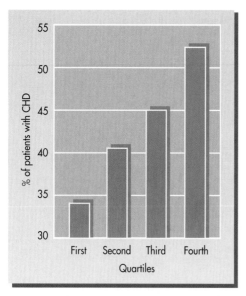

Figure 5-13 Percentage of patients with coronary heart disease as a function of spouses' ratings of partner's hostile outlook. The first quartile includes the lowest ratings of hostility; the fourth includes the highest.

SOURCE: Based on Kneip et al., 1993.

In addition to the investigation of the role of hostility and anger, another possible reformulation of the Type A pattern is suggested by evidence that Type As are more physiologically reactive than other people. This excitability might be the most active ingredient in the Type A personality (Manuck et al., 1995). It has been hypothesized that perhaps there are two groups of people, hot and cold reactors, with the cold reactors showing normal cardiovascular responses (blood pressure, heart rate) to stress, and hot reactors displaying abnormally intense cardiovascular responses (Eliot & Buell, 1983). Hot and cold reactors might not differ in terms of their overt behavior, but the hot reactors might experience steep blood pressure surges under stress. If this proves to be the case, measurements of the Type A pattern by means of questionnaires and interviews may not be as direct a predictor of cardiac disorders as measurements of actual cardiovascular responses under stressful conditions.

Most of the research on personal characteristics, such as Type A and hostility, and coronary heart disease has focused attention on human beings. While this is understandable, animal studies may have much to contribute to an understanding of the causes of heart attacks (Shively et al., 2000). An example of this contribution is research studying the role of several psychosocial factors in CHD among monkeys. In one study, there were two experimental conditions, differing in the stability of group relationships (Manuck et al., 1995). In "unstable" groups, the members were reorganized on a regular basis so that animals had to reestablish their dominance and affiliative relationships periodically. In "stable" groups, the initial group membership was maintained without disruption throughout the 22-month experiment. Repeated behavioral observations permitted identification of monkeys as relatively more dominant or subordinate in their social groups. Monkeys housed in reorganized social groups developed about twice the amount of coronary atherosclerosis as that seen among animals in a stable environment. However, this increase held only for dominant monkeys. This finding suggests that the behavioral demands of retaining preeminence in an unstable social environment accelerates the process of atherosclerosis.

The role of social losses and social isolation in recovery from heart attacks has been explored in a large number of studies. In one investigation, 2,320 male survivors of myocardial infarctions were assessed to identify factors that were predictive of how long they would live after having had a heart attack (Ruberman et al., 1984). One important factor in the outcome was education, with the better-educated subjects living longer. Life stress and social isolation, both alone and in combination, also emerged as significant predictors of mortality. Life stress was defined by subjects' reports concerning such problems as job difficulties, divorces and separations, accidents, and criminal victimization. Social isolation was defined in terms of contacts with friends and relatives and membership in social, church, and fraternal organizations.

In Figure 5-14, graphs (a) and (b) show that when the effects of life stress and social isolation were evaluated separately, each of these factors was significantly associated with increased probability of mortality. The risk of death for men who were high in life stress was double the risk for men who were low in life stress. A similar relationship was found when men who were high and low in social isolation were compared. The combined effect of these two factors is shown in graph (c) of Figure 5-14. For men who were high in both life stress and social isolation, the risk of dying was four times greater than for men who were low in both life stress and social isolation. The middle line in graph (c) presents the risk of dying for men who were high in either life stress or social isolation.

As Figure 5-14 makes clear, it is valuable to have evidence concerning the relationship between sudden personal cataclysms, such as the death of a loved one or the loss of a job, and coronary heart disease; equally significant is information about the effects of less intense, but persistent, aspects of a person's life-style.

The mechanism by which stress contributes to heart disease has not yet been worked out. One possibility is that high levels of autonomic nervous system activity caused by stressful life events underlie many cases of CHD. Heightened autonomic activity can come about either because of the extraordinary nature of the stressors or because of personality characteristics, such as a tendency to react with high levels of hostility and anger to perceived insults or rejections.

Stressful Events and CHD Researchers have found that particularly stressful episodes—trying to meet a deadline, for example, or getting fired—affect the cardiovascular system temporarily (as by raising blood pressure). Also, some sudden, personally meaningful events seem to set off major cardiovascular reactions. For example, separations from and losses of loved ones often bring about the need for sudden life-style changes and may culminate in a heart attack, as shown in the following case:

Harry Allen's wife had suffered from lung cancer for many months. Her death came slowly and painfully. For Allen, aged 54, the loss and grief were overwhelming. Everyone knew that the cancer was incurable and that death was approaching. Yet it came as a terrible shock to Allen. Four months before his wife's death, Harry had had a thorough physical examination that included an electrocardiogram. The electrocardiogram as well as the other studies relevant to heart function were completely normal. Yet two days after his wife's death, Allen collapsed and died of a massive heart attack.

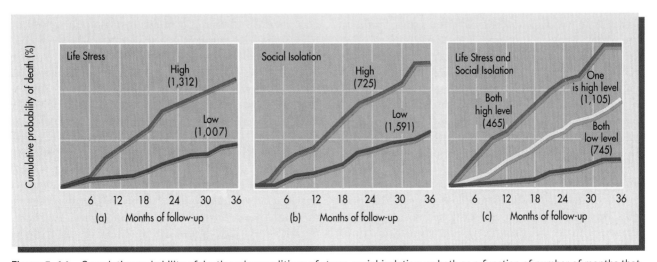

Figure 5-14   Cumulative probability of death under conditions of stress, social isolation, or both as a function of number of months that subjects were followed up after myocardial infarction.

Source: Adapted from Ruberman et al., 1984, p. 555. Reprinted by permission of *The New England Journal of Medicine.*

While the roles of social networks and social support have been examined in many studies of illness, these factors have much more consistently been linked to CHD in men than to CHD in women (Berkman et al., 1993). Interestingly, social support provided by women seems to reduce cardiovascular responses to stress for both men and women to a greater extent than is the case for support provided by men (Glynn et al., 1999).

Community Life-Style and CHD *Life-style* refers to a way of life that reflects the values and attitudes of an individual or group. Our jobs, interests, and social relationships show the effects of our life-styles, but the type of community in which we live may also play a role. A recent study has provided evidence that there may be an important relationship between the general pace of life in a community and the incidence of cardiovascular disorders (Levine et al., 1989). Thirty-six small, medium, and large metropolitan areas across the United States were compared using four indicators of pace of life:

1. How fast people walked
2. How fast people talked
3. The speed with which bank tellers worked
4. The proportion of individuals wearing watches (presumed to be an indicator of concern with time)

The researchers found that pace of life was strongly related to death rates from coronary heart disease, both across cities and across regions of the country. A faster life pace was associated with higher rates of CHD, while communities with slower paces of life had lower rates of CHD. Consistent with these findings is the fact that the death rate due to heart disease in New York City is higher than would be expected for both residents and visitors (Christenfeld et al., 1999).

Cultural Factors and CHD Studies that compare different cultures and the process of social change also provide evidence concerning the role of life-style factors in disease. In general, low rates of CHD tend to be found in parts of the world where tradition and family ties are strong. Cross-cultural data have provided a broader perspective on the relationship between psychosocial experience and physical breakdown. Japan, for example, has one of the lowest rates of heart disease in the world, while the United States has one of the highest. The rate of death from CHD for Japanese men between the ages of 35 and 64 is 64 per 100,000 population; the comparable figure for American men is 400 per 100,000.

There are also wide regional and cultural differences in rate of CHD within a large country like the United States. For example, according to a survey done many years ago, the town of Roseto, Pennsylvania, had a remarkably low death rate, especially from heart attacks. These low rates might seem surprising, since both the men and women of Roseto tended to be overweight and their dietary, smoking, and exercise patterns were similar to those in other communities. What seemed to contribute most to the relatively low death rate was the way in which the people lived. Almost all of Roseto's residents were of Italian descent, and the town's neighborhoods were very cohesive. Family relationships were extremely close, supportive, and traditional. Men were likely to be the uncontested heads of their families. Personal and family problems tended to be worked out with the help of relatives, friends, and the local priest.

Although Roseto had these stable features, like all American communities, it had begun undergoing constant change. Young men and women were marrying non-Italians from other towns. The birthrate was declining, church attendance was down, and people were moving outside the old areas into more distant suburban neighborhoods. By the mid-1970s, after many of these changes had occurred, a striking increase in the rate of heart attacks and sudden death was noticed, particularly among men under 55 (Egolf et al., 1992; S. Wolf & Bruhn, 1993). Apparently this social change was weakening Roseto's sources of social and emotional security, with important consequences for the health and longevity of its inhabitants.

Can CHD-Prone Life-Styles Be Changed? Researchers are exploring the possibility of reducing susceptibility to CHD through the use of psychological training. A variety of cognitive and behavioral techniques have been tried with Type As, including self-control training, learning to think about situations in less intense ways, and being attentive to the problems created by personal beliefs that emphasize urgency and the need to gain immediate control over events. There is some basis for believing that learning to think and act differently exerts a positive influence on the health of Type As. For example, one study found that Type A men who had already had a heart attack were less likely to have another attack if they had participated in a cognitive-behavior counseling program after the first heart attack (Thoresen et al., 1982). In regard to the connection between hostility and CHD, perhaps angry people can become more aware of their hostile tendencies and modify them, or perhaps they can learn to be more trusting of and empathize more with other people.

Another group of researchers has tried to help healthy, successful Army colonels engage in fewer Type A behaviors (J. J. Gill et al., 1985). The colonels participated in a series of counseling sessions that dealt with ways of modifying beliefs and attributions that underlie Type A behavior. They were also given advice on how to avoid potentially stressful situations, and they engaged in role play in which they practiced less highly pressured ways of coping with situational stress. The findings support the conclusion that the Type A attributes of anger, irritation, and impatience are not necessary aspects of the drive, ambition, creativity, and hard work needed by military leaders. The study showed that the colonels became less prone to Type A behaviors and that their ability to function as leaders was in no way impaired, but actually might have been improved.

Hypertension **Hypertension** is what most people describe as high blood pressure. A blood pressure level that is over 140 when the heart contracts (systolic pressure) and does not fall below 90 when the heart relaxes (diastolic pressure) is usually considered high. High blood pressure indicates that there is resistance to the flow of blood through the cardiovascular system. This condition places pressure on the arteries and forces the heart to work harder to overcome the resistance. Among younger adults (aged 25 to 44), men have higher blood pressures than women. Among older adults (aged 65 to 74), this pattern is reversed. Blood pressure readings of African American adults typically exceed those of White adults. The basis for higher rates of hypertension among African Americans has not yet been identified. Contributing to these higher rates may be a genetic factor (Ergul et al., 1996). African Americans with high blood pressure have four times as much of a potent protein, endothelin-1, as Whites with high blood pressure, and eight times the amount of endothelin-1 as healthy Blacks.

High blood pressure is a major contributor to cardiovascular disorders and is one of the conditions that creates increased risk of heart attacks. Usually it is a silent or symptomless risk because the hypertensive individual might show no observable signs of a medical problem for many years. Hypertension may well be the most common major, chronic disease in the United States today.

Clinical observations indicating that many hypertensives show wide variability in blood pressure readings and seem emotionally on edge much of the time have led to speculation about the causes and treatment of this disorder. Chronic anger and anger suppression have been identified as particularly important factors. While everybody is exposed to anger-provoking situations, according to one theory hypertensives experience chronic anger because of their inability to express it or assert themselves in a socially desirable manner. Psychotherapists believe that within the warm acceptance of the psychotherapeutic setting, angry, anxious people can gain insight into and mastery over their tendency to experience strong emotional reactions. While firm empirical support for this approach is not yet available, there is growing evidence that personality constellations including anxiety, anger, and depression contribute to elevated blood pressure (Jorgensen et al., 1996).

Some support is emerging for a behavioral approach to hypertension that directs attention to the specific types of situations associated with elevated blood pressure. Lack of competence in dealing with situations that call for assertiveness may be a specific behavioral deficit of many hypertensives. Assertiveness, defined as the ability to stand up for one's rights, express feelings, and avoid mistreatment by others, is a vital interpersonal skill and an indicator of social competence. People who are low in assertiveness tend to be mistreated, fail to express their feelings, and are frequently unable to have their needs met. Researchers have been able to show that hypertensives respond positively to behavioral training that involves the modeling and role-playing of appropriate assertiveness. As the social competence of these individuals increases, in many cases their blood pressure declines; thus, strengthening the social skills of hypertensives may prove to be of clinical value.

Another line of research concerns the relationship between relaxation and blood pressure. Some reduction in blood pressure can be achieved by teaching relaxation skills to hypertensives. Herbert Benson (1977) has developed relaxation exercises that involve four elements: a repetitive mental device, a passive attitude, decreased muscle tension, and a quiet environment. His approach uses instructions like the following:

> *Sit quietly in a comfortable position. Close your eyes. Deeply relax all your muscles, beginning at your feet and progressing up to your face. Keep them deeply relaxed.*
>
> *Breathe through your nose. Become aware of your breathing. As you breathe out, say the word "one" silently to yourself. Continue for 20 minutes. You may open your eyes to check the time, but do not use an alarm. When you have finished, sit quietly for several minutes, at first with closed eyes and later with opened eyes.*
>
> *Do not worry about whether you are successful in achieving a deep level of relaxation. Maintain a passive attitude and permit relaxation to occur at its own pace. Expect distracting thoughts. When these distracting thoughts occur, ignore them and continue repeating "one."*
>
> *Practice the technique once or twice daily, but not within two hours after a meal, since the digestive processes seem to interfere with elicitation of anticipated changes. (Benson, 1977, p. 153)*

The simple method outlined by Benson often leads to lower blood pressure, as well as to other bodily changes that accompany relaxation. Figure 5-15 shows the types of results that have encouraged clinicians to use relaxation techniques with hypertensives. As the figure makes clear, relaxation led to lower systolic blood pressure during the day, and also while the subjects were asleep. Similar results were obtained for diastolic pressure.

There is also evidence that the combined use of relaxation and biofeedback has particularly good long-term effects on blood pressure (Jacob et al., 1987). These benefits must be considered along with certain drawbacks, including cost, side effects, and difficulty in getting some patients to take antihypertensive medications. These medications have been shown to be effective in reducing blood pressure.

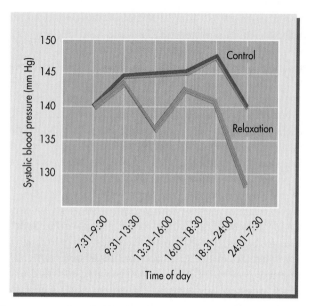

Figure 5-15 Systolic blood pressures for hypertensives who were given relaxation training and for an untreated control group. Blood pressure readings were taken during six time periods, beginning in the morning (7:31 A.M. to 9:30 A.M.) and ending after midnight.

Source: Adapted from Agras et al., *Archives of General Psychiatry, 37,* p. 861. © 1980 by the American Medical Association.

One study relating job stress to blood pressure elevation focused attention on the environment's role in hypertension (Schnall et al., 1990). In a study of 215 male workers (ranging from garbage collectors to stockbrokers) who were between the ages of 30 and 60, difficult work environments were found to have sustained round-the-clock effects on hypertension. The most problematic work environments were relatively low-level jobs in which high psychological demands were combined with little control over the work process and little use of skills. Inability to exert an influence on the work situation increased the likelihood of high blood pressure. If a high-stress job included latitude to control the situation, there was no increase in blood pressure. Twenty-one percent of all subjects suffered job strain. These men faced as much as three times greater risk of having high blood pressure than did those without job strain. The men aged 30 to 40 who had high-stress jobs showed a thickening of the heart's left ventricle, or chamber, a condition that often precedes coronary disease and heart attacks. These men had all worked on the job for at least 3 years, none was more than 20% overweight, and none had suffered heart disease before the study began. The finding of a significant relationship between high job stress and increased heart mass held regardless of the subject's alcohol intake and whether or not the subject was a smoker.

For some people with hypertension, stress is the main cause, and relaxation and biofeedback may solve the prob-

lem entirely. For others, stress is not a factor at all, and medication may be the best approach to the problem. Hypertension has many possible causes, and the relaxation response should be expected to help only in cases when stress is at least a significant component.

Cancer

A growing number of research efforts are investigating whether psychological variables are related in some way to the occurrence and growth of cancer and to recovery from the disease. **Cancer** is not a single disease but a group of different diseases sharing a common pattern of destructive, uncontrolled cellular growth. Psychosocial factors could theoretically affect at least two different stages of cancer: the initiation of a new cancer and the progression of an established cancer.

Animal studies suggest that certain early life experiences (e.g., daily handling by laboratory caretaking personnel or separation of young rats from their mothers) result in decreased or increased cancer susceptibility. Another critical factor is the animal's ability to develop an adaptive coping response. Exposure to acute *escapable* stress does not influence tumor growth appreciably; however, the identical amount of *uncontrollable* stress markedly exacerbates tumor growth (A. O'Leary, 1990). Both animal studies and clinical observations of humans have revealed that uncontrollable stress is related to cancer growth (Sklar & Anisman, 1981). Stimulated by such findings, research is now being carried out on the roles of stress and personality in human cancers. One of these studies has shown that medical students whose psychological profiles indicated a relatively restricted capacity for close interpersonal relationships were especially prone to develop cancers 20 to 25 years later (J. W. Shaffer et al., 1987).

One hypothesis that has been suggested is that people who have difficulty handling strong feelings are more likely to develop cancers than people who can appropriately ventilate their emotions. Some researchers have focused particular attention on feelings of depression. In one study, the MMPI (see Chapter 3) was administered to more than 2,000 middle-aged employed men. Two decades later, only the MMPI depression score was associated with increased risk of death (Persky et al., 1987; Shekelle et al., 1981). Whether psychological depression can be described as a direct or an indirect cause of increased risk of death from cancer was not answered by this study. To answer that question, we will need more information about the biology of psychological depression and its relationship to the growth of cancer cells.

While the role played by psychological factors in the development of cancer remains to be clarified, there is no question about the stressful impact of receiving a cancer diagnosis and having to live with the illness:

Figure 5-16   Bald but beautiful: The classmates of 11-year-old Ian O'Gorman (center), a cancer patient, shaved their heads so that Ian would not feel out of place. Ian's teacher was so inspired that he, too, shaved his head.

Source: *Seattle Times*, March 10, 1994, p. A3.

I knew from the outset that I had some form of cancer because the doctor didn't equivocate. I took the news calmly, agreeing that immediate hospitalization was the most prudent course of action. The tears, the terror, didn't hit until hours later, sometime deep in that first, sleepless hospital night. And it was months before the real subtlety of his statement hit me. "We can cure you" doesn't necessarily mean "We will cure you."

Beyond the anxiety engendered by the illness itself, cancer exposes patients to physical and emotional stress from painful and sometimes emotionally difficult treatments and their side effects. Counseling and psychotherapy may lighten the load. For example, one clinical study suggested that group psychotherapy may be useful in helping cancer patients cope with their disease (D. Spiegel et al., 1989). The lives of women with advanced stages of breast cancer were lengthened by a year and a half when they participated in group psychotherapy; these women also reported significant reductions in their anxiety and pain. This study is particularly impressive because the 86 subjects had been randomly assigned to therapy and control groups, and all patients in both groups received standard medical treatment, including surgery and radiation or chemotherapy.

While further research will be needed to specify the most beneficial elements of group psychotherapy, the social support it provides is probably among them. Having supportive social ties contributes to resilience and helps people cope with traumatic experiences of various types (see Figure 5-16). Cancer tends to stigmatize its victims and this often leads to social isolation and strong negative emotions.

As the following account demonstrates, well-intentioned people can add to stress when their supportive efforts do not meet the needs of the ill person:

People get upset when they hear that someone they know has been diagnosed with cancer. A number of people I told began to cry. People said they would pray for me. All this might sound like an outpouring of love and support, but it was also scary. For a while I reacted to any expression from others with anger, feeling that everyone thought I was dying. At times I worried that my understanding of my illness was incorrect, reasoning that others must know something that I don't about my prognosis or that I was denying the seriousness of my condition. I spent a lot of time reassuring others, trying to feel that they weren't viewing me as a person with "one foot in the grave."

These reactions make social support a more complex issue than it might at first appear. . . . While having people around me to help and support me was invaluable, it also was a burden, taking energy I needed for other things. There is, however, one exception to this ambivalence. I quickly discovered the comfort of being with other people who were diagnosed with cancer.

. . . One day some colleagues asked about my chemotherapy. After telling them about the regimen one listener invited me to agree with her that it was wonderful that such potentially lifesaving drugs were available. I couldn't respond. You see, I hate my chemotherapy drugs. I loathe ordering them from the pharmacy, smelling them, feeling them in my hand, and taking them. But to express this to her would involve a lot of explaining, assuring her that I don't intend to stop my treatments, stating that, of course, I am glad we have these drugs, etc. I don't have to do that with another cancer patient. When

a woman also being treated for breast cancer fairly spit out the name of one of her drugs I understood what she was feeling. When I complained that I was tired of being bald, a colleague with cancer didn't tell me I looked great, urge me to hang in there, or get teary. He simply said "I know." Similarly, when he and I joke about our experiences we are being funny, not poignant, touching, or brave. It's good to be able to gripe and joke unselfconsciously. (Shore, 1989, p. 25)

As Elsie Shore's account of her experience with cancer conveys, psychological stress frequently accompanies serious illness regardless of its cause. Social support can be most helpful in such situations, but the support must take account of what the ill person is going through.

The evidence implicating psychological factors in cancer acquisition is still tentative and not always consistent, but it is stronger with regard to adaptation to the disease and survival (Denollet, 1999). Emotional distress may adversely affect the clinical course of cancer, with depression being the emotion that creates the most noticeable roadblock to recovery. Aiding recovery are good coping skills and an optimistic attitude (Faller et al., 1999).

One of the greatest needs in cancer research is for longitudinal studies that begin before people develop cancer symptoms. Obviously, such studies are difficult to conduct because no one can tell in advance that a person will develop a malignancy. The ideal study would be one in which a large representative sample of apparently healthy people is assessed psychologically and then followed up to determine those individuals who develop cancer and find out whether its incidence can be predicted by psychological data collected before the cancer was identified.

Researchers who study possible behavioral factors in cancer suggest that the main behavioral contributions to cancer initiation include smoking and poor nutrition. And although current research—such as some of the studies discussed in this section—point to a link between psychosocial factors and cancer outcome, the role of morale, mood, and attitude remains less well established and is controversial. The complexity of interacting factors in survival and recovery from cancer is shown by evidence that there are significant ethnic differences. In general, African Americans have worse survival outcomes and Japanese have better survival outcomes than most other groups (Meyerowitz et al., 1998). These differences may not be due to ethnicity per se; they might be mediated by differences among ethnic groups in socioeconomic status, access to health care, attitudes, knowledge, and adherence to prescribed medical regimes.

The leads provided concerning the role of psychological factors in cancer may have some applicability to **human immunodeficiency virus (HIV)** infections and **acquired immune deficiency syndrome (AIDS).** Immune system failures are involved in these conditions, as they are in cancer. The progression from HIV to AIDS seems to be quite variable, but stress, social support, and coping skills play important roles in the transition.

Diagnostic Dilemmas

Although numerous questions remain unanswered, conditions like coronary heart disease and cancer are usually identifiable and several of the processes involved are known. Less is known about what is going on in many other diseases. These pose **diagnostic dilemmas.**

Whether a condition is "purely" medical often cannot be determined in a yes-or-no fashion. There are gray areas stemming from lack of medical knowledge, the way in which patients describe their problems to doctors, and doctors' skills at eliciting pertinent information from their patients. Also contributing to diagnostic difficulties is the assumption that mind and body are separate and that therefore illness needs to be categorized as either physical or mental. In some conditions that are especially difficult to explain, definite physical symptoms are evident but cannot be conveniently explained in terms of traditional diagnostic classifications. An example of this is fatigue, a clinical condition in which the patient complains of extreme tiredness accompanied by poor concentration, irritability, and muscle pain. Many family physicians believe that the symptoms of most patients suffering from chronic severe fatigue are not readily explained, either by recognized organic disease or by depression, anxiety, anger, or some other emotional reaction.

Chronic Fatigue Syndrome

Shirley Finley is a patient in the infectious disease department of the local hospital. Her principal complaints are of fatigue, poor concentration, and muscle pain. These symptoms, which seem to be exacerbated by physical and mental exertion, have led to a substantial reduction in her daily activities. Her case history describes an acute onset of symptoms after a viral illness. While she does mention feeling depressed and anxious at times, she does not display prominent or unusual mood states. She believes her illness to be medical rather than psychological. When she feels "stressed out," she explains it as a result of an illness rather than its cause.

A clinical syndrome in which the complaint of fatigue is severe and accompanied by symptoms similar to those seen in Shirley Finley has been recognized at least since the nineteenth century. In the late 1800s, this syndrome received the diagnosis of *neurasthenia,* a condition of uncertain cause but attributed to the effect of the stresses of modern life on the human nervous system. As the years passed, the diagnosis of neurasthenia became too broadly defined to be useful, and by the early 1900s it was beginning to fall out of common use. However, increasing numbers of physicians have recently been confronted with symptoms like those of Shirley Finley in many patients, especially White females in early and mid-adulthood.

Although it is not yet part of the official diagnostic nomenclature, **chronic fatigue syndrome (CFS)** is now gaining considerable attention. While there is disagreement about the definition of CFS, at the present time it can be characterized by the presence of certain symptoms (inclusion criteria) and the absence of others (exclusion criteria). Table 5-10 lists inclusion and exclusion criteria for CFS. Research is needed to determine the nature and cause of chronic fatigue syndrome. One limitation of the studies that have been carried out is that they often lack comparison groups and detailed information about the patients studied. So far, no single definitive cause of the disorder has been identified. However, viral infection seems to be a frequent precipitating agent. Immunological abnormalities are common in CFS, as are abnormalities of autonomic functioning and feelings of depression and anxiety. One interesting finding is that, while CFS patients often report having difficulty in concentration and memory, their actual cognitive performance is normal (Wearden & Appleby, 1997). It seems likely that multiple factors play roles in CFS. Thus, we probably have yet an-

other example of the need for a broad interactional perspective on biopsychosocial determinants. At the present time, CFS is best regarded as a descriptive term for a frequently reported disorder that seems to involve heterogeneous variables. Regardless of what is ultimately discovered about the causes of CFS, the attention it is receiving offers an opportunity to gain insight into the nature and classification of human illnesses whose origins are uncertain.

Headaches

Headaches are very common and often are not associated with significant organic disease. Who doesn't have a headache once in a while? Nonetheless, headaches can be debilitating and are probably the most commonly reported painful bodily signal. Even though they often are not easy to diagnose and despite gaps in knowledge about the mechanisms involved, the various types of headaches are good examples of how stress and vulnerability can influence physical symptoms.

Every year an estimated 80% of Americans suffer from at least one headache, and 10% to 20% of people who go to physicians give headaches as their primary complaint. Headaches also are a major reason given for absenteeism from work or avoidance of other undesired social or personal activities.

The pain of a headache has three components:

1. Physiological changes (usually either muscular contractions or blood vessel dilation)
2. The subjective experience of pain (aching, distress, fatigue, and so on)
3. Behavior motivated by the pain (e.g., pill taking, withdrawal from family and social activities, absence from work).

Not all headaches are alike, and there are wide differences in people's sensitivity to the physiological changes that signal the beginning of a headache (see Table 5-11).

Tension (or muscle-contraction) headaches, distinguished by changes in skeletal muscles, are probably the most common form of head pain. The person reports an aching, dull, pressing feeling; the scalp may feel tender if pressed with the hand; and there are persistent sensations of bandlike pain or tightness in the head. The exact cause of muscle-contraction headaches has not yet been pinpointed. Research suggests that tension headache sufferers are emotionally hyperreactive to pain and stress.

Migraine headaches are localized on one side or at the front of the head. They are severe, tend to recur, and are often accompanied by a variety of somatic symptoms. The throbbing, pulsating pain characteristic of migraines may last for several hours. Nausea and vomiting are common. In some cases, the dilated cranial artery is visible and tender.

Table 5-10

Definition of Chronic Fatigue Syndrome (CFS)

Inclusion Criteria

1. Medically explained fatigue of at least 6 months' duration
2. Acute onset of symptoms, not resulting from ongoing exertion
3. Not substantially alleviated by rest
4. Substantially reduced activity level in patient
5. Presence of four or more of the following symptoms:
   - Sore throat
   - Tendor lymph nodes
   - Muscle pain
   - Joint pain
   - Headache
   - Unrefreshing sleep
   - Patient reports of memory impairment
   - Worsening of symptoms after exertion

Exclusion Criteria

1. Active, unresolved, or suspected disease
2. Psychotic disorders
3. Severe depression
4. Dementia
5. Alcohol or other substance misuse
6. Eating disorder (such as anorexia or bulimia nervosa)
7. Severe obesity

Table 5-11

Differentiating Features of Common Types of Headaches

Feature	Tension Headache	Migraine Headache	Cluster Headache
Sex of sufferer	No difference between men and women	More frequent in women	More frequent in men
Quality of pain	Bandlike pressure, tightness	Throbbing	Piercing, burning, excruciating
Time of onset	Often afternoon or evening	Often early mornings and weekends	Soon after onset of sleep; also daytime
Mode of onset	Gradual	Abrupt or gradual	Abrupt
Duration	Hours, days, or weeks	Hours, 1 to 2 days	20 minutes to 2 hours
Precipitating or aggravating factor	Either emotional stress or not apparent	Emotional stress, menstruation, alcohol, certain food, change in weather	Alcohol, lying down, REM sleep
Associated symptoms or signs	No specific symptoms except tenderness of scalp or neck muscles	Nausea, vomiting, irritability, tender scalp	Tearing of eyes, nasal stuffiness and discharge
Personality traits	Competitive, conscientious	Perfectionistic, neat, efficient	Specific traits not identified
Age at onset	Adolescence; early adulthood	Puberty to menopause	20 to 50 years of age

Unlike muscle-contraction headaches, migraines are usually preceded by a sensory, motor, or mood disturbance called an **aura.** There may be ringing in the ears; tingling, numbness, or weakness of a limb; extreme sensitivity to light; visual blurring; distorted depth perception; nausea; or unaccountable emotional changes.

Many migraine sufferers have a family history of such headaches, but whether this is due to heredity or to common living experiences is unclear. Migraine attacks may begin with stressful life changes such as puberty, going to college, or starting a job. One study found that migraine attacks were most likely to be experienced after a pileup of minor but annoying and arousing life stressors (Sorbi et al., 1996). Hyperalertness, tenseness, irritability, reduced quality of sleep, and tiredness associated with daily hassles all seem to trigger the attacks.

Migraines occur more often in women than in men. A significant percentage of migraine sufferers are prone to experience feelings of depression and anxiety, although the basis for this relationship is unclear.

To someone unfamiliar with migraines, the agony of experiencing one may be hard to appreciate. An account by the prominent novelist Joan Didion (Figure 5-17) describes what the experience is like:

Three, four, sometimes five times a month, I spend the day in bed with a migraine headache, insensible to the world around me. Almost every day of every month, between these attacks, I feel the sudden irrational irritation and the flush of blood into the cerebral arteries which tell me that migraine is on its way, and I take certain drugs to avert its arrival. If I did not take the drugs, I would be able to function perhaps one day in four. . . .

Once an attack is under way, no drug touches it. When I am in a migraine aura (for some people the aura lasts fifteen minutes, for others several hours), I will drive through red lights, lose the house keys, spill whatever I am holding, lose the ability to focus my eyes or frame coherent sentences, and generally give the appearance of being on drugs, or drunk. The actual headache, when it comes, brings with it chills, sweating, nausea, a debility that seems to stretch the very limits of endurance. That no one dies of migraine seems, to someone deep into an attack, an ambiguous blessing. (Didion, 1979, pp. 168–172)

In the past, it was believed that migraine was caused by narrowing followed by dilation of blood vessels. This idea is now being replaced by the idea that a wave of cerebral electrical activity may cause the aura, or warning sensation, and that headaches develop when the wave reaches pain-sensitive blood vessels. What triggers this wave? Stress, hunger, hormone fluctuations, foods, alcohol, too much sleep, caffeine withdrawal, or noise are chief suspects. It has recently been found that serotonin, a nerve cell messenger, becomes depleted in

Figure 5-17 Joan Didion, a prominent novelist, suffers from frequent migraine headaches. Her description of them conveys a clear picture of what the experience is like.

the brain during a migraine attack. Some disturbance in serotonin function seems to be a central component, if not the primary culprit, in producing the pain and other symptoms of migraines. Drug companies are now working on the development of compounds that can correct a dysfunction in the brain chemistry of migraine sufferers.

Migraine headaches often respond positively to drugs that constrict the arteries in the scalp. Psychotherapy has also produced significant improvement in some chronic migraine sufferers, but little or no improvement in people who have migraines only occasionally. There have also been reports of the successful use of behavior therapy and biofeedback in some cases of migraine.

Cluster headaches are often confined to one side of the head. The pain is excruciating, hitting a peak in 3 to 5 minutes and disappearing within an hour or two or less. Patients often are pain-free for long periods of time but then experience a series of headaches over several weeks, sometimes several in one day. The headaches often occur at night and wake people from sound sleep. Patients often pace and sometimes bang their heads against the wall in an attempt to quell the pain. Cluster headaches are more common in men than in women.

Irritable Bowel Syndrome

Often when a patient comes to a physician with gastrointestinal symptoms, such as abdominal pain, gas, bloating, or a feeling of abdominal distension or altered bowel movements (hard, loose, watery), a few tests may be performed and medications for symptom relief prescribed. Often symptoms persist and additional tests may be performed. Frequently, these tests do not reveal the cause of the symptoms. At this point, the patient might be advised to "relax" or see a mental health professional. When this

happens, the patient is confronted, not only with a set of embarrassing and socially undesirable symptoms, but also the implication that the problem is psychological and "nothing is really wrong."

These sorts of gastrointestinal problems are common and symptoms compatible with a diagnosis of **irritable bowel syndrome (IBS)** are reported by 9% to 22% of medical patients (Toner et al., 2000). The costs of diagnosis and treatment are considerable and, in addition, IBS is responsible for much industrial absenteeism. So far, no clear physiological or psychosocial predictors of the syndrome have been identified. However, stress, strong emotions, and maladaptive thoughts are frequently observed in cases of IBS. Studies have shown a high prevalence of psychiatric disorder, especially depression and anxiety disorders in IBS patients. This comorbidity has raised chicken-or-egg questions about the meaning of the correlations observed. The following case illustrates what is seen in many cases of IBS:

R. S., the spouse of a prominent musician, frequently had to entertain guests as part of her husband's work. She was a meticulous homemaker and always ensured that all aspects of the evening went smoothly. She found such events anxiety provoking and frequently felt that she had embarrassed her husband and failed as a hostess and wife. Her stomach would frequently rumble in what she experienced as a painfully loud fashion. She assumed that guests heard her stomach rumbles but were too polite to ever say anything. She also had to leave the room quite frequently, for whenever she was anxious, she would have mild diarrhea and more frequent bowel movements.

After such parties, R. S. would feel depressed and experience a strong sense of shame. She felt guilty that she could not be a gracious hostess, that her noisy bowel sounds and frequent departures from the living room had made a spectacle of herself and her husband. She was always surprised and somewhat incredulous when guests said how much they had enjoyed the evening. (Toner et al., 2000, p. 128)

In the midst of the uncertainty concerning the causes of IBS, there is evidence that psychological interventions can be valuable. Sometimes it is helpful simply to point out to the patient that symptoms like "passing gas" are common (many people—especially women—find gastrointestinal symptoms to be quite stigmatizing). Training in relaxation may also be helpful. There is growing evidence that short-term cognitive-behavioral therapy can be beneficial (Toner et al., 2000). Effective ingredients of this therapy include education; questioning maladaptive automatic thoughts; and helping patients become less embarrassed about their symptoms, acquire more effective coping skills, and feel less anxious and depressed about their symptoms and perhaps other aspects of their lives. Symptom reduction often occurs when the patient can reconceptualize their IBS from helplessness and hopelessness to resourcefulness and hopefulness.

Concluding Comment

We have reviewed a very diverse group of problems traditionally regarded as being medical ones, that have significant psychological and social dimensions. While the concepts of stress and vulnerability certainly cannot explain all medical disorders, they do seem pertinent to a number of types of bodily dysfunction. Beliefs and attitudes, whether about a specific physical difficulty or more generally about oneself can influence the course of physical disease. As we pointed out earlier, a sense of personal control, and seeing meaning in one's life can have protective consequences for health, whereas anxiety, anger, and conflict (within oneself or with other people) often have negative effects. Psychological therapies can help a person cope more effectively with bodily dysfunction. Important questions remain about exactly how psychological factors contribute to illness and how they contribute to its reduction. However, what is significant is that a start has been made in specifying, understanding, and using these factors in improving each individual's quality of life. It is no longer rational to try to determine whether psychological or physiological factors cause a given set of symptoms. Both are almost always operational and the task is to determine the degree to which each contributes and is remediable. Health and illness need to be received from a multifactorial perspective (see Box 5-3).

Chapter Summary

PSYCHOLOGICAL, SOCIAL, AND BODILY INTERACTIONS

The **psychosomatic hypothesis,** which became popular some 50 or 60 years ago, linked a person's development of certain bodily symptoms with the lack of emotional expression. Contemporary research has focused on bodily reactions to various emotion-arousing stimuli or stressors.

The Biopsychosocial Model The **biopsychosocial model** considers the interaction of a person's biological, psychological, and social subsystems. In this view, psychological factors usually play indirect roles in illness in that they combine with biological vulnerabilities of the person. The product of this interaction determines the effects of different levels of stress on the individual. The biopsychosocial view emphasizes the concept of **homeostasis,** according to which a living organism attempts to restore its dynamic equilibrium when it is exposed to stressors. **Behavioral medicine** and **health psychology** are concerned with reducing the stressfulness of illness and, wherever possible, preventing it.

Stress and Illness Stress occurs when a person feels unable to control important aspects of life. There is growing evidence that stress can play a role in illness. Skills whose presence decreases stress and risk of illness include ability to adapt to environmental change, handle strong emotions, interpret situations correctly, and form positive close relationships.

EATING DISORDERS

Psychological factors play important roles in eating disorders. The major eating disorders are: **anorexia nervosa,** in which the individual seems obsessed with thinness and loses a great deal of weight; **bulimia nervosa,** in which excessive quantities of food are eaten followed by purging (e.g., through vomiting or laxatives); and **binge eating** in which large quantities of food are eaten but there is no purging. The prevalence of eating disorders appears to have increased over the past 50 years. Personality, family, and cultural factors play roles in these disorders. Because cognitive distortions are common, a cognitive-behavioral approach to treatment is often pursued.

SLEEP DISORDERS

There are several types of sleep disorders which involve various stages in the sleep process. Sleeping problems are common in people with many kinds of mental disorders defined by DSM-IV. Sleep research is concerned with the basic processes involved in sleep and, also, with the treatment of individuals suffering from sleep disorders. In **narcolepsy,** the individual may fall into a deep sleep too easily. Some people suffer from **hypnogogic hallucinations** in which there are vivid, terrifying sleep states. **Sleep apnea** is one of a group of conditions in which there are disruptions in breathing. **Primary sleep disorders** are conditions that are not attributable to other mental or physical conditions. There are two types of primary sleep disorders. **Dyssomnias** involve abnormalities in the amount, quality, or timing of sleep. **Parasomnias** are conditions marked by abnormal behavioral or psychological events occurring in association with sleep, specific stages of sleep, or transitions between being asleep and awake. In **hypersomnia** there is excessive sleep. A common sleep disorder is **insomnia,** in which the individual has difficulty initiating or maintaining sleep. In **nightmare disorder,** the individual has long terrifying nightmares. **Sleep terror disorder** involves even more vivid dreams as result of which there is partial awakening, confusion, disorientation, and a high level of activity of the autonomic nervous system. In **sleepwalking disorder** there are repeated episodes of complex motor behavior that begin while the person is asleep and many continue while he or she is awake.

PSYCHOPHYSIOLOGICAL DISORDERS

Psychophysiological disorders refer to physical conditions in which psychological experiences, usually stressful, are closely related to bodily malfunction. **Chronic stress** may have different effects on the body than **acute stress.**

Cardiovascular Disorders Cardiovascular disorders are pathological conditions related to the functioning of the heart and blood vessels. In **coronary heart disease,** deposits—called **plaques**—thicken the walls of the coronary arteries and decrease the supply of blood available to the heart. This produces a condition called **atherosclerosis.** This buildup can result in **angina pectoris** (chest pain) or in a **myocardial infarction** (what is usually called a heart attack). **Stress** is thought to contribute to the risk of coronary heart disease because in stressful situations the body secretes more of certain hormonal substances, the **catecholamines.** Two of these, **epinephrine** and **norepinephrine,** accelerate the rate of arterial damage. Many personal life-style factors can increase stress, as can separation from or loss of a loved one. Living in a fast-paced society also increases risk of heart disease, presumably because it increases stress. When stress and social isolation are both present in a person's life, the risk of dying from heart disease is much higher than it is for people who do not have stress experiences and who have enough social support. People who have **Type A personalities** are very demanding of themselves and others and tend to operate under high pressure. Their higher risk for coronary heart disease may be due primarily to the hostility that permeates their lives. **Hypertension,** or high blood pressure, is also a risk factor for heart disease. Behavioral methods, including assertiveness training, relaxation training, and biofeedback, are helpful in lowering blood pressure in some cases.

Cancer Uncontrollable stress may be related to cancer growth. Some research indicates that both depression and inability to express strong feelings may be associated with greater risk of cancer. Although evidence linking psychological forces and cancer is still tentative, supportive group psychotherapy has been shown to be associated with longer life expectancy for women with breast cancer. There is some evidence that stress–immune system relationships are related to cancer and that stress reduction can enhance immune functioning.

DIAGNOSTIC DILEMMAS

Many patients come to physicians with symptoms that are difficult to pin down objectively and that seem to have a strong psychological component. These conditions pose **diagnostic dilemmas.**

Chronic Fatigue Syndrome Chronic Fatigue Syndrome **(CFS)** is marked by complaints of fatigue in the absence of great exertion and medical indicators of disease. Viral infection is often part of the picture. Immunological abnormalities, self-reports of cognitive difficulties, and feelings of depression contribute to the heterogeneity of the clinical picture.

Headaches There are several types of headaches, including **tension** or **muscle-contraction headaches, migraine headaches,** and **cluster headaches.** Both bodily and psychological factors play roles in the pain people experience when they have headaches.

Irritable Bowel Syndrome Many medical patients have gastrointestinal complaints for which physical causes cannot be found. Common symptoms involve abdominal pain, a bloated feeling, and altered bowel movements. Stress, strong emotions, and maladaptive thoughts are frequently observed in these cases. There is a high frequency of psychiatric disorders, particularly those involving anxiety and depression. Short-term cognitive-behavioral therapy helps many of these people. The therapy includes providing pertinent information, relaxation training, and learning how to be less embarrassed by socially undesirable symptoms, such as passing gas.

Key Terms

Biopsychosoical model, p. 153
Behavioral medicine, p. 154
Health psychology, p. 154
Eating disorders, p. 157
Anorexia nervosa, p. 158
Bulimia nervosa, p. 162
Binge eating, p. 166
Sleep disorders, p. 166
Sleep processes, p. 166
REM sleep, p. 167
Polysomnography, p. 167
Narcolepsy, p. 169
Hypnogogic hallucinations, p. 169

Sleep paralysis, p. 169
Dyssomnias, p. 168
Parasomnias, p. 169
Primary sleep disorders, p. 169
Hypersomnia, p. 169
Insomnia, p. 169
Nightmare disorder, p. 170
Sleep terror disorder, p. 170
Sleepwalking disorder, p. 171
Psychophysiological disorder, p. 171
Cardiovascular disorder, p. 172
Coronary heart disease (CHD),
    p. 172

Type A personalities, p. 174
Type B personalities, p. 174
Hypertension, p. 179
Cancer, p. 180
Diagnostic dilemmas, p. 182
Chronic fatigue syndrome (CFS),
    p. 183
Tension headaches, p. 183
Migraine headaches, p. 183
Cluster headaches, p. 185
Irritable bowel syndrome (IBS),
    p. 185

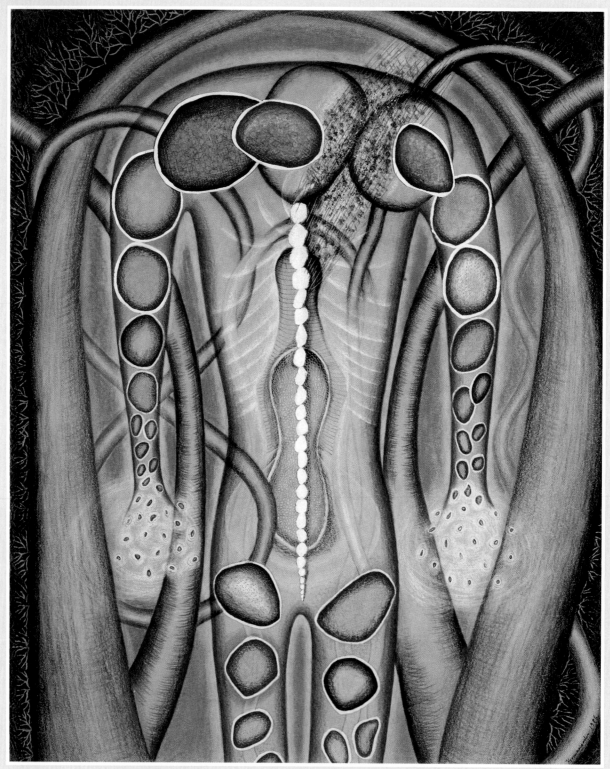

6

Disorders of Bodily Preoccupation

*A*lice Kenton, aged 22, worked part-time as a book-keeper in an accounting office. Since becoming a teenager, she had been excessively preoccupied with her facial acne, the size of her nose, and her height. She frequently compared her appearance with that of others, and continually sought reassurance that her skin was not horrible to look at, her nose was not bulbous, and her height not extremely unusual (she is 5′10″). As a result of her concerns, she did not date, avoided most social situations, had difficulty concentrating on her work, and was under-employed. She occasionally had suicidal thoughts. As a result of psychotherapy sessions with a clinical psychologist, Alice came to see that, while some of her physical features might be mildly unusual, her biggest problem was that she was too critical of herself. As her anxiety level and preoccupation decreased, she was able to allow herself to take some social initiatives, such as asking co-workers to go for coffee with her. Eventually she developed a dating relationship with a young man who lived in her apartment house. ■

Alice Kenton and Valerie Harris, whose case introduced Chapter 5, have in common the central role that bodily functioning plays in their lives. However, they differ in several important respects. Valerie suffers from a diagnosed medical condition, whereas Alice does not. Valerie's condition involves a set of clearly observable physical symptoms that are reduced somewhat by medication; Alice does not have a diagnosed medical condition, but she feels stigmatized by what she perceives to be her ugly physical features and negative reactions from other people. Both Valerie's and Alice's problems can be conceptualized in terms of stress and vulnerability. They both experience stress: Valerie's stems from having a physical problem that the reactions of her parents seem to make worse; Alice's is, in a sense, self-imposed because of her sensitivity about her physical attributes. Valerie's asthmatic condition makes her especially vulnerable to her parents' overprotection; Alice's insecurity makes her especially vulnerable to people's noticing and responding condemningly to her physical appearance.

It would be convenient if it were possible to distinguish easily between medical conditions to which personality and stress may make contributions and bodily complaints that cannot be diagnostically pinned down but in which personality and stress seem to be implicated. The diagnostic dilemmas discussed in the previous chapter (e.g., chronic fatigue syndrome) illustrate the ambiguities connected with many of the problems patients bring to their physicians. Given these ambiguities and the current state of knowledge, hard and fast distinctions between "real" and "unreal" physical illnesses often must be regarded as very tentative. Still, it is worth contrasting (1) physical conditions (such as coronary heart disease and cancer) in which psychological factors may play roles either as contributors to illness or aids in recovery and (2) bodily complaints that appear to be related to psychological makeup and stress, but cannot be medically diagnosed. This chapter deals with the second of these two sets of conditions.

The **bodily preoccupations** that mark this second set of conditions can take many forms. We will examine several somatoform disorders, including pain disorders, as well as factitious disorder and malingering. Of course, bodily preoccupation often accompanies genuine physical disease in the form of excessive worry and disproportionate disability. However, in other cases, there is no observable tissue damage and the problem seems to be almost a purely psychological one—for example, the individual who thinks his or her nose is abnormally large when, in fact, it is not. Bodily preoccupation often expresses itself as **somatization,** an individual's conscious or unconscious use of the body or bodily symptoms for psychological purposes or personal gain. The fact that there is no organic disease does not mean that the individual's suffering is not real. However, the causes and paths to cure the condition may be harder to find.

Somatoform Disorders

DSM-IV deals with conditions in which there are physical symptoms in the absence of physical disease. Many of the bodily complaints that physicians are asked to treat suggest physical pathology, but no actual impairment can be found. Although failure to diagnose a case medically might be due to a doctor's lack of knowledge or to a faulty laboratory test, in a large group of cases psychological rather than physiological factors are responsible for the symptoms. These cases, which do not seem to be produced consciously, are characterized as **somatoform disorders.** This category includes several conditions in which bodily complaints play an important role. Table 6-1 summarizes the major types of somatoform disorder described in DSM-IV.

Pain Disorders

Severe, prolonged pain, either without organic symptoms or greatly in excess of what might be expected to accompany organic symptoms, is classified as a **pain disorder.** There is often a temporal relationship between the occurrence of an actual, threatened, or fantasized interpersonal loss and complaints of pain. The complaints may be used to evoke social responses, such as attention, from others. Examples of impairment resulting from the pain include inability to work or attend school, frequent use of the health care system, the pain's becoming a major focus of the individual's life, substantial use of medications, and interpersonal problems such as marital discord and disruption of the family's normal life-style.

Table 6–1

Somatoform Disorders Described in DSM–IV

- *Pain disorder.* Pain as the predominant feature of the clinical picture; psychological factors are judged to have an important role in the pain's onset, severity, exacerbation, or maintenance.
- *Somatization disorder.* Multiple somatic complaints that may extend over a period of years; characterized by a combination of pain, gastrointestinal, sexual, and pseudoneurological symptoms.
- *Conversion disorder.* Unexplained symptoms or deficits affecting voluntary motor or sensory function that suggest a medical condition; psychological factors are judged to be associated with the symptoms or deficits.
- *Hypochondriasis.* Preoccupation with the idea that one has or might get a serious disease, along with misinterpretation of bodily symptoms or bodily functions.
- *Body dysmorphic disorder.* Preoccupation with an imagined or exaggerated defect in physical appearance.

Important factors that appear to assist recovery from pain disorder are the individual's participation in regularly scheduled activities (e.g., work) despite the pain and resistance toward allowing the pain to become the determining factor in his or her life. Pain disorder can be acute or chronic, and it can be difficult to diagnose because, while in some cases either psychological or physical factors seem to predominate, often the picture observed by the clinician is mixed. Table 6-2 lists the DSM-IV criteria for pain disorder. An acute pain disorder has a duration of less than 6 months. A chronic pain disorder is defined as having a duration of 6 months or longer.

What Is Pain? Saying "It hurts" is the result of an appraisal process that often leads to going to the doctor. Pain is influenced by biological, psychological, and social factors. The condition of our bodily systems obviously plays an important role in how we interpret signals coming from within our body. But our psychological state is also involved, and for this reason pain is one of the more mysterious and elusive aspects of illness and its treatment. Social factors influence the perception of pain as well. When one member of a family reports pain, the other members may respond with attention and expressions of concern. This response may serve as a stimulus for more reports of pain.

For decades, scientists had assumed that pain was a simple biological-alert mechanism, necessary to inform the brain that the body was injured. Pain signals were thought to shoot directly from the site of tissue damage to the brain, producing a pain sensation corresponding to the severity of the injury. But that theory failed to explain why people can tolerate pain better at some times than at others—for example, instantly dropping a hot cooking spoon, but holding on to a fine china cup overflowing with scalding tea long enough to set it down safely. We now know that electrical pain signals actually move from the injury to sites in the spine, where they can be amplified or diminished before being relayed to the brain. In trying to intercept pain, some researchers are now targeting these spinal control centers, which contain an abundance of nerve-cell receptors that can receive painkilling instructions from drugs. Box 6-1 describes some theories of pain that have been influential over the years.

By the middle of the twentieth century, it became clear that pain was a complex, multiply determined experience. One barrier to the treatment of pain is the difficulty people have describing it objectively. If you have a lump, you can point to it, or if a bone is broken, it can be seen in an X-ray. Pain does not have these objective indicators. Yet almost everyone must cope with periods of acute or chronic pain. Table 6-3 lists topics covered by clinicians in conducting interviews intended to assess the presence and intensity of a pain disorder.

Coping With Pain How much our bodies are hurt or damaged does not bear a one-to-one relationship with how much pain we experience. Knowledge is accruing concerning how people cope with hurt or damaged bodies so as to reduce or increase the pain that is experienced. How someone interprets the hurt or damage influences how much attention he or she focuses on feeling pain. How others respond to a person when he or she communicates pain also affects whether the pain diminishes or increases and whether significant disability results (e.g., not being able to go to work).

Active coping, such as remaining active and ignoring the pain, may be associated with better psychological and physical functioning, whereas **passive coping,** such as resting and social withdrawal, may be associated with poorer functioning (Boothby et al., 1999) (see Figure 6-2). (Obviously, how active or passive a patient is must be consistent with medical advice.) Table 6-4 describes coping strategies that can reduce or intensify pain. Active,

---

Table 6-2

DSM-IV Criteria for Pain Disorder

1. Pain exists in one or more anatomical sites of sufficient intensity to warrant clinical attention.
2. The pain causes clinically significant distress or impairment in social, occupational, or other important areas of functioning.
3. Psychological factors are judged to have an important role in the onset, severity, exacerbation, or maintenance of the pain.
4. The pain and deficits related to it are not intentionally produced or feigned.

Table 6-3

Questions Asked in Clinical Interviews to Assess the Presence and Intensity of a Pain Disorder

1. When does the patient experience the pain?
2. What are the conditions that lead to the onset of pain?
3. How intense is the pain?
4. Where in the body is the pain felt?
5. What factors are associated with the pain's exacerbation or relief from the pain?
6. How impaired is the individual in daily living, social relationships, and work?
7. Does the patient have a history of other types of maladaptive behavior (such as drug addiction or depression)?

Resilience and Vulnerability   Box 6–1

Perspectives on Pain

Discussions of what pain is and how to treat it have been found in ancient texts and treatises. For example, these topics are mentioned in Egyptian papyri dating back to 4000 B.C. In the fifth century B.C., Hippocrates theorized about the problem of pain in a person's body joints. In 1644, Descartes conceptualized pain as a specific phenomenon occurring in the nervous system. He viewed it as a kind of "straight-through" channel from the skin directly to the brain. He used the analogy of an individual pulling the rope at the bottom of a tower causing the bell in the belfry to ring. By the late nineteenth century, specificity theories of pain were offered according to which there are specific sensory receptors responsible for the transmission of specific sensations, such as, pain, warmth, touch, and pressure.

With the acceleration of scientific research in the twentieth century concerning pain, its complexities became more evident. Clinicians noted that similar bodily injuries resulted in widely differing reports of pain depending upon characteristics of the patient and circumstances. A person's emotional state and secondary gain (benefit he or she might receive from being sick or in pain) were identified as contributing to many cases of pain in the absence of a physical condition that would explain it. While a biopsychosocial model of pain is now widely accepted and reflects the movement away from the traditional descriptions of pain in purely physical terms, how psychological and social factors trigger the sensation of pain has not yet been worked out (Gatchel & Turk, 1999). Stress may play an important role in the triggering process (Melzack, 1999). For example, the stress effects of injury (such as loss of self-esteem, employment, or other security symbols) can influence the severity and pattern of pain experienced by the individual. Typically, pain is not just a figment of the imagination of the individual, but stresses of various types are capable of greatly intensifying it. It is possible that psychological stress alone can become a cause of chronic pain because it can produce substances that have destructive effects on body tissues. When pain is experienced, it may add to stress if the individual interprets the pain as a danger or as threatening (Figure 6-1).

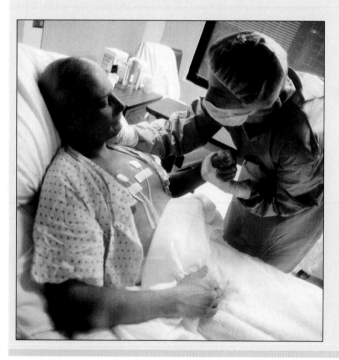

Figure 6-1   Stress and pain. This patient experienced a high level of pain following surgery and, perhaps, concluded that the surgery might not have been successful. After the surgeon explained that pain following surgery is normal and to be expected, the patient's experience of pain declined. Worry over the meaning of pain can lead to its intensification.

optimistic self-statements (such as "I don't think about the pain," "I pretend it's not part of me," "Although it hurts, I just keep going") are especially helpful as cognitive coping strategies.

Treating Pain Disorders The treatment of an **acute pain disorder,** one that is relatively recent and related to a specific event (such as surgery), is generally aimed at reducing the patient's anxiety through a trusting doctor-patient relationship and, perhaps, antianxiety medication. These approaches are usually successful. If not, a **chronic pain disorder,** one in which the experience of pain becomes an enduring, central aspect of a person's life, may result in a diagnosable psychiatric disorder (see Table 6-2). A number of treatment approaches have been found useful in chronic cases.

Operant Conditioning Clinicians who use operant conditioning in treating pain focus on pain behaviors (e.g., com-

   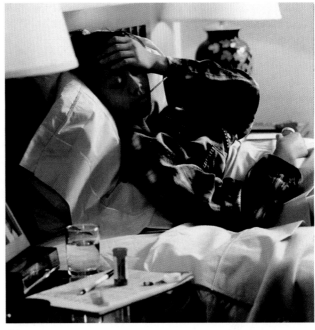

(a)   (b)

Figure 6-2   Active and passive coping. These two individuals have lower back pain resulting from comparable lower back injuries. One person (a) says, "I'm not going to let my pain dictate how I live my life" and is engaging in active coping by continuing to work full time despite continual pain. The passive coper (b) believes that rest is necessary to live with pain caused by the back injury and resorts to self-medication and unnecessarily checking her temperature. The active coper reports greater self-esteem and more enjoyment in life than does the passive coper.

Table 6-4
Coping Strategies

1. *Ignoring pain* can help a person lead a more active, satisfying life.
2. *Distraction and diverted attention* (e.g., reading a magazine or book) helps some people attend less to pain (especially acute pain) or disability.
3. *Positive self-statements,* such as, "I won't let it bother me," are often associated with lower levels of self-reported pain severity.
4. *Catastrophizing,* use of excessive or exaggerated negative self-statements, such as, "My condition is going to get progressively worse" is negatively correlated with adjustment to pain.
5. *Hoping/praying,* "I have faith in doctors who someday will find a cure for my pain," is negatively associated with adjustment to pain.

plaining about pain) and the conditions that strengthen or weaken these behaviors. In some cases, pain is related to a physical disorder that can be identified—for example, pain related to a deterioration of the discs that separate and cushion the bones in the spinal column. Even in situations where the source of the pain can be identified in bodily changes, some people experience incapacitating pain whereas others with what seem to be very similar changes do not. Psychological approaches have focused on these behaviors and the conditions that strengthen or weaken them. Another class of pain behaviors has no such clear antecedents: despite careful medical investigations, no organic changes can be found. The following case shows how operant conditioning procedures are clinically effective in bringing about behavioral changes related to pain when no physical cause can be identified:

> *The patient was a 19-year-old man who had been admitted to a hospital with complaints of pain in the lower back, hips, and both legs, and great difficulty in walking, sitting, and standing. An exhaustive medical study determined that his symptoms were unrelated to physical causes, and the case was diagnosed as a psychological disorder.*
>
> *The operant therapy consisted of visits by a young assistant to the patient's room three times daily. During these visits the assistant spent approximately ten minutes talking to the patient about topics unrelated to his disorder. During an initial three-day period she encouraged him to walk but provided him with no reinforcement for doing so. During the next three-day sequence she instructed the patient to walk and reinforced him when this happened. Reinforcement consisted of comments such as "Good," "That's great," and "You're doing fine," accompanied by attention, friendliness, and smiling. Reinforcements were not given during the following three-day period,*

but they were reinstituted during the final three days of the experimental therapeutic program. (Hersen et al., 1972, pp. 720–721)

This pattern of intervention is called an *A-B-A-B research design*. Such a design is useful in assessing the reasons for clinical change in a particular case because it can be carried out with only one subject who also serves as his or her own control in the period when no reinforcement is given. The A-B-A-B approach is used most often to determine whether operant conditioning procedures are effective in bringing about behavioral changes. It consists of obtaining a baseline measure of the target behavior (A), instituting reinforcement-contingency procedures (B), removing the contingency so that the conditions that were present during the baseline period are reinstated (A), and reintroducing the phase-B contingency (B). This *repeated-measures design* is a very powerful method for isolating the conditions that control behavior.

Figure 6-3 summarizes the results of the program described in the foregoing case. During the instruction

period there was no increase in walking, but the addition of reinforcement resulted in increased walking. When reinforcing contingencies are discontinued, there is usually a gradual decrease in the target behavior. In this case, however, contrary to what might be expected, improvement continued during the second period in which no reinforcement was given. Uncontrolled and unscheduled reinforcement by other patients may have contributed to this continued improvement. The greatest improvement occurred during the final phase of the program, when reinforcement by the assistant had resumed.

Cognitive-Behavioral Therapy From a conditioning perspective, pain is a learned response. The cognitive-behavioral perspective recognizes that the acquisition of pain behaviors also occurs by means of observational learning and modeling. That is, expectancies regarding pain intensity and actual behavioral responses to pain are based, at least partially, on prior learning history (e.g., children's observations of how their parents respond to pain.) Most cognitive-behavioral interventions include the following components:

1. The therapist explains to the pain sufferer the relevance of situations, thoughts, emotions, and behaviors to the pain experience.
2. The patient is encouraged to recognize and challenge maladaptive thoughts (such as catastrophizing and undesirable attitudes) that might be contributing to his or her pain and suffering.
3. The patient might be taught, as needed, a combination of specific skills, including self-relaxation, exercise, distraction techniques, pacing of activities, self-monitoring, and assertiveness. These skills are practiced and rehearsed in treatment sessions.
4. The patient is helped to identify high-risk situations that lead to emotional upset and pain flare-ups.
5. Finally, if the patient has retreated from normal life, encouragement is given to returning to prior daily life patterns.

Cognitive-behavioral therapists focus their attention on strengthening coping strategies that are useful in modifying the pain experience, elevating mood, and improving overall quality of life. A major goal of cognitive-behavioral therapy is to help the patient achieve adaptive self-management (see Table 6-5).

Biofeedback Pain has to do with bodily signals that are so amplified they hurt us. Some other types of bodily signals are not so readily perceived and require amplification. **Biofeedback** has been used in behavioral medicine to treat such problems as hypertension, highly volatile blood pressure, and epilepsy (see Figure 6-4). This technique provides a way of extending self-control procedures to deal with a variety of physiological behaviors that were formerly thought to be involuntary responses, such as heart rate, blood pressure, and brain waves. Such behaviors were

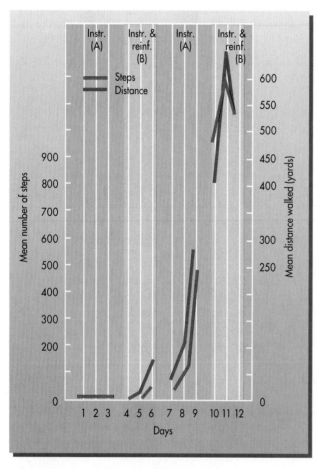

Figure 6-3   The chart shows changes in walking behavior during the four conditions of the repeated-measures design. Mean number of steps and distance walked are shown as a function of instructions and reinforcements.

Source: Based on Hersen et al., 1972.

Table 6-5
Self-Management Strategies for Coping With Pain

- *Relaxation and biofeedback.* Muscle relaxation decreases or prevents muscle spasms, reduces and controls muscle tension, and helps control other physiological mechanisms (such as changes in brain chemicals) involved in nervous system arousal and pain production. Relaxation and biofeedback, described elsewhere in this chapter, can help reduce common forms of chronic pain.
- *Cognitive restructuring.* Cognitive restructuring entails revising the way one thinks about a pain problem by rewriting one's internal "script." Pain sufferers have found it useful to record in diaries when their pain is particularly severe; what the situation was at the time of the pain; what they thought about and felt before, during, and after the pain episode; and what they tried to do to decrease the pain. In doing this, they have sometimes been able to (1) identify thoughts and cues that trigger tension and anxiety and (2) restructure or revise those of their thoughts that heighten stress and pain.
- *Distraction.* Conjuring up pleasant, painfree visions and thinking about topics not related to pain can help distract pain sufferers from becoming overly preoccupied with how much it hurts. Focusing on the environment and specific tasks (e.g., how to study for an upcoming exam) instead of paying attention to one's body can also help.
- *Exercise.* There is some evidence that physical workouts can ease pain by facilitating the release of neurotransmitters that serve as natural painkillers in the body. Exercise regimens for people with chronic pain usually entail working each day toward a specific goal—one that is difficult but still attainable.

thought to be beyond conscious control until researchers became aware of individuals who apparently are able to control them. One such person, a yoga practitioner named Swami Rama, was studied intensively at the Menninger Foundation (Green, 1972). Laboratory tests showed that, among other things, Rama was able to speed up and slow down his heart rate at will, to stop his heart from pumping blood for 17 seconds, to cause two areas of his palm a few inches apart to change temperature in opposite directions until their temperature differed by 10° F (the "hot" side of his palm became rosy, whereas the "cold" side became ashen), and to produce widely differing brain wave patterns at will.

Rama was not unique, although the extent of his control is startling. Humans and animals can learn to control their heart rate, blood pressure, brain waves, and other behaviors. For humans, no external reinforcement of the behavior seems to be necessary. All that is required is that the individual be given information in the form of feedback from the response system in question. Just as we could never learn to shoot a basketball accurately if we did not receive visual feedback and feedback from our muscles, we cannot learn to control our heart rates or brain waves unless we receive some kind of feedback on physiological changes as they occur. The feedback then serves as a reinforcer for the desired change.

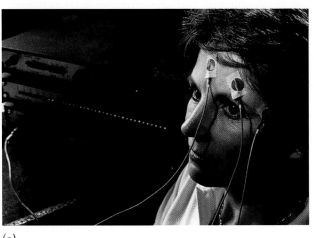

(a)

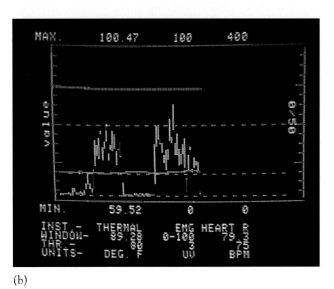

(b)

Figure 6-4   Biofeedback training can help clients control a variety of physiological responses. Photo (a) shows a client with the biofeedback apparatus. Photo (b) shows the video monitor that visually presents the responses as they occur.

Ordinarily we do not get feedback on such responses as blood pressure and brain waves, but through biofeedback—which precisely measures physiological events and converts the electronic signals into visual or auditory signals—we can be made aware of our own physiological responses. This process has been used to train people to control the physiological responses of the brain, muscles, and cardiovascular and glandular systems, and has been applied to a variety of clinical problems, including cardiac disorders, high blood pressure, headaches, anxiety, and neuromuscular disorders such as cerebral palsy. Clients come in for regular biofeedback sessions until they learn to recognize and control their bodily responses reliably without the help of the biofeedback apparatus.

Although there is no longer any question that people can learn to control a wide range of bodily functions, there are questions about the overall effectiveness of biofeedback. For example, there is evidence that skills learned through biofeedback training are lost rather quickly when training stops. As researchers continue to identify the limitations of biofeedback, how it can be used effectively will become more apparent (Schwartz, 1995). Biofeedback can be successfully applied to certain problems. An important goal of current research is to determine how and when biofeedback techniques can be used most effectively to enhance control over physiological and psychological responses.

Psychotherapy A large number of patients with chronic pain disorders are not psychologically oriented and for them insight psychotherapy is not efficacious. However, supportive psychotherapy may be helpful in reassuring and encouraging patients suffering from pain to comply with recommended rehabilitation programs. When a pain disorder is comorbid with another psychiatric condition, and if that condition is amenable to psychotherapy (e.g., as might be the case with anxiety disorder), the psychotherapy might be indirectly helpful in relation to the pain disorder.

Medication Pain-relieving medication is often prescribed for pain. However, some of the drugs that relieve pain are addictive and patients may demand increasingly larger dosages of them. Many clinicians explain to their patients that medications are often not helpful in the long run in relieving pain and that other techniques (described previously) are preferable. Patients who are prescribed pain-relieving medication on an as-needed basis often engage in pain behavior to indicate the need for medication. However, antidepressant medications can be helpful to pain patients when indications of depression are present.

The Realities of Pain Disorders Pain disorders are usually not simply figments of the imagination. They are biobehavioral phenomena. For that reason, it is not wise to focus only on symptoms and bodily pathology, even though these are important. The focus should be on the patient and how he or she is responding to physical trauma and the social environment. The patient's vulnerabilities (e.g., having certain personality characteristics, motivations, and needs), the precipitating factors (what brings on the experience of pain), and maintaining processes (e.g., the attention derived from being in pain) are all pertinent to understanding and treating pain patients. For most pain disorder patients, pain is out of proportion to what would normally be expected and becomes the central focus of their lives. Persistent pain creates a demoralizing situation that confronts the individual with the stress created by pain and often a cascade of ongoing stressors that affects all aspects of their lives.

There is much that is not known about pain as a biopsychosocial problem. However, we now know that pain is not simply a matter of a pure sensation. It is a subjective perceptual experience to which negative emotions (e.g., anxiety and depression) can quickly become attached. Pain as a biopsychosocial phenomenon is now being studied intensively. The results of this research are likely to enlighten our understanding of pain and lead to valuable treatments.

Somatization Disorders

Somatization disorders are marked by multiple somatic complaints that are recurrent or chronic. This condition is often referred to as **Briquet's syndrome** because a physician by the name Briquet described it in detail in 1859. The most common complaints are headaches, fatigue, heart palpitations, fainting spells, nausea, vomiting, abdominal pains, bowel troubles, allergies, and menstrual and sexual problems. With this wide assortment of complaints, it is not surprising that somatizing patients are continually going to the doctor, changing doctors, and undergoing probably unneeded surgery (see Table 6-6). Figure 6-5 compares the frequency of major surgical procedures for patients who were classified as somatizers with those of normal controls.

Individuals diagnosed with this disorder have a several-year history, beginning before age 30, of seeking treatment for or becoming impaired by multiple physical complaints that do not appear to be intentionally feigned. DSM-IV's criteria for this disorder include at least four pain symptoms in different bodily sites, two gastrointestinal symptoms without pain, one sexual symptom without pain, and one symptom or deficit suggesting a neurological symptom.

Patients with somatization disorders believe that they are sick, provide long and detailed histories in support of their belief, and take large quantities of medicines (see Table 6-7). Almost always, the chronic multiple complaints of somatizers are accompanied by a characteristic personality pattern and by difficulties in social relationships. They share many of the features of histrionic per-

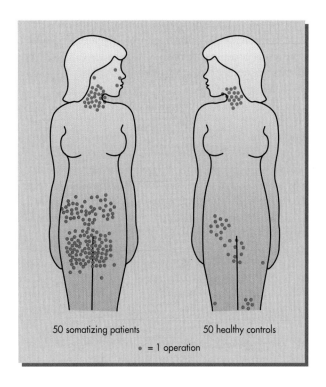

Figure 6-5 The complaints of somatizing patients often lead to unnecessary surgery. These two figures compare the number and location of major surgical procedures in 50 somatizing patients and 50 control subjects. Three times as much body tissue was removed from the somatizing patients as from the controls.

Source: Based on Cohen et al., 1953.

sonality disorders, including a self-centered attitude and exaggerated expressions of emotion. Anxiety and depression are common features, as is manipulativeness, which may take the form of suicide threats or attempts. Soma-

tizers impress people as being immature and overly excitable. Somatization disorder differs from hypochondriasis (discussed later in this chapter) in that hypochondriacs focus on the *fear* of having a specific disease or diseases whereas the person with a somatization disorder tends to be preoccupied with the *symptoms*.

The complaints in somatization disorders are usually presented in a dramatic, vague, or exaggerated way. Somatizers tend to use vivid images in describing events and their reactions to them. For example:

"I wake up in the morning stiff as a board."
"My heart feels as if iron bands were being tightened around it."
"I throw up every half hour."
"I can't even take liquids."
"I feel as weak as a cat."
"I really can't take it much longer."

Somatizing disorders seem to occur mainly in women; approximately 1% of women have the condition. It is not uncommon for a family to have more than one somatizer. Since people who are classified as having a somatizing disorder tend to be suggestible, the high prevalence of the disorder in certain families may reflect the influence of a somatizing parent (usually the mother) rather than heredity. The vagueness of somatization complaints makes it difficult to do good research on the disorder (e.g., the researcher is frequently left to wonder about possible organic causes of the symptoms).

It has frequently been said that patients with somatization disorders are unsuitable for psychotherapeutic treatment because they are not psychologically minded and are poorly motivated. However, both cognitive and psychodynamic therapies have been shown to be effective in treating these disorders (Guthrie, 1996). At the outset of psychotherapy, most somatizing patients believe that their complaints are caused by an organic disease. In building rapport, it is helpful if the therapist gives the patient the opportunity to describe his or her symptoms in detail and makes it clear that the symptoms are being taken seriously.

Conversion Disorders

People with **conversion disorders** report that they have lost part or all of some basic bodily function. The disturbance does not seem to be under voluntary control and cannot be explained in terms of the principles of medical science. Paralysis, blindness, deafness, and difficulty in walking are among the symptoms reported by these patients. The onset of symptoms in conversion disorders often follows a stressful experience and may be quite sudden. Psychodynamic theorists believe that the symptoms represent an underlying psychological conflict.

Conversion symptoms seem to be naive inventions developed without regard for the actual facts of anatomy. In the case of **glove anesthesia**, for example, the individual may be unable to feel anything in one hand, although the arm has normal sensation. This is anatomically implausible because the sensory nerve supply to this part of the body is organized so that glove anesthesia could not be a result of a neurological disorder (Halligan et al., 2000).

Although conversion symptoms often seem to appear for no obvious reason, they can frequently be traced to specific precipitating events. Complicating the task of diagnosing conversion disorders is the fact that at times they cannot easily be distinguished from somatically rooted symptoms. One clue that helps make the distinction is a characteristic feature of conversion disorders that has been termed *la belle indifférence* (beautiful indifference): whereas the individual may experience intense anxiety in other areas of life, his or her lack of concern about what seems to be an incapacitating physical disturbance is remarkable and not typically associated with similar symptoms caused by true somatic disorders.

Clinical conversion cases usually involve a single disturbance during any one period. Different bodily sites might be affected in subsequent episodes. The symptoms often allow the person to escape from frustrating or challenging situations through physical incapacity. When the pressures of these situations wane, the physical symptoms weaken. Secondary gain may also occur when the person derives something from a physical symptom (such as attention, affection, or a pension) that he or she might not get otherwise. Because histrionic tendencies and excitability are characteristic of people who have these bodily reactions, their symptoms often tend to be highly dramatic as well as incapacitating.

Conversion disorders illustrate how concepts of maladaptation can change over the years. Until relatively recently, these disorders were considered to be one type of a broader category called **hysteria** or **hysterical disorders.** The origin of the concept of hysteria can be traced back to at least the Middle Ages when it referred to disorders of the uterus, which it was believed were related to what is now called conversions. Hysteria was somehow viewed as a condition caused by a defect in the female reproductive system. In modern times, this broad category of hysteria included individuals who showed emotional immaturity and affective instability as predominant traits. In older terminologies these individuals might display dissociative reactions, multiple personality, and several other disorders in addition to conversion reactions. Today, DSM-IV limits the diagnosis of conversion disorder to conditions in which there are one or more symptoms of motor or sensory dysfunction that suggest but cannot be related to a medical problem. The symptoms, while not intentionally produced, are judged to be associated with psychological factors. Thus, the diagnosis of hysteria no longer occupies the important place it once occupied in psychiatric classification (see Box 6-2).

Hypochondriasis

Hypochondriasis is diagnosed if a person has a persistent (lasting 6 months or longer) belief that she or he has a serious illness despite medical reassurance, a lack of physical findings, and failure to develop the disease. Such persons often show poor insight in that they do not recognize that their concern is excessive. They are likely to say things like, "I consult a doctor as soon as possible when I have bodily complaints" and "If something seems wrong with my body, it upsets me at once" (Rief et al., 1998).

Hypochondriacs have an obsessive preoccupation and concern with the condition of their bodily organs and continually worry about their health. Because they fear developing a disease, they carefully track all potential symptoms by keeping themselves attuned to even the most minute changes in bodily functioning. They tend to misunderstand the nature of the significance of physiological activity and to exaggerate symptoms when they occur. Here is a physician's account of one of his hypochondriacal patients:

| Q&A | Box 6–2 |

Q. You say that the idea of hysteria has fallen into disuse, but I've read from time to time about something called mass hysteria. What's that?

A. The term **mass hysteria,** while not part of the psychiatric classification system, continues to be used to refer to somewhat mysterious outbreaks of illness in crowd or group settings. The symptoms—often headache, dizziness, nausea, and breathing difficulty—appear to be real but are not caused by a toxin. Rather, stress and anxiety seem to be the key factors. Schools, factories, and offices where people are under stress and share common space are common sites of mass hysteria. For example, on November 12, 1998, in Warren County High School located in McMinnville, Tennessee, teacher Susan Davis was preparing for her first class in food management when she noticed a gasoline-like smell. She felt dizzy, nauseated, short of breath, and developed a headache. Soon, several students in her room began to feel the same symptoms. When the school principal came to the room he also noticed an odor, which smelled to him like insecticide. He, too, got a headache. School officials sounded a fire alarm, evacuating the building. Still more students reported symptoms. Several people were taken to the hospital by ambulance; 100 people went to the emergency room.

Fire, gas company, and state health and safety experts spent 2 days inspecting, but found nothing wrong. When school reopened 4 days later, there was a new wave of complaints about odors. The day after the reopening, a half-dozen students were lying down in the lobby because the clinic was already packed. Ambulances returned, the school was again evacuated and closed, and 71 people went to the emergency room. This time, government agencies launched an extensive investigation that necessitated closing the school for 2 weeks. The investigation failed to find anything that could have caused the mass illness. After the school reopened the students showed high levels of anxiety for the rest of the school year. When the investigators concluded that no toxin, chemical, or virus spread the illness through the school, many students became upset and said things like: "They said we were crazy." "It makes me mad." "When I'm sick I don't want someone to say I'm faking." "They wouldn't have taken me to the hospital and my blood pressure wouldn't have been sky-high if I wasn't sick."

While some hidden cause not uncovered by the investigators might have been present, studies of the students suggested that, in any case, mass hysteria had occurred at Warren County High School. Victims were about three times more likely than others to have seen another sick person or to know that a classmate was ill. This illustrates a kind of social or emotional contagion, which spreads like a cold through a group of people. While social psychologists are studying this sort of phenomenon, it remains poorly understood (Bartholomew, 2000).

Harold Yocum kept the most extensive diary of any patient I have ever seen. Harold was a dapper little guy, standing perhaps five feet four. A local retail clerk, he was always impeccably dressed: sharp creases on his suit trousers (always a suit), carefully knotted ties, handkerchief in the breast pocket just so, highly polished wing tips, carefully clipped nails, and sharply parted hair with the long sweep over the bald spot. Harold was single and I could never get much social history from him—perhaps he didn't have much social history. He had some college education and had worked as a clerk for many years, but he never chatted about personal activities, friends, or hobbies. Efforts to engage him in such conversation made him uncomfortable, so after a few visits, I stopped trying. Indeed, after a few visits there was no opportunity to try. We had to review the diary. . . . He began to include more and more in his diary—time and dose of medication, general feelings, minor aches and pains, food-stuffs consumed, coffee and cola intake. He even developed his own stress scale and described evacuations in great detail—time, quantity, color.

Soon the volume of material was too much for his spiral-bound notebook and he began to bring in laboriously typed reports. (Burnside, 1987, p. 1802)

The diagnosis of hypochondriasis is considered when the individual (1) persistently believes that a serious illness underlies the symptoms presented to the physician and (2) disregards the physician's advice that no serious physical illness or abnormality is underlying the symptoms. Hypochondriacal individuals have three major characteristics: (1) physiological arousal, (2) a bodily focus, and (3) behaviors designed to avoid or check for physical illness. The physiological arousal is often reflected in increased tension and anxiety and sleep disturbances. The bodily focus is illustrated by close monitoring of bodily features, attention to information that is consistent with worries about illness, and preoccupation and rumination about physical complaints. The avoidance and checking is seen in repeated self-inspection, repeated medical consultation and reassurance-seeking, rigid views and behaviors regarding diet or lifestyle, and efforts to avoid physical exertion or contact with people who seem to have a disease.

Treatment strategies for hypochondriasis will vary from one individual to the next depending on the particular problems presented. Generally, however, these are components of most therapeutic approaches:

1. Establish a therapeutic relationship. This step is important because many individuals are reluctant to view their problems as being caused by anything other than a medical condition.

2. Acknowledge the distress caused by the individual's concerns.
3. Elicit the individual's fears and beliefs about his or her physical health.
4. Present alternative rational explanations and explain why the individual's ideas may be mistaken.

Cognitive-behavioral therapy may be especially helpful in treating hypochondriasis (Bouman & Visser, 1998). This approach emphasizes, consistent with Beck's cognitive therapy approach (Chapter 2), gently questioning the patient's beliefs—for example, the patient's statement, "My abdominal pain is a sign of stomach cancer." In addition, the patient is encouraged to resist going to the doctor as soon as bodily complaints are identified. Accomplishing this obviously requires the individual's cooperation in exposure to his or her symptoms without taking action in seeking a medical consultation. The individual is also encouraged to take note of the fact that the symptoms usually disappear.

Body Dysmorphic Disorders

Individuals with a **body dysmorphic disorder (BDD)** have a preoccupation with an imagined defect or morbidly excessive concern about a minor unwanted feature of their physical appearance. Alice Kenton, who was described at the beginning of the chapter, was diagnosed as having this type of disorder. Acne, hair thinning, wrinkles, scars, and excessive facial hair are examples of the unwanted features. Other common preoccupations include the shape, size, or some other aspect of the nose, eyes, mouth, teeth, or head. Most individuals with this disorder experience marked distress over their supposed deformity, often describing their preoccupations as "intensely painful" and "devastating." Feelings of self-consciousness about their "defect" may lead to avoidance of work or public situations.

One study found that when patients with BDD consult mental health professionals, they often emphasize their feelings of depression, phobias, obsessions, and compulsions, but fail to mention their bodily preoccupations (Veale et al., 1996). This seems to result from strong feelings of embarrassment and the belief that other people will not understand the concern or take the concern seriously. There is growing reason to believe that these feelings are outgrowths of personality, such as preoccupations about the need to be acceptable or even perfect (Cohen et al., 2000).

Body Image The essential feature of BDD is belief in an imagined defect in appearance. If a slight physical anomaly is present, the person's concern is markedly excessive. Unlike normal concerns about appearance, the preoccupation with appearance in BDD is time-consuming and causes significant distress or impairment in social situations. Beyond knowing that BDD is related to the presence of certain personality characteristics, little is known about this condition. It typically seems to become evident in adolescence, a developmental period marked by concern with how one appears to others and the need to minimize physical imperfections and maximize appealing bodily features.

While BDD is a disorder of **body image,** the perception of one's bodily features, it is worthwhile to think of it within the context of the diversity of bodily perceptions in a given population. We touched on this point when we discussed eating disorders in Chapter 5. We noted that individuals with anorexia nervosa place high value on achieving what they judge to be an ideal level of thinness. As with many human attributes, there are wide individual differences in what is regarded as desirable and undesirable. A fair amount of unhappiness is due to inaccurate or idiosyncratic personal judgments about body image—What is normal? What is realistic? What is admired? What is despised? Many women believe that being slender and not being muscular are desirable feminine characteristics. However, Jenny Thompson, who won several Olympic gold medals in swimming in 1992, 1996, and 2000, is much admired for her muscular physique and prowess. Her achievements would not have been possible if slenderness and nonmuscularity were ideals that guided her life. Thompson is 5'11", weighs 160 pounds, and while training eats six meals a day. She is a densely muscular person who takes pride in her appearance and achievements (see Figure 6-6). While there are few "rights" and "wrongs" concerning body image, there are many opinions about it. It is these opinions that influence whether one's body is perceived as admirable or defective.

Research on body image is turning up some interesting findings. One of these relates to the discrepancies between the bodies people want or think they should have and the bodies they have. In one study carried out with men in the United States, France, and Austria, the subjects desired to have a much leaner and more muscular body than the body they actually had or perceived themselves to have (Pope et al., 2000). Furthermore, they believed that women preferred a male body much more muscular than theirs. When asked for their preferences, women did not prefer highly muscular men. The wide discrepancy between men's actual muscularity and their body ideals may play a role in the apparent rise in disorders in which some men show a pathological preoccupation with their muscularity. A condition called **muscle dysmorphia,** in which these preoccupations play an important role, has been proposed as a form of BDD. In one study of a group of male weightlifters, a subgroup was identified in which there were high levels of body

(a)

(b)

Figure 6-6   How muscular should a woman be? Jenny Thompson, an Olympic swimming champion, sees her muscular body as admirable and a means by which she can live up to her potential.

Source: *New York Times,* August 7, 2000, pp. D1, D7.

dissatisfaction, use of anabolic steroids, the presence of eating disorders, and troubling anxiety and depression. These were taken as indicators of muscle dysmorphia (Olivardia et al., 2000). Normal weightlifters had few of these characteristics and, in fact, seemed very similar to a comparison group of men who did not lift weights. Further research on muscle dysmorphia in men and ideal-self discrepancies in body perception among both men and women is needed.

Treatment   Since BDD is a recently identified condition, research on effective treatments is just getting underway. Cognitive-behavioral therapy seems to be a promising approach. This type of therapy usually begins by providing the patient with basic information on the psychology of physical appearance, the concept of body image, and the development of BDD. At the outset, most patients believe that their psychological status (e.g., feeling tense and unworthy of the interest of others) cannot change until their "defect" (e.g., long nose, misshapen body) has been eliminated. The therapist typically responds to this by stressing that the problem in BDD is how patients view themselves and that therapy is designed to change body image, not appearance. After pinpointing dysfunctional attitudes and the situations in which they occur, patients are helped to restructure their cognitions by alerting them to the need to recognize maladaptive thoughts and to replace them with better alternatives. To overcome distress, patients must examine their assumptions about bodily characteristics in a more objective, dispassionate manner. It is sometimes helpful to use exposure therapy by having patients look at their bodies at home and encouraging them to question their evaluations of their bodies. Table 6-8 illustrates the application of exposure to BDD for a person who is overly self-conscious about his hands.

The treatment of BDD can be expected to improve as it becomes better understood.

Table 6-8
Exposure Exercises for a Man Who Is Ashamed of His "Awful" Hands

The patient is encouraged to:

1. Keep his hands out of pockets while in the presence of others.
2. Allow a stranger to greet him by shaking his hand.
3. Wear a wristwatch and rings to attract attention to his hands.
4. Sign checks in front of bank tellers and store merchants.
5. Try on rings in a jewelry store in front of the salesclerk.

Factitious Disorders and Malingering

Although somatoform disorders and various types of medical problems are different in a number of respects, they have in common the fact that the person with the disorder assumes the role of a patient—someone who receives attention and care. Another group of conditions that are characterized by the same feature is **factitious disorders** (the word *factitious* is defined as "artificial or unnatural"). But in these conditions, physical and psychological symptoms are voluntarily self-induced by the patient. This may involve either a total fabrication or an exaggeration of a preexisting condition.

In a factitious disorder, the only apparent goal is the desire to assume the role of patient. People with factitious disorders often have a history of uncontrollable lying, demands for attention from professional people, and dramatic accounts of vague pains. Classifying a set of symptoms as factitious may be quite difficult. The dramatic way in which the patient presents his or her problems usually arouses suspicion; however, many individuals with this disorder have managed to gather quite a bit of medical information and, as a consequence, may be good enough actors to make their symptoms seem credible.

Factitious disorders typically begin during early adulthood and are often stimulated by hospitalization for a genuine physical problem. Because of their dramatically presented but vague symptoms, individuals with factitious disorders often undergo frequent hospitalizations, during which unnecessary surgery may be performed. Although the symptoms of somaticizers and those with factitious disorders are the same, the somaticizers believe they are really ill, whereas those with factitious disorder are merely seeking attention by manufacturing symptoms. A review of childhood events in factitious disorders often reveals a history of childhood emotional insecurity, emotionally neglectful or rejecting parents, and broken homes leading to foster home placement or adoption (Folks et al., 2000).

The term **Munchausen syndrome** refers to an extreme type of factitious disorder marked by repeated, knowing simulation of disease for the sole purpose of obtaining medical attention. The syndrome is named after Baron von Munchausen, an eighteenth-century German cavalry officer who became legendary for concocting elaborate lies. A patient with Munchausen syndrome may travel great distances to appear at hospitals with dramatic and plausible, yet false, histories that convince physicians and staff members that he or she is suffering from an acute illness.

Patients with this syndrome tell incredible tales about their medical histories. They also fake symptoms; for example, they may pretend to be in pain, put blood in a urine sample, or manipulate a thermometer to create an impression of fever. Sometimes they go even further, inflicting real injury on themselves by burning or cutting themselves, taking dangerous drugs, or injecting foreign material into their veins. Often they persuade doctors to perform unnecessary surgery. They may spend most of their lives moving from one hospital to another, trying to be admitted. Once in a hospital, they refuse to comply with its rules and make constant demands for attention. The following case illustrates a typical example of Munchausen syndrome:

> A woman staggered into the emergency room of a New York City hospital bleeding from the mouth, clutching her stomach, and wailing with pain. It was some entrance. Even in that setting, forever serving bleeders and clutchers and wailers, there was something about her, some terrible star quality that held stage center. Her pain was larger than life.
>
> She told a harrowing story: A man had seduced her, then tied her up, beaten her, forced her to surrender money and jewelry on threat of death. She had severe pain in her lower left side and an unbearable headache.
>
> She was admitted, and exhaustively tested. Nothing could be found; no reason for the bleeding or the pain; the specialists were left scratching their heads.
>
> Then, one day, a hospital aide came upon these items in her bedside table: a needle, syringe, and a blood thinner called heparin. Eureka. Inject yourself with enough blood thinner and you, too, can take stage center in an emergency room.
>
> Confronted, she denied all charges. The stuff was not hers; someone was trying to frame her; if nobody believed her, she would check out of this place and find doctors who really cared. And off she went. Later, it was learned that she had recently been in two other hospitals: the same story, same symptoms, and same sequence of events. (Lear, 1988, p. 21)

A particularly disturbing variant of Munchausen syndrome is one in which a mother produces symptoms of disease in her child and then presents the child for treatment. When this happens, it is referred to as **factitious disorder by proxy.** The mother's concern may be convincing because she herself feels a need to be cared for; it is as though she regards the child's body as an extension of her own. The child goes along with the mother because the relationship is so close and intense and the activity so exciting.

Having a factitious disorder is not the same thing as **malingering.** People with factitious disorders simply crave attention and want to be taken care of. Malingerers, on the other hand, seek medical care and hospitalization in order to achieve some specific goal such as compensation, a disability pension, or evasion of the police. Whereas multiple complaints and hospitalizations seem almost a continuous pattern in factitious disorders, malingering often ends abruptly when the patient gets what he or she wants. In contrast, people with factitious disorders seem incapable of stopping their lying and manufacturing of symptoms. However, both of these conditions are self-induced, and both increase in response to high levels of stress.

Distinguishing factitious disorder or malingering from other conditions can be difficult. The judgment that a particular symptom is under voluntary control occasionally is made by excluding all other possible causes. Distinguishing between a factitious disorder and malingering also poses problems. When the clinician is not fully aware of the particular purpose for which the malingerer manufactures his or her symptoms, the chances of misdiagnosis increase. An act of malingering might, under certain circumstances, be considered adaptive (e.g., when a prisoner of war fakes an illness), but factitious disorders are almost always seen in people with severe, lifelong personality disturbances.

Chapter Summary

SOMATOFORM DISORDERS

Somatoform disorders are bodily complaints for which no actual physical impairment can be found. Somatization, conversion, body dysmorphic, and pain disorders, as well as hypochondriasis, are included under this classification.

Pain Disorders **Pain disorders** involve reports of extreme and incapacitating pain, either without any identifiable organic symptoms or with symptoms that are greatly in excess of what would be expected based on the organic symptoms found. These disorders can be acute or chronic and are difficult to diagnose. How people interpret pain influences their overall adjustment. Some pain sufferers can learn to use **active coping** (remaining active and ignoring the pain). Others engage in **passive coping,** which leads to relatively reduced activity and social withdrawal. While pain-reducing medications can be helpful in short-term **acute pain disorder, chronic pain disorder** is often most effectively treated using a psychological approach. Operant conditioning, cognitive-behavioral therapy, biofeedback, and psychotherapy are components of this approach. From a conditioning standpoint, pain is a learned response that can be influenced by changes in reinforcement contingencies. Cognitive-behavioral therapists use education, encouragement, and specific skills (e.g., self-relaxation, exercise, and distraction). Biofeedback provides patients with visual information concerning their ongoing physiological reactions. The technique helps them use self-control procedures to regulate body functions such as muscle tension and other reactions to stress. While insight psychotherapy is usually not an effective treatment for most pain problems, supportive therapy may be helpful in reassuring and encouraging pain patients to comply with recommended rehabilitation programs.

Somatization Disorders Patients with **somatization disorders** (also called **Briquet's syndrome**) have multiple and recurrent or chronic bodily complaints. These complaints are likely to be presented in a dramatic and exaggerated way.

Conversion Disorders The symptoms of **conversion disorders** are the reported loss of part or all of some basic body function, for instance the paralysis of some portion of the body or the loss of a sensory function such as ability to see. This loss does not seem to be under voluntary control, although the symptoms cannot be explained physically. One symptom of conversion disorder is *la belle indifférence,* a lack of concern about what seem to be incapacitating physical symptoms.

Hypochondriasis People affected with **hypochondriasis** show unrealistic fears of illness and are excessively preoccupied with their health. They are often helped by a therapist who gently questions their beliefs and motivates them to resist going to the doctor with hypochondriacal concerns. The patient is encouraged to observe that their symptoms usually disappear over time.

Body Dysmorphic Disorders People with **body dysmorphic disorders** are preoccupied with imagined or exaggerated bodily defects. They experience great distress over their supposed deformity. Their distress is an outgrowth of their personality and preoccupations with their **body image,** which includes the concern that they have an observable physical anomaly. Information showing that this concern is unwarranted may be helpful, as is encouraging them to question some of the components of their body image.

FACTITIOUS DISORDERS AND MALINGERING

Factitious disorders have symptoms that are voluntarily induced by the patient, presumably in an effort to receive attention and care. **Munchausen syndrome** is an extreme form of this disorder in which the person deliberately simulates the symptoms of disease by faking symptoms and even manipulating the results of medical tests. **Malingering** differs from factitious disorders because the person reports the symptoms in order to achieve some specific goal, such as an insurance settlement.

Key Terms

Bodily preoccupations, p. 192
Somatoform disorders, p. 192
Pain disorder, p. 192
Active coping, p. 193
Passive coping, p. 193
Acute pain disorder, p. 193

Chronic pain disorder, p. 193
Biofeedback, p. 196
Somatization disorders, p. 198
Conversion disorders, p. 200
Hypochondriasis, p. 200
Body dysmorphic disorder (BDD), p. 202

Body image, p. 202
Muscle dysmorphia, p. 202
Factitious disorders, p. 203
Munchausen syndrome, p. 204
Malingering, p. 204

Anxiety
Disorders

SUSAN: I wish I could tell you exactly what's the matter. Sometimes I feel like something terrible has just happened when actually nothing has happened at all. Other times I'm expecting the sky to fall down any minute. Most of the time I can't point my finger at something specific. Still, I feel tense and jumpy. The fact is that I am tense and jumpy almost all the time. Sometimes my heart beats so fast, I'm sure it's a heart attack.

Little things can set it off. The other day I thought a supermarket clerk had overcharged me a few cents on an item. She showed me that I was wrong, but that didn't end it. I worried the rest of the day. I kept going over the incident in my mind, feeling terribly embarrassed at having raised the possibility that the clerk had committed an error. The tension was so great, I wasn't sure I'd be able to go to work in the afternoon. That sort of thing is painful to live with.

PAUL: It happened without any warning, a sudden wave of terror. My heart was pounding like mad, I couldn't catch my breath, and the ground underfoot seemed unstable. I was sure it was a heart attack. It was the worst experience of my life.

SHARON: I can't tell you why I'm afraid of rats. They fill me with terror. Even if I just see the word *rat,* my heart starts pounding. I worry about rats in restaurants I go to, in my kitchen cupboard, and anywhere I hear a noise that sounds like a small animal scratching or running.

MIKE: Before I come home from work I spend half my time wondering whether a burglar has broken into the apartment. As soon as I get home I check every room, under the bed, and in the closets. Before going to sleep I probably check the lock on the front door fifty times. I feel better after each check, but then my concern wells up and I have to go check again.

PHILIP MANHARD: I dwelt on the good things. I refused to succumb to self-pity. I'd go back and relive the happiest moments. I had a wonderful marriage and family. I played over golf courses I knew in my mind. When a baguette replaced the rice in my meals, I molded bits of the bread into a chess set. Playing chess with myself was good therapy; the problem was that I always knew what move the other player was going to make. (Manhard, 1996–1997, p. 6) ■

If you feel that Philip Manhard is somehow different from the first four individuals, you are on the right track. The problems experienced by the first four individuals have one feature in common: the experience of strong anxiety. In Susan's case, which illustrates a generalized anxiety disorder, the anxiety is chronic and is felt in a variety of situations. Paul is describing a panic attack, in which the anxiety is sudden and overwhelming. People who experience one or more panic attacks worry a great deal about whether and where another attack may take place. Sharon has a phobic disorder, in which anxiety is aroused by a specific type of situation, animal, or object. Mike's case is an example of an obsessive-compulsive disorder, in which thinking certain thoughts and neglecting to do certain things (like checking the lock on the front door) arouse intense anxiety and concern.

What is Philip Manhard's problem? Actually, his self-description is an account, not of a problem, but of exemplary functioning under what might seem to be overwhelming stress. Manhard is describing how he coped with 5 years (1968–1973) of solitary confinement as a prisoner of war in Vietnam. When asked in 1996 how he looked back upon his imprisonment, he said, "I feel that what is past is past. There's too much that is interesting and worthwhile now to worry about yesterday" (Manhard, 1996–1997, p. 6).

What perhaps most distinguishes Philip Manhard from Susan, Paul, Sharon, and Mike is the absence of worry, tension, self-preoccupation, and catastrophic thinking in how he describes himself. Of course, from time to time everyone experiences these kinds of thoughts and feelings. However, in an anxiety disorder, they are not just occasional occurrences. Rather, they characterize huge chunks of the person's life. In this chapter, we describe and discuss these disorders.

The Experience of Anxiety

Everyone has worries and fears, even the rich and famous (see Figure 7-1). Freud argued that anxiety can be adaptive if the discomfort that goes with it motivates people to learn new ways of approaching life's challenges. But whether it is adaptive or maladaptive, the discomfort can be intense. The anxious person who is waiting for the worst to happen is often unable to enjoy a personal life or gain gratification from work. Anxious people may thus prevent themselves from experiencing positive outcomes in life.

The term **anxiety** is usually defined as a diffuse, vague, very unpleasant feeling of fear and apprehension. The anxious person worries a lot, particularly about unknown dangers. In addition, the anxious individual shows combinations of the following symptoms: rapid heart rate, shortness of breath, diarrhea, loss of appetite, fainting,

Figure 7-1 Even successful people known for their toughness and daring may have powerful fears that dictate their behavior. Tony Dorsett, one of football's greats, makes no secret of his fear of sleeping in the dark: "I've always been a person afraid of the dark. I was taught that when you have complete darkness, that's when spirits walk. In our house when I was growing up, all the doors were always cracked a little bit at night so you could get light into the room. You come in my house now and you're gonna see light everywhere. Even now when I sleep, I leave the bathroom light on and leave the door cracked. And I'm not ashamed to tell you."

dizziness, sweating, sleeplessness, frequent urination, and tremors. All of these physical symptoms accompany fear as well as anxiety. Fear differs from anxiety in that people who have fears can easily state what they are afraid of. People who feel anxious, on the other hand, are not aware of the reasons for their fear. Thus, even though fear and anxiety involve similar reactions, the cause of worry is readily apparent in the former case but is not at all clear in the latter. Examples of common fears include fear of being evaluated in a negative way by others (e.g., in a job interview) and fear of bodily injury or illness (e.g., thinking about the possibility of a crash during an especially bumpy airplane flight).

For persons suffering from anxiety disorders, intrusive thoughts often take the form of worries about possible future events and outcomes or catastrophic interpretations of past events that emphasize the negative, especially with regard to mistakes an individual might have made. These intrusive worries and exaggeratedly distressing interpretations are characteristic of the anxiety experience and often seem to have an automatic quality that emanates more from the individuals themselves than from what is actually going on in their lives. The characteristics of anxiety include feelings of uncertainty, helplessness, and physiological arousal. A person who experiences anxiety complains of feeling nervous, tense, jumpy, and irritable. Often he or she has difficulty falling asleep at night. An anxious person becomes fatigued easily and can have "butterflies in the stomach," as well as headaches, muscle tension, and difficulty in concentrating. There is growing evidence that people suffering from anxiety disorders are overly sensitive to threat cues. Such individuals may exhibit a heightened sensitivity, vigilance, or readiness to attend to potential threats. Table 7-1 lists common symptoms of anxiety and self-descriptions given by people with high levels of anxiety. In addition to occurring after an event has taken place or in anticipation of a future event, the experience of intense anxiety may occur when a person decides to resist a preoccupying idea, change an undesirable aspect of behavior, or approach a fear-arousing stimulus.

This chapter focuses on the serious maladaptive aspects of anxiety, but it is useful to remember that anxiety has many causes and that all people experience it at some time in their lives. It is normal for people to experience anxiety when faced with stressful, threatening situations, but it is abnormal to feel strong, chronic anxiety in the absence of an obvious cause.

In Chapter 4, we discussed several disorders that occur after traumatic events, such as serious accidents and natural disasters, and we saw that recovery from them usually is good. In this chapter we discuss four types of disorders— generalized anxiety, panic, phobic, and obsessive-compulsive disorders—in which anxiety is chronic and its cause not so clear, and one type (posttraumatic stress disorder) in which there has been a major stressor but the anxiety reaction to it is protracted.

A *generalized anxiety disorder* is marked by chronic anxiety over a long period (at least several months). A *panic disorder* consists of recurrent, sudden anxiety attacks in which the individual experiences intense terror and dread. In *phobic disorders*, the anxiety has an identifiable cause— for example, being near dogs or having to speak to a group. When the stimulus is not present, the phobic person's tension level is relatively low. In *obsessive-compulsive disorder*, anxiety results from efforts to prevent undesirable outcomes. The individual is plagued with a recurrent need to ward off disaster by thinking about certain ideas and/or performing certain acts. In *posttraumatic stress disorder*, intrusive thoughts, numbness, and anxiety persist long after the stressful event has ended.

Many clinicians used to describe people who were suffering from anxiety disorders as neurotic. In DSM-II, an early version of the DSM classification system that was strongly influenced by the psychodynamic perspective, the word *neurosis* was used to describe disorders marked by anxiety, personal dissatisfaction, and inappropriate (but not psychotic) behavior. These disorders were grouped together because it was thought that they all arose from somewhat similar unconscious mental processes and mo-

Table 7-1
Common Anxiety Symptoms and Self-Descriptions Indicative of High Anxiety
Symptoms

- Nervousness, jitteriness
- Tension
- Feeling tired
- Dizziness
- Frequency of urination
- Heart palpitations
- Feeling faint
- Breathlessness
- Sweating
- Trembling
- Worry and apprehension
- Sleeplessness
- Difficulty in concentrating
- Hypervigilance

Self-Descriptions

- "I am often bothered by the thumping of my heart."
- "Little annoyances get on my nerves and irritate me."
- "I often suddenly become scared for no good reason."
- "I worry continuously, and that gets me down."
- "I frequently get spells of complete exhaustion and fatigue."
- "It is always hard for me to make up my mind."
- "I always seem to be dreading something."
- "I feel nervous and high-strung all the time."
- "I often feel I can't overcome my difficulties."
- "I feel constantly under strain."

tivations. Although this view may someday be substantiated, today it is not widely held.

Most current schemes for classifying maladaptive behavior involve identifying its source and using the obvious presence of marked anxiety as the criterion for including maladaptive behavior in the group of **anxiety disorders.** This chapter is restricted to a discussion of disorders in which the individual is abnormally anxious, either generally or under certain circumstances, but still has adequate contact with reality and is rarely incapacitated enough to require institutionalization. The role of anxiety in several other disorders is described in later chapters. We will look first at specific characteristics of the various anxiety disorders and examine some similarities and differences among them. In the latter part of the chapter we will discuss particular therapeutic approaches to these disorders.

Although the anxiety disorders include a wide range of maladaptive behavior, the various conditions can usually be categorized into one of two groups: (1) the frequent experience of anxiety, worry, and apprehension more intense

Table 7-2

Prevalence of Anxiety Disorders

Anxiety disorders are common. This table shows the percent of the U.S. population that suffers from anxiety disorder during any given year.

Disorder	Percent (1-year prevalence)
Any anxiety disorder	13.3
Generalized anxiety disorder	2.8
Panic disorder	1.7
Phobic disorder	8.0
Obsessive-compulsive disorder	2.3
Posttraumatic stress disorder	3.6

Source: National Institute of Mental Health (1999).

and longer lasting than the anxiety experienced by the average person in everyday life; and (2) the frequent development of avoidance, ritual acts, or repetitive thoughts as a means of protecting the individual from experiencing the anxiety. Table 7-2 shows that the anxiety disorders affect a large number of people each year. Perhaps one-third of the United States' mental health bill is for the treatment of anxiety disorders.

We turn now to a review of the anxiety disorders from the standpoints of the clinical problems presented and diagnoses. The concluding section of the chapter will discuss how the anxiety disorders are interpreted and treated.

Generalized Anxiety Disorder

Generalized anxiety disorder might best be described as consisting of prolonged, vague, unexplained, but intense fears that do not seem to be attached to any particular object. They resemble normal fears, but there is no actual danger, and in most cases danger is not even imagined to be present. In one study, patients with various types of anxiety disorders were asked, "Do you worry excessively about minor things?" Ninety-one percent of those diagnosed as having generalized anxiety disorder answered yes to this question, a much higher percentage than for any of the other anxiety disorder groups (Sanderson & Barlow, 1990). Not only do individuals suffering from anxiety disorders worry about minor things that have happened, they also feel worried and tense even when nothing even mildly alarming has occurred. They seem to spend a lot of time anticipating alarms that probably will not sound (Figure 7-2).

Table 7-3 lists the major features of generalized anxiety disorder. This diagnosis is not used if there is evidence that the features listed in Table 7-3 are due to substance abuse or a general medical condition, or if they occur exclusively in connection with another major Axis I diagnosis.

In generalized anxiety disorder, anxiety persists for 6 months or longer and is not attributable to recent life experiences. The symptoms of generalized anxiety disorder usually include motor tension, hyperactivity of the autonomic nervous system, dread of the future, and hypervigilance. These symptoms, which are described as follows, may be experienced individually or in combination:

- *Worry and apprehensive feelings about the future.* People with generalized anxiety disorders worry about what the future holds for them, for people close to them, or for their valued possessions.
- *Hypervigilance.* People who suffer from generalized anxiety adopt a sentrylike stance in their approach to life. They constantly scan the environment for dangers (not necessarily of a physical nature), although often they cannot specify what the dangers might be. This excessive vigilance is related to their hyperaroused state. Because they are always alert to potential threats, they are easily distracted from tasks on which they are working. Their hypervigilance also contributes to difficulty in falling asleep.
- *Motor tension.* Individuals with this symptom are unable to relax; they are keyed up and visibly shaky and tense. Strained facial expressions are common, as are furrowed brows and deep sighs. Such individuals are easily startled.
- *Autonomic reactivity.* In individuals with this symptom, the sympathetic and parasympathetic nervous systems seem to be working overtime. There is some combination of sweating, dizziness, pounding or racing heart, hot or cold spells, cold and clammy hands, upset stomach, lightheadedness, frequent urination or defecation, lump in the throat, and high pulse and respiration rates.

One study conducted in three cities found that between 4.1% and 6.6% of the population had experienced a generalized anxiety disorder during their lives (Robins & Regier, 1991). It is more common among women than men. The course of generalized anxiety disorder for both men and women is usually protracted, with durations of as long as 20 years being common. The disorder tends to become evident between the late teens and early twenties. However, experiences early in life in which children feel they do not have control over what is happening in the environment or what might happen tend to make them especially vulnerable to the development of anxiety (Chorpita & Barlow, 1998).

The following case illustrates several of the general anxiety disorder symptoms we have described:

John Valle, a 32-year-old manager of a section of a department store, sought professional help because he was worried

Table 7-3

Clinical Features of Generalized Anxiety Disorder

1. Excessive anxiety and worry occuring for at least 6 months and affecting many areas of a person's life
2. Inability to control the worry
3. The presence of 3 or more of the following symptoms (only one type of symptom is required for DSM-IV in the diagnosis of children):
    a. Restlessness; feeling on edge
    b. Being easily fatigued
    c. Difficulty concentrating; mind goes blank
    d. Irritablity
    e. Muscle tension
    f. Sleep disturbance (difficulty falling or staying asleep; unsatisfying sleep)
4. Considerable distress or impairment in social, occupational, or other important areas of life

that he was "going insane." For almost 10 years he had had attacks of dizziness, feelings of weakness and fatigue, irritability, and—as he put it—"worry about everything." For the past year, his restlessness had grown so marked that he could scarcely stand, sit, or lie still. He felt driven to overactivity and wore out the people with whom he worked. Recently he had started taking sleeping pills because of difficulty falling asleep. While his main complaints at the time he started psychotherapy concerned his bodily symptoms, his worries about his life situation and the future came to dominate the content of his therapy sessions. He came to be aware of his intense anxiety,

and after three months of therapy realized that he was continually increasing this anxiety by getting into problematic situations and accepting responsibilities that, in retrospect, he believed were unreasonable.

John Valle improved somewhat as a result of his psychotherapy, which was psychodynamically oriented. However, generalized anxiety disorder is often difficult to treat, and there is no one clinical technique that regularly results in a cure. Cognitively and psychodynamically oriented psychotherapy can be helpful in some cases, as can

Pepper ... and Salt

THE WALL STREET JOURNAL

"My children are all happily married, for the time being."

(a)

"I've got the bowl, the bone, the big yard. I know I should be happy."

(b)

Figure 7-2 These cartoons illustrate the anxiety that can occur in the absence of a stimulating event.

behaviorally oriented treatment. The available medications designed to counteract anxiety are often helpful while the patient is taking them, but when they are discontinued symptoms usually return. Furthermore, prolonged use of these medications can have significant side effects. At the end of the chapter we shall compare the various theoretical influences in the study of all the anxiety disorders and their treatment.

Panic Disorder

Pan, the Greek god of woods and fields, was blamed for the inexplicable dread sometimes felt by travelers in lonely places. His name has been given to a disorder identified by sudden, overwhelming, apparently senseless terror. **Panic disorder** may attack with no warning (see Figure 7-3). The indicators of panic disorder are similar to those of generalized anxiety disorder, except that they are greatly magnified and usually have a sudden onset. However, there are differences between generalized anxiety disorder and panic disorder in their risk factors, rates of occurrence, and family incidence rates.

The term **panic attack** denotes an abrupt surge of intense anxiety rising to a peak that either is cued by the presence, or thoughts, of particular stimuli or that occurs without obvious cues and is spontaneous and unpredictable. In the former case (which is more common), persons experiencing panic often have phobic fears that the stimuli evoke. People who have panic attacks when evoking stimuli are not present typically do not have phobias as well.

Stressful life events such as a new job, marriage, or moving can trigger a panic attack. In panic disorder, there is intense fear of having another attack. DSM-IV defines **panic disorder** as including recurrent, unexpected panic attacks and at least 1 month of persistent concern over having them again. Worry over the implications and consequences of having panic attacks is a key aspect of this disorder, which is a chronic and debilitating condition. Although more research on the topic is needed, there are some suggestions that individuals who have panic attacks may be at a somewhat higher risk than the general population for sudden cardiac death later in their lives (Fleet & Beitman, 1998). However, the basis of this added risk has not been identified and it is possible that successful treatment of panic disorder reduces or eliminates the risk.

People with panic disorder need not be anxious all the time. Instead, they have unanticipated panic attacks that recur after periods (perhaps several days) of normal functioning. Severe palpitations, extreme shortness of breath, chest pains or discomfort, trembling, sweating, dizziness, and a feeling of helplessness mark the panic attacks. The victims fear that they will die, go crazy, or do something uncontrolled, and they report a variety of unusual psychosensory symptoms (see Table 7-4). In addition to recurrent unexpected panic attacks, panic disorder patients also display persistent concern about having additional attacks and what the attacks might imply. Panic disorder affects women more than men, and younger age groups more than the elderly (Robins & Regier, 1991).

Panic attacks range in length from a few seconds to many hours and even days. They also differ in severity and

Figure 7-3   John Madden, a 6'4" 240-pound former football player and head coach of the Oakland Raiders professional football team, is now a well-known TV sports personality. While he was flying across the country one day, Madden experienced a severe panic attack, disembarked at a stop halfway across the United States, and has never flown again. He is shown here in the luxury bus—donated for his use by Greyhound—that now serves as his home as he travels across the country.

Table 7–4

Clinical Features of Panic Attacks

- Shortness of breath or the feeling of being smothered
- Dizziness, unsteadiness, or faintness
- Trembling, shaking, or sweating
- Heart palpitations or a racing heart rate
- Choking, nausea, or stomach pain
- Numbness or tingling; flushing or chills
- Chest pain or discomfort
- A sense of "strangeness," of being detached from oneself or one's surroundings
- Fear of going crazy, losing control, or dying

in the degree of incapacitation involved. In the following case, frequent panic attacks had a definitely incapacitating effect:

A 30-year-old housewife comes to a psychiatric clinic complaining that she is afraid she will no longer be able to care for her three young children. In the past few months she has suffered repeated episodes of dizziness and shortness of breath, with chest pains, heart palpitations, headaches, and uncontrollable trembling. During these episodes the world seems strange and unreal, and she has a sense of impending doom. Once she went to a hospital, irresistibly convinced that she was having a heart attack. Her doctor told her that she was physically healthy and suggested that she relax, work less hard, and develop more interests outside her family, but the attacks became more intense and frequent, and finally he referred her to the clinic.

Although she used to be gregarious and outgoing, she is now afraid to leave home except in the company of her husband or her mother. She avoids supermarkets and department stores, and says that any crowded place makes her uneasy. When she has to be in an unfamiliar building, she tries to stay near the door and checks for windows and exits. She will no longer drive a car, ride a train, or board a boat. Bridges terrify her. She says that she trembled with fear even on the way to the clinic. Last summer, the family did not take their usual vacation because she did not think she could tolerate being so far from home. Now she wants her mother to stay with her when the children are at home, because she is afraid that if one of the children had an accident she would be unable to help.

This case illustrates an important feature in many cases of panic disorder: avoidance of certain activities or situations associated with panic attacks. This phobic avoidance, called agoraphobia, will be discussed further when we re-

view the major types of phobias in the next section of this chapter.

Compared to other anxiety disorders, panic attacks appear to be particularly distressing experiences. Generalized anxiety and panic disorder both run in families, although the family incidence rate is much higher for panic disorder. There is no evidence that any specific type of childhood experience predisposes people to these states. Problems often arise in classifying these disorders, because many cases are complicated. Several types of maladaptive behavior may occur simultaneously. Obsessions, compulsions, and phobias might all be observed in a given individual. Severe panic states are sometimes followed by periods of psychotic disorganization in which there is a reduced capacity to test reality.

Box 7-1 presents a case of both anxiety and panic disorder along with an interpretation of its major features. A person who has had a panic attack develops anticipatory anxiety: he or she becomes worried and tense, and is afraid that the panic will recur. In some cases, this type of anticipatory anxiety seems to be a quite realistic fear. Recent research has revealed that persons who experience panic attacks perceive themselves as having impairments in their physical health and emotional well-being, and in occupational and financial functioning. They are heavy users of health care facilities and emergency departments, and they are much more prone than the general population to think about committing suicide. Twenty percent of patients with panic disorder report that they have attempted suicide (Klerman et al., 1991). In addition to studying suicidal cognitions of people who experience panic attacks, research has revealed certain cognitive processes that occur during these attacks. Ottaviani and Beck (1987) asked persons who had had panic attacks about the types of thoughts they remembered having during the attacks. Subjects reported thoughts of humiliation, losing control, helplessness, and failure.

There is reason to believe that panic and anticipatory anxiety have different sources. Imipramine, a drug used in the treatment of depression, has been shown to prevent the recurrence of panic attacks. However, it seems to have no effect on the anticipatory anxiety that panic attacks almost always arouse. That is, subjects treated with imipramine may feel anxious in anticipation of a panic attack but not experience one.

In the past, relatively few attempts had been made to identify and compare generalized anxiety and panic disorder. Now their similarities and differences are being examined and investigated more intensively. For example, one group of researchers has compared the patterns of symptoms, family characteristics, type of onset, and clinical course in generalized anxiety disorder and panic disorder (D. J. Anderson et al., 1984). Their findings support the assumption that these conditions are distinct from one

Case Study

Box 7–1

An Anxious, Precise, Demanding Man Seeks Help

Mr. E., 40 years old and recently married, sought clinical help because he was nervous and worried about his health. These lifelong concerns became worse during his courtship and honeymoon. To quote from his case history:

Mr. E. has trouble falling asleep if the room is too dark or too light, if he has eaten too much or too little, if the sheets are cold or wrinkled, if he forgets his nose spray, or if there is any noise. He fears nightmares, nocturnal asthma attacks, or dying in his sleep. He often awakes in a panicky sweat with nightmares, typically of being chased or suffocated. He worries that his lost sleep is shortening his life and ruining his work efficiency.

Mr. E. had always been anxious and worried. He expects the worst, dreads each time the phone rings lest it be bad news, and suspects that he has a serious illness. He experiences frequent palpitations, shortness of breath, dizziness, and numb fingers and has had numerous physical exams and electrocardiograms. The negative findings do not reassure him, as Mr. E. is convinced that his doctors are withholding information, and he is determined to have additional checkups until his condition is diagnosed. He also has gastrointestinal flutters, frequent diarrhea or constipation, and occasional nausea and vomiting. His father died of heart disease and his mother of cancer, and he feels confident that he already has, or soon will have, one or both conditions.

Mr. E. is also extremely anxious about his work. He is a stockbroker responsible

for large financial transactions and cannot ever relax his concentration, even on vacations. He has also felt considerable performance anxiety about his recently more active sex life and has suffered from consistent premature ejaculation. There are many specific situations that make him intolerably nervous—waiting in line, sitting in the middle of a row at a movie, riding public transportation, wearing a pair of pants a second time without having them cleaned, having dirty dollar bills, and so forth—but he is able to avoid most of them without great inconvenience. Mr. E. has panic attacks at least every few weeks. They tend to occur whenever something new is expected of him, when he is forced to do one of the things he fears, when he must give a talk, and, at times, for no apparent reason.

Mr. E. is a very precise and demanding man who is difficult to live or work with (or to treat). He is controlling, self-absorbed, maddeningly fastidious, and meticulous. He did not marry previously because he had very demanding expectations of a woman, and his worries and habits are intolerable to many women. His wife had begun to complain to him, and he is afraid she may leave unless he is able to change quickly. (Frances & Klein, 1982)

An Evaluation of Mr. E.'s Condition

Because this is a real-life case, it is more complicated than a textbook outline of a disorder. Mr. E. might be described in

terms of either generalized anxiety disorder or panic disorder. However, because of the definite recurring panic attacks, panic disorder seems the more likely primary diagnosis. Mr. E.'s concerns about being precise and meticulous also raise the possibility of an obsessive-compulsive personality disorder. Despite Mr. E.'s protestations to the contrary, he suffers from no apparent physical disorder. A reasonable rating of Mr. E.'s psychosocial stress (his recent marriage) would seem to be moderately severe, Mr. E. might be described as having a fair level of adaptive functioning in the past year. Despite his superior work performance, his social and leisure-time difficulties now suggest a decreased level of functioning.

Thus, Mr. E. might be described as having a panic disorder, features of an obsessive-compulsive personality disorder, no apparent physical disorders, moderately severe stress in the recent past, and moderate but increasing difficulty in functioning.

It is important to remember that experienced clinicians might disagree about this description either because of gaps in what is known about Mr. E. or because of emphasis on different known facts. With additional information, the classification might change. A clinician treating Mr. E. would want to better understand his sexual problems, his conviction that he has cancer or heart disease, and his somatic complaints for which no bodily cause has been found.

Case study from A. J. Frances and D. F. Klein: "Anxious, Precise, Demanding Man Seeks Help Soon After Marriage," in *Hospital and Community Psychology, 33,* 89–90, 1982. Copyright © 1982 by the American Psychiatric Association. Reprinted by permission.

---

another. Table 7-5 compares these disorders with regard to several bodily symptoms. Subjects with generalized anxiety disorder have fewer bodily symptoms than do those with panic disorder. Their histories also show an earlier, more gradual onset. A generalized anxiety disorder has a more chronic course and is more likely to have a favorable outcome. Members of families in which a person suffers from a panic disorder tend to have a relatively high percentage of panic episodes. The comparable percentage

for family members of those with a generalized anxiety disorder is lower.

Panic and generalized anxiety disorders differ most clearly in the diffuseness of the anxiety seen in the latter and its focused intensity in the former. But research has shown that the two disorders differ in a number of other ways as well (Woodman et al., 1999). Table 7-6 lists some of these differences. In addition to investigating the characteristics of panic disorders, researchers are also con-

Table 7-5

Percentages of Patients With Panic Disorder and Generalized Anxiety Disorder Reporting Particular Symptoms

Symptom	Panic Disorder (%)	Generalized Anxiety Disorder (%)
Sweating, flushing	58	22
Heart palpitations	90	61
Chest pain	69	11
Faintness, lightheadedness	52	11
Blurred vision	31	—
Feeling of muscular weakness	48	11

Source: Based on D. J. Anderson et al. (1984).

Table 7-6

Characteristics of Panic Disorder in Comparison With Characteristics of Generalized Anxiety Disorder

1. Clinical onset is later.
2. The role of heredity seems to be greater.
3. The ratio of women to men is greater.
4. Alcoholism is more common.
5. While depression is common in both, it is unusually more common in panic disorder.

ducting experiments designed to better understand how the attacks come about. It has been discovered that sodium lactate, when administered intravenously to patients with panic disorder, will often provoke a panic attack, whereas this does not happen to the general population. A number of research teams are seeking to identify the mechanisms by which sodium lactate causes panic attacks. Imipramine significantly decreases the frequency of sodium lactate–provoked panic attacks.

There have been a number of theoretical and therapeutic approaches to panic disorder. One approach assumes that an underlying biological dysfunction causes the disorder and that this dysfunction has some similarities to a cause of some types of depression. This idea has led to efforts to correct the dysfunction using drugs, such as imipramine, originally employed in the treatment of depression. Some of these drugs are capable of reducing the occurrence of panic attacks. Psychological approaches focus attention on the role of psychosocial factors in panic disorder, particularly the patients' tendency to make catastrophic interpretations of their panic attacks (Clark et al., 1997). For example, many patients misinterpret heart palpitations as signaling an impending heart attack, or they misinterpret jittery, shaky feelings as indicating that they will lose control or go crazy. When patients can be helped to put their panic attacks in a more realistic perspective, they often find that they are less troubled by them when they occur, are less likely to avoid situations associated with the attacks, and have fewer attacks. An increasing number of clinicians and researchers now agree about the need for a conceptual framework that recognizes that both biological and psychological factors play important roles in panic disorders. We know that stress is often a triggering factor in panic attacks. How well an individual copes with stress (in this case, whether the person has a panic attack) depends on vulnerability factors (e.g., biological dys-

function) as well as the individual's resilience (e.g., the ability to place panic attacks in a realistic perspective). This integrated view of panic disorder is consistent with the interactional theoretical approach discussed in Chapter 2.

Phobias

Phobos was the Greek god of fear. His likeness was painted on masks and shields to frighten enemies in battle. The word **phobia,** derived from his name, came to mean fear, panic, dread, or fright. Unlike people who have generalized anxiety disorders, people who have **phobic disorders** know exactly what they are afraid of. Except for their fears of specific objects, people, or situations, phobic individuals usually do not engage in gross distortions of reality. Nothing physical seems to be wrong with them. However, their fears are out of proportion with reality, seem inexplicable, and are beyond their voluntary control.

One question that inevitably arises in discussions of anxiety is why people spend so much time brooding about vague menaces when there are so many real dangers to worry about. Perhaps the degree of fear we feel about a potentially harmful event is linked not primarily to the degree of threat (in terms of the probability that it will actually happen to us), or even to the amount of injury that we imagine we might sustain if the worst did happen, but to the disturbing quality of the event or situation itself. For example, even though there are three times as many traffic fatalities as there are murders, our thoughts are rarely preoccupied by the danger of an automobile accident. Fear of violent crime, on the other hand, touches many of us. Crucial to the experience of fear is whether people feel that they will be able to respond meaningfully to a situation—that is, whether they will be able to cope.

One of the most interesting aspects of phobias is that the stimuli that evoke them are not random. The most common fear-arousing stimuli tend to be animals, objects, or events that presented real dangers in earlier stages of human evolution. Although extreme fear of dogs, snakes, and spiders seems maladaptive today, such fears may have been highly adaptive in earlier times.

Some researchers believe that human beings are instinctively predisposed (or prepared) to like or dislike and fear or not fear certain stimuli—snakes, for example (Seligman, 1971). Presumably fears for which we are prepared are products of millions of years of evolution. While this theory seems consistent with some evidence—for example, the many fears of childhood that do not appear to be products of conditioning—many questions remain unanswered. Why do people develop fears of objects that have no evolutionary significance? Why are therapeutic interventions effective in treating phobias that might be regarded as being linked to instincts?

Phobic individuals do not need the actual presence of the feared object or situation to experience intense tension and discomfort. The following account by a psychiatrist with an airplane phobia shows that simply imagining a phobia-related event can elicit strong psychological and bodily reactions:

I was pampering my neurosis by taking the train to a meeting in Philadelphia. It was a nasty day out, the fog so thick you could see only a few feet ahead of your face, and the train, which had been late in leaving New York, was making up time by hurtling at a great rate across the flat land of New Jersey. As I sat there comfortably enjoying the ride, I happened to glance at the headlines of a late edition, which one of the passengers who had boarded in New York was reading. "TRAINS CRASH IN FOG," ran the banner headlines, "10 DEAD, MANY INJURED." I reflected on our speed, the dense fog outside, and had a mild, transitory moment of concern that the fog might claim us victim, too, and then relaxed as I picked up the novel I had been reading. Some minutes later the thought suddenly entered my mind that had I not "chickened out" about flying, I might at that moment be overhead in a plane. At the mere image of sitting up there strapped in by a seat belt, my hands began to sweat, my heart to beat perceptibly faster, and I felt a kind of nervous uneasiness in my gut. The sensation lasted until I forced myself back to my book and forgot about the imagery.

I must say I found this experience a vivid lesson in the nature of phobias. Here I had reacted with hardly a flicker of concern to an admittedly small, but real danger of accident, as evidenced by the fog-caused train crash an hour or two earlier; at the same time I had responded to a purely imaginary situation with an unpleasant start of nervousness, experienced both as somatic symptoms and as an inner sense of indescribable dread so characteristic of anxiety. The unreasonableness of the latter was highlighted for me by its contrast with the absence of concern about the speeding train, which if I had worried about it, would have been an apprehension founded on real, external circumstances. (Nemiah & Uhde, 1989, p. 973)

The onset of many phobias is so gradual that it is difficult to tell whether there were any specific precipitating factors. In other cases, the apparent time of onset, although not necessarily the cause, can be pinpointed:

I was riding in my husband's car and I suddenly became terrified. I felt as if I would die. I made him turn around and take me home. I ran into the house and suddenly felt safe. I could not understand what had happened. I had never been afraid of cars. The next day it happened again, and it kept getting worse. Finally, just being on the street and seeing a car would bring on a terrible feeling. Now I just stay at home. (De Nike & Tiber, 1968, p. 346)

Phobias may begin with a generalized anxiety attack, but the anxiety then becomes crystallized around a particular object or situation (e.g., elevators, snakes, or darkness). As long as the feared object or situation can be avoided, the anxiety does not reach disturbing proportions. Some objects of phobias—such as cats, cars, and stairs—are considered aspects of everyday life by most of us. Other objects and situations—snakes, death, and heights—are disliked to some extent by most people. However, phobias involve levels of fear that, in addition to being overly intense, interfere with normal living patterns. One study of phobic patients showed that their fears fell into five categories related to (1) separations, (2) animals, (3) bodily mutilation, (4) social situations, and (5) nature (Torgersen, 1979). Table 7-7 gives examples of phobic content that fall into these categories.

Phobias tend to grow progressively broader. For example, one woman had a subway phobia that began with an inability to ride an express train between two fairly distant locations. Gradually the phobia developed until she

---

Table 7-7

Examples for Five Categories of Phobias

Separation fears	Social fears
▪ Crowds	▪ Eating with strangers
▪ Traveling alone	▪ Being watched while writing
▪ Being alone at home	▪ Being watched while working
Animal fears	**Nature fears**
▪ Mice	▪ Mountains
▪ Rats	▪ The ocean
▪ Insects	▪ Cliffs, heights
Mutilation fears	
▪ Open wounds	
▪ Surgical operations	
▪ Blood	

Source: Based on Torgersen (1979).

would have to get off the train at each local stop, wait until her anxiety diminished, get on the next train, get off again at the next stop, and so on, until her destination was reached.

Phobic individuals usually develop ways of reducing their fears. The subway rider was able to get from one place to another. However, the cumbersome procedures people with phobias devise do not eliminate their fear; indeed, the fear seems always to be one step ahead of them. In one sense, phobic individuals who cannot cross the thresholds of certain rooms or cannot work may be as incapacitated as people with severe psychotic symptoms. In another sense, they are more fortunate than people who exhibit free-floating anxiety, since at least their fears are directed toward a specific object and they can reduce their anxiety by simply avoiding that object.

Phobias, like other forms of maladaptive behavior, do not occur in isolation. They are usually intertwined with a host of other problems. In consequence, it is difficult to estimate their frequency accurately. One survey of randomly selected residents of a medium-sized Canadian city found that 61% of the respondents reported being much or somewhat more fearful than other people in at least one of several types of situations (Stein et al., 1994). While fears reaching clinical proportions occur much less frequently, phobias are relatively common, being even more prevalent than generalized anxiety disorders (Robins & Regier, 1991).

Rates of phobic disorder are about twice as high for females as males. In both sexes, Blacks have higher rates than Whites or Hispanics. Phobias typically have their onset in childhood or young adulthood, and there is a sharp decline in new cases with age. The mean duration for phobias varies from 24 to 31 years—in other words, the condition tends to be chronic (Boyd et al., 1990). Phobias do not require hospitalization. Professional treatment, when it is given, is usually carried out on an outpatient basis.

Traditionally, phobias have been named by means of Greek or Latin prefixes that stand for the object of the fear, as shown in the following examples:

- *Acrophobia:* fear of heights
- *Agoraphobia:* fear of open places and unfamiliar settings
- *Aquaphobia:* fear of water
- *Claustrophobia:* fear of closed places
- *Xenophobia:* fear of strangers

Recently, however, such names have been avoided. People's knowledge of Greek and Latin is not what it once was, and in any case, a staggering number of labels would be needed to take account of the great variety of phobias that have been observed. Today, therefore, phobias are grouped into three general categories: specific phobias, social phobias, and agoraphobia.

Specific Phobias

Specific phobias are a miscellaneous category of marked, persistent, irrational fears. Some examples of specific phobias are intense fears of particular types of animals (e.g., snakes, dogs, or rats), claustrophobia, and acrophobia (see Figure 7-4). These phobias range from very general to highly specific. For example, although Jenny Dibley has successfully operated the elevator to the top of Seattle's 605-foot-tall Space Needle for more than 20 years (Figure 7-5), she can't bear to look through the crack where the observation-level floor meets the elevator floor. In addition, she cannot get on a ladder or even stand on a chair because of fear of heights.

Specific phobia is the most common type of phobia, with about 11% of the population meeting the criteria for

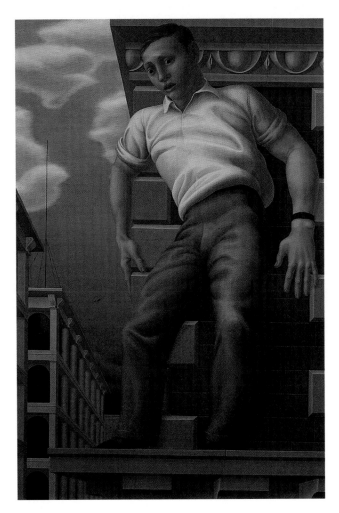

Figure 7-4 This painting by George Tooker, titled *Cornice*, captures the fear of heights that acrophobic people feel even when they are in situations much less threatening than the precarious perch shown in the painting—for instance, when they are climbing ladders or standing near the railings of observation platforms.

SOURCE: George Tooker "Cornice", tempera on panel 24 × 15½. Columbus Museum of Art, Ohio; Museum Purchase: Howard Fund II.

Figure 7–5   Space Needle operator Jenny Dibley jokes with riders as they head for the observation deck.

Source: *Seattle Times*, November 10, 1996, p. M1. Photo by Jimi Lott.

specific phobia during their lifetimes. (The comparable figures for agoraphobia and social phobia are 5.6% and 2.7%, respectively.) Unreasonable fears of heights and bugs or other small animals are the most common fears, with over 18% of a large surveyed population responding positively to questions about these fears (Robins & Regier, 1991). Two other phobias—unreasonable fear of water or of public transport—were reported by over 10% of the sample surveyed. Some specific phobias are related to having had traumatic experiences earlier in life. This seems to be the case with regard to the acquisition of dental fears. However, fears of water and heights have not been linked to conditioning based on prior experiences (Poulton et al., 1999).

For the person with a specific phobia, the degree of distress varies with the prevalence of the avoided situation. For example, a hospital employee who fears blood may be in a constant state of fear because the probability of encountering blood in a hospital setting is high. When the probability of the feared stimulus is low, people with specific phobias are usually free of symptoms. The person who is phobic about drowning is usually not affected by that phobia except in the presence of water or when a beach party is being planned.

Children eventually overcome many of their fears. And while it is not unusual for adults with specific phobias to overcome their fear as a result of a positive experience involving contact with the fear-arousing stimulus, specific phobias tend to be chronic.

DSM-IV provides for the diagnosis of a specific phobia when there is a marked and persistent fear that is excessive; when the person suffering from the phobia recognizes that the fear is unreasonable but continues to avoid the frightening situation; and when the avoidance of, anxious anticipation of, and distress caused by the feared situation

create problems in the areas of social relationships, work, and the carrying out of normal routines.

A variety of therapeutic approaches have been used in treating specific phobias. Procedures that promote association between the fear-arousing stimulus and nonanxiety responses, and at the same time provide information countering mistaken beliefs about the stimulus (e.g., that all dogs are ferocious), often have positive effects.

> *Mary, aged 29, had fainted at the sight of blood or injury ever since she was 4 years old. She and her therapist agreed on specific targets for treatment: watching blood samples being taken from someone else and from herself, coping with her children when they needed first aid for minor injuries, and getting her own varicose veins treated. In her first session, Mary was able to watch a blood sample being taken from her therapist's finger and then have her own finger pricked and a blood sample taken. In the next session, she was asked to imagine situations involving injury and to watch films depicting injuries to others. Between sessions, at home, Mary dealt successfully with some small emergencies with her children, and she had her varicose veins injected. At follow-up 8 months later, she reported that she was free of her problem. She was able to enroll in a first-aid class and went freely to movies depicting blood and injury. (Adapted from Marks, 1978, pp. 135–136)*

This case illustrates two important points. One is that exposure to fear-arousing stimuli contributes to overcoming specific phobias. The other is that high motivation on the part of the client increases the likelihood of success. Social support can be an additional contributor to overcoming certain fears (Figure 7-6).

Social Phobias

Social phobias are less common than specific phobias—they occur at only about 25% the rate of specific phobias—but they can attack with no less force. **Social phobias** are characterized by fear and embarrassment in dealings with others (see Figure 7-7). Often the individual's greatest fear is that signs of anxiety such as intense blushing, tremors of the hand, and a quavering voice will be detected by people with whom he or she comes into contact. Fear of public speaking and of eating in public are frequent complaints of socially phobic individuals. These problems often begin in late childhood or early adolescence and may crystallize into a phobia in late adolescence (Beidel & Turner, 1998).

> *I sometimes don't get to class because I think the teacher might call on me. My fear doesn't have anything to do with being unprepared if he asks me a question, because I'm almost always well prepared. My grades on exams are always near the top of*

Figure 7-6 For some people, fear of flying can be petrifying and, because it may keep them from doing things they want to do, disabling. Support from others, together with exposure to stimuli associated with flying, can be helpful to individuals with sufficient motivation to confront their fears. In this photograph, a fearful person (center) is on a flight with the head of a Fly Without Fear program (left) that uses support groups to provide encouragement. The person on the right is a support group member. Exposure is used in a graduated way, often starting with simply sitting in a plane on the ground and eventually culminating in a flight.

Source: *New York Times*, June 23, 1999, p. A21.

Figure 7-7 Individuals with social phobia avoid situations requiring interpersonal contact. If they cannot avoid contact with other people, they often experience physical symptoms such as nausea, trembling, and profuse perspiration as well as disabling feelings of anxiety.

the class. What I keep thinking about is that the teacher and all the students will see how red my face gets whenever I have to say something in a group.

Shyness is often mistaken for social phobia. Shy people, however, don't experience the terror felt by those with social phobia when they find themselves in situations where they might be exposed to criticism from others. The personal lives of social phobics is typically bleak. They often have no friends, for example. Having no one with whom to share experiences increases their risk for stress-related disorders.

Most phobias about interpersonal relationships involve one or more of the following fears: fear of asserting oneself, fear of criticism, fear of making a mistake, and fear of public speaking. People who are afflicted in these ways have much in common. They go through life feeling generally inadequate and have many social and interpersonal difficulties. They attempt to compensate by immersing themselves in school and then in their work, never being really

---

Table 7-8

Examples of the Two Types of Phobia-Arousing Situations in Social Phobia and the Phobic Concerns

Social Situations

- Meeting someone for the first time
- Attending social gatherings (e.g., parties or weddings)
- Asking someone for a date
- Conversing on the telephone
- Dealing with people in authority (e.g., boss or teacher)
- Returning items to a store
- Making eye contact with unfamiliar people

Performance Situations

- Speaking in public
- Performing in public (e.g., playing a musical instrument)
- Eating in public
- Urinating in a public bathroom
- Writing in public

Concerns Stimulated by Phobia-Arousing Situations

- Making a poor impression or being negatively evaluated by others
- Doing or saying something embarrassing or humilitating
- Having the hand tremble when writing in front of others
- Saying foolish things
- Blushing or showing other signs of anxiety that will be noticeable to others
- Mind going blank when speaking to others

Table 7-9

Interpersonal Self-Help Techniques for the Person With a Social Phobia

1. Respond to anxiety symptoms by approach rather than withdrawal.
2. Greet people properly, with eye contact.
3. Listen carefully to people and make a mental list of possible topics of conversation.
4. Show that you want to speak; initiate conversation (asking questions is easier, as it switches attention to the person expected to reply).
5. Speak up without mumbling.
6. Tolerate some silences.
7. Wait for cues from others in deciding where to sit, when to pick up a drink, and what to talk about.
8. Learn to tolerate criticism by introducing controversy deliberately at an appropriate point.

---

sure of their skills and talents. They dismiss their successes, if any, by saying, "My work isn't really good enough" or "I was just lucky—being in the right place at the right time." They may feel like impostors, fearing that they will be discovered and that the rug will be pulled out from under them.

The DSM-IV criteria for social phobia include marked and persistent fear of one or more social or performance situations. These situations usually involve unfamiliar people or scrutiny or evaluation by others, and the phobic reaction includes intense concern over being humiliated or embarrassed. The person recognizes that the fear is excessive and unreasonable. Avoidance of the feared situation, anxious anticipation, and distress interfere significantly with personal life and prevent the individual from effectively dealing with the situation. Table 7-8 provides examples of the two types of situations (social and performance) seen in social phobia and the concerns phobic individuals often display.

Two features of social phobia are particularly stubborn: the fears of blushing and of eating. Some people are terrified that they will blush in the company of others and are convinced that they will be highly visible and the center of painful attention. If questioned, these people cannot say what is so dreadful about blushing, but it is often evident that shame is an important component of their anxiety. In some cases, a change of color may not be at all evident to the observer, even though the individual insists that he or she feels bright red. The force of their fear, unfounded as it may be, often leads these people to restrict their social lives severely. Fear of eating often involves a dread of eating in the company of others. Even this fear may be very specific. For instance, Emma, aged 26, became very anxious when she had to eat or drink in the company of anyone she knew. However, she was able to eat or drink in public places without undue distress as long as the other people present were strangers. Table 7-9 gives some guidelines concerning interpersonal behavior that have been found to be helpful in building up the resilience of people with social phobias, and Table 7-10 provides some hints that might be useful for a friend or spouse who wants to help the phobic person.

The following case illustrates a number of the characteristics of social phobia:

The patient was a 39-year-old married African American female physician who described a long-standing history of becoming "really nervous" in large crowds, especially if the people were unfamiliar. Although unable to recollect the specific onset, she remembered being extremely shy in elementary and junior high school. At social functions, she typically would "hide out" in the bathroom, feigning illness in order to avoid social interactions. She reported no close friends or confidants, was unwilling to get involved with people unless certain of being liked, and did not date until after college. She occasionally would consume alcohol prior to, and frequently

Table 7-10

Hints for Helping a Phobic Person

1. Never make the assumption that you know what is best; do not force your beliefs.
2. Always provide a way out if the phobic person is having difficulties (e.g., leave the party).
3. Be aware of excuses to avoid the feared situation ("I'm not feeling well today"). Provide encouragement, but do not make it a big issue if your suggestion is met with resistance.
4. Don't assume that because something was accomplished successfully one time, the next time will also be easy.
5. Never play tricks by doing something that is different from what you initially agreed upon.
6. If things are going well, suggest trying something a little more difficult.
7. Approach feared situations in gradual steps, never making the decision to go on to the next step by yourself.
8. Encourage the phobic person to practice responses to the feared situation (such as a party or a dog).
9. While the phobic person is practicing or in the feared situation, don't constantly ask about the person's feelings.
10. If the phobic person practices alone and reports successes to you, share in his or her excitement.

during, social events to cope with her discomfort. When in stressful situations, she stuttered. For example, saying her name during introductions, whether to professionals or patients, was particularly difficult. Consequently, she avoided speaking on the telephone and introducing herself to others, often being perceived as brusque and somewhat rude. (Fink, et al., 1996, p. 202)

A feature of this case was the patient's concern that being an African American caused her to stand out as different and subject to ridicule. One element of her therapy involved a series of exercises in which she imagined situations similar to the ones she feared. After a number of these sessions, at least some of her fear had decreased. This is an example of a scene used in this therapeutic approach directed toward achieving extinction of the phobia:

You quickly glance around and realize that you are in the middle of the circle. You are the only Black person on the team. . . . You can't say your name! You feel hot and begin to sweat. Everyone is looking at you with smug "I knew it" expressions. You really screwed up. Everyone is thinking that the only reason you are in medical school is because you are a Black female. The department had a certain quota that needed to be filled. Your mouth becomes dry and you feel

nauseous. . . . You feel absolutely stupid—everyone knows that the only reason you got this far is because you are Black. You see the chairman lean to the person next to him, and hear him say, "This is what happens when we let a Black girl into the program." Everyone continues to stare at you. You feel incredibly inferior. You know that the only reason you are still in the program is because you are Black. You do not deserve to be a physician and everybody knows it. (Fink, et al., 1996, p. 204)

Figure 7-8 shows how one indicator of this patient's anxiety, heart rate, declined over a series of extinction sessions in which imaginary situations similar to those she feared were presented.

Earlier we noted the difference between shyness and social phobia. However, it is important to remember that there is a continuum of social anxiety. Many people experience some anxiety in certain types of social situations. Usually the anxiety is fairly specific to particular types of situations and does not cripple the individual's social relationships (see Figure 7-9). The diagnosis of social phobia refers to anxiety that is chronic, pervasive, and disabling across diverse situations that involve contact with others.

Agoraphobia

One ordinary day, while tending to some chore, taking a walk, driving to work—in other words, just going about his usual business—Leo Green was suddenly struck by a wave of awful terror. His heart started pounding, he trembled, he perspired profusely, and he had difficulty catching his breath. He became convinced that something terrible was happening to him—maybe he was going crazy, maybe he was having a heart attack, maybe he was about to die. He desperately sought safety, reassurance from his family, and some type of treatment program. His doctor could find nothing wrong with him, so he went about his business, until a panic attack struck him again. As the attacks became more frequent, he spent more and more time thinking about them. He worried, watched for danger, and waited with fear for the next one to hit.

He began to avoid situations where he had experienced an attack, then others where he might find it particularly difficult to cope with one by escaping and getting help. He started by making minor adjustments in his habits—going to a supermarket at midnight, for example, rather than on the way home from work when the store tended to be crowded. Gradually, Leo Green got to the point where he couldn't venture outside his immediate neighborhood, couldn't leave the house without his spouse, or sometimes couldn't leave at all. What started out as an inconvenience turned into a nightmare. Like a creature in a horror movie, fear expanded until it covered the entire screen of his life.

This case illustrates **agoraphobia,** fear of entering certain fear-evoking or unfamiliar situations, which often accompanies

Figure 7-8   Reduction in heart rate over sessions in which the patient described imagined scenes in which being an African American was the key feature. This patient's physiological reactivity showed great variability, but the figure reflects a generally downward trend in her heart rate over time, suggesting that extinction of fear was taking place.

SOURCE: Fink et al. (1996), p. 206.

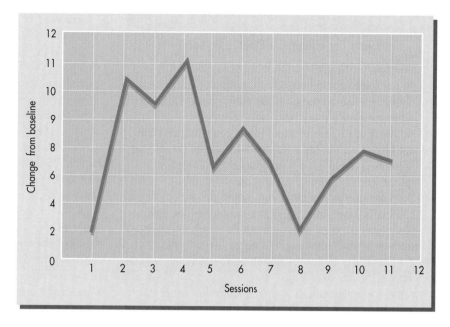

panic attacks. To the outside observer, a person with agoraphobia may look no different from one with a social phobia. Both may stay home from a party. But their reasons for doing so are different. While the socially phobic individual is afraid of the scrutiny of other people, the agoraphobic individual is afraid of his or her own internal cues. The agoraphobic person dreads the awful anxiety of a panic attack and is afraid of losing control in a crowd. Minor physical sensations may be interpreted as the prelude to some catastrophic threat to life. In severe cases, the individual may have an irrational fear of leaving the familiar setting of the home; in the most extreme cases, the victim is unable even to walk down the street or go shopping. Like most other intense fears, agoraphobia is more common among women than among men.

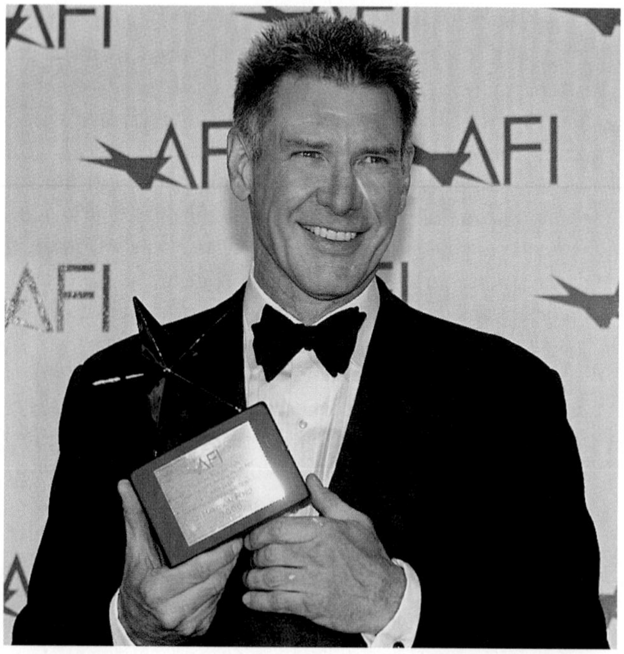

Although DSM-IV focuses particular attention on agoraphobia as a factor in many cases of panic disorder, cases of agoraphobia without panic attacks have also been reported (Eaton et al., 1994). In these cases, the agoraphobia often begins in the late teens, although it is also observed in older people. And, like other phobias, it waxes and wanes, and it is not uncommon for the object of the fear to change.

About 50% of people who experience panic attacks go on to develop agoraphobia unless they are treated early with certain drugs. One theory regarding the panic attack–agoraphobia linkage is that an individual is born with a biological vulnerability to panic attacks. Psychosocial factors, such as a pileup of stressful life events and upsetting situations, can trigger a panic attack in a vulnerable individual. According to this theory, many patients, unaware of the biological roots of panic attacks, conclude that the situations in which the attacks take place must be the culprit. They become increasingly preoccupied with avoiding such situations and constrict their life-styles—often at considerable economic and social expense—in the hope of eluding these attacks. One patient confided that she had accumulated hundreds of dollars in fines by parking her car illegally in front of her office rather than face the anxiety associated with walking across the parking lot.

Figure 7-9   Leading-man Harrison Ford often plays confident, intrepid characters in the movies. Yet he describes himself as being terrified of public speaking. When he was given a lifetime achievement award by the American Film Institute, he was not able to express his thanks at the banquet honoring him in the manner he would have liked to display. He spoke in barely audible tones.

As we pointed out earlier, panic attacks can be treated with certain drugs that are effective in treating depression (e.g., the tricyclic antidepressants and monoamine oxidase inhibitors). To a significant extent, agoraphobia is a complication of panic attacks that are not treated and therefore are allowed to recur. Antidepressants are effective in suppressing panic but not in reducing anticipatory anxiety and agoraphobia. Behavioral techniques, including graduated exposure to the situation the individual is afraid of, are effective in treating agoraphobia. Some highly motivated agoraphobics are able to carry out this exposure themselves without the constant aid of a therapist. The following case illustrates the successful use of this approach:

Ms. A., a 40-year-old woman, had been virtually housebound for five years because of classic agoraphobia. In a 1 1/2-hour session, she, her husband, and I delineated her avoidance profile (those places she avoided regularly because they evoked panic) and worked out an exposure-homework program in which she would slowly habituate to one situation after another. I explained how she should keep a diary of her exposure-homework exercises and asked her to mail them to me. This she did regularly. She diligently carried out her exposure program and within weeks was mobile for the first time in years. She kept up her progress for four years without seeing me again, but then she had some family difficulties, which depressed her, and quickly relapsed. She saw me once more for an hour and was encouraged to revive her original exposure-homework program. On doing this she recovered her gains, which continued through follow-up for nine years, when I last heard from her—a gratifying result for 2 1/2 hours of time from a clinician. (Marks, 1987, pp. 1163–1164)

Agoraphobic individuals are often clinging and dependent. Studies of the histories of severely impaired agoraphobic persons have shown that 50% of the patients exhibited separation anxiety in childhood, well before the onset of the agoraphobia (Gittelman & Klein, 1984). The association between childhood separation anxiety and agoraphobia is much stronger in women than in men. Perhaps, in some sense, agoraphobia is a delayed outbreak of childhood separation anxiety. Because separation anxiety is almost always measured by means of retrospective self-reports, there is a need for longitudinal studies that allow for the observation of subjects' behavior in addition to self-reports.

Obsessive-Compulsive Disorder

A man who suffered from fears of contamination from AIDS felt a drop in his eye as he looked up while passing under a building. He became obsessed with the thought that the drop was actually from someone with AIDS spitting out of a window. He

felt compelled to go to every office on the 16 floors of that side of the building and ask if anyone had spit out the window.

This man, diagnosed as having **obsessive-compulsive disorder,** shows the driven quality of the thoughts and rituals seen in people with this condition. While the specific features of the condition vary from case to case, they have in common recurrent obsessions or compulsions that are severe enough to be time-consuming (i.e., they take more than 1 hour a day) or cause marked distress or significant impairment. People with **obsessive behavior** are unable to get an idea out of their minds (e.g., they are preoccupied by sexual, aggressive, or religious thoughts); people with **compulsive behavior** feel compelled to perform a particular act or series of acts over and over again (e.g., repetitive hand-washing or stepping on cracks in the sidewalk).

Obsessions usually involve doubt, hesitation, fear of contamination, or fear of one's own aggression. The most common forms of compulsive behavior are counting, ordering, checking, touching, and washing. A few victims of obsessive-compulsive disorder have purely mental rituals; for example, to ward off an obsessional thought or impulse, they might recite a series of magic words or numbers. About 25% of people with an obsessive-compulsive disorder have intrusive thoughts but do not act on them. The rest are both obsessive and compulsive; compulsive behavior without obsessional thoughts is rare.

Compulsive rituals may become elaborate patterns of behavior that include many activities. For example, a man may require that his furniture never be left an inch out of place, while also feeling a need to dress and undress, brush his teeth, and use the toilet in a precise, unvarying order, all the time doubting whether he has performed this sequence of actions correctly, and often repeating it to make sure. Some theorists believe that compulsive behavior serves to divert attention from obsessive thoughts. In any case, compulsive rituals become a protection against anxiety, and so long as they are practiced correctly, the individual feels safe.

Therapists say there are enormous differences between healthy people with compulsive streaks and those suffering from obsessive-compulsive disorder. Truly obsessive-compulsive people often have family histories of psychiatric difficulties, suggesting a genetic component to the disorder. They are wracked by self-doubt and often are unable to make even simple decisions (see Figure 7-10).

By contrast, healthy people with a few compulsive tendencies tend to work efficiently and organize their daily activities to avoid confusion. They also take pride in their ability to control their emotions—an impossibility for those with obsessive-compulsive disorder. Although obsessive-compulsive people are wracked by guilt over their strange behavior's effects on their families, they continue because they believe their compulsive acts keep themselves and

Pepper . . . and Salt

THE WALL STREET JOURNAL

STEIN

"Your decision has to be either 'guilty' or 'not guilty' I can't accept 'too close to call.'"

Figure 7-10 Although decisions about guilt and innocence are far from simple or trivial, this cartoon conveys how difficult decision making is for individuals with obsessive-compulsive tendencies.

SOURCE: *The Wall Street Journal*, permission, Cartoon Feature Syndicate.

their families safe. Box 7-2 contains three first-person accounts, the first dealing with the development of a compulsion, the second with the experience of obsessive thoughts in a particular situation, and the third with a relapse after an encouraging period of improvement.

The exact incidence of obsessive-compulsive disorder is hard to determine. The victims tend to be secretive about their preoccupations and frequently are able to work effectively in spite of them; consequently, their problems are probably underestimated. Obsessive-compulsive disorder is more common among upper-income individuals who are somewhat more intelligent than average. It tends to begin in late adolescence and early adulthood, and males and females are equally likely to suffer from it. A relatively high proportion of obsessive-compulsive individuals—some surveys report up to 50%—remain unmarried.

Lifetime prevalence studies of obsessive-compulsive disorder in the United States and Canada have yielded figures ranging from 1.9 to 3.1 cases per 100 people, with the usual age of onset occurring in the 20s (Bebbington, 1998). While this figure is lower than for phobias and generalized anxiety, it is higher than for panic disorder and several other diagnostic groupings. As public awareness of the prevalence of obsessive-compulsive disorder increases, the social stigma associated with it may decrease and encourage those who suffer from it to seek professional help (Figure 7–11).

An example of the need for people who are disabled by obsessions and compulsions to receive professional help is the case of Jerrold Kaplan, a middle-aged man who has difficulty throwing away newspapers, scraps of paper, and information that he might want in the unspecified future.

As a boy, he collected stamps and coins. Now he collects everything because he feels anxiety when he doesn't save things. Describing his collecting as "a real time waster," Kaplan has been unable to work for several years and survives on Social Security and disability insurance. He holds a bachelor's degree and began collecting newspapers for want ad listings after he had lost a job. He ended up saving entire newspapers because they contained articles he might want to read. His bed is covered with newspapers, magazines, and bills. Every night he removes them from half the bed so he has room to sleep. In the morning he repeats the ritual in reverse. Kaplan is now receiving psychia-tric treatment for his obsessive-compulsive problems.

The most common features of obsessive-compulsive disorder are the following:

1. The obsession or compulsion intrudes insistently and persistently into the individual's awareness.
2. A feeling of anxious dread occurs if the thought or act is prevented for some reason.
3. The obsession or compulsion is experienced as foreign to oneself; it is unacceptable and uncontrollable.
4. The individual recognizes the absurdity and irrationality of the obsession or compulsion.
5. The individual feels a need to resist it.

The language used by those with an obsessive-compulsive disorder conveys their exaggerated attention to details, their air of detachment, and the difficulty they have in making decisions, as these two examples illustrate:

I seem to be stuck with them—the thoughts, I mean. They seem so unimportant and silly. Why can't I think about things I really want to think about? But I can't stop thinking about trivia like, Did I lock the garage door when I went to work this morning? I've never not locked it and my wife's home anyway. I get depressed when I realize how much time I waste on nothing.

I feel under such pressure, but I can't make a decision. I write out on 3-by-5 cards all the pros and cons; then I study them, consider all the complications that perhaps might bear on the decision, and then I do it again—but I never seem to be able to make up my mind.

Obsessional thoughts often seem distasteful and shameful. Their content generally involves harming others, causing accidents to occur, swearing, or having abhorrent sexual or religious ideas. People with these thoughts are often very fearful that they might act on them and as a

First Person

Box 7–2

Obsessive-Compulsive Disorder

The Development of Compulsions

The compulsive person feels compelled or driven to act a certain way.

I'm 18 now, and I've had OCD [obsessive-compulsive disorder] since I was 8 or 9. That's when my special "routines" for getting dressed in the morning started. I'd often miss the school bus, and my mother would have to drive me to school.

Before I could take my morning shower, I had to be sure everything was just right. The folds in the shower curtain had to hang a certain way. The sink, tub, and faucets had to be perfectly clean. I had to remove everyone else's towels from the racks and put them in the hall. Before I even stepped into the shower, I had spent more than half an hour cleaning and organizing the bathroom.

When I turned the shower on, I had a rule that only the cold water could run while I washed my hair. I also had a ritual for washing my hair—I used 30 circular motions, and if I touched either of my ears, I had to start over.

I had more routines for getting dressed. My clothes had to be organized a certain way and put on in a certain order. If any piece of clothing touched the floor, I'd have to take everything off and start again. Eventually my morning routines took so long that I had to set my alarm for 5 A.M. Even then, I'd be late some days.

At school I had rules about touching things and washing my hands. It was not unusual for me to go into the bathroom 20 times a day to wash my hands. I was afraid my friends would find out about my secrets—so I began to avoid them.

My parents knew something was wrong, but they thought I was just going through an "awkward stage." I knew all my weird routines didn't make sense, but I felt that something horrible would happen if I didn't give in to them.

Obsessive Thoughts While Driving

Obsessions are persistent and unwanted thoughts, ideas, or images that the person does not intentionally produce.

I'm driving down the highway doing 55 MPH. I'm on my way to take a final exam. My seat belt is buckled and I'm vigilantly following all the rules of the road. No one is on the highway—not a living soul.

Out of nowhere an Obsessive-Compulsive Disorder attack strikes. It's almost magical the way it distorts my perception of reality. While in reality no one is on the road, I'm intruded with the heinous thought that I might have hit someone . . . a human being! God knows where such a fantasy comes from.

I think about this for a second and then say to myself, "That's ridiculous. I didn't hit anybody." Nonetheless, a gnawing anxiety is born. An anxiety I will ultimately not be able to put away until an enormous emotional price has been paid.

I try to make reality chase away this fantasy. I reason, "Well, if I hit someone while driving, I would have felt it." This brief trip into reality helps the pain dissipate . . . but only for a second. Why? Because the gnawing anxiety that I really did commit the illusionary accident is growing larger—so is the pain. . . .

I start ruminating, "Maybe I did hit someone and didn't realize it . . . Oh my God! I might have killed somebody! I have to go back and check." Checking is the only way to calm the anxiety. It brings me closer to truth somehow. I can't live with the thought that I actually may have killed someone—I have to check it out.

Now I'm sweating . . . literally. I pray this outrageous act of negligence never happened. My fantasies run wild. I desperately hope the jury will be merciful. (J. L. Rapoport, 1989, pp. 21–22)

Relapse

I felt I was making real progress. Recently there had only been a glimmer of my obsessions breaking through.

I'd begun to think that perhaps they were behind me, that my life was on the brink of returning to normal.

And then, whammo. There I was spiraling downward into the dark heart of my old obsessions about cancer.

At first I felt only the deep anxiety that always accompanies this obsession, but it was quickly joined by a deep anger and frustration—I couldn't believe this was happening again. Was I never going to be free of this terrible obsessiveness?

But once beyond the initial shock, I began to notice a couple of things about this latest attack. First, my anxiety was not quite as bad as when my obsessions were at their peak a few years ago and that, in itself, was a small comfort. Second, I found I had a little perspective on them this time that I was able to use as a foundation for recovery.

For example, in looking back at the weeks preceding the attack, I realized they had been filled with stress—the Christmas season. Now, I like Christmas, but as befitting my personality, I go at it each year with a gung-ho attitude. This year, I shopped till I dropped. When I wasn't shopping, I was obsessing about "perfect" gift ideas. I baked too many cookies, made too many ornaments, and spent too much time fussing about an annual Christmas Day dinner with my neighbors. By the time the holidays were over, I was in an ideal mental state for a return of my symptoms.

I tried to reduce my stress by lowering my expectations for my household duties for awhile. I also made a greater effort to get out by myself more—I am an at-home parent of two young children, and if you've ever had that responsibility, I don't need to tell you what it can do to your stress level. Finally, I reviewed some of the behavioral techniques that I hadn't had to employ for some time, and found that they were still just as effective.

The result is that I'm improving—not quite back to the level I was at before the attack, but definitely better.

Figure 7-11 Many obsessive-compulsive people do not seek therapy either because of embarrassment or an inability to imagine living without their rituals. For example, many hoarders find their acquisitive behavior anxiety-reducing. Hoarders differ from collectors in that a real collector (for example, of paintings or books) acquires and discards, while a hoarder collects, but fails to discard. Hoarders are afraid that "there is something here that I might lose, something that could change my life if I throw it away." This is the bedroom of a hoarder who has difficulty plowing through the obstacles her hoarding has created in order to reach her king-sized bed. The bed is usually heaped so high with stuff that she changes the sheets only every few months.

SOURCE: *The Washington Post*, December 12, 2000.

result spend a great deal of time avoiding situations they fear might provoke such actions or checking that everything is all right.

> Susan, a quiet 30-year-old college graduate who has held the same responsible job for eight years, worries that she might put razor blades in other people's food. She refuses to drive a car because she fears she would deliberately smash it into another vehicle.
>
> When she makes coffee at work, she worries that she might have slipped poison into it. She checks her clothing when she leaves work to make sure she hasn't tucked a razor blade into a pocket. She is afraid to hold babies or be around small children. She worries that she might suddenly commit some violent act, such as hurling them to the floor.
>
> She won't shop by herself, afraid that she might slip something into the products on the store shelves. Even when accompanied by her boyfriend, she finds herself needing reassurance. "I was okay, wasn't I?" she asks.
>
> Despite her fears Susan has never put sharp objects in food, hurt a baby, or poisoned coffee.

Depending on the situation and the nature of the obsession, obsessive individuals may feel some pride in their unwillingness to make premature decisions or may feel self-contempt when indecisiveness prevents them from acting. The founder of evolutionary theory, Charles Darwin, is an example of an obsessive person. Only when Darwin faced the possibility that a colleague would publish a book on evolution was he able to overcome his obsessive indecisiveness and put *On the Origin of Species* into the hands of a publisher.

The variety of obsessive-compulsive rituals and thoughts is practically unlimited, but investigators have identified four broad types of preoccupations: (1) checking, (2) cleaning, (3) slowness, and (4) doubting and con-

scientiousness. The following statements illustrate each type:

- *Checking:* "I frequently have to check things like gas or water taps, or doors several times."
- *Cleaning:* "I avoid using public telephones because of possible contamination."
- *Slowness:* "I am often late because I can't seem to get through everything on time."
- *Doubting and conscientiousness:* "Even when I do something very carefully, I often feel that it is not quite right."

When the compulsive rituals or obsessive thoughts begin to interfere with important routines of daily life, they become significant problems that require professional attention. Their bases frequently are not well understood, but because all of us have had some persistent preoccupations with particular acts and thoughts, their interfering effects can easily be appreciated. Obsessive-compulsive preoccupations—checking details, keeping things clean, and being deliberate—often increase during periods of stress. They can have undesirable effects when speedy decisions or actions are required. In some cases, the onset of obsessions and compulsions can be traced to particular traumatic experiences (deSilva & Marks, 1999).

Attempts to find out what obsessive-compulsive individuals are afraid of usually fail. Many clinicians believe that fear of loss of control and the need for structure are at the core of the obsessions and compulsions. Whether the disorder reflects the impact of environmental factors or heredity, its incidence is greater among members of some families than among the general population.

A common feature of psychotic behavior is irrational thought, but obsessive-compulsive people are not considered psychotic, since they are usually aware of the irrationality. In some cases, however, the border between obsessive-compulsive disorder and true psychosis is imprecise.

People who suffer from obsessive-compulsive disorder are very cautious. Like victims of phobias and other anxiety disorders, they unreasonably anticipate catastrophe and loss of control. In general, victims of phobias fear what might happen to them, whereas victims of obsessive-compulsive disorders fear what they might do. There are mixed cases; for example, fear of knives might be associated with the obsessional thought that one will hurt someone if one picks up a knife, and fear of elevators might be brought on by a recurrent impulse to push someone down the shaft. An obsessional thought about shouting obscenities during a sermon might lead the victim to avoid attending church, just as a phobia about the sound of church bells would. Normally, the object of a phobia can be avoided whereas that of an obsession cannot be, but again there are mixed cases; a dirt phobia may be as intrusive as an obsession, because dirt is everywhere.

Obsessive thoughts and compulsive rituals shade into phobias to the extent that anxiety accompanies the thoughts or rituals and there is avoidance of situations that evoke them. For example, someone who has a washing ritual will try to avoid dirt, much as a person with a dog phobia avoids dogs. Clinical workers often observe that both obsessive-compulsive and phobic individuals have an unusually high incidence of interpersonal problems. The two disorders differ in that the obsessive-compulsive person's fear is directed not at the situation itself, but rather at the consequences of becoming involved with it—for example, having to wash afterwards. Another difference is that obsessive-compulsive persons develop a more elaborate set of beliefs concerning their preoccupying thoughts and rituals than phobics do about their fears. Cognitions seem to play a larger role in obsession-compulsion than in phobia. This point is illustrated by the case of a 40-year-old man with a checking compulsion.

> *The other night my wife and I went to the movies. It was torture even though the movie was great. For about an hour before going I couldn't stop thinking about this need I have to check the doorknob in order to make sure it's locked. I had to get out of the car four times to check the doorknob. When I do that sort of thing, my wife tries to be understanding, but I know she is thinking, "How come once isn't enough?" On the way to the theater I kept worrying about whether the door was locked. I would bet I had similar thoughts a hundred times while at the theater. You can't enjoy yourself under those circumstances, can you?*

The DSM-IV criteria for obsessive-compulsive disorder include having recurrent and persistent thoughts, impulses, or images that are not simply general worries and real-life problems. Patients recognize that the unwanted thoughts and rituals are the products of their minds, but distress persists and personal routines are seriously disrupted.

For many years, obsessive-compulsive disorder was considered to be very resistant to treatment, but the outlook is beginning to be more hopeful. Certain serotonin-related drugs (e.g., Prozac) are helpful with some patients, and promising psychological interventions include exposure and response prevention. Psychological therapies are helpful when the patient is exposed to stimuli that usually evoke compulsive rituals and the patient actively inhibits the rituals. This type of behavioral therapy requires that the patient be highly motivated to resist obsessive thoughts and compulsions. Recent evidence suggests that many people suffering from obsessive-compulsive disorder feel an excessive sense of responsibility that produces automatic negative thoughts like "I might cause a fire"; these, in turn, produce discomfort. Cognitive therapists seek to help patients become aware of their excessive sense of responsibility as a step toward overcoming obsessions and compulsions.

Posttraumatic Stress Disorder

In our discussion of stress in Chapter 4, we described several disorders that may follow traumatic experiences, for example, adjustment and acute stress disorders. As we have noted, one of the features of these disorders is their relatively good prognosis, with affected people getting over their difficulties relatively quickly. **Posttraumatic stress disorders (PTSD)** have both similarities to and differences from these conditions. The major similarity is that the individual has experienced something traumatic. However, in the case of posttraumatic stress disorder, the stressor is outside the range of common experience (e.g., it is not just being involved in or observing a minor, fender-bender type of car accident). PTSD involves an extreme experience, such as war or a natural catastrophe, whose effect may extend over a long period. The traumas range from those that are directly experienced (e.g., being threatened with death) to those that are witnessed (e.g., a family member being threatened with death). The onset of the clinical condition in posttraumatic disorders varies from soon after the trauma to long after. Table 7-11 summarizes the major DSM-IV criteria for PTSD. In DSM-IV, these disorders are considered to be acute if the condition begins within 3 months of the trauma and delayed if symptoms emerge more than 6 months after the event. The chances of complete recovery are better in the acute form than in the delayed form. However, questions have been raised about the desirability of having two distinct diagnoses, acute stress disorder and PTSD (Marshall, Spitzer, & Liebowitz, 1999) (see Box 7-3).

PTSD differs from less serious trauma-related disorders, not only in the extremity of the traumatic experience, but

Table 7-11

Diagnostic Criteria for Posttraumatic Stress Disorder

1. Exposure to a traumatic event that involved actual or threatened death or serious injury, or a threat to the physical integrity of self or others
2. A response to the event that includes intense fear, helplessness, or horror
3. Persistent reexperiencing of the traumatic event in the form of recurrent and distressing thoughts or dreams, or behaving or feeling as if the traumatic event were actually happening again, or intense psychological or physiological reactivity when exposed to cues that symbolize or resemble the event
4. Persistent avoidance of stimuli associated with the trauma, along with numbing of general responsiveness
5. Persistent symptoms of increased arousal—such as hypervigilance, irritability, sleep difficulties, difficulty in concentrating, and exaggerated startle response—not present before the trauma
6. Symptoms of more than 1 month's duration that cause significant distress or impairment (e.g., in the spheres of interpersonal relationships and work)

also the seriousness of the condition, its duration, and its poorer prognosis. In addition, evidence is accumulating that personal vulnerabilities play an important role in PTSD. Most people who have traumatic experiences get over them relatively quickly and without extensive professional help. Why do PTSD victims develop delayed and often prolonged symptoms? What role do their vulnerabilities play in the maladaptive way in which they cope with trauma?

Vulnerability Factors

There is growing evidence that preexisting emotional and behavioral difficulties constitute significant vulnerabilities and increase the likelihood of PTSD (van der Kolk, et al., 1996; Wilson & Keane, 1997). In one study, 72% of individuals with PTSD diagnoses had prestress histories of psychological disorders (E. M. Smith et al., 1990). Prominent among the prestress diagnoses of adult PTSD patients were depression and alcohol abuse. Another study that dealt with the aftermath of the 1991 fires in the Oakland, California, hills has provided information concerning certain conditions conducive to the development of PTSD (Koopman et al., 1994). The major finding was that those who react with an apparently unwarranted calm may be particularly prone to posttraumatic distress problems, such

---

 Q&A   **Box 7–3**

Q: Posttraumatic stress disorder is discussed in this chapter on anxiety disorders, while acute stress disorder was discussed in Chapter 4, which dealt with maladaptive responses to stress. Why aren't they in the same chapter? Aren't they pretty much the same thing?

A: *A very perceptive question. They aren't in the same chapter because acute stress disorder (ASD) is a relatively short-term condition, lasting from a few days to no more than 4 weeks, whereas posttraumatic stress disorder (PTSD) persists for longer than a month— often much longer. PTSD can also have a delayed onset, defined as at least 6 months after the traumatic experience. DSM-IV classifies PTSD with the anxiety disorders because PTSD has many of the symptoms seen in anxiety disorders. But your question is a good one because there is a degree of arbitrariness in*

DSM-IV's placement of ASD and PTSD. This is understandable given that ASD is a very new diagnosis and more research is needed to verify its usefulness. We wouldn't be surprised if ASD and PTSD were treated differently in a future edition of DSM. A possibility would be to have one diagnosis, posttraumatic disorder with subtypes such as, acute, chronic, and delayed.

PTSD is marked by hyperarousal, numbing, avoidance and reexperiencing symptoms over an extended period of time. ASD was added to DSM to provide a diagnostic category for distressed trauma victims during the days immediately after the trauma. Although there is a great overlap in the symptoms of ASD and PTSD there are some differences. In addition to the time course, an important difference is that dissociative symptoms (amnesia, depersonalization, derealization) are often present in ASD but not PTSD. An im-

portant methodological difference is that much of the research on PTSD has been conducted on male combat veterans years after trauma exposure, whereas many studies of ASD have been conducted on motor vehicle accident survivors and, to a lesser extent, violent crime witnesses or victims, and survivors of natural disasters.

The question you ask points up the fact that a classification system is a work in progress. As new information is revealed by researchers it becomes more rooted in empirical evidence and less a product of what has to be a degree of arbitrariness that is inevitable when all the pertinent evidence is not yet available. While ASD is a more recent diagnostic classification, PTSD was only defined in 1980. Both these disorders involve stressors that produce symptoms in certain people. We need to know more about which stressors produce which symptoms in which people.

as severe anxiety, sleep disruptions, or flashbacks, which may not surface until months or even years later. There was also evidence that such people may also be inclined to put themselves in danger during a disaster because they ignore the reality of the peril. The heightened risk occurs particularly in those whose steadiness during a catastrophe is a result of symptoms of dissociation that include lack of emotional reaction, a feeling that the events are unreal, or disorientation. Thus, those who tend to shut out reality in a stressful situation are at heightened risk for developing severe posttraumatic disorder.

Support for the idea that what a person brings to the traumatic event and its aftermath is a major factor in PTSD was provided by a study of soldiers' memories of combat trauma in the Gulf War (Southwick et al., 1995). Soldiers' recollections of combat were obtained 1 month after they had returned from the Gulf and collected again 2 years later. A key finding was that most soldiers' recollection of specific features of combat were inconsistent. Seventy percent of them recalled traumatic events 2 years afterward that they had not reported at 1 month. Those with greater PTSD symptom levels were significantly more likely to amplify their memory of combat trauma at the 2-year assessment. This association of changes in memory with greater PTSD symptom levels brings into question the methodology traditionally used to demonstrate a link between the severity of combat exposure and the development of PTSD. There may be considerable distortion in the recollection of past trauma, and what PTSD patients describe should be recognized as their current version of the past.

There are some indications that individuals who are socially withdrawn, inhibited, irritable, pessimistic, and impulsive, as well as those with tendencies toward dissociation, may be more vulnerable to traumatic experiences (Shalev, et al., 1996). A family history of these tendencies also increases the risk of posttraumatic problems, suggesting a possible genetic contributor to vulnerability. A hypothesis that merits serious consideration is that if individuals do not possess adequate coping skills or social support, they will become fearful about a repetition of the stress, and this fear contributes to a cycle of chronic overarousal and anxiety. This preoccupation with and anticipation of future stress may be at the core of PTSD.

Epidemiological Evidence

Epidemiological evidence suggests that the prevalence of PTSD typically ranges from 1% to 14% of the population, depending on the population sampled and how PTSD symptoms were assessed. Recent findings suggest that PTSD is more prevalent than has been thought to be the case (Solomon et al., 1992). About 20% of wounded Vietnam veterans showed some symptoms of PTSD (Helzer et al.,

1987). A study of people who had been present at a mass-murder spree in a cafeteria found that 20% of the men and 36% of the women later met the criteria for PTSD (North et al., 1994).

The combination of vulnerability factors and exposure earlier in life to traumatic experiences increases the likelihood of PTSD. Having been abused as children or having had other previous traumatic experiences increases the risk for PTSD, especially for individuals who generally have emotional difficulties, such as anxiety and depression.

The Posttraumatic Experience

A frequent characteristic of posttraumatic disorders is a tendency to reexperience the event. Painful and intrusive recollections and recurrent dreams or nightmares are common. The reexperiencing of a traumatic event may have an aura of unreality about it. When this happens, the person feels emotionally anesthetized amid an unstoppable flood of thoughts about the event.

In addition to reexperiencing the stressor, people who are suffering from posttraumatic disorders may show excessive autonomic arousal, hyperalertness, difficulty in concentrating on or completing tasks, and difficulty falling asleep. A symptom that often occurs in children who have experienced trauma is an exaggerated startle response. These symptoms may increase when the individual is exposed to cues related to the traumatic event (e.g., when a victim of a serious automobile accident sees a car crash in a movie). Preoccupation with the traumatic event may also lead to decreased interest in social relationships, intimacy, and sexuality. Painful guilt feelings are common, as are depression, restlessness, and irritability. In some cases, there may be outbreaks of impulsive behavior, usually of a nonviolent nature (e.g., unexplained absences from work), and abuse of alcohol or drugs.

In the following case, there was a short interval between the stressor and the onset of the posttraumatic condition. This case illustrates how denial can be used to blunt the strong feelings aroused by a stressful event.

Harry is a 40-year-old truck dispatcher. He had worked his way up in a small trucking firm. One night he himself took a run because he was shorthanded. The load was steel pipes carried in an old truck. This improper vehicle had armor between the load bed and the driver's side of the forward compartment but did not fully protect the passenger's side.

Late at night Harry passed an attractive and solitary girl hitchhiking on a lonely stretch of highway. Making an impulsive decision to violate the company rule against passengers of any sort, he picked her up.

A short time later, a car veered across the divider line and entered his lane, threatening a head-on collision. He pulled

across the shoulder of the road into an initially clear area, but crashed abruptly into a pile of gravel. The pipes shifted, penetrated the cab of the truck on the passenger's side and impaled the girl. Harry crashed into the steering wheel and windshield and was briefly unconscious. He regained consciousness and was met with the grisly sight of his dead companion.

The highway patrol found no identification on the girl. The other car had driven on, and Harry was taken by ambulance to a hospital emergency room. No fractures were found; his lacerations were sutured and he remained overnight for observation. His wife, who sat with him, found him anxious and dazed that night, talking fitfully about the events in a fragmentary and incoherent way, so that the story was not clear.

The next day Harry was released. Against his wife's wishes, he returned to work. From then on, for several days, he continued his regular work as if nothing had happened. There was an immediate session with his superiors and with legal advisors. The result was that he was reprimanded for breaking the rule about passengers but also reassured that the accident was not his fault and he would not be held responsible. As it happened, the no-passenger rule was frequently breached by other drivers. This fact was well known throughout the group.

For several days after the accident, Harry thought about it occasionally, but he was surprised at how little emotion he felt. However, despite his good performance at work, Harry's wife reported that he thrashed around in his sleep, ground his teeth, and seemed tenser and more irritable than usual. A month after the accident, he had a nightmare in which mangled bodies appeared. He awoke in a state of anxiety. During the following days he had recurring, upsetting images of the girl's body. He developed a phobia about driving to and from work, increased his consumption of alcohol, had outbursts of temper at minor frustrations, and began feeling intense guilt about the accident.

In psychotherapy an effort was made to understand the significance of the accident for Harry. Initially Harry resisted describing to the therapist the circumstances surrounding the accident. After this resistance subsided, his strong feelings—the guilt, fears, and anger—emerged and were discussed. Because of complex defensive motives, Harry could not accept and integrate his traumatic perceptions of the accident. They were stored, but not forgotten. He came to understand that two aspects had been most upsetting to him: guilt over his relief at the fact that the girl had been the victim instead of him, as well as guilt over his sexual fantasies about her; and anxiety over the realization that he had come so close to being the victim. Bringing these themes into focus enabled Harry to be more open about himself and to take a problem-solving rather than a defensive stance toward his situation. Psychotherapy enabled him to look at himself in a more realistic way, to feel comfortable doing so within the supportive therapy situation, and to achieve an improved adaptation. (Adapted from Horowitz, 1974, pp. 769–771)

What happens in posttraumatic stress? In coping with trauma, an individual uses a huge amount of psychologi-cal energy to fend off thoughts about it. Although the event has ended, it is relived daily, and there is an irrational fear that it will happen again. It is this fear that causes hypervigilance and agitation. Intrusive thoughts, images, and dreams may become so preoccupying that the person cannot engage in normal work or relationships.

In some cases of maladaptive reactions to trauma there may be an alternation of intrusive thinking and denial. In the intrusive state, the individual cannot stop having frightening thoughts related to the traumatic event. In the denial state, the individual ignores the implications of threats and losses, forgets important problems, and may show a withdrawal of interest in life. Table 7-12 lists symptoms of the intrusive and denial phases of posttraumatic disorders.

A variety of treatment approaches have been taken in regard to PTSD. While several of them seem to reduce PTSD symptoms and improve the patient's quality of life, the effects of treatment are often limited, and complete recovery is not common (Shalev et al., 1996). Antidepressant and antianxiety drugs may have some therapeutic effects in PTSD, but the results tend to be less impressive than the results of psychological therapies (Solomon et al., 1992). Psychotherapy can often be helpful in reducing the severity of PTSD because it helps victims not only to view the experience in a more objective way but also to express the strong emotions they may have felt forced to suppress in conversations with friends and relatives. Behavioral therapies designed to reduce anxiety by means of repeated or extended, real or imaginary exposure to objectively harmless yet feared stimuli have been used successfully in some cases of PTSD. Psychodynamic and cognitive therapy approaches have also been found to be helpful. Research suggests that some combination

---

Table 7-12

Symptoms of Intrusive Thinking and Denial in Posttraumatic Stress Disorders (Symptoms May Alternate)

Symptoms of Intrusive Thinking

- Sleep and dream disturbances
- Awareness of ideas and feelings related to the traumatic event
- Preoccupation with the event
- Compulsive repetitions of actions related to the event

Symptoms of Denial

- Selective inattention
- Amnesia (complete or partial)
- Use of fantasy to escape from real conditions
- Withdrawal

of psychological therapy and medication may yield better results than either alone (Marshall & Pierce, 2000). No matter which therapeutic approach is employed, the sooner the treatment begins, the better the outcome.

Interpreting and Treating Anxiety Disorders

There are two important tasks facing clinicians as they strive to diminish maladaptive behavior and enhance life satisfaction. One is understanding the nature of the clinical problem and the other is treating it. As we saw in Chapter 3, it sometimes is not easy to figure out how a problem can best be conceptualized. This is well illustrated by the anxiety disorders because, despite their diverse symptoms, there are common elements. This means that the same symptom might be present in two different disorders that require different types of treatment. For example, avoidance behavior is a feature of several of the anxiety disorders but requires different therapeutic tactics depending on why and what the individual is avoiding. Table 7-13 shows some of the ways in which avoidance behavior can manifest itself in anxiety disorders. Overlap among the anxiety disorders and between them and other problems represents a diagnostic challenge and an issue to be considered in planning treatment (Box 7-4).

Of course, anxiety is the common thread that runs through the anxiety disorders. Anxiety and the things that people do to avoid anxiety or keep it at manageable levels have been looked at from several theoretical perspectives. We will discuss the theories used to explain anxiety disorders that are currently most influential in clinical practice and research.

The Psychodynamic Perspective

Psychodynamic theorists and many other clinicians believe that the major determinants of anxiety disorders are intrapsychic events and unconscious motivations. They believe that anxiety is an alarm reaction that appears whenever a person is threatened. How an individual adapts to the anxiety alarm depends on its intensity, the cue that evokes it, and the person's characteristic response to alarms. It is normal to experience some overt anxiety; the amount of anxiety and the nature of the threat determine whether an instance of anxiety is normal or pathological.

Psychodynamic theorists frequently mention the following as causes of anxiety that reaches clinical proportions: perception of oneself as helpless in coping with environmental pressures, separation or anticipation of abandonment, privation and loss of emotional support as a result of sudden environmental changes, unacceptable or dangerous impulses that are close to breaking into consciousness, and threats or anticipation of the disapproval or withdrawal of love. The following case, diagnosed as a posttraumatic stress disorder, was treated with short-term (12 sessions) psychodynamic psychotherapy in which these types of unconscious processes were the primary focus (Krupnick, 1997):

> Susan, a 54-year-old African American woman, sought treatment for symptoms of PTSD 5 months after her husband Tom's death in a plane crash. Tom, a computer salesman, had been returning from a business trip when his plane exploded in midair, leaving no survivors. Susan was notified of her husband's death by airline officials who also requested Tom's dental records, as most of the bodies were burned beyond recognition.
>
> Susan's first reaction to the news of her husband's death was shock and disbelief. He had been in perfect health only days before and now she would never see him again. Furthermore, it was difficult to feel that the corpse she had buried was really her husband, because the body parts returned to her bore no real resemblance to Tom. The suddenness of the death and the strangeness of the circumstances provided a surreal quality to events. Susan could not believe that her husband was dead. She kept expecting him to call, apologizing for having missed his flight, and promising to take the next plane out.
>
> After her husband's death, Susan entered a denial phase in dealing with her grief. Her friends had remarked on the extent to which she appeared strong and capable of coping with her feelings, but Susan knew, from early on, that she felt more dazed than strong. Soon after the funeral, Susan returned to her work as a manager at a retail store. She spent an inordinate amount of time at her office, leaving little time to contemplate her feelings about, and reactions to, the death. This behavior served the purpose, at least for a while, of keeping her so busy that she was able to postpone feelings of grief that seemed too overwhelming.
>
> In the weeks before seeking treatment, however, this strategy was no longer working. Susan began to experience episodes of intrusive thought and emotion, comparing the feeling to going

---

Table 7-13

Examples of How Avoidance Manifests Itself in Anxiety Disorders

1. *Social phobia:* fear and avoidance of social situations
2. *Specific phobia:* fear and avoidance of nonsocial stimuli
3. *Agoraphobia:* avoidance of situations in which escape may be difficult (absence of panic attacks)
4. *Panic disorder with agoraphobia:* panic attacks precede avoidance of situations in which escape may be difficult
5. *Obsessive-compulsive disorder:* fear and avoidance of certain types of situations related to obsessions and compulsions (e.g., avoidance of dirt)

Research Close-up

Box 7–4

Comorbidity

Patients with anxiety disorders often have features of other mental disorders, especially the disturbances of mood found in depression. Although such co-occurrences of thoughts, behaviors, and symptoms appear in a number of other disorders as well, surprisingly little attention has been paid to this phenomenon. Table 7-14 shows the wide range of comorbidity, the co-occurrence of clinical symptoms, among various types of maladaptive behavior. The table indicates, for example, that 77% of cases of schizophrenia and paranoid disorders in the population studied had only that diagnosis, while 23% of these cases had multiple diagnoses (i.e., diagnoses in addition to the primary one). Comorbidity estimates vary from study to study for several reasons, including the methods employed in making diagnoses and characteristics of the sample surveyed. For example, while 30% of the cases of anxiety disorder in Table 7-14 involved multiple diagnoses, other studies using different populations and diagnostic methods have found greater comorbidity

for anxiety and depressive disorders. One study found that, while the risk of suicide in people with panic disorder is high, the risk is even higher in panic disorder cases that involved comorbidity with other disorders (Johnson et al., 1990).

Studies of comorbidity have led clinicians to attend to the fact that more than one disorder can be diagnosed in the same individual. In addition, an individual who meets the full diagnostic criteria for only one disorder may still have an increased frequency of symptoms from other categories—but to an extent that is insufficient to diagnose another disorder. Depending on the disorder, patients diagnosed as having a particular disorder may have relatively greater or lesser risk of having other disorders or other symptoms.

Comorbidity can occur within a given diagnostic category as well as between different ones. For example, there is evidence that the presence of one type of anxiety disorder increases the likelihood of the presence of another. We know persons diagnosed as having social phobias often re-

ceive a secondary diagnosis of panic disorder. Knowing that comorbidity may be high in certain types of cases is valuable to clinicians because it alerts them to the need to probe carefully regarding the possibility of co-occurrences.

Evidence of high comorbidity within a diagnostic category also leads to consideration of the possible need to revise classification criteria. For example, noting that generalized anxiety disorder has been associated with extremely high rates of comorbidity with other types of anxiety disorder, some researchers have suggested that generalized anxiety disorder might be conceptualized as a trait conducive to vulnerability to other types of anxiety disorders rather than as a discrete disorder in its own right (T. A. Brown et al., 1994).

Epidemiological studies of anxiety and mood disorders have revealed several intriguing findings. One is that the risk of depression in individuals with chronic anxiety disorders is greater than the risk of anxiety in individuals with depressive disorders (Maser & Cloninger, 1990). Another is that depressive disorders are more likely to remain free of comorbid anxiety, while anxiety disorders are more often complicated by depression after long-term follow-up. There are many issues raised by the comorbidity of mental disorders. One pertains to the role of heredity. Is there a common genetic cause or predisposition for both depression and anxiety, or are different environmental exposures responsible for comorbidity? At present we do not have an answer to this question. The association between anxiety and depression could be due to one of the disorders causing or leading to the other. Another possible explanation is that the two disorders have some common cause.

Future research needs to be directed toward distinguishing "true comorbidity" (separate disorders occurring in the same individual) and "false comorbidity" (such an intimate relationship between disorders that they are really one and the same).

Table 7-14

Percentages of Single and Multiple Diagnosis for Various Diagnostic Categories

Diagnostic Categories	Single Diagnoses (%)	Multiple Diagnoses (%)
Anxiety disorders	70	30
Affective disorders (depression)	57	43
Dissociative disorders	50	50
Adjustment disorders	69	31
Alcohol-use disorders	14	87
Psychosexual disorders	14	86
Schizophrenia and paranoid disorders	77	23
Mental retardation	15	85
Organic brain disorders	67	33

Source: Based on Mezzich et al. (1990).

to the dentist and having the Novocain wear off. She found herself snapping at co-workers and, once she arrived home, experiencing episodes of uncontrollable sobbing. Susan felt tense much of the time and started having nightmares about explosions and burning bodies. She learned after the crash that Tom

had not been required to make this particular trip, but he had insisted on going. Susan now felt angry at him for that decision.

Susan's developmental history revealed that, although she got along well with her father, her relationship with her mother had always been a source of tension. Her mother had been severely *depressed while Susan was growing up, and Susan had always felt neglected and abandoned by her. In response to Susan's traumatic bereavement, her mother again seemed preoccupied and self-absorbed.*

A number of themes and pieces of information emerged in the psychotherapy. Susan felt deeply guilty that she had not been with her husband at the time of the plane crash. She imagined how frightened he must have felt. At the same time, she blamed him for dying because he really didn't have to go on the trip. In one session, Susan revealed that she and Tom had had an argument the morning he left. Because they were both upset over the argument, Tom told Susan that he would take an earlier flight home that evening. This earlier flight was the one on which he was killed. Susan felt that because of the argument she was responsible for her husband's death. By the end of psychotherapy, Susan reported that she no longer had persistent morbid thoughts of her husband and that she was again deeply involved in her work and was beginning to develop new social relationships. Contributing to the positive outcome was a good patient-therapist relationship that (1) permitted Susan to express her deeply conflictful thoughts and emotions, and (2) showed the understanding and acceptance from the therapist that led Susan to question the condemnation with which she had viewed herself. The therapy helped Susan become less self-critical, more caring toward herself and others, and less tense and anxious.

Psychotherapy, the main clinical tool of the psychodynamically oriented clinician, is intended to help people expose and deal with the psychodynamic roots of their maladaptive behaviors. Most psychotherapists believe that such behaviors occur when a person becomes preoccupied with relieving or eliminating anxiety. They feel that by gaining insight into the unconscious roots of anxiety, the person can direct his or her activity toward altering or abandoning unwanted behavior.

Beyond their emphasis on the accepting therapeutic environment, psychodynamic clinicians interpret particular symptoms in certain ways. For example, they believe that obsessive ideas and compulsive rituals may direct attention away from significant, distressing unconscious thoughts. Psychoanalysts believe that these thoughts often involve aggression and rage that may have first been aroused in the battle for autonomy between the growing child and the mother. When the mother is especially demanding and has unreasonably high expectations about when the child should meet certain developmental challenges (such as toilet training), the child may be forced to bottle up his or her anger. This unacceptable anger expresses itself deviously later in life.

Freud emphasized the roles of several defense mechanisms in the development of obsessive-compulsive disorders. These include isolation, undoing, and reaction formation. Through **isolation,** emotions are separated from a thought or act, which then becomes obsessive or compulsive. However, the emotion is not completely barred from consciousness and constantly threatens to break through the controls that have been imposed upon it. **Undoing** is illustrated by an individual who thinks obsessively "My father will die" whenever he turns off a light. This thought compels him to turn around, touch the switch, and say, "I take back that thought." The compulsive act could be said to "undo" what he feared might result from the initial obsessive thought, which might be rooted in an underlying aggressive impulse toward the father. **Reaction formation** is illustrated by a mother who compulsively checks her children's rooms dozens of times while they are asleep; she is overly solicitous about her children because of her underlying resentment toward them.

The Behavioral Perspective

Instead of speaking of symptoms caused by underlying events, behavioral psychologists focus on acquired responses and response tendencies. They believe that the general principles of learning can be applied to the understanding of all behavior, including anxiety disorders. According to behavioral theorists, anxiety that reaches clinical proportions is a learned or acquired response, a symptom that has been created by environmental conditions, often within the home.

Learning concepts such as conditioning, reinforcement, and extinction have increasingly been applied to the study of anxiety disorders. Several new, clinically useful techniques, collectively referred to as **behavior therapy,** are the most valuable outcomes of these applications. Research in behavior therapy has been directed at discovering the variables that help defuse highly emotional responses.

Exposure Therapies As we have noted throughout this chapter, a common element in many behavior therapies is exposing the client to stimuli that evoke discomfort until he or she becomes used to them. Much research has been carried out in which clients are exposed to feared stimuli and are prevented from making an avoidance or escape response. The client is strongly urged to continue to attend to the anxiety-eliciting stimuli despite the stressful effects that usually accompany this effort.

Exposure therapy can be particularly effective in treating both phobic and obsessive-compulsive disorders. A critical element of the treatment is motivating the client to maintain contact with the actual noxious stimuli or with their imagined presence until he or she becomes used to them. This might mean, for example, exposing a compulsive hand-washer to dirt until the hand-washing no longer occurs, or encouraging such a person to think about dirt, perhaps imagined first as household dust and later as particularly noxious dirt such as vomit or feces. The therapist's task is to identify all components of the stimulus that evoke an avoidance or escape response and to continue the exposure until the evoked response no longer occurs.

Three types of therapy based on the exposure principle are systematic desensitization, implosive therapy, and in vivo exposure. In **systematic desensitization,** a series of fear-arousing stimuli, carefully graded from mild to strongly fearful, are used. Only when a client is comfortable with one level of fear-producing stimuli is the next, slightly stronger stimulus introduced. **Implosive therapy** refers to therapist-controlled exposure to the imagined re-creation of a complex, high-intensity, fear-arousing situation. **In vivo exposure** means that the individual experiences the actual feared situation rather than imagining it under the therapist's direction. In vivo exposure may be conducted gradually, beginning with low levels of stimulus intensity, or rapidly, by exposing the client immediately to high-intensity and prolonged stimulation. This rapid, intense exposure is called **flooding.**

Systematic desensitization, which is used primarily in the treatment of strong fears, is based on conditioning principles. The client is taught to relax and then is presented with a series of stimuli that are graded from low to high according to their capacity to evoke anxiety. The treatment of a death phobia illustrates how systematic desensitization is used. The patient's fears are arranged in a hierarchy, with the items in the hierarchy ranging, in descending order, from human corpses to funeral processions, black clothes, and floral wreaths. The therapy begins with items that are low in the hierarchy, such as seeing a wreath. The therapist tries to teach the client to remain relaxed while imagining or actually seeing a wreath. When the client can maintain a relaxed state consistently, the therapy proceeds with stimuli that are higher in the hierarchy.

A therapist does not try to produce cures overnight with conditioning procedures. Usually, the process of reducing the level of an emotional response to a stimulus that should be neutral is a gradual one. Clinical applications of systematic desensitization have shown that clients who are treated in this way become less upset by previously feared situations and better able to manage their anxiety. It is possible that the most effective part of systematic desensitization is the client's exposure to gradually increasing levels of fear-arousing stimuli under nonthreatening conditions. Individuals who can mentally rehearse being exposed to the upsetting, fear-arousing situations show particularly high levels of improvement.

Implosive therapy is based on the belief that many conditions, including anxiety disorders, are outgrowths of painful prior experiences. For the patient to unlearn them, the original situation must be re-created so that it can be experienced without pain. Therapists who use implosion ask their clients to imagine scenes related to particular personal conflicts and to re-create the anxiety felt in those scenes. The therapist strives to heighten the realism of the re-creation and to help the patient extinguish the anxiety that was created by the original aversive conditions. In addition, the client is helped to adopt more mature forms of behavior. Implosive therapy uses the methods and ideas of both behavioral and psychodynamic theories. Although implosive therapy is not uniformly effective in reducing anxiety, research to date suggests that it, like desensitization, can reduce many intense fears.

The term *in vivo exposure* means that the exposure is carried out in a real-life setting, not simply in the imaginations of the client and the therapist as they sit in the therapist's office. The difference between in vivo exposure and flooding might be compared to the difference between wading into a swimming pool and jumping in at the deep end. An example of flooding might be asking an agoraphobic client who experienced intense anxiety anywhere outside her home to go to a crowded shopping center with the therapist and remain there until her desire to escape disappeared.

In the treatment of most anxiety disorders, exposure has produced consistently good results, with improvements lasting up to several years. The longer the exposure to the critical stimulus, the better the results. How well exposure treatment works depends on the client's motivation and on how specific it is to the situation. For example, when compulsive rituals are triggered by home cues (which happens in many cases), treatment needs to be conducted in the home setting. Failure to improve can usually be traced to a patient's failure to comply with treatment instructions, particularly by not seeking exposure to fear-arousing stimuli. In one study, compulsive people received exposure therapy in their homes (Emmelkamp et al., 1980). The clients' task was to avoid responding compulsively when the evoking stimuli were present. Figure 7-12 shows changes in the clients' ratings of their levels of anxiety when exposed to the evoking stimuli. If the client refrained from compulsive behavior in the presence of the stimuli, the level of anxiety decreased immediately after exposure. The decrease was maintained 1 and 6 months later in the presence of the formerly compulsion-evoking stimuli.

An important task for future research is to find out why exposure is effective. When a client "gets used to" an upsetting stimulus, what is going on? One possible explanation is that as clients find that they can handle a little exposure to upsetting stimuli and note that their anxiety levels subside, they quickly gain confidence in themselves and develop the courage to persist in their efforts to overcome their problems.

The most effective behavioral technique for treating compulsive rituals is a combination of exposure and response prevention. The therapist asks the patient to disclose all obsessions and compulsive patterns, and then prohibits them. A compulsive washer, for example, is

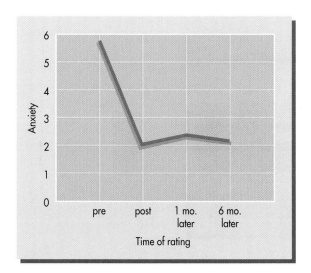

Figure 7-12 Changes in rated anxiety before in vivo exposure ("pre"), immediately afterwards ("post"), and at 1-month and 6-month follow-up points.

SOURCE: From Emmelkamp et al. (1980). Reprinted with permission from *Behavior Research and Therapy.* © 1980 by Pergoman Journals, Ltd.

allowed to become dirty, or is even made dirty, and then is ordered not to wash. A typical treatment might allow one 10-minute shower every fifth day. Exposure reduces hypersensitivity to dirt as well as its associated anxiety; response prevention eventually eliminates the compulsive ritual. Exposure usually has to be done outside the psychotherapist's office, and trained helpers may be needed—wives, husbands, friends, or nurse-therapists. Exposure in fantasy is less effective, but sometimes it is the only possible way—for example, a patient with a fear of causing a traffic fatality cannot actually run over someone.

Exposure therapy and other behavioral approaches are not highly effective with people who are "pure obsessives," that is, people who do not engage in rituals or avoidant behavior.

Modeling Another behavioral approach, **modeling,** is often combined with exposure to anxiety-provoking stimuli. While exposure therapies emphasize removing some of the overwhelming emotional response that may inhibit people who have an anxiety disorder, modeling emphasizes *acquiring* behavioral skills and a feeling of competence.

In addition to acting as a disinhibitor, modeling can help in the acquisition of new skills and response capabilities. For example, a therapist might model a response and then provide corrective feedback as the client performs the same behavior. In addition to the information provided by the modeled behavior, the client receives guidance on his or her own performance. Modeling works especially well with complex behaviors, such as those involved in certain social situations. A therapist can guide the client toward mastery over frightening situations and maladaptive behavior. Modeling and guidance help the client attain a sense of mastery and self-efficacy.

The Cognitive Perspective

Although they are based on learning principles, the methods developed by behavioral therapists have important implications for our understanding of cognitive processes, that is, private or internal processes such as imagery and how we think about ourselves and the world. Therapies such as systematic desensitization, exposure, and modeling affect not only clients' behavior but also how they think about themselves. Furthermore, cognitive activity is often a specific step in behavioral therapy; for example, in systematic desensitization the client is asked to visualize, think about, or imagine certain fear-arousing situations. Cognitive rehearsal in combination with in vivo exposure has been used successfully with phobic and obsessive-compulsive individuals. Available evidence suggests that this procedure is highly effective in ultimately reducing anxiety, regardless of whether the client feels relaxed or anxious during exposure.

Modeling can also have an important cognitive element. Someone who overcomes intense fears as a result of a behavioral therapy program such as participant modeling acquires more self-confidence and may begin to think about new ways of behaving in situations that were not covered in the modeling program. The way people think about things often changes when they acquire new response capabilities. These cognitive changes can then lead to important behavioral advances. As we have seen, the term **cognitive-behavioral therapy** refers to clinical procedures based on principles of learning, such as extinction and reinforcement, that emphasize cognitive behavior.

Cognitive Interpretation of Maladaptive Behavior In addition to increased interest in cognitive aspects of behavior therapy, there has been a rapid increase in the influence of the cognitive perspective on efforts to understand the anxiety disorders. This perspective emphasizes the ways in which certain thoughts and styles of thinking have undesirable effects on behavior. Thoughts that preoccupy people interfere with attention to the task at hand. Worries, daydreams, and ideas that have nothing to do with the immediate task are distracting and reduce behavioral effectiveness.

According to cognitive theorists, thinking disturbances that occur only in certain places or in relation to specific problems are often sources of anxiety. These thoughts may include unrealistic appraisals of situations and consistent overestimation of their dangerous aspects; for example, the degree and the likelihood of harm may both be exaggerated. Thus, a person's train of thought and mental set can be viewed as vulnerability factors that interact with the characteristics of certain situations. From this point of view, precipitating events (the situation) elicit or magnify an underlying attitude or fear (the vulnerability factor) and give rise to hypervigilance. As this attitude strengthens, danger-related thoughts become more easily activated by less specific, less avoidable situations ("If you look for it, you're sure to find it"). As a result, the anxious individual continually scans internal and external stimuli for danger signals.

An example of this sort of disturbance may be seen in an obsessive person who experiences intense anxiety when having to cross the street and may actually be unable to attempt crossing. Most people would use the following train of thought:

1. Streets are safe for crossing at green lights or when free of traffic.
2. This street has a green light or is free of traffic.
3. Therefore, this street can be crossed.

The obsessive person's thinking, on the other hand, might go as follows:

1. Streets are safe for crossing at green lights or when free of traffic.
2. This street has a green light or is free of traffic, but if the light suddenly changes or a car appears unexpectedly . . .
3. Then this street is not safe for me to cross.

Studies of obsessive thinkers have revealed unreasonable beliefs and assumptions. Such people believe that they should be perfectly competent, must avoid criticism or disapproval, and will be severely punished for their mistakes and imperfections. In addition, at some level they seem to believe that thinking certain thoughts or performing certain rituals will help them avoid the disastrous outcomes they imagine are just around the corner. Obsessive-compulsive individuals make arbitrary rules that they must follow (e.g., stepping on every seventh crack in the sidewalk). Phobic people also make up rules for themselves that are not reality-based (e.g., "Elevators get stuck. If I use one it will get stuck and I might suffocate; therefore, I won't go in an elevator."). Unfortunately, "protective" rituals and rules become very intrusive and can interfere with normal activity (Salkovskis, 1999).

Figure 7-13 illustrates the cognitive view of one anxiety disorder, social phobia. A particular social situation evokes these individuals' assumptions about the nature of the situation and of themselves (what is going on or expected in the situation and how they appear to others), and these assumptions lead to perceptions of social danger ("They might find out what an inadequate person I am"). In turn, these appraisals stimulate catastrophic thinking ("Everyone has seen me for the boring person that I am"). Not surprisingly, this overestimation of a situation's requirements, coupled with an underestimation of one's personal resources, is likely to lead to behavioral symptoms

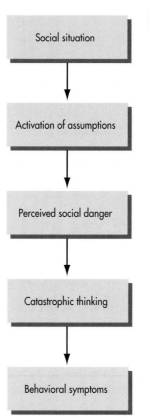

Figure 7-13   Cognitive interpretation of social phobia.

and to unrewarding social experiences that further contribute to fear of social situations and confirm one's social ineptness.

Cognitive Therapy   Cognitive therapists employ a number of techniques. One of these is **cognitive restructuring.** Developed out of the rational-emotive therapy of Albert Ellis (see Chapter 2), cognitive restructuring calls the client's attention to the unrealistic thoughts that serve as cues for his or her maladaptive behavior. The therapist helps clients review their irrational beliefs and expectations and develop more rational ways of looking at their lives. For example, many people with anxiety disorders are perfectionists who expect too much of themselves and others and become overly emotional when their unattainable goals are not realized. During therapy sessions, emphasis is placed on how the irrational things that people say to themselves can affect their emotions and behavior.

By means of cognitive restructuring, people develop more realistic appraisals of themselves and others. For example, when taking an exam, a person might think: "This test is hard. Everyone else seems to think it's going to be simple. They all must know a lot more than I do." Such thoughts are likely to lead to a high degree of anxiety. A cognitive therapist would help this client concentrate on a more adaptive type of thought, such as: "I studied hard. I'll just try to answer one question at a time. If I don't know the answer, I'll go on to the next one. No reason for panic. Even people who do well don't know the answer to every question."

Thought stopping is another cognitive technique. It works on the assumption that a sudden distracting stimulus, such as an unpleasant noise, will serve to terminate obsessional thoughts. The client is asked to get the thought firmly in mind; then the therapist loudly says, "Stop!" This sequence—obsessional thought followed by "Stop!"—is repeated several times with the client, rather than the therapist, yelling "Stop!" Finally, the client simply mentally says "Stop!" If it is successful, this procedure provides the client with a specific self-control technique for removing an obsessional thought when it occurs.

A third cognitive technique is **cognitive rehearsal,** through which the client can mentally rehearse adaptive approaches to problematic situations. Cognitive rehearsal is particularly useful for problems that cannot be conveniently simulated in a clinical setting. For example, behavioral rehearsal of social skills by socially phobic individuals requires the presence of a large group of people. However, someone who suffers from a social phobia can imagine being in a group and can mentally rehearse behaviors and internal statements designed to improve his or her interpersonal relationships.

Aaron Beck has developed one of the most influential types of **cognitive therapy** (A. T. Beck & Emery, 1985). He believes that the core psychological problem in anxiety disorders is a vulnerability that grows out of the individual's tendency to devalue his or her problem-solving ability as well as to exaggerate the degree of threat in a problematic situation. Such an individual perceives anxiety-provoking threats to social relationships, freedom, and self-identity.

Beck's cognitive therapy typically consists of 5 to 20 sessions. A minimal amount of time is spent acquiring background information, searching for the original causes of anxiety, or engaging in unfocused conversation with the patient. Most of the therapy is task-oriented, devoted to solving problems brought up by the patient. The therapist encourages the patient to talk openly about his or her fears and concerns, and conveys empathy for the patient's anxiety. The Socratic method is used to help the patient become aware of what his or her thoughts are, examine them for cognitive distortions, and substitute more realistic thoughts.

The following exchange occurred in a therapy session in which Beck's approach was applied to a case of panic disorder. Because catastrophic misinterpretation of physiological sensations is a central component of panic disorder, the therapist ("T") sought a precise description of the patient's typical attack and helped the patient ("P"), an 18-year-old female, become more aware of her misinterpretations.

P: *I've felt a couple of times like I was going to have a heart attack.*

T: *Tell me about that.*

P: *It's just like, it starts to beat so hard, and so fast, that, I mean, it hurts, and you just think, you're just like*

sitting there going [breathes rapidly to demonstrate how she hyperventilates].

T: *What was the effect, do you think, of that particular image or idea on the symptoms themselves?*

P: *Oh, well, they get worse, as soon as you think . . . [pause].*

T: *So you have a bodily sensation here at this point in the spiral of anxiety [pointing to diagram]. The next step, thoughts that the sensation is a sign of catastrophe, that you're going to have a heart attack. What do you think happens to your thoughts when your heart rate does in fact go up? Because you said it would increase when you had this fear . . .*

P: *Uh-huh.*

T: *What would you think then?*

P: *I just get really scared, and I have to get out of the situation that I'm in. I mean, I have to.*

T: *O.K. So you see what's happening there. You perceive a danger, which would lead to more anxiety; the anxiety would make the symptoms worse, would make the heart rate even faster; and you interpret that, then, as "I really am going to have a heart attack." Right?*

P: *Yeah, but only fleetingly, you know, and then I go "I'm not going to have a heart attack, but I've got to get out of here!"*

T: *O.K.*

P: *But, I mean, fleetingly, I've also thought all kinds of, you know, I'm sure . . .*

(Alford et al., 1990, pp. 231–232)

Upon identification of her physiological sensations and negative automatic thoughts associated with the sensations, the patient was able to rapidly obtain some distance from her fearful thoughts. At a 5-month follow-up, she reported having no panic attacks after the cognitive therapy ended.

Combining Cognitive and Behavioral Approaches

Some of the most promising efforts to apply psychological techniques to clinical problems involve combining approaches suggested by a variety of theoretical perspectives. Research on the treatment of anxiety disorders illustrates these attempts. For example, one anxiety-management training program has the following components (Butler, 1989):

1. Information about the nature of anxiety and what might be expected from treatment
2. A cognitive component to help with self-identification and response to specific anxiety-provoking thoughts
3. Use of distractions and relaxation to cope with situations in which anxiety is anticipated

4. Exposure training for overcoming avoidance behavior
5. A component designed to instill self-confidence by identifying the person's strong points, by having the person engage in rewarding and pleasurable activities, and by asking the person to pay attention to aspects of life in which he or she is functioning relatively well

The treatment program is described in an easy-to-understand self-help booklet that the client follows. Clients play an active role in setting goals, planning homework assignments, and monitoring their progress. The program has been used in a series of studies with social phobia and generalized anxiety disorder patients. In a study of generalized anxiety disorder, clients were randomly assigned to either the treatment or control conditions. The program, which typically extended over fewer than nine sessions, resulted in significant reductions of anxiety. The therapeutic improvement was maintained at a 6-month follow-up. The significance of these results is reflected in the finding that at posttreatment the anxiety ratings of half of the clients had fallen below the cutoff point that distinguishes a normal from a clinical population. There was some evidence that people with panic disorders also responded favorably to this type of treatment.

In general, cognitive-behavioral therapies begin by identifying pertinent idiosyncratic negative appraisals of events, situations, and other people. For example, an individual with PTSD might have these thoughts:

"The next disaster will strike soon."
"I'm going mad."
"I can't rely on other people."

Therapy typically involves the therapist providing the patient with the rationale for treatment (e.g., the need to reduce or eliminate intrusive thoughts). Identification of triggers for intrusive thoughts and behavior, modeling, cognitive restructuring, exposure, and practice in adaptive responding are used as components of therapy as needed (Ehlers & Clark, 2000).

The Biological Perspective

Over the years, several different types of anxiety reactions have been found to be influenced by an individual's biological state. Some of these discoveries have led to the development of medical treatment methods. Although no direct organic cause has been found for most types of anxiety disorders, the findings of physical causation in other conditions suggest the possibility that there are some links between anxieties and biophysical functioning. People whose nervous systems are particularly sensitive to stimulation seem more likely to experience severe anxiety.

Genetic Factors Inbreeding experiments with animals have shown that heredity has a strong influence on such characteristics as timidity, fearfulness, and aggressiveness. Anxiety disorders tend to run in families, and children of people treated for anxiety disorder tend to be more anxious and fearful, have more difficulties in school, worry more about family members and themselves, and have more somatic complaints than children of normal parents. They may also spend more time engaged in solitary activity and be more likely to meet the criteria for an anxiety disorder than children whose families have no history of anxiety disorder. One study of nearly 4,000 pairs of adult twins attempted to evaluate the separate effects of genetic and environmental factors in anxiety and depression (Kendler et al., 1986). There was strong evidence of a genetic factor and a statistically significant, but weaker, effect for a family environment factor.

At present, there is a lack of solid evidence concerning how genetic factors shape human personality. However, some clues are being uncovered. For example, one group of researchers found a modest but measurable link between anxiety-related behavior and a gene that controls the brain's ability to use serotonin, an essential neurochemical (Lesch et al., 1996). Serotonin is one of the small molecules that carry signals between nerve cells. It is involved in movement, appetite, sleep, reproduction, cognition, and emotion. In particular, it is involved in anxiety and depression, and several drugs (such as Prozac) are known to influence its role in neurotransmission.

Brain Function Studies with animals and humans have focused on pinpointing the specific brain areas and circuits involved in anxiety disorders. Fear, an emotion that evolved to deal with danger, causes an automatic, rapid protective response that occurs without the need for conscious thought. It has been found that the body's fear response is coordinated by a small structure deep inside the brain, called the **amygdala.** The amygdala, although relatively small, is a very complicated structure, and different anxiety disorders may be associated with abnormal activation of particular parts of the amygdala. Animal studies have shown that another area of the brain, the **hippocampus,** which is known to play an important role in emotion-laden memories, appears to be smaller in traumatized animals. Brain imaging in humans indicates a similar finding for PTSD patients.

A person's history of experiences may play a role in how parts of the brain involved in emotions function. For example, when PTSD patients are exposed to slides or sounds related to traumatizing experiences there are decreases in blood flow in certain brain areas (Bremner, 1998). There are also some suggestions that stress can result in hippocampal atrophy and dysfunction in certain individuals. It would seem that biological factors are not simply causes of anxiety and exaggerated responses to stress. Rather, bidirectional processes are becoming increasingly apparent: biology can influence behavior, and the experiences a person has can influence biological structures and processes. This bidirectionality applies to hormonal secretions, as well as brain function. **Cortisol,** a hormone released by the adrenal gland, influences how individuals respond to stressors, and its production is influenced by prior exposure to high levels of stress (Yehuda, 1999).

Drug Therapies During the 1950s, new medications for the treatment of severe psychotic disorders were found to have dramatic positive effects. Subsequently, much biological research has also been directed toward developing medications that might be effective for less severe—and often more common—disorders such as anxiety disorders.

Benzodiazepines Tranquilizing drugs are the most commonly used somatic therapy in the treatment of anxiety. Although placebo reactions may account for some of these drugs' effectiveness, psychiatrists and other physicians who prescribe tranquilizers have found them valuable in reducing states of great tension. The literature on the behavioral effects of tranquilizers and antianxiety drugs suggests that these agents reduce the intensity of responses to stimuli that signal punishment and frustration.

In 1960 a group of drugs called **benzodiazepines** were introduced. They are marketed under trade names such as Librium and Valium and are used for the treatment of anxiety, tension, behavioral excitement, and insomnia. Although benzodiazepines have been proven effective in reducing anxiety, they have some troubling side effects. These include drowsiness, lethargy, motor impairment, and reduced ability to concentrate. The drugs also produce physiological and psychological dependence. Furthermore, excessive use may lead to undesirable behavior, including disorientation, confusion, rage, and other symptoms that resemble drunkenness. When taken with alcohol, slowing of physical movements and lack of alertness may intensify dangerously.

Recently, one benzodiazepine derivative, **alprazolam,** was approved by the U.S. Food and Drug Administration for the treatment of panic disorders. Alprazolam is fast-acting and has fewer unpleasant side effects than other drugs used in the treatment of panic disorders. Its side effects include drowsiness and withdrawal symptoms if a patient stops taking it after long-term use.

Antidepressants Some drugs developed as antidepressants have proven to be effective in treating panic and obsessive-compulsive disorders. One group of antidepressants, the tricyclic drugs (such as imipramine and clomipramine), appear to have therapeutic effects on many people with these disorders. The tricyclics may be effective in up to two-thirds of those suffering with obsessive-compulsive disorder by reducing the obsessions and feelings of anxiety and increasing the likelihood of a positive response to behavior therapy designed to eliminate ritualistic responses. Possible side effects of the tricyclic drugs include dry mouth, drowsiness, blurred vision, and seizures.

The successful use of drugs to treat anxiety disorders has not only been of practical value and served as a stimulus for developing biological theories of anxiety, but has also raised some important questions. For example, why might drugs developed for the treatment of depression be helpful in cases of anxiety? Evidence that antidepressant drugs are useful in treating anxiety disorders suggests that the relationship between anxiety and depression needs careful examination (see Box 7-4, which discusses the comorbidity of anxiety and depression).

Combining Psychological and Biological Treatments

Various theoretical perspectives and the treatment approaches derived from them have often been discussed in competitive terms: Which is the most valid and effective? Of course, it would not be surprising if certain techniques were superior to others in treating particular types of disorders. Research comparing the various treatment approaches to maladaptive behavior is valuable theoretically as well as clinically.

The anxiety disorders illustrate the value of research suggesting the possibility that *combinations* of treatment approaches might be optimal for certain kinds of clinical problems. For example, one study showed that the combination of the benzodiazepine drug alprazolam and cognitive-behavioral treatment was especially effective for panic disorder patients (Spiegel et al., 1993). While the alprazolam was effective in reducing the number of panic attacks, a cognitive-behavioral program that included cognitive restructuring, exposure, and relaxation training was effective in preventing relapses after discontinuation of the alprazolam. As we noted earlier there is evidence that treatment combinations are helpful for many patients with anxiety disorders.

Chapter Summary

THE EXPERIENCE OF ANXIETY

Anxiety involves worry, fear, apprehension, intrusive thoughts, physical symptoms, and feelings of tension. It often seems to have an automatic quality that comes more from within the individual than from situational factors. The reasons for the anxiety are often not clear to the anxious person.

GENERALIZED ANXIETY DISORDER

A person with **generalized anxiety disorder** experiences vague but intense concerns and fearfulness that persist over a long period—at least 6 months. The symptoms include motor tension, autonomic reactivity, apprehension about the future, and hypervigilance.

The course of generalized anxiety disorder is usually protracted, with durations as long as 20 years. Cognitive, psychodynamic, and behavioral therapy can be helpful, as can medications intended to reduce anxiety. However, prolonged use of drugs can have significant side effects.

PANIC DISORDER

Panic attacks are severe anxiety attacks that occur unexpectedly and involve severe physical symptoms as well as very strong fears that often involve concern over dying, going crazy, or behaving in an uncontrolled way. Persons with **panic disorder** experience panic attacks unexpectedly and therefore become very anxious as they worry that another attack may occur. Some panic attacks can be prevented by imipramine, a drug used to treat depression. Both generalized anxiety disorder and panic disorder seem to run in families.

PHOBIAS

People who have **phobias** have fears related to specific objects, people, or situations. Phobias often develop gradually or begin with a generalized anxiety attack. Phobias are common disorders that affect women about twice as frequently as men. Phobias often begin before adulthood and are likely to become chronic. Phobias can be grouped into three main types: specific phobias, social phobias, and agoraphobia.

Specific Phobias **Specific phobias** are the most commonly occurring type of phobia. This group includes miscellaneous irrational fears such as intense fear of a certain type of animal or of being in an enclosed place. Specific phobias may arise from an earlier frightening or anxiety-producing situation that involved the type of person or situation that later became associated with the phobia. Procedures that use the classical conditioning approach of pairing the phobic stimulus with a nonanxiety response are often used successfully to treat specific phobias.

Social Phobias Intense and incapacitating fear and embarrassment when dealing with others characterize **social phobias.** Fear of blushing when in a social situation and fear of eating when others are present are two social phobias that are especially difficult to treat successfully.

Agoraphobia **Agoraphobia** is the term used when people develop a fear of entering unfamiliar situations. Many agoraphobics are afraid to leave their homes, so their ability to carry on normal life activities is severely limited. There are two major types of agoraphobia: the kind with panic attacks and the kind without them. In the former group, panic attacks often begin first and lead to agoraphobia. As noted, panic attacks can often be treated with antidepressant drugs. Agoraphobia can be successfully treated with behavioral techniques in which the agoraphobic is exposed to the feared stimulus, under controlled conditions, with the support of a therapist.

OBSESSIVE-COMPULSIVE DISORDER

People affected by an **obsessive-compulsive disorder** are unable to control their preoccupation with specific ideas or are unable to prevent themselves from repeatedly carrying out a particular act or series of acts that affect their ability to carry out normal activities. **Obsessive behavior** is the inability to stop thinking about a particular idea or topic. The topic of these thoughts is often felt by the person involved to be unpleasant and shameful. **Compulsive behavior** is the need to perform certain behaviors over and over. Many compulsions deal with counting, ordering, checking, touching, and washing. Compulsive rituals may become very elaborate and contain many activities. Obsessive-compulsive disorder tends to begin in late adolescence and early adulthood and is equally common in men and women. Serotonin-related drugs are helpful with some patients, as are psychological interventions that include exposure and response prevention.

POSTTRAUMATIC STRESS DISORDER

Posttraumatic stress disorder (PTSD) may occur after an extreme stress such as a natural disaster, a serious accident, or participation in a battle or other war-related situations. PTSD symptoms vary widely but may include recurrent dreams, flashbacks, impaired concentration, and emotional numbing. Those who experience PTSD after a stressful experience are likely to have had previous histories of psychological disorder.

While PTSD is now recognized as a stress-linked reaction to trauma, it is a controversial diagnosis because frequently it is difficult to evaluate the relative contributions of the traumatic situations and the psychological vulnerabilities the individual has brought to the situation. DSM-IV distinguishes PTSD from other acute stress disorders in that the symptoms persist for more than 1 month.

Psychotherapy and behavior therapy can help PTSD patients view their traumatic experience more objectively.

INTERPRETING AND TREATING ANXIETY DISORDERS

The Psychodynamic Perspective Psychodynamic theorists suggest several possible causes of anxiety disorders. These include perceptions of helplessness and inability to cope with life situations, fear of abandonment or loss of love, sudden loss of emotional support, and unacceptable impulses that, while still unconscious, are threatening to break into awareness. Freud defined several defense mechanisms that may play a role in obsessive-compulsive disorders. The mechanisms include **isolation, undoing,** and **reaction formation.** Psychodynamically oriented therapists typically deal with anxiety disorders by psychotherapy directed at helping clients gain insight into the unconscious roots of their anxiety.

The Behavioral Perspective The behavioral-learning concepts of conditioning, reinforcement, and extinction are all applied in **behavior therapy.** Behavioral therapists commonly use **exposure therapy** in treating phobic and obsessive-compulsive clients. Three types of therapy based on the exposure principle are **systematic desensitization,** in which fear-arousing stimuli are presented in a graded series paired with relaxation exercises; **implosive therapy,** in which the client imagines a complex and highly arousing fear situation; and **in vivo exposure,** in which the person actually is present in the feared situation. **Flooding** refers to a rapid, intense exposure to stimulation in an in vivo exposure situation. **Modeling** is used to help clients acquire adaptive responses and correct maladaptive ones.

The Cognitive Perspective Many of the behavioral therapies such as systematic desensitization include cognitive rehearsal. **Cognitive-behavioral therapy** is based on the learning principles of extinction and reinforcement that emphasize cognitive behavior. Cognitive therapy focuses on a number of techniques that are usually combined with various behavioral exercises. These include **cognitive restructuring, thought stopping,** and **cognitive rehearsal.**

The Biological Perspective Strong evidence for a genetic factor in anxiety disorders is shown in studies of both animals and humans. There is also some weaker evidence for an environmental factor. A number of drugs are now used for treating specific anxiety disorders. The **benzodiazepines,** tranquilizing drugs such as Valium, are the most frequently prescribed drugs used in the general treatment of anxiety. One benzodiazepine derivative, alprazolam, has recently become popular for treating panic disorders. A group of antidepressant drugs, the tricyclics, are also used successfully in treating obsessive-compulsive disorder, especially in combination with behavior therapy. It is thought that one reason antidepressant drugs are useful in treating anxiety is because of the overlap in symptoms and certain other conditions in the different disorders. This overlap is referred to as **comorbidity.** Combinations of biological and psychological treatment techniques have often been found to be more effective than either approach alone.

Key Terms

Anxiety, p. 208
Anxiety disorders, p. 209
Generalized anxiety disorder, p. 210
Panic attack, p. 212
Panic disorder, p. 212
Phobia, p. 215
Phobic disorders, p. 215
Specific phobias, p. 217
Social phobias, p. 218
Agoraphobia, p. 221

Obsessive-compulsive disorder, p. 223
Obsessive behavior, p. 223
Compulsive behavior, p. 223
Posttraumatic stress disorder (PTSD), p. 227
Isolation, p. 233
Undoing, p. 233
Reaction formation, p. 233
Exposure therapy, p. 233
Systematic desensitization, p. 234

Implosive therapy, p. 234
In vivo exposure, p. 234
Flooding, p. 234
Cognitive restructuring, p. 236
Thought stopping, p. 237
Cognitive rehearsal, p. 237
Amygdala, p. 238
Hippocampus, p. 238
Benzodiazepines, p. 239
Alprazolam, p. 239

Sexual Variants and Disorders

Gina R. is 25 years old and, for as long as she can remember, has always felt uncomfortable with her body. She feels she should have been a man. Her clothes generally have a masculine quality (jeans, flannel shirts, sturdy shoes), as do her voice and manner. Dissatisfaction with her sexual identity intensified when she became a teenager. She didn't like menstruating or the development of her breasts. She has had no sexual experiences with men, but she has had several same-sex relationships. In these relationships she took the initiative in bringing her partner to orgasm, but she would not allow her own breasts to be touched. While in high school she often thought of herself as being homosexual, but she finally came to realize that she was transsexual. She would like to undergo a sex change operation, marry a woman, and be a father to her partner's children.

Arnold M., a 38-year-old married man, becomes intensely sexually aroused by women's nylon stockings. As a college student, he used the stockings to masturbate. When he got married, he convinced his wife to wear nylons to bed before they had sex. Initially she complied, but she finally refused to do so. Arnold finds it difficult to get fully aroused without the stockings, and his wife has commented on this to him.

Jim P. is 47 years of age, married and the father of two children. For years he has been attracted to young girls, frequently masturbating while imagining himself frolicking with 5- to 7-year-old naked girls. Sometimes he has tried to take photographs of naked little girls, and on two occasions the police have received complaints from the girls' parents. He has encouraged girls to slip down their panties so he could look at, and perhaps photograph, them. Recently a teenage boy discovered him trying to observe a naked girl. The boy contacted the girl's mother, who pressed charges against Jim. In the course of the trial, several neighborhood girls who had been victimized by Jim in the past provided testimony that contributed to his conviction. The day after his conviction, Jim's wife filed for divorce. He is now in the penitentiary. ■

There is much that we do not know about these three people, but one point is clear. While each of them has certain unusual sexual interests and preferences, only in the case of Jim do these interests and preferences clash directly with social conventions. This chapter deals with expressions of sexuality that range widely from private idiosyncrasies and concerns to serious problems for the community. We will discuss three broad groups of problems. *Sexual dysfunction* (such as a man's inability to maintain an erection) is usually a very private matter that is very important to the person and the person's partner, but is usually not known by other people. The world outside the family of Arnold M. might have no clues whatever about his need for the sexual stimulation that nylons provide for him. Sexually dysfunctional individuals tend to suffer in silence, or they seek help from a professional expert such as a clinical psychologist or a psychiatrist. *Sexual victimization*, exemplified by Jim P., is *not* a private matter, because in one way or another a deviant sexual preference has an impact that extends into the community and may involve the violation of laws. A third group of problems consists of those arising from *violations of social conventions*. Violations of social conventions are matters of opinion. Some people may disapprove of an individual's having the transsexual change that Gina R. desires—and may even ridicule or discriminate against people with unusual expressions of sexuality—but there is no reason to believe that someone like Gina R. will do harm to others after having had sex change surgery.

This chapter deals with many variations in sexual behavior, ranging from behavior that is universally regarded as disturbed to behavior that some people simply don't like. Although the focus of this book is primarily on abnormal behavior, it is important to have a broad frame of reference in reviewing highly charged and often controversial topics like sexual variation.

Changing Views of Sexual Behavior

Sexual behavior of all types has never ceased to be a topic of great interest. Over the centuries, ideas about sexuality and sexual deviance have undergone drastic changes. During the fourth century B.C., the Greeks regarded sex as a pleasurable part of nature, to be enjoyed with partners of either sex. This open view of sexuality contrasts sharply with the prevailing view during the period between the fall of Rome and the eighteenth century, when church authorities were obsessed with the notion of sex as a sin. During that period many thousands of Europeans were tortured into confessing erotic encounters with the Devil, after which they were publicly burned alive. Entire villages in southern Germany and Switzerland were exterminated in this way.

The price that women had to pay to be rescued from this fate was to renounce all sexual or erotic thoughts. By the mid-nineteenth century, the idea of women as morally pure, erotically apathetic, and sexually inert had reached a peak. Women were expected to engage in sexual behavior only as a way of satisfying their husbands and carrying out their obligations to become mothers. Despite these expectations, however, pornography, prostitution, and venereal disease flourished.

From time to time, some brave souls have been willing to question popularly held ideas about the role of sexuality in human behavior. One of these individuals, Sigmund Freud, used material gathered from many patients to illustrate the negative effects of a repressive view of sexuality. Freud traced the sexual deviations of adults to significant events in childhood. Although some aspects of his theories continue to be controversial, Freud stimulated a rethinking of the role of sexual feelings in development. He argued that all people are innately bisexual. Although psychosexual development usually progresses along a heterosexual course, some circumstances, such as inability to resolve the Oedipus complex, might result in adult homosexual behavior. In general, Freud's view of homosexuality was that it is simply a variation of sexual development. In a letter to a mother who had written to him asking for therapy for her son, he wrote:

> Homosexuality is assuredly no advantage, but it is nothing to be ashamed of, no vice, no degradation, it cannot be classified as an illness; we consider it to be a variation of sexual function produced by a certain arrest of sexual development. Many highly respectable individuals of ancient and modern times have been homosexuals, several of the greatest men among them (Plato, Michelangelo, Leonardo da Vinci, etc.). It is a great injustice to persecute homosexuality as a crime, and cruelty too.
>
> (Freud, 1935/1951, p. 786) ■

Havelock Ellis was another important influence on views about sexuality. Ellis wrote books and articles focusing on the range of sexual behavior that occurs in the lives of ordinary people. He recognized that it was common for both men and women to masturbate, and emphasized the psychological rather than physical causes of many sexual problems. It was Ellis who suggested that objective surveys be taken to find out what happens in ordinary sexual relationships. This useful suggestion was not acted upon until fairly recently.

Surveys of Sexual Behavior

While the frequency with which people engage in various sexual practices has for a long time been of great interest and much discussed, it is only recently that concerted scientific efforts have been made to gather pertinent facts. It is virtually impossible (as well as socially unacceptable) to obtain direct measures of the sexual behaviors of members of a community. Consequently, we must rely on **sex surveys,** that is, individuals' self-reported sexual behavior. As with all surveys of sensitive issues, these self-reports are likely to contain some bias. Intentional misreporting (i.e., nonreporting or overreporting), incomplete recall, misunderstanding of survey questions, and selective participation in a survey can reduce the reliability and validity of the data (Seidman & Rieder, 1994).

Alfred Kinsey, a biologist at Indiana University, conducted a series of in-depth interviews with volunteers about their sex lives and published his findings for men in 1948 and for women in 1953. His research was the first major objective survey of sexual practices. However, his data were limited by the fact that his subjects were self-selected people who were probably more sexually interested and interesting than a randomly selected group. While scientists have recognized the need to improve on Kinsey's pioneering studies and obtain information about current sexual practices, the federal government has been reluctant to provide financial support for surveys of sexual behavior.

Fortunately, the National Opinion Research Center at the University of Chicago carried out a study of 3,432 randomly selected American men and women between the ages of 18 and 59 (Laumann et al., 1994). The participation was high for a survey—80% agreed to discuss the facts of their sexual lives. Table 8-1 shows some of the survey results.

The survey found that the median number of sexual partners over a lifetime reported by men was six. For women, the median number was two. More than 80% of Americans had only one partner or no partner in the past year, and just 3% of women and men said they had had five or more partners in the past year. Seventy percent of married men and 85% of married women say they had remained faithful to their spouse. The people who had the most sex and reported the most happiness with their sex lives were monogamous couples.

Depending on how the question was asked, people had a variety of responses on their sexual preferences. More than 5% of men reported having had a sexual encounter with another man as an adult, while 2.8% said they are homosexual or bisexual. Having had a sexual encounter with another woman was reported by 3.5% of women, while 1.4% said they are homosexual or bisexual (see Table 8-2). Geography plays an important role in the formation of homosexual communities. About 9% of the men and 3% of the women living in the nation's largest cities identify themselves as homosexual or bisexual. These findings help explain why the incidence of homosexuality has been subject to such dispute. Homosexuals are likely to cluster in large cities, but overall, they are a tiny fraction of the population.

In order to inform debates over combating teen pregnancies, Americans need to know why teenage girls have sex for the first time. The reasons have changed over the decades. In previous generations, most women said they had sex for the first time because of affection for their partner, and only a small number said the reason was peer pressure. In contrast, 37% of the younger women who participated in the survey said the reason they had sex for the first time was peer pressure, and only 35% said it was out of affection for their partner.

Table 8-1

How Often Do People in Different Age Groups Have Sex? Percentages of Various Age Groups Reporting Frequencies of Sex

Age Range	Four or More Times a Week		A Few Times a Month		Not at All	
	Men (%)	Women (%)	Men (%)	Women (%)	Men (%)	Women (%)
18–24	12	12	24	32	15	11
25–29	11	10	31	38	7	5
30–34	7	8	35	35	10	8
35–39	5	3	40	38	7	11
40–44	6	7	44	46	7	15
45–49	6	3	33	41	13	16
50–54	5	2	45	40	8	19
55–59	1	2	42	30	16	41
All Ages	8	7	36	37	10	14

Source: Laumann et al., 1994

Table 8-2

Percentages of Men and Women Who Described Themselves as Having Had Homosexual Experiences

Description	Men (%)	Women (%)
Identified themselves as homosexual or bisexual	2.8	1.4
Had sex with person of same sex at least once since puberty	5.3	3.5
Felt desire for sex with person of same sex	7.7	7.5
Total reporting some same-sex desires or experiences	10.1	8.6

Source: Laumann et al., 1994

The survey also found that men think about sex more than women and are drawn to a wider range of sex practices (see Table 8-3). Compared to earlier surveys, the most recent findings show a widening range of sex practices for both men and women. Studies of college students reflect this trend. There appears to have been an increase in and acceptance of oral-genital sexual behavior among college students.

The passage of time has brought with it changes in social customs, especially those related to increased acceptance of sexual relationships of nontraditional types, increased frequency of cohabitation before marriage, and increased rates of divorce and remarriage. In addition, concerns about AIDS and contracting the HIV virus seem to have had an impact on the sexual behaviors of many individuals. For all these reasons there is a need for continuing surveys of sexual practices. (See Box 8-1.)

Homosexuality: An Example of Changing Views of Sexual Behavior

When it comes to sex, who decides what constitutes normal? Who decides what is too little or too much? While surveys are valuable and can influence views concerning sexual behavior, definitions of sexual normalcy are completely determined by and grow out of opinions, biases, and myths that may change over time in the absence of any objective information, such as the results of surveys and sexual practices. For example, in Classical Greece some people believed that women derived more pleasure from sex than men did. In the nineteenth century the idea that men have a stronger sex drive than women became popular. During the Christian era ideas concerning celibacy have changed at varying times for a variety of religious and societal reasons. Some nineteenth century physicians asserted that strong sexual desires in women could be pathological and might require removal of ovaries and the clitoris. Over the years, opinions about homosexual behavior have varied widely, and today there is great variance concerning whether it is simply an expression of personal preferences or a violation of sacrosanct social codes.

Table 8-3

The Appeal of Various Sexual Practices: Percentages of Respondents

	Degree of Appeal to Men Aged 18–44				Degree of Appeal to Women Aged 18–44			
	Very (%)	Somewhat (%)	Not really (%)	Not at all (%)	Very (%)	Somewhat (%)	Not really (%)	Not at all (%)
Vaginal intercourse	83	12	1	4	78	18	1	3
Watching partner undress	50	43	3	4	30	51	11	9
Receiving oral sex	50	33	5	12	33	35	11	21
Giving oral sex	37	39	9	15	19	38	15	28
Active anal intercourse	5	9	13	73	—	—	—	—
Passive anal intercourse	3	8	15	75	1	4	9	87
Group sex	14	32	20	33	1	8	14	78
Same-sex partner	4	2	5	89	3	3	9	85
Sex with a stranger	5	29	25	42	1	9	11	80
Forcing someone to do something sexual	0	2	14	84	0	2	7	91
Being forced to do something sexual	0	3	13	84	0	2	6	92

Source: Laumann et al., 1994

Q&A   **Box 8–1**

Q: I understand that surveys of sexual beliefs and practices are valuable. But where do the beliefs and practices come from? Parents are often not very helpful and kids don't really learn much about sex in school. Can the schools help kids have satisfying sexual lives when they grow up?

A: *Quite a question! Little is known about where people get their ideas about sex. Some parents talk to their children about the topic, many do not, and those who do talk often don't know what to say. The media are influential, but what they communicate may not be accurate or applicable because the media often are concerned with entertainment, not education. What conclusions do kids who watch TV soap operas draw when they notice the*

many sexual encounters between people who are not married to one another? Of course, peer influences are very powerful. However, the education children receive from their friends may involve a lot of shared ignorance and distortion.

As you review the sexual disorders in this chapter, you probably will find yourself wondering, "Where did that come from?" "How do people acquire such deviant—and wrong— ideas about sexual behavior?" Unfortunately, there are few answers to these good questions. One reason for this is the frequent reluctance of parents and teachers to deal openly with questions children might have. Some people believe that school settings are good ones for cutting away some of the ignorance and often wrong ideas that children develop about sex.

Although there have been some promising attempts at sex education in schools, during recent years the schools have been especially interested in topics related to sexual health—for example, safe sex practices that help prevent HIV infection. While this is an important topic, children also have questions related to their sexual identity and how they should interpret the sexual behavior of others. The cartoon in Figure 8-1 is cute, but it has a serious side too. Children—and adults—try hard to figure out what is going on sexually and in other areas in their lives. An interesting question with regard to maladaptive behavior is: Could sexual pathology be reduced by answering some of the questions people have about the nature of sexuality? Sex education is a tantalizing and controversial topic.

"*I think oral sex is when they only just talk about it.*"

Figure 8–1 What are some of the other ideas these children are carrying around in their heads?

Source: *New Yorker,* February 9, 1998, p. 31

Homosexual behavior is sexual behavior with a member of one's own sex. **Homosexuals** are individuals who prefer to engage in sexual activity with members of their own sex over an extended period. Female homosexuality is often called **lesbianism.** Many homosexuals engage in sexual activity only with members of the same sex and are not attracted to members of the opposite sex. However, many homosexuals have heterosexual fantasies and can be sexually aroused by members of the opposite sex. A person's belief that he or she is a homosexual does not depend on actual behavior. Someone with no sexual experience at all may think of himself or herself as a homosexual. In recent years the term **gay** has been used by homosexuals to describe their life-style because they feel that the term has fewer negative implications than *homosexual.* Individuals, both male and female, who wish to publicly acknowledge their homosexual orientation usually use the term *gay.*

Homosexuality illustrates the changing character of views about sexual behavior and the degree to which sexual behavior can become a sociopolitical issue. Society's stigmatizing of homosexuals can be very harmful and lead to anxiety, self-doubt ("What's wrong with me?"; "I'm not normal"), and a perceived need to be "cured."

In the bad old days, when homosexuality was considered a mental illness, a friend of mine was trying to go straight. He was seeing a distinguished psychoanalyst who believed (and still believes) that what some call a life-style and still others call a crime is a psychiatrically treatable disorder. Through six years of anguished analysis, my friend changed his sexual orientation and married. His wife was wonderful—they had been friends for years—but he died unexpectedly of a heart attack at the age of 42, six months after the wedding. I am not superstitious, and I don't blame anyone, least of all his wife: he was happy with her. But a nagging question remains: Is it possible that my friend's doctor was trying to change something that should have been left alone?

He had been homosexual for years, and had had at least one stable long-term relationship. But he lived in a society that condemned him on religious and medical grounds. He "freely" chose to change through psychoanalysis. But this was a limited sort of freedom, and though he in fact did change—as some have—he did not live to find out how the change would work. (Konner, 1989, p. 60)

Public attitudes have tended to stigmatize homosexual activity to such an extent that many of those engaging in it have suffered social and legal mistreatment far beyond the domain of sexual behavior. During recent years, gay activism has increased markedly as homosexuals have battled discrimination and social stigmatization (see Figure 8-2). The need for such battles varies from country to country and culture to culture. In many public opinion polls, a majority of American respondents say that gays cannot be considered good role models for children and that homosexual relationships between consenting adults are morally wrong. Contrasting with this negativism and ambivalence is the situation in Denmark, the first country in the world that legalized (in 1989) same-sex marriages—or *registered partnerships*, as they are called. More than 2,000 homosexual couples have wed under the Danish registered partnership law.

> Erik Ladefoged and Kim Norgaard, surrounded by 30 family and friends, finally were able to formally tie the knot in 1989 after living together for more than 20 years. "We were [married] between two heterosexual couples. Before us was a young couple, and after us came an elderly couple," recalls Mr. Norgaard, 47, an airline employee, showing off photographs of the ceremony and a champagne reception that followed.
>
> The couple found to their surprise that the wedding was an emotional experience, symbolic not only as a public declaration of their love, but of their nation's acceptance of them. "I thought it would be a formality. But our friends were singing a traditional Danish wedding song. I was happy all over. It was great to be gay and have the official handshake and smile of the state," notes Mr. Ladefoged, a 49-year-old school teacher. 'It's extremely important that society said, " 'It's different but it's OK for you, there's a place for you.' "
>
> (*Wall Street Journal*, June 8, 1994, p. 1) ■

Research evidence may be playing a role in changing attitudes toward homosexuality. Although not too long ago homosexuality was considered to be a diagnosable disorder, it is not listed as a psychiatric condition in DSM-IV.

Figure 8-2 Gay Pride activities provide social support for homosexual individuals by visibly demonstrating their numbers. They also provide a way for homosexuals to publicly state their sexual preferences rather than hide them.

Both the American Psychiatric Association and the American Psychological Association have voted to remove homosexuality from the list of mental illnesses. Contributing to this diagnostic change has been evidence indicating that lesbians and gay men do not differ in psychological adjustment from heterosexual women and men (Rothblum, 1994). Furthermore, the adjustment of children with lesbian or gay parents does not appear to differ from that of children with heterosexual parents (C. J. Patterson, 1992). One study found that the large majority of children who grew up in lesbian families identified themselves as heterosexual (Golombok & Tasker, 1996).

Homosexuals, like heterosexuals, may be anxious or depressed, and are not always emotionally stable, but homosexuality is clearly not a form of mental illness. However, the psychological impact of the current high AIDS-associated death rate in the gay community, along with the personal loss of friends as a result of AIDS, is likely to result in an increased amount of stress experienced by gay individuals. Research has shown that mean levels of psychological distress among gay men at risk for AIDS are significantly higher than in the general population (Chuang et al., 1989; Joseph et al., 1990). As we have stated throughout this book (see especially Chapters 1 and 4), high stress is associated with a higher rate of disorders of various types. Thus, some homosexual individuals may be at higher risk for disorder, not because of their homosexuality itself, but because of current stress factors disproportionately affecting those in the gay community.

Origins of Sexual Orientation

All human behavior has causes and reasons, whether the behavior is arbitrarily regarded as normal or abnormal. The origins and determinants of sexual orientations, both heterosexual and homosexual, pose unanswered questions of genuine scientific interest. Sexual orientation, like any other human behavior, is experienced in complex and variable ways. Recently researchers have focused attention on the roles of biological factors and learning in the development of sexual preferences. For example, one study suggested that there may be anatomical differences between the brains of homosexual and heterosexual men (LeVay, 1991). The study found that among homosexual men who had died from AIDS-related diseases, a part of the hypothalamus (a brain region that influences sexual behavior) had the anatomical form usually found in women rather than the form typical of heterosexual men. This finding is not direct evidence that brain structure causes homosexuality, but it suggests the need to explore areas of the brain that might relate to sexual preference. One problem in this study is that because the subjects had AIDS, the results might not apply to the overall population.

Arguments for a genetic basis for sexual orientation are often based on findings such as those of Bailey and Pillard (1991), who measured sexual orientation in brothers of gay men. They found that for adoptive and nontwin brothers of gay men, about 10% were also gay. The rate of "double" homosexuality for fraternal twins was 22%, and for identical twins, 52%. The fact that fraternal twins of gay men were found to be roughly twice as likely to be gay as other biological brothers of gay men suggests that environmental factors play a role, since fraternal twins are no more similar biologically than are other biological brothers. It does not seem surprising that an even larger proportion of identical twins would have similar behaviors, since the world thinks of them as "the same" and treats them accordingly, and they often share such feelings of sameness.

So how much of sexual orientation is determined by genes and/or hormonal levels? While these and other biological factors related to sexual preference are intriguing, it is most likely that sexual orientation grows out of the interplay of multiple determinants in which both psychosocial factors and biological factors are important. An interactional approach opens the possibility of multiple pathways to the development of sexual orientation.

Bisexual behavior, in which partners of either sex may be preferred at different times, is a sexual orientation that is beginning to receive scientific attention. **Bisexuals** engage in sexual activity with both men and women. The incidence of bisexuality in Western societies is difficult to estimate. At present, the relevant factors in the development of bisexuality remain to be identified. Sometimes the bisexual individual has a long heterosexual relationship and then a long homosexual relationship. Or the order might be reversed. Sometimes both relationships go on during the same period. One 23-year-old woman described her bisexual experience as follows:

I had been dating a guy I was very friendly with for about a year with a good sexual relationship. Then I suddenly found myself making it with my roommate, who slowly but expertly introduced me to how two women make love. I really enjoyed both kinds of sex and both personal relationships, so I continued them for some while until my graduate school career was over and I moved to a new town. (Masters, Johnson, & Kolodny, 1988, p. 439)

Sexual Dysfunction

The human sexual response cycle begins with sexual desire and moves through a physiological process related to arousal/excitement, orgasm, and resolution. **Sexual dysfunctions** are problems that occur in the cycle. These problems are illustrated by disturbances in desire and by pain associated with penetration and sexual intercourse. Occasional or episodic difficulties with sexual function are common.

A sexual dysfunction can be generally defined as persistent impairment of sexual interest or response that causes interpersonal difficulty or personal distress. Sometimes the dysfunction is independent of, and sometimes it results from, other psychological disorders or physical conditions. If the problem is due *entirely* to organic factors, it is not given this diagnosis. A predisposition may be created by upbringing, personality, lack of information, or early sexual trauma. More immediate precipitating causes include conflict with the partner, infidelity, age, depression, and accidental failure produced by fatigue, stress, anxiety, or alcohol. The dysfunction may be sustained by anticipation of failure, the partner's reaction, poor communication, and limited sexual skills. Because of the large number of factors that might be involved in sexual dysfunctions, clinicians must sensitively inquire about many aspects of sexual activity (see Table 8-4).

For a dysfunction to be diagnosed in DSM-IV it must be persistent or recurrent and must cause distress or interpersonal difficulty. Clinicians who work in the area of sexual dysfunction emphasize the interacting roles of psychological, physiological, social, and interpersonal variables. Most of the dysfunctions have multiple causes, ranging from predominantly organic to predominantly psychological, and there are many possible contributing factors in both the organic and the psychological domains. Many of the causal factors are nonspecific, that is, they may be found in the histories of patients with different problems or persons with no dysfunction. The specific dysfunction that becomes manifest in a particular case is the result of a complex interplay between the individual's life history, psychological factors, and preexisting biological and psychological predispositions.

Table 8-4
Information Needed in Diagnosing and Treating Sexual Dysfunction

1. The nature of the dysfunction (e.g., lack of interest in sexual activity, inability to achieve orgasm)
2. When the sexual difficulty first became apparent (How long ago? In what situation?)
3. How frequently the difficulty has been encountered (With each sexual partner? Frequently or occasionally?)
4. The course of the dysfunction (Acute or gradual in onset?)
5. What the patient thinks the cause of the difficulty is (e.g., "Maybe I'm just getting older")
6. What the patient and partner have done to correct the dysfunction, and with what results.

Types of Sexual Dysfunction

There are a number of types of sexual dysfunction, many of which fall into three broad groups. One group consists of problems of sexual desire. **Sexual desire** is a complex construct involving physiological, cognitive, and behavioral components and shaped by development and cultural influences. Problems of sexual arousal comprise another group. **Sexual arousal** is characterized by a subjective sense of sexual excitement and pleasure and by swelling of the external genitals. Sexual desire and sexual arousability are intimately related, and the distinction between them is often unclear. Variations in sexual drive are usually inferred by asking about the person's frequency of sexual thoughts and fantasies, interest in initiating sexual experiences, awareness of sexual cues, and frustration due to lack of opportunity for sexual expression. Another group of sexual dysfunctions relates to orgasm. **Orgasm** is characterized in both sexes by an acme of sexual pleasure, cardiovascular and respiratory changes, and a release of sexual tension. Sexual desire, sexual arousability, and ability to experience orgasm decrease with age. Attainment of orgasm leads to what is referred to as the **resolution phase** of the sexual response cycle. Resolution consists of muscular relaxation and a feeling of general well-being.

Certain problems of sexual desire are caused by physical conditions such as high blood pressure and diabetes. However, some people simply seem to be at the low end of the normal distribution of sexual desire. These problems usually come to the attention of a clinician only when they become a source of concern to the individual or the individual's partner.

Sexual problems can also occur at the arousal stage of the cycle. The male may fail to attain an erection, or fail to hold an erection until the completion of intercourse. This problem is called **erectile dysfunction.** In females, a problem at this stage is inability to attain or maintain the swelling-lubrication response until the sex act is completed. This inability is often brought about by **inhibited sexual arousal.** Problems at each stage of sexual response may be a function of the individual and occur no matter who the partner is, or they may be a function of some aspects of a particular relationship and occur only with a specific partner.

Inhibited sexual desire in either men or women was not regarded as a distinct problem or even named as a separate diagnosis until relatively recently. This diagnosis now encompasses both lack of interest in and active aversion to sex. Low sexual desire is not always easy to define and cannot be judged merely by the frequency of sexual activity, which varies a great deal.

In women, inhibited sexual arousal means insufficient lubrication of the vagina to allow entry of the penis.

Women who persist in having intercourse with little arousal, particularly if intercourse becomes associated with pain because of inadequate lubrication, run the risk of progressing to **hypoactive sexual desire disorder,** in which the individual may come close to suppressing sexual desires completely. Problems of hypoactive sexual desire are usually subjectively defined by individual or couple dissatisfaction with the frequency of sexual activity. Hypoactive sexual desire disorder is usually amenable to psychotherapy (e.g., there may be important relationship issues), but a medical evaluation is needed to evaluate the possibility of a hormonal deficiency or some other physical condition.

Inhibited arousal in men means failure to attain or hold an erection sufficiently to complete coitus (sexual intercourse). It may be either primary (the man has never been able to sustain an erection long enough for coitus) or secondary (the man has been able to complete intercourse successfully in the past). The former is rare, the latter common. About one-eighth of men fail to retain an erection long enough to permit entry into the vagina and ejaculation at least a quarter of the time, and the proportion rises with age. Erectile dysfunction is the main problem of more than half of the men who request treatment for sexual disorders.

Some of these men report never, under any circumstances, having attained an erection sufficient for intercourse. These cases tend to be the most resistant to treatment. Others are men who have a history of satisfying function but now cannot function with a particular partner, although they perform well in other circumstances. Some men experience a gradual onset of erectile difficulty, whereas others experience a sudden onset, often with a well-remembered traumatic experience. Some can attain erections and function well during masturbation but cannot become erect in the presence of an intended partner. Some do achieve erections with their partners, but lose them before penetration or during thrusting before orgasm. It has been estimated that about 30 million men in the United States have some form of erectile impairment (Mulcahy, 1997). One study found that 43% of women in the general population had at some point in their lives experienced sexual dysfunction for several months (Laumann, Palk, & Rosen, 1999). The comparable figure for men was 31%. Lack of interest was the most common problem for women, with about a third saying they regularly did not want sex. Twenty-six percent said they regularly did not have orgasms, and 23% said sex was not pleasurable. About a third of men said they had persistent problems with climaxing too early, while 14% said they had no interest in sex, and 8% said they consistently derived no pleasure from sex.

As we have already noted, distress caused by sexual dysfunction is usually a very private matter about which other people have no knowledge. Both heterosexuals and homosexuals can experience sexual dysfunction. It often can

be traced to a personality problem or some difficulty in the partners' relationship. However, as Box 8-2 shows, it should not be assumed that marital and sexual satisfaction always go together.

The following are some of the frequent psychological contributors to sexual dysfunction:

1. A restricted ability to express warm and tender emotions
2. Worries about rejection or criticism
3. Inhibitions about nakedness or displaying one's body
4. Difficulty with authority and concerns about being dominated
5. Feelings of low self-esteem

Sexuality is a biological function like digestion or respiration, and adequate sexual functioning, like good digestion or normal breathing, requires freedom from agitated feelings or excessive tension and control. A psychophysiological disorder may develop through the mutual reinforcement of fears, excessive expectations, physical responses, and the partner's reaction. For example, a man may become anxious when his female partner is slow to achieve orgasm; his anxiety may make it still more difficult for her, which may increase his anxiety level further and lead to erectile dysfunction.

One technique that is used in evaluating a man's capacity to have an erection is measurement of changes in penis size during sleep, or **nocturnal penile tumescence (NPT).** Erection normally occurs during rapid eye movement (REM) sleep—the period of sleep associated with dreaming and indicated by the rapid darting of the eyeballs beneath the closed lids. Researchers have developed physiological recording instruments to measure NPT. A fairly reliable test for nocturnal erections is the use of a snap gauge—a device that springs open when the penis enlarges. There are also several techniques for measuring blood flow and blood pressure in the penis. If the man experiences NPT, the cause of the erectile problem is likely to be psychological rather than physiological.

Anxiety stemming from personal conflict or from concern over a physical problem is often an important psychological factor in erectile dysfunction. Physical causes include early undiagnosed diabetes, hormonal imbalances, and the use of narcotics and alcohol. In the past, hidden psychopathology or psychodynamic conflict was believed to be the main psychological cause of this type of sexual dysfunction. More recently, however, recognition has been given to **performance anxiety,** in which a man's preoccupation with sexual adequacy interferes with his performance. One 34-year-old man's comment is typical:

After a while, the problem becomes so predictable that you start to make excuses in advance. It's as though you lose any

Research Close-up

Box 8–2

The Marital Relationship, Psychological Adjustment, and Sexual Dysfunction

While many people think that marital and sexual satisfaction go together, research on these topics reveals a surprising and more complicated picture. Significant levels of sexual dysfunction are found even in "normal" samples and among patients at general medical clinics. For example, Ellen Frank and her colleagues (1978) recruited couples as the "normal control sample" for a broader investigation and found that sexual dysfunction (problems of desire, arousal, orgasm, and genital pain) was reported by 40% of the men and 63% of the women, with 50% and 77%, respectively, reporting sexual "difficulty." Of special note, 83% of subjects described themselves as happily married.

Marital researchers have often found a close relationship between one person showing "withdrawal" and the other person expressing "hostile" or "demanding" behaviors, with wife demand–husband withdrawal occurring more frequently than the reverse pattern. These elements can produce a vicious cycle of increasing demands met by further withdrawal. Furthermore, the more partners differ from each other in the amount of intimacy and distance they prefer, the greater their marital distress. As a result, we could expect marital distress in a situation where a woman did not feel that her husband was intimate enough with her. We might also expect perceived male withdrawal (also a common response to a sexual problem) to be associated with higher levels of female hostility.

Ellis and Heiman (1992) designed a study to look more closely at these issues. Participants were 36 men seeking treatment for sexual dysfunction and their wives (see Figure 8-3). All men reported erectile dysfunction, with several also reporting low sexual desire (thought to be secondary to the erectile problem) or premature ejaculation. None of the female partners reported a sexual dysfunction. The couples had been married for an average of 21 years (range: 1–44 years) and had an average of two children.

The couples' scores on indexes of marital adjustment were well within normal limits, suggesting that couples' marital functioning overall was intact. Scores on a measure of psychological symptoms were also within the normal range, though husbands scored slightly higher than wives on a few of the subscales (depression, hostility, and somatization, or a concern about physical functioning). Spouse scores were generally similar on the marital and psychological symptom scales, and on a self-reported stress rating (averaging 5 on a 10-point scale).

Ellis and Heiman looked at the variables that were most closely associated with overall marital adjustment. In the more distressed marriages, wives had higher ratings of depression and husbands had higher ratings of loneliness or alienation.

Interestingly, wives' marital adjustment was correlated with both their own and their husbands' psychological functioning, while husbands' marital ratings were related more to their own psychological functioning than to that of their wives.

The available evidence is consistent with two conclusions:

1. Sexual problems can occur in the context of a well-functioning marriage and with psychologically healthy individuals. A sexual problem does not necessarily signify a problem with an individual or a relationship.
2. The responses of men and women to a sexual problem within marriage are likely to differ. Within the context of a male sexual problem, women's depression and men's loneliness or alienation may be the most closely related to marital functioning. These psychological responses make sense in the context of a male erectile problem, since both partners may feel rejected. One can suppose that the two patterns—male withdrawal and female depressive symptoms—react with and maintain each other.

Figure 8-3   The participation of both partners is important in cases of sexual dysfunction because clinicians need to know not only about the presenting symptoms, but also about the context in which they occur and how each partner views the problem.

chance of having sexual pleasure because you become preoccupied with the notion of failure. And that failure hits you right in the gut—you don't feel like much of a man. (Masters et al., 1988, p. 502)

Table 8-5 lists major sources of stress that may interact with biological vulnerabilities to result in problems of sexual performance. Both males and females may experience problems in the orgasm phase of the sexual response cycle.

Table 8-5
Major Types of Stress, Both Remote and Immediate, That Contribute to Sexual Dysfunction

1. Performance anxiety
2. Sexual or life-style problems
3. Inappropriate concerns and attitudes learned early in life
4. Stress in the relationship

In the male, these take the form of premature ejaculation or delayed or absent ejaculation. In the female, they take the form of a delay or absence of orgasm after a normal excitement phase. **Premature ejaculation,** in which the man is unable to inhibit ejaculation long enough for his female partner to experience orgasm through intercourse, is probably the most common type of male sexual dysfunction. The man's failure to control his orgasm often results in his feeling sexually inadequate. According to one viewpoint, the male experiences anxiety as he reaches high levels of erotic arousal, and the anxiety triggers the involuntary orgasm. The majority of premature ejaculation cases have a psychological basis and psychotherapy either for the individual affected or couples therapy—and/or sex therapy—is likely to be employed. However, medical evaluation is needed because of the possibility of a physical condition that might be contributing to the problem.

In **retarded ejaculation,** on the other hand, the ejaculatory response is inhibited. Men with this problem respond to sexual stimuli with erotic feelings and a firm erection, but they are unable to ejaculate. Although physical injuries may be responsible for the problem, psychological factors that contribute to retarded ejaculation include ambivalence toward the sexual partner, strongly suppressed anger, and a religious upbringing that engenders sexual guilt.

For women, the chief disorder of the orgasmic phase of sexual activity is **female orgasmic disorder,** an inability to experience orgasm or a persistent or recurrent delay in orgasm following normal sexual excitement. This diagnosis is based on the clinician's judgment that the woman's orgasmic capacity is less than would be reasonable for someone of her age and sexual experience and for the amount of sexual stimulation she receives. It is not used if her difficulty is better accounted for by another Axis I disorder such as major depressive disorder or is the result of either a general medical condition or one of a variety of medications.

For most women, orgasmic disorder seems to be a lifelong condition rather than something that is acquired. Even chronic medical conditions such as diabetes or pelvic cancer tend to leave orgasmic capacity relatively intact although they may impair the arousal phase of the sexual response. Once a woman learns how to reach an orgasm, it is unusual for her to lose that ability unless there is poor sexual communication, relationship conflict, or a sexually related traumatic experience such as rape. One important issue for investigation is whether the woman is receiving inadequate stimulation during lovemaking. If this is the case, the therapist attempts to sensitize both partners to each other's sexual needs. It is also important for couples to know that most women do not have an orgasm each time they have intercourse.

If female orgasmic disorder is judged to be predominantly psychological, or due to an interaction of psychological and organic factors, psychotherapy is often recommended. If the disorder is lifelong, sexual education and guided masturbatory practice are often helpful. Self-help manuals are useful supplements to this approach. Couples therapy is also useful, helping to integrate the orgasmic response into the couple's sexual repertory once it has been achieved through masturbatory practice.

Although female orgasmic disorder may have a negative affect on a woman's body image, self-esteem, or satisfaction in her relationship, it has not been found to be associated with specific personality traits. As one 19-year-old college student said:

> There's so much talk about orgasms that I've been wondering what's wrong with me, that I don't have them. I used to enjoy sex a lot, but lately it's a bad scene because I just get reminded of problems. (Masters et al., 1988, p. 506)

Other problems can also occur that often make sexual intercourse difficult. Both men and women may experience **dyspareunia,** a recurrent or persistent genital pain that occurs before, during, or after intercourse. Women also may be affected by **vaginismus.** This disorder makes intercourse difficult or impossible because of involuntary spasms of the outer portion of the vagina.

There are many types of sexual dysfunction that can occur during the sexual response cycle. Table 8-6 describes major sexual dysfunctions included in DSM-IV that evoke marked distress or interpersonal difficulty and do not have identifiable medical causes. However, it is important to remember that various types of medical conditions and substances can be important factors in sexual dysfunction. Neurological illnesses, endocrine diseases, cardiovascular conditions, antihypertensive medications, steroids, estrogens, and antipsychotic and antidepressant drugs can all contribute to sexual dysfunction, as can substance abuse (including alcohol, cocaine, and opiates).

Treatment of Sexual Dysfunction

Clinicians who treat sexual disorders understand that these problems often involve complex psychological, interpersonal, and physiological interactions. Patients with

Table 8-6

Types of Sexual Dysfunction Covered by DSM-IV

Each type of dysfunction is described in terms of its duration (e.g., lifelong or recently acquired) and the context in which the problem occurs (to what degree is its occurrence limited to certain situations). None of these disorders has an identifiable biological cause.

- *Hypoactive sexual desire disorder.* A deficiency or absence of sexual fantasies and desire for sexual activity.
- *Sexual aversion disorder.* Aversion to (with anxiety, fear, or disgust) and active avoidance of genital sexual contact with a sexual partner.
- *Female sexual arousal disorder.* Persistent or recurrent inability to attain, or to maintain until completion of the sexual activity, an adequate lubrication-swelling response of sexual excitement.
- *Male erectile disorder.* Persistent or recurrent inability to attain, or to maintain until completion of the sexual activity, an adequate erection.
- *Orgasmic disorders.* Women: persistent or recurrent delay or absence of orgasm following a normal arousal phase (women exhibit wide variability in the type or intensity of stimulation that triggers orgasm). Men: persistent or recurrent delay in, or absence of, orgasm following a normal arousal phase.
- *Premature ejaculation.* Persistent or recurrent onset of orgasm and ejaculation with minimal sexual stimulation before, on, or shortly after penetration and before the person wishes it.
- *Dyspareunia.* Genital pain associated with sexual intercourse, experienced by a man or a woman.
- *Vaginismus.* Persistent or recurrent involuntary contraction of muscles surrounding the outer third of the vagina when penetration is attempted.

sexual problems may be strongly affected by shame, guilt, embarrassment, or anxiety. Lack of information and highly charged emotions relating to sexuality are common. Education with regard to gaps in the person's fund of information concerning sex is often surprisingly effective.

Most present-day **sex therapy** represents an integration of procedures stemming from psychodynamic approaches, family systems therapy, and cognitive-behavioral techniques (LoPiccolo, 1994). The decision to request help for a sexual disorder is difficult for most people, and the attitude of the person who hears the complaint is important. Whether a sexual problem is ultimately mentioned at all and how explicitly the problem is presented often depend on whether the therapist seems to have some knowledge of sexual problems and can discuss them without embarrassment. Once the client has indicated that the problem involves sexual activity, it is important for the interviewer to get detailed information about the patient's medical history and physical symptoms as well as family background, early sexual development, work history, and use of drugs or alcohol. For some disorders both a physical examination and a psychological evaluation are necessary. Although great advances have been made in the medical treatment of sexual dysfunction, particularly erectile dysfunction, psychological and relationship therapy generally continue to be the most effective treatments for sexual problems within relationships. The therapist should have a clear and detailed idea of the patient's physical acts, emotional responses, fantasies during sex, and expectations. For instance, Figure 8-4 suggests that the man's ex-

pectations do not mesh with the experience of his sexual partner.

Usually sex therapy is requested by a couple. It is important to know how the partners feel about each other apart from the sexual relationship, how the relationship has changed (sexually or otherwise), how well the partners communicate, whether one partner is more interested in sex than the other, and which one is more eager for treat-

"Multiple? Are you kidding? It wasn't even fractional!"

Figure 8-4

ment. The therapist must see each partner separately in case there are subjects they do not want to discuss in each other's presence, such as fantasies, masturbation, infidelity, or feelings about their partner's sexual attractiveness.

In addition to dealing with factors specific to a given case, sex therapists have three general goals for the couple:

1. To engender an atmosphere of mutual communication
2. To decrease the fear of failure
3. To shift attention away from the fear of failure to the experience of sensory pleasure

The Masters and Johnson Approach Over a 10-year period, the research team of William Masters (1915–2001), a gynecologist, and Virginia Johnson, a behavioral scientist, studied the sexual responses of 694 men and women under controlled laboratory conditions. Masters and Johnson's studies (1966, 1970) have been largely responsible for giving the laboratory study of human sexual behavior and the treatment of sexual dysfunctions scientific credibility and respectability.

Since the publication of Masters and Johnson's first two books in 1966 and 1970, sex therapy has emerged as a discipline in its own right. While they recognized that many sexually dysfunctional people are dysfunctional in other areas of their personal and social lives, Masters and Johnson believed that short-term treatment directed primarily at sexual problems can help most people who experience such dysfunctions. They had observed that becoming sexually functional had a positive influence on a person's anxiety level, as well as on his or her self-esteem. A man who is anxious but has a good sex life is probably happier than a man who has to deal with a sex problem in addition to anxiety.

Masters and Johnson emphasized the treatment of couples, not just the person who seems to have a problem. This does not mean that the partner is seen as the cause of the difficulty, but rather that both members of the relationship are affected by the problem. The **Masters and Johnson approach** uses a man and a woman working together as therapists. The therapy program is intensive and takes place daily over a 2-week period. It emphasizes instruction in the sexual needs of both partners, together with exercises in erotic stimulation. Specific homework assignments are given that are designed to help couples become more aware of their own sexual sensations. The therapy procedure includes basic information about the sexual organs and the physiology of the sexual response for clients who lack this information (which is most of the people who come for treatment, in fact). The presentation of this basic information often has important therapeutic benefits in itself.

Emphasis is also placed on communication between partners, nonverbal as well as verbal. Because couples who seek treatment typically place lovemaking exclusively under the man's control, sexual intercourse may be attempted only when he indicates that he is interested. The belief of many women that they will be rejected if they are sexually assertive continues to be widespread. In many cases of sexual dysfunction, the most effective treatment may not be complex physical or psychotherapeutic tactics, but simply providing information about sexual relationships and encouraging meaningful communication between sex partners.

Sensate focus is probably the best known of Masters and Johnson's sexual-retraining techniques. The rationale behind sensate focus is that sexually dysfunctional couples have lost the ability to think and feel in a sensual way because of the various stresses and pressures they associate with intercourse. They therefore have to be reacquainted with the pleasures of tactile contact. Each partner learns not only that being touched is pleasurable, but also that exploring and caressing the partner's body can be exciting and stimulating in itself. The couple is encouraged to engage in sensate focus under conditions that are dissimilar to those associated with the anxieties, frustrations, and resentments of their former lovemaking. Intercourse is prohibited throughout the early stages of treatment because that simple requirement can reduce tension in both sexual and nonsexual areas of the relationship. Masters and Johnson thought this ban on intercourse made sensate focus particularly effective in treating performance anxiety. However, some therapists believe that a de-emphasis rather than a ban is more helpful to couples.

The couples technique of therapy is especially appropriate in treating premature ejaculation, since this is often more upsetting to the woman than to the man. If premature ejaculation is the problem, the therapists often introduce a method, known as the "squeeze technique," that helps recondition the ejaculatory reflex. The woman is taught to apply a firm, grasping pressure to the penis several times during the beginning stages of intercourse. This technique reduces the urgency of the man's need to ejaculate.

When the couple's problem is related to an orgasmic dysfunction in the woman, the treatment includes an exploratory discussion to identify attitudes that may be related to the woman's inability to attain orgasm. Then the couple is given a series of graduated homework assignments. If the woman is willing, she begins by exploring her own bodily sensations, stimulating herself by masturbating. As she becomes more comfortable with this technique, her partner begins to participate in the sessions through kissing and tactile stimulation. The importance of the woman's clear and assertive communication of her reactions and desires to her partner is strongly emphasized.

Masters and Johnson have reported very low failure rates of their treatment programs for both heterosexual and homosexual couples. However, their research reports are not completely clear on such topics as who is selected

Case Study

Box 8–3

A Cognitive-Behavioral Approach to Sexual Dysfunction

Treatment in the following case involved both cognitive and behavioral elements. The elements included identifying thoughts and situations that were upsetting to the client, modeling, and rehearsal.

The client was a 24-year-old lawyer who after six months of marriage was upset by his frequent inability to obtain or retain an erection. His history suggested that his mother had been a dominating woman of whom he was fearful and that he was also unwilling to challenge or criticize his wife in any way even though he often felt considerable resentment toward her. He seemed to feel that expressing his feelings was not manly. After several therapeutic sessions directed at his irrational attitudes, he and the therapist composed a carefully worded speech for the client to deliver to his wife:

"Grace, I have something very important and very serious to discuss with you. It concerns you, me, our marriage, and life in general. I want you to please hear me out without interrupting me. . . . I was raised by my mother to bottle up my feelings, especially in relation to women. In thinking over this attitude, I now realize that this is crazy and even dishonest. I feel, for instance, that if I resent the fact that you turn to your father for advice in matters about which I have more knowledge than he, I ought to express my resentment instead of hiding it from you. I feel that when you order me about and treat me like a child, I ought to tell you how I really feel about it instead of acting like an obedient puppy dog. And most important of all, when you go ahead and make plans for me without consulting me, and especially when you yell at me in front of your parents,

maybe I should quit acting as if I didn't mind and let you know how strongly I really react inside. What I am getting at is simply that in spite of my love and affection for you, I would really rather be unmarried than be a henpecked husband like my father."

This little monologue was rehearsed several times during a one-hour session until playbacks on a tape recorder convinced the therapist that the client was ready to confront his wife and that he would do so in a forthright and sincere manner. Rehearsal techniques were used in preparing the patient to cope with tears, interruptions, denials, counterallegations, etc. His assignment was then put into effect. The patient reported that his wife "heard me out without interruption. . . . [She] seemed a little upset, but agreed that I should not withhold or conceal my feelings. I felt incredibly close to her and that night we had very good sex."

SOURCE: Lazarus, 1971, pp. 156–157

---

and who is rejected for the program and how success and failure are defined. Nevertheless, their techniques are far superior to earlier methods of treating sexual disorders.

Cognitive–Behavioral Approaches Looked at from a behavioral perspective, the Masters and Johnson technique of sensate focus is reminiscent of systematic desensitization in that it leads to the substitution of a pleasurable response for anxiety. Sex therapists often create a sort of hierarchy in which certain parts of the body initially are designated as "out of bounds" and then are gradually included as progress is made. Although orthodox systematic desensitization can be used to eliminate specific anxieties (such as feeling uncomfortable while looking at a man's genitals), the more global sensate focus appears to be appropriate in dealing with the various diffuse anxieties experienced by sexually dysfunctional individuals.

The methods used by Masters and Johnson have been further refined by many cognitive and behavioral therapists. For instance, relaxation, modeling, and a variety of cognitive elements have been introduced into treatment plans. The case presented in Box 8-3 illustrates this combined **cognitive-behavioral approach** to the treatment of sexual dysfunction.

Researchers are paying increasing attention to both the cognitive and fantasy underpinnings of sexual behavior.

Sexual fantasies can occur while daydreaming or during masturbation or sexual intercourse (see Figure 8-5). It is now recognized that being aroused by a given fantasy (e.g., linking sex to physical violence or an exotic locale or someone other than one's partner) is not necessarily a sign of maladaptation. Fantasies can be a means of self-stimulation that heighten the experience of sex with another person. Among the most common sex fantasies are thinking of an imaginary lover, imagining being overpowered or forced to surrender, pretending to engage in a sex act that is usually regarded as repugnant, and reliving a previous sexual experience. Analyzing the emotional meanings of sexual fantasies and how the fantasies become linked to behavior is a challenge being taken up by researchers. Fantasy can be a useful technique for some individuals with sexual dysfunctions. They may be able to utilize it to heighten their level of arousal during sexual activity.

Psychodynamic Approaches Some clinicians believe that the approaches taken by Masters and Johnson and cognitive-behavioral therapists are useful for many problems of sexual dysfunction, but that some problems require attention to psychodynamic difficulties for one or both partners. Kaplan (1974, 1979) argued that standard sex therapy methods were effective when sexual problems were based on mild and easily diminished anxieties and

Figure 8-5 This block print by eighteenth-century Japanese artist Suzuki Harunobu shows a young girl fantasizing about her lover while she masturbates.

conflicts. However, there are many individuals whose symptoms are rooted in more profound conflicts. Kaplan believed that this was especially true in the cases of men and women who lacked sexual desire and men who had difficulty maintaining an erection. For these problems, Kaplan developed a lengthy and individualized treatment program that often combined traditional sex therapy and psychodynamically oriented sessions, sometimes with just one of the clients and sometimes with both partners. The case of Sam and Susie illustrates this **psychodynamic approach.**

Susie, 28, and Sam, 30, had been married four years and had 3-year-old twin sons. The chief complaint was Susie's lack of desire. The couple had a good relationship, each felt in love with the other, and they were judged to be good parents. During their marriage they had had intercourse only three times. During the last two years they had had no physical contact because any attempt by Sam to hold or kiss Susie resulted in "hysterics," that is, she had an anxiety attack. The couple were referred to Kaplan after nine months of weekly sessions at a sex therapy clinic had not produced improvement.

The ordinary sensate focusing or pleasuring activities threw Susie into an anxiety state. In addition, when there was any improvement Susie would effectively resist or sabotage the treatment by trying to do too much. For example, if the assignment were to lie next to Sam in bed and hold his hand, she might try to have him caress her breast as well. This would then precipitate her anxious feelings. The therapist discussed this behavior with Susie and gave her the job of controlling the progress of desensitizing her anxiety. She was to select only tasks that were

within her comfort zone, that is, only those that produced tolerable anxiety.

Susie also had a more general problem with fun and pleasure. Whenever she allowed herself to experience them, she developed sharp headaches. As the desensitizing of her phobic avoidance of sexual contact progressed, Susie had a series of dreams about "dead relatives buried in the basement that needed to be removed." A central threatening figure was her deceased father. After discussions with the therapist about Oedipal feelings toward her father and the transfer of some of these feelings to her husband, Susie's father disappeared from her dreams.

After further sessions along with her husband that focused on her guilt over experiencing pleasure, Susie's pleasure anxiety had decreased, her relationship with her husband was more open, and the couple was having satisfying intercourse at least once per week. (Adapted from Kaplan, 1979, pp. 73–75)

Effectiveness of Treatment for Sexual Dysfunction

While research studies have shown great variations in the success rate for sex therapies, there is growing evidence of their usefulness (Sarwer & Durlak, 1997). For example, studies of erectile dysfunction using Masters and Johnson and cognitive-behavioral techniques have shown favorable outcomes, defined as some improvement, in as many as two-thirds of the patients treated (Segraves & Althof, 1998). In a study of Viagra, a pill used to treat erectile dysfunction, 50% of the patients were able to have intercourse after taking the medication (Pallas et al., 2000). Other conditions for which positive results have been obtained are premature ejaculation, male and female orgasmic disorders, dyspareunia, and vaginismus.

Despite these encouraging findings, well-controlled research on the evaluation of sex therapies is really only just beginning and there are important methodological problems that researchers must contend with. One problem is that the measurement of therapeutic success is often poorly defined. Another problem is the need for long-term follow-ups to determine whether a treatment technique has lasting effects. A difficulty of some of the studies that have been carried out is that dropout rates have often been high. While achieving 100% retention of research participants for follow-up is desirable, this usually isn't possible. Still, researchers often make strenuous efforts to achieve continuing cooperation from participants in studies. Beyond these sorts of methodological challenges, the complexity of many problems of sexual dysfunction needs to be recognized. Sexual dysfunction can occur because of difficulties in the relationship, differences between partners' hidden motivations for treatment (and compliance with it), the presence of psychological disorders, a lack of physical attraction between the partners, and medical problems (such as hormonal deficiencies).

Even if sex therapy is unsuccessful, its effects and the feelings it arouses may provide new insight for both the patient and the therapist. Some patients find the exercises mechanical or boring; this reaction may indicate hostility toward the partner, fear of rejection, or even performance anxiety about touching and caressing. Some people feel guilty about their own fantasies or are jealous of their partner's fantasies. The partner may sabotage the therapy by a critical attitude, detachment, or loss of interest. A common source of sexual problems is the relationship between the partners. Sometimes they have greatly differing expectations of the marriage or love affair. They may be chronically angry at each other or engaged in a power struggle. Sometimes both partners are unsure about how close they want to be, but this ambivalence takes a peculiar form in which one demands sexual intimacy and the other retreats. The recommended treatment for such problems is psychotherapy. The type of psychotherapy depends more on the therapist and patient than on the specific sexual disorder.

Some types of self-help, alone or in combination with therapy should be noted. A couple's efforts to improve their communication can enhance the quality of their sexual relationship. Communication that strives to accept (rather than criticize) the feelings and concerns of each partner can be especially helpful. Communication can also be improved when a special effort is made not to dismiss what one's partner is saying as selfish, crazy, or irrational. It is useful to bear in mind that small changes can be valuable first steps. For example, if you want your partner to be less inhibited, start slowly, perhaps by suggesting having sex in a different room or place.

One reason for optimism is that clinicians and researchers are increasingly viewing sexual dysfunction from a broad perspective that includes the biology of desire (e.g., the physical aspects of the various stages of sexual behavior), the motivations that play roles in sexual relationships, need for intimacy, desire to satisfy one's partner, and cultural influences (what individuals think about, what goes on in normal sexual relationships). This broad perspective, together with improved methodologies, and more ambitious studies that objectively compare or combine different therapeutic approaches are likely to enhance the understanding of sexual dysfunction and improve the effectiveness of its treatment.

Gender Identity Disorder

Gender identity, a basic feature of personality, refers to an individual's feeling of being male or female. Children become aware that they are male or female at an early age, and once it is formed, their gender identity is highly resistant to change. Gender identity is different from sexual preference. Sexual preference refers to whether a person desires a sexual partner of the same or the opposite sex; it does not refer to the person's sexual self-concept.

Gender Identity Problems in Children

In **gender identity disorder of childhood,** children who have not yet reached puberty may show considerable distress at being male or female and will express intense desire to be of the opposite sex. For instance, a girl may vehemently state her desire to be a boy or even insist that she is a boy. She may refuse to wear ordinary feminine clothing and insist on wearing the clothing typical of males, including boys' underwear and other accessories. She may also deny her gender by such behaviors as refusing to urinate while in a sitting position or by the insistence that she either already has or will grow a penis. Boys show the same types of behavior in reverse. In addition to playing with girls' toys and wanting to dress as a girl, a boy may say that he wants to be a woman when he grows up and that his penis and testes are disgusting or that they will disappear as he grows older.

Problems that may relate to gender identity come to clinical attention when parents become concerned because their child's behavior and social relationships are not like those of other children of the same sex and age. For instance, this mother is worried that her son is and will continue to be sexually abnormal:

My boy is showing feminine tendencies and has ever since he was two years old. It started out real cute. His sister had dress-up clothes at her grandparents', and when he got to be about two years old, he'd dress up in these clothes and hats and high heels, and he was just real cute. We thought it was something he'd pass. Now he will be eleven years old this month, and he does this in secret. I just felt like now was the time to investigate it. (R. Green, 1974, p. xxi)

If a young child's behavior is typical of that of children of the opposite sex, it does not always mean that the child has a gender identity problem. Often parents are not aware of how much their own behavior contributes to the behavior of their children. The mother quoted earlier may have encouraged her son to dress in women's clothes by telling him how cute he was then, and at no other time. When this is the case, counseling may be helpful. Parents can be trained to reinforce sex-appropriate behavior in the home—for example, by giving the child special attention or a material reinforcer when he or she is behaving appropriately. This approach has been found to be effective in helping children acquire new sex roles (Rekers, 1977).

Despite advances in the study of sexual practices, questions frequently arise as to how maladaptive a certain type of behavior is. Children who act out inappropriate sex roles early in their development may drop this behavior as they get older. The 5-year-old tomboy or sissy may simply be going through a phase. However, children who dress in the clothes of the opposite sex, and whose play follows the patterns of the other sex, have an increased likelihood of developing a homosexual orientation in adulthood (Money, 1987). A longitudinal study compared boys with extremely feminine interests and behavior in childhood with boys in a control group (R. Green, 1987). Eleven years later, 75% of the previously feminine boys were either bisexual or homosexual in fantasy and/or behavior. All but one of the boys in the control group were heterosexual.

Gender Identity Disorder in Adults

Until a few years ago, Sara Buechner was David Buechner, a successful concert pianist who had played with the New York Philharmonic, the National Symphony in Washington, and performed to rave reviews around the world. Although he had been admittedly bisexual, the majority of Buechner's relationships had been with women. At 21, he married a Korean pianist. The marriage ended with divorce. Freed by the divorce, Buechner began cross-dressing. He decided that his true self was a woman and embarked on a sex change program that included daily doses of estrogen that shrunk his male genitals and enlarged his breasts, electrolysis sessions to remove hair, and finally sex change surgery. As Sara, Buechner remains a highly ranked pianist. He believes strongly that his sex change has worked out well and feels confident and happy about his new sexual identity. He has faced unpleasantness related to becoming Sara, including cancelled teaching appointments and concert appearances. Nevertheless, Buechner feels he is a better person and a better pianist as Sara (See Figure 8-6).

(*Baltimore Sun*, October 13, 1999) ▪

Because Buechner's sex change took place only a few years ago, lasting conclusions cannot yet be drawn regarding its success. Are sex changes adaptive or maladaptive? Many clinicians believe that some sex changes—or perhaps simply the desire for them—are linked to personality, social, and biological idiosyncrasies.

Figure 8-6 As a man, David Buechner was unhappy and full of conflict, but as a woman, Sara, feels free and fulfilled.

SOURCE: *New York Times Magazine*, September 13, 1998, p. 51.

Gender identity disorders in adults can take two forms: **transsexualism** and **nontranssexual gender identity disorder.** Transsexuals experience an intense desire and need to change their sexual status, including their anatomical structure. In contrast, although adults with nontranssexual gender identity disorder feel a discomfort and inappropriateness about their assigned sex and often cross-dress, they are not preoccupied with getting rid of their primary and secondary sexual characteristics and acquiring those of the other sex.

The number of cases of transsexualism is very small, its prevalence ranging from 1 per 100,000 men and 1 per 400,000 women in the United States to 1 per 37,000 men and 1 per 103,000 women in Sweden (Landen et al., 1996). Scientific interest in transsexualism derives mainly from the light that such cases may shed on the general nature and development of gender identity. When a child's strong desire to be a member of the opposite sex continues into adulthood, transsexualism may result. The problem begins to surface at puberty, when maturational changes in the body emphasize biological gender. In the follow-up study of feminine boys described in the previous section (R. Green, 1987), one boy seemed to have transsexual feelings. Though clinicians agree on the value of studying the lives of transsexuals, the use of medical techniques to bring about bodily changes that conform to the transsexual's gender identity remains controversial.

Changing a male transsexual into a female involves administering female hormones to reduce hair growth and stimulate development of the breasts, removing the male genitals, and creating an artificial vagina. Changing a female into a sexually functioning male is more difficult because the artificially constructed penis cannot become erect by natural means or feel tactile stimulation. An inflation device is sometimes implanted in the penis to make artificial erection possible. The long-term success of this method, however, is still in doubt.

A number of the candidates who apply to clinics for what is called sex reassignment surgery show considerable psychological disturbance. In one group of patients who applied to a university gender identity clinic, 92% of the males and 60% of the females showed other psychological disturbances in addition to problems with sexual identity (S. B. Levine, 1980). For this reason, clinicians stress the need to assess each candidate carefully before deciding whether to carry out the medical steps needed for a sex change. After people who are emotionally stable and likely to adjust well to surgery are selected, most reputable centers still require a number of preliminary steps before the surgery is carried out. This degree of caution is needed because the surgical procedures are irreversible. This is important because the desire for sex change can wax and wane (Marks et al., 2000).

After patients have been selected, they usually are required to spend 1 or 2 years prior to the surgery living in the community as a member of the opposite sex. During this period, hormone injections are used to alter secondary sex characteristics such as breast size and muscle definition. This period serves as psychological preparation for life as a member of the other sex and also provides a realistic experience of what that life may be like. Psychotherapy is also often required during the presurgical period. Sometimes clients have what might be called "magical" hopes regarding the surgery. The psychotherapeutic sessions can give them a chance to look at their underlying feelings and perhaps become more comfortable as hetero- or homosexuals.

What happens to those who undergo the surgery? We noted that only a short time period has passed since the Buechner sex change. However, in the long term, several transsexuals have written about their experiences. One is Jan Morris, whose autobiography is titled *Conundrum* (1974). James Humphrey Morris was a highly regarded English foreign correspondent. At age 17 he had been an officer in one of Britain's crack cavalry regiments. As a correspondent for *The Times* of London, he covered the successful attempt by Hilary and Tenzing to climb Mount Everest. He covered wars and rebellions the world over and also wrote 15 books on history and travel. Then James became Jan. Jan Morris refers to her former self as a woman trapped in a man's body.

At age 3 or 4, James Morris realized that he was a girl who had been born into the wrong body. As an adult he enjoyed the company of women but did not desire to sleep with them. He married at 22, and he and his wife had five children. As middle age neared, he became depressed, had suicidal thoughts, and finally sought a transsexual change. Hormones were used to enlarge his breasts and soften his body to more feminine lines. After surgery to complete the process begun by the hormone pills, Morris divorced his wife. Jan Morris reports that she feels like the person she always wanted to be (see Figure 8-7). She says that the children of her former marriage treat her as an aunt.

Jan Morris appears to have had a rewarding transsexual experience. A study conducted in the Netherlands found that only 5 of a group of 1,285 transsexuals expressed regrets over their sex reassignments (van Kesteren et al., 1996). However, some clinicians have been disappointed by the results of sex reassignment and have stopped doing transsexual surgery. A 5-year follow-up Swedish study found that about 30% to 40% of those who undergo this surgery do not show a significant beneficial effect (Bodlund & Kullgren, 1996). In another long-term follow-up study of male-to-female transsexuals, only one-third were judged to have a fair or good sexual adjustment (Lindemalm et al., 1986). More than half of the patients were unchanged

(a)   (b)

Figure 8-7   (a) James Morris in 1960. (b) Jan Morris in 1974. (c) A note written by Morris to the authors.

in social adjustment. Almost one-third considered their sex reassignment surgery to have been a mistake.

Transsexualism is a prime example of the interactional point of view. Sex is a matter of anatomy and physiology, but gender identity is strongly influenced by psychological, social, and cultural factors. It is likely that there may be a small group of transsexuals for whom sex reassignment therapy is an effective treatment. For many more, who are likely to have significant personality problems and other psychopathology, the surgery does not provide an answer to their mental health problems; instead, the problems may worsen (Haertsch & Heal, 1997). Some individuals become deeply depressed after surgery, while others have transient psychotic episodes.

Nontranssexual gender identity disorder also produces discomfort about one's assigned sex. However, people with this disorder lack the preoccupation with acquiring the sexual organs and other physical characteristics of the opposite sex that is characteristic of transsexuals. Instead, they focus on fantasizing that they are of the opposite sex or actually acting out that role through cross-dressing. This cross-dressing differs from that of transvestites, discussed later. Although transvestites obtain sexual gratification from cross-dressing, they are not dissatisfied with their biological sex. They wish to remain male but become sexually excited by wearing women's clothes.

The Paraphilias

Not everyone is sexually excited by the same stimuli. Some individuals can gain sexual gratification only from particular objects or situations. While many of these sexual behaviors are practiced in private or with consenting adult partners and do not cause harm to other people, paraphilic imagery may be acted out with a nonconsenting partner in a way that does cause harm.

Paraphilias are characterized by specialized sexual fantasies, masturbatory practices, sexual props, and requirements of the sexual partner. Nonnormative sexual interests and practices have been known since antiquity, but it was not until the nineteenth and twentieth centuries that efforts were made to categorize and understand them.

DSM-IV describes three general classes of *paraphilia* (which means attraction to the deviant):

1. Preference for the use of a nonhuman object for sexual arousal
2. Repetitive sexual activity with humans that involves real or simulated suffering or humiliation
3. Repetitive sexual activity with nonconsenting partners

DSM-IV classification of the paraphilias takes into account the duration of the fantasies, urges, or behavior, which must be present for at least 6 months; and the level of distress or impairment of function they cause. In a mild condition, the individual may be distressed by the imagery but not have ever acted on it; in a moderate condition, imagery may have been transformed into action leading to impairment of social or occupational functioning; and in a severe condition, the urges may have been repeatedly acted upon and have come to occupy a central role in the person's life. Table 8-7 summarizes the most important clinical features of major paraphilias.

Table 8-7
Clinical Features of Major Paraphilias

The clinical features must be present for at least 6 months and cause significant distress or impairment in social, occupational, or other important areas of functioning.

- *Fetishism.* Recurrent, intense, sexually arousing fantasies, sexual urges, or behaviors involving the use of nonliving objects (such as female undergarments).
- *Transvestic fetishism.* Recurrent, intense, sexually arousing fantasies, sexual urges, or behaviors in heterosexual cross-dressing men.
- *Sexual sadism and masochism.* Recurrent, intense, sexually arousing fantasies, sexual urges, or behaviors involving, in masochism, real or simulated humiliation, beating, and suffering; and in sadism, actually causing psychological or physical suffering (including humiliation) to the victim.
- *Voyeurism.* Recurrent, intense, sexually arousing fantasies, sexual urges, or behaviors involving the act of observing an unsuspecting person who is naked, in the process of disrobing, or engaging in sexual activity.
- *Exhibitionism.* Recurrent, intense, sexually arousing fantasies, sexual urges, or behaviors involving the exposure of one's genitals to an unsuspecting stranger.
- *Pedophilia.* Recurrent, intense, sexually arousing fantasies, sexual urges, or behaviors involving sexual activity with a child or children who have not yet gone through puberty (generally 13 years or younger). (The perpetrator is at least 16 years of age and at least 5 years older than the child or children.)

Fetishism

Fetishism, a psychological state in which a nonliving object (fetish) serves as a primary source of sexual arousal and consummation, is an example of a sexual deviation that is not usually addressed by the law. Most fetishists are solitary in their activities, although in some cases they commit crimes to acquire their favorite fetishes (often undergarments, boots, or shoes). Fetishists are almost always male, and the fetishes vary widely, from the clearly erotic (such as an article of women's underwear, especially underwear that has been worn, stained, and not yet laundered) to objects with little apparent connection with sexuality. Fetishism often begins in adolescence (see Figure 8-8).

Rubber fetishes are particularly popular. Some rubber fetishists derive sexual excitement merely from wearing rubber garments. Others dress in them or want their partner to wear them during sexual activity because the garments are necessary for them to become sexually aroused. One rubber fetishist describes the role played by rubber boots in his sexual behavior.

> *I always seem to have been fascinated by rubber boots. I cannot say exactly when the fascination first started, but I must have been very young. Their spell is almost hypnotic and should I see someone walking along with rubber boots, I become very excited and may follow the person for a great distance. I quickly get an erection under such circumstances and I might easily ejaculate. I often will take the boots to bed with me, caress them, kiss them, and ejaculate into them. (Epstein, 1965, pp. 515–516)*

Fetishism is one of the most puzzling of all forms of sexual behavior. It is chronic, and in some cases the collection of fetishistic objects is the main activity in the individual's life. No one has been able to explain adequately fetishists' sexual attachment to diverse objects. Although theories range from those that stress unconscious motivation to those that hypothesize impaired neural mechanisms such as those found in epileptics, the causes of this unusual type of sexual behavior remain shrouded in mystery.

Fetishists do not often seek therapy. In one large London hospital, only 60 cases were diagnosed in a 20-year period (Chalkley & Powell, 1983). Of these, about 30% were referred by the courts, mainly because of their theft of fetishistic objects. About a third of the patients came for treatment because of anxiety about their fetishistic behavior. About 20% came for other reasons; the fetish was identified only after they had begun treatment. Treatment based on learning principles has been applied to fetishism with some success. In aversion therapy, for example, the object of the fetish is paired, either in actuality or in fantasy, with an unpleasant stimulus such as electric shock or an imagined situation in which discovery of the fetish causes a sense of overwhelming embarrassment.

Transvestic Fetishism

A transvestite often uses clothing as a sexual stimulant or fetish. *Transvestism* literally means "cross-dressing." Figure 8-9 shows a male cross-dresser. Transvestic behavior in men ranges from occasional solitary wearing of

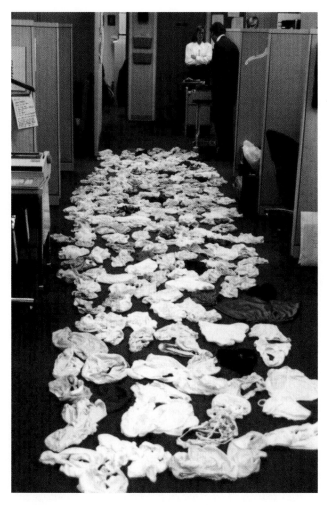

Figure 8-8 240 pairs of women's underwear stolen by a 17-year-old fetishist.

SOURCE: Bellevue, Washington, Police Department photo published in *The Seattle Times*, May 5, 1995, p. D1.

female clothes to extensive involvement in a transvestic subculture. Some males wear a single item of women's apparel (e.g., underwear or hosiery) under their masculine attire, while others dress entirely as females and wear makeup. While cross-dressed, male transvestites often masturbate.

DSM-IV describes **transvestic fetishism** only in heterosexual males. Women are not usually considered to be transvestites, probably because our society allows them to dress in most masculine styles. However, cases of female cross-dressing have been described. For example, Billy Tipton was a successful jazz musician who began his career in jazz clubs in the 1930s. Tipton had been married and had adopted three sons. When he died in 1989, the funeral director discovered that he was biologically a woman (see Figure 8-10).

References to cross-dressing can be found throughout history. King Henry III of France, who reigned from 1574 to 1589, cross-dressed publicly and wished to be addressed and treated as a woman. Joan of Arc (1412–1431) wore her hair short and preferred to dress as a man. Most transvestic fetishists are heterosexual men who dress in women's clothes, often starting in adolescence. When not cross-dressed, the transvestite usually exhibits masculine behavior and interests.

Although some clinicians have contended that transvestism and transsexualism are basically similar, there are a number of differences between these two conditions. Transsexuals wish to change their genitals and live as members of the opposite sex. They do not experience sexual arousal when cross-dressing. Transvestites, on the other hand, may become sexually aroused when cross-dressing but continue to identify themselves as members of their biological sex.

A male transvestite gave this explanation for his behavior in a letter to his wife:

Figure 8-9 Many transvestites, also known as cross-dressers, are in committed and satisfying relationships with female partners. A married couple, Davida (left) and Corinne, are shown here with Davida in cross-dress. Although some male transvestites gain sexual gratification while cross-dressed, others, particularly those who have passed adolescence and early manhood, seem to experience aesthetic pleasure and release from the responsibilities of the male role.

SOURCE: Photo by Mariette Pathy Allen, New York City. From her book, *Transformations*.

Figure 8-10 The Billy Tipton Trio: Tipton (center), Ron Kilde, and Dick O'Neill. "I never suspected a thing," O'Neill said after he found out, on Tipton's death, that Tipton was a woman.

The personal masculine attributes that first attracted you to me are, as you know, an integral part of my personality, just as my transvestism is. It has always been a part of me. . . . We are only make-believe girls, and we know always that we are really men, so don't worry that we are ever dissatisfied with manhood, or want to change forever into a woman. When we are dressed in feminine clothes and attain as close a resemblance as possible to a real girl, we do certainly pretend that we are girls for that short time, but it is a pretense and definitely not a reality. (Prince, 1967, pp. 80–81)

An unusual study some years ago of a nationwide sample of transvestites provided comprehensive descriptions of their behavior and attitudes (Bentler & Prince, 1969, 1970). Compared with a nontransvestite group, the transvestites were more inhibited in their interpersonal relationships, less involved with other individuals, and more independent. In general, they gave evidence of being less able to seek sympathy, love, and help from others and seemed to be happier when they temporarily shed the responsibilities of the male gender role. However, in many areas of personality they did not differ significantly from nontransvestites.

Psychologists have emphasized several perspectives—psychodynamic processes, conditioning, and biological predisposition—in discussing transvestism. Many clinicians believe that transvestism develops in the context of disturbed parent-child relationships. Others see it as a product of aberrant psychosexual development. Behaviorists see it as a conditioned response that is susceptible to aversion therapy in which dressing in women's clothing is paired with an aversive stimulus. Behavioral training aimed at fostering confidence and adequacy in playing a conventional sex role has also been suggested. Some recent therapy is focused on reducing the guilt and anxiety associated with cross-dressing.

Covert sensitization seems to be particularly useful in treating transvestism and other paraphilias. In this procedure, clients are first asked to imagine as vividly as possible the sexually arousing behavior that they are trying to eradicate, and to follow these thoughts with equally vivid aversion imagery (e.g., being discovered and embarrassed). This approach was used for a 31-year-old transvestite, a married police officer who sought help for uncontrollable urges to dress in women's clothing and appear that way in public. The client had a 16-year history of transvestism that had earlier resulted in his discharge from the Marine Corps. His wife had threatened to divorce him because of his cross-dressing. In treatment, he was asked to form images of deviant sexual scenes as well as aversive images of their undesirable consequences. The following is an example of the material used in the covert sensitization for this case:

You are in your house alone, and you are feeling lonely. You get the urge to put on the clothing, so you enter the bedroom and open the closet. You begin to get aroused as you decide what to wear. As you put on the clothing, you can see the colors and feel the clothing on your hands. You really are turned on as you put on the bra, panties, nylons, wig. You feel like playing with yourself as you apply your makeup, but you can't wait to go out. As you leave the house, you get very excited. You are touching your penis through the panties as you're driving. And then you hear sirens! The police pull you over, and it's your fellow policemen. They start to laugh and call for other police cars. A crowd is gathering, and they know you're a man. The officers throw you around and take you to the station. The women are disgusted, and the chief will take your gun and badge. You are humiliated, and they call you "sick." Your kids are crying as they return from school because others tease them about having a perverted father. Look what you've done to yourself! (Brownell et al., 1977, pp. 1146–1147)

Covert sensitization has been successful in treating transvestic fetishism. Figure 8-11 shows the average percentages of full erection (measured by penis circumference) during a baseline period, during covert sensitization, and upon follow-up. The figure also shows self-reported changes in sexual arousal to transvestic stimuli. Both the physiological and self-report measures revealed a sizable decrease in sexual arousal. In addition, physiological and

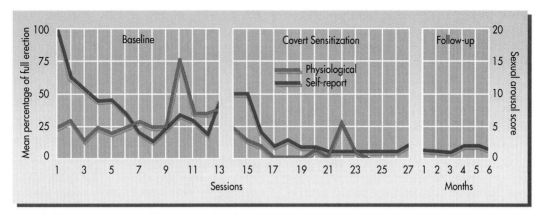

Figure 8-11 Mean percentages of full erection and sexual arousal scores (based on actual measurements and self-reports) for a transvestite man during baseline, treatment (covert sensitization), and follow-up periods.

Source: Adapted from Brownell, Hayes, and Barlow, 1977 © by the American Psychological Association. Adapted by permission of the authors.

self-reported arousal in response to heterosexual stimuli increased. The client, who had received prior treatment for his sexual difficulties, was surprised at the effectiveness of the covert sensitization.

For some transvestic fetishists it is not the clothes themselves that are exciting, but rather the ability to fool the public and be taken for a woman. One transvestic fetishist was asked if he would feel happier if social custom allowed people to dress as they wished in public.

"Heavens, no," he smiled. "Merely to be allowed to wear women's clothes in public is nothing. It is the challenge of being so much like a woman that no one knows I'm a man that turns me on. The combination of doing something that I want to, that everyone says is impossible and is forbidden anyway, produces in me an arousal which, because it is in a sexual context, becomes sexual arousal." (Gosselin & Wilson, 1980, p. 67)

Sexual Sadism and Masochism

For some people, inflicting or experiencing pain and indignity is linked to sexual gratification. Many people incorporate mildly painful acts—such as biting, nipping, and spanking—into their sexual practices. When both partners enjoy them, these activities can enhance sexual pleasure. However, sadists and masochists often go beyond mild pain and, moreover, cannot enjoy sex any other way. To the **sadist,** achieving orgasm depends on humiliating others or inflicting pain on them. This is often referred to as "discipline." To the **masochist,** sexual satisfaction depends on "bondage"—suffering, humiliation, pain, and ill treatment at the hands of others. **Sadism** and **masochism** occur

in both heterosexual and homosexual relationships, but like other sexual deviations, they are poorly understood. Both sexual masochism and sadism are chronic conditions. When they are severe, serious injury or death may result for the victim. Some clinical workers have conjectured that the roots of sadism and masochism are to be found in childhood; others have mentioned possible biological factors. One area that would seem to merit study is the fantasy life of these individuals—for example, the thoughts associated with their sexual activities.

The sexual masochist experiences arousal through his or her own suffering, preferably by being humiliated and beaten. Masochists have fantasies, often beginning in childhood, in which they are bound, tortured, raped, or otherwise abused in ways that they cannot prevent. These fantasies and acts are far more common in males than in females. *Sadomasochism* refers to interaction in which one person enjoys inflicting suffering on the other, who derives pleasure from experiencing pain. Five features are found in most cases of sadomasochism: (1) agreement as to which partner is to be dominant and which one submissive; (2) awareness by both partners that they are role-playing; (3) the consent of both participants; (4) a sexual context; and (5) a shared understanding by both participants that their behavior is sadomasochistic (Weinberg et al., 1984).

In sadomasochistic relationships the participants agree on the limits beforehand:

My wife and I do play dominance and submission games, and maybe we have the marks to prove it on occasion. But the one playing top dog watches like a hawk to make sure we stop when the other one doesn't like it any more. (Gosselin & Wilson, 1980, p. 69)

Often a signal is set up so that the submissive partner can stop the session at any time if the agreed-upon boundaries are exceeded. One sadomasochistic prostitute explained her approach:

When you have a new client, what I used to do was I used to sit down and I would talk to them first and find out exactly what they wanted. Because sometimes you can get into a session with somebody and get very brutal and that's not what they want. There's heavy dominance and there's light dominance and there's play acting, roles, all different kinds. So the best thing to do is to sit down and talk to somebody first, initially. (Weinberg, 1978, p. 290)

When sadomasochism is a person's predominant sexual style, the most common way of reaching other sadomasochistic devotees is the use of ads in sadomasochistic magazines. For example:

Beautiful Dominatrix, 24. A true sophisticate of the bizarre and unusual. I have a well-equipped dungeon in my luxurious home. You will submit to prolonged periods of degradation for my pleasure. Toilet servitude a must. I know what you crave and can fulfill your every need.

A very pretty 30-year-old female has fantasies about receiving hand spankings on her bare behind. I've never allowed myself to act out any of the fantasies. Is there anyone out there who'd like to correspond with me about their fantasies or experience with spanking?
   (Weinberg & Falk, 1980, pp. 385–386)

As these examples show, the ads contain code messages. "Toilet servitude," for instance, refers to handling feces or being defecated on. Sadomasochistic experiences can also be enhanced by hoods, paddles, enema equipment, adult diapers, and other paraphernalia sold in sex shops (see Figure 8-12). Many of these "sex boutiques" can be found in middle-class neighborhoods.

Sadomasochists may be heterosexual, bisexual, or homosexual in their choice of partners. A questionnaire study showed few differences among these groups (Breslow et al., 1986). In general, subjects in all three groups felt that their sadomasochistic interests were natural ones that were present in childhood. People in all three groups used ads to make contact with others with similar interests. Few subjects in any of the groups reported being sexually abused as children, although a sizable minority felt emotionally abused. In general, the homosexual respondents sometimes tended to take the dominant and sometimes the submissive role in their sadomasochistic activities. Heterosexual and bisexual subjects were about equally divided into "predominantly dominant," "predominantly submissive," or "adopting either" roles. Although more men than women seem to be interested in sadomasochism,

Figure 8-12 This model is wearing the leather garments, chains, and restraints that many sadists and masochists find sexually stimulating.

in one survey using questionnaires placed in a sadomasochistic contact magazine, 40% of those who responded were female (Breslow et al., 1985).

Voyeurism

Some sexual variations are not physically harmful but may victimize innocent people. One example is **voyeurism,** the impulse to spy on others, usually strangers. The French word *voyeur* means "watcher." The voyeur is subject to an irresistible, repetitive urge to spy on others through windows or doors, in public toilets, in parks, or on beaches, and particularly enjoys watching other people have sex. Like the exhibitionist (to be described shortly), the voyeur, or "peeping Tom," is male and achieves sexual gratification from doing something forbidden. Also like the exhibitionist, the voyeur is usually harmless and will run if he is discovered. In some cases, however—usually after feeling intensely stimulated or provoked—the voyeur will let his presence be known: for example, he may exhibit his genitals and ask his victim to touch him or even to masturbate him. Cases have been known in which the voyeur tried to force the victim to have sexual intercourse with him, but such cases are exceptional.

Voyeurism begins in early childhood and usually continues over a long period. Fifty percent of those arrested for voyeurism are later rearrested for similar acts. About one-fourth of the men who are arrested for peeping are married. When voyeuristic acts are related to life stress, the impulse to commit them usually decreases when the stress dissipates. While voyeurs show few signs of serious mental disorders, they usually have unsatisfying heterosexual relationships.

Exhibitionism

Exhibitionists, who are always males, repeatedly expose their genitals to unsuspecting strangers in public places as a way of experiencing sexual arousal. The exhibitionist does not want to harm anyone; his act of exposure is done for his own sexual gratification. His arousal is apparently heightened by seeing people react with amazement or shock when he unexpectedly shows his penis. **Exhibitionism** involves exposing one's genitals mainly to women and children. One-third of all people arrested for sex offenses are exhibitionists, and about 20% of these are arrested more than once.

Exhibitionism can begin between preadolescence and middle age, but it occurs most frequently during the 20s. An exhibitionist has an irresistible, compulsive need to expose his genitals, and he does so despite the anxiety, depression, and shame he feels as a result. Acts of genital exposure often seem to be triggered by feelings of excitement, fear, restlessness, and sexual arousal. When overcome by these feelings, the exhibitionist is driven to find relief. Both psychodynamic and behavioral therapies (particularly aversion therapy) have been tried with exhibitionists. Although both methods seem to achieve some success, the results are unpredictable.

Pedophilia

Pedophilia is the term used to describe a disorder that includes intense and recurrent sexual urges and sexually arousing fantasies involving some form of sexual activity with a child who has not reached the age of puberty. To be classified as a **pedophile,** a person must be 16 years or older, at least 5 years older than the child or children, and either have acted on these urges or be very distressed by them. The sexual attractions of pedophiles are very specific. For instance, the only children who may be seen as arousing may be girls from the ages of 8 to 10. The behavior is usually a chronic one that continues over a long time. However, periods of high stress tend to increase the frequency

of pedophilic behavior. In the majority of cases, the pedophile is someone whom the child knows.

Pedophilic behavior may take a variety of forms, including exposure of the pedophile's sexual body parts to the child; kissing, hugging, and fondling the child in a sexual way; touching sexual parts of the child's body or inducing the child to touch or fondle the pedophile's sexual organs; or attempted or actual intercourse with the child. Most of the victims do not seek the assistance of public services. Clearly, better preventive and therapeutic measures are needed. Youngsters need to be taught to protect themselves, and the public needs to be educated about the nature of the problem.

Pedophiles are likely to repeat the behavior after being apprehended. Some, but not all, child sex abusers can be classified as pedophiles. In most cases, a pedophile will have had sexual contacts with children both in and outside of the family and prefers children rather than adults as sexual targets. Many pedophiles do report being sexually abused as children, although researchers do not have much data on this disorder.

Perspectives on the Paraphilias

Human sexual behavior is varied. It has its underpinnings in a biological substrate for physiological expression and is strongly influenced by the socialization process. When sexual behavior greatly diverges from the norm, and especially when it is harmful to others, researchers attempt to understand it better by defining its characteristics. Defining and classifying these deviant sexual behaviors has been difficult, however, because they are (1) committed by a small percentage of the population; (2) usually concealed by their participants; and (3) constantly modified by adaptation to social changes. One hallmark of the paraphilias that researchers have been able to identify is that these unusual or bizarre acts are insistently and involuntarily repetitive.

No single theory has so far been able to explain the development of paraphilic behavior. Each of the theoretical perspectives has implications for research in terms of definition of the variant behavior, preferred type of treatment, appropriate treatment goals, and ways of assessing treatment outcome.

The Psychodynamic Perspective This perspective views paraphilic behavior as a reflection of unresolved conflicts during psychosexual development. It calls for long-term treatment that aims to change personality structure and dynamics and also alter overt behavior and sexual fantasies.

Particular emphasis is placed on (1) strengthening what is often a quite unstable body image, and (2) identifying unconscious components of fantasy life that contribute to a perverse outcome. Conventional psychotherapy or counseling has not been very effective in modifying the behavior of paraphiliacs. The reasons for resistance to treatment are unclear.

The Behavioral Perspective The behavioral perspective views sexual variance as something learned by the same rules as more ordinary sexual behavior—through conditioning, modeling, reinforcement, generalization, and punishment. From this perspective, the definition of variant sexual behavior would be based on the individual's personal discomfort with the behavior and any conflict between this behavior and the rules of society. The treatment, which can be as short as one day or much longer, is based on understanding the immediate antecedents and consequences of the behavior and on developing alternate forms of sexual arousal. Treatment effectiveness is based on overt behavior, as measured by self-monitoring and psychophysiological measures.

Various types of aversion therapy have been tried with individuals with paraphilias, but this approach has generated a great deal of controversy because of the pain and discomfort created. There is evidence that behavioral treatment may be effective in reducing or eliminating some paraphilic sexual behavior and increasing appropriate sexual behavior instead (Kilmann et al., 1982). Many of the therapeutic efforts reported used a variety of behavioral treatments that included aversion therapy. The programs were most effective when they were tailored for the specific problems of the individual paraphiliac.

The Cognitive Perspective The cognitive perspective, incorporating social learning principles, explains the variant behavior as a substitute for more appropriate social and sexual functioning, or as resulting from an inability to form a satisfactory marital relationship. The treatment goal is to help clients form satisfactory relationships through teaching them interpersonal skills.

Covert sensitization that involves imagining unpleasant events seems to avoid some of the ethical questions surrounding the use of physical punishment. It seems to be particularly effective in cases of sadism, exhibitionism, and pedophilia. Measures of outcome here are clients' self-reports of satisfying sexual and nonsexual relationships with significant others.

The Biological Perspective The biological perspective focuses on heredity, prenatal hormonal environment, and the biological causes of gender identity. Because the paraphilias seem to be largely male conditions, emphasis is often placed on the possible role of events in fetal development that might contribute to them. Other foci of attention have been organic disturbances such as the malfunctioning of parts of the brain; abnormal hormone levels and neurological function; and chromosomal abnormalities. Unfortunately, it is often not clear whether these types of abnormalities are causal, correlated with, or incidental to paraphilic interests. Biological treatment approaches may be hormonal or surgical, and treatment goals include suppression, not only of the variant behaviors, but also of sexual responsiveness in general. The outcome is usually measured in terms of psychophysiological responses as well as sexual activity. However, until the side effects of hormonal treatments and long-term behavior changes can be assessed accurately, it is difficult to draw any conclusions about the therapeutic effects of this type of treatment for paraphilias.

The Interactional Perspective The interactional view has intellectual appeal because no one treatment seems to be clearly superior for the paraphilias. It is possible that treatment approaches integrating a number of theoretical perspectives will be more effective than any one approach. However, it should be reiterated that research on the paraphilias is often difficult to carry out; for example, many people with paraphilias do not seek professional help. As a consequence, much of the available research has severe shortcomings, consisting often of single-subject studies without control subjects. Nevertheless, it is important to attend to the multiple factors that may play significant roles in the paraphilias. These include biological and environmental factors as well as personality development. The paraphilias might be viewed as composite products of psychological development. Identifying the factors contributing to the composite and learning how they interact require exploration.

Sexual Victimization

Some sexual deviations involve a participant who is either unwilling, uninformed, vulnerable, or too young to give legal consent. Among the clearest examples of this **sexual victimization** are rape and child sexual abuse. When individuals who practice these deviations come into contact with the law, they are usually known as **sex offenders** and are subjected to a variety of treatments as well as to imprisonment. Some cases of rape and child sexual abuse are examples of paraphilias; others are examples of gratification through aggression or, in the case of child sexual abuse, desire for an easily obtainable and easily coerced sexual partner. As a result of sexual assaults, the victims often suffer from a variety of persistent problems—including anxiety, posttraumatic stress disorder and depression—that require the help of mental health professionals. Sexual assaults may create psychological problems for victims over and beyond the fact of having been assaulted. One study found that sexually abused women differed from nonsexually abused women in their greater negative evaluations of themselves and low levels of self-esteem (Meston & Heiman, 2000). Even if sexual victimization does not result in a serious clinical problem, it often leaves its mark on the victimized person, often as hypervigilance with regard to cues associated with the victimization. Nancy Raine, a rape victim, has provided an illustration of this:

> On an October afternoon in 1985 I was raped by a stranger who crept through the open back door of my apartment while I was taking out the trash. My back was turned to that door for less than a minute as I shoved the slippery green bags down into the garbage cans. Seven years to the day and hour, I carried trash out of another home thousands of miles away from that place, and as I bent over the barrels with my back to the street, the fear of that day returned to me as if no time had passed. I spun around and scanned the driveway, my heart pounding. No one was there. Just dry leaves, caught up in the wind, rattling along on brittle edges in light filtering through the trees. (Raine, 1998, p. 1)

Sexual Victimizers

Sexual violence is a major societal and public health problem with approximately 500,000 victims each year. Research has shown a relationship between being a sex offender and having a mental illness. Paraphilias, antisocial personality, psychosis, mood disorder, and substance use disorder are frequently seen in perpetrators of sexual assault, and DSM-IV Axis I and Axis II classifications are common (McElroy et al., 1999). Sexual violence tends to begin early in life, be repetitive, and be associated frequently with other types of criminal behavior. Almost all sex offenders are men.

The number of sex offenders in state prisons has increased by more than two-thirds in the last decade, and a variety of efforts have been made to reduce the likelihood of repeated offenses. Cognitive-behavioral techniques have shown some therapeutic promise (Grossman et al., 1999). The goal of this approach is to change sex offenders' belief systems, eliminate inappropriate behavior, and increase appropriate behavior by modifying reinforcement contingencies so that offensive behavior is no longer reinforced. Cognitive restructuring (e.g., modifying distorted cognitions used to justify paraphilic behavior), social skills training, encouraging empathy for potential victims, and conditioning regimens are components of this approach. In covert sensitization, deviant sexual fantasies are paired with mental images of distressing consequences. Offenders may verbalize detailed sex fantasies and, when they become aroused, begin verbalizing equally detailed fantasies of highly aversive consequences, such as being arrested. This technique requires them to focus attention on negative consequences that they find upsetting.

Although some forms of treatment for sex offenders appear promising, little is known definitely about which treatments are most effective, or for which offenders, over what time span, or in what combinations. The fact that some therapeutic approaches seem promising has provided encouragement for further rehabilitation research that is more methodologically sound than most existing studies have been. To date, support for scientific study of sexual offenses has not been adequate, in part because of the widespread negative attitudes toward sex offenders.

Chapter Summary

CHANGING VIEWS OF SEXUAL BEHAVIOR

A look at history shows that views concerning sexuality have at some times been permissive and at other times restrictive. Individuals such as Freud and Ellis had an important influence on views of sexuality.

Surveys of Sexual Behavior Most information concerning sexual practices comes from survey research. Because patterns of sexual practices are known to have changed over time, there is need for frequent surveys that focus on representative samples of the population.

Homosexuality: An Example of Changing Views of Sexual Behavior Homosexual behavior refers to sexual behavior with members of one's own sex. Surveys indicate that it is not unusual for people to have at least some experience with homosexual behavior in their lifetimes. **Homosexuals** are

individuals who prefer to engage in sexual activity with members of their own sex over an extended period. The term **gay** is increasingly used to refer to this behavior because of the feeling that the term has fewer negative associations. Many people who identify themselves as gay adopt this self-label during adolescence.

Origins of Sexual Orientation It is likely that sexual orientation is the result of multiple determinants in which both psychosocial and biological factors play a role. **Bisexual behavior** is a sexual orientation in which preferred partners are sometimes of one sex and sometimes of the other.

SEXUAL DYSFUNCTION

A persistent impairment of sexual interest or response is called a **sexual dysfunction.** A sexual dysfunction is often associated with anxiety about performance or cultural inhibitions.

Types of Sexual Dysfunction Sexual problems can occur in any of four stages of the sexual response: arousal, excitement, orgasm, or resolution. **Erectile dysfunction** refers to the inability of a man to maintain an erection until the completion of intercourse. Women may have problems of **inhibited sexual arousal** that result in an inability to maintain a swelling-lubrication response. A problem that often brings women to clinics is the frequent inability to achieve orgasm.

Treatment of Sexual Dysfunction When a person seeks therapy for a sexual dysfunction or disorder, the clinician should get detailed information about medical history, physical symptoms, developmental history, drug and alcohol use, present relationships, and stressors. Sex therapy is often carried out by working with the couple rather than one person. The therapist attempts to decrease fear of failure and to focus on sensory pleasure rather than on the sex act itself. A frequent way of carrying this out is to use **sensate focus,** a sexual retraining technique developed by Masters and Johnson in their pioneering work on sex therapy. Behavioral and cognitive elements are widely used in current treatments of sexual dysfunction. Some therapists use an approach that combines these elements with a more traditional psychodynamic approach.

Although more research is needed to be completely confident about the success of sex therapy, the Masters and Johnson and cognitive-behavioral approaches seem promising. Many therapists believe that aspects of the relationship between the members of the couple may be a major force in a negative therapeutic outcome.

GENDER IDENTITY DISORDER

Gender identity refers to a person's sexual self-concept, the feeling of being male or female.

Gender Identity Problems in Children In **gender identity disorder of childhood,** children who have not yet reached puberty express extreme distress at their gender and intense desire to be of the opposite sex.

Gender Identity Disorder in Adults **Transsexualism** refers to the intense desire by adults to change not only their sexual identity but also their anatomical status. Adults who have **nontranssexual gender identity disorder** are uncomfortable with their assigned sex and may frequently cross-dress, that is, wear clothes of the opposite sex. However, they are not preoccupied with changing their physical sexual characteristics the way that transsexuals are.

THE PARAPHILIAS

The term **paraphilia** means attraction to the deviant. There are three general classes of paraphilias: preference for use of nonhuman objects for sexual arousal, sexual activity with humans with sexual arousal based on real or simulated suffering or humiliation, and repetitive sexual activity with nonconsenting partners.

Fetishism **Fetishism** refers to the use of a nonliving object as a primary source of sexual arousal and consummation.

Transvestic Fetishism **Transvestic fetishism** refers to the practice of seeking sexual stimulation through cross-dressing. Transvestic fetishists continue to identify with their biological sex, and when not cross-dressed show behaviors and interests consistent with their sex. **Covert sensitization** has been used successfully in treating transvestic fetishists.

Sexual Sadism and Masochism A **sadist** achieves orgasm through humiliating or inflicting pain on others. A **masochist** achieves sexual gratification and orgasm under circumstances of humiliation and ill treatment by others. Sadism and masochism occur in both heterosexual and homosexual relationships.

Voyeurism **Voyeurism** refers to the achievement of sexual gratification through watching or spying on others, particularly when they are dressing, undressing, or engaging in sexual activity. The socially forbidden nature of the activity seems to be a major factor in producing the voyeur's sexual excitement.

Exhibitionism **Exhibitionists** are males who gain sexual arousal from exposing their genitals to strangers in public settings.

Pedophilia A **pedophile** targets children as the main source of sexual gratification. Pedophilic behavior includes a variety of types: exposing the pedophile's sexual body parts to the child, forcing the child to fondle the adult's sexual organs, the sexual fondling and caressing of the child by an adult, and attempted or actual intercourse.

Perspectives on the Paraphilias Each of the perspectives has something to offer in understanding the paraphilias. Because many of the paraphilic behaviors are carried out in private and only occasionally come to public attention, and because they vary so greatly, little research has been carried out on them and their causes are poorly understood. Conventional psychotherapy seems ineffective in treating paraphilias. Biological treatments involving hormones have been used but long-term effects have not yet been evaluated. Behavioral therapy using aversion techniques has been tried but is found objectionable by many people on ethical grounds. Cognitive-behavioral approaches involving covert desensitization may be helpful in some cases. The interactional view of paraphilic sexual behavior maintains that biological and environmental factors as well as personality development all may play a role. From this perspective effective treatments need to consider all of these aspects of paraphilic behavior rather than focusing on any single causal factor.

SEXUAL VICTIMIZATION

Sex offenders are those who come into contact with the law because their sexual deviations (e.g., rape and child sexual abuse) involve a participant who is unwilling, uninformed, vulnerable, or too young to give legal consent. Some of these sexual offenses are examples of paraphilias, while others are related to gratification of aggressive impulses or the desire for an easily obtainable sexual partner.

Sexual Victimizers Each year there are about 500,000 victims of sexual assaults. Many of the victimizers have Axis I and Axis II diagnoses. Although research on the development of treatments for sexual victimizers is just getting under way, several cognitive-behavioral techniques seem promising.

Key Terms

Sex surveys, p. 245
Homosexual behavior, p. 247
Bisexual behavior, p. 249
Sexual dysfunctions, p. 249
Sexual desire, p. 250
Sexual arousal, p. 250
Orgasm, p. 250
Erectile dysfunction, p. 250
Inhibited sexual arousal, p. 250
Hypoactive sexual desire disorder, p. 251
Nocturnal penile tumescence, p. 251
Premature ejaculation, p. 253

Female orgasmic disorder, p. 253
Dyspareunia, p. 253
Vaginismus, p. 253
Sex therapy, p. 254
Masters and Johnson approach, p. 255
Cognitive-behavioral approach, p. 256
Psychodynamic approach, p. 257
Gender identity disorder of childhood, p. 258
Transsexualism, p. 260
Nontranssexual gender identity disorder, p. 260

Paraphilias, p. 261
Fetishism, p. 262
Transvestic fetishism, p. 263
Covert sensitization, p. 264
Sadism, p. 265
Masochism, p. 265
Voyeurism, p. 266
Exhibitionism, p. 267
Pedophilia, p. 267
Sexual victimization, p. 268

9

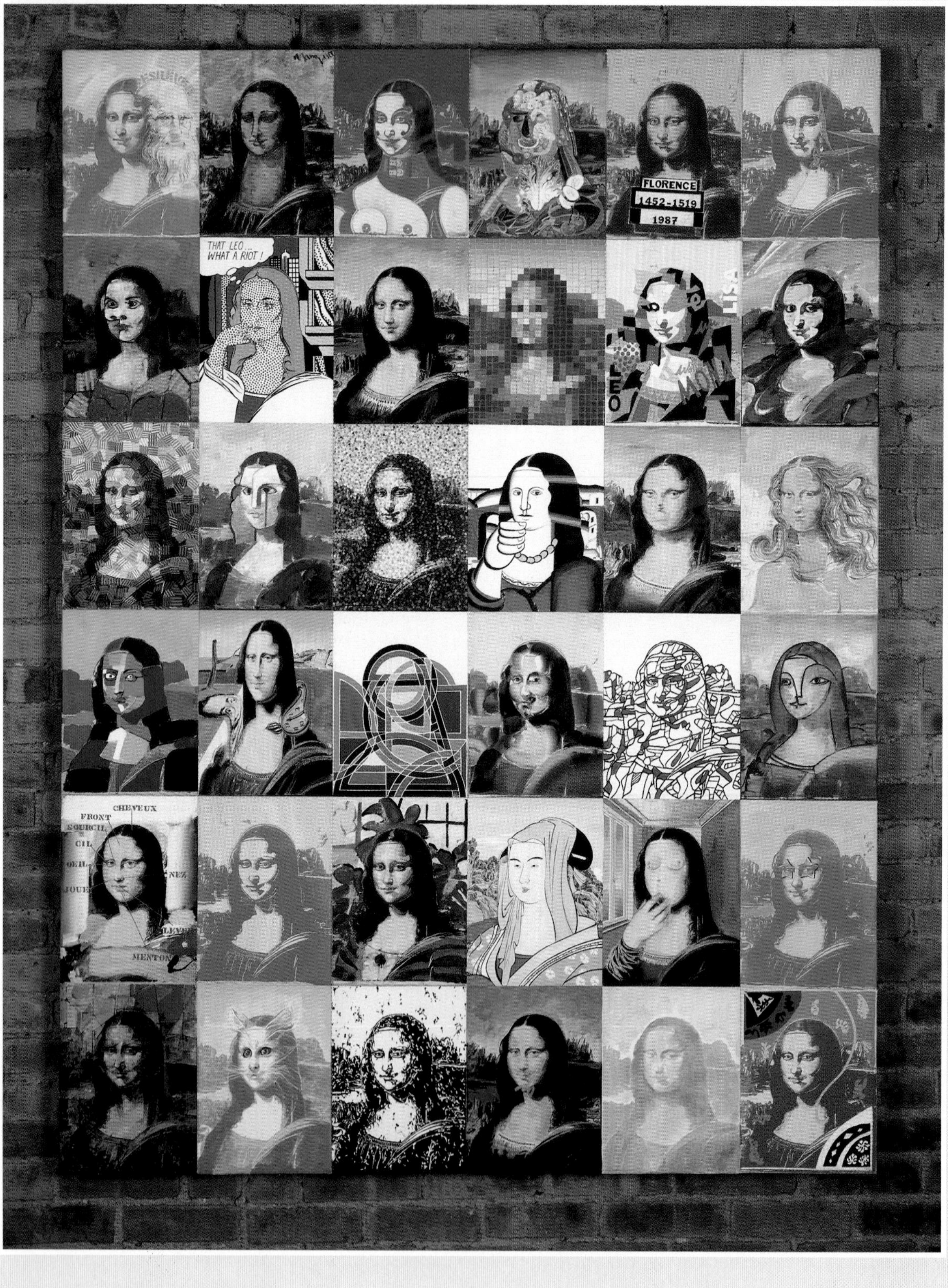

"Mona Lisa" 1988 Paul Giavanopoulos.

Personality Disorders

John, a 50-year-old retired policeman, sought treatment a few weeks after his dog had been run over and died. Since that time he had felt sad and tired and had experienced trouble sleeping and concentrating.

John lived alone, and for many years had had virtually no conversational contact with other human beings beyond "Hello" or "How are you?" He preferred to be by himself, found talk a waste of time, and felt awkward when other people tried to initiate a relationship. He occasionally spent time in a bar, but always off by himself and not really following the general conversation. He read newspapers avidly and was well informed in many areas, but took no particular interest in the people around him. He was employed as a security guard, but was known by fellow workers as a "cold fish" and a "loner."

John floated through life without relationships except for the one with his dog, which he dearly loved. At Christmas he would buy the dog elaborate gifts and, in return, would receive a wrapped bottle of Scotch that he bought for himself as a gift from the dog. The loss of his pets had been the only events in his life that had caused him sadness. He experienced the death of his parents without emotion and felt no regret whatever at being completely out of contact with the rest of his family. He considered himself different from other people and regarded emotionality in others with bewilderment. (Adapted from Spitzer et al., 1989, pp. 249–250)

Dr. B., a 41-year-old family practitioner, was getting ready to leave his office at 6 P.M. to rush home and have supper before attending his son's final high school basketball game. The hospital called to inform him that one of his obstetric patients had arrived in Labor and Delivery and was currently showing 5 cm of cervical dilation. He knew that one of his partners was covering obstetrics that night, but he felt compelled to run by the hospital to check her before going home. After checking her, he decided to stay through the delivery, necessitating his missing his son's last game. After the delivery, the physician sat in the locker room and wept. He felt terribly guilt-ridden over missing the game, and as he reflected on the evening, he could not understand why he had not simply handed the case over to his partner. He poignantly stated later that he was not even emotionally attached to this particular patient. ∎

What do these two men have in common? How are they different? Do they have problems of clinical proportions?

John sought treatment because he felt terribly distraught. However, most clinicians would be confident that John also has some sort of mental disorder because of the extreme intensity of his reaction to the death of his dog and the amount of time the reaction has lasted. His Axis I diagnosis (see Chapter 3) would probably be adjustment disorder with depressed mood because his distress is clearly linked to an identifiable stressor, the dog's death. But this Axis I classification does not completely capture all the major features of John's life. His long-standing pattern of not wanting or enjoying close relationships with other people, including his family, always choosing solitary activities, and only rarely experiencing strong emotions, coupled with an absence of oddities and eccentricities of behavior, speech, or thought, is indicative of schizoid personality disorder, an Axis II classification. Clinicians would maintain that it was the presence of the schizoid personality disorder that made John particularly vulnerable to the stress of his pet's death.

Dr. B. is probably not suffering from a mental disorder of any kind, but he may be somewhat compulsive when it comes to feeling responsible for his patients' welfare. When that compulsivity gets out of hand, it can cause him temporary distress, as it did in this case. Yet he seems to be functioning well in his medical practice, and his personality style is shared by many physicians who often feel an exaggerated sense of responsibility.

John's and Dr. B.'s cases illustrate what both clinicians and the general public would agree on—that everyone has a distinctive set of personal characteristics and that these traits affect behavior. John's life-style seems to have contributed to his protracted bereavement, while Dr. B.'s compulsivity probably makes him the dedicated doctor he is (although, along with that dedication, there are occasional temporary personal upsets, such as missing his son's game).

A person's characteristic ways of responding are often referred to as his or her **personality.** Personality is both complex and unique in that individuals differ greatly from one another in multiple components of behavior. Most people's personality styles do not affect their behavior similarly in all situations. Personality styles can be maladaptive if an individual is unable to modify his or her behavior when the environment undergoes significant changes that call for different approaches. If personality characteristics are not flexible enough to allow an individual to respond adaptively to at least an ordinary variety of situations, a disorder may be present.

When personality styles become pathological, they can impair an individual's functioning in important situations and can lead to anxiety, feelings of distress, and unhappiness. The point at which a personality style becomes a personality disorder is unclear. **Personality disorders** are long-standing, maladaptive, inflexible ways of relating to the environment. Such disorders can usually be noticed in childhood, or at least by early adolescence, and may continue through adult life. They severely limit an individual's approach to stress-producing situations because his or her characteristic styles of thinking and behavior allow for only a rigid and narrow range of responses. The general population prevalence for personality disorders is estimated to be between 10% and 15% (Clarkin, 1998).

Classifying Personality Disorders

Personality disorders pose problems for people who construct classification systems, as well as for textbook writers and teachers of abnormal psychology. They seem important, and their existence can easily be recognized even by nonprofessional observers, yet little is known about their origins and development. With the exception of the antisocial personality disorder, and until recently the borderline personality disorder, very little research has been done on these problems, probably because they often are not dramatic or severely incapacitating and because many people who might have such disorders do not seek help in dealing with their problems.

A major characteristic of personality styles is their ingrained quality. They are deeply rooted and firmly established. Individuals usually do not raise questions or worry much about these sorts of habitual ways of functioning. The two cartoons in Figure 9-1 illustrate the seemingly unthinking way in which personality reflects itself in behavior.

Although the maladaptive behavior that is typical of personality disorders sometimes causes great distress to the people involved, they find it difficult to change the way they think about and respond to situations. The clinical problems are intensified when, as is usually the case, the person does not regard his or her behavior patterns as maladaptive or undesirable, even if the unpleasant and counterproductive consequences of those behaviors are obvious to others. As we will see in this chapter, this situation is perhaps most evident in cases of antisocial personality.

Personality disorders are diagnosed on DSM-IV's Axis II. Mental retardation is also diagnosed on this axis. Because these two conditions have in common a lifetime or near-lifetime duration and stability, there are not likely to be periods of improvement or change. A diagnosis of personality disorder can be made only when a person's inflexible, long-lasting behavior pattern or personality style causes important problems in social situations or on the job, or when it results in a high level of personal distress.

(a)

(b)

Figure 9-1 These two cartoons show both personality in action and personality manifesting itself in a quite unthinking, unreflective way. (a) The man with the whip seems very much wrapped up in himself and doesn't seem to be worrying very much about the effect of using his whip on the rowers. (b) The person also seems personally focused and inquires about the 911 caller's problem almost as an afterthought.

SOURCE: (a) *Barron's*, September 11, 2000, p. 55. Cartoon by Roy Delgado. (b) *Barron's*, September 11, 2000, p. 57. Cartoon by Nick Downes.

Table 9-1 lists the central features of a personality disorder. Table 9-2 lists three groups of major personality disorders; Figure 9-2 shows their frequency, as well as how that frequency is divided between men and women.

Unlike the near-permanent disorders diagnosed on Axis II, Axis I disorders, called **symptom disorders,** may come and go. Symptom disorders may be triggered by events or environmental factors and may disappear when conditions change, or when a person is taught new behaviors. People with Axis I disorders often see themselves as having personal problems (symptoms) that are troublesome and require treatment. People with Axis II disorders are far more

Table 9–1

Features of Personality Disorders

1. Early onset; evident at least since late adolescence
2. Stability; no significant period when not evident
3. Pervasive; evident across a wide range of personal, social, and occupational situations
4. Clinically significant maladaptation, resulting in personal distress or impairment in social and occupational functioning

likely to say that their difficulties are attributable to the environment (e.g., their family or co-workers) and that they do not need clinical treatment.

Frequently a person has both a personality disorder and a symptom disorder. The relationship between person-

Table 9–2

Major Personality Disorders and Their Characteristics

Odd or Eccentric Behavior

- *Paranoid:* Tense, guarded, suspicious; holds grudges.
- *Schizoid:* Socially isolated, with restricted emotional expression.
- *Schizotypal:* Peculiarities of thought, appearance, and behavior that are disconcerting to others; emotionally detached and isolated.

Dramatic, Emotional, or Erratic Behavior

- *Histrionic:* Seductive behavior; needs immediate gratification and constant reassurance; rapidly changing moods; shallow emotions.
- *Narcissistic:* Self-absorbed; expects special treatment and adulation; envious of attention to others.
- *Borderline:* Cannot stand to be alone; intense, unstable moods and personal relationships; chronic anger; drug and alcohol abuse.
- *Antisocial:* Manipulative; exploitive; dishonest; disloyal; lacking in guilt; habitually breaks social rules; childhood history of such behavior; often in trouble with the law.

Anxious or Fearful Behavior

- *Avoidant:* Easily hurt and embarrassed; few close friends; sticks to routines to avoid new and possibly stressful experiences.
- *Dependent:* Wants others to make decisions; needs constant advice and reassurance; fears being abandoned.
- *Obsessive-compulsive:* Perfectionistic; overconscientious; indecisive; preoccupied with details; stiff; unable to express affection.

ality disorders and symptom disorders is unclear, but the relationship is obviously a close one. One theory holds that personality disorders may be thought of as vulnerabilities, with each personality disorder associated with vulnerability to only some of the symptom disorders. For example, schizotypal personalities are thought to be susceptible to schizophrenia, dependent personalities to depression, avoidant personalities to social phobias, and borderline and antisocial personalities to drug and alcohol abuse. While this idea of increased vulnerability has some support, it is not a certainty. Another classification scheme might consider personality disorders as milder forms of symptom disorders. For example, schizotypal disorder might be a mild form of schizophrenia and borderline disorder might be a form of mood disorder.

In some instances, the classification statements of Axis II are used to provide information that bears on the primary diagnosis of Axis I. In other cases, a personality disorder referred to on Axis II is the individual's major problem. Many combinations are possible. A person may have a diagnosis on both Axes I and II. For example, Henry A. had psychotic symptoms that called for a diagnosis of schizophrenia. Before his present schizophrenic episode, however, Henry A. had shown several characteristics—odd speech, social isolation, suspiciousness, and hypersensitivity to real or imagined criticism—that had significantly impaired his effectiveness in a variety of situations. Because of the different types of behaviors Henry A. showed, he was diagnosed using both Axis I and Axis II:

- Axis I: Schizophrenia, paranoid, chronic
- Axis II: Schizotypal personality disorder (premorbid)

The term *premorbid* means that before the schizophrenic symptoms developed, the personality disorder already existed.

In another case, Gerry B. showed similar personality characteristics, but there was no basis for an Axis I diagnosis. Her diagnosis would be as follows:

- Axis I:———
- Axis II: Schizotypal personality disorder

A third individual, Deborah C., had characteristics of the same personality disorder seen in Henry A. and Gerry B. However, she had additional characteristics that fit another personality disorder. In this case, both personality disorders would be diagnosed:

- Axis I:———
- Axis II: Schizotypal personality disorder; borderline personality disorder

Personality disorders produce relatively unreliable diagnostic classifications. Research has shown that when cli-

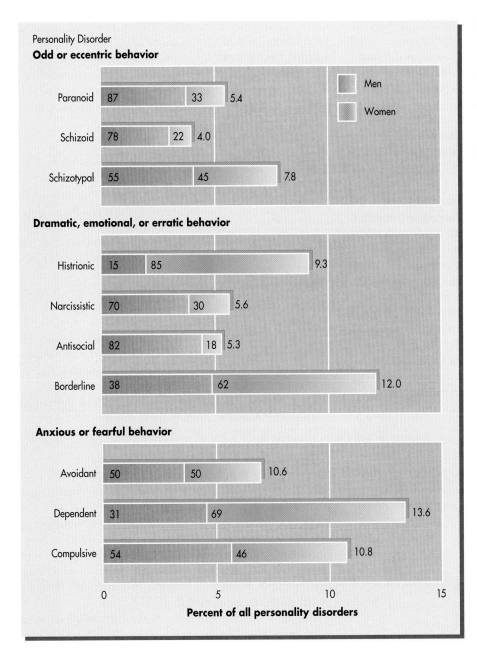

Personality Disorder

Odd or eccentric behavior

Paranoid   87 | 33 | 5.4
Schizoid   78 | 22 | 4.0
Schizotypal 55 | 45 | 7.8

☐ Men
☐ Women

Dramatic, emotional, or erratic behavior

Histrionic   15 | 85 | 9.3
Narcissistic 70 | 30 | 5.6
Antisocial   82 | 18 | 5.3
Borderline   38 | 62 | 12.0

Anxious or fearful behavior

Avoidant   50 | 50 | 10.6
Dependent   31 | 69 | 13.6
Compulsive 54 | 46 | 10.8

0   5   10   15
Percent of all personality disorders

Figure 9-2 Not all personality disorders occur with equal frequency, and not all affect men and women equally. Each bar shows which percent of all personality disorders is represented by each disorder. The different-colored portions of each bar represent the proportion of men and women given this diagnosis. The total does not add up to 100 percent because some personality disorders do not fit any of these categories.

SOURCE: Data from Millon, 1986.

nicians use standardized interviews (interviews following a structured format), their interrater reliability is higher than for clinicians who conduct relatively freewheeling interviews (Loranger et al., 1994; Zimmerman, 1994).

One difficulty in deciding on the appropriateness of an Axis II diagnosis is the unclear boundary between those personality characteristics within normal limits and those representing disordered behavior. Another problem is that some of the Axis II categories overlap a great deal. Rather than being separate disorders, they represent different degrees of the same general behaviors. In fact, about two-thirds of the patients who meet the criteria for one personality disorder will also meet the criteria for at least one more (Widiger, 1991). A third problem is that some

personality disorders also overlap Axis I categories. For instance, in one study more than half of the individuals who were diagnosed as borderline also had a major affective disorder (A. J. Frances & Widiger, 1986).

If disorders are to be classified into separate types, their criteria should be distinct and mutually exclusive, and the number of ambiguous cases should be relatively few. Some DSM categories—for example, schizophrenia, the affective disorders, and the organic disorders—are relatively distinct from each other, although there are some fuzzy areas between them. But, as we have seen, this is not true of personality disorders, many of whose diagnostic criteria overlap.

Some of these classification problems come about because so little is known about most personality disorders.

Another difficulty stems from the so-called **prototypal approach** used in DSM-IV. Each disorder has a list of possible characteristics, and if more than a specific number are met, the diagnosis of that disorder is given. This means that no single listed characteristic must necessarily be shared by everyone diagnosed with a particular personality disorder. For instance, for a diagnosis of paranoid personality disorder, a person must have any four from a list of seven characteristics. This means that any two people given this classification might have quite different characteristics.

Despite the drawbacks and uncertainties associated with the disorders listed in DSM-IV Axis II, the attempt to incorporate personality disorders into the classification process still represents a major advance. Prior to DSM-III, the diagnosis of mental disorders gave primary attention to the more obvious conditions now classified on Axis I. DSM-III's placement of the personality disorders on a separate axis highlights their importance to, coexistence with, and contribution to other disorders. In this way, Axis II represents a pioneering step toward a classification system applicable to the whole person. As research proceeds on this novel approach to diagnosis, it is likely that ways will be found to solve some of the classification problems mentioned previously (Millon & Davis, 2000).

In this chapter, we will discuss the personality disorders in terms of the three groupings outlined in Table 9-2: odd or eccentric behavior; dramatic, emotional, or erratic behavior; and anxious or fearful behavior. While there are a number of other reasonable categorizations, this grouping provides an approachable structure for understanding these disorders.

Odd or Eccentric Behavior

Disorders in this group are marked by odd, eccentric, reclusive, or suspicious behavior. Individuals with a diagnosis falling within this group may read hidden demeaning or threatening meanings into benign remarks, seem detached from social relationships, and have difficulty forming close relationships. They are often characterized as being withdrawn, cold, and irrational.

Paranoid Personality Disorder

People with **paranoid personality disorder** have several outstanding characteristics: unwarranted feelings of suspiciousness and mistrust of other people; hypersensitivity; the expectation—without sufficient justification—that they will be exploited or harmed by others; and a ten-dency to read hidden demeaning or threatening messages into benign remarks and events (e.g., suspecting that a neighbor has put out trash early just to annoy them). It is very difficult for such people to have close relationships with others because they are constantly expecting treachery. The following case provides an account of a typical paranoid personality:

> A 36-year-old single white male engineer was referred for psychiatric evaluation, with his grudging cooperation, by his project manager. He described his current work situation as very tense because his co-workers had been "ganging up" on him, giving him the most difficult assignments and sometimes removing the crucial information he needed from the relevant files. He said they did this "because they like to see me sweat." He had changed jobs four times in the past six years because of similar problems at previous jobs. Aside from his frequent contact with a sibling, the patient was socially isolated. He stated, "I've never trusted people. All they want to do is take advantage of you." He was tense, aloof, and obviously very angry at his co-workers. He was hypervigilant and made several comments indicating that he felt that the interviewer might not "see things my way." There was no evidence of psychosis or depression. (Siever & Kendler, 1986, p. 199)

Paranoid individuals rarely seek clinical help. If a situation becomes so difficult that they are forced to seek help (e.g., if they are required to work closely with other people), the therapist's hardest task is to penetrate the barrier of suspiciousness. They are also hypersensitive to criticism, making it especially difficult for them to function in subordinate positions. They have a strong fear of losing independence and the power to shape events. Just the feeling of being in a position of lower rank or lesser power might be intolerable.

People with paranoid personality disorder often seem cold, humorless, devious, and scheming. These characteristics do not promote close, rewarding relationships. Perhaps because people with this kind of personality keep to themselves and rarely become intimate with others, many of their unusual ideas remain unnoticed. Their performance is often impaired because their preoccupation with searching for hidden motives and special meanings limits their ability to consider and understand situations. When problems occur, they are often work-related, since work is an area in which interpersonal contacts are difficult to avoid.

Table 9-3 lists the major clinical features of paranoid personalities in DSM-IV Axis II. As we stated earlier, all of the features do not have to be present for this classification to be used—four or more of the characteristics might justify the diagnosis.

Table 9-3
Clinical Features of Paranoid Personality Disorder

A person having at least four of these characteristics might be considered to have a paranoid personality disorder.

1. Expects, without sufficient basis, to be exploited or harmed by others.
2. Questions, without justification, the loyalty or trustworthiness of peers and associates.
3. Reads hidden demeaning or threatening meanings into benign remarks and events.
4. Bears grudges or is unforgiving of insults or slights.
5. Is reluctant to confide in others because of unwarranted fear that the information will be used against him or her.
6. Perceives attacks on his or her character or reputation that are not apparent to others and is quick to react with anger or to counterattack.
7. Has recurrent suspicions, without justification, regarding fidelity of spouse or sexual partner.

Schizoid Personality Disorder

Individuals with **schizoid personality disorder** are reserved, socially withdrawn, and seclusive (see Figure 9-3). They prefer solitary work activities and hobbies and lack the capacity for warm, close relationships. Such people rarely express their feelings directly. Not only do they have few relationships with others, but they also seem to have little desire for them. In any case, they often have poor social skills, although their speech and behavior patterns are not unusual or eccentric. They also lack a sense of humor and seem detached from their environment. When,

Figure 9-3 Spending time alone, withdrawn from others, is typical of people with the schizoid personality disorder. They often appear quite detached from the life around them.

in her book *The White Album*, Joan Didion uses the phrase "only marginally engaged in the dailiness of life," she could be describing the detachment of people with schizoid personality disorders. Perhaps because of this detachment, men with schizoid personality disorder seldom marry. Women with this disorder are more likely than men to marry, possibly by accepting a marriage offer rather than seeking it.

John, whose social isolation was portrayed at the beginning of the chapter, would probably be described as having a schizoid personality disorder. Although the man in the following example did not complain of social isolation (schizoid individuals rarely do), his stable solitary existence was a central part of his personality. He also showed a rigidity in his personal life and was not concerned about others' opinions of him as long as they let him alone.

A 46-year-old single white male accountant sought professional consultation on the advice of a colleague because of persistent feelings of dissatisfaction and depression following a change in his work situation. Although he retained his position at his firm, where he had worked for 20 years, many of his more important responsibilities had been shifted to a younger colleague. He had always worked well in a rather autonomous position in the firm but now felt that his daily work routine had been disrupted and he no longer had meaningful tasks to accomplish. It turned out that he had always been socially isolated, with social contacts limited to acquaintances at work, and followed a rather prescribed pattern of reading the newspaper and watching television as his evening recreation. He at times saw a married sister and her family on weekends. This limited life style had been tolerable for him for some time and he appeared relatively indifferent to the opinions of co-workers as long as he could count on being assigned his quota of accounts. His redefined position left him with less work to do and an unclear role in the firm. He felt as if "the rug had been pulled out from under me." In the consultation, he was a quiet man who, although cooperative, was difficult to engage affectively. He spoke with little emotion and mumbled at times, exhibiting no sense of attachment to other people in his life, but only to his "way of doing things," which he had great difficulty in changing. (Siever & Kendler, 1986, p. 192)

The emotional responses of schizoid individuals seem rather flat as well as cold. The kinds of frustrations that arouse expressions of anger in most people elicit little observable hostility from these individuals. They often seem vague, self-absorbed, absent-minded, and not very aware of or interested in what is going on around them. Some of these people can support themselves if they find socially isolated jobs. Many of them, however, have problems at work because of the contact with other people that most jobs require. Since schizoid people are not bothered by their lack of personal relationships, they are poor prospects for therapy.

Table 9-4 lists the clinical features of schizoid personalities described in DSM-IV. As with all the personality disorders, the presence of every feature is not required for use of the classification.

Schizotypal Personality Disorder

People with **schizotypal personality disorder** are characterized by oddities of thinking, perceiving, communicating, and behaving. These deviations are never as extreme as those found in cases of full-blown schizophrenia. Still, clinicians often feel the need to probe for the possibility of major distortions, such as hearing voices and having ideas that do not seem to make sense. Box 9-1 shows how clinicians explore these possibilities.

People with schizotypal personality disorder, like schizoid individuals, are seclusive, emotionally shallow, and socially unskilled. However, the speech patterns of the two groups are quite different. People with a schizoid personality disorder have no oddities of speech, although they may lack social skills. Those with a schizotypal personality disorder, on the other hand, often are not understood because they use unusual words and phrases or use common words in unusual ways. They also are likely to express ideas unclearly. At times—usually when they are under stress—their thinking deteriorates and they may express ideas that seem delusional. These cognitive and perceptual characteristics are probably the most important ones in distinguishing schizotypal personality disorder from the borderline (discussed later) and schizoid personality disorders.

Table 9-4

Clinical Features of Schizoid Personality Disorder

A person having at least four of these characteristics might be considered to have a schizoid personality disorder.

1. Neither desires nor enjoys close relationships, including being part of a family.
2. Almost always chooses solitary activities.
3. Obtains pleasure from few, if any, activities.
4. Indicates little, if any, desire to have sexual experiences with another person.
5. Appears indifferent to the praise or criticism of others.
6. Has no close friends or confidants (or only one).
7. Shows emotional coldness, detachment, and little variation in emotions.

The behavior of people with a schizotypal personality disorder may, at times, border on the bizarre. Much of the time they seem suspicious, superstitious, and aloof. The following case illustrates a number of the characteristics of schizotypal personality disorder:

A 41-year-old man was referred to a community mental health center's activities program for help in improving his social skills. He had a lifelong pattern of social isolation, with no real friends, and spent long hours worrying that his angry thoughts about his older brother would cause his brother harm. He had previously worked as a clerk in civil service, but had lost his job because of poor attendance and low productivity.

On interview the patient was distant and somewhat distrustful. He described in elaborate and often irrelevant detail his rather uneventful and routine daily life. He told the interviewer that he had spent an hour and a half in a pet store deciding which of two brands of fish food to buy, and explained their relative merits. For two days he had studied the washing instructions on a new pair of jeans. Did "Wash before wearing" mean that the jeans were to be washed before wearing the first time, or did they need, for some reason, to be washed each time before they were worn? He did not regard concerns such as these as senseless, though he acknowledged that the amount of time spent thinking about them might be excessive. When asked about his finances, he could recite from memory his most recent monthly bank statement, including the amount of every check and the running balance as each check was written. He knew his balance on any particular day, but sometimes got anxious if he considered whether a certain check or deposit had actually cleared.

He asked the interviewer whether, if he joined the program, he would be required to participate in groups. He said that groups made him very nervous, and he was unsure if he could "stand" participating in them. (Spitzer et al., 1989, p. 154)

Noteworthy features of this case include the absence of close friends or confidants, the man's belief that he has magical powers (worrying that his angry thoughts would cause his brother harm), constricted affect (reflected in his being "distant" in the interview), odd speech (providing elaborate and often irrelevant details), and social anxiety. Because of this man's eccentricities of thought and speech, he would be classified as schizotypal rather than schizoid.

Schizotypal individuals probably have more than the average risk of an episode of schizophrenia later in life. A 15-year follow-up of patients with schizotypal personality disorder suggests that this category represents a borderline group between health and schizophrenia (McGlashan, 1986). Since many cases of schizophrenia are presumed to have a hereditary biological component, schizotypal individuals probably share this genetic characteristic. There is evidence that schizotypal personality disorder is

Case Study

Box 9–1

Probing for Schizotypal Thinking

The following interview was productive because of the interviewer's sensitivity and ability to communicate empathy for the patient's feelings and thoughts. (I is the interviewer; P is the patient.)

I: Where shall we begin?

P: I may as well start with them, the character disorders.

I: Tell me about them!

P: I think the people who give you the most trouble—that's who they are.

I: It sounds as if some people bother you a lot.

P: You see, it all depends. I hate the character disorders who are cruel and who hurt you. You can feel their aggressive thoughts, but I quit my job so they can't get at me anymore.

I: It must feel awful to be harassed by those people.

P: I just have to stay away from them.

I: Did they try to harm or persecute you?

P: It's their thoughtlessness that hurts you.

I: Have they ever tried to follow you, observe your house, tap your phone, bug your bedroom or living room?

P: No, but I'm surprised that you ask. Are you in tune with them?

I: I want to understand how they bother you, how they get to you.

P: The way they look at you, the way they don't talk to you.

I: Have you heard any voices ever?

P: My own thoughts, I think them in words. I imagine how they would sound if I were to speak them out loud. There is the quality of sound in thoughts.

Thoughts go beyond people. They interconnect and survive.

I: Do you have access to those interconnecting thoughts? Are you familiar with ESP?

P: I can sense them, I can sense the hostile thoughts of the character disorders.

I: Tell me about these character disorders! Who are they?

P: Those people who impose on your thoughts—you meet them everywhere. These thoughtless, callous mental morons.

I: Do you think they are like a fraternity? Sticking together and conspiring against you?

P: No, they are not like a conspiracy—more here and there, you know, just like people you meet and don't like. I don't think they are organized. It's more like a mind game.

Source: Othmer & Othmer, 1994, pp. 414–415.

common among individuals who have a twin or close relative with schizophrenia (Torgersen et al., 1993).

Table 9-5 lists clinical features of schizotypal personality disorder. Persons with paranoid, schizoid, and schizotypal personality disorders have in common a degree of social detachment and the presence of "odd" or idiosyncratic behavior that can be observed in much more extreme form in schizophrenia. Paranoid personality disorder is characterized by suspiciousness and mistrust of others; schizoid personality disorder by the preference for solitary activities, without there necessarily being distortions in perceptions of reality; and schizotypal personality disorder by eccentricity and cognitive-perceptual distortions. Because of overlaps among these odd and eccentric behaviors and between them and some other Axis II and Axis I classifications, there is no complete agreement about their clinical uniqueness. Agreement is probably least for schizotypal personality disorder because research has shown that it is often closely related to schizophrenia and might simply be a weak form of that disorder (Siever et al., 1991). However, the schizotypal classification does meet the Axis II requirements of enduring patterns of perceiving, relating to, and thinking about the environment and oneself. The criteria for schizotypal personality disorder include persistent disturbances in the perception and cognition of relations between the self and others. These

Table 9-5

Clinical Features of Schizotypal Personality Disorder

A person having at least five of these characteristics might be considered to have a schizotypal personality disorder.

1. Inappropriate ideas of reference (the belief that other people's conversations, smiles, or actions have reference to oneself).
2. Excessive social anxiety that does not diminish with familiarity and tends to be associated with paranoid fears rather than negative judgments.
3. Odd beliefs or thinking that one has magical powers (e.g., "Others can feel my feelings").
4. Unusual perceptual experiences, including bodily illusions.
5. Odd speech and thinking (e.g., very vague, circumstantial, overelaborate).
6. Paranoid ideas or suspiciousness.
7. Odd or eccentric behavior or appearance (e.g., unusual mannerisms, talking to self, odd speech).
8. No close friends or confidants (or perhaps only one) other than relatives, primarily because of lack of desire for contact, pervasive discomfort with others, or eccentricities.
9. Inappropriate or constricted affect (e.g., coldness, aloofness).

disturbances are not limited to periods of stress; they are present virtually all the time. Research is needed to establish the contribution this Axis II classification can make to the diagnostic process.

Dramatic, Emotional, or Erratic Behavior

The first group of personality disorders, which we have just reviewed, is composed of individuals with withdrawn behavior. The second category contains people who seek attention and whose behavior is often highly noticeable and very unpredictable.

Histrionic Personality Disorder

For people with **histrionic personality disorder,** getting the attention of others is a high priority (see Figure 9-4). Their motto might be "All the world's a stage"; in interpersonal relationships, they often act out a role, such as "the star" or "the victim." These people strike others as vain and immature and tend to speak in a dramatic, exaggerated, and gushing manner.

This classification is used in cases that are marked by exaggerated expression of emotion, stormy interpersonal relationships, a self-centered attitude, and manipulativeness. The manipulativeness might manifest itself in suicidal gestures, threats, or attempts, as well as in other attention-getting behaviors such as dramatic physical complaints. Histrionic patients often come to the attention of therapists because of a drug overdose or other form of suicide attempt.

Figure 9-4 Histrionic personalities may be overly concerned with physical attractiveness and making a striking or dramatic impression.

Histrionic individuals often react too quickly to situations that require some analysis and thought. They don't always focus their attention long enough to perceive the details of a situation, and as a result they tend to respond with emotionally tinged generalities. When people with histrionic personalities are asked to describe something, they generally respond with impressions rather than facts. For example, a therapist who was taking a case history from a client and had made repeated efforts to get a description of the client's father reported that the patient "seemed . . . hardly to understand the sort of data I was interested in, and the best she could provide was, "My father? He was wham-bang! That's all—just wham-bang" (Shapiro, 1965, p. 111).

Histrionic individuals often operate on hunches and tend to stop at the obvious. Not only are they suggestible and easily influenced by the opinions of others, but they are also easy to distract. Their attention is easily captured and just as easily turned toward something else. Thus, their behavior has a scattered quality. These problems of attention also lead histrionic people to appear incredibly naive about many commonplace things.

Psychoanalyst Anthony Storr (1980) has interpreted histrionic behavior as a pattern that is often adopted by individuals who do not feel able to compete with others on equal terms and believe that no one is paying attention to them. Storr thinks that such people may have been disregarded by their parents as children. According to this theory, although the child had repeatedly tried to get the parents to think of him or her as an individual, those attempts had failed. The child then became demanding and resorted to all kinds of dramatic behaviors in order to be noticed. This interpretation may help to explain another characteristic of these histrionic individuals—their frequent complaints of poor health, for example, weakness or headaches. The less attention the parents paid to the child, the more the child had to shout or dramatize to get their attention. Histrionic individuals carry these extreme behaviors into adulthood.

Perhaps because of such childhood experience, histrionic people may also feel unlovable and may react to this feeling by trying to make themselves sexually irresistible. Women in particular may dress and behave seductively yet not really desire intimate sexual activity. Women are more likely than men to be diagnosed as histrionic. Table 9-6 lists several clinical features frequently observed in cases of histrionic personality disorder. In the following case, the interviewer (I) inquires about a sleep problem for which the patient (P) was seeking clinical consultation:

I: *Tell me about your sleep problems.*

P: *Oh, it's terrible. There are whole nights when I can't sleep at all. I toss and turn, and I get up in the morning without having closed my eyes for even a second.*

Table 9-6

Clinical Features
of Histrionic Personality Disorder

A person having at least five of these characteristics might be considered to have a histrionic personality disorder.

1. Rapidly shifting but basically shallow expressions of emotion.
2. Overconcern with physical attractiveness.
3. Inappropriate sexual seductiveness in appearance or behavior.
4. Discomfort when not the center of attention.
5. Excessively impressionistic speech, which lacks detail.
6. Intolerance of, or excessive frustration over, situations that do not work out exactly as desired.
7. Apparent view of relationships as possessing greater intimacy than is actually the case (e.g., referring to an acquaintance as "dear, dear friend").
8. Exaggerated expression of emotion, with much self-dramatization.

"I'm looking for a job that satisfies my lust for power."

Figure 9-5 People with narcissistic personalities show grandiosity, a need for admiration, and lack of appreciation of how others might react to their grandiosity.

Source: *Wall Street Journal,* February 22, 1996, p. A19. Cartoon by Joseph Farris.

I: *This happens only some nights?*

P: *It happens when I have these terrible, terrible fights with my husband. He just tears me to pieces. [Patient rolls her eyes dramatically upward.]*

I: *Does he or anybody else notice what you are going through?*

P: *They don't have the foggiest idea. I can scream and yell and they still don't understand.*

I: *When you have these fights, is your mood affected?*

P: *I get these devastating depressions and I have to cry the whole time.*

(Othmer & Othmer, 1989, p. 402)

Even though this patient talks freely, she isn't able to provide the needed information. For example, she is unable to describe precisely the circumstances of the fights with her husband. She expresses her suffering in an exaggerated way typical of histrionic personality disorder, and she is reluctant to furnish the facts.

Narcissistic Personality Disorder

The word *narcissism* comes from the classical myth about a young man, Narcissus, who fell in love with his reflection in a pond. Because he could never grasp his own image, he despaired and died of anguish.

Several critical factors play roles in **narcissistic personality disorder**: an extreme sense of self-importance and the expectation of special favors, a need for constant attention, fragile self-esteem, and lack of empathy or caring for others (see Figure 9-5). People with narcissistic personality disorder are often preoccupied with fantasies of unlimited success, brilliance, power, beauty, and ideal love relationships. They may think of their problems as unique and feel that only other equally special people are able to understand them. The case of Robert Graham illustrates many of the characteristics of narcissistic personality disorder.

Graham, a successful 30-year-old actor, contacted a therapist because he was having trouble with a new stage role. In it he had to play a character who was deeply depressed by the death of his wife. As Graham said, he had trouble portraying "a character who was so involved with a woman that his life essentially ended simply because she died."

In his first interview he told the therapist what a good actor he was. "I don't wish to be immodest, but I am uniquely talented." Throughout his life he had been told he was "uniquely cute" and "gifted." He could be charming and entertaining and used these abilities to make other people feel "special" as a way of furthering his career. He seemed to respond to others with a feeling of contempt and remarked that other people were gullible and "easily taken in by experiences."

Graham's relations with women puzzled him. He began dating and had sexual activity early and had romances with a

Table 9-7

Clinical Features
of Narcissistic Personality Disorder

A person having at least five of these characteristics might be considered to have a narcissistic personality disorder.

1. Grandiose sense of self-importance, exaggeration of personal achievements and talents, and need for recognition of one's superiority by others.
2. Preoccupation with fantasies of unlimited success, power, and beauty.
3. Sense that one's specialness and uniqueness can be appreciated only by other special or high-status people or institutions (e.g., employers).
4. Need for excessive admiration and attention.
5. Sense of entitlement; expects especially favorable treatment or automatic compliance with personal expectations.
6. Exploitation of other people; takes advantage of them.
7. Lack of empathy for other people's needs and feelings.
8. Often, envy of others or belief that others are envious of him or her (resents privileges or achievements of those regarded less special or deserving).
9. Arrogance; haughty behavior or attitudes.

Figure 9-6 This sign suggests that Dr. Holgdbrn may have become a specialist in narcissistic personalities from observing his own behavior.

SOURCE: Harley Schwadron.

series of women as he grew older. However, in each romance he would gradually lose interest after a short period and usually start an affair with another woman before breaking off with the first. He gave little thought to his former partner after breaking off each relationship. "It is almost as if people are playthings and I need lots and lots of new toys." His account of his life sounded as if he had never grieved or been depressed. (Adapted from Spitzer et al., 1983, pp. 71–74)

Table 9-7 lists characteristics frequently seen in narcissistic personality disorder. As with other personality disorders, all clinical features do not have to be present for the classification to be used. Rather, the characteristics in the table can be viewed as a prototype or composite of narcissistic disorders. The presence of more than half the features in a given case would justify use of the diagnosis.

The category of narcissistic personality disorder was introduced into DSM because mental health professionals were seeing an increase in cases in which the problem seemed to be excessive self-concern and an inflated sense of self-importance and uniqueness (see Figure 9-6). In addition, in recent years several psychoanalysts have focused on personal development in the early years of life, the development of the self as a separate entity, and narcissism as an aspect of self-development. Relatively little research has been done on the classification of narcissistic personality disorder.

Borderline Personality Disorder

Borderline personality disorder was officially recognized as a diagnosis in 1980. Since that time, the borderline category has been used so widely that 20% of psychiatric patients are given this diagnosis and it is estimated to occur in 3% to 5% of the general population (A. J. Frances & Widiger, 1986). About two-thirds of those with borderline personality disorder are female. A heterogeneous group of individuals receive this diagnosis, but they share a number of characteristics, including unstable personal relationships, threats of self-destructive behavior, a chronic range of cognitive distortions, fears of abandonment, and impulsivity.

Intense clinging dependency and manipulation characterize the interpersonal relationships of those with borderline personality disorder and make interaction with these people very difficult. They seem to wish for a dependent and exclusive relationship with another person. This desire for dependency is clear to outside observers but vehemently denied by the borderline individual. As a part of this vehement denial, such individuals devalue or discredit the strengths and personal significance of others. This often takes the form of extreme anger when the other person sets limits for the relationship or when a separation is about to occur. In addition to anger, the borderline individual uses manipulative behavior to control relationships, such as complaining about physical symptoms and making and carrying out self-destructive threats. Table 9-8 lists major clinical features of borderline personality disorder.

Self-destructive behaviors have been called "the behavioral specialty" of those with borderline personality

Table 9–8
Clinical Features of Borderline Personality Disorder

A person having at least five of these characteristics might be considered to have a borderline personality disorder.

1. Employment of frantic efforts to avoid real or imagined abandonment.
2. Unstable and intense interpersonal relationships.
3. Persistent and markedly disturbed, distorted, or unstable sense of self (e.g., a feeling that one doesn't exist or that one embodies evil).
4. Impulsiveness in such areas as sex, substance use, crime, and reckless driving.
5. Recurrent suicidal thoughts, gestures, or behavior.
6. Emotional instability, with periods of extreme depression, irritability, or anxiety.
7. Chronic feelings of emptiness.
8. Inappropriate intense anger or lack of control of anger (e.g., loss of temper, recurrent physical fights).
9. Transient, stress-related paranoid thoughts or severe dissociative symptoms.

Table 9–9
Total Number of Self-Destructive Acts Described by 57 People With Borderline Personality Disorder

Category	Number of Acts	Behavior Pattern
Suicide threats	42	To get attention; to cause trouble; in rage
Overdose	40	No usual pattern; barbiturates most frequent
Self-mutilation	36	Wrist-slashing most frequent; then body banging; then burning, puncturing, or hair removal
Drug abuse	38	Polydrug abuse most frequent; next amphetamines or alcohol binges; then marijuana
Promiscuity	36	Usually under the influence of drugs or alcohol
Accidents	14	Reckless driving

Source: Adapted from Gunderson, 1984, p. 86.

disorder. Table 9-9 shows the frequency of self-destructive acts in one group of borderline individuals. Overdosing with drugs and self-mutilation are common as are suicide threats. In recent years severe bulimia has become a common self-destructive tactic. Such behaviors are designed to call forth a "saving" response from another significant person. Persons with borderline personality disorder often are a continuing burden for the police and hospitals.

Self-destructiveness is the characteristic of borderline individuals that generates the most discomfort in those who attempt to help them. The therapist's hope of saving an endangered life is alternately encouraged and then dashed by the patient's spiteful efforts at self-destruction. Therapists often experience intense feelings of responsibility for borderline patients. The therapist's initial efforts to be supportive when the patient threatens suicide can lead to increased responsibility for the patient's life and increased involvement outside of the therapy sessions. Unless the controlling nature of the patient's responses are interpreted in the therapy sessions, the situation may become unworkable for the therapist. It is necessary to make the patient understand that the therapist cannot be manipulated by threats of suicide and that the patient must work to understand these self-destructive urges without acting them out. If this effort is not successful, the threats of self-destruction will recur, and the risk to the patient will be even greater if the therapist fails to respond on cue. This danger is illustrated by the following example.

A borderline patient periodically rented a motel room and, with a stockpile of pills nearby, would call her therapist's home with an urgent message. He would respond by engaging in long conversations in which he "talked her down." Even as he told her that she could not count on his always being available, he became more wary of going out evenings without detailed instructions about how he could be reached. One night the patient couldn't reach him due to a bad phone connection. She fatally overdosed from what was probably a miscalculated manipulation. (Gunderson, 1984, p. 93)

Their strong need for a relationship leads borderline persons to have chronic and long-lasting fears that the people on whom they are dependent will abandon them. These fears are related to the extreme panic they feel when alone. As a defense against this fear, borderline people are compulsively social. But despite this need for social interaction, many of their behaviors repel people. These include their intense anger and demands, their suspiciousness, and their impulsivity. They deal with stress by being sexually promiscuous, getting into fights, and binge eating and purging.

Marked emotional instability with sudden shifts to anxiety and continued depression or irritability—which may last only a few hours and never more than a few days—are typical of borderline personality disorder, as is illustrated in the following account by a patient:

"I was alone at home a few months ago; I was frightened! I was trying to get in touch with my boyfriend and I couldn't. . . . He was nowhere to be found. All my friends seemed to be busy that night and I had no one to talk to. . . . I just got more and more nervous and more and more agitated. Finally—bang!— I took out a cigarette and lit it and stuck it into my forearm. I don't know why I did it because I didn't really care for him all that much. I guess I felt I had to do something dramatic."
(Stone, 1980, p. 400)

Borderline individuals also show disturbance in their concepts of identity: they are uncertain about self-image, gender identity, values, loyalties, and goals. They may have chronic feelings of emptiness or boredom and be unable to tolerate being alone. The following anecdote illustrates the behavior of a borderline individual:

A 27-year-old woman was married and had two small children. She had had a stormy adolescence, having been forced into sexual relations with a brother six years her senior whom she at first idolized and later feared. Their relationship continued until just before she left home for college, when she told her parents of it. In the ensuing emotional turmoil, she made a gesture of suicide (overdose of aspirin) but was not hospitalized. . . . Outwardly flirtatious, although inwardly shy and ill at ease, she felt intensely lonely and went through a period of mild alcohol abuse and brief sexual affairs in an effort to cope with her anxiety and sense of inner emptiness. At age 19, she married a classmate and dropped out of school.

Fairly at ease in the first years of her marriage, she became anxious, bored, and given to fits of sadness and tearfulness after the birth of her second child. Her mood fluctuated widely from hour to hour, day to day, but negative feelings were greatly intensified on the three or four days before her period. Her husband had grown less attentive as the family expanded, in response to which she became increasingly irritable, provocative, and at times abusive (smashing plates, hurling insults). Her husband began to carry on an extramarital relationship, which she eventually discovered. At that point, she became seriously depressed, lost sleep and appetite, began to abuse alcohol and sedatives, and made several gestures of suicide, including one instance of cutting her wrist. On two occasions she hid for several nights in motels without informing anyone where she was. Each time she took her 8-year-old daughter with her, as though to protect her from the "designs" she imagined her husband had on their elder girl. After the wrist-cutting incident, when she had also left a note apologizing for being a "failure" as a wife and mother, she was hospitalized. She understood the unrealistic nature of her suspicions, as she explained to the hospital staff, but could not shake off the morbid doubts she experienced. (Stone, 1986, p. 210)

Distinguishing Borderlines From Other Groups The word *borderline* suggests a marginal level of functioning, something that borders on becoming something else. Originally the term was used to describe a marginal or milder form of schizophrenia. Today, some researchers argue that borderline patients actually represent the boundary between personality disorders and mood disorders. Indeed, about half of those with borderline personality disorder can also be diagnosed as having a mood disorder. Such individuals are also likely to have a family history of mood disorder. However, people with several other types of personality disorders are equally as likely to be depressed. Relatives of those with borderline personality disorder are more likely to share this diagnosis than are family members of those with other personality disorders—that is, the disorder seems to "breed true."

Despite the evidence obtained from family studies, some researchers have been unable to distinguish borderline disorder from histrionic personality disorder and antisocial personality disorder (Pope et al., 1983). Figure 9-7 shows the overlapping characteristics between borderline personality disorder and the other personality disorders in the same diagnostic cluster. Overlap may also occur with a personality disorder in another cluster. Sometimes patients who are diagnosed as borderline and those who are diagnosed as schizotypal seem similar. However, the schizotypal and borderline categories have different emphases. The schizotypal category stresses cognitive symptoms: suspicious thought and thinking that one has magical powers. The borderline category stresses affective, or emotional, symptoms: feelings of emotional instability, emptiness, boredom, and inappropriate and intense anger. Schizotypal individuals are socially isolated; in contrast, borderline individuals cannot stand being alone. Not only is there overlap between borderlines and other types of personality disorder, but there also is considerable comorbidity with Axis I disorders (Zimmerman & Mattia, 1999). For example, borderlines are much more likely than nonborderlines to have Axis I diagnoses of mood anxiety, eating, somatoform, and substance use disorders.

Research Into Causes of Borderline Personality Disorder Probably because of the relatively large number of cases diagnosed as borderline personality disorders, and also because borderline individuals are likely to make frequent suicidal gestures, more research on causes and treatment has been carried out with this disorder than with many of the other personality disorders. Most of the theories about its cause focus on a disturbed early relationship between a preborderline child and his or her parents. There are a variety of descriptions of what this relationship might be like (Gunderson & Zanarini, 1987). Some focus on the attachment experience in early childhood, while others point to parents who fail to provide adequate attention to the child's own feel-

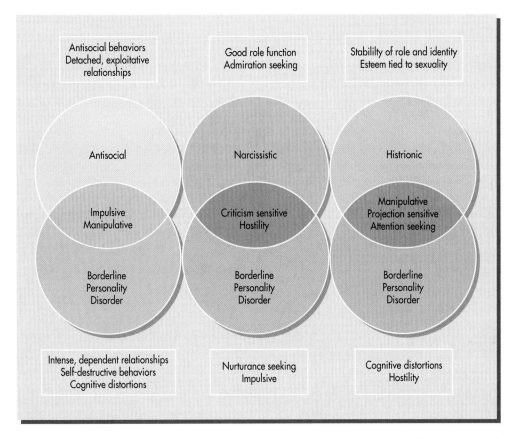

Figure 9-7   The borderline personality disorder has some characteristics that overlap with other personality disorders in the "Dramatic, Emotional, or Erratic Behavior" category. The similar characteristics are shown in the overlapping circle segments. Characteristics that are not shared are shown in the boxes above and below each overlapping segment.

SOURCE: Adapted from Gunderson and Zanarini (1987), "Current Overview of the Borderline Diagnosis." *Journal of Clinical Psychiatry,* 48(8) Supplement, p. 7.

ings so that he or she never develops an adequate sense of self. Some theorists focus on parental abuse (both sexual and physical) in adolescence, as well as on divorce, alcoholism, and other stressors (Linehan, 1987). It is clear from all these examples, however, that such stressors in the family occur often without children developing borderline personality disorder. This finding suggests that borderline disorder may be associated with some genetic vulnerability.

Intolerance of being alone is a frequently observed core problem of borderline personality disorder (Gunderson, 1996). There is no firm answer as to why this is so. Being alone may be intolerable to borderline patients because it is associated with a profound sense of being evil and evokes such intense feelings of guilt and shame that these patients often question their worthiness to live. Intolerance of being alone is a serious psychological deficit that may be an outgrowth of basic failures within the family, particularly those related to parent-child relationships. For whatever reason, the main problem may be the child's inability to see primary caretakers as consistently, reliably, durably available. Clearly there is a need for in-depth studies of the families of borderline patients. One study found that

adult borderline patients and their parents differed widely in their descriptions of what went on within the family when the patients were growing up (Gunderson, 1996). The patients were much more negative in their descriptions than were their parents.

Borderline personality disorder probably develops through a combination of neurobiological, early developmental, and later socializing factors. **Splitting** is Otto Kernberg's (1975) theoretical explanation of the extreme changeability that can be seen in the borderline person's relationships to others. He defined splitting as the failure to integrate the positive and negative experiences that occur between the individual and other people. Rather than perceiving another individual as a loving person who sometimes accepts and sometimes rejects—for example, a mother who sometimes hugs and sometimes disciplines a young child—the borderline individual shifts back and forth between these contradictory images.

Clinical Treatment of Borderline Personality Disorder

A first step in planning treatment for any disorder is to identify its most distinctive features. There seem to be three especially important problems in cases of borderline personality disorder (Hurt & Clarkin, 1990):

1. *Identity disturbances*, reflected in borderline individuals' chronic feelings of emptiness or boredom and their intolerance of being alone. These people have a strong need for involvement with others and a reliance on external support for self-definition.
2. *Affective disturbances*, reflected in their intense, inappropriate anger, emotional instability, and unstable interpersonal relationships. Borderline individuals often lead stormy, dramatic lives.
3. *Impulse disturbances*, reflected in their self-damaging acts and impulsive behaviors.

Various therapeutic approaches deal with these core issues in different ways. Psychodynamically oriented clinicians believe that most borderline individuals can best be treated in intensive face-to-face psychotherapy sessions at least three times a week over a period of several years. In these sessions the therapist plays a more active structuring role than is usual in classical psychoanalysis. At the beginning the emphasis is on present behavior rather than childhood experiences, and rather than allowing the transference relationship to develop fully, the therapist explicitly describes and discusses the patient's apparent distortions of reality—for example, the patient's perceptions of the therapist.

Therapists differ in the importance they attach to going beyond the here and now of the borderline patient's life to explore traumatic childhood relationships. Some clinicians believe there is no convincing evidence that therapies focused on eliciting histories of trauma are effective (Paris, 1995). Indeed, according to one school of thought, borderlines, like people with other personality disorders, seek therapy because of their desire for relief but unconsciously avoid, evade, or undermine therapeutic programs (Strand & Benjamin, 1997). Decisions about therapeutic approaches to borderline patients need to be informed by research that identifies factors in the present and past lives of these patients that are linked to their current problems.

Although psychoanalysts were among the first clinicians to describe and treat borderline personalities, clinicians of several theoretical perspectives are now developing therapies for these people. Cognitively oriented therapists focus on the borderline individual's limitations in three areas: automatic thoughts, cognitive distortions, and unrealistic underlying assumptions (e.g., that people are either all good or all bad). Cognitive therapy thus concentrates on identifying and changing cognitions so as to permit better reality testing. Behavior therapists direct attention elsewhere, to the borderline person's defective behavioral repertoire. They try to teach patients better social skills and to help them manage their anxiety so as to not become overwhelmed with affective reactions. Biologically oriented clinicians make use of various types of medication in treating borderline individuals. In general, medication alone is mildly effective, with patients perhaps improving from severely to moderately impaired. Combinations of several therapeutic approaches may prove to be particularly effective. For example, medication together with psychotherapy and family support could be useful in dealing with the borderline persona's multiple problems. Further research is needed in developing therapeutic approaches that will help these unstable people, who lead such chaotic lives (see Box 9-2).

Long-Term Prospects for Borderline Individuals It was originally thought that because of their depressive and sometimes psychoticlike symptoms, borderline individuals would eventually develop a traditional illness such as schizophrenia or a major mood disorder. However, several follow-up studies show that this rarely happens; instead, borderline personality disorder tends to remain roughly the same over time (Plakun et al., 1985).

Follow-up studies of borderline individuals show that their unstable relationships, poor work performance, and symptom levels usually continue relatively unchanged. However, long term follow-ups found that borderline individuals of a high socioeconomic level who had received intensive treatment improved in their interpersonal relationships after their young adult years and had a fairly good chance of full time employment (Stone et al., 1987). About a third of these borderline patients eventually marry and establish their own families. However, the range of outcomes is wide, and many of those with borderline personality disorder continue to have severe interpersonal and occupational problems. One negative outcome is suicide. Probably 8% to 10% of borderline individuals actually kill themselves, although this figure is small compared to the number of suicide attempts by people with this diagnosis. Another frequent negative outcome is alcohol abuse.

Antisocial Personality Disorder

Antisocial personality disorder is associated with crime, violence, and delinquency occurring after the age of 15. This diagnosis is not given until age 18; however, its essential characteristics include a history of continuous and chronic conduct disorder in the period before the age of 15. After the age of 15, the individual must have shown a pervasive pattern indicating disregard for the rights of others and violations of those rights. Such behaviors must include at least three of the types of actions

Research Close-up   Box 9-2

Does Dialectical Behavior Therapy Help Patients with Borderline Personality Disorder?

Given the complexities of borderline personality disorder, it would not be surprising if a treatment approach incorporating elements of several of the traditional therapies were needed to help people with this condition. Marsha Linehan (1993) has developed a new approach, called *dialectical behavior therapy (DBT)*, that builds on a variety of cognitive, behavioral, and psychodynamic concepts. The word *dialectical* describes the contradictions that dominate the borderline person's thinking and the need for him or her to learn that human relationships are not just a matter of love or hate and that there is a middle ground.

Linehan's approach is aimed particularly at the suicidal threats, gestures, and attempts seen in many borderline individuals. This approach uses a combined format of individual and group psychotherapy that is time-limited (usually to 1 year) and makes explicit what the patient's, as well as what the therapist's, responsibilities are (e.g., the patient's missing four sessions of group or individual therapy in a row results in termination of the treatment). Linehan's therapy is active in that she deals directly, and early, with several key issues in the lives of the borderline individual—for example, coping with anger and impulses toward self-destructive behavior. Therapeutic sessions provide patients with opportunities to learn ways of tolerating and expressing distressing emotions. Emphasis in therapy is placed on the patient's acquiring a better understanding of her or his vulnerabilities and strengths, developing more reasonable expectations regarding other people, and improving stress-coping skills.

Dialectical behavior therapy has three stages. In the first, the therapist focuses on reducing the most dysfunctional and out-of-control aspects of the patient's current life (such as suicide attempts and self-injury). In pursuit of that objective, emphasis is placed on the patient's learning alternatives to the extreme thoughts and behaviors that are causing the current problems. The second stage explores past traumatic experiences associated with maladaptive processing of emotional ties. In the third stage, patients are encouraged to value themselves more than they have in the past and to have more confidence in themselves.

Linehan has asked two questions that are pertinent to therapy in general and her own approach in particular: (1) What is the theory behind the therapy? and (2) Does the therapy work? She describes her therapy in the following way:

Many borderline patients react to themselves with extreme loathing, bordering on self-hate. All but a few feel enormous shame in general, and shame about their own abuse history, the troubles they have caused, and their present emotional reactivity in particular. Cherishing oneself is the opposite of these emotional reactions. Thus, the therapist must target the self-hate, the self-blame, and the sense of shame. Although work on this target is a lifelong process, substantial progress should be made before therapy ends.

One thing the therapist must be especially careful to do before therapy ends is to reinforce patient self-respect that is independent of the therapist. That is, the therapist must ultimately pull back and

relentlessly reinforce within the therapeutic relationship self-validation, self-care, self-soothing, and problem-solving without reference to the therapist. I hasten to add, however, that this stance does not suggest that patients should learn to be independent of all people. Interpersonal dependence, asking for and accepting nurturing, soothing, and active assistance from others are crucial for most people's well-being. . . .

My patients often ask me whether they will ever get better, whether they will ever be happy. It is a difficult question to answer. Surely they can get better and happier than they are when they first come to see me. And, yes, I believe that life can be worth living even for a person who has at one time met criteria for BPD. I am less certain, however, whether anyone can ever completely overcome the effects of the extremely abusive environments many of my patients have experienced. . . . The relationship with the therapist may be the best one an individual ever finds—not necessarily because of deficiencies on her part, but because the ability of our society to provide community and companionship is limited, even for many of its best members. (Linehan, 1993, pp. 160, 461).

Although research on DBT is in its early stages, results to date seem promising. One study followed patients during treatment that lasted 1 year and comparable patients receiving therapies other than DBT. The DBT patients were less likely to drop out of therapy and less likely to make suicidal threats and gestures (Linehan et al., 1991). A later study did follow-ups a year after completion of treatment and also found a reduction of suicidal threats and gestures (Linehan, et al., 1993). A more recent study found that DBT reduced patients' anger levels and increased their social competence (Linehan et al., 1994).

---

listed in Table 9-10. Convicted murderer Gary Gilmore fits this description well (see Box 9-3).

Although Gary Gilmore's antisocial traits may have led him to commit crimes, it is important to distinguish between criminal or aggressive behavior and antisocial personality disorder.

From the standpoint of abnormal psychology, the defining properties of antisocial personalities are not so much

the particular acts they perform (e.g., robbing a bank or shoplifting) as their distinctive, deeply ingrained approach to life. They always seem to be participating in a game in which other individuals exist as pieces to be manipulated and utilized, and it is this game-playing that leads these people to get into trouble with the law. At their worst, people with antisocial personality disorder can be cruel, sadistic, and violent. They seldom show anxiety and don't

Case Study

Box 9–3

Antisocial Personality Disorder

The case of Gary Gilmore (Figure 9-8) illustrates many characteristics of antisocial personality disorder. While Gilmore experienced short-term distress when things did not go well, the distress usually concerned "How can I get out of this fix?" rather than any long-term personal anxieties, fears, or worries.

Gilmore was convicted of two murders and sentenced to death. When he was executed in 1977, he was the first person to be put to death in the United States in 11 years. Although he refused to appeal his conviction, several appeals were made on his behalf and his execution was delayed three times. During this period, while newspapers featured stories on his

Figure 9-8   Gary Gilmore in 1977.

"fight for the right to be executed," he attempted suicide twice.

Gilmore reported that he had begun drinking at the age of 10 and later had used a variety of illegal drugs—amphetamines, cocaine, and LSD. He displayed an antisocial personality pattern very early. In spite of his high intelligence, his school grades were poor, he was often truant, and he was repeatedly accused of stealing from his schoolmates. At age 14 he was sent to a juvenile center for stealing a car; after his release he was sent to jail several times for burglaries; and at age 20 he was sent to the state penitentiary for burglary and robbery.

It seems like things have always gone bad for me. It seems like I've always done dumb things that just caused trouble for me. I remember when I was a boy I would feel like I had to do things like sit on a railroad track until just before the train came and then I would dash off. Or I would put my finger over the end of a BB gun and pull the trigger to see if a BB was really in it. Sometimes I would stick my finger in water and then put my finger in a light socket to see if it would really shock me. (cited in Spitzer et al., 1983, p. 68)

Gilmore was evaluated to determine whether he was competent to stand trial. His IQ was found to be 129, in the superior range. His general knowledge was surprisingly good for someone with so little education. He was proud of his vocabulary and read both fiction and news magazines avidly. There was no indication of any organic problems. He reported no bizarre or unusual thoughts except when on drugs.

Personality tests revealed no thought or mood disturbances. He slept soundly, had a good appetite, and was not depressed or worried. "I almost never get blue. Though I've made a mess of my life, I never stew about the things I have done."

Gilmore showed the characteristic behaviors of an antisocial personality. He disobeyed rules at home and at school, drank, and used illegal drugs at an early age. By 14 he had been arrested for car theft. While he was in prison he was known for his cruel and violent behavior. He seemed to lack sympathy and felt no guilt. He never had a steady job or a long-lasting relationship.

Although Gary Gilmore shared some of his early experiences with professionals who interviewed him, he said very little about his early life in terms of family relationships. This appeared to be an area he was reluctant to discuss or even think about. Seventeen years after Gary Gilmore's death, his younger brother, Mikal Gilmore, a professional writer and columnist, wrote a book in which he discussed some of the Gilmores' family life and provided some clues that might help to understand Gary's behavior (Gilmore, 1994). Mikal Gilmore described a family in which violence and child abuse were daily occurrences, a family in which the children lived in fear of the consequences of their misdeeds and experienced both physical punishment and extreme psychological mistreatment at the hands of their father. Mikal makes the point in his book that these events were never discussed in the family and that he, himself, felt he could not be free of their influence until he had confronted them by writing the family story, which ended in the violent deaths of his father and both of his brothers.

feel guilt. Freudians would maintain that the mind of the antisocial personality is totally lacking the "moral police officer" role of the superego. Antisocial personalities do not see themselves as the cause of their problems; instead, they see the tough spots they find themselves in as due to flaws in other people. Despite their frequent violation of the rights of others, many individuals with antisocial personality disorder do not have criminal records. A large community-based epidemiological survey found that more than half the people whose histories caused them to be classified as having antisocial personality disorder did not

have a significant history of arrests, despite continuous and chronic antisocial behavior (Robins & Regier, 1991). Such people were also unlikely to have sought help in traditional clinical settings except under circumstances when it seemed to them that seeking help would enable them to avoid legal consequences arising from their actions.

The case of Bert is not as dramatic as that of Gary Gilmore, but is representative of many people who are diagnosed as having an antisocial personality disorder yet who never come in contact with the law—or, if they do, are not convicted of a crime. These people treat others

Table 9-10
Clinical Features of Antisocial Personality Disorder

A person having at least three of these characteristics might be considered to have an antisocial personality disorder. If he or she is at least 18 years old and has shown evidence of conduct disorder before age 15.

1. Failure to conform to social norms (violating laws).
2. Deceitfulness; manipulativeness.
3. Impulsivity; failure to plan ahead.
4. Irritability, aggressiveness.
5. Reckless disregard for the safety of self or others.
6. Consistent irresponsibility.
7. Lack of remorse after having hurt, mistreated, or stolen from another person.

Table 9-11	
Characteristics of Subjects Interviewed by Widom[a]	
Characteristic	Percentage of Subjects
Arrest records:	
Detained	18
Arrested as an adult	64
Convicted as an adult	18
Incarceration:	
As a juvenile	11
As an adult	32
Psychiatric hospitalization:	
Hospitalized at some time	21
Treated as an outpatient only	46
Suicide attempts	29
Number with both psychiatric and arrest records	46
Parental separation:	
Broken homes	21
Divorce	7
Parental psychopathology	7
Parental alcoholism	18

[a]The subjects averaged 25 years of age (from 19 to 47 years old). All except one were White.
Source: Widom (1978).

callously, without any apparent concern. They seem to feel no guilt, even at harming those closest to them. The excitement of taking chances and manipulating others seem to be their prime motivators. They either lack an ability to foresee consequences or they consider the consequences unimportant.

After graduating from high school and having a few dead-end jobs, Bert wanted to go into business for himself. He asked his parents, who had a modest income and some savings for their retirement, to lend him the money he needed to get started. Within five months, Bert was out of business, his parents' money "lost," as he put it. Several months later, having found a new business opportunity, Bert again pleaded with his parents to lend him the money he needed. They agreed, and again Bert's opportunity fizzled. His parents desperately wanted to help Bert and to believe in him. So great was their need and so successful was Bert in "conning" his parents that they repeatedly helped him engage in activities that were doomed to failure. Bert craved the excitement of going into business for himself, but was unable either to attend to all the details involved in running a business or to plan ahead. He was magnificent in playing the role of the charming young man on the way up. When he failed, he felt no regrets concerning his failure's implications for his parents and others who had helped him.

Research Into Causes of Antisocial Personality Disorder Researchers of antisocial personality disorder have been hampered by the fact that it is much easier to identify antisocial personalities among individuals who have been convicted of crimes than among the general population. Consequently, the group on which research is based may not be typical of all people with an antisocial personality disorder. One researcher approached this methodological problem in a unique way—she inserted the following ad in a Boston counterculture newspaper:

> Wanted: charming, aggressive, carefree people who are impulsively irresponsible but are good at handling people and at looking after number one. Send name, address, phone, and short biography proving how interesting you are to . . . (Widom, 1978, p. 72) ■

Widom's ad drew 73 responses, of which about two-thirds were from males. About one-third of the respondents seemed to meet the criteria for a diagnosis of antisocial personality disorder. The respondents were interviewed and given a battery of psychological tests. Some of the characteristics of the group are shown in Table 9-11. The researcher concluded that the main difference between her sample and prison samples was that the people who answered her ad had somehow been able to avoid conviction after arrest or detention by the police. In other respects they seemed very similar to prison inmates.

Researchers have looked at many aspects of antisocial individuals—their life histories, psychological and physiological functioning, and personality characteristics—in order to understand why these people behave as they do. The biological perspective has yielded a number of interesting findings. There is increasing evidence that heredity may play a role in both criminality and antisocial behavior (Gottesman & Goldsmith, 1994; Lykken, 1995). A Swedish study revealed that adopted children who were separated at birth from biological parents meeting the criteria for antisocial personality disorder showed more antisocial behavior later in life than control subjects (Bohman et al., 1982).

How antisocial behavior might be inherited is not yet clear. Researchers have connected habitually violent and antisocial tendencies with neurochemistry. Impulsive physical violence and aggression in humans is related to very low levels of one of the neurotransmitters, serotonin, and one of its metabolites in the spinal fluid (Virkkunen, 1983). Other research has focused on patterns of brain wave activity. For example, some researchers have demonstrated a relationship between one type of electrical brain activity, slow alpha waves, and later antisocial behavior (Volavka, 1990). In normal individuals, alpha-wave frequency is known to decrease with relaxation and drowsiness and to increase with tension, so the slow alpha waves suggest that some antisocial individuals have a lower-than-normal arousal level. This may mean that sensory inputs that would be disturbing to most people are not strong enough to excite antisocial individuals. Such people may crave increased stimulation and may therefore seek out unusual forms of excitement. The brain wave patterns found in people who fit the criteria of antisocial personality disorder have some resemblance to those that occur normally in children and adolescents rather than those of adults. This similarity suggests that at least one subgroup of people with this disorder may have delayed cerebral maturation (Reid, 1986).

Another physiological factor—anxiety—has been studied in antisocial individuals. It had seemed reasonable to assume that people who met the criteria for antisocial personality disorder would also show little anxiety compared to other individuals. But this assumption may be true only in a limited sense. Schalling (1978) found that while antisocial personalities seem to worry less than other people, they nevertheless experience all of the common somatic and muscular indicators of anxiety (high heart rate, shortness of breath, tense muscles). If we divide anxiety into its cognitive part—worry—and its physiological components—the body's responses to fear—antisocial individuals seem to lack the cognitive component of anxiety.

From a cognitive perspective, the study of antisocial behavior focuses on moral development (Kegan, 1986). Just as in the case of psychophysiological factors, the idea of a delay in moral development has been suggested. Between the ages of 7 and 11, normal children can tell when someone else treats them unfairly. If they have been treated unfairly in the past, when an opportunity arises they will "make up" for the past unfairness by striking back when someone else is vulnerable. For example, after being teased for being the shortest player on the peewee basketball team and then growing several inches, instead of feeling empathy for smaller kids a child may think, "Now it's my turn," not "I'll treat younger kids differently."

A new morality normally begins to develop at about the age of 13. Then children think about the fairness of their own actions rather than concentrating on getting even. Cognitive theorists describe this as the development of the ability to reason in abstract terms and to understand the concept of partnership. From this point of view, those with antisocial personality disorder are developmentally arrested at the 7- to 11-year-old level because they are not concerned about the effects of their behavior on others.

In general, antisocial personality disorder cannot be explained simply by social class, bad associates, membership in a deviant subgroup, residence in a high-crime neighborhood, or brain damage. However, there is evidence that abused and/or neglected children are at greater risk of being diagnosed as having antisocial personality disorder when they are adults (Luntz & Widom, 1994). Childhood victimization may be a significant predictor of antisocial personality disorder symptoms. In all likelihood, an adequate explanation of antisocial personality disorder will require approaches that simultaneously examine environmental, physiological, genetic, and temperamental variables.

Clinical Treatment of Antisocial Personality Disorder

The following excerpt from a therapy session with 29-year-old Brett illustrates some of the important features of antisocial personality disorder. For most of his late adolescence and early adult life, Brett had frequently schemed to cheat "the system" and to take what he wanted without paying for it. He used this approach not so much from lack of money as for the excitement and pleasure that resulted when he was successful. Notice how the cognitively oriented therapist deftly tries to get Brett to think about costs associated with "beating the system."

Therapist: How well has the "beat-the-system" approach actually worked out for you over time?

Brett: It works great . . . until someone catches on or starts to catch on. Then you have to scrap that plan and come up with a new one.

Therapist: How difficult was it, you know, to cover up one scheme and come up with a new one?

Brett: Sometimes it was really easy. There are some real pigeons out there.

Therapist: Was it always easy?

Brett: Well, no. Sometimes it was a real bitch. Like beating the phone system. That really ended up in a big hassle. There was really no way to cover it up, and everyone gave me such a hard time.

Therapist: Was it very easy to come up with an alternative plan?

Brett: Not for the phones. I never did come up with another plan.

Therapist: How about at other times? Did beat-the-system plans come to you very easily—I mean, ones that actually worked?

Brett: Well, I came up with lots of good ones, but it was tough coming up with something that would really pay off.

Therapist: Did a good plan last a long time, or were new ones frequently required?

Brett: Seems like I'm always needing a good plan to beat the system.

Therapist: Do you think it's ever easier to go with the system instead of trying to beat it in some way?

Brett: Well, after all that I have been through, I would have to say yes, there have been times that going with the system would have been easier in the long run. By the time I'm done paying legal fees, I will have shelled out more than my tuition would ever have cost me. But . . . it's such a challenge to beat the system. It feels exciting when I come up with a new plan and think I can make it work. Going with the system might not even occur to me.

(A. T. Beck, Freeman, and Associates, 1990, p. 171)

The following excerpt from an interview with a person diagnosed with antisocial personality disorder illustrates the sensitivity with which clinicians must approach aspects of a patient's life that the individual might prefer not to admit to or discuss. In this case, the clinician needs to inquire into the patient's fighting. Does he get into fights because he lives in a violent neighborhood, or is he frequently the instigator?

Clinician: Do some of them try to hassle you?

Patient: Yeah sure, but that's all part of the game.

Clinician: Have any of them tried to push you around?

Patient: Yeah, a couple of them but I set them straight.

Clinician: How do you mean?

Patient: I kicked their asses.

Clinician: Well, you look like you're in pretty good shape. I imagine you can take care of yourself pretty well. What about in the past, what types of fights have you been in?

Patient: Oh, I been in a few now and then. People know not to mess with me. I grew up in a tough neighborhood and you had to know how to fight to survive.

Clinician: When you were fairly young, let's say between the ages of say 15 and 25, how many fights do you think you were in, 20, 30?

Patient: I'm bad but not that bad . . . oh, let's see, maybe about 15, who knows, it could have been as high as 20.

Clinician: Did you ever get hurt?

Patient: Nah, not really, but I did a number on a few of those guys.

Clinician: Did you ever put anyone in the hospital?

Patient: Yeah, there was one dude that I cut up pretty good, but he really deserved it, trust me.

Clinician: Earlier you told me that you drank a fair amount in the past but have completely stopped now, which you deserve a lot of credit for. Back when you were drinking, did you sometimes feel on edge, almost like you needed a good fight, so you went looking for one, perhaps the alcohol making it a little more difficult to control your anger?

Patient: Sometimes, yeah, sometimes . . . especially if I was pretty strung out, I would be just plain nasty, and I started my fair share of fights. But usually I was just protecting myself or the guy really had it coming to him.

Clinician: It certainly sounds like you know how to handle yourself in a fight. Did you use to run in a gang, or how did you learn how to defend yourself so well?

Patient: Like I said, where I grew up you had to learn how to fight, and I did hang out with a gang for a couple of years.

(Shea, 1998, pp. 405–406)

In this interview, the clinician discovers that while the patient comes from a tough neighborhood, he is a frequent instigator of fights. The clinician enters the potentially loaded topic of fighting by asking, "Do some of them try to hassle you?"—referring to the patient's fellow residents at a drug rehabilitation center. Asking the question in this way enables the topic of fighting to be brought up without attributing blame to the patient. Once the patient is talking freely about fights, the clinician focuses on his history of fights and his role in them. Had the clinician prematurely asked, "Do you pick a lot of fights?" he probably would have gotten a defensive answer. The clinician skillfully compliments the patient ("Well, you look like you're in pretty good shape . . .") and makes it easy for the patient to admit to fighting by associating it with the use of alcohol. This approach not only provides needed diagnostic information, but also helps the clinician build a working relationship with the patient.

People with antisocial personality disorder are not usually helped by traditional methods of psychotherapy. Their lack of empathy and social responsibility are major deterrents to establishing therapeutic rapport and commitment to change. The antisocial patient may at times experience a greater investment in outwitting the therapist than in effecting positive changes. Whenever possible, the therapist tries to raise questions in the patient's mind about beliefs that might result in antisocial behavior and negative outcomes—for example, the idea that wanting something or wanting to avoid something justifies a particular course of action.

A correctional facility or other type of highly structured, well-controlled setting may be the only means of managing some antisocial patients. An effective residential treatment center forces antisocial personalities to stay for months or years in a program with rigid rules so firm that they cannot talk their way out. In such a situation, the participants initially become depressed because they are forced to face their lack of inner feelings and their inability to establish meaningful relationships with others. The major goals of such programs are to increase the patients' ability to feel emotions, to encourage them to think constructively about the future and to trust other people, and to help them develop empathy. These programs emphasize **milieu therapy,** an approach in which all the staff work together to provide consistent support and long-term stable relationships.

Another type of program has similar goals but can be carried out in the community. A judge may offer young male first offenders, or other men who are good prospects for improvement, such programs as an alternative to prison. The offender is required to begin schooling or a job immediately and to remain in an unlocked treatment center when not in school or at work. Gradually he is given more physical freedom. Throughout the program he is also expected to be responsible for his behavior and that of others in the program. He is also expected to repay his victims for their losses and to pay for his living expenses. If he fails in the program, his alternative sentence, prison, immediately takes effect. Many people with antisocial personalities find this type of program very stressful. Often as many as 50% drop out and return to prison. For those who do successfully complete the program, however, the rearrest rate has been significantly lower than the rate for similar people from traditional prison or halfway house settings.

All in all, the development of treatment, for and rehabilitation of antisocial personalities have been discouraging. However, conduct problems in children have been shown to be highly predictive of later antisocial behavior (Lynam, 1996). A current focus of research is the development of practical prevention programs focused on such at-risk children. As yet, reliably effective interventions have not been developed.

Anxious or Fearful Behavior

Disorders in this group share many characteristics with the personality disorders already described. What sets them apart is that each of these disorders has a prominent component of anxiety or fear.

Avoidant Personality Disorder

Avoidant personality disorder is characterized by low self-esteem, fear of negative evaluation, and pervasive behavioral, emotional, and cognitive avoidance of social interaction. In therapy, avoidant personalities express a desire for affection, acceptance, and friendship; yet frequently they have few friends and share little intimacy with anyone. Fear of rejection plays a key role in influencing these people to keep away from personal attachments. They won't enter into a relationship unless the other person provides unusually strong guarantees of uncritical acceptance. Table 9-12 lists clinical features of this disorder.

The seclusiveness of avoidant personalities differs from that of people with schizoid personality disorder because, unlike the latter group, avoidant people do want to enter into relationships. The conflict they feel is over wanting affection and, at the same time, doubting their acceptance by others. They cannot seem to rid themselves of the belief that any overtures of friendship will end in pain and disillusionment. They are caught between wanting human contact and dreading it. People with avoidant personality disorder seem timid and withdrawn, and perhaps also cold and strange, to those who have superficial contact with them. However, to those who know them well, they appear anxious and extremely sensitive. Some of these feelings come from doubts about their own competence.

One coping mechanism that those with avoidant personality disorder are likely to use is hypervigilance. They continuously assess all their human contacts for signs of deception, humiliation, and negative reactions. As a result, they are able to detect the most minute traces of indifference or annoyance. They make mountains out of molehills. This technique of constantly scanning the environment is a self-defeating one, however, because it increases the likelihood that they will pick up just the

---

Table 9-12

Clinical Features of Avoidant Personality Disorder

A person having at least four of these characteristics might be considered to have an avoidant personality disorder.

1. Anticipates and worries about being rejected or criticized in social situations.
2. Has few friends, despite the desire for them.
3. Is unwilling to get involved with people unless certain of being liked.
4. Avoids social or occupational activities that involve significant interpersonal contact.
5. Inhibits development of intimate relationships (despite wishing for them) because of fear of seeming foolish, being ridiculed, and feeling shamed.
6. Possesses low self-worth because of self-perceived social ineptness and lack of personally appealing qualities.
7. Is unusually reluctant to engage in new situations or activities for fear of embarrassment.

kind of negative response they expect. In addition, their nervousness can result in making their companions uncomfortable, which can further damage the quality of their relationships with others.

Another maneuver that avoidant personalities use is to narrow their range of activities in order to cut off upsetting stimuli. Someone with an avoidant personality disorder may patronize only a small number of shops and restaurants so as to avoid encountering unfamiliar people and situations, or may even avoid shopping and other everyday activities because they seem too tiring or uncomfortable. Such people may also exaggerate the potential dangers of certain situations; for example, they may refuse to ride on buses or trains even though others do not doubt their safety. The lives of people with avoidant personality disorders are controlled by fear of looking foolish or being embarrassed. One unfortunate consequence of this retreat from contact with others and from new experiences is that it gives these individuals more time to be preoccupied with their own thoughts and to relive earlier painful experiences. The retreat also inhibits the development of social skills that might provide increased feelings of self-efficacy in dealing with interpersonal situations. Both these factors lead to a vicious cycle that makes new social contacts harder.

Avoidant personality disorder was added to the official DSM classification system in 1980. As yet little research has been done that gives insight into its causes or the most effective treatment approaches. One question concerning this disorder has to do with how it is discriminated from social phobia (discussed in Chapter 7). One study compared individuals with social phobia and those diagnosed as avoidant personality disorder as they performed in a social role-play test and gave a speech (Turner et al., 1986). Although the two groups reported equal levels of anxiety and similar anxious thoughts, those patients diagnosed as avoidant personality showed poorer social skills than those with social phobia. Further research is needed to evaluate overlaps between avoidant personality disorder and other classifications.

Dependent Personality Disorder

People with **dependent personality disorder** have two basic characteristics. First, they passively allow other people to make all the important decisions in their lives because they lack confidence and feel that they are unable to function independently. Second, to ensure that they will not lose this dependent position, such people subordinate their own needs to the needs and demands of others. Dependent personalities fear separation and have an excessive need to be taken care of. As a consequence, they are submissive and clinging.

Dependent individuals try to make themselves so pleasing that no one could possibly wish to abandon them. If left on their own, they feel empty, extremely anxious, and unable to function. They may feel anxiety even when the dependent relationship is intact because of the pervasive worry that the dominant figure might be lost in some way—for example, through death or divorce. Table 9-13 lists the clinical features of dependent personality disorder.

Dependent individuals feel that they must act meek and obedient in order to hold on to other people. They also behave affectionately and admiringly toward their protectors. In many cases this behavior functions as a coping technique. The dominant partner will then feel useful, strong, and competent and will want to encourage the relationship. Sometimes, however, things go wrong. The dominant individual may tire of the constant need to demonstrate affection and support and may behave abusively or seek to be rid of the leechlike attachment of the dependent partner.

There is evidence that, despite their efforts at ingratiation, individuals with dependent personalities have difficulties in the area of social behavior (Overholser, 1996). They may be trying hard to gain the support, direction, and nurturance they desire from other people.

The following case is an example of a dependent personality. The subject has allowed his mother to make the

---

Table 9-13

Clinical Features of Dependent Personality Disorder

A person having at least five of these characteristics might be considered to have a dependent personality disorder.

1. Is unable to make everyday decisions without excessive advice and reassurance from others.
2. Allows or encourages others to make their own important life decisions (e.g., whether to get married, where to live, whether to have children).
3. Has difficulty expressing disagreement with others because of fear of their anger or loss of support.
4. Has difficulty independently initiating activities because of lack of confidence in personal judgment or abilities.
5. Goes to excessive lengths to obtain nurturance and support from others.
6. Feels uncomfortable or helpless when alone because of exaggerated fears of inability to care for himself or herself.
7. Indiscriminately seeks another relationship to provide nurturing and support when a close relationship ends.
8. Is frequently preoccupied with fears of being left to care for himself or herself.

important decision as to whether he should marry his girlfriend.

Matthew is a 34-year-old single man who lives with his mother and works as an accountant. He sought treatment because he was very unhappy after having just broken up with his girlfriend. His mother had disapproved of his marriage plans, ostensibly because the woman was of a different religion. Matthew felt trapped and forced to choose between his mother and his girlfriend, and since "blood is thicker than water," he had decided not to go against his mother's wishes. Nonetheless, he was angry at himself and at his mother, and believed that she would never let him marry and was possessively hanging on to him. His mother "wore the pants" in the family and was a very domineering woman who was used to getting her way. Matthew was afraid of her and criticized himself for being weak, but also admired his mother and respected her judgment. "Maybe Carol wasn't right for me after all." He alternated between resentment and a "Mother knows best" attitude. He felt that his own judgment was poor. (Adapted from Spitzer et al., 1989, pp. 123–124)

The causes of dependent personality disorders are unclear. One suggestion is that dependent individuals had overprotective parents who made life so easy for them as children that they never learned coping skills. Other theorists have suggested that dependent children were insecurely attached to their mothers or other caregivers or did not have close and trusting relationships with others during childhood. So far both of these ideas are interesting but untested hypotheses.

Although there have been a number of discussions of dependent personality disorder as a clinical problem, much-needed empirical information has been lacking. However, one study examined a large sample of hospitalized individuals with this diagnosis in order to obtain basic data about their background and comorbidity (Loranger, 1996). The majority were women over 40 years of age, much older than patients with other personality disorders. In addition, the dependent patients were more likely to have Axis I diagnoses in the area of depression than those with other personality disorders. Further research will be needed to determine whether this picture also applies to outpatients.

As with avoidant personalities, assertiveness training may be useful in treating dependent people. It may be difficult to convince these individuals that their coping styles need to be changed; sometimes consciousness-raising therapy groups are used before direct treatment is attempted.

As with other personality disorders we have discussed, more research is needed on this disorder's overlap with other conditions, its causes, and effective treatment strategies. Working with clients who have dependent personality disorders can be rewarding to the therapist when they develop the ability to function independently, but reaching that point can be difficult and frustrating. Many

dependent people revel in the early stages of therapy. Then, at some point, they come to the realization that therapy isn't a passive experience. They begin to understand that therapy isn't just a matter of someone (the therapist) showing an interest in them. What happens then can be a turning point in therapy—or the therapy can turn into a dead end.

Obsessive–Compulsive Personality Disorder

Obsessive-compulsive personality disorder is similar to obsessive-compulsive anxiety disorder (discussed in Chapter 7), but the two disorders are believed to be different. People with obsessive-compulsive personality disorder are rigid and restricted in their behavior, but they do not show obsessional thinking that seems to force itself into consciousness, nor do they engage in the kinds of irrational rituals that are performed by people with obsessive-compulsive anxiety disorder. People with the anxiety disorder see their behavior as nonadaptive and distressing, but they cannot stop behaving that way. People with a personality disorder, on the other hand, usually exhibit behavior that is rigid and nonadaptive, but they feel this behavior is under their control. More research is needed on the degree of overlap between Axis I obsessive-compulsive anxiety disorder and Axis II obsessive-compulsive personality disorder (Diaferia et al., 1997).

Compulsive people have been described as "living machines" (Reich, 1933/1949). As one patient put it, his life was like "a train that was running efficiently, fast, pulling a substantial load, but on a track laid out for it" (Shapiro, 1965). An obsessive-compulsive personality disorder has several characteristics. One is lack of ability to express many warm and tender emotions. Instead, a person with this disorder seems stiff, formal, and unusually serious. Such an individual is likely to be overly conscientious and inflexible about matters of morality. Extreme perfectionism is also a problem because it focuses on small details, lists, and rule-making rather than on getting the job done. This rigidity leads to an inability to grasp the "big picture." For instance, in the following example, two friends are discussing a house that K is interested in buying. L shows his rigidity in not really listening to what K says but going by his own "rule of house ownership."

K: *So you think I shouldn't buy it?*

L: *Never buy a house with a bad roof. It will cost you its price again in repairs before you're finished.*

K: *But the builder I hired to look it over did say it was in good condition otherwise.*

L: *The roof is only the beginning. First it's the roof and then comes the plumbing and then the heating and then the plaster.*

K: *Still, those things seem to be all right.*

L: *And, after the plaster, it will be the wiring.*

K: *But the wiring is . . .*

L: *[Interrupts with calm assurance] It will cost double the price before you're finished.*

(Shapiro, 1965, p. 25)

This example also illustrates another aspect of compulsive personalities: insistence that their way of doing things be followed, without any awareness of the feelings this creates in other people. K probably really wants to buy the house, and if L's criticisms are, as we suspect, simply evidence of his compulsive personality without any facts attached, K's self-esteem and his positive feelings toward L are not likely to increase as a result of this encounter. People with this disorder focus on rules and neatness and may be disturbed by anything out of place (see Figure 9-9). Excessive concentration on work and productivity is also typical. Even pleasure becomes work:

One such person carefully scheduled his Sundays with certain activities in order to produce "maximum enjoyment." He determinedly set about enjoying himself and became quite upset

Figure 9-9 Housekeeping routines or other cleaning or straightening rituals occupy a great deal of time for some obsessive-compulsive people. This person's home library is a source of worry and frustration because of her concern about how to arrange the books. If they are arranged alphabetically by author, then she finds that the different sizes mixed together are visually unpleasing. If she arranges them by size, although they look better, she cannot find a particular book quickly. The result is that this woman spends a great deal of time both arranging the books and feeling dissatisfied with what she has done.

if anything interfered with his schedule, not merely because he missed the activity, but because his holiday had been spent inefficiently. Another compulsive patient always tried hard, in his social life, to be "spontaneous." (Shapiro, 1965, p. 32)

Finally, obsessive-compulsive personality disorder is characterized by indecisiveness. Individuals with this disorder have great difficulty making decisions because they might be wrong. Their inability to make decisions can be so extreme that they can accomplish relatively little. Their pleasure comes from planning a job, not from doing it.

Despite job problems such as those referred to previously, obsessive-compulsiveness is relatively less likely than other personality disorders to inhibit job performance and is least often confused with misbehavior. Table 9-14 lists the clinical features of this personality disorder.

Someone with an obsessive-compulsive personality disorder usually seeks treatment only when his or her carefully built-up life-style is threatened. This may happen when a spouse is exasperated and leaves, when a boss decides to fire the difficult employee, or when there is an accumulation of stressful events that make it impossible to carry on as usual. Psychotherapy is often recommended in such circumstances. Although in the past the therapeutic approach was usually psychodynamic and focused on unconscious processes that might underlie the disorder, in recent years other approaches have also come to the fore. A cognitive approach directs attention to the content, style, and structure of the individual's thought processes in the belief that it is irrational and dysfunctional thoughts that lead to maladaptive behavior (A. T. Beck et al., 1990). For example, automatic thoughts such as "I need to

Table 9-14
Clinical Features of Obsessive-Compulsive Personality Disorder

A person having at least four of these characteristics might be considered to have an obsessive-compulsive personality.

1. Perfectionism that interferes with completing tasks.
2. Preoccupation with details, rules, lists, and schedules.
3. Reluctance to delegate tasks or to work with others unless they follow exactly his or her way of doing things.
4. Excessive devotion to work and productivity to the exclusion of leisure activities and friendships.
5. Overconscientiousness and inflexibility about matters of morality or ethics.
6. Perception of money as something to be saved for future catastrophes; miserliness regarding spending for self and others.
7. Inability to discard worn-out or worthless objects even when they have no sentimental value.
8. Behavior that is typically rigid and stubborn.

get this assignment done perfectly" may inhibit spontaneity and the expression of feelings. Behavioral approaches that use techniques like exposure therapy are also being employed, as is group therapy.

Treatment of Personality Disorders

Our knowledge of personality disorders is limited because professionals see a restricted sample of people with these disorders and often lack appreciation of cultural factors related to the clinical problem (see Box 9-4). Unless their difficulties become overwhelming, such individuals tend to be satisfied with their behavior, not intensely unhappy

the way an anxious or depressed person might be. As we have seen, people with personality disorders perceive their environment—not their rigid behavior patterns—as the cause of any difficulties they may encounter.

It is important to remember that even individuals who are classified as having a personality disorder may behave appropriately or normally some of the time. However, when coping behaviors are called for, each personality disorder is distinguished by the frequency and intensity with which certain characteristic behaviors appear. For example, someone with a paranoid personality disorder does not always appear to be suspicious, but he or she is much more likely than most people to be inappropriately suspicious. Many people with personality disorders go through

---

Q&A   Box 9-4

Q: Several times throughout the book you have emphasized the need to take cultural factors into account when working clinically with people whose cultures are not mainstream American. I guess the reason is that people with different cultural backgrounds often have different perspectives on life, different values, and different sets of ingrained attitudes. People who have personality disorders also seem to be different from others in their unusual ingrained attitudes, needs, and desires. Does that mean that, like cultural values, we have to accept their different ways of thinking and not label them as "crazy"? Where does culture fit in when we consider the personality disorders?

A: You obviously have been thinking hard about both personality disorders and the role of cultural factors in mental health. You, no doubt, agree with us that labeling someone as "crazy" is not very precise or helpful. The two reasons why cultural considerations are important for all types of maladaptive behavior are that (1) cultural factors might play a role in the maladaptation and need to be kept in mind in working clinically with individuals, and (2) what seems like maladaptation might be regarded as normal in the individual's culture. For these reasons, DSM-IV urges clinicians to be sensitive to differences in language, values, behavioral norms, and styles of expressing distress. People from cultures that are distinctive in these respects may be deviant (different), but not necessarily abnormal or pathological.

Whether a personality trait or a life-style pattern is maladaptive or causes impairment depends on the cultural context. Defining or labeling deviations from the norm is culture-relative. The uniqueness of childhood experiences across cultures may play a role in shaping certain personality traits, emphasizing some while suppressing others. It is conceivable that a Vietnamese refugee who is Buddhist might exhibit certain traits that could be taken as religious inspiration to Vietnamese but that could lead to consideration of a diagnosis of schizoid personality disorder in an American clinic. Many Mediterranean people believe in the power of the "evil eye," bear grudges, and are unforgiving of insults. Unless the cultural context were taken into account, an immigrant who came from this area might be considered for the diagnosis of paranoid personality disorder. Some individuals in severely oppressed minority groups are reluctant to express themselves in social situations because of fear of saying something inappropriate. They also might show anxiety in front of others, be unwilling to get involved with people unless certain of being liked, and be easily hurt by what they interpret as criticism. Labeling such individuals as having an avoidant personality would mask real problems related to acculturation.

What these examples suggest is that the diagnosis of personality disorder should not be made just on the basis of an individual's behavior. The cultural context needs to be considered for the purposes of both classification and treatment.

The personality disorders are an especially good illustration of the need to take culturally relevant factors into account in clinical work. How to do this represents a challenge for a clinician who doesn't know about the patient's culture. Although assessing how important cultural factors might be is often not easy (there are no uniform guidelines regarding how to do this), simply keeping in mind the possibility of relevant cultural considerations provides a good start. The point is that the clinician needs to be informed and have an open mind in drawing inferences from a patient's behavior. A patient's silence in an interview might be taken as an indication of conscious or unconscious conflict or of reluctance to talk about upsetting matters. However, some people with Chinese or Japanese backgrounds might use silence as an indication of a desire to continue speaking after making a particular point or as a sign of respect and politeness. In these cases, a silence would not indicate a lack of desire to continue speaking. Clinicians who work with people from other cultures should make it a point to understand their cultural characteristics.

A personality disorder needs to be culturally dissected so that a culture's value as a predisposing, complicating, or therapeutic factor in the patient's overall clinical condition can be duly assessed. Individuals' accounts of their cultural contexts (e.g., religious values and conceptions of mental illness) and, when possible, information obtained from their families or persons in their cultural group can be helpful (Mezzich et al., 1996).

life without ever coming into contact with a mental health professional. However, their rigid response styles often lead them to cope ineffectively with their environment. If the environmental stresses become too great, their response styles may become clearly ineffective.

When patients with personality disorders come to therapy because of their general dissatisfaction with themselves and/or with life, they often show ambivalence (Newman, 1998).

Jerry, a 38-year-old unmarried computer programmer and diagnosed as having an avoidant personality disorder, sought help as a result of his continuing unhappiness. He did not see himself as an active contributor to his own misery in life. After his therapist gently raised some questions about Jerry's description of himself as simply being "unlucky," Jerry came late to the next session. With the support of his therapist, Jerry stayed in therapy. Using a cognitive-behavioral approach, the therapist found out that Jerry was avoidant in many aspects of his life, not just therapy. Jerry rarely returned phone calls, often failed to come to meetings and social events he had promised to attend, frequently took "sick leave" from work coincidental with the busiest times in the office, hadn't made a new friend in years, and could not maintain a dating relationship with a woman.

The therapist focused attention on cognitions, such as, "I should avoid unpleasant situations at all costs," "If I ignore a problem, it will go away," and "If I keep my expectations low, I can never be disappointed." The therapist questioned these sorts of assumptions that guided Jerry's life. The therapist gave Jerry homework assignments, but emphasized that it was up to Jerry to decide whether or not to use them. (The therapist was concerned that if he was too forceful in making the assignments, Jerry might drop out of therapy.) The assignments involved punctuality, opening mail, meeting obligations, and seeking social interactions. While he was far from being completely cured, he did start opening some mail, began paying his bills on time, came to therapy sessions on time, and began to think about seeking social contacts. At one point, Jerry said with a broad, knowing grin, "You mean I have to actually show up for my life?"

After Jerry had achieved some successes in his homework assignments, his therapist presented him with the following story as a metaphor of his avoidant style:

"Jerry, you are a man who is trying to run away from his own shadow. You run and you run and you run, until you can run no more. But when you look down your shadow is still there. Now you're upset, and you're very fatigued. You hate your shadow. You keep thinking, 'Why can't I get rid of this darned thing?' You hit upon this idea—'I'll close my eyes. Then I won't have to see my shadow.' So you close your eyes, and then you find that you can't see anything at all, and your life has no light, no direction, and no beauty. So you open your eyes, and there is your shadow once again. You cry 'I give up! No matter what I try, it doesn't work. I'm doomed!' But then you realize

something—something that will change your life in ways that you could not have imagined. You decide to make peace with your shadow. You decide to hold your head up high. You decide to look at everything in your life, both the shadows and the light. You decide to live your life as if it is the middle of a sunny day, when your shadow is strong, but actually quite small, because the sun is directly overhead. You don't have to run anymore. You can relax. You don't have to close your eyes anymore. You can see the world. You can accept yourself, and enjoy your day, and enjoy your life. And you can see where you're going. And you go there." (Newman, 1998, pp. 67–68)

The therapist was gratified when in later sessions Jerry made the comments, "I'm tired of running away" and guessed that the shadow story had made an impact on Jerry's everyday thinking. Jerry made a number of small, consistent changes that resulted in fewer daily problems and developed more pride in himself. How much further progress was possible remained an open question.

A variety of therapies have been used in treating personality disorders. Although most of these disorders have not been found to be very responsive to drugs in the past, clinicians have recently been using certain psychoactive drugs to treat some people with personality disorders. The drugs currently being assessed include certain antipsychotic drugs; one group of antidepressant drugs, the MAO inhibitors; and lithium. So far the results of drug therapy are not entirely clear. Behavioral techniques such as assertiveness training and systematic desensitization may be helpful for avoidant and dependent patients. Although cognitive therapies seem to be appropriate for deviant cognitive styles, little information on their effectiveness is available. However, as Jerry's case suggests, dealing with the cognitions that underlie the personality disorders would seem to be a promising approach.

As Box 9-2 showed for borderline personality disorder, there may be considerable merit in developing therapies that combine several treatment approaches. Psychodynamic therapy has to some extent been used successfully with personality disorders in which anxious or fearful behaviors play a prominent role (Winston et al., 1994). An intensive milieu therapy that provides clear rules and a stable environment—as well as clear penalties for failure to take personal responsibility for behavior—is being tried as a way to help those with antisocial personality disorder.

Because personality disorders affect interpersonal relationships, they also tend to elicit certain patterns of behaviors from family members and friends. For this reason, any behavior changes that come about through therapy will have an impact on the patterns of these relationships. Group or family therapy thus may be a useful part of the treatment of many individuals with personality disorders. Therapists need to focus the patient's attention on the effect of his or her behavior on the behavior of others.

The Outlook for Personality Disorder Classification

The idea of personality disorders as independent conditions (listed on DSM-IV's Axis II) that might or might not be related to the more traditional disorders (listed on Axis I) is relatively new. Even though many clinicians have responded positively to this new system of classifying various personality patterns, many questions and issues remain. As we mentioned in Chapter 3 (Box 3-1), Axis II might be regarded as a first step.

We have referred several times in this chapter to the need to distinguish among the various personality disorders, and the need to find ways to conceptualize and treat them. Studies of borderline and antisocial personality disorders far outnumber those of all the other Axis II personality disorders, but there are still large gaps in knowledge about them.

Two questions that inevitably arise are (1) Are the personality disorders included in DSM-IV the right ones—that is, are they defined in ways that contribute to diagnostic reliability and validity? and (2) Are there personality disorders not included in DSM-IV that should be part of the classification system? It has been difficult for professionals to answer these questions because, except for a few of these disorders (most notably the borderline classification), research has been quite limited. With increased use of Axis II by clinicians, and as research evidence accrues, it seems likely that conceptualizations of the personality disorders will change, along with the diagnostic criteria.

Clinical experience and research may also suggest adding to Axis II some classifications of personality patterns not currently represented. For example, some people show a pervasive sadistic pattern of cruel, demanding, and aggressive behavior to other people; others show a self-defeating or masochistic pattern that leads to disappointment, failure, and mistreatment by others; and still others show a mild but persistent depressive mood that is dominated by dejection and cheerlessness. Whether these or other personality patterns should also be included within Axis II is a topic of considerable discussion among clinicians and researchers.

Another important topic concerns how information about the personality disorders can most effectively be presented. Currently, Axis II uses a **categorical model** of classification, in which a disorder is considered to be diagnosed if a certain threshold of criteria is reached or exceeded. As we have seen in the clinical features tables presented in this chapter, it is not necessary for all listed criteria to be present in order to use a particular classification.

In contrast with this classification model, a **dimensional model** focuses attention on patterns of personality characteristics. In a dimensional approach, an individual would be classified not as having a dependent or antisocial personality disorder, but rather as having a personality pattern that reflects the individual's standing on a variety of dimensions. The value of a dimensional approach is that it results in a profile for each person classified. One possibility would be a profile of ratings of the severity of various types of maladaptive personality patterns. Widiger (2000) recently stressed the need to recognize (1) the continuous nature of personality functioning and (2) the fact that personality disorders are maladaptive variants of common personality traits. While the time for dimensional classification may not yet have come (it involves somewhat novel and complex procedures), with further research to support its value, it might be incorporated into future DSMs.

Understanding and treating personality disorders can be advanced by recognizing their multiple causes. People with these disorders have varied combinations of vulnerability and risk factors on the one hand, and resilience features on the other. Their traits can best be understood as developing from the interaction of biologically rooted factors, such as temperament, and their many types of life experiences. Social influences can act either as protective factors against personality disorder that buffer the effects of biological and psychological risk, or as risk factors in their own right. Personality disorders are highly complex phenomena, and their multidimensional character needs to be borne in mind by researchers and clinicians.

Chapter Summary

CLASSIFYING PERSONALITY DISORDERS

Personality disorders are long-standing, maladaptive, inflexible ways of relating to the environment. These disorders are diagnosed on Axis II of DSM-IV. Many people with personality disorders also have a diagnosis on Axis I. Personality disorders can be grouped into three categories: odd or eccentric behavior; dramatic, emotional, or erratic behavior; and anxious or fearful behavior.

ODD OR ECCENTRIC BEHAVIOR

Paranoid Personality Disorder People with **paranoid personality disorder** are suspicious and mistrusting of others and hypersensitive; they expect to be taken advantage of, and they read hidden meanings into benign remarks and events.

Schizoid Personality Disorder Those diagnosed with **schizoid personality disorder** are withdrawn and seclusive, prefer to work alone, and do not seem interested in warm, close relationships with others.

Schizotypal Personality Disorder

Schizotypal personality disorder is associated with odd ways of thinking, perceiving, communicating, and behaving—although these deviations are not as extreme as those seen in people diagnosed with schizophrenia. Some research suggests that this disorder may be a weak form of schizophrenia.

DRAMATIC, EMOTIONAL, OR ERRATIC BEHAVIOR

Histrionic Personality Disorder

People with **histrionic personality disorder** are self-centered, manipulative, and have stormy interpersonal relationships.

Narcissistic Personality Disorder

Factors that are important in the diagnosis of **narcissistic personality disorder** are an extreme sense of self-importance, need for constant attention, fragility of self-esteem, and a lack of empathy for others.

Borderline Personality Disorder

Those diagnosed as having a **borderline personality disorder** have unstable personal relationships, often threaten and frequently engage in self-destructive behavior, are very impulsive, and tend to have relationships characterized by intense clinging dependency and manipulation of others. Because of the frequency of the borderline diagnosis, more work is done on treatment of this disorder than on the other personality disorders.

Antisocial Personality Disorder

Antisocial personality disorder is typified by a chronic and continuous history of behavior that violates the rights of others. This history begins before age 15 and continues into adulthood. In adulthood these individuals continue to have a history of antisocial acts against property and other people, and they are likely to be reckless and irresponsible and to lack remorse for hurting others. However, many acts of criminal and antisocial behavior are committed by people who do not fit the classification of antisocial personality disorder. Traditional psychotherapy does not seem effective with individuals with antisocial personality.

ANXIOUS OR FEARFUL BEHAVIOR

Avoidant Personality Disorder

People diagnosed as having **avoidant personality disorder** have low self-esteem, worry about negative evaluation by others, and avoid social interactions. Although they desire affection and close relationships, fear of rejection seems to keep these people from seeking such relationships.

Dependent Personality Disorder

People with **dependent personality disorder** lack confidence in their ability to function independently. In order to maintain their dependent relationships, they are willing to subordinate their own needs and wishes to those of others.

Obsessive–Compulsive Personality Disorder

Obsessive-compulsive personality disorder is characterized by lack of ability to express warm emotions, extreme perfectionism, and a rigid approach to the way things "should" be done.

TREATMENT OF PERSONALITY DISORDERS

Because many people with personality disorders never come to clinicians' attention, researchers have studied only a limited sample of this group. People with personality disorders may not seek clinical help because they see the environment as the source of their problems. They are also likely to behave appropriately much of the time; thus their problems do not cause others to refer them for treatment. Therapeutic approaches from each of the perspectives, sometimes in combination, are used for treating these individuals. These include a variety of psychoactive drugs, behavioral techniques such as assertiveness training and systematic desensitization, cognitive therapies, and psychodynamic therapies. Family or group therapies focus on the effects of the behaviors on others.

In the diagnosis and treatment of personality disorders it is necessary to attend to cultural factors that might influence how maladaptive behavior is evaluated. Unless the cultural context is taken into account, it is possible that a person might be considered for an Axis II classification while in actuality the behavior is understandable and acceptable within a particular group in the population.

THE OUTLOOK FOR PERSONALITY DISORDER CLASSIFICATION

Because the current classifications of personality disorders overlap with one another, it is likely that as more research is done the conceptualizations of the disorders may change and new categories may be added. Another possibility is that a dimensional model focusing on personality patterns might be preferable to the categorical model in current use.

Key Terms

Personality, p. 274
Personality disorders, p. 274
Symptom disorders, p. 275
Prototypal approach, p. 278
Paranoid personality disorder, p. 278
Schizoid personality disorder, p. 278

Schizotypal personality disorder, p. 280
Histrionic personality disorder, p. 282
Narcissistic personality disorder, p. 301
Borderline personality disorder, p. 283
Splitting, p. 287
Antisocial personality disorder, p. 288

Milieu therapy, p. 294
Avoidant personality disorder, p. 294
Dependent personality disorder, p. 295
Obsessive-compulsive personality
    disorder, p. 297

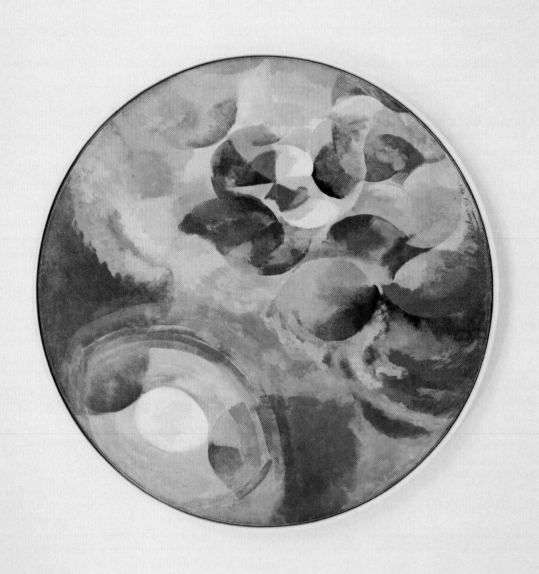

10

Robert Delaunay "Simultaneous Contrasts: Sun and Moon (Soleil, lune, simultane 2)" 1913, dated on painting 1912, oil on canvas, 53 in. (134.5 cm) diameter. The Museum of Modern Art, New York. Mrs. Simon Guggenheim Fund. Photograph © 2002 The Museum of Modern Art, New York.

Mood Disorders

"It is difficult to put into words how I felt at that time. I guess my major reaction was one of despair—a despair of ever being human again. I honestly felt subhuman, lower than the lowest vermin. Furthermore, I was self-deprecatory and could not understand why anyone would want to associate with me, let alone love me. I became mistrustful and suspicious of others and was certain that they were checking up on me to prove that I was incompetent myself. . . . I had become increasingly concerned about finances. On one hand, I thought that I was receiving extra money that I didn't deserve and, on the other, I was certain that we were going bankrupt. In any case, I was positive that I was going to wind up in jail. When I received my July salary statement it appeared to me that the total was larger than it should be. This frightened me and I told my wife that we should phone the university immediately and arrange to return the extra money before I got into trouble. Gently, my wife told me that she thought the amount of money was correct and there was nothing to worry about. Of course, she was right. . . . I not only pondered my current situation but my whole career as well. I was positive that I was a fraud and a phony and that I didn't deserve my Ph.D. I didn't deserve to have tenure; I didn't deserve to be a Full Professor . . . I didn't deserve the research grants I had been awarded; I couldn't understand how I had written the books and journal articles that I had and how they had been accepted for publication. I must have conned a lot of people." (Endler, 1990, pp. 41–42) ∎

These were the thoughts of a well-known psychologist during a period of severe depression. They illustrate how drastically depression may alter mood, perception, and behavior. A period of mania, on the other hand, leads to quite different thoughts and feelings, as described here by another psychologist who later became an expert on bipolar disorder:

When I am high I couldn't worry about money if I tried. So I don't. The money will come from somewhere, I am entitled, God will provide. . . . So, I bought twelve snake bite kits, with a sense of urgency and importance. I bought precious stones, elegant and unnecessary furniture, three watches within an hour of one another (in the Rolex rather than Timex class: champagne tastes bubble to the surface, are the surface, in mania), and totally inappropriate siren-like clothes. During one spree I spent several hundred on books having titles or covers that somehow caught my fancy. . . . Once I shoplifted a blouse because I could not wait a minute longer for the woman-with-molasses-feet in front of me in line. I imagine I must have spent far more than $30,000 during my two manic episodes, and God only knows how much more during my frequent hypomanias. I haven't any idea where most of the money went. (Goodwin & Jamison, 1990, p. 29)

The periods of depression in bipolar disorder are often similar to those experienced in a major depressive episode. The same person whose description of a manic episode appears above, described a period of depression this way:

The bottom began to fall out of my life and mind. My thinking, far from being clearer than a crystal, was tortuous. I would read the same passage over and over again only to realize that

I had no memory at all for what I just had read. Each book or poem I picked up was the same way. Incomprehensible. Nothing made sense. I could not begin to follow the material presented in my classes, and I would find myself staring out the window with no idea of what was going on around me. . . . [My mind] was incapable of concentrated thought and turned time and again to the subject of death: I was going to die, what difference did anything make? Life's run was only a short and meaningless one, why live? I was totally exhausted and could scarcely pull myself out of bed in the mornings. It took me twice as long to walk anywhere as it ordinarily did, and I wore the same clothes over and over again, as it was otherwise too much of an effort to make a decision about what to put on. I dreaded having to talk with people, avoided my friends whenever possible, and sat in the school library in the early mornings and late afternoons, virtually inert, with a dead heart and a brain as cold as clay. (Jamison, 1995, pp. 37, 38)

Mood Disorders

The examples given here illustrate the variety of behaviors that may be produced by **mood disorders.** DSM-IV divides mood disorders into three general types, which are listed in Table 10-1. In this chapter we will discuss two of these types of mood disorder: depressive disorders and bipolar disorders. Each of these types reflects a disturbance in mood or emotional reaction that is not due to any other physical or mental disorder. The third general type of mood disorder, which comprises about 10% of all mood disorder diagnoses, is caused either by medical illness, prescribed medication, or abuse of a variety of illegal drugs or other chemical substances (Clinton, 1993). Medically

Table 10-1

Types of Mood Disorder

Depressive Disorders

- *Dysthymic disorder:* — History of depressed mood a majority of the time.
- *Major depressive disorder:* — One or more major depressive episodes.

Bipolar Disorders

- *Bipolar I disorder:* — One or more manic episodes, and usually one or more major depressive episodes.
- *Bipolar II disorder:* — At least one hypomanic episode and one or more major depressive episodes but no manic episode or cyclothymia.
- *Cyclothymic disorder:* — Numerous hypomanic episodes and numerous periods of depressive symptoms that do not meet criteria for major depressive episode.

Other Mood Disorders

- Mood disorder due to a general medical condition.
- Substance-induced mood disorder.

related mood disorders may coexist with general medical conditions such as cancer, diabetes, or a recent heart attack. Some of these disorders are discussed in Chapter 5. Mood disorders associated with medication, illegal drugs, and other chemical agents are discussed in Chapter 13.

Facts About Mood Disorders

How often do mood disorders of the two major types shown in Table 10-1—depressive disorders and bipolar disorders—occur in the overall population? About 10% of the adults in the United States have experienced one of these types of mood disorder (Thase & Kupfer, 1996), but a majority of these people receive no treatment. These large numbers of untreated individuals represent a serious social problem because untreated mood disorders have an important impact, both on the quality of life of those affected and on their economic productivity. For example, major depressive disorder is the second greatest cause of disability affecting quality of life and productivity, worldwide. The only more frequent cause of disability is heart disease (Murray & Lopez, 1997). In addition, suicide, a leading cause of death across many age groups, is closely tied to mood disorders. Depression seems to be related to up to one-third of all suicides (Angst et al., 1999).

Overall, treatment of mood disorders not only decreases human misery, but also increases economic productivity and decreases the general use of health care facilities. Under these circumstances, why are mood disorders so often not treated? Several reasons have been identified: (1) personal feelings of being socially stigmatized by treatment; (2) failure of health care providers to recognize the disorder (this is especially true of depression, which can produce a variety of bodily symptoms); and (3) lack of awareness of the potential effectiveness of treatment and its benefits to the individual (Wells et al., 1994).

Mood disorders often are comorbid (exist together) with other kinds of disorders. For example, about half the people diagnosed with a major depressive disorder also have an anxiety disorder (Barbee, 1998). Substance abuse disorder is also very common among people with mood disorders (Merikangas et al., 1998). This is particularly troubling because substance abuse seems to make mood disorders worse. Personality disorders are also likely to coexist with mood disorders.

The best way to get information about the number of people who have been affected with a mood disorder sometime in the past or who are currently affected is to carry out an epidemiological study. Most epidemiological studies use a large sample selected scientifically to be representative of the population. These selected individuals are contacted and interviewed with the use of a standard survey form. The epidemiological approach makes it possible to identify both people who have come into contact with the health care system and those who have, or have had,

a disorder but have never sought treatment. Using this approach, researchers have concluded that, within the United States, the reported rate of mood disorder is generally similar for all Americans, whether they were White, Hispanic, or African American (Regier et al., 1993). However, there is a pronounced sex difference in mood disorders: they affect more than twice as many women as they do men. This sex difference in mood disorders is entirely accounted for by the higher rate of *depressive* disorders among women. Men and women do not differ substantially in their rate of *bipolar disorder*.

When epidemiologists study rates of major depression and bipolar disorder in other countries, they find a considerable difference in rate and also in the male-female ratio of those affected across these different cultures (Weissman et al., 1996). For example, the lifetime likelihood of being diagnosed with major depression ranged from 1.5 per 100 adults in Taiwan to 19.0 per 100 adults in Beirut, Lebanon, but in every country the rate was higher for women than for men. The lifetime likelihood for bipolar disorder ranged from 0.3 per 100 adults in Taiwan to 1.5 per 100 adults in New Zealand, with an approximately equal ratio of women to men in all sites studied. Despite these differences in the proportion of people affected, the symptoms found in these very different settings were quite consistent. Thus, it seems that cultural, economic, or environmental factors may affect the rates of depression and bipolar disorder, but they do not appear to influence the types of behaviors and symptoms that result from these disorders.

Depression

The term **depression** covers a variety of negative moods and behavior changes. Some are normal mood fluctuations and others meet the definition of clinical problems. The mood change may be temporary or long-lasting. It may range from a relatively minor feeling of melancholy to a deeply negative view of the world and an inability to function effectively. In this section we discuss several kinds of depression—temporarily depressed mood, long-lasting downward or negative mood that may interfere only mildly with effective behavior, and severely depressed mood accompanied by a marked but usually temporary inability to function effectively.

Symptoms of depression are also likely to occur in bipolar disorders. For this reason, the term **unipolar disorder** is often used when discussing different types of depressive disorders to distinguish between people who have experienced one or more episodes of depression but no manic or hypomanic episode and those who have a past history that includes at least one episode of mania or hypomania. Individuals who have one or more episodes of mania or hypomania as well as periods of depression are diagnosed as having bipolar disorder. Bipolar disorder is discussed later in the chapter.

Depressed Mood

Because the word *depression* is part of our everyday language, it is important to realize that feeling depressed is not the same thing as having a depressive disorder. Technically, when people say they feel depressed, "low," or "down," they are experiencing a depressed mood. Usually these feelings are based on a temporary situation and fade quickly when the situation changes. For instance, people often feel sad around the holidays, when they believe that others are enjoying closeness and pleasant companionship. These feelings, though unpleasant, are quite different from the feeling of being under a black cloud that accompanies a depressive episode or major depressive disorder.

People also use the term *depression* to describe the sadness that comes from a death in the family. After the death of someone they care deeply about, most survivors experience a depressed mood that is usually called grief. Common features of grief include physical distress such as sighing, tightness of the throat, an empty feeling in the abdomen, and a feeling of muscular weakness. In addition, there may be preoccupation with the visual image of the dead person, along with guilt and hostile reactions. These feelings of grief are entirely normal and are not classified as a depressive disorder.

The breakup of a dating relationship, or divorce or separation, may also bring about these feelings, which are likely to occur to both participants regardless of who wanted to end the relationship. Such feelings often represent a short-term response to stress.

A 24-year-old single female nursery-school teacher terminated brief psychotherapy after ten sessions. She had entered treatment two weeks after she discovered that the man she had been involved with for four months was married and wanted to stop seeing her. She reacted with bouts of sadness and crying, felt she was falling apart, took a week's sick leave from her job, and had vague thoughts that the future was so bleak that life might not be worth the effort. She felt that she must be in some essential way "flawed"; otherwise she would not have gotten so involved with someone who had no intentions of maintaining a long-term relationship. She felt that others "would have seen it," that only she was "so stupid" as to have been deceived. There were no other signs of a depressive syndrome, such as loss of interest or appetite or trouble concentrating. She responded to mixed supportive-insight psychotherapy and, toward the end of treatment, began dating a law student whom she met at a local cafe. (Spitzer et al., 1981, p. 261)

Other kinds of life events—losing a job, being turned down for a graduate school program, or losing everything in a fire—may also bring on a depressed mood. If such feelings of loss not due to bereavement are not severe enough to be called mood disorders, they are classified as an **adjustment disorder with depressed mood** (adjustment disorders are discussed in Chapter 4).

Vulnerability Factors for Depression

As we have said throughout this book, the chance that any person may develop a particular disorder is related to risk factors in the environment, that person's biological vulnerabilities, and the presence or absence of factors that promote resilience. Risk factors affecting depression include heredity, age, gender, negative life events, and lack of social support.

Heredity An important risk factor for mood disorders is heredity. Studies of twins and of families clearly suggest a genetic component in both major depression and bipolar disorders.

The importance of heredity in mood disorders is shown by the strong association between the closeness of the biological relationship (the percent of shared genes between two people) and the likelihood that if one of them has a mood disorder, the biological relative will also be diagnosed with such a disorder. For instance, there is a much greater risk of developing a major depression if one's identical twin has had this disorder than if one's parent, brother, or sister has experienced it. The chances of developing the disorder are even less if a person has no close relatives that have ever been given this diagnosis. Figure 10-1 shows how the closeness of relationship to a person with a major depressive disorder affects a person's risk. Figure 10-1 also shows that both major depression and bipolar disorders may be associated with the same genetic makeup. Those having relatives with a bipolar diagnosis have almost three times as great a chance of developing a major depression as those who have no close relative with either a diagnosis of depression or bipolar disorder.

Family studies have shown that the younger people are when their first major depression occurs, the more likely it is that their relatives will also experience periods of depression. For instance, relatives of people whose first depressive episode had occurred before the age of 20 had an eight-times-greater chance of becoming depressed than relatives of normal subjects. In contrast, relatives of people who were over 40 when they first had a major depression had little more than the normal risk of depression (Weissman et al., 1984).

Although major depression has consistently been shown to run in families, much less is known about how heredity affects the clinical features of the disorder, such as the number and type of symptoms and the length of the severely depressed mood. A study comparing monozygotic (MZ) and dizygotic (DZ) twins investigated the effect of genetic simi-

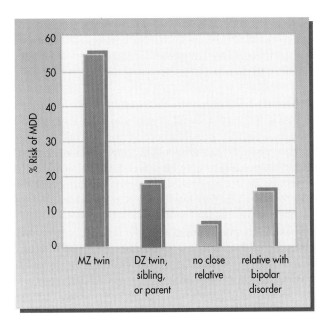

Figure 10-1   The hereditary risk of developing a major depressive disorder (MDD) varies, depending on the closeness of the biological relationship to any affected family members.

Source: Data from Gershon, Berrettini, & Goldin (1989).

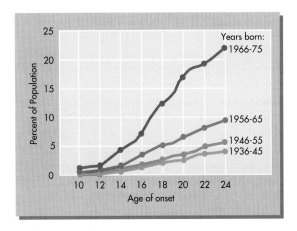

Figure 10-2   The lifetime prevalence of major depression in the United States has increased with every decade beginning in 1936, and the age at which symptoms appear had dropped.

Source: U.S. National Co-morbidity Survey.

larity on such questions (Kendler et al., 1992). What are called the negative symptoms of depression (changes in weight, appetite, and sleep) and whether or not the depression recurred after the first diagnosis both seemed more influenced by heredity than by events in the twins' lives, because these symptoms occurred more often in both members of the MZ twin pairs than they did in the DZ pairs. In contrast, within the group experiencing recurrent episodes of depression, the actual number of episodes seemed to be related to stressful life experiences not shared by the other twin of the pair rather than to heredity.

Age   Another risk factor for depression is age. The risk for a first episode of any degree of depression is highest in women between the ages of 20 and 29. For men, the similar risk period is between the ages of 40 and 49 (Rorsman et al., 1990). In addition to age, another factor is year of birth, or the birth cohort to which a person belongs. Figure 10-2 shows that by age 24, those born in the years 1966 to 1975 had a much greater chance of experiencing a depression than those born from 1936 through 1965. It shows further, that for those born in each succeeding decade during this period the rate of depression was greater and the age of onset of depression became steadily earlier, as shown by how steeply each curve rose with age.

Overall then, the rate of depression increased during the twentieth century and, in addition, the average age at the time of first diagnosis declined. No one knows why depression has increased worldwide and why younger people are more likely to be at risk than they would have been in the past. Explanations given include increasing alcohol and drug abuse, changes in the stability of marriages and in the structure of families, fewer employment and promotion opportunities, urbanization, and the effects of increasing pollution. So far, although many studies in each of these areas are being conducted, the role these factors play in the increase in depression is unclear.

Gender   One of the greatest risk factors for depression is simply being female. Women are at least twice as likely to experience all types of depressed states as are men. Past researchers have tried to understand this difference in cultural terms. In American culture it has been thought to be more acceptable in general for women than for men to seek help for emotional problems. Women are more likely to consult physicians or mental health experts and to take a psychological view of their problems than they are to see them only in terms of physical symptoms. However, these explanations of why more women *seek treatment* for depression do not explain the higher overall *rate* for depression, because the same difference in rate of depressive disorder for women and men has been consistently found in community surveys where people are contacted on a randomized basis and not because they have sought help.

One explanation suggested by researchers interested in social support and its effect on health is that while women in general receive more social support than do men, they are also expected to offer more support (Shumaker & Hill, 1991). Because support-giving often involves them in the problems and stressors experienced by others, women may on average experience more stress than men. During the age period from 25 to 45, married women have a particularly high rate of depression, while unmarried women in this age bracket have a much lower rate, more similar to the rate for men (Paykel, 1991). This difference may reflect the greater stress for married women from both heavy child-care responsibilities and support provision for extended families, in addition to job stress.

Low income and economic need are additional stressors that affect women more often than men and may be related to the higher rate of depression for women (Beekman et al., 1999). Poor young women (including African American, Hispanic, and White) are at greater risk for depression than other groups (Miranda & Green, 1999). Overall these women have poorer support systems than those with higher income and are likely to have been victims of crime and sexual and physical abuse in the past. They are also likely to have more difficulty in obtaining treatment for depression. Older African American women also report a significantly higher rate of depressive symptoms than White women in the same age group (Cochran et al., 1999). Again greater stress may be a factor because older African American women are more likely to be poor and to have more family responsibilities as care providers for grandchildren and other relatives than White women of the same age.

The way men and women cope with depressed mood may also be a factor. Men tend to have an action-oriented approach that may distract them from their symptoms, but women tend to have a more cognitive style in which they discuss problems with others and ruminate (continue to think) about them (Butler & Nolen-Hoeksema, 1994). This ruminative response style is associated with more lengthy periods of depression and with more severe depression. Men's more action-oriented response style may result in a different expression of mood disorder among men, for instance an increased tendency to abuse alcohol and behave in an antisocial way. This explanation is supported by the finding that in families where one or more members developed depression at a relatively young age there was also a much higher than expected rate of alcoholism and antisocial personality, especially among the male members of the extended family (Winokur, 1997). Men and women may simply have different ways of expressing a genetic vulnerability to depression rather than differing in the vulnerability itself.

Researchers have also followed up on physiological differences between men and women that may be responsible for the difference in rate of depression. Women experience hormonal changes connected to childbirth as well as to menstrual cycles and menopause. Each of these situations has been thought to increase the chances of depression. Treatment for depression that involves administration of hormones suggests that they may play a role. For example, one hormone, estrogen, has been used successfully in therapy for depression experienced by menopausal women (Caranza-Lira & Valentino-Figueroa, 1999). These physiological differences may be less impor-

tant than the social ones, however, because depression related to these periods in women's lives contributes only a little to the greater frequency of depression in women compared to men.

Life Events Environmental factors such as life events, especially a pileup of stressful events in a short time period, may play a significant role in producing an episode of depression, especially in vulnerable people. Life events and genetic vulnerability may be interrelated. Neither genes nor family environment is likely to produce life events directly, but both factors may predispose a person to negative life events.

Stressful life events are not usually random but are often associated with a person's vulnerability and life circumstances, not simply with "bad luck" (Kendler et al., 1999).

Many stressful life events are associated with relationships in the person's social network. One study of twins found that more than half of all personal stressful life events were rated as being in some way dependent on the person involved rather than on factors outside of the person's control (Kendler et al., 1999). Although independent events, those over which the person was likely to have no control, often resulted in depression, an episode of depression was much more likely to occur after one or more dependent events. People's choice of relationships and the way they interact with others close to them seem more apt to create stressful events that produce depression than do events based on outside forces.

Lack of Social Support The negative effect of life events related to close personal relationships is made even stronger because it is usually accompanied by a decrease in social support. **Social support,** the belief that one is cared about by others who are also available to provide help or emotional support when needed, has been shown to be an important protection from depression (Henderson, 1992). Behaviors of others that convey criticism or imply that a person is unworthy of love or friendship are more likely to be related to depression than is the mere absence of support (Harris, 1992).

One close relationship that is generally considered to provide support is marriage. Both divorce and the quality of an ongoing marriage are associated with depression as well as with worsened mental and physical health in general (Prigerson et al., 1999). Figure 10-3 compares the rate of depression for married and divorced men and women in an epidemiological study of several countries. Two things are clear from the findings of this study: (1) those who are divorced or separated are more likely to be depressed than those who are married, and (2) women are more likely to be depressed than men. Marital status and sex have consistent effects across countries, even though the overall rate of depression differs (Weissman et al., 1996).

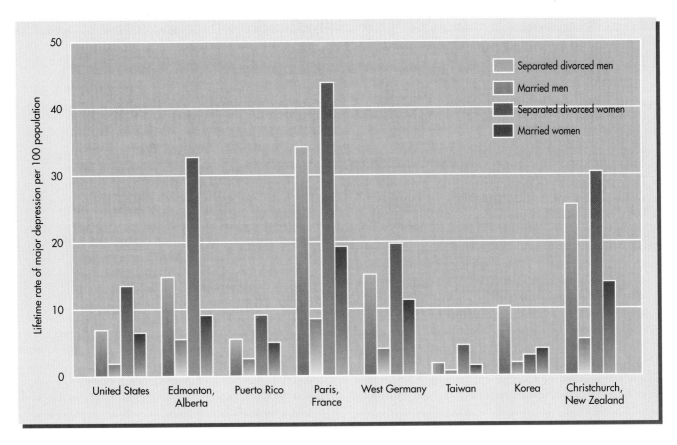

Figure 10-3   The lifetime rate of major depressive disorder per 100 people, by marital status, for men and women 26–64 years of age shows a similar pattern but different rates for various countries. In most countries, the rate for those who were divorced was considerably greater than for those currently married. All the data are standardized to the U.S. age distribution by sex and adjusted by age.

Source: Weissman et al. (1996), *Journal of the American Medical Association, 276*, p. 298.

Depressive Disorders

Dysthymic Disorder

Most people who have a **dysthymic disorder** would tell you that they have felt depressed for many years, or for as long as they remember. Feeling depressed seems normal to them; it has become a way of life. They feel helpless to change their lives. **Dysthymia** is defined as a condition characterized by mild and chronic depressive symptoms. Periods of dysthymia have been found to last from 2 to 20 or more years, with a median duration of about 5 years (Keller, 1990). About 3% of the general population and about 30% of those seen at outpatient clinics can be classified as dysthymic.

Table 10-2 summarizes the conditions that must be met for dysthymic disorder diagnosis. Note that other problems must be present in addition to depressed mood. Some researchers have criticized the DSM-IV criteria because they believe they do not give enough emphasis to what these researchers consider the most characteristic symptoms of dysthymia: the cognitive symptoms, including low self-esteem,

feelings of guilt or thinking about the past, and subjective feelings of irritability or excessive anger. Because the depressed mood is so long-lasting, dysthymia has sometimes been considered a personality disorder. However, most researchers include it in the group of mood disorders and believe it is biologically related to depression.

Dysthymia and major depressive disorder (discussed next) have been found to have a high degree of comorbidity (D. N. Klein et al., 1996). This means that both types of mood disorder are likely to occur in the same individual.

If a person with dysthymic disorder develops symptoms of major depression as well, he or she is said to have "double depression," because the criteria for both diagnoses are met. This dual state occurs quite frequently. In one large epidemiological study, almost half of the people who had dysthymic disorder also had had at least one episode of major depression (Weissman et al., 1996).

Although dysthymia seems to make people more vulnerable to major depression, dysthymia itself is different from major depression in terms of the ages at which people are most likely to be affected. In major depression, rates increase in certain age groups, but in dysthymia, the

Table 10–2
Summary of Diagnostic Criteria for Dysthymic Disorder

- Depressed mood most of the day, more days than not, for at least 2 years.[a]
- Two or more of the following symptoms while depressed: poor appetite or overeating, insomnia or sleeping too much, low energy, low self-esteem, poor concentration or difficulty in making decisions, and feelings of hopelessness.
- The symptoms described above have never been absent for more than 2 months in a 2-year period.[a]
- During the first 2 years of the disturbance,[a] there has never been a major depressive episode. If one of these episodes has occurred in the past, there has been a complete remission, or disappearance of symptoms.
- There has never been a manic or hypomanic episode, and the criteria for cyclothymic disorder have not been met.
- The disturbance is not part of a chronic psychotic disorder, or the result of some chemical substance (medication or drug abuse) or a general medical condition.
- The symptoms cause clinically significant distress or impairment in important areas of functioning.

[a]One year for children and adolescents.
Source: Adapted from DSM-IV.

rate is stable from about age 18 until at least age 64. Figure 10-4 shows a comparison of symptoms of patients with a "pure" dysthymic diagnosis (i.e., they had no additional DSM-IV diagnoses) with symptoms of people who were diagnosed as having recurrent episodes of major depression. In every case, the frequency of the symptoms differed significantly for the two diagnostic groups. Dysthymic disorder tends to be chronic, persisting for long periods. In contrast, periods of intense depression are usually described as time-limited, which means that even without treatment the symptoms naturally tend to lessen over time.

The following case describes a woman who had continued to show dysthymic symptoms throughout her adult life. Despite extensive psychotherapy, she continually felt inferior and unattractive to others. Even when events should have suggested to her that she was attractive and competent, she seemed to go out of her way to prove to herself that this was untrue.

The 28-year-old junior executive. . . . told the therapist in her initial interview that she had had extensive psychotherapy previously, but that she was "depressed" about everything: her job, her husband, and her prospects for the future.

Her complaints were of persistent feelings of depressed mood, inferiority, and pessimism, which she claims to have had since she was 16 or 17 years old. Although she did reasonably well in college, she consistently ruminated about those students who were "genuinely intelligent." She dated during college and graduate school, but claimed that she would never go after a guy she thought was "special," always feeling inferior and intimidated. Whenever she saw or met such a man, she acted stiff and aloof, or actually walked away as quickly as possible, only to berate herself afterward and then fantasize about him for many months. She claimed that her therapy had helped, although she still could not remember a time when she didn't feel somewhat depressed.

Just after graduation, she married the man she was going out with at the time primarily because she felt she "needed a hus-

band" for companionship. Shortly after their marriage, the couple started to bicker. . . . She began to feel that she had made a mistake in marrying him. Her social life with her husband involves several other couples. The man in these couples is usually a friend of her husband's. She is sure that the women find her uninteresting and unimpressive, and that the people who seem to like her are probably no better off than she.

Recently she has also been having difficulties at work. She is assigned the most menial tasks at the firm and is never given an assignment of importance or responsibility. She admits that she frequently does a "slipshod" job of what is given her, never does more than is required, and never demonstrates any assertiveness or initiative to her supervisors. (Spitzer et al., 1981, pp. 10–11)

Major Depressive Disorder

Someone who has **major depressive disorder** has experienced one or more major depressive episodes without ever experiencing a manic or hypomanic episode. Table 10-3 summarizes the criteria for this diagnosis.

Major Depressive Episode A **major depressive episode** is marked by either depressed mood or a loss of interest or pleasure in almost all activities and at least four additional symptoms from the following group: marked weight loss or gain when not dieting; constant sleeping problems; agitated or greatly slowed-down behavior; fatigue; inability to think clearly; feelings of worthlessness; and frequent thoughts about death or suicide. These symptoms must last at least 2 weeks and represent a change from the person's usual functioning.

Mrs. B., who was brought to a psychiatrist's office by her concerned husband, provides a typical example of a major depressive episode. When her husband had called to make an appointment and was told that the first one available was in 10 days, he had responded that he didn't

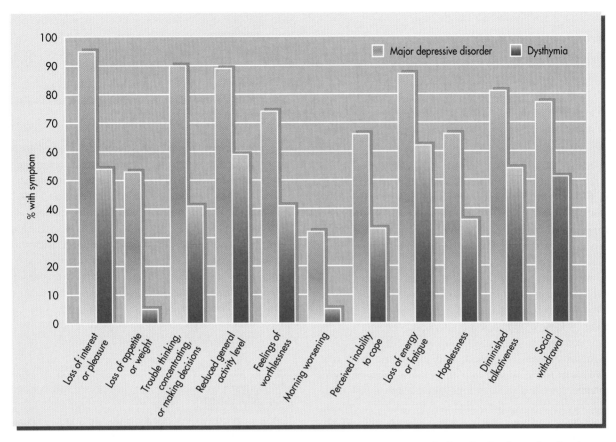

Figure 10-4 Symptom differences between dysthymic patients and those with recurrent episodes of major depressive disorder. All differences are statistically significant.

SOURCE: Keller et al. (1995).

think his wife could wait that long. Mrs. B., the mother of two children, was a 45-year-old legal secretary.

Mrs. B. was dressed in wrinkled and slightly soiled clothing. Her hair was carelessly combed and there was a faint body odor

---

Table 10-3

Summary of Diagnostic Criteria for Major Depressive Disorder

- The presence of a major depressive episode, with or without a history of past major depressive episodes.
- The episode cannot be accounted for by some other disorder.
- There has never been a manic episode or a hypomanic episode, except for any that may have been the result of substance abuse, medication, or the direct physiological effects of a general medical condition.
- If either hallucinations or delusions are present, the major depressive disorder is diagnosed as having psychotic features.

Source: Adapted from DSM-IV.

about her. Her face was drawn and expressionless. She was helped by her husband into the office where she sat motionless, staring at the floor and occasionally sighing audibly. She said nothing unless asked a simple direct question. Even then her answers were delayed, spoken slowly, and of a droning, monotonous quality. A portion of the interview went as follows:

Dr. R: *What's the trouble that brings you in?*

Mrs. B: *I don't care about anything.*

Dr. R: *What do you mean?*

Mrs. B: *[No response]*

Dr. R: *You look sad.*

Mrs. B: *Yes . . . not sad . . . just nothing.*

Dr. R: *How long have you been like this?*

Mrs. B: *About three weeks . . . getting worse.*

Dr. R: *Has anything like this ever happened to you before?*

Mrs. B: *No.*

Dr. R: *How's your appetite?*

Mrs. B: *No appetite.*

Dr. R: *Have you lost weight these three weeks?*

> *Mrs. B:* *I don't know . . . maybe 10 or 12 lbs.*
>
> *Dr. R:* *How's your sleeping?*
>
> *Mrs. B:* *Bad, I wake up every morning about 3 and just lay there.*
>
> *Dr. R:* *Do you feel bad about anything?*
>
> *Mrs. B:* *Everything . . . I wish I were dead.*
>
> (Tomb & Christensen, 1987, p. 198)

After her interview, Mrs. B.'s husband spoke with the psychiatrist. He said that he and his wife had been married 26 years and that this behavior was very different from any she had ever shown before. He thought the trouble had begun about a month earlier. At that time she was too tired to take part in her favorite activity, boating.

> *"Gradually she has withdrawn. She doesn't want to see anybody, just wants to rest but I never see her sleeping. I force her to eat. I guess I panicked yesterday when she said she wanted to die." (Tomb & Christensen, 1987, p. 198)*

A major depressive episode may end completely in a few weeks or months or it may merely lessen, with some symptoms continuing for a long period. For a few individuals the symptoms may continue to meet the criteria as much as a year later. Although bereavement or loss of a close loved one can result in behavior similar to that classified as a depressive disorder, a bereaved person who experiences such symptoms for 2 months or less is not considered to have experienced a major depressive episode.

Up to 12% of those who initially have a single episode of major depressive disorder will eventually have a manic or hypomanic episode as well (Akiskal et al., 1995). The initial diagnosis of major depressive disorder will then change to bipolar disorder.

Recurrent Major Depressive Disorder At least half of the people who experience a major depressive episode will later have a recurrence of major depression (Thase & Sullivan, 1995). If they have three or more episodes, then the chance of one or more additional episodes within the next 3 years is almost 80% unless there is appropriate treatment. This means that for many people an initial episode of major depression will develop over time into a recurrent illness. Although a severe life stress may be important in the occurrence of the first or even the second episode of depression, later episodes seem less likely to be related to additional stressful events.

Major Depressive Episode With Psychotic Features
About 15% of people with a major depression have some psychotic symptoms, usually delusions (false beliefs about reality). The delusions typically include guilt ("It is my fault that she is ill"); punishment ("I am suffering because I am a terrible person"); or poverty ("I will go bankrupt and starve in my old age"). Sometimes, but more rarely, the delusions do not have depressive themes.

Behavior typical of depression with psychotic features is illustrated by the case of a 58-year-old man brought to the emergency room by his wife and son:

> *. . . He was working as an architect and doing well until three weeks ago. At that time, he became noticeably more quiet and began to withdraw to his room immediately after dinner. One week ago he refused to go to work, stopped eating, and began to pace the floor at night. He would wring his hands, clench his fists, and cry. He talked of many minor life events as being "major sins" and today began to warn his family that he was really "the devil." "All these years you've mistaken me for your father. I am the devil, Satan himself. No one is more evil and wretched than me. I bring death and disease to the world and I will burn in Hell forever." This is the third time in five years . . . he has professed the belief that his identity has been mistaken and he is really the devil. (Tomb & Christensen, 1987, p. 49)*

Whether psychotic features are present or not, severe depression is highly visible to others. Not only are those who are severely depressed unable to work or carry on other normal life activities, but they also seem immersed in their own misery. The well-known American artist Jacob Lawrence depicted these attributes of severe depression in his painting of hospitalized depressed men painted after his own hospitalization for depression (see Figure 10-5).

Causes and Treatment of Depression

The causes of depression are still not well understood (*Mental Health: A Report of the Surgeon General*, 1999). Many times depression is triggered by stressful life events, yet not all people who experience such events become depressed. How long the stress continues and its intensity, as well as a person's coping skills and the social support available, all seem to interact with genetic factors that contribute to vulnerability to depression. The relative importance of each of these factors in producing some type of depressive disorder may also vary from person to person.

Many theoretical perspectives have contributed to an understanding of depression. Probably none of these perspectives in itself can adequately explain the causes of depression, but when biological, genetic, and psychosocial factors are considered together, progress can be made in understanding and treating depression of different types.

Figure 10-5 In his painting *Depression*, artist Jacob Lawrence showed the downcast eyes, the drooping head and shoulders, and the shrunken posture of people who are deeply depressed.

SOURCE: Jacob Lawrence, *Depression*, 1950. Tempera on paper, 22 × 30 1/2 in. (55.9 × 77.5 cm). Gift of David M. Solinger. Collection of Whitney Museum of American Art, New York. Photo by Geoffrey Clements.

Biological Factors in Depression

Although the specific genetic causes of vulnerability to depression have not yet been identified, it is clear that depression is related to biochemical factors. The lack or the insufficiency of certain chemical neurotransmitters at particular sites in the brain is related to depression. One relatively early hypothesis, called the **monoamine hypothesis,** focused on the activity of several neurotransmitters, including those related to **serotonin** and three **catecholamines** (dopamine, norepinephrine, and epine-phrine), which were thought to be the most important in producing depression.

One problem with this hypothesis is that many other neurotransmitters seem to be involved in depression, including **gamma-aminobutyric acid** (usually referred to as **GABA**) and **acetylcholine** (Rush et al., 1998). Another problem is that insufficiency of monoamines is not consistently present in depression (Dunman et al., 1997). Although these problems indicate that the monoamine hypothesis is not the primary cause of depression, it remains important for treatment purposes.

Neurotransmitters are important because each of the billions of neurons in the brain interacts with other neurons by electrochemical means. When a neuron is stimulated, a chemical substance (the neurotransmitter) is released from **vesicles** or storage areas in one neuron, called the presynaptic neuron. The neurotransmitter dif-

fuses across the synaptic cleft or space between two neurons (see Chapter 2) and interacts with receptors on the outside surface of the postsynaptic neuron. Figure 10-6 is a greatly simplified diagram that illustrates how one of these neurotransmitters, serotonin, crosses the synapse from one neuron to another. The arrival of an electrical impulse or action potential in the presynaptic neuron results in the release of serotonin from vesicles where it has been stored after it has been synthesized from the amino acid tryptophan. The serotonin then moves into the synaptic cleft. Some of it finds its way to specialized receptors in the postsynaptic or receiving neuron, and as a result the postsynaptic neuron alters its electrical and chemical activity. Serotonin can also be removed from the synapse in two other ways besides moving it to the postsynaptic neuron. Reuptake mechanisms in the presynaptic neuron can remove the serotonin from the synapse by taking it back. Another way serotonin is deactivated is by the enzyme **monoamine oxidase (MAO),** which causes serotonin to change chemically into another form, 5-hydroxyindole acetic acid (5-HIAA). Both MAO and the reuptake mechanisms decrease the amount of serotonin available at the synapse.

A great deal has been learned about the role of the monoamines, especially serotonin, through studies of the actions of different types of antidepressant drugs. Each group of drugs has a different approach to regulating the

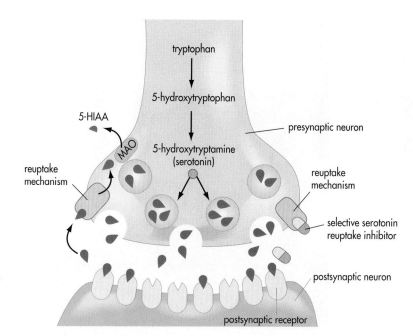

Figure 10-6   This simplified diagram of a serotonin synapse shows the release and reuptake of serotonin as well as its binding to postsynaptic receptors.

SOURCE: Adapted from Jacobs (1994).

amount of serotonin in the synapse. Antidepressants called **monoamine oxidase (MAO) inhibitors** work by inhibiting or lessening the ability of MAO to change serotonin into 5-HIAA. This MAO inhibitor action leads to a buildup of serotonin in the brain. However, because MAO performs a number of vital chemical functions in the brain, MAO inhibitors can be very toxic because they affect these other functions in addition to altering the amount of serotonin available. Newer versions of MAO inhibitors called **reversible inhibitors of monoamine oxidase (RIMAs)** have been developed that seem to greatly reduce the risk of the dangerous side effects of MAO inhibitors by having more focused, selective effects. However, initial testing of RIMAs also indicates that they may not be as effective in reducing symptoms of depression as MAO inhibitors (Lotufo-Neto et al., 1999).

In contrast to MAO inhibitors, **tricyclic antidepressants** work by blocking the reuptake of serotonin back into the presynaptic neuron. This results in a larger supply of serotonin in the synapse. Although tricyclic antidepressants do not have the more dangerous side effects of MAO inhibitors, they cause side effects because they also block the reuptake of norepinephrine and dopamine as well as serotonin. The resulting increase in these monamines may produce a variety of side effects, including dryness of the mouth, constipation, and headaches. A newer group of drugs, called **selective serotonin reuptake inhibitors (SSRIs)** limit their action to serotonin and thus cause fewer side effects. Each of these categories of antidepressant drugs is described later in this chapter, in Table 10-6.

Research using antidepressant drugs has shown that their use changes levels of norepinephrine and serotonin rather quickly after the drugs are taken. However, the mood-elevating effects of these changes often cannot be observed for several weeks.

Markers of Depression   Since most scientists agree that not all depressions have similar causes, a great deal of effort has been spent on finding subgroups of depressed patients who have similar characteristics. The study of such subgroups should not only make it easier to understand the causes of depression but, even more important, provide clues to the most effective treatment for a particular individual. A major focus of research in this area is the effort to develop a test that could be used to identify various subgroups, just as laboratory tests are used to identify particular strains of bacteria in order to diagnose types of infection.

Scanning Techniques   Findings from a variety of scanning techniques—computerized tomography (CT), magnetic resonance imaging (MRI), positron emission tomography (PT), and single photon emission computed tomography (SPECT)—done on individuals with depression suggest that the disorder is associated with some type of regional brain dysfunction. Dysphoric mood, inability to experience pleasure, helplessness, and feelings of sadness all are shown by these scanning techniques to be associated with changes in blood flow in the cerebrum and/or with differences in metabolism in the frontal-temporal areas of the cortex and other specific brain areas (Cummings, 1993).

Because the MRI scanning technique does not expose the person scanned to any potential harmful effects even with repeated use, it has spurred a considerable amount of research on biological abnormalities in the brain and how they correlate with behavioral and emotional patterns that distinguish different patterns of symptoms in major depression (Rush et al., 1998).

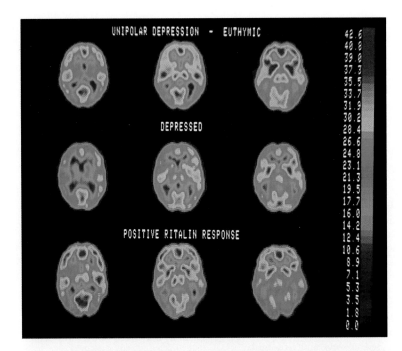

Figure 10-7 Each row of PT scans depicts three views of a portion of the brain of a patient diagnosed with unipolar depression. They illustrate how the PT scanning technique can be used as an objective measure of changes in biological activity that accompany certain behavior changes. The center row of scans illustrates the decreased glucose metabolism typically found in unipolar depressed patients (in the scan, the more to the blue-green end of the spectrum the area is, the less the metabolic activity). The top row shows an increase in glucose metabolism after the patient has naturally recovered from a period of depression. The bottom row shows an increase in glucose metabolism similar to that seen in natural recovery, but which is produced when the patient has been treated with an antidepressant.

Source: Photo from O. Lingjaerde (1983). "The Biochemistry of Depression," in *Acta Psychiatrica Scandinavica Supplementum, 302*, pp. 36–41. © 1983 by Munksgaard International Publishers Ltd., Copenhagen, Denmark.

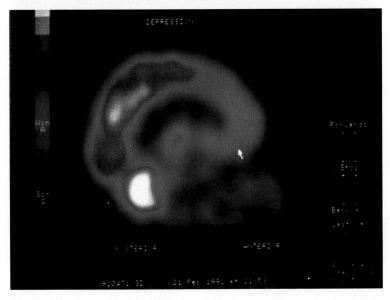

Figure 10-8 A SPECT scan showing the low level of frontal activity (see dark area at right of scan) in a clinically depressed patient.

Source: From M. S. George, H. A. Ring, & D. C. Costa (1991), *Neuroactivation and Neuroimaging With SPECT*, London: Springer Verlag, as reprinted in *Journal of Clinical Psychiatry 54, Sup. 11*, 1993, p. 9.

Figure 10-7 shows how PT scans of the brain of a patient with a major depressive disorder indicate changes as the depression decreases, as well as the effects of a drug that produces a lessening of depressed behaviors. Figure 10-8 shows a SPECT scan of a vertical interior view of the brain that is similar to the PT findings in showing decreased blood flow in the frontal brain region. An important area of future research using these imaging techniques involves finding whether any of these differences continue after patients have recovered from an episode of depression. If the blood flow and metabolism return to normal, this suggests that they are a result rather than an initial cause of the depressive episode.

Biological Rhythms The study of biological rhythms may be another way to clarify how biological functioning differs for people who are depressed as compared to those who are not. Regular daily rhythms in the functioning of human beings and other animals have been recognized for a long time. Seasonal changes may also affect biological rhythms. **Seasonal affective disorder (SAD),** described in Box 10-1, is a type of depression related to seasonal rather than daily rhythms.

Biological rhythms are controlled or influenced by internal factors, including neurotransmitters, as well as by external factors, such as light. Some circadian rhythms, such as body temperature and sleep activity, are usually synchronized so that their peaks occur at the same time. When these rhythms get out of synchrony, other changes occur. For instance, sleep lasts a long time if a person goes to sleep at the top of the body temperature curve. If, instead, the person goes to sleep near the bottom of the

Research Close-up

Seasonal Affective Disorder

Most of us would feel more cheerful strolling through spring flowers, with balmy breezes and brightly shining sun, than battling through a winter sleet storm in the late afternoon when darkness is already coming on. Many people respond to seasonal changes with changes in affect, bodily responses, and behavior. This seasonal phenomenon has been recognized for thousands of years. For example, Aristotle and Hippocrates both mentioned it (Wehr, 1989). Yet these changes may have to do not so much with temperature or bad weather as with the amount of daylight during the seasonal period.

Most people live in regions of the world where the number of hours of light per day vary with the season. This has the most extreme effect in the farthest northern and southern parts of the globe, where winter daylight is short. In 1984, it was first formally recognized that some people suffered recurrent depression that started in the fall, lasted through the winter, and ended in the spring, in a regular pattern associated with the number of hours of seasonal light and darkness (N. E. Rosenthal et al., 1984). The researchers called this disorder **seasonal affective disorder (SAD).** The current DSM-IV criteria for SAD, now called recurrent mood disorder with seasonal pattern, are shown in Table 10-4. Figure 10-9 shows the difference in the percentages of people affected by SAD in the different latitudes of the United States. The seasonal effect of this disorder has been supported by findings that if those affected move from northern to more southern latitudes in the United States, their symptoms improve.

Although latitude and the shortness of winter daylight may be important in the prevalence of SAD, this relationship is much higher in the United States than in other countries. In European countries there is a relationship but it is much lower (Mersch et al., 1999). In Iceland, a country far to the north of the United States, no change in the preva-

lence of depression in the winter and summer months has been found (Magnusson et al., 2000). These differences in pattern of seasonal depression from that found in the United States suggest that other factors such as climate, genetic vulnerability, and sociocultural factors may play a more important role than latitude in SAD.

For the typical individual with SAD, the symptoms may begin in November and last for an average of 5 months. Figure 10-10 shows the average yearly profile for a group of SAD patients who were studied for a period of at least 7 years. Symptoms of SAD include mood change, loss of energy, increased anxiety and irritability, weight gain apparently resulting from a craving for foods high in carbohydrates, and an increase in hours of sleep. The pattern of symptoms seems to be the reverse of some aspects of the symptom pattern most characteristic of depression, which is usually accompanied by weight loss and difficulty in sleeping.

It is not clear whether SAD is more closely related to unipolar or bipolar mood disorder (Dalgleish, et al., 1996). It has also been linked to eating disorders, especially bulimia (Braun et al., 1999). For those affected, the pattern of seasonal change is consistent across a multiyear period. In one 7-year follow-up of the first 59 SAD patients treated at the National Institute of Mental Health, about 40% continued to have pure seasonal affective disorder, 40% developed some nonseasonal depression as well, and 10% no longer had symptoms. All these individuals had been treated for SAD, and most who had symptoms were currently receiving treatment (P. J. Schwartz et al., 1996).

The disorder is most likely to begin in early adulthood, although substantial numbers of children and adolescents seem to be affected. The majority of those diagnosed with the disorder are female. The ratio is higher than the 1-to-2 ratio for men and women found in the depressive

Table 10–4

Summary of Diagnostic Criteria for Recurrent Mood Disorder With Seasonal Pattern (SAD)

- A regular temporal relationship between the onset of major depressive episodes and a particular time of year (this does not include cases in which particular psychosocial stresses, such as a heavy work load, tend to occur at a particular time every year: e.g., the work load of accountants prior to income tax deadlines). These episodes may occur either in people with diagnoses of recurrent major depressive disorder or in people with bipolar disorder.
- Full remission (or disappearance of symptoms), or a change from depression to episodes of mania or hypomania, that also occurs at a particular time of the year.
- The occurrence in the last 2 years of two major depressive episodes showing the temporal seasonal relationships described above, but no nonseasonal major depressive episodes during the same period.
- Substantially more seasonal major depressive episodes in the individual's lifetime than any nonseasonal major depressive episodes that may have occurred.

Source: Adapted from DSM-IV.

disorders. Families of people diagnosed with SAD are likely to have a higher than average rate of psychiatric disorder (Kasper et al., 1989). Twin studies also show that there is a strong genetic effect for both men and women (Sher et al., 1999).

Box 10-1

Several theories have focused on physiological processes. Of these, the most likely seem to relate to neurotransmitter function. Dopamine, serotonin, and noradrenaline have all been thought to be related to SAD. Another research approach is the study of out-of-phase circadian rhythm (Rosenthal & Wehr, 1992). Styles of negative thinking and depressive attributions may also prolong the seasonal depression once it occurs (M. Marks & Hodges, 1993).

Phototherapy (light therapy) is the therapy most often recommended for treatment of SAD. It consists of exposure to a high-intensity light source for a prescribed period of time once or twice a day. Light therapy is known to be very effective for patients with typical symptoms of SAD and appears to have no long-term negative effects even if used for 7 years or more (P. J. Schwartz et al., 1996). However, there is no agreement on what pattern of light exposure is best or what portion of the wavelength is most beneficial. It may be the exposure to infrared light that is most effective rather than the visible component of light (Meesters et al., 1999). Some researchers think intense light in the early morning is best; others prefer light gradually increasing in intensity each day in a simulation of dawn. However, those who have typical symptoms show the most improvement with more intense light. For those with atypical symptoms (e.g., having a reverse pattern of greater depression in summer than winter) the intensity of the light seemed to make no difference (Lee & Chan, 1999). For those who have severe SAD symptoms, a combination of light treatment and use of one of the SSRI group of antidepressants seemed to produce the best long-term effects (Thorell et al., 1999).

continued

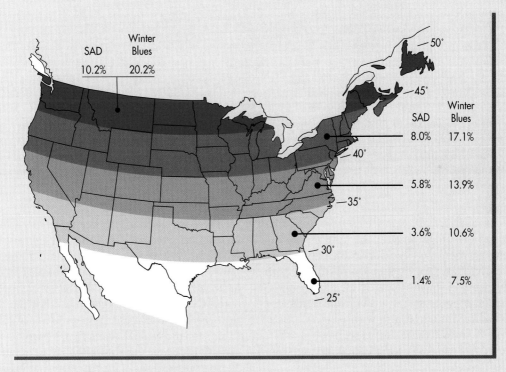

Figure 10-9   The estimated percentages of seasonal affective disorder and its milder form, "winter blues," vary by latitude and the resulting differences in the hours of winter sunlight.

SOURCE: *The New York Times,* December 29, 1992, p. B7.

Research Close-up

Box 10-1

continued

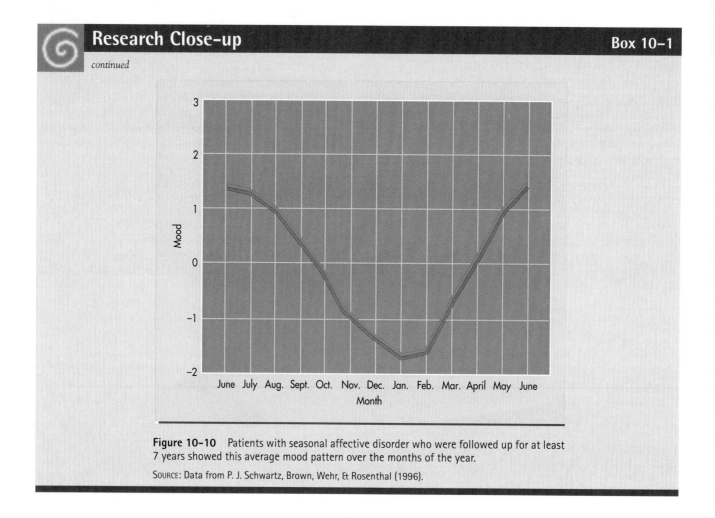

Figure 10-10 Patients with seasonal affective disorder who were followed up for at least 7 years showed this average mood pattern over the months of the year.

SOURCE: Data from P. J. Schwartz, Brown, Wehr, & Rosenthal (1996).

temperature curve, sleep lasts a much shorter time. Depression researchers are interested in how biological rhythms affect sleep because sleep disturbance is frequent in depressed individuals. They tend to have trouble both in going to sleep and in staying asleep. Researchers studying the causes of depression had noted that treatment with antidepressant drugs and also with electroconvulsive therapy (ECT) causes these sleep disturbances to disappear. Table 10-5 lists some of the characteristic sleep disturbances of depressed people.

Sleep has a number of phases that can be measured by monitoring the electrical impulses of the brain. The one that is of most interest from the standpoint of depression is REM sleep, during which the eyes rapidly move from side to side and brain wave patterns indicate a peak in brain activity. In some depressed individuals there is a shortened period between falling asleep and the beginning of the first REM period, as well as increased length and intensity in the first REM period of the night. During REM sleep the serotonin-transmitting neurons become completely inactive (Jacobs, 1994). It may be that the increased REM period may be related to a decrease in available serotonin. The causal factors in this relationship, however, are unclear.

These connections between REM sleep and serotonin production have led some researchers to study the effect of sleep deprivation on depression. In one study, 15 depressed and 15 control subjects experienced a night of total sleep deprivation (Wu et al., 1992). PT scans were taken the day before and the day after the sleep deprivation. Although not all the depressed patients improved, those who did had PT scans that showed hyperactivity in some limbic areas of the brain before sleep deprivation, and normal patterns of limbic activity afterward. Depressed individuals who did not improve showed normal limbic patterns both before and afterward. Thus sleep deprivation appeared to affect abnormal limbic function. Research such as this is important in understanding biological factors in depression and may help clinicians predict which type of treatment would be most helpful for each particular subgroup of depressed individuals.

Biologically Based Treatment

Basic research both on chemical compounds that alter neurotransmitter action and on changes in brain activity that accompany depression have led to two major biologically based treatment approaches: antidepressant medi-

Table 10–5
Major Sleep Disturbances Common to Depression

Shallow Sleep

- Decreased Stage 3 and 4 (Delta) sleep
- Increased Stage 1 sleep
- Greater sensitivity to noises

Fragmented Sleep

- Increased awakenings
- Increased stage shifts
- Decreased sleep efficiency

Short Sleep

- Decreased total sleep time
- Increased time to fall asleep
- Increased early morning wakening

"Intense" REM Sleep

- Increased REM density (increased eye movement during REM sleep)

REM Sleep Advanced Toward Sleep Onset

- REM beginning sooner after falling asleep
- Increased length and REM density of first REM period
- Increased proportion of REM in first half of night

Source: Adapted from Campbell & Gillin (1987).

cation and electroconvulsive therapy. Of the two, the use of antidepressant drugs is far more common.

Antidepressant Medication In severe depression in which a depressed person must be initially hospitalized, the current standard of care specifies the use of **antidepressant medication** (American Psychiatric Association, 1994). However, many people do not recover completely with the use of these drugs. Only about 29% to 46% of depressed patients respond fully to antidepressant treatment in which they receive both an adequate dosage and an adequate length of treatment with the medication (Fava & Davidson, 1996). Another 15% seem to be helped somewhat, and the remainder seem not to respond to the treatment at all.

As Table 10-6 shows, many types of antidepressant medications exist and many new medications are being developed. Because depressive disorders are serious and disabling illnesses and because they may affect one in five individuals in his or her lifetime, it is important to know how effective antidepressant medications are. The Agency for Health Care Policy and Research (1999) commissioned a review of research on the effectiveness of antidepressant medications. The review showed that many people recover from episodes of depression on their own. In the control group, an average of 32% improved considerably although

they received only a placebo. Overall, the use of antidepressants increased the number who improved considerably to 50%. In addition, if the medication was continued for at least 6 months after recovery from the depression, the overall risk of relapse was decreased by 70%. The review showed that the newer antidepressant drugs are about equally as effective as the older tricyclic antidepressants in treating major depression but that the new drugs are preferable in many cases because they have fewer side effects. This study also showed that these drugs were similarly effective in treating dysthymia. However, all currently available groups of antidepressants do not work equally well for every individual, so one challenge is to determine how to select the best medication for any one patient.

In choosing an antidepressant for a particular person, psychiatrists and other physicians usually consider the person's past treatment history, the likelihood of side effects, the safety of the medication if taken in overdose, and the expense of the drug chosen. On the basis of these criteria, a drug in the SSRI group is often the first choice (Vanderhoff & Miller, 1997). Not only do these drugs have fewer bothersome side effects, they are also easy to use and are safer than drugs in other groups if taken in overdose. The safety issue is an important one, because by giving depressed people access to drugs that could be toxic in high doses, physicians might inadvertently make it easier for those who feel suicidal to kill themselves. In addition to safety concerns, side effects are important in determining whether those who are prescribed a given medication will continue to use it even if it is helpful in reducing depressive symptoms. If side effects are too unpleasant, many people will not want to take a medication regularly, and thus will not receive its full benefit.

One of the SSRI group, fluoxetine (Prozac), has become one of the best-selling drugs in the world. Claims for this drug extend to its use for many other problems in addition to depression (see Figure 10-11). Some advocates have argued that fluoxetine is also appropriate for people who are not clinically depressed because it makes them "still happier" and "better than well" (M. W. Miller, 1994). Most researchers view such claims with skepticism. Scientific proof of a drug's effectiveness for a particular disorder or set of symptoms, along with consideration of possible short- and long-term side effects, needs to be considered in making the choice to prescribe Prozac or any other medication.

In considering treatment of depressive disorder, it is important to consider the pattern of the disorder. A typical pattern often consists of initial symptoms and a progression into the disorder, followed by a lessening of the symptoms without a return to completely normal functioning. If the symptoms then reappear, the individual is said to have experienced a **relapse.** If the symptoms lessen so that the person returns to his or her normal state, the depression is said to be in **remission.** A relapse can still occur during the remission. However, if the remission continues for at least

Table 10–6

Examples of Some Classes of Medication Used to Treat Mood Disorders

"Older" Antidepressants	Trade Names (Examples)	General Description of Effects
First-generation tricyclics		
Amitriptyline	Elavil	Variable effectiveness in moderating symptoms. Slow-acting.
Doxepin	Sinequan	Many side effects. Dangerous in overdose.
Imipramine	Tofranil	
Trimipramine	Surmontil	
Second-generation (secondary amines)		
Desipramine	Norpramin	Somewhat less dangerous side effects than first generation.
Nortriptyline	Aventyl, Pamelor	
Protriptyline	Vivactil	Protriptyline may cause irregular heart beat.
Other older antidepressants		
Amoxapine (disbenzoxazepine)	Ascendin	Likely to cause drowsiness.
Maprotiline (tetracyclic)	Ludiomil	Maprotiline and tradazone can dangerously lower blood
Trazadone (trizolopyridine)	Desyrel	pressure.
MAO inhibitors (nonselective)		
Phenelzine	Nardil	Require restrictions in diet because of serious interactive
Tranylcypromine	Parnate	effects with certain food chemicals. Slow-acting.
"Newer" Antidepressants		
Selective serotonin reuptake inhibitors (SSRIs):		
Citalopram	Celexa, Vitalopram	Fewer side effects than tricyclics or MAO inhibitors. More
Fluoxetine	Prozac	specific focus on serotonin receptors. Slow-acting. Safe in
Paroxetine	Paxil	overdose. Expensive.
Sertaline	Zoloft	
Reversible inhibitors of monoamine oxidase A (RIMAs)		
Medifoxamine	Cledial	Less dangerous, more selective, fewer side effects.
Moclobemide	Aurorex	Increase concentrations of norepinephrine, 5-HT, and dopamine.
Other Types of Medication for Depression		
Bupropion	Wellbutrin	Blocks dopamine reuptake, relatively few side effects.
Venlafaxine	Effexor	Affects serotonin/norepinephrine reuptake inhibitors.
Nefazodone	Serzone	Affects 5-HT receptors.
Hypericum (St. John's wort)	Valeriana, Kava	Herbal remedy, sometimes used for mild depression, effects
	Kava	unclear.
Medication for Bipolar Disorder		
Lithium carbonate	Eskalith, Lithane	Mood stabilizer, highly toxic, used when family history of
Valproate		bipolar disorder.
	Depacon	Anticonvulsant, used for bipolar disorder.

6 months, the patient may be considered to be **recovered.** If another episode of depression occurs after recovery, then the new symptoms are termed a **recurrence.** Figure 10-12 shows these periods graphically.

The use of antidepressant medication, its combination with psychotherapy or another psychosocial therapy, or the use of the psychosocial therapy alone may differ in effectiveness across these time periods. **Maintenance therapy**—that is, continuing the medication for some time after the patient shows an improvement in or a remission

"How about that! I take Prozac too."

Figure 10-11   The widespread knowledge about Prozac makes this cartoon funny.

SOURCE: "Pepper . . . and Salt," *The Wall Street Journal*, November 4, 1996, p. A23.

of symptoms—is usually recommended for those who have had three or more depressive episodes, who have a chronic depression, or whose depression is part of a bipolar disorder (Prien & Kocsis, 1995). Although antidepressants are currently the treatment of choice in the acute phase of a major depressive disorder, research suggests that other types of therapy we will discuss later—either cognitive-behavioral therapy or interpersonal psychotherapy (IPT)—may be effective in reducing the relapse rate after medication is withdrawn or may be an effective substitute for medication during a remission (Evans et al., 1992). For patients who are severely depressed but who do not need hospitalization, four major studies have shown that cognitive-behavioral therapy may be equally as effective as antidepressant medication (DeRubeis et al., 1999).

Electroconvulsive Therapy One of the problems in treating a severe episode of depression with antidepressant drugs is the time lag between their initial use and the first signs of improvement in the patient's mood. Several weeks may go by before any improvement is seen. If there is concern about suicide, a wait of 3 weeks or so may seem too great a risk. In such situations, or if drugs are not effective, electroconvulsive therapy may be the treatment used because it produces a more rapid effect. Although electroconvulsive therapy is not effective in dysthymia and adjustment disorder with depressed mood, it is more effective than other treatments in very severe depression (Rudorfer et al., 1997).

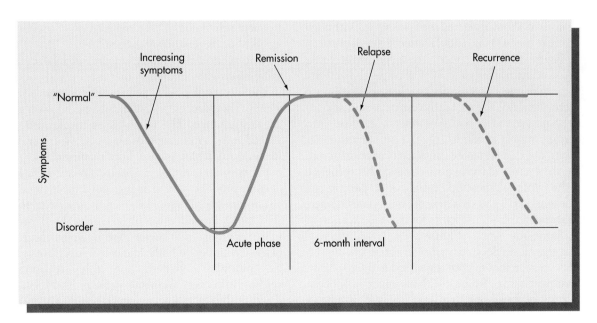

Figure 10-12   Either with or without treatment, mood disorders usually have an episodic pattern. This means that symptoms appear and after a time may lessen, either as a result of treatment or in the natural progress of the disorder. If the person again functions at the old "normal" level, he or she is said to be *in remission.* If, after some improvement, the symptoms again worsen, the affected individual has had a *relapse.* A relapse can also occur during the acute phase when symptoms worsen before the remission stage is reached. If the remission lasts at least 6 months and then symptoms reappear, the patient is said to have experienced a *recurrence* rather than a relapse.

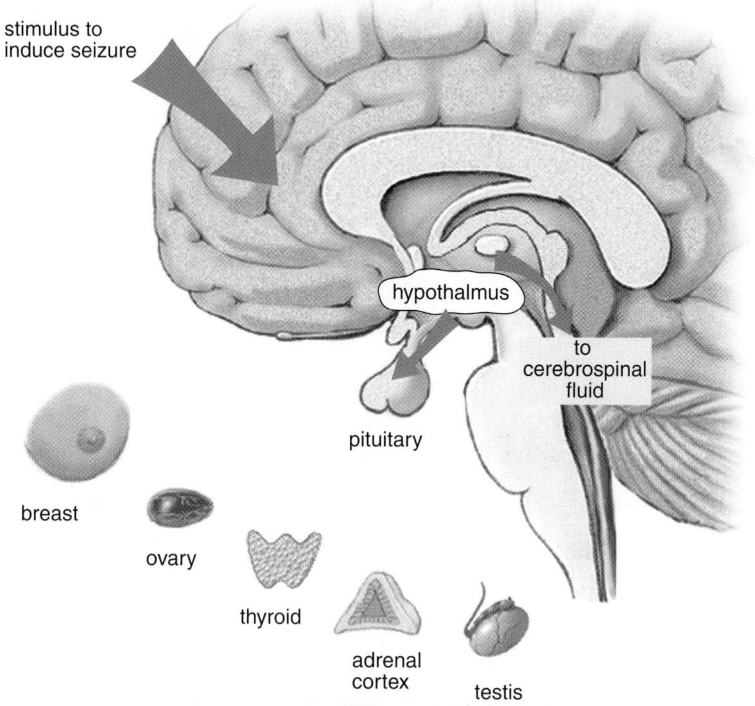

Figure 10-13 One hypothesis of how ECT produces changes in the brain. Here the seizure caused by the ECT makes the hypothalamus release peptides (red arrow) into the cerebrospinal fluid of the ventricles and the hormone-releasing factors (green arrow) into the anterior pituitary. The peptides released into the cerebrospinal fluid diffuse to many parts of the brain and can alter brain function. The hormone-releasing factors stimulate the anterior pituitary to release hormones (blue arrows) that stimulate activity in various glands of the body. These glands then release other hormones.

SOURCE: M. Fink (2000). Electroshock revisited. *American Scientist, 88*, p. 166.

Electroconvulsive therapy (ECT) involves producing a series of brief generalized seizures by passing an electric current through the brain by means of two electrodes placed on the scalp. A typical ECT treatment involves 6 to 12 sessions at about three sessions per week. Although it is not clear precisely how ECT affects the depression process, Figure 10-13 illustrates one hypothesis (Fink, 2000). According to this view, ECT changes the activity of the hypothalamus by causing it to release peptides into the cerebrospinal fluid of the brain ventricles and also increases the movement of hormone-releasing factors into the anterior pituitary (Fink, 1999). The pituitary then releases hormones that stimulate the activity of other glands as well as the brain and the hypothalamus. This sequence "resets" the hypothalamus and possibly other parts of the brain. Although ECT does readjust the hormonal balance, whether this change is responsible for the effectiveness of ECT on depression is not yet known.

ECT is the most effective treatment for severe depression and depression that has not responded to the use of antidepressants (Thase & Rush, 1995). However, only about half the cases of depression that have not responded to a range of antidepressant medications then respond to ECT. ECT is also effective in treating severe depression in which there is a great deal of delusional thinking and where no precipitating event or events can be identified (Rush & Weissenburger, 1994). It is particularly difficult to protect patients against relapse after a course of ECT administration has improved their symptoms. Antidepressants offer no protection for those who were initially not helped by those medications. A continuation of ECT on a less-frequent schedule has been tried, but that has not yet been established as generally beneficial.

The safety of ECT has been improved by the use of brief-pulse electrical stimulation that uses only about one-third of the electrical power used in older methods (Andrade, 1998). This reduces the potential for confusion and memory disturbance. The stimulus electrodes are generally placed only on one side of the head (the nondominant hemisphere, which is away from the primary learning and memory brain centers). These modifications in ECT procedure produce virtually no detectable memory loss (Rudorfer et al, 1997). However, these new methods were sometimes less effective in lessening the depression. A newer approach that seems to work well is the placement of the electrodes on both sides of the very front of the head. This bifrontal placement seems to lessen depression and yet has little effect on memory (Fink, 2000). Figure 10-14 diagrams the placement of electrodes and a variety of physiological monitors on a patient prior to ECT treatment.

At present, because of public concern about the safety of this treatment, ECT is ordinarily administered only after the patient gives consent. In cases where the patient is not considered to be capable of giving consent because of

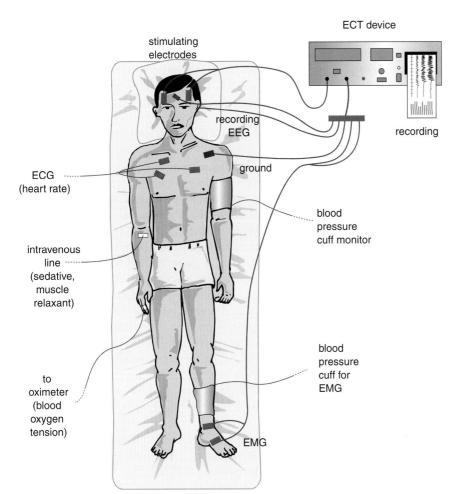

ECT device

stimulating
electrodes

recording
EEG

recording

ground

ECG
(heart rate)

blood
pressure
cuff monitor

intravenous
line
(sedative,
muscle
relaxant)

blood
pressure
cuff for
EMG

to
oximeter
(blood
oxygen
tension)

EMG

Figure 10-14   This diagram shows the setup for ECT and the various monitoring methods used to assess the patient's status during the treatment. In this diagram the electrodes are placed on both sides of the forehead, a position thought to greatly reduce negative effects of ECT without reducing its effectiveness.

Source: M. Fink (2000). Electroshock revisited. *American Scientist, 88,* p. 165.

the severity of the symptoms, consent must be obtained through a court hearing in which the patient is entitled to legal representation. Because ECT tends to lead to shorter hospital stays and cuts medical costs, there has been fear that low-income patients will be forced to undergo this treatment as a cost-saving measure. However, the legal requirements make this unlikely and, in fact, poor and minority patients are less likely to receive ECT than more affluent patients. This may be an unfortunate consequence for those affected by the severe mental disorders for which ECT seems to be the best treatment choice.

Sometimes ECT can produce dramatic changes in mood. Norman Endler, the psychologist whose description of his own depression (later diagnosed as a bipolar type) appears at the beginning of this chapter, also described his experience with ECT after both tricyclic and MAO-inhibiting drugs had proved ineffective and the depression was still incapacitating him after 5 months. Endler was faced with a choice between ECT and hospitalization; he reluctantly chose ECT.

Dr. Persad met us on the sixth floor at seven forty-five. He tried to calm me down, and I recall his saying that he had never seen anyone so agitated as I. The prospect of ECT really frightened me.

Beatty [Endler's wife] remained in the waiting area and Dr. Persad and I went into the ECT room. I changed into my pajamas and a nurse took my vital signs [blood pressure, pulse, and temperature]. The nurse and other attendants were friendly and reassuring. I began to feel at ease. The anesthetist arrived and informed me that she was going to give me an injection. I was asked to lie down on a cot and was wheeled into the ECT room proper. It was about eight o'clock. A needle was injected into my arm and I was told to count back from 100. I got about as far as 91. The next thing I knew I was in the recovery room and it was about eight-fifteen. I was slightly groggy and tired but not confused. My memory was not impaired. I certainly knew where I was. Shortly after eight-thirty, I got dressed, went down the hall to fetch Beatty, and she drove me home. At home I had breakfast and then lay down for a few hours. Late in the morning I got dressed. I felt no pain, no confusion, and no agitation. I felt neither less depressed nor more depressed than I had before the ECT. . . . After about the third or fourth treatment I went up to Dr. Persad's office and spoke to him briefly. He asked me if I had noticed any improvement and to what degree. I believed that I had improved 35 to 40 percent. Dr. Persad believed that the improvement was more likely to be 70 to 75 percent. (Endler, 1990, pp. 74–75)

After the fifth and sixth treatments had been completed, Endler returned to his office. A colleague who had been helping to manage the psychology department in his absence was there.

I asked her to remain. She stated that she would be glad to stay as long as I needed her assistance. By early afternoon Kathy looked at me and said "Norm, you are perfectly fine, you do not need me here." She left and I stayed the rest of the day. As of then I resumed the chairmanship full time. A miracle had happened in two weeks. I had gone from feeling like an emotional cripple to feeling well. (Endler, 1990, p. 75)

Like many people who have a bipolar disorder, Endler experienced another depression about a year after the first. This time, although ECT produced improvement and made it possible for him to work effectively, the depressed mood hung on for several months. Treatment with a combination of antidepressants and lithium led to a quick recovery.

Psychodynamic Theories

The psychodynamic view of depression considers both the causes of the depressed person's problems and the treatment to help those problems quite differently than the biological perspective. Although the psychodynamic approach—especially in terms of the early psychoanalytic theories and therapeutic approaches of Freud and others—is rarely used today for the treatment of depressive disorder, some of the basic ideas from these theories have influenced two of the therapeutic approaches most often used today, interpersonal psychotherapy and cognitive-behavioral therapy. For that reason, it is important to understand some basic ideas stemming from the original psychoanalytic perspective as well as later modified views that continue to stress psychodynamic factors but depart from the original theories.

The psychological study of depression was begun by Sigmund Freud and a German physician named Karl Abraham. Each of them described depression as a complex reaction to loss (Abraham, 1911/1968; Freud, 1917/1957). Depression (or melancholy, as Freud called it) was grief gone haywire—excessive, drawn out, often unrelated to the environment, and seemingly unjustified. Freud described both normal mourning and depression as responses to the loss of someone or something that was loved. However, in contrast to the mourner, Freud believed that the depressed person suffered "an extraordinary diminution of his self-regard, an impoverishment of his ego on a grand scale" (Freud, 1917/1957, p. 246). Freud thought that a depressed person had a strong and punishing conscience, or superego and that one reason the conscience became so strong was to control the anger and aggressive feelings that otherwise might come forth to hurt others (Freud, 1930).

Much later, a different way of conceptualizing depression from a psychodynamic view was suggested by Edward Bibring (1953), an Austrian psychoanalyst. He viewed depression as the emotional expression of the ego's helplessness in maintaining a desired sense of self. He changed the focus from Freud's emphasis on internal conflict to feelings of helplessness associated with particular situations. This idea became important in later efforts to understand and treat depression from a cognitive perspective.

Psychoanalytic theorists have suggested that clinical episodes of depression happen because the events that set off the depression revive dimly conscious, threatening views of the self and others that are based on childhood experience. These assumptions appear to be related to a childhood belief that one will never be loved by others, will never become worthwhile, and will always lack the ability to control what happens. John Bowlby, a British psychoanalyst, was one of the prominent theorists who emphasized the importance of childhood loss or separation to later development. Bowlby (1980) believed that the childhood experiences that contribute to these feelings were not single events, but developed from long-term patterns of familial interaction.

Research supports the view that a combination of traumatic childhood experiences and acute external stressful events in adulthood is associated with the occurrence of a major depressive episode (Alnaes & Torgersen, 1993). The following case illustrates how past experiences may contribute to depression and anxiety in the present:

One depressed woman stated that she became symptomatic when she could no longer keep up with her work and felt herself to be a failure. This explanation was partially true but did not go far enough in describing her actual situation. Later it [became clear] that she began to feel anxious and dysphoric when her boss, upon whom she depended for a sense of worth . . . hired another female assistant. This threatened the patient's imagined special status with the boss, and she anticipated that he would favor the new employee, who was erroneously perceived as more able, attractive, and likable than the patient. Much of this reaction was a recapitulation of the events surrounding the birth of a younger sibling when the patient was five years old. Just as in childhood, she attempted to win back the father's preferential regard by working harder and harder, in order to obtain praise and reassurance.

However, in contrast to her father, the boss did not sufficiently recognize her increased effort, causing her to apply herself even harder so that her work did become too much for her. Therefore, she did become depressed as a result of being overwhelmed by her work; however, the initiative to do more and more was of her own choosing, and the basic reason for it was to become reinstated as the boss/father's favorite. (Bemporad & Vasile, 1990, pp. 57–58)

With the help of the therapist, this client gradually began to understand that her beliefs originated in childhood. As she became aware of these distorted views, other distortions in her reactions to the therapist became clear. These are called "transference distortions" because the client reacted to the therapist as if he behaved toward her as her father did, although this was not the case. For example, although she was unaware of doing so, she began to defer toward the therapist as a parental figure. But the therapist, instead of acting out the parental role she expected, helped her to identify and examine the reactions she anticipated. As these old assumptions began to alter, the client was able to be comfortable with the idea that perfection either in one's own eyes or in the eyes of others is not necessary for happiness or love.

Interpersonal Psychotherapy

Current emphasis on short-term therapies has focused interest on a variation of psychodynamic therapy, **interpersonal psychotherapy (IPT).** Interpersonal psychotherapy was originally designed to prevent relapse following an acute episode of depression that had been treated with antidepressant medication (Frank & Spanier, 1995). Since that time it has become a well-researched psychotherapeutic intervention useful both in the treatment of acute depression and as a way to prevent a relapse in those who were recovering from a major depressive episode (Weissman & Markowitz, 1994). IPT developed from the ideas of Adolf Meyer, a psychiatrist who argued that the way a person responds to changes in the adult environment is, in part, a direct reflection of his or her interpersonal experiences in early life, especially experiences within the family. Another contributor to this viewpoint was John Bowlby, who believed that many forms of psychopathology were the result of inability to form or to maintain positive emotional bonds (Bowlby, 1977a). Bowlby suggested that psychotherapy should emphasize the connections between these early attachment bonds with parents and current adult relationship patterns with significant others (Bowlby, 1977b).

Another contribution to the development of IPT was early work on the association between the onset of depression and stressful life events, especially events that involved the loss of important people, either through death or by divorce or other factors (Paykel, 1985). Research showing that social support protected people who had experienced such negative events from becoming depressed (G. W. Brown & Harris, 1978) also played a role in the development of IPT.

IPT has been described by some of its proponents as a therapy that one's grandmother would find sensible (Frank & Spanier, 1995). It focuses on teaching people to be more socially effective as a way to improve their relationships with their significant others. It integrates the psychodynamic perspective, which emphasizes early childhood experiences, with the cognitive-behavioral perspective, which emphasizes current psychosocial stressors such as chronic marital discord, and with research-based evidence linking difficulties in the immediate social environment with the onset of depression. IPT works well when paired with the use of antidepressant medications and has been demonstrated to be effective, both in lessening depressive symptoms and in extending the period of remission for individuals who have a history of recurrent depressions (Elkin et al., 1989). Currently, with cognitive-behavioral therapy, IPT is one of the most effective psychological therapies used in the treatment of depression.

The Humanistic-Existentialist Perspective

Although the ideas of humanist and existential theorists are usually combined into a general **humanistic-existentialist perspective** because they have many similarities, theorists of these two groups differ somewhat in their major emphases. Existentialist theorists tend to focus on loss of self-esteem, and humanistic theorists focus on the discrepancies between a person's view of the ideal and view of his or her actual self.

For existentialist theorists, instead of emphasis on the loss of a loved object or an important person as central to depression, the loss can be symbolic—power, social rank, or money, for example. Whether the lost object is real or symbolic, the loss itself is not as important as the change in an individual's self-assessment as a result of the loss. Many people base their self-concepts on who they are or what they have: I'm the leader of the factory assembly team; I'm the boss; I'm a member of the exclusive city athletic club; I'm the husband of a famous movie star. Identifications of this kind offer external verification of people's worth in their own minds.

Humanistic theorists such as Carl Rogers (1951, 1980) emphasize the difference between a person's ideal self and his or her perceptions of the actual state of things as the source of depression and anxiety. They believe that depression is likely to result when the difference between the ideal and the real selves becomes too great for the individual to tolerate. This discrepancy occurs frequently, especially among people who have high aspirations for achievement and are trying to fill several roles simultaneously. An example of this problem is the dilemma of many women today. These women may be trying to fill multiple roles—success in a job or career, effectiveness as a wife and household manager, and the role of an attentive mother involved in her children's lives. In such a situation, it is inevitable that each role is not carried out to its highest potential. The resulting discrepancy between the ideal self and the actual self in each of the multiple roles is likely to create stress and depressed feelings as well as possible clinical depression in those women who are especially vulnerable.

The Behavioral Perspective

Behaviorists view depression in a very different way than do either existential or humanistic theorists. Behaviorists are concerned with people's skills in getting social reinforcement and their typical ways of dealing with stressful situations.

When depressed people find themselves in stressful situations, they tend to cope by delaying (seeking more information before taking any action) and attempting to get emotional support from others. Such excessive support seeking may make other people feel uncomfortable and guilty. Depressed people may also complain frequently in order to elicit sympathy and affection. After a while those who are on the receiving end of this behavior may begin to be annoyed or frustrated. Eventually a vicious cycle develops in which the display of the depressed person's symptoms and the frustration of the depressed person's companions increase until the companions begin to say things like "You could get better if you try" or "No one has to act like that!" These statements merely serve to worsen an already bad situation. Such feelings of frustration, whether expressed or not, are probably one reason why people tend to avoid the company of depressed individuals.

Although people who are depressed often seem to take a negative view of their interactions with others, there is considerable evidence that they also make a negative impression on others because of deficits in their social skills (Dykman et al., 1991). A negative spiral results. Not only are depressed people likely to think others respond to them negatively, but others are more likely to respond negatively because of the depressed person's lack of social skills.

Behavioral Treatment for Depression

Because people who are depressed often lack skills necessary to develop satisfying relationships with others, one behavioral approach to this problem is through **social skills training.** Social skills training consists of several parts. First clients are taught basic verbal and nonverbal skills. When these are learned, the clients practice gradually putting the basics together. Then clients are given "homework" assignments in which the goal is to adapt the new skill so it is useful in the everyday environment. Clients are also trained to be more perceptive about cues other people in the environment give, and they learn how to change their own behavior in response. Finally, clients learn to adopt realistic criteria for evaluating their performance and are

taught how to be self-reinforcing. The following case illustrates the effectiveness of social skills training:

> Ms. S. J. is a 43-year-old single woman with a master's degree in chemistry. She has worked as a laboratory assistant for a number of years. She came to the clinic complaining of (a) sad mood, (b) low energy, (c) trouble making decisions, (d) feeling worthless, (e) pessimism about her future, and (f) guilt about her unsuccessful past. She was involved in a three-year intimate relationship, which has just ended. This event has rekindled symptoms of depression and a fear that this new episode would be as bad as a previous one ten years earlier.
>
> Standardized role plays revealed difficulties with display of positive and negative assertion, as well as with conversation. She could not give a compliment to another person, particularly a male, and she could not touch a person. . . .
>
> The first focus of clinical treatment was greeting people. Role plays focused on making eye contact with the other person, saying "Hello, I'm Sarah," and smiling. This behavior contrasted sharply with her current style of avoiding eye contact, not smiling, and only speaking if directly spoken to. . . .
>
> As she began to improve in this skill, touching the other person was added. Reverse role plays were first used, and her initial response to a touch on the hand was to become quite scared, to be silent, and to withdraw as fast as possible. Several practices were carried out in conjunction with a homework assignment. . . . After one week of observational data, she was astounded at how often people touched. . . .
>
> Conversation role plays were repeated to include touching. After many repetitions, she became comfortable and began to enjoy the contact. Two further existing conversation behaviors were addressed before the first homework. . . First, she never wore a name tag. . . . Second, she would always position herself to be out of the way in order not to impede other people. . . . She attended her meetings with instructions (a) to introduce herself and say "Hello, I'm Sarah" to everyone, (b) to wear her name tag, (c) to locate herself in high traffic areas, and (d) to smile with her greeting and with her departure. . . .
>
> This homework assignment resulted in an astonishing response. People were friendly to her, included her in their conversations, and invited her into some of their activities. . . . This was such a success for her that she wondered why she had not done it before. (Becker, 1990, pp. 99–100)

Therapists who use a social skills training approach usually find it works well with depressed clients (Becker, 1990). Role play is necessary so that the client gets the practice needed to use new behaviors in the real-life situations called for in the homework assignments. The practice gained from these assignments is in turn critical for success in learning new habits.

The Cognitive Perspective

Probably the most influential psychological theories of depression today are derived from the cognitive perspective. According to this view, people who are depressed consistently perceive causes of events in a way that is unfavorable to themselves. For example, a person who does not receive an expected promotion might think: "I am a worthless person. Everyone thinks poorly of me. If they did not, I would have been selected for the job." A second person in the same situation might think: "R. was chosen for that job I wanted because he had more experience in negotiation. I know I could have done the job, but my qualifications didn't look as impressive on paper." The first causal attribution is more characteristic of depression than the second.

One cause of unjustified negative interpretations may be the presence of **schemata,** or ways of coding and interpreting behavior. These schemata are thought to have arisen early in life, but they continue their influence into adulthood. Cognitive therapy techniques are used to counter the effects of these schemata and to help the client create new behavioral approaches and alter schemata to make them more adaptive.

Cognitive Distortion The **cognitive distortion model** of depression developed by Aaron Beck (A. T. Beck, 1967, 1976; A. T. Beck et al., 1979) has been the most influential of the cognitive approaches to depression. Beck believes that depression can best be described as a **cognitive triad** of negative thoughts about oneself, the situation, and the future. A person who is depressed misinterprets facts in a negative way, focuses on the negative aspects of any situation, and also has pessimistic and hopeless expectations about the future.

Table 10-7 illustrates some categories of cognitive errors that Beck believes are common in depression. Beck maintains that these cognitions are specific to depression and thus differ from the thoughts of people with anxiety disorders (A. T. Beck et al., 1987). He thinks that the anxious person worries about what *might* happen and *whether* he or she will be able to deal with it. In contrast, the depressed person thinks about how he or she *has* failed in the past, how terrible the future *will* be and how he or she *will be unable* to deal with it or improve it.

Beck believes that a person who is depressed attributes any misfortune to his or her personal defects. Awareness of these presumed defects becomes so intense that it completely overwhelms any positive self-concepts. Any ambiguous situation is interpreted as evidence of the defects, even if there are more plausible explanations. A good example is provided by Norman Endler's description of his thoughts during his bout of depression (Endler, 1990). Endler went through a period of fear (not at all based on reality) that his family would desert him and that he would be unable to cope with everyday living.

> I recall a time during the end of August when I took the subway with my wife. She had gone through the turnstile before I did and I was positive that she was going to desert me. She probably had had enough of me and my shenanigans and was fed up with my behavior. (p. 44)

After his recovery from this period of depression, Endler recognized the irrationality of such a thought.

> Of course nothing could have been further from the truth. Her kindness and devotion, her concern, compassion, and her love, more than anything else, sustained me during my ordeal. If I had to single out the one person who was most instrumental in my getting better, it would be my wife. (p. 44)

Beck also thinks that depressed people tend to emphasize self–other comparisons, which further lower their self-esteem. Every encounter with another person becomes the opportunity for a negative self-evaluation. For instance, when talking with others the depressed person thinks: "I'm not a good conversationalist. I'm not as interesting as other

---

Table 10-7

Cognitive Errors and the Assumptions From Which They Are Derived

Cognitive Error	Assumption
1. Overgeneralizing	1. If it is true in one case, it applies to any case that is even slightly similar.
2. Selective abstraction	2. The only events that matter are failures, deprivation, etc. Should measure self by errors, weaknesses, etc.
3. Excessive responsibility (assuming personal causality)	3. *I am responsible for all bad things, failures, etc.*
4. Assuming temporal causality (predicting without sufficient evidence)	4. If it has been true in the past, then it is always going to be true.
5. Self-references	5. *I am the center of everyone's attention, especially of bad performances or personal attributes.*
6. "Catastrophizing"	6. *Always think of the worst. It is most likely to happen to you.*
7. Dichotomous thinking	7. *Everything is either one extreme or another (black or white; good or bad).*

Source: A. T. Beck (1976). *Cognitive Therapy and the Emotional Disorders.* New York: International Universities Press. © 1976 by Aaron T. Beck, M. D. Reprinted by permission of the publisher.

people." Beck thinks that the tendency to have these negative cognitions may be related to particular ways of evaluating situations that grow out of childhood experiences. These schemata affect all the elements of the cognitive triad in later life.

Attributional Models of Depression One of the cognitive maneuvers Beck discusses is **attribution** or assigning a cause. He predicts that depressed individuals' attributions will be personal—that is, depressed people will blame themselves when anything bad happens. When something good happens, it will usually be attributed to luck. For instance, one woman was not especially pleased when a short story she had written was accepted for publication; she attributed the acceptance to sheer luck. On the other hand, when one of her articles was rejected, she was distressed because she thought the rejection reflected badly on her. Most nondepressed people do the opposite: they accept responsibility for the good in their lives but tend to blame the situation on others when things do not work out. Figure 10-15 illustrates this difference in attributional thinking. Attributional models of depression do not claim that attributional style alone is enough to cause depression. These models suggest that attributional style is important only when a person experiences stress from intense or frequent negative events in his or her life (Abramson et al., 1989).

People who are depressed seem to feel helpless to control their environment. They think that, no matter what they do, they will be unable to affect the way things turn out. It is possible that such people learn to be helpless as a result of certain situations they have encountered in the past. Martin Seligman (1974, 1975) first popularized this concept, which recalls Edward Bibring's explanation of depression mentioned earlier in this chapter and is termed **learned helplessness.** Research on the concept of learned helplessness soon showed that some people feel generally helpless and others feel helpless only in certain situations. The explanation of this difference appears to lie in the kinds of attributions people make about stressful situations (Abramson et al., 1989).

Some researchers have suggested that there is a subtype of depression, **hopelessness depression,** that links attributional style in a causal chain that leads to the occurrence of depression (Abramson et al., 1989). This chain starts with the perceived occurrence of negative life events or the nonoccurrence of positive life events. It also includes a person's characteristic way of viewing the causes and consequences of events as well as the person's self-evaluation. These personal characteristics work together to determine how the person will respond to a life event. The theory maintains that if the response is one of hopelessness, either about dealing with the event or changing oneself, depression will result.

The hopelessness theory is more similar to the other cognitive theories of depression than is the helplessness theory. It closely resembles Beck's ideas, though with some differences. The hopelessness theory describes a particular subclass of depression, whereas Beck focuses on the role that cognitions play in depression in general. The hopelessness theory also suggests that some people may be invulnerable, or at least much less vulnerable, to depression because of their tendency to attribute negative events, not to themselves or to ongoing conditions in their environment, but to specific causes or situations that can be expected to come to an end soon.

Cognitive Accuracy in Depression Both Beck's theory and Seligman's learned helplessness hypothesis stress the inaccuracy of self-perception in depression. But the attributions of depressed people may be more accurate than these theories predict. Experimenters, studying how well people assessed their own social competence, found that depressed patients were quite realistic about their own social skills (Lewinsohn et al., 1980). In contrast, other psychiatric patients and control subjects tended to see themselves as more competent than other people saw them. Even more interesting, the realism of the depressed patients' self-perceptions tended to decrease as therapy progressed. As they became less depressed, the patients became less realistic about their effect on others. According to this view, the result of cognitive therapy may actually be to encourage a normal lack of realism (Sackeim & Wegner, 1986). Many aspects of the cognitive theory of depression have been supported by research on the depressed person's increased negativity of cognitions about the self, increased hopelessness, and focus on themes of loss. However, evidence that depressive thinking is especially inaccurate or illogical is still weak (Haaga et al., 1991).

Cognitive–Behavioral Therapy

Cognitive therapy is often referred to as **cognitive-behavioral therapy (CBT)** because it makes use of both behavioral and cognitive theoretical perspectives. The main focus of CBT is to help clients think more adaptively and, as a result, to experience positive changes in mood, motivation, and behavior (A. C. Butler & Beck, 1996). The proportion of cognitive and behavioral techniques that are used depends on the client's skills and degree of depression as well as on the chosen goals of therapy. In general, the more severely depressed the client, the more likely the therapist is to use behavioral techniques at the beginning of the treatment process. Clients are taught how to self-monitor their experiences, noting which gave pleasure and feelings of mastery and which lowered their mood. On the basis of this information, they may be given graded task assignments to help them increase their motivation to engage in activities or situations that may be potentially rewarding.

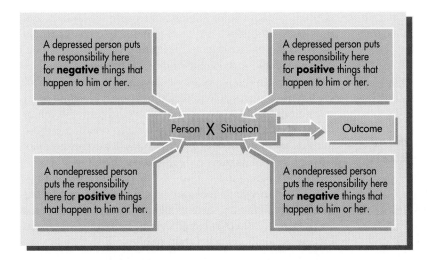

Figure 10-15 The attribution process is thought to differ for depressed and nondepressed people. The personal responsibility depressed people take for the negative things in their lives may have the effect of prolonging their depression.

Clients are also taught to monitor and to record their negative thoughts. Special emphasis is put on **automatic thoughts,** recurring thoughts that come into a person's mind almost as if by habit rather than as a specific response to what is currently going on. For cognitive therapy to be effective, the client must be able to identify these automatic thoughts when they occur. Therapists use several techniques to help clients identify these thoughts, including direct questioning, asking the client to use imagery to evoke the thoughts, or eliciting them by means of a role-play situation. These automatic thoughts are important because they are the link between an outside event and the client's reaction to the event. However, because these thoughts occur so quickly and so frequently, they are often unnoticed. After clients learn to identify the thoughts, they are asked to keep a daily record of them. The record includes notes on the situation, emotions, automatic thoughts, and the outcome. The client and therapist then use this record to approach each of these thoughts as a testable hypothesis. In this way the client learns that a person's view of reality can be quite different from the reality itself. The therapist can help change dysfunctional thinking, and thus alleviate the depression, by challenging parts of the client's belief system.

Cognitive-behavioral therapy sessions tend to be active, structured, and focused on specific problems. They usually involve a check on the client's current mood and symptoms, the setting of an agenda for the session, a review of the self-help homework assignments that were agreed on during the previous session, a discussion of the issues on the agenda, agreement about new homework, and feedback from the client about the session. Usually the therapy is expected to include about 16 sessions. Often an improvement in symptoms occurs at least by the twelfth session. Clients often return for a few booster sessions during the first year after the therapy is completed.

Even when clients can identify automatic thoughts and can recognize and correct their cognitive distortions, they are vulnerable to a return of the depression if their early maladaptive schemata have not been modified. The therapist tries to link past experiences with present emotions by probing into the client's childhood and identifying events that were linked to the beginning of difficulties with depression. For example, Michelle came to the clinic after she had stopped working and begun to leave the house only rarely except for shopping (J. E. Young et al., 1993). Her depression appears to have begun when, after visiting her gynecologist, she found she was not pregnant. She reported being happily married until a few months earlier and had been successful as a real estate salesperson. She also said she currently felt worthless, unloved, and unappreciated.

After a period of treatment in which she learned to identify and test her dysfunctional thoughts and had successfully completed homework assignments, her depression lessened. The therapist then began the schemata-focused phase of the treatment to help prevent a recurrence:

Michelle's recollection of her early family life was sketchy. She remembered her father as very bright and a good provider who was "hardly ever around." Her mother she recalled as gentle but seemingly passive. While growing up she could not confide in either of them for fear of engendering anger, ridicule, or "worse," especially on the part of her father. A sister, two years her junior, was favored by her parents and "she has remained their darling even up to now."

Michelle reported no "real" depressive episodes until she started dating and began experiencing feelings of "being terribly lonely and discarded" whenever her relationships suffered. Further questions about her past and her previous experience with psychotherapy revealed several minor episodes of depression, and at least one major depressive episode. Perceived or actual fluctuations in her relationship with Jim, her husband, seemed to have triggered many of her depressive reactions, during their marriage as well as during their courtship.

*Her previous major depression was triggered by Jim's an-
nouncement, after months of dating, that he was breaking up
with her. (J. E. Young et al., 1993, pp. 269–270)*

The therapist worked to change Michelle's schemata by
examining the evidence for Michelle's feeling that her
husband might leave her:

T: *Is it possible, based on some of these schemas that we
     talked about, some of the feelings of being defective or
     that people will leave you, that you have tended to
     exaggerate how little Jim is attracted to you?*

M: *That would be wonderful if it were true, but I don't
     think so.*

T: *Well, let's look. What could you point to as evidence
     that he is attached and committed to you?*

M: *He says he loves me. Often he's happy to see me, to be
     around me. . . . He compliments me at times when we
     go out so I know he's attracted to me. He buys me
     very nice gifts—rings, jewelry, pocketbooks—and he
     takes me out on weekends. He asks me where I want
     us to go on vacation. I guess he does think of me.*

T: *Is there any evidence about his leaving you? Has he
     ever left you or threatened to leave you?*

M: *When we dated he left several times.*

T: *And since you've been married?*

M: *No, not since we've been married. He's never left.*

T: *Did he ever say anything about wanting to leave?*

M: *No.*

(*Ibid, pp. 272–273*)

The therapist also asked Michelle to imagine dialogues
with her father in which she expressed anger at him for
making her feel abandoned. This helped her see the connection between these feelings and how her schemata
were activated, both with her husband and in her sessions
with the therapist.

The Vulnerability–Resilience Perspective

Thus far we have discussed the role in depression of heredity and other biological factors—such as neurotransmitter
activity, brain structure, and metabolism—that may be,
but are not necessarily, a result of genetic inheritance. We
have also talked about other personal factors that may play
a role in depression, including misattributions of the causes
of events and the strength of the supportive relationships a person has. Both biological factors and these other
personally related factors can contribute to vulnerability
or resilience. Together they often determine the outcome
when people encounter environmental stressors or what
we often call negative life events. Highly personally relevant stressful events, especially those that occur in the

context of chronic problems or ongoing difficulties and
low levels of support, are especially likely to result in depression (G. W. Brown, 1993; Patten, 1991).

An example of the vulnerability and resilience approach
can be seen in the life of Abraham Lincoln, an American
president who was able to function effectively amid great
stress despite a lifetime of what we would now call major
depressive episodes. Lincoln was able to overcome these
periods of melancholy to effectively lead the country
through one of its most trying periods, the Civil War.

In 1841 Lincoln wrote to his law partner in Washington, D.C.: "If what I feel were equally distributed to the
whole human family, there would not be one cheerful face
on the earth. Whether I shall ever be better, I cannot tell.
I awefully [sic] forebode I shall not."

Despite his apprehension about the future, Lincoln, of
course, did carry on. However, even during his presidency
he experienced periods of depression. The terrible loss of
life in the Civil War and the defeats of the Union forces
in the early part of the war affected him greatly. During
this period, the public and many members of Congress
turned against him and doubted his leadership. His visits
to the wounded in military hospitals also upset him deeply.
He often sat silent, his "soul filled with sadness" (cited in
Grinker, 1979). He felt guilty and full of self-reproach,
wanted to die, and had dreams about assassination.

Lincoln's personal life was also filled by negative life
events. His marriage to Mary Todd was an unhappy one,
his wife was bitterly criticized and villified by Washington society, and two of his children died in childhood. His
early life also had been difficult: he grew up in extreme
poverty, his mother died when he was young, and his father had treated him harshly. Despite these adverse conditions, and despite his episodes of depression, Lincoln
showed amazing resilience, managing to educate himself,
become a successful lawyer and politician, be elected to
Congress and the presidency, and become one of the most
revered U.S. presidents.

How Should Depression Be Treated?

Although we have reviewed many therapeutic approaches
to depression, what do we know about which kinds of
treatment are most effective? Practical limitations in terms
of cost make it impossible to compare all types of treatment and to investigate their effects on all types of depression. People who are seeking treatment for dysphoric
mood often opt for psychological therapy, although there
is an increasing tendency to treat milder types of depression with medication, in part because of the increased emphasis on cost of treatments under managed medical care.
The relative merits of psychological and biologically based
treatment approaches have not been systematically assessed in these milder types of depression. The two psychological therapies most often used in milder cases are

cognitive-behavioral therapy (CBT) and interpersonal psychotherapy (IPT). Both CBT and IPT appear to be effective in such cases.

So far, the most intensive research efforts aimed at comparing therapeutic results of different treatment approaches have focused on the treatment of people who are experiencing severe depressive episodes or who have experienced a series of these episodes. Most of the people in this group were initially treated with antidepressant medication, which may be used alone or combined with a psychological therapy (either CBT or IPT). One of the questions addressed in these comparisons has been the frequency of relapse or recurrence with the use of different treatment plans. These plans differed in the length of the initial treatment with antidepressants as well as the period of time a psychological therapy continued after the medication period had ended. Some evidence suggests that CBT during the posttreatment period reduces the risk of relapse for patients who were treated with antidepressants during the acute period of depression (M. D. Evans et al., 1992) Other studies have looked at subgroups of patients with certain characteristics, such as particular patterns of brain waves during sleep. Patients with normal profiles of sleep patterns were likely to have a positive response to IPT, and in such cases IPT was as successful as antidepressant medication in preventing the recurrence of depression (Thase & Kupfer, 1996). In another study, patients who had normal sleep profiles were likely to improve with ITP alone, without initial medication (Thase et al., 1997). However, those who did not improve with IPT and who had abnormal sleep profiles, which probably indicate a greater disturbance of the central nervous system, were more likely to improve after receiving antidepressant medication. EEG sleep profiles thus may be a marker indicating the most appropriate treatment approach.

An ambitious and comprehensive study of the relative effectiveness of antidepressant medication and different types of psychological therapy for severe depressive disorder was the Treatment of Depression Collaborative Research Program funded by the National Institute of Mental Health (Elkin 1994; Elkin et al., 1989). This study was conducted at three research sites, each of which used identical research protocols. There were four treatment conditions at each site: (1) cognitive-behavioral therapy (CBT); (2) interpersonal psychotherapy (IPT); (3) the antidepressant imipramine, combined with clinical management; and (4) a placebo combined with clinical management. ("Clinical management" refers to the usual care given patients who are not part of a special study. It includes supportive meetings with a clinician and checkups of symptoms and progress.) A total of 250 patients were enrolled in the study. Each treatment site randomly assigned patients to each of the four treatment conditions. All the patients had been diagnosed as having a current major depressive disorder in each of two evaluations over

a 2-week interval before they were admitted to the study. This was done to make sure the symptoms observed were relatively stable over time. All treatments were planned to be 16 weeks long and to include from 16 to 20 sessions.

The initial article published on the outcome of this large study (Elkin et al., 1989) reported that all four of the conditions resulted in a significant reduction in symptoms of depression and an improvement of general functioning after the course of the treatment. The different treatments resulted in few statistically significant differences in measures of outcome. Because the data from such a complex study call for a variety of analyses, both the original researchers and others have analyzed many aspects of the findings. Because any differences found between groups were relatively small, and because the number of subjects in each group was also small when they were divided by both research condition and study center, findings from statistical analyses varied according to the specific measures of depression that were used. As a result, a dialogue is still being carried out among researchers as to exactly what the findings mean and whether some treatments actually are more effective than others (DeRubeis, et al., 1999; Elkin et al., 1996; Jacobson & Hollon, 1996; Klein, 1996).

One large ongoing study's early findings suggest that for people who are chronically depressed, a combination of medication and a form of cognitive-behavioral therapy was more effective than either medication or therapy alone (Rush & Trivedi, 2000). Patients who were given both treatments had an 85% improvement rate compared with about a 50% improvement rate for either the medication or the cognitive-behavioral therapy.

Despite a considerable amount of comparative research, questions still arise regarding the merits of the currently widespread treatment of severe depression primarily with antidepressant medication. Some of these questions are: If medication is used, how long should it be continued? What is the appropriate level of medication? Does a combination of medication and some psychologically based therapy (usually either IPT or CBT) promote faster recovery from the acute episode? Does either IPT or CBT perform an important role in preventing relapse, either after medication is no longer used or if it is continued? At present, there are no clear answers to these questions.

Another important question is, what should the treatment choice be for those who, for a variety of reasons, should not use antidepressant medications, or those for whom they are not effective? A sizable group of patients (5% to 10%) refuse to take medication; others (10% to 15%) cannot tolerate the medications' side effects; others do not improve with medication; and still others (e.g., pregnant women, those who have a variety of medical problems, and very old adults) cannot be safely prescribed these medications (Clarkin et al., 1996).

For people with milder depression or dysthymia, the picture is even less clear. Evidence suggests that these disorders can often be treated effectively with psychological therapy, but the trend, at present, seems to be toward increased use of antidepressant drugs for these cases as well. One reason for this may lie in the growth of managed health care in the United States. Half of the depressed individuals who are in treatment receive care in general medical settings and are not treated by specialists, so medication is often the first treatment suggested. In general, treatment by nonspecialists in general medical settings is not desirable for those affected with depression. One study concluded that care of depression by general medical providers worsens outcomes and decreases the value of health care spending, as measured by health care improvement per dollar spent (Sturm & Wells, 1995).

The Bipolar Disorders

Bipolar disorder, often called manic-depressive illness in the past, is a mental illness involving episodes of mania and depression. People affected by this disorder usually experience swings in mood from overly "high" and often irritable to sad and hopeless and back again with periods of normal or near-normal mood in between. Table 10-8 illustrates the moods found in the bipolar disorders.

At least 1.6% of Americans have a bipolar disorder, and the number of cases in the United States seems to be rising. Many epidemiologists think that the number of people affected is underestimated because some people whose manic symptoms are relatively mild are never diagnosed with this disorder. Symptoms of bipolar disorder usually appear when a person is young; the peak age at which symptoms begin is during adolescence and the early 20s. The actual number of people affected during this age period may be an underestimate for two reasons. First, early symptoms are often diagnosed as some type of

attention or hyperactivity disorder (see Chapter 14). Second, many people's initial symptom is depression and only later when they experience some type of mania are they reclassified from a unipolar disorder to a bipolar disorder. In one follow-up study, 18% of those classified as having a depressive disorder experienced a manic episode within the following 6 years and their classification then changed to bipolar disorder (Winokur et al., 1995). After age 30, the chance of newly developing this disorder is very low.

Mania and depression are usually thought to be opposite ends of a continuum with normal mood lying somewhere in the middle. However, manic and depressive symptoms often occur together in patients, and both may worsen or improve together. DSM-IV has divided bipolar disorders into four groups: Bipolar I disorder, Bipolar II disorder, cyclothymic disorder, and a miscellaneous category for bipolar disorders that does not clearly fit into any of these categories.

Bipolar I Disorder

A person with **Bipolar I** disorder will experience episodes of mania and usually major depressive episodes as well. A very small number of people may experience one or more periods of mania without ever experiencing depression (F. K. Goodwin & Jamison, 1987). Because this happens so infrequently, people are classified as having a bipolar disorder after an episode of mania with the expectation that a period of depression will ultimately occur. **Mania** is characterized by a flight of ideas, elevated mood, and increased psychomotor activity. Table 10-9 gives diagnostic criteria for a manic episode.

Manic behavior is illustrated by the life of the well-known American poet Robert Lowell (1917–1977), who was affected by bipolar disorder for much of his life. Over a 15-year period his manic episodes followed a repeated pat-

Table 10-8

Moods Found in Bipolar Disorder

Mania—episodes characterized by abnormally or persistently elevated, expansive, or irritable mood that include at least three of the following: inflated self-esteem or grandiosity, decreased sleep, extreme talkativeness, flight of ideas, distractibility, increase in goal-directed activity, excessive involvement in pleasurable activities.

Hypomania—a milder elevated state that may not be recognized as dysfunctional by the patient or sometimes even by others.

Depression—a state in which the person experiences diminished interest, energy, and ability to experience pleasure and sometimes profound pessimism, despair, irritability, anger, and anxiety. There is often a slowing of mental activity, feelings of fatigue, insomnia, and loss of appetite.

Mixed mania—a condition affecting about 40% of bipolar patients, in which mania or hypomania occur simultaneously with depressive symptoms.

Cyclothymia—mood swings between hypomania and less severe depression. Often develops into a more severe bipolar disease over time.

Rapid cycling—a condition affecting 20% of bipolar patients. Characterized by four or more episodes in the past twelve months of depression, mania, or hypomania that are separated from each other by periods of relatively normal mood or which represent a dramatic switch from mania to depression or the reverse.

tern. Each time, just as his manic behavior became obvious, Lowell, a married man, started an affair with a young girl.

> With his immense charm and erudition, his stature as a famous poet and his quality of infectious enthusiasm, he would court a girl many years his junior. Always successfully. . . . He would then summon his circle of friends to a party to announce the exciting change in his life, and that he was leaving his wife forever. Over the ensuing days his elation would become increasingly frantic until he would be hospitalized and, after 1953 when it first became available, he would be treated with chlorpromazine [an antipsychotic drug]. The elation would be followed by several weeks or months of what he called his "dark, post-manic and pathological self-abasement." The girl would be abandoned and he would return to Hardwick [his wife]. She, for her part, would protest over the intense public humiliation she had been put through, but always took him back. No treatment modality, including attempts at psychotherapy, seems to have altered this pattern until the time he was eventually given lithium. (Powell, 1991, p. 378)

Bipolar disorder has been found to occur with a higher frequency in highly creative people such as artists and poets than in the general population (Jamison, 1989). For instance, of the 36 American poets born since 1900 who are recognized by inclusion in the *New Oxford Book of American Verse*, 8 have well-documented histories of bipolar disorder. Epidemiological data would lead us to expect, at most, only one of this group to have a bipolar diagnosis. Bipolar disorder is also associated with a high risk of suicide. Two well-known writers who were affected by bipolar illness are shown in Figure 10-16.

The extremes of mood that are characteristic of bipolar disorders may in some way fuel the creative process.

For example, Virginia Woolf, a highly creative writer who was affected by bipolar disorder and ultimately killed herself while depressed, described the relationship of her disorder to her creativity this way:

> As an experience, madness is terrific, I can assure you, and not to be sniffed at; and in its lava I still find most of the things I write about. It shoots out of one, everything shaped, final, not in mere driblets, as sanity does. (V. Woolf, 1978, p. 180)

Her husband, Leonard Woolf, seemed to agree:

> I am quite sure that Virginia's genius was closely connected with what manifested itself as mental instability and insanity.

Figure 10-16 Virginia Woolf and Ernest Hemingway are two well-known writers who experienced some form of bipolar illness. Both Woolf and Hemingway killed themselves while in the depressed phase of this disorder. Suicide is frequent in bipolar disorder, especially in Bipolar II disorder.

Table 10-9

Summary of Diagnostic Criteria for a Manic Episode

- A distinct period of abnormally and persistently elevated, expansive, or irritable mood lasting at least 1 week (less if hospitalization is necessary).
- During the period of mood disturbance, three or more of the following symptoms are present to a significant degree and persist (if the mood is only irritable, four or more symptoms are required).
  - Inflated self-esteem or grandiosity
  - Decreased need for sleep
  - Greatly increased talkativeness, or pressure to keep talking
  - Flight of ideas or subjective experience of racing thoughts
  - Distractibility
  - Increase in goal-directed activity or psychomotor agitation
  - Excessive involvement in pleasurable activities that have a high risk of negative consequences
- The mood disturbance causes marked impairment in occupational or social functioning or relationships with others, or requires hospitalization to prevent self-harm, or there are psychotic features (hallucinations or delusions).
- The symptoms are not the result of the direct effects of some substance (drug abuse, medication) or a general medical condition.

Source: Adapted from DSM-IV.

Table 10-10
Summary of Diagnostic Criteria for Bipolar II Disorder

- The presence or history of one or more major depressive episodes.
- The presence or history of at least one hypomanic episode. A hypomanic episode is similar to a manic episode but does not meet all the criteria: it is not severe enough to cause marked impairment in functioning or hospitalization, but it is observable to others.
- There has never been a manic episode or a mixed episode.
- The mood symptoms are not better accounted for by another disorder.
- The symptoms cause clinically significant distress or impairment in social, occupational, or other important areas of functioning.

Source: Adapted from DSM-IV.

The creative imagination in her novels, her ability to "leave the ground" in conversation and the voluble delusions of the breakdowns all came from the same place in her mind . . . that in itself was the crux of her life, the tragedy of her genius. (L. Woolf, 1964, p. 80)

Before classifying someone who has experienced a manic episode as having a bipolar disorder, it is important to rule out other causes for the manic behavior. Mania may be caused by biochemical factors not related to bipolar disorder. For instance, certain drugs can cause people with no history of affective disorders to experience episodes of mania. Drugs that produce this response include steroids, MAO inhibitors and tricyclic drugs used to treat depression, and L-dopa (used to treat Parkinson's disease). Mania can also result from infections, metabolic disturbances, and tumors. Mania in these cases is considered a symptom of the change in a person's biochemical state and is not classified as a mood disorder.

Bipolar II Disorder

Bipolar II disorder differs from Bipolar I disorder in that manic behavior is present to a lesser degree, called **hypomania** or a **hypomanic episode,** instead of in the florid, dramatic manic episodes that Robert Lowell experienced. Table 10-10 summarizes the criteria for Bipolar II disorder. A hypomanic episode occurs when there is a distinct period of elevated, expansive, or irritable mood and other manic behaviors, but social or on-the-job functioning is not greatly impaired and the person does not have to be hospitalized. This ability to function makes hypomania very different from mania. Bipolar II seems to be a separate type of disorder and not a preliminary problem that will later develop into a typical bipolar disorder (Dunner, 1987).

People who experience a hypomanic episode may not see it as pathological, although those around them may be concerned about the erratic behavior they see. For the person affected, the feelings of elation and creativity and the driving energy characteristic of the hypomanic state can be positive forces.

Although Kay Redfield Jamison, the psychologist whose descriptions of manic and depressive episodes appeared early in this chapter, would be diagnosed as having a Bipolar I disorder because of the intensity of the manic periods she experienced, she also gives a good description of a hypomanic episode that occurred early in her illness:

I was a senior in high school when I had my first attack of manic-depressive illness. . . . At first, everything seemed so easy. I raced about like a crazed weasel, bubbling with plans and enthusiasms, immersed in sports, and staying up all night, night after night, out with friends, reading everything that wasn't nailed down, filling manuscript books with poems and fragments of plays, and making expansive, completely unrealistic, plans for my future. . . . I felt I could do anything, that no task was too difficult. My mind seemed clear, fabulously focused, and able to make intuitive mathematical leaps that had up to that point entirely eluded me. Indeed, they elude me still. At the time, however, not only did everything make perfect sense, but it all began to fit into a marvelous kind of cosmic relatedness. . . . I found myself buttonholing my friends to tell them how beautiful it all was. They were less than transfixed by my insights . . ., although considerably impressed by how exhausting it was to be around my enthusiastic ramblings: You're talking too fast, Kay. Slow down, Kay. You're wearing me out, Kay. Slow down, Kay. And those times when they didn't actually come out and say it, I still could see it in their eyes: For God's sake, Kay, slow down. . . .

Unlike the very severe manic episodes that came a few years later and escalated wildly and psychotically out of control, this first sustained wave of mild mania was a light, lovely tincture of true mania; like hundreds of subsequent periods of high enthusiasms it was short-lived and quickly burned itself out: tiresome to my friends, perhaps; exhausting and exhilarating to me, definitely; but not disturbingly over the top. (Jamison, 1995 pp. 36–37)

Cyclothymic Disorder

Like dysthymic disorder, a type of depressive disorder discussed earlier in the chapter, **cyclothymic disorder** is a chronic state of mood disturbance that is most noticeable as a change in energy level. In cyclothymic disorder, both hypomanic behavior and depressive behavior occur and continue over at least a 2-year period, but neither type of behavior meets the DSM-IV criteria for a manic episode or a major depressive episode. Table 10-11 defines the characteristics of cyclothymic behavior. Episodes of cy-

Table 10-11

Summary of Diagnostic Criteria for Cyclothymic Disorder

- The presence of numerous periods of hypomanic symptoms and numerous periods of depressive symptoms for at least 2 years.[a] The depressive symptoms must not meet the criteria for a major depressive episode.
- The symptoms described above have never been absent for more than 2 months at a time during the 2-year period.[a]
- No major depressive episode, manic episode, or mixed episode in which these episodes alternate has been present during the first 2 years of the disorder.

[a]One year for children and adolescents.
Source: Adapted from DSM-IV.

clothymia often have a seasonal pattern and are more common in spring or fall. Although the first episode is often associated with a stressful situation, later episodes do not seem to be related to stress level. In some cases the hypomania and depressive symptoms alternate, whereas in other cases one of these moods is predominant and the other appears less often.

People who are classified as having cyclothymic disorder seem to be a diverse group. Some will later develop bipolar disorder (Thase & Howland, 1995). People who are diagnosed with a cyclothymic disorder are more likely to have a close relative with a bipolar disorder than either normal controls or people diagnosed with a unipolar disorder. This difference suggests that bipolar disorder may have genetic causes different from unipolar depression.

Causes and Treatment of Bipolar Disorder

Genetic Factors

The evidence for an inherited predisposition to bipolar disorder is very strong. Nearly two-thirds of those who develop this disorder have a family history of mood disorders. The risk can be even higher if family members in earlier generations also had bipolar disorder. The importance of genetic factors is shown in studies of pairs of MZ twins in which at least one twin has bipolar disorder. In such twin pairs, the chance that the other twin will also have bipolar disorder is very high (40% to 70%), much higher than the risk of bipolar disorder for a DZ twin when the other twin has this diagnosis (5% to 10%). This reflects the lesser genetic similarity of DZ twins, which is equal to that of ordinary siblings (5% to 10%) (Craddock & Jones, 1999).

What may be inherited, however, is not the disorder itself but rather a vulnerability to the disorder. Despite the clear hereditary risk, stress also plays a role in bipo-

lar disorder. People who have this genetic vulnerability are more likely to develop symptoms of the disorder if there is a great deal of stress in their lives. For example, in MZ twin pairs who were discordant for bipolar disorder (*discordant* means that one had the disorder and one did not), the children of the twin who did not develop the disorder still had the same risk for the disorder as their cousins, the children of the twin who had developed the disorder (Bertelsen & Gottesman, 1986). The fact that the unaffected twin did not develop symptoms but could pass on the genetic vulnerability to the next generation shows clearly that situational factors including stress play a role in bipolar disorder. In the same way, stress can also bring on new bipolar episodes in people with a history of the disorder who are currently functioning normally.

Although genetics seems to play an important role in causing bipolar disorders, researchers are still trying to determine important details concerning genetic inheritance and the development of bipolar disorder. Researchers have yet to determine whether the disorder inherited is part of a general tendency toward mood disorders or is specifically for either unipolar or bipolar disorder.

Studies of Bipolar I disorder show that there is a strong hereditary component that is specific to bipolar disorder (Winokur et al., 1995). Patients with a diagnosis of Bipolar I had significantly more close relatives with bipolar disorder than did members of a control group of patients with unipolar mood disorder. However, the same study also showed that in families of both unipolar and bipolar patients there was an equal chance of having family members who have a severe unipolar disorder. This finding suggests that there is some overlap between the two disorders even though Bipolar I disorder seems to have somewhat different genetic determinants than unipolar disorder.

Another unanswered question is whether there are gene locations on particular chromosomes that are associated with bipolar disorder. In order to understand more about the genes that cause bipolar disorder, researchers have studied a number of large extended families that contain a larger than might be expected number of members with bipolar disorder. Families chosen for study were those that tended to marry within their own ethnic or religious group so that their genetic inheritance was more concentrated. Through the use of DNA technology, genes of both affected and unaffected family members have been compared. Several studies of family groups have suggested a particular chromosome that might be the site of the genes identified but the same chromosome was not singled out in the different family groups. For example, in a large family group from Quebec, where records were available back to the 1830s, several gene locations on chromosome no. 12 seemed to predict inheritance of bipolar disorder (Morissette et al., 1999). In a large Scottish extended family, gene locations on chromosome no. 4 were linked to both unipolar and bipolar disorder (Visscher et al., 1999). A study of German families suggested a linkage based on chromosome no. 18 (Nothen et al., 1999). Other studies have shown linkages based on gene sites on other chromosomes including chromosome nos. 16, 21, and the X chromosome (Craddock & Jones, 1999). This variety of findings suggests either that several different combinations of genes may interact to produce the symptoms of bipolar disorder or that the genetic factors involved are very complex. What is clear is that no single gene can account for susceptibility to this disorder.

These family studies have also suggested that members of families in which bipolar disorder is a high risk also have a higher than average risk for several other disorders (Edmonds et al., 1998). Relatives of those who have bipolar disorder are more likely than average to have a unipolar depression, substance abuse disorders including alcohol-related disorders, panic disorder, or phobias, or some combination of these disorders.

Biologically Based Treatment of Bipolar Disorder

Bipolar disorder cannot be cured; it is a lifelong or chronic condition. However, effective treatment is possible in many cases, although even the most effective treatment does not prevent new episodes. The frequency of episodes is usually reduced, however, and this is important because the more episodes a person experiences the poorer the long-term outcome.

The most common treatment for bipolar disorder used today is lithium. It is especially effective in reducing manic activity but can also decrease the depression experienced in bipolar disorder. However, treatment with lithium has several important limitations (El-Mallakh, 1997). Lithium may have dangerous side effects. There is only a slight difference between an effective and a toxic lithium dosage, the smallest difference found for any drug routinely prescribed for psychiatric illness. In addition to this danger, lithium treatment is inadequate for about half the people affected by bipolar disorder. Lithium also has unpleasant side effects and as a result many patients either wholly or temporarily discontinue their lithium medication against medical advice. Patients may abandon lithium during low, though not depressed, periods in the hope that stopping its use will elevate their mood. Patients may also be unwilling to give up some of the pleasant cognitive and behavioral changes that come with an elevated mood (F. K. Goodwin & Jamison, 1990). These changes include increased sensitivity to the environment, sexual intensity, creativity, and social ease. Psychologist Kay Jamison, whose experiences with bipolar disorder have been described earlier in this chapter, presents a clear picture of her reluctance, for many years after her illness began, to use lithium regularly:

Even though I was a clinician and a scientist, and even though I could read the research literature and see the inevitable, bleak consequences of not taking lithium, I for many years after my initial diagnosis was reluctant to take my medications as prescribed. Why was I so unwilling? Why did it take having to go through more episodes of mania, followed by long suicidal depressions, before I would take lithium in a medically sensible way? . . .

My family and friends expected that I would welcome being "normal," be appreciative of lithium, and take in stride having normal energy and sleep. But if you have had stars at your feet and the rings of planets through your hands, are used to sleeping only four or five hours a night and now sleep eight, are used to staying up all night for days and weeks in a row and now cannot, it is a very real adjustment to blend into a three-piece-suit schedule, which, while comfortable to many, is new, restrictive, seemingly less productive, and maddeningly less intoxicating. People say, when I complain of being less lively, less energetic, less high-spirited, "Well, now you're just like the rest of us," meaning, among other things, to be reassuring. But I compare myself with my former self, not with others. Not only that, I tend to compare my current self with the best I have been, which is when I have been mildly manic. When I am my present "normal" self, I am far removed from when I have been my liveliest, most productive, most intense, most outgoing and effervescent. In short, for myself, I am a hard act to follow. (Jamison, 1995, pp. 91–92)

Because of the limitations of treatment with lithium, other drugs have been tried (see Table 10-6). Two other mood stabilizers, valproic acid and carbamazepine are also considered standard treatment. These are anticonvulsant medications, developed to prevent seizures. Because these drugs have fewer side effects than lithium, patients with bipolar disorder may be less likely to stop using these medications. Despite this, lithium is still the most effective treatment choice in decreasing the number of episodes of bipolar disorder and is also effective in decreasing the mortality rate in patients with bipolar disorder (Muller-Oelinghausen et al., 1992). People with bipolar disorder have a shorter life span than the average person mainly because the probability of suicide is very high.

Antidepressants are also used to treat bipolar disorder, especially when the first episode is depression. This is a risky approach because instead of decreasing depression, the antidepressant medication may hasten a switch to manic behavior. The development of this so-called rapid switching makes the long-term outcome much less favorable because this form of bipolar disorder is not helped much by medication.

Psychosocial Factors and Bipolar Episodes

Although bipolar disorder has generally been considered to be a biologically based disorder, psychosocial factors play a role both in triggering new episodes and in preventing them. Even when patients are receiving state-of-the-art pharmacotherapy, relapse rates are high. They range from 40% in the first year after an episode has ended to 73% over the first 5 years (Gitlin et al., 1995). Even if there is no relapse, at least half of the patients do not function as well as they did before the initial episode because they still have some symptoms. Only 20% perform as well in their job as they did before the first episode. Divorce rates are high among bipolar patients, and their children often have problems of adjustment (Miklowitz & Alloy, 1999). Another risk for bipolar patients is suicide. The rate of suicide in this group is 30 times greater than in the normal population (Guze & Robbins, 1970).

Environmental Stressors Environmental stressors can sometimes be important in setting off either an initial or an additional manic episode in a vulnerable person. Two-thirds of all manic episodes experienced by patients in one study were preceded by a life-related stress of some kind (Ambelas, 1987). Although many of the stressors that can lead to a manic episode involve relationships with other people, sometimes an environmental happening such as a tornado, hurricane, or flood can be the trigger. Manic or hypomanic episodes are more likely to follow stressors that disrupt the person's sleep-wake cycle, whereas depressive symptoms are more likely to follow loss events (Malkoff-Schwartz et al., 1998).

Stressful events can also cause a manic episode in people with a past history of manic episodes or bipolar disorder. For example, when a major hurricane struck Long Island, New York, in 1985, there was a dramatic increase in manic episodes among patients being treated for bipolar disorder (Aronson & Shukla, 1987). All the people who relapsed had already had a high level of stress in their lives, and most lacked social support from a close, confiding relationship. For each of these people, the hurricane resulted in additional stress besides stress from the storm itself. Two people had to move into their parents' homes, where there was a high tension level; another person went into a temporary shelter where she knew no one; and yet another wrecked her boyfriend's new car during the storm, causing their relationship to deteriorate. There is a need for studies of the interaction between genetic vulnerability to bipolar disorder and stressful environmental factors.

Family Stressors Positive and negative occurrences in relationships can be important in the development of bipolar symptoms. Most people who are affected by bipolar disorder are low in social support (Johnson et al., 1999). Even when they are not experiencing an episode of mania or depression, people with this disorder reported fewer contacts with friends than either a control group or a group of people with unipolar depression. Unfortunately, the episodic nature of bipolar disorder is likely to make social support more necessary rather than less needed. Although

in this study, social support did not seem to lessen life stress, people who had high social support recovered more quickly from the episodes of depression or mania they did experience and their later depressed episodes tended to be less severe than for those low in social support. In particular, negative family interactions and attitudes predict relapse rates in bipolar patients (Hooley & Hiller, 2001).

Both mania and severe depression can make family relationships stressful. In addition, the episodic nature of bipolar disorder makes it hard to know just what is going to happen next. Mania can be hard to tolerate: "No other difficulty, not even homicide in the family, has such a high degree of enduring familial chaos nor such a high likelihood that [the] family will be unable to tolerate the patient and give up on him or her" (Lansky, 1988, p. 216). Living with a person who is experiencing a depressed episode is also stressful. In one study, 40% of those living with a person in the midst of a depressed episode were sufficiently distressed themselves to meet the criteria for needing psychological intervention. However, when the family member was not in the midst of such an episode, their own distress faded as well.

A person with a bipolar disorder usually experiences relapses alternating with periods of normal or nearly normal functioning. When these changes occur, roles shift within the family (Moltz, 1993). Responsibilities for everday decision making need to be redistributed and the hierarchy of authority changes. As one patient's son said "I have to take myself away from the fact that I'm her son and I have to be a parent. It's hard to do that " (Moltz, 1993, p. 416).

Psychoeducational Treatment for the Family

Psychoeducational treatment programs for the family can be a useful addition to patient treatment with lithium or other medications. It has been known for some time that family psychoeducational interventions help prevent relapses in patients affected by schizophrenic disorder. These programs help the family learn about the disorder and coach family members in how to interact with the patient. Like families with a schizophrenic member, families that include a bipolar patient often show high levels of family discord, but until recently no one has tried the psychoeducational approach with these families.

In one of the few studies that have investigated the impact of psychoeducational treatment on families, researchers from the University of Colorado recruited families of patients who were being treated with the standard medications for bipolar disorder (Simoneau et al., 1999). Some of the families participated in 21 sessions of home-based family therapy over a 9-month period. These sessions involved the patient as well as his or her close relatives (parents, siblings, or spouse). During the sessions the nature of symptoms, prognosis, and treatment of bipolar disorder were discussed. The participants were also given communication enhancement training, which involved delivering positive and negative feedback, ways to request changes in behavior of other family members, and training in problem-solving skills. As part of this training the family members participated in modeling and behavioral training sessions in which they role-played situations and homework assignments to practice the skills from the training sessions. A control group of families received only standard help with crisis management as it was needed. The patients in both groups continued to receive appropriate medication. One year after the study began, both verbal and nonverbal positive and negative behaviors were counted during a family interaction. Families in the psychoeducational treatment group had significantly more positive behaviors during the interaction, but the number of negative behaviors did not differ. When the researchers looked at the results more closely, they found that the difference in the groups was due mostly to an increase in positive nonverbal behaviors of the bipolar *patients*. These same behaviors also changed for the relatives, but not by as much. Even more important, the change in the psychoeducational group of patients' positive nonverbal behaviors from the start of the study to the 1-year point also predicted a decrease in the patients' mood disorder symptoms at the 1-year point. It is not clear why only positive nonverbal behaviors were affected by this type of intervention. That is a question that only further research can help answer. What is important is that a psychosocial intervention with a family group can add to the effects of medication for bipolar disorder to produce an improvement in symptoms.

One problem with this kind of intervention is that many bipolar patients are unmarried, divorced, or alienated from their families. This is not surprising, considering the strain that bipolar illness can put on relationships.

Family members often believe that a person with a bipolar or unipolar disorder can control his or her feelings and behavior. This misunderstanding can lead to anger and a sense of failure for all concerned. Family members can also become hypervigilant and interpret any expression of emotion as a signal that another episode of mania or depression is about to begin.

Box 10-2 illustrates how bipolar disorder can affect behavior and shows how judgment during a hypomanic episode can be impaired, although outside observers may not be aware of the degree of the impairment.

Despite all the negative outcomes described here and the stress experienced by family members, it is worth remembering, though, that at least in the case of Bipolar II disorder, the abnormal mood state may include some positive aspects. Although certainly all those with bipolar disorder are not creative people and all creative people do not have bipolar disorder, a sizable proportion

of highly creative artists and writers seem to have been affected. For these people, mood changes that preceded or accompanied intense creative episodes have often been indistinguishable from hypomania.

Suicide

Suicide has been declared a major health problem in the United States by the Surgeon General, David Satcher (1999). He noted that the suicide rate among children has doubled since 1980 and that the elderly account for one in five suicides. In 1997, the last year for which complete figures were available, suicide was the eighth leading cause of death in the United States and about 30,000 people killed themselves. In addition, about 500,000 Americans were treated in emergency rooms after trying to kill themselves. The problem is not confined to the United States. It is estimated that nearly half a million people worldwide kill themselves each year.

Although countries around the world have different overall rates of suicide, this increase in suicide rate seems to hold true worldwide. In most countries the young adult group seems to be at the highest risk. In Denmark and Japan, countries with very different cultural histories, suicide is the number one cause of death among the 25- to 34-year-old age group and accounts for 30% of all deaths among men and 25% of all deaths among women.

Mental Illness and Suicide

Although not everyone who attempts suicide is mentally ill, mental illnesses, particularly those with psychotic symptoms, greatly increase the probability of a suicide attempt (Radomsky et al., 1999). Among the mood disorders, the lifetime risk of a suicide attempt is highest for Bipolar II disorder, intermediate for Bipolar I, and lowest for unipolar depression (Rihmer & Pestality, 1999).

Parasuicide is a term used to describe suicidal behavior that does not result in death. One question that has been raised is whether those who survive a suicide attempt have a different motivation, perhaps to gain attention or call for help rather than to end their lives. In general this does not seem to be true. Reasons given by parasuicides for their attempts and the reasons deduced from information available about those who died from the suicide attempt are very similar. The difference seems to be in lethality of the method used. The use of firearms is the most lethal, and nonprescription medication such as aspirin among the least life threatening even without medical attention.

Risk Factors for Suicide

Several risk factors in addition to mental health status predict the likelihood of suicide. These include age, sex, marital status, ethnicity or race, and recent occurrence

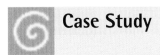

Bipolar Disorder and a Pyramid Scheme

Alice Faye Redd was sentenced to 15 years in prison as the result of what seemed, when the details were known, to be a bizarre investment scheme. More than a hundred people, many of them elderly, had invested more than $10 million in what they thought was partial ownership in a medical complex. At one point, Mrs. Redd was paying as much as 90% interest per month to the investors. How-ever, much of the money she was given was simply used to continue the pyramid scheme she had developed. She used some of the money from later investors to pay the interest on earlier investors' shares. Much of the remainder of the money she collected was used for lavish entertainment and gifts. Investors lost a total of $3.6 million dollars in the cycle of interest payments, loans, and lavish spending that took place over a 9-year period.

Mrs. Redd seemed an unlikely person to be the originator of such a scheme. She had been president of many local organizations, such as the PTA and the Junior League. She was a successful fund-raiser for many civic, religious, and political causes;

was regarded as a pillar of the community, had been honored by the Nixon White House as one of 10 outstanding young women in America; and even had her own radio program, *The Happy Homemaker*, on a local radio station. Her family was wealthy and respected in the community. To those who knew her, Mrs. Redd seemed to be a "superwoman." Not until one day, when she broke into tears while having lunch with her daughter and told her, "Nobody likes me, I'm better off dead," did this myth begin to shatter. As Mrs. Redd's husband and daughter began to investigate why she might feel so distressed, they began to ask questions of friends and go through closets and drawers. One thing they discovered was 4 years of unopened bank statements. After learning something about Mrs. Redd's investment scheme, they called a meeting of the investors to see if they could work out some settlement and committed Mrs. Redd to a mental hospital, because they assumed that her bizarre behavior indicated a loss of contact with reality. There her condition was diagnosed

as a Bipolar II disorder. Later, two court-appointed psychiatrists agreed with this diagnosis. Although the psychiatric evidence concerning her disorder was strong, she was not granted leniency by the court because of the judge's view that the facts of her illness did not overweigh the loss of scores of people's life savings.

Alice Redd's case illustrates the strong genetic factor in bipolar disorder. Investigation showed that she came from a family in which mental illness could be traced through five generations (see Figure 10-17). Mrs. Redd's case also illustrates the energy and accomplishments that often accompany the hypomanic phase of Bipolar II disorder as well as the lapses in judgment that frequently occur during hypomanic periods. One question that our society finds difficult to answer is how such individuals should be treated if they commit a crime. Should treatment for the disorder take precedence over prison? What degree of responsibility should those with serious mental disorders bear for their behavior? Chapter 17 discusses this issue in further detail.

SOURCE: Based on article by Fox Butterfield in *New York Times*, April 21, 1996, p. 104.

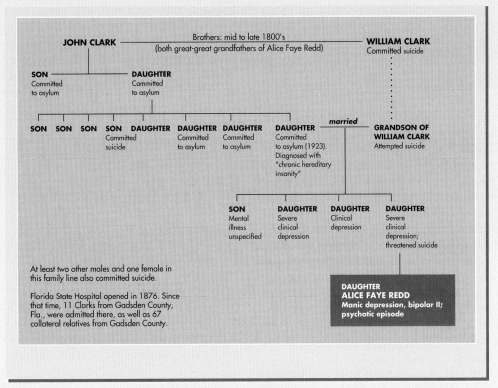

Figure 10-17   The family of Alice Faye Redd, who pleaded guilty to conducting a pyramid scheme and who has also been diagnosed with bipolar disorder, shows a pattern of mental illness through several generations. Since the Florida State Hospital opened in 1876, 11 members of the Clark family, as well as 67 of their more distant relatives, have been hospitalized there.

SOURCE: *New York Times*, April 12, 1996, p. 10Y. Chart by Rebecca Hagelen.

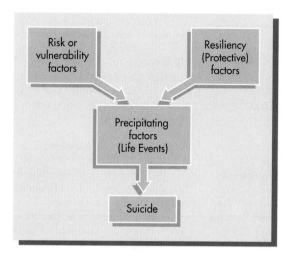

Figure 10-18 Whether or not a suicide occurs is related to individuals' vulnerabilities and resiliencies as well as to negative life events.

of severe life events, particularly those related to loss. Other factors such as personality characteristics, cognitive style, easy access to a means of suicide, and presence or absence of social support are also important. Drug and alcohol abuse also make suicide more likely. Because the factors that determine whether a person will attempt suicide are complex, a model that includes both personal vulnerabilities and resilience factors makes sense (See Figure 10-18).

Age Two age groups are particularly at risk for suicide: (1) adolescents and young adults and (2) those over age 70. For the United States population as a whole, suicide is the third most frequent cause of death for people of ages 10 to 14 and 15 to 24. It climbs to second place for the 25 to 34 age group and declines to sixth place at ages 45 to 54 and ninth place for those in the 55 to 64-year bracket. Although suicide is not in the top 10 causes of death for those over 65, this is not because the number of suicides is low but rather because in this age range the death rate is high from a variety of diseases, led by heart disease and cancer. For example, the number of suicides among white men over 85 is six times the national suicide rate. Figure 10-19 shows changes in suicide rate by age for men and women of several racial/ethnic groups.

College students are often thought to have a particularly high risk for suicide. However, after a review of all available studies of student-age suicide in the United States, the average rate of suicide for college students was found to be about half the rate of that for nonstudents of comparable age (A. J. Schwartz & Whitaker, 1990). It

may be, however, that the student rate is higher than it appears. In a study of suicides at Oxford University researchers found authorities were more likely to classify student deaths as "of undetermined cause" or accidental than they were for deaths in the general population (Hawton et al., 1995b).

Sex Figure 10-19 also shows that in the United States the suicide rates for men and women are very different. Men are much more likely to kill themselves than women are, although women make many more suicide attempts. Although firearms are the most common method of suicide for both men and women, accounting for 58% of all suicides in 1997 (National Institute of Mental Health, 1999), men are more likely to use firearms than women. Women often choose a potentially less lethal means—poison or an overdose of medication. Recent purchase of firearms is highly related to suicide. One study compared suicide rates for the people who purchased a handgun in California in 1991 with that of the general adult population of the state (Wintemute et al., 1999). In the first week after the gun purchase the rate of suicide by means of firearms was 57 times as high as the general population rate. In the first year, handguns accounted for one-quarter of all suicide deaths. These findings suggest that many people who are considering suicide make a gun purchase with that in mind.

Worldwide, however, women seem to choose drug overdoses or poisons as the preferred suicide method. This difference in choice of method also results in a difference in likelihood of suicide by men and women depending on the availability of firearms and lethal poisons. In countries where firearms are less available, poisons more easily procured, and medical help less available, the rate of suicide for women is higher than that for men, the reverse of the pattern seen in the United States.

Race and Ethnicity The rate of suicide consistently differs across race and ethnic groups. Figure 10-20 shows the average suicide rate for men and women by more specific racial/ethnic groups. The figure makes it clear that the rate for women in all racial/ethnic groups is less than that for men. What stands out in this figure is the very high rate for Native American and Alaskan native men. It is not clear why these racial/ethnic differences exist, but they are consistent across time periods. None of the frequently suggested predictors of suicide can be related consistently to these racial/ethnic differences.

Cultural Attitudes Cultural factors may account for some differences in suicide rate, but this may be more true when comparing national suicide rates than rates for those within a country. For example, in Japan, suicide is traditionally viewed as a culturally appropriate way to deal with

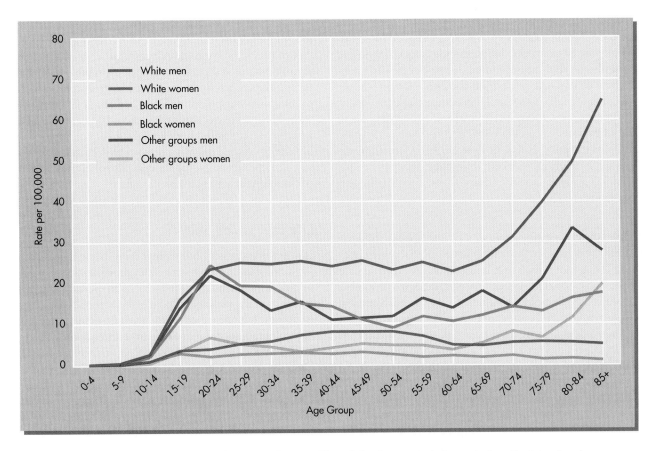

Figure 10-19   Rate of suicide per 100,000 for men and women. These "other" groups include people from the Asian American, Hispanic American, and Native American populations.

SOURCE: Data based on National Center for Injury Prevention report, 2000.

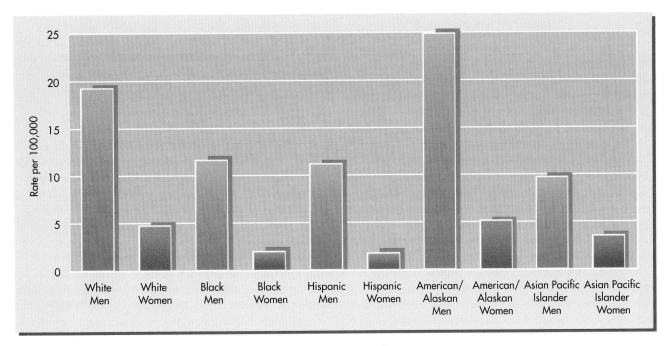

Figure 10-20   Age-adjusted suicide rates for men and women of several racial/ethnic groups.

SOURCE: National Center for Health Statistics, 2000.

feelings of shame and of being personally disgraced, perhaps about failure to achieve or having behaved in an unethical way. Seen in this light, suicide may compensate for the shame that an individual, his or her family members, and others will suffer from the behavior. In a study comparing Japanese and Canadian college students, Japanese students were more likely to think about suicide, to have formulated a suicide plan, and to have attempted suicide in the past (Heisel & Fuse, 1999). Canadian students were much more likely than their Japanese counterparts to have sought help from mental health professionals.

Hopelessness Negative expectations and hopelessness are important themes for those who have suicidal preoccupations. These individuals may come to believe that suicide is their only possible strategy for dealing with insoluble problems. The Beck Hopelessness Scale has been used in both inpatient and outpatient populations to predict whether a person is at increased risk for suicide (A. T. Beck et al., 1985, 1990). In a study of nonhospitalized patients, all but 1 of the 17 who killed themselves (94%) had scores above 9 on the Beck Hopelessness Scale. People whose scores were above 9 were 11 times more likely to commit suicide than those with lower scores.

Although many people who have a high score on the Beck Hopelessness Scale do not kill themselves, the scale is useful in signaling the possibility of increased risk. It has also provided insight into aspects of depressed thinking that might be related to the greatest risk of suicide. Because Beck and his co-workers have shown that hopelessness can be modified by cognitive therapy, his approach has also promoted more effective treatment.

Perfectionism Some people have a tendency to set unrealistically high standards for themselves and are likely to be overly critical in their self-evaluations. Perfectionism may increase the chances of suicide even more than hopelessness (Blatt et al., 1995a, 1995b). For example, perfectionism seemed to play a role in the death of British writer Alasdair Clayre. Clayre ended his life by jumping into the path of a subway train on the day his new book, on which he had worked for years, was to be published (Goleman, 1995). According to his friends, Clayre, a man with many previous accomplishments and winner of a prestigious fellowship, was extremely fearful about what reviewers might say about his book.

Roy Baumeister (1990) has developed the escape theory of suicide which views it as an attempt to escape aversive self-awareness. He believes that a causal chain of events leads to suicide. The chain begins with one or more stressful life events in which the person's standards and expectations are not met. The individual attributes these failures internally, which then generates negative emotions and may produce depression. Escape from these negative emotions is sought by a retreat into a cognitive state focusing only on immediate or short-term goals. As a result of this separation of feelings from cognitions, drastic measures such as suicide become acceptable. Baumeister's escape theory has been supported by research on a clinical outpatient population (Dean & Range, 1999). The patients' level of perfectionism predicted level of depression, which then predicted hopelessness. Level of hopelessness, in turn, predicted negative reasons to continue living and suicidal thoughts. Negative reasons for living also contributed directly to suicidal thoughts.

Life Events and Suicide

Just as very stressful life events have been related to depression, they are also sometimes precipitating factors for suicide. Life events that involve loss are particularly devastating to many people. Of course most people who experience these events do not try to kill themselves; nevertheless in a vulnerable person, a suicide may result. One of the most important factors is the breakup of a romance or a marriage. Overall, divorced people have a higher suicide rate than those who are married, however, epidemiological studies that consider many additional factors in prediction show that the rate of death from suicide is increased by divorce only among men (Kposowa, 2000). Job loss is another life event that increases the likelihood of suicide. Even without loss, stress on the job is also a predictor of suicide. There is a long-term difference in suicide rate among occupations that appears related to job stress (Murphy, 1985). Physicians, dentists, and lawyers are among the highly trained professionals whose suicide rate is high. A quite different group, unskilled laborers, also has traditionally had a high rate of suicide. Of course it is also possible that some personal characteristics that lead to the choice of one of these occupations are responsible rather than the job itself.

Suicide Contagion

Sometimes when the suicide of a well-known person makes headline news, an increase in suicides occurs shortly afterward. This has been called **suicide by contagion** or the "Werther effect," named after Goethe's fictional hero who killed himself with a pistol as the result of a failed love affair. After the publication of Goethe's poem, an epidemic of suicides of young men who shot themselves, as Werther did, was reported in Europe. In the United States, when film star Marilyn Monroe killed herself with an overdose of medication, the national suicide rate increased by 12% (Philips, 1974). This copycat phenomenon has been investigated scientifically by doing a time series analysis of daily overall suicides and relating the results to the suicides of prominent individuals that were widely publicized in the press (Jonas, 1992). The analysis supported the idea of an imitative

(a) Marilyn Monroe

(b) The body of a Heaven's Gate cult member

(c) Mementos commemorating the death of two South Boston teenagers.

Figure 10-21 The possibly accidental death by prescription drug overdose of film star Marilyn Monroe, the mass suicide of members of the Heaven's Gate cult, and the death by self-inflicted hanging, within a short time period, of six young men from South Boston, all illustrate the copycat effect that is likely to occur after well publicized self-inflicted deaths. In cases such as these the rate of suicide, attempted suicide, and concerns about suicidal thoughts rise shortly after the event.

effect. Sometimes, however, an intervention can counteract this effect. For instance, after the highly publicized suicide of Kurt Cobain, a rock star, in Seattle in 1994, authorities were braced for a similar rash of copycat suicides, but these did not occur. It may be that the media emphasis on the outreach efforts of the Seattle crisis center provided an alternative way for potential copycats to deal with their feelings.

A suicide may provoke a copycat effect even if the person involved was not famous (see Figure 10-21). Six young men from South Boston killed themselves by hanging in an 8-month period. In addition, about 70 teenagers from the area, mostly male, were hospitalized in the same period for suicide attempts or acute suicidal thoughts. Although other factors may have been involved, this huge increase in suicides, many by the same method, as well as suicidal attempts, is a clear illustration of the copycat effect.

Some other instances of multiple suicides appear to be related more to shared beliefs or group pressure than to contagion. Examples include the death of 39 members of the Heaven's Gate cult in California and the recent mass suicide of religious cult members in Africa.

Prevention of Suicide

There are several approaches to suicide prevention: increasing awareness of possible suicidal thinking, providing crisis centers and other facilities, and changing cultural expectations about how people should deal with their problems. Table 10-12 lists some warning signs that adolescents may be considering suicide. Many of these same signs apply to all ages.

Table 10-12

Warning Signs of Suicide in Adolescent Behavior

Because suicides among young people have increased dramatically in recent years, possible warning signs have been listed to help parents and others recognize indications that someone may be thinking about suicide. Many of the signs may signal depression and suicidal feelings for which there are appropriate treatments.

Major Signs

- Changes in eating and sleeping habits
- Withdrawal from friends, family, and regular activities
- Violent actions, rebellious behavior, running away
- Drug and alcohol use
- Unusual neglect of personal appearance
- Marked personality change
- Persistent boredom, difficulty concentrating, decline in quality of schoolwork
- Complaints about physical symptoms such as stomachaches and headaches
- Loss of interest in pleasurable activities
- Inability to tolerate praise or rewards

Additional Signs

- Complaints of being a bad person
- Verbal hints such as "Nothing matters anymore" and "I won't be a problem for you much longer"
- Putting affairs in order, for example, giving away or discarding favorite possessions
- Becoming suddenly cheerful after a period of depression
- Signs of hallucinations or bizarre thoughts

First Person

Box 10–3

Suicide and the Survivors

Suicide has a strong impact on the families of those who kill themselves and on others who knew them. It is more painful for the family than other kinds of death, and often harder to accept or acknowledge. Parents may think of the suicide of their adolescent child as an accidental death. They may also experience strong feelings of guilt and shame that may make normal mourning impossible. Young children of a parent who commits suicide are also likely to be seriously disturbed. The surviving parent may claim that the suicide was an accident. The child then begins to distrust the parent, doubt the reality of what he or she had observed, or both. Children often feel responsible for a parental suicide or think they should have prevented it. The result of these misperceptions may be a child who is depressed, passive, and self-destructive. Because of the social stigma that surrounds suicide, the survivors often avoid talking to others.

In the following paragraphs a wife describes her reactions and those of her 12-year-old son, Richard, to her husband's death.

For me the days that followed [her husband's suicide] were full of pain. The questions pounded at me. Why? Why? But shock numbs; somehow I could cope with memorial-service plans. Like a robot, I did what I had to do. People came and went, and I sat for hours without moving much. I remember not taking my clothes off for two days. I didn't want to move or change anything. Talking was an effort. Eating was an effort.

At the end of a week, after the service was over, the relatives had left, the real loneliness set in, and the guilt. Each night I dreamed that I was soothing Dick, telling him how much I loved him and still love him, feeling in my dreams that if only he knew, then he would be back and

safe. . . . Two months later on the plane as we came home from a Christmas trip to visit Dick's family, Richard said, "I feel like I really miss somebody and I don't even know who." I said, "Don't you think it's Dad?" and the only tears I saw him cry came then. We talk often and he tells me that now he mostly feels mad. "When I start to feel angry or sad," he says, "I try to concentrate really hard on whatever I happen to be doing at the time, like playing ball or riding my bike."

I've found it difficult to be that sensible, to avoid guilt and constant questioning. The notes Dick left said it was his job, that I had nothing to do with what he did. Still, why couldn't I have seen what was happening? Why couldn't I have saved him? He had been the best friend I ever had. I must not have been a good enough friend to him. I wanted to piece it together; I relived every conversation. But there were no answers, and it didn't fit together.

SOURCE: Kenyon (1979), p. 17.

Crisis centers can play an important role in suicide prevention by giving a troubled person an opportunity to express concerns, assuring them that effective help and treatment is available, and providing referrals to hospitals and clinics that offer immediate help. Changes in cultural attitudes toward dealing with stress are also important so that people will not interpret their feelings of hopelessness as a weakness but rather as signs that it is important and acceptable to seek help. A good example of this need for change is reflected in the high rate of suicide among police officers. Not only is the rate more than twice that of the total population, but more than twice as many police officers die by suicide as are killed in the performance of their active duties including being killed by criminals (Violanti et al., 1996). Critics have argued that the police subculture teaches people to suppress emotions as a psychologically necessary way to deal with the violence officers regularly encounter. However, officers are reluctant to seek help and their departments do not generally encourage them to do so (Karel, 1995). The U.S. Air Force developed a program aimed at decreasing the resistance of Air Force personnel to seeing a therapist and talking about personal problems. The program, required for all personnel, also provided suicide awareness training. After the program was initiated, the suicide rate for Air Force personnel was cut in half over a

5-year period. Suicide had been the second leading cause of death in the Air Force, but as a result of the program the suicide rate dropped to a level lower than the national average (*New York Times*, November 26, 1999).

Schools often try to give students more information about warning signs of suicide. Because students often seek help first from peers, these school programs try to alert other students to signs of potential suicide risk. The programs often encourage students to turn to adults for help, but many students, especially some at potential risk, lack supportive adult as well as peer relationships. Because suicide, although a major cause of death in adolescence, is still infrequent in any one school, it is difficult to evaluate whether these school programs are effective.

Another type of school program that can be helpful is a **postvention program,** which occurs after a suicide has taken place. Those close to the person who died often experience high levels of grief over a long period (see Box 10-3). Postvention can help survivors deal with their grief and possible feelings of responsibility and guilt, and may discourage other students from viewing suicide as a way of dealing with personal difficulties. Such programs often include information like that in Box 10-4, which lists some commonly asked questions about suicide.

Q: What should you do if someone tells you he is thinking about suicide?

A: *Take his distress seriously, listen without being judgmental, help him get to a professional for evaluation and treatment. Remove firearms and other potentially lethal means of suicide. If someone is in immediate danger of self-harm, do not leave the person alone. Take emergency steps, for instance, call 911.*

Q: What are the most common methods of suicide?

A: *Firearms are the most common method and are used in nearly 60% of all suicides, more frequently by men than by women. A firearm in the home is an additional, independent, risk factor for suicide. Hanging is the second most common method for men; for women the second most common method is self-poisoning including drug overdose.*

Q: Who is at the highest risk for suicide in the United States?

A: *Although men in the 15 to 24-year-old age group have a high risk, the elderly, especially older White males, have the highest risk. Many of these people have seen their primary care physician within the previous month and many had a depressive illness that was not detected. Another group that has a high risk of suicide is Native American and Alaskan native men. In this group, suicide is often associated with problems with drugs, especially alcohol.*

Q: Are gay and lesbian youth at high risk for suicide?

A: *There are no national statistics on this, although for completed suicides—once substance abuse and mental disorders are taken into account—there does not appear to be any difference. However, many people may not be open about their sexual orientation so it is difficult to know if this finding is accurate. High school students who report they are homosexually and bisexually active also report a higher rate of both suicide attempts and suicidal thoughts in the previous year.*

Q: Can the risk for suicide be inherited?

A: *Genetic factors can contribute to the risk. Major depression, bipolar disorder, schizophrenia, alcoholism, substance abuse, and some personality disorders tend to run in families and all these increase suicide risk. This does not mean that suicidal behavior is inevitable in these families. Instead it means that family members may be especially vulnerable and should take steps to reduce their risk, such as by getting treatment at the first sign of mental illness.*

Q: Is it possible to predict suicide?

A: *Right now there is no effective way to predict suicide. Risk factors have been identified, but few people with these risk factors will actually commit suicide. Some of the ways that an increased possibility of suicide can be recognized are listed in Table 10-12.*

SOURCE: Adapted from National Institute of Mental Health, Frequently Asked Questions About Suicide (December, 1999).

Chapter Summary

MOOD DISORDERS

A wide range of behaviors are seen in mood disorders. The three main types of **mood disorder** are depressive disorders, bipolar disorders, and other mood disorders which are substance-induced or due to general medical conditions.

Facts about Mood Disorders Depressive disorder is relatively common. Bipolar disorders are much less common than depressive disorder. The overall rates of both depressive and bipolar disorders, but not their typical symptoms, seem to be affected by a variety of cultural, economic, and environmental factors.

DEPRESSION

Depression can refer to a symptom or a disorder. The symptom of depressed mood does not necessarily mean a person has a **depressive disorder.** Although some symptoms of depression occur frequently in people who "have the blues" but are not clinically depressed, those who do meet DSM-IV criteria experience more symptoms and symptoms that are more severe. Depressive disorders are sometimes referred to as **unipolar dis-** orders to differentiate these types of depression from that found in bipolar disorder. There are several categories of depressive disorder.

Depressed Mood In everyday language, we often use the term *depression* to refer to normal feelings experienced after significant loss, such as the breakup of a relationship or the failure to attain a significant goal. These feelings are not classified as a depressive disorder by DSM-IV. Symptoms of grief over the death of a loved one also are not classified as depression unless they continue for an unusually long period.

Vulnerability Factors for Depression Genetic makeup, or heredity, is an important risk factor for both major depression and bipolar disorder. Age is also a risk factor. Women are particularly at risk during young adulthood, while for men the risk is highest in early middle age. Gender is also related to risk. Twice as many women as men in the general population report a depressive disorder. Other risk factors are experiencing negative life events and a lack of social support, particularly from close relationships. This support may be especially valuable if stressful life events have recently occurred.

DEPRESSIVE DISORDERS

Dysthymic Disorder A **dysthymic disorder** is a stable condition in which a depressed mood is dominant over long periods of time even if it is interrupted by short periods of normal mood.

Major Depressive Disorder A **major depressive disorder** is diagnosed when a person has experienced one or more major depressive episodes but has never experienced either a manic or hypomanic episode. A **major depressive episode** is defined as a period of depressed mood and/or loss of interest or pleasure in most activities, together with some other symptoms, which may include marked change in body weight, constant sleep problems, tiredness, inability to think clearly, agitation or greatly slowed behavior, and thoughts of death. When a person who has experienced one major depressive episode develops the symptoms again at a later time, the diagnosis is changed to **recurrent major depressive disorder.** At least half of those who experience a first episode experience a recurrence. If someone experiences delusions or other psychotic symptoms during a major depressive episode, the diagnosis then becomes a **major depressive episode with psychotic features.**

CAUSES AND TREATMENT OF DEPRESSION

Depression is generally thought to result from an interaction between biological characteristics, psychological vulnerabilities, and stressful events or ongoing stressful life situations. Each of the theoretical perspectives has contributed to the understanding of and the treatments available for depression.

Biological Factors in Depression The mechanism for depressed or manic behavior may be the activity of the neurotransmitter systems. An early theory, the **monoamine hypothesis** focused on the neurotransmitters **serotonin** and the **catecholamines,** but other neurotransmitters including **GABA** and **acetylcholine** also seem to be involved in depression. The study of the effects of various antidepressant drugs—including **MAO inhibitors, tricyclics,** and **selective serotonin reuptake inhibitors**—has led to hypotheses about the role of the neurotransmitters in producing behaviors associated with depression. The search for markers of depression has been an important research strategy. The markers investigated include specific receptor sites in the brain, studied by various scanning devices, and the role of biological rhythms, especially in **seasonal affective disorder (SAD).**

Biologically Based Treatment Treatments based on biological theories include **antidepressant medication** and **electroconvulsive therapy (ECT).** Biologically based treatments of depression are often successful in lessening depression. ECT is faster-acting than antidepressant medication and also is often used if an effective medication cannot be found.

Psychodynamic Theories Freud's view of depression focused on a decrease in self-regard and a punishing conscience that was an attempt to control feelings of anger and aggression. Later psychodynamic theorists believed feelings of helplessness in coping with loss were central to depression. They also stressed the importance of expectations based on early relationships to the development of satisfying current relationships.

Interpersonal Psychotherapy Interpersonal psychotherapy (IPT) is a therapy based on psychodynamic ideas concerning the importance of relationships and on the protective role of social support when life stress occurs. IPT is often used to help prevent relapse after recovery from a depressive episode.

The Humanistic–Existentialist Perspective Existentialist theorists view depression as a loss of self-esteem. Humanistic theorists emphasize the difference between the person's ideal self and his or her perception of the actual self. If the difference is too great, depression is likely to result.

The Behavioral Perspective Behaviorists are concerned with people's skills in getting social reinforcement, particularly as it relates to stress. Depressed people may engage in excessive support-seeking, which eventually causes distress in those who have contact with them. In both their own estimation and in the view of others, some of those who are depressed may lack important social skills.

Behavioral Treatment for Depression An effective behavioral approach to treating depression is **social skills training,** focused both on appropriate behavior and on improved skills in understanding the cues other people give in social interactions.

The Cognitive Perspective Unjustified negative interpretations of events or interactions are likely to be caused by **schemata,** or customary ways of interpreting behavior that are based on experiences earlier in life. Beck's **cognitive distortion model** of depression was the original cognitive view of depression and remains highly influential. The model explains depression as a **cognitive triad** of negative thoughts about oneself, the situation, and the future. Many measures of cognitions have developed as a result of interest in a cognitive theory of depression. Attributional models of depression focus on the causal **attributions** people make, for instance, whether they blame themselves or others. The interest in these attributions originally stemmed from **learned helplessness** theory. A subtype of depression may be **hopelessness depression,** in which the attribution process is important in initiating the depression. Although originally it was believed that depression was associated with negative **cognitive distortions** of reality, some researchers believe that depressed people may distort less than those who are not depressed.

Cognitive-Behavioral Therapy Therapy from the cognitive perspective utilizes both cognitive and behavioral elements and is often called **cognitive-behavioral therapy (CBT).** Although initially a behavioral approach may be used, as the client improves, the therapist works with the client to change his or her dysfunctional thought patterns. One aim of the therapist is to elicit clients' **automatic thoughts** and eventually to modify their early maladaptive schemas.

The Vulnerability–Resilience Perspective Biological and personally related factors combine to produce vulnerability or resilience to stressful life events. Personally relevant stressful events, especially in the context of ongoing or chronic problems and lack of social support, are likely to result in depression.

How Should Depression Be Treated? Antidepressant medication is often effective in treating depression. Little research has compared the effectiveness of medication and various other therapies in dysthymic disorder or mildly depressed mood. In major depressive disorder, the evidence is not clear as to whether medication alone or a combination of medication with either CBT or IPT is more effective in preventing relapse.

THE BIPOLAR DISORDERS

Bipolar disorders, formerly referred to as manic-depressive disorders, include phases of both depression and mania or hypomania. DSM-IV lists four bipolar disorders: Bipolar I disorder, Bipolar II disorder, cyclothymic disorder, and a miscellaneous group.

Bipolar I Disorder Bipolar I disorder includes episodes of mania and usually also major depressive episodes. **Mania** is a state of elevated mood, flight of ideas, and increased psychomotor activity. Episodes of bipolar disorder tend to recur. The number of recurrences is greater in those who have a family history that includes bipolar disorder.

Bipolar II Disorder Bipolar II disorder is a variant of bipolar disorder in which there has been no manic episode but at least one hypomanic period as well as a major depressive episode. A **hypomanic episode** refers to a period of manic behavior that is not extreme enough to greatly impair function.

Cyclothymic Disorder Cyclothymic disorder includes both hypomanic and depressive behavior that extends over at least a 2-year period.

CAUSES AND TREATMENT OF BIPOLAR DISORDER

Genetic Factors Twin studies show genetic factors create a vulnerability for bipolar disorder. Family studies have identified some gene locations that may play a role, but these locations differ from study to study.

Biologically Based Treatment of Bipolar Disorder Bipolar disorder is most commonly treated with lithium, but sometimes with anticonvulsant drugs. Lithium may dampen enjoyable moods and can have dangerous side effects but is still the most effective treatment.

Psychosocial Factors and Bipolar Episodes Psychosocial factors play a role both in triggering and preventing episodes of bipolar disorder. Both environmental stress and family stress resulting from the symptoms of bipolar disorder can make new episodes more likely.

Psychoeducational Treatment for the Family Family psychoeducational programs may be helpful in reducing stress. One study found that families, and particularly the bipolar patients, showed an increase in positive nonverbal behavior following psychoeducational treatment. This type of intervention can add to the effects of medication to improve symptoms of bipolar disorder.

SUICIDE

Mental Illness and Suicide Mental illnesses greatly increase the probability of a suicide attempt. Among the mood disorders, the suicide rate is highest for Bipolar II disorder and lowest for unipolar depression. **Parasuicide** is the term used for suicidal behavior that does not result in death.

Risk Factors for Suicide Teenagers and young adults are at high risk for suicide, as are those who are well past middle age. Sex is also a factor: men have a higher rate of completed suicide than women. Rates of suicide also differ among racial and ethnic groups. Native American and Alaskan native groups have the highest rates and Whites (especially men) have the next highest rate. Other factors that affect suicide rates are cultural attitudes toward suicide, feelings of hopelessness, and perfectionism.

Life Events and Suicide Stressful life events are sometimes precipitating factors for suicide. Events that involve loss are particularly important.

Suicide Contagion When a well-known person's suicide is widely publicized, an increase in other suicides usually occurs shortly afterward. This contagion may also occur within members of a group, when one person kills him- or herself.

PREVENTION OF SUICIDE

Prevention of suicide can involve increasing public awareness of warning signs, providing crisis centers and other help facilities, and changing cultural expectations about how people should solve their problems. **Postvention programs** are often used to help survivors deal with the impact of the suicide of a member of their group.

Key Terms

11

Diana Ong (B. 1940) "Confusion of Shapes". Private Collection. SuperStock.

Schizophrenia and Other Psychotic Disorders

"I live in a closet. Unlike most closets, mine is invisible. . . . Nevertheless, its imprisoning walls and terrifying darkness are very real.

"The 'closet' is schizophrenia, a major mental illness or, as some professionals now refer to it, a neurobiological disorder. I have suffered from schizophrenia for a good part of my adult life. It is treatable but is, as yet, without a cure. . . .

"Despite two hospitalizations, I managed to graduate from Brown University a Phi Beta Kappa and go on to attend the University of Connecticut Medical School. But after little more than a year, I could not function any longer. By this time the voices had made their appearance. . . . To this day, [I] am not sure that I was not in fact responsible for JFK's assassination as well as other international catastrophes. . . . Once, the title of a book so preoccupied and disturbed me that I . . . spent almost my last cent getting to Orlando, Florida, because I believed the book had told me to do so.

"I was, and despite medication at times still am, sensitive to casual remarks. Sometimes even a 'Hello' or 'How are you?' can feel threatening or of cosmic significance. I hear the voices of abusively cruel people talking to me constantly, even when no one is present. . . . Listening to the radio is impossible because of the personal messages I am sent, either by the DJ or by the sequence of music and advertisements.

"Although I still have symptoms, I have not been hospitalized (except very briefly for a medication reaction) in a year. . . . At 42, I think I'm slowly getting better or at least getting better at dealing with the difficulties that remain. I feel stronger and more stable now than ever before. Bad days, days when I cannot write or even read a word, are becoming rarer, while the good days filled with productive writing hours are more frequent. Just recently, in fact, I had an article published in the *Hartford Courant,* while one I wrote in 1993 won the Connecticut Mental Health Media Award, an award limited to professional journalists." (Wagner, 1996, pp. 399–401) ■

Although she still is severely affected by symptoms of schizophrenia, the woman whose account you have just read is able to live a productive life. Even though medication, treatment, and support have not enabled her to live without some manifestations of her disorder, she has learned ways of coping with these so that she is able to function.

Not all people who develop schizophrenia have such a good outcome, as other examples, later in this chapter illustrate.

Psychotic Disorders

Schizophrenia is a prominent part of the category of mental disorders known as psychotic disorders. A **psychotic disorder** is defined by its effects in altering perception, thoughts, or consciousness; these alterations are called hallucinations or delusions. Someone who makes incorrect inferences about reality on the basis of these alterations and believes that the inferences are real and actual has a psychotic disorder. Symptoms of psychotic disorders may also include disorganized speech and behavior. Psychotic symptoms often produce the kind of behaviors that were formerly called madness, lunacy, or insanity. Table 11-1 lists the principal psychotic disorders as DSM-IV classifies them.

Not all hallucinations and delusions indicate the presence of a psychological disorder. Sometimes hallucinations or delusions result from temporary causes such as the effect of medication, the reduced availability of oxygen to the brain during a high fever, or extreme vitamin deficiencies. In other cases the symptoms are caused by permanent changes that result from infections such as syphilis. Sometimes they are also found in major depressive disorders. However, if no specific cause can be found for the disordered thoughts and perceptions, they are considered to be the defining aspects of one of the psychotic disorders discussed in this chapter: schizophrenia, schizoaffective disorder, delusional disorder, and shared psychotic disorder.

Schizophrenia

Of all the psychotic disorders, schizophrenia has the most severe impact on people's lives and on the health care system. About 20 million people worldwide meet the criteria for schizophrenia (Sartorius & de Girolamo, 1991). In the United States more than 2 million Americans, or more than 1% of the population, suffer from this chronic and disabling disease any given year (Sperling, 1999). Despite the relatively small percentage of the total U.S. population affected, the seriousness and incapacitating consequences

of schizophrenia mean that about 50% of those affected will become severely and permanently disabled and dependent on public assistance funding. Individuals diagnosed with schizophrenia make up 10% of the permanently and totally disabled population and constitute as much as 14% of the homeless population of some large urban centers (Rupp & Keith, 1993). When lost productivity, social welfare expenses, and the estimated value of family caregiving are included, in addition to the cost of treatment, the total cost of schizophrenia in the United States has been estimated to exceed $70 billion annually.

In addition to the cost in money, the social and psychological costs of schizophrenia are tremendous, both to patients and their families and to society. The psychological cost to patients is shown in the very high rates of attempted and completed suicide by those with schizophrenic diagnoses. About 1 in every 4 patients with schizophrenia will try to kill himself or herself, and 1 in every 10 will succeed (Roy, 1992). Those who choose suicide are in some ways similar to those in the general population who turn to suicide. They tend to be unmarried and unemployed, live alone, feel hopeless, and have made previous suicide attempts. However, people with schizophrenia who kill themselves are also likely to have some additional characteristics not typical of others who kill themselves. They are likely to be young and college educated, have a course of illness that is chronic with many worsenings and improvements, are afraid of further mental disintegration, and have a nondelusional negative view concerning the future (Caldwell & Gottesman, 1990).

Schizophrenia, as defined in DSM-IV, probably includes several disorders with different causes that are currently lumped together because there is not enough knowledge of the critical factors that differentiate them (Maj, 1998). The traditional way of categorizing schizophrenia is to divide it into subtypes derived from historical views of schizophrenia. Box 11-1 discusses these historical views in more detail. A more recent way of creating subgroups that may represent different disorders within the general category of schizophrenia has been through statistically analyzing schizophrenic signs and symptoms to obtain groupings that seem to occur together (Andreasen et al., 1995). These signs and symptoms seem to fall into two groups that are referred to as positive symptoms and negative symptoms. In the next sections we will discuss first the DSM-IV categories and then the positive and negative symptom grouping.

DSM-IV Subtypes of Schizophrenia

Box 11-1 describes how Emil Kraepelin divided schizophrenia (or as he called it, dementia praecox) into three subtypes—*paranoid, catatonic,* and *hebephrenic.* Later, Eugen Bleuler broadened the description of the disorder and added a fourth category, *simple schizophrenia.* Current DSM-IV

Table 11-1	
The Principal Psychotic Disorders	
Name	Characteristics
Schizophrenia	Disturbance lasts 6 months or more. At least 1 month of active phase, usually including at least two of the positive symptoms listed in Table 11-3 or one positive and one negative symptom. A decline in social or occupational function must also occur. (Five subtypes include paranoid, disorganized, catatonic, undifferentiated, and residual.)
Schizophreniform disorder	Same symptoms as schizophrenia, but lasts between 1 and 6 months. It is not necessary that there be a decline in function for this diagnosis.
Schizoaffective disorder	The active-phase symptoms of schizophrenic disorder occur, together with an episode characteristic of a mood disorder. These are preceded or followed by at least 2 weeks of delusions or hallucinations.
Delusional disorder	Nonbizarre delusions lasting at least 1 month without the other symptoms that characterize the active phase of schizophrenia.
Brief psychotic disorder	A psychotic disturbance lasting more than 1 day but less than 1 month.
Shared psychotic disorder	A disturbance that develops in a person influenced by someone else who has an established delusion with similar content.
Psychotic disorder due to general medical condition	Psychotic symptoms thought to be physiological results of a general medical condition or illness.
Substance-induced psychotic disorder	Psychotic symptoms thought to be the physiological result of toxin exposure, medication, or drug abuse.

categories reflect a modification of these traditional types. These include the *paranoid*, *catatonic*, and *disorganized* subtypes and a catchall, or *undifferentiated*, group. In addition, there is a *residual* category for cases in which the psychotic features are no longer prominent. Table 11-2 lists

and briefly describes these DSM-IV subtypes. Although the DSM-IV subtypes have a historical basis, they have some important limitations for researchers interested in understanding more about the causes of schizophrenia. The classification by subtype is only moderately stable for

Table 11-2	
DSM-IV Subtypes of Schizophrenia	
Subtype[a]	Characteristics
Paranoid type	Preoccupation with delusion(s) or auditory hallucinations. Little or no disorganized speech, disorganized or catatonic behavior, or inappropriate or flat affect.
Disorganized type	All the following—disorganized speech, disorganized behavior, and inappropriate or flat affect—are prominent in behavior, but catatonic-type criteria are not met. Delusions or hallucinations may be present, but only in fragmentary or noncoherent form.
Catatonic type	At least two of the following: extreme motor immobility; purposeless excessive motor activity; extreme negativism (motionless resistance to all instructions) or mutism (refusing to speak); peculiar or bizarre voluntary movement; echolalia or echopraxia.
Undifferentiated type	Does not fit any of the subtypes above, but meets the symptom criteria for schizophrenia.
Residual type	Has experienced at least one episode of schizophrenia, but currently does not have prominent positive symptoms (delusions, hallucinations, disorganized speech or behavior). However, continues to show negative symptoms and a milder variation of positive symptoms (odd beliefs, eccentric behavior).

[a]In assigning a subtype to the diagnosis, DSM-IV uses the following rules: Paranoid type is assigned if delusions or hallucinations are prominent unless the person also meets the criteria for the catatonic or disorganized type. If criteria for either of those types are met, then that diagnosis takes priority. If criteria for both disorganized type and catatonic type are present, then catatonic is the type assigned. This means that the catatonic-type diagnosis is used if catatonic symptoms are present, even if behaviors characteristic of another type are also seen. If a person shows symptoms characteristic of the active phase of schizophrenia but does not meet the criteria for any of these three types, a subtype diagnosis of undifferentiated type is used.
Source: Adapted from *DSM-IV*.

Research Close-Up

Changing Views of Schizophrenia and Their Implications for Classification, Research, and Treatment

Despite the fact that many of the historic views concerning schizophrenia are no longer accepted, many early ideas, such as the subgroups or types of the disorder and the characteristics of symptoms essential for diagnosis, still have an influence seen both in the DSM-IV and in the way researchers go about formulating questions for their studies. Psychotic disorders were not clearly defined until the nineteenth century, although brief descriptions of what today would probably be called schizophrenia are found in writings as early as the Hindu *Ayur Veda* (1400 B.C.) (Kendell, 1983).

Dementia Praecox

One of the first writers to classify schizophrenia as a distinct disorder was Emil Kraepelin (1856–1926) (see Figure 11-1a), a German physician, who called it **dementia praecox.** Kraepelin was the author of the most influential psychiatric textbook of his time. He emphasized that classification depended on the cause of the illness, not just the symptoms observed at a particular time. Kraepelin used the term *dementia praecox* (premature madness) because the onset of the disorder occurred

early in life, typically in adolescence. He noted that problems with attention were important symptoms of schizophrenia. He noted that one sign of the disorder was the loss of the inclination and ability on the patient's own initiative to keep attention fixed for any length of time (Kraepelin, 1971). Kraepelin believed the cause of dementia praecox was irreversible organic deterioration, which would eventually be found to have a specific organic cause and pathology. Although he considered recovery from dementia praecox impossible, 16 of the 127 cases he studied seemed to have ended in complete recovery (Kraepelin, 1909, vol. 2, p. 865).

His entire focus was on the symptoms of the underlying deterioriation. He ignored the person's life history, personality, and experiences with the illness. When he did mention psychological features, Kraepelin considered them temporary expedients, expecting that findings from microscopes and test tubes would make it possible to investigate the disease objectively. Kraepelin divided schizophrenia into three subtypes: *paranoid, hebephrenic,* and *catatonic*. These categories have influenced diagnostic systems up to the present time.

The Schizophrenias

One of the first people to emphasize the psychological aspects of the disorder was Eugen Bleuler (1857–1939) (Figure 11-1b), a Swiss physician who was influenced by Freud's work on the neuroses. According to Bleuler, whatever the underlying process might be, many of the symptoms had a psychological cause. Bleuler spoke of "the schizophrenias" instead of using the term *dementia praecox* and broadened the concept of the disorder as well as changing its name. He also added another subtype of the disorder, which he called *simple schizophrenia*, to the three subtypes Kraepelin had suggested.

Bleuler believed that the symptoms might represent a group of disorders with different causes and outcomes, not a single cause and outcome as Kraepelin had thought.

Bleuler noted that although some people with psychotic disorders deteriorate, others remain unchanged, and some even improve. Bleuler also emphasized the role of the environment. In his view, some individuals might have the potential for developing these disorders, but because particular types of environmental situations did not occur, the illness remained latent and these people never showed visible signs of schizophrenia. This idea is still current in the concept of vulnerability, discussed later in this chapter.

Bleuler spoke of this group of disorders as characterized by loss of integration of thinking, emotion, and motivation rather

Figure 11-1 Emil Kraepelin (a), Eugen Bleuler (b), and Kurt Schneider (c), three pioneer clinician-researchers whose influence is still felt in present-day definitions of schizophrenia.

than by gradual deterioration. He summed up the primary characteristics of schizophrenic behavior as the "four A's"; alterations in affect (mood), alterations in association, ambivalence, and autism. Bleuler argued that although hallucinations and delusions were the most noticeable and dramatic features of the schizophrenic disorder, they were secondary to these primary characteristics and did not reflect the real causes of the disorder. Thus using a classification system that emphasized these aspects would not be helpful either in treating patients or in increased understanding of the causes of the schizophrenic process.

From the 1930s until the 1960s, several important figures in American psychiatry, such as Adolf Meyer and Harry Stack Sullivan, emphasized a broad concept of schizophrenia and psychosis in general. They were concerned with the psychodynamics of the behavior and emphasized interpersonal relationships as causal factors. As a result, differential diagnosis—discriminating, for example, between mood disorders and schizophrenia—was thought to be of little importance, and the proportion of people who were called schizophrenic increased sharply. Because such a large number of people with different symptoms and different outcomes of illness were given the same diagnosis, the chances of effective treatment greatly decreased. As a result of this problem, work began to be focused on narrowing the definition of schizophrenia.

First-Rank Symptoms

Kurt Schneider (1887–1967) (Figure 11-1c) was one of the leaders in the effort to make the definition of schizophrenia more concise and easier to reach agreement over. Schneider did not deny that Kraepelin's idea of organic deterioration was correct, but he believed that since these changes had not been identified, it was more useful to divide people into types on the basis of their psychological symptoms. Schneider also felt that Bleuler's characterization system of the four A's was too vague to be reliable.

Schneider dealt with these problems by describing a series of first- and second-rank symptoms. If first-rank symptoms were present and no organic cause was evident, a diagnosis of schizophrenia was justified.

First-rank symptoms were all related to hallucinations and delusional thinking; they are now described as positive symptoms. These hallucinations were likely to be auditory, such as voices keeping up a running commentary on the person's current behavior, and the delusions would include the belief that thoughts are no longer confined only to the person's mind but are simultaneously broadcast for all to hear. For example, Schneider would have considered the following account by a 21-year-old student a good example of first-rank symptoms:

As I think, my thoughts leave my head on a type of mental ticker-tape. Everyone around has only to pass the tape through their mind and they know my thoughts. (Mellor, 1970, p. 17)

First-rank symptoms also included experiences of external control, such as having thoughts inserted into one's head or arbitrarily taken away. Patients might report feeling hypnotized or having become robotlike, under the control of others, as in this female patient's report:

I cry, tears roll down my cheeks and I look unhappy, but inside I have a cold anger because they are using me in this way, and it is not me who is unhappy, but they are projecting unhappiness into my brain. They project upon me laughter, for no reason, and you have no idea how terrible it is to laugh and look happy and know it is not you, but their emotions. (Mellor, 1970, p. 17)

Schneider's classification system attempted to identify behavioral symptoms of abnormal inner experiences of the individual that would be readily noticed by an examiner, could be easily agreed upon by several observers, and could occur only in schizophrenia.

Schneider was only partially successful in meeting his goals. The first-rank symptoms are easily noticed and are easy for examiners to agree on. However, although they occur frequently in schizophrenia, they are not unique to it. At least one-fourth of patients with bipolar affective disorders also show some of these symptoms (Hoenig, 1984). In addition, the presence or absence of these symptoms does not seem to be related to later func-

tioning and improvement (Silverstein & Harrow, 1981).

Implications

Viewing the changing ideas concerning schizophrenia across time makes it clear that each of them has implications for classification, treatment, and research. Kraepelin's view implied that researchers should be most interested in examining the brain tissue of deceased patients to understand more about how brain anatomy might be related to symptoms. This view did not encourage treatment, since it was thought to be useless, but it was the beginning of the formal classification process of mental disorders because it distinguished dementia praecox from disorders involving depression, and perhaps mania. Bleuler's view had quite different implications, including treatment approaches that focused on decreasing environmental stress. We can still see the influence of his views, as well as those of Meyer and Sullivan, in the emphasis on vulnerability and the stress on both environmental factors and aspects of interpersonal relationships that is current today. These views have stimulated research, particularly on family relationships, such as the work on expressed emotion discussed later in the chapter. Schneider's emphasis on improving the description of symptoms and developing a reliable classification system for them was a forerunner of the extensive work on classification systems that is continuing today. The widespread use of a classification system such as the DSM-IV has made communication easier for clinicians and enabled researchers to utilize older findings. However, the criteria used today may also interfere with understanding the causes and processes of schizophrenia because the criteria chosen are likely to represent secondary signs of the disorder that are not part of the basic disease process (Maj, 1998).

Research as we see it today is tied closely to the continuing influence of theories of the past. As in other areas of research in the field of abnormal psychology, the emphasis shifts back and forth between biological and social-psychological processes. The interactional view and the vulnerability-and-resilience approach that are the focus of this book combine these emphases.

individuals over the course of their illness. The types of symptoms they show tend to move from paranoid to disorganized and undifferentiated, and from the positive symptoms toward the negative symptoms as time goes on. These changes seem to be associated with increasing functional decline and neurological impairment (McGlashan & Johannessen, 1996). Most of the deterioration in behavior takes place in the first year after symptoms appear, and after 3 to 5 years the symptoms seem to reach a plateau, or they may decrease (Eaton et al., 1992). Some researchers believe that grouping the symptoms into positive and negative types may help researchers to understand more about the causes and processes of schizophrenia.

The diagnosis most often given to patients with schizophrenia on their first admission to a mental hospital is schizophrenia of the paranoid type, or **paranoid schizophrenia.** This disorder displays itself primarily in cognitive behavior, characterized by delusions and sustained, extreme suspiciousness. Well-defined systems of delusional paranoid thinking can also exist in people who in other respects show well-integrated behavior. Such people are diagnosed as having a delusional disorder rather than schizophrenia of the paranoid type. Delusional disorder is discussed later in the chapter.

It is important to realize that paranoid elements can be observed in the average person as well as in a range of disorders. Everyone engages in paranoid thinking at one time or another. You could probably think of at least one occasion when you have felt that you were being discriminated against or talked about or were suspicious of someone else's motives without adequate proof that such things had actually occurred. We can consider paranoid thinking to be a kind of cognitive style that can be expressed as a continuum extending from everyday types of fleeting thoughts to severe delusional thinking that affects all of a person's life. (The case at the beginning of the chapter describes one person's account of her delusional thinking.) Illness, drugs, damage to the brain, some effects of aging, and the experience of severe stress can also produce paranoid thinking even when no disorder is present.

Catatonic schizophrenia is characterized by psychomotor disturbance that may range from immobility or stupor to excessive motor activity that seems purposeless and unconnected to what is going on in the environment. A person with this type of schizophrenia may refuse to speak and may remain stiffly immobile or may be extremely agitated. Waxy flexibility is an extreme form of immobility in which the person's arm or leg remains passively in the position in which it is placed. In contrast, a person with agitated catatonic behavior shows extreme psychomotor excitement, talking and shouting almost continuously. Patients who experience prolonged catatonic excitement may be very destructive and violent toward others.

A person diagnosed as having **disorganized schizophrenia** shows incoherence in expression, grossly disorganized behavior, and either flat or extremely inappropriate emotional reactions. Such people behave actively but aimlessly, and they may show a childish disregard for social conventions and may resist wearing clothes, or urinate or defecate in inappropriate places. Usually the long-term outlook for recovery is poor. People with disorganized schizophrenia are likely to have shown symptoms at an early age and to have been poorly adapted even before that.

If someone has previously met the diagnostic criteria for schizophrenia and no longer has prominent positive symptoms but still continues to have negative symptoms or some very mild residual positive symptoms such as eccentric behavior or odd beliefs, he or she is classified as having **schizophrenic disorder of the residual type.** Behavior of the residual type may represent any of the following situations: a transition between an active psychotic episode and a complete remission, an interlude between psychotic episodes, or a long-term state that may last over many years.

Positive and Negative Symptoms

Positive symptoms reflect a distortion or excess of normal functions and tend to be most frequent in the first stages or early episodes of schizophrenia. **Negative symptoms,** which are behavioral deficits or the loss or decrease of normal functions, tend to be infrequent at the beginning of the disorder but may be more prominent later. In the early stages of schizophrenia, both positive and negative symptoms are likely to fluctuate in severity and may respond to treatment. In later stages of schizophrenia, the negative symptoms usually dominate and tend to be quite stable (McGlashan & Fenton, 1992). Table 11-3 lists the categories of behavior classified as positive or negative symptoms.

Table 11-3

Positive and Negative Symptoms of Schizophrenia

Positive Symptoms

- Delusions
- Hallucinations
- Disorganized speech
- Disorganized and bizarre behavior

Negative Symptoms

- Flat affect
- Poverty of speech
- Loss of directedness or motivation
- Loss of energy
- Loss of feelings of pleasure

Positive Symptoms At least one positive symptom must be present in the active or acute phase of schizophrenia in order for a diagnosis of schizophrenia to be made. The most important positive symptoms of schizophrenia are delusions and hallucinations.

Delusions A **delusion** is essentially a faulty interpretation of reality that cannot be shaken despite clear evidence to the contrary. Delusions occur in other disorders besides schizophrenia, but in each disorder they have a somewhat different content (see Table 11-4).

Delusions can be expressed in many ways. Some types of delusions occur more often in schizophrenia than in any other type of psychosis. Among these are bizarre delusions, for example, the belief that everyone can hear the person's thoughts; the belief that others are either inserting thoughts into the person's mind or removing them; and the belief that the person's thoughts, feelings, and impulses are controlled by some external force. Bizarre delusions are considered very characteristic of schizophrenia, so if even one bizarre delusion is present, the criterion for symptoms in DSM-IV is satisfied. Another kind of delusion is referential. The person believes that certain gestures or comments, song lyrics, passages in books, and so forth are specifically intended for him or her. Additional delusions that are typical of schizophrenia but that occur less often include the belief of being persecuted, grandiose thoughts about being an extremely important person, and ideas with a religious theme. For example, a common delusion is a person's belief that he or she is an important religious figure, such as Jesus Christ.

Delusions can result in violent behavior that harms others. In 1994, a stagehand working on the *Today* show was shot and killed after he tried to alert police to an armed man who was trying to enter the NBC studios in midtown Manhattan (see Figure 11-2). William Tager, the 46-year-old man who was later convicted of the shooting, told police that the television networks had been spying on him and sending rays through his television set into his brain. He brought an assault rifle to the studio as a result of these delusional thoughts. At the time he was arrested, he also told police that he had been responsible for the attack on TV news anchor Dan Rather 8 years earlier. Although his claim was not investigated at the time because so many years had passed, the psychiatrist who examined him was curious to know if it was true. The psychiatrist was able to match up details given by Tager with those that had been given by Rather, and later Rather identified a photo of Tager as his assailant. In both cases, the motive appeared to be suspicion of the news media. The assailant believed that the media had intruded into his car, his home, and his workplace (Bruni, 1997). This example illustrates how stable and persistent delusions may be.

Although delusions such as Tager's may seem highly illogical, some behavior based on delusional thinking can be highly organized and appear quite logical. For example, the Army journal *Military Review* published an article, titled "Hell in a Hand Basket: The Threat of Portable Nuclear Arms," that focused on the growing peril from hand-held nuclear weapons that could easily come into the possession of terrorists. C. T. Harrison, the author, was identified in the journal as a commercial pilot with a science degree; a member of the Mensa society, an organization open only to those of superior intelligence; and a freelance researcher for several government agencies. However, Harrison was later identified, to the embarrassment of the journal's editors, as someone who was confined to a mental health institution with a diagnosis of paranoid schizophrenia after having been given the verdict of not guilty by reason of insanity for the killing of his mother 9 years earlier. After the journal staff received this information, they made further inquiries about the author and discovered that both the FBI and the Secret Service had been investigating him for at least 12 years in connection with death threats against political figures and with a stream of letters in which he identified himself as a member of a fictional terrorist group that claimed responsibility for assassination plots against many world leaders, including the Pope. Yet despite the apparent delusional nature of his thinking, he was able to communicate clearly

Table 11-4	
Typical Content of Delusions in Different Types of Psychoses	
Disorder	Typical Delusional Content
Schizophrenia	Variety of bizarre content: being controlled by others; being persecuted by others; finding reference to oneself in others' behaviors and in printed materials
Depression (in either unipolar or bipolar disorder)	Unjustified guilt; perceived bodily changes (e.g., rotting, putrefaction)
Mania	Great self-importance; grandiosity
Delusional Disorder	Loved by celebrity/high-status person; unfaithful behavior by spouse/lover; possession of special (unrecognized) talent

Figure 11-2 William Tager, escorted by police after being charged with the shooting death of an NBC stagehand outside the *Today* show, was later identified by TV news anchor Dan Rather as his assailant in an earlier attack.

and logically enough to convince the journal that his paper was worth publishing. In the course of considering the article, the editor had spoken with Harrison several times over the phone but did not realize he was conversing with someone who was hospitalized.

Hallucinations Hallucinations account for most of the difficulties a person with schizophrenia experiences in perceiving reality. **Hallucinations** are projections of internal impulses and experiences onto perceptual images in the external world. Although they may occur in other disorders—for example, during the delirium associated with a high fever or as a result of the effects of drugs or other chemicals on the nervous system—only in schizophrenia do hallucinations occur when the person is in a clear, conscious state. Hallucinations can be associated with any of the senses. Auditory hallucinations are the most common type found in schizophrenia. Many individuals with schizophrenia report voices making a running commentary on their behavior, or speaking directly to them and issuing orders, or accusing them of terrible crimes or actions. Hallucinations may also be related to touch. For instance, the person may feel burning or tingling sensations. Hallucinations associated with smell, while less common, are also typical. Foul odors may be perceived as coming from one's body as a sign of decay and death or of some sexual change.

The frightening quality of hallucinations is illustrated by the following experience of a medical student in response to a highly stressful personal situation:

One night, after weeks of bunking with anxiety, I was lying in bed, . . . when from the room, barely audible, came a whisper. Calmly, I looked around. Dormitories are noisy. There could be someone walking around outside. I opened my door, peeked side to side at the empty hall, then returned to bed. I rested within my sheets and attempted to relax, when again came a definite whisper. My eyes flashed open and there, al-

most expected, beside my bed, without certain form, rose a warm shadowy figure, a vibration in the dark that stood nearly motionless, then, after a moment, spoke.

"I am here to help you," was the first it said. . . . My visitor softly crossed the room and sat lightly on my desk. I could see it had a head and a mouth. Looking close, I saw it grin. I lunged from the room, slamming the door behind me. . . .

During the next week, my specter returned every night. I dropped out of school and began visiting a psychiatrist. . . .

Up till now, I've told only two trustworthy (medical student) friends about my experiences and, curiously, they both reacted by eagerly asking the same question: "What was it like?" As if it were some psychedelic, amusement-park hallucination, a thrilling fun-for-the-whole-family adventure. One asked, "Was it like having a movie inside your head?"

No, it wasn't. It was the fright of close lightning; it was waking up thinking you're blind, with your eyes wide open in the dark. It's lonely seeing what no one else sees. Frightening and lonely. Terror can also isolate. What I have seen and heard I know are not there. But these things I have seen and heard. . . . What is real to the mind is real to the person. Hallucinations can talk, they can walk, they can blind, mute, maim, and they can kill. (Name withheld, 1993, pp. 149, 151)

Although many hallucinations are frightening, not all are accusatory or unpleasant. Sometimes those who experience hallucinations find them so comfortable they are unwilling to give them up because they serve as protections from negative aspects of reality.

Brain activity during hallucinations has been investigated using scanning techniques. The results show that, during auditory hallucinations, the blood flow in Broca's area (the brain's speech center) was significantly greater during the time the hallucination was occurring than when it was not (McGuire et al., 1993). Researchers also found that activity decreased in Wernicke's area (the brain's hear-

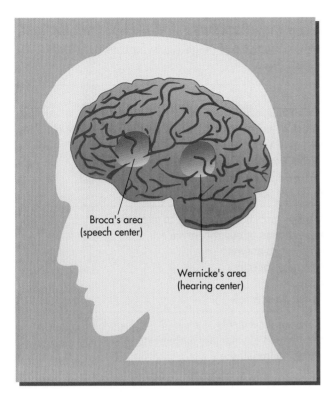

Figure 11-3 Auditory hallucinations, such as hearing voices, are common in schizophrenia. Research using scanning techniques to track the blood flow in the brain has shown that the greatest brain activity during these auditory hallucinations is in Broca's area, the brain's speech center. At the same time, the scans show a decrease in activity in Wernicke's area, the hearing center of the brain.

Broca's area
(speech center)

Wernicke's area
(hearing center)

ing center) during the hallucination. Figure 11-3 shows the location of these two areas of the brain. These findings surprised researchers because they suggested that auditory hallucinations in schizophrenia are associated with increased activity in cortical areas specialized for language, not for hearing as might be expected. In people who do not have schizophrenia, Broca's area is activated when they silently talk to themselves. It appears, from these research findings, that the schizophrenic process somehow makes it difficult to distinguish between one's own silent speech and hearing words that come from others.

Disordered Speech Disordered thinking has frequently been considered to be the most important characteristic of schizophrenia. Because disordered thinking is difficult to measure objectively, DSM-IV lays stress on disordered speech instead. **Disordered speech** is often described as a *loosening of associations* in which the speaker's ideas shift from one topic to another in a way that seems unrelated to everyone listening. When the loosening of association is severe, the person's speech becomes incomprehensible. An example of loose associations is the answer given by this person to the question "What does this proverb mean: 'Strike while the iron is hot'?"

It could mean [pause] Hercules! (Could you say more?) I saw the movie Hercules. (Yes . . .) And it means don't iron over your hands and don't strike anybody before you cast the first stone. (Marengo et al., 1986, p. 498)

Some of the difficulty in understanding the meaning of schizophrenic speech comes from the tendency toward **perseverative speech,** or the repetition of words or phrases, often by inserting them in subsequent statements. The incoherent speech of the patient quoted here illustrates this perseverative tendency:

Yes I mean er I mean are you from London I mean do you like London particular of London I think that London is wild buses wild buses in London and wild trains underground is wild in London bus I mean it is Lebanon bus of London and Lebanon train of London so we are the chancellor if it is the underground. (Cutting, 1985, p. 250)

Hard-to-follow communications may also come from people who have been given diagnoses other than schizophrenia. The following excerpt was produced by a patient who was experiencing a hypomanic episode (hypomanic behavior may be seen in bipolar disorder, discussed in Chapter 10):

Women of America, it behooves you one and all to help at this, the most interesting epoch of the World's History, in every way possible, the march of civilization, the march of victory! I will play you Beethoven's Great Symphony with its four fateful opening notes—sol, sol, sol, mi. . . . V.V.V.V. the Day of the Century has dawned. (R. A. Cohen, 1975, p. 1020)

It is important to remember that not all people with schizophrenia display peculiar speech. The majority speak coherently most of the time, and peculiar speech is found in other patients about as frequently as it is in those with schizophrenia (Andreasen & Grove, 1979). To appreciate this point, rate the following examples on a 5-point scale from 1 (schizophrenic) to 5 (normal):

Then, I always liked geography. My last teacher in the subject was Professor August A. He was a man with black eyes. I also like black eyes. There are also blue and gray eyes and other sorts, too. I have heard it said that snakes have green eyes. All people have eyes. There are some, too, who are blind. These blind people are led by a boy. It must be terrible not to be able to see. There are people who can't see, and in addition, can't hear. I know some who hear too much. One can hear too much. There are many sick people in Bürgholzli; they are called patients. (Bleuler, 1915/1950, p. 17)

Yes, of course, the whole thing wasn't my idea. So, I suppose I'd be perfectly happy if he came back and decided to do it all on his own. If I could make two trips myself, I don't see why he can't. (Laffal, 1965, p. 309)

When these excerpts were informally rated by several psychologists, the first example was usually rated as characteristic of schizophrenic speech. It represents the way people think those with this disorder speak. The second example was rated as normal because it is neither bizarre nor obscure. How do these ratings agree with yours? The results may cause you to readjust your ideas about those with schizophrenia, because both examples were produced by patients who had a diagnosis of schizophrenia.

Disorganized Behavior Behavior of those with schizophrenia varies widely, is unpredictable, and may seem unrelated to the surroundings. This **disorganized behavior** may be due to hallucinations, experiences that the observer does not share. Another inappropriate emotional response that may occur in schizophrenia is sudden, unpredictable, and seemingly inexplicable outbursts of anger. Whether all these inappropriate expressions of emotion are connected to hallucinations and delusions is not known. Some of the angry outbursts may be a result of the ideas of reference mentioned earlier, in which behaviors of others or written materials may be falsely interpreted by the person who has schizophrenia as referring to him or her, usually in a derogatory way. The example that began this chapter illustrates these misinterpretations, although in that case the author could control them. However, some individuals may become wildly aggressive as a result of the misinterpretations.

The following comment by a person diagnosed as having schizophrenia illustrates another type of unpredictable behavior:

> *I get shaky in the knees and my chest is like a mountain in front of me, and my body actions are different. The arms and legs are apart and away from me and they go on their own. That's when I feel I am the other person and copy their movements, or else stop and stand like a statue. I have to stop to find out whether my hand is in my pocket or not. (Sass, 1987, p. 16)*

This description shows both the tendency to excess or seemingly random motor activity, called **catatonic excitement,** as well as the complete lack of activity called **catatonic rigidity,** or posturing. In the latter case the person may remain motionless in strange postures for many hours, to the point where circulation is impaired and swelling occurs in the feet, ankles, or other body parts.

Negative Symptoms The characteristics discussed so far—hallucinations, delusions, and disorganized speech or behavior—are usually called the positive symptoms of schizophrenia. **Negative symptoms** can be described as behavior deficits, and include such behaviors as flattened affect, poverty of speech and of speech content, and lack of directedness. Although they are not found only in people with a diagnosis of schizophrenia, negative symptoms do appear to be more common among these patients than among other diagnostic groups (McGlashan & Fenton, 1992). Table 11-5 provides examples of several categories

Table 11-5
Examples of Negative Symptom Behavior

Flat Affect

- Avoidance of eye contact
- Immobile, expressionless face
- Lack of emotion when discussing emotional material
- Apathy and noninterest
- Monotonous voice
- Low voice, difficult to hear

Poverty of Speech

- Long lapses before replying to questions
- Restriction of quantity of speech
- Failure to answer
- Slowed speech
- Blocking

Loss of Directedness

- Slowed movements
- Reduction of voluntary movements
- Inability to initiate
- Little interest in social participation

of the negative symptoms listed in Table 11-3. The following description characterizes a patient with negative symptoms predominating:

> *He is a single male who has had problems socializing throughout adolescence and does not date. He has a mediocre-to-poor school achievement record and, at best, a sporadic work record. He appears uncoordinated physically and conveys an aura of being different or unusual. Although he may show both positive and negative symptoms in a fluctuating pattern when the disorder just becomes apparent, later a poor level of functioning and a dominance of negative symptoms are seen. The disorder results in a chronic and disabling condition that is likely to require some form of institutionalization or housing in a sheltered environment, such as a group home, for his lifetime.*

Genetic family studies show that those diagnosed with schizophrenia who have predominantly negative symptoms are less likely to have relatives diagnosed with either schizophrenia or other disorders in the schizophrenic spectrum than patients who have a predominance of positive symptoms (Baron et al., 1992). This finding has suggested to some researchers that negative symptoms are more likely to be related to nongenetic causes such as pre- or postnatal virus infection, birth complications, and brain damage.

Negative symptoms are often difficult to evaluate because they are more like the end of the continuum of nor-

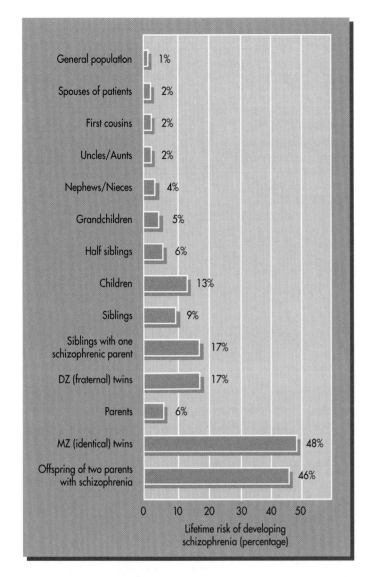

General population | 1%
Spouses of patients | 2%
First cousins | 2%
Uncles/Aunts | 2%
Nephews/Nieces | 4%
Grandchildren | 5%
Half siblings | 6%
Children | 13%
Siblings | 9%
Siblings with one schizophrenic parent | 17%
DZ (fraternal) twins | 17%
Parents | 6%
MZ (identical) twins | 48%
Offspring of two parents with schizophrenia | 46%

Lifetime risk of developing
schizophrenia (percentage)

Figure 11-8   The degree of risk of developing schizophrenia correlates highly with the degree of genetic relationship with someone who has that disorder. These higher risks contrast with the general population's risk of from 1% to 1.4%. The column on the left shows the degrees of relationship, and the lengths of the corresponding bars indicate the lifetime percentage of risk of developing schizophrenia.

SOURCE: From *Schizophrenic Genesis: The Origins of Madness* by Irving I. Gottesman. Reprinted with permission of W. H. Freeman and Company.

mal behavior than positive symptoms are. Sometimes antipsychotic medications produce as side effects behavior that is very similar to the flat affect that is a typical negative symptom, so if the symptoms are observed some time after the initial diagnosis, they may be a result of medication rather than of the disorder itself.

What Causes Schizophrenia?

The cause of schizophrenia is not known, although it seems likely that symptoms of schizophrenia are produced by the interaction of vulnerability factors with some kind of environmental stress. Thus, in studying schizophrenia it is important to utilize many perspectives, to look at genetic factors, other biological variables, and environmental conditions that may be related to whether or not symptoms of the disorder appear. Also important are the interactive effects of vulnerability with other factors.

The case study in Box 11-2 describes quadruplets with schizophrenia whose lives were investigated from many perspectives.

Genetic Factors

The importance of genetic factors in the development of schizophrenia has emerged from the results of many family, twin, and adoption studies conducted over at least 75 years. These studies have shown that the risk of development of schizophrenia is correlated with the closeness of genetic relationship, or genetic overlap with the **index case,** as the person under study is often called. Genetic overlap, or the percentage of genes that the relative has in common with the index case, ranges from 100% for identical twins to 12.5% for great-grandchildren, first cousins, and great-nieces and great-nephews.

Figure 11-8 shows the average risk for developing schizophrenia when family members with different degrees of

Case Study

Investigating Schizophrenia from a Variety of Perspectives

Investigation of schizophrenic behavior from several perspectives can help in understanding both the disorder and its symptoms. The case of the Genain sisters illustrates how investigations of heredity, brain anatomy and activity, psychophysiological measures, and family interactions can complement one another.

The sisters, who were identical quadruplets, shared the same heredity (see Figures 11-4 and 11-5). Because the odds for identical quadruplets are 1 in 16 million births, they became celebrities in their hometown soon after their birth in 1930. During their childhood, they performed song and dance routines and were so popular that they had a police escort on one early local tour. As they grew older, however, it became clear that they were not developing in a normal way. One sister dropped out of high school. The other three graduated but had trouble holding jobs. During their twenties, all four sisters developed schizophrenia.

Because of the uniqueness of this case (four individuals with identical heredity who all showed schizophrenic behavior could be expected to occur only once in tens of billions of births), a local physician

alerted scientists at the National Institute of Mental Health (NIMH). The sisters came to Washington, D.C., and were hospitalized there for intensive study in the mid-1950s. During the three years that they spent at NIMH, they were examined from a number of perspectives. To protect their privacy, the sisters were given pseudonyms, corresponding to NIMH's initials—Nora, Iris, Myra, and Hester—and the family was given the name Genain, from the Greek word meaning "dire birth."

Several of the quadruplets' family members had histories of psychological problems. Not only was their father's behavior often bizarre, but his brother, his mother, and his paternal uncle had all had nervous breakdowns.

Even though they had the same genetic risk, the sisters' schizophrenia could have been at least partly the result of environmental factors. For example, as is usual in multiple births, they were all small at birth. All of them spent time in incubators and did not go home from the hospital until they were 6 weeks old. They grew up in the glare of publicity and constantly heard comments about their similarity. Their father restricted their interactions

with other people by refusing to allow them to play with other children, or later to take part in school activities or date.

The girls' father also objected to their stay at NIMH and often threatened to take them out of the hospital. Although he was cooperative and cordial at times, he also had considerable hostility toward people. His wife reported that he had tried to choke her several times and said that she had considered leaving him. At times he accused his wife of having sexual relationships with his daughters' psychiatrists. During the quadruplets' third year at the hospital, he died.

This report, which reflects the psychodynamic perspective, describes the family relationships in detail:

> Mrs. Genain's unfulfilled needs for maternal nurturing found expression in her closeness to Nora. It was the symbiotic tie of mother and infant, one in which the mother does not see the infant as a separate individual but as part of herself. . . . The closeness between them supported a report that Nora was not only her father's "favorite," but her mother's also. . . . Nora was always the first of the babies to be burped after feeding. . . . Nora was also the daughter Mrs. Genain took home for trial visits from the hospital, although Iris' adjustment was also appropriate for home visits.
>
> The central role for Myra was the "independent positive." Mrs. Genain identified Myra with her own independent strivings and actions. . . . Myra was the daughter upon whom Mrs. Genain was prone to lean in times of stress, who often strove for the favored position (which in

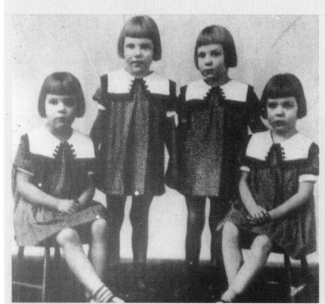

Figure 11-4   The Genain sisters as young children.

Figure 11-5   The Genain sisters as adults performing for an NIMH party.

Box 11-2

this family was the protected one) with her mother. . . . She tried to live out the role her mother assigned to her of becoming independent, and the dependent-independent conflict became acute for her when she tried to move out on her own.

The central theme of the role Mrs. Genain assigned to Iris was the "repressed" one. She identified in Iris her own feeling that she must put up with anything. . . . In areas that concerned Iris as an individual, e.g., her abilities and appearance, Mrs. Genain was neither concerned nor interested.

The central theme assigned to Hester was the "negative" one. . . . Hester personified that which Mrs. Genain regarded as undesirable—hostility and sexuality, for example. The perception of these feelings

in Hester appeared to have blocked her mother's perception of other human qualities in her. She was the last to be regarded as sick (she had been "bad") and she was not hospitalized before coming to the Clinical Center. Later Mrs. Genain did not even consider a time when Hester might come home for home visits from the hospital. (D. Rosenthal, 1963, pp. 463–465)

The Genains were invited back to NIMH for a follow-up in 1981. During that period Myra had lived the most normal life. She went to business college and later worked as a secretary. She was the only one of the four sisters to marry and have children. Nora was next best in adjustment. She had worked for at least 7

years, partly in government training programs. Hester and Iris had each spent more than 15 years in hospitals and had received more antipsychotic drug treatment than either Myra or Nora.

Researchers wondered if scanning techniques, developed after the early study of the sisters, could shed light on the differences in their behavior. The sisters' CT scans appeared normal, but other types of scans showed abnormal patterns. Their PT scans, made when the women were resting, showed activity in the visual areas (see Figure 11-6). Scientists wondered if this was an indication of hallucinations. The PT scans of Myra and Nora, the two sisters who had made the best adjustment, were closer to the normal PT scans than those of the two sisters whose behavior was

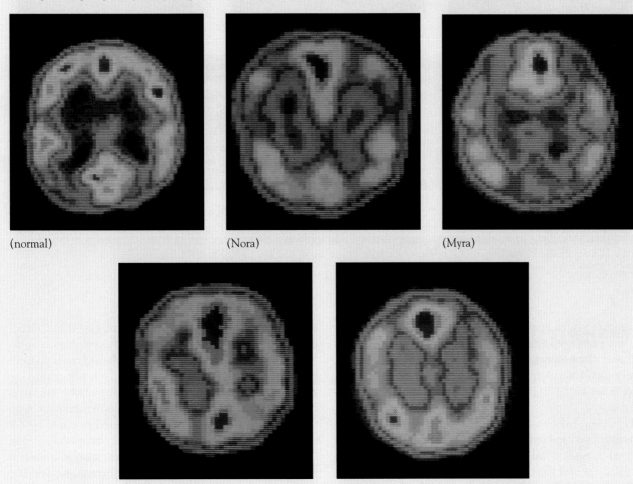

Figure 11-6 The PT scans of the Genain sisters differ from the normal PT scan. Energy use is highest in the frontal lobes of the normal scan (higher energy is indicated by the yellow-orange-red part of the spectrum and lower energy by the blue-green-purple end). In contrast, the visual areas of the sisters' scans are most active, possibly as a result of hallucinations.

less adaptive. The Genains also showed much less alpha brain wave activity than is normal. Since alpha waves appear when people relax or let their minds go blank, the low frequency of alpha waves may also suggest hallucinations.

The sisters were also given computer electroencephalographic tomography scans (CET). CET scans show the electrical activity in the brain, in contrast to PT scans, which show chemical activity (see Figure 11-7). Since CET scans are much cheaper and safer for the subject than PT scans, they can be repeated at frequent intervals. All four Genain sisters showed low levels of alpha waves on the CET scans as compared to a control subject. The correspondence between PT and CET scan patterns both in this case and in general research findings seems fairly close (Buchsbaum & Haier, 1987). These findings, when matched with the sisters' behavioral histories and with the earlier test data, may prove helpful in relating specific behaviors with environmental factors and biological functioning.

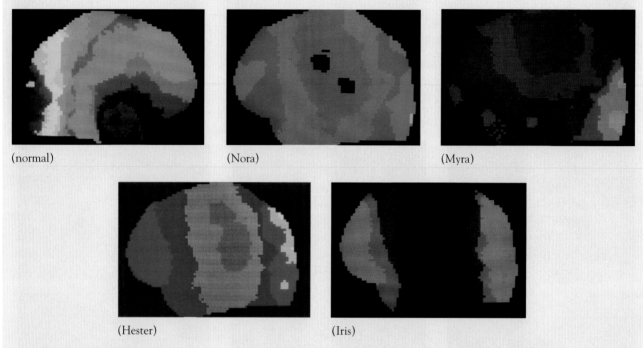

(normal)   (Nora)   (Myra)

(Hester)   (Iris)

Figure 11-7 CET scans of the Genain quadruplets show low levels of alpha rhythm as compared to the normal scan. All of these CET scans were made while the subjects were resting, with their eyes shut.

relationship have been diagnosed with the disorder. The lifetime risk of developing schizophrenia correlates quite well with the proportion of genes shared with an affected family member (Gottesman, 1991). In other words, the more genes that two people have in common, the higher the risk.

However, other factors seem to be at work besides heredity. Even for **monozygotic (MZ)** twins, sometimes referred to as identical twins, who originate from the same fertilized egg and thus should have identical heredity, the risk is a little less than 50% that if one twin develops schizophrenia, the other twin will also develop it. A large study of Finnish twins found that the greater part of the risk of developing schizophrenia could be attributed to genetic effects while the remaining risk did not seem to come from

environmental experiences the twins shared but rather individual-specific environmental effects (Cannon et al., 1998). Another important, well-established research finding also shows that genetic inheritance is not enough to explain schizophrenia: 89% of all people who are diagnosed with schizophrenia have no known relative with that disorder so this suggests that if heredity is involved it is not inheritance of the disorder itself (Cromwell, 1993).

Although, as Figure 11-8 illustrates, genetic transmission seems to be a factor in schizophrenia, no specific mode of genetic transmission has been identified as yet (Portin & Alanen, 1997). This means that no particular gene locations have been associated with schizophrenia in at least several studies of different family groups. It may be that many genes, acting together, constitute a risk factor for schizophrenia and that a number of different combinations of genes may produce vulnerability. Whether or not a person with a certain genetic inheritance experiences some disorder in the schizophrenic spectrum is dependent on the interaction of this with both physical and psychosocial factors in the environment.

Before discussing the genetic hypothesis further, we will briefly review the common models used in genetic theory and research. In studies of heredity, predictions based on theoretical models are compared with the observed frequency of occurrence of various characteristics. If the model is a good one, the agreement between prediction and observation should be close. There are two major types of models showing the transmission of inherited traits: the monogenic model, showing transmission by one gene, and the polygenic model, showing transmission by more than one gene.

Monogenic Models

Researchers in the area of genetics have developed several possible genetic models. The simplest of these is the *Mendelian pattern of heredity*. This pattern is called a **monogenic model** because one gene pair is all that is needed to determine a particular characteristic. Some genes are **dominant** and some are **recessive.** Because one gene of each gene pair is inherited from each parent, the Mendelian pattern could be expressed in one of three possible ways. Consider an example that follows a Mendelian pattern, the case of eye color. If both parents have brown eyes (brown is dominant), this means they each must have a brown-eyed gene. However, when a dominant gene is paired with a recessive gene, the dominant gene is said to be expressed, in this case meaning that if the parent has brown eyes, we don't know whether that parent's other gene is for brown or blue eyes. Thus if each parent has a recessive gene for blue eyes paired with his or her dominant brown-eyed gene, their child may have two brown-eyed genes; or one brown-eyed gene and one blue-eyed gene and thus have the **expressed trait** of brown eyes like the parents; or the child might receive the recessive gene from each parent and thus have blue eyes. In the last case, the child would have no possibility of passing on a brown-eyed gene to his or her own children. The first researchers who investigated the genetics of schizophrenia looked for results to support a monogenic model but did not find them. They found that the number of cases of schizophrenia in relatives of people with schizophrenia was always less than would be predicted by a monogenic model.

Polygenic Models

Another possible model, the **polygenic model,** assumes that several gene pairs found at specific locations on particular chromosomes must interact to produce a trait or a disorder. Many basic characteristics of humans—such as height, weight, and skin color—are thought to be influenced by more than one gene pair and thus can be predicted from this polygenic model. Some of these models suggest that a limited number of gene locations are involved and that these can be identified.

Multifactorial Polygenic Models

More complex or multifactorial polygenic models seem to be the best fit to the findings from genetic research in schizophrenia. **Multifactorial polygenic models** do not specify which gene locations (called *loci*) or how many of them are involved. These models assume that gene pairs for any number and combination of loci may be involved and that each pair may have a small additive effect on a person's vulnerability to schizophrenia. According to this view, many people have some predisposition to develop schizophrenia. Although this built-in vulnerability is not in itself enough to determine who will develop the disorder, the higher the gene loading, the greater the risk. This idea is compatible with the vulnerability concept discussed later in the chapter.

Recent advances in molecular biology have made it possible to study variations in DNA sequence to identify gene locations related to particular disorders. This new technology has been used to understand genetic contributions to various illnesses such as Huntington's disease and muscular dystrophy. A number of studies have identified gene locations associated with schizophrenia by studying the DNA from several generations of family groups in which there was more than one member with a diagnosis of schizophrenia (Ezzell, 1995). So far the findings differ. Figure 11-9 shows regions on chromosome nos. 6 and 8 that so far seem to have the strongest linkage, although these findings have not yet been sufficiently confirmed (Gottesman & Moldin, 1998). On each chromosome, the region identified is indicated by a bracket in the figure. Other chromosomes, including nos. 3, 9, 20, and 22, have also been found, in various family studies, to contain regions where genes may be linked to schizophrenia (Portin & Alanen, 1997). The lack of compelling findings so far even for chromosome nos. 6 and 8 may have several causes. One possibility is that even if these locations are correct, genes on these chromosomes may produce susceptibility to schizophrenia but the size of the effect is so small that a very large sample size is required to obtain clear and statistically significant evidence. Another possibility is that these genes may be related to susceptibility to schizophrenia in only a small proportion of families and in other families different gene locations are involved. This would mean that different study samples produce different results as a result of this genetic heterogeneity. Yet another possibility is that the findings regarding chromo-some nos. 6 and 8 were the result of chance. Although further study of the genome holds promise for understanding more about the genetic causes of schizophrenia, we still are a long way from identifying the genetic components of this disorder.

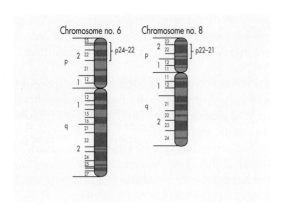

Figure 11–9 Chromosome nos. 6 and 8 have been rather consistently linked to schizophrenia in family studies. The bracket to the left of the diagram shows the regions of these chromosomes that may be involved.

SOURCE: Adapted from Ezzell (1995), p. 25.

Prenatal Factors

Infants born from January through March, in urban, but not rural, areas have been found in some studies to have a higher risk of developing schizophrenia than children born at other times of the year (Verdoux et al., 1997). One possible cause of this seasonal effect might be the increased prevalence of influenza and other viral diseases during winter and spring. Some studies have found that if the mother had influenza while pregnant, the child born of that pregnancy had an increased risk of schizophrenia. One test of this hypothesis was made possible by an unusually severe and time-limited influenza epidemic in Helsinki, Finland in 1957. An estimated two-thirds of the population had some signs of flu during a 5-week period. The researchers determined the rates of schizophrenia in adulthood for babies born to Helsinki women in the 9 months after the epidemic of 1957 (Mednick et al., 1988). Because of the clear dates for the beginning and end of the epidemic they were able to divide these births into three groups. Those in the first group were born in the 3 months after the epidemic so their mothers would have been likely to have had the flu in the third trimester of pregnancy. The second group, born 4 to 6 months after the epidemic would have been exposed to flu in the second trimester of pregnancy, and those born 7 to 9 months later would have been exposed in the first trimester. The ability to divide the subjects in this way was important because different aspects of development occur in each pregnancy trimester and these developments have been extensively studied. What the study showed was that the risk in the first and third trimesters of pregnancy was the same for those involved in the flu epidemic and for a control group (see Figure 11-10). However, for those born 4 to 6 months after the epidemic and exposed to the flu in the second trimester of pregnancy, the risk of a diagnosis

of schizophrenia was much higher than that for the control group. The results of this study not only clarified earlier findings relating schizophrenia and month of birth, but it helped to pinpoint the phase of prenatal development when the effects occurred. Exposure to the flu virus may lead to disruption of neural development that takes place during the second trimester, and this disruption may affect vulnerability to schizophrenia in adulthood.

Other kinds of stress experienced by a mother during the second trimester of pregnancy have also been found to create additional vulnerability to schizophrenia. In 1939 the Russian army invaded Finland, and in a little over 3 months later 25,000 Finnish soldiers had been killed. Researchers compared the outcome for children of women pregnant at that time whose husbands had been killed in the fighting with the outcome for those whose husbands had been in the military but survived (Huttunen & Niskanen, 1978). There were significantly more cases of schizophrenia among the children of the widowed women and all of these cases occurred in children of women who had been in the second trimester of pregnancy when they received the news of the death. Like the influenza study, the Finnish research indicates that what occurs in the second trimester of pregnancy may be implicated in vulnerability to schizophrenia.

In some—but not all—studies, individuals diagnosed with schizophrenia in adulthood have also been found to be more likely to have had obstetric complications at birth (O'Callaghan et al., 1992). These complications might have been a causal factor themselves, or they may have been the result of other developmental or environmental problems experienced by the fetus. Nevertheless, birth complications suggest possible damage to the brain or nervous system.

The Neurodevelopmental Model of Schizophrenia

Although it is accepted that heredity is an important factor in schizophrenia, it is not the whole story. The most clear evidence of this is that about half of identical twins whose co-twin develops schizophrenia do not also develop full-blown symptoms of the disorder and many of them have no unusual symptoms at all even after many years of follow-up (Gottesman & Moldin, 1997). This finding, together with the observation that the majority of those who develop schizophrenia do not have a close relative with the disorder, has led to the view that schizophrenia is a long-term consequence of an early, often prenatal, abnormality in neural development, which may or may not be associated with genetic factors. The **neurodevelopmental model of schizophrenia** assumes that the abnormality in neural development occurs early in life and then is not generally noticeable until the affected region of the brain matures and is called upon to function in the normal

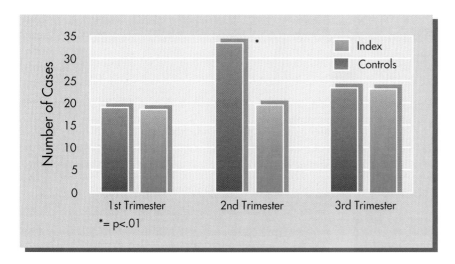

Figure 11-10 Adults whose mothers were exposed to the influenza virus during the second trimester of pregnancy were at significantly greater risk for developing schizophrenia than adults whose mothers were exposed to the virus during the first and third trimesters. These two groups had no more risk than if their mothers had not had exposure to influenza during pregnancy.

SOURCE: From Mednick, Machon, Huttunen, & Bonnett (1988), pp. 189–192.

course of development (Weinberger, 1987). It is only at that time that clinical symptoms of schizophrenia appear. One problem in investigating this perspective is that the period when the developmental problem occurs (usually before or at birth) is many years before any symptoms appear. Although there are many research findings related to some of these biological factors, many of them disagree. One explanation for this lack of agreement may be that biological factors alone do not increase the chances of developing schizophrenia unless some genetic vulnerability already exists. A number of inventive methods have been used to investigate the neurodevelopmental model. These include epidemiological studies, studies of cell orientation and placement, home movies of infants or young children, and investigation of markers of abnormal neurodevelopment such as minor physical deviations. Box 11-3 highlights the importance of the neurodevelopmental model.

Prenatal Developmental Processes In the second trimester of pregnancy, cells migrate from their original position into more distant locations where they establish connections with other neurons. This made researchers wonder if the brains of patients who had been diagnosed with schizophrenia would show a different organization of cells from what is generally expected. Even with sophisticated methods of neuroimaging like those discussed in this chapter and elsewhere in this book, the primary way to answer this question is still by examination of brain tissue at autopsy. Several studies of this brain tissue have shown displacement of neurons in the brains of patients who had been diagnosed with schizophrenia. In each case the researchers found that compared with control patients, the distribution of neurons was different. More cells were in the deeper layers of the cortex and fewer toward the surface (Akbarian et al., 1996). Because the cortex develops from the inside to the outside, this finding suggests that many neurons failed to migrate as far as they should have.

This in turn could disrupt the process of synaptic pruning. **Synaptic pruning** is a developmental process in which neurons selectively reduce the number of branches of their dendrites. If it occurs abnormally it can result in either too many or too few synapses and can result in problems in cognitive function, an important difficulty in schizophrenia. Normal synaptic pruning starts in late childhood, and scientists believe that the process is essential for handling the explosive growth of information to which children are exposed, especially during their adolescent years. Essentially the pruning readies the brain for the more complex mental activities demanded of adults. One theory suggests that the brains of individuals who develop schizophrenia may either experience over-aggressive pruning or, because of developmental problems during the second trimester of pregnancy, their brains may have fewer dendrite branches to begin with and therefore the normal pruning process leaves them with an inadequate number (McGlashan & Hoffman, 2000). Figure 11-11 shows some of the brain areas where this pruning is thought to occur. If this theory is correct, then intervention when the earliest symptoms of schizophrenia occur may help prevent further destruction of these neural connections. Treatment based on this idea is discussed later in the chapter.

Prenatal developmental abnormalities are often reflected in minor physical abnormalities, often referred to as **minor physical anomalies,** that can be detected at and after birth. These anomalies include minor abnormalities of the head, feet, hands, or face such as malformed ears, unusual spacing of tear ducts, or abnormalities of the interior of the mouth such as a highly arched palate. Many infants have a single anomaly, but those who are later diagnosed with schizophrenia may have several (see Figure 11-12). Although it is not known exactly at what stage of prenatal development these anomalies occur, it is thought that they reflect processes in neurodevelopment that occur in the second trimester of pregnancy (M. F. Green et al.,

Q. You talk about the neurodevelopmental model of schizophrenia. Why is that so important?

A. *The neurodevelopmental model helps to integrate and make sense of many research findings that have accumulated over a long period of time. It is focused on developmental changes that naturally occur and how these may be disrupted. The two periods of change that it emphasizes are the second trimester of* *pregnancy and late childhood and adolescence. During each of these periods important changes in the brain and nervous system occur as part of the normal developmental process. If something interferes with these normal processes, one result may be increased vulnerability to schizophrenia. Many researchers, but not all, had found that a mother's viral infection during pregnancy increased the risk of schizophrenia. This model shows what period of pregnancy may be crucial and what devel-* *opmental process may be affected. It also helps explain why many people who develop schizophrenia may seem to have no signs of the disorder until adolescence or early adulthood. Another result of these processes may be the problems with attention that have been noticed by clinicians and researchers in people who have schizophrenia. Finally, the model suggests that early treatment even before any clear symptoms occur may be helpful for people at high risk for schizophrenia.*

1994). The number of anomalies does not seem to have a genetic basis because siblings of patients with schizophrenia do not have an excess number. This excess of anomalies often found in schizophrenia is not found in other psychotic disorders, but are found in some disorders in which prenatal neural involvement is clear, for instance in Down syndrome.

In addition to developmental abnormalities in the brain, development of the neuromotor system also seems to be affected in schizophrenia. Children who may later develop schizophrenia often show unusual expressions of emotion and motor behaviors, for example, atypical hand postures like those shown in Figure 11-13. These behaviors may be relatively subtle and may not be noted at the time.

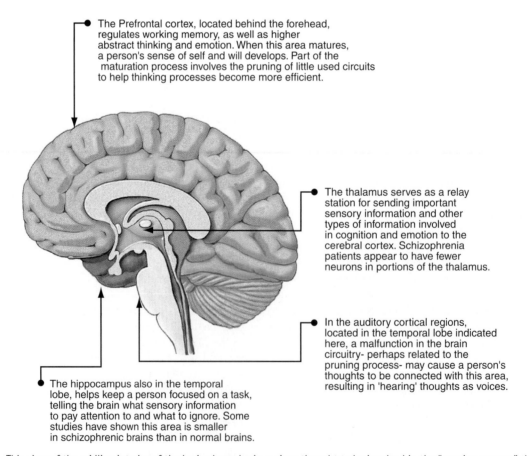

The Prefrontal cortex, located behind the forehead, regulates working memory, as well as higher abstract thinking and emotion. When this area matures, a person's sense of self and will develops. Part of the maturation process involves the pruning of little used circuits to help thinking processes become more efficient.

The thalamus serves as a relay station for sending important sensory information and other types of information involved in cognition and emotion to the cerebral cortex. Schizophrenia patients appear to have fewer neurons in portions of the thalamus.

In the auditory cortical regions, located in the temporal lobe indicated here, a malfunction in the brain circuitry- perhaps related to the pruning process- may cause a person's thoughts to be connected with this area, resulting in 'hearing' thoughts as voices.

The hippocampus also in the temporal lobe, helps keep a person focused on a task, telling the brain what sensory information to pay attention to and what to ignore. Some studies have shown this area is smaller in schizophrenic brains than in normal brains.

Figure 11-11 This view of the midline interior of the brain shows brain regions thought to be involved in the "pruning process" that is part of the late adolescent and early adult development.

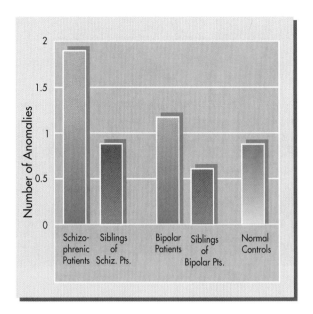

Figure 11-12 Individuals with a diagnosis of schizophrenia are likely to have a larger number of physical anomalies than their siblings, which suggests that more than genetic factors may be involved in the disorder. They also have more anomalies than either those diagnosed with bipolar disorder or normal controls. These anomalies are thought to reflect processes occurring in the second trimester of pregnancy.

SOURCE: From M. F. Green (1998), p. 12.

However, the use of old home movies, such as those from early birthday parties, often show clear differences between the child who later develops schizophrenia and his or her siblings. The following recollection about a brother later affected by schizophrenia illustrates this clearly:

Despite the differences in the way we perceived and coped with the world, Andy and I were unusually close as children. . . .

I adored and emulated my older brother . . . he was my daily companion, my playmate, and so I believed, my protector.

However, a recent look at old family photos . . . belie my memories of Andy as my caretaker. . . . In each and every one . . . I am sturdy and smiling; Andy is frail, his handsome features scrunched up into a scowl. He holds his body in an odd, concave position, sucking in the center of his body, with his head pitched awkwardly forward. Thin arms, bent at the elbows, hang lank behind his torso as if he holds onto a set of invisible supporting bars. Occasionally, he smiles but . . . my brother's taut, clenched smile, baring most of his upper and lower front teeth, conveys only great tension and pain. . . . (Brodoff, 1988, pp. 114–115)

These abnormalities in motor behavior are thought to be a result of lack of regulation of the dopamine system that later in life may lead to the development of psychotic symptoms (Walker & Diforio, 1997). In a study of five families where one sibling was diagnosed with schizophrenia as an adult, trained observers studied home movies of the siblings that covered the period from infancy until at least age 5 (Walker & Lewine, 1990). Although the observers were not told the later psychiatric status of the children, they could reliably identify which child would receive the diagnosis of schizophrenia by taking into account responsiveness to others, amount of eye contact, positive affect, and motor coordination in both fine and large movements. These differences were apparent to raters before the children were 8 years old. Many times these unusual behaviors become less noticeable as the child grows older, but the underlying problem remains.

Biochemical Brain Abnormalities There are strong arguments for the assumption that biochemical factors play a role in schizophrenia. Antipsychotic drugs are known

Figure 11-13 This young boy shows some of the abnormal hand postures that may indicate a vulnerability to schizophrenia.

SOURCE: From Walker, Savoie, & Davis (1994), pp. 441–455.

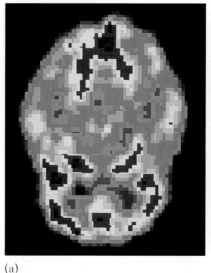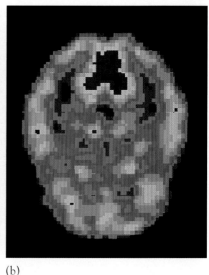

Figure 11-14 PT scan photos show brain metabolism, the chemical activity that takes place in a living brain. Photo (a) shows a PT scan of the brain of a normal individual, and photo (b) shows a PT scan of a person affected by schizophrenia who is not currently receiving antipsychotic medication. Colors toward the yellow-orange-red end of the spectrum indicate a higher rate of metabolic activity, and those at the green-blue-purple end a lower rate. Notice the relatively higher frontal metabolism in the normal person and the higher posterior metabolism in the patient.

(a) (b)

to produce certain biochemical changes in the brain, as well as positive changes in behavior. Recent developments in scanning technology have enabled researchers to look for abnormalities in biochemical functioning. For example, research using PT scans shows that people whose schizophrenic behavior is long-standing and chronic tend to have a lower level of metabolism in their frontal and temporal lobes and a somewhat higher flow at the base of the skull than control subjects do (see Figure 11-14).

The Dopamine Hypothesis Just as neurotransmitters are currently thought to be important in at least some types of mood disorders (see Chapter 10), biologically oriented research on schizophrenia also stresses the importance of neurotransmitter functioning. In schizophrenia, current research focuses on dopamine. The **dopamine hypothesis,** simply stated, says that an excess of dopamine at certain synapses in the brain is associated with schizophrenia.

The effectiveness of antipsychotic drugs in reducing psychotic symptoms is directly related to their success at binding to (i.e., blocking) postsynaptic dopamine receptors. Excessive receptor activation in several parts of the brain, especially parts of the cortex, is correlated positively with psychotic symptoms, especially hallucinations (Vollenweider et al., 1997). Antipsychotic drugs that effectively block brain receptors for dopamine are able to reduce positive symptoms of schizophrenia in about 80% of patients, although this control is usually not sufficient to remove all symptoms. However, the dopamine hypothesis is too simple to explain all the findings of the effects of antipsychotic drugs on the symptoms of schizophrenia. For instance, even though the drugs may quickly block the dopamine receptors in the brain, the changes in behavior usually do not appear for several weeks. Thus far, the reason for this delay is not understood.

Because dopamine receptors can now be identified using PT scans, researchers have been able to identify several types of these receptors, called D1, D2, D3, D4, and D5. One puzzle is that, although schizophrenia is characterized mainly by cognitive and emotional disturbance, several of these dopamine receptors are located in areas of the nervous system that control movement. However, D3 and D4 are located in parts of the brain that have more relevance to cognitive and emotional functioning. Thus far, no genetic linkage has been established between schizophrenia and any of the dopamine receptors (Hartman & Civelli, 1996).

One finding that has emerged from the use of scanning techniques is that some individuals with schizophrenia have significantly larger **cerebral ventricles** (cavities that contain cerebrospinal fluid) than the ventricles found in the brains of people without this diagnosis. However, some enlargement of ventricles seems to occur naturally; in general, people's ventricles become larger with age. Enlarged ventricles are also found in other conditions such as alcoholism, traumatic head injuries, and severe mood disorders involving psychosis. Another difficulty in understanding the meaning of enlarged ventricles is that these and other significant brain effects occur in only about one-third of people with schizophrenia whose brain scans have been studied.

The results of a study of 15 sets of MZ twins in which only one of each pair had been diagnosed with schizophrenia were of particular interest in understanding the role of enlarged ventricles, because the anatomy of the brains of each pair would be expected to be highly similar (Suddath et al., 1990). The twins with schizophrenia not only had enlarged lateral and third ventricles compared to their twins who did not have this diagnosis (see Figure 11-15), but they were also found to have a reduction in size of areas of the brain that are involved with thinking, concentration, memory, and perception, all aspects of behavior that are affected in schizophrenia. In all but one of the twin pairs, the twin with the diagnosis of schizophrenia also had reduced brain volume when compared to his or her healthy twin. A particularly interesting finding in this study was that, in many cases, the ventricular enlargement found in the twin with the diagnosis of schizophrenia was not large enough to have been considered abnormal by a specialist. It was only in comparison to the healthy twin that the ventricle enlargement could be seen. This suggests that even subtle changes in ventricle size may be important in vulnerability to schizophrenia.

The increasing use of ultrasound and MRI scanning of fetuses has also led to the finding that even in MZ twins, brain development is not identical. In addition to differences in ventricular size, there was also a difference in the amount of cortical folding (Kulynych et al., 1997). Shallower cortical folds or creases, which mean that there is less total cortical area, have also been linked to vulnerability for schizophrenia.

Schizophrenic Spectrum Disorders

As researchers learn more about the genetic basis of schizophrenia, it has been pointed out the "Disease comes in all sizes and we should move away from asking, 'Has this person got it?' toward 'How much of it do they have?'" (Rose, 1993). One way to follow this advice is to consider schizophrenia as part of a spectrum of disorders that may be associated through differential loadings of the same group of genes. When the families of individuals diagnosed with schizophrenia are studied, they seem to include more than the expected number of relatives who are somewhat unusual in their behavior. These relatives dress eccentrically, behave in unusual ways, and seem somewhat limited emotionally or else somewhat asocial. This excess of individuals with unusual behaviors in the extended families of those with diagnoses of schizophrenia has been observed in a variety of cultures (Varma & Sharma, 1993). A greater-than-anticipated number of relatives in these families may also show peculiarities in thinking—believing one has magical powers, for instance. Many researchers believe that there is some genetic relationship between these behaviors and the schizophrenia and that all of these disordered behaviors should be investigated under the label of schizophrenic spectrum disorders.

Schizophrenic spectrum disorders include not only unusual emotional responses and cognitive behavior, but also some personality disorders (Jones & Cannon, 1998). Of all the spectrum disorders *schizotypal personality disorder* seems to be closest genetically to schizophrenia. Odd speech patterns, social dysfunction and aloofness, odd communication, and suspiciousness all suggest milder forms of symptoms of schizophrenia. The qualities of eccentricity, constricted affect or emotion, and excessive so-

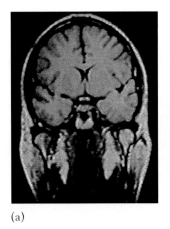
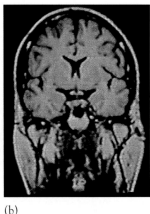

(a)   (b)

Figure 11-15   When one identical (MZ) twin develops schizophrenia and the other twin of the pair does not, one difference found between them is likely to be enlarged ventricles. The MRI scans shown here point out the differences in ventricle size between an unaffected twin (a) and her twin sister (b) who has a diagnosis of schizophrenia. One possible explanation of this difference in MZ twins is that the twin with the enlarged ventricles might have experienced some injury before birth.

cial anxiety in this personality disorder may have the same biological origin as schizophrenia. Other personality disorders—*paranoid personality disorder* and *schizoid personality disorder*—also occur more frequently in the families of people who have been diagnosed with schizophrenia. In addition to these personality disorders, the schizophrenia spectrum includes *schizoaffective disorder*—a category including individuals who show significant depression or manic symptoms along with the development of thought disorder and other types of psychotic disorders. Schizoaffective disorder is discussed later in the chapter.

The study of the relationships among these disordered behaviors may provide clues to the genetic causes of schizophrenia. A gene locus on chromosome no. 8 has been linked to increased risk of schizophrenic spectrum disorders in more than one study (Kendler et al., 1996). The schizophrenic spectrum does not appear to include all types of behavior disorders. For instance, relatives of those with schizophrenia do not seem to be at increased risk for most forms of mood disorders, anxiety disorders, or alcoholism (Kane, 1993).

The idea of spectrum disorder fits in well with the multifactorial polygenic model discussed in the preceding section. Such a model can be expanded to include two different levels of liability. Figure 11-16 illustrates such a model. People to the right of the right-hand threshold (for severe symptoms) would develop a severe form of schizophrenia, whereas those to the left of the left-hand threshold (for mild symptoms) would not have symptoms of schizophrenia. Those between the two thresholds would develop a mild form of the disorder. Using a complex statistical technique called *path analysis*, this model seems to predict outcome fairly well for

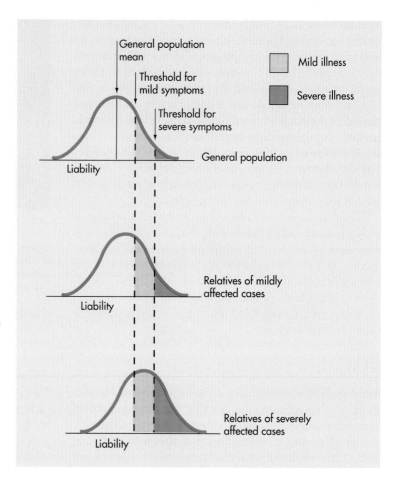

Figure 11-16   These distributions show the likelihood of mild and severe disorders within the schizophrenic spectrum for the general population and for relatives of those with mild and severe disorders. If the likelihood is greater than the threshold, the disorder can be observed. Relatives of those who are severely affected have a greater risk for both mild and severe diagnoses than the relatives of those who are mildly affected.

SOURCE: Adapted from *Journal of Psychiatric Research, 21,* M. Baron and N. Risch, "The spectrum concept of schizophrenia: Evidence for a continuum," © 1987. Reprinted with permission.

several large sets of data (Faraone & Tsuang, 1985; McGue et al., 1985).

Studying Vulnerability to Schizophrenia

So far in this chapter we have discussed both genetic and nongenetic, but still biological, factors that contribute to schizophrenia. What role does each of these play in the development of schizophrenia? It is possible that they play independent roles and schizophrenia may develop as a result of either, but what we know at present suggests that prenatal neurodevelopmental problems, in particular, may add to genetic vulnerability to make schizophrenia more likely. In addition, a third factor, the degree of stress in the environment, plays an important role. Researchers have worked for many years to understand the contributions of each factor to the development of schizophrenia. In this section we will highlight some of the principal research methods used to study the combined effect.

A number of methods have been used to study the role of genetics in schizophrenia. These include family, twin, adoption, and cross-fostering studies. Although twin and

adoption studies, in particular, have also been used to learn about hereditary patterns in other disorders, the serious consequences of schizophrenia have stimulated many large studies, often with long-term follow-up.

Family Studies

A common first step in studying the genetics of any disorder is to determine whether relatives of an affected person are more likely to have that same disorder than are members of the general population. One way to begin a **family study** is to construct a diagram of the family tree going back several generations. Next, all those people in this family tree who showed symptoms of the disorder being studied are identified. In this way it is possible to see whether a disorder seems to occur in any particular pattern over the generations. This pattern can then be matched with predictions based on theoretical models. One example of a family tree, shown in Figure 10-17, provided information about possible hereditary influences in bipolar disorder.

In addition to highlighting patterns of heredity for specific disorders, family studies provide information about the relationships between schizophrenia and other disorders. If several different disorders all typically occur in the same family, this suggests that those disorders may be genetically similar and may represent a spectrum of disorders that are closely associated. This so-called spectrum concept was discussed earlier in this chapter.

One factor that may affect the risk for schizophrenia and other disorders is assortative mating. **Assortative mating** refers to the tendency to choose a mate who is genetically similar more frequently than would be expected by chance. Assortative mating occurs with physical traits, psychological traits, and behavior disorders, and it is sometimes seen in families of patients with schizophrenia. Because of assortative mating, the spouses of people who have schizophrenia are more likely than members of the general public to have genes associated with that same diagnosis. As a result, the children of these marriages may get "double doses" of genes associated with schizophrenia.

Although families with both a mother and father diagnosed with schizophrenia are rare, at least five studies of the adult offspring of such parents have been carried out (Gottesman, 1991). The results of all these studies are similar. In each study, about one-third of the children of these parents had developed schizophrenia. Because some of the children studied were not yet old enough to have passed through the entire period of risk for developing schizophrenia, the estimated lifetime maximum risk for the group as a whole was 46%. This risk is much higher than the 17% lifetime risk of developing schizophrenia for children with only one parent affected. Even children of these marriages who did not develop schizophrenia had a considerably higher risk of having some other psychiatric diagnosis than the average child. The studies also were in agreement about another, and perhaps quite surprising, finding: about one-quarter of the children in these families showed neither schizophrenia nor any other type of disordered behavior. This finding is startling, not only in view of their genetic inheritance, but also because of the likelihood that these children had experienced a good deal of stress from living in a family with two parents who have this disorder.

The following account conveys the stress in a household in which the mother had schizophrenia:

My mother is a paranoid schizophrenic. In the past I was afraid to admit it, but now that I've put it down on paper, I'll be able to say it again and again. . . .

I have been teaching inpatient children on the children's ward of Bellevue Psychiatric Hospital in New York City for 13 years, and yet I'm still wary of revealing the nature of my mother's illness. . . .

On the outside our house resembled those of our neighbors, but on the inside it was so different that there was no basis of comparison. Our house was a disaster. Everything was a mess. . . . I was ashamed of our house. It was impossible to bring friends home. I never knew what my mother might be doing or how she would look.

She was totally unpredictable. At best she was working on a sculpture or practicing the piano, chain smoking and sipping stale coffee, with a dress too ragged to give to charity hanging from her emaciated body. At worst she was screaming at my father, still wearing her nightgown at six o'clock in the evening, a wild look on her face. I was never popular as a youngster, and I blamed my lack of popularity on my mother. . . .

Mother was quite interested in music and ballet, and she took me to every ballet and concert in Kansas City. She always looked terrible when she went out, and more than once she arrived at the theater in her bedroom slippers. I was embarrassed to be seen with her, [but] I loved music and dance as much as she did. I even gave up Saturday afternoons to stay home with her and listen to the Metropolitan Opera broadcasts, and I loved her most and felt closest to her . . . as we listened to the music together. . . .

When I was in high school, Mother and I shared a room with twin beds. When Mother was lying down, she would start to moan as if she were talking in her sleep. "I can't stand that girl. She's evil; she's a bitch. She's just like her father." . . . I used to lie in bed, wishing I were dead, believing that I was the worthless girl she was describing. (Adapted from Lanquetot, 1984, pp. 467–471)

Twin Studies

While family studies can give an overall picture of hereditary risks in schizophrenia and the possible genetic relationships among disorders, **twin studies** provide a way to focus on the environmental factors that contribute to schizophrenia while controlling for hereditary factors. This is possible because **dizygotic (DZ) twins** are produced from two fertilized eggs, and as a result have the same genetic relationship as any other pair of siblings, whereas, as mentioned in the section on genetic causes, **monozygotic (MZ) twins** are produced from the same fertilized egg and therefore can be expected to begin life with identical genetic makeup. It is possible that a few pairs of MZ twins may not be genetically identical because of chromosome alterations or gene mutation that may occur in only one MZ twin after the original cell division, but this is very rare and should have little effect on the findings based on large samples of twins.

About a dozen major twin studies of schizophrenia have been carried out and all of them show that MZ twins have a much greater chance of being concordant for schizophrenia than DZ twins have. However, as we saw in Figure 11-8, the concordance rate for schizophrenia in MZ twins is less than 50%. This finding makes it clear that heredity alone is generally not enough to produce schizophrenia.

One way to learn more about the nongenetic biological factors and environmental factors that may increase vulnerability to schizophrenia is through the study of MZ twins, one of whom is affected by the disorder and one of whom is not. A 6-year study of 27 MZ twin pairs who differed or were **discordant** for schizophrenia has been carried out by the National Institute of Mental Health (Torrey et al., 1994). These discordant pairs were compared with 13 twin pairs in which both twins had been diagnosed with schizophrenia and 8 normal pairs who served as a control group. This study represents an opportunity to learn more about risk factors, vulnerability, and resilience, even if these twins represent a distinctly unique group, one from which the findings may not generalize to the larger population. One question that interested the researchers in this study was the age at which the affected twin was first observed as becoming "different." This information is important in understanding the development of schizophrenia. In many cases the difference was apparent early. One-quarter of the twin pairs discordant for schizophrenia were already seen as different by age 5. However, the remainder did not show differences until age 13 or later and the most likely age for a difference to emerge was around ages 14 to 16, a time when symptoms of schizophrenia are likely to first appear. This peak in observation of differences suggests that some of the neurocognitive processes related to schizophrenia, although probably based on abnormal prenatal development, do not show their effects until they are activated by a later developmental stage (Green, 1997).

Adoption Studies

Another way of studying the effects of heredity on the development of schizophrenia is through adoption studies. Adoption studies can give researchers a clearer understanding of the roles environment and heredity may play in schizophrenia. There are two basic kinds of **adoption studies** in research on schizophrenia: those that compare adopted children whose biological parents were diagnosed as having schizophrenia with adopted children whose parents did not have this disorder and those that examine the incidence of schizophrenia in the biological and adoptive families of adopted children who later develop this disorder.

One of the first large adoption studies ever conducted was reported by a group of Danish and American researchers working in Denmark (Cannon & Mednick, 1993; D. Rosenthal et al., 1968, 1975). Because Denmark and a few other countries have excellent national medical and psychiatric registers as well as adoption registers, marriage registers, and other such records, many of the large studies tracing the heredity of disorders have been carried out in those countries. In this study, the researchers first searched the government adoption register of the Copenhagen area to find the names of parents who had given up their children to nonfamily members for adoption. Then they searched the official psychiatric register to see if they could find the names of any of those parents. The records of those who were found were rated, and those parents who clearly fit a strict definition of schizophrenia were selected. The children who had been given up for

adoption by these parents were called the index cases. The control group consisted of adopted children whose parents had no psychiatric history. Three of the 39 index cases and none of the 47 controls were given a definite diagnosis of schizophrenia by the time they reached adulthood. This high rate (8%) in the index group, compared with no cases in the control group, points to a hereditary factor.

In another kind of adoption study, Seymour Kety and his colleagues (1978, 1994) took advantage of the Danish government's comprehensive records to locate people in Denmark who had been adopted and had later developed schizophrenia. They then compared the frequencies of schizophrenia or other disturbances in the adoptees' biological and adoptive relatives. In both of these studies—the one confined to the urban Copenhagen area and one covering an area of Denmark that included less urban areas—the researchers found that adoptees who developed schizophrenia were twice as likely to have biological relatives who were diagnosed with schizophrenia.

The 1978 study also contained an important subsample: half-brothers and half-sisters who had the same father, but not the same mother, as the adopted children. Half-siblings share 25% of their genes, rather than 50% as full siblings do. More important, half-siblings with a common father do not share the environment in the uterus before birth, nor do they share the same early mothering experience. Both the paternal half-brothers and half-sisters were found to have a greater risk of schizophrenia and schizophrenic spectrum disorders than the control group. This finding gave increased weight to the importance of genetic factors in schizophrenia as compared to prenatal factors.

Vulnerability and the Environment

Although genetic factors and other biological vulnerabilities are thought to be important in the development of schizophrenia, environmental factors can play a role in whether biologically vulnerable individuals develop schizophrenia or one of the schizophrenia spectrum disorders. The **diathesis-stress theory of schizophrenia** presumes that the disorder is a result of an interplay of genetic and environmental factors. (The word *diathesis* means "predisposition.") According to this theory, only people who have some genetic vulnerability may possibly develop schizophrenia, but they will experience schizophrenic symptoms only if they are exposed to so much stress that they are unable to cope. This theory, developed by Joseph Zubin (Zubin et al., 1983; Zubin & Spring, 1977), was originally questioned by many researchers, but today it is commonly accepted because evidence is clear that environmental and interpersonal stress make a difference in whether or not symptoms of schizophrenia will appear. Zubin's hypothesis assumes that schizophrenia is not a permanent disorder but rather a permanent vulnerability to a disorder. He believed that each person has a level of **vulnerability** to schizophrenia determined both by genetic inheritance and by prenatal and postnatal factors. This level of vulnerability, which may range from no risk to high risk, interacts with stressful events or conditions in a person's life. If the combination exceeds a certain critical level or wellness/illness threshold, schizophrenic behavior will occur. This concept of vulnerability offers one way of understanding why, if one identical twin has schizophrenia, the other twin's chances of also having the disorder are not 100%, but slightly less than 50%.

Vulnerability and Adoptive Family Characteristics

An adoption study carried out in Finland supports the diathesis-stress theory (Tienari et al., 1990, 1994). Adopted children whose biological mothers were diagnosed with schizophrenia were paired with adopted children whose biological parents did not have this diagnosis. In order to carry out this study, the researchers collected information about the nearly 20,000 women who had been treated in psychiatric hospitals in Finland at some time during a 10-year period. From this group they found 171 women who had been diagnosed with schizophrenia and who had given birth to a child who was adopted by a nonrelated Finnish family before the child was 4 years old.

The complex and time-consuming procedures necessary to carry out a study like this illustrate why, although such studies are extremely valuable, more of them are not carried out. First, before the study could even get under way, a large number of cases had to be investigated to determine which of the women in the original sample had been diagnosed as schizophrenic, had had a baby, and had given up the baby for adoption. Fewer than 1 in 100 of the original cases qualified.

Some of the other tasks the researchers faced were as follows:

1. Selecting two adopted children as matched controls for each index case (an adopted child whose mother was diagnosed with schizophrenia).
2. Checking the psychiatric histories of the control children's parents.
3. Administering structured interviews to all the biological mothers, thus providing a diagnosis to compare with the diagnosis in the hospital records.
4. Interviewing the biological father of each index group member to evaluate whether he also had a psychiatric disorder that would add to risk for the child.

In addition, the research team performed an evaluation of the child-rearing environment of each adoptive family for each index and control child, which included the following steps:

1. An interview with the entire family.
2. A joint interview with both adoptive parents.
3. Psychological testing of adoptive parents together, and then also with their adoptive child.
4. A comprehensive test battery for each child and each adoptive parent, separately.
5. Follow-up assessments 5 to 7 years after the initial assessment.

As might be expected from the importance of biological factors in schizophrenia, the researchers found that people in the control group were much healthier than those in the index group. Only 1 1/2% of the control group had developed a psychotic disorder, as compared to more than 7% of the index group. In addition, 15% of those in the control group had a schizophrenic spectrum disorder, as compared to 30% of the index group. However, the most interesting finding in this study is the relationship between the adoptive family environment and frequency of psychological problems of the index cases.

The study's findings, shown in Figure 11-17, support the idea that healthy family environment has a protective effect for children who may be at risk for schizophrenia. In the group of index children reared in psychologically healthy families, none had become psychotic and only 4% had a severe psychological disorder. For the index children brought up in severely disturbed families, 11% were psychotic and 41% had a severe psychological disorder. The index children were less likely to be psychologically healthy and also were more likely to have a psychosis compared to the control children within each corresponding family type. These findings support the view that genetically transmitted vulnerability may be necessary for, or at least increase the likelihood of, occurrence of schizophrenia, but that disturbed family environment may play an important role in the expression of that vulnerability as schizophrenia.

Community Factors and Stress

More than 50 studies conducted in Europe, Asia, and North America have found that people of lower socioeconomic status (SES) are diagnosed with schizophrenia more frequently than people of middle or upper SES. However, researchers have not been able to discover why social class is related to schizophrenia. Two theories—the social selection theory and the social causation, or increased-stress, theory—have been posed to explain this relationship. The **social selection theory** assumes that people who cannot make it in society gradually become lower in SES because of their poor coping skills. Whereas the social selection theory points to flaws in the individual as the cause of schizophrenia, the **increased-stress theory** points to flaws in the society itself. The increased-stress theory focuses on the amount of stress experienced

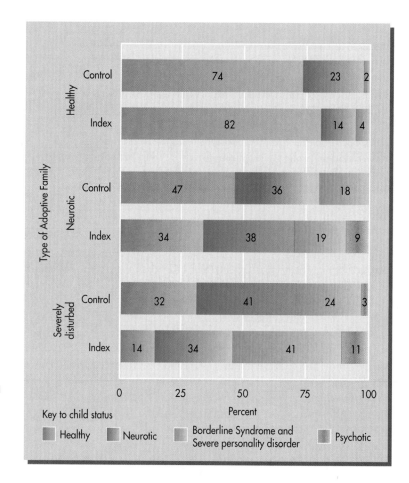

Figure 11-17 Even though adopted children whose biological mothers were diagnosed with schizophrenia (the index group) are more at risk for schizophrenia and other disorders than adopted children whose biological mothers had no such diagnosis (the control group), the atmosphere in the families into which children are adopted is important to their psychological outcome.

SOURCE: Adapted from Tienari et al. (1990), p. 327.

by people in different socioeconomic classes. Living in areas with high crime rates, run-down housing, and inadequate schools may be more difficult and stressful than living in more affluent communities. At the same time, lower-SES people have little money or power to cope with the stresses they encounter.

The results of many studies have supported each of these theories. A study of schizophrenia in inner London supported the social selection theory. It showed that the higher prevalence of schizophrenia in the poor inner areas of London, as compared to other parts of the London urban area, was explained by the movement of people affected by schizophrenia to inner London from other parts of the city (McNaught et al., 1997). Those with the diagnosis who moved into the area were more likely to be male, to have prominent hallucinations, and to be without a regular physician. In contrast, evidence from a study of almost 50,000 Swedish men called to serve their military obligation supports the increased-stress theory (Lewis et al., 1992). The study found that the incidence of schizophrenia was 1.65 times higher for men brought up in cities than for those who grew up in rural areas of Sweden. The difference remained even after the researchers had controlled for factors that might have differentiated

between urban and rural settings, such as drug use, family finances, parental divorce, and family history of psychiatric disorder. The researchers found that the increase in the rate of schizophrenia varied with the size of the city. Small towns showed a lower rate than large towns, and large towns had a lower rate than cities. This supports the idea that environmental factors found in cities are associated with an increased risk of schizophrenia. This may be because of the higher overall level of stressful life events that have been found to occur in cities. Another possibility is that pregnant women living in cities are more likely to be exposed to a variety of viral infections, especially during certain seasons of the year, than those in more rural settings. As a result, their children may be more exposed to negative effects of these viruses on prenatal development (Mortensen et al., 1999). The conflicting findings regarding why risk for schizophrenia is greater in urban areas may indicate that both theories have some usefulness.

Another finding that implicates increased stress in the development of schizophrenia in vulnerable individuals comes from research on immigrant populations, especially those who become ethnic minorities in their new home (see Figure 11-18). Immigrants of African ancestry who

Figure 11-18 These new immigrants are likely to experience stress not only because they need to learn many new behaviors including how to shop for their families in large supermarkets, but they also are confronted with many cultural customs quite different from those in which they were raised.

moved from the Caribbean area to one of two large cities in England have been found to have a much larger risk of schizophrenia than those of similar background who remained in their home country (Bhugra et al., 1997; Harrison et al., 1997). The same is true for immigrants to Holland from the former Dutch possessions in South America (Selten et al., 1997). These immigrants are of a different racial background than the Afro-Caribbean group, but like the immigrants to England, they form a distinguishable racial minority in Holland. In each case, most of these immigrants live in poverty in their new country, but the additional difficulties of adapting to a new culture and facing racial discrimination may help explain the greatly increased likelihood of developing schizophrenia for those whose genetic background makes them vulnerable (Jablensky, 1999).

High-Risk Studies and the Search for Markers

The purpose of **high-risk studies** is to identify *markers*, or signs of, schizophrenia and other serious disorders before the disorder becomes apparent. Knowledge of these predictors could be important in what is called *primary prevention*: an intervention that may help keep the disorder from developing. Researchers interested in prevention have problems in targeting their efforts because only about 1 in every 100 people in the general population is likely to develop schizophrenia. This means that researchers taking a study sample from the population as a whole would initially have to include many thousands of individuals in order to include enough people who later develop the disorder so that the results would be statistically meaningful.

High-risk studies deal with this problem of low incidence in the general population by selecting for study a group considered to have a higher potential or risk of schizophrenia, so that for the same number of subjects studied, more cases of the disorder will be expected to occur. One difficulty with high-risk studies is that because the population studied is expected to be at high risk, it is a special one, which raises the question of how much the findings can be generalized or extended to the overall population.

Although high-risk studies may have some disadvantages, they have a great advantage over other types of studies because they are *prospective*, that is they select and begin to study the participants before symptoms appear. This prospective method is much better than a *retrospective* approach in which the patients and their families are asked to recall earlier behaviors and past events. This is especially important because once a diagnosis of schizophrenia has been made, everyone in the family may see past events in a different light. Studying the person and his or her family after schizophrenia has developed tells us more about the consequences of having the disorder than about its causes. The diagnosis of schizophrenia means that the person is likely to have already suffered educational, economic, and social failure and may also have experienced hospitalization and extensive drug therapy. These factors alone may explain many of the differences that researchers find between groups with a diagnosis of schizophrenia and control groups.

Many high-risk studies define risk status in genetic terms; that is, they select biological children of parents who have been diagnosed with schizophrenia. An advantage of this type of study is that it provides ideal control cases: children within the study population who do not develop schizophrenia but who have been selected on the same genetic basis as children who do. High-risk studies also encourage the study of gene-environment interactions like those in the Finnish adoption study described earlier. It is important in the study of disorders such as schizophrenia, for which clear symptoms often do not appear until young adulthood, to continue a longitudinal study of high-risk individuals throughout the period of risk for the disorder. Up to now only a few studies have extended for that long. Participants in the Copenhagen study whose mothers had been diagnosed with severe schizophrenia were studied at least through age 40 (Mednick et al., 1987; Parnas et al., 1993). At that age, about 20% of them had developed schizophrenia or a schizophrenia-associated psychosis. But just as important for learning more about schizophrenia, an even larger number in this group had been diagnosed with either schizotypal or paranoid personality disorder. All these disorders occurred at a much greater frequency in the high-risk group than in the control group where only about 1% of the participants were diagnosed with a psychosis of any type, and only 5% were diagnosed with either schizotypal or paranoid personality disorder. The results of this and other high-risk studies demonstrate that genetic inheritance greatly increases the risk of developing either schizophrenia or one of the personality disorders from the schizophrenic spectrum even when the child is not reared by a parent with schizophrenia or a schizophrenic spectrum disorder.

The results of the Danish high-risk studies have identified several distinctive characteristics of children who have a parent with schizophrenia and who ultimately develop schizophrenia themselves. Of these characteristics, the most predictive was impaired attention. Social dysfunction and behavioral deviance reported by teachers was also a reliable predictor of later schizophrenia (Cannon et al., 1990). Other characteristics that increased the risk of developing schizophrenia included the mother's having influenza during the second trimester of pregnancy, birth complications, and the child's early separation from the mother (Olin & Mednick, 1996). None of this last group of characteristics predicted schizophrenia in the control group, however. This suggests that they add to the risk of developing schizophrenia only in those who already have a genetic vulnerability.

A well-known longitudinal study that has continued for many years differs in some important respects from the high-risk studies based on adopted children. The New York High-Risk Project has studied two groups of children: children in one group were at risk because one of their parents had schizophrenia and those in the second group because one of their parents had a serious form of mood disorder, either major depression or Bipolar I disorder (disorders discussed in Chapter 10). These two groups were selected so that the researchers could investigate whether parental mood disorder and schizophrenia had similar or different effects on the children involved. A group of low-risk children was also included as a control

group. The study began in 1971 and has followed the children from childhood to midadulthood. One important finding has been that children of a parent with a mood disorder did not share the symptoms of children who had a parent with schizophrenia (Erlenmeyer-Kimling et al., 1995). This suggests that the basic causes of the two types of disorder are different and not simply different symptoms all stemming from a general category of serious psychological disorder. By the time they reached adulthood, 11% of the children of a schizophrenic parent also were diagnosed as schizophrenic and an additional 5% were diagnosed with some unspecified psychosis. This rate of diagnosis is much higher than the 1% rate found in the overall population. None of the other children in the study, either in the mood disorder parent group or a control group, had either of these diagnoses.

In addition to this finding regarding the genetic specificity of schizophrenia, an even more important finding was that abnormal attention in childhood served as a marker of biological susceptibility to schizophrenia. These unusual attentional characteristics served as markers that predicted later illness in the at-risk children (Cornblatt et al., 1996). This conclusion fits in very well with the findings concerning prenatal development difficulties in children who are later at risk for schizophrenia, which were discussed earlier. The abnormal distribution of neurons that is thought take place in the second trimester of pregnancy is thought to disrupt the process of synaptic pruning that starts in late childhood. Attentional deviance appears to be a key factor mediating the relationship between risk for schizophrenia and later social dysfunction (Freedman et al., 1998). Some measures of attentional deviance will be discussed in the section that follows.

High-Risk Markers of Attention and Cognition

Patients often report disorders of attention and perception in the early stages of their schizophrenia (McGhie & Chapman, 1961). These attentional problems have been noted for many years. In 1921 Emil Kraepelin (see Box 11-1) commented on a "certain unsteadiness of attention" in patients he identified by the diagnosis dementia praecox (the forerunner of the present category of schizophrenia). Eugen Bleuler (1913/1950) also noted that "acute attention is lacking" in schizophrenic patients. In their attempt to understand the schizophrenic process, many psychological researchers have focused on quantifying information-processing and attentional deficits.

These studies have operated on the assumption that patients with schizophrenia have important deficiencies in their information-processing abilities and that these deficiencies are shown most clearly when the total task involves efficient and rapid information processing and high processing loads, as well as distraction or other stressors.

Although some attentional deficits may be state-linked; that is, they may be associated with an active psychotic process, the researchers were most interested in those that were trait-linked; that is, they may be stable personal characteristics even when a disorder is not apparent. Studies of high-risk children and family members of patients diagnosed with schizophrenia, for example, are based on that assumption. As knowledge about the role of prenatal brain development and its relation to vulnerability to schizophrenia has grown, researchers have begun to link these attentional deficits to specific biological factors described earlier in the chapter.

In the New York High-Risk Project, several measures of attentional dysfunction, administered when the children under study were age 7, detected attentional deficits several years before other risk markers—such as social insensitivity, indifference to others, and social isolation—appeared. One of the measures used was the Digit Span Subtest from the Wechsler Intelligence Scale for Children. This subtest requires children to repeat a series of numbers either forward or backward. The longer the series the child can repeat correctly, the higher the score. Low scores on the Digit Span Subtest were associated with later development of schizophrenia (Erlenmeyer-Kimling et al., 1995).

Continuous Performance Test Another measure used in the New York High-Risk Project was the **Continuous Performance Test (CPT)**. This test measures sustained visual attention for periods of up to 20 minutes (Rosvold et al., 1956). The person tested is instructed to respond to one particular type of stimulus by pressing a key and is then exposed to a series of different stimuli. For instance, the possible stimuli might include the numbers 0 through 9, and in each trial, a video monitor displayed three of these numbers in random sequence. The task of the test participant is to press the response button only when a 1 in the middle position of the three-number display was followed in the next stimulus set by a 9 in that same position. The numbers in the left and right positions merely served as distractors. Two kinds of errors were recorded. If the person being tested failed to press the button after the correct series in the middle position, this was called an *error of omission*. If he or she pressed the response button after a different sequence of numbers (say, 7 and 1) or after the correct sequence of numbers appeared in the left or right position rather than the middle position, this was called an *error of commission*.

Children of mothers who had a diagnosis of schizophrenia scored more poorly on the CPT than either children of mothers who were seriously depressed or children in the control group whose mothers had no known disorder (Nuechterlein, 1983). This finding suggests that the attentional difficulties the CPT measures are trait-linked characteristics that are not a function of a current psychotic process, because none of the children had symp-

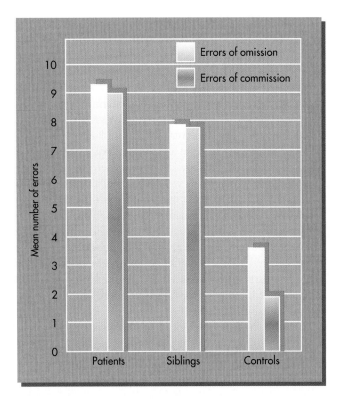

Figure 11-19 Mean errors of omission and commission as a measure of attentional dysfunction for patients with a diagnosis of schizophrenia, their siblings, and a no-diagnosis control group. Mean errors of patients and siblings both differ significantly from mean errors of the control group.

SOURCE: Adapted from Finkelstein et al. (1997), pp. 203–212.

toms of psychosis when they were first tested. These CPT scores for the children in the New York High-Risk Project also predicted whether or not they would be diagnosed later with schizophrenia or a schizophrenic spectrum disorder (Erlenmeyer-Kimling et al., 1995). This measure of attention in a complex task shows that CPT scores can be markers to determine which children are most at risk for later development of schizophrenia.

More support for the idea that the attentional problems revealed on the CPT test indicate a continuing trait rather than a state based on current psychotic symptoms comes from a study of the CPT performance of both patients diagnosed with schizophrenia and their relatives (Finkelstein et al., 1997). This study compared the patients, their siblings, and normal controls. Figure 11-19 shows that both patients and their siblings made significantly more errors than did the controls. These errors were both of omission (not responding when a correct stimulus was shown) and commission (responding to a stimulus that was incorrect and thus should have been ignored).

Eye Tracking Smooth-pursuit eye movements are not believed to be under voluntary control. They normally occur only when a person tracks a slow-moving target such as a pendulum. Tests of patients diagnosed with schizophrenia showed that about 85% of them exhibited abnormal patterns of smooth-pursuit eye-tracking movements (Siever & Coursey, 1985). Figure 11-20 illustrates the difference between the typical tracking pattern of a normal control and the pattern typically found in someone with schizophrenia. About 50% of the close relatives of these patients also showed this deviant pattern, but in contrast, only 13% of relatives of other types of patients showed abnormal tracking patterns. Eye-tracking and other eye-movement abnormalities seem to follow a consistent hereditary pattern when families of patients with schizophrenia are studied (Grove et al., 1992). However, this genetic link may not be specific to schizophrenia, or even to the schizophrenic spectrum of disorders, but may indicate poor motor control, which is predictive of a variety of disorders. Poor trackers, even among people who have not received any psychiatric diagnosis, are likely to have interpersonal difficulties and neurological impairment.

Despite the lack of specificity of eye-tracking problems to schizophrenia, in children who are at risk because a parent has been diagnosed with the disorder, an abnormal pattern of eye tracking may serve as a marker of vulnerability to schizophrenia. Like attention problems on the CPT, abnormal eye-tracking patterns seem to be a trait measure rather than a measure of a person's clinical state (Schlenker & Cohen, 1995). Some researchers have argued that the use of attentional measures such as the CPT and eye tracking would be valuable in understanding the genetic pattern of schizophrenia. These markers occur much more frequently than the diagnosis of schizophrenia, so using them in constructing a family tree for genetic analysis might reveal hereditary patterns that are currently hidden when individuals are described only in terms of diagnosis. Because the diagnostic category of schizophrenia as it is currently defined is generally considered to include a number of disorders that may stem from different causes, constructing a family tree may not lead to clear conclusions and may make the search for specific genetic factors in schizophrenia more difficult.

Therapeutic Approaches

We have described how some people are vulnerable to developing schizophrenia as a result of genetic inheritance, or problems during prenatal development, or both, and that this vulnerability may interact with stress to produce the symptoms of the disorder. The greater the vulnerability, the less stress seems to be needed to produce this outcome. However, because the specific biological causes of vulnerability are not yet known and because the DSM-IV category of schizophrenia may include disorders with several causes, a wide range of treatment approaches have been developed over time that reflect several of the per-

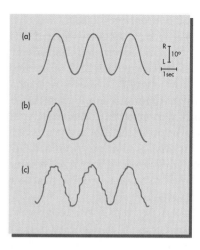

Figure 11-20   Normal and abnormal eye tracking. Figure (a) shows the movement of the target and figure (b) a normal eye-tracking record. Figure (c) illustrates a qualitatively abnormal tracking of the type that may suggest vulnerability to schizophrenia.

Source: From Levy, Holzman, Matthysse, & Mendell (1993), pp. 461–536.

spectives considered in this book—biological, behavioral, cognitive, and psychodynamic—as well as several family-centered approaches. Currently the biological, behavioral, and family-centered approaches show the most promise, although none of the treatment approaches, alone or in combination, can be said to cure schizophrenia. What they can do is decrease symptoms, particularly the positive symptoms, for many patients, thus allowing them to function more effectively. However, with many of these patients, relapse and a worsening of symptoms occur periodically, even if treatment is not interrupted.

Despite the distressing and dramatic nature of some of the symptoms of schizophrenia, there is often a substantial time lag between the first onset of these symptoms and the diagnosis and beginning of treatment. One review of studies of first-episode schizophrenia found that, on average, treatment began a year after the first clearly psychotic symptoms had been observed (Birchwood et al., 1977). Delay in recognizing these early symptoms as the beginning of a schizophrenic process may have a negative effect on the patient's ultimate degree of improvement. An increasing number of researchers believe that an untreated psychosis is "biologically toxic" and that a delay in treatment results in a poorer lifetime outcome than prompt treatment does, even when the later treatment is effective (Bustillo et al., 1999). However, beginning treatment early may not be as easy as it sounds. Often, individuals who do not end up with a diagnosis of schizophrenia also show these prodromal symptoms. **Prodromal symptoms** are changed behavior prior to the clear onset of schizophrenia. As a result, these symptoms are not predictive of a specific risk for schizophrenia.

The following account, written by a psychoanalyst, shows how hard it may be, even for an expert observer, to understand the implications of these early changes until after a diagnosis is made. The psychoanalyst and his wife, knowledgeable and close to their children, saw only in hindsight that what at the time seemed like explainable behavior on the part of their son was in fact the beginning of the schizophrenic process.

I have often been asked, "When did Gary's illness begin?" If I were his psychiatrist writing up the case history, I would say, "When he dropped out of Harvard during his sophomore year" or "At the time of his first hospitalization two years later." But when the onset of the illness is so insidious . . . , it is an impossible question to answer. In retrospect, we have reason to believe that his illness started much earlier.

At age 13, while at summer camp, he became depressed for about a month. At age 14, he asked to see a psychiatrist, whom he saw for four years. I later learned that Gary was experiencing certain unusual visual imagery in his fantasy life at that time. Otherwise, the psychiatrist thought he was having some not-untypical adolescent conflicts and never . . . had any suspicion of any kind of psychosis. During high school Gary quit the tennis team, saying that he wanted to concentrate on his drumming and band work. At the time it seemed reasonable, but in retrospect it was the beginning of a tendency toward isolation. He asked for a single room at Harvard, although he had always been quite gregarious. During his senior year of high school he sent in his application to Amherst College late; not so unusual for many teenagers, but quite unusual for him. . . . His well-written college essay was preoccupied with issues of moral integrity and concerns about being phony. Weren't these also concerns appropriate for an adolescent?

It was only when his illness was full-blown that we realized that his ambivalence about his college choice was the early manifestation of the profound ambivalence so characteristic of this illness. At its height he might spend many minutes opening and closing the refrigerator door, each action accompanied by a delusional fear and the attempt to avoid it. Only when his illness was diagnosed did we see that the preoccupation with morality and phoniness which he displayed in his essay was the early form of the typical delusions with which he is still struggling. Despite the fact that these symptoms were already beginning to plague him, he was selected as the leading drummer for the Harvard jazz band during his freshman year and was able to maintain a B average. The next year, however, he could no longer do the work and his condition deteriorated. (Willick, 1994, pp. 708–709)

Gary subsequently was hospitalized three times, received a variety of antipsychotic medications, and 10 years after leaving Harvard was living in a halfway house.

Because the changes in the function of the nervous system that are associated with schizophrenia may be most damaging in the early stages of onset, a recent, somewhat controversial approach has been to treat young people who are at high risk with low doses of antipsychotic drugs even though they show only small changes in behavior and not clear symptoms of illness. Two studies using this approach, one in the United States and one in Australia, are investigating whether those who receive these low doses of antipsychotic drugs have a better outcome than other high-risk subjects who do not (Goode, 1999). Although the drugs prescribed were those that have the fewest negative side effects of all those available for treating schizophrenia and the doses used were small, the safety and ethics of the approach have been questioned by some researchers. Opponents worry that, because no one yet knows exactly what the early symptoms of schizophrenia are, many of those treated may be treated unnecessarily or given the wrong treatment. Also, the long-term effects of such treatment for people who do not have the disorder are not known and may have permanent negative effects. Despite these concerns, many researchers believe that the development of schizophrenia may be the result of neural changes that are believed to take place in the brain during late adolescence and young adulthood, the so-called "natural pruning" discussed earlier, and that the use of antipsychotic medication for high-risk individuals might help modify these changes (McGlashan & Hoffman, 2000). So far preliminary results from a small Australian study of early intervention medication and intensive psychotherapy for high-risk individuals have been encouraging. They indicate that the number of control group members who developed psychosis in the first 6 months was greater than that in the research group who received both medication and psychotherapy (Tanouye, 1999).

Detection of early signs that predict later schizophrenia is making some progress. Researchers examined the results of the compulsory testing of Israeli 16- and 17-year-olds by the Israeli Draft Board Registry (Davidson et al., 1999). They found that they could accurately identify almost 88% of those who later developed schizophrenia by subtle differences in intellectual and social functioning on the screening tests. The tests dealt with personal relationships, ability to organize life activities, and evidence of maturity by asking questions such as: How many good friends do you have? How often are you late for school? Who cleans your room? and Do you tend to be the center of attention at parties? Although more research needs to be done and the predictors need to be tested on other groups, development of valid measures of early symptoms of schizophrenia is important for treatment.

Antipsychotic Drugs

Antipsychotic medications are the mainstay of treatment for schizophrenia and reflect the importance of the biological perspective in understanding and treating this disorder. However, at the same time, there is considerable evidence that psychosocial interventions accompanying these medications—especially after the first acute episode of the disorder—are very helpful in preventing relapse and improving social functioning (Lehman, 1995).

About two-thirds of patients who are experiencing their first episode of schizophrenia improve considerably after 6 weeks of administration of conventional antipsychotic drugs (phenothiazines) (Beaumont, 2000). However, antipsychotic medications may produce only a temporary improvement in the positive symptoms of schizophrenia (symptoms of thought disorder, hallucinations, and delusions) and have little effect on attention and cognitive functioning. They do not alter biological vulnerability but only weaken its expression. Within the first year after treatment begins relapse and a worsening of symptoms are likely to occur in about half of those treated, even if the medication is continued regularly during that period. Improvement of symptoms after the first relapse is not as great as the initial improvement. Some researchers believe that with every successive relapse, the potential for recovery is lessened because of the progressive effects of the disease process on the person's nervous system (McGlashan & Johannessen, 1996). Although in the initial period of the disorder both positive and negative symptoms occur in an unstable and fluctuating pattern, as the disorder progresses the negative symptoms become more stable and usually dominate the clinical picture.

Until a few years ago, the antipsychotic drugs used to treat schizophrenia, while often effective in moderating symptoms, had two significant disadvantages related to their effect of blocking the D2 dopamine receptors. One of these disadvantages was their negative effect on the individual's motivation and the numbing of sensory input. These effects are illustrated by the comments of callers to a mental health help line, which indicate that the medication made the callers' lives less pleasant. One young man said, "When I take my medication, I feel as though I am walking with lead in my shoes." Another composed a poem in which he compared the effect of the medication to drowning—"I was always under the water gasping for air and sunshine" (Wallace, 1994, p. 35).

Other more serious disadvantages of traditional antipsychotic drugs are some of the serious and often irreversible side effects they produced. One of these is **tardive dyskinesia,** or involuntary movements of the mouth, lips, tongue, legs, or body. Other side effects include mental unease and depressed feelings that were accompanied by uncontrollable restless movements such as rocking from foot to foot, swinging one leg on the other while sitting, and rapid pacing, sometimes with an inability to sit or stand in any one position.

Because of these negative aspects of traditional antipsychotic drugs, new types of antipsychotic drugs were developed. The first of these to have wide use was clozapine (Clozaril). Clozapine lessened some of the problems of the traditional antipsychotic drugs because it was more selective in the types of receptors it affected. It also was effective for a large number of patients whose symptoms had not been helped by the traditional antipsychotic drugs and in general was more effective for all patients (Wahlbeck et al., 1999). However, for up to 10% of those who were given it, it had a potentially fatal effect on their production of white blood cells. As a result it is not safe to use unless blood samples are monitored regularly. Because of this danger it was slow to be widely adopted despite its effectiveness. Other atypical antipsychotic drugs have been developed that have fewer harmful side effects. These include risperidone, olanzapine, and quetiapine. Some of them seem promising because their side effects, especially those related to movement, are less severe. However, because they are relatively new, extensive trials are needed to assess whether they are as effective as clozapine or older antipsychotic drugs (Schulz, 2000).

Those who improve as a result of antipsychotic medication are likely to be advised to remain on a medication program after discharge from the hospital in the hope that continuing the medication may dampen symptoms and reduce the chance of relapse. Despite this advice, about half of all discharged patients discontinue using the prescribed medication (H. Weiner et al., 1989). One recent development that may help this situation, at least for discharged patients willing to take antipsychotic medication, is the availability of some of these medications in longlasting injectable form so that patients do not have to remember to take them orally on a daily basis. Another way to get patients to continue taking medication after their symptoms lessen may be to reduce the amount of medication prescribed. Numerous studies have shown that discharged patients whose acute symptoms have receded are often prescribed larger dosages of medication than are necessary to keep their symptoms under control (Schulz, 2000). An appropriate decrease in the amount of medication prescribed should lessen side effects and might make taking the medication more acceptable.

A major problem in carrying out treatment that relies on antipsychotic drugs is the question of whether a patient is competent to agree to or refuse the medication. Although the law is clear that no patient should receive medication without his or her informed consent, the cognitive impairment and loss of insight that are primary effects of schizophrenia make the issue of competence a difficult one. Then the question arises, when should a person have the right to refuse treatment? Because of the informed consent–competence issue, the families of patients who refuse medication and clinicians who believe that medication is necessary to those patients' welfare are often forced to wait until after medication is discontinued and the patients' psychoses worsen and they become dangerous to themselves or others. Only then can rehospitalization and medication be required. When such patients again improve with medication and are judged to be legally competent, they may again refuse medication and another cycle of worsening symptoms and active psychosis may begin.

One mother eloquently described this situation. Her son had been first hospitalized 12 years earlier but was currently living in a halfway house. His present medication seemed ineffective, and he often refused medication for long periods.

> *Over the past year, my husband and I had been observing a marked deterioration in our son's behavior and thinking, even on medication. He stopped his weekly visits to our apartment in Manhattan after the voices forbade him to take the elevator to the eighth floor. He told us we wouldn't see him anymore, because the CIA was preparing to send him out of the country.*
>
> *The only hope was for him to try one of the newer medications . . . which might be more effective in decreasing the psychotic symptoms. But he refused to return to the hospital, where the drugs would be administered and their potential side effects monitored. It was the standard Catch-22: When he was taking the old medication, he didn't feel the need to be hospitalized; when the drug gradually lost its effectiveness, or he stopped taking it, he no longer had the insight to recognize his own deterioration and stubbornly refused to hospitalize himself.*
>
> *Involuntary hospitalization was out of the question, we learned. Since Serge wasn't dangerous, his civil rights were inviolable. Although he was completely crazy, he had the right to remain without proper treatment. He could be committed only if he harmed himself or someone else. (Lanquetot, 1994, p. A12)*

Although progress is being made in finding more effective antipsychotic drugs with fewer side effects, frequent relapses generally occur in the early years of schizophrenia, even when there is ongoing treatment with the most effective drugs available and even among those people who show an initially good response to antipsychotic drug therapy. Thus, though antipsychotic medication is considered to be the basic standard treatment, other approaches accompanying drug therapy can greatly add to the quality of life of someone affected by schizophrenia. The additional treatment approaches include focusing on improving the patient's social, self-care, and cognitive skills; educating both the family and the affected individual about schizophrenia, thus helping to improve relationships within the family; and providing a safety net of community support that allows the affected person to function at the highest level possible.

Skills Training

Many people affected by schizophrenia, especially those for whom the disorder appears to be chronic, lack a variety of skills. Skill deficits can be seen in a number of areas: social interactions; cognitive skills that appear linked to some of the attention problems discussed earlier; self-care and symptom identification skills related to independent living; and finally, coping with stress in general.

Social Skills Up to two-thirds of those with chronic schizophrenia are seriously deficient in generic social skills such as assertiveness, compromising when socially appropriate, and symptom management (Mueser et al., 1991). Social perception abilities that are important in social interactions are also likely to be inadequate. These include self-awareness, affect regulation, and social cue recognition. In addition, schizophrenia seems to lead to deficits in problem-solving skills, including appraising social and other situations, thinking of possible alternative responses, and predicting the effects of these responses.

There are three general categories of social skills training: basic skills, social problem solving, and cognitive effectiveness. Early efforts in the area of skills training tended to concentrate on training programs that combined instruction, modeling, rehearsal of behaviors, and verbal reinforcement. Studies generally showed that these interventions led to short-term improvement in these skills when patients were tested using tasks very similar to those in the original training. An important question is whether social skills training helps prevent relapse and an increase in symptoms after the training has ended. In one study in which intensive social skills training on an individual basis was used, the relapse rate of the control group after 1 year was 46% but only 30% in the social skills training group (Hogarty et al., 1991). However, after 2 years there was no difference in the relapse rate of the two groups.

A broader approach to social skills is through the use of a social learning approach. This training is based on the belief that the limited social competence that is characteristic of schizophrenia is a result of problems in information processing. Topics included may be management of medication, management of symptoms, basic conversation, and self-care skills, depending on the needs of the patient. This kind of training has produced gains in some aspects of social adjustment when compared to the outcome for supportive group therapy, but the differences between the two groups were very small (Marder et al., 1996).

Cognitive Skills Cognitive skills training has also been tried as a means of improving outcome in schizophrenia. It seems clear from the results of high-risk studies that cognitive impairments in attention, memory, and planning are not simply a result of any symptoms in the active schizophrenic process or medication, but are general characteristics of those at risk. Although intensive training in elementary cognitive functions such as concept formation by using computer games can produce some modest gains, as yet this training has not been shown to have much effect on symptoms or social competence (Brenner et al., 1992). A different approach to helping people with schizophrenia deal

Table 11-6	
Remedial Strategies for Some Cognitive Deficits of Schizophrenia	
Cognitive Deficit	**Remedial Strategy**
Hyperarousal from overstimulating milieu.	Diminish external distractors, ambient noise, and likely interruptions.
Difficulty sustaining attention over time.	Keep training tasks brief and focused. Use frequent prompts to regain attentional focus. Use incentive programs and self-management techniques to improve prearranged attention goals.
Distraction from irrelevant cues.	Keep training site uncluttered by stimuli not germane to modular skill areas.
Misinterpretation of learning points.	Post charts that explain skill areas.
Difficulty with speeded tasks.	Proceed slowly through training steps.
Overload from complex tasks.	Conduct task analysis and break tasks down into simpler substeps.
Distraction from immediate stimuli in the environment.	Avoid accidental pairing of extraneous variables by providing immediate feedback and reinforcement. After overlearning has occurred, gradually fade feedback and reinforcers.
Distraction from hallucinations and associations.	Adopt thought-stopping techniques. Self-monitor disordered thought and hallucinations and avoid stressors that may exacerbate them.

Source: Based on Liberman & Corrigan (1993), p. 246.

with some cognitive deficits characteristic of the disorder is focused not on correcting or lessening these deficits but rather developing strategies for dealing with their effects. Some of these remedial strategies are illustrated in Table 11-6.

Cognitive-behavior therapy has been used experimentally to deal with some of these deficits in processing skills—for example, to decrease chronic auditory hallucinations to make them less upsetting. These efforts focus on the idea that these hallucinations, arising from inside the patient, are misattributed by him or her to an external source (Norman & Townsend, 1999). For instance, by using this cognitive approach some patients became aware that it was not the voices that were so distressing, but their own thoughts about the voices. When they were able to recognize situations that caused the voices to become worse, they sometimes were also able to understand that the voices reflected feelings they were unable to express. This allowed them to begin addressing some of these problems with the therapist. Although the application of cognitive therapy techniques to the treatment of schizophrenia has not yet been adequately demonstrated, the cognitive approach to stress reduction is consistent with the diathesis-stress theory and thus may help vulnerable individuals prevent or reduce their delusional thoughts.

Self-Care and Symptom Identification Skills In addition to poor social skills, chronic patients are likely to have inadequate self-care skills and awareness of symptoms that tend to predict relapse. They are often poorly groomed, fail to wash regularly, have poor table manners, and are unable to use public transportation, manage their money, or prepare meals. Behavioral training methods can focus on the improvement of these skills. Successful tran-

sition from the hospital to the community is predicted better by these skills than by any characteristics of behavior at or during hospitalization. One series of modules focusing on a variety of social and self-care skills needed for independent living was developed by the UCLA Clinical Research Center. It includes such skills as patient management of medication, self-monitoring for symptoms of relapse, conversational and self-grooming skills, and skills related to recreational activities. Table 11-7 illustrates the skills areas for medication and symptom management. Both sets of skills are important in helping the patient prevent a relapse into psychotic behavior or, if a relapse occurs, in helping the individual recognize its signs and seek help.

Skills for Dealing With Stress A somewhat different focus on skill training for those with schizophrenia is a focus on each person's characteristic response to stress in general rather than to any specific category of stress (Hogarty, et al., 1997a). In this approach, participants were taught to identify their own cognitive, affective, and bodily indicators of distress and the appropriate relaxation and cognitive techniques to use when these signs of stress occurred. This focus on coping with stress was successful in reducing the chance of relapse, but only for participants who were living with their families (see Figure 11-21). Those who were living independently were affected negatively by this therapeutic approach and experienced a significantly increased rate of relapse compared to the control group. The evidence suggested that this negative outcome was a result of a cognitive overload. The group living away from their families experienced more instability in their living conditions and more stressors and as a result probably found the added demands of the training program more than they could handle.

Table 11-7	

The Skill Areas and Goals from Two of the UCLA Modules for Training Social and Independent Living Skills

Skill Areas and Goals for Medication Management

Skill Areas	Goals
1. Obtaining information about antipsychotic medication.	To gain an understanding of how these drugs work, why maintenance drug therapy is used, and what benefits result from taking medication.
2. Knowing correct self-administration and evaluation of medication.	To learn appropriate procedures in taking medication and to learn how to evaluate responses to daily medication.
3. Identifying side effects of medication.	To learn the side effects that sometimes result from taking medication and what can be done to alleviate these problems.
4. Negotiating medication issues with health care providers.	To practice ways of getting assistance when problems occur with medication; for example, how to call the hospital or doctor and how to report symptoms and progress.
5. Using long-acting injectable medication.	To desensitize fears of injection and learn benefits of biweekly or monthly injectable medication.

Skills Areas and Goals for Symptom Management

Skill Areas	Goals
1. Identifying warning signs of relapse.	To learn how to identify personal warning signs and monitor them with assistance from others.
2. Managing warning signs.	To learn to use specific techniques for managing warning signs and develop an *emergency plan.*
3. Coping with persistent symptoms.	To learn how to recognize persistent symptoms and use techniques for coping with them.
4. Avoiding alcohol and street drugs.	To learn about the adverse effects of alcohol and illicit drugs, and how to avoid them.

Source: Based on Liberman & Corrigan (1993), p. 242.

Family Programs

Just as the stress-coping skills study demonstrated, the patient's family can play an important role in reducing the frequency of psychotic symptom relapses. One approach to helping the family help the patient is through psychoeducational family interventions, especially when combined with continuing treatment of the patient with antipsychotic drugs. These interventions can reduce the relapse rate of patients who had earlier experienced an acute episode of schizophrenia (Dixon & Lehman, 1995). There is also reason to believe that these interventions improve overall family well-being. Family interventions usually include different combinations of several elements: (1) education about what schizophrenia is (diagnostic criteria, symptoms, future course); (2) information on how it is treated (both medication and family management), (3) identification of probable causes; and (4) instruction in problem-solving and crisis management skills for family members. In some family intervention programs, the patient is included in some or all of the discussions. Sometimes the program is conducted with one family at a time; in other cases, several families meet together.

For most patients, a combination of medication and family intervention clearly delays a relapse into acute psychosis and may even prevent it in some cases. However, this kind of intervention may not have a long-term effect unless it is continued for a long period, perhaps in the form of less frequent meetings or booster sessions. For instance, 2 years after one such intervention ended, the relapse rate for the patients in the family intervention group was no different from the relapse rate for the control group, even though a year earlier their relapse rate had been much lower (Lam, 1991). If the intervention continues, the probability of relapse may continue to be low. In one case, the benefits of continued intervention were still seen at an 8-year follow-up (Tarrier et al., 1994). In addition to helping to lower the frequency of relapse, family interventions may improve patients' functioning to at least a modest degree and may increase the probability that these patients will be able to find and keep jobs (McFarlane et al., 1995).

Information given to families about the psychobiology of schizophrenia seems to be particularly helpful. It helps them understand the underlying mechanisms that create vulnerability and produce the symptoms they see in their family member. Because one of the major goals of these

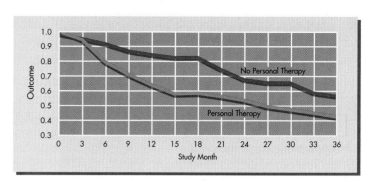

Figure 11-21 Among patients with schizophrenia or schizoaffective disorder who lived with their families, those who received personal therapy that focused on dealing with stress had fewer relapses, affective episodes, and terminations of treatment than patients receiving supportive or family-focused therapy. All patients received antipsychotic medications during this period.

Source: From Hogarty, Kornblith, et al. (1997b), p. 1510.

programs is to decrease the guilty feelings of family members who think that their behavior may in some way have caused the illness, most programs emphasize the genetic aspects of schizophrenia and discuss the difficulty these vulnerable patients have in coping with stress (see Box 11-4). The role of the family in managing the stress the patient experiences is emphasized as a possible way to decrease symptoms and prevent a relapse.

Some research indicates that including patients in at least some of the family sessions may be important to the effectiveness of the intervention (Tarrier & Barrowclough, 1995). Other research findings suggest that interventions with groups of families may be more effective than working with one family at a time. Monthly multifamily educational group meetings have been shown to greatly reduce the frequency of relapse compared to the use of antipsychotic drugs alone (Schooler et al., 1997).

The most effective family intervention seems to be a combination of a positive approach focused on the present; an emphasis on cognitive restructuring for family members in regard to their attributions regarding the patient; a behavioral approach; and attention to improved communication within the family (Lam, 1991). This kind of intervention can help participants learn how to cope with schizophrenia. They learn constructive ways to handle guilt, embarrassment, frustration, and anger at their relative's behavior. They also learn to evaluate their behavioral tactics in dealing with the patient and to understand why some of the tactics they use may not work as well as other, more effective ways of interacting.

Expressed Emotion Many of the first studies to use a family intervention approach were focused on the effects of expressed emotion. **Expressed emotion (EE)** is a measure of the attitudes expressed by family members when talking about the person whose behavior is disturbed (Leff & Vaughn, 1985). Table 11-8 lists the categories of expressed emotion that are measured.

Researchers have consistently found that patients hospitalized for schizophrenia who were subsequently discharged and who returned to families high in negative EE were not likely to stay out of the hospital as long as patients whose families were less critical. This was true whether or not the patient was also taking antipsychotic

drugs (Leff & Vaughn, 1981) (see Figure 11-22). Studies carried out in England and Los Angeles produced similar results (Vaughn et al., 1984).

Negative EE includes criticism, hostility, and emotional overinvolvement (exaggerated emotional response to the illness or extreme overprotectiveness). Relatives who were rated high in negative EE made such remarks as the following:

"I always say, 'Why don't you pick up a book, do a crossword or something like that to keep your mind off it.' That's even too much trouble." (Hooley, 1985, p. 134)

"He went round the garden 90 times, in the door, back out the door. I said, 'Have a chair, sit out in the sun.' Well, he nearly bit my head off." (ibid.)

Relatives who were low in negative EE were likely to make very different comments:

"I know it's better for her to be on her own, to get away from me and try to do things on her own." (Hooley, 1985, p. 134)

"I just tend to let it go because I know that when she wants to speak she will speak." (ibid.)

As research on EE has continued, several findings have emerged:

1. EE in a family may change over time. It may be a product both of the degree of agitation in the patient and of the family interaction style. EE can be considered as part of the diathesis-stress or interactional framework (Hooley & Richters, 1995). Certain as yet unidentified characteristics of some family members may place them at greater risk for developing critical attitudes when they are exposed to the disturbed behavior of the relative with schizophrenia, and even greater exposure to that disturbed behavior will result in more and more relatives eventually being classified as high in EE. This also suggests that during periods of the illness in which there are decreased symptoms, the relatives' EE levels may decrease. Thus, EE may reflect an interaction of traitlike factors of relatives, the patient's

First Person   Box 11–4

Lessening a Family's Guilt over Schizophrenia

Donna Lee has 25-year-old twin sons, Malcolm and Michael. Malcolm has been hospitalized with a diagnosis of schizophrenia. Donna, Malcolm, and Michael were participants in a twin study at the National Institute of Mental Health (NIMH). NIMH had identified approximately 150 twin pairs in Canada and the United States in which one twin had been diagnosed with either schizophrenia or bipolar disorder and the other one had not developed the disorder. Sixty-four of these twin pairs and their parents came to Washington, D.C., for an intense battery of tests and interviews. Among these were the Lees.

Some of the comments made by the Lees during their interviews show how important knowledge about schizophrenia is to families in which one member is affected by the disorder:

When Malcolm was first hospitalized, Donna said, "I was taken into a room, told he has schizophrenia, and asked if I had any questions. Well, you go into a total state of shock. And nobody sat there and explained exactly what schizophrenia is."

Relatives should receive a thorough explanation of the illness after they've recovered from the initial shock, because at that point, she said, "you're really not hearing anything—all you're hearing is that one word and you can't think of anything else." . . .

"Don't blame the families," Michael said adamantly, emphasizing the "psychological and emotional damage" such an approach causes. "You're making a bad situation terrible." His mother agreed[:] . . . "I didn't know anything about schizophrenia and I blamed myself totally and thoroughly. . . . I thought, I've done this to him."

In Washington the Lees spoke openly about their experiences with mental illness. But at home, Michael said, "I don't really talk about it at all. If I have to say anything, I just say that [Malcolm] has a brain disease."

"I've got relatives that I haven't even gotten in touch with," Donna said, "because I know . . . they have the general view that it's caused by your being a bad parent . . . and also they wouldn't want Malcolm near them."

"It's really helped all of us in our family, coming here," Donna commented. Learning that schizophrenia has a biological basis "made me feel better, made my ex-husband feel better. Even my youngest son is starting to accept it now. And it's made me feel easier with Malcolm to realize that this is just an illness."

Both Donna and Michael Lee had experienced many frustrations in trying to deal with Malcolm after his disorder became apparent, but they were also aware of how much more difficult it had been for him than for them.

"No matter what any of us has gone through, Malcolm has gone through ten times worse," said his mother. He's "tried to commit suicide I don't know how many times since he found out about [his diagnosis]. Because when you think you're different and people avoid you and some are even afraid of you . . . what kind of life have you got to look forward to?"

Still, Michael observed that his twin recently obtained his high school equivalency[:] . . . He's doing better than some people who aren't plagued with mental disease."

The experience of the Lees shows the importance of helping family members understand that there are biological causes of schizophrenia in order to spare them needless and crippling guilt. It illustrates how this knowledge can aid families to deal more effectively with the problems that a schizophrenic disorder creates and thus help both the person with the disorder and themselves.

SOURCE: Extracts adapted from *Psychiatric News*, March 17, 1989, pp. 2, 23.

current clinical condition, and other influences such as length of exposure to the pathological behavior.

2. The culture in which people live or from which they come plays a role in the amount of EE they express. In India, relatives show relatively lower levels of negative expressed emotion toward patients than that shown by relatives of Anglo-American patients in the United States. Mexican Americans who live in the United States but who follow traditional cultural practices also show typically lower levels of negative expressed emotion toward their relatives than do Anglo Americans (Jenkins et al., 1986; Leff & Vaughn, 1985). However, despite these cultural differences, the association between EE and elevated risk for relapse in schizophrenia has been replicated in many cultural settings (Hooley & Hiller, 1997).

3. EE research also has implications for patients who do not live with their families. High negative expressed emotion is associated with treatment that makes too many demands and high expectations for behavior in foster homes and day-treatment centers, which in turn may lead to high rates of relapse.

EE research has become a focus of controversy because some practitioners and family members believe that it blames families for the development of a family member's schizophrenia. The research should not be thought of in this way, however. It is focused not on the cause of schizophrenia, but on conditions that increase the chance of rehospitalization. The term *expressed emotion* became associated with a negative interactive style because early work showed how negative aspects of EE predicted a high relapse rate. Later research has shown that warmth and positive comments may help protect against relapse (Leff & Vaughn, 1985). The most important result of the work on EE has been the development of training programs to help families learn how to interact more effectively with family members when they return from the hospital after an acute episode of schizophrenia.

Table 11–8
Scales of Expressed Emotion

1. *Critical comments about family members.* Criticisms are rated on the basis of content and/or tone. Remarks are considered to be critical if there is a clear and unambiguous statement that the relative dislikes, disapproves of, or resents a behavior or characteristic. The dissatisfaction is expressed intensely and emphatically; the relative must use phrases such as "It annoys me" or "I don't like it." Vocal aspects of speech such as pitch, speed, inflection, and loudness are used to identify critical tone.

2. *Hostility.* Hostility is rated as present when the patient is attacked for what he or she *is* rather than for what he or she *does.* Negative feeling is generalized in such a way that it is expressed about the person him- or herself rather than about particular behaviors or attributes.

3. *Emotional overinvolvement.* Emotional overinvolvement is rated when there is either an exaggerated emotional response to the patient's illness, marked concern reflected in unusually self-sacrificing and devoted behaviors, or extremely overprotective behaviors.

4. *Warmth.* Ratings of warmth are based on the sympathy, concern, and empathy relatives show when talking about the patient, the enthusiasm for and interest in the patient's activities, the number of spontaneous expressions of affection, and the tone of voice used when talking about the patient.

5. *Positive remarks:* Positive remarks are statements that express praise, approval, or appreciation of the behavior or personality of the patient.

Source: Leff & Vaughn (1985). Reprinted with permission from the *British Journal of Psychiatry.*

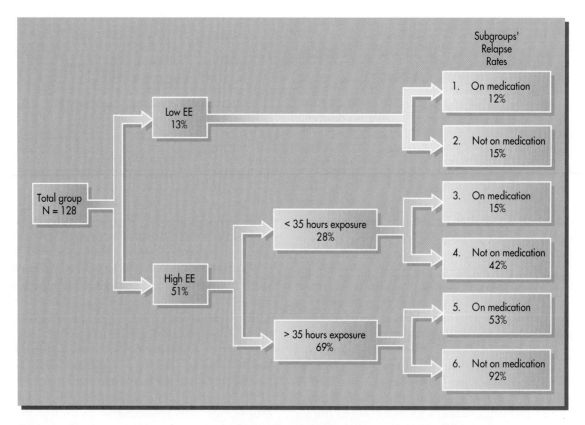

Figure 11–22   The relapse rates (after 9 months) of 128 patients affected by schizophrenia. Patients were grouped according to whether their families were high or low in negative expressed emotion (EE), the amount of time per week they were exposed to family members, and whether or not they were taking antipsychotic medication.

SOURCE: From Vaughn & Leff (1976), p. 132. © 1976 by the *British Journal of Psychiatry.* Reprinted by permission.

The term *expressed emotion* can also be misleading because research on negative EE may suggest that families should not express their emotional reactions to each other. What has been found is quite the reverse: in general, a high level of emotional expression in the sense of communicating feelings with other family members has been found to help prevent relapse (D. Spiegel & Wissler, 1986). This finding indicates that some expression of feelings creates a healthier emotional atmosphere for everyone and prevents the festering of anger and irritation that leads to full-blown emotional flare-ups.

Relapse Recognition Acquiring the ability to detect early warning signs of a potential relapse (i.e., **relapse recognition**) is an important skill for those affected by schizophrenia and for their family members. The cognitive and perceptual symptoms that appear or intensify when a relapse begins often happen in several stages. First comes a period of dysphoria (depressed mood), followed by increasing psychotic symptoms such as delusions. When these cognitive and perceptual symptoms appear or intensify, the person affected is likely to react by seeking help from a doctor or clinic for symptoms that can only be vaguely described. Effective coping may be made even more difficult by the stress caused by these vague forebodings. Fears and increased stress work together to hasten the relapse process.

Because an increase in symptoms is often accompanied by a decrease in insight, people affected by schizophrenia often conceal these symptom changes from others. Also, because many of these individuals continue to have some symptoms (called **residual symptoms**) even after their psychosis has improved, it is not always clear to others that the unusual behaviors observed are not just due to ongoing cognitive deficits or the side effects of antipsychotic medication. Because the characteristics of a beginning relapse may vary greatly from person to person, an effective approach is to train both patients and relatives to watch for changes similar to those that led to the initial diagnosis or to past relapses. One way to identify these changes is through a structured interview with the person with the schizophrenic diagnosis and with relatives. Sample questions asked of relatives might include:

> *"When did you decide he [or she] needed help?"*
>
> *"What was his [or her] behavior like at that time?"*
>
> *"Were there changes before that, even any that might not seem important?"*

(Adapted from Birchwood, 1992, p. 273)

Table 11-9 illustrates the kind of information obtained from one interview of this type. Having this sort of information available beforehand can help relatives or the affected person seek help more quickly.

Community Support

Because former patients may not have a family to return to, community-based support programs are needed. These programs—such as halfway houses or group homes, day-care facilities, and mental health clinics—can be sources of both treatment and practical help. Some of this support may be transitional, helping the discharged patient readjust to life in the community. Others may help people who are functioning at a low level to stay out of the hospital. Most support programs aim to help people maintain the same level of adaptive behavior they had at the time of their hospital discharge but do not expect to increase their level of performance.

Residential facilities such as halfway houses or group homes provide a sheltered setting that reduces the residents' need to cope with many of the social and financial stressors they would face if they were trying to function alone in the community. Ideally, these residential facilities would also offer a therapeutic, homelike environment that provided support for and protection of the residents, along with some structure for their day-to-day living. The staffs of these facilities can provide needed supervision to ensure that residents follow their antipsychotic medication plans. This is important in order to combat the tendency (discussed earlier) of many patients to stop taking their medications, thus increasing their chances of experiencing a relapse. In a properly functioning mental health system, these residential treatment facilities, in combination with crisis teams, should be able to take over the functions of the traditional psychiatric hospital. Unfortunately, these facilities are in very inadequate supply.

Another important aspect of community support is the **nonresidential support approach.** One of the most comprehensive of these approaches is the **assertive case management program,** which has repeatedly been shown to be effective. This form of case management ideally involves an interdisciplinary team of mental health professionals and social workers. The team aims to deliver all services as needed at any time, 24 hours a day, over a long period of time. Because each team has only a small number of patients with whom to deal, someone is available to monitor whether these patients are taking antipsychotic medication as prescribed, and whether symptoms of a relapse are present; to help them find housing, a job, or a sheltered workshop placement if suitable; and to assist them in dealing with the many stressful situations that arise in peoples' lives but with which those affected by schizophrenia are particularly ill-equipped to cope. Unfortunately this approach is usually not available because

Table 11–9	
Results of an Interview to Establish a Symptom Pattern Prior to a Relapse or Renewed Period of Psychosis	

Informant:	Parents
Date admitted:	5/25/90
Date of relapse:	March 1990 (first episode)
Change first noted:	October 1989

Early Sign	Period Prior to Relapse
Spending more time alone in bedroom Avoiding contact with family; talking less Stopped interests/hobbies—listening to music and rawing wildlife Stopped work—"people were picking on him" Accused friends of same	12–20 weeks
Neglecting personal hygiene—not washing or changing clothes Stood in front of mother naked Stealing money from family Irritable and argumentative toward family	8–12 weeks
Accusing family of reading his mind Said he thought the phone was being interfered with Laughing for no reason Very preoccupied with TV—sat and stared but did not appear to be watching	4–6 weeks

Key: Withdrawal/Dysphoria   •
       Disinhibition   •
       Incipient Psychosis   •

Source: Adapted from Birchwood (1992), p. 274.

it is often thought to be too costly. Because assertive case management avoids the costs of repeated hospitalizations, the costs may be less than are often supposed.

Assertive case management enhances the outcome for many individuals diagnosed with schizophrenia, especially those who have no family members available to provide support (Lehman et al., 1997). Overall, assertive case management has been shown to reduce the number of days of hospitalization and to increase patient and family satisfaction compared to standard community care. The assertive case management approach recognizes the strong evidence that managing schizophrenia with antipsychotic drugs alone is insufficient. Family interventions (where possible), community treatment facilities, skills training, and sheltered employment are all necessary to keep people with this disorder functioning. Probably the most important aspect of assertive case management is the continuity it provides. The case of "Sylvia Frumkin," discussed in Chapter 17, shows the very negative effects of a lack of coordination in the care for one individual affected by schizophrenia who experienced many relapses over a long period of time.

Combined Treatment Approaches

What is the optimal treatment program for schizophrenia? Current opinion suggests that initial treatment with antipsychotic drugs is important and that drug treatment should begin as soon as possible. However, if the psychotic symptoms subside and are no longer in evidence—as may be the case for some, but not the majority, of those affected by schizophrenia—there is some disagreement on whether medication should be discontinued, at least until new symptoms appear. Although antipsychotic medication, even with the use of the newest drugs, usually has undesirable side effects as well as unknown long-term effects from its use, new episodes of schizophrenic symptoms seem to have a negative long-term effect on a person's functioning, so a decrease or cessation of the antipsychotic medication is usually made with great care.

The recurrent nature of the psychosis, even with the use of medication, makes it clear that the preferred treatment includes both medication and interventions based on several psychological perspectives. Efforts to improve the patient's skills, to educate the patient and the patient's family about schizophrenia, to provide family support, and to provide a social safety net for all patients—especially the many individuals with a chronic form of the disorder—and their families are all important in assuring the best possible outcome. Unfortunately, such treatment combinations are very rare. However, even relatively simple family interventions as well as more comprehensive community treatment programs have been shown to be effective for preventing relapse and reducing the "revolving door syndrome" where the affected person shuttles back and forth between living in the community and hospitalization and experiences little coordination in treatment from different agencies and other service providers. The symptoms of a sizeable group of patients are not helped by medication, so for them the psychosocial treatment approach is even more important (Bustillo et al., 1999).

Most studies of treatment outcome focus on a lessening of symptoms. Although this is certainly important, psychosocial adjustment, particularly between relapses is also of great importance. Psychological therapies combined with medication have been shown to improve work performance and relationships with others for people living independently of their families (Hogarty et al., 1997a). Among patients living with their families, those who received psychologically based therapy were more competent and interpersonally effective. Also of importance was the lasting effect of these changes. While changes based on medication tended to last a year or less after hospitalization, changes associated with intensive psychosocial treatment combined with medication were still apparent after several years.

Long-Term Outcome Studies

There are two schools of thought regarding the outcome or prognosis for schizophrenia. One is derived from Kraepelin's original concept of dementia praecox (see Box 11-1). This view of schizophrenia as a nonreversible deteriorative disorder assumes that the prognosis is negative. The second viewpoint stems from Bleuler's concept of schizophrenia, which emphasizes the symptoms rather than the course of the disease. From this viewpoint, a certain number and kind of symptoms are necessary for the diagnosis, but the outcome may range from complete recovery to permanent and severe disability. Currently, a generally accepted view is that some individuals who have been affected by schizophrenia do fully recover, but that this percentage is low (Rund, 1990). Note that mental health professionals make a distinction between *recovered* and *cured*. Most of those in the mental health

field do not think that those who recover from schizophrenia can be "cured" because they believe that any person who has had the disorder must live with a vulnerability toward new psychotic episodes for the rest of his or her life.

One frequently asked question is, What happens to people who are diagnosed with schizophrenia? Whether or not there ever can be complete recovery from schizophrenia is a very important issue for individuals who have been diagnosed with the disorder and for their families. Studies that investigate outcomes for individuals a long time after the diagnosis is made can provide important answers to this question.

A review of studies of outcome at least 10 years after the diagnosis of schizophrenia showed that, as compared to the outcome for those with other mental illnesses, the outcome for people with a diagnosis of schizophrenia is generally poor (McGlashan, 1988). This review also confirmed that the course of schizophrenia should not be described as a continuous process of deterioration, as some researchers had thought. In most of the studies reviewed, the level of recovery achieved 5 to 10 years after the diagnosis was likely to continue unchanged in subsequent years. In addition, the diagnosis of schizophrenia was associated with an increased risk for physical illness, suicide, and premature death not associated with suicide.

Review of these long-term follow-up studies also showed that none of the treatment approaches used was consistently beneficial in promoting improvement. However, outcomes for individuals within each study varied greatly, ranging from continuous incapacity to recovery of the previous level of functioning. The important point to recognize is that a substantial number of patients—not just a few unusual cases—showed so much improvement that they no longer met the criteria for schizophrenia.

Because the diagnostic criteria for schizophrenia have changed in successive editions of the DSM, long-term follow-up studies are not useful unless more than diagnoses were recorded in medical records. Complete information about all symptoms exhibited by each patient is needed to allow patients diagnosed under the old systems to be rediagnosed on the basis of their original hospital records. In addition to the problem of inadequate hospital records, researchers in long-term follow-up studies can rarely interview or personally evaluate former patients because of the high costs involved. This problem introduces a good deal of potential error into the conclusions. However, despite these problems, long-term follow-up studies provide important information.

One example of a well-done follow-up study was focused on patients from a hospital in Vermont (Harding et al., 1987a, 1987b). In this study, long-term hospital patients who had participated in a comprehensive rehabilitation program and been deinstitutionalized 20 to 30 years earlier were rediagnosed from their records. Those whose records met the current diagnostic criteria for schizophrenia were traced, and they or their families were interviewed. Between half and two-thirds of these individuals had recovered or were significantly improved. Figure 11-23 shows how many were functioning at least fairly well.

Although many of the people in the study had made a poor adjustment for at least 5 years after the rehabilitation program, later on many had improved their level of functioning. Some of those who were classified as functioning well apparently did so only because they had learned to live with certain symptoms (another example of adapting to symptoms is given in the account that begins this chapter). These better-functioning people were employed and had good social relationships but still experienced some hallucinations or delusions. Other former patients in the better functioning group did not work but had developed extensive social networks. Because the patients in this study had been hospitalized for up to 25 years and were middle-aged when the rehabilitation program began, these results suggest that for younger, more recently hospitalized patients, the outcome might be even better.

One intriguing finding is that long-term outcome for schizophrenia seems to vary from country to country. This suggests that environmental factors may play a role. In 1967 the International Pilot Study of Schizophrenia, sponsored by the World Health Organization (WHO), unexpectedly found that people living outside Europe and the United States seemed to have a more favorable short- and medium-term outcome than people living within these areas, despite having had the same symptoms at the time of the original assessment. Although these conclusions were criticized by several other researchers, WHO has since carried out a series of international studies that have confirmed these findings (Sartorius et al., 1996). None of these studies has made clear the reasons for this difference, although they have provided many possible explanations—most of them relating to the differences in demands and stressors in industrialized societies as opposed to those in less-industrialized developing nations. Family structure, religious or cultural beliefs, and treatment approaches have also been considered. Because these differences in outcome have not yet been satisfactorily explained, WHO is currently involved in a follow-up study that will assess outcome 15 to 25 years after the original assessment.

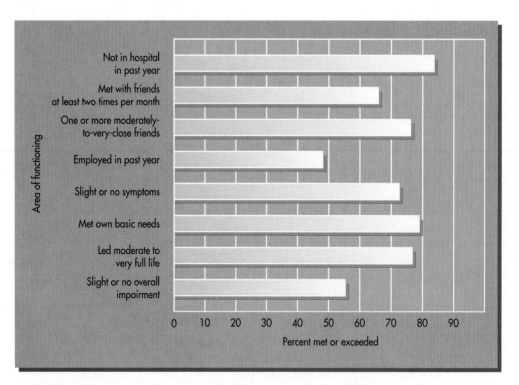

Figure 11-23 Many of the long-term hospital patients who had participated in a rehabilitation program and were followed up 20 to 30 years after they had been deinstitutionalized had at least a marginally adequate level of functioning. This figure shows the percentage of 168 patients studied who met or exceeded each criterion.

Source: Data from Harding et al. (1987a), pp. 718–726.

Other Psychotic Disorders

Several other psychotic disorders are described in DSM-IV. We will briefly describe three—schizoaffective disorder, delusional disorder, and shared psychotic disorder—in this section. The clinical characteristics of each, as described in DSM-IV, are shown in Table 11-1.

Schizoaffective Disorder

The behaviors and symptoms of some individuals do not fit neatly into either the category of major mood disorder or schizophrenia in the way Emil Kraepelin had divided them when he first described these disorders (see Box 11-1). Instead, they seem to have characteristics that belong in both of these categories. **Schizoaffective disorder** is the diagnostic category that deals with this "real-world messiness" observed by clinicians because it combines some of the characteristics of psychosis with those of a major mood disorder. In a study comparing three groups of outpatients who had the respective diagnoses of schizoaffective disorder, schizophrenia, and mood disorder, one study found that the patients with either schizoaffective disorder or depression were more depressed than those with schizophrenia and had less severe positive symptoms (Evans et al., 1999). Both the outpatients with schizophrenia and schizoaffective disorder had poorer neuropsychological performance (measures of psychomotor skills, attention, and learning and memory) than the depressed outpatients.

For schizoaffective disorder to be diagnosed, delusions or hallucinations must occur even when symptoms of depressed or manic mood are not present. In addition, there must be an uninterrupted period of illness in which either a major depressive episode, a manic episode, or an episode containing both mania and depression occur during the same period in which the person meets the criteria for schizophrenia. The mood characteristics must be present both during the acute, or active, periods of the disorder and in periods when the acute symptoms have subsided.

It is estimated that the lifetime prevalence of schizoaffective disorder is between 0.5% and 0.8%, somewhat less than the prevalence of schizophrenia. Like schizophrenia, the age at which schizoaffective disorder typically begins is late adolescence or early adulthood, but, in general, the outcome for those with schizoaffective disorder is more favorable than for those diagnosed with schizophrenia. Schizoaffective disorder may be thought of as part of the schizophrenic spectrum and affected by the same diathesis-stress model that is the basis of the interactional view of schizophrenia. It may occur in people who have a moderate vulnerability to schizophrenia and who, when they experience the stress of a major mood disorder, show some symptoms of schizophrenia as well (Siris & Lavin, 1995). Antipsychotic medication and lithium are the biological treatments most used if there are clear manic symptoms in the schizoaffective disorder. Based on this observation it might seem logical that if the person has prominent depressive symptoms, adding an antidepressant medication during the acute stage of the schizoaffective disorder would be helpful, but this is not true. During these periods of acute symptoms, schizoaffective disorder with depression as the predominant mood seems best treated by using the same antipsychotic medications used in schizophrenia. Only after the acute symptoms fade are antidepressants helpful. A long-term study of outcomes for patients who had been hospitalized more than 50 years ago showed that people diagnosed with schizoaffective disorder were likely to have a better outcome than those who were originally diagnosed with schizophrenia (Stephens et al., 1997).

Delusional Disorder

Delusional disorder is thought to be a very rare condition, and the cause is unknown. As DSM-IV defines **delusional disorder,** it includes what was formerly referred to as paranoia, but it is not limited to delusions with paranoid or accusatory elements. Whereas delusions in schizophrenia are generally bizarre (beliefs that the person's culture would regard as totally implausible), those in delusional disorder, though not accurate representations of the situation, reflect situations that could occur in real life. For delusional disorder to be diagnosed, the person must never have met the criteria for schizophrenia.

Typical delusions found in delusional disorder include being followed, poisoned, infected by disease, or loved by someone the person has never met (usually a person who is famous), or being especially chosen for some important mission such as introducing a new religious belief to the world. Generally these delusions are well systematized. This means that, apart from the particular topic involved in the delusion, the person's thinking seems to follow logical patterns and he or she is able to function at least relatively effectively in other areas of life. Examples of delusional disorder might include believing that a film star was in love with you even if you had never met that person, or quitting a job because of a belief that fumes in the office were causing lung cancer even though there was no objective evidence of this and other workers did not share the belief.

It is likely that the delusional disorder category consists of a group of disorders with different causes, although some researchers think that social isolation or stressful experiences such as immigration may be factors in most cases. Another possible cause is reduced blood flow to the temporal and parietal lobes of the brain (Wada et al., 1999b). Because delusional disorder is relatively rare, there are no controlled studies evaluating different treatments (Manschreck, 1995). Clomipramine has been found to be effective in some cases, especially those of the somatic type

(Wada et al., 1999a). Appropriate psychosocial treatments include cognitive therapy and general supportive therapy to enhance the fragile self-esteem common in these individuals (Alford & Beck, 1994). One group particularly affected by delusional disorder is older adults. This may be related to stress created by increasing sensory impairment such as hearing loss and feelings of social isolation (Maher & Spitzer, 1993).

Shared Psychotic Disorder

Shared psychotic disorder, sometimes referred to as *folie à deux*, was first described more than 100 years ago. It is probably very rare, and most information about it is available only from reports on single cases seen in clinical settings. In this disorder, delusions seem to have been transferred from one person to another. For example:

> *A middle-aged woman made recurrent visits to her doctor complaining about a vile body odor that she noticed despite diligent attempts to remove it by bathing and other cleansing measures. The physician could find no physical cause for the disorder, and neither she nor other medical personnel could smell the odor. The woman's husband also complained about the odor, which he claimed pervaded the room whenever his wife was present. After being reassured that the odor did not exist, the couple seemed somewhat relieved but a few weeks later started on another round of physician visits, again complaining about the wife's foul body odor.*

Typically, both people affected by the shared psychotic disorder, almost always from the same family, live together in relative social isolation. One seems to play a dominant role and the other—often of lower intelligence, more passive, and more gullible, and perhaps younger—takes on the beliefs of the first. Sometimes, if the two are separated, the secondary person may abandon the delusion. After separation, the dominant person may be treated with antipsychotic drugs and the secondary individual may be helped by psychological support to compensate for the loss of the partner. One study that examined over 90 cases of shared psychotic disorder in Japan found that the most common combinations of people involved were mother and child or a married couple. The dominant partner was most often diagnosed with schizophrenia and the submissive partner as experiencing a paranoid reaction (Kashiwase & Kato, 1997). When the shared delusion includes a religious delusion of some form, there can be a high risk of a fatal or near-fatal outcome (Kraya & Patrick, 1997).

Chapter Summary

PSYCHOTIC DISORDERS

A **psychotic disorder** has symptoms that involve alterations in perceptions, thoughts, or consciousness. These alterations are called hallucinations or delusions. Schizophrenia is the most important subgroup of psychotic disorders. Other DSM-IV categories of psychotic disorders are schizophreniform disorder, schizoaffective disorder, delusional disorder, brief psychotic disorder, shared psychotic disorder, and psychotic disorder related to general medical conditions or brought on by drug abuse, effects of medication, or exposure to toxins.

SCHIZOPHRENIA

Schizophrenia is a debilitating disorder affecting more than 1% of the population. A DSM-IV diagnosis of **schizophrenia** requires that the disturbance last at least 6 months, with at least 1 month of an active phase that includes at least two positive symptoms or one positive and one negative symptom. There must also be a decline in social or occupational function.

DSM-IV Subtypes of Schizophrenia DSM-IV divides schizophrenia into several subtypes: **paranoid, catatonic, disorganized, undifferentiated,** and **residual.** Schizophrenia as defined in the DSM-IV probably includes several different disorders.

Positive and Negative Symptoms In order to investigate differences in subgroups of persons with schizophrenia, researchers have divided symptoms into two categories, *positive* and *negative*. Delusions, hallucinations, disordered speech, and disorganized behavior are all categorized as **positive symptoms. Delusions** are faulty interpretations of reality. **Hallucinations** are faulty perceptions that can be associated with any of the senses; auditory hallucinations are the most common type. **Negative symptoms** are behavior deficits, including flattened affect, poverty of speech, and lack of motivation or directedness.

WHAT CAUSES SCHIZOPHRENIA?

The causes of schizophrenia are not known.

Genetic Factors Genetic factors seem important, but the genes involved have not been reliably identified. It is likely that heredity in schizophrenia is best understood using a multifactorial **polygenic model.**

Prenatal Factors Prenatal factors such as viral disease of the mother during pregnancy (especially in the second trimester), the prenatal environment, and birth injuries seem to increase the risk of schizophrenia.

The Neurodevelopmental Model of Schizophrenia During the second trimester of pregnancy, brain cells migrate and establish connections with other neurons. If neurons fail to migrate properly, the process of **synaptic pruning** that normally begins in late childhood may also be abnormal and result in problems of cognitive function. Prenatal developmental abnormalities are often reflected in **minor physical anomalies,** which tend to be more frequent in those who develop schizophrenia. Enlarged cerebral ventricles have also been identified in some cases of schizophrenia, as have biochemical abnormalities in the brain's neurotransmitter system. These abnormal neurotransmitter functions have led to the **dopamine hypothesis.**

Schizophrenic Spectrum Disorders Several different disorders are more common in extended families in which cases of schizophrenia occur. These **schizophrenic spectrum disorders,** which may be of the same biological origin as schizophrenia, include *schizotypal personality disorder, paranoid personality disorder, schizoid personality disorder,* and *schizoaffective disorder.*

STUDYING VULNERABILITY TO SCHIZOPHRENIA

Family Studies Although they provide some information about the genetic transmission of schizophrenia, **family studies** do not separate out environmental and genetic effects. Family studies sometimes show **assortative mating** patterns, meaning that people tend to choose mates who are more similar to them genetically than might occur by chance.

Twin Studies By studying pairs of MZ and DZ twins in which at least one twin has been diagnosed with schizophrenia, **twin studies** help researchers do a better job of understanding the effects of heredity as opposed to those caused by environmental factors.

Adoption Studies Another way to study the effects of heredity is in **adoption studies,** usually those in which the outcomes of being adopted into healthy families are compared for children whose biological mothers had been diagnosed with schizophrenia, and for children whose biological mothers had no such diagnosis.

VULNERABILITY AND THE ENVIRONMENT

The **diathesis-stress theory** predicts that only people with some genetic vulnerability will develop schizophrenia.

Vulnerability and Adoptive Family Characteristics Adoption studies show that the environment in the adoptive family is important in determining whether adoptive children with a schizophrenic biological parent will develop symptoms of schizo-

phrenia or one of the spectrum disorders. The less the stress in the adoptive family, the less likely the child is to develop one of these disorders.

Community Factors and Stress In many studies, the diagnosis of schizophrenia is found to be more common among people of low socioeconomic status (SES) than those of higher SES. The **social selection theory** assumes that the decreased coping ability associated with schizophrenia causes people to drift to a lower SES group. The **increased-stress theory** argues that people living in low SES groups experience more stress, and therefore those who are vulnerable are more likely to develop symptoms. Some support has been found for each theory.

High-Risk Studies and the Search for Markers **High-risk studies** focus either on children at risk because of family history, birth complications, or negative environmental factors; or else on groups who show potential signs of mental illness before adulthood. The aim of high-risk studies is to identify markers of the disorder before it becomes apparent.

High-Risk Markers of Attention and Cognition Problems of attention and cognition seem to be markers of potential disorder especially for those at high risk for schizophrenia. Two measures of attention that may identify markers of schizophrenia are the **Continuous Performance Test (CPT)** and eye tracking of **smooth-pursuit eye movements.**

THERAPEUTIC APPROACHES

Treatment with antipsychotic drugs is the first step in treating schizophrenia, although the addition of psychosocial treatment is recognized as important in preventing relapse and improving social functioning. Treatment as soon as the first signs of schizophrenic process occurs is now recognized as very important in later outcome. Researchers are developing assessment tools to indicate early signs of increased risk.

Antipsychotic Drugs Traditional antipsychotic drugs sometimes cause **tardive dyskinesia** and other involuntary motions, in addition to other negative side effects, which may be irreversible. The newer drug clozapine is less likely to cause these problems but it can have dangerous side effects. Still newer antipsychotic drugs seem to have fewer harmful side effects but their effectiveness needs further assessment. One problem with medication is that many people with schizophrenia stop taking it, either because of negative side effects or because of the cognitive impairments caused by the disorder.

Skills Training People with chronic schizophrenia are likely to be deficient in generic social skills and social perception abilities. Cognitive skills training is aimed at decreasing cognitive deficits in processing information and attention. Self-care and symptom identification skills can help keep people with schizophrenia out of the hospital. Cognitive and relaxation techniques are used to help people with schizophrenia identify and respond better to stressful situations.

Family Programs Family education programs are effective in preventing the need for rehospitalization. These programs can help reduce harmful **expressed emotion** (**EE**) and negative feelings about the patient by increasing the family's understanding of schizophrenia. They also help the patient and family improve their **relapse recognition** skills so that additional treatment or changes in medication can be sought to help prevent a worsening of symptoms or the need for rehospitalization.

Community Support Especially for patients without family members to provide support upon discharge from hospitalization, residential facilities such as halfway houses or group homes, day-care facilities, and mental health clinics can provide both treatment and practical help. The most important nonresidential support may be assertive case management by a constantly available interdisciplinary team of professionals. Unfortunately, this approach is not always available.

Combined Treatment Approaches Optimal treatment approaches usually combine medication with other treatments such as those described previously.

LONG-TERM OUTCOME STUDIES

Follow-up studies of those diagnosed with schizophrenia a number of years ago show that a few people with this diagnosis seem to regain or nearly regain their previous level. They also show that the deteriorative effects of schizophrenia seem to plateau after 5 or 10 years; from that time on, the person's condition does not worsen. Some individuals are able to function reasonably well by adapting to their symptoms.

OTHER PSYCHOTIC DISORDERS

Schizoaffective Disorder A **schizoaffective disorder** is one that combines delusions or hallucinations with symptoms of depression or manic mood. It may be part of the schizophrenic spectrum disorder group.

Delusional Disorder The difference between delusions in schizophrenia and in **delusional disorder** is that, in the latter diagnosis, the delusions are less bizarre than those seen in schizophrenia, and while not accurate could possibly reflect situations in real life. These delusions are usually systematized, or related only to a particular topic.

Shared Psychotic Disorder A rare disorder, shared psychotic disorder usually involves two people, most often from the same family, who share the same delusional beliefs. One of those affected is the originator of these beliefs; the other seems to be a passive follower but still holds firmly to the same delusions.

Key Terms

Psychotic disorder, p. 350
Schizophrenia, p. 350
Paranoid schizophrenia, p. 354
Catatonic schizophrenia, p. 354
Disorganized schizophrenia, p. 354
Schizophrenic disorder of the residual
    type, p. 354
Positive symptoms, p. 354
Negative symptoms, p. 354
Delusions, p. 355
Hallucinations, p. 356
Disordered speech, p. 357
Perseverative speech, p. 357
Disorganized behavior, p. 358
Index case, p. 359
Monogenic model, p. 359
Polygenic model, p. 362

Multifactorial polygenic models, p. 362
Neurodevelopmental model of
    schizophrenia, p. 364
Synaptic pruning, p. 365
Minor physical anomalies, p. 365
Dopamine hypothesis, p. 368
Cerebral ventricles, p. 368
Schizophrenic spectrum disorders, p. 369
Family studies, p. 370
Assortative mating, p. 371
Twin studies, p. 371
Dizygotic (DZ) twins, p. 371
Monozygotic (MZ) twins, p. 371
Adoption studies, p. 372
Diathesis-stress theory of schizophrenia,
    p. 372
Vulnerability, p. 373

Social selection theory, p. 373
Increased-stress theory, p. 373
High-risk studies, p. 375
Continuous Performance Test (CPT),
    p. 377
Smooth-pursuit eye movements, p. 377
Prodromal symptoms, p. 378
Tardive dyskinesia, p. 380
Expressed emotion (EE), p. 384
Relapse recognition, p. 387
Residual symptoms, p. 387
Assertive case management program,
    p. 387
Schizoaffective disorder, p. 390
Delusional disorder, p. 391
Shared psychotic disorder
    (*folie à deux*), p. 391

Cognitive Impairment Disorders

Bob Oxley, aged 39, had been a long-distance runner and, until recently, seemed to be in excellent condition. One morning he awoke with the worst headache he had ever had, became too nauseated to eat, and lay in bed caught between dreams and delirium. After a great effort, he dragged himself to his office, but the pain intensified and he could barely call his wife to take him home. When she got him to the hospital, a CT scan detected a white haze of blood in the fluid-filled spaces around his brain. Swollen tissue cast a shadow across both of his frontal lobes. A dye injected into his blood vessels filled a grapelike enlargement that ballooned out from a weakened artery in the front of his brain. Blood had leaked from a tiny tear in this bulge, causing the severe headache, and then clotted—preventing Bob from dying. However, he was left with a condition called aphasia, which meant that he had a problem finding words and expressing what he might want to say. The aphasia resulted from an injury to the language center in his left frontal lobe. When Bob wanted to refer to his doctor, he said "blotcher." When asked to name 10 animals, he could not utter the names of more than two ("dog" and "cat"). When asked about his work, he said that he worked with "climates" (he was a stockbroker and worked with his clients). In most cases, Bob did not look distressed after his errors.

Ann Martin used to have an enviable memory. Now at age 58, she forgets recent events and shows poor judgment (she recently threw out a pair of valuable sterling silver salt and pepper shakers). Because she can no longer balance her household budget, plan her meals, or take care of herself in other ways, she now lives in a retirement home, even though she is still relatively young. Her condition has been diagnosed as Alzheimer's disease, which is caused by physical degeneration of the brain. This disease results in loss of intellectual ability and changes in personality and behavior. ■

These two cases show both similarities and differences. They are different because Ann Martin's behavior was the result of a deterioration of brain tissue as the result of a disease process that affected many aspects of her intellectual functioning. Bob Oxley's problem was due to an injury that affected a specific brain function—his ability to translate thoughts into speech. Despite these differences, these two people are similar in that they are each experiencing the effects of changes in the brain.

DSM-IV categorizes mental disorders in terms of clusters of behavioral and psychological features that are associated with distress or disability. The causes of the disorders are usually either unknown or only imperfectly understood. For example, while there is some evidence of central nervous system dysfunction in schizophrenia, affective disorders, and obsessive-compulsive and other disorders, not enough is known to say that they are organically caused. On the basis of future research, organic factors may come to be regarded as defining features of these disorders and others, or they may be ruled out as specific causes. In contrast, the disorders we review in this chapter compose one of the few groupings in DSM-IV that involve both specific behavioral symptoms and known causative factors. In each of them there are characteristic disturbances of consciousness, memory, and/or other cognitive functioning in association with a medical condition or substance (injected, ingested, or inhaled) that is causally related to the disturbance. Establishing the link between the behavioral symptoms and the medical condition or substance is the key element in diagnosing the cognitive impairments we will be describing.

Our knowledge of the conditions that cause these disorders and their specific effects on brain function is increasing, not only because of new tools for study of the living brain, but also because of new information about the interactions between organic functioning, personal characteristics, and environmental variables. Despite these new techniques and this new knowledge, for the many people like Bob Oxley and Ann Martin who develop organic brain disorders, their lives will never be the same again.

The Brain: An Interactional Perspective

The brain is an organ, like the kidney, the heart, or the liver, and organs are known to fail because of hereditary factors as well as environmental ones. Yet to believe that the brain is merely a series of chemical reactions is to remove humans from any effects of their environment and their own actions. In fact, some brain functions are "hardwired" in advance of birth, and some are designed to be shaped by experience.

At one time the prevailing view held that the brain grew through childhood, took its final shape during adolescence, and then slowly aged. New work shows, however, that each area of the brain develops in unique ways throughout life. While some parts of the brain deteriorate, most brain cells continue to form new connections.

Three areas of brain research seem especially pertinent to an understanding of both normal and abnormal behavior:

1. Specifying how the brain grows and maintains itself
2. Identifying the mechanisms by which the brain acquires, stores, and uses information at the cellular and molecular levels, as well as at the level of behavior and social interaction
3. Making clear the role played by the brain in monitoring and regulating internal bodily processes

In the past, people looked for physical causes for all forms of maladaptive behavior. If people behaved in odd ways, it was because there was something physically wrong with them. People could be "born criminals" or have "bad blood." Then scientists became aware of the psychological and social causes of behavioral problems. As a result, physical explanations came to be seen as inadequate, and even as somewhat simple-minded. Today, however, psychologists are developing a more complete picture of how intertwined the psychological, social, and physical domains of human behavior are.

We learn social skills, interact with others, and acquire personal attitudes within a framework of physical development. Human functioning is influenced by organic events that occur during intrauterine life, the birth process, and the long period of development after birth. The brain may become damaged suddenly—for example, when a person has a stroke or receives a head injury in an accident (see Box 12-1). In other cases, certain diseases cause slow deterioration in the brain. These changes in the brain's physical nature, whether they happen quickly or slowly and whether they involve large or small areas, are often the cause of unusual behavior. Damage to the brain can lead to a wide variety of behavioral problems, depending on what part of the brain is affected and the extent of the damage.

What is known today about brain disorders is consistent with what we have said throughout this text about the interactions between personal and environmental factors, vulnerability, and stress. It would simplify the lives of clinicians and researchers if they could assume that certain types of maladaptation were due solely to personal variables, others solely to physical factors, and still others solely to situational pressures. Unfortunately, such assumptions would be incorrect. Behavior is a joint product of individual differences and environmental variables. The particular mix of these variables determines how people

Case Study

Box 12-1

Sarah Fell and Her Life Was Changed

One April day 10-year-old Sarah Monahan lost control of her bike and fell. She landed on a spiked piece of farm equipment and a 2-inch spike punctured her left temple. Today, there is only a small scar, nothing to show the quarter-size hole where the spike shattered Sarah's skull and drove bone splinters into her brain. The accident left Sarah permanently brain-damaged, emotionally like a 2-year-old, and academically at the third-grade level (see Figures 12-1 and 12-2). Her moods change in an instant, and she is increasingly aggressive toward her family and classmates. Her parents have been advised to lock up scissors and knives. Sarah once pushed her 2-year-old brother into a rock pile, cutting his head and requiring a trip to the emergency room. She had no concept she had done anything wrong. Sometimes Sarah hears voices. One evening while the family was watching television, she stood up and yelled, "If you say that again, I'll kill you." No one had said a word.

Based on *Seattle Times,* March 15, 1991.

Figure 12-1 Sarah's external wounds have healed, and she appears unaffected by her injury.

SOURCE: Jim Berry/*Seattle Times*

Figure 12-2 Sarah and her teacher rejoice at Sarah's success in completing a computer problem.

SOURCE: Jim Berry/*Seattle Times*

act and what they think about. There is no standard type of psychological effect for each type and degree of brain defect.

Vulnerability to Brain Disorders

Not only are there many differences in the actual damage to the brain that occurs in different individuals through injury or disease, but the same amount of brain damage or deterioration can have varying effects in different people. To some degree, these effects depend on each individual's personality and abilities and the social supports available to cushion the organic blow. Thus there are many cases in which the psychological and behavioral effects of brain injuries and tumors do not conform to what would be expected on the basis of the amount of brain damage suffered.

The following are among the factors that influence vulnerability to brain damage and brain disorders:

1. *Age.* The age at which a brain condition develops can have both long- and short-term effects. Although in some instances an infant brain is better able to compensate for an injury than an adult brain, the infant brain may also be more susceptible to a variety of pathological conditions. Many behavioral deficits that are caused by damage to the brain in infancy are not noticed until considerably later.

2. *Social support.* The presence of caring, accepting people on which the individual can rely usually eases adjustment to a brain condition. Social isolation, on the other hand, increases cognitive deficits and thus, abnormal behavior.
3. *Stress.* The greater the stress, the greater both the cognitive and the behavioral deficits will be. Elderly people with chronic brain conditions often show marked deterioration following a piling up of stressful life events such as retirement or the death of a spouse.
4. *Personality factors.* It is a common clinical observation that some people react with intense anxiety, feelings of depersonalization, paranoid thinking, defensiveness, and hallucinations to any condition that causes even mild clouding of consciousness and impairment of cognitive and perceptual functioning.
5. *Physical condition.* The site of the brain disorder, the rate of onset, and the duration of the disorder all influence the clinical picture. In addition, the individual's general level of health plays a role in his or her adjustment.

An individual's psychological state and social relationships at the onset of an organic condition can influence the impact of the condition on his or her behavior. A person with a stable personal life, for example, usually responds differently, and more adaptively, to treatment than does someone in the throes of marital turmoil or financial reversal. When personal problems complicate an organic condition, both medical and psychological treatment may be necessary. In addition to its personal effects, impairment of brain function has a profound influence on interpersonal relationships. For example, people with epilepsy suffer from undesirable social consequences as well as from the seizures themselves.

Because determining the presence and extent of brain damage is complicated by the need to isolate its effects from those caused by personal and social factors, clinicians must avoid overly simple diagnoses. Clearly, a person who is noticeably disoriented, has trouble solving problems, and displays shallow or very changeable moods and emotions is suffering from some sort of behavioral problem. But the primary aspects of the diagnosis—an estimate of the roles played by organic damage, personality, and life stress in causing the disturbance—are not so easily determined.

Assessing Brain Damage

While the list of rare brain disorders is long, many brain disorders that have major impacts on thought and behavior are fairly common. For example, brain injuries, epilepsy, and acute cerebrovascular diseases are more common than schizophrenia and panic disorders (Silver et al., 1990). Consequently, the task of correctly identifying conditions that might be due to brain malfunction is an important

one. This task is complicated by the fact that damage to a particular area of the brain can have diverse effects. This point is illustrated in Table 12-1, which lists symptoms often seen in patients who have disorders related to malfunction of the brain's frontal lobes. Some of these symptoms are evident in the following case:

> *Mrs. L., a 58-year-old housewife, was brought to the hospital by her daughter, who reported that for the past year her mother has shown a decreased interest in caring for her house and personal needs. The patient lived alone in a rural area with few neighbors. The daughter, during an infrequent visit, had noticed a change in her mother's behavior; she showed a lack of interest in conversation and had an unkempt appearance, with a lack of concern about family affairs and total neglect of personal and household cleanliness. Neighbors had noticed that the patient had stopped attending church, did very little shopping, and no longer made social visits. On examination at hospital admission, Mrs. L. was awake but markedly apathetic. She offered no spontaneous conversation and answered all questions with only single-word responses. She walked with a slow, shuffling gait and had several episodes of incontinence. A computerized tomography (CT) scan revealed a large frontal lobe cyst. Surgery to remove the cyst produced a marked behavior reversal. Within 2 weeks, the patient was walking well, was conversing spontaneously, and was no longer apathetic or incontinent.*

A variety of procedures are used in assessing the extent of brain damage or deterioration. In addition to a general physical evaluation, clinical tests may include a mental status examination, neuropsychological testing, traditional X-rays and scans that provide information on the brain's soft tissues and chemical activity.

Mental Status Examination and Neuropsychological Testing The **mental status examination** consists of an interview, which is useful for clinical observation as well as

Table 12-1
Personality and Cognitive Changes in Patients With Disorders Related to Frontal Lobe Malfunctions

- Apathy; loss of interest in social interaction
- Inattention to personal appearance
- Boisterousness; profanity; increased volume of speech
- Irritability; violence
- Increased risk-taking
- Overeating; overdrinking
- Reduced capacity to use language, symbols, and logic
- Diminished ability to concentrate
- Loss of orientation to time or place

Source: Adapted from Silver, Hales, & Yudofsky (1990).

for evaluating any statements the individual might make. As we noted in Chapter 3, the mental status examination provides information about a patient's current behavior and thought. Its questions and tasks deal with orientation to reality, memory, and the ability to follow directions. Table 12-2 gives examples of questions and tasks used to detect brain disorders.

The mental status examination is often supplemented by psychological testing and a neurological examination. Clinicians use the mental status examination to elicit the following information:

1. Level of consciousness—how aware is the individual of what is going on?
2. General appearance (behavior, dress, cooperation)
3. Attention span
4. Orientation with regard to time and place
5. Short-term memory (events of past life or common knowledge)
6. Language (spontaneous speech, comprehension, repetition, reading, writing)
7. Stream of thought—do the individual's ideas fit together logically?
8. Mood
9. Judgment and insight

As we saw in Chapter 3, use of the mental status examination is not limited to cases of suspected brain damage. It is employed generally to describe patients' behavior at the time they are seen clinically. It provides an objective record that is important for diagnosing and assessing the course of a disorder and its subsequent response to treatment. Careful and precise descriptions of behavior, without speculations or inferences, are necessary in recording the results of the mental status examination. These results are interpreted in conjunction with information about a patient's history, data from a physical examination, and the results of laboratory tests.

Neuropsychologists use various techniques to assess brain damage and its cause. As we mentioned in Chapter 2, **neuropsychology** is a relatively new branch of psychology that deals with relationships between behavior and the condition of the brain. Clinical neuropsychologists are particularly interested in the effects of brain lesions on behavior. **Neuropsychological tests** are used to assess impairment in such areas as awareness of and responsiveness to sensory stimulation, ability to understand verbal communication and to express oneself, and emotional expression. Neuropsychological testing is sensitive to impaired functioning of various regions of the brain.

Brain Imaging Progress in constructing tests to measure disturbances in various regions of the brain has been limited by the lack of direct information about what actually goes on in the brain. As we have seen in previous chapters, new technology using a variety of **brain imaging** techniques is rapidly changing this situation. This technology helps clarify the relationship between damage to specific regions of the brain and the effects of the damage on psychological functioning. Studies using both brain imaging techniques and neuropsychological tests have often found that conclusions drawn from them often are comparable (Ritchie & Richards, 1999). This chapter, which focuses on brain disorders, is a good place to review some of the information about scanning techniques. Figure 12-3 shows the basic principles involved in three of the most widely used scanning techniques—computerized tomography (CT scan), positron emission tomography (PT scan), and magnetic resonance imaging (MRI).

The CT scan provides images that show where injuries, deterioration, or enlargement occurred. The PT scan allows researchers to visualize the activity of different parts

Table 12-2

Questions and Tasks Used in Mental Status Examinations for the Assessment of Brain Disorders

Types of Question or Task	Examples
Time orientation	"What year is this?"; "What day is today?"
Place orientation	"What city are we in?"; "What state are we in?"
Immediate memory	"Repeat these words: ball, flag, tree."
Attention	"Subtract 7 from 100. Continue subtracting 7s."
Recall	"Repeat the words [ball, flag, tree] I mentioned earlier" [a few minutes after the original presentation].
Naming	"What is this?" [Show pencil, watch, etc.]
Repetition	"Repeat: East, west, home's best."
Following command	"Take this pencil and put it over there on the table."
Visual construction	"Copy this figure." [Show triangle and then two intertwined pentagons]

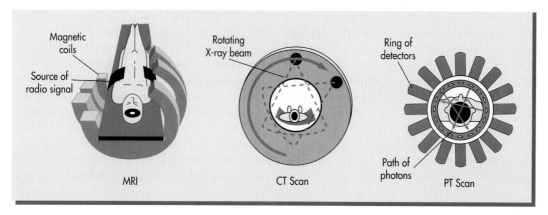

Figure 12-3 Each of the three major scanning techniques used to study the brain produces images in a different way, and as the text explains, each type of scan may have somewhat different uses.

Magnetic resonance imaging (MRI) uses energy in the form of radio waves. After the patient is placed inside the imaging device, a strong magnetic field is created. Under these conditions, atoms in each type of tissue resonate differently. A computer uses these resonance patterns to recreate a composite picture, or scan.

Computerized tomography (CT) operates through a narrowly focused X-ray that is rotated rapidly around the patient's body as the patient lies in the scanner. A computer then builds images of thin slices of the body from measures of the radiation passing through the patient as the X-ray source moves from one location to another.

In order to use positron emission tomography (PT) scanning procedures, radioactive chemicals must first be injected into the patient. As these chemicals are metabolized and move through the patient's body, they emit positively charged electrons, or positrons. Electrons and positrons then collide and emit pairs of photons that create signals by hitting detectors in the apparatus. These signals are then converted by a computer into a map of chemical activity.

of the human brain. Much as weather maps show various levels of rainfall, a PT scan shows the levels of glucose metabolism in different brain areas as they vary with the person's mental state and behavior. Thus the PT scan enables scientists to study biochemical changes that could never be charted before. The PT scan is the most elegant of the available imaging techniques because of its sensitivity and flexibility. PT scans permit the assessment of metabolic activity and the measurement of neurotransmitter function.

Magnetic resonance imaging (MRI) uses arrays of sensitive detectors placed over the head to locate and measure precise sites of neural activity deep within the brain's furrows and creases. Both the MRI and the CT scan provide visualizations of brain anatomy and possible structural abnormalities. Unlike the CT, which is limited to imaging brain regions in a transverse plane, the MRI can image in all planes.

The Brain and Cognitive Impairment

Many conditions marked by cognitive impairment are basically outgrowths of bodily conditions. From this perspective, the observed psychological syndromes are secondary to physical factors. A **syndrome** consists of symptoms that tend to appear together. These symptoms include disturbances in perception, memory, imagination, thought processing, problem-solving skills, and judgment. The most common syndromes involve delirium, dementia, amnesia, intoxication, and withdrawal. This chapter emphasizes dis-

orders marked by delirium, dementia, and amnesia; Chapter 13 focuses on intoxication and withdrawal.

Delirium affects a person's state of consciousness or attention, whereas *dementia* refers to loss of intellectual ability. Delirium is often a short-term condition that is reversible; dementia generally implies a nonreversible and often progressive condition. Amnestic disorders are memory disturbances due either to a medical condition or the effects of a substance (e.g., abuse of an illegal drug or a medication).

Delirium

The symptoms of **delirium** include relatively global cognitive impairment, disorientation, and confusion. In delirium, an individual has difficulty mobilizing, focusing, shifting, and sustaining attention. A wide and changeable range of strong emotions that do not seem related to environmental events may be evident.

DSM-IV's diagnostic criteria for delirium are as follows:

1. Disturbances of consciousness (e.g., reduced awareness of what is going on in the environment) and reduced ability to focus, sustain, or shift attention
2. Cognitive deficits and perceptual disturbances (e.g., memory loss and disorientation)
3. The development of symptoms over a short period of time (usually from hours to days), and fluctuation during the course of a day

4. Evidence that the condition is caused by the direct physiological consequences of a medical condition or intoxication attributable to a psychoactive substance such as alcohol

Delirium can occur as a result of either an acute or a chronic brain condition. There are four general organic causes of delirium:

1. Brain disease (e.g., an infection or tumor)
2. A disease or infection in another part of the body that affects the brain (e.g., a metabolic condition)
3. Intoxication (e.g., with alcohol)
4. Withdrawal from a substance to which an individual is addicted (e.g., drugs)

Delirium generally accompanies some other serious physical problem; about 10% of hospitalized medical and surgical patients (especially those who are elderly) become delirious (Lipowski, 1987). A person who is hospitalized after a heart attack may become delirious because the amount of oxygen the brain receives could depend on whether the patient was sitting up or lying down. Inadequate excretion of body wastes can also cause delirium. For example, if the kidneys fail to function, the toxins that are usually filtered out by the kidneys and excreted in the urine will accumulate in the bloodstream and the blood will have less room for oxygen. As a result of such physical disturbances, the brain will begin to starve for oxygen, and symptoms of delirium may occur. The symptoms generally disappear shortly after the precipitating condition has been corrected.

Psychological stress, sleep and sensory deprivation, prolonged immobilization, and severe fatigue are likely to contribute to the onset of delirium and to increase its severity. It is believed that a general derangement of brain metabolism, coupled with an imbalance in the neurotransmitters, underlies all cases of delirium.

Although everyone has the potential to develop delirium, there appear to be wide variations in susceptibility. Some people become delirious in response to metabolic changes or medications that do not produce delirium in others, whereas others fail to become delirious under metabolic conditions that are likely to produce delirium in most people. The incidence of delirium is highest among old people. It is not known to what extent this increase is a function of age itself rather than the frequency of brain and systemic disease in old age.

Patients with brain lesions are especially liable to develop delirium, as are people with long histories of alcohol or drug addiction. Delirium following surgery—either immediately afterward or after a lucid period of several days—is common and seems to be due to the physical stress of the surgery itself and to the psychological stress of the surgery and postoperative period. In a sense, delirium is a threshold phenomenon; that is, each individual may have a specific threshold for this condition. Preexisting brain damage, addiction, and certain chronic medical disorders may bring people close to this threshold even if they do not cross it; relatively small metabolic changes may then push the patient over the threshold.

Delirium Tremens

One of the most dramatic examples of delirium can be seen in an acute brain condition called **delirium tremens** (or "the DTs") that may sometimes result from excessive alcohol consumption. People with the DTs may be unable to follow directions like "Stick out your tongue" or to attend to events going on around them. In addition to delirium, the DTs are characterized by tremors and visual hallucinations that result in a state of terror.

The symptoms of delirium tremens usually are not evident until after a person has stopped drinking. Several aspects of the mechanism that causes its symptoms are not well understood, but the DTs seem to be due to the prolonged interference of alcohol with the metabolism of the brain. The condition occurs in about 5% of alcoholics. Regardless of the cause (alcohol, infection, or something else), diffuse slowing of brain wave patterns is a regular finding.

Delirium tremens can last for a week or longer, and the affected person usually must be hospitalized. During an episode of the DTs, the patient's physical condition deteriorates and he or she becomes highly susceptible to infections. Tranquilizing drugs and a quiet and orderly environment are essential, since even routine conversations among hospital personnel may frighten the patient and heighten his or her hallucinatory experiences. Renewed ability to sleep and rest usually indicates that an episode of DTs is coming to an end. However, recovery depends on restoration of metabolic equilibrium. In some cases equilibrium cannot be restored and death occurs.

Dementia

> *I fear I am not in my perfect mind.*
> *Methinks I should know you, and know this man;*
> *Yet I am doubtful; for I am mainly ignorant*
> *What place this is; and all the skill I have*
> *Remembers not these garments; nor I know not*
> *Where I did lodge last night. . . .*
> (Shakespeare, King Lear, Act IV, Scene 7)

The onset of King Lear's madness shows the symptoms of dementia that people have witnessed for centuries. The essential feature of **dementia,** or *brain deterioration,* is a gradual loss of intellectual abilities that is sufficient to interfere with social or occupational functioning. Memory impairment, decline in ability to exercise good

Figure 12-4 Dementia was not a major public health concern prior to the twentieth century because few people lived beyond the age of 75, and dementia is largely a problem associated with advanced age. Today, more than 50% of the entire U.S. population reaches 75 years of age, and 25% live to be 85. A large number of older people in nursing homes have some degree of dementia. The economic impact of dementia is great, running into the billions of dollars each year.

judgment and engage in abstract thinking, loss of self-control, confusion, language and motor problems, and personality changes also occur. Dementia may be progressive, static, or even reversible if an effective treatment is available. Because individuals with dementia are not able to think clearly and often have difficulty making rational judgments, they are particularly vulnerable to physical, psychological, and social stress. Individuals with dementia are more likely than other people to experience delirium.

The onset of dementia is insidious, and the course of the disorder is usually gradual. The term *senile dementia* is often used to refer to the condition when it occurs in people over 65 (see Figure 12-4). Autopsies show that most senile dementias have the characteristics of *Alzheimer's disease*, which will be discussed later in the chapter. If dementia occurs in younger individuals, it is termed *presenile dementia*. In people with dementia, there is a progressive atrophy (degeneration) of brain tissue, and the brain wave patterns are almost invariably abnormal. The individual becomes increasingly subject to lapses of memory, poor judgment, and disorientation. Deterioration in personal habits is common, and behavior may become unpredictable and impulsive. Because the person often remembers past events better than recent ones, he or she seems to live in the past much of the time.

The rate at which behavior is affected and the manner in which it changes are influenced by many factors, not the least of which is the individual's reaction to the physical and psychological deterioration. A sizable percentage of people with dementia seem to undergo profound personality changes. However, these changes may be in degree rather than being basic alterations of personality. In such cases, reconstruction of the earlier personality traits may uncover the presence of maladaptive behavior patterns before the onset of senility, including actual and severe psychotic or neurotic reaction patterns—or more likely,

tendencies in those directions. These tendencies are made worse by the onset of senility, but they are not caused by it. One common symptom is **confabulation:** when faced with loss of particular memories, the individual fills in memory gaps with detailed, but inaccurate, accounts of his or her activities.

Over half of the cases that are diagnosed as senile dementia show various combinations of agitation, paranoid thinking, and schizophreniclike reactions. Depressive features are especially common in cases of dementia; they include restlessness at night, irritability, narrowing of interests, and loss of initiative. Table 12-3 lists some of the ways to differentiate dementia from depression.

Dementia is primarily distinguished by impairments of memory and cognitive functioning (see Box 12-2). While there are many causes of dementia, DSM-IV recognizes certain core criteria regardless of the cause. Table 12-4 lists these core criteria.

A large survey of Canadians over age 65 resulted in an estimated prevalence of dementia of about 8% (Costa, 1996). The female-to-male ratio was 2:1. The prevalence for both men and women ranged from 2.4% among those aged 65 to 74 to 11.1% for those between 75 and 84 years of age and 34.5% for those 85 or older. Fifty-six percent of all persons over 65 living in institutions of various types were diagnosed as having dementia. The figure for institutionalized persons in the 65–74 age group was 40%, and the rate was 66% for those over 85.

Alzheimer's Disease

On rare occasions, he says my name. More frequently, he'll simply press my arm and hold me there in front of him and look hard in my eyes. His hand is still strong, his grasp still firm. The nurses tell me that his recognition of my face is now the only bond that still connects him to the life he lived. (Kozol, New York Times, August 22, 2000, p. 27)

Table 12-3

Signs and Symptoms That Help Distinguish Dementia From Depression

Dementia	Depression
Even progression over months or years	Uneven progression over weeks
Attempts to hide memory loss	Complaints of memory loss
Worse later in day or when fatigued	Often worse in morning, better as day goes on
Unawareness of or minimizing of disability	Awareness of and exaggeration of disability
Abuse of drugs rare	Possible abuse of alcohol or other drugs

Source: Based on Heston & White (1991).

In this way, author Jonathan Kozol described his aged father who for nearly 50 years had taught neurology at Harvard Medical School and who now suffers from Alzheimer's disease. Dementia is primarily a problem of the aged. For many years, most of the problems were lumped together in the category of "senile disorders." We now know that several different types of psychological and behavioral problems occur among old people. The elderly are vulnerable both to serious consequences of brain changes such as senile dementia and to certain other psychological conditions such as those in which the role of organic factors is much less clear-cut. For example, depressive episodes increase in both frequency and depth in the later years of life. Depression is likely to be provoked by the beginning of an illness or disability, or the death of a spouse; but given time, most people adjust to these changes. The majority of severe depressions in old age are relapses, although new cases may occur even after the age of 75. Paranoid and hypochondriacal disorders are also common in older people.

Generally, the major clinical challenge facing the elderly is the greater likelihood of disorders in which there is brain degeneration. The following account was written by a medical student who had been working with a patient with Alzheimer's disease who showed significant cognitive impairment. It conveys some of the reality of this insidious, heartbreaking malady that is associated with advancing age.

I visited Margo at her home each day. On my way, I'd pick up whatever she needed from the store, or sometimes a treat. Her favorite is peanut butter and jelly sandwiches on white bread. She can devour two in one sitting, especially if milk is at hand. Given her size, this always amazes me.

At the apartment, Margo's Jamaican home attendant, Louise, welcomed me with giggles and smiles, probably because my visit signaled a relief from her duties. It took Louise a few minutes to open the door since it was rigged with an array of locks and chains designed to keep Margo from slipping out in the night. Before the locks were installed, Margo had, on occasion, satisfied her understandable desire to explore the city on her own. We usually found her a couple of days later when we learned of a police report describing a woman in a nightgown seen roaming Central Park. Bad things have happened during these excursions. Does Margo understand that she is locked inside for her own safety? . . .

Margo never called me by name. I never figured out if she just forgot it from one day to the next or whether she ever actually remembered me at all. If I asked her, she would say she knew who I was. But that could have just been adaptive politeness. I probably looked like I wanted to be remembered. (Firlik, 1991, p. 201)

Alzheimer's disease is marked by memory lapses and confusion. Compared with short-term memory, long-term memory remains relatively intact. However, dementia associated with this disease inevitably worsens. One woman said that she did not understand her husband's Alzheimer's condition until the night they gave a dinner party at their home. "It was a very nice evening; we all had a wonderful time. And then, as people were getting ready to leave,

Table 12-4

Core Criteria for Dementia

1. Memory impairment (inability to learn new information and to recall previously learned information)
2. One or more of the following cognitive disturbances:
   a. Deterioration of language function (speech becomes vague or empty; comprehension of spoken or written language may deteriorate)
   b. Impaired ability to execute motor activities despite intact motor function, sensory function, and comprehension of the required task (e.g., impaired ability to pantomime using an object, such as combing hair)
   c. Failure to recognize or identify objects despite intact sensory function (e.g., loss of the ability to recognize objects such as chairs or pencils despite normal visual acuity)
   d. Disturbance in executive functions such as planning, organizing, sequencing, and abstracting (executive dysfunction includes inability to recite the alphabet or state as many animals as possible in 1 minute).

Q&A

Box 12–2

Q. I've noticed that both my mom and dad occasionally can't remember something and seem to get upset and worried when it happens. They are in their 50s. Are they in an early stage of dementia?

A. *Probably not. But it is understandable that they become concerned when memory failures occur. Newspapers, magazines, and TV are full of stories about severe memory impairments as people get older. For middle aged people that can be pretty scary news.*

Researchers are trying to figure out when minor memory failures earlier in life are and are not predictive of the extensive memory losses that characterize senility. Many memory lapses are not associated with the prediction of extensive cognitive impairment. For example, most people who experience trouble calling up names or other similar information are having a problem with speed of retrieval. It's not that the memories are fading or disintegrating in the brain's memory banks; it just takes a bit more time to activate the circuits. This is what accounts for the "tip of the tongue" sensation that is consistent with a

healthy memory search. Another indication that a memory lapse is probably benign is if the person who has a memory lapse shows what is called the "aha! phenomenon." The person knows the correct recollection has been recaptured ("Oh yes, that's what I was searching for"). People with brain disorders experience neither the "tip of the tongue" sensation nor the "aha! phenomenon."

Much of normal age-related memory loss has to do with loss of processing speed, not loss of ideas. Normal aging often does bring with it certain declines in attention that can be mistaken for loss of memory skills. Neither time nor cues appear to help people suffering from brain disorders like Alzheimer's disease. As conditions like Alzheimer's disease progress, dementia may occur rapidly. However, the deficits of normal aging either do not progress or progress very slowly over time.

One type of memory deficit that does seem to be a bad omen has to do with what is called "executive functioning." This is the kind of memory required for fairly complicated tasks that involve a sequence of steps— for example, planning and preparing a

multicourse dinner. Perfectly normal people can show memory disruption when they are under stress. Perfectly normal people also may have to pause to remember what step comes next, but serious disruptions of such memory often indicate that something could be seriously awry.

The following examples indicate the differences in normal age-related memory loss, mild impairment, and dementia:

Normal

- Misplacing keys, checkbook
- Blanking on a new acquaintance's name

Mild cognitive impairment

- Missing important appointments
- Difficulty learning new names

Dementia

- Forgetting close relatives' names
- Inability to plan and execute a meal

---

my husband put on his coat to leave with them. He didn't know he was in his own home." Diagnosis of the disease is based in part on the patient's inability to answer simple questions such as "What is the (year), (season), (date), and (month)?" and to perform assigned tasks such as "Count backwards from a given number (like 100) by subtracting 7s" and "Spell the word *world* backwards."

Alzheimer's disease is by far the leading cause of mental deterioration among the elderly. It is responsible for more than 100,000 deaths each year in the United States, where it is the fourth leading cause of death after heart disease, cancer, and stroke. Mean survival time following its diagnosis is about 8 years. There appear to be two types of the disease: sporadic and familial. While the symptoms of both are similar, the **sporadic type** (the majority of cases) does not run in families, whereas the **familial type** does.

Because most Alzheimer's patients must eventually be placed in institutions, the disease places tremendous demands on health care resources. Alzheimer's victims constitute 50% to 60% of the 1.3 million people in nursing homes, accounting for more than half of the many billions of dollars spent annually on nursing home care. The disease will become more common and take an even greater toll

as the average age of the U.S. population continues to rise. By the year 2040, the number of people over the age of 85—the fastest-growing segment of the U.S. population— is expected to be five times greater than it is currently. From the proportion of cases currently in that age group, it has been estimated that at that time the number of cases of Alzheimer's disease may exceed 6 million.

Alzheimer's disease is also the most common form of presenile dementia, which can occur as early as a person's 30s. In these cases, it also usually causes intellectual deterioration with growing lapses of memory. However, the rate of disease progression tends to be faster in early-onset cases and tends to involve genetic mutations.

In both early-onset and senile Alzheimer's disease the progressive destruction of nervous tissue leads to slurring of speech, involuntary movements of arms and legs, and in some cases, seizures. When the disease manifests itself primarily in the intellectual sphere, the individual may experience great anxiety about the deterioration of his or her abilities (see Table 12-5). The patient, described here—a woman who died at age 47 of familial Alzheimer's—had shown a progressive memory loss for 8 years before her death:

Table 12-5	
Phases in the Cognitive Decline Accompanying Alzheimer's Disease	
Phase	**Examples**
1. Complaints of memory deficit	Forgetting names that one formerly knew well
2. Increased cognitive decline and signs of confusion	Losing or misplacing an object of value
3. Moderately severe cognitive decline and intensified confusion (early dementia)	Inability to recall major aspects of one's life, such as the names of close family members
4. Severe cognitive decline and confusion (middle dementia)	Being largely unaware of all recent events and experiences
5. Very severe cognitive decline and confusion (late dementia)	Loss of all verbal abilities; need for assistance in eating and using the toilet

At the onset of the disease, she often repeated the same questions or stories, and she often forgot where she had left objects. She had no formal education and worked as a housewife. Over the ensuing years, she developed difficulty in preparing meals, neglected her family obligations, and appeared apathetic. She did not complete activities that she began and became isolated from others. Four years after the onset of memory loss, she developed agitation, became aggressive at times, and began wandering. She neglected her personal hygiene, and her language function deteriorated. By 6 years after the onset of her illness (2 years before her death), she developed urinary and occasional fecal incontinence.

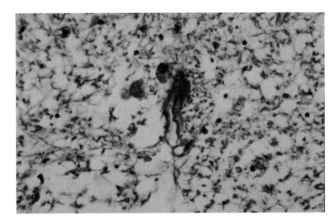

Figure 12-5 A brain section from a 57-year-old familial Alzheimer's disease patient showing plaques in the frontal cortex.

Source: Lopera, et al. 1997, p. 797.

Research Directions Alzheimer's disease was first identified in 1906 by a German physician, Alois Alzheimer. His patient, a 51-year-old woman, suffered loss of memory, disorientation, and later, severe dementia. After her death, Alzheimer performed an autopsy on her brain and found the two distinctive characteristics of the disease: tangled clumps of nerve cells and patches of disintegrated nerve-cell branches called *plaques* (see Figure 12-5). Because the patients Alzheimer studied were relatively young, he thought the disease was one of middle age; similar symptoms in elderly people were generally regarded as a natural consequence of aging by Alzheimer and his contemporaries. Today this view has been discarded. Dementias of the Alzheimer's type seem to involve a specific pathological process rather than being a normal consequence of aging. Researchers have looked to many sources for information about possible causes of the disease. There is growing reason to believe that different cases of Alzheimer's disease can spring from different causes. Rather than being a single illness, the disease may be a group of closely associated disorders that involve both genetic and nongenetic factors.

Neurochemicals One of the keys to Alzheimer's disease may be a certain type of brain cell, the cholinergic cell, that is involved in memory and learning. These cells release the important chemical messenger *acetylcholine*. Acetylcholine is a key player in brain activity. When it is released by the cholinergic cell, it stimulates neighboring cells, causing them to release other chemicals. These chemicals in turn influence still other cells. Alzheimer's disease evidently throws a wrench into this process. For reasons that are not yet understood, people with advanced Alzheimer's disease lose up to 80% of their cholinergic cells in key brain areas. As a result, there also is a dramatic reduction in the amount of acetylcholine produced in the brain. There is a strong correlation between the amount of loss of acetylcholine or cholinergic cells in an individual's brain and the severity of that person's dementia. One focus of current research is the development of drugs that will increase the formation of acetylcholine, prevent its destruction, or directly stimulate acetylcholine receptors. Current research also suggests that biochemical abnormalities in Alzheimer's disease are not limited to the cholinergic system. There are deficiencies in other systems as well, for example, cell loss in the noradrenergic system, which is another chemical messenger system.

Genes The fact that Alzheimer's disease often occurs in several members of the same family suggests that a genetic factor is at work. The genetic basis for many cases of early-onset familial Alzheimer's disease has now been established (Lopera et al., 1997). Clinically, the symptoms in these cases resemble those seen in the sporadic type, except that headaches preceding and during the disease characterize the early-onset variety.

Some studies have linked the disease to abnormalities on chromosome no. 21, which has been identified as the location of the gene for a protein called **beta amyloid,** which is found in the characteristic clumps and plaques of Alzheimer's disease. Laboratory studies have shown that beta amyloid fragments can kill nerve cells. However, it is not completely clear whether the presence of beta amyloid in the brains of those with Alzheimer's disease is the *cause* or the *result* of the process of brain cell degeneration. The degeneration might be due to a protein called *apolipoprotein E (Apo E)*. A high percentage of Alzheimer's patients have at least one gene coding for the type of Apo E protein known as E4. Apo E4 may be a risk factor for Alzheimer's disease, just as high cholesterol is a risk factor for heart disease.

Screening for hereditary influences in Alzheimer's disease might reveal genetic markers, and it might be possible to identify environmental factors that influence the age of onset and the progress of the disease. However, research on the genetic aspects of Alzheimer's disease is complicated by the fact that the disease occurs so late in life, and thus many people who might be destined to get it die from other causes first. Work on this topic is accelerating, though, and there is reason to hope that the various forms of the disease will be reliably identified, along with the genes associated with them. Thus far, all the known genetic alterations underlying familial Alzheimer's disease increase the production of the beta amyloid protein in the brain (Selkoe, 1997). More research on the correlates of being at high risk in the development of Alzheimer's disease is needed (see Box12-3).

Alzheimer's Effect on the Family The challenges confronting those who live with and take care of Alzheimer's patients are considerable. Some of caregivers' most common behavioral concerns about those for whom they are responsible are as follows:

- *Depression.* Unhappiness and withdrawal are common in individuals with Alzheimer's disease.
- *Hostility, belligerence, and aggression.* Alzheimer's individuals can be selfish and hostile.
- *Disorientation.* The person with Alzheimer's will become increasingly confused about people, places, and time.
- *Wandering.* Wandering and restlessness are common problems.

- *Anxiety and suspiciousness.* Worries and paranoid thinking occur.

In addition to searching for the causes of Alzheimer's disease, researchers are attempting to find ways of treating not only patients, but caregivers as well. Those who care for people with Alzheimer's disease often experience severe stress. Marian Roach provided the following description of her reactions and those of her sister, Margaret, to their mother's deterioration as a result of Alzheimer's disease:

> I noticed that she had stopped taking phone messages. One friend said she sounded "jealous and hostile." She would abruptly hang up on people. She became obsessed with the plumbing: She would look under the sinks and start to take apart the pipes, convinced there was a drip. She would walk away in the middle of conversation. She became repetitive, depressed. (Roach, 1983, p. 23)

As the deterioration continued, the pressures and emotional strain worsened:

> Margaret and I have no relatives but my mother. The decisions we make are made together. Margaret works until 11 at night and on weekends. We have a young woman who lives in the house from Monday through Friday. Another woman comes on Friday and Saturday nights. Yet another takes my mother out—for rides or to the movies—three afternoons a week. But the burden of care is on my patient sister, who manages the schedules and sees my mother daily. I work during the day. I am with my mother on Sundays.
>
> As I have gotten to know this disease, I have felt ashamed at my own embarrassment. I find myself explaining her condition to people, to excuse her behavior. Sometimes I do this in front of her and, for an instant, my mother will look terribly embarrassed. I see it in her face and I feel very unlike a daughter. I feel like a traitor. And then she will forget my explanation of her "memory problem," and her questions and repetitions, along with my embarrassment, will continue. Alzheimer's victims are likely to say or do anything during the stages just before they can do literally nothing for themselves. It is difficult to know what to expect. The anticipation is sometimes the worst part.
>
> I sometimes dread the weekends. I try not to cry in front of Margaret, who tries not to cry in front of me. Margaret and I have discussed the possibility of our contracting the disease. If I get it, I have said that I'd want Margaret to kill me; she has said the same. (Roach, 1983, p. 31)

Research on the particularly stressful aspects of caring for Alzheimer's victims has shown that the sense of lack of control over what will happen next is of great importance (Gonzalez-Salvador et al., 1999). In addition, caregivers feel isolated, unable to deal effectively with the continuing stress, and confused about their own reactions. Support

Research Close-up
Box 12–3

Indications Early in Life of Alzheimer's Disease

Long before the terminal phase of the deterioration process, Alzheimer's disease can exert a powerful influence over many aspects of life. A study of the brains of elderly drivers killed in automobile accidents in Sweden and Finland found that an unusually high percentage—as many as half—showed signs of early Alzheimer's disease (Lundberg et al., 1997), although the condition had not been diagnosed before their deaths. It was inferred that even in its preliminary stages, Alzheimer's disease can cause enough mental impairment to make driving dangerous. In this way, dementia contributes to societal problems. Future research is likely to shed light on the point in the dementia process at which Alzheimer's disease affects driving and other types of performance.

If it were possible to find indicators of Alzheimer's disease early in the lives of genetically vulnerable people, it might be possible to develop ways of preventing its serious effects later in life. For example, early drug treatment might prove to be beneficial. A recent study focused on a group of individuals at high genetic risk for Alzheimer's (Bookheimer et al., 2000). When tested, they had normal memory function. While this high-risk group performed as well on early memory tests as a comparable group at normal risk for the disease, magnetic resonance imaging scans found that their brains had to work harder. Table 12-6 shows one of the memory items and Figure 12-6 shows examples of MRI brain scans from the high-risk and normal groups. This might indicate that the brains of those at high risk were compensating for a subtle deficit. The subjects whose brains worked hardest during the memory testing were more likely to show marked declines in verbal recall ability when tested 2 years later.

The results of this brain imaging study are consistent with other studies providing evidence of physical changes in the brain years before unusual memory problems occur. Future research is likely to be concerned with how this evidence of early physical changes can be used preventively. For example, it might be possible to develop neurochemical compounds that prevent the clumping of amyloids known to be important in Alzheimer's.

Table 12-6

An Item Used in Memory Test

Subjects are read seven word pairs and then given the first word of each pair and asked to recall the second. The exercise is repeated five times with the pairs in different orders.

small	tap
water	envelope
girl	arm
shoe	milk
egg	under
day	valley
out	hammer

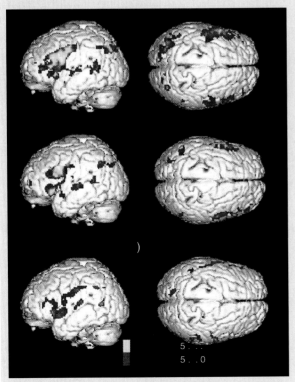

Figure 12-6 Brains of people at risk for Alzheimer's (images at top) compared with normal brains (at bottom) during a memory test. Yellow indicates the most intense exertion, followed by orange and red.

SOURCE: Bookheimer et al., 2000.

Figure 12-7   Family members of those affected by Alzheimer's disease also feel the impact of the behavioral and cognitive changes brought about by the disorder. Counseling sessions for patients and their families can help caretakers develop strategies for care and reduce the stress experienced by all family members.

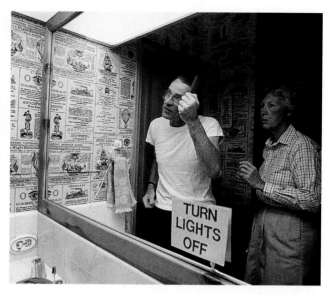

Figure 12-8   Alzheimer's disease has a profound effect, not only on the person who develops it, but also on the lives of all the members of the family. In this home, written reminders are used to help the patient cope with the memory problems Alzheimer's disease creates.

groups and group therapy can be valuable in allowing family members to express their feelings, particularly those that they consider unacceptable (e.g., anger and disappointment). The opportunity to compare their experiences with those of other people who are going through the same trial often makes them aware that such feelings are normal and understandable (see Figure 12-7).

The following coping strategies can be useful aids to Alzheimer's caretakers:

1. Try to increase activities that patients formerly enjoyed and can still manage. Try to involve them in such activities, perhaps with another family member or a friend. Talk with them; reminisce about family, friends, and activities.

2. Confronting the situation head-on and trying to reason with Alzheimer's patients will not work. Being reassuring and calm may help to reduce the hostility. Trying to distract the patient with questions about the problem and gradually moving his or her attention to something else may also help.

3. Labeling items and color-coding rooms such as the bathroom or bedroom can alleviate some problems in the early stages of the disease (see Figure 12-8). Talking in a calm voice and reminding patients of where they are and whom they are with may help ease their feelings of being lost and alone.

4. Keeping the household free of clutter is a major consideration so that there is not added confusion or harm to the patient as he or she wanders through what was once a familiar environment. Identification bracelets and safety locks are other useful devices for individuals given to wandering. Walking and other

physical exercise may help alleviate the patient's desire to wander.

5. A patient's fears and anxieties cannot really be dealt with in a rational and normal manner. Identifying what is frightening the patients may be helpful, but directly confronting them and telling them there is nothing to their concerns will not work. It is often useful to develop calming reassurances about the frightening situation and then to distract the patient by changing the subject.

Because there is no cure and because of the daily stress experienced by caretakers, Alzheimer's disease is a source of great anxiety for many people. All too often, anxiety leads to efforts to deal with a concern or problem by hiding it from other people. It is as if it were something to be ashamed of. There is a need to bring concerns about Alzheimer's disease into the open so that its reality can be accepted and dealt with in as constructive a way as possible. For this reason, former president Ronald Reagan's announcement in November 1994 that he had the disease was a valuable contribution to public education about Alzheimer's (see Figure 12-9). Earlier in their lives, President and Mrs. Reagan's sharing of information about their medical problems proved to be valuable, not only from an educational standpoint, but also as a boost to the morale of other affected people.

Treatment Little progress has been made in the treatment of Alzheimer's disease since Alois Alzheimer's day, and even diagnosis remains difficult. While the patient is alive,

Figure 12-9 Former president Ronald Reagan and his wife, Nancy, pose for pictures during his first public appearance after his announcement that he had been diagnosed with Alzheimer's disease. In 1998, Patti Davis, Ronald Reagan's daughter, wondered whether her father understood Christmas and observed:

Although my father is not in pain, he loses more of himself each month to Alzheimer's. For him, as for anyone who has this disease, time is the enemy. It becomes jumbled, confused, compressed and emptier all the time—hollowed out. (New York Times Magazine, December, 27, 1998, p. 58)

the diagnosis must be arrived at by a careful process of elimination. Through brain imaging and other tests, it is possible to determine that the patient has not suffered a series of small strokes and does not have Parkinson's disease, a brain tumor, depression, an adverse drug reaction, or other disorders that can cause dementia. The chances of making an accurate diagnosis of Alzheimer's disease in the living patient have been improved by the finding that 70% to 80% of patients with the disease show a characteristic pattern of decrease in metabolic function or cerebral blood flow in certain areas of the brain. Because no other illness with symptoms of confusion and intellectual deterioration has so far been found that shows this pattern, scanning techniques provide a valuable clue to diagnosis, although they do not as yet provide enough information to be certain that the patient has Alzheimer's disease. The only way to be absolutely certain that a patient has the disorder is to examine the brain after death. An autopsy is needed because so far it is the only way to determine whether the plaques and tangles characteristic of the disease are present.

There are more than 4 million Alzheimer's disease patients in America. Presence of an affected parent or sibling is associated with a fourfold increase in the risk of developing Alzheimer's disease. It is well known what the brain of a patient looks like at death. Equally well documented are the losses of abilities that occur in a predictable way.

What is not known is the mechanism that triggers the illness and when it starts.

Although much remains to be discovered about this disease, two critical crossroads reached in the approach to treatment for Alzheimer's disease have been (1) the recognition of Alzheimer's disease as a disorder distinct from the normal aging process, and (2) the realization that in developing therapeutic and social interventions for a major illness or disability, the concept of *care* can be as important as that of *cure*.

Increasing knowledge about the role of genetic abnormalities in Alzheimer's disease may lead to effective treatment methods. There are several ways in which formation of beta amyloid might be stopped from killing nerve cells in the brain. For example, certain drugs might accomplish this task. However, progress in treating the disease does not necessarily depend on stopping the process of beta amyloid formation. Drugs that simply slow the process could be of enormous value. Because Alzheimer's symptoms don't usually become apparent until late in life, simply delaying its onset by 5 years could reduce the number of cases by as much as 50% (Marx, 1996).

In addition to drug therapy, psychosocial interventions may be useful in postponing institutionalization and improving the quality of life for patients and their caretakers. Support groups and skills training for caretakers seem to be promising approaches. Some of the techniques used in skills training are modeling, role-playing, and corrective

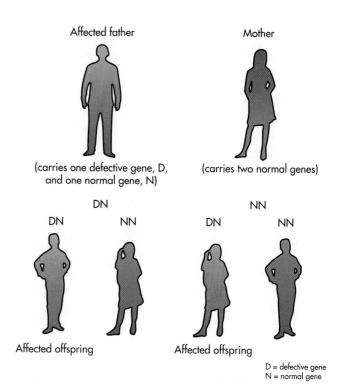

Figure 12-10 Autosomal dominant disorders are inherited when one parent who carries the defective gene passes this gene on to the next generation. This illustration shows how offspring have a 50-50 chance of inheriting a disorder from a carrier parent. In any given family it is possible for all or none of the offspring to inherit the defective gene.

feedback. Providing pertinent information about the behavioral effects of the disease can also be helpful.

Four scientific and clinical care challenges now face researchers and clinicians who deal with Alzheimer's disease:

1. Determining the fundamental neurobiological causes of the disease
2. Developing more effective treatments that would prevent its occurrence and impede or reverse its progression
3. Providing sensitive clinical care for those already diagnosed
4. Providing family members with expert advice, treatment, and support throughout the course of the disease

Pick's Disease

Pick's disease is much less common than Alzheimer's disease. Whereas the risk of Alzheimer's disease increases steadily throughout adult life, Pick's disease is most likely to develop between the ages of 60 and 70. After that period, the risk decreases (Heston & Mastri, 1982). Its symptoms are so similar to those of Alzheimer's disease that it takes an autopsy to tell the two disorders apart. People who have died from Pick's disease show a characteristic form of brain atrophy. Among people over age 40, 24 out of 100,000 can be expected to die of the disease. There appears to be a strong genetic factor, and men are at greater risk of developing the disease than women (Heston et al., 1987).

As is the case with Alzheimer's disease, there are no known cures for Pick's disease or any of the other senile and presenile dementias. The usual treatment consists

mainly of emotional support and sedative drugs. Efforts are made to organize the patient's life so that his or her days are uncomplicated and structured so as to avoid pressure and tension. This can also improve the quality of life for those affected by these disorders.

Huntington's Disease

Huntington's disease, also known as *Huntington's chorea,* is a rare hereditary disorder transmitted by a single dominant gene and characterized by progressive degeneration of brain tissue. It can begin at any time from childhood to late in life, but most commonly the onset occurs between the ages of 30 and 50. Although the disease was described as far back as the Middle Ages, George Huntington, an American physician, gave the first detailed account of it in 1872. He and others used the word *chorea* to describe the disorder because its unusual movements bore some similarity to *choreography,* the Greek word for dance. Today there are about 30,000 cases in the United States. At least 150,000 others have a 50% hereditary risk of developing the disease. Huntington's disease is an **autosomal dominant disorder,** a non-sex-linked disorder that can be inherited even if only one parent passes on the defective gene (see Figure 12-10). Since the disease is inherited through a single dominant gene, each child of an affected parent has a 50% chance of inheriting the disorder. There is no skipping of generations, and until recently there has been no way of distinguishing carriers of the gene from noncarriers until the symptoms appear. The fact that Huntington's disease does not manifest itself until

Figure 12-11 Some of the members of a large Venezuelan family, the Soto family, whose members are at exceptionally high risk for Huntington's disease are shown here enjoying a watermelon party. By donating their DNA for study, family members have helped in the search for the location of the gene that causes this disease.

midlife has meant that family members who might be affected by it must spend their childhood, adolescence, and early adult years not knowing whether they will develop the disorder or not.

Four types of symptoms are observed in Huntington's disease: dementia, irritability and apathy, depression, and hallucinations and delusions. In addition, there are *choreiform* movements—involuntary, spasmodic jerking and twisting movements of the neck, trunk, and extremities, and much facial grimacing.

The psychological and behavioral symptoms of Huntington's disease are even more devastating than the physical ones. As the disease develops, the person experiences increasing difficulty in memory storage and retrieval. There is also evidence that intelligence test scores get progressively lower in the period just before the appearance of the characteristic choreiform movements. This suggests that the gene for Huntington's disease does not suddenly "turn on" at the time that the involuntary movements appear.

Impulsiveness in behavior and paranoid and depressive thinking are likely to occur as the disorder progresses, and family life becomes disrupted. It is not clear whether these behavioral components of Huntington's disease are organically caused or whether they are psychological reactions to physical deterioration. Recently it has become known that people with Huntington's disease have a deficiency of one neurotransmitter, **gamma-aminobutyric acid (GABA),** and that the death of brain cells in persons with the disease has caused accumulations of protein to form in the cell nuclei.

Huntington's disease usually begins in midlife, although the onset can occur much earlier. The folksinger and composer Woody Guthrie died in 1967 at the age of 55 after suffering from Huntington's disease for 13 years. As a result of a misdiagnosis, Guthrie had been considered an alcoholic and had been placed in a series of mental hospitals for years before the correct diagnosis was made.

In the San Luis region of Venezuela, the prevalence of Huntington's disease is 700 times higher than the general prevalence rate in the United States. Within a population of about 3,000, about 150 people have been stricken by the disease and 1,500 more have a substantial risk of developing it. This is because San Luis is the home of a handful of families with many affected members. By far the largest of these families is the Soto family, which has the highest known concentration of Huntington's disease of any family in the world. This high incidence of the disease in one family has given scientists an unusual opportunity to study this rare disorder (see Figure 12-11).

By carefully studying the blood of Iris del Valle Soto and other members of her extended family of almost 4,000 people covering eight generations, researchers achieved a startling breakthrough. They identified the location in the chromosome pair (chromosome pair no. 4) at which the gene for Huntington's disease is located. In 1993 the specific gene was identified (Gusella & MacDonald, 1994). This identification was an important first step toward developing a diagnostic test for the disease, and perhaps eventually a treatment. The diagnostic genetic test is now being used at several clinical centers in Canada and the United States on an experimental basis. As a result of the gene discovery, an even more direct and accurate test for Huntington's disease should be possible, and ultimately, researchers hope, we should have a better understanding of what causes the nerve degeneration that characterizes the disease. A key leader in organizing research on Huntington's disease has been Nancy Wexler, a clinical psychologist and president of the Hereditary Disease Foundation (see Figure 12-12).

Figure 12–12 Ever since learning that her family was affected by Huntington's disease, Nancy Wexler has been a leader in encouraging research into its cause. In 1993 she was given the prestigious Albert Lasker Public Service Award. This citation accompanied the award: "Learning that her family was affected by the disease, she did not bemoan her situation, but rose to the challenge and used her adversity to set her life goal to conquering this late-onset, invariably fatal genetic disorder." In this photograph she is seen with her sister Alice (right), a historian, and her father, Milton, a psychoanalyst.

At present many people who have been offered the currently available genetic test have not chosen to take it. In a study carried out in Canada, those at risk who volunteered to be tested also were assessed for psychological well-being both before the genetic testing and at several intervals afterward (Hayden, 1991). As might be expected, those who learned that they were likely to develop the disease were very distressed when they first learned the result. However, 6 months later, their psychological state was better than it had been prior to testing, although they became distressed whenever they noticed something about their behavior—stumbling over a curb, for instance—that could possibly be an early symptom. People for whom the test indicated freedom from the Huntington's gene were elated at first, but then seemed to go into a slump for a variety of reasons. Those who had previously made irreversible decisions based on concern about genetic status—for example, by being sterilized in order to avoid passing on the Huntington's gene—were particularly negatively affected. Another group negatively affected by the news that they did not carry the gene were those who had had unrealistic expectations about how the predictive testing would change their lives. There were similar numbers of negative psychological reactions in the groups that got good and bad news. In general, people who had experienced psychological problems prior to the test had the worst outcome regardless of the test results. The find-

ings of the study show clearly the importance of including counseling and support services in genetic testing programs.

Various behavioral disturbances have been described in persons with Huntington's disease. While some of these symptoms may be part of the psychological reaction to having this neurological condition, there is evidence that many patients show psychiatric symptoms *before* the physical symptoms are noticed. Depression is one of the psychological symptoms often found to be associated. Obsessions and compulsions are also seen in cases of Huntington's disease (DeMarchi & Mennella, 2000). The explanation for these linkages of neurological and psychological conditions has not yet been uncovered.

Parkinson's Disease

Like Huntington's disease, **Parkinson's disease** is progressive and may begin by the age of 50. Its symptoms include tremor; rigidity; an expressionless, masklike facial appearance; and loss of vocal power. Parkinson's disease affects about 1% of the population and up to 2.5% of the population over age 70 (Marsh, 2000.) A person with Parkinson's disease typically exhibits social withdrawal, reduced intellectual ability, and rigidity in coping with his or her problems. Parkinson's patients seem emotionally overcontrolled. As with Huntington's disease, it is difficult to determine how much of the behavioral maladaptation associated with Parkinson's disease is due to organic processes and how much to the patient's psychological reaction to them.

There is evidence that the brains of Parkinson's patients are deficient in the neurotransmitter dopamine. Unlike the dementias discussed so far, this disorder can be treated. A drug called *L-dopa* is used to relieve some of the symptoms. A promising advance in understanding Parkinson's disease has been the discovery of a new protein (glial cell line–derived neurotrophic factor, or GDNF) that may promote the secretion of the neurotransmitter dopamine and thereby counter the degeneration seen in Parkinson's disease (Weiss, 1993).

Surgeons have carried out tissue implantations, including tissue from aborted fetuses, into the human brain as a possible way of relieving Parkinson's symptoms. Success with tissue implantation has been reported in some cases, there have also been a number of failures. While there have been better results with younger (less than 40 years old) patients than with older patients, but some cases of deterioration have also occurred.

Brain Trauma: Injuries, Tumors, and Infections

Brain injuries, tumors, and infections can cause dementia and other serious acute and chronic conditions. Damage to the brain is of central importance in influencing how a person functions.

Injuries and Tumors Traumatic brain injury is a common cause of mental disorders (Varney & Roberts, 1999). Each year in the United States, more than 500,000 people suffer severe injuries to the brain. As the case of Sarah Monahan, presented in Box 12-1, makes clear, major brain injuries can have profound cognitive and behavioral consequences. Patients with less severe injuries also may suffer from prolonged psychological disability. They may have difficulties in a number of areas of functioning, including work, school, and leisure activities, and may show extreme personality changes.

In addition to head injuries, intracranial growths (**brain tumors**) can lead to both acute and chronic disorders. In many cases it is difficult to determine how much of the abnormal behavior is a result of damage and how much represents a lifelong behavior pattern or simply a reaction to knowledge of the injury. These factors can interact in many ways. A startling or traumatic event, whether or not it involves physical injury, usually has some specific symbolic significance for the individual. The term **traumatic neurosis** has been used to describe reactions that follow such an event. A blow to the head that caused little physical damage might be exploited by the injured person, as in some hysterical disorders. The reaction may be reinforced by secondary factors, such as sympathy from one's family or permission to quit one's job. Table 12-7 lists some of the factors that contribute to the effects of a brain injury.

Brain injuries are usually classified into three groups: (1) **concussions,** or transient states that momentarily change the physical condition of the brain but do not cause structural damage; (2) **contusions,** in which diffuse, fine structural damage—for example, the rupturing of tiny blood vessels—takes place; and (3) **lacerations,** which involve major tears or ruptures in the brain tissue.

Although a concussion might include a temporary loss of consciousness, complete recovery can be expected within 24 to 48 hours. Sometimes it is difficult to diagnose precisely the extent of brain injury and its potential effect on brain functioning. A variety of tests and observations are used to analyze each case, including X-ray evidence of skull fracture; a CT scan to determine tissue damage; a test for blood in the spinal fluid, and observation of symptoms such as bleeding from the skull orifices (e.g., the ears), throbbing headaches, prolonged loss of consciousness, and sluggish cognitive behavior. Head injuries can lead to highly specific losses in motor or cognitive functioning, with the extent of the loss depending on the kind of injury and where it is located.

Sometimes the brain is injured, not by an accident or a blow, but by pressure inside the skull, perhaps from a tumor. In such cases the speed with which the intruding body develops also influences the amount of loss. A tumor might grow slowly for a long time before there is evidence of

Table 12-7
Factors That Contribute to the Effects of a Brain Injury

- Age
- Site of injury
- Extent of damage
- Emotional reactions to resulting physical and mental deficits
- Personality and social competence
- Social support available after injury

intracranial pressure or behavioral change (see Box 12-4). A good prognosis in cases of brain injury or tumor depends on how early and how accurately the condition is diagnosed and whether an effective treatment for the condition exists.

In some cases in which there is known physical damage, only minor behavioral deficits develop. Apparently some people adapt to minor brain damage better than others do. While brain damage can directly cause maladaptive behavior, it is also possible that the maladaptive behavior can occur simply as a response to the knowledge of having a damaged brain. Furthermore, any type of major injury or traumatic condition might set off a maladaptive psychological reaction.

Tumors produce a variety of physiological and psychological changes because their presence causes a rise in intracranial pressure and interferes with the blood supply to the brain. As with head injuries, the symptoms of a tumor depend on its location in the brain. For example, tumors growing in or near the frontal lobes frequently lead to a gradual onset of mental changes, but again, the symptoms depend on the site of the tumor. One group of people with frontal-lobe tumors may become exuberant and euphoric, with their conversation punctuated by laughter and jokes. Another group may show general apathy and slowness in responding. Memory disorders are very common in people with cerebral tumors and are often the first noticeable indication that a problem exists. Researchers are investigating the degree to which training in attentional and cognitive skills can aid in the rehabilitation of brain-damaged individuals.

Early in their development, some brain tumors result in changes that neurologists can assess. However, in the absence of other evidence to suggest the presence of a tumor, emphasis on personality and behavioral changes often results in misdiagnosis and the attribution of the symptoms to nonorganic factors; the role of organic factors may become evident only later. For example, the composer George Gershwin underwent psychoanalysis because he

First Person Box 12–4

A Malignant Brain Tumor

I don't really understand myself these days. I am supposed to be an average, reasonable, and intelligent young man. However, lately (I can't recall when it started) I have been the victim of many unusual and irrational thoughts. These thoughts constantly recur, and it requires a tremendous mental effort to concentrate on useful and progressive tasks. In March when my parents made a physical break I noticed a great deal of stress. I consulted Dr. Cochran at the University Health Center and asked him to recommend someone that I could consult with about some psychiatric disorders I felt I had. I talked with a doctor once for about two hours and tried to convey to him my fears that I felt overcome by overwhelming violent impulses. After one session I never saw the doctor again, and since then I have been fighting my mental turmoil alone, and seemingly to no avail. After my death I wish that an autopsy would be performed on me to see if there is any visible physical disorder. I have had some tremendous headaches in the past and have consumed two large bottles of Excedrin in the past three months.

This letter was written by Charles Whitman, a student at the University of Texas, on the evening of July 31,

Figure 12-13 Charles Whitman, shown here in a college photo, killed his wife, mother, and 14 strangers who were hit by bullets he sprayed from a perch high in the tower of the administration building at the University of Texas.

1966. Later than night Whitman killed his wife and his mother. The next morning he went to the tower of the administration building on the university campus with a high-powered hunting rifle and opened fire. Ninety minutes later he was shot to death, but by that time he had shot 38 people, killing 14 (see Figure 12-13).

Because of the shocking nature of this incident, it attracted widespread attention.

There were many attempts to explain Whitman's murderous acts. The letter that Whitman had written provided a number of clues. It referred to intense headaches, and a postmortem examination revealed a highly malignant tumor in a region of the brain that is known to be involved in aggressive behavior. Some experts suggested that Whitman's actions had been caused by brain damage. Most brain tumor victims don't become violent, but the behavioral effects of brain injuries and tumors can sometimes be puzzling and dramatic.

Other experts viewed Whitman's actions as products of the "unusual and irrational thoughts" to which he referred in his letter. A study of Whitman's life revealed that he had had many positive experiences with guns, and some authorities on violent behavior pointed to these experiences as a possible causal factor. Still others cited Whitman's reference to "overwhelming violent impulses" and suggested that those impulses had been bottled up for many years and had finally exploded into action because of the recent life stresses described in his letter.

We cannot be certain which of these potential causes was most important. Perhaps all of them contributed to his actions to varying degrees. The Whitman case dramatically illustrates the many perspectives from which a single act can be viewed and explained.

---

suffered severe headaches. It was not until shortly before his death that the diagnosis of a brain tumor was made.

George Gershwin's experience underlines a point we have made several times: the value of an integrative approach toward symptoms. Symptoms can arise for a variety of reasons. Figure 12-14 provides an example of what repeated blows to the head can do to psychological and motor functions. In general, it is always valuable to investigate all the possible contributions to a condition. An example of this point is provided by a study of boxers, some of whom did and others of whom did not recover from traumatic head injuries (Jordan et al., 1997). Is it just bad luck that determines which boxers wind up with permanent brain damage? The study found that the Apo E gene, which is already known to predispose people to Alzheimer's disease, also seems to be associated with failure to recover from traumatic head injuries. Failure to recover from a head injury is often attributed solely to the injury itself, but a genetic predisposition may interact with

the pounding boxers give each other's heads in determining whether permanent brain damage occurs. One hypothesis is that head injuries can elicit Alzheimerlike changes in the brain, specifically deposits of the protein beta amyloid, and that people with an Apo E gene are less able to repair those injuries.

HIV-Associated Cognitive Impairment Many AIDS patients display cognitive impairment (Catalan & Burgess, 1996). Individuals who are infected with HIV but do not have AIDS show no evidence of clinically relevant cognitive impairment. Indicators of **HIV-associated cognitive impairment** include forgetfulness, concentration difficulties, mental slowness, mild motor difficulties, and apathetic, withdrawn behavior. The early symptoms are similar to the dementias of the elderly and may closely resemble a major depression. (See Table 12-3 for noticeable differences between the dementias and depression.) As the cognitive impairment progresses, the majority of pa-

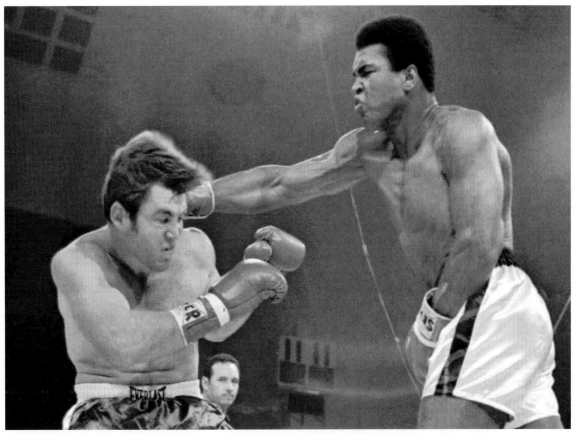

Figure 12-14   Jerry Quarry, a heavyweight contender of the late 1960s and early 1970s, died in 1999 at the age of 53. Here he is in a fight with Muhammad Ali in 1970. In his final years, Quarry was severely debilitated by boxing-induced brain damage. He experienced severe memory loss, hallucinations, and crippled motor skills as a result of repeated blows to the head during his boxing career.

Source: *New York Times,* January 5, 1999, p. A20.

tients develop a severe dementia with global loss of cognitive functions, severe psychomotor retardation, mutism, and motor weakness. Psychotic symptoms develop in some patients. CT scans often reveal cortical atrophy.

This type of dementia has only recently been recognized. Because the disorder usually appears in younger people who are not normally expected to develop dementing illnesses, the problem may be misdiagnosed. The typical psychological reactions to a diagnosis of AIDS may further hinder a correct diagnosis. Because many young individuals have a variety of self-defeating behaviors such as drug abuse and promiscuous sexual activity at the time they develop the condition, it is particularly difficult to treat and to research carefully.

General Paresis   Infectious disorders often have an acute onset, although the possibility of slow-acting viral infections should not be ruled out. The central nervous system often is more susceptible to bodily infections than other tissues of the body. Some of these infections do not last long, and successful treatments have been worked out for many of them. If left untreated, however, some infections can lead to irreversible brain disorders.

Untreated **syphilitic infections** are an example of this type of condition. If syphilis is diagnosed before its terminal stages, it can be treated with drugs, usually penicillin. The aim of the drugs is to return the cerebrospinal fluid to normal, which may require many months. These drugs may cure the patient, but the degree of improvement depends on how many neurons were destroyed before the treatment began. When the destruction is great, losses in intellectual functioning cannot be restored.

One of the results of untreated syphilis in its late stage is **general paresis,** or *dementia paralytica,* a progressive deterioration in psychological and motor functioning that results in paralysis, psychosis, and ultimately death. Among the symptoms of general paresis are loss of cognitive functions, slurring of speech, tremors of the tongue and lips, and poor motor coordination. These symptoms are progressive and eventually lead to a helpless condition. Before the cause and treatment of syphilis were discovered, patients with general paresis represented between one-tenth and one-third of all admissions to mental hospitals.

Because of the negative relationship between the degree of possible improvement and the extent of irreversible brain damage, prompt diagnosis and medical treatment of syphilitic infections is clearly the best approach to reducing the incidence of general paresis.

Amnestic Disorders

Amnestic disorders are disturbances of memory due to either the direct physiological effects of a medical condition or the persisting effects of a substance (drugs, medications, exposure to toxic chemicals). Individuals with an amnestic disorder are impaired in their ability to learn new information or are unable to recall previously learned information or past events. The impairment is particularly evident in the areas of social and occupational functioning and most apparent for verbal and visual tasks that require spontaneous recall. While amnestic disorders have a common core of symptoms, the causes vary depending on the area of the brain affected. An amnestic disorder is often preceded by a period of confusion and disorientation. Most patients with severe amnestic conditions do not have insight into their memory deficit and may actually deny the presence of impairment, even though its presence is obvious to others. The impairment could be chronic or transient and short-lived. In the case of head injuries that cause brain trauma, the patient may be amnestic for the time period before, during, and after injury. Even after relatively minor injuries, many patients complain of headaches, dizziness, fatigue, lack of concentration, and anxiety. In most cases these complaints are of short duration.

The Diversity of Cognitive Impairment Disorders

Delirium, dementia, and amnesia are the three categories of cognitive impairment emphasized in DSM-IV. However, there is a wide diversity of impairments that result from the varied nature of the events causing brain dysfunction (e.g., an injury to the brain), the location of the injury or the type of illness, and the age of the individual. For this reason, many patients with cognitive impairment do not fit neatly into standard diagnostic categories. Cerebrovascular accidents and epilepsy illustrate the diversity of dysfunctional brain-behavior relationships.

Cerebrovascular Disorders

Cerebrovascular accidents (CVAs), or **strokes,** are blockages or ruptures of the blood vessels in the cerebrum. When these blood vessels break or are blocked by a clot, a portion of the brain is deprived of its supply of oxygen and blood. Extensive damage to the brain and obvious changes in behavior may result. When the affected blood vessels are small and the interference with blood flow is temporary, the symptoms are milder—perhaps only confusion, unsteadiness, and excessive emotionality. Some of the behavioral effects of a stroke may be similar to the dementia that occurs in cases of brain deterioration. However, the symptoms of stroke characteristically have an abrupt onset and often include **aphasia,** partial or total loss of speech, and paralysis of part of the body.

Strokes are the third-ranking cause of death after heart attacks and cancer. There are approximately 500,000 new strokes and 150,000 deaths due to strokes in the United States each year. Over 80% of these involve people over the age of 65. In addition to age, high blood pressure plays a major role. The single most important way in which strokes can be prevented is through the treatment and control of high blood pressure. Many clinicians have observed that strokes occur especially often in people who live pressured lives. These people tend to have their strokes while they are relaxing or vacationing. Why strokes occur when stress apparently decreases is unclear.

Poststroke depression and anxiety inhibit physical recovery from stroke (Chemerinski & Robinson, 2000). Successful treatment of these psychological conditions (often using antidepressant medications) improves the likelihood of favorable coping with the effects of stroke.

Vascular Dementia Vascular dementia, also called *multi-infarct dementia,* is caused by a series of minor strokes that occur at different times. The onset is abrupt, and the course of the disorder is fluctuating rather than uniformly progressive. The pattern of deficits is "patchy," depending on which areas of the brain have been destroyed. As the condition worsens, the relatively intact areas of intellectual functioning decrease and there is increased disturbance in several functions, including memory, abstract thinking, judgment, and impulse control. Hypertension may be a major factor in multi-infarct dementia. Controlling high blood pressure helps prevent this type of dementia and reduces the likelihood of additional minor strokes when multi-infarct dementia is already present. Vascular dementia is more likely to occur after age 65 than before.

Korsakoff's Syndrome

Vitamin and other nutritional deficiencies can affect the nervous system. **Korsakoff's syndrome,** which occurs in some chronic alcoholics, results from a combination of vitamin B_1 (thiamine) deficiency and alcoholism. This irreversible disorder was described by Sergei Korsakoff in 1887. Recent and past memories are lost, and the person seems unable to form new memories. In addition, there are perceptual deficits, loss of initiative, and confabulation. Delirium tremens frequently is part of the patient's medical history. The longer the vitamin deficiency has persisted, the less responsive the individual will be to vitamin therapy.

Epilepsy

Epilepsy is a transitory disturbance of brain function that develops suddenly, ceases spontaneously, and is likely to recur. The form that this disturbance takes depends on the site in the brain in which it originates, the extent of the brain area involved, and other factors. Epilepsy is not a disease but instead is a symptom consisting of recurrent episodes of changes in state of consciousness with or without an accompanying motor or sensory involvement.

An **epileptic seizure** is a result of transient electrical instability of some cells in the brain, which sometimes triggers an "electrical storm" that spreads through part or all of the brain. This electrical activity culminates in a seizure, which can take one of many forms. Many people with epilepsy have only one type of seizure, but a sizable minority experience two or more types. The major types include *grand mal* and *petit mal* seizures and *psychomotor epilepsy*.

The most severe form of epileptic disorder is the **grand mal** (French for "great illness") **seizure** that typically lasts from 2 to 5 minutes. This type of attack leaves a painful impression on anyone who witnesses it. The victim of a grand mal seizure displays a set of very striking symptoms. The seizure often begins with a cry, followed by loss of consciousness, falling to the floor, and extreme spasms. These uncontrollable spasms can cause serious harm to the victim. Among the greatest dangers are head injuries and severe biting of the tongue or mouth. The muscular movements of a grand mal seizure are usually preceded by an *aura*, in which the individual experiences an altered state of consciousness, including feelings of unreality and depersonalization (feelings of strangeness about oneself). The aura may last only a few seconds, but it is often remembered very vividly.

In the **petit mal** ("small illness" in French) **seizure**, which is particularly common in children, there is no convulsion. Rather, there is a lapse of consciousness characterized by blank staring and lack of responsiveness lasting up to about half a minute. The individual usually does not appear to others to lose consciousness. These seizures may occur many times a day.

In **psychomotor epilepsy**, a type that includes 15% of epilepsy cases and is rarely seen in children, the patient retains control of his or her motor functioning but loses the ability to exercise good judgment in carrying out activities. During a psychomotor attack, the individual is in a kind of trance; his or her movements may be repetitive and highly organized but are in fact semiautomatic. Psychomotor seizures may resemble those of petit mal epilepsy, but they last longer (up to 2 minutes), involve muscle movements related to chewing and speech, and show more clouding of consciousness. The occasional visual hallucinations and the confused state that characterize psychomotor epilepsy are similar to some symptoms of psychosis.

The prevalence of epilepsy is approximately 0.5% and approximately 5% to 10% of the population will have a seizure at some time in their lives (Schwartz & Marsh, 2000). The incidence of epilepsy is highest in the first years of life, remains steady through midlife, and then peaks in elderly persons.

Changing Views of Epilepsy Throughout history, epilepsy has inspired awe, fear, a sense of mystery, and puzzlement. The Greek physician Hippocrates argued that epilepsy was a naturally caused disease, but for much of modern history it was seen as a sign of demonic possession. Many famous people—including Julius Caesar, the elder William Pitt, and Fyodor Dostoyevsky—had epilepsy. Dostoyevsky, one of the world's great novelists, suffered his first epileptic seizure while he was in prison in Siberia. He believed that the agony of living in chains, the stench, and hard labor had precipitated his attacks, which persisted for years even after he was permitted to leave the prison.

It was the English neurologist Hughlings Jackson (1834–1911) who first accounted for epileptic seizures in terms of brain lesions. We now know that epilepsy is caused by intermittent disruption of the brain's neurophysiology. Understanding epilepsy is important, not only because it is a human problem, but also because it provides a path to discovering how the brain works.

Medical Treatment Antiepileptic drugs are now available to reduce the frequency and severity of seizures. Clinical attention must be directed toward establishing optimal dosage levels and identifying possible side effects of medication. If the seizures are a result of some identifiable structural defect and drugs either are not effective or have strong side effects, surgical intervention may be considered. However, because brain surgery entails obvious risks, it is used only when it is clear which area of brain tissue is causing the seizures.

Psychological Factors While most cases of epilepsy can be controlled with anticonvulsant medications, psychological factors often play important roles. The rate of depression in epilepsy is high (perhaps in the range of 30% to 50%). While sadness and demoralization would be understandable reactions to having seizures, underlying brain pathology may contribute to higher rates of depression in epilepsy relative to comparison groups. Antidepressant medications are helpful in treating the depression experienced by persons with epilepsy.

Operant conditioning procedures have been tried successfully with some individuals who cannot be helped by medication. For example, children with epilepsy have been rewarded with attention and care following seizure-free periods. After a seizure occurs, these reinforcers are withdrawn or reduced in strength. Avoiding or changing certain cognitive cues can also be helpful because it is known that the aura preceding a grand mal seizure can be induced by thinking certain thoughts. People with epilepsy who have this form of the disorder can be trained to direct their attention to pleasant thoughts when they feel an aura coming on. Desensitization and relaxation training have been found to be helpful in reducing the frequency of epileptic attacks. Biofeedback, in which patients receive visual or auditory information about their brain wave patterns, can also be an effective treatment.

Many people with epilepsy need help in order to cope with their condition. Because the disorder frequently begins before adulthood, the emotional responses of the affected person's family must also be dealt with. Often the patient and the family see epilepsy as a kind of disgrace and react to it with shame and guilt. Because an atmosphere of emotional tension and frustration can increase the severity of epileptic seizures, psychotherapy and counseling are frequently recommended both for those who have epilepsy and for their families. Many people still view epilepsy as frightening and mysterious. As a result of such attitudes, a person with epilepsy often feels socially stigmatized.

An Integrative Approach to Brain Disorders

Because the conditions discussed in this chapter involve actual organic defects, it is tempting to see them as purely medical problems. Why do we consider brain disorders to be different from other organic problems, such as broken arms or gallstones? A physical defect lies at the root of all of these conditions, but the brain has a complex effect on our behavior as well as on our body. This effect is not as clear and predictable as the effects of damage to other parts of the body. Once a broken arm has been set and healed, for example, the person can return to the condition he or she was in before the accident. This is not the case with brain injuries, and it is for this reason that they are of interest to psychologists.

To comprehend the effects of a brain injury on behavior, we require information about the person's life history, personality, and environmental and biophysical factors. We need to identify vulnerability factors in the person's life and indications of his or her ability to be resilient. Purely physical conditions such as broken arms can be treated successfully without such data. However, although brain disorders can be treated medically, the psychodynamic, behavioral, cognitive, and community approaches are also

important in understanding and treating these conditions. Thus, the most fruitful approach to brain disorders is one that integrates knowledge from these diverse fields.

From a psychodynamic perspective, although certain forms of maladaptive behavior may be organically caused, the way people respond to their condition involves psychological factors such as personality, earlier experience, and characteristic ways of coping. For example, the more outgoing a person is, the greater the likelihood of improvement in his or her condition. Many cases of brain disorder have shown that an individual's personality at the time of the organic damage has an effect on the degree and form of his or her behavioral deterioration. For example, the content of hallucinations and the ease with which they are expressed depend on personality characteristics.

Behavioral psychologists are less interested in the effects of personality and experience than are psychologists who emphasize other perspectives. Behaviorists focus instead on people's ability to adapt to even the most drastic situations. Teaching new responses to compensate for those that have been lost is seen as more important for adjustment than simply helping people accept their new lot in life. Moreover, the way people respond to such training can provide more relevant information about their present psychological state than an examination of their personality before the illness occurred. Because of their emphasis on revising people's maladaptive responses as quickly as possible, behavioral psychologists have a major contribution to make in the treatment of organic brain disorders.

Cognitively oriented psychologists have contributed a variety of techniques to help people in the early stages of dementia deal with the deterioration in their abilities. Memory-aiding techniques such as making lists can help Alzheimer's disease victims, for example. Cognitive techniques are also useful in countering the depression that often accompanies the development of physical problems and declining intellectual competence.

Damage to the brain and central nervous system would not seem to be a condition that is influenced by community variables. Yet, from all indications, central nervous system dysfunction is not randomly distributed. Cases of brain damage are highly concentrated in the segments of the population lowest in socioeconomic status. Within this group, such problems seem to be most prevalent among African American children. This is true for sociological, not biological, reasons. Poor African American infants may become biologically vulnerable shortly after the moment of conception. Inadequate nutrition and prenatal care result in complications of pregnancy, which take their toll in high rates of premature births and congenital defects. These abnormalities include neurological damage that results in impaired intellectual functioning and in behavioral difficulties such as hyperactivity and short attention span. No single complication of pregnancy is more clearly associated with a wide range of neurological dysfunctions than premature birth. For these reasons, those who focus on the community perspective emphasize the prevention of brain disorders through preventive medical care, especially good prenatal care.

The stigma attached to many of the behavioral maladaptations stemming from brain damage often makes the situation worse. People tend to avoid and isolate individuals who are markedly deviant. The behavior of old people provides one of the clearest illustrations of the effects of this social rejection. Mild brain deterioration in a socially rejected older person may lead to greater behavioral maladaptation than moderate deterioration in a person who lives in a friendlier, more accepting environment. From the community perspective, changing people's attitudes toward those who behave differently because of brain disorders can sometimes lessen the behavioral effects of these biological changes.

Cognitive impairment, as seen in delirium, dementia, and amnesia, is a product of events occurring in the brain, but several other factors also play important roles. Psychological and social variables interact with physical condition in determining the individual's level of functioning. A variety of vulnerability and resilience factors (such as general health, the availability of social support, personality characteristics, coping skills, and interests) can influence the impact of brain dysfunction.

Chapter Summary

THE BRAIN: AN INTERACTIONAL PERSPECTIVE

Areas of brain research that are especially important in understanding normal and abnormal behavior are those dealing with how the brain grows and maintains itself; the mechanisms by which it acquires, stores, and uses information; and the role it plays in monitoring and regulating internal bodily processes.

Vulnerability to Brain Disorders Factors that influence vulnerability to brain damage are age, social support, stress, personality factors, physical conditions of the disorder, and overall health.

Assessing Brain Damage Brain disorders that have important effects on thought and behavior are fairly common, occurring more frequently than such disorders as schizophrenia or panic disorder. The presence of brain damage is assessed by clinical tests, neuropsychological testing, and a variety of scanning techniques. The **mental status examination** is an interview that assesses a person's general awareness, appearance, mood, and a number of aspects of cognitive functioning. **Neuropsychology** is a branch of psychology that deals with relationships between behavior and the condition of the brain. Noninvasive imaging techniques are useful in specifying abnormalities in brain anatomy and biochemical processes in different areas of the brain that are linked to disturbances in perception, memory, imagination, thought processes, problem-solving skills, and adjustment.

The Brain and Cognitive Impairment Conditions marked by cognitive impairment may be due to changes in brain function.

DELIRIUM

Delirium is a state of relatively global cognitive impairment, disorientation, and confusion in which a person has difficulty with all aspects of attention. It can occur as a result of many factors, including an acute brain disease or infection, a disease or infection in another part of the body that affects the brain, intoxication, or withdrawal from an addicting substance. People differ widely in their vulnerability to delirium.

Delirium Tremens Delirium tremens, or "the DTs," sometimes result from excessive alcohol consumption. The symptoms—delirium, tremors, and visual hallucinations—usually are not evident until after a person has stopped drinking.

DEMENTIA

Dementia or *brain deterioration* involves a gradual loss of intellectual abilities that interferes with normal functioning. Depending on its cause, dementia may be progressive, static, or reversible. *Senile dementia* refers to this condition if it first occurs after age 65. In younger people, it is called *presenile dementia*. A common symptom of dementia is **confabulation,** in which a person compensates for loss of particular memories by filling in the gaps with inaccurate details.

Alzheimer's Disease Elderly persons are at greater risk than the general population for developing disorders involving brain degeneration. They are also at greater risk for depression as a result of increased life stress that may be age-related. It is important to remember, however, that there are many examples of successful aging.

Alzheimer's disease is the most common form of both senile and presenile dementia. This disease's characteristic tangled clumps and disintegration of nerve cells in the frontal and temporal lobes of the cerebral cortex leads to memory lapses, confusion, and eventual physical and mental deterioration. Research on Alzheimer's disease has focused on neurochemical changes in the brain and on genetic factors. Researchers also have explored ways to help families adapt to the stress of caring for a person with this disease.

Pick's Disease

Pick's disease is much less common than Alzheimer's disease. This disorder can be diagnosed only at autopsy by a characteristic form of brain atrophy.

Huntington's Disease

Huntington's disease is a rare hereditary disorder transmitted by a single dominant gene. It results in a progressive degeneration of brain tissue. Its symptoms have been found to be related to a deficiency of one neurotransmitter, GABA, and are thought to be related to a gene defect in chromosome pair no. 4.

Parkinson's Disease

Symptoms of **Parkinson's disease** are progressive deterioration of intellectual ability, increased rigidity in coping, tremor, and masklike facial appearance. This disease is believed to be related to a dopamine deficiency and can be treated with the drug L-dopa.

Brain Trauma: Injuries, Tumors, and Infections

Brain injuries, tumors, and infections can result in profound cognitive and behavioral consequences. Some of the changed behavior may be the result of psychological factors related to the injury. Such changes are referred to as **traumatic neurosis.** Brain injuries are classified into three groups: **concussions,** which result in transient problems; **contusions,** where there is diffuse damage; and **lacerations,** which involve major tears or ruptures in the brain tissue. **Brain tumors** can result in a variety of behavioral changes depending on the location of the tumor. **HIV-associated cognitive impairment** and **general paresis** are examples of dementia caused by infections.

AMNESTIC DISORDERS

Amnestic disorders are disturbances of memory due either to a medical condition or to the effects of drugs, medication, or exposure to toxic chemicals. People with amnestic disorders have difficulty learning new material and/or recalling previously acquired information. Amnestic impairments can be transient or chronic.

THE DIVERSITY OF COGNITIVE IMPAIRMENT DISORDERS

Many cognitive impairment disorders do not fit neatly into established diagnostic categories. There is wide diversity of cognitive impairments.

Cerebrovascular Disorders

Cerebrovascular accidents (CVAs) or **strokes** are blockages or ruptures of the blood vessels in the cerebrum. Some of the effects may be similar to those of dementia, but the onset is sudden rather than gradual. **Vascular dementia** is caused by a series of minor strokes that occur over a period of time.

Korsakoff's Syndrome

Korsakoff's syndrome is the result of a combination of alcoholism and vitamin B_1 deficiency. It causes loss of memory and initiative, perceptual deficits, and confabulation.

Epilepsy

Epilepsy is due to an abnormality in brain cell behavior that may have many causes. Some epilepsies are related to generalized seizures, while others can be traced to a source in a specific area of the brain. **Grand mal seizures** last several minutes and include loss of consciousness and convulsions. **Petit mal seizures** are lapses of consciousness that last less than a minute and do not include convulsions. **Psychomotor epilepsy** involves a trancelike state lasting up to 2 minutes and may include outbursts of emotions. Epilepsy can be treated with drugs, surgery, or psychological management, depending on the symptoms.

AN INTEGRATIVE APPROACH TO BRAIN DISORDERS

Although brain disorders involve organic problems, knowledge of psychological factors is very important in predicting exactly how a person's behavior will be affected. Each of the psychological perspectives is useful in understanding the impact of these disorders.

Key Terms

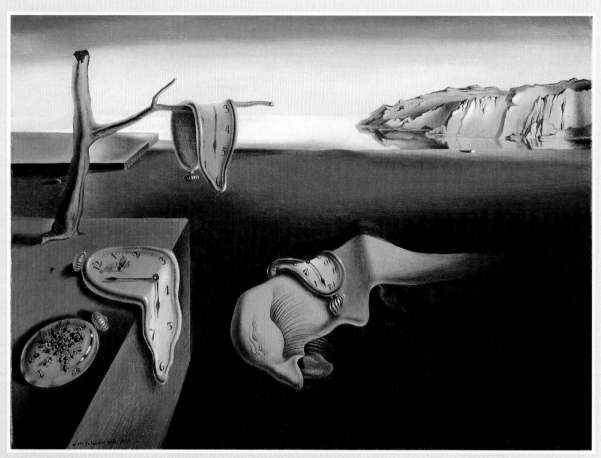

Salvador Dali "The Persistence of Memory (Persistance de la memoire)" 1931, oil on canvas, 9½ × 13 in. (24.1 × 33 cm). The Museum of Modern Art, New York. Given anonymously. Photograph © 2002 The Museum of Modern Art. © 2002 Kingdom of Spain, Gala-Salvador Dali Foundation/Artists Rights Society (ARS), New York.

Substance-Related Disorders

"My alcoholism took years to develop into a chronic affliction, and during much of that time I went to bars after work, one of the guys. The delusion was gradually reinforced by gravitation. I mingled more and more with other persistent drinkers who took longer and longer to call for their bar tabs. Most of us were actually alcoholics in varying stages of development. The nonalcoholics had long ago selected themselves out. Those of us who remained agreed that we were 'normal.' Unhappy, but normal.

"Alcoholic perceptions are like that, in a hundred insidious and distorting ways. All of them are aimed at protecting a drunkard's notion that he is possessed of free will. My drinking buddies and I agreed that we did not have a drinking problem. Everything in our increasingly narrow world, though, was a problem that required drinking: the wife, the kids, the boss, the government. In dingy watering holes from which everyone with a healthy life to lead had gone home, we conspired to overlook the obvious, that our bodily cells were addicted, and our minds were along for the ride.

"Inexorably, the need for alcohol grew, while the lies wore thin. As my alcoholism accelerated, I abandoned most drinking partners and joined the ranks of solitary topers bellied up to countless bars. I lost any sense at all of what would happen after I started drinking; I became completely unpredictable. Sometimes I would go home after a couple of drinks (there was usually more booze there). More often, I would join the lineup of other alcoholics at the bar telephone stalls, fumbling with worn-out excuses about unexpected visitors and urgent business meetings.

"Sometimes I would simply hole up in my office with a bottle after everyone else had gone home. There simply wasn't anything else in my life. Most frightening of all, I began to suffer alcoholic blackouts during drinking episodes. I would swim back into consciousness with no recollection of where I had been or what I had done. Once, I came to late at night on a downtown city street with my suit trousers slashed down one side by a razor." ■

425

This first-person account illustrates a number of features seen in substance-related disorders. This man, who is struggling with alcoholism while denying that he has an alcohol problem, develops an increasingly strong linkage between social interaction and drinking, moves on to solitary drinking, and finally displays symptoms that leave no doubt that his drinking is out of control.

Alcohol is one of a group of substances that have ruined the lives of countless numbers of people. Although there are many differences among them, all of these substances are **psychoactive drugs**; that is, they affect thought, emotions, and behavior. A generalized reduction in goal-directed behavior (e.g., going to school or work), together with cognitive deficits (such as inability to concentrate), is a common consequence of prolonged heavy use of a psychoactive substance. Other consequences are changes in motivation, lessened ability to concentrate and think clearly, and frequently serious physical symptoms.

The scope of the problem of substance abuse is suggested by the fact that 13.8% of the U.S. population aged 18 and older meet DSM criteria for an alcohol-related disorder (Robins & Regier, 1991). In addition, 6.2% meet the criteria for abuse of or dependence on a substance other than alcohol or tobacco. *Addiction* is a term that has been used to describe the harmful effects of excessive reliance on drugs for pleasure and relief of tension. This term is not used in DSM-IV, which instead focuses attention on *substance dependence*. DSM-IV contains two broad categories of substance-related disorders: the substance-use disorders and the substance-induced disorders.

Substance-Use Disorders

Substance-use disorders include problems associated with using and abusing such drugs as alcohol, cocaine, and heroin, which alter the way people think, feel, and behave. There are two subgroups of substance-use disorders: those related to substance dependence and those related to substance abuse.

Substance Dependence

DSM-IV defines **substance dependence** as a maladaptive pattern of substance use that leads to clinically significant impairment or distress. Table 13-1 presents the criteria for this disorder. Cognitive, behavioral, and physiological symptoms define the condition of substance dependence. Most individuals with substance dependence have an intense craving for a particular substance. They continue to use it even though doing so exacerbates their substance-related problems. There are alterations in their bodily systems (particularly the nervous system) when drug use is discontinued, and a need for increased

---

Table 13-1

Diagnostic Criteria for Substance Dependence

The presence of three or more of the following criteria in the same 12-month period establishes the existence of substance dependence:

1. Tolerance, as defined by the need for markedly increased amounts of the substance to achieve the desired effect and a markedly diminished effect with continued use of the same amount of the substance.
2. Withdrawal, as defined by the characteristic withdrawal syndrome for the substance and use of the substance to relieve or avoid withdrawal symptoms.
3. Ingestion of larger amounts or over a longer period than was intended.
4. Persistent desire or unsuccessful effort to cut down or control substance abuse.
5. A great deal of time spent in activities necessary to obtain the substance, use the substance, or recover from its effects.
6. Elimination or reduction of important social, occupational, or recreational activities that are given up or reduced because of substance use.
7. Continued substance use despite knowledge of having a persistent or recurrent physical or psychological problem that is caused or exacerbated by the substance.

---

frequency and amount of the substance to get the same effects as previously. Withdrawal symptoms occur if use of the drug is discontinued. Substance-dependent individuals show a distinctive pattern of repeated use that usually results in tolerance, withdrawal symptoms, and compulsive drug-taking.

In the context of substance use, **tolerance** refers to the need to use more and more of a substance to get the same effect because the same-size dose has progressively less effect as time goes by. Reactions to morphine and alcohol are examples of tolerance build-up. The pain-reducing power of morphine decreases if the drug is given over a long period. As alcoholics consume increasing amounts of alcohol, their cell membranes are altered so that less and less of the alcohol permeates the membranes. If less alcohol is actually penetrating cell membranes, an alcoholic may have less alcohol in his or her brain than a nonalcoholic person with the same blood level of alcohol would. This is interesting in view of the fact that some alcoholics can perform well after consuming an amount of alcohol that would put a nonalcoholic into a coma. Whereas tolerance for alcohol is considerable, it is usually much less extreme than tolerance for some other substances, such as amphetamines. The degree to which tolerance develops varies greatly from substance to substance.

Withdrawal refers to a particular set of physical symptoms that occur when a person stops or cuts down on the use of a psychoactive substance. The severe physical reaction that occurs when heroin use is curtailed is probably the best-known example of withdrawal. Withdrawal symptoms vary greatly, according to the class of substance. Marked and generally easily measured physiological signs of withdrawal are common with alcohol and anxiety-reducing drugs. Withdrawal symptoms are often present, but less apparent, with stimulants such as amphetamines and cocaine.

Compulsive substance use involves behavior directed toward obtaining the substance, frequently called *drug-seeking behavior*, and behavior associated with the actual ingestion or use of the substance. Someone who is dependent on a drug gives its use a much higher priority than other behaviors that once had higher value. Substance-dependent individuals may expend inordinate effort and time trying to obtain the substance on which they are dependent, and frequently when it is available they are unable to control the amount they use or the length of time they use it. This lack of control may be manifested by unsuccessful efforts to reduce or stop using the substance despite a persistent wish to do so. They may continue to use the substance, often in situations in which it is physically hazardous to do so, despite an awareness of the serious problems this causes.

Substance Abuse

In **substance abuse** there are recurrent and significant adverse consequences related to the use of substances. These consequences include repeated failure to fulfill major obligations (e.g., as a parent), repeated use of the substance in situations in which it is physically hazardous to do so, legal problems, and recurrent social and interpersonal problems. The criteria for substance abuse do not include tolerance, withdrawal, or a pattern of compulsive use. Instead, its outstanding features are only the harmful consequences of repeated use. Table 13-2 presents DSM-IV criteria for this disorder.

The concepts of substance dependence and substance abuse have long been controversial, and this controversy has been reflected in DSM changes over the years. In DSM-II the term *dependence* included both psychological and physiological dependence. Psychological dependence had to do with psychologically based substance-seeking behavior that resulted in a fairly regular schedule of daily or continuous usage, while physiological dependence referred to substance-seeking behavior in which physiologically based tolerance and withdrawal played key roles. In DSM-III, *dependence* was used only in the physiological sense and required evidence of either tolerance or withdrawal.

Table 13-2

Diagnostic Criteria for Substance Abuse

The presence of three or more of the following criteria within a 12-month period establishes the existence of substance abuse:

1. Recurrent substance use resulting in a failure to fulfill important obligations (e.g., at work, school, or home).
2. Recurrent substance use in situations in which it is physically hazardous to do so (e.g., driving an automobile when under the substance's influence).
3. Recurrent substance-related legal problems (e.g., arrests).
4. Continued substance use despite having persistent or recurrent social or interpersonal problems caused or exacerbated by the effects of the substance (e.g., physical fights).

As we have seen, DSM-IV distinguishes between substance dependence and substance abuse. The current criteria for substance dependence include tolerance, withdrawal, and compulsive use, whereas the criteria for substance abuse are essentially psychological problems and maladaptive behavior (e.g., failing to fulfill social or work responsibilities). However, some writers have argued that there is no meaningful distinction between substance abuse and substance dependence and that substance abuse is simply a less severe (and overlapping) variant of substance dependence (Widiger & Smith, 1994). While there is agreement that drug usage becomes a substance-use disorder when control is impaired, increased knowledge concerning the physiological and psychological aspects of the process will no doubt influence future efforts to classify these disorders.

Substance-Induced Disorders

Recent ingestion of certain substances can lead to serious behavioral, psychological, and physiological signs and symptoms. Different substances have quite distinctive effects. **Substance intoxication** is usually associated with substance abuse or dependence. However, one or more episodes of intoxication alone are not sufficient for a diagnosis of either substance dependence or abuse.

Evidence for recent ingestion of the substance is obtained from physical evidence (e.g., the smell of alcohol on the breath), case histories, and analyses of bodily fluids (e.g., urine or blood). DSM-IV's criteria for substance intoxication include the development of reversible substance-specific symptoms due to recent ingestion of or exposure to a substance and clinically significant maladaptive behavioral or psychological changes due to the

Table 13-3

Diagnostic Criteria for Substance Intoxication

1. Development of a reversible substance-specific syndrome due to recent ingestion of (or exposure to) a substance.
2. Clinically significant maladaptive behavioral or psychological changes due to the effect of the substance on the central nervous system (e.g., cognitive impairment, mood lability, belligerence, impaired judgment, impaired social or occupational functioning). These changes develop during or shortly after use of the substance.
3. The symptoms are not due to a general medical condition and are not better accounted for by another mental disorder.

effect of the substance on the central nervous system (see Table 13-3).

The most common indications of intoxication are disturbances of perception, wakefulness, attention, thinking, judgment, motor behavior, and interpersonal behavior. The substance, the dose, the history of using the substance, the person's tolerance for the substance, the period of time since the last dose, the person's expectations regarding the substance's effects, and the environment or setting all can influence level of intoxication. **Substance-induced disorders** cause a variety of symptoms that are characteristic of other mental disorders. These symptoms include delirium and psychotic behavior.

Psychologists are interested in substance-use disorders and substance-induced disorders because each person's response to drugs seems to be due to a combination of physiological and psychological factors. Some people can control their use of many psychoactive substances; others seem unable to do so. Some individuals have severe withdrawal symptoms; others do not. The effects that drugs produce also differ from one user to another.

People differ in their vulnerability to the negative effects of particular substances and in their resilience after an experience of substance use. The personality and physiological characteristics of the user and the environment or setting in which the substance is used probably combine to influence the reaction. This is another case in which the interaction between the person and the situation, which has been referred to so often throughout this book, is important in understanding individual behavior. However, although individual characteristics have a major influence on a person's response to a mood- or behavior-modifying substance, such substances do have certain general effects that are experienced by most people who use them. Table 13-4 describes some of the typical effects and symptoms caused by six types of psychoactive substances, along with the consequences of overdose.

Most adults use some substances; most do not use them pathologically. What is pathological use? It is use beyond which any positive effects are outweighed by negative effects. Often this point comes early—for some people and substances, with their first exposure. Typically, the use is frequent and leads to symptoms and maladaptive changes in behavior.

To gain an appreciation of the diversity of substance-related disorders, we turn now to a review of the major ones, beginning with problems related to the use of alcohol. In most cultures, alcohol is the most frequently used

Table 13-4

Several Types of Substances, Their Effects and Symptoms, and the Consequences of Overdose

Substance	Typical Effects and Symptoms	Consequences of Overdose
Alcohol	Tension reduction followed by depressed physical and psychological functioning.	Disorientation, loss of consciousness, and death at extremely high blood-alcohol levels.
Tranquilizing drugs	Depressed reflexes and impaired motor functioning; tension reduction.	Shallow respiration, dilated pupils, clammy skin, weak and rapid pulse, coma, possible death.
Amphetamines	Increased alertness, excitation, euphoria, increased pulse rate and blood pressure, sleeplessness.	Agitation, hallucinations, paranoid delusions, convulsions, death.
Heroin	Initial euphoria followed by apathy, drowsiness, "rush" of pleasure, impaired judgment.	Slow, shallow breathing, nausea, clammy skin, vomiting, convulsions, coma, possible death.
LSD	Illusions, hallucinations, distortions in time perception, loss of contact with reality, palpitations.	Psychotic reactions.
Marijuana	Euphoria, relaxed inhibitions, increased appetite, possible disorientation, dry mouth.	Fatigue, possible psychosis.

brain depressant and a cause of serious and widespread interpersonal and health problems.

Alcohol-Related Disorders

Alcohol has been used for recreational, medicinal, and ceremonial purposes for at least ten thousand years. The oldest of all archaeological records contain reference to its use. The alcohol that is contained in beer, wine, and hard liquor is a chemical compound known as ethyl alcohol, or ethanol. Only ethanol is safe for human consumption. Other kinds of alcohol are isopropyl alcohol (rubbing alcohol) and methyl alcohol (wood alcohol).

Ethanol is manufactured by two methods, distillation (hard liquors) and fermentation (beer and wine). Despite these different production methods, the ethanol contained in all these beverages is the same drug. The only difference is in the amount of alcohol as a percentage of total volume. In beer and wine, the percentage usually varies from 3% to 14%. In hard liquor, sometimes called *distilled spirits*, the percentage varies from 40% (80 proof) to 75% (150 proof). The amount of pure ethanol is generally about the same in a 1-ounce shot of whiskey (or other hard liquor), a 4-ounce glass of wine, and a 12-ounce bottle of beer.

In the short term, alcohol acts on the central nervous system as a "blocker" of messages transmitted from one nerve cell to the next. It first affects the frontal lobes of the brain, the seat of inhibitions, reasoning powers, memory, and judgment. After continued consumption, it next affects the cerebellum, the seat of motor muscle control, balance, and the five senses. Finally, it affects the spinal cord and the brain's medulla, which govern involuntary functions such as breathing, heart rate, and body temperature control. If enough alcohol is consumed—to the point of a blood-alcohol level of 0.50% or more—the involuntary function system can shut down and the person may die from acute alcohol poisoning.

Excessive Alcohol Use

Negative effects from the overuse of alcohol have been considered a serious problem for many years. About 70% of adults in America drink alcohol on occasion; 12% of these Americans are heavy drinkers, people who drink almost every day and become intoxicated several times a month. More men than women are heavy drinkers. For both men and women, the prevalence of drinking is highest and abstention is lowest in the 21- to 34-year age range.

Alcohol consumption and problems related to its excessive use vary from country to country, and in a particular country often from region to region. In addition, there are important cultural and ethnic differences in how alcohol and other substances are used and the occurrence of substance-related disorders (see Box 13-1). Overall, within the United States, per capita alcohol consumption has been decreasing for several years. Nationwide, the growth of abstinence and the decline of heavy drinking are often attributed to rising health consciousness and greater caution about the hazards of drinking and driving. However, a hard-drinking minority consumes a lot of alcohol. About half of all the alcohol drunk in the country is consumed in sprees of five or more drinks at a time. This binge drinking may be a major factor in the large number of alcohol-related traffic deaths. The top 10% of drinkers—averaging more than 2.5 drinks a day, or just over the limit for healthy intake—account for over 60% of the alcohol consumed in the United States.

Over the years, the terminology used to describe the excessive use of alcohol has ranged widely. It has been characterized in terms of alcohol dependence or alcohol abuse, as a disease that is essentially an involuntary disability, and as alcoholism. Characterizing it as alcoholism usually recognizes that excessive drinking involves multiple causes, signs, and symptoms that usually include dependence and abuse. DSM-IV defines **physiological dependence on alcohol** in terms of tolerance and symptoms of withdrawal. **Alcohol abuse** is defined in terms of behavioral indicators such as lowered job performance and poor interpersonal relationships. In **alcohol intoxication** there are clinically significant behavioral and psychological changes (e.g., inappropriate sexual or aggressive behavior, slurred speech, lack of coordination, impaired attention or memory, or coma) (see Table 13-5).

Table 13–5

Diagnostic Criteria for Alcohol Intoxication

1. Recent ingestion of alcohol.
2. Clinically significant maladaptive behavior or psychological changes (such as inappropriate sexual or aggressive behavior, mood liability, impaired judgment, impaired social or occupational functioning) that develop during, or shortly after, alcohol use.
3. One or more of the following signs that develop during, or shortly after, alcohol ingestion:
   a. Slurred speech
   b. Incoordination
   c. Unsteady gait
   d. Nystagmus (involuntary spasmodic motion of the eyeballs)
   e. Impairment in attention or memory
   f. Stupor or coma
4. The symptoms are not due to a general medical condition and are not better accounted for by another disorder.

Q. You have emphasized throughout the book the roles of culture and ethnicity in maladaptive behavior. How do they relate to the use of alcohol? I'm under the impression that alcohol is an especially big problem for some groups, such as Native Americans. Is that correct?

A. *The use of alcohol and other drugs varies considerably across racial, ethnic, and cultural groups. However, it is necessary to bear in mind that each of these groups is far from homogeneous. Many of the generalizations that have been drawn about differences among various groups have been based on studies of limited subsets of them, for example, males, the unemployed, and people with low incomes.*

With regard to alcohol use, it is highest among European Americans and Native Americans, followed by Latino/Hispanic Americans and African Americans (Jung, 2001). It is lowest among Asian Americans. But, as we mentioned, there is quite a bit of variability within these groups, for example, Latino American fathers and Asian American fathers are much more likely than mothers to use alcohol. Drinking is much more acceptable among European American mothers than among Latino American and Asian American mothers. Higher educational and socioeconomic levels reduce the risk of substance use disorders in virtually all groups. Many studies of Hispanic alcohol and other drug use have combined data from such diverse groups as Mexicans, Puerto Ricans,

Cubans, and Central and South Americans. However, there may be significant differences among these groups.

The minority group with the highest rate of alcohol abuse is Native Americans, with the highest rates among those who live in cities. There are a number of significant differences among the various Native American groups in the reasons for drinking and the social contexts in which it occurs. Some forms of intoxication have traditionally been an integral part of certain Native American sacred ceremonies. Contrasting with Native Americans, Asian Americans come from cultures that have emphasized Confucian ideals of moderation. As a result, moderate use of alcohol for males and little or no alcohol consumption for females have traditionally been the norm. However, there are significant differences among Asian Americans, with Chinese American groups having high rates of abstention and low rates of alcoholism. Alcohol use seems to be greater among Japanese Americans and Korean Americans than among Chinese Americans. What is common to Asian cultures is that they discourage public intoxication.

*While there is some information about the complex factors involved in the use of alcohol and other substances, many variables need much more study. For example, **acculturation,** the modification of members of one culture as a result of contact with another culture, is quite likely relevant to substance use because use tends to move away from*

those in the country of origin toward those for the U.S. general population. Complicating the picture is the fact that immigrants come in waves often with different patterns of acculturation. For example, immigrants from Japan to the United States at the turn of the twentieth century came from a different background than those coming at the turn of the twenty-first century, and the United States was certainly very different at these two points in time.

The use of other drugs besides alcohol also varies among different groups. For example, cigarette smoking is highest for Native Americans and lowest for Asian Americans, with men generally smoking at higher rates than women. Among high school students, those with Caucasian backgrounds have high rates of illicit drug use, but Hispanics and Native Americans also have high rates. African Americans, Asians, and Pacific Islanders tend to have lower rates. Patterns of illicit drug use are less clear.

What these similarities and differences suggest is that an understanding of them requires attention to many factors that are often neglected in particular kinds of comparisons. Some of the commonly accepted differences and their explanations may be incorrect because of heterogeneity within and between minority groups and the relevance for particular groups of historical factors, acculturation patterns, and demographic factors, such as socioeconomic level, education, and gender differences.

Alcohol and Risk Regardless of the terms employed, there is agreement about the harmful effects for individuals and the community of excessive intake of alcohol. Forty percent of all traffic fatalities (the leading cause of accidental death) are alcohol-related (see Table 13-6). Highway accidents in which alcohol is involved are the primary cause of death for young people. After 18-year-olds received the right to vote in 1971, the legal drinking age was lowered in many states. Studies of auto accident statistics from these states produced convincing evidence that the age reduction had resulted in an increased proportion of auto crashes and fatalities involving youthful drivers. After 1976, therefore, many states raised the drinking age. In the 12 months after Michigan raised the drinking age, accidents resulting in death or injury among 18- to 20-year-olds dropped by 28%.

Alcohol is also involved in a high percentage of non-traffic accidents: almost 50% of people who die from falls

had been drinking; 52% of the fires that lead to adult deaths involve alcohol; and 38% of drowning victims had been drinking (*Alcohol and Health*, 1990).

Alcohol and Health Perhaps 20% of the total national expenditure for health is alcohol-related. A recent survey found that over 10 million Americans had major problems with alcoholism, most of which involved physiological dependence (tolerance, withdrawal, and drinking to relieve or avoid withdrawal symptoms). Alcoholism shows several typical patterns: regular daily intake of a large amount, regular heavy drinking confined to weekends, and unpredictable binge drinking (long periods without alcohol interrupted by episodes of heavy drinking lasting for weeks or months). Much of the excessive use of alcohol that has not reached clinical proportions might be called **problem drinking.** While problem drink-

Table 13-6

Is It Safe to Drive?

The amount of alcohol that seriously interferes with driving skills varies from person to person, and even one individual's tolerance can vary at different times. In general, however, impairment increases with each drink and the subsequent rise in blood-alcohol level. As little as one drink—especially if you do not drink regularly or if you drink on an empty stomach—can make you an unsafe driver.

Blood–Alcohol Concentration (%)	Effects on Driving
0.05	Blood-alcohol concentrations of 0.05% and above can mean lax thought, judgment, and restraint. There may be a significant increase in mistakes in tasks requiring divided attention. Steering errors increase and vision is affected.
0.10	Around 0.10%, virtually all drivers are significantly impaired. Reaction time to novel situations requiring choices is slowed, as are reactions to sounds and visual stimulation. Voluntary motor activity is affected, with arm movements, walking, and speech usually becoming noticeably clumsy. At this blood-alcohol level, the likelihood of being involved in a crash is six times that of a sober driver.
0.20	At 0.20% the entire motor area of the brain is significantly depressed, and the person is very drunk. Staggering is likely. Reactions time is even slower, especially in tasks requiring divided attention. The person may become loud, incoherent, and emotionally unstable. At this level, the risk of a crash is 100 times that of a sober person.

ing should not be viewed as an inevitable step on the way to alcoholism, one study found that over a 4-year period 30% of people initially categorized as problem drinkers and alcohol abusers had become alcohol dependent (Hasin et al., 1990).

As the case with which this chapter began suggests, drinking that begins as a social activity often evolves into the solitary drinking behavior typical of alcoholism. Figure 13-1 illustrates this pattern.

Alcohol abuse and dependence are linked to physical, as well as behavioral, impairment. Table 13-7 describes the negative effects of alcohol on various organs and systems in the body. When alcohol is abused extensively, brain damage can result. For example, CT scans of chronic alcoholics show reductions in the density of their left brain hemispheres compared to those of nonalcoholic individuals. In addition to damage to regions of the brain involved in sensory, motor, and cognitive functions,

(a)

(b)

Figure 13-1 Drinking takes place in many different settings. (a) These couples have incorporated a drink with friends as one aspect of a pleasant social interaction. (b) This solitary drinker, who is likely to be using alcohol as a way of dealing with worries or depressed feelings, probably began drinking in social situations like the one at left.

Table 13-7	
The Effects of Alcohol on the Body	
Organ or System	Effect
Brain	Brain cells are altered, and many die; memory formation is blocked; senses are dulled; physical coordination is impaired.
Stomach and intestines	Alcohol can trigger bleeding and can cause cancer.
Heart	Deterioration of the heart muscle can occur.
Immune system	Infection-fighting cells are prevented from functioning properly; risk of bacterial disease is increased.
Reproductive system	In men: hormone levels change, causing lower sex drive and enlarged breasts; in women: menstrual cycles become irregular and ovaries malfunction.

chronic use of too much alcohol can result in decreased blood flow and metabolic rates in certain brain regions. Results of autopsies show that individuals with a history of chronic alcohol consumption have smaller, lighter, more shrunken brains than nonalcoholic adults of the same age and sex. Brain dysfunction is present in 50% to 70% of detoxified alcoholics at the beginning of treatment.

The damaging effects of alcohol use by pregnant women on their unborn children has also been clearly documented. Because alcohol freely crosses the placenta, the developing fetus's blood-alcohol level will be equal to that of the mother. As a result, the child may develop *fetal alcohol syndrome*, which produces physical malformations and mental retardation. It was at first thought that fetal alcohol syndrome was related to the mother's heavy alcohol use and to binge drinking in particular. More recent research has shown that even light to moderate alcohol use may have negative effects on the unborn child. (Fetal alcohol syndrome is discussed in detail in Chapter 15.)

In addition to what alcohol does to the body, its role in behavioral maladaptation is also powerful. This fact is reflected in comorbidity data showing that among people with alcohol disorders, another mental disorder appears in 37% of cases (Robins & Regier, 1991). Alcohol disorders in men are associated with an eightfold risk for psychotic episodes; in women, there is a threefold risk (Tien & Anthony, 1990). The highest comorbidity rates are for affective, anxiety, and antisocial personality disorders. Comorbidity rates are generally higher in women than men. The causes of high comorbidity rates related to alcohol abuse and dependence have not yet been discovered. When two disorders are associated, the one that occurs first might be a risk for the other. Generally, alcoholism precedes depression in the majority of cases. However, among women, depression usually comes first (R. Meyer, 1989).

Surprisingly, alcohol may also have some beneficial effects. Moderate use of alcohol (2 ounces per day) may lessen the chances of a heart attack. It is not clear why this should be the case, but researchers have suggested a

number of possibilities. Alcohol may reduce psychological stress, or it may promote the formation of substances that help prevent or remove the plaque that can clog coronary arteries. Some public health officials are concerned that announcing that alcohol use can have positive effects will be interpreted as a suggestion that drinking is desirable for everyone. What is a moderate amount for one person may be too much for another because of individual differences in tolerance for alcohol. This is discussed in the next section under "Metabolism of Alcohol."

Women appear to be more vulnerable than men to some of the adverse consequences of alcohol use. Many of these differences in the consequences of alcohol consumption are due to differences in certain bodily processes. Women achieve higher concentrations of alcohol in the blood and become more impaired than men after drinking equivalent amounts of alcohol because women absorb and metabolize alcohol differently than men. This is related to the fact that women have less body water than men of similar body weight resulting in the higher concentrations of alcohol in the blood. Where women and men drink at the same rate, women are at higher risk for certain serious medical consequences of alcohol use, including liver, brain, and heart damage. In addition to metabolism, research to better understand gender differences in the effects of alcohol use is also being focused on brain chemistry and genetic risk factors.

Theories and Treatment

Alcohol-related disorders do not have just one cause. There are many, and they often combine to produce bodily, psychological, and behavioral effects. Therefore, it is not surprising that several theoretical perspectives have contributed to research on these disorders and their treatment.

Regardless of the theoretical perspective, the first step in treating alcohol dependence is usually **detoxification,** or "drying out." Many alcoholics can withdraw on their own, but some are so severely dependent that they have to be detoxified-supervised as they go through a gradual withdrawal. Detoxification, which usually is carried out in a protected, well-supervised setting such as a hospital, is aimed at removing the effects of a toxic substance (e.g., alcohol) from the body. Physiological withdrawal symptoms often begin 6 to 24 hours after heavy drinking has stopped, although they can occur as soon as alcoholics simply reduce their intake of alcohol. Withdrawal symptoms can include tremors, delirium, sweating, confusion, increased blood pressure, and agitation. There is no established sobering agent—nothing that counteracts the effects of alcohol or speeds its breakdown and passage out of the body.

Once detoxification is complete, insomnia, depression, and anxiety may persist for weeks or months. However, these conditions usually receive no treatment after the detoxification period has ended.

Most recovery from alcoholism is not the result of treatment (L. C. Sobell et al., 1996). Probably no more than 10% of alcohol abusers are ever treated at all, but as many as 40% recover on their own. Alcoholics with a stable job and family life have the best chance of recovery; age, sex, and the duration of alcohol abuse matter less for them.

An important step in overcoming alcoholism is the alcoholic's acknowledgement of the disorder. Unfortunately, many alcohol abusers feel ashamed and guilty: they may refuse to admit the problem to themselves and try to conceal it from their families and friends, who in turn may avoid acknowledging it for fear of being intrusive or having to take responsibility.

James B., a 62-year-old man, had denied his drinking problem, and so had his family and friends. He had been depressed over the death of his wife and the loss of his business and had been presenting different excuses to his family and friends for his growing isolation. When confronted by loved ones about his drinking, he said, "My problems have nothing to do with alcohol."

It is valuable in clinical interviews to determine the patient's willingness to admit the seriousness of his or her drinking problem (see Table 13-8).

Table 13-8

Determining Extent of a Drinking Problem and the Alcoholic's Willingness to Admit the Problem— The Initial Steps in Treatment Planning

It is not necessarily useful simply to ask how much a person drinks, because the response is likely to be vague and may be influenced by denial. One of the best ways of determining the extent of denial of the symptoms is a series of questions that can be addressed to alcoholics. Here are some helpful questions.

Questions About Drinking Patterns or Habits

- Do you sometimes drink heavily after a disappointment or quarrel?
- Do you always drink more heavily when you feel under pressure?
- Are you drinking more often without eating?
- Do you try to sneak in extra drinks on social occasions?
- Have you attempted various ways to control your drinking?
- Have you failed to keep promises to yourself to cut down?
- Do you avoid your family and close friends while drinking?

Questions About Feelings

- Do you feel guilty about your drinking?
- Do you want to go on drinking when your friends have had enough?
- Do you often regret what you have said or done while drinking?
- Do you feel uncomfortable if alcohol is not available in certain situations?
- Are you annoyed by the way others talk about your drinking?

Questions for Friends and Family Members

- Does this person's drinking ever worry or embarrass you?
- Does it spoil family holidays?
- Does it create a tense atmosphere?
- Do you lie to conceal it?
- Does he or she try to justify the drinking or avoid discussion of it?
- Do you or your children fear physical or verbal assault from this person when he or she is drinking?
- Does this person become remorseful and apologize after a drinking episode?
- Do others talk about this person's drinking?

Denial and obliviousness are not the only sources of misunderstanding about drinking. In a society that has so many heavy drinkers, it is not always easy to decide when a drinking problem has become so serious that special help is needed. Alcoholism can be hard to observe day by day, even if it's easily recognizable over a period of years. Patterns of abuse through a lifetime are variable; the symptoms come and go. Alcoholics do not always drink uncontrollably; some drink only on weekends, and many succeed in remaining abstinent or nearly abstinent for months at a time.

The Biological Approach After the first drink, the average person experiences a lessening of anxiety. As more alcohol is consumed, the depressant action of alcohol affects brain functions. The individual staggers, and his or her mood becomes markedly unstable.

Influenced by evidence that heavy drinking leads to a variety of bodily changes, writers have often characterized alcoholism itself as a disease. E. M. Jellinek (1960), often referred to as the father of the modern study of alcoholism, believed that alcoholism is a permanent and irreversible condition and that alcoholics are essentially different from nonalcoholics. Alcoholics, he contended, experience an irresistible physical craving for alcohol. Satisfaction of this craving leads to loss of control as a result of increasing physical dependence. Alcoholic individuals feel compelled to continue drinking even after ingesting only a small amount of alcohol. Jellinek believed that the only way alcoholics could return to a normal life was through complete abstinence.

Some of Jellinek's ideas have been questioned on the basis of research findings that seem inconsistent with them. However, Jellinek's concept of alcoholism as a disease did succeed in changing the public attitude toward alcoholics from one of condemnation and blame to one of concern. In addition, it focused researchers' attention on biological aspects of alcohol abuse, such as hereditary influences, the effects of alcohol on the brain and nervous system, and differences among individuals and groups of people in sensitivity to alcohol.

Biological approaches to the effects of alcohol have identified a number of factors pertinent to what alcohol does to the body, particularly metabolic, genetic, and neural processes. We have already touched upon some of the pertinent research.

Metabolism of Alcohol Individual sensitivity to the effects of alcohol varies greatly. As noted earlier, some people can remain conscious after drinking a quantity of alcohol that would cause others to pass out, become comatose, or even die. Others are so sensitive to alcohol that just one or two drinks can produce acute discomfort accompanied by obvious physiological changes. These individual variations are probably due to differences in the ability to metabolize alcohol or to innate differences in the central nervous system's **sensitivity to alcohol**.

When compared with men, women have much less of a specific stomach enzyme (alcohol hydrogenase) that neutralizes and breaks down alcohol. As a result, when a woman and a man drink the same amount, proportionately, for their size and weight, about 30% more alcohol enters the woman's bloodstream. When women drink too much alcohol, the small amount of the enzyme that they do have loses its ability to break down alcohol in the stomach. For alcoholic women, drinking alcohol is essentially the equivalent of injecting it intravenously, bypassing stomach digestion entirely. In male alcoholics, however, the enzyme still can neutralize alcohol, but not so well as in men who do not drink to excess. This enzyme may be one reason that women's livers get diseased more quickly than men's.

A comparison of people of different races may shed light on the genetic component of differences in alcohol metabolism. There is evidence of a high prevalence of sensitivity to alcohol among people of Asian descent. Signs of sensitivity—rapid facial flushing, elevated skin temperature, and increased pulse rate—after consuming moderate amounts of alcohol appear to be common among these groups but are seen in only 5% of Caucasians. These differences are based on genetic variations in the enzymes involved in alcohol metabolism.

Genetic Factors Studies using animals have shown that it is possible to breed strains of mice or rats that differ in the way they metabolize alcohol. It has been demonstrated many times that alcoholism runs in human families as well. For example, sons of alcoholics are about four times more likely to be alcoholic than are sons of nonalcoholics, and adoption studies show that this is true even when children have no exposure to their biological parents after the first few weeks of life. Furthermore, concordance rates for alcoholism in monozygotic twins are much higher than in dizygotic twins.

Evidence for genetic predisposition to alcoholism is growing, and it is now widely accepted by researchers that alcoholism can result from the interaction of heredity and environment. Researchers are attempting to identify the specific gene or genes that might be linked to alcoholism. Although some researchers believe there are genes specific to alcoholism, others think alcoholism results from a set of biological factors that are heavily influenced by environmental events.

Knowledge that alcoholism has both genetic and environmental components can have important practical applications. If reliable biological indicators of a predisposition toward alcoholism can be found, individuals who have those indicators could know the risks they face and could make informed choices about drinking. Another practical application is improved treatment. It is already clear that alcoholism is not a single disease. By clarifying the nature of various subcategories of alcoholism, genetic studies can point the way to more specific and effective therapies based on the genetic characteristics of every individual. It has been established that the liver can metabolize only a certain amount of alcohol per hour, regardless of the amount that has been consumed. The rate of alcohol metabolism depends, in part, on the amount of metabolizing enzymes in the liver, which varies among individuals and appears to have genetic determinants. Genetic molecular variations in alcohol-metabolizing enzymes are a major area of research on the heredity of alcoholism because a mutation that produces a slight alteration in the molecular structure of these enzymes could be expected to have a pronounced effect on their ability to remove alcohol from the body. As information concerning genetic factors accrues, it may become possible to identify genetic indicators of susceptibility to alcohol.

The Brain and Nervous System Alcohol affects every system of the body, but its greatest, most immediate, and most visible effects are on the central nervous system. All the complex features of an individual's thoughts, emotions, and actions are based on chemical and electrical processes that occur in billions of nerve cells at any instant. Several features of this system could be involved in inherited predisposition to alcoholism.

As we saw in Chapter 2, all brain functions involve communication among nerve cells (neurons). Neurotransmitters are chemicals that carry messages across synapses. Although there are many different neurotransmitters, each neuron releases only one or a few types. After its release, a neurotransmitter crosses the synapse and activates a receptor protein in the outer membrane of the receiving neuron. Each receptor type responds preferentially to one type of neurotransmitter. However, most neurotransmitters can activate different subtypes of the same receptor, producing different responses in different brain cells or in different parts of the brain. Alcohol could interfere with numerous processes involved in nerve cell function, and if there is inherited variation in these processes it could result in either neurochemical vulnerability or resistance to alcoholism. Determining the specific neurotransmitters and receptor subtypes that may be involved in the development and symptoms of alcoholism is probably the first step in developing medications that might be useful in treating it.

Among the leading neurochemical hypotheses about alcoholism are the following:

- Individuals who are predisposed toward alcoholism might have nerve cell membranes that are less sensitive to the permeability-altering effects of alcohol, which would affect the movement of sodium and potassium ions and the propagation of nerve impulses.

- Predisposition toward alcoholism might be based on inherited variations in the sensitivity of certain enzymes to inhibition by alcohol. This also would affect the transmission of nerve impulses, which depend on the enzyme's regulation of the flow of ions through the nerve cell membrane.

- Predisposition toward alcoholism may be based on inherited variations in the neurotransmitter release and uptake systems involved in the chemical propagation of nerve impulses between nerve cells.

- People who are predisposed to alcoholism may produce abnormal amounts of certain morphine-like compounds that may be involved in alcohol addiction.

- Predisposition toward alcoholism may be based on inherited variations in the brain's neurochemical mechanisms for reinforcing certain behaviors.

Central to several biological theories of the effects of alcohol is the idea that a reward center exists in the brain that mediates all types of reinforcement, including reinforcers such as food and various types of drugs (including alcohol). Consequently, the inherent abuse potential of a given substance is likely to reflect its ability to activate this reward pathway. Controversy exists concerning the precise site of this reward center. Brain imaging studies may make important contributions to understanding the brain regions involved in the extraordinarily good feelings some people experience after ingestion of psychoactive substances and cravings for the substances (Hommer, 1999).

Biological Treatment In the past decade research into the pharmacological treatment of alcoholism has become increasingly active. Several drugs have been developed for the treatment for alcohol dependence that are used in the management of withdrawal symptoms, the treatment of certain psychological problems (e.g., anxiety) in heavy drinkers, and in other aspects of rehabilitation. Research is also being conducted with the aim of developing a pharmacological agent that might reduce alcohol cravings. Achieving this goal will require more knowledge concerning the behavioral and biological factors that regulate alcohol intake.

One promising drug is **naltrexone,** which was originally developed for the treatment of opiate addiction. Naltrexone has been shown to suppress the amount of work an animal will perform to self-administer alcohol. In humans, it has been shown to reduce relapse to heavy drinking in persons receiving treatment for their drinking problems.

Another biological approach to alcohol problems is to alter the body's response to alcohol. The drug *disulfiram* provides one way to do this because it causes extreme and sometimes violent discomfort (nausea, vomiting, cold sweats) when a person drinks alcohol within 12 hours of taking it. Since disulfiram is self-administered, the success of this technique depends on the individual's motivation to reduce or eliminate drinking. If the person wants to drink, disulfiram therapy will fail. It may be useful, however, as part of a therapeutic approach that also deals with motivations or situational cues that lead to alcohol use.

The Psychodynamic Approach Although there is no conclusive evidence that personality factors are involved in the development of alcoholism, a study reported by Jones (1981) demonstrated a consistent set of personality attributes among some alcoholics. The study drew upon data from a longitudinal research project that had begun when the subjects were 10 1/2 years old. In middle age the subjects were interviewed about their drinking patterns. Jones found that as adults, male problem drinkers were likely to be described as relatively hostile, submissive, socially unsuccessful, and anxious. In general, these men had been rated as rather extroverted in adolescence. However, at that time they also described themselves as having less satisfactory social relationships and greater feelings of inferiority than did other males in the study. Jones believed that these men were rather impulsive and unsure of themselves in adolescence and that they had difficulty forming deep and lasting friendships. Additional longitudinal studies are needed to clarify the roles of personality and psychodynamic factors in alcohol use.

Psychoanalysts see overuse of alcohol and other psychoactive substances as products of neurotic conflict, doubt and anxiety about one's self-worth, and attempts to make up for an impaired self-concept. Psychodynamically oriented therapists believe that individuals become addicted to alcohol or some other substance because they are trying to correct or counteract negative emotional states from which they want relief. While they judge certain characteristics (e.g., a condemning view of oneself) as constituting a vulnerability to substance overuse, psychoanalysts tend to neglect physiological and social variables that may be vulnerability factors.

Psychodynamic Treatment Clinicians who take a psychodynamic perspective advocate psychotherapy for alcoholics. Although there have been some encouraging clinical reports on the usefulness of psychotherapy, research on the topic has not yet produced definitive conclusions. Most studies of psychotherapy with alcoholics are not comparable with respect to such important variables as the setting in which the treatment was applied, the duration of the therapy, and the criteria by which the therapy was evaluated.

In the past, psychotherapists believed that alcoholism was merely a symptom of underlying psychological difficulties. The logical conclusion was that such patients would improve in regard to their drinking if such difficulties were successfully addressed. Today it is widely recognized that psychotherapeutic exploration for someone who

is still drinking not only provides very little benefit, but may be barely remembered from one session to the next.

An increasing number of psychodynamically oriented clinicians recognize the value of looking at alcohol problems from the standpoint of the family rather than the individual. These therapists acknowledge that alcohol abuse not only affects families but is also influenced by how the family interacts and functions as a system. For this reason, it is necessary to find out whether family behavior patterns have been altered to accommodate the unique demands of the alcoholic member. Family therapists view the whole family, not the alcoholic member alone, as the primary patient. While treatment goals vary from case to case, family therapists often focus their attention on restabilizing family behavior after cessation (or reduction) of drinking has taken place. In some cases, a major effort is needed to restructure relationships within the family.

The Cognitive-Behavioral Approach The cognitive-behavioral approach to alcohol-related problems recognizes the roles both learning and cognition play in problem drinking and alcoholism.

Behavioral Factors One reason people drink is that alcohol is reinforcing. People experience effects from drinking alcohol that can cause them to drink again to repeat the experience. Through its effects, alcohol can be a positive reinforcer, producing positive sensations in the brain, or a negative reinforcer, alleviating negative feelings such as anxiety. Studies have shown that some of alcohol's actions in the brain and bloodstream can cause an animal to seek alcohol and even to work to get it (e.g., to press a lever) in order to repeat the experience it elicits.

Consuming alcohol is generally believed to reduce anxiety and to be a way of coping with stress and problems of living. This behavior may be acquired through reinforcement (being accepted by friends who value drinking), modeling (seeing others "solve" their problems with alcohol), and other learning mechanisms. The more severe and chronic the stressor, the greater the alcohol consumption. However, whether an individual will drink in response to stress appears to depend on many factors, including possible genetic determinants, an individual's usual drinking behavior, expectations regarding the effect of alcohol on stress, the intensity and type of stressor, the individual's sense of control over the stressor, the person's range of responses to cope with the perceived stress, and the availability of social support to buffer the effects of stress. High levels of stress may lead to drinking when alternative resources are lacking, when alcohol is accessible, and when the individual believes that alcohol will help to reduce the stress.

It is also possible that alcohol is sought for its short-term excitatory action and that it is reinforcing because it makes people "feel good." Like all psychological phenomena, reinforcement has underlying neurochemical mechanisms. Several studies have implicated certain neurochemicals in the reinforcing properties of alcohol. Alcohol may make many people feel good because it alters the levels of dopamine and norepinephrine, as well as opioid peptides, in a specific brain region. Subjectively, these neurochemical changes are experienced as excitation, and because that experience can be pleasurable, people will seek alcohol again.

Short-term use of alcohol may be reinforcing for many people because of the pleasurable feeling of relaxation it produces. But since drinking is not an effective coping mechanism, their life situations do not improve. Feeling even less able to cope constructively, they increase their maladaptive coping behavior.

Cognitive Factors Behavior is influenced by expectations about the consequences of acting in a particular way as well as by what actually does happen. Behavior thus can be shaped and maintained by cognitive appraisals of what has happened and what is likely to happen. A problem drinker learns to expect positive effects from drinking and interprets the experience in that way, despite the fact that the predominant quality of the actual experience is negative.

The importance of expectancy is illustrated by an experiment reported by Marlatt and others (1973). These investigators used a taste-rating task to determine whether drinking rates are affected by the actual presence of alcohol or merely by the expectancy of alcohol. The taste-rating task was an unobtrusive measure of drinking because the person's attention was focused on the taste of the drinks. The drinks used were vodka and tonic, and tonic alone. The subjects were permitted to drink as much of the beverages as they wished in the time allotted. The researchers found that the only significant determinant of the amount of beverage consumed was the subjects' expectations regarding what they were drinking: those who

expected alcohol drank more. This finding supports a cognitive interpretation of drinking. Figure 13-2 shows a naturalistic setting for experiments on drinking behavior.

A person's belief about the alcohol content of a drink, regardless of its actual content, can be a significant determiner, not only of alcohol consumption, but also of various behaviors that may accompany or result from drinking, such as depression, inability to delay gratification, social anxiety, and sexual responsiveness. This evidence comes from studies, like the one just described, using the **balanced placebo design,** in which half of the subjects are given a drink containing alcohol and half are given a nonalcoholic beverage. By varying both drink content and expectancy set, this design permits joint and separate evaluation of the behavioral consequences of a subject's belief that he or she has consumed alcohol and the consequences of actual alcohol consumption (see Figure 13-3).

Cognitive-Behavioral Treatment Although primarily behavioral or primarily cognitive approaches to the treatment of persons with alcohol-related problems continue to be employed, it is increasingly common for therapists to combine behavioral and cognitive techniques in therapy. In cognitive-behavioral therapy, therapists teach and coach skills to enable patients to cope with situations and emotional states known to result in alcohol abuse. Patients practice drink-refusal skills, learn to manage negative moods, and learn to cope with urges to drink.

Aversive conditioning is a behavioral technique employed in treating alcoholism. It is based on the principles of classical conditioning (see Chapter 2). If a glass of alcohol (conditioned stimulus) regularly precedes an aversive stimulus such as a nausea-producing drug (unconditioned stimulus), the alcohol will eventually elicit some part of the unconditioned response—in this case, vomiting. Once the unpleasant response has been conditioned

Figure 13-2 Student volunteers pose as research participants for an Alcohol Skills Training Program study conducted at the Behavioral Alcohol Research Laboratory (BARLAB) at the University of Washington.

THE WALL STREET JOURNAL

Figure 13-3 What might lead someone to go to the Control Group Bar and Grill between 5 and 7 P.M.? Research using the balanced placebo design suggests that knowing that the drinks contain no alcohol would inhibit drinking.

SOURCE: *The Wall Street Journal*, 12/7/95, p. A19. Reprinted with permission.

to alcohol, the habit of avoiding alcohol will be established through operant conditioning. The response of abstinence is strengthened because it reduces the unpleasant feeling (nausea) that the conditioning situation has associated with alcohol. Electric shock is sometimes used in place of nausea-producing drugs in this procedure, but it seems to be less effective. Aversive conditioning approaches often require "booster sessions" because the threat of an unpleasant reaction tends to weaken over time. Long-term follow-up studies are needed to establish the success rate of this therapeutic method.

Another behavioral approach, **covert sensitization,** uses aversive images and fantasies rather than shocks or drugs. Alcoholic patients are told that they can eliminate their "faulty habit" by associating it with unpleasant stimuli. They are instructed to close their eyes and imagine that they are about to drink an alcoholic beverage. They are then taught to imagine the sensations of nausea and vomiting. If it is repeated often enough, the association between nausea and the sight, smell, and taste of alcohol is presumed to establish a conditioned aversion to alcohol.

Many cognitively based alcohol programs are focused on controlled drinking rather than on abstinence. The **controlled drinking approach** means that the emphasis is on building participants' coping skills so that they can keep their alcohol consumption to a level they have previously determined is acceptable. In this approach, clients are oriented toward monitoring their own behavior by noting the situational and environmental antecedents and consequences of heavy drinking. Their past learning in relation to drinking is reviewed, and their expectations about the effects of alcohol are discussed. Participants in controlled-drinking programs are encouraged to ask themselves questions such as the following:

- At what places am I most likely to overdrink?
- With which people am I most likely to overdrink?
- When am I most likely to overdrink?
- How do I feel emotionally just before I begin to overdrink?

Special emphasis is placed on drinking as a response to stress. This approach makes sense, since a high percentage of people with alcohol problems report that their heavy drinking often begins when they are faced with unpleasant, frustrating, or challenging situations. Improved problem-solving skills, particularly in the area of interpersonal relationships; learning how to anticipate and plan for stressful experiences; and acquiring the ability to say "No, thanks" when offered a drink have all been shown to have therapeutic value for alcoholics.

One reason that learning approaches may not be effective is that the short-term effects of alcohol often are positively reinforcing. Only the effects of overconsumption ending in intoxication, dangerous or socially frowned-upon behavior, or a period of binge drinking have negative-reinforcement properties. The cognitive perspective deals with this problem by focusing the client's thoughts on the consequences of the drinking behavior as well as on the specific situations in which drinking is most likely to appear tempting. The patient and the therapist work together to develop cognitive coping techniques to deal with these situations.

While the goal of therapeutic efforts is to help alcoholics stop drinking, or drinking to excess, maintaining sobriety over the long term is also of great importance. Alcoholics who undergo treatment have a high relapse rate. Many go through treatment a number of times or through a number of treatments and still relapse into uncontrolled drinking (see Box 13-2).

For those who view alcoholism as a disease, a relapse is a failure that the victim is powerless to control. From the cognitive viewpoint, a relapse is a slip or error. The cognitive approach views a relapse as a fork in the road. One fork leads back to the abusing behavior, the other toward the goal of positive change.

Relapse prevention programs combine a cognitive approach with a variety of treatment procedures designed to change the individual's drinking pattern (Daley & Marlatt, 1992). Such programs can be used whether the goal is abstinence or controlled drinking. The only requirement is that the client make a voluntary decision to change. The relapse prevention approach assumes that the person experiences a sense of control over his or her behavior as long as the treatment program continues. If the person encounters a high-risk situation, this sense of control is threatened and a relapse is likely. High-risk situations include negative moods such as frustration, anger, or depression; interpersonal conflicts such as an argument with

Research Close-up   Box 13–2

Abstinence Versus Controlled Drinking

A sometimes intense and angry dispute arises when the merits of controlled drinking versus a complete rejection of alcohol use by alcoholics are discussed. Most advocates of controlled drinking are behavioral or cognitive-behavioral therapists who see alcohol abuse as a bad habit or a personal or social problem. Defenders of abstinence, including Alcoholics Anonymous and many medical and mental health professionals, believe that loss of control is inevitable for an alcoholic once drinking starts. They tend to regard alcoholism as a disease whose progress can be arrested only by removing the poison that causes it.

Critics of the disease perspective argue that while abstinence can work well for some individuals, it is very hard to live up to; moreover, recovery from alcoholism may not require such a drastic step. One study found that alcohol abusers can re-

turn to drinking on a controlled basis without abusing alcohol (Vaillant & Milofsky, 1982). However, subjects who were alcohol-dependent and/or had many alcohol-related problems generally achieved successful results only if they become abstinent (see Figure 13-4).

These findings suggest that there may be two groups of alcohol abusers (M. G. Sobell & L. C. Sobell, 1995). Some can successfully resume drinking on a controlled basis. Others must abstain entirely if they are to cope with their alcohol problem. Both studies show that level of abuse before treatment plays an important role in the success of various treatment strategies. However, most researchers in this area would agree that the success rates of treatment are not high enough.

Further research on such issues as the value of abstinence versus controlled drinking needs to be sufficiently complex

to take into account not only subjects' drinking histories, but also their motivations and expectations about what would constitute success in coping with their drinking problem. For example, how much does abstinence change the life of an alcoholic? Alcoholics in the first few years of abstinence have been compared with returning prisoners of war. Their world is unfamiliar, because they have been living in an environment created by alcohol. Feelings that have been blunted or suppressed come back to trouble them. They have lost a great deal of time and must start where they left off. Being sober, like being free after imprisonment, entails new responsibilities. Alcoholics in the early stages of abstinence thus often suffer from anxiety and depression and may find it difficult to hold a job or preserve a marriage. The resolution of these problems comes when they establish new personal relationships, rebuild old ones, and begin to develop confidence in their power to control their lives (Rosenberg, 1993).

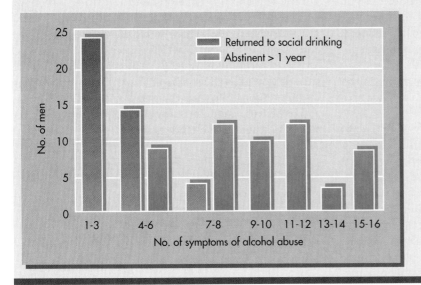

Figure 13-4 A return to controlled social drinking has a greater chance of success if the person has only a few symptoms of alcohol abuse. Only four men who had seven or more problems were able to return to social drinking. Most of these multiproblem people who did not resume alcohol abuse eventually became abstinent.

SOURCE: *Archives of General Psychiatry, 39,* 127–133. © 1982 by American Medical Association.

an employer or family member; and social pressure to indulge in drinking. If the person is able to make an effective coping response—for example, refusing the offer assertively when friends suggest "just one drink"—the probability of a relapse decreases. Figure 13-5 illustrates the cognitive-behavioral approach to the relapse process.

An important factor in relapses is the **abstinence violation effect.** When a relapse occurs, the individual has a

choice between two kinds of cognitive and emotional responses. One is conflict and guilt; the other is an attribution to temporary situational factors rather than to a permanent personal weakness or lack of self-efficacy. An alcoholic who breaks abstinence for the first time may continue to drink after the lapse in order to relieve the conflict and guilt related to the first drink. The individual may also reduce the conflict between the drinking behavior and the

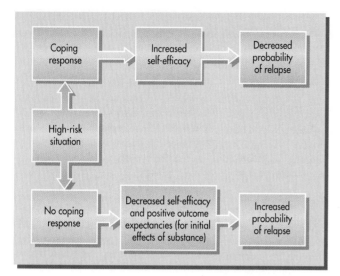

Figure 13-5 A cognitive-behavioral analysis of the relapse process begins with exposure to a high-risk situation. A high-risk situation is any situation that arouses stress, negative emotions, strong urges and temptations, or interpersonal conflict. Having a coping response increases the sense of self-efficacy (feeling that one is in control) and decreases the probability of relapse. Not having a coping response decreases self-efficacy, thus heightening the feeling of not being in control, and, together with positive expectations about the favorable effects of the substance, increases the probability of relapse.

goal of avoiding relapses by thinking: "This just proves I'm an alcoholic. I can't control my drinking once I start it." Rather than attributing the lapse to the difficult situation, people who use these cognitions are likely to blame themselves for lack of willpower or inability to resist temptation. Such thoughts increase the probability that a single drink may snowball into a full-strength alcoholic binge and a total relapse.

In addition to viewing any slip into drinking as a temporary lapse and not necessarily a permanent relapse and a sign of personal failure, one of the primary goals of the relapse prevention program is to train the individual to recognize the early-warning signals that may precede a relapse and to plan and carry out a series of intervention or coping strategies before it is too late. The relapse prevention technique holds promise, not only for alcohol abuse, but also for drug use, smoking, and other problems of self-control such as dieting. Its main components—identifying high-risk situations and learning effective coping and behavioral skills—are applicable to many types of situations. Table 13-9 lists some ways in which lapses can be handled in a positive manner. Many relapse prevention programs recommend that individuals carry a card with them listing some coping techniques. Further research is needed that explores short- and long-term effects of relapse prevention techniques.

Evaluating Treatment Approaches As we have seen, the various theoretical orientations have led to different ap-

proaches in treating alcohol-related problems. How do they compare with regard to treatment effectiveness? While studies comparing particular approaches with appropriate control groups are useful, it is also important to compare the treatment approaches with one another. However, because they are costly and complex, not many treatment comparison studies have been carried out. In evaluating treatment approaches, it is necessary to compare them, not only with each other, but also with community programs that do not involve professional clinicians.

Alcoholics Anonymous (AA) is the most widely used community-based approach to alcoholism. There are more than 89,000 groups throughout the world with more than 2 million members in 141 countries. Most members are referred to AA by other AA members and by rehabilitation and counseling programs. AA expects recovering alcoholics to admit their personal powerlessness over alcohol and seek help from a higher power, which can be understood in any way an individual member chooses. Members are urged to pray or meditate to get in touch with that power. They are asked to make a "moral inventory," confess the wrongs they have done, beg forgiveness, make amends, and carry the message to other alcoholics. AA takes the position that anyone who has once been an alcoholic is always an alcoholic; the disease can be arrested, but the vulnerability is permanent.

The most famous AA slogans are "It's the first drink that gets you drunk," which states the goal of abstinence, and "One day at a time," which places present action before long-term planning. AA members are told that although alcohol is the source of their problems, they must assume responsibility for their own recovery. They must also resolve to devote themselves to helping others in need as part of their own rehabilitation.

Table 13-9
Learning From a Lapse

A temporary lapse can be used as an opportunity for learning and need not signal defeat. The first priority is to prevent slips by anticipating high-risk situations and preparing ways to handle them. When a lapse does occur, it helps to carry a card listing coping tactics tailored to personal needs. Such advice might include the following suggestions:

1. Treat the slip as an emergency requiring immediate action.
2. Remember that a slip is not a relapse.
3. Renew your commitment.
4. Review the actions that led to the lapse so you won't repeat them.
5. Make an immediate plan for recovery.
6. Ask someone for help.

The effectiveness of AA has not been scientifically documented, and methodological problems make such an evaluation difficult. Because many alcoholics drop out of the program, presumably as failures, they are not counted when the percentage of members who successfully abstain is calculated. In addition, not all people with alcohol problems are willing to join AA. Because the organization is committed to the idea of total abstinence from alcohol, individuals who believe they have a problem with alcohol but want to reduce rather than cease their drinking probably would not join the group. Because its members represent a selected population of those with alcohol-related problems, their rate of success in remaining abstinent does not necessarily represent the potential success rate for all alcohol-dependent people if they follow the AA program.

One of AA's most important rehabilitative ingredients is the social support it provides for members. Members know they can call upon fellow members at any time for aid in resisting the temptations of alcohol. Although AA may not be the right approach for every alcoholic, for those who find it congenial it can be a valuable source of support, belongingness, and security. While not formally affiliated with any professional organization or institution, AA now represents a major referral resource for alcoholic patients.

One ambitious study compared three treatments: (1) cognitive-behavioral therapy that sought to help participants develop skills to manage their desire for alcohol (e.g., learning how to refuse drinks and to acquire methods of avoiding situations leading to drinking); (2) a program designed to prepare and encourage patients to affiliate with Alcoholics Anonymous (this program emphasized the problem drinkers' need for a spiritual reawakening and encouraged them to admit their powerlessness over alcohol and to acknowledge the need to make amends to people who had been harmed by their alcoholism), and (3) a therapeutic approach focused on enhancing alcoholics' motivation to take personal responsibility for their condition and change their behavior (Project MATCH Research Group, 1997). The participants were randomly assigned to the treatment groups and their status evaluated 1 year after their participation in the study.

All three therapies produced good and comparable results, with most patients remaining abstinent for approximately 80% of the follow-up period. There were indications that the cognitive-behavioral approach worked best for women and patients with severe psychological, cognitive, and social adjustment problems. The Alcoholics Anonymous program seemed to help particularly the patients who drank the most, were looking for meaning in their lives, and had too many friends who encouraged them to drink. Prime candidates for the motivational enhancement therapy seemed to be those with little initial readiness to change their drinking-related behavior. Thus,

while all three therapies were effective, each one seemed to be especially helpful with a particular type of patient. Before treatment in all three groups, the patients had on average drunk on 25 of 30 days. After treatment, this was reduced to 6 drinking days per month.

While encouraging, these results need to be confirmed by other evaluations. It would also be useful to explore the effects of combining features from different therapies. For example, it might be productive to evaluate incorporating both psychological treatment and medication in therapy programs. In practice, this sort of integrated program is employed with problem drinkers, but there is usually no evaluation of these programs' components. For example, naltrexone is typically prescribed for alcoholics who also receive psychological counseling and rehabilitation services. Evaluating various therapy components would help the development of optimal programs for each particular type of patient. One important factor of all therapies is the clinicians who administer them. One study found that the clinician's ability to communicate both authoritativeness and interpersonal warmth exerted a significant influence over the clinical progress of alcoholic clients (Cartwright et al., 1996).

Research on treatment for alcoholism is improving and should yield practical results. Although some research has not been helpful in analyzing the effectiveness of various treatments because different types of patients have been lumped together in study populations, a general picture of which alcohol abusers are likely to do well, regardless of the treatment, is emerging: they are people with jobs, stable relationships, minimal psychopathology, no history of past treatment failures, and minimal involvement with other drugs. One difficulty in interpreting the available evidence is that many people (perhaps more than 50%) who enter alcohol treatment programs drop out of them, and no one knows what happens to these dropouts.

Future research on the treatment of alcohol-related problems will need to deal with a number of issues, such as the dropout problem, and ask important questions like: (1) what are the elements of effective therapeutic approaches? and (2) what should be the goals of treatment? With regard to the first question, the therapeutic value of such elements as providing patients with feedback on their risks for alcohol problems, giving advice to reduce or stop drinking, and showing empathy for and understanding of the patients' problems needs to be determined. It is likely that no one therapeutic element is going to be sufficient to meet the needs of all patients. Some individuals may especially require treatment for underlying personality problems; others may need help in dealing with their relationships with others, such as spouses; and still others may need to become more confident concerning their ability to handle relapses. Treatment programs should be tailored to deal with the problems of particular pertinence to each individual.

An Interactional Perspective During recent years, an interactional view of alcoholism has developed. At the core of this concept of alcoholism is viewing it as a cycle that results in a perpetuation of harmful drinking. This cycle involves the following steps:

1. Certain vulnerable individuals are more likely to develop alcohol dependence because of biological, psychological, or social predisposing factors (e.g., genetics, depression, or peer influence).
2. Heavy drinking is intensified by precipitating factors such as stressful life events or psychological instigators (e.g., anxiety or insomnia).
3. The vulnerable individual finds alcohol rewarding, either because of the euphoria produced or the dysphoria assuaged.
4. Alcohol abuse develops as a consequence of these rewarding experiences, resulting in tolerance and increased drinking.
5. Physical dependence follows, along with the need to drink to prevent withdrawal symptoms.
6. The addictive cycle is further intensified by persistent physiological craving.
7. Physical dependence mechanisms tend to become reactivated by alcohol ingestion after a period of abstinence, with accompanying reinstatement of the self-defeating cycle.

Perhaps the greatest need in research on substance-related disorders is for consideration of the simultaneous effects of a number of personal, social, and cultural factors on alcohol consumption. It is important to examine the interactive effects of these factors in order to explain current levels of alcohol consumption. For example, two individuals with similar biological vulnerabilities (such as sensitivity to alcohol) might consume quite different amounts of alcohol depending on social (peer) pressure to participate in drinking.

One set of potentially pertinent factors and processes may involve the cultural and community setting from which an individual comes. The problem of excessive use of alcohol has sociocultural as well as psychological dimensions. The values and customs of the community influence attitudes toward drinking. In the past, problems of alcohol use were extremely frequent among certain ethnic groups, such as the Irish and Swedish; relatively infrequent among Italians; and particularly infrequent among Jews. Today, however, alcoholism is decreasing among Irish and Swedish Americans but rising among second- and third-generation Italian Americans and Jews. Changing social customs within these cultural groups seem to be a significant factor in these changing patterns of alcohol consumption.

Rates of alcoholism are low in groups in which drinking customs, values, and sanctions are well-known, agreed to by all, and consistent with the rest of the culture (see Figure 13-6). Among the sociocultural conditions that minimize alcohol problems are the following:

- Exposing children to alcohol at an early age in a strong family or religious setting.
- Serving the alcoholic beverage in diluted form (e.g., wine as opposed to distilled spirits) and in small quantities.
- Treating the beverage as a food and serving it mainly at meals.
- Not considering drinking a virtue—(e.g., a proof of manhood or virility) or a sin.

Figure 13-6 The context in which alcoholic beverages are consumed is an important factor in alcoholism. Drinking wine at family gatherings, as in this Jewish Passover ceremony, is much less likely to lead to problem drinking than imbibing in situations in which there is pressure for the individual to "excel at drinking."

■ Considering abstinence socially acceptable, but not excessive drinking or drunkenness.

A variety of social and interpersonal factors also influence alcohol consumption. These include the level of stress in the community and in the individual's personal life. Among the personal factors are friendships, family situation, and employment and financial status.

Preventing Alcohol-Related Disorders

Preventing alcohol abuse is obviously better than having to treat it. Unfortunately, less is known about prevention than about treatment. According to some studies, taxes that raise the price of alcohol and therefore reduce a society's total consumption have a more than proportionate effect on serious alcohol abuse. There are usually fewer alcohol problems in countries where the price of alcohol is high relative to the average income. It is less clear whether merely limiting alcohol advertising is effective.

Other community-level strategies that can be useful from the standpoint of prevention are raising the minimum drinking age, regulating the types of outlets and the hours during which alcohol may be sold, establishing tough drinking-and-driving laws, and carrying out various types of educational programs directed at important target groups. Box 13-3 presents information about the scope of the alcohol-abuse problem in one setting—the college campus—and suggests some practical approaches to prevention.

The overuse of alcohol and other drugs during adolescence and early adulthood continues to be a public health problem. The problem is serious because for the developing young adult these substances undermine motivation, interfere with cognitive processes, contribute to debilitating mood disorders, and increase risk of accidental injury or death. Researchers have had difficulty developing preventative interventions with long-term staying power and are seeking ways of devising prevention programs that are likely to be successful. One way of approaching this task is to identify risk factors for overuse and then develop programs aimed at reducing them. Addressing the following risk factors for overuse of alcohol and other psychoactive substances might significantly reduce the problem:

■ Extreme economic deprivation
■ Neighborhood disorganization
■ Early and persistent behavior problems, including aggressive behavior and hyperactivity
■ Poor family management practices
■ Family conflict
■ Lack of cohesion within the family
■ Academic failure
■ Social pressure to use drugs

■ Alienation and rebelliousness
■ Early rejection by peers

Other Drugs

Strictly speaking, alcohol is a drug—it is a chemical substance that leads to physiological and psychological changes when ingested. But for most people, the word *drugs* means pills, powders, and marijuana. In addition to alcohol, psychoactive drugs may be classified into several groups: barbiturates and tranquilizers, the opioids, cocaine, amphetamines, hallucinogens, phencyclidine (PCP), inhalants, marijuana, and nicotine. There is growing evidence that alcoholism is frequently comorbid with the use of other drugs, such as opioids and nicotine (Enoch & Goldman, 2000). The greater the severity of alcoholism, the more likely it is that other substance dependencies will also be present. It is possible that a portion of genetic vulnerability to alcoholism may be common with other addictive disorders. Substance abuse also has significant comorbidity with a variety of other conditions.

Barbiturates and Tranquilizers

Barbiturates (such as phenobarbital) and tranquilizers (such as Valium) are grouped together because they both have a depressing effect on the central nervous system. They probably do this by interfering with synaptic transmission: either they inhibit the secretion of excitatory neurotransmitters or they cause the release of inhibitory transmitter substances. Both types of drugs reduce anxiety and insomnia and affect a wide range of bodily functions. They are both very popular. Each year Americans consume over 300 tons of barbiturates; tranquilizers are an even bigger business.

Barbiturates, or derivatives of barbituric acid, are prescribed by physicians for relief of anxiety or to prevent convulsions. Mild doses of barbiturates are effective as sleeping pills, although they may actually cause sleep disorders if used over a long period. Higher doses, such as those taken by addicted individuals, trigger an initial period of excitement that is followed by slurred speech, loss of coordination, severe depression, and impairment of thinking and memory. Illicit use of barbiturates often occurs in conjunction with the use of other drugs, notably alcohol and heroin. The effects of alcohol and barbiturates are addictive, and this combination is especially dangerous.

The body quickly develops a tolerance to barbiturates and tranquilizers. As tolerance develops, the amount of the substance needed to maintain the same level of intoxication is increased. The margin between an intoxicating dose and a fatal one also becomes smaller. These drugs can cause both physical and psychological dependence. After addiction has developed, sudden abstinence

Research Close-up

Drinking on Campus

In stark contrast to the purposeful bustle along the hospital corridor that crisp February dawn, a cluster of bewildered students glanced silently at each other as they waited to find out whether Jim Callahan was dead or alive. Full of fear, for him and for themselves, the fraternity brothers replayed the previous night in their minds, again and again. The initiation ritual was supposed to have been funny—a test of the fraternity's power over its new pledges. Wasn't it a good job, to order them to drink "kamikazes" in the frat house basement until they were sick? The freshmen could sleep it off, after all. But when 18-year-old Jim Callahan passed out early on the morning of February 12, 1988, he never woke up.

Later, doctors would explain that Callahan died from acute alcohol poisoning caused by drinking a huge quantity of alcohol in a very short time. He drank about 24 ounces—nearly three-fourths of a liter—in 30 to 45 minutes following a Lambda Chi Alpha pledge-pinning ceremony.

This tragedy took place at Rutgers University, but there have been similar events at other educational institutions (see Figure 13-7). Many colleges and universities seem to be continually dealing with the problem of **binge drinking,** which is often defined as the consumption of five or more drinks in a row for men and four or more for women. Regardless of the exact way in which it is defined, binge drinking seems to be increasing. One study found that on college campuses the percentage of frequent binge drinkers increased from 23.4% in 1993 to 28.1% in 1999 (Wechsler et al., 2000). Among the students most likely to binge drink were fraternity and sorority house residents. Lower rates of binge drinking were found for African

American and Asian American students, students 24 years of age or older, and those who were married.

There is great interest in the development of programs that might prevent binge drinking and other alcohol-related problems. One prevention approach taken by two University of Washington researchers, G. Alan Marlatt and John Baer, has been the development of a 6- to 8-week college course on sensible approaches to alcohol. Can merely taking a class alter harmful drinking habits? Marlatt and Baer found that course participants significantly reduced their alcohol consumption and had maintained that reduction as long as 2 years later. Further-

more, two other groups—one that only read the class manual and another that received only brief oral instruction—also cut their drinking significantly. These results are even more impressive because all those selected for the class were at high risk for alcohol problems through heavy drinking or factors such as a family history of alcoholism.

This prevention program does not tell students they must abstain from liquor (except for those who are alcoholics), which may be a contributing factor to the program's success. The course provides information from which students can assess whether they have a problem and decide what, if anything, they want to do about it. Emphasis is placed on sensible drinking as a skill. Drinking is compared with driving, both of which can be dangerous if

Figure 13-7   Sometimes a tragedy in the family prompts social action. Larry Wooten, a university junior, died as a result of a challenge from an old friend with whom he competed in sports, for grades, and in social activities. While watching a football game in a bar, the boys challenged each other to see who could drink more in an hour. Larry drank one more drink than his friend—a total of 23 shots of liquor—but died as a result. His parents, shown here, have mounted a campaign against alcohol abuse. Their efforts are part of many by parents, fraternities, and universities to try to control the trend toward abusive drinking by college students.

can cause withdrawal symptoms including delirium and convulsions, and can even result in death.

There are three types of barbiturate abuse:

1. *Chronic intoxication,* in which people obtain prescriptions, often from more than one physician. Initially they seek barbiturates to reduce insomnia and anxiety,

and they may then become addicted to the drugs. Chronic use leads to slurred speech and decreased effectiveness on the job.
2. *Episodic intoxication,* in which individuals take barbiturates orally to produce a "high," or state of well-being.
3. *Intravenous injections,* in which the drug is injected, often in combination with other drugs (such as heroin).

Box 13–3

practiced by an unskilled person. The course tells students that, as with driving, one must learn to drink by experience—what, when, where, and how much—and that one can't learn simply be being told how. The course also asks students to monitor their own drinking behavior by providing answers to questions such as those in Table 13-10.

In a related approach, Marlatt (1994) used a one-on-one procedure. Called *motivational interviewing,* this method avoids confrontation. Counselors meet individually with freshmen college students who were heavy drinkers in high school (five drinks in at least one setting during the previous month) to give them feedback on their drinking patterns, their beliefs about the effects of alcohol, and the risks they face. Sessions are followed by annual check-ups on changes in drinking behavior. Students who participated in this program saw a 68% drop in the average quantity of alcohol they consumed 2 years later. Consumption by a control group of heavy drinkers fell by a moderate 16%.

The Social Side of College Drinking

Drinking is a preferred way to socialize; few students drink alone. Those whose drinking is getting out of hand often feel threatened by those who don't drink. As long as others are consuming alcohol in large amounts, heavy drinkers rationalize that the amount they consume must be all right. Motives for drinking can vary quite a bit, however. For most students, college years are a time of experimentation with a range of adult behaviors; drinking, especially when it is not one's family pattern, is one of these. For some students, college years are also a time for rebellion; underage drinking is a way to flout the rules they say they are "too young." For some, too, on campus as in society in general, drinking is a popular way to relieve stress. Other factors, such as ethnic patterns and heredity, may also play a role in drinking habits.

What Can You Do?

Here are some ways students can help themselves before they drink.

- Before a party, agree as a group on a designated driver—someone who will stay sober.
- Agree on ways to let someone know that he or she is drinking too much.
- Before drinking alcoholic beverages, provide and eat foods high in protein and carbohydrates.
- Pace drinks to one per hour.
- Have nonalcoholic beverages available, and switch to them after you reach your alcohol limit.
- Focus an event on dancing, dining, or other activities, not on drinking.
- If someone becomes intoxicated, strongly suggest that he or she not drive, and drive the person home yourself or call a taxi. If necessary, let the person sleep overnight on the couch.
- If someone passes out, keep the person on his or her side, not on the back, and call for medical help.

Table 13-10

Understanding Personal Drinking Patterns as the First Step to Sensible Alcohol Use

In order to help students understand the personal reasons for their alcohol use and the kinds of situations that are likely to lead to more drinking, one assignment to a class on sensible approaches to drinking involves thinking about and answering the following questions. The answers may give each student some important insights into his or her drinking patterns.

- Are there any *places* where you are more likely to overdrink? [Yes/No] Where?
- Are there any *people* with whom you are more likely to overdrink? [Yes/No] Who?
- Are there any *times* or *days* when you are more likely to overdrink? [Yes/No] When?
- Are there any *activities* that make it more likely that you will overdrink? [Yes/No] Describe them.
- Do you think that you overdrink when you are *feeling* certain ways? [Yes/No] Describe those feelings.
- Could you take a "vacation" from (avoid) any of the places or people involved in your overdrinking? [Yes/No] Which ones?
- Are there *places* where you are *less likely* to overdrink? [Yes/No] Where?
- Are there *people* with whom you are *less likely* to overdrink? [Yes/No] Who?

Intravenous use produces a "rush" of pleasant, warm, drowsy feelings. Many complications are associated with prolonged use of the drug in this manner.

Relapses are common among barbiturate users because use of the drug is an easy way of escaping tension, anxiety, and feelings of inadequacy.

Some tranquilizers act like barbiturates, while others act quite differently. **Tranquilizing drugs** are derived from several chemical groups. Overuse of tranquilizers is common. They are frequently prescribed to reduce anxiety, and perhaps half a million Americans use them for nonmedical purposes. As with barbiturates, the body develops a tolerance to many tranquilizers. Physical and psychological dependence and serious withdrawal symptoms may occur. Apparently unaware that they are addictive or that they can cause death, many people use tranquilizers freely. Just as they do with barbiturates, the undesirable effects of these substances increase when they are used in combination with alcohol and other drugs.

Valium is a member of the *benzodiazepine* group of tranquilizers. Drugs in this group produce less euphoria than other tranquilizing drugs, so the risk of dependence and abuse is relatively low. Nevertheless, tolerance and withdrawal symptoms can develop.

The Opioids

The term **opioid** refers to any natural or synthetic substance that acts on the body in a way that is similar to the action of derivatives of the opium poppy. These substances bind to and act upon opioid receptor sites in the brain. The opioids include a variety of substances, some of which occur naturally while others are synthetic. Heroin is the most well-known synthetic opioid.

The opioids are sometimes called **narcotics,** but because this term is used differently by those who study drugs and by the legal system, it does not always have the same meaning to law enforcement personnel, laypeople, physicians, and scientists.

Natural Opioids Several forms of opioids that resemble opium and heroin in their effects are manufactured by the brain and the pituitary gland. Three such distinct opioids are the **endorphins,** the **enkephalins,** and the **dymorphins.** Some of these substances can also be made artificially for experimental use. Research using natural opioids may provide insights into the mechanisms of pain, pleasure, emotion, and perception. The endorphins have been the most widely studied.

Study of the endorphins has led to the mapping of the entire opioid-receptor system. The nerves of the brain and spinal cord have been found to contain specific receptor sites to which opioids must bind in order to produce their effects. Morphine and similar drugs block pain signals to the brain because they fit into these receptor sites like a key into a lock. Some scientists suspect that addiction may stem from a deficiency disease: the addict's craving for and dependence on opioids may be caused by chronic underproduction of natural endorphins. If this is the case, it may be possible to use synthesized endorphins to correct the underlying cause of addiction. Two possibilities might account for endorphin deficiencies. One is that the opioids themselves suppress endorphin production; the other is that some people have a genetically caused deficiency in endorphin production.

Ever since the endorphins have been isolated and examined directly by biochemists, behavioral researchers have been able to study their action, either by injecting these substances into subjects and observing their analgesic (pain-killing) effects or by injecting a drug called **naloxone,** which blocks the effects of the endorphin. If a procedure produces analgesia when naloxone is not used but does not affect pain when naloxone is present, there is indirect evidence that endorphins mediate the pain-reducing effects of the procedure.

The Opiates The word **opiate** refers only to opioid drugs derived from or chemically similar to the juice of the opium poppy, *Papaver somniferum.* Archaeologists think that the opium poppy's seemingly miraculous powers were first discovered by Neolithic farmers on the eastern shores of the Mediterranean Sea. This knowledge spread from Asia Minor across the ancient world as the drug manufactured from the poppy, opium, became a valued commodity. In the seventeenth century, opium was praised by a prominent physician as God's greatest gift to humanity for the relief of its sufferings.

In 1804 the most important active ingredient of opium, **morphine,** was identified. Physicians applauded it as a painkiller of known reliability. Opium and its derivatives were also used to treat coughs, diarrhea, fever, epilepsy, melancholy, diabetes, skin ulcers, constipation, and a variety of other ills well into the 1800s. When opiates are used to control pain, they usually do not produce the kind of intense orgasmic rush characteristic of high doses and do not produce addiction.

Just as morphine was at first considered a safe substitute for opium, **heroin,** which was produced for the first time in 1874 by boiling morphine in acetic acid, was at first hailed as a safe and effective substitute for morphine. This assertion soon proved to be horribly untrue, and today heroin is involved in over 90% of narcotic-addiction cases.

Heroin can be injected, smoked, or inhaled (see Figure 13-8). Heroin addicts go through a characteristic sequence of experiences. After the drug is injected, the user feels a "rush" or "flash" as the nervous system reacts to its presence. Addicts describe the rush as an extraordinarily pleasurable sensation, one that is similar in many ways to sexual orgasm, only more intense and involving the whole body. Following the rush, the user experiences the "nods," a lingering state of euphoric bliss. Fatigue, tension, and anxiety fade away. Feelings of inadequacy are replaced by relaxed contentment. One young addict reported that after experiencing his first heroin high, he had exclaimed to himself: "Why didn't they tell me such wonderful feelings existed?" A significant number of heroin addicts have stated that unless the world could provide them with a feeling to compensate for the loss of the high, they would never be able to give up heroin. The negative consequences of heroin, however, far outweigh the temporary feelings of well-being.

Figure 13-8 A heroin addict about to self-inject.

The Effects of Opioids Opioids have both sedative and analgesic effects. They cause mood changes, sleepiness, mental clouding, constipation, and slowing of the activity of the brain's respiratory center. An overdose may cause death due to cessation of breathing. The withdrawal reaction can be severe and is manifested by sweating, muscle pains, nausea, vomiting, diarrhea, and other symptoms that may last for 2 or 3 days; less-severe symptoms may persist for 4 to 6 months. Heroin use is likely to be associated with serious deterioration of both the individual's social life and family relations. Table 13-11 summarizes the major features listed in DSM-IV for opioid intoxication and opioid withdrawal. In addition, opioid intoxication involves significant maladaptive behavioral or psychological changes developing during, or shortly after, the initial euphoria resulting from the opioid. These changes include apathy, impaired judgment, and impaired social or occupational functioning. In opioid withdrawal, persons who have stopped (or reduced) using an opioid after prolonged and heavy use show the features listed in Table 13-11.

The following case illustrates opioid intoxication:

Jamie is a 17-year-old high school dropout whose boyfriend, Matt, has recently joined a local motorcycle gang. The gang members use drugs extensively, and Matt's initiation to the gang required that he receive a "fix," or injection, of intravenous heroin. It was his first experience with heroin, and he

enjoyed it. He tried to convince Jamie to try heroin. She was fearful and initially resisted.

One night Matt and Jamie were riding with the gang and stopped at a local gang hangout. Several of the female gang members gathered around Jamie and started teasing her about not trying heroin. She finally agreed to try a "fix." One of the women dissolved some heroin in a spoon, drew it into a syringe, put a tourniquet on Jamie's arm, and injected the heroin into her vein. Jamie felt a sudden "rush," or "high," that she later described as akin to an orgasm. This was followed by a sense of euphoria. Matt glanced at her face and noticed that she had a slightly dazed look, with tiny pupils. After a few minutes Jamie became lethargic and began to nod off. The effects peaked in about 20 to 30 minutes and gradually began to wear off.

Opioid withdrawal is quite different:

Sean is a 27-year-old man who arrived at a local hospital emergency room late one night complaining of feeling depressed and suicidal. He was admitted to the psychiatric ward for observation. A few hours later, in the middle of the night, he began vomiting and complaining of muscle aches, stomach cramps, diarrhea, and difficulty sleeping. The nurse initially thought that he was developing a viral syndrome. However, when she examined his arms, she discovered several needle "tracks." Sean admitted that he had begun injecting heroin a few weeks ago. He had injected his last heroin approximately 6 hours before his admission to the hospital. The nurse called

Table 13-11
Clinical Features of Opioid Intoxication and Opioid Withdrawal

Opioid Intoxication

In addition to constriction of the pupils, one or more of the following:

1. Drowsiness or coma
2. Slurred speech
3. Impairment in attention or memory

Opioid Withdrawal

Three or more of the following:
1. Depressed mood
2. Nausea or vomiting
3. Muscle aches
4. Running eyes and nose
5. Dilation of the pupils
6. Sweating
7. Diarrhea
8. Yawning
9. Fever
10. Insomnia

Source: DSM-IV.

the ward psychiatrist, who examined Sean and prescribed medication to treat the symptoms of his withdrawal syndrome.

Causes of Opioid-Related Disorders A study of Vietnam War soldiers who used heroin heavily during the war found that a high percentage stopped using it when they returned home (Robins, 1993). This showed that, contrary to the widespread assumption that when a person uses heroin extensively he or she becomes "hooked" on it, heroin addicts are not doomed for life. A study conducted in California found that ceasing to use opiates is easier for individuals who are in their early 30s or younger (Hser et al., 1993). While the precise meaning of these findings is not yet clear, the fact that many veterans who used opiates in Vietnam were able to abstain upon returning home has stimulated interest in the idea that controlled use of at least some substances is possible for some people. Additional support for this view was provided by reports of people who have used opioids in a controlled manner for long periods. Although some users require drugs in increasingly large dosages every day, other daily users seem able to limit their intake. Perhaps the reason that controlled use of opioids has received relatively little attention is that people who are able to limit their use do not come to the attention of clinicians. In any case, a better understanding of the process of opioid addiction is necessary so that effective social policies—for example, drug use laws and treatment procedures—can be formulated.

At present there are two competing views of opioid addiction: the exposure orientation and the interactional orientation. According to the **exposure orientation,** the cause of addiction is simply exposure to opioids. When a person experiences stress, endorphins are secreted and produce a stress-induced analgesia (increased tolerance for pain). The use of heroin and other opioids may cause a long-term breakdown in the biochemical system that synthesizes the endorphins. An addict may continue to use opioids because drug use has broken down the body's normal pain-relief system. It is also thought that opioid drugs are reinforcing because they postpone painful withdrawal symptoms. This view does not explain why some addicts have severe withdrawal symptoms while others do not. Moreover, some people become seriously addicted to other drugs that do not produce severe withdrawal symptoms, such as nicotine and coffee.

According to the **interactional orientation,** both the person and the situation are important factors in the development of addiction: people's characteristics (their expectations, worries, etc.) and the situations they face in life, particularly those that create stress, jointly influence their need for and reactions to drugs. The available evidence is consistent with this interpretation. This can explain why some military personnel who had served in Vietnam could so easily leave heavy drug use behind when they returned to the United States. In Vietnam, they were faced with strange people and places, boredom, danger, feelings of helplessness, and other emotions and situations that made their coping mechanisms appear inadequate. Once they had returned home, the situational cues that were related to a craving for opioids were absent.

One recurring finding of research on opioid addicts is that they frequently have severe personality problems (Krausz, 1999). They suffer particularly from depression, and their suicide rate is much higher than the average. Depression often continues after withdrawal and even becomes worse. Some authorities believe that the drugs cause depression, and others think that more often depression—or at least a vulnerability to depressive symptoms under stress—leads to opioid abuse when the drugs are available. Depression in addicts may have been overestimated, since there is some evidence that the ones who seek treatment are more depressed than those who do not.

Treatment for Opioid Dependence The first step in treatment for opioid dependence consists of detoxification in a hospital, removal of the drug from the body by metabolism, while withdrawal symptoms are also being treated. In a great many cases, this represents just about the entire treatment program and does not contribute to reducing the likelihood of relapse. Clinicians do not agree on how opioid-dependent individuals should be treated beyond these necessary physical steps. Some clinicians believe that, once an opiate addict, always an opiate addict and that treatment for this addiction is unlikely to be helpful in the long run. Complicating treatment is the fact that opioid dependence is now rarely the sole clinical problem; most patients with opioid dependence also abuse drugs other than opioids and commonly have severe psychological problems as well. Depression, antisocial behavior, and anxiety disorders are among the comorbidity features found in opioid dependence.

Methadone maintenance is the most widely used treatment for opioid addicts. **Methadone** is a synthetic substance that blocks the effects of heroin. It can be taken orally, prevents withdrawal symptoms for 24 hours, and prevents or decreases the euphoric effects or rushes that occur if heroin is taken while the methadone is active. Its withdrawal effects are also less intense (though somewhat more prolonged) than those of heroin, and their appearance is delayed. While the biochemical and physiological properties of methadone are not fully understood, it apparently blocks all the ordinary effects of morphinelike drugs by competing with them at receptor sites in the central nervous system. Through the use of methadone, the craving for heroin is relieved. Methadone allows a heroin-dependent person to function in society.

Methadone maintenance programs seem suitable to a wide range of opioid-dependent individuals, and since they can be carried out on an outpatient basis, they cost less than institutional treatment. However, despite its relative effectiveness, methadone maintenance is not universally supported. Critics claim that it does not really cure addicts but merely transfers their dependence from one drug to another.

Another drug (mentioned earlier in the treatment of alcoholism) that may be helpful in achieving abstinence is *naltrexone*, which specifically blocks opioid receptors. While the drug is present, it prevents readdiction to heroin and other opioid drugs. It is relatively safe and nontoxic and one dose can last for up to 3 days. Unfortunately, although it is an excellent treatment for highly motivated patients who prefer to be opioid-free, most street heroin addicts are not interested in naltrexone because it keeps them from getting high. Naltrexone will effectively block the effects of opioids, but it does not stop the psychological craving for opioids. The optimum duration of naltrexone therapy has not yet been established, but motivated patients should probably take it for at least 3 months after detoxification.

Most addicts need help in a variety of areas in their lives. Family therapy, psychotherapy for depression, vocational counseling, and other types of treatment, along with drugs such as methadone and naltrexone, can play useful roles in the attainment of abstinence and a satisfying life.

Cocaine

Cocaine is the main active drug in the leaves of the coca bush, which grows on the eastern slopes of the Andes in South America. The Indians of Peru and Bolivia have used its leaves for centuries to increase endurance and decrease hunger so that they can better cope with the rigors of their economically marginal high-altitude existence. In 1860 cocaine was isolated and purified.

Like heroin, cocaine initially had a positive, even benign, image. Sigmund Freud, who periodically used cocaine himself, recommended its use for treating depression and other conditions, including morphine withdrawal. The use of cocaine as a local anesthetic led to the discovery of synthetic substitutes with low toxicity, while its use in treating morphine withdrawal led indirectly to self-administration of the drug. From about 1880 to 1900, cocaine was actually an ingredient in some popular brands of soda. Cocaine can be "snorted," or sniffed; smoked (often in a water pipe); or injected intravenously. Cocaine taken by injection is associated with the highest levels of dependence (Gossop et. al., 1994).

Cocaine is a central nervous system stimulant. Whereas the opioids are "downers" that slow the body's responses, cocaine is an "upper" that increases heart rate, raises blood pressure and body temperature, and decreases appetite. It puts the body in an emergency state in much the same way that a rush of adrenaline would in a stressful situation. Although it isn't clear how cocaine produces this effect, it is likely that it causes the release of large amounts of dopamine in the brain. Cocaine also affects at least three parts of the brain itself: the cerebral cortex, which governs reasoning and memory; the hypothalamus, which controls appetite, body temperature, sleep, and emotions such as fear and anger; and the cerebellum, which regulates motor activities such as walking and balance.

High doses of the drug can result in a condition called "cocaine psychosis":

After a while, I was convinced that there were people trying to break into my house. I didn't know who they were, but I was sure that people were after me. There was probably some reality to it too, since I really was scared that the police would come in and bust me. The only way that I felt that I could protect myself was by getting a knife. So I started sleeping with a butcher knife next to me. That didn't work for long, though, because I still feel insecure. So I felt that I had to get a gun. Every night, I went to bed with a gun on one side of me and a butcher knife on the other side. I was just waiting for someone to come in the house so that I could blow his brains out. God knows what I was going to do with the knife. I swear, I was a maniac. It wouldn't have mattered who had come to the door. If someone had come to my door at the wrong time to borrow a cup of sugar, I can tell you with 100 percent certainty, he would have been dead. (R. D. Weiss & Mirin, 1987, p. 39)

Persons with *cocaine intoxication* have recently used cocaine and, following a period of euphoria, show clinically significant maladaptive behavioral or psychological changes (such as anxiety, impaired judgment, and impaired social or occupational functioning) during or shortly after use of the drug. Cocaine withdrawal occurs in persons who have stopped (or reduced) the consumption of cocaine after prolonged and heavy use. The withdrawal syndrome is marked by dysphoric mood accompanied by other psychological changes. Table 13-12 lists features of the DSM-IV diagnoses of cocaine intoxication and cocaine withdrawal.

With the wide availability of **crack,** a concentrated form of the drug, the potency of cocaine products now available is much greater than in the past. Crack differs from other forms of cocaine primarily because it is easily vaporized and inhaled, and thus its effects have an extremely rapid onset. Crack has greatly increased the use of the drug among adolescents because of its relatively low price. People who use crack experience high-dose, high-intensity effects that greatly increase the probability of extremely negative long-term effects such as panic states, toxic psychoses, and paranoid schizophrenia. High-dose effects also include markedly altered perceptions of reality, including imagined persecution by others. This can lead to aggressive or homicidal behavior. Crack represents a serious problem because dependence develops extremely rapidly.

The use of crack has produced one of the great tragedies of the last decade, the birth of thousands of "crack babies."

Table 13-12
Clinical Features of Cocaine Intoxication and Cocaine Withdrawal

Cocaine Intoxication

In addition to an initial period of euphoria, significant maladaptive behavioral or social changes (such as anxiety, impaired judgment, and impaired social or occupational functioning) and at least two of the following during or shortly after cocaine use:

1. Abnormally rapid or slow heart beat
2. Dilation of the pupils
3. Elevated or lowered blood pressure
4. Perspiration or chills
5. Nausea or vomiting
6. Weight loss
7. Psychomotor agitation or retardation
8. Muscular weakness or chest pain
9. Confusion, seizures, and coma

Cocaine Withdrawal

Significant distress or impairment in social or occupational functioning following cessation or reduction of cocaine use that has been heavy and prolonged. Accompanied by dysphoric mood (feeling depressed) and at least two of the following within a few hours to several days of cessation or reduction:

1. Fatigue
2. Vivid, unpleasant dreams
3. Sleep abnormalities (too much or too little)
4. Increased appetite
5. Psychomotor retardation or agitation

Source: DSM-IV.

Women who use cocaine in any form during pregnancy are likely to place the fetus at risk because of the greater chance of spontaneous abortion or fetal death late in pregnancy, or the reduction of infant birth weight if the pregnancy is carried to term. These effects are thought to be related to a lack of oxygen and reduced blood flow to the fetus as a result of the intense vasoconstriction (temporary narrowing) of the mother's blood vessels induced by the cocaine. Some crack babies are born with visible birth defects, but many more have neurological defects. Nearly all these infants are irritable and difficult to soothe, and as a result are less likely to receive adequate mothering. As these crack babies enter the school system, it appears that they have cognitive difficulties in structuring information and also have low tolerance for frustration. Estimates of the number of babies affected by crack use range from 50,000 to 200,000 births per year.

Cocaine produces hyperalertness and the feeling that one is being witty, and it is often praised by users as being almost risk-free: they say there are no hangovers like those produced by alcohol; no injection scars like those caused by heroin use; and no lung cancer, which is associated with use of marijuana and tobacco. Unfortunately, its action is more complex and less benign than most users believe. Since cocaine's effects are highly reinforcing and psycho-

logically addicting to the user, desire for it is hard to control. A damaging habit usually develops over a period ranging from several months to several years. Compulsive users cannot turn the drug down; they think about it constantly, dream about it, spend all their savings on it, and borrow, steal, or deal drugs to pay for it.

Physical tolerance also develops quickly, so an increased dose is needed to produce the same effects, thus increasing the danger of overdose. Users often say that they never quite recapture the euphoria of the first snort.

High doses or repeated use of cocaine can produce a state resembling mania, with impaired judgment, incessantly rambling talk, hyperactivity, and paranoia that may lead to violence or accidents. There is also an acute anxiety reaction that is sometimes severe enough to be called panic. In addition, people who have high blood pressure or damaged arteries may suffer strokes as a result of cocaine use. A common cause of death is intravenous injection of a "speedball"—a combination of heroin and cocaine.

Treating Cocaine Dependence The cocaine-dependent person must first become convinced that treatment is necessary. As in all types of drug and alcohol dependence, more or less subtle forms of denial are common; for example, abusers may want relief from some of the side effects without giving up the habit itself. Sometimes they are convinced to come in for treatment only by pressure from family members, employers, or the law. People seek treatment at different stages of dependency, and the severity of symptoms varies greatly.

Many cocaine users have joined mutual-help groups such as Cocaine Anonymous or Narcotics Anonymous. These programs use more or less the same approach developed by Alcoholics Anonymous: they encourage their members to confide in others who have the same problem, to share their feelings, to make a resolution to overcome dependency, and to support the resolutions of other members. Members admit their powerlessness to control their drug use and seek help from a higher power while taking a "moral inventory" of themselves and pledging abstinence "one day at a time."

Many cocaine users have histories of dysfunctional family lives. Cocaine use has been associated with family patterns of alcoholism, domestic violence, separation, and divorce, as well as with physical, sexual, and emotional abuse within the family (B. C. Wallace, 1991). In such cases psychotherapy can be an important part of treatment—although psychotherapy alone rarely solves drug problems. *Supportive therapy* is a relationship with a sympathetic professional who provides comfort and encourages the abuser to stay away from sources of cocaine. Interpretive or exploratory psychotherapy can help some abusers understand which functions cocaine has been filling in their lives and find other ways of coping.

A serious problem in treating cocaine dependence is preventing relapse. Abusers usually return to cocaine because it has become a familiar response to certain cues—daily annoyances; family conflict; feelings of boredom, loneliness, anger, and depression; sexual stirrings; alcohol intoxication; and the places, people, sights, and sounds that have become associated with the drug. People dependent on cocaine need to learn to avoid places where the drug is available and to stay away from friends who use it. Sometimes that means finding a new job and a new place to live. Usually they must give up other drugs that arouse a desire for cocaine or reduce the ability to resist it. Behavioral principles can be helpful, for example, by using desensitization to eliminate craving. The cocaine-dependent person might repeatedly be shown hypodermic needles, glass pipes, or films of people using cocaine in the hope that desire for the drug will fade when it is no longer satisfied after exposure to the cues that have come to provide it. In general, however, recovery is difficult unless a cocaine-dependent person has a stake in something besides the drug.

There is evidence that providing incentives for abstinence can be helpful for cocaine users. One study showed that men and women who were cocaine dependent achieved increased abstinence when rewarded with vouchers that could be converted into money (Higgins et al., 2000). Positive effects of this reinforcement could be observed in a 1-year follow-up. Another study showed that cognitive-behavioral therapy helps crack cocaine abusers achieve abstinence (Maude-Gridden et al., 1998). Components of the therapy included dealing effectively with urges and high-risk situations, managing negative moods, increasing positive moods and social support, and strengthening commitment to abstinence. One national survey showed that better outcomes were associated with being in a cocaine dependence treatment program for 90 days or longer (Simpson et al., 1999). Although many more studies of psychological interventions for cocaine abuse are needed, results such as these provide encouragement for continued efforts to create effective treatments for cocaine abuse.

Amphetamines

Amphetamines, like cocaine, are potent psychomotor stimulants. Various drugs in this group are called "speed," "crystal," "pep pills," "beanies," "meth," and many other names, depending on the specific active agent. Despite their dissimilar chemical structures, amphetamines and cocaine have many similar properties. They both probably act by influencing the norepinephrine and dopamine receptor systems. This has been demonstrated in research studies using antipsychotic medications that are known to block not only the dopamine receptors but some of the norepinephrine receptors as well. If these antipsychotic medications are given prior to amphetamine or cocaine use, they inhibit most of the behavioral effects of either drug. This suggests that the blocked receptors were those that would otherwise transmit the nerve impulses that produce the drug-related responses.

Moderate amphetamine use results in increased wakefulness, alertness, and elevation of mood. Psychomotor performance is improved temporarily, but the improvement may be followed by a compensatory rebound or letdown in which the user feels fatigued, less alert, and somewhat depressed.

The medical uses of amphetamines include suppression of appetite and improvement of mood in mild depressions. Amphetamines are also helpful in treating certain neurological and behavioral disorders. College students who use amphetamines when cramming for exams not only notice increased energy and tolerance for sleeplessness, but also increased productivity on the next day's exam. Although this may be useful at times, the "improved" performance may not actually be better. Many students have the disillusioning experience of looking at their wondrous performance later and finding it to be of poor quality. The drug impaired their critical thinking at the same time that it increased their output.

High doses of amphetamines have significant effects on the central nervous system and the cardiovascular system: they lead to nervousness, headache, dizziness, agitation, apprehension, confusion, palpitations, and elevated blood pressure. Regular use of large amounts leads to greater tolerance for the drug and increased intolerance for being without it. Users become malnourished, exhausted, careless, and indifferent to normal responsibilities. Their thinking is often characterized by a paranoia that may develop into a full-blown psychosis accompanied by hallucinations. Withdrawal symptoms, if they occur, are mild compared with those that often accompany cessation of opioid use; they also differ qualitatively. Since tolerance for amphetamines develops rapidly, many users inject it into a vein to obtain more intense effects. This high-dose, long-term use of amphetamines is dangerous and self-destructive. Since the initial effects are stimulating and pleasant, unwary individuals often proceed to higher doses and eventually to a state of dependence.

Methamphetamine is closely related chemically to amphetamine, but the central nervous system effects of methamphetamine are greater. It is made in illegal laboratories and has a very high potential for abuse and dependence. It is often described as the "poor man's cocaine" because it can cost half as much. Although scientific research on methamphetamine is in its infancy, available evidence suggests that its prolonged use not only modifies behavior but also changes the brain in fundamental and long-lasting ways. (Cocaine, by contrast, doesn't stay long in the brain because it almost completely metabolizes in the body.)

Hallucinogens

Hallucinogens, or *psychedelics*, act on the central nervous system to produce alteration of consciousness. They change the user's perceptions of both the internal and the external world. There is usually sensory displacement, which can drastically alter color perception and hearing. Auditory, visual, and tactile hallucinations accompany the experience, along with a changed perception of self. Among the natural hallucinogenic substances are mescaline and psilocybin. Synthetic psychedelics include diethyltryptamine (STP), and **lysergic acid diethylamide (LSD).** The following case describes some of the effects of LSD:

A 21-year-old woman was admitted to the hospital after ingesting a large amount of LSD. About half an hour after ingestion she perceived that light affected her strangely and that the bricks in the wall had begun to move in and out. She became frightened when she realized that she was unable to distinguish her body from the chair she was sitting on or from her lover's body. Her fear became more marked as she began to think that she would not get back into herself. At the time of her admission she was hyperactive and laughed inappropri-

ately. Her stream of talk was illogical and her emotions extremely variable. After two days this reaction had ceased, but she was still afraid of the drug and convinced that she would not take it again because of her frightening experience. (Adapted from Kolb & Brodie, 1982, p. 666)

In many cultures hallucinogens have been used for hundreds of years. Mescaline, which is derived from the peyote cactus, and psilocybin, which is obtained from certain mushrooms, are used for religious ceremonies by Indians in Mexico and Central America. West Africans and Congolese have traditionally chewed the "bogain" root, which contains tryptamine, to "release the gods." While epidemiological surveys have found a decline in use of most substances that are abused, major hallucinogenic drugs, predominantly LSD, have maintained a steady, somewhat increasing trend.

LSD (popularly called "acid") is a colorless, odorless, and tasteless material. Effects are produced by as little as 50 micrograms (a microgram is a millionth of a gram), an amount that in pure form would not be visible to the naked eye. No legally manufactured LSD is available to the general public, and the output of illegal, often amateur, laboratories is rarely pure LSD. LSD was first synthesized in 1938 by Albert Hoffman, a Swiss chemist, in the course of research on certain groups of therapeutic compounds. His description of the drug's effects on him in the laboratory presents a more benign view than the case described previously.

I was forced to stop my work in the laboratory . . . and to go home, as I was seized by a particular restlessness associated with the sensation of mild dizziness. On arriving home, I lay down and sank into a kind of drunkenness which was not unpleasant and which was characterized by extreme activity of imagination. As I lay in a dazed condition with my eyes closed (I experienced daylight as disagreeably bright), there surged upon me an uninterrupted stream of fantastic images of extraordinary plasticity and vividness and accompanied by an intense, kaleidoscope-like play of colours. This condition gradually passed off after about two hours. (Hoffman, 1971, p. 23)

The immediate effects of LSD usually last from about 8 to 12 hours. The mechanism of its action is not well understood, but it is known to stimulate the sympathetic nervous system and to produce physiological changes like those seen in a person who is aroused, excited, or under stress. The most common subjective effects are euphoria, quick shifts from one mood to another, and altered awareness of the color, size, and shape of stimuli. Time perception is so altered that minutes may seem like hours. Bizarre sensations may be experienced, frequently including feelings of separation or disintegration of some part of the body. The user typically realizes that these effects are due to the drug and are not "out there." Some users experience bewilderment, disorganization, personal and sexual identity confusion, and fears of losing control. They may experience intense emotions that they cannot label. In fact, one of the most unfortunate effects of LSD is the feeling of being overwhelmed by confusing emotions that cannot be sorted out because they are going by so fast.

LSD sometimes produces extreme anxiety or panic reactions. Such "bad trips" are generally short-lived and can often be modified by supportive reassurance. Bad trips may be terminated by appropriate medication and occasionally by hospitalization. The most serious effects of LSD are paranoid symptoms (feelings of being followed, spied on, or persecuted), psychosis resembling that found in schizophrenia, and severe depression that occasionally leads to suicide attempts. Negative effects of a single large dose of LSD may persist for months, require long hospitalization, and resist the usual forms of treatment. The frequency of such reactions is difficult to determine but is probably less than 1%. When such problems arise, it is often difficult to separate the effects of LSD from those of prior drug use, personality characteristics, and a variety of other factors. While users of hallucinogens develop dependence, withdrawal symptoms usually do not occur.

In **post-hallucinogen perceptual disorder** there are "flashbacks": spontaneous recurrences of parts of the LSD experience long after the action of the drug has ceased. Such recurrences can take place in the first few weeks and have been reported as long as 2 years after the last dose of the drug. It is not clear why these flashbacks occur. One possibility is that LSD causes biochemical changes in the body that last long after drug use. The aftereffects may have serious consequences if they occur in situations that require attentive thinking and decision making.

Treatment for abuse of hallucinogens depends on the severity of the reaction. Severely affected people must have medical attention to prevent cardiovascular or respiratory collapse. If psychotic behavior is present, antipsychotic drugs of the type used to treat schizophrenia may be helpful, although about 10% of drug users who become acutely psychotic never recover. Psychologically based therapy, particularly group psychotherapy and supportive drug-free groups, can be helpful because users of hallucinogens often have feelings of low self-worth and use the drugs to improve their relationships with other people. Many of these abusers need psychological help with their social responses so that they can substitute rewarding experiences for the reinforcement they get from drugs.

Phencyclidine (PCP)

The drug **phencyclidine (PCP)** was introduced in 1957 as an experimental intravenously administered surgical anesthetic. Researchers found that 10% to 20% of the patients who received PCP experienced drug-related delir-

ium and hallucinations. As a consequence, its use was discontinued. Because it is easily manufactured in illicit laboratories, it has become a street drug that goes by several names, including "angel dust" and "crystal." It is available in a number of forms—as a pure, white crystalline powder, a tablet, or a capsule. PCP is sometimes sprinkled on marijuana or parsley and smoked. It also can be swallowed, sniffed, or injected. Although PCP is illegal, it is easily manufactured. Users can never be sure what they are buying, since it is manufactured illegally. Sometimes it may not even be PCP, but a lethal byproduct of the drug.

The effects of PCP depend on how much is taken, the way it is used, and the individual. Effects include increased heart rate and blood pressure, flushing, sweating, dizziness, and numbness. As with hallucinogens, adverse reactions to PCP tend to be more common among individuals with preexisting mental disorders. When large doses are taken, effects include drowsiness, convulsions, and coma. Taking large amounts of PCP can also cause death from repeated convulsions, heart and lung failure, or ruptured blood vessels in the brain.

PCP is classified as a dissociative anesthetic because it makes the individual feel dissociated or detached from the environment. In small doses, it produces insensitivity to pain; in large doses, it produces a comalike state and blank stare. People who take larger doses feel as if they are being bombarded by stimuli. They may lose the ability to distinguish between fantasy and reality and suffer severe intellectual and emotional disorganization. PCP users sometimes develop severe depression or a severe psychotic state that is not easily reversible. Whether these outcomes are a result of the drug alone or of underlying personality characteristics is not clear.

Researchers studying areas of the brain affected by PCP have discovered that PCP can protect the brain from permanent damage after a stroke or heart attack. Scientists do not yet fully understand this process, but they have proven that it works in a series of animal studies. PCP has diverse effects because it works at two different sites on nerve cells, named PCP and sigma receptors, that have quite different characteristics. Pharmaceutical companies are working to develop new synthetic drugs with the same action as PCP but without its undesirable qualities.

Inhalants

The extensive capillary surface area of the lungs makes inhalation a favored method of administration of many psychoactive substances. In some cases, the effect of inhalation can resemble intravenous injection in its intensity. There is one group of substances for which direct inhalation is virtually the only route of self-administration. The **inhalants** are volatile substances or organic solvents such as gasoline, lighter fluids, spray paints, and cleaning fluids. Most of these substances are hydrocarbons of some type. Once inhaled, blood levels of most inhalants peak within minutes. Users report distortion in their perceptions of size, color, and the passage of time. They may briefly develop delusions and hallucinations. As with alcohol, intoxication is accompanied by muscular incoordination and dizziness. Headaches, nausea, coughing, and abdominal pain are often present.

Because of their low cost, easy availability, and ease of concealment, inhalants may for many be the first psychoactive substance used. Inhalant use is generally considered to be more common among younger people. One study found the median first-time use of inhalants to be 13 years (McGarvey et al., 1999). Tolerance of the effects of inhalants and withdrawal symptoms have been reported among heavy users. Recurrent inhalant use may result in the individual giving up or reducing important social, occupational, or recreational activities.

Cannabis

The **cannabis** plant (see Figure 13-9) has been harvested throughout history for its fibers, oils, and psychoactive resin. **Marijuana,** which consists of the dried leaves and flowering tops of the plant, is the form in which it is most often used in the United States. The solidified resin, called **hashish** (or, colloquially, "hash"), can also be used to produce psychoactive effects.

Many Americans have used marijuana at least once, in spite of the fact that it is classified as an illegal substance and its cultivation, possession, distribution, and use are prohibited. Despite the prohibitions and the controversy over its safety, the use of marijuana increased sharply during the 1960s and 1970s. This was followed by a decline in the 1990s.

Figure 13-9 Leaves from a cannabis plant.

Marijuana is not pharmacologically a narcotic, although in the United States it has been legally classified as one since 1937. The mechanisms of its action are not well understood, but its more common effects have been identified. An important advance in research was the isolation of the major active ingredient in marijuana, **THC (tetrahydrocannabinol).** Only barely detectable concentrations of THC are present in the brain of a rat after one dose. But with repeated administration, THC and the products of its metabolism gradually build up so that administration of a single dose is detectable for as long as 8 days afterward.

Marijuana can be used by either eating or smoking parts of the cannabis plant. Smoking is the fastest way to feel the drug's effects. When the smoke is inhaled, it is spread across the surface of the lungs, quickly absorbed into the bloodstream, and carried to the brain in a few seconds. When marijuana is ingested, THC enters the bloodstream from the digestive system and is carried to the liver. There enzymes break it down into other substances, which are carried to the brain by the circulatory system.

Cannabis intoxication usually begins with a "high" feeling followed by such symptoms as inappropriate laughter and grandiosity, lethargy, impairment in short-term memory, impaired judgment, distorted sensory perceptions, impaired motor performance, and distortions in time perception (usually time seems to pass very slowly). These are the reactions of some people who had used marijuana for the first time:

> *The first time I smoked I had the feeling of being entirely outside of my body, hovering above it, and as I was lying on the bed, I was exceptionally conscious of my body for part of the time, realizing how, and feeling how, each individual part was working. (Berke & Hernton, 1974, p. 97)*

Marijuana became popular as a recreational drug, partly because it is cheap and readily available, but also because many people believe that when used in moderation it is not a risk to physical or mental health. Despite this widespread attitude, the federal government has conducted a vigorous and costly campaign to prevent the entry of marijuana into this country. As a result, a great deal of marijuana is grown illegally in the United States and Canada. Several authoritative reports have been issued on the effects of marijuana on health, but scientific controversy and public confusion still exist as to whether marijuana should be legalized or whether the laws against it should be strengthened.

Marijuana use causes changes in the heart and circulation that are similar to those caused by stress. These changes might be a threat for individuals with high blood pressure or heart disease. Marijuana smoke causes changes in the lungs that may lead to respiratory problems, but cancer-producing agents in marijuana smoke are even more of a problem. Marijuana smoke contains about 50% more carcinogens than does tobacco smoke.

In males, marijuana suppresses the production of male hormones, decreases the size and weight of the prostate gland and testes, and inhibits sperm production, although these effects appear to be reversible. Marijuana blocks ovulation in women and can cause birth defects in animals. In pregnant women. THC crosses the placental barrier and may harm the unborn child. It can also be secreted in breast milk, thereby affecting nursing infants. The belief that marijuana use is associated with chromosome breaks, which are thought to be indicators of genetic damage, does not appear to be correct. Contradictory evidence exists as to whether the drug causes atrophy or other gross changes in the brain. One particularly important point is that behavioral or cognitive impairment from marijuana use lasts for 4 to 8 hours after the feeling of intoxication is over. This means that behavior may be affected even when the user is no longer aware of the presence of the drug.

One positive aspect of marijuana and its chemical derivatives is its therapeutic potential. Evidence suggests that marijuana is useful in the treatment of glaucoma, an eye disorder that may cause blindness, and that it helps control the severe nausea and vomiting that accompany chemotherapy for cancer. It may also be useful in treating asthma and certain types of epileptic seizures. However, the stress it puts on the cardiovascular system may make marijuana an inappropriate drug for treating older people.

Government agencies are reluctant to legalize the sale and use of marijuana because of vocal public opposition. Some opponents of legalization argue that the most potent deterrent of marijuana use is the possibility of arrest and imprisonment. However, while enforcement of marijuana laws is a major drain on the resources of the criminal justice system, it does not seem to be effective. Some people have proposed licensing the sale of marijuana, as is done with alcohol, and writing laws regulating its potency. Endangering the lives or well-being of others—for example, by operating a motor vehicle while intoxicated—would be penalized, but safe recreational use would not be illegal. Others have suggested eliminating criminal penalties for users but not for sellers of marijuana. Several states permit the use of marijuana for certain medical purposes.

There is a great need to base laws and social policies concerning marijuana and other drugs on facts rather than on opinions and fears. Laboratory research and studies of the longer-term effects of drugs and therapies are a first step toward providing the facts. Because marijuana is the most frequently used illicit drug in the United States, there is a particular need to develop treatment programs for the disorders it causes. One controlled study evaluated the effects of two treatments on the ability of people with marijuana problems to achieve abstinence (Stephens et al., 1994). The treatments were (1) a relapse prevention program similar to those described earlier in the chapter and

(2) social support groups. The support groups included opportunities to get and give support and dealt with such topics as coping with mood swings, relating to friends who continue to use marijuana, and maintaining motivation to be abstinent. As Figure 13-10 shows, both treatment approaches were effective. There were significant reductions in marijuana use: nearly two-thirds of the subjects were able initially to achieve abstinence, and one-third showed signs of improvement throughout a 12-month posttreatment period.

Use of marijuana seems to be related to family disorganization and stress. Adolescents not living with two biological or adoptive parents are from 50% to 150% more likely to use marijuana and other substances than adolescents living with two biological or adoptive parents. Young adults who used alcohol, marijuana, and other illegal substances as teenagers tend to cut down or quit when they assume the responsibilities of marriage and family. But divorce and other types of family stress can drive them back to their old habits (Bachman et al., 1997). Thus, substance use may increase as commitment to close interpersonal relationships decreases.

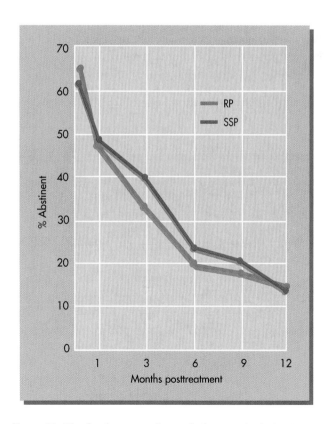

Figure 13-10 Continuous marijuana abstinence rates by treatment condition (RP = relapse prevention; SSP = social support.) Both treatment approaches were effective in reducing marijuana use.

SOURCE: Stephens, Roffman, & Simpson (1994), p. 97.

Nicotine

I can quit smoking if I wish; I've done it a thousand times.
(Mark Twain)

Nicotine and cancer-causing tars are the only pharmacologically active ingredients in tobacco. Nicotine acts at least in part by directly stimulating certain receptors that are sensitive to the neurotransmitter acetylcholine, and as a result exerts powerful effects on the brain and spinal cord, the peripheral nervous system, and the heart. Its initial use causes nausea and vomiting by stimulating the vomiting center in the brain stem as well as receptors in the stomach, but sensitivity to this effect diminishes quickly. Normal doses of nicotine can increase heart rate and blood pressure, and the heart's need for oxygen. If this increased need for oxygen cannot be met—for instance, in people who have atherosclerosis, or hardening of the arteries—the result may be angina, chest pains, or a heart attack. Smoking by pregnant women tends to reduce the birth weight of their babies. In addition to the effects of nicotine, the tars contained in tobacco are a major cause of lung cancer.

Despite these consequences, smoking is a difficult habit to give up even for those who try (see Figure 13-11). Some smokers experience psychological distress in the form of anxiety and guilt because they cannot stop smoking. The difficulty of giving up tobacco use on a long-term basis may be due to the unpleasant nature of the withdrawal experience, the importance of social or environmental cues, and the highly overlearned nature of the habit (the pack-a-day smoker is reinforced by the rapid effects of nicotine in each of about 75,000 puffs per year). Withdrawal symptoms—irritability, anxiety, headache, excessive appetite, and difficulty in concentrating—do not occur in all smokers, but in some heavy smokers withdrawal symptoms can be detected within 2 hours after the last cigarette. Since many smokers use cigarettes as a way of coping with stress, it is not clear whether these symptoms are related to the withdrawal of nicotine or whether some of them may be due to psychological characteristics that helped start the addictive behavior.

Nicotine seems to work by releasing dopamine and increasing the strength of messages running through the brain. These messages take the form of electrical impulses. In order to cross the synapse, neurotransmitters are needed that can diffuse across this gap. Nicotine binds to receptors on a transmitting neuron and speeds message transmission. While in the short run smoking a cigarette can speed memory, the 400 known carcinogens associated with tobacco and its negative effects on the individual's life can create serious problems. Within 4 hours after the last cigarette, heavy smokers experience measurable declines in many cognitive functions, such as the ability to do mental arithmetic and logical reasoning. They frequently become confused, restless, irritable, or drowsy. For

Figure 13-11

Source: Drawing by Handelsman. © 1985 by *The New Yorker Magazine, Inc.*

"Phil suddenly decided to give up everything that was bad for him—no more smoking, drinking, or junk food—and he feels absolutely <u>terrific!</u>"

those most seriously addicted to nicotine, the withdrawal symptoms can last for months.

The degree to which perceptions of smoking have changed in recent years becomes clear when cigarette ads of prior times are examined. For a long time these ads accurately reflected the public's lack of concern regarding smoking as a threat to health. Table 13-13 contains some early cigarette ad slogans.

Primarily owing to more public awareness of the negative effects of tobacco, smoking rates have declined in the United States and Canada. Many long-term smokers have given up the habit. Most cigarette smokers who try to quit do so on their own, and they are more likely to be successful than those who seek help in quitting through formal programs. This may be because those who seek help tend to be heavier smokers and to have made more cessation attempts than those who quit unaided. While stopping smoking unaided is a simple, direct, and effective path to getting rid of nicotine dependence, special smoking cessation programs have an important role to play.

Therapeutic efforts to help people stop smoking take several forms. Some of these methods use the biological perspective. From this viewpoint, the problem is not so much that smoking calms the nerves as that nonsmoking sets up the negative reinforcement of withdrawal symptoms, which can be ended by having another cigarette. By resuming the use of cigarettes, the individual is attempting to regulate the nicotine level in his or her body. This may have important physiological effects because nicotine stimulates the release of central peptides, hormones that have a powerful effect on key mental and physical functions. This suggests that smokers who are heavily dependent but want to quit smoking may require, on a temporary basis, some pharmacological substitute for the nicotine they are deriving from cigarettes.

Chewing gum containing nicotine was developed to ease withdrawal from tobacco by providing both an alternate source of nicotine and a substitute oral activity. **Nicotine gum** probably does not give the same positive pleasure as smoking a cigarette because nicotine is absorbed more

slowly through the lining of the mouth than through the lungs. However, the gum may enable a smoker to break the habit in two stages. First the smoker can focus on overcoming the behavioral and psychological components of tobacco dependence without having to cope with nicotine withdrawal at the same time. Linked with each smoker's puffing habits are the many other actions involved in handling cigarettes and responding to cues that call for lighting up. Because smoking is a complex behavior, all components of that behavior need to be addressed in helping a person stop smoking. Once these behavior patterns are controlled, withdrawal from the nicotine gum might be accomplished more easily. Research is needed to evaluate the effects of nicotine gum by itself and in combination with other factors. The available evidence indicates that it makes a positive contribution to smoking cessation and an even more positive one when used in conjunction with counseling programs (Cepeda-Benito, 1993; Orleans & Slade, 1993).

The use of the nicotine patch also seems promising. A **transdermal nicotine patch** is a multilayered pad containing the active ingredient nicotine, which is applied to the skin via a pressure-sensitive adhesive (see Figure 13-12).

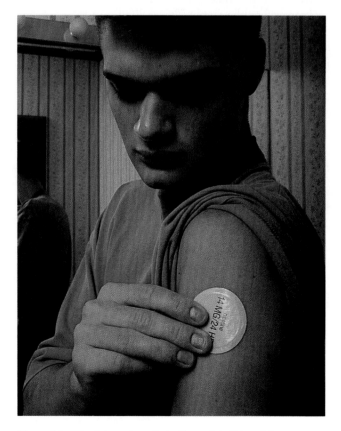

Figure 13-12 A transdermal nicotine patch. This patch administers 14 milligrams during a 24-hour period.

SOURCE: *Alcohol, Drug Abuse, and Mental Health Administration News,* May–June, 1992, p. 6.

Table 13-13	
Some Early Cigarette Slogans	
Year	
1919	"You never tasted such mellow mildness."
1935	"They don't get your wind!"
1938	". . . so smooth and mellow you can smoke them in any number without cigarette hangover."
1946	"More doctors smoke Camels than any other cigarette."
1951	"Notice that Philip Morris is definitely less irritating, definitely milder!"

The patch, which must be prescribed by a doctor, administers a controlled dose of nicotine over a 16- or 24-hour period. Doses are maintained for a specified number of weeks and reduced in stages to gradually wean the smoker from nicotine dependence. The total course of nicotine replacement treatment is approximately 90 days but depends on the patch used. A number of pharmaceutical companies manufacture a nicotine patch.

The available evidence suggests that the nicotine patch is effective and there are few side effects. One study showed that it significantly reduces craving and sensitivity to smoking cues (Tiffany et al., 2000). The positive effects of both the gum and the patch seem to be maximized when they are combined with counseling that provides support, information about the process of quitting, and training in useful skills such as relaxation.

Cognitive research has identified three "stages of change" relevant to smoking cessation. The first stage involves the individual's commitment to making a change and setting goals—for example, stopping smoking. Unfortunately, smokers are often ambivalent about quitting and reluctant to take personal responsibility for quitting. They need help in developing their commitment and motivation to change. Once the individual has made the commitment to stop smoking, a specific plan can be developed and implemented. This second stage is an action phase for actual change. The third stage involves maintenance of the change, with relapse prevention playing an important role. Change is facilitated when people can identify the situations in which they are most likely to be tempted to smoke, learn cognitive coping techniques as al-

Table 13–14
Stages of Change
1. *Contemplation and commitment.* This stage is usually preceded by a precontemplation stage in which people do not see themselves as having a problem ("What's bad about smoking?").
2. *Action.* A specific plan for change is established and implemented (e.g., use of nicotine substitutes, activating social support from friends, family, and co-workers).
3. *Maintenance.* Changing smoking patterns takes time, and self-monitoring and relapse prevention strategies are necessary during the action and maintenance phases.

ternatives to smoking, and use self-reinforcement when they are successful in resisting the temptation to smoke. Table 13-14 summarizes these stages of change. Can smokers proceed through these stages themselves, or do they require professional assistance? While some people may need professional assistance, available evidence indicates that for many people self-help approaches can be effective (Curry, 1993). Box 13-4 provides some tips that might be useful to smokers who are thinking about quitting. Quitting smoking is not just a matter of willpower. It requires awareness of one's vulnerabilities (e.g., people are more likely to feel they need to smoke in certain tension-arousing situations) and one's ability to be resilient (e.g., to continue efforts to stop smoking even after a relapse).

Resilience and Vulnerability

Box 13–4

Thinking About Quitting?

Quitting smoking is not just a matter of willpower. Planning and effective cognitive strategies can aid in achieving cessation goals.

You Are Not Alone

- Remember that most adult smokers want to quit.

Getting Ready to Quit

- Notice when and why you smoke.
- Change your smoking habits.

- When you want a cigarette, delay having it for 1 minute.
- Buy one pack of cigarettes at a time and switch to a brand you don't like.
- Set a date for quitting.
- Have a friend quit smoking with you.

Quitting Day

- Change your morning routine.
- Get rid of all cigarettes. Put away your ashtrays.
- When the urge to smoke hits, remember the four "Ds": drink water,

delay, deep-breathe, and do something else.
- Carry gum, hard candy, or a cinnamon stick with you.
- Reward yourself for getting through the day without smoking.

Staying Smoke-Free

- Take one day at a time.
- If you relapse, don't feel you've failed. Try again. Most smokers try to quit several times before quitting for good.

Caffeine

Is **caffeine** in the same league as such substances as cocaine and marijuana? Researchers have recently shown that caffeine exhibits the features of a typical psychoactive substance that cause dependence. Coffee, tea, and cola drinkers are addicted to caffeine in the same way that others are addicted to cigarettes, alcohol, or intravenous drugs. This means that caffeine is the world's most widely used mind-altering drug. Most people consume per day about the amount of caffeine in two cups of coffee. This amount produces a mild positive effect, including a feeling of well-being and alertness. Higher doses can produce anxiety and nervousness, but these negative effects do not in themselves constitute serious health risks. Using DSM-IV's criteria, a person is caffeine-dependent who develops tolerance, has withdrawal symptoms, uses the substance in spite of aggravation of medical or mental problems, and makes repeated unsuccessful attempts to quit. Symptoms of caffeine intoxication include excitement, insomnia, restlessness, nervousness, and a high heart rate. Many coffee, tea, and cola lovers meet these criteria, are physically dependent on caffeine, and will suffer temporary headaches, lethargy, and depression when they stop using it. But of the millions of people who like and use caffeine, only a small, but as yet unknown, percentage are true addicts.

Is There a Final Common Pathway?

Why do certain substances have the power to make us feel so good (at least at first)? Do some, most, or all drugs lead to a final common pathway—that is, do they have similar biological consequences that might explain the maladaptive behavior seen so often in drug abusers? Using a variety of techniques, researchers are beginning to develop tentative answers to and hypotheses concerning these questions. Recent research may ultimately lead us to some important general principles and valuable therapies.

When asked for their opinions about why drugs are abused, most people are likely to mention a failure of character as an important contributing factor. This stereotype is beginning to give way to the recognition that drug dependence has a significant biological basis. Influencing the debate about the causes of drug abuse are more—and improved—research studies and powerful new techniques. For example, for the first time, scientists have captured images of the brains of addicts in the throes of craving a drug. In so doing, they come closer to revealing the neural basis for addiction.

It is now becoming evident that no matter what the addictive substance is—amphetamines, heroin, alcohol, nicotine, or marijuana—all seem to activate a single circuit for pleasure located in the brain. This circuit, for the neurotransmitter dopamine, may be the site of the high that addictive drugs bring. This is not to say that dopamine is the only chemical involved or that the deranged thought processes that mark drug abuse are due to dopamine alone. A study of early-onset substance abuse found that boys whose mothers lacked warmth and nurturant behavior were most likely to begin using drugs at an early age (Dobkin et al., 1997). Another early-onset study showed that greater life stress, lower parental support, and poorer coping skills were predictive of adolescents' substance abuse (Wills et al., 1996). It is known that dopamine can be elevated by a hug, a kiss, a word of praise, or a winning poker hand—as well as by the potent pleasures that come from drugs. So our experiences and how we live our lives have significant impact on biological states such as a dopamine level. Still, the possibility that dopamine may be a common pathway or outgrowth of drug ingestion is an important concept. A genetically encoded trait—such as a tendency to produce too little dopamine—might interact with environmental influences to create a serious behavioral disorder.

Might an inability to absorb enough dopamine, with its pleasure-giving properties, cause someone to seek gratification in drugs? While we do not yet have a solid answer to this question, evidence is mounting that dopamine is involved in the exhilarating rush that reinforces the desire to take drugs. The evidence is particularly strong in cocaine addicts for whom the reinforcing effect of cocaine is associated with highly elevated dopamine levels (Volkow et al., 1997). Rather than saying that addicts crave heroin or cocaine or alcohol or nicotine per se, it might be more accurate to say that what they want is the rush of dopamine that these drugs produce.

It is not yet clear where recent developments will lead. One direction is likely to be research on medication that might reduce intense cravings for drugs. Another is a focus on reversing the biochemical abnormalities associated with addiction through psychosocial interventions that provide useful learning experiences and coping skills to help people resist cravings.

Substance Dependence and Public Policy

Substance dependence continues to be a major problem throughout the world. Recent developments in the study of pain regulators and pain receptors in the body are providing some valuable clues, particularly in the area of opioid abuse. Information about the health consequences of using some substances—for example, marijuana and tobacco—has decreased their overall use. Some therapeutic procedures, especially those that emphasize cognitive techniques for relapse prevention, show promise as treatments for alcohol and tobacco abuse. Still unanswered, however, is the question of whether public policy should be changed—for example, whether to decriminalize marijuana. Because we cannot know the consequences of such actions—would they increase or decrease use of these substances?—and because of philosophical differences among citizens, lawmakers, and scientists, these policy issues seem likely to remain unresolved.

Are There Behavioral Addictions? The Dilemma of Pathological Gambling

In Chapter 5 we discussed diagnostic dilemmas, clinical problems that are not well understood and consequently difficult to diagnose with confidence. So far, all the disorders reviewed in this chapter involve substances ingested into the body that create or are part of maladaptive behavior. They are often referred to as addictions. Although it is an imprecise word, an addiction generally has four properties: (1) craving, (2) compulsion, (3) loss of control, and (4) continuing the behavior in spite of associated adverse consequences. **Pathological gambling** has all of these properties but does not involve an ingested substance. It was first recognized diagnostically in DSM-III in 1980 as a disorder of impulse control, failure to resist the impulse to gamble despite serious personal consequences.

Many clinicians see some significant similarities between pathological gambling and substance abuse disorders and, in fact, up to 48% of pathological gamblers also have documented alcohol and drug abuse problems (Black & Moyer, 1998). They also have a greater than average number of other conditions, including various personality disorders, mood disorders, attention-deficit disorder, and anxiety disorders. Because research on pathological gambling is just getting under way, it is difficult to predict how it will be handled diagnostically in the future. For the present, perhaps the most important question is not in which part of the DSM should pathological gambling be placed, but rather, what is the phenomenon and how prevalent is it?

Pathological gambling is persistent and recurrent maladaptive gambling behavior that disrupts the personal, family, or vocational aspects of a person's life. The individual who engages in pathological gambling is preoccupied with gambling (e.g., reliving past gambling experiences, planning the next gambling venture, or thinking of ways to get money with which to gamble).

When money is not available, the person may resort to illegal activities designed to obtain it. Pathological gambling may result in jeopardizing or losing a significant relationship, job, educational, or other desired opportunity.

The prevalence of pathological gambling has been estimated to range from 0.5% to 1.5% of the U.S. population, with approximately one-third of the gamblers being women (Black & Moyer, 1998). Its impact may not be readily apparent since many of its consequences, such as financial problems and marital discord, remain out of the public's view. It typically begins in early adolescence in males and later in life in females. The gambling pattern may be regular or episodic, but the problem is usually chronic. There is generally a progression in the frequency of gambling and preoccupation with it. The urge to gamble generally increases during periods of stress or depression. Pathological gamblers tend to see gambling as a solution to any problem. They are often highly competitive, often overly generous, and strive to impress others. Once they start to lose, gamblers often lie about their gambling. Table 13-15 contains a list of questions clinicians ask if they think someone's major problem may be pathological gambling. Although various types of therapies (such as cognitive therapy, behavioral therapy, and psychodynamic therapy) have been used for pathological gamblers, there is a paucity of scientific studies concerning their effectiveness.

While pathological gambling is a personal problem, it is influenced by public policy. Gambling is legal in some form in virtually all states. While gambling results from personal decisions made by individuals, it is important to determine how ease of gambling opportunities influences those decisions.

Table 13-15

Finding Evidence of Pathological Gambling

Affirmative answers to these questions suggest the presence of pathological gambling.

1. Do you feel stimulated and intensely alive while gambling?
2. Do you gamble even though you lose more than you win?
3. Have you borrowed money or sold possessions to pay off gambling debts?
4. Do you try to hide your gambling from friends or relatives?
5. Do you gamble more money in riskier ways to win back your losses?
6. Are you increasingly worried about gambling?

Chapter Summary

Substance-related disorders involve psychoactive substances that affect thought, emotions, and behavior. Two categories of disorders are related to these substances: substance-use disorders and substance-induced disorders.

SUBSTANCE-USE DISORDERS

There are two subgroups of substance-use disorders, those related to **substance dependence** and those related to **substance abuse.**

Substance Dependence In substance dependence there is intense craving for the substance to which the person is addicted, and that person shows tolerance, withdrawal symptoms, and compulsive drug-taking. **Tolerance** means that the person has to use more and more of a substance to get the same effect. **Withdrawal** refers to physical symptoms that occur when a person stops or cuts down on the use of a psychoactive substance. **Compulsive substance use** involves drug-seeking behavior—behavior related to obtaining the substance.

Substance Abuse Substance abuse refers to recurrent and significant adverse consequences related to use of substances.

SUBSTANCE-INDUCED DISORDERS

Ingestion of different substances can lead to serious behavioral, psychological, and physiological symptoms. In **substance intoxication** there are reversible substance-specific symptoms due to recent ingestion. Indications of substance intoxication include disturbances of perception, attention, and thought.

Alcohol-Related Disorders

Ethanol is the only type of alcohol intended for human consumption. The ethanol contained in various types of alcoholic drinks—beer, wine, and hard or distilled liquor—is the same drug. However, these types of drinks differ in the percentage of their total volume that is made up of alcohol.

Excessive Alcohol Use Negative effects from the overuse of alcohol are a serious problem. Alcohol is involved in 40% of all traffic fatalities and a high percentage of nontraffic accidents. Perhaps 20% of the total national expenditure for health is alcohol-related.

Theories and Treatment Alcohol-related disorders have multiple causes, and there are a number of theories concerning known and possible determinants. Ingestion of alcohol first reduces anxiety and then has a depressant effect on the body. The biological perspective views alcoholism as a result of the operation of metabolic, genetic, and neural processes. People vary greatly in their sensitivity to the effects of alcohol. Women may be more sensitive to alcohol than men because they have less of a specific enzyme that neutralizes alcohol and because of their

lower body weight. Brain imaging studies may help identify the regions of the brain most influenced by excessive alcohol use. Several drugs have been developed for the treatment of alcohol dependence.

Psychodynamically oriented clinicians see addiction to substances like alcohol as part of an effort to correct or counteract negative emotional states. The cognitive-behavioral approach to treating alcohol-related disorders recognizes the roles played by learning and cognition. From a behavioral point of view, people learn to use alcohol as a result of modeling and social and psychological reinforcement. **Aversive conditioning** is used in the behavioral treatment of alcoholism. The cognitive point of view takes a **controlled drinking approach** and focuses on people's expectations about the effects of alcohol. Increasingly these two perspectives are being integrated in **cognitive-behavioral** treatment programs.

A growing number of researchers are evaluating the various treatment approaches and seeking to identify their major components. Treatment approaches need to be tailored to deal with the problems (such as the tendency for relapse) of particular relevance to each individual. The **interactional view** considers some individuals as having a predisposition toward alcohol dependence and focuses on stress as a precipitating factor in drinking. In this view, an addictive cycle develops. Cultural factors can play important roles in this cycle.

Preventing Alcohol-Related Disorders Community-level programs regulating access to alcohol and penalizing driving after alcohol use may be helpful. Prevention programs that teach young people about alcohol's effects and help them to learn effective coping responses in situations where alcohol is served may be even more useful. Development of effective prevention approaches can be facilitated by identification of risk factors for overuse of alcohol (e.g., family conflict and neighborhood disorganization).

OTHER DRUGS

Barbiturates and Tranquilizers Both barbiturates and tranquilizers have a depressing effect on the central nervous system. Both groups of drugs are especially dangerous in combination with alcohol. **Barbiturates** are often prescribed by physicians to decrease anxiety or prevent convulsions. **Tranquilizing drugs** are derived from several chemical groups. They are overused in the United States. Both barbiturates and tranquilizers are dangerous because tolerance develops and the user often increases the dose to dangerous levels in order to get the desired effect.

The Opioids Opioid is the term used to describe all drugs with morphinelike effects that bind to the opioid receptors in the brain. Some opioids occur naturally and some are chemically synthesized. Opioids are sometimes called **narcotics,** but this term does not have the same meaning to law officers, physicians, scientists, and the public. Natural opioids include **endorphins,**

enkephalins, and dymorphins, all of which are manufactured by the brain and the pituitary gland. **Opiates** are members of the opioid group that are derived from the juice of the opium poppy—for example, **morphine** and **heroin. Opioids** cause mood changes, sleepiness, mental clouding, constipation, and slowing of the activity of the respiratory center in the brain. The withdrawal reaction from opioid use can be severe. According to the **exposure orientation** theory of opioid addiction, the use of opiates shuts down the body's synthesis of natural opioids. The **interactional orientation** holds that the situations in which drugs are used are significant. The most widely used treatment for opioid addicts is **methadone maintenance.** *Naltrexone*, a drug that blocks opioid receptors, can be used effectively as treatment to prevent readdiction after detoxification.

Cocaine Cocaine, a drug from the leaves of the coca bush, stimulates the central nervous system and increases heart rate, raises blood pressure and temperature, and decreases appetite. It can produce feelings of hyperalertness, but in larger doses can produce a maniacal state, paranoia, and impaired judgment. **Crack** is a more potent form of cocaine that is highly addictive. Many cocaine users have dysfunctional families. Mutual help groups similar to Alcoholics Anonymous can be an effective way to provide the social support that is lacking. Incentives for abstinence can be helpful in treating cocaine abusers.

Amphetamines Amphetamines are powerful psychomotor stimulants that affect both the central nervous system and the cardiovascular system. In moderate doses they result in wakefulness, alertness, and elevated mood. Tolerance develops rapidly, so many users begin injecting amphetamines to get more intense effects. High doses lead to nervousness, dizziness, confusion, heart palpitations, and elevated blood pressure. **Methamphetamine** is chemically similar to amphetamine but has a greater impact on the central nervous system.

Hallucinogens Hallucinogens, or psychedelics, produce alterations in consciousness by their action on the central nervous system. Natural hallucinogens include mescaline and psilocybin. Synthetic hallucinogens include STP and LSD. Natural hallucinogens have been used in religious ceremonies by many primitive cultures for hundreds of years. Abuse of hallucinogenic drugs can result in respiratory or cardiovascular collapse or in psychotic behavior. Support groups and teaching of social skills seem effective in preventing the recurrence of hallucinogen use.

Phencyclidine (PCP) PCP is a synthetic chemical that may cause disorientation and hallucinations and make the user feel dissociated from the environment. Users sometimes develop a severe depression or a severe psychotic state that may be difficult to reverse.

Inhalants Inhalants are volatile substances or organic solvents (such as gasoline or spray paints) that can be used to produce changes in perception. Their recurrent use may cause withdrawal from social, occupational, or recreational activities. Inhalants are more commonly used by young people because of their accessibility. Tolerance and withdrawal symptoms occur when inhalants cause dependence.

Cannabis Cannabis is most often used in the form of **marijuana** in the United States. **Hashish** is a solidified resin of the cannabis plant. The major active ingredient in cannabis products is **THC.** Marijuana use impairs motor coordination and perception and affects short-term memory and learning even after the feeling of intoxication from the drug has passed. Treatments involving relapse prevention and social support groups have been found to be effective in helping people with marijuana problems achieve abstinence.

Nicotine Nicotine, a chemical found in tobacco, acts at least in part by directly stimulating certain receptors that are sensitive to the neurotransmitter acetylcholine. Normal doses of nicotine can increase heart rate and blood pressure, and the drug increases the heart's need for oxygen and may cause chest pains or a heart attack in people with atherosclerosis. Despite their knowledge that smoking is hazardous to health, many people find the habit of smoking difficult to give up. This difficulty may be due to withdrawal symptoms, social and environmental cues, the overlearned nature of the habit, and the frequent reinforcement that is delivered with every puff. Although many smokers are able to quit on their own, smoking cessation programs can be effective for those who would like to quit. Cognitive research has identified three stages of change relevant to smoking cessation. These are commitment to change, implementation of the change, and maintenance of the change with emphasis on relapse prevention. When used along with a counseling program, **nicotine gum** and **transdermal nicotine patches** can be helpful in reducing tobacco use.

Caffeine Caffeine can be addictive. It has mind-altering properties and in high doses can cause anxiety and nervousness. Tolerance and withdrawal symptoms also can occur. Symptoms of caffeine intoxication include excitement, insomnia, restlessness, nervousness, and high heart rate.

IS THERE A FINAL COMMON PATHWAY?

Researchers are exploring the possibility that the effects of drugs are mediated by certain neurotransmitter pathways in the brain, particularly those that involve dopamine. Chemicals that reduce cravings for drugs and psychosocial interventions that strengthen coping skills useful in resisting cravings might be clinically valuable.

SUBSTANCE DEPENDENCE AND PUBLIC POLICY

Society and its governmental units play significant roles in shaping policies regarding the availability and use of various substances.

ARE THERE BEHAVIORAL ADDICTIONS? THE DILEMMA OF PATHOLOGICAL GAMBLING

Pathological gambling does not involve substance abuse, but has a number of properties characteristic of substance-use disorders. Pathological gambling overlaps with several other conditions, as well. Although how it might be best thought of diagnostically is not yet clear, pathological gambling is quite common and more research on its determinants and treatment is needed.

Key Terms

Substance-use disorders, 426, 461
Substance dependence, 426, 461
Tolerance, 426, 461
Withdrawal, 427, 461
Compulsive substance use, 427, 461
Substance abuse, 427, 461
Substance intoxication, 427, 461
Substance-induced disorders, 428, 461
Physiological dependence on alcohol, 429
Alcohol abuse, 429
Alcohol intoxication, 429
Problem drinking, 430
Sensitivity to alcohol, 434
Detoxification, 432
Naltrexone, 435, 462
Balanced placebo design, 437
Aversive conditioning, 437, 461
Covert sensitization, 438

Controlled drinking approach, 438, 461
Relapse prevention programs, 438
Abstinence violation effect, 439
Alcoholics Anonymous (AA), 440
Barbiturates, 443, 461
Tranquilizing drugs, 445, 461
Opioids, 446, 461
Endorphins, 446, 461
Enkephalins, 446, 462
Dymorphins, 446, 462
Naloxone, 446
Opiates, 446, 462
Morphine, 446, 462
Heroin, 446, 462
Exposure orientation, 448, 462
Interactional orientation, 448, 462
Methadone maintenance, 448, 462
Methadone, 448

Cocaine, 449, 462
Crack, 449, 462
Amphetamines, 451, 462
Methamphetamine, 452, 462
Hallucinogens, 452, 462
Lysergic acid dimethylamide (LSD), 452, 462
Post-hallucinogen perceptual disorder, 453
Phencyclidine (PCP), 453, 462
Inhalants, 453, 462
Cannabis, 454, 462
Marijuana, 454, 462
THC (tetrahydrocannabinol), 454, 462
Nicotine, 456, 462
Nicotine gum, 457, 462
Transdermal nicotine patch, 457, 462
Caffeine, 459, 462
Pathological gambling, 460, 462

Milton Dacosta "Menina Ajoelhada". Photograph, Christie's Images.

Disorders of Childhood and Adolescence

Jack's mother described him as a "handful." From the time he was very young he had had trouble sitting still, and whoever took care of him had to be constantly vigilant because he was likely to "get into trouble," which meant that he was likely to engage in activities that would hurt himself or other people. Despite the comments of some of his parents' friends that he "was just being a boy," Jack's behavior didn't change much as he grew older and went to school. His teachers complained that he was difficult to deal with in the classroom because he didn't sit still, made a lot of noise, and seemed to enjoy teasing and hurting other children. As he grew older, it also became clear that he was not learning to read and to do simple arithmetic nearly as fast as other children in the class. Tests given by the district school psychologist showed that Jack scored in the average range of intelligence but was more than a year below his age level in various reading skills.

Julie, in contrast to Jack, was described by her teacher as achieving well in class, even though she seemed rather sad and expressionless and didn't interact much with other children. She spent a lot of time during the school day worrying about whether her crayons and coloring paper were arranged correctly in her desk and didn't volunteer in class, even though her teacher was certain she knew the answers. Julie's mother reported that when Julie came home, she went right to her room and began to arrange her Barbie doll's shoes in neat rows. This seemed to occupy her for hours. When her sisters went out to play with the children in the neighborhood, Julie always wanted to stay in her room. ■

Many families have children like Jack or Julie. Even though children like Jack are much more likely to be taken to see mental health professionals than children like Julie because their behaviors are more disturbing to others, often a troubled child will not receive any professional help unless some crisis occurs. If Jack or Julie were your child, would you seek professional help?

Childhood and adolescence are notable for the many changes in physical, cognitive, and social-emotional skills and abilities that occur in this 20-year period. The pattern of changes is marked by periods of transition and re-organization or what is referred to as the process of development. Understanding maladaptive behavior in childhood must be based on an understanding of these developmental patterns. If children are considered to be little adults for the purpose of understanding their behavior, then some of what is really normal behavior for the child's present developmental state might be considered to be abnormal. For instance, if an adult had frequent temper tantrums that might be a symptom of a disorder. However, for very young children, temper tantrums are an expected behavior.

However, if children deviate greatly from the expected developmental norms, this may cause great distress to the child and the family. If their behaviors suggest that development is not proceeding smoothly, it is important to recognize and deal with the problem. Because children go through many developmental changes as they grow, many parents are likely to see potentially problematic behavior as "just a stage." Other parents may be reluctant to seek professional help for their children because they feel that, as parents, they must have caused the problem. Children's problem behaviors and feelings of sadness or isolation are important, even though they are often neglected. This is especially true because behavioral problems may interfere with children's development by delaying the learning of both social and academic skills. Once children have experienced a series of failures in either the social or academic areas, it may be harder for them to see themselves as worthwhile people and it may be difficult for them to "catch up" with the knowledge they have lost so they can begin to behave more adaptively.

The percentage of young children who meet DSM criteria for at least one disorder is quite high. In a sample of several thousand American children aged 2 to 5, over 1 in 5 of the children surveyed was tentatively classified as having a DSM disorder, and 1 in 10 of all the children surveyed was considered to be severely affected by his or her symptoms (Lavigne et al., 1996). From age 9 through age 17, about 21% of all children meet the criteria for a diagnosable disorder with at least minimum impairment. If the problems result in a significant impairment in function either at home or at school, this number is reduced to about 11% (Surgeon General's Report, 1999). Table 14-1 shows the percent of children from ages 9 to 11 who meet

Table 14-1	
Percent of Children and Adolescents Ages 9 to 17 With at Least Mild Impairment From a Mental Disorder	
Disorder	Percent Affected
Anxiety disorders	13.0
Mood disorders	6.2
Disruptive disorders	10.3
Source: Report of the Surgeon General, 1999.	

the criteria for mental disorders at any one time. As children grow older, some of these symptoms seem to change. In children between the ages of 5 and 17, there is a general decrease in the types of behavior we describe in this chapter as externalizing behaviors and an increase in behavioral problems we have classified as internalizing. However, across this age span, boys are more likely than girls to be diagnosed with a disorder, either in the externalizing or internalizing categories (McDermott, 1996).

Attention should be paid to children's disorders, not only because the lives of the children affected could be improved and their later development enhanced, but also because these disorders do not seem to disappear—instead, they continue into adulthood as disordered behavior. In a longitudinal epidemiological study in New Zealand, three-quarters of young adults who met the DSM criteria for mental illness at age 21 also had a history of childhood or adolescent problems that met DSM criteria (Newman et al., 1996). This means that, for most people, mental illness in adulthood is based on long-standing psychological problems. Figure 14-1 shows that people who met the diagnosis for an anxiety, mood, or substance use disorder at age 21 were much more likely than not to have had some psychiatric disorder during adolescence. This suggests that most of these disorders tend to be chronic, or at least to have recurring episodes.

Only about two out of five children who need mental health treatment receive it and only half of those who receive it are treated by people knowledgable about children's mental health (Surgeon General's Report, 1999). Most of the remaining children with mental health problems receive no treatment at all. In contrast, 74% of children suffering from physical handicaps are treated professionally (U.S. Office of Technology Assessment, 1990). In other words, maladaptive behavior in children is a major problem that society is addressing inadequately. Many untreated children are likely to develop into seriously mentally ill adults who, if untreated, may have difficulties in their personal lives and in holding jobs. A number of risk factors for childhood disorders have been identified. These factors include parental psychopathology, family discord and divorce,

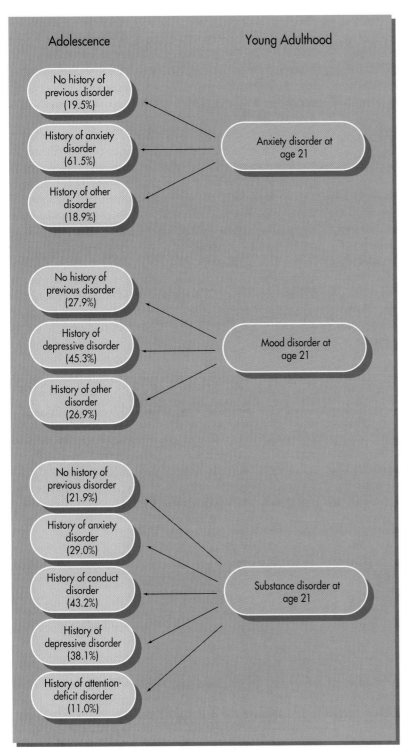

Figure 14-1 Although some people who are diagnosed with one of three major groups of psychiatric disorders at age 21 had no diagnosable disorders earlier, the majority had already shown significant maladaptive behaviors, at least by adolescence. The figure shows the history of disorders for a large group of patients diagnosed with anxiety, mood, or substance abuse disorders at age 21.

SOURCE: Adapted from Newman et al. (1996), pp. 552–562.

low socioeconomic status, the child's temperamental characteristics, and stressful experiences. Child abuse is an especially damaging stressor: abused children have a very high rate of psychological problems (Egeland et al., 1993). For many of these children, problems will extend into adulthood.

Helping troubled youngsters is often problematic because the nature of many childhood disorders and their causes are not well understood. For example, it is not known whether some disorders of childhood—such as psychoses, depression, and anxiety disorders—are extensions of these same disorders in adults or whether they are separate disorders with different causes. One piece of evidence that suggests that many childhood disorders are distinct from their adult versions is the difference in the sex ratios in these disorders for children and adults. In childhood, boys are affected more often than girls in almost all categories. In adulthood the ratios vary depending on the disorder.

Externalizing Disorders

The term **externalizing disorders** includes disorders with behaviors that are disruptive and often aggressive. A high level of externalizing behavior is an obvious indication of a potential problem. Children who behave disruptively are of special concern to parents, teachers, and clinicians, as are children who do not pay attention and seem exceptionally active and children who behave aggressively, break rules, and cause significant harm to other people and their property. Several disorders in which children typically display these disruptive or externalizing behaviors are described in this section. These include *attention-deficit/hyperactivity disorder, tic disorders, Tourette's syndrome, oppositional defiant disorder,* and *conduct disorder.*

Attention–Deficit/Hyperactivity Disorder

The impact of attention-deficit/hyperactivity disorder is very large whether measured in terms of stress experienced by families and effect on children's self-esteem or by fi-nancial costs and interference with academic and vocational achievement. **Attention-deficit/hyperactivity disorder (ADHD)** is defined by symptoms of inattention, hyperactivity, and impulsivity. ADHD frequently occurs together with learning disabilities, depression, anxiety, conduct disorder, or oppositional defiant disorder so that the overall effects of the problem can be large. Figure 14-2 shows graphically the many disorders that are likely to occur along with ADHD. The causes of ADHD are unknown, despite a great deal of research, and it is likely that there may be several different basic causes for the disorder.

The percent of schoolchildren diagnosed with ADHD is much higher in the United States than in most other countries (Klasen, 2000). This is in part because of a different attitude toward the disorder. In the United States it is often considered to be a medical condition whereas in many other countries, especially those that use a different diagnostic system (*The International Classification of Diseases,* which has a much narrower definition of the disorder than the DSM-IV). The all-inclusiveness of the criteria in the United States has been criticized in the past by professionals and parents alike who believed that many active and energetic, but normal, children were being categorized as having ADHD. As a result, when DSM-IV was developed, the diagnostic criteria for ADHD were narrowed by requiring that the child must experience some performance impairment as a result of the behaviors leading to the diagnosis. Even using this more rigorous standard, almost 7% of children were diagnosed with ADHD in a study of a large school-age sample who were rated by their classroom teachers (Wolraich et al., 1998). Even more

Figure 14-2 Attention-deficit/hyperactivity disorder is likely to occur together with one or more other disorders.

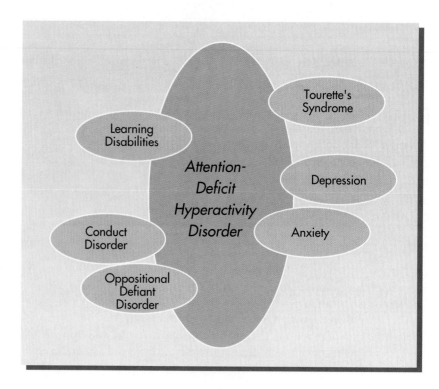

preschool children (almost 10%) met the criteria for ADHD when the diagnosis was based solely on parent ratings (Gimpel & Kuhn, 2000).

ADHD, as DSM-IV defines it, has three subtypes: problems of attention, overactive behavior, and a combination of attentional problems and hyperactvity. The first subtype is characterized primarily by difficulty in keeping attention focused on tasks, a problem that interferes not only with learning but also with correctly completing assignments in school and work because of failure to listen to instructions or pay attention to details. The second subtype is marked by overactive and sometimes impulsive behavior. The third, the combined subtype, includes both difficulties. Table 14-2 gives the DSM-IV criteria for each of these types. One study based on teacher ratings found that of children classified as meeting the overall criteria for ADHD, almost half of them were classified as the inattentive type and only about 9% met the criteria for the predominantly hyperactive-impulsive type (Wolraich et al., 1998). The remainder were classified as the combined type. These ratings also showed that if the criterion of impaired behavior was not used, the number of children in the inattentive category increased to 55% and the number in the hyperactive-impulsive category increased to 16%.

These same three subtypes of ADHD are found in many different cultures including North and South America and in Europe (Power & DuPaul, 1996). Children in the inattentive group were found to be prone to daydreaming and

---

Table 14-2

Diagnostic Criteria for Attention-Deficit/Hyperactivity Disorder

Either the criteria for (1) inattention, or (2) hyperactivity-impulsivity must be met. If the criteria for both are met, the diagnosis would be for ADHD combined disorder.

1. *Inattention.* At least six of the following symptoms must occur often and must have persisted for 6 months or more to a degree that is both maladaptive and not consistent with the developmental level:
   a. Fails to pay close attention to details, or makes careless mistakes in school or work assignments or other activities.
   b. Has difficulty keeping attention on tasks or play activities.
   c. Does not seem to listen when directly spoken to.
   d. Does not follow through on instructions, and fails to finish tasks.
   e. Has difficulty in organizing activities and tasks.
   f. Avoids or is reluctant to engage in tasks that require sustained mental effort.
   g. Loses things necessary for tasks or activities.
   h. Is easily distracted by other stimuli.
   i. Is forgetful in daily activities.

2. *Hyperactivity-impulsivity.* At least six of the following hyperactivity or impulsivity symptoms must occur often and must have persisted for 6 months or more to a degree that is both maladaptive and not consistent with the developmental level:

Hyperactivity Symptoms:
   a. Fidgets with hands and feet or squirms in seat.
   b. Leaves seat in situations where staying in seat is expected.
   c. Runs about or moves excessively in inappropriate situations or, if an adult, has strong feelings of restlessness.
   d. Finds it hard to play or do other leisure activities quietly.
   e. Is "on the go" or appears "motor-driven."
   f. Talks excessively.

Impulsivity Symptoms:
   g. Blurts out answers before questions are completed.
   h. Has difficulty awaiting his or her turn.
   i. Interrupts or intrudes on others (e.g., by butting into ongoing conversations or games).

In addition to meeting the criteria for inattention or hyperactivity-impulsivity in (1) or (2) above:
3. Some of the same symptoms must have been present before age 7.
4. Some impairment from these symptoms is present in two or more settings, for example, at school or work and at home.
5. The impairment that the symptoms produce must be marked enough to be of clinical significance.
6. The symptoms cannot be part of another disorder, for example, a psychotic disorder, mood disorder, personality disorder, autism, or mental retardation.

Source: Adapted from DSM-IV.

were cognitively sluggish. They seemed to have problems in focusing attention, were more socially withdrawn, and were likely to have symptoms of depression and anxiety. Children in the hyperactive-impulsive group were more aggressive, were likely to have difficulty dealing with authority figures, and were more likely to be rejected by their peers than children in the first group. Those with the combined type of ADHD were more likely to be placed in classes for children with emotional disturbances, to be suspended from school, and to be referred for psychological treatment.

The case of Bobby is a good example of the difficulties that both children with ADHD and their parents may encounter, although many children who have much less severe difficulties have received this diagnosis. Bobby, a 10-year-old boy, was referred to a psychiatrist for an evaluation because he had been suspended from fourth grade because of fighting. His mother commented on the phone as she made the appointment that he had been a problem all his life. When the family came for their appointment, his parents told the clinician that during his first 3 months he had colic and would waken crying every few hours. Even after these problems lessened he still had difficulties in sleeping. Although toilet training had been started when he was 2, he still wet the bed at night. They described in detail Bobby's history of problem behavior.

At age 3 years, Bobby entered a part-time nursery school. He ran around the room and refused to sit during story time or rest period. His parents were told that he was not ready for nursery school. . . . When Bobby was 4, his parents enrolled him in another nursery school. Throughout the year, his teachers complained that he would not sit still during circle time or pay attention to the group activities. Often he would get up and wander around the room. If another child did not do what he wanted, he would hit the child. . . . Bobby's second grade teacher complained that he would not stay on task or complete his work. He got in trouble with the other children, especially during unstructured and less supervised times. . . . [In third grade he] distracted the class by the noises he made or by tapping his pencil. He called out in class and forgot to raise his hand. He always seemed to be "doing something." (Silver, 1999, pp. 104–105)

When Bobby was in fourth grade his parents were called to school for a conference.

Bobby's teacher told them that he was moving around the room and bothering other children. His calling out or interrupting her disrupted the other children who were trying to work. He did not complete his classwork and appeared to be daydreaming. . . . The other children did not like him and avoided him during lunch and recess. (Silver, 1999, p. 105)

The teacher told Bobby's parents that they needed to talk to him and tell him that because he was now in fourth

grade he needed to "grow up." His parents weren't surprised by what the teacher said because he behaved in the same way at home although they felt they had tried in every way to help change his behavior. Then in December a classmate teased Bobby and Bobby hit him. As a result the classmate's mother called the principal to complain and Bobby was suspended from school for 3 days. His parents were told that unless they got help he would grow up to be a delinquent. It was at this point that Bobby's parents sought professional help.

ADHD is most often diagnosed during the early school years for two reasons. First, it is usually hard to establish a positive diagnosis of ADHD before a child is 4 or 5 years old because during this developmental period, some normal behaviors seem similar to the DSM-IV criteria. Second, the school situation makes demands on children that may not have been present in their earlier environments. For instance, children in school are frequently expected to sit quietly, to complete intellectually challenging tasks, and to pay attention while the teacher gives instructions or explains new concepts. These demands, which increase at higher grade levels, may highlight attention difficulties and inability to control activity level.

How Common Is ADHD? ADHD is the most frequently diagnosed behavioral disorder of childhood and is very common in the school-age population. Even using the DSM-IV criteria that specify that some impairment is necessary to give the diagnosis, it is estimated that 7 out of every hundred children meet the criteria for this diagnosis (Wolraich et al., 1998). In both children and adolescents, ADHD has traditionally been more common in boys than in girls: the ratio is about 4 boys to 1 girl in general population surveys and 9 boys to 1 girl in clinical studies. The difference between the figures for the general population and the figure for clinical cases suggests a bias in referral—girls with the disorder are less likely to be referred for treatment than are boys. This may be because boys with ADHD are more likely to show aggressive-impulsive behavior, whereas girls with the disorder are more likely to be primarily inattentive (Cantwell, 1996). Another sex difference is the change in the number of individuals who meet the diagnosis at different ages. Figure 14-3 shows that the rate for girls decreases only slightly from age 10 to age 20, whereas the rate for boys exhibits a sharp drop over that period. Because girls tend to display more attentional problems than disruptive behavior, the changes in diagnostic criteria in DSM-IV to include three subtypes of ADHD may result in a future increase in the proportion of girls who meet the diagnostic criteria for the attentional subtype of ADHD.

The frequent diagnosis of ADHD among schoolchildren has raised concern among many parents. What is normal childhood behavior? Where is the boundary or threshold that separates normal behavior from a classifiable disorder?

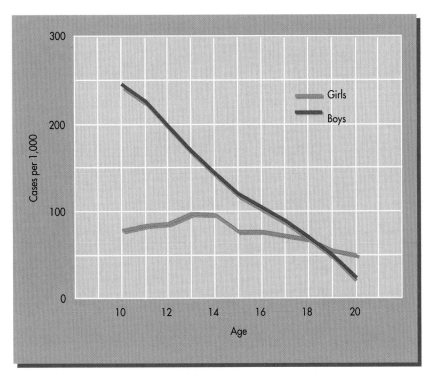

Figure 14-3 The rates of ADHD in children vary according to age and sex.

SOURCE: P. Cohen et al. (1993b), p. 858.

This is an important question, because diagnosis brings several consequences. A positive one is that the child's behaviors may then be treated, aiding the child's development. On the negative side, the child may receive a label that will be disadvantageous then or later in life. Further, the label may be incorrect and the treatment inappropriate. This is a particular concern when the labeling is done only the basis of reports of school behavior.

As you can see in reviewing the ADHD criteria in Table 14-2, many children without ADHD behave in some of these ways some of the time. For instance, in one study of preschool children, almost 30% of their mothers endorsed the item "is on the go or acts as if driven by a motor" (Gimpel & Kuhn, 2000). Mothers of male preschool children and mothers who had less formal education are more likely to describe their child in terms of the criteria in Table 14-2. This suggests that parents' expectations of what is normal behavior are related both to the sex of their child and to their knowledge of child development. Thus, a diagnosis of ADHD may depend on the frame of reference used in evaluating a child's behavior. For this reason, questions have been raised about whether this diagnosis and medication to treat it are given too readily. Some parents and professionals have raised the question of whether boys are being penalized by the diagnosis for behavior that is typical for them at a certain period in their development.

Researchers have found that both the method used to make the diagnosis of ADHD and the people who provide information about the child's behavior affect the likelihood of a child's being diagnosed with the disorder. For instance, in one study a comparison was made of the results obtained by a number of methods and information from both parents and teachers (Boyle et al., 1996). First parents and teachers were asked to fill out a checklist regarding the same child's behavior over the past 6 months. The checklist included such items as "Fidgets," "Cannot stay seated when required to do so," "Talks excessively," "Does not seem to listen," and so on. Each item could be scored 0 (never, or not true), 1 (sometimes, or somewhat true), or 2 (often, or very true). These ratings were compared with ratings based on a structured face-to-face interview with the parents and a telephone interview of teachers conducted by a psychiatrist. Two classification methods were used in deciding whether a child would be diagnosed with ADHD. In the first, only those children whose parent or teacher ratings fell at least one standard deviation above the mean were selected, and from this group only those who were rated as needing professional help were given the diagnosis of ADHD. In the second, the children were again selected only if their scores were one standard deviation or more above the mean, and only those who were rated as showing impairment in school or in social relationships were considered to meet the ADHD criteria. Figure 14-4 shows the results of this study. The percentage of children who received the diagnosis varied greatly, depending both on the method and the person reporting. The study also showed when the ratings were repeated 6 months later, their reliability (especially for the parent ratings) was rather low, no matter which set of criteria was used. This low reliability suggests that the behaviors these individuals were observing

Figure 14-4   Estimates of the percentage of children affected by ADHD vary greatly, depending on the criteria used to define the presence of the disorder.

Source: Adapted from Boyle et al. (1996), p. 1444.

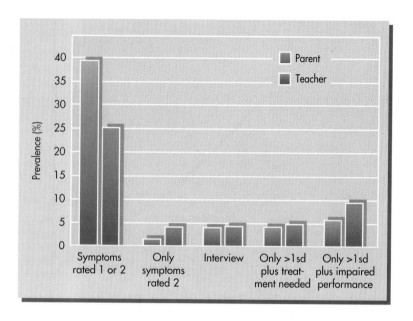

are somewhat unstable. Agreement between parents and teachers about the ADHD status of particular children was also quite low for all the methods used. These findings show that the ADHD diagnosis is largely subjective and depends on who is asked and which criteria are used. Without some agreement on standards for meeting the DSM criteria, there will continue to be wide variation in estimates of the frequency of the disorder, and whether or not a child is treated may depend on who is asked to evaluate the child's behavior.

Consequences of ADHD   ADHD produces two important consequences for children—deficiencies in both academic and social skills. Deficits in attention characteristic of ADHD may have a negative effect on learning because they make it more difficult for children to pick up basic information and concepts. In a school setting, this problem is compounded by distraction and lack of organization in school assignments. In turn, these difficulties may result in lack of practice of basic skills, such as those gained by completing sets of arithmetic problems or spelling exercises. As a result of the lack of skill development, school achievement becomes a problem, continuously setting up a spiral of decreasing achievement that can encourage a negative self-view, lowering the child's belief that he or she can succeed at school-related tasks.

Learning by observation in social settings may also be impacted by behaviors characteristic of ADHD. One research project that took place at summer camp illustrates the difficulty (Whalen & Henker, 1985). Pairs of boys, one with ADHD and one a control, played a game in which they alternated playing the roles of an astronaut and of mission control. The astronaut was to be the follower, to listen carefully to mission control messages, comply with instructions, and give appropriate feedback.

Mission control was to be the leader, conveying the needed information and guiding the astronaut. Each boy played the game twice in each role, each time with a different partner. The most interesting finding was that unlike the boys in the control group, the ADHD boys did not seem to benefit from the opportunity to observe other boys in the more difficult role of mission control before playing the role themselves (see Figure 14-5).

The ability to interact successfully with peers in a social setting is one of the most important aspects of a child's development. Children diagnosed with ADHD may experience social roadblocks because they are not well liked, either by their classmates or their teachers. Children categorized as having the inattentive subtype or the combined subtype of ADHD seemed to be the least well liked by their peers and teachers (Lahey et al., 1994a). In addition to experiencing negative feedback from others and holding negative views of themselves, children with ADHD seem to elicit maladaptive behaviors from others around them. In one study, boys with ADHD were each paired with a boy without that diagnosis. The pair's interactional behavior was then compared to that of control pairs in which neither boy had been diagnosed with ADHD (Cunningham & Siegel, 1987). In the pairs that included a boy with ADHD, both boys showed more frequent demands, command statements, and negative responses than did the boys in the pairs in which neither boy had this diagnosis. This suggested that behaviors characteristic of ADHD elicit more demanding and negative behaviors in normal peers that may then serve to reinforce and escalate these behaviors in the child with the ADHD diagnosis.

This interaction between a child's behavior and the behavior of another person is frequently seen in family settings as well as in school. Problematic interpersonal

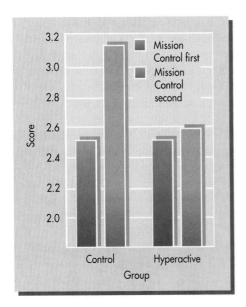

Figure 14-5 Boys with ADHD and boys in a control group were differently affected by the opportunity to observe their partners play the role of mission control first. The performance of boys in the control group was much better when they played the role of mission control the second time, but the boys in the ADHD group didn't show much difference in performance whether they played the role of mission control first or second. They seemed to learn little from watching another boy carry out the task.

Source: Whalen & Henker (1985), p. 469.

interactions are often observed among family members in families that include a child with ADHD. Parents of children with this disorder often experience marital difficulties, high levels of stress, and conflict-laden parent-child interactions (Bernier & Siegel, 1994). While sometimes these characteristics are seen as probable causes of the child's difficulties, they may instead be a result of the catalyzing effect of interacting with a child with an ADHD diagnosis. In laboratory settings, at least, after children's behaviors change as a result of medication, parents' behaviors also alter. Parents of children with ADHD experience more stress and fewer gratifications as parents than most other parents do (M. Weiss et al., 1999). Although much of this stress arises from parent-child interactions, another important source of stress comes from people outside the family who may respond negatively to the parents by expressing disapproval either of their parenting skills or of their child's behavior.

When parents of hyperactive children were interviewed, they tended to focus on the effects that living with a hyperactive child had on their own physical and mental well-being, on their family and social relations, and on their confidence about their parenting skills (Klasen, 2000). They described life with a hyperactive child as ex-

tremely exhausting because the children were always on the go, had a short attention span, and were likely to behave in dangerous ways because of failure to think before acting. The following excerpts from interviews make clear the difficulties that parents reported:

I don't know how my marriage survived. My husband couldn't cope with it at all. He worked longer and longer hours, and although he would probably not admit it, I think he did it to stay away from home. . . . (Klasen, 2000, p. 337)

It's tiring and very, very hard. . . . Other people can be very, very hurtful. You see they are blaming you. "What sort of mother is she? Why can't she control that child?". . . Sometimes the pressure from other people is worse than dealing with him. (Ibid., p. 337)

A lot of the time you think it's something you have done or not done. . . . I felt very guilty. I never felt very warm to him. . . . I thought it was a punishment because I hadn't wanted him. (Ibid., p. 337)

In many instances parents feel a sense of relief after their child is diagnosed with ADHD.

It was like a big weight being lifted off my shoulders. Everything the doctor gave me about hyperactivity was my "Sarah," and I came home thinking, "I've got a hyperactive child. That's what's wrong with her." It just takes the pressure away. (Ibid., p. 338)

Sometimes, however, they were worried that their child would be stigmatized by the label or find it hard to accept the diagnosis because of its long-term implications. Even with treatment, hyperactive behavior is likely to persist and may have a negative effect on the child's future.

I was very relieved about the diagnosis, but I am worried what effect it has on "Tom." One day he drew a picture and wrote on it "from the ADHD child." I was so upset and tried to explain that "ADHD is something you have, not something you are." (Ibid., p. 339)

We tried to avoid giving this child a label . . . because we thought that once he has a label, he won't get rid of it. The child is always thought of in the context of the label rather than in the context of the child he is. (Ibid., p. 339)

Possible Causes At present the causes of attention-deficit/hyperactivity disorder are unknown. Although it is a common disorder, it is probably the result of a complex set of factors, including genetic inheritance, environmental factors, function in several brain regions, and level of neurotransmitter activity. Studies of twins have shown that there is greater similarity in ADHD status for MZ (identical) as opposed to DZ (fraternal) twins (Biederman, 1998). Studies of parents also support the idea that ADHD is transmitted in families, because both mothers and fathers of children with ADHD are much more likely to be classified in this category than are parents of children in the control group, and siblings of children with ADHD are two to three times as likely to be diagnosed with ADHD as controls (Faraone & Biederman, 1994). Second-degree relatives (aunts and uncles) of those with ADHD diagnoses have also shown higher rates of hyperactivity diagnosis than did relatives of a control group. Even biological relatives who did not meet the criteria for an ADHD diagnosis were found to have higher rates of school failure, learning disabilities, and intellectual impairment. Adoption studies also suggest a genetic component. They show that the adoptive relatives of a child with ADHD are less likely to have ADHD than the children's biological relatives.

Family and twin studies suggest that ADHD may have a stronger genetic component for girls than boys. In two-thirds of the families who had a girl with this diagnosis, at least one parent had a lifetime diagnosis of ADHD while in boys' families less than half contained a parent with this diagnosis (Smalley et al., 2000). This may be because boys are more likely to receive this diagnosis because of high activity levels, which may be characteristic of their developmental stage rather than be a true indication of a disorder. Although ADHD seems to run in families, it is important to distinguish between familial and genetic causes. The closer the genetic relationship, the more the environment also tends to be shared. Thus environmental factors cannot be ruled out by the data so far.

Understanding the role of genetic factors in ADHD is complicated because ADHD often occurs together with one or several other disorders including conduct, mood, and anxiety disorders as well as specific learning disabilities. Table 14-3 shows the percentage of time that one of these other disorders is also diagnosed along with the diagnosis of ADHD. The table also shows that each of the three subtypes of ADHD shows a different pattern of comorbidity with each of these disorders. These differences have led many researchers to conclude that a variety of genes at different gene locations may combine to produce the behaviors associated with ADHD.

Since the first descriptions of ADHD early in this century, it has been speculated that the disorder has a neurological basis, or is at least in part biologically based. This idea has been investigated by brain-imaging studies focused on both the anatomy of the brain and patterns of brain activity as well as EEG studies, with the idea that abnormal EEG activity might reflect signs of seizure activity in the brain. Within the past decade, the use of many types of neuroimaging in ADHD research has produced conflicting results. Some differences between ADHD and control groups have been found but there seem to be no consistent findings across studies (M. Green, 1999). No studies have found any serious EEG abnormalities in children with ADHD, although many found significant differences in brain wave activity between such children and children without any diagnosis. Abnormal neurotransmitter activity, especially for the neurotransmitters dopamine and norepinephrine, has also been studied as a possible cause of ADHD. So far this research shows differences between children with ADHD and children in the control group, but like the EEG findings, the types of differences are not consistent across studies. Thus, although neurotransmitter activity may be a factor in this disorder, so far it is not clear how it plays a role.

Findings from neurological studies are currently not sufficiently specific to allow any kind of biologically based measure to be used as a diagnostic instrument or screening tool for ADHD (M. Green, 1999). At present the best diagnostic tool seems to be a checklist measure. Studies have been carried out to see whether the use of behavioral checklists would discriminate between children who had been diagnosed with ADHD and normal controls. A review of these studies showed that at least two checklists focused specifically on ADHD behaviors could discriminate between the groups (Connors, 1997). General behavior checklists, however, were not useful. The usefulness of the ADHD specific checklists to discriminate ADHD from other disorders has only been verified under rigorous laboratory conditions (M. Green, 1999). More work must be done before even the ADHD specific checklists can be accepted as an effective diagnostic tool for use by general physicians or school personnel.

Table 14–3

Extent of ADHD Comorbidity With Other Disorders

DSM–IV Diagnosis	Prevalence (%)			
	Oppositional Defiant Disorder	Conduct Disorder	Anxiety/ Depression	Learning Disability
ADHD, predominantly inattentive type	11.1	3.7	21.3	13.6
ADHD, predominantly hyperactive-impulsive type	36.3	8.0	11.5	2.7
ADHD, combined type	49.8	21.5	24.9	10.9

Source: Adapted from Wolraich et al., 1998.

Treatment Both stimulant and antidepressant drugs of the tricyclic group are used to treat ADHD. By far the most common treatment for hyperactive children is the use of stimulant drugs that affect the central nervous system, such as methylphenidate (Ritalin), dextroamphetamine (Dexedrine), and pemoline (Cylert). Between 80% and 90% of all children diagnosed with ADHD are thought to have been treated with one of these central nervous system stimulants at some time. Antidepressant drugs, because of their potential side effects, are generally used only if none of the stimulant drugs seems effective. Mood stabilizers such as lithium do not seem to have positive effects on basic ADHD symptoms. Before a child is given a stimulant drug, it is important to investigate whether the family has a history of mood disorder or suicide, or whether any family member shows even a low level of manic symptoms such as racing thoughts, euphoria, or changeability in mood. What appears to be ADHD may be a result of vulnerability to bipolar disorder. If this vulnerability exists, the use of stimulant drugs may produce acute agitation. In one case an 8-year-old whose mother and father both had bipolar disorder hanged himself shortly after being diagnosed with ADHD and given stimulant medication (Krehbiel, 2000).

A large number of studies show that stimulant drugs have positive short-term effects (Pelham, 1993). They take effect quickly (behavioral effects can often be seen within 30 minutes) and wear off quickly (within 4 to 6 hours). Their effectiveness follows a general bell curve or normal curve pattern, with the maximum effect at about 2 to 4 hours, depending on the medication used. This pattern of effectiveness has important implications for children in classroom settings. The administration of medication should take into account the timing of school

activities that cause a child particular difficulties. For example, if a child has problems with social interactions at noon recess, a pill given at breakfast 5 hours earlier and another administered 10 minutes before recess will not provide much benefit.

Many children treated with these medications show improved classroom behavior, with a reduction in class disruption and increased on-task performance. In addition, they may complete more of their assigned work and do it with greater accuracy (Pelham, 1993). Figure 14-6 illustrates measures of classroom behavior in a special summer treatment program for children with ADHD who received a placebo (nonactive medication) as compared to ADHD children who received methylphenidate medication. The figure shows that several aspects of classroom performance were clearly improved by the medication. Medication also seemed to have an effect on behavior in social group interactions. Figure 14-7 shows that medication decreased negative behaviors but did not increase the number of positive behaviors. Generally, preschool children and older children and adults do not benefit as much from medication as young schoolchildren do (Cantwell, 1996).

Because information about the long-term effects of medication is lacking, many experts recommend that a behavioral intervention be established and evaluated before any medication is given. This behavioral approach should include both classroom intervention and parent training (Pfiffner & O'Leary, 1993). Only if the child does not show sufficient improvement after such an approach is established should medication be used. The most effective way to monitor behavioral changes as a result of these interventions is to use rating scales for specific behaviors rather than general overall teacher ratings. Since the criteria used in making a diagnosis of ADHD may vary

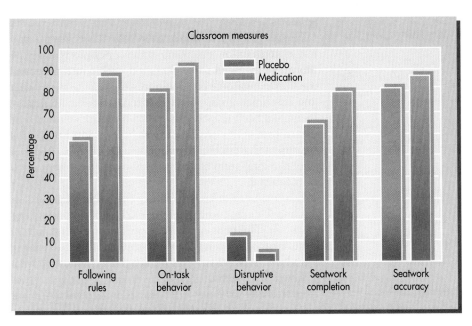

Figure 14-6 Differences in classroom behavior and performance between children with ADHD diagnoses who received doses of methylphenidate twice daily and children with ADHD who received doses of a placebo. Children were given 0.3 milligrams of methylphenidate per kilogram (2.2 pounds) of their body weight.

Source: Pelham (1993), p. 202.

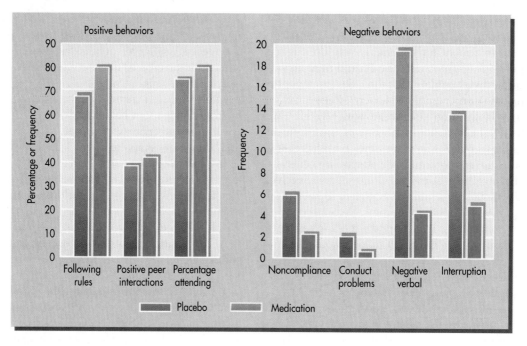

Figure 14-7 Differences in behavior during recreational activities between children with ADHD disorder who received 0.3 milligrams of methylphenidate per kilogram (2.2 pounds) of their body weight and children who received placebos. The figure makes clear that while positive behaviors were not greatly affected by the medication, negative behaviors were dramatically decreased for the medicated group.

SOURCE: Pelham (1993), p. 205.

depending on the information used (parents' or teachers' descriptions or observations of the child's behavior), many children whose problems are primarily behavioral rather than stemming from some biological vulnerability may be receiving unnecessary medication. This is another advantage of starting treatment with behavioral interventions rather than medication. Sometimes the need to take medication, especially in school, stigmatizes a child. Here is an excerpt from a young boy's description of himself:

> My name is Denis Rousseau, and I live in Montreal. I am a child with ADHD and am writing this story of my life for people to find out what it is like to be a child with ADHD. As you will find out while you are reading this, my life is not the ordinary rose garden . . . [A problem I have is] making friends in school. I never really knew why; it was just that people sort of avoided me. . . . There is only one other thing that if I could fix it would make my life perfect, and it is probably the same with many other children. That problem is that I am a child with ADHD and I have to take pills to help me concentrate and to help me not be so hyper, and I get bugged about it a lot. . . . My best friend once said to me: "My family is too perfect. I wish we had just one or two problems, like your family." His family seems like paradise to me. I think mostly about one thing, though: If only I could be normal like everyone else. (M. Weiss et al., 1999, pp. 298, 300)

In 1995 the National Institute of Mental Health began sponsoring a long-term study of the relative effectiveness of medication, behavioral treatment, and a combined approach in the treatment of 7- to 9-year-old children diagnosed with ADHD. The study was based at five different academic sites and was intended to compare behavioral treatment, medication, combined behavioral treatment and medication, and what was called community treatment, the usual care given in the community. Some important findings are already available, although because of the complexity of the study and the many variables assessed only a few of the results have been published so far (Pelham, 1999). Eventually there will also be results from longer-term follow-up. Some of the conclusions at the 14-month point need to be accepted with caution because medication was still being administered in the medication and combined groups but the intensive behavioral treatment had been discontinued 4 to 6 months earlier. This means that active treatment was being contrasted with a treatment that had been withdrawn considerably earlier so only the long-term effects of behavioral treatment could be measured.

The major findings of the study show that all groups, including the community treatment control, improved dramatically. The behavioral treatment–alone group and the community group had similar results. The researchers found that most of the children in the community group, although they did not receive treatment through the study, were treated by their own physicians with medication and often with either formal or informal behavioral techniques as well. The outcome in the medication-only group in the study was superior to the community group despite the fact that most of the children in the community group received medication. This result may be due to the higher doses of medication used in the study compared to that typically used in the community sample. On the majority of measures, the combined treatment seemed the most effective although the medication-alone group received better parent and teacher ratings on inattention and better teacher ratings on hyperactivity. Children in the combined treatment group also were receiving lower doses of medication by the end of the study. Both parents and teachers were most likely to rate the children as "normalized" if they were receiving the combined treatment. Parent attitudes toward the treatment were also measured. Parents were found to prefer either the behavioral treatment alone or the combined treatment. For low-income children in the study, those on public assistance, the medication-only treatment had an unexpected effect; it was associated with worsening parent-child relationships over time (The MTA Cooperative Group, 1999). Parents in this group reported a decrease of feelings of closeness and of positive interactions with their children. In contrast to the results of medication alone, the combined treatment was better than all other treatments for this group in terms of teacher ratings of the children's social skills.

One question not answered by the results so far is how the groups will compare when medication is discontinued. Past research has shown that although the use of stimulant medication is beneficial while it being administered, the improvements do not last after medication is terminated. However, most children stop taking this medication sometime during childhood or adolescence. So far the results from this study and others show that behavioral therapy and psychostimulant medication each have areas of effectiveness and areas of weakness. As a result, for many children, stimulant medication should be combined with a psychosocial approach. Medication seems most effective in the areas of academic accuracy and productivity, while behavioral modification, including parental training, is more effective in changing social behaviors. Both medication and behavioral modification seem to be essential ongoing aspects of treatment in the long-term treatment of ADHD.

Researchers also have concluded on the basis of many studies that counseling the parents of children with ADHD and involving them in the treatment plan and behavioral aspects of the treatment are extremely important. Parents need to be informed about the disorder—including its natural course, possible causes, and likely prognosis with and without treatment. They also should be given practical suggestions for the daily management of their child. For example, parents must learn the importance of avoiding stressful situations known to cause difficulty, overstimulation, and excessive fatigue. Almost all parents

can be taught the general principle of structuring the child's environment to include regular routines and proper limits set on the child's behavior. Parental involvement is particularly valuable because complete reliance on drugs may reduce the interest of parents and teachers in finding other ways to help.

Long-Term Outcomes Although the rate of ADHD decreases in adolescence, this seems primarily due to a decrease in level of overactivity. For those people who had problems with attention, ADHD is likely to persist as people grow older. This persistance is also found when there is comorbidity, that is, when a person meets the diagnostic criteria for both ADHD and some other disorder. In studies of people who were first diagnosed with ADHD as children, as many as 50% to 80% still meet the criteria in adolescence, and 30% to 50% in adulthood (G. Weiss & Hechtman, 1993). As a result of such findings, the criteria for this disorder were modified in DSM-IV so that they would also be applicable to adults. For example, references to "play" and "school" were expanded to include "work" as well.

Studies that follow children diagnosed with ADHD into early adulthood show that it frequently persists and is accompanied by significant psychopathology and dysfunction in later life (Biederman, 1998). For example, the young adult with ADHD is at risk for school failure, emotional difficulties, poor peer relationships, and trouble with the law. Overall, adults with ADHD have more emotional difficulties, more interpersonal problems with peers, more marriage breakdowns, poorer work and school records, and more car accidents. Medication in childhood does not seem to improve outcome in adulthood. When adolescents or adults who received stimulant medication for hyperactivity in childhood are compared with their peers who were hyperactive as children but did not receive such medication, their current adjustment and behaviors do not differ (McMahon, 1994).

If ADHD is not originally diagnosed in childhood, it may be difficult to make the initial diagnosis in adulthood because DSM-IV criteria require that certain behaviors must have been observed before the age of 7. Adults may have trouble recalling these early behaviors accurately. A study of adults who had received hyperactive diagnoses as children showed that one-fifth of them could not remember being hyperactive at that period (Mannuzza et al., 1993). Another difficulty in identifying ADHD in adults is the high rate of comorbidity of ADHD and other disorders, such as conduct disorder and learning difficulties. Aggression or conduct problems in childhood make it more likely that ADHD will persist into adulthood.

Often adults realize they have this disorder when one of their children is diagnosed with ADHD. In one case, after her child, Howard, had been diagnosed with ADHD, Howard's mother telephoned the clinician and confided that after the diagnosis she had begun to wonder if her husband also had ADHD. She described him this way:

> [He was] explosive at home. He would yell, throw things, and "explode." On several occasions he punched holes in the wall with his fists. She also commented that he dropped out of college and that he had difficulty keeping jobs because of complaints about his not getting his work done. (Silver, 1999, p. 231)

As a result of her call, after describing Howard's problem and a proposed treatment plan, the clinician mentioned that it was likely that if a child had ADHD a parent might also have the disorder. Howard's father then commented that he had been thinking about how he had behaved much like Howard as a child and had realized that he still was hyperactive, distractible, and impulsive. He agreed to come in for an evaluation and, when it became clear that he met the diagnosis for ADHD as an adult, was prescribed stimulant medication. He also began to work with a therapist who helped him with his work-related problems. His wife later reported that he seemed much more relaxed and was not losing his temper at home.

Henry is an example of someone who did know that he had a problem but neither he nor professionals identified it until his son was diagnosed with ADHD.

> Although he loves puttering around in his shop, for years Henry has had dozens of unfinished carpentry projects and ideas for new ones he knew he would never complete. His garage was piled so high with wood, he and his wife joked about holding a fire sale. Every day Henry faced the real frustration of not being able to concentrate long enough to complete a task. He was fired from his job as stock clerk because he lost inventory and carelessly filled out forms. Over the years he was afraid he might be losing his mind, he had seen psychotherapists and tried several medications, but none ever helped him concentrate. (National Institute of Mental Health, 1996)

If problems with attention are the main symptom as was true for Henry, ADHD is less likely to be identified in adults. Once the problem was identified, Henry found that stimulant medication made a big difference in his ability to concentrate.

Tic Disorders and Tourette's Disorder

Two disorders that often occur together with ADHD in children are tic disorders and Tourette's disorder. These disorders also tend to occur with *obsessive-compulsive disorders*, discussed in a later section of this chapter.

Tics are involuntary, sudden, recurrent, stereotyped motor movements or vocalizations that are rapid and not rhythmic. A tic behavior rarely lasts more than a second at a time. People affected by tic behaviors experience them as irresistible, but can often suppress the behavior for a relatively short length of time. Chronic tic disorders, once thought to be rare, are now believed relatively common (Hanna, 1995). **Tic disorders** generally begin in childhood and can include motor tics, vocal tics, or both. Some motor tics are simple behaviors such as eye blinking, nose twitching, and tooth clicking, but others—sticking out the tongue, hand clapping, and so on—are more complex. Vocal tics include grunting, sniffing, barking, and throat clearing. Table 14-4 gives the DSM-IV criteria for chronic tic disorder.

One type of tic disorder, **Tourette's disorder,** which may begin as early as age 2, can cause significant social and functional difficulties for children. It occurs four times more frequently in boys than in girls (Freeman et al., 2000). About 88% of those who have Tourette's disorder have at least one comorbid disorder; more than half of these also have ADHD symptoms. Tourette's disorder, when it occurs alone, does not affect the skills involved in attention. Attentional skills such as the ability to ignore visual distractions seems to be affected primarily when Tourette's disorder occurs together with either ADHD or obsessive-compulsive disorder (Ozonoff et al., 1998). Table 14-5 gives the diagnostic criteria for Tourette's disorder.

Tourette's disorder often begins with a single tic or multiple tics of the eyes, face, or head, and then is likely to progress to tics involving the shoulders, trunk, and arms and legs. An unusual symptom that is part of Tourette's disorder is **coprolalia,** the uttering of obscenities. This occurs only rarely during the initial period, but as the disorder progresses it may occur in 30% to 60% of all cases.

Table 14-4

Diagnostic Criteria for Chronic Tic Disorder

1. The presence of one or more tics, either motor or vocal, but not both.
2. The tics occur many times a day, either daily or intermittently, during a period of more than a year, and without any tic-free period of 3 or more consecutive months.
3. The tics cause marked distress or significant impairment in one or more important areas of functioning, such as social or occupational.
4. The symptoms began before age 18.
5. The tics are not due to the direct effects of some chemical substance or some general medical condition.
6. The person has never met the criteria for Tourette's disorder.

If the tics occur many times, either daily or nearly every day, for at least 4 weeks but not for as long as 12 consecutive months, then a diagnosis of transient tic disorder may be made.

Source: Adapted from DSM-IV.

Table 14-5

Diagnostic Criteria for Tourette's Disorder

1. Both multiple motor and one or more vocal tics have been identified at some time during the disorder, although it is not necessary for them to occur in the same period.
2. The tics occur many times a day and nearly every day, or else they occur intermittently, for a period of more than a year, with never more than 3 consecutive months free of tic behavior.
3. The tics cause marked distress or significant impairment in important areas of functioning.
4. The symptoms began before age 18.
5. The behavior is not due to the direct effects of some medication or drug or a general medical condition.

Source: Adapted from DSM-IV.

Tourette's disorder is found in many cultures and one of its most interesting features is that if coprolalia is present, the content of the utterances is similar, no matter what the culture. For example, coprolalic utterances in both Chinese and Arabic were the literal equivalents of Western profanity and concerned subjects that are taboo in all three cultures: words referring to sexual and bodily functions (Staley et al., 1997).

In the first few years after Tourette's disorder is diagnosed, the tics usually become increasingly worse until about age 10. In almost one of four children involved in one follow-up study, the tics and other symptoms reached such an extreme level by age 10 that school functioning was either very difficult or impossible (Leckman et al., 1998). However, by the time the children in the study were 18, almost half of them had very few tics. In addition to the motor and verbal tics found in this disorder, sudden explosive outbursts of rage are frequent in children who have both Tourette's disorder and either ADHD or obsessive-compulsive disorder (Stephens & Sandor, 1999).

Tourette's disorder has been found to run in families, and both family and twin studies suggest a genetic basis. Gene studies thus far suggest that at least several gene sites may be involved (Seuchter et al., 2000). Treatment with antidepressant medication can often lessen the symptoms of Tourette's disorder, probably because it affects the dopamine receptor system, which seems to be involved in the disorder. Relaxation therapy has also been tried but has not been shown to be very helpful (Bergin et al., 1998).

Oppositional Defiant Disorder

At times, children or adolescents are likely to behave in negativistic, defiant, disobedient, and hostile ways toward authority figures. If this behavior is severe enough to interfere with the child's functioning and relations with others, the child may be diagnosed as having **oppositional defiant disorder (ODD)**. As you read the DSM-IV criteria for ODD in Table 14-6, it may strike you that all children act in some of these ways sometimes. The boundaries between what is normal arguing, for example, and something that would meet this diagnostic criterion are not clearly defined. For this reason, DSM-IV also requires that these behaviors not only occur frequently, but also that they occur *more* frequently than is typical for children of a comparable age and level of development. Because the degree and frequency of each of these behaviors that is considered normal is not defined, here again, as with the ADHD criteria, a great deal depends on what the person making the diagnosis thinks is normal behavior for children of certain ages. This can be a problem when a clinician uses only the reports of parents or teachers rather than combining this information with other sources of data, especially behavioral observations.

It is important in evaluating young children's behavior, in particular, to keep in mind the normal changes in behavior that occur across developmental stages. For example, in the age period known as "the terrible twos" children normally behave in a very oppositional manner at many times and their parents sometimes come to think that "no" is their favorite word. This behavior is usually a reflection of the children's increasing sense of competence and while possibly hard to live with temporarily is a sign of normal development. Unless parents are aware of these

Table 14-6

Diagnostic Criteria for Oppositional Defiant Disorder

1. A pattern that includes negativistic, defiant, and hostile behavior that lasts at least 6 months and *includes the frequent occurrence* of *at least four* of the following behaviors during that period (note that *frequent* means *more frequently* than the behavior is typically observed in people of comparable age and development):
   a. Loses temper
   b. Argues with adults
   c. Actively defies or refuses to comply with adults' rules or requests
   d. Deliberately annoys others
   e. Blames others for own mistakes or misbehaviors
   f. Is easily annoyed by others, touchy
   g. Is angry and resentful
   h. Is spiteful or vindictive
2. These behaviors cause clinically significant impairment in social, academic, or work-related functioning.
3. The behaviors do not occur exclusively as part of a psychotic disorder or mood disorder.
4. Criteria are not met for conduct disorder or, if 18 years or older, for antisocial personality disorder.

Source: Adapted from DSM-IV.

developmental patterns, they may risk mislabeling their child and may create rather than solve a problem. When ODD occurs in the later preschool years, from ages 4 to 5 1/2, it may be an indicator of high risk for later problems, especially if it occurs together with ADHD (Speltz et al., 1999). However, in a 4-year follow-up of a group of children who had initially been diagnosed with both ADHD and ODD, only half were still classified with ODD and only one of the group (2.3%) was found to have developed conduct disorder (August et al., 1999). Thus although conduct disorder, which is discussed in the next section, is usually preceded by ODD, only a minority of children who have been diagnosed with ODD go on to develop conduct disorder.

Figure 14-8 shows the rates for ODD by age and sex. Two things stand out in this graph. The first is that the disorder is not commonly diagnosed before the age of 10, that it peaks in the midteen years, and that it is rarely diagnosed in adults. The second thing the figure illustrates is that there is not a great deal of difference between the rates of ODD for girls and for boys, even though generally boys have a somewhat higher rate. This sex ratio contrasts strongly with that reported for ADHD, in which the number of cases for boys is much greater than that for girls throughout late childhood and adolescence.

The following case illustrates the level of seriousness of oppositional behavior necessary to justify a diagnosis of ODD. Jeremy's mother brought him to a mental health clinic at the age of 9 because of his increasing disobedience and problems at school.

Several events that occurred during the previous month had convinced [Jeremy's] mother that she must do something about his behavior. Several weeks ago he had sworn at his teacher and was suspended from school for three days. Last week he was reprimanded by the police for riding his three-wheeler in the street, something his mother had repeatedly cautioned him about. The next day he failed to use his pedal brakes and rode his bike into a store window, shattering it. He has not been caught in any more serious offenses, though once before he broke a window when he was riding his bike with a friend. Jeremy had been difficult to manage since nursery school. Since that time the problems slowly escalated. Whenever he is without close supervision, he gets into trouble. He has been reprimanded at school for teasing and kicking other children, tripping them, and calling them names. He is described as bad-tempered and irritable, even though at times he seems to enjoy school. Often he appears to be deliberately trying to annoy other children, though he always claims that others have started the arguments. He does not become involved in serious fights, but does occasionally exchange a few blows with another child. (Spitzer et al., 1989, pp. 307–308)

Family factors may play a role in ODD. It seems to be more common in families in which at least one parent has a history of ODD, conduct disorder, ADHD, antisocial personality disorder, substance-related disorder, or mood disorder. Serious marital conflict in a family is also associated with ODD. Parent-child relationship factors that may be related to ODD include harsh parental discipline or inconsistent discipline, as well as the parents' lack of involvement with their children and the children's education. Other factors that may be important are the ways parents help their children to become socialized and to learn to modulate their behavior according to the demands of the situation. In general, negative parenting practices

Figure 14-8 The frequency of oppositional defiant disorder varies according to the ages of the children assessed. Although there are some sex differences, they are less marked than those found in some other disorders.

Source: P. Cohen et al. (1993b), p. 859.

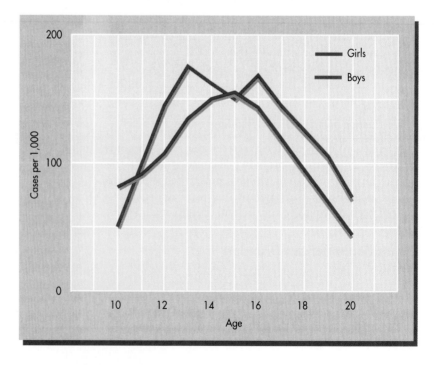

and mothers' psychiatric disorders predict that ODD will continue over time (August et al., 1999). Parent training programs can reduce oppositional child behavior and also improve parenting skills and reduce mothers' feelings of stress. In one study, for example, 6 months after the training program ended, the improvements for both parents and children remained stable (Danforth, 1998).

Conduct Disorder

Another category of aggressive behavior that often is more serious in its consequences than ODD is conduct disorder. In **conduct disorder,** important societal norms are violated, and the basic rights of others are often severely violated as well. The persistent behaviors typical of conduct disorder include aggressive actions that cause or threaten harm to people or animals, nonaggressive conduct that causes property damage, major deceitfulness or theft, and serious rule violations. Several of these characteristic behaviors must have occurred in the past year, and at least one in the past 6 months. Table 14-7 lists behavioral characteristics of conduct disorder.

The case of a 12-year-old boy, Jake, is a typical example of the behaviors found in conduct disorder. Jake was brought to an outpatient mental health clinic for a comprehensive evaluation by his mother and stepfather who reported that they had tried many forms of discipline but that none seemed to be helpful in bringing about changes in his behavior. They were also concerned because he was doing so poorly academically that he was currently re-

---

Table 14-7

Behavioral Features of Conduct Disorder

Three or more of these behavioral criteria have been present in the last 12 months, and at least one in the past 6 months.

1. *Aggression toward people* including bullying, intimidating, use of weapons, physical cruelty, forced sexual activity, mugging, purse-snatching, and aggression toward animals.
2. *Destruction of property* including fire-setting and other deliberate property destruction.
3. *Deceitfulness or theft* including breaking into a building or car, conning others to obtain goods, stealing items of value.
4. *Serious rule violation* including staying out at night without parents' permission before age 13, running away from home, and school truancy before age 13.

These behaviors must be severe enough to cause impairment in some area of functioning—social, school, or at work. For those over 18 years of age, conduct disorder is diagnosed only if the individual does not meet the criteria for antisocial personality disorder.

---

peating the sixth grade. Because he seemed to have difficulty in paying attention and showed the kind of overactive behavior often associated with ADHD, Jake had been treated with the stimulant medication Ritalin the previous year. However, because this treatment seemed to have little effect on his behavior, the medication had been discontinued by his physician.

Jake had a long history of behavior problems in school beginning in kindergarten. He had received frequent detentions and in-school suspensions throughout his school career, for such things as disobeying teachers, talking back and arguing with teachers, and breaking class rules (e.g., not staying in his seat, talking without being called on). However, these behavior problems had been increasing in severity as Jake got older, progressing into more severe conduct problems like fighting and lying. His parents were so frustrated with his behavior and his lack of response to their discipline attempts that they were considering sending him to a military boarding school, pending the outcome of the psychological evaluation. (Frick, 1998, p. 124)

The prevalence of conduct disorder has been increasing over the last 50 years, at least in industrialized countries (Robins, 1999). Although conduct disorder seems to occur in all cultures, its level of occurrence may vary from one culture to another. Despite this difference, the factors that predict conduct disorder and its long-term outcome are very similar across both place and time. Not only are boys much more likely than girls to receive this diagnosis, but the age pattern is different. For boys aged 10 to 20, the rating is highest at age 10 and decreases thereafter. For girls, the midteens represent a peak for this behavior although the overall rate is still lower than that for boys (P. Cohen et al., 1993b). Those who continue to meet the criteria for conduct disorder at the end of their teens are at high risk for the development of serious antisocial behavior and substance abuse. Figure 14-9 shows that rates of conduct disorder have a different pattern from rates for ODD as shown in Figure 14-8.

Comorbidity of Conduct Disorder With Other Disorders

Both ADHD and ODD are often associated with the later development of conduct disorder in adolescence. Children diagnosed with the combined subtype of ADHD are more likely to develop conduct disorder than children in the inattentive subgroup (Eiraldi et al., 1997). Conduct disorder, once established, seems to be very stable; children diagnosed with conduct disorder by the age of 8 have a 75% chance of having the same problems in adolescence. Children whose conduct disorder is severe, meaning that it began early and there was a high rate of antisocial behavior across different settings, have a high likelihood of continued problems in adulthood. A diagnosis of conduct disorder strongly predicts a later diagnosis of antisocial

Figure 14-9 The rate of conduct disorder for boys drops gradually from age 10 to age 20. For girls, the pattern is different: their peak rate is reached at age 16.

SOURCE: P. Cohen et al. (1993b), p. 859.

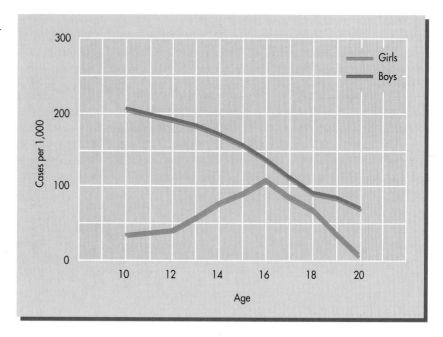

personality disorder, as well as drug and alcohol abuse disorders in adulthood. In addition, there is a high probability that a child with conduct disorder will become an adult criminal offender. In one study, 76% of the males and 30% of the females with a history of childhood conduct problems had either a criminal record, a diagnosis of mental disorder (usually for severe substance abuse), or both by the age of 30 (Kratzer & Hodgins, 1997). Children with conduct disorder are also likely to have other disorders besides ADHD and ODD. They are frequently diagnosed with some of the internalizing behaviors discussed later in this chapter, including withdrawn behavior, anxiety, and depression. It is estimated that around 70% of children with conduct disorder also have one of these other diagnoses (Hemphill, 1996).

Causes of Conduct Disorder The rate of conduct disorder is much higher in families that are stressed by conflict and poverty and in which one or both parents have a psychiatric disorder, such as antisocial personality or alcoholism. Several factors have been investigated to determine what specific factors put children growing up in such a family at special risk. These include genetically influenced predisposition or vulnerability, lack of social and academic skills, and factors in the family environment such as poor parenting skills. Figure 14-10 shows how all these factors may interact to produce conduct disorder.

Genetic Factors Antisocial behavior in childhood predicts similar behavior in one's offspring. This effect may continue over several generations. The grandparents of delinquents are more likely to have engaged in delinquent or criminal behavior than are the grandparents of nondelinquents (Glueck & Glueck, 1968). Such findings do not make clear whether family environment or genetic factors or some combination of the two is producing this effect. The role of genetic factors is supported by adoption studies that have shown that adoptees' conduct disorder (as well as antisocial personality disorder and drug abuse) is more related to their biological background than to conditions in their adoptive families (Cadoret et al., 1995). However, data from a large study of twins who were called up for military service in the Vietnam era found that genetic factors did not seem to contribute to conduct disorder symptoms although they did predict twin similarity in alcohol and marijuana dependence (True et al., 1999). Family environment contributed strongly to conduct disorder and somewhat less to risk for alcohol or marijuana dependence. How much genetic factors contribute to conduct disorder not occurring with other disorders is not clear at present. When conduct disorder occurs together with either ADHD or with substance dependence, or with disorders such as oppositional defiant disorder, the genetic link may be stronger (Comings, 2000). It is likely that there are two types of conduct disorder—one that is transient and fades toward the end of adolescence and one that persists. This second type often occurs with other disorders and is likely to have some genetic determinants. The first type appears to be related more to parenting, peers, and other aspects of the environment.

Parenting Factors Researchers have investigated the contribution of quality of the family environment to the stability of conduct-disordered behavior in families across generations. Families of children with conduct disorder are likely to have experienced more than the average amount of negative life events—financial hardships, unemployment, and other disruptions. They are also likely to

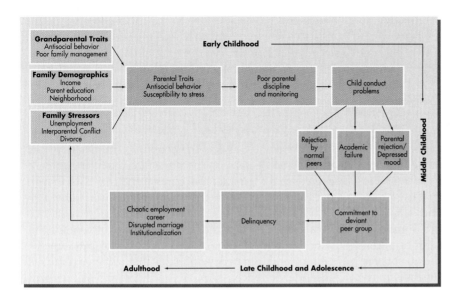

Figure 14-10 A developmental model of conduct disorder.

SOURCE: Wenar & Kerig (2000), p. 210.

have few sources of social support and are likely to be involved in chronic conflict with others in the community (McMahon & Estes, 1997). In addition, or perhaps in part because of this level of life stress, parents of children with conduct disorders are likely to display large deficits in parenting skills. Thus children and adolescents with conduct problems and delinquent behaviors seem to have different family experiences than children without these problems. Perhaps as a result, children in these families appear to learn to use coercive behaviors in family interactions and to transfer these techniques to their contacts with others outside the family circle. For parents who are willing to participate, behaviorally based parent training programs can be effective in helping decrease conduct disorder–related behaviors, particularly if the children involved are young or preadolescent.

Lack of Social and Academic Skills Children with conduct disorder generally have poor relationships with their peers. This is not surprising, given the antisocial nature of their behavior, but they seem to be at an even greater disadvantage because they also lack adaptive social skills. Their lack of social skills covers several areas. They have difficulties in paying attention to and perceiving social information; instead, they respond quickly to a problem situation without considering available social cues (Dodge, 1993). They also seem to have biased and inadequate mental representations of social cues given by others. Because of this, they tend to label others' emotions inaccurately and they tend to attribute hostile intentions to others, especially when the situation is somewhat ambiguous. Another difficulty associated with conduct disorder is a lack of adaptive problem-solving skills. Rather than using socially appropriate problem-solving strategies, children with conduct disorder typically respond to difficulties with aggressive responses and other violations of

codes of socialized behavior, for instance, using bribery to attain a goal.

Children with conduct disorders are likely to have little positive reinforcement, either from their peers or in school-related settings, because in addition to inadequate social skills, they tend to be academic underachievers. In particular, difficulties in reading and especially in paying attention interfere with academic performance. Some of the academic problems may be related to some problems in functioning in the brain or nervous system. One study of 7- to 12-year-old children who were diagnosed with conduct disorder found that, compared to a control group, the children with conduct disorder performed significantly more poorly on a neuropsychological test battery (Toupin et al., 2000). These tests included tests of attention and of abstract reasoning as well as tasks that required planning and organizational skills. This lack of attentional skills may be a lifetime characteristic. When adults who had been diagnosed with conduct disorder before the age of 15 were tested on the Continuous Performance Test, a measure of attention discussed in detail in Chapter 11, they responded much more quickly than those in the control group but also made more errors. The errors were both in failing to identify the correct stimuli (errors of omission) and identifying incorrect stimuli as correct (errors of commission) (Dougherty et al., 2000).

An Interactional View Although both parenting and child-related factors, behavioral and genetic, have been related to conduct disorder and antisocial behavior in children, a more fruitful way of understanding these disorders may be by considering both child and parent in an interactive model. One way to investigate this interaction is in adoption studies, which allow environmental and genetic factors to be disentangled. An interactive model predicts that genetic characteristics associated with conduct disorder in adolescents have systematic effects on the adolescents' interactions with their adoptive parents. These effects increase the negative parenting the adolescents receive, and this negative parenting then puts the adolescents at further risk for antisocial behavior.

In addition, an important factor in the adoptive parents' environment—their marital relationship—might play a role in the effects of the family environment on the child. One test of this interactional model was in a study in which 12- to 18-year-old adoptees whose biological parents had diagnoses of alcohol abuse or dependency, antisocial personality, or drug abuse or dependency were compared with a control group of adoptees whose records showed no mention of parent psychopathology (Ge et al., 1996b). All the subjects had been adopted before they were 1 year old, generally in the first 2 months of their lives. The study found that adoptive mothers' disciplinary practices significantly influenced their adopted children's antisocial or hostile behaviors, while at the same time the children's antisocial or hostile behaviors had an effect on the mothers' disciplinary practices, increasing their harsh and inconsistent disciplinary behaviors. The mothers' disciplinary practices were also affected by the warmth in their marriages, as rated both by them and by their husbands. There was a genetic effect as well: the children's antisocial or hostile behaviors were also predicted by their biological parents' psychiatric disorders. This complex relationship is shown in Figure 14-11. Although this

model was most applicable to the child–adoptive mother relationship, it also fit with aspects of the child–adoptive father relationship. Adolescents' antisocial or hostile behavior predicted harsher discipline from their adoptive fathers, although these harsh disciplinary behaviors were not good predictors of an increase in the adolescents' antisocial or hostile behaviors. This study demonstrated that genetically related characteristics of adolescents did have systematic effects in increasing the negative parenting and decreasing the nurturant parenting they received from their adoptive parents and that this, in turn, put the children at further risk for antisocial behavior.

Treatment Probably the most effective treatment for conduct disorder is prevention. Preventive measures involve helping children to develop skills that will give them successful experiences, both as youngsters and as they grow older. A project designed to enhance the cognitive development of preschool children provides an example of the importance of learning skills in preventing later delinquent behavior. In a follow-up to this study, the children, then adolescents, were compared to a group of similar background who had not attended the special preschool program (Schweinhart & Weikart, 1980). Although the intelligence test scores of children who had been in the preschool group did not differ from those of children in the control group, their motivation and achievement in school and their classroom behavior were superior to those of the controls. Even more important in terms of the treatment of conduct disorders, their self-reports of delinquent behavior were much lower than those reported by the controls. These findings suggest that skill building may be an important tool for modifying the aggressive behavior typical of conduct disorder. If family members are involved in the skill-building program so that they know how to reinforce the child's skills at home, school-based programs that teach cognitive or social skills are especially likely to be effective (G. E. Miller & Printz, 1990).

For skill building to be helpful, the way the child customarily evaluates situations must be taken into account. One interesting difference between aggressive and nonaggressive children is that the former show more bias in interpreting the causes of social interactions. In situations in which the cause was not obvious—for example, being hit on the back with a ball—aggressive children are more likely to interpret the act as hostile. Sometimes this response may be caused by past experiences. For example, a psychologist reported the following incident:

I was treating an aggressive adolescent boy named Rocky twice per week on a long-term basis. We had built a good, warm relationship. One day I saw Rocky in the hallway and approached him from behind as he talked to a peer. I touched him on the shoulder and began to say hello when he turned around and impulsively punched me in the jaw. As soon as he realized

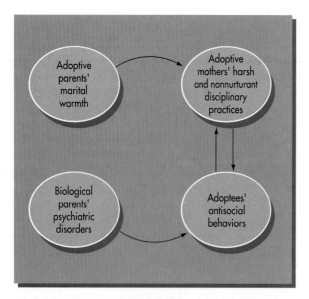

Figure 14–11 Antisocial and hostile behaviors of adopted children may be influenced by several factors. This diagram shows how genetic influence from the biological parents indirectly affects the adoptive mother's disciplinary practices, although these are also influenced by the degree of warmth in her marriage.

SOURCE: Adapted from Ge et al. (1996a), p. 585.

whom he had hit, he apologized profusely, saying that he thought I must have been another patient on the ward. It was painfully clear to me that Rocky had been perceptually ready to perceive an attack from another. (Dodge, 1985, p. 93)

This typical response by aggressive boys can be see in laboratory studies as well as in real-life situations. In one study aggressive and nonaggressive boys were selected and then paired so that each pair contained one aggressive and one nonaggressive boy (Lochman & Dodge, 1998). The boys completed three interaction tasks—in two each boy was told that winning was important and in one the boys were told that their score depended on their cooperation. The boys made ratings of themselves and their partners after each task and raters scored their videotaped interaction. The aggressive boys rated their partners as more aggressive and themselves as less aggressive than the observers' evaluation based on the videotapes. In contrast, nonaggressive boys saw themselves as more aggressive than their partners and the tape evaluation. Whether the task was to win or to cooperate, the results were the same. The perceptions of the aggressive boys were accompanied by more dominant behavior in each of the situations compared to the behavior of the nonaggressive boys. This pattern of results was found for both African American and Caucasian boys and for both younger boys and adolescents. These results suggest that these expectations might be formed by aggressive children at an early age and continue to affect their behavior as they grow older. The results make very clear the maladaptive effect that distorted perceptions can have on behavior.

One way of dealing with these aggressive responses might be to devise interventions that aim at "de-biasing" perceptions (Kendall et al., 1990). In this type of cognitive-behavioral intervention, children learn to mentally review the answers to a series of questions before acting. These questions include not only what led up to the situation and what happened, but also the long- as well as the short-term outcomes of the response that might be made. The children practice the skill of cognitive review by first listening as the instructor reviews appropriate thoughts for a particular situation aloud and then verbally rehearsing appropriate thoughts themselves. As the children learn to apply this technique in other situations, they are taught to begin by saying their thoughts aloud. A child might be taught to use the following "think-aloud" procedure when he or she finds that a pencil is missing:

"Uh-oh, my pencil is missing. There, I see that Ronald has it. Now before I go and get it back, let me think about what happened. I'll do it out loud, like my skills leader has told me. Let's see, first I'll say to myself 'What happened?' Well, I lost my pencil and Ronald has it. Ronald could have stolen it. Or maybe he just found it and was using it. Or maybe he doesn't know that it is mine. I wonder what Ronald is thinking. I guess

I could ask him. I'm not sure which of these is right, but I don't want to get into a fight. I'd rather stay friends with Ronald, because we play basketball together. So I'll give him the benefit of the doubt. Maybe he just found it. I'll go ask him to return it." (Dodge, 1985, p. 101)

For this kind of approach to be effective, the child must have a warm working relationship with a clinician or some other person with whom he or she can have a series of positive social encounters. The positive encounters must happen over and over again to demonstrate to the child that his or her initial negative expectations were not accurate. Even then it may be difficult for the child to generalize the experience to other people, especially peers.

Parents can be effective forces for behavior change, but they may need help. Parent training has been effective in preventing progression of the problems of oppositional defiant disorder into the more serious ones of conduct disorder or adult disorders related to aggressive and antisocial behavior. One of the first and best-known parent training programs, developed by Gerald Patterson (1975, 1982), uses the social learning approach. This approach, designed to help prevent coercive interactions between parents and children, works most effectively with preschool and elementary school children. Such family-based interventions do not seem to be as successful with adolescents (McMahon, 1994).

Working with both children and parents may be particularly important in preventing conduct disorder. In a study of 4- to 8-year-old children with early-onset conduct problems, several kinds of interventions were evaluated (Webster-Stratton & Hammond, 1997). These included parent training only, child training only, and a combined parent-training and child-training condition. Although each of these treatments was more effective than a control or waiting-list condition, the combined child-and-parent training condition produced the most significant improvement in child behavior at a 1-year follow-up. Behavioral assessments based on observations of the children interacting with friends showed that both conflict management and problem-solving skills were superior in children from the combined training group. Results such as this indicate that working with children with conduct disorders or other disruptive behavior is not nearly as effective as working with both children and parents. Improvement in parenting skills seems to be a key factor in reducing conduct problems, especially in younger children. One great advantage of parent-training programs is that they enable parents to act as therapists in the child's natural environment. However, a problem with this type of program is that, in many cases, the multiple problems existing in families with a child at risk for conduct disorder make it difficult to enlist the parents' interest and—even if parents are interested—it can be hard for them to carry out the program.

In all of these interventions, a common factor seems to be positive, prosocially inclined social support from one or more close relationships. Social support appears to be one of the principal ways to prevent conduct disorder initially and to keep it from developing into a more serious disorder in adulthood. Although conduct disorder appears to be part of a chain leading to association with a deviant peer group in the midteens, followed by more serious antisocial behavior as an adult, conduct-disordered individuals from harmonious families are less likely to move into deviant peer groups. Choice of a nondeviant romantic partner is also associated with a more supportive relationship and less deviance in adulthood (Quinton et al., 1993). Despite the protection such relationships can afford, individuals with conduct disorder are less likely to achieve supportive relationships because of their negative behaviors toward others, their lack of interpersonal skills, and their frequent association with deviant peers.

Internalizing Disorders

The externalizing disorders we have just discussed are hard to ignore because the behaviors involved are disruptive to social relationships and often harmful to others. In contrast, internalizing disorders are often overlooked—or at least not brought to clinical attention for long periods of time—because they are less easy to detect and their potential seriousness is often discounted by parents and teachers. **Internalizing disorders** refer to conditions whose most important feature is disordered mood or emotion. They include several kinds of anxiety disorders—separation anxiety disorder, generalized anxiety disorder, social phobia and other phobias, and obsessive-compulsive disorders—and depression. Of these, only *separation anxiety disorder* is a DSM-IV category unique to children.

One important question about internalizing disorders is whether they are transient, that is, whether they will disappear as the child grows older, or whether they predict continued problems in adulthood. Evidence suggests that having an anxiety or depressive disorder in childhood increases the probability of similar difficulties in adulthood (Kovacs & Devlin, 1998). Although adult outcomes for these disorders are varied and some adults with a diagnosis of internalizing disorder in childhood do not have any disorder and others had a different type of internalizing disorder or an externalizing disorder, for many children these difficulties continue into adulthood despite the many developmental changes that occur between. The increased likelihood of continuing difficulty has been explained in several ways, including a genetically mediated tendency toward difficulties in emotional regulation, temperament in general, and style of information processing. One way the change in diagnosis from childhood to adulthood may occur is that there is a high degree of comorbidity between depression and anxiety disorders and between depression

and externalizing disorders. A large study in New Zealand, in which children were assessed at the age of 11, again at age 15, and finally in adulthood at age 21, investigated whether the diagnosis changed from preadolescence to early adulthood (Newman et al., 1996). Of the children who were diagnosed with depression at 11, 80% also had other diagnoses, often both anxiety disorder and an externalizing disorder. By the age of 21, almost half of those who met the diagnosis for mood disorder also had an anxiety disorder. The degree of comorbidity with externalizing disorder, however, decreased between late adolescence and adulthood.

Researchers have been puzzled about why internalizing disorders such as anxiety and depression occurred together with externalizing disorders because by definition they are very different. One reason might be that externalizing behaviors may lead to difficulty in social interactions. The problems may negatively affect children's self-esteem and may lead to the development of cognitive schema or expectations that increase the risk of depression (Capaldi, 1992). If this idea is correct then it is important to determine which diagnosis came first. If the anxiety and depression came first the cause of the comorbidity might be problems with affective dysregulation. If the externalizing disorder appeared first, then focus on problems of behavioral dysregulation might be most important.

Separation Anxiety Disorder

Children with **separation anxiety disorder** show excessive anxiety or even panic when they are not with major attachment figures, usually parents, or in familiar surroundings. They may be unable to stay in rooms by themselves and may refuse to go to school or visit friends' houses. When these children are asked why they are afraid, they may express fear of getting lost and never finding their parents again. They may also have greatly exaggerated fears of animals, monsters, kidnappers, muggers, and accidents or illness that may strike them or their parents. Very often such children complain of nausea, headaches, abdominal pains, or rapid heart rate. Sometimes, especially in older children, feelings of anxiety or panic are anticipated when thinking about a coming separation and manifest themselves when the time for the separation approaches. Table 14-8 describes the characteristics of separation anxiety disorder.

In early childhood all children experience some separation anxiety (see Figure 14-12). They may cry or clutch a parent who has to leave even temporarily. Older children may also react strongly at the time of a separation from a parent or another person with whom they have a close relationship without being diagnosed with separation anxiety disorder. Unrealistic fear about harm to attachment figures or to themselves is relatively common through childhood although it decreases after about age 10. These normal, developmentally related fears are different from the excessive reaction to separation that occurs in

Table 14–8

Diagnostic Criteria for Separation Anxiety Disorder

1. Excessive anxiety concerning separation from home or from individuals the child is attached to that is developmentally inappropriate. At least three of the following criteria must be met, and they must be excessive and persistent or recurrent:
   a. Distress when the separation occurs or is anticipated.
   b. Worry about harm coming to attachment figures or about losing them.
   c. Worry about some event, such as getting lost or being kidnapped, that will result in such a separation.
   d. Reluctance or refusal to go to school or other places because of fear of separation.
   e. Fear or reluctance about being alone or without major attachment figures at home or elsewhere.
   f. Reluctance or refusal to go to sleep without an attachment figure near or to sleep away from home.
   g. Nightmares involving the idea of separation.
   h. Complaints about physical symptoms such as headaches or stomachaches when separation from these attachment figures is anticipated.
2. In addition, the disturbance must extend over at least 4 weeks, must begin before the age of 18, and must result in clinically significant distress or impairment in an important area of functioning.
3. The disturbance must not be related to a pervasive developmental disorder [discussed in Chapter 15], schizophrenia or other psychotic disorder, or, in adolescents or adults, to panic disorder with agoraphobia.

Source: Adapted from DSM-IV.

Figure 14–12 For the age period from 12 to 18 months, most children experience distress when they are about to be separated from a parent. This desire to stay in contact with an attachment figure may have biological roots: through natural selection, infants of all species who stay close to their mothers have been more likely to survive.

children who develop a separation anxiety disorder, and they do not interfere with normal functioning.

The diagnosis of separation anxiety disorder is given only if the disturbed behavior lasts an unusually long time—at least 4 weeks—and results in clinically significant distress or impairment in important aspects of functioning, such as school or social relationships. It is this lasting quality, rather than the occurrence of distress and concern about separation when it occurs, that distinguishes this disorder. Figure 14-13 shows the steep decline

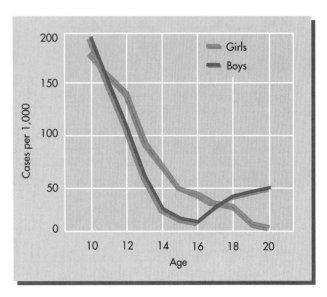

Figure 14–13 For both boys and girls, the rate of separation anxiety disorder decreases sharply with age.

Source: P. Cohen et al. (1993b), p. 856.

in the rate of separation anxiety after age 10. Although separation anxiety disorder is uncommon in adolescence, if it does begin then it may result in substantial and chronic psychopathology.

Many times, separation anxiety disorder develops after the child experiences some life stress. This could be a loss through death of a relative or pet or a threatened loss such as a serious illness in the family. Figure 14-14 shows a creative way that one child dealt with the separation anxiety resulting from the death of her brother. Parental separation or divorce, or moving to a new neighborhood, also may help precipitate this disorder. Why some children have this reaction to stress and others do not is unclear. Children with this disorder are likely to come from families that are caring and close-knit; neglected children are not

likely to develop separation anxiety disorder. Some tendency to experience separation anxiety may run in families because it seems to be more common in close biological relatives of children with the disorder than in the general population. Another possible cause for this reaction to stress is that children who develop a separation disorder have experienced some difficulties during the attachment process that usually occurs early in a child's life (Bowlby, 1980). The type of attachment achieved between parent and child differs for children with externalizing and internalizing disorders. If the children and parents establish a secure attachment bond during that period, this may decrease the children's vulnerability to later psychological disorders, especially depression. Research on children who were securely attached in infancy shows that as they grow

Figure 14-14 A sister tries to deal with the separation anxiety resulting from her brother's death by symbolically seeking to be close to him.

Source: *A Birthday Present for Daniel: A Child's Story of Loss,* by Juliet Rotheman, illustrated by Louise Gish, Amherst, NY: Prometheus Books, 1996.

Lots of times, I wear his clothes under mine.
I pick his favorite lunches, pizza and hot dogs,
in the school cafeteria.

older, they become more independent and better able to form good social relationships than children who were anxious or ambivalent in their early attachment.

Other Anxiety Disorders Found in Childhood

Anxiety disorders that are not specific to children, but occur both in childhood and adulthood, are *social phobia, generalized anxiety disorder* and *obsessive-compulsive disorder* (Mattison, 1995). Often one of these disorders is also found to be present in older children who have been diagnosed with separation anxiety disorder.

Social Phobia Children with **social phobia** show an excessive shrinking from contact with unfamiliar people that makes it hard for them to function normally in daily social contacts. However, their relationships with familiar people—for instance, family members—are generally warm and satisfying. Children with social phobia show symptoms most clearly when they are under pressure to perform or when they interact with other children or anticipate that others will be paying attention to their behavior. They seem to anticipate embarrassment and humiliation. Their peer relationships seem overly inhibited and tentative and they are likely to be very tense and to show signs of discomfort such as blushing in social situations.

Although children of all ages may experience both separation anxiety disorder and social phobia, when children in the community are studied the relative severity of the two disorders changes with age. Separation anxiety disorder is likely to be the more prominent in younger children and social phobia becomes the stronger in adolescents. Between these two age periods, from ages 8 to 12, children with anxiety problems are likely to be high on both separation anxiety and social phobia (Compton et al., 2000). There also seem to be racial/ethnic differences in the percent of children affected by social phobia. African American children have the highest prevalence rate and Hispanic children the lowest, with White children's rate in between (Fones et al., 1998). Social phobia in childhood or adolescence increases the chances of social phobia in adulthood and has also been linked to both adult general anxiety disorder and depression (Compton et al., 2000).

Generalized Anxiety Disorder To be diagnosed with **generalized anxiety disorder,** children must have been affected by symptoms of the disorder for at least 6 months. Although some of the symptoms—such as stomachaches, nausea, vomiting, and so on—are similar to those of separation anxiety disorder, the precipitating factors in bringing on these symptoms are not separation from attachment figures or the threat of that separation. Instead, like the types of problems associated with social phobia, generalized anxiety disorder is related to situations that involve pressure for performance or that carry the risk of loss of self-esteem or feelings of lack of competence. However, unlike the response to these situations in social phobia, children who experience generalized anxiety disorder seek out peers and attempt to establish dependent relationships with them, often by being overly eager to please the other children.

One important stressor and source of anxiety for many children is school. For some children the stress of school-related experiences becomes so unbearable that they refuse to attend. Children may want to get away from school because they feel a general dread connected with it. School causes them to feel upset and experience strong symptoms of anxiety. Sometimes this may be the result of specific problems, for instance, difficulty making friends and feelings of being isolated, or finding the frequent evaluations such as tests and oral presentations very tension-provoking. A child may refuse to attend school for reasons other than anxiety as well—for instance, for positive attractions outside of school or as a means of getting attention from parents. **School refusal,** described in Box 14-1, may be related to generalized anxiety disorder or to separation anxiety disorder, although it may have other causes.

Obsessive-Compulsive Disorder **Obsessions** involve the persistent intrusion of intense, unwanted, senseless thoughts, while **compulsions** are marked by repetitive, ritualistic behaviors. The majority of children diagnosed with **obsessive-compulsive disorder** have multiple obsessions and compulsions. The younger the child is when severe symptoms develop, the more likely the disorder is to continue into adulthood. Although not every child who is diagnosed with obsessive-compulsive disorder has the same problems as an adult, the majority of adults diagnosed with obsessive-compulsive disorder first developed these symptoms in childhood (Thomsen, 1998).

Despite this apparent relationship between the disorder in children and adults, there are some important differences between child and adult obsessive-compulsive disorder (Geller et al., 1998). The number of newly diagnosed cases peaks at age 10 and again at age 21, but the proportion of male to female cases differs between the two groups. Among children, boys are diagnosed with this disorder twice as often as girls, but among adults, men and women are about equally affected. Children also are more likely than adults to have other disorders that are comorbid with obsessive-compulsive disorder. Adults may also be diagnosed with mood and anxiety disorders but children, in addition to these, are highly likely to have additional disorders such as tics. The presence of tics usually predicts less of a chance of improvement in obsessive-compulsive symptoms with antidepressant treatment.

Just as is true with separation anxiety disorder, it is important to realize that in a mild form obsessive-compulsive behaviors are seen in many children. Children often

Research Close-up

School Refusal

Although most children feel some degree of fear or anxiety about school, some children experience such excessive anxiety that they refuse to attend school at all. This can be a serious problem because it not only causes much distress to the child but also interferes with his or her social and educational development. School refusal also causes distress both to parents and to teachers. If school refusal is left untreated, children with severe symptoms are at increased risk of problems with anxiety and depression in adulthood as well as difficulties in social adjustment and employment. This means that early identification and successful treatment is essential.

School refusal is different from school truancy. Children who are habitually truant from school tend to have problems of antisocial behavior. Children who are given the diagnosis of **school refusal** show signs of anxiety or even panic when pressure is placed on them to attend school, but they show no antisocial behavior. They usually show marked physiological changes when forced to go to school, including muscular tension and irregular breathing. They are also likely to appear pale because of a high level of arousal of their sympathetic nervous system. If children with a problem of school refusal do leave for school, they may refuse to enter the building or they may telephone home and request that one of their parents come for them. These children use verbal protests, temper tantrums, and whining as strategies to avoid or leave school.

School refusal is not a DSM diagnostic category, but instead it is a symptom that may be related to a number of possible diagnoses or school or social problems. Most researchers believe that a biological vulnerability factor or predisposition to emotional problems is important (King et al., 1995). Stress as a result of a new school setting or because of some family-related situation such as divorce or death of a family member often triggers school refusal. Problems of school refusal seem to peak at 5 to 6 years, when the child is first entering school and again at about age 10, the time when many children move from elementary to middle school. In addition, when school refusal occurs there are several more specific causes that need to be considered (Elliott, 1999). These include:

- Fearfulness or anxiety related to some particular aspect of the school setting. This includes fears related to some particular feature of the school (specific teachers, test taking, corridors, or toilets).
- Aversive social situations at school from negative relations with peers or teacher, especially those that include evaluation.
- Attention-getting behavior that is related to separation anxiety. This includes somatic complaints or tantrums when the child anticipates going to school.
- Rewarding situations and the opportunity for preferred activities, such as watching television, that occur when staying at home. These motivations may be related to truancy as well as school refusal.

School refusal is most often treated with a cognitive-behavioral therapy (CBT) although an SSRI-class antidepressant is sometimes added. However, because a review of studies conducted so far does not show a clear benefit from antidepressants, the safer psychological therapies are generally preferred (Elliott, 1999). Brief but intensive treatment with CBT in

---

engage in mild rituals and obsessions as part of their normal development. Bedtime and dressing rituals are common in toddlers, preschool children, and younger grade-school children. Compulsions in the form of trivial motor acts are also common. A young child may stroke a blanket continuously before falling asleep or may suck his or her thumb only at bedtime. Even children's games reflect these rituals. Children often chant rhymes or songs in a repetitive fashion or feel compelled to avoid certain objects, such as sidewalk cracks. Such childhood behaviors are normal rather than maladaptive. Sometimes, however, in childhood certain acts develop into more disruptive obsessive-compulsive and ritualistic behaviors that require treatment.

Children affected by obsessive-compulsive disorder are likely to spend much of their day in rituals and obsessive thoughts and as a result their functioning may be severely restricted. The most common obsessive-compulsive symptoms seen in children are concerns about dirt and contamination and complex and time-consuming washing rituals. They may feel compelled to wash their hands or shower up to 100 times per day. Checking behavior is also a common symptom. Table 14-9 shows the most common obsessive and compulsive symptoms. Children who have obsessive-compulsive disorder often have problems in school because of slowness or indecisiveness. For example, they have problems finishing their assignments, even those that are quite short. Although such a severe degree of obsessive-compulsive behavior in childhood is rare, most adults diagnosed with this disorder report that their compulsive or obsessive behaviors had begun at least by adolescence and had continued relatively unchanged into adulthood (Zeitlin, 1986).

Two adolescent patients who were hospitalized because of the severity of their problems are described in the following excerpt:

Patient A was a 14-year-old boy who began washing eight to ten times a day after his family moved to a new neighborhood when he was 4. After that, he had only occasional episodes until about two years ago, when he began washing excessively because of fear of sperm on his body.

Box 14-1

a total treatment package that focuses both on the child and on training parents and teacher in child behavior management skills has been shown to be effective. In one study using this approach over a 4-week period, school attendance was improved for the children receiving CBT compared to a control group (King et al., 1998). In addition, the children's self-reports of fear, anxiety, and depression decreased and their reports of coping strategies improved. Their teachers and caregivers also reported improvements. When the children were reassessed 3 months after the therapy was discontinued, they continued to show these gains. The case of Charise illustrates the use of the CBT approach with a case of school refusal that seemed to stem from a separation anxiety disorder.

Charise was a 10-year-old girl who had refused to go to school unless her mother accompanied her and stayed throughout the day. Her parents and the therapist had come up with a plan, and the therapist had also asked for cooperation from the teacher and other school staff. The first day of the treatment plan her parents firmly told her that she was going to school and that her father would take her so that her mother could go to her own job. Her father brought her to school early before her classmates arrived, and after she was seated at her desk, and although she was crying and protesting, he kissed her, told her he would be back at the end of the day and left the school. As soon as her father left, Charise began telling the teacher she wanted to go home. The teacher asked her to return to her desk. This happened several times until her teacher, who had been informed about the therapy, took her to the school nurse who had also been instructed how to deal with Charise.

After several hours, lying on a cot in the nurse's office began to seem boring and Charise asked to go back to the classroom. After a short time she again told the teacher she wanted to go home, but the teacher reminded her that her father would soon be arriving. In the meantime the teacher suggested that she help her by erasing the board, a job that many children enjoyed. When it was time for her father to arrive, her teacher took Charise down to meet him and gave him a brief summary emphasizing how helpful Charise had been and how she was sure she would continue to do well.

As soon as Charise got in the car she began to scream and cry and continued this at dinner. Her parents told her that unless she stopped her tantrum she would have to go to her room. She shouted that she would never go to school again, ran to her room, and slammed the door. The next morning she refused to get dressed and finished only after her parents matter-of-factly began to dress her. Her father took her to school as before, and after he left the initial events of the day before repeated. However, Charise spent a much briefer time in the nurse's office before she asked to go back to class. The teacher again tried to provide her with some enjoyable tasks in the classroom.

At the same time that these school events were occurring, Charise had several individual sessions with the therapist in which she worked on coping skills to deal with anxiety-provoking situations such as being separated from her mother or being teased by children at school. She was taught the difference between anxiety-arousing thoughts and the kinds of self-talk she could use to reduce anxiety. Her parents also received several hours of training in behavior management skills. After about 2 months Charise was going to school regularly without her mother although during that period there were many ups and downs in her behavior.

He also had obsessive thoughts of death and compulsively checked light switches. He had been treated both by psychotherapy and with antipsychotic drugs. At school, he was quiet and unaggressive, participated in many activities, and was a good student. His parents had a mutually supportive re- lationship and were of middle-class socioeconomic status. All his siblings were well; however, his father was mildly depressed.

Patient B was also 14 years old. For the last two years, she had washed herself excessively, and was preoccupied by number rituals, such as the compulsion to perform all her daily acts

Table 14-9

Most Common Obsessive–Compulsive Symptoms in Children and Adolescents With OCD

Obsessions Regarding	Seen in appr. (%)	Compulsions Regarding	Seen in appr. (%)
Dirt and infections	40	Washing rituals	50
Something terrible happening	20	Checking	40
Disease	20	Compulsive behavior	40
Death	20	Fixing/arranging	30
Symmetry	15	Other rituals	25
Sex	10	Counting	20
Religious thoughts	10		
Anxiety of harming oneself or others	8		

Source: Adapted from Thomsen (1998), p 3.

in multiples of six. Until her symptoms developed, she had no obsessive traits, was a good student, and had many friends. She had been treated by psychotherapy for one year. Her symptoms began suddenly at a time when her father's business failed. Both parents, of middle-class socioeconomic status, were alcoholic. (Adapted from J. Rapoport et al., 1981, p. 1548)

These adolescents were part of a long-term National Institute of Mental Health study of children with severe obsessive-compulsive disorder (Flament et al., 1990). Although when first admitted to the hospital none of the children could function effectively because of the severity of their obsessive-compulsive problems, none showed any signs of disordered thinking and all were able to discuss their problems sensibly. Before their symptoms began, their development had not been particularly unusual. In general, they were good, but not outstanding, students and seemed somewhat timid though not excessively withdrawn. The overall outlook for children who engage in severe obsessive-compulsive behavior is not promising. When followed up several years later, almost 70% of those in this long-term study still met the criteria for obsessive-compulsive disorder (Flament et al., 1990). In addition, more than half the group were diagnosed at follow-up with a major mood disorder, often with recurrent episodes, and almost half had some form of anxiety disorder. Eating disorders also are often found in children and adolescents affected by obsessive-compulsive disorder.

Obsessive-compulsive rituals may occur as a way of dealing with anxiety and other types of negative affect such as depressed mood or feelings of personal worthlessness. One type of compulsion that has only recently begun to be investigated in connection with this disorder is self-injury, for example, obtaining relief from these negative feelings by relatively superficial cutting or burning of one's own body. Although self-injury has been recognized to be associated with borderline personality disorder and also with suicidal attempts related to depression, the self-injury seen in obsessive-compulsive disorder appears to be focused on easing present emotional distress (Bystritsky & Strausser, 1996). This type of self-injury is often done in secret and the results kept concealed from family and peers by clothing. Figure 14-15 shows some of the results of this type of self-injury.

Although the exact cause of obsessive-compulsive disorder in children is not known, it has been shown that the neurotransmitter serotonin is involved. There is also a hereditary factor—children who have this disorder are much more likely than average to have relatives with the same disorder. However, because some children who develop the disorder have no such family history, other environmental factors such as stress may lead to obsessive or compulsive behavior in vulnerable people. At least half of the children with obsessive-compulsive disorder

Figure 14-15   Scars resulting from self-injury inflicted by teenagers as a way of dealing with overwhelming feelings of anxiety. One patient at a psychiatric hospital described her feeling about the scars this way: "I can look at different scars and think, yeah, I know when that happened, so it tells a story. I'm afraid of them fading."

Source: J. Egan, "The Thin Red Line," *New York Times Magazine,* July 27, 1997, p. 23. Photo by Lisa Spindler for *New York Times Magazine.*

who were studied in five large research projects first developed their symptoms after something very stressful happened in their lives (Geller et al., 1998). Although most of the children were treated with antidepressant medication, the symptoms usually persisted.

Treatment of Anxiety Disorders in Children

Anxiety disorders can have a negative effect on social adjustment. About 5% to 10% of all schoolchildren have an anxiety-related disorder—separation anxiety, social phobia, or generalized anxiety—that has a major impact on their functioning, and thus potentially on their development. Much of the research on effects of treatment for children's anxiety disorders has focused on the treatment of simple phobias and specific fears such as fears of school, nighttime fears, and fears related to medical procedures. This research often uses a single-subject design in which each child also serves as his or her own control. Cognitive-behavioral therapy that combines exposure to the feared stimulus with relaxation training and training in cognitive coping skills such as self-instructional training has been a successful treatment for these phobias and simple fears (Kendall, 1994). Because anxious children are likely to have parents with a variety of anxiety problems, the application of family treatment strategies can also be helpful.

In a study of the family treatment approach, children ranging from 7 to 14 years of age with one or more anxiety disorders were recruited from a variety of sources, including schools, clinician referrals, and referrals from parents (P. M. Barrett et al., 1996). The children were randomly divided into individual treatment, treatment including family, and waiting-list groups. No children who had only simple phobias were included. Children in both treatment groups took part in a 12-session program of cognitive-behavioral therapy in which they met with a therapist in individual sessions. A structured workbook was used that included activities such as recognizing anxious feelings, cognitive restructuring in anxiety-provoking situations, self-talk coping instructions, exposure to the feared stimuli, and other activities. Children in the family treatment condition also met with the therapist together with their parents in a family anxiety management session after the individual session with the therapist. In these family sessions, the same topic that the child had just covered in the individual session was dealt with again, using a structured approach. The parents were trained to reward courageous behavior and to extinguish excessive anxiety in their children by using several reinforcement strategies, including verbal praise, special privileges, and contingent rewards. They were taught to respond empathetically to anxious behaviors and complaints from their children the first time these occurred but then to ignore them if they were repeated and instead to respond by prompting the children to use coping strategies.

The results from both treatment groups showed that cognitive-behavioral therapy was very effective in treating young children with anxiety disorders. However, treating both child and family was more effective than treating the child alone: the positive effects of treatment lasted longer and appeared to increase over time. At the end of the treatment period, 57% of the children in the child-only treatment group and 84% in the child-plus-family treatment group had improved so much that they no longer met the diagnostic criteria for an anxiety disorder. Twelve months later, the improvement rates had increased to 70% for the child-only treatment group and 95% for the combined treatment group. The extra benefits of the family treatment applied to each of the specific anxiety disorders included—generalized anxiety, separation anxiety, and social phobia. Another treatment study, also using cognitive-behavioral therapy, found that children

who had been treated 2 to 5 years earlier continued to maintain their original treatment gains (Kendall & Southam-Gerow, 1996).

Medication, usually of an antidepressant rather than an antianxiety type, is the only systematically investigated form of treatment for children with severe obsessive-compulsive disorder (Thomsen, 1996). However, other types of treatment—especially family therapy, behavior therapy, and individual psychotherapy—are often used, either alone or together with medication. In a 7-year follow-up of children and adolescents treated with an antidepressant and some type of psychologically based therapy, almost half of the group still had enough symptoms to meet the diagnostic criteria for obsessive-compulsive disorder (Leonard et al., 1993). However, therapeutic interventions may be useful even if they do not show a great deal of effectiveness in treating the obsessive-compulsive behaviors. In a 9- to 14-year follow-up study of children with obsessive-compulsive disorder, the researchers found that having been treated either with behavior therapy or antidepressants was likely to improve adjustment in adulthood, even if obsessive-compulsive behaviors were still present (Bolton et al., 1995).

Some children who were followed up in the long-term NIMH study of children with obsessive-compulsive disorder reported that they had also utilized a "do-it-yourself" behavior therapy in which they exposed themselves to the feared situation while preventing themselves from carrying out their ritualizing behaviors (Flament et al., 1990). They believed that this approach was helpful when used over a long period. They also tried to "keep very busy" with almost any activity or thought, and they reported that this also helped keep the rituals away. These children believed the psychotherapy they had received was helpful for family problems and personal problems such as shyness, but they didn't think it was effective in helping them decrease their obsessive-compulsive behaviors.

Depression

DSM-IV does not contain a special diagnostic category or description for **depression in childhood;** instead, it uses the adult criteria with minor modifications. Figure 14-16 shows the change in frequency of depression across childhood and adolescence, as well as the different patterns for boys and girls. Although childhood is often pictured as a happy time of little responsibility, endless play, and infinite enjoyment, in fact, many children often think such thoughts as: "I'm dumb, ugly, and stupid," "I wish I were dead," and "You don't love me." Studies confirm that many youngsters often feel sad. In one study, about10% to 12% of the 10-year-olds in a school district population were described by parents and teachers as often appearing miserable, unhappy, tearful, or distressed. While probably most of these children do not meet the criteria for major

Figure 14-16 Boys and girls have very different rates of major depressive disorder during their midteens.

Source: P. Cohen et al. (1993b), p. 857.

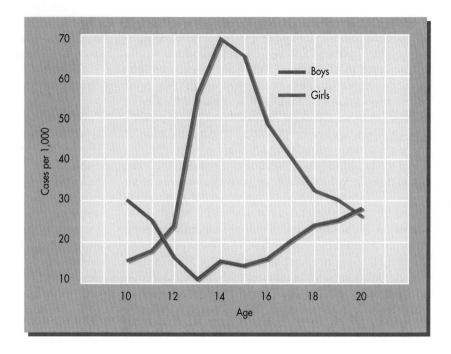

depression, they may meet the criteria for dysthymic disorder. The case of Alan, who is 13, illustrates how long-lasting a dysthymic disorder can be.

When Alan was asked what made him happy, he said, "nothing . . . I've not hardly been happy." When asked what made him sad, he said, "I'm just a sad kid." He could not think of anything he liked about himself. He reported having only one friend. (Kashani & McNaul, 1997, p. 348)

Sometimes the depression is more severe, and the diagnosis is depressive disorder.

Helen knew something was wrong with her 12-year-old daughter, but she couldn't quite put her finger on it. Some days Nancy moped in her room, other days she was just quiet. She seemed very unhappy, although she didn't share these feelings with her parents. There were times when she had angry outbursts for no reason at all, and she was terribly irritable. In addition, she seemed to be constantly eating even though in the past she had been proud of her slim figure. She also began to spend a lot of time "sleeping in" on days when she didn't have to go to school. At first, Helen wrote it off as typical "preteen stuff." When her husband disagreed, they took Nancy to her pediatrician, who referred her to a child psychiatrist. Nancy told the clinician that she wished she were dead and that she frequently had suicidal thoughts although she had not made a plan to kill herself.

Generally children's self-reported symptoms are stable over at least several months (Charmon, 1994). This suggests that children are not reporting temporary moods, but rather describing long-lasting conditions. When children's reports of depression are compared with reports by parents about the child, the number of depressive symptoms the children report is consistently higher than the number reported by their parents (Esau et al., 1999). There is better agreement on various observable behaviors such as sluggish behavior or sleep problems and much poorer agreement on the internal aspects of depression or feelings. However, the level of agreement on symptoms between parents and children improves when the child reaches adolescence. Because of this lack of agreement, both parents and child are usually interviewed when a child is brought to a clinician. Many questionnaires developed to assess depression with older children have both a child and a parent version for this same reason. If at all possible, teachers should also be asked about the child's depressed behavior because their observations may add important information.

Because children pass through different developmental states that affect the cognitive abilities and their ways of dealing with emotion, the behaviors associated with depression in children vary according to the child's developmental level. Table 14-10 describes the primary symptoms that accompany depression at different age levels. Children and adolescents with depression often describe themselves as feeling sad, mad, or bored. Younger children often complain of feelings of agitation and somatic symptoms such as headaches and stomachaches. They are more likely than adults or adolescents to describe auditory hallucinations that have themes such as being controlled and persecuted, although these hallucinations do not seem to predict the seriousness of the depression. Adolescents who are depressed are likely to begin sleeping excessive amounts of time and to use drugs and alcohol. Although both children and adolescents report suicidal thoughts, these are more frequent among adolescents than

Table 14-10	
Symptoms of Depression at Different Developmental Stages During Childhood	
Developmental Stage	Symptoms of Depression
Birth to 2 years	Whining, withdrawal, weight loss, slowed growth, unresponsiveness to social interaction, slow language development, lack of curiosity, poor cognitive development. Later, nightmares and night terrors, clinginess, oppositional behavior, excessive fears, decrease in play activity.
3 to 5 years	Sadness, weight loss, slowness in movement, tiredness, thoughts of suicide, anger, apathy, irritability, social withdrawal.
6 to 12 years	Similar to those of adults. Depressive verbalization of depressive thoughts and feelings. Failure to experience pleasure, apathy, low self-esteem, fatigue, suicidal thoughts, withdrawal from social interaction, irritability, lack of motivation. Sometimes delinquency, anger, oppositional behavior, fears, somatic symptoms, social problems, poor school performance.
12 to 18 years	Volatile moods, rage, intense self-consciousness, low self-esteem, poor school performance, delinquent behaviors, substance abuse, sexual acting out, social withdrawal, problems with overeating and oversleeping, suicidal thoughts.

Source: Adapted from Kronenberger & Meyer, 1996.

among younger children. Studies have shown that as many as 30% of seventh- and eighth-graders in a school sample report that they have thought about suicide in the past week (Pataki & Carlson, 1995). The older the child, the greater the risk of an actual suicide attempt.

Although major depressive disorder diagnosed in childhood has many of the same characteristics as major depressive disorder in adulthood, the early appearance of depression predicts (1) that the child will be more likely than someone first diagnosed as an adult to have a later manic or hypomanic episode, and thus "switch" from a diagnosis of depression to a diagnosis of bipolar disorder, and (2) that the child will have a recurrence of depression sooner than someone who first experiences an episode of major depressive disorder as an adult (Kovacs, 1996). An episode of major depressive disorder occurring in childhood predicts a 70% chance of another episode within the next 5 years. These differences in both the probability of a "switch" and the likelihood of a recurrence suggest that a diagnosis of depression in childhood predicts a more serious disorder than a similar diagnosis in adulthood.

One of the most striking aspects of major depression in childhood is the likelihood of coexisting disorders. Anxiety symptoms are found among almost all depressed children. At least 50% of children who were chronic school refusers also met the criteria for depressive disorder. Other childhood disorders that are likely to co-occur with depression are ADHD, oppositional defiant disorder, and conduct disorder. Children seen in diagnostic centers for learning problems and children with chronic illnesses also have high rates of depression.

The effects of childhood depression on future cognitive and social development are not yet clear, although it is known that depression in children and adolescents may be relatively long-lasting. In one study of major depressive disorder in children 9 to 13 years of age, it took 1 1/2

years before 92% of the children had recovered (Kovacs, 1985). The chance of another occurrence of depression was also high for this group: 72% of these children had a second episode within 5 years. Some of these children will probably continue to experience depression throughout much of their lives. In one longitudinal study, several children showed differing but long-continuing patterns of depression (Chess et al., 1983).

At 8 years of age, Harold had been having behavioral problems for a year. He disliked school, was shy, and had few friends. He was moody, quiet, and afraid of new situations. Because there had been several problems in his life—his parents had separated when he was 6 and his mother had been briefly hospitalized for severe depression—it was unclear whether his depression was due to these events or to other causes. Things improved, but at 12 Harold became depressed again and disliked school intensely. At 17 he reported that he could "step into an unhappy mood for no apparent reason" and then would feel tired and irritable and would avoid people. Shortly after this he became severely depressed for about two weeks and was treated with antidepressant drugs. At 22 he had moved to his own apartment. He made some money mopping floors but was basically supported by his mother. He spent most of his time practicing music—he had taught himself to play the piano, banjo, and guitar. He summarized his existence as going from "slow deadness to acute crises" and described recurrent depressions at ages 9, 15, 18, and 19, each of which lasted months even when treated with antidepressant drugs. (Adapted from Chess et al., 1983, pp. 413–414)

Sylvia's depression was not noted until she was 21, after months of an intense obsessive preoccupation that her skin and hair were terribly ugly, which was not true. She threatened to drop out of college, and although she had top grades and was attending a top-level school she had changed colleges twice. She was hospitalized briefly and for the next year made many suicidal threats and a few suicidal attempts and then gradually improved.

During her therapy sessions she reported that she had been depressed even as far back as age 8 and had always covered it over with a veneer of cheerfulness and friendliness. This was substantiated by some poems she had written from ages 12 to 15 which were filled with melancholy and hopelessness. She did not report any life events that could explain the cause of her depression, although she did have several family members who had been depressed. (Adapted from Chess et al., 1983, p. 415)

Causes Depression tends to "run in families" (Hammen, 1992). This means that many depressed children have depressed parents. Environmental factors are also important: undesirable family environments and poor relationships with parents, siblings, and peers are common in children with mood disorders. Sometimes family tensions and parental divorce bring on symptoms of depression. The symptoms may reflect the child's feelings of hopelessness and helplessness about the situation. Although the conflict of divorcing parents is not a problem a child can solve, the child's attributional style is an important vulnerability factor, just as it is in adult depression. Children tend to become depressed when they encounter stressful situations if they use an attributional style in which they blame themselves, or when they see general or unchanging factors as a cause of their problems. This was demonstrated by a study of children in grades 3 to 5 whose perceived rejection by peers, actual rejection by peers, and levels of depression were assessed at three different times over the year (Panak & Garber, 1992). Even after taking into account the children's initial levels of depression and actual and perceived peer rejection at the beginning of the study, as well as any increase in actual peer rejection over time, the children's attributional styles at the beginning of the study predicted the level of depression a year later. This finding illustrates the role of attributional style as a vulnerability factor in producing depression.

Treatment Very young children have difficulty describing their emotional states. While fear can be inferred from behavior, facial expressions, and psychological responses, depression is difficult to pinpoint because of the importance of its cognitive components. When interviewing a child about possible depression, it is essential to ask questions in simple, concrete language. For example, few preschoolers spontaneously state that they feel sad, but most preschoolers will express sad feelings when carefully questioned.

One way to get this information is through use of a structured interview. The "Kiddie SADS"—a child's version of an adult interview used in diagnosis of depression, the Schedule for Affective Disorders and Schizophrenia—has been shown to measure depression in children reliably (Chambers et al., 1985). However, because an individual interview with a child by a mental health professional is costly, other less expensive methods of getting information—such as questionnaires—are often used instead. One questionnaire frequently used for screening children is the Children's Depression Inventory (Kovacs & Beck, 1977).

Although antidepressant drugs are used to treat depression in children and adolescents as well as in adults, neither tricyclic antidepressants nor the SSRI antidepressant fluoxetine (Prozac) has been found to be effective for children or adolescents in double-blind studies in which neither the patient nor the physician knew the identity of the medication used for each child (J. Sommers-Flanagan & R. Sommers-Flanagan, 1996). So far it seems clear that tricyclic antidepressants may have serious side effects for children, so they are seldom a first choice. Although there are currently some larger-scale trials of SSRI antidepressants underway to study their effect on childhood depression, no consistent results are currently available (Kutcher, 1999). It may be that depression that begins in childhood or adolescence is a more severe illness and less responsive to treatment than a depressive disorder that begins in adulthood.

Two psychological approaches used to treat adult depression—interpersonal therapy and cognitive therapy—have produced promising results when used with depressed adolescents (Mufson, 1993; Mufson et al., 1994). Interpersonal therapeutic efforts are focused on problems in the child's or teenager's relationships. In this approach, the client is coached on how to express feelings more clearly in troubled relationships and assisted in other interpersonal problem-solving skills.

A promising approach designed to prevent the development of depression in vulnerable children is cognitive group therapy that may be administered in after-school classes (D. M. Clark et al., 1994). In these classes the children learn that they have some control over their moods and that they can change the way they feel by changing the way they think. For example, they might learn to tell themselves "I didn't study hard enough" when receiving a poor test score instead of thinking "I'm stupid." Other work using social skills training rather than a purely cognitive approach suggests that such training not only results in improvement immediately after treatment but that when compared to a group that received supportive therapy, the social skills group members continued to progress after the treatment had ended (Fine et al., 1991).

Therapy for Children and Adolescents

There are important differences in therapeutic work with children and adults. Often children are referred for therapy because they are deviating from the normal pattern of development. This means therapy must be at least partly directed toward helping them to attain those norms if at all possible. Unlike adults, children rarely see themselves as needing therapy or as "disturbed." Most of the time adults, usually parents, initiate the request for treatment, sometimes at the request of teachers or other adults. Parents also contract for the therapy, pay the bill, and have certain goals for the therapy that may not be the same as those the therapist might select. Because they often don't participate in identifying the goals of therapy, children sometimes begin the process with little motivation to cooperate with the treatment or even for personal change. Another difference between child and adult therapy is that the therapist gets most of his or her information about

the child and the problems from the parents. This information may be inaccurate or distorted, influenced by the parents' own agenda, presented in a way designed to conceal what they believe are their own failings as parents, or biased by the parents' own psychopathology. Even when parents do not make intentional distortions, their reports and opinions are biased by their degree of knowledge of child development as well as the values and practices of their cultural group. The examples in Box 14-2 make clear the importance of a cultural perspective.

Case Study

Box 14–2

Successful Assessment, Diagnosis, and Treatment of Children and Adolescents From Diverse Cultural Backgrounds

When children are referred for clinical evaluation or treatment, it is important to understand the cultural beliefs of the family and take these into account. In addition, it is important that the clinician not "jump to conclusions" by assuming a stereotyped view based on limited cultural knowledge rather than by investigating the actual facts concerning the family.

Grace, a withdrawn and overly shy Asian American 10-year-old, was accompanied to the clinic by her parents for an evaluation session. The clinician, who spoke to the parents to obtain a clinical history, had made the following initial assumptions:

- The family is Chinese because their address is near Chinatown.
- Their dress and demeanor indicate that this is a traditional first-generation family.
- The family's belief system is based on Confucianism.
- Although the child is withdrawn, she is probably doing well academically.
(*Canino & Spurlock, 1994, pp. 43–44*)

Acting on these assumptions without further investigation could have denied Grace the help she needed. Fortunately, the clinician took a thorough history. This information made it clear that the family were not immigrants but nontraditional third-generation Korean American Roman Catholics who believed that their daughter had a learning disability. Testing did show some specific learning difficulties, and treatment was begun promptly. The experience of this therapist shows that it is important to remember that minority group membership does not automatically imply certain beliefs and attitudes (see Figure 14-17).

Although clinicians should not make unwarranted cultural generalizations, at the same time they need to be aware that cultural beliefs can play an important role in both evaluation of the problem and the acceptability and outcome of treatment. For example, Maria was referred to a clinic because of her disrespectful behavior at home. She was 13 years old and from a Latino family.

[Her parents described her] as confrontational, assertive, and too autonomous. Maria demanded more freedom and openly talked about boys and sex. Her parents' traditional beliefs and child-rearing attitudes were in direct opposition to their child's behavior. (Canino & Spurlock, 1994, p. 46)

Although Maria's parents viewed her behavior as deviant, in contrast,

her teachers perceived her as an assertive and independent young woman who felt comfortable exploring difficult issues. They regarded her behavior as an indication of strength. At school Maria had been told to speak up, know her own mind, question what she heard, and be independent. (Ibid, p. 47)

After the clinician learned of Maria's parents' and teachers' discrepant views concerning her behavior, a series of meetings for both family and teachers was arranged with a biculturally sensitive clinician. As a result of these interactions, her family was able to understand Maria's behavior in a new way, her teachers became more aware of the family's beliefs and values, and Maria was able to begin to understand the conflicting messages from home and school and develop her own view.

Figure 14-17 Although Asian American families may participate in activities related to traditional Asian culture (a), they also engage in typically American activities (b). Clinicians need to be aware of both these dimensions in the lives of Asian Americans.

Although many of the therapeutic approaches developed for adults can be used directly or in slightly modified form with older children and adolescents, frequently the most effective approach to therapy for young children is to work with one or both parents instead of the child or, especially with slightly older children, with the child and parents together. Parental involvement in therapy has several purposes:

- To help parents understand the way children develop and the kinds of behavior typical of different ages.
- To show parents adaptive ways to deal with the child—for instance, how to play with a young child and how to use constructive methods of motivation rather than harsh discipline.
- To suggest ways to improve family interactions that may be causing stress for the parents or the child or both.

While many therapeutic approaches for adults have been adapted for use with children, researchers have also developed some methods uniquely suited to young children. Play therapy, storytelling techniques, and parent-administered behavior modification programs are some therapies specially tailored for children.

Play Therapy

Play is the natural means by which children communicate. Young children cannot be expected to spend a long period of time talking face-to-face with a therapist. **Play therapy** is a combination of play and talking that facilitates the therapeutic process. Figure 14-18 shows a typical play therapy session. Although therapists may enter into play with children, they do not take the role of a playmate. Instead, therapists communicate that they are trying to understand the children through play. By means of play, children can express their own concerns. The therapists then show interest in the play, acting nonjudgmental and asking the children what their play suggests. The therapist usually encourages the child to take the lead in play and may ask for instructions on how the child thinks the therapist should respond during the play sequence.

Another use of play therapy is with children who have experienced some kind of trauma, for example, a death, fire, or accident. In this type of play therapy, the child reenacts the event in play in a repetitive, often emotionless way. For example, the father of 4 1/2-year-old Cathy had recently killed himself. During one session, Cathy first played briefly with a doll and then made some "cookie faces" out of modeling clay. One face was misshapen, and when the therapist asked her if the faces were like people in her family, she put the faces in the bottom of a bowl and later rerolled the clay, destroying them. Then she walked to the sand table. The therapist described what happened next. When Cathy absentmindedly ran her fingers through the sand, she found a figure of a man buried in the sand:

C: *Look, I found a man in here.*

T: *You're surprised to find a man buried in the sand.*

C: *[Her attention focuses completely on the sand table now, her eyes focused and body turned. She proceeds with intent and with a sense of anxious excitement to check the sand very thoroughly with her fingers for more buried men but does not find another. She leans down and picks up a box of army-type men and tanks and dumps them into the sand. She is silent as she works to clear all the sand aside, and, as she works, it becomes apparent to the therapist she is making room for the box to fit.] I'm making a place for the box to stay.*

T: *You want it to have a spot there. [Cathy then takes the tanks out of the sand and places them carefully in the box.*

Figure 14-18   Children often communicate better through play than through speech. Play therapy is designed to take advantage of this fact and to give children a symbolic way to express their fears, aggressions, and insecurities.

With much effort, she piles up the sand and smoothes it up against the box, wedging and blending it into the sandbox.] It seems you're really working to smooth the sand up to hold the box in place. It's almost like a mountain.

C: *[with pride] You can see that right! [She then picks up some of the figures and carefully covers them up with sand with a look of satisfaction.]*

T: *Some of the people are buried.*

C: *Yeah . . . so they can't come out.*

T: *You want to be sure that they stay buried and no one will dig them up . . . like people in a cemetery are buried and they don't get dug up.*

C: *Like my dad. He's inside the coffin.*

T: *In the ground, and no one can dig it up. It stays there in the ground. Is your dad buried in a cemetery too?*

C: *I think so . . .*

T: *Where is your dad now?*

C: *His spirit goes from his body.*

T: *Where?*

C: *To heaven.*

T: *And what about his body?*

C: *It's in the ground. It's in the ground inside the coffin. The coffin stays in the ground buried. I'd like to see it again.*

T: *You'd like to see it again, but you can't. That makes us sad sometimes. (Hurley, 1991, pp. 247–248)*

Charlie, a 10-year-old boy, and his sister were living with their aunt and their mother, who had recently been divorced from Charlie's father after a marriage characterized by chronic violence. Charlie's mother expressed her anger at the breakup of her marriage by refusing to grant many of Charlie's requests and by threatening not to let him visit his father again. Charlie, on his first visit to the therapist, drew his dysfunctional family as occupants of a spaceship with a crisis in the making and his own foot next to the escape hatch (see Figure 14-19). He described the drawing this way:

It's a spaceship. My sister's at the controls. Mom is up here, reading. Dad is sleeping, and Auntie is below, working . . . she likes to be away from everybody. This is me. The spaceship is going to California [where Charlie's father lived] . . . but we are all going to crash . . . run into a star. (Robinson, 1991, pp. 223–224)

Charlie felt helpless and defeated and was frightened by his mother's hostility and anger. He acted out some of these feelings by playing war games with the therapist. He used toy soldiers to fight against the therapist's "troops," built forts from furniture, and made the whole therapy room into a battleground:

C: *I've blown away your bunkers. . . . Here come my men to attack.*

T: *I have nothing to protect me; anything can happen to me now.*

C: *You take all of these men [gives me the full complement of soldiers]. Captain [one Rambo-like soldier who grew in power with every battle] will fight them all!*

T: *The Captain is all by himself; how can he handle all these attackers alone?*

(Ibid., pp. 232–233)

The therapist played along by letting Charlie know that he recognized the lopsided odds over which Captain (Charlie) was going to triumph. In these play episodes Charlie always won, but that was not good enough—he had to "wipe out" the therapist in every play encounter. The interactions were used by the therapist to help Charlie

Figure 14-19 Charlie's family portrait.

SOURCE: Robinson (1991), p. 224.

express his aggression safely and begin to learn to master it in the presence of a nonreactive and trusted adult.

Behavioral and Cognitive–Behavioral Therapy

Probably the most often used treatments for children involve behavioral methods of various kinds. Gerald Patterson (1982, 1986) has developed a widely used behavioral therapy for families with a child who behaves overaggressively. The family members are taught the social skills needed to interact in positive reinforcing ways rather than aversively. They are also shown how to teach their child that such overaggressive behaviors will not be tolerated. This no-tolerance policy is demonstrated by their refusal to comply with or give in to the coercive demands and by subjecting their child to a time-out procedure in which he or she is removed to another room and required to stay there for a set period of time. This policy, coupled with positive reinforcement for desirable behaviors, has been effective for many families.

Cognitive-behavioral approaches have also been useful, especially in school settings. Children have been taught to identify problems, plan how to deal with them, and then self-monitor their behaviors, sometimes using "think-aloud" techniques in which they self-instruct by giving themselves audible verbal instructions. This training not only improves school performance, but also seems to improve peer relationships and behavior at home.

Family Therapy

The family-systems approach to therapy holds that it is the system of family interaction, not one individual, that is disturbed. (The family as a system is further discussed in Chapter 16.) Even though one person is usually identified as the member with the problem, that person's symptoms are a reflection of a disturbance in the larger family unit. For example, a boy whose behavior was hyperactive was referred for treatment. Although he was labeled as the problem, a look at the family showed a more pervasive difficulty:

> In this family the husband and wife did not get along. The husband spent all his time caring for his own dependent parents. He felt burdened by his wife and three children and felt no one looked after his needs. The wife felt neglected and uncared for and got satisfaction from the antics of her youngest child, the boy [referred for treatment]. The other two older children, who were well behaved, seemed excessively mature in their actions. The problems in this interconnected system could be seen by looking at any of the members, not just at the young boy labeled as hyperactive. (Andolphi, 1983)

Family therapy has much in common with the psychodynamic approach because it often focuses on the meanings behind the behavior of each of the family members. The family therapist seeks to get a picture of the actual experience of the problem by the family. What is going on in the family now? What was going on in the family when the problem developed? How have family members responded? The first task of the therapist often is to reframe the child's problem in terms of family dysfunction and help develop alternative, healthier ways of dealing with these issues.

Effectiveness of Therapy With Children

Through the use of a technique called **meta-analysis,** a method of quantitatively combining the findings of independent studies, over 300 research-based therapy studies of children and adolescents in which treatment groups were compared to controls have been summarized in four different analyses (Weisz et al., 1998). (Meta-analysis is discussed further in Chapter 16.) The studies represented a variety of therapeutic approaches, including behavior modification, cognitive-behavioral methods, group therapy, client-centered therapy, play therapy, and family therapy. The focus in meta-analysis is on **effect size** which refers to the average level of treatment benefits for the children in a study by showing what their percentile rank in terms of outcome would be if after treatment their scores were placed in a frequency distribution consisting of the scores of the untreated children in the control group. After the effect size for each study is calculated, the average effect size can then be obtained. This approach makes it possible to compare studies that differ in very important ways including the problem treated, the type of therapy used, and the age and gender of the children in the study. Although a way of combining studies is useful because therapy studies usually deal with a limited number of participants due to the high costs involved, many specific questions about what produces the helpful effects remain to be solved. The overall results showed that therapy in these research studies had consistently beneficial effects for the children involved, as compared to the outcome for the control groups. In general, the studies were in agreement that the average treated child functioned better than 75% to 80% of the controls. When the studies were divided into smaller groups based on type of therapy, behavioral treatments such as modeling and cognitive-behavioral therapy generated larger effects than nonbehavioral treatments in two of the meta-analyses while the others showed no difference. Adolescent girls were more likely to improve with therapy than adolescent boys or either boys or girls who were younger.

Even though this result is encouraging, it is important to realize that most of the 300 studies used in these meta-analyses involved samples, treatments, and treatment conditions that are not very representative of what usually happens when children are referred for therapy. Table 14-11 summarizes the way the studies differ from the ordinary therapeutic experience of children who are

Table 14–11

Typical Differences Between Research-Based and Clinic-Based Child Psychotherapy Research Conditions

Research Therapy	Clinic Therapy
Cases recruited, volunteers, often less severe problems	Clinic referred, usually more severe, some required to obtain treatment by courts, etc.
Groups tend to be homogeneous	Groups tend to be heterogeneous
Focus on single problems	Multiproblem focus
Treatment carried out in laboratory or school settings	Treatment carried out in clinic or hospital
Researchers as therapists	Career therapists
Small caseloads	Very large caseloads
Strong pretherapy preparation	Little pretherapy preparation for particular cases
Preplanned and highly structured treatment using treatment manuals	Flexible treatment approaches, no manual
Monitoring of therapist behavior to keep in conformity with plan	Little monitoring of therapist behavior
Behavioral methods generally used	Nonbehavioral methods predominate

Source: Adapted from Weisz et al. (1998), p. 60.

referred for treatment. Most of the studies available for analysis deal with research studies while there are many fewer studies that deal with clinical samples. When a meta-analysis was done only of studies using clinical samples, the effect sizes of the individual studies were much smaller. In these studies the children had been referred to a clinic, the treatment was conducted in service-oriented clinics as part of the regular services provided by the clinic not in research settings, and the therapy was carried out by practicing clinicians rather than spe-

cially trained researchers. Of the nine studies that could be found to include in the clinic-based meta-analysis, two showed clearly negative outcomes and three others showed very little change from the therapy. Even the most successful studies showed a very small effect size (Weisz et al., 1995). (See Box 14-3.)

Although we know from the research-based studies that therapeutic interventions can be very helpful, this meta-analytic study of conventional clinical treatments does not suggest that under real-world conditions therapy for

Q&A

Box 14–3

Q: Research-based treatment has been shown to be quite effective in helping children, whereas on average clinic-based treatment has not. How can this important gap in outcome be bridged?

A: *The differences spelled out in Table 14-11 suggest some, but only some, of the answers. Research studies usually focus on limited objectives, use a cooperative and less severely affected group, and provide more time and resources for those carrying out the treatment. The difference in the effectiveness of research and clinical studies means that several more things need to be done before treatment based on manuals created for research is exported to clinical sites. This would involve taking these treatments to clinical settings and experimenting with them. This would help uncover what modifications need to be made to make the treatments effective with more severely affected children who often have*

multiple problems. It would also provide information about how under the real-life constraints of scarce time and money the treatments could be modified and still be effective.

Some researchers have tried to treat children with severe problems. For instance, the work of Ivar Lovaas with autistic children is discussed in the next chapter. Although this was a large and well-funded study, it was focused on children who were considered very difficult to treat. We also need to know more about whether modifications need to be made so that treatments that are effective with a middle-class, predominantly White group of children are equally as effective for children of different racial, economic, and cultural backgrounds. As Box 14-2 indicates, therapists often make assumptions about parents and their motivations and beliefs that are inaccurate because of the therapists' unwitting use of stereotypes and lack of knowledge of cul-

tural beliefs. Another problem may be that for effective treatment of children's behavior disorders specialist training in behavioral techniques is especially important. We know that behavioral treatments generally produce better outcomes than nonbehavioral treatments. Evidence suggests, however, that behavioral therapies are used less frequently in the clinic than nonbehavioral therapies. Finally, more information about outcome in clinic-based studies is needed. The few formal studies that are available may not give a clear picture of the results. Even when they are focused on patients who would be treated anyway, clinic studies take extra time and money to provide records and test measures that can be used to assess the kinds of problems treated and their severity and the outcomes. Because clinic budgets generally don't cover this sort of expense, perhaps funding priorities for research need to be altered to make funds available for this purpose.

children is consistently effective. Yet even in the real-world setting there are many reports that show that children are significantly helped by therapeutic intervention. For example, in a study of children with conduct problems and their families, improvements for children, parents, and in family functioning were significant (Kazdin & Wassell, 2000). Not only did the children benefit consid-erably but the parents and the family as a whole benefited even though the focus of the treatment was on the child. One current task for researchers is to identify the key components of success in child and adolescent therapy studies and test the most effective ways of adopting these components to clinical settings.

Chapter Summary

On average, 1 in 10 American children is severely affected by one or more DSM disorders at some time during childhood. Research shows that although symptoms may change as children grow older, at least three-quarters of those who meet the criteria for a disorder in childhood or adolescence still meet the criteria for some DSM disorder in adulthood.

EXTERNALIZING DISORDERS

Children who have **externalizing disorders** often have trouble paying attention, are likely to behave aggressively, and may cause harm to people and property.

Attention–Deficit/Hyperactivity Disorder
Children diagnosed with **attention-deficit/hyperactivity disorder (ADHD)** show one or both of two kinds of behavior: (1) severe or frequent problems in paying attention, and (2) impulsive or overactive behaviors. Boys are four times more likely than girls to be given this diagnosis. ADHD can have serious negative effects on children's acquisition of academic and social skills. Although causes of ADHD are complex, genetic inheritance appears likely. The most common treatment is the use of stimulant medications such as methylphenidate (Ritalin). Behavioral therapy is also used successfully with many children. The disorder is so frequently diagnosed in schoolchildren that concern has been raised about the threshold for diagnosing the disorder. The frame of reference used by the person making the diagnosis often seems to determine whether a child's behavior meets the DSM-IV criteria for ADHD. This has led to concerns about the overuse both of this diagnosis and of medication to treat it. ADHD symptoms may change, but the disorder seems to persist into adulthood.

Tic Disorders and Tourette's Disorder
Tics are involuntary, sudden, rapid, recurrent, and stereotyped movements or vocalizations that are experienced as irresistible by those affected. Examples of motor tics include eye blinking, nose twitching, or more complex facial gestures. Vocal tics include grunting, sniffing, and throat clearing. One type of tic disorder, **Tourette's disorder,** which may begin as early as age 2, can cause significant social difficulties for children. One unusual symptom of Tourette's disorder is **coprolalia,** the uttering of obscenities. Antidepressant medication can lessen the symptoms of Tourette's disorder.

Oppositional Defiant Disorder
Children who frequently behave in a negativistic, defiant, disobedient, and hostile way may have **oppositional defiant disorder (ODD).** Unlike ADHD, the rates of ODD in boys and girls are not very different. ODD is more common in children where at least one parent has a history of ADHD, ODD, conduct disorder, or such adult disorders as antisocial personality disorder, substance-related disorder, or mood disorder. Both genetic links and parent-child relationships may help produce ODD in children.

Conduct Disorder
In **conduct disorder,** major societal norms are violated as well as the basic rights of others. Both ADHD and ODD are often associated with later development of conduct disorder. If the conduct disorder–related behavior occurs in many settings, there is a strong possibility that the person will later meet the diagnostic criteria for antisocial personality and drug and alcohol abuse disorders or commit criminal offenses in adulthood. A vulnerability or person-situation interaction model is useful in understanding conduct disorder because this disorder is thought to be caused by a combination of lack of social and academic skills, negative factors in the family environment, and genetic factors. The most effective treatment seems to be prevention of the disorder's development through skill building for both children and parents when children who show marked externalizing behavior are at an early stage of development.

INTERNALIZING DISORDERS

Internalizing disorders are often overlooked for long periods because adults tend to think of them as less serious than externalizing disorders. The problems in **internalizing disorders** tend to be covert, that is, related to worries and disturbing thoughts rather than to overt activities. Predominant symptoms of internalizing disorders include anxiety and depression.

Separation Anxiety Disorder
An internalizing disorder unique to children, **separation anxiety disorder** has as its most prominent symptom excessive anxiety or even panic experienced by children whose major attachment figure is about to leave or is absent.

Other Anxiety Disorders Found in Childhood Three anxiety disorders that occur in adulthood—social phobia, generalized anxiety disorder, and obsessive-compulsive disorder—are also found in children. Children with **social phobia** tend to shy away from unfamiliar people, especially other children, but do not show this same anxiety with members of their families. Children with **generalized anxiety disorder,** like adults affected by the same disorder, tend to have physical symptoms such as stomachaches, nausea, or vomiting when they are in situations that involve pressure for performance or that carry a risk of loss of self-esteem. Although children often show mild obsessive or compulsive behaviors in the normal course of development, **obsessive-compulsive disorder** involves persistent intrusion of unwanted thoughts and ritualistic behaviors that may affect children so severely that they may require hospitalization. Compulsive self-injury is sometimes used as a method of controlling anxiety.

Treatment of Anxiety Disorders in Children Cognitive-behavioral therapy is often effective for children with anxiety disorders. Family sessions can be a useful addition to child-only therapy sessions. Antidepressant medication is often recommended for obsessive-compulsive disorder, and behavior therapy can also have a positive long-term effect for this disorder.

Depression Depressive disorder in children tends to be relatively long-lasting. The appearance of depression in childhood or adolescence increases the risk that the child may (1) have a manic or hypomanic episode, and thus switch from depression to a bipolar disorder, and (2) have a recurrence of depression sooner than would someone whose first depressive episode had occurred in adulthood. Newer antidepressant medications from the class called SSRIs are sometimes used in treatment of older children, but no consistent results are yet available. Interpersonal therapy and cognitive therapy have produced promising results among depressed adolescents.

THERAPY FOR CHILDREN AND ADOLESCENTS

Because parents have such an important role in their children's lives, sometimes the most effective treatment for childhood behavior disorders involves working either solely with the parents or with both parents and children. Many therapeutic techniques for adults can be adapted for use with children. When working with families from diverse cultural backgrounds, clinicians need to avoid their own stereotypes and also take family cultural values into account.

Play Therapy Play therapy provides a way for young children with limited verbal skills to communicate with therapists. It also allows children to work through traumatic events through symbolic play.

Behavioral and Cognitive–Behavioral Therapy Behavioral methods can be effective when family members are trained to use them with aggressive children. Cognitive-behavioral approaches, often using a "think-aloud" technique, may improve school performance, peer relationships, and home behavior.

Family Therapy The family-systems approach focuses on patterns of family interactions rather than on a particular family member as the source of difficulty. The therapist tries to assess family dynamics and then help family members develop more adaptive ways to interact.

Effectiveness of Therapy With Children **Meta-analyses** of studies of a variety of psychological therapies have shown that, overall, therapeutic interventions for children conducted in a research setting have a clearly positive effect. The findings of these studies are usually expressed in terms of **effect size,** that is, where the average scores of the treated group would rank in a distribution of the scores of children with the same disorder who had not received treatment. The few clinic-based studies of therapy outcome that have been published, however, raise questions about how effective child therapy is in ordinary treatment settings.

Key Terms

15

Joan Miró "Painting" 1933, oil on canvas, 68½" × 6′ 5¼". The Museum of Modern Art. New York. Loula D. Lasker Bequest (by exchange). Photograph © 2002 The Museum of Modern Art, New York. © 2002 Artists Rights Society (ARS), New York/ADAGP, Paris.

Pervasive Developmental Disorders and Mental Retardation

John is five years old. He was referred to a child psychiatrist because of delayed speech development and poor peer relationships. His mother describes him as "living in a shell" and feels he never developed a close, loving relationship with her. He did not begin to speak until the age of three, and even now has a limited vocabulary of only about 200 words. Most of his speech consists of repetitive phrases heard on television, or simple requests or demands. He is unable to initiate or sustain a conversation with peers or adults.

John demonstrates a number of unusual behaviors and interests. For example, he is fascinated with water and often will spend long periods of time intently watching water dripping into a basin. He shows no interest in playing with toys in a usual way but would rather arrange objects in a straight line or else talk jargon to himself while rocking back and forth. . . . He becomes very upset if furniture is moved around in the house and was inconsolable when his parents bought a new car.

His nursery school teacher says he has an amazing facility for numbers and letters, but she is concerned because he would rather stay by himself than play with other children. John communicates little with his teacher and seems odd and aloof, "in his own world."

When John was three, his mother was told by the family doctor that John probably would grow out of these problems. John's mother senses now that John is suffering from a severe and chronic condition. (Institute of Medicine, 1990, pp. 26–27) ■

John's behavior is typical of *autistic disorder*, one of the pervasive developmental disorders we will be discussing in this chapter. The chapter is focused on pervasive developmental disorders and mental retardation, two general classes of disorders that typically are identified in infancy or childhood but which also have important and permanent effects on developmental progress and the level of functioning children can be expected to achieve as adults.

Pervasive Developmental Disorders

All the disorders in this group result in severe and long-lasting impairment in several aspects of a child's expected development. **Pervasive developmental disorders** are conditions that become apparent early in a child's development and affect all of the major systems that develop as the child becomes older (e.g., social, language, and cognitive systems). In some cases, children who are diagnosed with a pervasive developmental disorder appear to develop normally for some months and then either regress in their behavior or develop abnormal behavioral or physical symptoms. In other cases, children with these disorders appear to be abnormal in some respects from birth or very early in life.

Children who have pervasive developmental disorders lack the skills needed for ordinary social interactions, and their ability to communicate with others is either severely impaired or absent. In addition, children affected by these disorders are likely to behave in stereotyped ways and are not able to adapt their behavior to different situations. All in all, their social and cognitive behaviors are clearly different from those of most children of the same age. Pervasive developmental disorders include *autistic disorder, Asperger's disorder, childhood disintegrative disorder, Rett's disorder*, and a general category called *pervasive developmental disorder, not otherwise specified*. This last category is used for children who do not fit precisely the definitions in one of the other four groups but whose atypical behavior seems to be affected by the same general type of disorder. Table 15-1 shows the major similarities and differences among these pervasive developmental disorders. Pervasive developmental disorders often occur together with some degree of mental retardation. If mental retardation is also present, it is coded on DSM-IV Axis II, while the developmental disorder itself is coded on Axis I.

Table 15-1

Characteristics of Four Types of Pervasive Developmental Disorders

	Autistic Disorder	Asperger's Disorder	Rett's Disorder	Childhood Disintegrative Disorder
Age at onset	Before age 3; generally much earlier	Often not recognized until school	Usually between ages 1 and 2	Over age 2
Sex differences	More frequent in males	Probably more frequent in males	Typically females only	More frequent in males
Presence of mental retardation?	Often moderate, but child may be of average or above-average intelligence with uneven cognitive skill	No	Yes, severe or profound after symptoms begin	Yes, after symptoms begin
Difficulty in social interaction?	Yes, beginning early	Yes: qualitative impairments; restricted interests and activities	Yes, but not long-lasting	Yes, after symptoms begin
Early development normal?	Cognitive and social differences appear early	Generally	Yes, but head growth deceleration, and slowed development begin early	Yes, at least for 2 years
Language development affected?	Delayed and impaired	No	Severely impaired	Not initially
Unusual movements or behavior patterns?	Yes	Stereotyped and repetitive behaviors, motor delays, and clumsiness	Yes, after symptoms begin	Yes, after symptoms begin

Autistic Disorder

People with **autistic disorder** typically show an unusual pattern of social and cognitive development beginning in childhood, with marked difficulties in social interaction and communication. A very restricted repertoire of interests and activities is also typical of autism. This disorder affects 2 to 5 people, on average, in every 10,000. Autism originally was considered to be extremely rare, but more recent epidemiological studies find that the rate of autism has increased (Gillberg & Wing, 1999). Whether this increase is a result of an increased awareness of the disorder or whether it represents a real increase is unknown.

About 70% of people with autistic disorder are also mentally retarded, that is their IQ scores are 70 or lower. However, the other 30% have IQ scores that classify them in anywhere from the normal to gifted range in intelligence. Autistic disorder does not affect men and women equally. The rate of autistic disorder is four to five times higher in boys than in girls, although if girls are affected by autistic disorder they are likely to have more severe mental retardation than boys.

Autism was first described by Leo Kanner, a child psychiatrist, in 1943. Kanner presented cases of children who, from the beginning of life, exhibited a unique pattern of behavior in which they were unable to relate in an ordinary way to people and situations. In addition to this "extreme autistic aloneness," he stressed the children's "obsessive desire for the maintenance of sameness." Kanner thought of autism as a childhood psychosis and believed that most autistic children were basically very intelligent. However, we now know that children with autism fall into two groups: those who are normal or near normal in intelligence and those who function at a retarded level. One important area for future research is the separate study of these two groups, which despite some similarities may be very different, especially in social functioning.

Characteristics of Autistic Disorder Children with autistic disorder show impairment in social relationships, communication, and activities. The diagnostic criteria are listed in Table 15-2. People with autistic disorder generally show a noticeable lack of awareness of the existence or feelings of others. Autistic children do not seek out an adult for comfort if they are hurt or upset. They don't like to be held, and they avoid eye contact, prefer solitary play, and have a poor understanding of social conventions. Even when they are very young, autistic children do not enjoy the usual parent-child–kiss-and-cuddle routines. Figure 15-1 illustrates how much less infants

---

Table 15-2

Diagnostic Criteria for Autistic Disorder

To qualify for this diagnosis, a child must exhibit a total of six or more characteristics from categories 1, 2, and 3. Of these, there must be at least two from category 1 and at least one each from categories 2 and 3.

1. Qualitative impairment in social interaction, as indicated by at least two of the following:
   a. Marked impairment in the use of nonverbal behaviors such as eye contact, body posture, and gestures that regulate social interaction.
   b. Failure to develop the peer relationships that might be expected for the child's developmental level.
   c. Lack of spontaneity in seeking to share with other people enjoyment, interests, or achievement (e.g., by pointing things out to others).
2. Qualitative impairments in communication, as shown by at least one of the following:
   a. Delay in or lack of spoken language, not accompanied by compensatory attempts to communicate by gestures, mime, etc.
   b. For individuals with adequate speech, marked impairment in ability to initiate or carry on a conversation with others.
   c. Use of stereotyped and repetitive or idiosyncratic language.
   d. Lack of varied and spontaneous make-believe play or social imitative play appropriate to the person's developmental level.
3. Restricted, repetitive, and stereotyped patterns of behavior, interests, and activities, as shown by at least one of the following:
   a. Preoccupation with one or more stereotyped and restricted patterns of interest that is abnormal in intensity or focus.
   b. Seemingly inflexible adherence to specific, nonfunctional routines or rituals.
   c. Persistent preoccupation with parts of objects.
4. The delay or abnormal functioning, in at least one of the following—social interaction, language as it is used in social communication, or symbolic or imaginative play—must have begun before the age of 3.
5. Rett's disorder or childhood disintegrative disorder cannot better account for the disordered behavior.

Source: Adapted from DSM-IV.

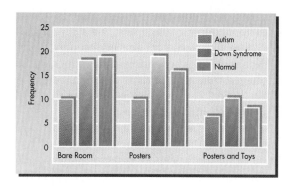

Figure 15-1 The average frequency with which infants with autism and Down syndrome gazed at their mothers in a laboratory setting compared to the frequency of gaze of normally developing infants. The settings included a room bare except for basic furniture, the same room with wall posters added, and the room with both posters and toys added.

SOURCE: Adapted from Dissanayake & Crossley (1996).

with autism made visual contact with their mothers than either Down syndrome babies or babies who were developing normally (Dissanayake & Crossley, 1996). Down Syndrome is discussed later in this chapter. In autism, impairment in speech is even more dramatic than impaired social behavior. About half of all autistic children do not develop speech at all. If they do learn to talk, autistic children's speech is likely to be unusual. For instance, they may simply echo what is said to them or repeat commercials they have heard on television. Another characteristic of autism is a very narrow range of interests and activities. Autistic individuals may spend a great deal of time spinning objects, flicking their fingers, or rocking their bodies.

Sameness and routine are very important. Children with autistic disorder may resist change by attempting to control the behavior of others. For instance, one girl began to cry each time her mother did not put her right foot on the step first when she started to climb the steps in front of their house. For another child, a minor re-arrangement of furniture, such as moving a living room chair to a different spot, resulted in outbursts of anger and tantrumlike behavior. One explanation of the importance of sameness and routine to those with autistic disorder, and also for their seeming lack of desire for social contacts, may be that these behaviors are an attempt to control exposure to overstimulation. The account by Temple Grandin in Box 15-1 highlights this kind of rigidity. Overall, the lives of autistic individuals are limited by their failure to develop peer relationships, their delay in or total lack of spoken language, and their adherence to specific inflexible routines or rituals that seem to have no obvious function. These developmental delays and behavioral abnormalities are usually noticeable before age 3.

A number of theoretical perspectives have contributed to many of the hundreds of research studies focused on autistic disorder. Topics of particular interest to researchers include cognitive deficits, language difficulties, deficits in interpersonal relationships, diagnosing autism, and biological factors that may help to explain autistic behavior.

Cognitive Deficits Researchers have been trying to understand the aspects of cognition that are the core deficits underlying autism. Deficits in *theory of mind* and in *executive functions* have been a special focus of research in recent years. **Theory of mind** refers to the ability to attribute mental states such as desire, knowledge, and belief to oneself or other people as a way of explaining behavior. This ability can be seen by the end of a child's first year but is better developed by age 3 or 4. Performance of autistic children of preschool age on the false-belief laboratory task is a good example of this cognitive deficit (Baron-Cohen et al.,1985). Children were introduced to two dolls, Sally and Anne, who were placed in a diorama in which the experimenter enacted a scene. Sally placed a marble in her basket, and left the room leaving the basket and marble behind. After Sally left, Anne took the marble from the basket and put it in a box. The child was asked to predict where Sally would look for the marble when she came back. The correct response was that Sally would look in the basket because that was the place where she last saw the marble. In order to be correct, however, the child being tested must disregard his or her own knowledge of where the marble actually was (now in the box rather than the basket) because Sally had not seen Anne move the marble. Although the autistic children could correctly answer questions about where the marble was originally and where it was moved, 80% of them answered incorrectly by saying that Sally would look in the box. Their failure rate was far higher than the failure rate in either of the control groups—Down syndrome children or normally developing children matched to the autistic children in intelligence level. This result, which has been replicated in many studies is strong evidence that autistic children have a specific impairment in interpreting the intentions, beliefs, or behaviors of others. This characteristic has sometimes also been called "mindblindness" (Baron-Cohen, 1995).

One problem in research on the cognitive functioning of those with autistic disorder is finding an appropriate control group. Because many autistic children are retarded, matching groups for intelligence level generally means the control groups are likely to be significantly younger. The variety of age-related developmental changes throughout infancy and childhood that interact with, but are not the same as, intelligence makes the comparison of groups of different chronological ages somewhat inexact, even if the groups are matched in some aspect of intellectual performance. That is one reason that children with

First Person

Box 15-1

Living With Autism—Two People's Experience

Autism has a profound effect on the lives of those born with this disorder. Many people with autism are also mentally retarded, but some are of average or above-average intelligence. Special interventions by professionals and by trained family members may enable autistic individuals to reach somewhat higher levels of performance. In some cases, those affected by autism, especially if they are above average in intelligence, may be able to invent special techniques to help compensate for the difficulties in language and abstract thinking that are part of the disorder. However, it is clear that despite the efforts of these individuals, their families, and helping professionals, some limitations cannot be overcome. The two individuals here, both of whom had the benefit of expert resources and supportive families, show very different outcomes. Until more is known about the causes of autism, it is impossible to say why their outcomes were so different. Although a great deal is written about autistic children, very little information is available about what life is like for those

children when they grow up. The two people whose stories are summarized here help provide information about living with autism as an adult or an older adolescent.

Temple Grandin

Temple Grandin, who has a Ph.D. in animal science, has built a professional reputation as one of the world's foremost designers of livestock handling facilities. She also has written two books on autism and spends time speaking to a variety of groups to help parents of children with autistic disorder as well as the general public understand the disorder. Figure 15-2 shows her viewing the behavior of cattle in a holding pen.

Grandin described growing up with autistic disorder and some of the cognitive problems she faced in this way:

At the age of 1 1/2 to 3 I had many of the standard autistic behaviors such as fixation on spinning objects, refusing to be touched or held, preferring to be alone, de-

structive behavior, temper tantrums, inability to speak, sensitivity to sudden noises, appearance of deafness and an intense interest in odors. . . .

At the age of 3 to 3 1/2 my behavior greatly improved, but I did not learn to speak until 3 1/2. At the age of 3 to 4 my behavior was more normal until I became tired. When I became tired, bouts of impulsive behavior would return. . . .

In college I was on the Dean's honor list, but getting through the foreign language requirement was difficult. I scraped by with D's and C's. Learning sequential things such as math was also very hard. My mind is completely visual and spatial work such as drawing is easy. I taught myself drafting in six months. I have designed big steel and concrete cattle facilities, but remembering a phone number or adding up numbers in my head is still difficult. I have to write them down. Every piece of information I have memorized is visual. If I have to remember an abstract concept I "see" the page of the book or my notes in my mind and "read" information from it. Melodies are the only things I can memorize without a visual image. I remember very little that I hear unless it is emotionally arousing or I can form a visual image. In class I take careful notes, because I would forget the auditory material. When I think about abstract concepts such as human relationships I use visual similes. For example, relationships between people are like a glass sliding door. The door must be opened gently, if it is kicked it may shatter. If I had to learn a foreign language, I would have to do it by reading, and make it visual. (Grandin, 1984, pp. 144–145)

Some of Grandin's experiences with autism have helped her to have unique insights about animal behavior, especially when animals are under stress. She observed that although, like most autistic children, she did not like to be touched or held by others, the feeling of being enclosed in a tight space was relaxing and gave her relief from anxiety.

When I was six, I would wrap myself up in blankets and get under sofa cushions, because the pressure was relaxing. I used

Figure 15-2 Temple Grandin, shown inspecting cattle in a holding pen, has combined a professional career designing facilities for the humane handling of animals in stockyards and meat processing facilities with an active role in educating the public about autism as an advocate for autistic individuals and an educator about autism.

SOURCE: From *Thinking in Pictures* by Temple Grandin. New York: Doubleday, 1995. Photograph © by Rosalie Winard.

First Person

to daydream for hours in elementary school about constructing a device that would apply pressure to my body. I visualized a box with an inflatable liner that I could lie in. It would be like being totally encased in inflatable splints.

After visiting my aunt's ranch in Arizona, I got the idea of building such a device, patterned after the cattle squeeze chute I first saw there. When I watched cattle being put in the squeeze chute for their vaccinations, I noticed that some of them relaxed when they were pressed between the side panels. I guess I had made my first connection between those cows and myself, because a few days later, after I had a big panic attack, I just got inside the squeeze chute at the ranch. . . .

I asked Aunt Ann to press the squeeze sides against me and to close the head restraint bars around my neck. I hoped it would calm my anxiety. At first there were a few moments of sheer panic as I stiffened up and tried to pull away from the pressure, but I couldn't get away because my head was locked in. Five seconds later I felt a wave of relaxation, and about thirty minutes later I asked Aunt Ann to release me. For about an hour afterward I felt very calm and serene. (Grandin, 1995, pp. 62–63)

This idea later developed into Grandin's famous "squeeze box," shown in Figure 15–3. The squeeze box has been used successfully by others with autistic disorder. The idea that prompted the squeeze box has also been useful to Grandin in her professional career as a designer of cattle pens.

Learning new things was usually only possible for Grandin if she visualized them. The spoken words themselves had only very literal meanings. Again, Grandin has been able to translate this deficiency into a positive attribute in her professional work because her difficulty with symbolism has made it easier for her to understand how cattle perceive their surroundings in slaughterhouses:

Spatial words such as "over" and "under" had no meaning for me until I had a visual image to fix them in my memory. Even now, when I hear the word "under" by itself, I automatically picture myself getting under the cafeteria tables at school during

an air-raid drill, a common occurrence on the East Coast during the early fifties. . . .

I also visualize verbs. The word "jumping" triggers a memory of jumping hurdles at the mock Olympics held at my elementary school. Adverbs often trigger inappropriate images—"quickly" reminds me of Nestle's Quik—unless they are paired with a verb, which modifies my visual image. For example, "He ran quickly" triggers an animated image of Dick from the first-grade reading book running fast, and "He walked slowly" slows the image down. As a child, I left out words such as "is," "the," and "it" because they had no meaning by themselves. Similarly, words like "of" and "an" made no sense. Eventually I learned how to use them properly, because my parents always spoke correct English and I mimicked their speech patterns. To this day certain verb conjugations, such as "to be," are absolutely meaningless to me. . . .

It is likely that Raymond, the autistic savant depicted in the movie Rain Man, used a similar strategy to memorize telephone books, maps, and other information. He simply photocopied each page of the phone book into his memory. When he wanted to find a certain number, he just

scanned pages of the phone book that were in his mind. To pull information out of my memory, I have to replay the video. Pulling facts up quickly is sometimes difficult, because I have to play bits of different videos until I find the right tape. This takes time. . . . (Grandin, 1995, pp. 30–31)

Another problem area for people with autism, even people as well adapted and successful as Grandin, is social relationships:

Social interactions that come naturally to most people can be daunting for people with autism. As a child, I was like an animal that had no instincts to guide me; I just had to learn by trial and error. I was always observing, trying to work out the best way to behave, but I never fit in. I had to think about every social interaction. . . .

I've remained celibate because doing so helps me to avoid the many complicated social situations that are too difficult for me to handle. For most people with autism, physical closeness is as much a problem as not understanding basic social behaviors. At conventions I have talked to several women who were raped on dates

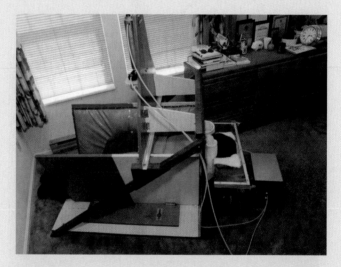

Figure 15–3   A version of the famous squeeze machine originated by Temple Grandin has been commercially produced for use in helping people with autism control their feelings of anxiety. A model illustrates how the padded side boards of the machine press tight against its occupant.

Source: From *Thinking in Pictures* by Temple Grandin. New York: Doubleday, 1995. Photograph © by Rosalie Winard.

Box 15-1

because they did not understand the subtle cues of sexual interest. Likewise, men who want to date often don't understand how to relate to a woman. They remind me of Data, the android on Star Trek. In one episode, Data's attempts at dating were a disaster. When he tried to be romantic, he complimented his date by using scientific terminology. Even very able adults with autism have such problems. (Grandin, 1995, pp. 132, 133)

Grandin's successes are not typical for a person with autistic disorder, but she exemplifies how someone with a biological vulnerability can capitalize on strengths not only to adjust, but to develop skills that most people do not possess.

Ted Hart

Like Temple Grandin, Ted Hart grew up in a supportive family (Figure 15-4 shows him with his father on a visit home). His uncle was also autistic but had never received a diagnosis or any therapeutic interventions because little was known about autistic disorder when he was growing up. Even though Charles Hart, Ted's father, had grown up with an autistic brother, in Ted's childhood, autistic disorder was still not readily recognized. Hart's parents, despite consulting many professionals over many years, had little information about how to deal with Ted's symptoms. Even as a young adult with a supportive family and expert help in communication and other skills, Hart has remained severely incapacitated. For a number of years he has lived in a residential facility for disabled youth. There his independent self-care skills were encouraged; he learned to make his bed and even to do his laundry.

Because of the unevenness of Hart's cognitive skills, even experienced houseparents in the residential facility sometimes misjudged his ability to understand. For example, once when his mother came to pick him up for the weekend and offered to help him pack, she noticed that all the clothes in his closet and bureau drawers were very wet, as if they had just left the washing machine. Unable to find out from him why they were wet, she and the houseparents slowly pieced together what had happened:

Unable to get any more information out of Ted, Sara [Hart's mother] asked one of the houseparents for help. Slowly they began to piece together an explanation for this mystery. They had spent weeks training Ted to do his laundry, gradually reducing supervision after he had memorized all of the instructions and demonstrated that he could follow them alone.

The task analysis included every step a person needed to take. It did not, however, include safeguards in case of mechanical failure. The day that Ted did his laundry without supervision, the dryer was broken.

Unconcerned by this change, he followed all of the memorized instructions to the letter. When the functional buzzer on the dysfunctional dryer signaled, he obediently removed the soggy clothing and placed the entire wet load in his chest of drawers.

No one had ever considered the possibility that he would do such a thing. No one realized that he had to be "programmed" to check the clothing in the dryer to ascertain whether it was dry. To the staff this was such an obvious step that no one had even considered the possibility that Ted would misunderstand.

Common sense should have told Ted something was wrong. But his autism prevented him from developing common sense or understanding the obvious. Although capable of memorizing rules and processing a string of instructions, he couldn't make a simple judgment. (Hart, 1989, pp. 195–196)

Hart's inability to deal with abstractions is similar to but much more severe than that of Temple Grandin. Like Grandin also, Hart has trouble with social interactions. He learned appropriate social expressions, but it was clear that he separated them from their meanings and used them mechanically.

Figure 15-4 Ted and Charles Hart during one of Ted's visits home. Charles Hart, who has both a son and a brother with autistic disorder, has been a leader in the state of Washington and throughout the country in creating a better understanding of autism and in improving community facilities that will benefit autistic individuals and their families. He has written a book describing his experiences with his son and brother.

SOURCE: Photo by Tom Reese/*Seattle Times.*

First Person

Box 15–1

As Ted grew older he learned that some social phrases, such as "How are you?" and "Fine, thanks" have no literal meaning. They are courtesies like "Please" and "Thank you" that have to be used in polite conversation. We didn't realize how totally Ted had separated the social use of these expressions from their literal origins until one evening Sara called him at Parkview.

A family friend had given Ted a terrarium with two lizards for Christmas. We taught Ted the care of his pets and he did very well. . . .

Ted had named the lizards Rick and Sasha and seemed to enjoy them more than

any other possessions. However, Sasha eventually died of unknown causes and Rick appeared lethargic and unhealthy.

Sara worried that Rick might die soon and we would have to buy a replacement, so she called Ted and asked, "How's Rick?"

"He's fine." Then Ted added, "Rick died today."

Ted has learned some gestures that make him appear courteous and eager to please. He assumed that the polite answer to Sara's question, "How's Rick?" had to be, "He's fine." (Hart, 1989, p. 281)

Both Grandin and Hart have handicaps that stem from autistic disorder. Al-

though the two of them differ greatly in their competencies, there are certain general similarities in the ways they think and interact with others. Grandin, whose autism is less severe and who has become a success in a demanding career, is able to say more about her own reactions. To understand Hart's abilities and difficulties, it is necessary to rely on others' descriptions. Like Grandin, Hart's father has become active in promoting an understanding of autism and improving the facilities and opportunities for those with this disorder.

Down syndrome are often used in control groups. They, too, are likely to be retarded.

Although the ability to understand what others are thinking and why they react in certain ways as described in the theory of mind is clearly important, it is only one of several types of deficits experienced by children with autism. Another cognitive deficit is found in executive functions. **Executive functions** are the cognitive operations—such as planning, inhibition of response, flexibility, and working memory—that are thought to be directed by the prefrontal cortex. Many children and adults with autism have problems in planning and organization, in using feedback from others, and in changing the focus of their attention. However, these deficits do not explain the obsessivelike preoccupations and repetitive patterns of behavior that are characteristic of autism. Researchers are now trying to go beyond this general concept of executive functions to the more specific areas of information processing and cognitive neuropsychology to try to understand which components of executive function are impaired and which are functioning as would be expected in normal development (R. M. Joseph, 1999). Neuropsychological research is focused on mapping relationships between brain structures and observable psychological and behavioral functions. Cognitive flexibility and working memory are two of the areas investigated in this type of research.

Most children with autistic disorder also show large deficits in symbolic play, although the exact nature of these deficits is not clear (McDonough et al., 1997). In the normal course of development, children usually progress from what is called functional play, such as scooting a car along the floor or placing a telephone receiver to the ear, to symbolic play, in which they may use other available objects to carry out these same actions. In this object substitution, as it is called, children show that they

can "pretend" that one object, such as a block, is substituting for or playing the role of another object, such as a car or a cup, in their play. They have progressed from using an object functionally to using it in a symbolic way. Although children typically engage in a great deal of spontaneous symbolic play, in autism symbolic play occurs very rarely. In normally developing children, the ability to use symbolic play seems to occur at the same time that the children are beginning to acquire language.

Children with autistic disorder are generally unable to engage in symbolic play because they cannot derive what are called *second-order representations*, or *meta-representations*. This doesn't mean that they aren't able to engage in symbolic play if they are in a structured situation and do not have to initiate the play themselves. For example, in one study children were first observed in their actions with toys involved in each of several familiar sequences of behavior and then given a demonstration by the experimenter. In this study, one sequence, "Teddy takes a bath," was demonstrated by the experimenter in the following steps. The experimenter's vocalizations for each step are indicated in brackets.

["Time to give the bear a bath"]
["Put him in the tub"] The experimenter places the bear in the toy bathtub.
["Wash the bear"] She washes the bear with a sponge.
["All done, let's dry the bear off."] She dries the bear with a towel.

(Adapted from McDonough et al., 1997, p. 30.) ∎

For some of the sequences, all the objects used were realistic. For other sequences, an object dissimilar to the one named in the experimenter's instructions was used to measure the effect of substitution of a symbolic component. For instance, children who saw the bath sequence with a symbolic component saw the experimenter use a red drawer handle to represent the sponge. After the experimenter finished the demonstration, the children were asked to reproduce the behavioral sequence using exactly the same equipment the experimenter had used. Their performance on this reproduction task was measured immediately after the demonstration, and then again 24 hours later. The researchers found that the performances of the control and autistic disorder groups did not differ. This result demonstrated that under certain conditions, especially when the situation is highly structured, children with autistic disorder are capable of at least a limited type of symbolic thinking. However, when their self-initiated efforts at play were measured, they were less likely to carry out symbolic sequences than children in the control group.

People who have autistic disorder seem to develop unevenly in their cognitive skills. Some of them, even those whose cognitive functions are generally impaired, have unusual abilities that seem limited to very specific areas, often in the area of factual memory. For example, although Ted Hart, who was described in Box 15-1, is severely affected by autism and is unable to live independently, he has unusual memory abilities:

> Nineteen-year-old Ted appeared to be developing normally until he was almost three. Then his parents became concerned because he still showed no interest in playing with other children and had begun to use unusual speech patterns and show other unusual behaviors. At nine he could read and remember the spelling of five-syllable Greek names for dinosaurs but he couldn't tie his shoes or differentiate the fantasy on television or in books from reality. He knows the number of toes on exotic animals and names the day of the week a person's birthday will fall on far into the future. (Adapted from the Seattle Times, 1990, p. H1)

The presence of these so-called *savant* abilities (areas of surprising talent in otherwise low functioning individuals) are at least 10 times more common in autism than in other forms of mental handicap (Scheuffgen et al., 2000). The best known skills include music, drawing, and calendar calculation. Other skills out of line with general development that may be even more frequent include skill at jigsaw puzzles, memory for routes or timetables, and superior word knowledge. Sometimes these skills give the impression of good or superior intelligence even in apparently retarded children with autism.

Language Difficulties Language is an important problem in autistic disorder. More than half of all autistic children remain mute, and many others have a significant developmental delay in beginning to talk. For most of those who

do speak, specific aspects of language disorder remain. Language of autistic children tends to be stereotyped, repetitive, and idiosyncratic. There is often difficulty in comprehending the meaning of what others say, ranging from understanding simple directions to an inability to understand jokes. Jokes usually require some symbolic thinking, and even in normally developing children, the humor of a joke often goes "over the head" of a young listener until sometime in the primary school years, when unsubtle jokes begin to be understood as funny. The theory of mind hypothesis of autism has also been important in understanding these language difficulties. The lack of ability to understand how others think and feel makes it hard to learn that language is a means of sharing information, thoughts, and feelings and interacting with others. Instead of taking the listener's perspective into account, people affected by autism tend to lecture about their own interests without considering their listeners' role in the conversation. Language difficulties are just one of the problems that contribute to the social difficulties in autism.

Social and Affective Deficits From very early in life, children with autistic disorder show difficulties in interacting with other people. As infants, children who are later diagnosed with autistic disorder may not be interested in games enjoyed by most children, like patty-cake and peekaboo. Ordinarily children seem to like these games because of their interactive nature. The games call for the use of **joint attention behaviors,** behaviors that involve the coordination of attention between the child, another person, and an object or event. These behaviors usually develop prior to language and are of two types, either following another's behavior or initiating the behavior. Children with autistic disorder are likely to have impairments in both of these types of joint attention behaviors.

The lack of these normal interactive interests and skills in infants and young children with autism can be a valuable clue to early diagnosis and treatment of this disorder. Researchers have found that it was possible to identify children who would later be diagnosed with autistic disorder by the time they were 1 year old. Earlier research has shown that about half the parents of autistic children suspected a problem before their infant was a year old and that most parents began expressing concern to their pediatrician by the time their child was 18 months old.

Diagnosis of Autism Diagnosis can be difficult because, even though many autistic children have some form of mental retardation, they usually appear physically normal and their motor development usually occurs at the proper time. At a very young age, a child with autistic disorder may seem like a normal child with a few abnormal behaviors. Staring off into space and rocking back and forth are stereotypical autistic behaviors, but normal kids also do them. Normal children even do head banging, which is common at an early age. But normal children also make eye contact and point at things, behaviors that are rare in autistic children. Because parental concerns about what they perceive as abnormal development in their child are often brushed off by professionals, researchers have developed a variety of checklists of child behaviors that, while they may not indicate autism and may be part of normal development, concern conscientious parents and are definitely worth exploring further as potential danger signs. Table 15-3 provides one such list of potential red

---

Table 15–3

Parental Concerns That Are Red Flags for Autism

Communication Concerns

Does not respond to his or her name
Cannot tell me what he or she wants
Delay in acquiring language
Doesn't follow directions
Seems deaf or not to hear sometimes, but not others
Doesn't point or wave bye-bye
Used to say a few words but no longer does

Social Concerns

Doesn't smile socially
Prefers to play alone
Gets things for himself
Is very independent
Has poor eye contact
Seems to be in his or her own world
Tunes us out
Is not interested in other children

Behavioral Concerns

Has frequent tantrums
Is hyperactive, uncooperative, or oppositional
Doesn't know how to play with toys
Gets stuck on things over and over
Toe walks
Has unusually strong attachments for specific toys
Lines toys and other objects up rather than playing with them
Is oversensitive to certain textures or sounds
Has odd movement patterns

Absolute Indications for Immediate Further Evaluation

No babbling sounds by 12 months
No gesturing (pointing, waving bye-bye, etc.) by 12 months
No single words by 16 months
No two-word spontaneous phrases by 24 months
ANY loss of ANY language or social skills at ANY age

Source: Adapted from Filipek et al. (1999), p. 452.

---

flags that parents may report. Screening tools such as this should be used whenever young children have routine pediatric examinations because identification of early signs of autism is very important. Many researchers believe that interventions must begin very early in the autistic children's lives if the children are to reach their full potential (Filipek et al., 1999). Despite this importance, the average age of diagnosis in the United States is 3 to 4 years and in many other countries much later. In one study carried out in England, the majority of parents of autistic children reported that they were either reassured that the child would "grow out of the symptoms" that concerned them or were referred to a second professional who provided such reassurances (Howlin & Moore, 1997). Even in cases where a diagnosis was given, no help was offered as to education, therapy, or referrals to parent support groups.

A creative assessment method for early identification of autism has been developed by some researchers who have been studying early signs of autism. The researchers knew that the most predictive behavior of autism is how seldom eye contact is made. They wanted to determine if this same behavioral characteristic would identify very young children who would later be diagnosed with autistic disorder. In order to do this, they compared first-birthday-party videotapes for 11 infants who were later diagnosed as having autistic disorder with those of 11 normally developing infants (Osterling & Dawson, 1994). Figure 15-5 shows an example of the types of pictures they used. Video footage of first birthdays was chosen for the study over tapes of other activities because parents often can't recall when they shot film or how old their child was at the time. The party setting also reduced somewhat the variability of the environments in which the children were observed.

The researchers developed a coding system to note the presence or absence of a number of developmentally appropriate behaviors and autisticlike behaviors. Raters who were unaware of the children's diagnoses viewed the party videos and coded the number of times each child exhibited certain behaviors. Using these videotape ratings, the results of the study showed that the absence of four behaviors—eye contact, showing an object to another person, pointing to objects, and responding to their own names—could identify children who were later diagnosed as autistic with 91% accuracy. A single behavior—the number of times a child looked at another person's face—could correctly classify 77% of the children into either the autistic or the nonautistic group.

Children with autistic disorder never seem to develop social play with other children. Box 15-1 shows that even for someone like Temple Grandin, who has overcome most of the difficulties of autism, interacting with others and following the general social conventions that most people seem to learn without being taught are obstacles that can be overcome only by diligent preparation and practice. As a result, many autistic children often prefer solitary activities.

(a)   (b)

Figure 15-5 Videotapes of children at their first birthday parties have been used to detect early signs of autism. Note the difference between the behavior of the child in photo (a), who was later diagnosed as having autistic disorder, and the child in photo (b), whose later development has been normal. The autistic child, in this frame and throughout the videotape, tended to focus on objects rather than people. In contrast, the child in frame (b) spent most of the time during the taped segment looking at the people gathered at the party and sharing their enjoyment.

Researchers have speculated that the inability of many autistic children to make emotional and physical connections with others would also result in a failure of the normal attachment process between mother and child. However, research has shown that this may not be the case. In a study of 15 autistic children 3 to 6 years old who were below average in intelligence, 40% were judged to be securely attached on the basis of a Strange Situation procedure modified from that originated by Mary Ainsworth to measure attachment (Capps et al., 1994). Children who were judged securely attached had mothers who behaved with more sensitivity to them. The securely attached children did not differ from the remainder of the group of children with autism in terms of their general social responsiveness, but they were more likely to initiate social interaction with their mothers than the children who were not securely attached. Intelligence test scores of the securely attached children and the remainder of the group did not differ except that the securely attached group scored higher on language comprehension. This finding supports a link between language and the cognitive representation and expectations of caretaker behavior that are a basic feature of attachment.

Biological Perspective on Autism The biological basis of autism has been investigated in a number of ways. Among these, two of the most relevant types of studies are those that focus on brain structure and function and those that investigate the genetic aspects of autism.

Brain Structure and Function There is general agreement that autistic disorder has a neurobiological basis, but so far there is little agreement among studies about which aspects of neurobiological makeup and function cause autistic behavior (Piven & O'Leary, 1997). Studies of the brains of autistic individuals, both by using scanning techniques to examine living brains and by laboratory studies of brain tissue and structure conducted after death, show a variety of brain abnormalities. The problem with these findings is that most of them are not found consistently from one study to another. About the only area of agreement from imaging studies is that the brains of those with autism tend to be larger than average and that this greater size is primarily accounted for by the greater size of the temporal, parietal, and occipital lobes (Folstein, 1999).

Despite the lack of consistency in research findings, some kind of brain pathology seems likely in people with autistic disorder. In a follow-up study of the condition of autistic persons who were first studied as many as 24 years earlier, researchers found that about one-third were reported to have had epileptic seizures at some times during their lives (Wolf & Goldberg, 1986). This is a much higher rate (up to 22 times as high, depending on age) than is found in the overall population. Children with autism who are also severely mentally retarded and never learn to speak are particularly likely to have epileptic seizures at puberty (Rapin, 1995). This connection between autism and epilepsy supports the idea that some brain abnormalities are involved in autism.

Genetic Research on Autistic Disorder Although no specific gene or gene combination associated with autism has been identified, studies of several types suggest that genetic factors may be important. One example is found in twin studies that compare monozygotic (MZ) and dizygotic (DZ) twin pairs in which at least one of the twins is autistic. The results of one such study are shown in Figure 15-6. In this study, the probability that if one twin is autistic the other would also be autistic was much greater for MZ than for DZ twin pairs (Folstein & Rutter, 1978). If the researchers broadened their definition from the criteria for autistic disorder to include cognitive abnormalities similar to those found in autism, then both twins were affected in 82% of the MZ twin pairs, but in only 10% of the DZ twin pairs. However, genetic inheritance cannot be the only necessary factor to produce autism because the probability of a diagnosis of autistic disorder for MZ twin pairs is not 100%. Researchers have also noted a correlation between autism and brain injury at or after birth. Among identical twins in which only one of each twin pair was autistic, the autistic twin was more likely to have experienced some type of brain damage at or shortly after birth than the unaffected twin (Folstein & Rutter, 1977).

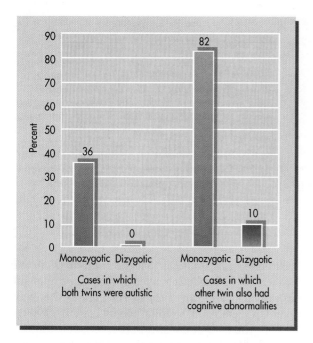

Figure 15-6 Twin studies have been used to study the influence of hereditary factors in autistic disorder. As these results show, in twin pairs where one of the twins meets the criteria for autism, there is a much greater chance among monozygotic twins that both twins will have autistic disorder than among dizygotic twins. This difference is even greater when cases were included in which the other twin had, if not autistic disorder, then at least some cognitive abnormalities.

SOURCE: Adapted from Folstein & Rutter (1978), p. 226.

Questions of heredity in autism are currently being investigated with molecular genetic methods, which can go beyond twin studies by investigating specific gene locations on particular chromosomes. One possible gene location has been found on chromosome no. 7 (International Molecular Genetics Study of Autism Consortium, 1998). However, as with other molecular genetic studies, different studies have not been in agreement about specific gene locations. Until several researchers obtain the same or similar results, it will not be clear which genes are important. However, it is likely that the problem is a complex one because it is probable that autism is related not to one gene but to several genes that each act independently but in combination increase vulnerability to autism (M. Rutter, 1999).

If families have an autistic child, the chances that another child born into the family will also be autistic are about 3 to 6 per 100 (Ritvo et al., 1989). Although this probability is much lower than the probability found for MZ twin pairs, it is much higher than that found in the general population. Thus the increased risk for siblings not only suggests a genetic factor but also strengthens the argument that several independent genes must be inherited together to cause the disorder. If each parent contributes one or more genes associated with vulnerability

to autism and three or four genes must be inherited to cause autism, it is relatively unlikely that all the genes will be inherited by an autistic child's sibling. However, it is also unlikely for the sibling to inherit none of these genes. This means that most siblings as well as parents of an autistic child are likely to have some genes that contribute to autism but in themselves are not enough to produce the disorder. As a result, each family member may have some behavioral characteristics found in autism but not in a strong enough form to meet the criteria for the disorder (Folstein, 1999). This prediction is supported by studies of relatives of autistic individuals. The relatives show an increased tendency to have unusual personality traits, especially shyness and aloofness, and very circumscribed or narrow interests (M. Rutter, 2000). These social deficits are milder than those found in autism but echo some of the autistic characteristics. Language problems alone were not more frequent among family members, but language problems accompanied by social deficits were found more often than in the general population. The following description of Mr. A presents a good example of someone who shows some of the characteristics of autism often seen in relatives of people with autistic disorder despite the fact that he is a reasonably well-functioning and successful professional.

Mr. A is a 35-year-old college professor of engineering. He spends most of his free time reading. He has been treated for anxiety and depression, including one hospitalization. Mr. A describes himself as very organized and a careful planner. . . . A colleague in his department notes that he spends more time than any other professor she knows in preparing lectures.

Mr. A is most comfortable with routine in his life. He says he would be happy if he could have a life with no surprises. He requests that his courses be scheduled at the same time each semester. . . . His wife says he protests when asked to drop off a letter on the way to work because it disrupts his routine. He prefers to use a certain bowl for his breakfast, tends to have the same thing for breakfast each day, and gets upset when his wife changes his toothbrush, saying that it takes him months to get used to using a new one. He has always been uncomfortable socially. He says he spent more time with books than people in his childhood. He doesn't see the point in "chit chat" or "small talk." He prefers there be a purpose to conversations. . . . He has a set of rules for different types of interactions (e.g., teacher-student) and when the roles are clearly defined he knows which rules to follow. Otherwise he is very uncomfortable. (Piven, 1999, p. 302)

Studies of relatives of those with autism are based on the idea that any genetic liability for autistic disorder of these nonautistic parents or other family members may be expressed in behaviors that are similar in quality, but milder, than the characteristics common in autism. Of course researchers who look for unusual behaviors in the parents and family members of autistic children need to take into account the possibility that any such characteristics in the parents' behavior and personalities may be a consequence of having a child with a severe disorder such as autism. One way to discount this factor is to use as a control a group of parents who also have children with a serious disorder, but one that presumably results from different genetic causes. An example of this approach was a study of the personality and language characteristics in parents who had more than one autistic child, as compared to those of parents of children with another type of disorder that causes mental retardation, Down syndrome (Piven et al., 1997). Results of this comparison demonstrated that parents of autistic children showed milder forms of several characteristics associated with autism, while parents of Down syndrome children did not. Personality and behavior characteristics found in the parents of the autistic children, as compared to the parents of the Down syndrome children, included higher rates of rigidity in behavior and thinking, aloofness, hypersensitivity to criticism, and anxiety. These parents also were more likely than the Down syndrome parents to have speech and other language deficits and to be less socially outgoing and have more limited friendships. Because these characteristics, though much less extreme than the behaviors found in autistic disorder, were generally similar in type, the findings support the idea of an autistic spectrum that is discussed at the end of this section on pervasive developmental disorders.

Autistic Disorder Versus Childhood Schizophrenia Although autistic disorder is now considered to be a developmental disorder, it was originally thought of as a psychosis similar to or the same as schizophrenia occurring in childhood. Some instances of autistic disorder were probably diagnosed as childhood schizophrenia in the past. **Childhood schizophrenia** rarely occurs until at least age 7 or 8, whereas autistic disorder begins much earlier. Like schizophrenia in adulthood, childhood schizophrenia includes hallucinations and/or delusions and seems to involve similarities in brain anatomy to those found in adult schizophrenia (Frazier et al., 1996). Although it is not clear whether schizophrenia that occurs before age 15 has the same outcome as schizophrenia in adulthood, research suggests that the disorder called schizophrenia in adults may begin in childhood. There are also enough differences between the DSM-IV definitions of autistic disorder and schizophrenia to suggest that autistic disorder and schizophrenia in children can be clearly distinguished. Table 15-4 highlights some of the differences between autistic disorder and childhood schizophrenia.

Treatment of Autistic Disorder Although many different treatments have been claimed to have a dramatic impact on children with autism, a review of available research makes it clear that there is little evidence of any cure for autism, although some structured programs—especially if begun very early in a child's life—can significantly enhance later functioning (Howlin, 1997). Children who begin receiving some kind of intervention between the ages of 2 and 4 make better progress than those who get similar help when they are older. To be successful, the interventions must be intensive (at least 15 hours per week), last 6 months or more, and utilize a high ratio of adults to children. In general, successful programs provide clear guidelines on what the parents can do to help, assist them to value their child as a person, and provide more attention and encouragement for parents than is typical in parents' interactions with professionals. Although it is important to avoid giving the parents false hopes, at the same time successful programs encourage parents to have reasonably high expectations about their child's ultimate capabilities.

Treatment for autistic disorder is usually directed at improving the life of the autistic person by helping to reduce problem behaviors and increase skills. These limited goals are appropriate because at present no cure for autism exists and fewer than 5% of those who receive this diagnosis will become normally functioning adults. The majority of people with autistic disorder live most of their adult lives under some type of custodial care or in institutions. Behavioral training and medication, often used jointly, are currently the most common treatment approaches.

Although in general the outcome in autistic disorder is not terribly positive, it has improved over time. Figure 15-7 compares the adult outcome for those with autistic disorder as shown in studies done before and after 1980. The differences in outcome between these two time periods may be related to both better treatments and to an increased emphasis on providing care outside of custodial institutions. For any particular individual several factors predict later outcome. The most positive outcomes are achieved by children who:

- By age 5 or 6 develop at least simple communicative language.
- Score in at least the mildly retarded range on nonverbal ability tests.
- Have additional skills or interests that make it easier for them to find a niche (e.g., special competencies in math, music, or computing).

Many questions about the most effective treatment approach have not been answered. These include understanding which of the aspects of the treatment are crucial for change, the comparative roles of parents and professionals, whether different approaches are best for different subgroups of children, and so on.

Behavioral Training Intensive behavioral training has been used extensively to reduce the behavioral symptoms of

Table 15–4		
Differences Between Autistic Disorder and Childhood Schizophrenia		
	Autistic Disorder	Childhood Schizophrenia
Age at onset	Before 30 months	Late childhood to adolescence
Incidence	2 to 5 per 10,000	Not known; possibly more rare than autistic disorder
Sex ratio (M:F)	3:1 or 4:1	Nearly equal; slightly more males
Family history of schizophrenia	Probably not	Greater than average
Socioeconomic status of family	Above average	Below average
Behavioral characteristics	Fails to develop relationships; poor social interaction skills; stereotyped speech; need for sameness; language disturbance; muteness; no hallucinations or delusions	Interacts socially to a greater degree than in autistic disorder; hallucinations and/or delusions are present
Level of intelligence	Majority in retarded range, IQ frequently between 35 and 50; markedly uneven in cognitive skills	Usually within normal range; relatively even in cognitive skills

autism and to help children with autistic disorder learn social skills. For some autistic children, particularly those who are only mildly retarded or of average or above-average intelligence, this approach can be very useful. Behavior modification procedures may be helpful in establishing desired behaviors and eliminating behaviors that create problems.

The behavioral modification techniques of *shaping* (gradually increasing response requirements), *prompting*, and *discrimination training* (learning when to make a response and when it is not appropriate), along with unambiguous instructions and positive reinforcement for desired performance, can be useful with young children who have

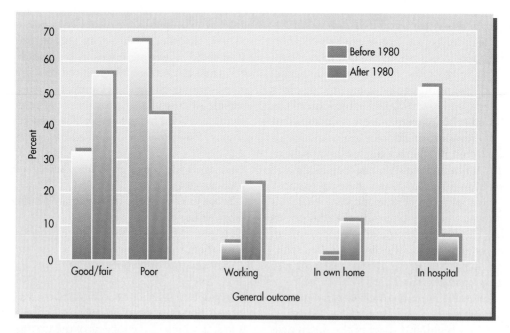

Figure 15–7 A summary of the results of many studies shows several aspects of the long-term outcome for those with autistic disorder. The differences in outcome before and after 1980 may be related both to better treatments and to the emphasis on providing care outside of custodial institutions that was part of the widespread deinstitutionalization movement that gathered momentum in the mid-1960s.

Source: Adapted from Howlin (1997), p. 56.

autistic disorder. For example, with these techniques a child might be taught to sit in a chair upon request as follows:

1. The therapist sits on a chair with the child standing (facing the therapist) between the adult's legs to reduce the possibility of the child's escaping from the situation. A helper holds a chair in place directly behind the child.
2. The therapist tells the child to sit, and if he or she fails to do so, the therapist gently pushes the child backward so there is no choice but to sit.
3. The child is then rewarded with a favorite food, applause, or some other thing the child is known to like.

This sequence is repeated almost continuously for up to 2 hours. Eventually, less prompting is required and the child sits for longer periods of time. Parents are trained to work with the child in similar exercises when the teacher is not present. Figure 15-8 shows two aspects of behavioral training: prompting and reinforcement.

Such methods can be successful with at least some children with autistic disorder. In a well-known study carried out by Ivar Lovaas and his co-workers at the University of California at Los Angeles, preschool-age autistic children were treated for 40 hours a week or more by teachers and parents trained by these teachers over a period of more than 2 years (Lovaas, 1987). The training and involvement of the parents was an important aspect of the program. The intervention included several aspects: reducing self-stimulatory behavior, teaching imitation behavior, and later emphasizing such skills as expression of feelings, observational learning, and preliminary reading and writing skills. The children in the intervention group gained about 20 IQ points on average over the 2-year period and were able to move to a normal kindergarten program. Half

of them passed successfully into a regular first-grade class. Comparable children who had been in a control group showed no change in IQ scores, and only one child in the control group was able to go into a regular school program. A later follow-up when the children were an average of 13 years old showed that the mean IQ of the intensively treated children was 85, as compared with a mean IQ of 55 in the control group (McEachin et al., 1993). A number of other measures used at the follow-up also showed that the experimental group was functioning at a much higher level than the control group. The researchers described 40% of the children in the experimental group as "indistinguishable from their normal peers." In contrast, all but one child in the control group were still in special schools.

In order to answer the question of whether such a program needed to be so time-intensive, the same program was used with another group of children with autistic disorder, but they were given the intervention for only 10 hours each week. Results from this limited intervention were no better than those for the control group. Figure 15-9 shows some results from this study. Thus, it seems that a successful training program must include intensive and extended contact.

Some researchers have questioned whether these results gave an accurate picture of the children's improvement (Mesibov, 1993; Mundy, 1993). They point out that many of the skills needed for normal functioning were not measured in the study. For example, social interaction, conceptual abilities, social communication, mood disturbances, and obsessional and ritualistic behavior—all of which are important problems in autistic disorder—were not assessed. People who do not have difficulties in these areas will be severely handicapped even if they are participating in a regular school program. The authors of the

(a)

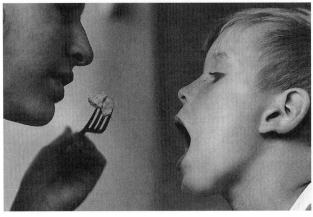

(b)

Figure 15-8 Behaviorally based training is effective in teaching basic skills to children severely affected by autistic disorder. As part of a special intensive learning program, one therapist (a) is hand-prompting a mute child to make the "wh" sound while another therapist (b) is using food as a reinforcer to encourage a child to make eye contact.

Figure 15-9   Results of a study comparing the effects of an intensive behavioral therapy intervention during the preschool period with a 10-hour-per-week intervention of a similar type and also with a control group. The results show a clear difference in school placement when these children reached second grade. The 10-hour-per-week intervention did not seem to produce better results than the control condition.

SOURCE: Data from Lovaas (1987). © 1987 by the American Psychological Association. Reprinted by permission of the author.

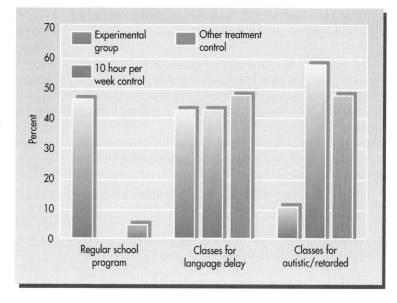

study themselves point out some concerns about the intervention program, especially the fact that the intensity of the therapy makes it very difficult for this program to be widely used (Lovaas, 1993). However, the results clearly show the power of behavioral interventions in working with those who have autistic disorder.

Despite the controversy over whether the intensive behavioral methods first used by Lovaas can produce large gains for children with autism, behavioral treatment can be useful in discouraging behaviors in young children with autism that will be viewed as unacceptable as they grow older. For example, a young child had what appeared to be a harmless obsession with watching the clothes move as washing machines went through their cycles (Howlin, 1998). This obsession seemed so benign that friends and neighbors were happy to encourage him to come in to see their machines in action. However, by the time he was 17 the obsession had become so strong that he was in constant trouble with the police because of breaking into others' property to watch the washing cycles in their machines. There is a danger that if rituals and obsessions common to autism are not brought under control when they first develop, they may steadily escalate and interfere with many other activities.

Another more common example of the use of behavioral methods is to help parents deal with the rigid behavior patterns of autistic children. If the child begins to scream or have a tantrum whenever there is a change in home routine or when the parents take a different route to the store, the parents may always give in to the child's demands because of a fear that their resistance will damage the child. However, if they let these controlling behaviors persist, parents may eventually find themselves

trapped in a set of routines that prevent the family from functioning effectively. To minimize the impact of the child's social, communicative, and obsessional problems in later life, parents need help in identifying these potential problems and the encouragement to deal with them consistently and firmly. Probably the most important skills for parents to focus on are simple communication strategies, even for children who are slow in learning to talk or who never develop speech.

In addition to teaching adaptive behaviors and skills, behavioral training can be used with children who are severely retarded to decrease the self-injurious behavior that is common in autism. Most autistic children have severe tantrums, and these may be accompanied by behaviors such as striking their heads with their fists up to thousands of times an hour if they are not restrained. It appeared to researchers that the behavior was not gratifying in itself but was being used to escape or avoid demands, and they thought that one way to approach this problem was to help children use appropriate alternative behaviors (Lovaas, 1989). Self-injury and other types of undesirable behaviors such as tantrums and aggressive behavior can often be significantly reduced if the child can learn more effective communication strategies (Durand & Carr, 1991).

Medication   Although thus far no consistently safe and effective drugs have been found, medication—especially antidepressant, antipsychotic, stimulant, and anticonvulsant drugs—is often used in treating autistic disorder (Rutter, 1999). Because the physiological abnormalities in autism have not been clearly identified, medication is not intended to treat the disorder directly. Instead the goal of medication use is to reduce some of the symptoms that interfere with behavioral and educational skills training and make it difficult for children with autism to live in a family setting. One exception to the role of medication in autism is the use of anticonvulsant drugs. Anticonvulsive medication may help to prevent the negative short- and long-term effects of frequent epileptic seizures for children and adults with autism who develop these.

In general, then, medication is frequently used to treat symptoms of autism despite the lack of knowledge of how it might affect the autistic process. Although some treatments can be helpful in improving particular aspects of behavior, many unscientifically proven treatments are also tried by parents as they search for new approaches that might help their children. One example is the administration of large doses of vitamins. A survey of parents who had children with autistic disorder found that more than half of the children were being treated with some form of drug or special vitamin treatment (Aman et al., 1995). According to the survey results, parents were most satisfied with the effects of antidepressant and stimulant medications that are aimed at difficult behaviors rather than at the basic problems of autism as well as with the results of anticonvulsant medications that prevent seizures.

Other Treatments Many other types of therapy are used in the treatment of autistic disorder. *Auditory integration training* is targeted at reducing the jumble of confusing stimuli that children with autistic disorder seem to experience. *Sensory integration training* is designed to improve sensory awareness and responsiveness by exposing the child to a variety of stimuli such as swings, balls, and objects with unusual textures. The deep pressure therapy advocated by Temple Grandin and described earlier in Box 15-1 is a part of sensory integration training. Some therapies focus directly on facilitating communication by training the child to use a keyboard or letter board. Still other therapies focus on exercise as a way of controlling what are thought to be the high anxiety levels of children with autistic disorder. Daily Life Therapy, developed by the Higashi schools in Japan and now also used in the United States, includes exercise in its program. Educational programs such as the TEACCH program are widely used in schools in the United States and Europe (Schopler et al., 1995). The TEACCH program emphasizes visual cues and individually based teaching as well as cognitive and behavioral approaches. Although some success is claimed for each of these programs, little objective and scientific evidence supports their use.

High Functioning Autism About 30% of those diagnosed with autism (nearly nine times as many autistic males as females) have **high-functioning autism;** that is, they have IQs above 70 and some of this group are clearly above average in intelligence. Even in the high IQ group, however, certain difficulties in language, cognition, and social skills remain so that the profile of the individual's skills

is much more uneven than would be expected for someone of his or her intelligence level. For example, the language behavior of those in the high-functioning autism group was characterized by inappropriate utterances especially in social situations, impaired ability to communicate what they intended, and stereotyped language. Some of these difficulties were described by Temple Grandin in Box 15-1. People with high-functioning autism may also appear to be aloof and rigid, are upset with changes in their routine or in their environment, and are often anxious. These characteristics may explain why primary and middle school children with high-functioning autism reported greater feelings of loneliness than the control group of normally developing children of the same ages and intellectual level (Bauminger & Kasari, 2000). These high-functioning children with autism reported that their friendships were of poorer quality than the normal developing children in the study did. Although each of the children in the high-functioning autistic group reported having at least one friend, they thought the friendships offered less companionship, security, and help than the children in the control group.

Asperger's Disorder

This disorder was first described by German psychiatrist Hans Asperger in 1944, but it was not included as an official diagnosis until the publication of DSM-IV in 1994. In many ways it seems similar to Kanner's description of autism that was developed independently but at about the same time. Like autistic disorder, the prominent characteristics of **Asperger's disorder** include severe and long-lasting impairments in social interaction and restricted and repetitive patterns of behavior and interests. However, unlike autistic disorder, there are no significant delays in language or cognitive development, curiosity about the environment in childhood, or self-help skills and other adaptive behavior aside from social interaction. Table 15-5 gives the diagnostic criteria for Asperger's disorder. There is still some dispute as to whether Asperger's disorder should be considered a separate type of disorder. Some researchers believe it represents the high-intelligence-end of a spectrum that includes autistic disorder as a more severe type (Bonus & Assion, 1997), but others point to research findings that demonstrate that Asperger's disorder and high-functioning autism can be differentiated in terms of their profile of deficits, even though some of these deficits may be shared (Siegel, 1998).

What little is known suggests that Asperger's disorder may occur in about 1 of 1,000 individuals and that it seems to be more frequent in men than in women. For every woman who is given this diagnosis, 9 men also received it. Unlike autistic disorder, which can usually be diagnosed

Table 15-5

Diagnostic Criteria for Asperger's Disorder

1. Impairment in the quality of social interaction, as shown by at least two of the following:
   a. Marked impairment in the use of multiple nonverbal behaviors customarily used to regulate social interaction, such as eye-to-eye gaze, facial expressions, body postures, and gestures.
   b. Failure to develop peer interactions that are appropriate for the person's developmental level.
   c. Lack of behaviors that indicate spontaneous seeking to share interests, enjoyment, or achievements with other people.
   d. Lack of social or emotional reciprocity.
2. Restricted repetitive and stereotyped patterns of behavior, interests and activities, as shown by at least one of the following:
   a. Preoccupation with one or more stereotyped patterns of interest that is of abnormal intensity or focus.
   b. Seemingly inflexible adherence to specific, nonfunctional routines or rituals.
   c. Stereotyped and repetitive motor movements such as hand or finger flapping.
   d. Persistent preoccupation with parts of objects.
3. Clinically significant impairment in social, occupational, or other important areas of functioning.
4. No clinically significant delay in cognitive development or in the development of age-appropriate self-help skills, adaptive behavior (with the exception of social interaction), or curiosity about the environment in childhood.
5. The criteria are not met for another specific pervasive developmental disorder or for schizophrenia.

Source: Adapted from DSM-IV.

by about 30 months of age, Asperger's disorder is usually not suspected or diagnosed until a child is of school age (Gillberg et al., 1996).

Characteristics of Asperger's Disorder Young children with Asperger's disorder usually enjoy physical affection from their parents, in contrast to the aversion children with autistic disorder show for cuddling and close body contact. Although the criteria for Asperger's disorder specify that there is no general delay in language, some children with this disorder have problems with the social use of language. Their speech appears to others to be stilted and repetitive, and is filled with unusual words that most children recognize in reading but seldom incorporate into their conversation. Children with Asperger's disorder do significantly better on verbal sections of intelligence tests than on performance sections, in contrast to children with autistic disorder whose performance test scores are generally higher than their verbal scores (Ehlers et al., 1997). Other characteristics of Asperger's disorder include motor clumsiness, as shown by an awkward way of walking, a seeming lack of coordination in throwing and catching balls, and trouble in childhood with fine motor movements such as tying shoelaces and buttoning clothes. One feature that children with Asperger's disorder and children with autism often share is high levels of anxiety.

Biological Factors In many disorders, differences in brain structure or function between diagnostic and control groups are often studied using brain scanning techniques.

One study of some individuals with Asperger's disorder assessed the brain activity shown on a CT scan when the subjects were given tasks related to their ability to attribute mental states to others, a deficit in what is termed theory of mind that is also characteristic of autism (Happe et al., 1996). The researchers found that an area of the left prefrontal cortex that was active when normal volunteers did one of these tasks was not active in those with Asperger's disorder who did the same task, even though normal activity was found in brain areas surrounding this location. Although this suggests that the functioning of this small and circumscribed area of the brain may be related to this disorder, much more research will be necessary to determine whether this finding can be replicated with other groups of children with Asperger's disorder.

Just as the genetic basis of autistic disorder has been studied by investigating whether parents of children with the disorder may show some mild forms of the symptoms, the same approach has been applied in researching Asperger's disorder. As the researchers predicted in one study of parents of children with Asperger's disorder, these parents showed deficits in two specific areas when their performance was compared to a control group of parents whose children did not have the disorder (Baron-Cohen & Hammer, 1997). The parents of children with Asperger's disorder were less able to understand the feelings of others when interpreting photographs that included only a portion of another's face, a deficit that might be expected if they were deficient in theory of mind. They also did significantly better than parents in the control group on an embedded-figure task that involved identifying figures hidden in a puzzlelike format. Above average performance on the embedded-figure task is similar to past research findings of performance of autistic children and their parents. Both of these groups also typically solve embedded-figure tasks more quickly than children and parents in control groups.

Childhood Disintegrative Disorder

Childhood disintegrative disorder begins after an initial period of normal development in which children show age-appropriate social relationships and adaptive behavioral and communication skills. The first signs of the disorder, which may appear either gradually or abruptly, begin between ages 3 and 4. Childhood disintegrative disorder is thought to be extremely rare, probably occurring only once in every million births. It is believed to be more frequent in boys than in girls. Table 15-6 lists the characteristics of childhood disintegrative disorder.

Like Asperger's disorder (and Rett's disorder to be discussed next) childhood disintegrative disorder is a newly included category in DSM-IV even though the characteristics of the disorder were first described early in the twentieth century. Initial testing of DSM-IV categories in clinical settings justified the inclusion of this disorder as a separate category because it could be clearly differentiated from autism. Although childhood disintegrative disorder seems to be associated with a deterioration of the central nervous system, the reasons for this deterioration are not known.

Rett's Disorder

Rett's disorder is a progressive disorder in which the symptoms usually begin at about 5 months of age. Before that time the infant appears to be developing normally. At about that time what had been the normal growth of the infant's head gradually slows so that the head becomes much smaller than normal for the child's age, a condition called **microcephaly.** During this period, children who are affected by Rett's disorder also lose various functions and skills they had acquired earlier, such as early language development and the ability to relate socially to other people. They also develop a peculiar walk, lose the ability to move their hands in a purposeful way, and develop stereotypic hand behaviors such as hand-wringing or hand-clapping or tapping. Table 15-7 lists the diagnostic criteria for Rett's disorder. In the next stage of the disorder children lose the verbal and motor skills that they had acquired earlier and may experience seizures. At this point evidence of mental retardation appears. This stage of the disorder may last up to 1 year and is followed by a period when some brief or relatively longer lasting improvement

---

Table 15-6

Diagnostic Criteria for Childhood Disintegrative Disorder

1. Apparently normal development for at least the first 2 years after birth, as shown by age-appropriate verbal and nonverbal communication, social relationships, play, and adaptive behavior.
2. Before age 10, the clinically significant loss of previously acquired skills in at least two of the following:
   a. Expressive or receptive language.
   b. Social skills or adaptive behavior.
   c. Bowel or bladder control.
   d. Play.
   e. Motor skills.
3. Abnormalities of functioning in at least two of the following:
   a. Impairment in the quality of social interaction.
   b. Impairment in the quality of spoken language, such as delay or lack of spoken language, inability to initiate or sustain a conversation, stereotyped and repetitive use of language, or lack of a variety of make-believe play.
   c. Restricted, repetitive, and stereotyped patterns of behavior, interests, and activities.
4. The behaviors cannot be better accounted for by another specific pervasive developmental disorder or by schizophrenia.

Source: Adapted from DSM-IV.

Table 15-7

Diagnostic Criteria for Rett's Disorder

1. All of the following:
   a. Seemingly normal development before and after birth.
   b. Seemingly normal psychomotor development for the first 5 months after birth.
   c. Normal head circumference at birth.
2. Onset of all of the following after an initial period of normal development:
   a. Slowing of head growth between the ages of 5 months and 48 months.
   b. Loss of previously acquired purposeful hand skills between the ages of 5 months and 30 months, followed by the development of stereotyped movements such as hand-wringing or hand washing.
   c. Loss of social interaction behavior early in the course of these changes (although some social interaction develops later).
   d. Poorly coordinated walk and movements of the body.
   e. Severely impaired language development, both in speaking and understanding, and severe psychomotor retardation.

Source: Adapted from DSM-IV.

in both communication and movement seems to take place. Despite this improvement the child does not return to a normal level of functioning and eventually deterioration again occurs, this time permanently. At this stage children with Rett's disorder usually become severely disabled and wheelchair bound.

Like Asperger's disorder, Rett's disorder was first introduced into the DSM in DSM-IV. It is unusual in that it typically affects only girls. Only a very few cases in which it affected boys have been reported (M. Campbell & Shay, 1995). It is also quite rare, with an estimated prevalence of 1 in 10,000 to 15,000 female children, or even less. Rett's disorder has been found worldwide, although it appears to be more frequent in small and isolated areas where marriages typically take place within a biologically related group rather than to outsiders. Over time, such a pattern of marriage limits the diversity of genes available and increases the chances of marriage between people who have recessive genes that may increase vulnerability to hereditary disorder.

Because the disorder typically affects only girls, the X-chromosome has been the most intensively investigated, but so far no gene locations have been identified. Attempts to find causes related to metabolism, hormonal function, and damage to chromosomes have all been in vain. It appears that Rett's disorder is the result of some kind of defect in the programmed normal growth of the nervous system that occurs during the early years of life. Both scanning techniques used with live patients and autopsies of those who have died show abnormalities in the development of the dendrites especially in some areas of the brain cortex (Belichenko et al., 1997). Because Rett's disorder occurs relatively infrequently, research studies are difficult to carry out.

There is no specific treatment for Rett's disorder. In some cases, antipsychotic drugs have been useful in decreasing stereotyped behavior, but these must be used cautiously because they may increase the frequency of seizures. Most children with this disorder become severely mentally retarded; for that reason, behavioral methods often seem the most appropriate therapeutic approach. For instance, behavioral methods have been used on an experimental basis to help children with Rett's disorder increase their ability to communicate which of two objects they preferred (Sigafoos et al., 1996). Although intensive work with the children produced a limited improvement, it was too small to be of practical significance in improving their functioning level.

Is There an Autistic Spectrum

The term *pervasive developmental disorders* is a relatively new one, and whether or not it is a useful overall category is not yet known. Some researchers believe that most of these disorders are part of an **autistic disorder spectrum** similar in concept to the schizophrenic spectrum disorders discussed in Chapter 11. The spectrum view assumes that the different disorders within the pervasive developmental disorder group stem from the same general causes and simply represent different manifestations of the same basic disorder. According to this view, individuals who have a heavier loading of the different genes that contribute to autistic disorder will be diagnosed with one of the more serious variants of the disorder. The experiencing of extreme or frequent stressful life events may also interact with gene loadings to produce more severe symptoms than the gene loadings themselves might predict. The autistic disorder spectrum is broader than the DSM-IV pervasive developmental disorder category and can include any level of ability from profound learning disability to average or even superior cognitive skills in areas that are not directly affected by the impairments common to the spectrum. If all the disorders thought to be part of the autistic spectrum (childhood autism, Asperger's disorder, disintegrative disorder, and atypical disorders that include autistic behaviors and Rett's disorder) are included, 4 or 5 of every 1,000 children may be affected by some form of autistic spectrum disorder (Gillberg & Wing, 1999).

Lorna Wing, one of the chief proponents of the autistic spectrum disorder view, argues that the disorders grouped within it have in common impairments in social interaction, communication, and imagination as well as a narrow repetitive pattern of behavior (Wing, 1997). Wing distinguishes four major groups within this spectrum. The *aloof* group includes children who seem indifferent to others, especially their peers. This group is most similar to the DSM-IV description of autism in which the children have a delay in beginning to speak and show the characteristics of autistic speech that includes stereotyped repetition of words or phrases. The *passive* group includes children who do not socially interact spontaneously but passively accept approaches of others. They have impairments in both communication and imagination. Unlike the passive group, the *active but odd* group makes social advances but these are unusual and do not fit the situation. Their conversation in these social interactions is repetitive and inappropriate, quite different from that of normally developing children. The fourth group are the *loners*, people of at least average ability and fluent speech who prefer to be alone, lack empathy, and are concerned primarily with their own interests. They may learn the roles of social interaction by memorizing them and often find school very stressful because of its demands for social conformity. Some individuals in this group go on to successful careers especially in areas where a great deal of social interaction is not required.

Mental Retardation

Epidemiological studies show that about 1 in every 100 individuals in the United States is mentally retarded (Bregman & Harris, 1995). The central characteristic of **mental retardation** is subaverage intellectual functioning that began before age 18 and exists together with significant limitations in adaptive functioning. These limitations may occur in two or more of a wide variety of basic skill areas listed in Table 15-8. Table 15-8 also provides the criteria that must be met for a diagnosis of mental retardation. It is important to note that these criteria include more than intelligence test scores; they also emphasize adaptive behavior. Thus people who score in the retarded range on intelligence tests but otherwise get along adequately at home, school, or work are not classified as mentally retarded. Those who have poor levels of adaptive behavior but who do not score poorly on intelligence tests also are not given a diagnosis of mental retardation.

DSM-IV divides mental retardation into four levels—*mild, moderate, severe,* and *profound*—on the basis of intelligence test scores. Table 15-9 shows these categories and the percentage of all retarded individuals who are classified into each. The table makes clear that most mentally retarded individuals are classified as mildly mentally retarded and that as the severity of the retardation increases, the percentage of cases decreases. Table 15-9 also includes some characteristics typical of individuals at each level of retardation, as well as brief examples.

Table 15–8

Diagnostic Criteria for Mental Retardation

To be classified as mentally retarded, a person must meet each of the following three criteria:

1. Significantly below-average intellectual functioning, with an IQ of approximately 70 or below on an individually administered IQ test or, for infants, a clinically based judgment of significantly below-average intellectual functioning.
2. Deficits or impairments in the person's effectiveness in meeting the standards expected for his or her age by his or her cultural group in at least two of the following areas: communication, self-care, home living, social/interpersonal skills, use of community resources, self-direction, functional academic skills, work, leisure, health, and safety.
3. These criteria must both be met before the age of 18 years.

Source: Adapted from DSM-IV.

If a diagnosis of mental retardation is made, it is entered on Axis II of DSM-IV. (Axis II is also used for the diagnosis of personality disorder.) If the person also meets the criteria for a DSM-IV diagnosis of some psychopathology—for instance, autism, bipolar disorder, or schizophrenia—that diagnosis is made on DSM-IV Axis I. The use of Axis II for mental retardation makes it more likely that both this condition and any Axis I disorder that is present will be included in the diagnosis. Although it was formerly believed that people who were mentally retarded did not have Axis I disorders as well, we now know that the two types of conditions frequently exist together.

Historical Views of Mental Retardation

Until the 1870s, what was then called *mental deficiency* was regarded as a homogeneous category, and no distinctions were made among the various forms that mental retardation might take. Then, in 1877, John Down published a monograph called *The Mongolian Type of Idiocy* in which he described what today we call *Down syndrome.* Although Down was incorrect in his ideas about what causes Down syndrome, which he thought represented regression to earlier racial forms, his work suggested that mental retardation was a condition that could have many causes, and interest grew in its classification. Two other scientists whose research and writings spurred interest in mental retardation were Gregor Mendel and Alfred Binet.

Mendel's work on the principles of genetic inheritance in plants led to interest in the effects of genetics in human beings, including the idea that mental retardation might be genetically transmitted. One of the consequences of this idea was the **eugenics movement,** which focused on improving the genetic stock of the population by sterilizing individuals who were mentally retarded in order to prevent them from passing along their genetic inheritance. Leaders in the eugenics movement also supported the idea that retarded individuals should be institutionalized because of what was believed to be their tendency toward delinquency and "loose sexual behavior."

In France, Alfred Binet and others worked to develop psychometric tests that could select students for specialized educational programs. The Binet tests became very popular in the United States because they were considered to be objective and scientific. However, rather than being used primarily to determine appropriate educational programs as Binet had intended, they were used to classify people by intelligence level. For example, in the United States the Binet tests were used to classify those incarcerated in prisons and correctional institutions to determine whether or not they were *mentally defective.* Many people imprisoned for drug abuse, prostitution, and other antisocial behaviors had low scores on the Binet test. The

Table 15-9			
Levels of Mental Retardation and Their Characteristics			
Level of Mental Retardation	IQ From Intelligence Tests	Percentage of Total Group	Characteristics
Mild	IQ level from 50–55 to approximately 70	85%	▪ Often not distinguishable from other children until school age. ▪ May attain 5th- to 6th-grade level of academic skills. ▪ Socioculturally may have few difficulties, but may have problems in coping and may need some supervision in living.
Moderate	IQ level from 35–40 to 50–55	10%	▪ Variable cognitive ability profiles; often higher spatial than language skills. ▪ Language development variable. ▪ May attain 2nd-grade level of academic skills.
Severe	IQ level from 20–25 to 35–40	3%–4%	▪ May participate in carefully structured work such as a sheltered workshop. ▪ Living independently usually is not possible. ▪ Significant number have marked motor deficits and deficits in communicative speech. ▪ May learn to read "survival" words such as "Stop," "Men," and "Women." ▪ Need protective living situation. May need nursing care, depending on associated problems.
Profound	IQ level from below 20 or 25	1%–2%	▪ Language and comprehension limited to simple requests and commands. ▪ Ability to take part in simple household tasks variable. ▪ Majority have brain abnormality and specific neurological disorder. ▪ Autisticlike behavior common.

interpretation of their scores to indicate a "mental defect" did not take into account the economic and social factors that might have contributed to their low scores but instead created in the public mind a strong connection between antisocial behavior and low intelligence. This very negative view of mental retardation and misuse of the Binet test resulted in considerable increase in the institutionalization of those classified as mentally retarded in order to "protect society."

Finally, after World War II, parent groups began organizing to work toward changing this stereotype and providing adequate training for children who were mentally retarded or had significant learning problems. In 1963, President John F. Kennedy contributed to a reevaluation of attitudes toward mental retardation when he presented to Congress a task force report on mental retardation and mental illness and called for a national program to help prevent mental retardation. Since that time, work in the field of genetics has helped to identify the causes of some disorders associated with mental retardation and has led to new interest in different causes of retardation.

Because of earlier attitudes about mental retardation, much of the terminology used in the field has reflected the stigma associated with this status. The term *idiocy* used by Down in the title of his book is one example of this. Until relatively recently, the term *mental deficiency* has been used, but this too has a negative implication. DSM-IV uses the term *mental retardation*. Many people feel that this term is also too negative and prefer terms such as *intellectual disability* or *learning disability*. However, because DSM-IV terminology is relevant to the field of abnormal psychology and to this book, we use the term *mental retardation* throughout this chapter.

Causes of Mental Retardation

Mental retardation is a heterogeneous classification, which means that the term covers conditions with many causes. Usually these causes are grouped into two categories: those resulting from some pathological condition that has an effect on the brain and nervous system and those that are thought to be psychosocial in origin. However, this grouping is far too simple. The cognitive impairment that leads to a classification of mental retardation is often a complex interaction between a person's genetic vulnerability and environmental factors that may have an effect before, during, or after birth.

There are a variety of biologically based causes of mental retardation. These include genetic and hereditary conditions; chemicals such as alcohol, radiation, and certain drugs that affect the development of the child prior to birth; factors that affect the nutrition of the fetus, such as circulatory abnormalities in the placenta or malnutrition of the mother while pregnant; trauma during birth related to prematurity, deprivation of oxygen, or other birth problems; traumatic effects after birth, such as diseases, poisoning, or accidents; and a variety of malformations of unknown origin.

Genetically Based Disorders Genetic disorders include those caused by specific dominant genes, by specific recessive genes inherited from both parents, by gene mutations, by chromosomal abnormalities, and by still-unidentified combinations of genes from both parents that bring the person over the threshold from normality to pathology. If the disorder is caused by a dominant gene, only one gene of that particular gene pair needs to be affected to produce the disorder. In contrast, in recessive disorders, both members of the gene pair must be affected.

The number of known dominant genes that cause severe mental retardation is small because people who are affected by these disorders do not usually have children. Often a mutation, or spontaneous variation in a gene, seems to be responsible for the first case of a dominant gene disorder recognized in a family. In many of these disorders, the symptoms do not become apparent immediately after birth.

Tuberous sclerosis is an example of a dominant gene disorder. In addition to severe mental retardation and seizures, this condition produces small fibrous tumors on the skin, often beside the nose, as well as internal tumors and other skin abnormalities. The seizures typical of this disorder may not begin until the child is 3, and the tumors may not appear until several years later. In some mild cases the tumors appear but retardation may be minimal or absent.

About two-thirds of children born with tuberous sclerosis are classified as mentally retarded. This retardation is progressive and increases as the child grows older. This may reflect additional deterioration of the nervous system because virtually all children in this mentally retarded group are affected by seizures as they grow older. Children with tuberous sclerosis in the nonretarded group are somewhat less likely to have seizures. There may be a genetic link between autism and tuberous sclerosis because autism is much more frequent among those who have tuberous sclerosis than among the general population (Fombonne, 1999).

Gene Mutation Often the first instance of a disorder that occurs in a family is the result of gene mutation rather than direct inheritance. **Phenylketonuria (PKU),** a metabolic disorder produced by a mutation of a gene that results in the impaired function of a specific enzyme, phenylalanine hydroxylase, is one example. This impairment results in the inability of the person's body to oxidize the chemical phenylalanine, which therefore accumulates in the body. If this accumulation is allowed to continue, severe mental retardation may result. Very few untreated PKU victims have IQs above 50. The only effective way to reduce this excess of phenylalanine in the blood is through a special low-protein diet. If a child is born with this disorder and treatment involving a restrictive diet is started early, most of these changes can be prevented. The sooner treatment is begun the better the chances that mental retardation will not result. Children who received treatment at an early age are usually in the normal range on intelligence tests and neurological examinations (Cabalska et al., 1996). However, even if treatment is not started until later in life, some improvement can result (Fitzgerald et al., 2000).

Because early treatment lessens the likelihood of mental retardation, PKU testing of newborn babies is required in many parts of the United States, as well as in other countries. An example of someone who was successfully treated by special diet therapy is shown in Figure 15-10. The majority of treatment centers in the United States and Canada recommend lifelong adherence to the restrictive protein diet necessary to control phenylalanine levels, although some researchers believe that somewhat higher phenylalanine levels are acceptable in older adults (Cerone et al., 1999).

Before treatment for PKU was developed, most people who had this disorder did not have children. Now that early dietary intervention for PKU has decreased the likelihood of retardation, childbirth is more likely for women with PKU. It has been estimated that because of newborn screening and dietary treatment there are now approximately 10,000 people who have developed normally neurologically but who have PKU (Moats et al., 2000). Unless women in this group continue to follow a special low-protein diet designed to control their blood phenylalanine level both before and during pregnancy, their children are at risk for mental retardation, congenital heart disease, facial abnormalities, and microcephaly (abnormally small skull size associated with retardation). These mental retardation and other problems do not come from inheritance of the mutated gene that causes PKU, but instead are the result of the chemical environment within the mother's uterus during the pregnancy. Even if pregnant

Figure 15-10 Jackie Gnecchi (left) is a member of the first generation of young people with PKU who have reached adulthood without cognitive damage that results from untreated PKU. She was born in 1970, soon after screening of newborn infants became standard practice in many hospitals in the United States. Because her PKU was identified early, she received a special diet from the time she was 2 weeks old. She is seen here talking with a social worker at the University of Washington Child Development and Mental Retardation Center who was part of the treatment team that worked with Jackie and her parents.

women have not controlled their diets prior to pregnancy, the earlier they begin to do so after pregnancy occurs, the fewer negative consequences for the child will result. For example, in one longitudinal study in which mothers' phenylalanine levels were monitored throughout pregnancy, researchers found that the likelihood of abnormalities in the newborn infants were related to how early in the pregnancy the level of phenylalanine in the mothers' blood was brought down to the recommended range (Rouse et al., 1997). Results from this and other studies have led to the recommendation that women with PKU who wish to become pregnant should begin a low-phenylalanine diet prior to conception if they have not continued it from childhood. This diet will help to reduce their blood-phenylalanine level and if the diet is continued throughout pregnancy the chances of birth defects in their children will be decreased. Even good control throughout this period does not entirely remove the risk to the child, but it greatly reduces it. For instance, in a group of pregnant women who had adhered to the recommended diet, two-thirds of their children were unaffected by the mother's PKU (Mowat et al., 1999). However, in the group of women who did not follow the diet during pregnancy, all their children were negatively affected by the prenatal chemical conditions in their mother's uterus.

Fragile X Syndrome

Many kinds of mental retardation are related to genes on the X chromosome. **Fragile X syndrome** gets its name from the fact that the X chromosome of the affected individual will show a fragile spot when it is grown in a laboratory culture. This malformation is shown in Figure 15-11. The X chromosome is part of the so-called sex chromosome pair that determines the sex of the individual. Women have two X chromosomes in this pair, and men have one X and one Y chromosome. If only one

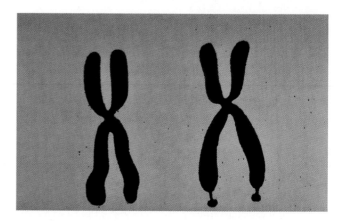

Figure 15-11 The fragile X chromosome on the right shows the malformation that gave fragile X syndrome its name. Compare the long arms of this chromosome with those of the normal X chromosome on the left.

of the mother's X chromosomes is affected by fragile X syndrome, the mother may not be retarded herself but may be a carrier who can transmit the chromosomal abnormality to her children. Because one of the sex chromosome pair comes from each parent, if a man has fragile X syndrome it must have been transmitted through his mother, since his Y chromosome must come from his father. Because girls have two X chromosomes, one from each parent, female children are less likely to be affected by fragile X syndrome. Not everyone whose X chromosome shows the fragile X syndrome is equally affected. One-fifth of the men and two-thirds of the women who carry a fragile X chromosome show no obvious signs of the disorder. These people who carry the fragile X gene but show no visible or behavioral effects carry what is called a premutation gene (Mazzocco, 2000). When the gene is passed to one of their children, it may mutate, which means that one set of gene components repeats

Figure 15-12 This young boy is mentally retarded as a result of fragile X syndrome. His long face, prominent forehead, and large ears are typical of the physical appearance that results from this disorder.

Figure 15-13 Enrichment activities early in life may help some children with Down syndrome achieve far more than might be expected. Jason Kingsley (left) and Mitchell Levitz (right) are well-functioning young men who in 1994 wrote a book, *Count Us In*, describing their experiences as people with Down syndrome. They and their parents attribute their triumphs over Down syndrome to their early exposure to mentally stimulating activities and exercise.

SOURCE: *The New York Times*, March 20, 1994, p. 13.

many times and the gene stretches in length. This increase continues from generation to generation. Once the number of repeats exceeds a threshold amount, the disease and its accompanying mental retardation result (Kooy et al., 2000).

Fragile X syndrome is the most common form of inherited mental retardation; it is estimated to have a prevalence of 1 in 1,000 for men and 1 in 2,000 for women. These affected individuals are likely to have mental retardation and various specific learning problems, impairments in language, and various other disorders such as ADHD (discussed in Chapter 14) and pervasive developmental disorder (discussed earlier in this chapter). For men in particular, fragile X syndrome may be accompanied by autisticlike behaviors, outbursts of aggressive behavior, and distinctive physical features. These physical features include longer-than-usual faces, large ears, and large testes in adulthood. Figure 15-12 shows facial features typical in young adults with fragile X syndrome.

Because the gene responsible for fragile X syndrome has been identified, it is possible through the use of DNA testing to identify people who may be carriers of the premutated gene but do not show clear signs of its effects. Using this technique it has been estimated that 1 of 600 women carry this gene. This knowledge is important because it

makes possible better genetic counseling as well as more precise prenatal diagnosis.

Down Syndrome

Down syndrome, named for the physician who first described this condition and whose work was mentioned earlier in this section, is a chromosomal abnormality involving the 21st chromosome pair. Down syndrome occurs about once in 1,000 births and is the most common individual cause of mental retardation. Although sometimes Down syndrome produces severe mental retardation, most persons with this disorder have mild or moderate mental retardation and a few may be classified in the normal range of intelligence (see Figure 15-13).

The characteristic physical features of Down syndrome make this disorder easy to recognize. These include a flat face and a small nose, eyes that appear to slant upward because of small folds of skin at the inside corners, slightly protruding lips and tongue, small ears, and small square hands with short fingers and a curved fifth finger. Children with Down syndrome tend to be shorter than average, with especially short arms and legs in proportion to their bodies. They also are likely to be somewhat obese in childhood and adolescence and have congenital heart abnormalities.

Three types of chromosomal abnormalities may cause Down syndrome. The most common form, which accounts for 80% to 90% of the cases, is the result of what is known as **nondisjunction.** This means that an extra chromosome exists at what is usually the site of chromosome pair no. 21 so there are three rather than two no. 21 chromosomes at this location. The probability of nondisjunction increases with the mother's age and is dramatically greater for mothers age 40 and older: the risk is less than 1 per 1,000 for pregnant women in their early 20s but increases to 18 per 1,000 after age 40. This form of Down syndrome is also called **trisomy 21.** Figure 15-14 shows the chromosome configuration for a female with trisomy 21. Trisomy in two other chromosome pairs, pair no. 13 and pair no. 18, may also produce mental retardation, but these conditions are much more rare than Down syndrome. For all these trisomies, however, once parents have conceived a child with a trisomy-based disorder, they face an increased risk of a trisomy in later pregnancies.

Two other kinds of processes can produce Down syndrome by affecting chromosome pair no 21. The first, called **translocation,** occurs when material from the 21st chromosome pair breaks off and fuses to another chromosome pair. In contrast to the trisomy process, transloca-

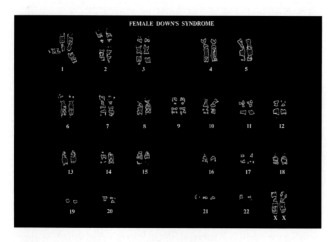

Figure 15-14 The most common cause of Down syndrome, accounting for 80% to 90% of the cases, is the presence of three no. 21 chromosomes rather than the normal chromosome pair at that location. This karyotype shows the chromosomes from a person with this type of Down syndrome.

tion is thought be an inherited pattern in at least a third of all cases in which it occurs. Translocations are found most often in mothers under 30 years of age, a reversal of the age pattern associated with the nondisjunction process in which the risk increases with age. The second alternative process that creates Down syndrome is known as mosaicism. **Mosaicism** is the result of an accident that occurs sometime during the development of the embryo and produces a child with a mixed chromosomal makeup in which some cells are affected and others have a normal configuration. Depending on how early in the developmental process this accident occurs, the level of mental retardation can vary from a normal range of functioning to severe impairment. For example, one study reported a 35-year-old man with signs of mild Down syndrome who performed well throughout his school career and reached university educational level (De Azevedo-Moreira et al., 2000). Tests showed mosaic trisomy 21 in only 3% of his cells. Although this man also had experienced early and continued intervention programs, it is likely that the small percent of cells affected was most important in his good outcome.

Intellectual Development Patterns As infants, children who have Down syndrome explore their environment in the same ways that other children do. During the preschool period, their development, although slower than average, seems to follow a generally normal pattern, although they show less exploratory behavior and are not as vigorous in investigating their surroundings. Through childhood and adolescence, Down syndrome children have poorer muscle tone and coordination than other children. As a result, they are less physically active, carry out tasks more slowly, and have poorer balance than other children do. As Down syndrome children reach school age, their delays in physical and cognitive development begin to cause more problems. Deficits in short-term memory often mean that information overload occurs and as a result poor school performance follows. Auditory memory is especially poor, making the child less able to learn from verbal information.

Common problems of children with Down syndrome that can be major hindrances in pursuing a normal life are inability to comprehend instructions, to pay attention to several things at once, and to express clearly what they are thinking or what they need. Even older Down syndrome children often use a kind of telegraphic speech in which connecting words like *and* or *but* and other classes of words such as prepositions and adverbs are missing. In general, children with Down syndrome seem especially weak in higher-level abstraction and reasoning and in auditory perception.

Programs to provide increased stimulation to very young Down syndrome children have attempted to modify the typical downward trend of development. Intervention often begins a few days after birth with physical therapy programs designed to increase muscle tone. Programs for young children provide a variety of activities to help develop both physical and cognitive skills. Parents are trained to take part in activities to intellectually stimulate their children. Parent involvement seems particularly important in improving the motor development of children who have less initial intellectual deficit (Torres & Buceta, 1998). Growth in communication skills, skills of daily living, and social skills can be increased by both the quality of the family environment and of parent-child interactions (Hauser-Cram et al., 1999).

Because Down syndrome children often learn better by seeing material rather than hearing it, some researchers have tried using computers to improve their language abilities. In one project, teenagers improved their language communication by using special computers that read back what they wrote. One boy, who before the project could only describe his father, who had recently died, by saying "Dad. Talk. Down. Boom" was able to write: "My father and I went to his office. We would eat lunch and drink Diet 7-Up. I love you, Dad" (Kolata, 1987). Such efforts cannot cure retardation, but can help people function more effectively. As a result of research on cognitive development in children with Down syndrome, teachers and parents can use educational interventions that are tailored to their intellectual strengths and weaknesses.

Aging in Down Syndrome People with Down syndrome typically begin to experience the physiological changes of aging relatively early in life. A decline in their cognitive abilities usually occurs by age 40 when many of them begin to experience deterioration in memory, problem solving, language skills, and general abilities in self-care (Holland, 2000). This decline in cognitive ability may be associated with the high risk of early dementia and Alzheimer's disease found in those with Down syndrome (Lai et al., 1999). The beginning signs of dementia also are likely to begin around age 40, much earlier than they might be found in people who did not have Down syndrome, and after age 50 about half of those with Down syndrome can be expected to develop dementia.

Autopsy studies have shown that the same type of senile plaques and neurofibrillary tangles that occur in the brains of those with Alzheimer's disease begin to occur before age 30 in people with Down syndrome. Figure 15-15 illustrates these brain lesions. Autopsies of Down syndrome patients who died after age 40 showed these indications of Alzheimer's disease in 95% of the cases. The regions of the brain most affected are also similar in Down syndrome and in patients with Alzheimer's disease. The hippocampus, an area of the brain that plays an important role in learning and memory, is especially likely to be affected by these changes. Positron emission tomography (PT) scans of living patients also support a relationship

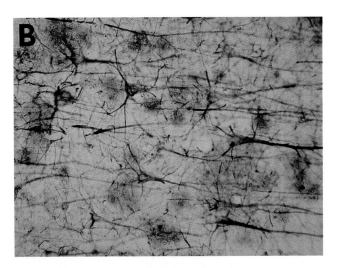

Figure 15-15 This micrograph of a tissue sample from the brain of a young Down syndrome patient shows that, although some normal neurons (blue) are still present, there are also a considerable number of senile plaques (brown) that are typical of those found in patients with Alzheimer's disease. It is thought that premature aging of the brain is one result of Down syndrome. Almost all adults who have Down syndrome and who live to be at least 30 years old develop the senile plaques and tangles that are characteristic of Alzheimer patients who are usually much older.

SOURCE: Courtesy of Drs. Brian Cummings and Patrick Kesslak, Institute for Brain Aging and Dementia, University of California, Irvine.

between Alzheimer's disease and Down syndrome because in both disorders there is a reduction in glucose metabolism in similar brain areas (Bregman & Harris, 1995). Although genetic research is being carried out to identify the regions of chromosome no. 21 that play a role in the abnormalities found in both Down syndrome and Alzheimer's disease, so far no gene locations have been consistently identified.

Prenatal Screening for Down Syndrome A large proportion of Down syndrome cases can be identified in prenatal diagnosis through the use of **amniocentesis.** In this technique amniotic fluid is extracted from the sac protecting the fetus and tested for genetic and chromosomal defects. Amniocentesis is now routinely offered to pregnant women in the United States if they are aged 35 or older. This age was chosen because the risk of having a child with Down syndrome increases only gradually until about the age of 30 but after that point the increase is increasingly rapid. The risk of having a child with Down syndrome is 1 in 1,300 for a 25-year-old woman; at age 35 the risk is 1 in 365; and at the age of 45 the risk increases to 1 in 30 (Newberger, 2000). The amniocentesis process itself slightly increases the chances of miscarrying the fetus, so it is typically not used if the risk for Down syndrome or other genetic disorders is considered low. Women under 35 are usually tested first using what is called a *triple screen* that measures maternal levels of certain proteins and hormones that normally vary with the stage of pregnancy. Amniocentesis is suggested only if the test is positive. The difficulty with this triple screen is that it detects only about 60% of the cases of trisomy 21 and also produces some false positive results, so it is not accurate enough to use with a high-risk group.

The results of the amniocentesis are used to counsel parents regarding the risk of Down syndrome as well as some other genetically related problems in the pregnancy. Given this knowledge, the prospective parents can decide to terminate the pregnancy, or they can prepare themselves for the birth of a child with a specific problem. Because amniocentesis cannot be performed until about the fourth month of pregnancy and the cells must be cultured for 2 weeks after the test, the pregnancy will be well advanced before the result is known. This means that if the tests show a defect in the fetus, the parents may face an especially difficult decision over continuing the pregnancy. However, in the majority of cases, the amniocentesis procedure reveals that the fetus does not have the defect, and the parents are spared months of needless anxiety.

The Fetal Environment and Mental Retardation

Sometimes disorders associated with mental retardation come about, not because of heredity, but because of conditions in the environment in which the fetus or unborn child lives prior to birth. A mother with PKU who does not control her diet may not pass on that heredity to her child, but the chemical condition in her uterus during the pregnancy may cause a variety of birth defects including mental retardation. Prenatal factors that have been linked to mental retardation include maternal infections and chronic conditions, blood incompatibilities between mother and child, chemicals in the fetal environment, radiation, malnutrition, factors associated with the age of the mother, and stress the mother may be experiencing. Each of these factors can have an important effect on development of the brain and nervous system and on later intellectual functioning. These factors often have their greatest effects if the problem occurs early in the pregnancy, particularly in the first few weeks after conception.

The placental sac surrounding the unborn infant acts as a barrier that prevents many infections from being transferred from the mother to the fetus, but a number of viruses may cross this barrier. About half of all fetuses whose mothers contract the **rubella virus** (German measles) in the first 3 months of pregnancy are also infected. The virus destroys cells and may interfere with the fetal blood supply. Approximately half of all children born to mothers who had rubella early in pregnancy are retarded. Those who are not retarded often have learning disabilities. Congenital heart disease, deafness, and other problems are also common results of rubella during the first 6 months of

pregnancy. Retardation can also result if the mother has a bacterial infection such as syphilis or a chronic viral illness such as herpes or human immunodeficiency virus (HIV). Children who are infected with HIV before birth have a high probability of developing seizures, brain atrophy, and mental retardation within their first year of life.

Some chronic medical conditions of the mother may also cause retardation in the fetus. Hypertension (high blood pressure) and diabetes are examples of chronic disorders that may interfere with fetal nutrition and lead to brain damage. Both of these conditions can be treated during pregnancy if they are diagnosed early. Sometimes biochemical substances in the fetus cause the mother to develop an immune system response to the baby. The antibodies her body produces may damage fetal tissues in much the same way that people sometimes reject organ transplants. An example of this antibody response is an incompatibility between mother and child in the Rh blood factor.

Drugs taken by the mother during pregnancy can also pass through the placenta to the fetus. Even mild tranquilizers such as Librium are associated with an increase in the rate of serious fetal malformations. In addition, chemicals in the air, food, and water may affect the child's development before birth. One example of a chemical factor in the fetal environment that may cause retardation is alcohol. The amount of cognitive impairment is related to the level of alcohol use, so that even children born of mothers who used alcohol at social drinking levels during pregnancy may have some cognitive and behavioral problems that persist throughout their lives (Olson et al., 1997). Some research suggests that even before ovulation, the potential hazard of exposure of human eggs to alcohol may be as great as that of exposure to alcohol of either a recently fertilized embryo or an unborn infant during the course of pregnancy (M. H. Kaufman, 1997). One result of alcohol use in pregnancy is *fetal alcohol syndrome*.

Fetal Alcohol Syndrome

The effects of maternal alcohol use on the unborn child were first recognized when a specific set of facial characteristics was noted in some children of women who were heavy alcohol users during pregnancy. These facial deformities, which identify **fetal alcohol syndrome (FAS),** include small eyes; drooping eyelids; a short, upturned nose with a low bridge; flat cheeks; a thin upper lip; low-set ears; bulging forehead; and unusually large distance between the nose and mouth. The face of the child shown at several ages in Figure 15-16 illustrates many of these characteristics. FAS is associated with mental retardation as well as retarded growth, a variety of physical defects and deformities, and abnormalities in brain functioning and behavior. It is estimated that more than 4% of the children of heavy drinkers have FAS (Abel, 1995).

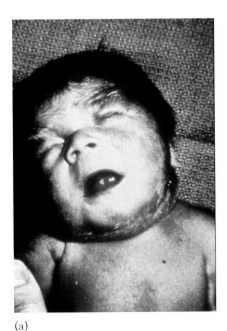
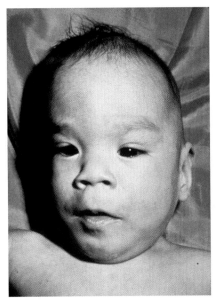
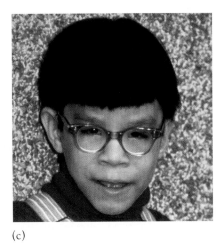

(a) (b) (c)

Figure 15-16 People affected by fetal alcohol syndrome generally have a number of characteristic facial features including tissues obscuring the inner corner of the eyes, a short nose and low nasal bridge, an underdeveloped groove in the center of the upper lip between the nose and lip edge, and a thin upper lip. This boy, pictured at three different ages in these photos, shows all these facial features. He was diagnosed with fetal alcohol syndrome at birth. Despite having spent all his life in an excellent foster home and attending a superior school program, his IQ has remained in the 40 to 45 range.

SOURCE: Dr. Ann Streissguth, The University of Washington.

Children affected with FAS face many problems because of their cognitive difficulties. Michael Dorris, who had adopted a boy who was later diagnosed with FAS, described his son Adam's life in this way:

> He did not learn from his mistakes, inconvenient or maddening as they often were. He clung to established order with tenacity, refusing to adapt to fluctuations in his external environment. If he had successfully worn a T-shirt and no coat in the summer, then by golly, he'd slip from the house in identical clothing in January, even though the temperature was well below zero. When he learned a new skill, he would more often than not focus on some extraneous detail within the overall structure, and drop anchor. The whole constellation of actions, the essential mixed with the accidental, would become entrenched, and no single part could be selectively jettisoned. There were no gradations, no interchangeable parts to a pattern once he embraced it. Right clothes = T-shirt. Period. . . .
>
> But his greatest problem, the day-in, day-out liability with which it was hardest for the world to cope, was his lack of a particular kind of imagination. He could not, cannot, project himself into the future. "If I do x, then y (good or bad) will follow." His estimation of consequences was so hazy that it translated into an approach to action so conservative that it appeared to be stubborn. He existed in the present tense, with occasional reference to past precedent. . . .
>
> And when he did venture forth, sometimes tentatively, sometimes with the brashness of having nothing to lose, he made wrong choices, saw only part of the picture, was either too literal or too casual in his interpretation of detail. If left to monitor his own medication, he might take all three of a day's doses at once in order to "get them all over with" or might sequester them in a drawer "so that I won't run out." He might take a dollar out of my wallet, even when he had ten of his own, "because I wanted to save mine." The question "why" has never had much meaning for Adam; the kind of cause-effect relationship it implies does not compute for him. (Dorris, 1989, pp. 200, 201)

As research on FAS has continued, it has become clear that even children who do not have the facial characteristics described earlier and whose mothers were much lighter drinkers also can have cognitive and behavioral problems associated with prenatal exposure to alcohol. These difficulties include problems in attention, information processing, and academic performance that continue through childhood and adolescence. One longitudinal study that assessed children at 4, 7, and 14 years of age showed a consistency across time in their performance on a task involving attention (Streissguth et al., 1995). For the 7- and 14-year-old children, one of the measures used was the Continuous Performance Test (CPT), described in Chapter 11. In this test the children were asked to watch as a series of stimuli were presented and to press a key whenever a particular stimulus (identified as the correct response) appeared. Both the reaction time and accuracy of performance were measured. The greater the mother's alcohol use in pregnancy, the shorter the child's reaction time and the poorer the child's correctness score, both in terms of identifying the correct stimuli and not responding to incorrect stimuli. These CPT scores also predicted teacher ratings of how well the child was able to pay attention. The more alcohol their mothers had used during pregnancy, the less able the children were, at all ages studied, to pay attention for a period of time and the more likely they were to perform poorly in school.

Exposure to alcohol prior to birth affects a number of cognitive skills. When the children in this longitudinal study were 14 years old, both their reading performance and their ability to solve arithmetic problems were negatively related to the degree of prenatal alcohol exposure (Streissguth et al., 1994). Mathematical skills and higher-order processes such as the ability to deal with abstractions seem particularly affected. These patterns of deficit may reflect either diffuse brain damage or an accumulation over time of learning deficits that interfere with complex problem solving.

Problems During and After Birth

Vulnerability to mental retardation can also be increased by environmental factors that occur during or after birth. A relatively large proportion of individuals who are mentally retarded—from 10% to 20%—have experienced some trauma or accident during the birth process. Another 5% to 10% of those who are mentally retarded experience some trauma or other condition after birth that leads to mental retardation.

Factors that can increase the probability of retardation through difficulties at birth include prematurity, low birth weight, lack of oxygen during the birth process, and too-rapid progress through the birth canal, which can result in bleeding and tearing of brain tissue. Neurological complications related to prematurity have become an increasingly important cause of cognitive impairment because of the development of medical technologies that allow more at-risk infants to survive.

Damage to the nervous system after birth can also result in mental retardation. The damage can be caused by infections such as encephalitis, extreme malnutrition, blows to the head, tumors, deprivation of oxygen (e.g., in near-drowning accidents or entrapment in a discarded refrigerator or other container), and poisons from the environment such as lead from flaking paint.

Psychosocial Disadvantage

Some people whose intelligence test scores place them in the mildly retarded range also have parents with IQs of a similar level. In many instances no specific factor can be identified as a cause of their retardation. It is often suggested that the intellectual level of these individuals merely reflects their heredity and represents one tail of the naturally occurring bell-shaped curve, or normal distribution, that represents intelligence. Before coming to this conclusion, it is important to realize that a very large proportion of those who score in the mildly retarded range have a **psychosocial disadvantage,** that is, they come from families of low socioeconomic status and limited educational and cultural opportunities. Because most intelligence test scores reflect both biological factors (including genetic endowment) and exposure to a stimulating environment and educational opportunities, it is difficult to assign a particular cause to the level of measured intelligence in this group. Heredity provides a range of possibilities for a developing child but the child's level of achievement within that range is the result of many factors, including aspects of the environment. Research studies have shown that 30% to 50% of variation in intelligence test scores can be attributed to environmental influences (Zigler et al., 1984). Early intervention and psychosocial enrichment programs such as those discussed in the following sections are often focused on children who may be disadvantaged, both because of heredity and because of the environments in which they grow up.

Types of Prevention and Intervention in Mental Retardation

Efforts to prevent mental retardation and to help those affected by it live up to their full potential take many forms. These include *primary prevention* (preventing the disorder from occurring in the first place), *secondary prevention* (treating the problem so that its effects are minimized), and *tertiary prevention* (helping the individual make the best use of his or her capabilities). These types of prevention are discussed further in chapter 17.

Primary Prevention Some types of mental retardation can be prevented from occurring. One outstanding example of such a **primary prevention** program is the campaign to inform women that using alcohol in pregnancy is potentially harmful to the developing child. Public health campaigns and warning signs on alcoholic beverages and in places where alcohol is served help to accomplish this. Figure 15-17 illustrates one such warning.

Another type of public health effort is aimed at reducing the chances of brain damage to children after birth. An example is the effort to reduce children's exposure to lead, which may have a negative effect on their intellectual functioning by requiring the use of unleaded gasoline and by removing lead as an ingredient of most paints, as well as by making parents aware of the dangers to children of chipping paint in older houses.

Probably the measure that has the most widespread effect in preventing mental retardation is educating people

Figure 15-17 Warnings about the effects of alcohol use by pregnant women are required to be displayed prominently on the labels of alcoholic beverages as well as in bars and restaurants that serve alcohol. This closeup of the label on one bottle illustrates the required warning about the use of alcohol during pregnancy, as well as other risks of alcohol consumption.

about the importance of prenatal care for pregnant women. Through prenatal care, physicians and other health care workers can monitor pregnant women to detect the development of such conditions as high blood pressure and a special type of diabetes called gestational diabetes that occurs only during pregnancy. If these disorders are not brought under control they can result in damage to the developing child. Mothers who already have disorders such as diabetes or PKU can be helped to prevent damage to their unborn children by advice about the need for a strict diet during the pregnancy. Good prenatal care can also help prevent premature births, which are associated with a greater risk of retardation.

Another type of primary prevention associated with prenatal care was made possible by the increasing ability to detect genetically based and developmental problems during pregnancy through the use of amniocentesis and ultrasound scanning. Information from these procedures allows the parents and the physician to discuss potential problems and to explore the desirability of terminating the pregnancy. One example of the use of amniocentesis is to detect Down syndrome. Although therapeutic abortion is legally accepted, it may present a dilemma for prospective parents who oppose the procedure for moral or

ethical reasons. However, the increasing use of prenatal screening makes it possible for these parents to make an informed choice about continuing the pregnancy.

New techniques in genetic research have been able to identify gene locations related to a variety of disorders. Eventually gene locations involved in other disorders currently believed to have a genetic factor will be identified. This genetic information can help prospective parents evaluate their risk of conceiving a child with mental retardation or another disorder so that, after consulting with a genetic counselor, they can make an informed decision about initiating or terminating a pregnancy.

Secondary Prevention Sometimes children are born with a disorder that may cause mental retardation if it is not treated. **Secondary prevention** efforts focus on providing that treatment. Some of these conditions may cause mental retardation very quickly after birth unless they are identified and treated. For example, PKU screening is now done routinely for newborn infants so that if the problem exists, dietary control can begin at once to prevent damage to the central nervous system.

Tertiary Prevention **Tertiary prevention** is aimed at improving an already existing situation. Intervention programs have been developed for specific disorders, particularly Down syndrome and autism, as a way of increasing children's skills early in the developmental cycle. Other examples are school-based educational programs, community living programs, and vocational and social skills training programs. An additional type of tertiary prevention is an increased recognition of the importance of treatment of psychological and family relationship problems for people who are mentally retarded.

Early Intervention Programs

Early intervention programs are tertiary prevention programs typically carried out with children who are judged to be at high risk for mild retardation as a result of an impoverished environment or parents whose IQ falls in the mildly retarded range.

Children at Psychosocial Risk Children who come from economically deprived homes, especially those who have mothers whose intelligence test scores are in the mildly retarded range, are particularly at risk for mental retardation. Many psychologists and educators maintain that for these children, the important question is not how to "cure" mild mental retardation, but rather how to encourage these children to fully utilize the intelligence they possess—in other words, to provide them with an enriched environment through early intervention (Zigler, 1995). Research has shown that intervention in infancy and early childhood, combined with health care and social programs aimed at families, can decrease the proportion of children whose test scores later fall into the mildly retarded group. A study named Project CARE (Wasik et al., 1990) was designed to compare the effectiveness of early home-based interventions in which mothers were taught how to provide developmental stimulation for their infants and toddlers with that of an intervention that took place in a special center with a trained staff but which was supplemented by home visits. There was also an untreated control group. Each child participating in the study was randomly assigned to one of these groups at birth. Children in all three groups received free health care and social services. The IQs of the children in the study were tested a number of times up through age 6. Children in the group that attended a child development center 5 days a week consistently tested much higher in intellectual performance than the children in either of the other groups. Researchers were disappointed to find that the average IQ of children in the home-based treatment group did not differ from that in the control group.

In another study conducted by the same research group, the Infant Health and Development Program (1990; Ramey & Ramey, 1992), the children participating were infants who were born prematurely and were of low birth weight (less than 5 1/2 pounds). Low-birth-weight children have a higher-than-average risk of poor subsequent development, including intellectual performance. This large study took place at eight child development centers across the United States and included more than 1,000 children and their families. Children who attended these centers were compared with control groups. Because many of the children were of low birth weight, attendance at the

centers did not begin until they were 12 months old. The majority of the families in the study had very low incomes and poor educational resources, although they represented a much wider range of incomes than the families in the Project CARE study. Because the number of subjects was large, the researchers were able to divide them into four different intelligence test score groups. Figure 15-18 shows that in both the intervention and the control groups, children were most likely to have test scores in the borderline or mentally retarded range when they were 3 years old if their mothers had IQ scores below 70. In both groups there was a downward trend in intelligence test scores as the children became older, although this was more marked in the control than in the intervention group. An earlier study of similar groups demonstrated that despite this downward IQ score trend, large differences still existed between the educational intervention group and the control group when the children were 12 years old (Ramey & Ramey, 1992). In this earlier study, almost half of the children in the control group had IQs of less than 85, but only about one-eighth of those in the early education intervention group scored this low. One-quarter of the intervention group had repeated at least one school grade by the time they were 12, as compared to more than half of the control group. These results show that intensive early intervention can have lasting effects on the intelligence test scores of children.

School–Based Programs Because public policy has changed its focus from institutionalizing retarded individuals to helping them live as independently as possible in the community, school programs for the mentally retarded have also changed greatly. Laws requiring free

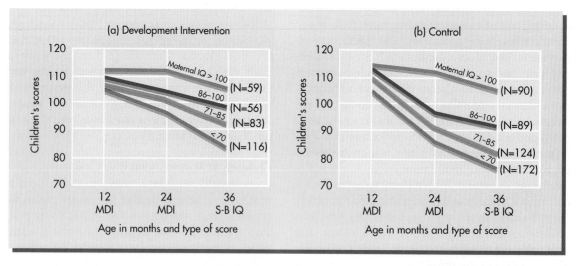

Figure 15-18 These figures compare intelligence test scores at 12, 24, and 36 months for children who took part in the Infant Health and Development Program. Within the intervention group (a) and the control group (b), the children were further divided into groups based on their mother's IQ score. Although all groups' average IQ scores declined with age, those in the intervention group declined less. Children whose mothers tested lower in IQ were helped most by the intervention. (MDI = Bayley Mental Development Index; S-B IQ = Stanford-Binet IQ.)

Source: Adapted from Ramey & Ramey (1992), p. 342.

public education for all children, including those who are retarded, date from the 1970s. However, the passage of the Individuals with Disabilities Education Act in 1990 strengthened this effort by requiring that the education of all disabled children, including mentally retarded children, be as much like that of normal children as possible. Because of these laws and a series of court decisions, school districts are obligated to provide training, not only for mildly mentally retarded children, but also for severely and profoundly retarded children and children with all types of physical disabilities. Although there is still not much evidence about whether these programs significantly improve severely and profoundly retarded children's performance, they do seem to make institutionalization of these children less likely.

For many years before these legal decisions, children who were mildly retarded were placed in special classes for slow learners. Children were often assigned to these classes on the basis of scores on group-administered intelligence tests. The use of paper and pencil test scores as a way of assigning children to special education was unfair to handicapped and minority children and children in lower socioeconomic classes because the test items were heavily biased in favor of information and skills that children of the middle-class majority group were likely to have acquired. Critics pointed out that as a result of this testing approach a disproportionately large number of minority children were assigned to these special slow-learner classes. Their teachers generally had low expectations for the children's learning and as a result the children made little educational progress. Assignment to these classes also stigmatized the children in the view of others and in their view of themselves. Another problem with these special education classes was that many of the children assigned to them were not retarded but instead had one or more of a variety of learning, communication, and motor skills disorders that required special teaching methods that the classes did not provide. Box 15-2 discusses these disorders, the growing use of this diagnostic category, and the controversy that surrounds their inclusion in DSM-IV.

As a result of the legal requirement that each child receive the "least restrictive" placement possible, pressure has grown for placement in regular classes, not only of children who may be at a psychosocial disadvantage or who have a specific learning disability, but also of children who have mental retardation as a result of biologically based disorders such as those discussed earlier in this chapter. These children may spend part of the school day in a regular classroom and the remaining time in classes where they can receive specialized help. This flexibility is important because despite their benefits, regular school classes may be unable to provide the special services and individual attention these children may need.

One concern that parents and teachers have about placing mentally retarded children in regular classes is the degree to which they will be socially accepted. Attitude studies have shown that schoolchildren of all ages are less likely to say they will befriend a hypothetical child labeled mentally retarded than a child without such a label (Rothlisberg et al., 1994). However, when 12-year-old children in a mainstreamed class were studied using sociometric ratings in which each class member identified preferred and nonpreferred classmates, the researchers found that some of the mentally retarded students were well accepted by the other students (Siperstein & Leffert, 1997). Children who were accepted had better social skills and different friendship strategies than those who were not considered part of the whole group. The accepted children attempted to play a submissive role in friendships and were not as likely to use positive outgoing strategies in making contact with other students. Those who were not accepted tended to be assertive in making contacts with other children. This pattern is different than that typically found in classes that do not contain retarded children. In those classes, children who were more friendly, assertive, and outgoing were also rated as more socially accepted. Such findings show that although social skills play an important role in acceptance, successful social approaches are somewhat different for mentally retarded and nonretarded individuals.

Vocational and Social Skills Training Programs

Although learning how to do a job is important, getting and keeping a job requires a combination of basic living skills including personal hygiene and awareness that it is important to come to work regularly and to finish jobs that are assigned. Basic social skills that include getting along with others and knowing how to avoid being exploited by others are also important. Job preparation for people with mental retardation usually includes training in all these skills. In a study of the relationship between social competence and the overall success of mentally retarded employees in a competitive workplace, the employee behaviors that most predicted the competence and quality-of-work ratings by supervisors and co-workers were polite social interaction and task completion (Butterworth & Strauch, 1994).

Behavioral methods are most often used in this training (Huang & Cuvo, 1997). For instance, in one training program several problem situations were modeled so prospective workers could learn to identify problem behaviors and appropriate ways of dealing with such situations:

You come to work in the morning and can't find one of the materials you need to do your job (for example, the napkins). Inappropriate solution: walk around, talking to co-workers; sit at table and do nothing. Appropriate solution: request help from supervisor politely.

Research Close-up

Learning, Communication, and Motor Skills Disorders

Barriers to the acquisition or performance of specific skills can have major consequences throughout life. DSM-IV includes diagnostic categories for three major areas of these skills: *learning disorder, communication disorder,* and *motor skills disorder.* Table 15-10 lists the types of specific disorders included in each category. All these disorders begin in childhood, and learning and communication disorders are usually first recognized when related skills do not appear as expected in the normal process of child development.

Successive editions of the DSM have greatly increased the number of these disorders included, from 6 in DSM-II to 10 in DSM-IV. The authors of DSM argue that it is important to include these because the classifications will lead to more research and increased understanding of the disorders and how they may be most effectively treated. The authors also believe the existence of these increasingly specific DSM categories will alert pediatricians and family physicians to the problems so that they will identify the disorders earlier and treatment can be begun.

Not everyone is happy about the increasing number of disorders included in the DSM. In Figure 15-19, cartoonist Roz Chast satirizes the increasing number of DSM categories. Although in general the DSM-IV has been criticized for including many disorders that others believe are not mental illnesses, there has been specific controversy over the inclusion of the categories of learning, communication, and motor skills disorders. Many critics, including speech pathologists and educational therapists, have argued that these problems are not true mental disorders and so are not appropriately included in the psychiatric classification system. One of the biggest concerns critics have about learning and communications disorders is the circularity of reasoning that may have led to the diagnosis. If a child does poorly in school, he or she may be diagnosed with one of these disorders, and then that disorder becomes the reason for poor performance. To avoid this problem, it is important to measure children's intellectual abilities by individual rather than group intelligence tests, to examine their motivation and their exposure to good teaching, and to determine whether there are any adjustment or family problems that may play a role in school performance. These classifications will be useful categories only if they lead to specific appropriate remedial interventions, not if they are used merely as explanations.

The most common way to identify one of these disorders is by a discrepancy between scores on a general intelligence or IQ test and achievement tests that measure the specific skill in question. However, there is no absolute agreement on how large a discrepancy is needed to define the presence of a disorder. This vagueness in definition means that there is little agreement about many children who might be identified as having one of these disorders and as a result be eligible for special educational attention. The advantage of the use of the discrepancy approach is that it helps to differentiate children with specific disorders from those who are low school achievers in general. A good definition is important because over 2 million children in the United States are labeled as having a learning disability.

For the most part, the causes of these disorders are not known, although the increased use of the various brain scanning techniques is beginning to provide some clues. For example, MRI scans of normal and dyslexic adult readers showed that the dyslexic readers had relatively less activation in the visual cortex, the angular gyrus, and Wernicke's area of the brain but a relative overreaction around Broca's area (Shaywitz et al., 1998). (Figure 15–20

Table 15–10

Learning, Communication, and Motor Skill Disorders Included in DSM-IV

Learning disorders—academic functioning substantially below what is expected based on chronological age, measured intelligence, and age-appropriate education

- Reading disorder
- Mathematics disorder
- Disorder of written expression
- Learning disorder not otherwise specified

Communication disorders—difficulty in speech or language not explained by other causes

- Expressive language disorder
- Mixed expressive-receptive language disorder
- Phonological disorder
- Stuttering
- Communication disorder not otherwise specified

Motor skills disorder—motor coordination considerably below what would be expected from chronological age and measured intelligence and not related to another disorder

- Developmental coordination disorder

Box 15-2

Figure 15-19 Cartoonist Roz Chast has modified the old nursery rhyme that categorizes children born on each day (Monday's child is fair of face. . .) and created "A Nursery Rhyme From the American Psychiatric Society."

SOURCE: *The New Yorker,* Sept. 18, 2000, p. 156.

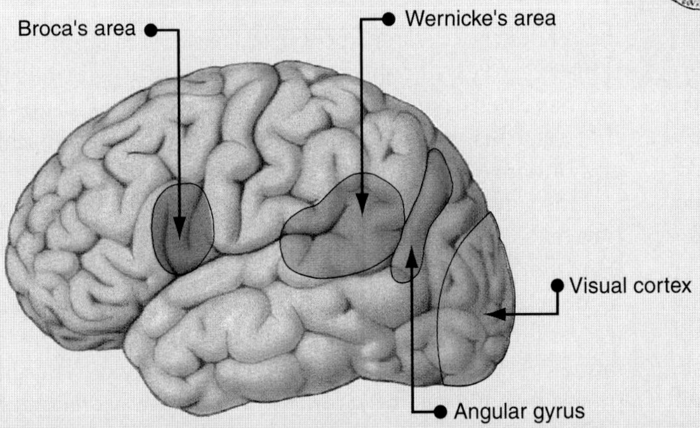

A NURSERY RHYME FROM THE AMERICAN PSYCHIATRIC SOCIETY

Broca's area • Wernicke's area • Visual cortex • Angular gyrus

Figure 15-20 Functional magnetic resonance imaging has been used to determine which brain areas differ in activity when normal and dyslexic individuals are reading (Shaywitz, et al., 1998). Several areas were less active when the dyslexic participants were reading. These include the visual cortex, which receives the visual input; the angular gyrus, which transforms this input into sound information; and Wernicke's area, which is involved in comprehension. Broca's area, which is associated with speech, was relatively more active in the dyslexic group.

shows the location of these areas.) Because a small number of participants is typically used in studies like this, caution is needed in interpreting the results. It is not only important to replicate the findings but to study children as well as adults.

Despite their unknown causes, the behaviors appear to be stable over time and the eventual outcome for children with these disorders is likely to be poor in terms of both psychological adjustment and occupational outcome. Children with learning disabilities are likely to be socially rejected by their classmates. In one study

of children in grades 4 through 6, these children were not only more likely to be socially rejected but they were also less likely to be seen as cooperative or as leaders than the other children in the class (Kuhne & Wiener, 2000). Of even greater concern, those children with learning disorders who had scored as *average* in social status at the beginning of the year were more likely than other children to change their status to *neglected* or *rejected* as the school year progressed.

The majority of students with learning disabilities (probably about 85% to

90%) have reading disability or **dyslexia** as it is commonly called (Bender, 1995). The particular types of reading problems vary greatly. Some students do not have enough basic knowledge and recognition of words. They have difficulty sounding out letters, searching their memories for similar words, and coming up with informed guesses about the meanings of novel words. They may not know common prefixes and suffixes, and they have trouble making analogies. Poor readers

continued

Research Close-up   Box 15–2

continued

also do not seem able to use contextual cues to figure out meaning. Part of their problem in using contextual cues seems to be an inability to understand the main ideas in the text. These students are likely to focus on peripheral information and minor details rather than understanding the general message the author wants to convey. Teaching specific learning strategies, such as how to summarize a paragraph and how to recognize the sounds of letters and letter combinations, can often produce great improvement in reading performance (Scruggs & Mastropieri, 1993). Sometimes reading problems may stem from perceptual problems such as an inability to copy from the chalkboard correctly or an inability to distinguish various geometric shapes, such as circles and

triangles. Other visual perception problems include seeing a visual stimulus as an assemblage of unrelated parts—for example, seeing a capital A as a set of three unrelated lines (/, –, and \)—and trouble discriminating a figure from the background. Sometimes children reverse letters, such as horizontally reversing *b* and reading "*d*," or vertically reversing *b* and reading "*p*." Such reversals are frequently made by young children, but they normally decrease with age. If they continue to occur beyond age 7 or 8, they may be the sign of a potential problem. Perceptual difficulties of this type have been attributed to neurological problems, but this assumption is largely inferred from observing the child's behavior and generalizing to what is known about brain dysfunction rather than from direct evi-

dence from scanning techniques or other tests. For this reason, caution is needed in assigning causes to these behaviors (Bender, 1995).

Those who support their inclusion in DSM-IV argue that because these disorders are associated with an increased risk of suffering or distress, it is appropriate to include them. Another reason given for their inclusion is that learning and communication disorders frequently occur together with other clinical disorders. For instance, learning disorders are likely to be associated with attention-deficit/hyperactivity disorder (ADHD), which was discussed in Chapter 14. Both learning and communication disorders also seem to make the later development of another Axis I clinical psychiatric disorder more likely (Baker & Cantwell, 1987).

You are working in the morning and the person working next to you is being very loud, talking and laughing. You are finding it hard to concentrate on your work because of the noise. Inappropriate solution: yell at co-worker to "shut up"; throw something at co-worker; insult co-worker; threaten co-worker. Appropriate solution: politely request quiet behavior; ignore co-worker. (LaGreca et al., 1983, p. 272)

The effectiveness of the modeling approach was shown by comparisons with both a coaching group and a control group. After 7 weeks on the job, only 1 of the 11 people in the modeling group had been fired as compared to half of the coaching group. In the control group, 10 had been fired and only 2 were still on the job.

Charitable organizations and other groups often subsidize sheltered workshops that provide appropriate job sites for people affected by mental retardation. These organizations usually contract with outside businesses for projects that fit with the skills of their employees. Figure 15-21 illustrates the personal supervision available in one sheltered workshop. However, even if workers are well trained in sheltered workshops they may not be able to hold jobs successfully in the open market. For example, mentally retarded adults who had participated in two sheltered workshops in Israel were followed up more than 20 years later. Only about 12% were employed in the open job market. More than half were still living with their parents, and 20% were in institutions (Katz, 1994). Such findings emphasize that, in spite of training and social support, many mentally retarded persons are not able to compete fully in the labor market.

When mentally retarded individuals are integrated into the community, they are vulnerable to personal, sexual, and financial exploitation. One source of this problem is

the tendency of retarded people to answer "yes" to all questions, regardless of content. This readiness to agree clearly can have negative consequences. For one thing, it means that retarded people are likely to agree to inappropriate and unfair requests.

One way to prevent exploitation of retarded individuals is to teach them what is expected of people and how to say "no." For example, participants in a training program for food service workers were taught how to handle their earnings and how to say "no" to people who asked to borrow money. Another problem area is sexual behavior. Training programs have taught retarded people how to recognize and escape from sexually exploitive situations. Mentally retarded individuals also need to be trained to understand what society views as appropriate sexual behavior and to avoid such acts as public masturbation and inappropriate sexual advances to others.

Recognition and Treatment of Psychological Problems

Although only a small proportion of people with mental retardation are also formally diagnosed as having emotional or behavioral disorders, epidemiological findings show that more than 40% of people with mental retardation also meet the criteria for some psychological disorder; that is, they have a dual diagnosis (Einfeld & Tonge, 1996). Some of the psychological disorders identified in mentally retarded individuals seem to be related to central nervous system damage that also plays a role in their mental retardation. This is particularly true for people who are severely retarded. If people in this group have a dual diagnosis, they are more likely to display a psychosis or

Figure 15-21 A sheltered workshop offers a place to learn job skills as well as a longer-term working environment for people who cannot compete for jobs on an equal basis.

hyperactivity and less likely to meet the criteria for a conduct disorder. Stereotyped and self-injurious behaviors are also frequently found among people who are severely retarded. In both severe and profoundly retarded groups, autism and other pervasive developmental disorders are also common. Among those in the mildly and moderately retarded groups who show no obvious nervous system damage, depression is a frequent problem. Up to 10% of mentally retarded persons have serious mood disorders, and as many as half meet the diagnostic criteria for dysthymic disorder.

About one-fourth of all mentally retarded persons have a personality disorder and up to half of all adults with mental retardation have dysfunctional personalities (Bregman & Harris, 1995). Personality characteristics frequently found in this group include overdependency, low self-image, limited levels of aspiration, and ineffective methods of problem solving (Zigler & Burack, 1989). Many of these personality characteristics become more pronounced during adolescence perhaps because social isolation and "friendship void" become more apparent at this developmental period.

Problems of social development that are more prevalent in mentally retarded adolescents than among other adolescents include temper tantrums, aggressive or destructive behavior, alcohol and drug abuse, and an increase in withdrawn behavior. These problems often appear to be related to mentally retarded adolescents' growing awareness

of the gap between their expectations for the future and their ability to be independent. Conflicts with parents over issues of independence and dating relationships are very common because of comparisons with the activities of other, nonretarded, teenagers.

In one study, adults with mental retardation who did not live in institutions were assessed for psychological and behavioral problems. Half of those tested were rated as having problems that would lead to a diagnosis on Axis I of DSM-IV in addition to the diagnosis of mental retardation on Axis II (Sturmey et al., 1996). In a study of community-based day programs for people with mental retardation, almost 40% of the participants were found to meet the criteria for a dual diagnosis although only about 12% of them had a psychiatric diagnosis in their files (Reiss, 1990). Findings such as these show not only that psychological and behavioral problems are underdiagnosed among those with mental retardation, but also that caregivers and community services need training in identifying these problems and getting appropriate therapy for them when it seems appropriate.

Psychopathology Specific to Certain Disorders Evidence is growing that people with specific developmental disorders are likely to have different probabilities of developing various kinds of psychopathology. For instance, there is some evidence that children and adults with Down syndrome have a lower overall rate of emotional and behavioral disorders than people with other forms of retardation. Children with Down syndrome are likely to form secure attachments with caregivers and are highly responsive socially. These characteristics may help prevent them from developing later psychological disorders, although mood disorders are relatively common in both adolescents and adults with Down syndrome. Children with fragile X syndrome have a high frequency of ADHD and stereotyped behavior. Compared to other retarded individuals, they have also been shown to exhibit more autisticlike behaviors and more characteristics associated with schizoid or schizotypal personality diagnosis (Kerby & Dawson, 1994). In general, children and adults with mental retardation do not receive adequate help for the psychological problems they experience. Knowledge of associations between some types of mental retardation, personality difficulties, and behavior disorders can be helpful in providing adequate treatment.

The Families of Mentally Retarded Children

From the parents' point of view, the birth of a mentally retarded child is a stressful and often devastating event. For 9 months they have looked forward to the arrival of a healthy, normal child. When those expectations are shattered, the parents often go through a grieving process similar to that following the death of a family member. In the past, many professionals, viewing the process as time-limited, emphasized the parents' need for help until they could accept the situation. One parent of a retarded child comments on this view:

Parents of retarded people, the theorists tell us, learn to live with their children's handicaps. They go through stages of reaction, moving through shock, guilt, and rejection to the promised land of acceptance and adjustment.

My own experience as the father of a retarded child did not fit this pattern. Instead, it convinced me that most people seriously misunderstand a parent's response to this situation. The standard view does not reflect the reality of parents' experience or lead to helpful conclusions. Professionals could help parents more—and they would be more realistic—if they discarded their ideas about stages and progress. They could then begin to understand something about the deep, lasting changes that life with a retarded son or daughter brings to parents. And they could begin to see that the negative feelings—the shock, the guilt, and the bitterness—never disappear but stay on as a part of the parent's emotional life.

Most parents, I believe, never fully resolve the complexity of feelings about their child's retardation. They don't "adjust to" or "accept" that fact, at least not in the way psychology books describe it. (Searl, 1978, p. 27)

Many parents who have a child affected by mental retardation retain some optimism about their child's future progress while the child is still young. They may overestimate the child's academic potential and underestimate problems in learning. Probably for this reason parents of young children are more supportive of the concept of mainstreaming (combining children of all abilities into one school program) than parents of older children, who see a greater need for special education programs. In general, just as the grieving process goes on over a lifetime, the parents' acceptance of the severity of their child's disability is not steady and gradual. Instead, problems of acceptance flare up acutely at particular stages in the child's development.

Families of retarded children go through a series of crises as the child reaches various developmental stages. In one survey, three-quarters of the parents described life with their retarded children as a series of ups and progressively greater downs (Wikler, 1986). Parents were asked to evaluate the extent to which they were upset at a number of specific times, including early events—such as the time of diagnosis, the time for walking and talking, and decisions on school placement—and later events—such as the onset of puberty, the 21st birthday, and discussion and decisions about the care of the child after the parents' deaths. When the parents' responses were compared with the predictions of social workers, the results showed that the social workers tended to overestimate the extent of parental upset over the earlier experiences and to underestimate the parents' distress extent over the later experiences. For example, the social workers overestimated the degree of the parents' upset at the times when the child would normally have been expected to walk, when the child entered a special-education class rather than the regular school program, and when younger siblings surpassed the retarded child in functioning. They markedly underestimated how upsetting the child's 21st birthday was to the parents.

The unmet needs of parents seem to form a U-shaped curve. These needs are high among parents of preschoolers, drop off when the children enter some kind of school program, and rise again, even beyond the original levels, when the children become young adults. Periods of transition in the children's lives are also associated with increased family stress. Both entry into adolescence and into young adulthood seem particularly stressful to the family. Figure 15-22 shows the stress levels of families with retarded children of different ages.

Figure 15-22 The amount of stress reported by families who have a mentally retarded child varies with the child's age. Age periods when normal developmental transitions can be expected for non–mentally retarded children seem to produce especially high levels of stress.

Source: Wikler (1986), p. 705.

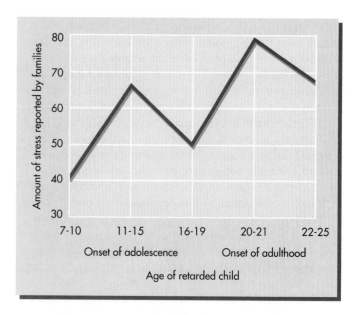

A Parental Dilemma

Q. My Aunt Mary and Uncle Bill have a 25-year-old daughter, Jessie, who has autistic disorder and is moderately mentally retarded. Through the efforts of an alert pediatrician her disorder was identified early and she received intensive behavioral training. However she never learned to speak and tends to be very rigid and stereotyped in her behavior. Because my aunt and uncle wanted her to have the best living conditions possible she has lived at home all her life. This was difficult at times for her older brother who is now a successful architect as well as for Mary and Bill. However they believe that

they had made the right choice. Because Mary was almost 40 and Bill was 50 when Jessie was born, they are now worried about her welfare when they cannot care for her any longer. They do not want to burden their son and his wife, who have young children, with her care, but they worry that she will not be able to adjust to life in an institutional setting. Do you have any suggestions?

A. *Clearly Mary, Bill, and their son and his wife, need to work this out together. In retrospect they may have made a poor choice in maintaining a home for Jessie even though that choice was made with her welfare in mind.*

Perhaps if she had been placed in a good institution or some kind of day-care setting sometime earlier she might have been able to make an easier adjustment. However, perhaps they still have time to help her adjust. They can utilize information from support groups formed by parents of autistic children. This may help them in two ways: by finding out how others have dealt with this problem and how satisfied they are with their solutions. Mary and Bill may get not only information on institutional possibilities but also valuable hints on helping Jessie adapt to a new living situation. The most important thing is to start working on the problem now before an emergency occurs and to make this a family decision in which all family members' psychological welfare is considered.

As parents age, problems develop in their ability to continue to serve as caretakers for their mentally disabled children. Researchers have found that many of these caregivers are committed to maintaining home care for their children as long as possible (Prosser & Moss, 1997). However, few of them have made any concrete plans for future residential care. These findings and others like them suggest that for many families, help is needed both in finding and in financing long-term care for retarded family members. Box 15-3 deals with this issue.

Brothers and sisters of retarded children may also be affected by the child's presence. Although there has not

been much research on this we do know that the parents of a retarded child often place increased demands on their other children and at the same time often have less time and attention to give them. The other children in the family are expected to help care for the retarded child and to subordinate their needs to those of their sibling. In addition, the other children sometimes feel pressure to excel in order to "make up" for the retarded sibling. In one study, children having siblings with autism, Down syndrome, or another type of mental retardation reported a greater stress level than did children with nonretarded siblings (Senel & Akkok, 1995).

Chapter Summary

PERVASIVE DEVELOPMENTAL DISORDERS

Pervasive developmental disorders appear early in a child's development and affect later development in important areas, including social, language, and cognitive abilities. Pervasive developmental disorders include autistic disorder, Asperger's disorder, childhood disintegrative disorder, Rett's disorder, and a general category called pervasive developmental disorder, not otherwise specified.

Autistic Disorder Children with **autistic disorder** have marked difficulties in social interaction and communication, a restricted range of interests, and strong desire for routine. About

70% of those with autistic disorder are also mentally retarded. Two deficits thought to be central to autism are in **theory of mind,** or the ability to infer the mental states of others and to think abstractly, and in **executive functions,** cognitive operations involved in planning and flexibility of response. Many autistic children never develop speech, and those who do often have stereotyped, repetitive, and idiosyncratic speech patterns. Another problem area lies in **joint attention behaviors.** Lack of attention behaviors, especially maintaining eye contact with another person, is a valuable early diagnostic sign of autism. Social interactions are a particular problem. Brain abnormalities have been suspected in autism because epileptic seizures are common among those with autistic disorder. However, the only consistent finding is that the brains of children with autism tend to be larger than average in size, especially in the temporal, parietal, and occipital lobes. Twin studies, the higher probability of having a second autistic child if there is an autistic sibling, and the tendency for relatives to have some autistic-like behaviors all suggest that genetic factors are important although specific genes have not yet been consistently identified. Stress or injury may interact with genetic vulnerability to produce an autistic disorder. Treatment for autistic disorder is usually focused on limited objectives, increasing skills and reducing problem behaviors. Intensive behavioral training seems to produce effective results. For children with autistic disorder who have minimal or no mental retardation, special learning techniques that take into account specific cognitive strengths and weaknesses typical of autistic disorder are effective. A variety of medications are also used to treat some of the symptoms of autistic disorder, but they do not appear to affect the basic disorder itself.

Asperger's Disorder

Like autism, **Asperger's disorder** includes impaired social interaction and restricted and repetitive patterns of behavior and interests. However, it does not include the delays or absence of language development and the impairment in cognitive development that are characteristic of autism. It is usually not diagnosed until a child is of school age. Some researchers have argued that Asperger's disorder is not a separate disorder but instead a mild form of autistic disorder.

Childhood Disintegrative Disorder

The first signs of **childhood disintegrative disorder** do not appear until age 3 or 4 and are preceded by a period of normal development. Although these changes are thought to be associated with a deterioration of the nervous system, the reason deterioration occurs is not known. Childhood disintegrative disorder is more common among boys than girls.

Rett's Disorder

Rett's disorder is a progressive disorder that occurs after at least 5 months of apparently normal development after birth. The infant's head stops increasing in size so that it becomes smaller than normal, a condition that is called **microcephaly.** During this period, children lose various developmental skills—including both language and social skills—that they had previously acquired. Motor behaviors are also affected. Rett's disorder typically affects only girls.

Is There an Autistic Spectrum?

Some researchers have suggested that all the pervasive developmental disorders are part of an **autistic disorder spectrum.** By this they mean that the disorders may all have the same basic causes.

MENTAL RETARDATION

Mental retardation is diagnosed if a person has subaverage intellectual function that began before age 18 and that is accompanied by significant limitations in adaptive functioning. DSM-IV divides mental retardation into four levels—mild, moderate, severe, and profound—on the basis of intelligence test scores. Axis II of the DSM-IV is used for the diagnosis of mental retardation.

Historical Views of Mental Retardation

Until the 1870s, no distinctions were made among various forms of what was then known as mental deficiency. After the 1877 publication of a monograph on what is today called Down syndrome, interest grew in the classification of mental retardation. Other factors that increased interest in understanding more about mental retardation were the work on heredity begun by Gregor Mendel and the development of the Binet tests. Mendel's work influenced the **eugenics movement,** which focused on sterilization of those considered defective in order to improve the genetic stock of the population.

Causes of Mental Retardation

Mental retardation results from many different causes that can be classified into two main categories: biologically based causes and those that are believed to be psychosocial in origin. Biologically based causes include genetic and hereditary conditions; exposure to harmful conditions in the fetal environment; trauma related to premature birth, deprivation of oxygen, or other birth problems; and traumatic effects after birth, such as diseases, poisoning, or accidents. **Tuberous sclerosis** and **phenylketonuria (PKU)** are examples of genetically caused disorders. Phenylketonuria often is the result of the mutation of a specific gene.

Fragile X Syndrome

Fragile X syndrome, the most common form of inherited mental retardation, is diagnosed when a laboratory culture of an X chromosome of the affected individual shows a fragile spot. Because this gene is located on the X chromosome, it is more common in men. Women are less likely to have this disorder because they have a second X chromosome that, if it is normal, will prevent the symptoms of the disorder. People with this syndrome have distinctive facial features, and affected men may have autisticlike behaviors and a tendency to have aggressive outbursts.

Down Syndrome

The most common single cause of mental retardation, **Down syndrome** is usually the result of a **chromosomal nondisjunction,** the occurrence of three chromosomes instead of the usual two in chromosome pair no. 21. Two other processes—**translocation,** or the breaking off of material from a chromosome in pair no. 21, which then fuses to another chromosome pair, and **mosaicism,** in which some, but not all, cells have an abnormality involving chromosome no. 21—can produce Down syndrome. Abnormal aging occurs in the brains of individuals with Down syndrome, and by the age of 30 most people with this syndrome have developed some of the same types of senile plaques and neurofibrillary tangles that are found in much older people who have Alzheimer's disease.

The Fetal Environment and Mental Retardation

Sometimes disorders associated with mental retardation develop because of conditions in the fetal environment. Prenatal factors linked to mental retardation include infections and chronic medical conditions in the mother, blood incompatibilities between mother and child, chemicals in the fetal environment, radiation, malnutrition, factors associated with maternal age, and maternal stress. These factors often have their greatest effects if the exposure occurs in the first few weeks after conception. Examples include viral diseases such as rubella (German measles), herpes, and human immunodeficiency virus (HIV). Chronic medical conditions such as high blood pressure and diabetes may also lead to fetal brain damage. The chemical conditions in the uterus of a woman with PKU can also cause retardation unless the mother follows a special diet. Chemical factors from use of both legal and illegal drugs may also cause fetal malformations and mental retardation.

Fetal Alcohol Syndrome Alcohol use in pregnancy can result in a set of physical deformities and brain abnormalities in the child, which is called **fetal alcohol syndrome.** Mental retardation is one likely consequence of fetal alcohol syndrome.

Problems During and After Birth Premature birth, low birth weight, lack of oxygen during the birth process, and too-rapid progress through the birth canal, which can result in bleeding and tearing of brain tissue, can increase the probability of retardation. A child's central nervous system can also be damaged in a number of ways after birth that can result in mental retardation. Among these causes are infections such as encephalitis, extreme malnutrition, blows to the head, tumors, deprivation of oxygen, and poisons from the environment.

Psychosocial Disadvantage Some children classified as mentally retarded have parents whose intelligence test scores are in the mildly retarded range. If both child and parents come from backgrounds of limited education and cultural opportunities, it is not easy to determine whether the similarity between child and parents results from heredity or from a lack of education and stimulating environment.

Types of Prevention and Intervention in Mental Retardation Some types of mental retardation can be prevented from occurring. Examples of **primary prevention** are public health campaigns to warn about potential hazards that can produce mental retardation, for instance, use of alcohol in pregnancy or

a child's contact with lead from paint or gasoline fumes. **Secondary prevention** of mental retardation is focused on providing treatment to prevent mental retardation in vulnerable individuals. An example is PKU screening and dietary treatment. **Tertiary prevention** involves improving possible outcomes for those already affected by a disorder, such as providing special intervention programs beginning in infancy for children with Down syndrome.

Early Intervention Programs Children who are thought to be at special risk for mild mental retardation as a result of poverty, premature birth, or having parents with low intelligence test scores, can be provided with an enriched environment in infancy and early childhood. Because of public policy changes, public education must now be provided for children who in the past might have been routinely institutionalized. These policies also require children who score as mentally retarded on IQ tests to be placed in regular classes whenever possible.

Vocational and Social Skills Training Programs Special programs, often using behavioral methods, help many mentally retarded individuals function in a variety of jobs, often in sheltered workshop settings.

Recognition and Treatment of Psychological Problems Many people who are mentally retarded also have some psychological disorder of the type diagnosed on Axis I of the DSM-IV. For many of these individuals, these disorders are not identified or treated.

The Families of Mentally Retarded Children Families who have mentally retarded children go through a series of crises that are often linked to the developmental landmarks. The degree of stress created by these problems often follows a U-shaped curve. Stress is initially very high, then decreases, then increases again as the child reaches adolescence and adulthood.

Key Terms

16

Karel Appel "Untitled" 1966, gouache, tempera and collage, 23 × 35³/₈". Signed and dated lower right. Jane Kahan Gallery, NYC.

The Therapeutic Enterprise:

Choices, Techniques, Evaluation

Kevin, a bright, appealing 6-year-old boy was refusing to go to school, seemed frightened much of the time, and demanded that his mother sit in the classroom with him. At home he was very jealous and aggressive toward his younger sister and was frightened of going to sleep. He had occasional contact with a few children outside of school but no real friends. Kevin was frightened in any new situation, for example, going on the bus to a place he had not visited before. He seemed especially fearful if he went with his father. He complained frequently that no one liked him and that other people were always seeking ways to get him to do what they wanted him to do. Because of his behavioral problems and obvious unhappiness, his parents decided to take him to a child clinical psychologist.

In the first session, the psychologist met with Kevin and his parents to find out how each saw Kevin's problem, observe how they interacted as a family group, and get an impression of each of them as a person. Kevin didn't say much, although his intelligence and verbal facility were obvious on the occasions when he did speak. Kevin seemed quite fearful. The parents mentioned how much he had been loved as a baby. They said he used to smile all the time, and seemed happy. He crawled when he was 7 months old, walked at 9, and had learned to read before he was 4 years old. Kevin's mother became pregnant with his sister when Kevin was 19 months old. After she was born, Kevin's mother for the first time began placing him occasionally in a child-care center for half days. Usually she did this in order to devote her full attention to the baby and, also, to meet her own need for relief from the pressures of being a parent.

Kevin agreed to come to the second session without his parents. After his mother had dropped him off, and upon entering the psychologist's office, Kevin immediately began playing with a number of cars, stuffed animals, trucks, and other things in a large toy box. He said little to the therapist and played increasingly violently with the toys. However, in his play there were brief moments when he showed tenderness and affection toward some of the animals. Kevin returned twice a week to see the therapist for 3 weeks and his play was frequently violent. In one session, Kevin asked the psychologist why he was being brought to see her.

At this point, the psychologist met with the parents without Kevin, having told him that she would like to do this. Kevin did not object to the meeting. The psychologist was particularly interested in the change that had occurred in Kevin from being a smiling, happy baby to a frightened angry boy. She was also interested in Kevin's hostility to his sister. The parents commented that Kevin was probably resentful that his sister interfered with receiving the individual attention he had been getting from his parents. In the course of the discussion, Kevin's father recalled that when his wife was 8 months pregnant with Kevin's sister, the family was vacationing in a cottage near a lake several miles from their home. On a few occasions, the father took Kevin to the lake and encouraged him to play in the water. In retrospect, the father felt he had "come on too strong" in encouraging Kevin to play in the water. On several occasions, he had picked Kevin up and placed him at the water's edge. Several times, he had gotten angry that Kevin was so fearful of the water. Each time they went to the lake Kevin screamed, ran away from the water, and withdrew from his father.

In subsequent therapy sessions, Kevin's play became even more violent. At times this extended to the psychologist. A few times he attempted to push or hit her and had to be held until he calmed down. The psychologist was unable to see Kevin for a 2-week period during which she went on a long-planned vacation. When their sessions resumed, Kevin became even angrier than he had been before the vacation and broke several of the toys. Most of the sessions consisted of Kevin's violent play. During a few of the rare quiet periods, the therapist asked Kevin about his experiences at lakes and with water and also about his sister. He was not very responsive to these questions although at one point he expressed anger at his father who "made him do things."

As the sessions proceeded, Kevin broke more trucks and sought to have the psychologist play more actively with him and the toys. The psychologist did not criticize Kevin for breaking the toys, but did note that the number of toys had diminished. As the number of cars and trucks dwindled, she would add a few new ones. As time went on, there were some positive developments. Kevin became less violent in his play and not at all aggressive toward the psychologist. He talked more and on one occasion observed that the psychologist did not tell him what he should do and had added cars to the toy box. On another occasion, he said that he had thought the psychologist would either not return from her vacation or would not see Kevin again. Kevin began bringing toys from home to show to the psychologist. When he did this he would invite her to play with them.

After 4 months, Kevin's violence was almost absent and it became possible for there to be some discussion of Kevin's negative feelings toward his sister and how he didn't like it when his father wanted him to do things Kevin didn't want to do. The psychologist listened to what Kevin said, did not criticize him for feeling as he did, but did observe that it was her impression that his father really liked Kevin. Kevin told his parents that he would like to go to school regularly so that he might play with the other children. When Kevin's family went on a vacation necessitating canceling a visit to the psychologist, he expressed regret that this was going to happen. However, he did not become more violent, rather he expressed his negative feelings verbally.

After 5 months, the psychologist decided that the therapy should end. She was aware of the financial strain on the family of the cost of the sessions. She discussed this with Kevin and he accepted the need to terminate the sessions. At the last session, he made positive comments about some school experiences he had enjoyed, a movie his parents had taken him to, and a toy he had taught his sister to play with.

Kevin's Therapist's Comments

"Obviously, there is a lot you can't be sure about when you work with a 6-year-old child. Much of what I did in my sessions with Kevin was in response to things he did that I could not have anticipated. But I did have a theory of what might be going on with Kevin and his family. I thought that his father's overeagerness to get Kevin to play in the water was a traumatic experience for Kevin. I also thought that anticipating the birth of his sister and her birth were traumatic because of what they did to his sense of security, being cared for, and being the center of his parents' attention. The unfortunate experiences at the lake and the frustrations his sister brought to his life combined to traumatize him and distort how he viewed himself and people in his life. I felt that what Kevin needed most was acceptance and an opportunity to express some of what he was feeling. I should note that other than his negativeness to his sister, he wasn't especially nasty to his parents. I felt he needed an understanding outlet and that's what I tried to give him. Kevin clearly improved and I think it was because in therapy he had an opportunity to form a relationship that enabled him to work through

some hurts he had experienced. I wouldn't pretend to be definitive about what brought about Kevin's improvement, because there is so much I don't know about him and his family. But I think that respect and caring have curative properties."

———

On a stormy November night, Garrett Cross, age 35, and his wife, Marge, also 35, were returning home from a visit to her parents when a car pulled into their lane (the passing lane) without having noticed that they were there. The ensuing accident killed Marge who was sitting in the passenger seat. Garrett was shaken up and bruised, but physically all right. However, psychologically he was far from all right. He just didn't seem able to accept and assimilate the death of his wife and the circumstances surrounding it. He couldn't get the memory of what had happened out of his mind, experienced waves of anxiety and depression, and had nightmares either about the car crash or something else equally horrifying. He relived many times each day what had happened that night including Marge's bloodied, broken, and mangled body; the arrival of the police and ambulance (she died before the ambulance arrived); his feelings of helplessness; and his sense of responsibility and guilt over not having attended carefully enough to the other car as it began to move into his lane.

The accident occurred 2 months before he began therapy. During that time his recurrent intrusive thoughts persisted. He could not bring himself to drive on the stretch of road on which the accident had occurred. Garrett's nightmares, if anything, were becoming worse. He continually found himself waiting for a phone call informing him of some disaster experienced by a loved one. He was unable to enjoy social relationships and sometimes went out of his way to avoid talking to people he knew and liked. He dreaded particularly seeing or talking with Marge's parents, who he had always enjoyed but toward whom he felt guilt because he was driving the car when their daughter was killed.

It didn't take long for his therapist to see that Garrett was undergoing a posttraumatic stress reaction. To find out how incapacitated Garrett was, he asked him if he was able to work. Garrett told him that he went to work every day but really didn't get much done. Images and thoughts related to the accident intruded throughout each day. Garrett commented that he was lucky that the company he worked for was understanding and everyone was very kind to him.

During the first session, the therapist asked few questions beyond ones that would stimulate Garrett to talk about the accident and its aftermath. By the end of the session, the therapist felt he understood fairly well what Garrett was going through and what needed to happen in therapy to help him live more in the present than in the past. As he saw it, Garrett was being haunted by the past and was continually anticipating the occurrence of other disasters. The therapist concluded that Garrett needed to find a way to integrate the terrifying events related to the accident and the death of Marge into the realities of the present. His therapeutic goals included reducing Garrett's high anxiety and depression levels and altering the way he viewed himself and what had happened. Achieving those goals would help Garrett reestablish a feeling of personal integrity and control over his life. At the end of the first session, he told Garrett that he thought their discussions in subsequent sessions would be helpful and that in the next one he would tell him about what was known about the type of reaction he was experiencing and describe some useful steps that could be taken. The therapist did this because he wanted to end the first session on an upbeat note so that Garrett would have some positive thoughts about overcoming his problems. At the same time that he was anticipating the next steps in the therapeutic process, the therapist let Garrett know that he appreciated what Garrett had been going through and, given what had happened, believed his reactions were understandable.

At the beginning of the second session the therapist acknowledged the terrible thing that had happened and went on to say that everything Garrett was going through (his nightmares, preoccupying thoughts, difficulty in concentrating, and emotional upset) could be observed in many people who had experienced similar traumatic events. He said: "Everyone has a breaking point. That is nothing to feel ashamed of." The therapist explained that traumatic past events can come to organize a person's life and when people encounter reminders of traumatic experiences, emotional reactions can be triggered. He explained that traumatic experiences can overwhelm an individual's sense of safety and lead to the assumption that other traumatic events are likely to take place. The therapist added: "You are on alert for the occurrence of terrible things. Being on alert isn't purely psychological; your body is also in a hyper-state of alertness. Your alertness and feelings of impending doom don't occur because you are telling yourself to have these reactions. The reactions occur automatically. We have to get you off automatic pilot. Contributing to your being on automatic pilot is that you are a responsible person who, perhaps, finds it easy to blame yourself when terrible things happen."

Part of the second session was devoted to a review of what happened that November night and its aftermath. The therapist showed particular interest in Garrett's recurrent thoughts and flashbacks. He suggested that Garrett might be able to catch these upsetting cognitions before they "take over" by directing his attention to do so. If he could do this, he might be able to control and reduce the occurrence of thoughts and images that elicit anxiety, depression, and emotional upset. He asked Garrett if doing this seemed useful and Garrett agreed. As they pursued the topic of controlling what were now automatic responses, the therapist emphasized that the purpose of gaining control was not to stamp out or forget the accident and death of Marge. He told Garrett that what had happened could not and should not be forgotten. "Your love for Marge will be an important part of you for the rest of your life. Your guilt over what happened is no memorial that Marge would ever want."

Garrett then said that a light seemed to come on in his mind when the word "memorial" was used. The therapist saw this and asked "What are you thinking about?" Garrett replied that he would have a really good feeling if he could do something that would recognize and memorialize his wife. He added: "The world should take some note of this fine person." The therapist suggested that Garrett think about what might be a fitting and feasible memorial. To himself, the therapist was happy that Garrett now had something that wasn't emotionally draining to think about and that might have lasting value for him.

The therapist then gave Garrett a homework assignment. It was to write an account of what had happened that November night. The account should not be a "police report," but rather be a full description of what had happened from his perspective. The account was to include pertinent facts, how and why the accident had occurred, and the images and thoughts associated with it. Garrett was not to worry about sentence structure or grammar, but rather focus attention on the realities. The therapist asked Garrett to write this account for three reasons. He thought it would be a reality-orienting project for Garrett, produce a document Garrett and he could review and discuss in subsequent sessions, and might provide opportunities to correct cognitive distortions contributing to Garrett's posttraumatic reactions.

Over the next several sessions, considerable time was devoted to Garrett's account and on two occasions the therapist asked Garrett to read it aloud. This was done to give Garrett opportunities for reliving the accident within a protected environment. In the course of discussing the account the therapist found several opportunities to gently confront personal schemas contributing to his maladaptive response to stress. For example, Garrett had written: "If my reflexes were better I could have seen the other car and swerved out of the way." The therapist commented: "You said that you were driving along passing several slow-moving cars. How could you have known that all of a sudden that car was going to pull into your lane? I guess if you were Superman you could have figured out how to stop that car. But you aren't Superman; no one is. I don't think you caused or contributed to the accident." The therapist also pointed out that Garrett earlier had said that the police concluded that the accident was totally the fault of the other driver. The therapist also expressed the opinion that it was important to distinguish between the facts of what actually happened and Garrett's grief and guilt. He made the point that it would be very valuable if Garrett could see the accident within a context that had a beginning, middle, and end.

They talked about a memorial to Marge several times. Garrett said that he had received $5,000 from an insurance policy on Marge's life. He felt he didn't really need the money and he was thinking about donating it in Marge's name to the local horticultural center. Marge had always loved plants and flowers and had bought plants and bulbs at an annual fund-raising sale at the center. He was going to direct the center to use the money to establish a small library of gardening books. When he discussed this idea with the center's director, she had commented that they very much needed a library and the only reason they didn't have one was lack of funds. At the entrance to the library room there would be a plaque on the wall saying: "Margaret Cross Library." Garrett said that the idea of the library was occupying a lot of his thoughts. He gave as an example the thought that he might in the future be able to make additional contributions to the library for the purchase of more books. When he mentioned this to the center's director, she had said that establishment of the library would in all likelihood stimulate contributions from other people interested in the center.

In one session as they were discussing Garrett's nightmares and flashbacks, the therapist commented: "Keep in mind that the accident shattered many of your assumptions about your life and Marge's. Maybe the flashbacks and nightmares reflect the fact that you haven't yet been able to develop a new set of assumptions and expectations consistent with current realities. Doing that takes time. I think the more you are able to think realistically about the accident the better the chance that your emotional reactions will become less intense. Maybe your flashbacks and nightmares are caused by emotions you don't have control over. I think you are coming closer to recollecting the events of that November night with less fear of being overwhelmed and a more realistic perspective that recognizes the present you are living in."

The therapist took every opportunity he could to question the blame and guilt Garrett assigned to himself and his fixation concerning the accident. At the same time, he encouraged Garrett to focus attention on good times he and Marge had had together. When possible he got Garrett to talk about aspects of his life other than Marge and the accident. He didn't do this to lessen the importance of Marge and the accident in Garrett's thoughts but rather to provide a context within which the particular meanings of the tragedy might be understood. Thus, two things went on in therapy: first, putting the tragedy into words and related imagery and, second, putting Garrett's narrative of the trauma in a context that included other aspects of his life. In doing the latter, Garrett came to be able to think about his parents, about whom he cared and toward whom he felt responsibilities; his brother, with whom he had always been close; his boss who was so thoughtful; and several friends with whom he and Marge had had warm relationships.

One other thing the therapist did was bring out into the open for discussion several questions that he was sure were occupying much of Garrett's thoughts—for example, why did Marge have to die? Why did this tragedy have to happen to Garrett? Whenever these questions arose, the therapist listened respectfully and with interest. He did not try to answer these questions, but rather to let Garrett know that he was with him while struggling with them. When Garrett commented: "I guess there really are no solid answers to these questions," the therapist agreed with him.

On several occasions, Garrett talked about his mourning over the death of his wife rather than his guilt, accident-related images, flashbacks, and nightmares. The therapist encouraged this and mentioned that mourning took courage. Twice Garrett's voice broke and he cried when talking about his mourning. Each of these occasions, the therapist thought, seemed to help Garrett take steps out of the limited world of the accident and its trauma into the real world. With increasing thoughts about his ties to significant others, he seemed also more able to forgive himself and realize that what had happened was, in fact, an accident beyond his control.

At the twelfth and last session, Garrett said: "I'm not so hard on myself now. Maybe it's because I'm thinking about other people in my life who are important to me and not feeling quite so guilty." Garrett was gratified that the previous Sunday he had driven up to have dinner with Marge's parents and some other members of their family. There were a few tears, but some laughter as well. Marge's parents felt wonderful about Garrett's donation to start the library. They felt that it was very appropriate—exactly what Marge would appreciate—and said they would make a contribution to the horticultural center library as well.

Garrett's Therapist

At the end of therapy, Garrett's therapist said, "I don't think Garrett is completely back to his old self—but he is on his way. Some of what happened in the therapy sessions grew out of research I knew about concerning strategies to help traumatized and bereaved individuals—for example, acceptance, listening empathetically, exposure, reconstructing traumatic narratives, enabling the expression of deep emotions, and directing attention to present realities and relationships. But there also were some unexplained, fortuitous occurrences, especially Marge's memorial. When they happen—and they happen fairly often in therapy—it is wonderful because they often provide a real opportunity to make a quantum jump forward."

Tom Martin, 34 years old, a real estate salesman, came to therapy because, as he put it, "I'm fed up with being on my guard and being mad all the time." The clinical psychologist he consulted was an experienced cognitive therapist. However, Tom didn't know that. He went to him because someone at work had mentioned that this clinical psychologist had helped a friend of his who was anxious all the time. (Tom hadn't said anything to his colleague about being interested in seeing a therapist).

In the first session, after a brief exchange of small talk, the therapist said, "Tell me about your concerns. Where do you think we ought to start?" The therapist asked this question because he hoped it would stimulate Tom to take the initiative, rather than passively answer a series of specific questions he (the therapist) might ask. He wanted Tom to tell his story in his own words, on his own terms. The story he told was of a man who feels his life is a constant battle for survival. From his perspective, it is a dog-eat-dog world, a world in which other people can't be trusted and where you have to be on guard against being taken advantage of. He said that living in a dog-eat-dog world, in addition to being unpleasant, did two things to him: it made him feel angry all the time and it depressed him.

As he told his story, Tom mentioned some examples of what he meant by a dog-eat-dog world. What was common to them was that you couldn't trust people. People are out to get what they want and they will say and do whatever is necessary to achieve their ends. Illustrations he provided included his father who would lie to him about a situation in which he wanted Tom to do something; someone he knew in high school who kept telling Tom—and other students—that it wasn't necessary to study hard for a particular teacher's tests in order to make his own exams (for which he studied hard) look better, and a suit salesman who told him the size 38 suit he wanted to sell Tom looked fine on him, even though Tom knew that 40 or 42 was his size. As a result of these sorts of experiences, Tom said he feels as though he cannot relax for a minute; he always has to be on his guard.

Tom said that he often didn't know how to handle the efforts of others to take advantage of him. In some cases, he could just listen to what the other person was saying and then ignore it. For example, he didn't buy the suit. But if doing something was required, he either had to do what the person wanted, or, if he didn't, let the other person know why he wouldn't comply. This might lead Tom to tell the other person off, that is, let them know that what had been said was manipulative and not true. This could lead to an argument, maybe even a fight. Always being ready for the possibility of a confrontation sometimes wore Tom out. It drained him and depressed him. He didn't want to live like that for the rest of his life.

At one point in the first session, Tom said: "For as long as I can remember, I've been preoccupied with getting swindled or screwed. I think it goes back to when I was

a kid. My mother was always screeching for money-money-money and my father felt he had to do anything that would provide the money. He was always coming home with stories of swindles, someone swindling someone else, someone trying to swindle my father. What neither my mother nor my father ever mentioned but what I saw many times was that they themselves wouldn't hesitate to do whatever was necessary to get money. And they didn't trust each other; they were always hiding money from each other. You can imagine the terrible fights they had, if they discovered what their spouse was doing. I guess it's easy to see how I got to be on guard all the time."

His "on guard" problem was greatest when he was working. He felt that his boss was trying to get him to work mainly on properties that had something wrong with them. He also felt that his boss was only concerned with what he could get out of Tom and didn't really care about him as a person. Tom also didn't trust most of the other salespeople with whom he worked. Frequently, there were disputes about how commissions should be split. Tom mentioned that he was "on guard" not only at work, but also frequently when he had to buy something—he recently had gone to a shoe store where the salesman tried to sell him a pair of shoes that were not right for Tom. He was sure this happened because the salesman got a higher commission for selling them than most other shoes in the store. Tom told this to the salesman and stormed out of the store.

With 15 minutes of the session remaining, the therapist realized that there was some basic information Tom hadn't provided, like whether he was single, married, or divorced. When he inquired about this factual information, Tom readily provided it. Tom said that he was in good health, had been selling real estate for several months and was married with two children, ages 3 and 6. He described his wife and children as the most important people in his life. He loved his wife and said he was lucky to have such a fine family life.

About 5 minutes before the session ended, Tom said: "I guess I should tell you that I don't just get angry, sometimes I sort of explode. A small example of this was what I said to that shoe salesman. But, of course, the shoe salesman doesn't mean anything to me and I don't care that much what he thinks of me. But I've had to leave three jobs either because I let someone have it (once I let them have it physically) or the boss simply thought I was a negative influence on everybody else. This job I have now has potential and I want to succeed at it. But, as I told you, I already have concerns about my boss and some other people in the office."

At the end of the session, the therapist drew some tentative conclusions. One was that Tom needed both acceptance and sympathy. Tom needed to know that the therapist appreciated the pressure he was under, particularly with regard to his new job and his need to be a good provider for his family. Another tentative conclusion was that a big contributor to Tom's "dog-eat-dog" view of life was distorted automatic thoughts, thoughts Tom wasn't directing himself to think; they just seemed to come automatically to the forefront of his thoughts. Finally, the therapist saw the importance of reinforcing Tom and helping Tom reinforce himself for success in overcoming his automatic thoughts.

Tom saw the therapist for 15 additional sessions during which a number of things happened. Perhaps the most important was the therapist's efforts to get Tom to the point where he would begin to question some of his distorted automatic thoughts, maladaptive assumptions, and negative schemas. Central to all of these were Tom's thoughts about the dog-eat-dog world and having to be on guard all the time. The therapist did two things. First, he let Tom know that he understood the stress and unhappiness these thoughts engendered. His comments concerning what Tom was experiencing and how he felt about his experience were intended to communicate acceptance and empathy. Second, the therapist took every opportunity to raise questions in Tom's mind about the validity of his automatic thoughts. All of this was done in a gentle manner. The questions were never confrontational or accusatory and the focus usually was not so much the therapist's opinions, but more what Tom thought about the therapist's observations.

Towards the end of one session the therapist asked Tom to prepare a list to be brought to the next session of people Tom completely trusted, individuals who really cared about him. Not surprisingly, Tom started the list with his wife, but several other people were also on the list. One was the priest at the church Tom and his family belonged to. Another was the man at the newsstand where Tom bought a newspaper every morning, and yet another was Tom's doctor. Others on the list included several people with whom Tom no longer had contact, but who he had liked a lot at some point in the past. One of these was Edmund

Burk with whom he had been friends for 2 years in high school before Edmund's family moved to another state. When Tom gave the list to the therapist, they spent a considerable amount of time talking about each individual. How did Tom know each person? What made him feel the person could be trusted and interested in Tom's welfare? Tom commented that he was impressed at the number of people on the list (he had listed 12 people) and the warmth of his feelings toward each person. He also commented that, while including his wife on the list was obvious, he was a bit surprised at some of the others—at least, in terms of the intensity of his positive feelings toward them. In terms of time, he dwelt most on the priest and Edmund Burk. Edmund especially intrigued Tom because they had not had contact for almost 20 years and he had no idea where Edmund was now.

In talking about Edmund, Tom mentioned Edmund's willingness to share his lunch with him and lend him money and his obvious desire to do things with Tom. They occasionally had disagreements, and in a few cases, arguments, but they had always worked things out.

The therapist commented that the list was an interesting one and that Tom must have something that brought out in others positive feelings toward him. He went on to say that it doesn't seem as though all aspects of Tom's life were of the dog-eat-dog variety. He wondered what Tom did that elicited such genuine liking from others. Tom said that he had never really connected how he behaved toward people with how they behaved toward him. Then, he made what the therapist regarded as a very insightful observation: Perhaps, his anxieties about money and getting gypped or swindled affected how he behaved in situations in which money was involved. He said: "Maybe money is for me what the color red is for a bull."

Throughout their sessions, the therapist asked questions like: "Are you thinking in all-or-none terms?" "What is the evidence for and against this idea?" "Are you oversimplifying what was going on in the relationship you just described?" and "Are you setting things up so that the other person will be on his guard?" The purpose of these questions was to help Tom consider all sides of an issue—not just what he wanted to happen or what he thought should happen. As these questions became real to Tom and as he became more empathetic toward those with whom he interacted, he felt his relationships were improving somewhat. As time went on, he became more aware that how he felt about other people was linked to the assumptions and schemas of his cognitive world and that schemas are not sunk in concrete. They can be reviewed and reframed.

As he became more questioning of his motives and needs and the motives and needs of others, Tom became a bit less certain of why they did or said certain things and he became more open to alternative possibilities. It was hard work going over a real estate plan or contract with his boss without simply assuming that the boss wouldn't mind taking advantage of Tom. But Tom persisted. As he did so, he became aware of some things he did that might turn people off. He gave as an example recently approaching his boss about a plan he had in mind for buying a parcel of land and building houses on it. He had presented the plan, which he had worked on for 2 weeks, and got angry when the boss raised some questions about what he wanted to do and how he intended to go about doing it. Tom got angry, but managed to suppress it. Afterward he realized that some of the points the boss had raised might be thought of as criticisms, but really they were alternative approaches that in a few instances made a lot of sense. He saw his boss again the next day and told him that he had thought over their discussion of the previous day and realized that the boss had offered a number of good ideas. Tom thanked him for the helpful ideas.

By the end of therapy, Tom had not yet hit a home run, but he had a few singles and doubles. He felt he and his boss had a better relationship—friendlier, freer, and more productive. Their discussions even had some humor in them. As therapy ended, Tom said he intended to be more attentive to what he brought to relationships as well as what other people brought to theirs with him. He said that he felt that it wasn't true that everybody was out to get him and he remembered Edmund Burk and the priest who not only weren't out to get him, but liked him and, in fact, were out to help him. Tom felt he was now less likely to get angry and fly off the handle than he had been.

Tom's Therapist's Comments

"Tom is not 'cured.' There is a lot about himself he hasn't explored. Still, in at least one respect he has made progress. He is less sure than he had been of the motives of other people. Before therapy he just accepted on faith that everybody with whom he dealt was out to get him. He didn't focus his attention on how solid the support was that he received or had received from his wife, Ed-

mund Burk, the priest, and in less significant ways, from the man at the newsstand. I tried to direct his focus of attention to the positive side of his personal relationships. I also tried to get him to think about what he brings to relationships with other people, especially his suspicions of the motives of others and his belief that they are out to take advantage of him. As therapy ended, I think Tom's self-esteem was increasing." ■

Each of these cases is unique. The challenges confronting the three clinicians were complex, involving many interacting variables. Kevin, Garrett Cross, and Tom Martin have in common their apparent improvement. This doesn't mean that they were "cured" and unlikely to have similar or different problems in the future. It also does not mean that all their major current problems necessarily have been dealt with. While the outcomes of the cases seem favorable, there is a certain indeterminate quality to each of them. In this way, they reflect the "real world" with all its ambiguities and unexpected, unpredictable twists and turns. What happened in Garrett Cross's therapy illustrates this in a very positive way. Could anyone have predicted that the use of the word *memorial* would set in motion thoughts and action that seem to have played an important role in Garrett's improvement? As Garrett's therapist's comment shows, the idea of a memorial for Marge was a fortuitous event that was taken advantage of.

The three cases are probably not representative of the many clinical interactions that occur every day in consulting offices. They couldn't be. There are too many diverse therapeutic approaches, too many clinicians, and too many people in need of help for both specific and general problems to be captured in three cases—or even in several times that number. But these cases do reflect the nature of the clinical enterprise—persons with problems and clinicians striving to transform maladaptation into adaptation. Kevin's, Garrett Cross's, and Tom Martin's therapists were not flying blind. They had theoretical orientations. While they had to make many instantaneous decisions with imperfect knowledge, they employed certain organizing principles that played roles in how they approached their cases. Kevin's therapist was strongly influenced by the conviction that her relationship with Kevin was the matrix within which he might be able to develop in the direction of positive growth. Garrett Cross's therapist saw as a major challenge helping him integrate the tragedy of his wife's death into his current life in such a way that his life could go on with less strain than was currently the case. Tom Martin's therapist saw Tom's cognitive schemas as, in a sense, the creator of his dog-eat-dog world and their modification would be needed to remove Tom from that world. Their theoretical perspectives led the three clinicians to see their cases in certain ways, make choices concerning what needed to be done, and decide which techniques were likely to be effective. In addition they brought their own personalities to the therapeutic enterprise. The three cases convey something of the richness, challenge, and idiosyncratic quality of the therapeutic enterprise. They also suggest the need to describe, understand, and evaluate what goes on in therapeutic settings.

All therapeutic relationships aim to provide patients with certain ingredients that are missing from their lives. Regardless of their therapeutic orientations, all clinicians must deal with the patient's psychological state and his or her expectation of receiving help. All therapists attempt to form some sort of supportive therapeutic relationship. All clinicians must create a problem-solving setting, communicate their views of the problems presented, and help the patients devise solutions to those problems.

In preceding chapters we have described major therapeutic approaches to specific types of maladaptive behavior. We have discussed the "talking therapies," such as psychoanalysis and client-centered counseling, in which conversations between the patient and the therapist are the vehicle for achieving change; cognitive-behavioral therapies, such as systematic desensitization and the building of social skills and confidence in using them, which involve applications of learning and cognitive principles in specially structured clinical situations; and biological therapies, such as antipsychotic, antidepressant, or tranquilizing drugs and electroconvulsive treatments, which are aimed at achieving behavior change through physical means.

Until now, we have focused attention primarily on the particular therapies that seem most pertinent to helping people with certain types of disorders overcome their difficulties. However, there are some general questions about the nature of therapeutic interventions and their effects that require special consideration. The questions include the following:

- Do most or all of the different therapeutic approaches have common elements? If so, what are they?
- Why is a particular therapy effective for certain types of problems but not for others?
- Would combining different therapeutic approaches yield better results than using each approach by itself?
- What is the process by which therapeutic change comes about?
- On what basis should judgments about the success of therapeutic efforts be made?
- How researchable are issues related to these efforts?

In the following pages, we will attempt to answer these and other questions about therapies for maladaptive behavior and try to separate what is known from what is not yet known. We will focus attention on what works, why, and under what circumstances. We will inquire into the nature of personal change.

Like the three cases with which the chapter began, the case of a 54-year-old man who participated in a clinical trial of the type described in Chapter 1 illustrates the importance of thinking about the nature of therapeutic change. The aim of the trial was to evaluate a new medication for depression. The trial, which lasted for 12 weeks, had a placebo control group. It was also double-blind which meant that neither patients nor the therapists knew whether the pills the patients were taking had active ingredients or were simply placebos.

His response during the first week was modestly positive. At Week 3 he was remarkably happy, saying he had not felt this way for 5 years. He was rated "markedly improved" with no symptoms of depression from Week 4 until completion of the study.

He was a lonely man who knew that he needed but one strong heterosexual relationship to sustain himself. Five years before entering the study, he had found the only woman whom he had ever loved. Because she was in the midst of a painful divorce and because he was so ardent in his declarations of affection, she ended their 2-month romance.

During his first week in the study he felt somewhat better and decided to call her. To his amazement, she said, "Maybe we should work on our relationship." He had dinner with her and was delighted that she wanted to continue to see him. He relaxed, stopped worrying, and became less affected by the little things that had been tormenting him. He attributed his dramatic increase in positive mood to "fate," namely, that she was ready to see him again. He reluctantly admitted that he had initiated the spiral of events associated with the improvement in his mood.

This man was receiving a placebo, not the medication for depression. What caused his improvement? It certainly was not the contents of the inert pills he was taking. A relevant fact is that the trial in which he was participating was conducted in a clinic. Each time he came to the clinic for a new supply of pills he had contact with a clinician who inquired as to how he was getting along. We will never know exactly why improvement took place in this case. It might have been a spontaneous remission—that is, the patient might simply have gotten better in the absence of active treatment. This seems unlikely, since the man's depression was long-standing. The improvement might have come about because participation in the clinical trial created hope that he would be helped by doing so. The clinician's questions about how the patient was getting along might have been quite supportive, given how lonely he was. The hope created by coming to the clinic and getting to know the clinician may have given the man enough courage to make an attempt at rekindling the romantic relationship he so desired. This attempt was his alone—and yet the clinical contacts probably played a facilitative role. This man's improvement shows the need for (1) well-controlled evaluations of therapies and (2) large enough numbers of participants so that occasional unexpected improvements of people in placebo conditions do not wash out the effect of whatever therapeutic effects the experimental condition might have.

To lay the groundwork for a discussion of how therapies are evaluated, compared, and in some instances combined, we shall briefly review the therapeutic approaches described earlier in the book as we considered the various diagnostic groupings. Doing this will highlight how much we have learned along the way and prepare us for a discussion of issues involved in research on therapeutic methods and their evaluation.

Psychotherapy

All forms of psychotherapy involve interchanges between a patient and a therapist. These interchanges, which are nonverbal as well as verbal, are aimed at understanding what is on the patient's mind. This understanding is then used as a basis for efforts to change the patient's maladaptive ways of thinking, reacting to situations, and relating to others.

In the course of their work, and regardless of their theoretical orientations, therapists must perform three tasks: (1) listening, (2) understanding, and (3) responding. The therapist listens to the patient in order to learn about his or her preoccupations, worries, and concerns. Listening serves two functions: it lets the therapist hear about topics that the patient brings up spontaneously, and it provides information pertinent to the therapist's hypotheses about the patient's problems. Listening provides a basis for the therapist's understanding of the patient's self-concept and view of the world.

Through listening and understanding, the therapist becomes able to respond. The response might be a question aimed at eliciting more information, or it might be a comment. The comment might be an interpretation of what has been going on in the session or in the patient's interpersonal relationships. As our review will demonstrate, there are many types of psychotherapy that differ in their theoretical bases, aims, and techniques. Yet there are also important similarities.

Psychodynamic Therapy and Psychoanalysis

While psychoanalysis might well be described as the granddaddy of virtually all forms of psychotherapy, its greatest influence has been in the field of psychodynamic therapy, which includes a variety of approaches. A **psychoanalysis** requires on average between 2 and 5 years, usually with four to five sessions per week. The patient lies on a couch, and the therapist sits out of the patient's line of sight in order to avoid distracting the patient from the process of **free association.**

Psychodynamic therapy is typically conducted with the patient and the therapist sitting facing or almost facing each other. The patient is encouraged to review early relationships with parents and significant others, but the therapist also directs attention to the situations facing the patient at present. The patient is expected to do most of the talking, while the psychodynamic therapist occasionally interjects clarifications to assist the patient in understanding the dynamics of the problem that led him or her to seek professional help.

An important feature of psychoanalysis and psychodynamic psychotherapy is **transference,** the displacement by the client of affect and feelings from one important person (mother, father, spouse) to another—specifically, the therapist. In **positive transference,** the patient feels predominantly friendly and affectionate toward the therapist. In **negative transference,** hostility predominates. **Countertransference** refers to the therapist's emotional reactions to a patient. It is important for the success of treatment that the therapist be aware of the countertransference reactions. Psychoanalysts must be analyzed themselves because of the belief that their self-insight will increase their awareness of their countertransference reactions (see Figure 16-1).

Insight is a major goal of both psychoanalysis and psychodynamic psychotherapy because of the belief that as people acquire a more realistic view of their motivations and the needs of other people, the likelihood of behavioral change increases.

Figure 16-1 Therapists may have negative reactions to patients because of countertransference.

SOURCE: Drawing by D. Reilly; © 1991 by *The New Yorker* Magazine, Inc.

After months of talking about her husband as a demanding, overbearing man who was always gloomy, Rose Francis, aged 50, remarked to her therapist: "You know, I guess I really don't like him." There was a tone of wonder and surprise in her voice when she said this. After recognizing her strong negative feelings toward her husband, Mrs. Francis found it possible to identify and sympathize with some of her husband's worries and concerns. She became better able to see the world through his eyes. The opportunity to tell her therapist, "You know, I guess I really don't like him," enabled Rose to be more accepting of her husband than she had been for years. Gaining insight into negative feelings often enables an individual to be more objective about the situation that gave rise to the feelings in the first place. In this case, Rose was able to ask herself the question, "Why does he behave as he does toward me?" and this thought then allowed her to think about the specific behaviors in the situation rather than about her angry feelings.

While Rose Francis's insight concerning her view of her husband seemed to influence her attitude toward him, the nature of the relationship between insight and behavior change is often unclear. Sometimes gaining insight leads directly to behavior change, while at other times it seems to be unrelated to what people do and how they live their lives. The patient in Figure 16-2 may be gaining an insight, but the acquisition doesn't seem to be modifying his behavior.

Recovered Memories Psychodynamically oriented therapists generally agree about the importance of making the unconscious conscious. They seek to recover repressed memories in the effort to achieve this. But are the **recovered memories** correct? Because trauma-linked material recovered often pertains to early childhood, it may not be possible to obtain objective confirmation that the recovered memories are true. Did the traumatic events the pa-

tient remembers really take place, or might the recovered memories be the patient's response to the therapist's suggestions that the traumatic experiences had occurred or might have occurred? Because of the possibility that the allegedly repressed memories are false, several writers have questioned the validity of the idea of the lifting of repression (Lynn & McConkey, 1988). The fallibility and malleability of memory is familiar to anyone who has had his or her vivid recall of a third-birthday party shattered by a grainy home movie. One's present bad life situation (e.g., being in an acrimonious marriage) and the need to explain it might well distort a person's memories. In addition, a therapist's beliefs about the causes of a person's psychological problems might also distort memories by directing a patient's thought in a particular direction.

Recovered memories about childhood sexual abuse and other traumatic experiences may well be correct, but what is often lacking is objective evidence of their validity. Without this type of verification, it becomes conjectural whether recovered memories are correct or are due to inadequacies of the therapeutic method, to the workings of the patient's or therapist's mind, or to some other factor. Such possibilities make it clear that a significant challenge confronts psychodynamic therapists and researchers: When can memories be trusted? There is some evidence that the brain processes traumatic memories differently from the way ordinary memories are recorded and stored (Nadel & Jacobs, 1988). Still, at the present time, the remembrance of things past can be a mysterious process, with realities and myths blending into a vivid—but perhaps incorrect—picture (see Box 16-1).

Hypnosis Hypnosis is an approach taken by some psychotherapists as a means of recovering repressed memories and helping patients deal with them. **Hypnosis** involves a process of inducing a trancelike state in which the person being hypnotized is receptive to suggestions made by the hypnotist. In addition to receptivity to suggestion, the hypnotic state is characterized by an altered state of consciousness in which focused attention and concentration appear to be maximized. The hypnotized person seems exceptionally attentive to inner experience during the hypnotic session. Some psychotherapists use hypnosis for a variety of purposes: to suggest specific changes in thinking or behavior; as an aid in psychotherapy (e.g., to help a client overcome anxiety or deal with upsetting ideas); and to enhance relaxation. Although the technique has been used clinically for years, research on hypnosis is in its infancy. There is controversy over what hypnosis actually is. However, because of its success in inducing states that appear to involve relaxation, it has aroused the interest of behavior therapists as well as psychotherapists.

It is now known that hypnosis is an altered state of consciousness—an intense alertness in which the mind can screen out extraneous matters and focus on particular details. The hypnotic state is characterized by heightened

"YOU'RE RIGHT, I'M ARROGANT AND BOSSY, AND RELATE TO OTHERS INAPPROPRIATELY. READ THAT BACK."

Figure 16–2 Insight does not always lead to behavior change.

First Person   Box 16–1

False Memories

Harold I. Lief, a respected and experienced psychiatrist, raises questions that many other clinicians are also raising about the recovery of unconscious material.

Imagine that you are consulted by parents whose adult daughter has just accused her father of incestuous relations a decade or more after the alleged sexual abuse occurred. Who to believe—the parents or the adult child?

On the one hand, sex abuse is a frequent and frightful experience with potentially disastrous consequences for adult adaptation. On the other hand, a false allegation of incest will rip apart a family, inflicting a blow from which few families can fully recover. What a dilemma for the psychiatrist.

What if you believe that the therapist treating the adult "victim" has unduly influenced the patient by a style of interviewing in which suggestion, perhaps even hypnosis, has been used to elicit

memories of abuse? How reliable are such memories?

The issue of real versus false allegations of child abuse, which haunted Freud, still haunts us today but for different reasons. We need to research the frequency of false accusations, the motives for making them, the role of the therapists in generating them, and the relationship between repressed memories and the process by which they are recalled. (Lief, 1992, p. 8)

In 1994, a special committee of the American Psychological Association issued a report on memories of abuse. The report acknowledges both the possibility of remembering long-forgotten memories of abuse and of constructing convincing pseudomemories for events that never occurred. These were the committee's conclusions:

- Controversies about adult recollections should not obscure the fact that child sexual abuse is a complex, per-

vasive problem in America that has historically been unacknowledged.
- Most people who were sexually abused as children remember all or part of what happened to them.
- It is possible for memories of abuse that have been forgotten for a long time to be remembered, although the mechanisms by which this might happen are not well understood.
- It is possible to construct convincing pseudomemories for events that never occurred, although the mechanisms by which this occurs are not well understood.
- There are gaps in knowledge about the processes that lead to accurate or inaccurate recollection of childhood sexual abuse.

The committee also noted that it was important (1) for therapists to approach questions of childhood abuse from a neutral position and (2) for individuals looking for a psychotherapist to seek a licensed practitioner who has training and experience in the issues for which treatment is sought.

---

susceptibility to suggestion. It allows people to suspend logical reasoning and draw upon psychological strengths that they do not normally command voluntarily. The focused concentration and heightened suggestibility of the hypnotic state help the individual accept the therapist's directions and come to grips with problems more rapidly.

Although the scientific study of hypnosis is a relatively recent development, much has been learned about how it works and its effects. We now know that there are wide differences among people in their susceptibility to hypnosis. Instances of post-hypnotic amnesia are commonly reported. That is, if told to forget what occurred under hypnosis, some suggestible subjects show an absence of recall until they are later told by the hypnotist that they can remember. Because hypnosis does not seem to be a distinct physiological state and because hypnotized and nonhypnotized subjects often behave in identical ways, psychologists have sought to understand hypnosis in terms of such psychological processes as dissociation, imagination, and role-playing.

Humanistic and Existential Therapies

Several schools of psychotherapy either disagree with the assumptions of psychoanalytic theory or modify them in

certain ways. The neo-Freudians accept most psychodynamic principles but reject the emphasis placed by psychoanalytic theory on instinctual unconscious impulses. **Humanistic therapies** emphasize people's desire to achieve self-respect. **Existential therapies** emphasize the need to confront basic questions of existence, such as: What is the meaning of my life? Am I hiding from myself?

Common to humanistic and existential approaches is a focus on the client's experience in the therapy situation and the view that each individual is the expert concerning his or her unique experience in life. These approaches seek to foster a person's potential for growth, self-determination, and choice. They hold that new awareness and the creation of new meanings are the basis of behavioral change. These therapeutic approaches share the view that an effective relationship with the therapist is crucial in bringing about this change.

Client-Centered Therapy **Client-centered therapy** is a leading example of humanistic therapy. Carl Rogers, the founder of client-centered therapy, saw the individual as seeking personal growth but needing the support of an appreciative, accepting therapist. The therapist is a nondirective facilitator who encourages the client's self-exploration and efforts to achieve greater maturity and self-confidence. Whereas in traditional psychodynamic therapy the therapeutic relationship—including transference and countertransference—and the therapist's interpretations help clients solve personal problems, in client-centered therapy a nonjudgmental therapist facilitates the process of self-understanding by serving as a mirror for the client.

Client-centered therapists emphasize the importance of **unconditional positive regard,** nonjudgmental acceptance and empathy shown by the therapist. Whereas a behavior therapist would concentrate on getting clients to change their behavior, a Rogerian therapist would focus on supplying an environment in which the client feels free to express thoughts and feelings. The client-centered therapists assume that unconditional positive regard will increase the client's self-acceptance and self-knowledge, which, in turn, will lead the client to change his or her behavior.

Gestalt Therapy Gestalt therapy focuses on patients' perceptions of themselves and the world. It is based on the recognition that people unconsciously organize their perceptions as a *Gestalt:* a meaningful, integrated whole. A Gestalt therapist uses a variety of techniques, including role-playing, in an effort to stimulate the client to express strong emotions. Fritz Perls, the founder of Gestalt therapy, stressed the relationships between distorted perceptions, motivations, and emotions. Unlike most humanistic therapists, who stress the importance of unconditional positive regard for the client, Perls (1969) believed that the therapist's main task was to frustrate the client, to make him or her angry enough to fight out conflicts with authority and thereby develop enhanced feelings of self-worth. Perls believed that instead of trying to reconstruct the history of the client's relationships with others, as is done in traditional psychodynamic therapy and psychoanalysis, the therapist should stress the client's moment-to-moment experiences as each session progresses.

Gestalt therapists believe that anxiety and personality disorders arise when people dissociate parts of themselves, particularly their need for personal gratification, from awareness. Because dreams often contain clues to dissociated parts of the self, Gestalt therapists encourage discussion and acting out of dreams.

Cognitive Psychotherapy

Conversation is the primary vehicle by which **cognitive psychotherapy** seeks to achieve change. However, this vehicle is aimed at cognitive errors rather than uncovering hidden memories or psychodynamics (see Figure 16-3). Since opinions, beliefs, and conceptions are ordinarily formed on the basis of evidence, adequate or inadequate, we can also assume that beliefs may be modified by evidence. Psychotherapy may, in fact, provide one of the few situations in which individuals are encouraged to think

Figure 16-3 Is this the real world? If this man believes he deserves this sort of hero's welcome all the time, he may need help in coping with the letdowns that will occur when he is not welcomed as a conquering hero.

SOURCE: Drawing by Frascino; © 1987 by *The New Yorker* Magazine, Inc.

somewhat systematically about their beliefs, particularly their beliefs about themselves. A number of psychotherapeutic approaches share the assumption that maladaptive behavior is a product of unrealistic perceptions and conditions. The various cognitive therapies use different tactics in redirecting the way people see and interpret their experiences, but they all generally reject the Freudian emphasis on the powerful role of unconscious drives (see Table 16-1).

In his widely used therapy, Aaron Beck emphasizes the irrational ideas that contribute to feelings of depression and thoughts of suicide. The approach basically consists of a collaborative inquiry into the validity of patients' false beliefs about themselves, the world at large, and the future. (Tom Martin's therapist took this approach.) For example, a patient who believes he or she is a worthless individual may be encouraged to offer evidence in support of that view and then be asked to consider possible alternative interpretations of such evidence.

Rational-Emotive Therapy Rational-emotive therapy, also directs the patient's attention to incorrect assumptions and self-debasing thinking. Such thinking is based on arbitrary, inaccurate assumptions about oneself and others. It is often marked by a preoccupation with "musts": "I *must* always be friendly to people," "I *must* not disappoint my parents," "I *must* be a big success." In rational-emotive therapy, these *musts* are seen as causes of emotional arousal, which, if maintained at too high a level for too long a time, result in psychological and physical wearing down. Therapists who adhere to this approach believe that most of these and other self-defeating *musts* are pounded into

Table 16–1
Principal Elements of Cognitive Therapy

1. *Presentation of cognitive rationale to patient.* The therapist explains that emotional states are derived from the interaction of events and the individual's interpretation of them. Emotions are experienced in response to a particular event or type of event as a function of interpretations made at the time of the event or in anticipation of it.
2. *Short-term intervention.* The number of therapy sessions is usually 20 or less. One aim of the short-term focus is to facilitate motivation and maintain a problem-centered orientation.
3. *Here-and-now focus.* Without implying that historical material is irrelevant or unimportant, a here-and-now focus directs attention to the need to interrupt the vicious cycle of maladaptive cognition, mood, and behavior. Emphasis is placed on identifying and addressing the thoughts and beliefs related to the problems that brought the patient to treatment.
4. *Patient-therapist collaboration.* Therapist and patient work together to identify and track target problems, generate and apply strategies for change, and evaluate the usefulness of the strategies.
5. *Questions and homework.* Through questioning, the therapist tries to expose the patient's cognitive schemata that contribute to behavioral problems and poor performance. Homework assignments take the form of (1) maintaining daily records of mood, behavior, and dysfunctional thoughts; (2) carrying out informal experiments that test the validity of patients' thoughts, beliefs, and assumptions; and (3) applying newly acquired cognitive schemata to real-life situations.

our heads as children and that we tend to accept them without question. Thus, rational-emotive therapy has two goals: to get people to question these fundamental, but mistaken, beliefs; and then to exchange them for more constructive ones (A. Ellis & Dryden, 1997).

During the course of therapy, the rational-emotive therapist actually demonstrates the ways in which unrealistic self-verbalizations can create or worsen emotional problems. The therapist also actively questions and contradicts faulty, unreasonable assumptions by the patients and suggests alternative ways of thinking. Role-playing is often used, with the therapist demonstrating the behavioral consequences of different types of beliefs.

Brief Psychotherapies

Although psychotherapy is often thought of as a lengthy, even leisurely, exploration of the inner life, in fact most psychotherapy is relatively brief (fewer than 12 sessions) (Hersen & Biaggio, 2000). During recent years there has been an increased trend toward limiting how long psychotherapy lasts. Contributing to this trend has been the growth of health insurance programs that pay for patients' psychotherapy but place a limit on the number of therapy sessions for which payments will be made. A large number of these programs, often referred to as managed care, were introduced in the 1980s to contain health care costs. A key factor in cost containment is the requirement that the insurance program review and approve interventions recommended by clinicians.

Brief therapies usually have specific goals or targets, such as helping an individual cope with a pressing problem or distressing life event (e.g., the death of a loved one). Today, many therapists who perform brief therapy

make use of a variety of techniques and theoretical approaches. As we have just seen, cognitive therapy is one such approach. Interpersonal therapy also illustrates the time-limited approaches that are increasingly being used.

Interpersonal Therapy Interpersonal therapy was originally designed for people suffering from depression. Because of its success with this group, its use is now being extended to other types of problems. It is usually conducted in weekly 50-minute sessions for 12 to 16 weeks. The first step is a structured interview dealing with symptoms, family history, and current and recent events in the patient's life. After this, the therapist makes a tentative diagnosis and discusses it with the patient so that they can agree on a therapy plan (Weissman & Markowitz, 1994).

Interpersonal therapists are especially interested in the interpersonal relationships that play a role in a person's thoughts or mood. For example, some depressed people feel abandoned and hopeless because they are undergoing a delayed or distorted form of mourning. Their lives may have changed radically after a marital separation or death in the family. Interpersonal therapists are also attentive to role disputes that may involve incompatible expectations of people who are constantly in one another's company— husbands and wives, parents and children, friends, coworkers, and so on. The word *dispute* may be misleading, since conflicting expectations are usually not made explicit and the resulting hostility is perpetuated by faulty communication as well as by unreconciled differences. Interpersonal therapists introduce these issues only if the patient hints at them, but they have to listen carefully, because many people are so preoccupied with themselves that they hardly notice other people's expectations and concerns. Where appropriate, the interpersonal therapist helps the patient to reinterpret complaints and examine suppressed feelings and thoughts. Other issues with which interpersonal therapists deal are role transitions (e.g., moving, graduating, the birth of a child) and interpersonal deficits (which are often reflected in social isolation).

How Effective Is Psychotherapy?

Many groups have a stake in the evaluation of therapeutic effectiveness. Patients, their families, therapists, researchers, insurance companies, legislators, and planners of mental health services all want to know about effectiveness.

One useful approach in evaluating therapeutic effectiveness is to ask the customer—the patient. This is exactly what the magazine *Consumer Reports* did when it surveyed a large sample of its 4 million subscribers. Approximately 184,000 randomly selected readers were sent questionnaires that included questions related to mental health services. Twenty-two thousand respondents returned the questionnaires. Of these, more than 31% reported having sought help for emotional problems sometime in the preceding 3 years. The sources of help were varied and included family, friends, clergy, and mental health professionals (such as psychologists and psychiatrists).

With regard to the services provided by mental health professionals, there were a number of noteworthy findings (Seligman, 1995). Most of the respondents judged themselves to be feeling much better as a result of their therapy experiences. For example, of those who were feeling very distressed when they began therapy, 87% reported feeling better at the time of the survey. Those who received long-term therapy (2 years or more) reported more improvement than those who had had short-term therapy. Nevertheless, there were also high improvement rates for people who had short-term therapy. There did not appear to be a significant difference between people who received psychotherapy plus medication and those who received only psychotherapy. There also did not appear to be any significant differences among different types of psychotherapy. Respondents whose choices of therapist or duration of treatment were limited by managed care reported less improvement than those who did not have this limitation.

While encouraging, these positive results are not the final word regarding the effectiveness of psychotherapy. They provide information from only one perspective, the patient's. Only a small proportion of subscribers who received questionnaires returned them, and those who described their mental status prior to starting therapy necessarily had to rely on their memory of events that had occurred many months ago. It would be interesting to compare patients' ratings of improvement with those of

the therapists, and also to compare responses to questions phrased in different ways (Brock et al., 1998).

Given that there are many types of psychotherapy, it is obvious that researchers have their work cut out for them. Obtaining information about therapeutic effectiveness is not easy for a number of reasons. For example, individual therapists differ in their ability to carry out particular therapies. Furthermore, some therapies may be more effective with certain types of patients than with others. Psychotherapy is not a single process applied to a single problem. Research on therapy is improving as studies become more complex and incorporate more relevant factors into their research designs. For many reasons, researchers cannot conduct studies on the effectiveness of different therapies in the same way that laboratory studies are usually carried out. Table 16-2 summarizes some of the practical differences between these types of studies.

Before a clinical research project is carried out, there must be agreement on how to measure the results. For example, suppose a researcher intends to assess the effectiveness of a type of psychotherapy designed to reduce the tendency to hallucinate. One way to measure the dependent variable would be to count the number of times people report having hallucinatory experiences. But people might have hallucinations that they did not report, or might make up such experiences just to have something to report. Thus, whereas some clinicians might contend that frequency of reported hallucinations is a reasonable index of the general tendency to hallucinate, others might not be satisfied with this conclusion.

In any research, all groups of subjects must be as similar or equal as possible before the experiment begins. The therapists in the various groups should also be comparable. Most studies of therapy techniques compare a group of people who receive treatment with one or two groups of people who do not. But such comparisons do not show how individuals within the treatment groups are affected by specific aspects of the treatment. Clinicians also need to know how changes in the patient's behavior are related to what the clinician does or says.

Because of these complexities, and despite hundreds of research studies, there are disagreements about the relative effectiveness of the different psychological therapies. Researchers with different criteria and expectations have obtained different results from such comparisons.

Meta-analysis The technique known as **meta-analysis** (discussed in chapter 14) can be used to summarize the results of many studies. Meta-analysis involves (1) grouping studies in which treatment conditions have been compared with an untreated control condition on one or more measures of outcome; (2) statistically determining the therapeutic effects on different groups using the available measures; and (3) averaging the sizes of the effects

Table 16-2		
Differences Between Experimental Laboratory Studies and Evaluation of Therapy		
Factor	Laboratory Study	Therapy
Independent variables	Usually quite clearly defined	Complex; often difficult to define clearly
Dependent variables	Usually quite clearly defined	Often involve complex sets of responses that change over time
Experimental situation	Well controlled	Impossible to eliminate unexpected events
Other situations	Researcher usually not concerned about what happens to subject outside experimental situation	Therapist is interested in outcome for patient outside therapy situation

across the studies that the researcher wants to compare. In this way, groups receiving psychotherapy can be compared with untreated control groups and groups receiving other therapeutic approaches, such as systematic desensitization and behavior modification. Figure 16-4 provides an example of a meta-analysis of 475 studies of the effects of psychotherapy. This meta-analysis showed that the average patient receiving therapy was generally better off in a measurable way than 75% of people who received no treatment, and was also better off with respect to the alleviation of fear and anxiety than were 83% of the untreated controls (M. L. Smith et al., 1980). Subsequent studies have also yielded results showing that patients given psychotherapy have better outcomes than people in untreated control groups. Whether meta-analysis is the best way to answer questions about therapeutic effectiveness is still being debated.

However, the number of meta-analytic studies is increasing, and so is their complexity (J. A. Hall & Rosenthal, 1995). Greater complexity is needed, in part because researchers do not want to be criticized for mixing studies that are not similar. The results of meta-analysis are harder to interpret if the effect sizes from fundamentally different types of studies are lumped together. Perhaps the sharpest criticism of meta-analysis is that comparisons of studies that are methodologically weak can add little to an ultimate evaluation of therapeutic effects. On the other hand, meta-analysis of tighter, more homogeneous studies could prove very enlightening. Unfortunately, so many factors are relevant to therapy outcomes that there are not enough studies incorporating all these factors to permit the most meaningful meta-analyses. For example, it is quite conceivable that certain types of therapy used with certain types of patients are highly effective when certain outcome measures, but not others, are used. The results might be different using other therapies, patients, clinical problems, and outcome measures.

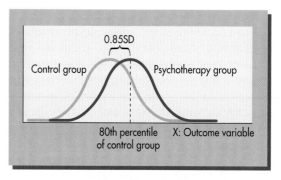

Figure 16-4 Meta-analysis involves the statistical combination of many separate and often very different studies. This figure illustrates the general findings of an analysis that combined 475 controlled studies of therapeutic effectiveness. The average person in the treated group was 0.85 standard deviations above the mean for the control group on the measures used to evaluate therapeutic outcome. This difference is a large one when compared to the effects of many experimental interventions used in psychology or education. For example, cutting the size of a school class in half causes an increase in achievement of 0.15 standard deviation units, and the effect of 9 months of instruction in reading is an improvement in reading skills of 0.67 standard deviation units.

SOURCE: M. L. Smith, Glass, and Miller (1980), p. 88.

Given all the complexities associated with the evaluation of psychotherapy, are any general summary statements possible? Overall, psychotherapy plays a positive role in the lives of those who receive it (Shadish et al., 1997). Borderline and obsessive-compulsive individuals are less likely to have favorable outcomes, as are people with severe interpersonal difficulties, and those who are poorly motivated or expect psychotherapy to be painless (Mohr, 1995). There is growing evidence that psychotherapy is helpful in regard not only to personal adjustment, but also to health, recovery from illness, and overcoming disability (Bennett, 1996). For example, one study found that psychotherapy is superior to the usual medical treatment of irritable bowel syndrome, a condition marked by abdominal cramping and diarrhea (Blanchard & Malamood, 1996). Psychotherapy also seems to play a positive economic role in reducing the cost of health care (Gabbard et al., 1997).

Ingredients of Effective Psychotherapy The evidence that in many instances psychotherapy, rather than a particular brand of a psychotherapy, has positive effects has contributed to interest in identifying factors common to different therapies that might be the "active ingredients." Particular emphasis is being placed on therapist variables and the therapist-patient match. The therapist's ability to instill hope in people who are upset may be especially important.

Research on the nature of psychological therapies has explored the characteristics, attitudes, and behavior of the patient and therapist in addition to the therapeutic technique used. What goes on in therapy sessions can be characterized in terms of the operation of two sets of factors. **Technique factors** are the procedures employed by the therapist, which may or may not match the descriptions of those procedures found in books and manuals. **Interpersonal factors** refer to the social chemistry, or dynamics of the relationship, between the therapist and the patient. While it would be convenient if technique factors were the only ingredients in therapy, interpersonal factors not only are important but also can be decisive in influencing the outcome. For example, a study of treatment for substance-use disorders found that therapists showed widely different rates of effectiveness and that high effectiveness was associated with the therapist's possession of strong interpersonal skills (Najavits & Weiss, 1994).

If psychological therapies are effective in treating specific clinical problems, an important question is, which events in therapy sessions are the active ingredients, the ones that actually bring about change? **Process research** is concerned with the elements of psychotherapy, that is, what actually happens in therapy. This research explores such topics as the following:

1. The therapist-patient relationship.
2. The patient's goals, and whether they change over time.
3. The therapist's goals, and whether they change over time.
4. The content of therapeutic sessions and changes in content over time.
5. Types of emotional expression at different phases of the therapeutic process.
6. How the patient and therapist perceive the sessions.
7. Whether the sessions focus on achieving insight or direct behavior modification.

Researchers who study the therapeutic process seek to identify the events, beliefs, and attitudes in psychotherapy that contribute to the patient's improvement.

In addition to providing support and acceptance, good therapists give their patients the opportunity to learn that the world may not be as punishing a place as they think it is. The therapist may serve as a model who disconfirms the patient's irrational or unnecessarily pessimistic beliefs about the nature of interpersonal relationships, as shown in the following case:

> *A patient complained that she could not feel close to men. She was burdened by the unconscious belief that unless she was totally compliant with a man's wishes, he would feel insulted and reject her. She soon began to respond to the male therapist in the same way, withdrawing from him out of fear that she might feel forced to accept damaging interpretations or follow bad advice. So she consciously decided that before confronting any other problems, she would have to change her belief in the need for compliance. Encouraged by her therapist, she decided to test the belief through trial actions.*
>
> *On one occasion she questioned some of the therapist's comments and felt relieved when the therapist was not upset; he had passed her test. He pointed out her exaggerated fear of hurting him. As a result, she felt less constrained by her unrealistic belief, less anxious and defensive. She relaxed some of the repression she had maintained in obedience to the belief and recalled that her father used to sulk whenever she challenged him. She then began to challenge the therapist more directly, and at the same time felt more able to cooperate with him. Once she knew that she did not have to agree with his ideas, she could like him and take his ideas seriously. She also began to feel more comfortable with her boyfriend and was able to work on problems she would have been afraid to confront before.*

Research on the process of psychotherapy requires evaluation of therapists' ability to form working alliances with patients. Study of therapists, as well as types of therapies, are needed in the scientific study of the therapeutic process.

Cognitive-Behavioral Approaches

So far, we have discussed only those therapies in which conversational interchange is the primary vehicle used to treat people with problems. We turn now to some psychologically based approaches that are more action-oriented, directed toward changing specific types of maladaptive behavior, and that usually follow a carefully laid out plan for strengthening or weakening target responses.

These approaches originally grew out of learning theories dealing with the acquisition and extinction of behavioral responses. They tended to be behavioristic, avoiding discussion of mental events and focusing on identifiable stimuli and responses. Since they were not amenable to direct observation, cognition, affect, and motivation were held to be beyond the purview of psychological inquiry. Terms such as *behavior therapy* and *behavior modification* were used to describe these approaches.

Behavior Therapy

Behavior therapy uses techniques based on operant and classical conditioning in an effort to change maladaptive behavior. Table 16-3 lists the basic assumptions of behavior therapy. The operant techniques used in behavior therapy led to an approach referred to as *behavior modification*. The classical conditioning approach resulted in a variety of desensitization techniques used to reduce people's fear of specific situations or particular objects. **Behavior modification** refers to the application of operant learning principles to bring about a specific change in behavior. Although behavior modification originated as a technique based on operant conditioning, combinations of behavioral and cognitive approaches are now the most commonly used techniques in programs for behavioral change. Operant conditioning methods use schedules of reinforcement and shaping to gradually achieve a desired response. Special prompts might be employed to highlight a situation that calls for a particular response. **Fading** refers to gradual elimination of these special cues when they are no longer needed. Positive reinforcers (such as praise or

money) are used to strengthen desired responses. The **token economy** method is one of the most common applications of operant principles to modify maladaptive behavior. In a token economy, patients are given reward tokens, such as poker chips, for socially constructive behaviors. The tokens can later be exchanged for desirable items or activities. Extinction procedures and punishment might be used to eliminate undesirable responses. When punishment is employed to eliminate a response, it is a good idea to positively reinforce an alternative, more desirable, response at the same time.

Biofeedback is an application of behavior therapy in which the individual is reinforced whenever a designated change in bodily functioning takes place. Through biofeedback the individual becomes better able to control internal processes, such as body temperature and heart rate, that are related to maladaptation.

Behavior therapy has made important contributions by emphasizing the need for fine-grained analysis of how individuals react to specific life situations. It has also shown the value of a skills-training orientation to therapy and of specifying therapy outcomes especially relevant for individual patients.

Cognitive–Behavioral Therapy

As psychology moved in a cognitive direction, it became clear that thought processes were frequently as important as environmental influences. As a consequence, interventions were developed to modify cognitions that contribute to maladaptive behavior. The term **cognitive-behavioral therapy** refers to these interventions that integrate cognitive and behavioral therapies.

Cognitive therapies, such as the one devised by Aaron Beck, were developed within traditional psychotherapeutic settings. Cognitive-behavioral therapy reflects the increasing interest of therapists in cognitive modification as a means of influencing emotions and behaviors. This approach to therapy makes use of a variety of behavioral techniques, such as a graded program of activities, homework, and role-playing, along with an effort to identify and modify unrealistic cognitions. In recent years, cognitive therapists and behavior therapists have freely borrowed techniques from one another. For example, Beck now employs homework assignments in his therapeutic work. Cognitive-behavioral therapy builds on behavior therapy.

Components of Cognitive-Behavioral Therapy   In one sense, cognitive-behavioral therapy is not as easily defined as certain other therapies. Psychoanalysts always focus on certain general aspects of their work with patients—for example, transference. On the other hand, cognitive-behavioral therapists will use one or more

---

Table 16–3
Basic Assumptions of Behavior Therapy

1. Most abnormal behavior is acquired and maintained according to the same principles as normal behavior.
2. Most abnormal behavior can be modified through the application of social learning principles.
3. The current determinants of behavior must be assessed.
4. People are best described by what they do in specific life situations.
5. Treatment methods are precisely specified and objectively evaluated.
6. Treatment outcome is evaluated in terms of generalization to the real-life setting and its maintenance over time.
7. Treatment strategies are individually tailored to different problems in different individuals.
8. Extensive use is made of psychological assistance, from parents and teachers and others, in order to modify problem behavior in the settings in which it occurs.

therapeutic interventions that seem appropriate to the needs of particular patients. Let's review some of these therapeutic components.

Relaxation Training **Relaxation training** often helps people who are tense and generally anxious. In one approach, emphasis is placed on learning to contrast muscular tension with muscular relaxation. In another, meditation procedures are employed. Relaxation therapies appear to be helpful for a variety of psychophysiological disorders, particularly tension headaches and migraine headaches. However, they usually are not sufficient by themselves. Life-styles, social environments, and views of the world can create or compound problems in living. Such factors as the quality and nature of available social support and the individual's goals, attitudes, and values often must be addressed. Table 16-4 lists a number of factors that bear on the advisability of using relaxation techniques in a given case.

Research on relaxation skills requires answers to two questions: (1) has the individual learned the relaxation skills? and (2) does use of the skills lead to beneficial clinical results? Obviously, if the skills were never learned, there would be little reason to expect positive results from relaxation training. Appropriate control groups are needed to provide an adequate basis for judging the effectiveness of training. There is also a need for studies that explore the effectiveness of relaxation training, both alone and in combination with other types of therapy.

Muscular relaxation involves tensing and then relaxing various muscle groups. The individual is encouraged to note the differences between feeling tense and feeling relaxed. Relaxation training is used in many methods, including natural childbirth and yoga. People who have difficulty falling asleep often find that relaxation exercises help them get to sleep more quickly. At first, individuals use relaxation exercises mainly in the therapeutic situation. But as their ability to relax themselves improves, they are encouraged to perform relaxation exercises in stressful situations that they encounter in everyday life.

Table 16–4
Factors in Successful Use of Relaxation Training

1. The individual's problems do not have an organic basis.
2. The individual is not psychotic, depressed, or subject to panic attacks.
3. The individual is able to assume responsibility for active participation in treatment, with special emphasis on home practice.
4. Family members are cooperative with and supportive of the individual's treatment.
5. The individual has reasonable expectations of the training's effectiveness.

In relaxation training involving **meditation,** the individual learns to concentrate on a thought, a sensation, a word, an object, or some mental state. Some techniques are very active and require that the person make a strenuous effort to focus on a specific thing. Certain yoga techniques, for example, require that the practitioner maintain specific postures and deliberately control his or her breathing or other bodily functions.

Exposure Therapy **Exposure therapy** is based on the principle that continued exposure to anxiety-provoking stimuli will decrease anxiety to manageable levels and reduce phobic responses. **Exposure** consists of a gradual approach to an anxiety-provoking situation. Under such conditions the distress experienced in the situation is kept at a relatively low level.

Exposure to fear-arousing situations is one of the most effective ways of overcoming fear. However, there are positive results only if patients are willing to expose themselves to the situations they are afraid of. Although **in vivo exposure** (actually being in the situation) usually works best, **fantasized exposure** (thinking about being in the situation) is also effective. Exposure treatment is appropriate for many unpleasant or disadvantageous emotional responses. If the treatment is effective, improvement can usually be observed within five or six sessions.

Flooding is a form of exposure therapy in which the patient is exposed to a flood of fear-arousing stimuli that is not terminated simply because the patient experiences a high level of tension. In flooding, the clinical session is saturated with frightening thoughts and images in the hope that emotional responses to them will be extinguished through "burnout." If this happens, **extinction** is said to have occurred.

In **implosive therapy,** the patient experiences higher and higher levels of anxiety through working with the therapist to vividly imagine scenes depicting behavior and situations that he or she has strenuously avoided in the past. The imagery used in treatment is intended to represent conflict areas that are thought to be the source of the avoidance behavior. The imagined situations used in implosive therapy tend to be much more intense than the stimuli used in flooding.

Systematic desensitization combines behavioral training (muscular relaxation) with cognitive activity. It begins with the induction of a relaxed state. While the patient is relaxed, he or she imagines scenes related to his or her specific fear. Desensitization begins with scenes or images that are only mildly fear-arousing. The patient is encouraged to concentrate on perpetuating the relaxed state while imagining those situations. Once the patient is able to remain relaxed, scenes that are progressively more upsetting are imagined.

The theory behind systematic desensitization is that the relaxation response competes with previously learned anxiety responses, such as fears and phobias. Research has shown that practicing relaxation when the fear-arousing stimulus is actually present (in vivo exposure) yields results superior to simply imagining the stimulus. Desensitization works best with people who habitually show noticeable increases in physiological arousal (e.g., accelerated heart rate, moist palms) when exposed to the fear-arousing stimulus.

Modeling   Often people are unaware that habit controls much of their behavior. Through **modeling,** they can be shown that there are other ways of doing things. Although modeling can take place when an individual observes someone demonstrating specific social skills, it also occurs informally—for example, when children imitate the heroes of television shows. In clinical applications of modeling, demonstrations by models are often combined with **guided rehearsals,** in which the individual is encouraged to imitate the behavior of the model with the model helping whenever necessary. When people imitate the adaptive behavior of models, their new responses are strengthened by positive reinforcement. The success of a modeling program depends on several factors:

1. How carefully the observer attends to the modeled behavior.
2. How well what was observed is retained.
3. The observer's ability to reproduce the modeled behavior.
4. How motivated the observer is to use the modeled behavior.

Live modeling involves direct observation of a model. **Participant modeling,** or **behavioral rehearsal,** goes one step further by requiring the client to practice the behavior, often in interaction with the model. **Symbolic modeling** refers to observation of a model who is presented indirectly through film, video- or audiotape, or the printed word. **Covert modeling** is a logical extension of symbolic modeling in which the individual is asked to imagine observing a model and a particular consequence. For example, a male cross-dresser was asked to engage in covert modeling by imagining the following scene:

> *You are standing behind a one-way mirror. You see a bare room except for two single beds with clothes on them. One bed has male clothes on it and the other has female clothes on it. Straight ahead at the other end of the room, you see a door open and a naked man about your age walks into the room. He walks toward the beds which are next to each other about four feet apart. He starts to go toward the bed with the female clothes on it. He looks at the clothes; suddenly you can see a painful expression on his face. He sits down on the bed. Now he starts to sweat and looks sick. He reaches for a bra and he starts to gag. As he puts the bra on he starts to vomit all over the clothes and on himself. He groans in agony as he doubles over and falls down to the ground. He is lying with the bra on and wallowing in vomit. (Cautela, 1985, p. 93)*

A covert modeling scene was then suggested in which the model put on the male clothes and looked happy. In general, covert modeling involves constructing scenes or situations in which the patient can picture the behavior that is to be changed.

Like other cognitive-behavioral therapies, modeling is often combined with other approaches. For example, while reinforcing adaptive overt behavior, the therapist might help the patient acquire more realistic ideas about problem areas. In treating a complex problem such as intense anger in a child, the therapist might (1) teach the parents to be more effective in reacting to temper tantrums (modeling might be used to accomplish this), (2) help the child identify the situations and thoughts that evoke the tantrums, (3) model cognitive and behavioral responses to stress and frustration that are more effective than anger, and (4) use guided rehearsal and praise to strengthen the child's adaptive behavior.

Lack of assertive behavior is often related to deficits in social skills or to interference from emotional reactions and thoughts. If appropriate behaviors are available but are not performed because of anxiety, a useful focus may be on enhancing the patient's anxiety management skills. **Assertiveness training** is specifically designed to enhance the interpersonal skills one needs to stand up for one's rights, such as refusing unwanted requests, expressing opinions, and making requests. Assertiveness training is preceded by a careful assessment of the patient's responses in certain types of situations. The assessment is designed to answer these questions: What situations are of concern to the patient? What does the patient typically do in these situations? What are the personal and environmental blocks to more assertiveness in these situations?

Modeling and behavioral rehearsal play important roles in assertiveness training programs (see Figure 16-5). Positive feedback is offered after each rehearsal, and prompting is

Figure 16-5   Modeling and behavioral rehearsal can be effective techniques in assertiveness training.

Case Study   Box 16-2

Therapy Using Several Cognitive-Behavioral Components

Lisa, a 29-year-old mechanical engineer, sought treatment for chronic anxiety and panic attacks. She had had only two panic attacks, but feared having another one. The first panic attack occurred when she was in the hospital waiting to go home with her new baby. About 2 weeks later, she had another attack. At the time of the second attack, she and her 7-year-old daughter were at home on a Saturday afternoon with the new baby. Her husband was playing basketball with friends.

Lisa's therapy extended over 15 sessions. Six months after the end of therapy, Lisa had had no recurrence of panic attacks. Several issues had emerged as the therapist discussed Lisa's problem with her. Lisa's husband had a job that required him to be away for two or three nights a week. Because of her husband's absences, Lisa had difficulty doing the overtime work required to meet her job's deadlines. Lisa frequently felt overwhelmed by the circumstances of her life.

The first thing Lisa's therapist had done was to give her a relaxation tape with the suggestion that she listen to it several times a week. The therapist thought that Lisa might be able to use some of the relaxation strategies presented on the tape to counteract anxiety when it occurred. At about the fourth week of therapy, Lisa reported much less anxiety. At that point, the therapist asked Lisa to keep a log of any negative feelings (such as anger) that she might experience. After 3 weeks of log-keeping, Lisa came to her therapy session saying that she had noticed for the first time that she felt distressed on the nights when her husband was away from home. Lisa then commented that, in addition to his absences, her husband, although loving and well-meaning, tended not to be very helpful when he was present; he seemed to expect Lisa to do most of the work of holding the family and household together.

Lisa's log-keeping led her to begin keeping a journal, which led to two positive changes. First, she realized that she needed more help around the house and hired a college student to come help her with the dinnertime bustle several nights a week. Second, when Lisa described some of the events included in her journal, the therapist concluded that Lisa needed to be more assertive in certain situations. The therapist helped Lisa cognitively restructure some of her beliefs. Instead of believing "There's no point in asking for help—I can't get it," Lisa was encouraged to think more positively. After Lisa realized that she might get help if she asked for it, during therapy sessions she and the therapist engaged in role-playing in which Lisa learned and practiced making assertive responses. She came to realize that she tended to ask for too little and to let people off the hook if her request was not immediately met.

This case illustrates the problem-solving approach taken by cognitive-behavioral therapists. After completing her cognitive-behavioral therapy, Lisa and her husband came together for 10 joint therapy sessions. This contributed to the positive development of their relationship and reduction of her distress level.

SOURCE: Based on Persons (1992).

---

provided when needed. Homework assignments are used if, as is desirable, the patient agrees to carry out tasks that require assertiveness outside the training sessions. If the assertiveness deficits extend over a broad range of social behaviors, a number of training sessions may be needed. However, if the problem is fairly specific, a few sessions may be sufficient.

A particular component of cognitive-behavioral therapy, such as assertiveness training, might be completely sufficient by itself in helping someone overcome a specific problem. However, multiple components are frequently required to achieve therapeutic success. Box 16-2 presents a case study that involved several therapeutic components.

How Effective Are Cognitive and Behavioral Approaches?

Cognitive-behavioral interventions aim to correct people's misconceptions, strengthen their coping skills and feelings of control over their own lives, and facilitate constructive self-talk, or the things people typically say to themselves as they confront different types of situations.

For instance, rather than saying "I'll never be able to do all that," they might tell themselves, "I'll just take it one step at a time."

There is growing evidence that cognitive-behavioral training can be quite effective in helping people overcome fears and inhibitions and increase their coping skills (Brewin, 1996). While the mechanism by which this training leads to improvements in behavior is not yet completely understood, an important factor seems to be the patient's sense of self-efficacy, that is, the patient's belief that he or she is effective at carrying out tasks. Feelings of self-efficacy increase when individuals acquire new skills, which in turn encourages them to strengthen their skills even further. Cognitive-behavioral interventions seem to be particularly effective in treating disorders in which anxiety and depression play prominent roles.

Integration and Extension of Psychological Therapies

Two issues related to therapeutic approaches that are currently being discussed by clinicians and researchers concern (1) the integration of elements from different therapeutic approaches in order to carry out the most ef-fective treatment of individual cases and (2) extension of approaches developed for individuals to groups. The in-tegration issue arises from the frequent observation that good therapists don't just do one thing—their therapeu-tic tactics are often complex, borrowing ideas from a va-riety of schools of therapy. The extension issue relates to the possibility that group therapy may be as effective as individual therapies and, if it is, working with groups would be more efficient than working with individuals—and would lower the cost of therapy.

Integrative Approaches to Treatment

We know that certain therapeutic approaches are particu-larly useful for certain types of problems (e.g., as we noted earlier, cognitive-behavioral interventions with individu-als suffering from certain types of anxiety and depression are especially effective). Would combining certain thera-peutic strategies that have grown out of different theoret-ical orientations enhance their applicability and effectiveness? This is a question that is increasingly being asked, and ongoing research should prove useful in pro-viding information about the range of applicability of var-ious clinical techniques.

The three cases with which the chapter began suggest that combining these techniques may be more common than might be expected. For example, Kevin's therapist's theoretical perspective was strongly psychodynamic and her use of the clinical relationship as the vehicle for achieving change was consistent with that point of view. However, in addition to the acceptance she showed to-ward Kevin, she also served as a model he might want to emulate (e.g., by her being patient and calm rather than

explosive and hostile.) She also sought to help Kevin re-organize his cognitive schemas in a way that would in-crease his self-regard and how he functioned behaviorally. Tom Martin's therapist practiced cognitive therapy and directed attention to Tom's automatic thoughts. But he also showed acceptance of and empathy for Tom's situa-tion. In addition, he effectively employed a homework as-signment (the list of people toward whom Tom had warm positive feelings) and, at appropriate points, made inter-pretations and observations about the contributions Tom was making to the situations in which he felt on guard. Garrett Cross's therapist also had a cognitive orientation but incorporated a variety of elements into the therapy, for example, education in the form of an explanation of posttraumatic stress disorder, homework, and positive re-inforcement of Garrett's ideas concerning a memorial for his wife.

What these three cases suggest and what the experi-ences of therapists of various persuasions point toward is the value of **multimodal therapy** in which a broad array of tools is used in treating individuals.

Group Approaches

Many therapists of various persuasions see group ap-proaches as vehicles for facilitating adaptive functioning. One appealing feature of group therapy is that patients can learn both by observing other group members' adap-tive and maladaptive attempts to solve personal problems and by comparing their own relationship with the thera-pist with those of the other members (see Figure 16-6).

Group therapy is usually seen as a means of broaden-ing the application of psychotherapeutic concepts. Some advocates of group psychotherapy believe it may actually

Figure 16-6 Members of a therapy group have opportunities to learn and gather support from one another and from the therapist.

produce better results than individual therapy. Groups are particularly effective when they give participants opportunities to acquire new social skills through modeling. Opportunities to rehearse or practice these skills in the group increase the chances that the participants will actually use their newly acquired skills in everyday life. The following are among the most frequently observed features of group therapy:

1. *Self-disclosure*—the opportunity to tell the group about one's personal problems and concerns.
2. *Acceptance and support*—feeling a sense of belongingness and being valued by the other group members.
3. *Norm clarification*—learning that one's problems are neither unique nor more serious than those of other group members.
4. *Social learning*—being able to relate constructively and adaptively within the group.
5. *Vicarious learning*—learning about oneself through the observation of other group members, including the therapist.
6. *Self-understanding*—finding out about one's behavior in the group setting and the motivations contributing to the behavior.

Although group therapy initially was carried out from a psychodynamic perspective, humanistic, cognitive, and behavioral therapists have developed their own group techniques (Beck & Lewis, 2000).

The experience of group therapy differs from person to person, not only because of the varying theoretical perspectives and methods of different group leaders, but also because of a number of other factors. These include the types of problems or disorders confronting the group members, the therapeutic goals that have been established, the role the leader takes, the setting in which the group meets, and the individual characteristics of the group members. Patients are usually screened before being admitted to a therapy group to ensure that they will be able to participate at an effective level and that they will not be disruptive to the group as a whole.

Group therapy provides an opportunity for members to observe how their behavior affects other people and to receive personally relevant feedback. To maximize the likelihood that this will happen, group therapists often emphasize not only what members reveal about themselves, but also how the others react to what is said in the group setting. The following account gives an example of this process:

John, usually a silent member, opened a group meeting with a carefully planned statement about an episode of sexual abuse he had experienced as a child. He told the story in a deliberate manner with a flat expression. When he finished, there were a couple of minutes of silence, whereupon John said, half-jokingly, that he didn't give a damn if the group responded to him or not. Soon the disclosure evoked many reactions in the rest of the group. Another member, Steven, began to weep, recalling a past experience of sexual molestation and its subsequent influence on his sexual identity. Two other members offered him some words of support, which fell on deaf ears: this permitted the leader to point out how hard it is for Steven to accept comfort from others. One member commented that she felt confused by the discrepancy between how much John revealed and his flat, rehearsed manner of revelation. Another member, Mary, had an entirely different set of responses to John: She felt that his overwhelming self-disclosure put pressure on other group members to respond in kind. She resented this pressure and felt manipulated by John. A lively and engaging session ensued, with many complex variations on the theme of self-disclosure. (Vinogradov & Yalom, 1990, p. 191)

How did John's revelation affect the other members? How did John feel about his self-disclosure? The group leader encouraged John to examine his feelings and to comment on the support offered to him by other group members (both the explicit support of other members and the implicit support of Steven, who revealed a similar painful experience). The leader also encouraged a discussion of observations about John's style of delivery and Mary's feelings of having been coerced and manipulated. A productive discussion took place, not so much about the content of John's early sexual abuse, but about how the group functioned in dealing with it. Later sessions suggested that John had benefited both from having made his self-disclosures and from learning about how the other members of the group reacted to them.

Cognitive–Behavioral Group Therapy Many of the originators of group therapy focused attention on the role of psychodynamic processes in how groups function. Today, while this orientation continues to flourish, there are also several other types of group therapy. For example, the focus of cognitive-behavioral group therapy is on increasing the skills and comfort of people in social situations. Group members role-play specific social situations that they find difficult. The themes of particular sessions are often selected by the therapist from prior knowledge of the members' problems. The therapist may model alternative ways of handling these situations. The role-playing is accompanied by social reinforcement and feedback, and homework tasks are assigned. Other techniques are used as well, including graded task assignments, examination of specific types of distortions that may arise in social interactions (such as overgeneralization and imagining catastrophes), and discussion of types of cognitions that have negative and positive influences in group situations.

Cognitive-behavioral group therapy is more highly structured than group therapy conducted along psychodynamic lines. From a psychodynamic point of view, group psychotherapy represents an opportunity to deal with transference in a social situation and to compare one's attitude toward participation in a group with those of other group members. The group is often seen as an extension of the family. For example, a frequent topic that arises in group therapy is the competition of group members for the therapist's attention. A psychoanalyst might see echoes of the members' relationships to parents and siblings in their performances in the group. A cognitively oriented clinician, on the other hand, would be interested primarily in the often irrational ideas of group members concerning what goes on, or should go on, in social situations. Client-centered therapists see the therapist's role in groups as basically the same as in individual counseling; in both situations the therapist is a facilitator of personal growth. Cognitive-behavioral therapists are increasingly using techniques such as modeling and behavior rehearsal in groups.

Family and Marital Therapy Sometimes therapy focuses on individuals who already constitute a group. Two examples are *family therapy* and *marital therapy*.

Family Therapy Family therapy is based on the idea that many problems not only arise from family behavior patterns but also are affected by them. The following are some of the core problems that family therapy addresses:

1. Inability to resolve conflicts, make decisions, or solve problems.
2. Chaotic family organization and lack of agreed-upon responsibilities.
3. Too rigid an organization, resulting in an inability to respond to changing circumstances and stress.
4. Overcloseness to the point that individual family members may lose a sense of individuality.

5. Lack of emotional ties and communication among family members.
6. Failure of the parents to agree on child-rearing practices.

Instead of treating family members individually, the therapist encourages the family to work as a group, dealing together with their attitudes and feelings toward one another and their resistance to cooperation and sharing (see Figure 16-7). Family therapy often provides a valuable forum for airing hostilities, reviewing emotional ties, and dealing with crises. It is important for the therapist to be fair and impartial in discussing disagreements between family members and to bear in mind that families usually are characterized by a hierarchy in which parents are expected to assume some authority and responsibility for the behavior of their children. The degree of hierarchy will vary, depending on the parents' philosophy of child-rearing and the ages of the children. For adolescents and young adults, one important problem may be that their growing independence requires modification of the hierarchical structure.

Most family therapists begin by focusing on here-and-now problems. For example, a 12-year-old boy may be intermittently truant from school, tell lies, and seek out parties on weekends where he has been known to drink beer. The child may complain of parental pressure and repeated criticism, whereas the parents express their fears about the child's unreliability and poor school performance. The therapist seeks to help the family develop plans for dealing with these problems that the parents and child then can implement together. The therapist's approach is designed to minimize guilt, scapegoating, and blame among family members and to maximize open-mindedness and cooperation among them (Papp, 2000).

Figure 16–7 During family therapy sessions, the therapist observes how the members of the family interact. Here, the therapist is using what has just been said by a family member to help the others see how one person's behavior affects other family members.

Roles in the drama of family life, possibly assumed out of loyalty or a need for belonging, may become destructive over time yet hard to abandon because they help to maintain the family. For example, a child who takes on the role of a parent because of a mother's or father's incapacity is likely to play this adult role poorly, using authority too harshly or making it a vehicle of rivalry with younger brothers and sisters. Another child may be assigned the role of "bad boy" so that one of the parents can play disciplinarian. Such roles must be openly recognized and the assignments altered if the family is to become more healthy. The family members often develop an unspoken family mythology that has important effects on all family members. The mythology may be something like "John is the stupid one" or "Father can't work." These myths are especially likely to create conflict when they are incompatible with family ideals or are not accepted by all members of the family. Therapists often find that bringing the myths out in the open in family discussion is helpful in focusing on the problems these distorted role assignments create.

Two frequent characteristics of family therapy are that (1) it is time-limited, and (2) at least at the beginning, it is concerned primarily with a particular problem or crisis being faced by the family. The success of family therapy depends on the therapist's flexibility and ability to improvise useful therapeutic strategies. A family therapist working with an individual who has a substance abuse problem, for example, recognizes and explores the effects of family relationships on the patient's drug-seeking behavior and the potential consequences on these relationships were the patient to achieve and maintain sobriety. The therapist might raise the question, How could the patient accomplish sobriety without a shift in family patterns to ones that would support this change? In the following case, related by the therapist, the problem was a 9-year-old boy's refusal to talk in school and the factors related to his refusal. There were only a handful of sessions, some of which took place in the clinic and some in the boy's home.

George is a 9-year-old boy who refused to talk in school. He was referred by the school, which had decided that he might need to be transferred to a special class for emotionally disturbed children. George came to the clinic with his mother for an evaluation. On a second visit, George was brought to the clinic by his aunt; she was accompanied by her 4-year-old son. The aunt explained that George's mother had to work, and went on to describe a large, close-knit family network. George lived with his mother, little brother, grandmother, and great-grandmother, along with one aunt and her two children. His grandmother was one of eight children, many of whom lived in the neighborhood. His mother was one of 15 children. There were too many cousins in George's generation to count, and most of them lived in the same block.

We held two more sessions, both of them at George's house. We had hoped to meet a number of the family members, but instead hit pay dirt with George's grandmother. He was her oldest grandchild. To her, he was "Man"—the nickname she used for him. At the first session, she needed to be filled in on what the problem was—that George did not talk in school and that the teachers were concerned that he could not make progress. She argued that none of the men in the family were good in school but that George was clever, a leader in the neighborhood, and good with the computer they had bought for him. Her argument seemed to be that George did not need to perform well in school because he performed well in the family. At that visit, George showed us a clubhouse he and his friends had built. He spoke to us.

We made one further visit. At this time the family presented the following reasons for George's silence: first, they thought George's silence in school was an act of protest for being bused out of his neighborhood for integration purposes, and second, they had extracted a promise from George that if he were allowed to return to his neighborhood school, he would talk. They discussed what they would do to George if he did not keep his word: his grandmother would go down to the school and "read him the riot act."

The follow-up in 4 months found that George's mother and grandmother had met with the school officials armed with a letter of support from the clinic and that George had been transferred to a regular class in his neighborhood school and was talking.

If any single idea could be said to guide family therapy, it is probably the notion of a family system. Human life can be organized hierarchically into systems of varying size and complexity: the individual, the family, the society, the culture. The **family systems approach** sees the family as a self-maintaining system which, like the human body, has feedback mechanisms that preserve its identity and integrity by restoring homeostasis—the internal status quo—after a disturbance. A change in one part of the family system thus is often compensated for elsewhere. Families have mechanisms for adapting to changed circumstances, and, like individuals, they have biologically and socially determined states of development.

A family that functions poorly cannot adjust to change because its mechanisms are either inflexible or ineffectual. The family's daily habits and internal communication—its *transactional patterns*, as they are called—harm its individual members. The pathology is in the system as a whole. Individual disorders not only serve as a source of protection and power for the disturbed person but may also preserve the family system and act as a distorted means of communication within that system. They fulfill the same function that neurotic symptoms are said to fulfill for individuals in psychodynamic theory.

Some families are highly interdependent: everyone in them is overresponsive to everyone else. They develop habits of intimate quarreling and complaining that become difficult to change. In other families, the family members have little mutual contact or concern; their boundaries are rigid. Family systems that are too closely knit, or enmeshed, respond too intensely to change; every disturbance may turn into a crisis. Systems in which the family members are distant, or disengaged, do not respond strongly enough; serious problems are ignored and issues are avoided.

Acculturation and ethnicity may pose special challenges for family therapists (Javier & Herron, 1998; McGoldrick, 1998). For example, immigrant families face problems related to adjustment to a new culture, and there may be conflicts among different generations within the family concerning the new society. Family therapists who work with Hispanics have commented particularly on the need to deal with issues of personal identity, cultural identity, gender roles, the extended family, parenting styles, and expressions of affection and sexuality (Flores & Carey, 2000). Similar issues are probably also common in other ethnic groups.

Marital Therapy Marital difficulties contribute not only to personal unhappiness and family instability, but also to a wide range of mental health and physical problems. **Marital therapy** is directed toward helping couples overcome their difficulties and discuss differences between them without having emotional explosions (see Figure 16-8). Couples frequently seek marital therapy because one or both of the partners believe that the relationship is troubled or are contemplating ending it through divorce or separation. By seeing the therapist together, the partners can more easily identify problems and alter the ways in which they relate to each other.

The main advantage of couples therapy is that the therapist, as an impartial observer, can actually witness the couple's interactions rather than hearing about them in a secondhand and perhaps one-sided report. Both family therapy and marital therapy can be carried out from one of several perspectives. Family therapy is likely to use a cognitive-behavioral or a psychodynamic approach. Couples therapy often utilizes a cognitive approach as well. Regardless of the type of marital therapy practiced, a current trend is to focus attention on specific relevant issues such as helping the couple increase communication, express feelings, help each other, and enjoy shared experiences.

Marital therapists report distinct patterns of symptoms among couples. In some cases, each partner in a marriage demands too much of the same thing from the other: service, protection, care, and so forth. In other cases, spouses compound each other's problems by complementing each other. One partner takes charge and the other becomes incompetent: an overbearing and emotionally distant husband has a "hysterical" wife whose erratic behavior makes him still more overbearing; a strong, angry wife has a passive, alcoholic husband who is a suitable object of her anger, and that anger makes him even more passive; the husband of a depressed and hypochondriacal woman needs to be a healer and savior. Often marital therapy aims to reveal what is hidden: the passive partner's suppressed anger, the savior's feelings of helplessness.

When a couple comes for treatment, the following steps can be taken:

1. Identifying specifically what the couple would like to see changed.
2. Identifying how they would know if these changes took place.
3. Identifying patterns in their interaction that perpetuate the current situation and that, when changed, would support the preferred situation.
4. Assigning tasks within the sessions and for homework that will facilitate the desired changes; allowing time between sessions for the couple to try out new ways of being together.
5. Performing a running evaluation of the couple's response to treatment and revising goals and plans as the therapy progresses.

"Let's stop this before we both say a lot of things we mean."

Figure 16-8 A major aim of couples therapy is helping the couple discuss major issues openly, but rationally.

SOURCE: *The New Yorker* Magazine, 1995.

Psychodrama In the 1920s, Jacob Moreno created an interesting form of group therapy called *psychodrama*. Using role-playing techniques, he had been leading impromptu activity groups for children in the public gardens of Vienna. He noticed that when the children were encouraged to act out stories instead of merely reading or listening to them, they often displayed unexpected depths of feeling and understanding. He later experimented with a form of theater, which he called the "theater of spontaneity," in which players were encouraged to draw upon their inner resources in creating the dramatic action rather than following a script.

Moreno saw psychodrama as a vehicle for expressing strong emotions, acquiring insight into one's own behavior, and realistically evaluating the behavior of others. Psychodrama is a directive treatment in that the therapist controls the mechanics of the therapy situation. However, it is nondirective in that the emotional content of sessions arises spontaneously from the activities of the participants.

In **psychodrama,** a group of individuals assembles under the leadership of a therapist (often called the director). The group enacts events of emotional significance in order to resolve conflicts and release members from inhibitions that limit their capacity for spontaneous and creative activity, particularly social activity. Behavior therapists use role-playing to give patients practice in new social skills, but in psychodrama role-playing tends to be more spontaneous and oriented toward expressing strongly felt emotions.

How Effective Are Group Approaches?

In discussing individual psychotherapy and cognitive-behavioral therapies, we noted that each approach seemed to be effective but that information was lacking on the treatment components that were the "active ingredients" and the clinical groups for which particular therapies might be most appropriate. For example, while cognitive-behavioral approaches are often quite helpful with people for whom anxiety is a major problem, their effectiveness with many other clinical groups has not yet been demonstrated. Group therapy is even more complex than individual therapy because of the number of people involved. Not surprisingly, less is known about its processes and effectiveness. Lack of agreement about the basic concepts that underlie the processes involved in group therapy has hampered research on its effectiveness. Questions about which treatments work and when and why they work have not yet been answered.

The lack of answers to these questions is more an indication of the complexity of the processes involved and lack of accepted conceptualizations than of demonstrated lack of effectiveness. An increasing number of clinicians and researchers believe that group approaches are promising and likely to be effective and efficient. There is growing evidence that marital and family therapies produce statistically significant results (Lebow & Gurman, 1995). The evidence is particularly strong for cognitive-behavioral approaches to these types of therapy. Not only do marital and family therapies appear to be generally effective, they seem to be useful in dealing with several specific types of clinical problems (Szmuckler & Dare, 1996). For example, therapies aimed at helping families of persons with schizophrenia cope better with the many problems associated with the disorder seem to be valuable, as are therapies aimed at supporting and strengthening the coping skills of nonalcoholic members of families where there are problems of heavy drinking.

While past research on the effectiveness of group therapies has been methodologically weak, it is rapidly becoming more rigorous (Johnson & Lebow, 2000). Descriptions of what goes on in various types of therapy are becoming clearer; more specific types of therapeutic outcome are being assessed; more follow-up studies are being carried out; and efforts are increasing to specify the processes involved in group approaches.

Research on the Psychological Therapies

There are over 400 psychological therapies for adults and over 200 for children and adolescents. These therapies are being used to treat approximately 300 different forms of abnormal behavior. It is not surprising that we do not yet have answers to all the questions raised about the therapies. Nevertheless, it is a step forward to be aware of the questions for which answers are needed. Table 16-5 lists the major questions for which researchers are seeking answers. Because the future of psychological therapies relies on these answers, we will mention four of the most important issues in research in this area. The first concerns features unique to particular treatments or common to all treatments. The second concerns the criteria by which therapeutic effectiveness is judged. The third relates to comparisons among different therapeutic approaches. The fourth issue concerns the way cultural and ethnic diversity relates to therapy, a topic that is beginning to receive the attention it deserves.

Table 16–5
Questions for Which Psychotherapy Researchers Are Seeking Answers

- Does psychological treatment produce therapeutic change?
- What components constitute necessary, sufficient, and facilitative therapeutic change?
- What components or other treatments can be added to enhance therapeutic change?
- What changes can be made in the treatment to increase its effectiveness?
- Which treatments are more or most effective for particular conditions and populations?
- On what characteristics of patient, family, or therapist does treatment depend for its effectiveness?
- What processes occur in treatment that affect performance within a session and that may contribute to the treatment outcome?

Common and Unique Features of Therapies

We have already pointed out that the various therapies have both unique and common features. An example of a common feature is the therapist's ability to instill hope in patients. This ability, regardless of the formal therapeutic techniques used by the therapist, is an important common feature of all therapies. Given the evidence that people who are treated tend to do better than nontreated controls, no matter what the therapy, and that differences in the effectiveness of various types of therapy are often not large, it is reasonable to consider the possibility that the therapist, rather than the treatment per se, is the active ingredient. To the extent possible, research on treatment techniques needs to separate the effects of the therapist's personal characteristics and the therapist-patient relationship from those attributable to the technique employed. This can be accomplished by careful planning, use of appropriate statistical methods, and large enough samples. However, to date most research on the outcome of psychotherapy has compared particular therapeutic approaches and has not taken account of therapists as independent variables, that is, as agents of change (Glass et al., 1998). Another need in psychotherapy research is study of various combinations of therapeutic techniques, such as we noted with regard to the three cases presented at the beginning of the chapter.

Contributing to better specification and standardization of therapeutic techniques has been the development of procedural manuals that clinicians can use in applying different types of therapies (Wilson, 1996). These manuals often describe treatment programs that have been evaluated in controlled trials. Thus far, most therapy manuals have dealt with cognitive and behavioral treatments, although manuals have also been devised for a wide variety of other therapies. Manuals help define the independent variables in treatment outcome studies and allow independent corroboration of whether the way a treatment approach was implemented was consistent with its procedural specifications.

While efforts at specifying the unique features of therapies are increasing, so also is interest in determining factors contributing to therapeutic effectiveness that might be independent of or cut across the particular clinical approaches taken. For example, one study dealing with treatment for depression found that differences in therapeutic effectiveness were independent of the type of therapy provided and the clinical experience of the therapists (Blatt et al., 1996). More-effective therapists had a psychological rather than biological orientation to the clinical process and were less likely to combine medications with psychotherapy. Another study showed that psychiatric inpatients preferred therapists who were able to express their interest in and caring about the patient, as opposed to therapists with certain professional qualifications such as

certain types of advanced training (Barker et al., 1996). A therapist's expressiveness may be a key factor in therapeutic effectiveness because it contributes to building rapport and the establishment of a strong alliance between patient and therapist. The strength of this alliance has been demonstrated to play an important role in successful therapy outcomes (Castonguay et al., 1996).

Therapeutic Outcomes

One of the most important questions in outcome studies is what the criteria for improvement should be. Which are more important, changes in how the patient feels and behaves or changes in what he or she thinks about? Would the opinions of the patient's family or co-workers be helpful in evaluating improvement? How important is the therapist's evaluation of the outcome? Sometimes the therapist and the patient don't agree. Anthony Storr, a British psychoanalyst, gives this example of what he had considered an "unsuccessful" case:

> Some time ago I had a letter from a man whom I had treated some 25 years previously asking whether I would see, or at any rate advise treatment for, his daughter. He assumed, wrongly, that I would not remember him, and, in the course of his letter, wrote as follows: "I can quite truthfully say that six months of your patient listening to my woes made a most important contribution to my life style. Although my transvestism was not cured, my approach to life and to other people was re-oriented and for that I am most grateful. It is part of my life that I have never forgotten."
>
> Looked at from one point of view, my treatment of this man was a failure. His major symptom, the complaint which drove him to seek my help, was not abolished. And yet I think it is clear that he did get something from his short period of psychotherapy which was of considerable value to him. A man does not write to a psychotherapist asking him to see his daughter, 25 years after his own treatment was over, using the terms employed in this letter, unless he believes that what happened during his period of treatment was important. (Storr, 1980, p. 146)

If all the measures of improvement do not agree, then which is most important? How can we compare studies that use different outcome measures to evaluate the effectiveness of various therapies? Clearly, although outcome research is progressing in sophistication, many of the important questions will be difficult to answer. Personal accounts of experiences in psychotherapy provide researchers with hypotheses for future research. Identifying the elements of personal growth and the factors that foster it will contribute to the development of better formal and informal therapies.

It is not unusual for patients to see themselves as cured while their therapists see them as unimproved or even as being worse. Studies of improvement, therefore, should include three independent measures: the patient's evaluation of the progress made; the therapist's evaluation; and the judgments of people who know the patient well, such as family members and friends.

Another approach to evaluating the effectiveness of therapy is to assess the resultant behavior change. Although one of the goals of psychotherapy is enhancement of the patient's self-awareness and insight, most people would consider therapy a failure if the person's behavior remained the same. It is not enough for therapy to be a source of insight.

Changes in overt behavior are easier to describe and assess objectively than changes in attitudes, feelings, and beliefs. But questions remain. To what degree should behavioral change be used as a criterion? Who should determine the kinds and amounts of change desired? How lasting should the change be? How long-standing and disabling has the patient's condition been? It seems reasonable that criteria for success should be related to the difficulty of the hurdle to be overcome. Implicit in this conclusion is the recognition that criteria that are appropriate in one case may be inappropriate in others.

Comparing Therapies

Most of the treatment outcome studies we have mentioned so far involved comparisons between treatment and nontreatment (control) groups. We noted that there is growing support for the conclusion that psychological therapies are worthwhile for many people. What have been the results of head-to-head comparative studies of two or more therapies? Meta-analyses of these studies have revealed a mixed picture. There is a strong tendency for measurements to show no difference among techniques in amount of change produced. However, this is countered by indications that, under some circumstances, cognitive and behavioral methods have superior results, although they do not generally differ in efficacy among themselves (Lambert & Bergin, 1994). Research carried out with the intent of contrasting two or more treatments has often shown few small differences between outcomes for the groups compared.

In one widely cited comparative study (Sloane et al., 1975), the subjects were college students who had applied for treatment—mostly for anxiety and personality disorders—at a psychiatric outpatient clinic. The goal of the study was to compare the relative effectiveness of behavioral therapy (desensitization, assertiveness training, and so on) and more traditional short-term psychodynamically oriented therapy. In addition to these two groups, there was a control group whose members were told that they would have to wait about 4 months to receive treatment. The students were followed up 4 months and 12 months after completing therapy. The measures used in the treatment comparisons were derived from interviews with the students at these times, from the students' ratings of their own improvement, and from improvement ratings made by an independent assessor. At 4 months, the psychotherapy and behavioral therapy groups had improved equally, and significantly more than the waiting-list group. At the 1-year follow-up, the students receiving behavioral therapy, but not the psychotherapy group, showed some significant improvement with regard to the problems that had led them to seek therapy. However, there were no significant differences between the two groups with regard to social adjustment. The 1-year follow-up results were complicated by the fact that some of the students had continued to receive treatment even though the therapy sessions were supposed to end after 4 months. The researchers concluded that their study provided no clear evidence that behavioral therapy was superior to psychotherapy.

The same researchers reported an interesting additional set of comparisons for some of the students in their treatment study (Sloane et al., 1977). One year after beginning treatment, the students were mailed questionnaires in which they were asked to rate the importance of 32 factors in the success of their treatment. What was most striking about their responses was the similarity between the psychotherapy and behavioral therapy groups. Both groups emphasized the importance of gaining insight into one's problems, the relationship with the therapist, the opportunity to give vent to emotions, a sense of trust in the therapist, and the development of confidence. Thus, even though the two treatment approaches are based on different assumptions and use different methods, they were described similarly by the students. This similarity held both for the sample as a whole and for subgroups of students who were judged to have responded most positively to the treatments offered them.

In another project, researchers analyzed four studies on the outcome of psychotherapy and concluded that who performs the therapy matters much more than what kind of therapy it is (Luborsky et al., 1986). The studies were conducted at Johns Hopkins University, the University of Pennsylvania, the University of Pittsburgh, and McGill University. Altogether, 25 therapists and 240 patients were involved. In three studies, the patients were average psychiatric outpatients; in the Pennsylvania study, they were heroin addicts taking methadone. The techniques included individual psychodynamic therapy, cognitive-behavioral therapy, and group therapy, all in various combinations and for varying lengths of time. Among the many measures of outcome were judgments of improvement by both patients and therapists and ratings of interpersonal behavior, social adjustment, depression, severity of addiction, and other symptoms.

In all four studies, some therapists had a significantly higher success rate than others. Differences among therapists were much greater than differences among therapies in producing a favorable outcome. There was little evidence to show that any individual therapist did better with a particular kind of patient. The researchers suggested that more might be learned about how psychological therapies work by studying the most effective therapists than by comparing different forms of treatment.

Conclusions about the relative effectiveness of therapeutic techniques cannot be drawn from research that is too limited in scope or methodologically weak (see Table 16-6). We noted earlier that there is no best index of clinical outcome. That being the case, research studies should include several measures of outcome, such as patients' self-reports and behavioral measures gathered before and after therapy, as well as expert judgments of clinical progress. There might be significant differences between therapeutic approaches to specific problems with respect to some outcome measures but not others. Furthermore, a therapeutic procedure may be valuable even if it doesn't bring about a complete cure. A person who is less anxious after therapy will be grateful for that benefit despite the failure to achieve a total release from anxiety.

Arguments over the effectiveness of therapeutic programs can be expected to continue for several reasons: people's problems, expectations, and the extent to which their lives can be changed vary; therapists use different methods and have different expectations; and there are no uniform criteria for judging therapeutic effectiveness. Many people are helped by therapy, but some get worse. Even though psychological therapies are not for everyone, they seem to help a sizable number of people sort out their problems and develop new ways of handling stress and the challenges of life.

Recognizing Cultural and Ethnic Diversity

Asian American immigrant parents were concerned that the grades of their only son, a 15-year-old, were falling. The therapist decided that the parents were overcontrolling, overanxious, and overdemanding with a timid adolescent boy who was reluctant to stand up to his parents about his social isolation. The therapist encouraged the boy to argue to convince his parents to allow him to join the school band, participate in after-school sports, choose his own school schedule, and listen to rock music. His mother did not speak English and his father was deferential and seemed to accept the therapist's suggestions. But the parents then terminated the appointments. They said it was because of transportation problems, but the boy indicated that his parents felt the therapist was "too American" and was encouraging disrespect toward them. The therapist had ignored the cultural issues by working with the boy with little attention to the parents' feelings and customs. The approach was not successful. (Ayres, 1994, p. vi)

We have seen how important it is to compare therapeutic approaches and identify the similarities and differences among them. It is also important to determine the degree to which factors usually not dealt with by psychological theories might be important to the process and outcome of therapy. While most psychological theories have tended to ignore the issue of cultural and ethnic diversity, there is growing reason to believe that the various

---

Table 16-6

Key Features of Research on Therapies

1. *Control and comparison groups.* These groups are needed in therapy studies because many influences beyond those that are of special interest to the researcher may be at work during the period covered by therapeutic intervention. Without adequate control or comparison groups, researchers cannot rule out the possibility of alternative explanations such as spontaneous remission.

2. *Sample size.* Because of the need to incorporate a large number of factors into the design of therapy research, sufficiently large sample sizes are needed to allow for appropriate statistical analyses and justifiable inferences from results.

3. *Patient specificity.* Firm conclusions are more likely if subjects are relatively homogeneous in terms of factors that are not the target of the treatment intervention. So many factors may influence outcome that it is important to control as many extraneous variables as possible.

4. *Treatment specificity.* The more clearly defined the treatment or treatments, the more likely it is that reasonable inferences can be drawn from the research. This requires careful specification of the therapeutic techniques used in the research.

5. *Outcome measures.* The more relevant the outcome measures are to the type of case being treated, the more useful the study will be. For example, since people with obsessive-compulsive disorder rarely hallucinate, there would be little value in using the frequency of hallucinations as an outcome variable. A more useful variable would be the frequency of obsessive thoughts and compulsive behaviors.

types of diversity in the population are highly relevant to carrying out treatment and doing research. This issue is important in itself as well as because of the growing diversity of the population. The United States population includes millions of people, Native Americans, African Americans, Hispanics, and Asian Americans, whose cultural beliefs may differ from those of the majority group. Different cultural groups frequently differ with regard to specific beliefs, attitudes, behaviors, and the types of psychological problems they experience. Cultural differences also are likely to be reflected in how people perceive emotional and physical states. For example, there is evidence that African Americans often blame themselves for their problems, whereas Puerto Ricans often blame others (Casas, 1995).

Cultural and ethnic diversity is particularly relevant to therapeutic practice because different groups within the population frequently have different values and may see themselves and others in disparate ways. For example, insight is not highly valued by all cultural groups; in fact, many Asian American elders believe that thinking too much about something can cause problems. People from lower socioeconomic classes frequently do not perceive insight as appropriate to their life situations and circumstances. Traditional psychodynamic psychotherapy might be less effective for these segments of the population than for middle- and upper-class White people. The usefulness of particular therapies needs to be demonstrated for various cultural and ethnic groups. Research is needed to substantiate the applicability or limitations of traditional and new therapies with respect to minority individuals.

Three steps that would improve mental health services for members of minority groups would be (1) to increase accessibility to therapy by locating mental health clinics in minority group neighborhoods close to public transportation; (2) to employ mental health workers who share the linguistic and cultural backgrounds of the patients; and (3) to provide clinicians with training that increases their awareness of the needs of particular groups.

One example of this last point is the need for therapists working with Asian Americans to be sensitive to issues of shame and guilt when probing for personal information. To avoid leaving patients with the impression that they have "caused" their own problems, therapists must help them understand that people often encounter difficult situations as the result of inevitable and unavoidable circumstances. Another example is that because African American families often have extended kinship networks, some therapists have found it appropriate and useful to include members outside the immediate family in group therapy (Canino & Spurlock, 2000).

To provide useful mental health services to children and adults, the therapist should know enough about their culture for them to feel accepted and understood and also to feel they are active participants in their treatment. That understanding a patient's ethnic background is important is suggested by a study showing that therapists whose ethnicity was the same as that of their patients rated the psychological functioning of the patients higher than did therapists whose patients' ethnicity was different from their own (G. L. Russell et al., 1996).

Integration of Psychologically Based Therapeutic Approaches

When therapists who base their techniques on different perspectives discuss their work, there are inevitable differences of opinion. The issues that separate the various schools of thought seem substantial. Should therapists actively direct patients toward behavioral change, or should they focus on the patients' development of insight? Should therapy delve into the past or examine the present? Should therapy's duration be long or short? Despite the different ways in which these questions are answered, there is evidence of a movement toward the integration of therapeutic approaches. "Talking therapies," such as psychodynamic therapy, are placing more emphasis on patients' need to take responsibility for themselves and develop self-mastery. Behavioral therapies are giving increased attention to the cognitive underpinnings of behavioral change. Often this means helping patients acquire insight into their misconceptions about themselves and their social relationships. Many cognitive-behavioral therapists rely heavily on imagery as a means of achieving therapeutic goals. The use of imagery for treatment purposes clearly acknowledges the potentially crucial role of private events.

There is growing evidence that performance-based therapies, in which individuals concretely deal with problematic situations, can be very effective. However, cognitive processes such as insight may play an important role in helping people develop more adaptive approaches to problems of living. As more therapists attend to the relative roles of cognition, emotion, and behavior, steps toward greater integration of therapeutic approaches are being taken.

Biological Therapies

In Chapter 2, we discussed the biological orientation to maladaptive behavior and the therapies that have developed from this point of view. The most widely used biological therapies today are electroconvulsive therapy and a growing variety of drugs that influence psychological functioning.

Electroconvulsive Therapy (ECT)

Until recently, use of **electroconvulsive therapy (ECT)** had been declining for about 20 years. The basis for the decline was the public's perception (shared by many clinicians) that ECT is dangerous, inhumane, and overused. Some municipalities have urged that its use be restricted. Nevertheless, ECT has experienced a quiet revival. In improved forms, it has emerged as the treatment of choice for the most severe depression when drugs and other therapy fail to help (see Chapter 10). Patients for whom ECT is recommended are so severely depressed that they do not eat, sleep very little, and are suicidal. Many suffer from delusions. In about 80% of cases, ECT can lift depression within a few weeks (Andreasen & Black, 1991). Norman Endler's response to ECT, described in Chapter 10, is an example of the method's effectiveness.

Available evidence suggests that ECT is a relatively safe procedure, particularly when used with anesthetics and muscle relaxants that substantially lessen the traumatic effects of the treatment. Risks are further reduced by changes in the amount and duration of the electric charge. Several such improvements in reducing ECT's side effects have contributed to its comeback (see Table 16-7). There has been concern about the cognitive consequences (e.g., memory loss) of passing an electric current through a person's head. However there seems little likelihood of permanent memory loss due to modern ECT (Hales et al., 1999).

Even though it has been used for many years, the mechanism by which ECT works is not yet clear. However, evidence suggests that the active ingredients in ECT are the electrical-biochemical events that follow the seizures triggered by the electrical impulses. Progress is now being made in understanding these events.

A clinician who is considering the use of ECT must perform a risk-benefit analysis. On the benefit side is the probability of rapid improvement and, for those who are depressed, the reduced likelihood of death due to suicide. On the risk side, however, are the possibility of death in the course of receiving ECT (this risk is low, with an incidence of about 1 in 10,000 treatments), the chance of memory impairment (which is short-term and becomes less noticeable with time), and the risk of spontaneous seizures (which are infrequent). In weighing the advantages against the risks, clinicians might reasonably consider ECT when there is severe depression or a possibility of suicide, or when drugs and other therapies are ineffective or seem inappropriate.

Drug Therapies

Many drugs have been used clinically and in research. **Drug therapy** has been notably effective with four types of disorders: those in which schizophrenia, mania, depression, and anxiety play important roles:

1. **Antipsychotic drugs** (e.g., phenothiazines) are used primarily to treat people who have schizophrenia. (These drugs are described in Chapter 11.)
2. **Antimanic drugs** (e.g., lithium) are used to treat those who have a bipolar disorder. (Chapter 10 includes a description of these drugs.)
3. **Antidepressant drugs** (e.g., tricyclics, MAO inhibitors, SSRIs) are used to treat patients who have been diagnosed as having a mood disorder of the unipolar type, that is, characterized by relatively long-lasting depression but without any history of manic or hypomanic episodes. (More information about these drugs is found in Chapter 10.)
4. **Antianxiety drugs** (e.g., benzodiazepines) are used with people who have a high level or prolonged state of anxiety that is strong enough to incapacitate them, or at least cause them difficulty in carrying out many activities of daily life. (See Chapter 7 for more information about these drugs.)

These types of medication differ in their effectiveness, mechanisms of action, and side effects. The antipsychotic drugs usually produce improvement in 4 to 6 weeks. Antimanic drugs are often effective by themselves, but at times they need to be combined with an antipsychotic drug in highly agitated patients. The effects of antimanic drugs are usually noticeable within a week. Among the antidepressants, drugs from the SSRI group are often tried first, with other types of antidepressants reserved for those patients who do not respond to these. The therapeutic

---

Table 16-7

Improvements in ECT That Have Increased Its Safety

1. *Length of electrical charge:* reduced from one second to one twenty-fifth of a second.
2. *Intensity of electrical charge:* reduced greatly.
3. *Timing sessions:* reduced from as often as every day or even two or three a day to no more than three times a week.
4. *Length of treatment:* formerly up to 20 sessions or more; now typically 10 or fewer.
5. *Use of anesthetics and muscle relaxants:* formerly no anesthetics or muscle relaxants were used; now both are employed.
6. *Monitoring:* both brain waves and the electrical functioning of the heart are now monitored through EEG and EKG.
7. *Placement of electrodes:* formerly on both sides of the head; now on the nondominant side only or on the right and left sides of the forehead.

effects of the antidepressants usually require between 2 and 4 weeks to be apparent. Antianxiety drugs, whose therapeutic effects may be noticed within a week, are usually employed for limited time periods (up to a few months) to avoid the problem of drug dependence.

Although psychoactive drugs have helped many people live normal or almost normal lives and their safety has improved, there are many unanswered questions about them. A number of risks must still be considered, including a variety of side effects. Depending on the drug employed, side effects may include drowsiness, confusion, nightmares, poor appetite, insomnia, blurred vision, lethargy, and changes in blood pressure. Some of the drugs may be fatal if the patient's condition is not monitored regularly, and some of the drugs expose the patient to the risk of having a fatal overdose available.

Like those of psychological therapies, the effects of drug therapy are not always predictable. Factors such as age, sex, and genetic background can influence a person's response to a drug. The effectiveness of a particular drug may also depend on how it is metabolized, whether the patient takes it as prescribed, and whether other drugs are being taken at the same time.

Earlier in the chapter, we mentioned that managed care health systems usually prefer to reimburse the cost of brief, rather than long-term, psychotherapy. In managed care programs, the final decision regarding type and duration of treatment rests with the insurer rather than the clinician. The insurer understandably must pay attention to the economic costs of different types of therapy. Because drug therapies are often demonstrably effective (particularly with severe disorders), require only minimal contact between patient and therapist, and are relatively inexpensive compared to the cost of psychotherapy, they are popular with managed care programs. While managed care programs do seem to have been successful in containing the costs of treatment for physical and mental health problems, some observers have expressed concern that organizations such as insurance companies (rather than the treating clinicians) are making decisions about how patients are treated. Because managed care is a relatively new development in the American health care system, the philosophical and practical aspects of managed care are currently being widely debated (see Figure 16-9).

Research on Medications Clinicians who prescribe medications want to maximize their therapeutic effects and minimize their undesirable consequences. These goals require the use of carefully designed research procedures. First, extensive preliminary research is done to study the effects of varying doses of a drug on laboratory animals. If these tests suggest that the drug is effective and does not have harmful side effects if properly used, the drug is administered to human beings under carefully controlled conditions. If these results are also positive, the drug may

"IT'S YOUR INSURANCE COMPANY, THEY SAY YOU'RE CURED."

Figure 16-9 In managed care programs, insurers make the final decisions concerning treatment and its duration.

Source: *Wall Street Journal*, 1997, p. A 15. Drawing by Ron Delgado.

be approved for large-scale clinical trials in which its effectiveness is scientifically compared with that of other treatment methods.

Clinical trials involving drugs and other therapeutic procedures can be complex and costly, and may extend over many years (see Chapter 1). They often include samples of subjects located throughout the country, and even throughout the world. They require careful planning, decisions about dependent measures, recruitment of subjects and their random assignment to the various treatment conditions, use of placebo conditions if possible, and assuring that all clinical personnel are "blind" to the assigned treatment whenever possible.

Controlled clinical trials of most drugs used in the treatment of maladaptive behavior indicate an average effectiveness rate of about 70% (Erickson & Goodwin, 1994). Although several drugs in a category (e.g., antidepressants) may be rated about equal in effectiveness, there still are significant variations in individual responses to a particular drug.

How Effective Are Biological Therapies?

Many disorders can be treated effectively with biological therapies. ECT may alleviate severe depression. Antidepressant drugs can also be helpful in treatment of depression. Panic disorders are successfully treated with tricyclic antidepressant drugs. Anxiety symptoms, especially after trauma, may be helped by antianxiety drugs or tranquilizers. The extreme mood swings of bipolar disorder can be moderated by lithium. Some symptoms of schizophrenia can be lessened by antipsychotic drugs; however, even with these drugs many people with schizophrenia remain chronically and socially impaired. Even if the medications prove effective in reducing symptoms of schizophrenia and bipolar disorder in particular, they have potential negatives, for example, the possibility of causing tardive dyskinesia. Many people decide on their own to discontinue medication use because of unpleasant side effects (see Box 16-3).

Combining Therapeutic Approaches Although evidence suggests that various psychological approaches to treating cases not involving extreme psychopathology can all be effective, one should not conclude that it makes no difference which techniques are employed in clinical work. Psychological therapies used alone have been relatively unsuccessful with serious conditions such as schizophrenia, some types of affective disorders, alcoholism, and drug abuse. However, psychological therapies can play an important role in treating some of these conditions when used in combination with biologically based treatments like drug therapy and ECT. The value of the psychological component of these combinations frequently lies in helping the patient deal realistically with problems of day-to-day living. For example, social skills training has been used effectively to help psychotic individuals taking antipsychotic drugs adjust better to hospital or community settings. Perhaps, as more is learned about the distinctive features of particular therapies, it will be possible to combine them in ways that are optimal for patients.

Researchers are devoting increasingly greater efforts to studying the effectiveness of therapeutic programs that include both medications and psychological interventions. Depression and panic disorders have received the most attention. Medications and psychological interventions often seem to be equally effective, but combined treatment may have advantages for some patients. One study found that providing cognitive therapy while patients were taking antidepressant medications resulted in half the relapse rate compared to patients who received only medications (M. D. Evans et al., 1992). Another study found that a family therapy intervention combined with drug therapy for hospitalized bipolar disorder patients yielded better results than did drug therapy alone (Clarkin et al., 1990). A similar facilitative effect for unipolar patients was not obtained. **Multimodal treatment** that combines different approaches to clinical intervention has been recommended for several conditions, including substance-use disorders, borderline disorders, anxiety disorders, and schizophrenia.

Combined therapies need not be limited to integrating biologically and psychologically based treatments. There often is considerable merit in combining features of different psychological interventions. Some members of a family might not only participate in family therapy, but also receive some form of individual therapy. This seems a reasonable approach when we note that individual psychopathology and family dysfunction are almost always interdependent. In the following case, drug therapy for a wife led to the couple's therapy, and ultimately to family therapy:

> *A 43-year-old depressed married woman with two children responded positively to imipramine after 3 weeks of treatment. She denied that her relationship to her husband played any role in her symptoms and, in fact, claimed, "We have excellent communication." Her psychiatrist asked about her husband's response to the imipramine. She replied, "He hasn't said anything." This response was at odds with her claim that they had excellent communication. The psychiatrist asked her husband to come to the next session. In that session, the husband reported that he had told her how pleased he was with the change in her mood but [said,] "Perhaps I didn't state it very clearly." In couples therapy they explored the husband's dysphoria about work, and his fear of burdening his depressed wife with more difficulties. They had difficulty communicating at home because their children repeatedly interrupted their conversations. Their children also dominated much of the decision making. Their psychiatrist worked with them in regaining a parental hierarchy over the children by suggesting that they exclude the children from major decisions and by fostering parental discussion and agreement about managing the children's behavior. (Beitman, 1993, p. 651)*

As we suggested earlier in the chapter, utilizing techniques derived from many different perspectives, clinicians may be able to improve significantly the quality of the treatments they provide.

Hospitalization

Serious psychological illness may require **hospitalization,** not only because the hospital provides round-the-clock care, but also because it can offer all the complex therapies that a patient might need. But while some comprehensive mental hospitals provide enriched programs offering such benefits as psychotherapy, drug therapy, and active social, educational, and recreational programs, the budgets of most state hospitals do not permit such varied fare. As a result, many patients in state hospitals receive drugs but few psychological therapies, and live in a relatively impoverished, unstimulating social environment. This is unfortunate, because a hospital can be a place that helps the patient cope with a crisis and experience personal growth.

The major reasons for psychiatric hospitalization are as follows:

- Behavior that poses a threat to self or others.
- Behavior that is intolerable to members of the patient's community.

Q&A Box 16–3

Q. If many people decided not to take medications or to discontinue using them, the patients would not be the only ones with problems. Clinicians and researchers would have problems as well. The clinicians wouldn't be helping their patients, and the researchers couldn't be as confident about their conclusions concerning the effectiveness of drugs as they would like to be. How serious an issue is this?

A. *You are right that clinicians and researchers are concerned about this issue, which is usually described in terms of* **adherence** *to a prescribed regimen or compliance with a clinical program. Clinicians and researchers strive to keep non-adherence to a minimum. In Chapter 11 we noted the serious problem of psychotic individuals who stop taking their medications. Some people have a fairly negative view of medicines, perceiving them to be generally harmful substances that are overprescribed by doctors. Failure rates as high as 50% to 60% in adherence to prescribed clinical programs are not uncommon (McNamara & Trotman, 1997). In the realm of mal-adaptive behavior, it is now widely recognized that failure to take prescribed medications is especially common for a number of serious chronic conditions, such as schizophrenia and bipolar disorder. Adherence failures are more common among outpatients than inpatients because hospital staff have the opportunity to observe inpatients and encourage them to take their medications. They are particularly common in disorders that do not have symptoms (e.g., high blood pressure) and in individuals who may not understand either their condition or why a medication has been prescribed. Impaired concentration, poor memory, thought disorder, or anxiety all interfere with adherence. Depression, apathy, and the negative symptoms of schizophrenia often are strong barriers to the motivation and persistence necessary for long-term treatment. In most acute illnesses people take medicine until they feel better and stop. However, in many psychiatric disorders, treatment must continue beyond the restoration of normal function, often for months or even indefinitely.*

A good relationship between clinician and patient can foster adherence. It is important

for a clinician to inquire into the patient's knowledge, attitudes, beliefs, and questions about the particular disorder and its treatment. The benefits to patients of medication are often unclear to them unless they are explained in plain language (e.g., restful sleep, increased energy, and absence of voices or alien ideas). The presence of concerned persons (family, friends) is a potent facilitator of adherence to a clinical program. What this means is that prescribing medication is often necessary but not sufficient. Coercion (trying to force the patient to take a medication) is usually ineffective. It is increasingly recognized that medications need to be seen as part of an alliance between clinician and patient that pays attention to pertinent beliefs, experience, and lifestyle. This alliance can serve as the vehicle for identifying factors related to medication adherence and for integrating psychotherapy with biological treatment. Psychotherapy might be limited to increasing the patient's understanding of the need for medication and the importance of adherence, or it might deal more generally with the patient's motivations, concerns, and quality of life. Patients whose clinicians listen carefully to their problems and concerns and toward whom there is a feeling of trust are more likely to adhere to a medication program than patients who simply get a prescription. Patients are less likely to discontinue taking a drug if, before starting the medication, they are informed about possible side effects of the drug and are given a realistic account of what to expect while taking it (e.g., understanding that the drug might not have an effect immediately).

Culture and ethnicity can play significant roles in adherence. Ruiz (1998) presented an account of a 55-year-old Hispanic American woman, Mrs. A., of Cuban extraction who developed the symptoms of early morning awakening, crying spells, loss of appetite, and weight loss after the death of her mother in Cuba. A psychiatrist diagnosed her as being depressed and prescribed an antidepression medication. Mrs. A. would neither take the medication nor return to the psychiatrist who did not speak Spanish and did not seem to appreciate the cultural context of the woman's problem. When Mrs. A.'s condition wors-

ened, she was taken to another psychiatrist, who could communicate in Spanish (although the woman could comprehend and speak English fairly well) and inquired into the circumstances surrounding the depression that was so easy to observe. Mrs. A. was able to express her unhappiness and guilt over not being able either to visit her mother in Cuba before she died or attend her funeral. She thought her symptoms were the result of God's punishment for the abandonment of her mother in Cuba. The psychiatrist expressed to the family the importance of showing respect for Mrs. A.'s feelings and thoughts concerning her mother. The psychiatrist also urged Mrs. A., who was Catholic, to attend church regularly and to speak with the priest. The psychiatrist also prescribed an antidepressant drug, which he told her would help her sleep better. Probably because Mrs. A. viewed the second psychiatrist as understanding of her situation, she took the medication and recovered completely. One year after seeing the second psychiatrist several times and taking the medication, Mrs. A. seemed fine. Lack of sufficient attention to cultural factors probably accounted for her nonadherence to the medication prescribed by the first psychiatrist. A treating clinician does not necessarily have to share the patient's ethnic background but needs to be knowledgeable about and sensitive to the main aspects of the patient's culture.

One additional point related to ethnicity is pertinent both to treatment failures and non-adherence. Asian Americans can have a unique metabolic response to drugs prescribed by mental health practitioners (Lin & Cheung, 1999). They often respond to substantially lower doses of many psychoactive drugs than are usually prescribed. As a consequence, it is preferable to start an Asian patient on a relatively low dose and, if necessary, increase it rather than to start with the dose usually recommended for Caucasians. Prescribing too strong a dose could lead to an adverse reaction as a result of which the patient might decide to discontinue the prescribed medication and be less open to taking any other medication that might be prescribed.

■ Failure of outpatient treatment and the hope that in-patient treatment will reverse the process.

■ A treatment procedure that requires a degree of control possible only in a hospital.

■ Withdrawal from alcohol or drugs.

■ Physical illness that is complicated by a mental disorder requiring continuous care.

Researchers have studied the kinds of hospital activities that are helpful to patients when they are not in an acute phase of their disorder. One experiment compared a fairly traditional mental hospital routine with a routine based on social learning principles (Paul & Lentz, 1977). Under the traditional routine, patients spent most of their time in unstructured activities and only 5% in classes and meetings. As a result there was a great deal of boredom and a waste of therapeutic opportunities. In contrast, under the social learning routine, 59% of the patients' time was devoted to classes, meetings, and structured activities. The ward employed a token economy to motivate the patients to engage in productive behavior. A comparison of the effects of the two approaches showed that the social learning group had a significantly higher percentage of discharges to the community than the traditional group. However, regardless of the treatment used, only a small percentage of the patients were able to function in a self-supporting way.

Research on the process of resocialization may contribute answers to such questions as, what steps could help chronic patients adjust successfully to the community? Long ago Gordon Paul suggested 10 steps that mental hospitals might take to provide greater happiness and better functioning among patients, higher morale among staff members, and a more positive social rehabilitation role for the institution. However, even today few institutions meet these standards completely.

1. Emphasize a "resident" rather than "patient" status through informal dress of staff, open channels of communication in all directions, and broad (but clear) authority structure.

2. Make clear, through a set of rules and attitudes, that the residents are responsible human beings; are expected to follow certain minimal rules of group living; and are expected to do their share in participating in self-care, work, recreational, and social activities.

3. Utilize step systems which gradually increase the expectations placed on the residents in terms of their degree of independence and level of responsibility, with community return emphasized from the outset.

4. Encourage social interactions and skills and provide a range of activities as well as regular large and small group meetings.

5. Emphasize clarity of communication, with concrete instruction in appropriate behavior and focus on utilitarian "action" rather than "explanation."

6. Provide opportunity to practice vocational and housekeeping skills, with feedback, and specific training in marketable skills when needed.

7. Reacquaint residents with the "outside world" by exposing them to the community and bringing in community volunteers for discussions.

8. Identify the specific unique areas for change and support in concrete terms for each individual.

9. Prepare residents and significant others to live in mutually supportive ways in the community through prerelease training and scheduled aftercare.

10. When no significant other exists, train and release residents in groups of two to three as a "family" to provide significant others for one another. (Paul, 1969, p. 91)

The effectiveness of a hospital depends on the needs of its residents, the quality and scope of its programs, and the community and family resources available to the patients. Because of variations in all of these areas, it is not surprising that there are strong differences of opinion about the effectiveness of hospitalization. When all factors are considered, it seems reasonable to conclude that some severely disturbed people can benefit from life in a socially active therapeutic hospital. The precise percentage of currently institutionalized individuals who might benefit from this experience is very difficult to estimate.

If a ward is run mainly to satisfy the staff, or if a latent goal of the hospital is to maintain order and stability in the institution, the patients get the message. No therapy takes place; instead patients' behavior is managed to minimize conflict with the system and disruption of routine.

The effects of a bad hospitalization experience may be felt long after a patient is discharged. A negative experience can increase the patient's sense of bearing a stigma and make it easy to assume a "sick role"—that is, to come to see oneself as a sick person who will always have to be taken care of. It can also lead to a weakening of social and work skills. When these things happen, patients become less able to function in the community.

When complete hospitalization is not required, **partial hospitalization** may be employed. This may involve either day or night hospitalization, and perhaps evening and weekend care in the hospital.

Day hospitalization is used to provide treatment for patients who can live at home but need the structure and social interaction available in the treatment center. Day hospitalization also allows members of the patients' families to function more normally because they can carry on their usual activities during the day. Day hospitalization often concentrates on teaching patients social and interpersonal behaviors as well as helping them learn practical skills such as how to use the bus system or a pay telephone. It may also include training in basic work skills so that patients can get jobs in sheltered workshops that will provide the satisfaction of doing useful work and some payment as well.

Evening, night, and weekend programs are designed primarily to help hospitalized patients make the transition from the hospital to the community. Such programs are especially useful for people who are able to return to their jobs, schools, or training programs but do not have adequate family or social support to go from inpatient to outpatient status without a partially protected transition period. The concept of night hospitalization has gained some acceptance, but relatively few such programs have been established on a formal basis.

Over the past few decades, hospitalization for mental illness has become less frequent. While this in itself is not necessarily undesirable, public hospital beds available to people with low incomes have declined in number, while there has been an increase in private hospital beds (Dorwart et al., 1991). As a consequence, access to hospital care is unevenly distributed in the population. Patients in public hospitals are being discharged after shorter periods of hospitalization, largely because of the effectiveness of psychoactive drugs and an increase in efforts to return patients to the community as quickly as possible. This **deinstitutionalization** process can be a boon to personal development if the individual has a good place to live, sufficient social support, and supervision when needed. Unfortunately, many people who have been discharged from mental hospitals live in furnished rooms in undesirable neighborhoods, are socially isolated, and receive little professional help beyond brief contacts with physicians who prescribe antipsychotic drugs.

The lack of adequate community care for chronic mental patients has contributed to the large numbers of homeless people in American cities. Thousands of deinstitutionalized people have nowhere to live. They wander about city centers, sleep where they can, and carry their belongings with them. While the problem of homelessness is complex, the "dumping" of deinstitutionalized people on a community only contributes to human misery. We will look further at this problem in the next chapter.

Chapter Summary

PSYCHOTHERAPY

No matter what their theoretical orientations, psychotherapists perform three tasks: listening, understanding, and responding to the patient.

Psychodynamic Therapy and Psychoanalysis Psychoanalysis is a special type of **psychodynamic therapy** carried on by specially trained therapists who use the technique of **free association** and place special emphasis on the examination of both dreams and fantasies. All psychodynamically oriented therapists emphasize **insight,** the understanding of one's motives and the needs of others, as the goal of psychotherapy. They use **transference,** the patient's displacement of affect and feeling about others onto the therapist, as an important part of therapy. They also take into account **countertransference,** the therapist's emotional response to the patient. Some psychotherapists use the trancelike state of hypnosis to uncover and deal with material their patients have repressed.

Humanistic and Existential Therapies Humanistic therapies place emphasis on people's desire to achieve self-respect. An example of a humanistic therapy is Rogers's **client-centered therapy,** which stresses a nondirective, nonjudgmental approach in which the therapist provides an atmosphere of **unconditional positive regard.** The therapy is focused on increasing self-acceptance and self-knowledge as a way to facilitate changes in behavior. **Existential therapies** emphasize patients' needs to confront basic questions regarding the meaning and direction of their lives. Perls's **Gestalt therapy** is based on the view that problems arise when people dissociate parts of themselves, especially their needs for personal gratification, from awareness.

Cognitive Psychotherapy The theory of **cognitive psychotherapy** is that the best way to solve emotional problems is to alter the patient's thinking through cognitive restructuring. Aaron Beck's widely used cognitive therapy focuses on automatic thoughts that may govern behavior although they are not produced by rational considerations. The patient and therapist jointly explore the validity of the patient's false beliefs about himself or herself, the world at large, and the future. **Rational-emotive therapy** emphasizes the need for patients to question and change their self-defeating thinking and mistaken beliefs.

Brief Psychotherapies Most psychotherapy involves fewer than 12 sessions. Health insurance programs that pay for patients' psychotherapy put pressure on health care providers to keep psychotherapy as brief as possible. Brief psychotherapy usually has specific goals or targets, such as helping patients deal with currently important problems in their lives. **Interpersonal therapy** is a type of brief psychotherapy that originally was used for depression but is now being extended to other problems. It emphasizes the key social relationships in a person's life.

How Effective Is Psychotherapy? Research on the effectiveness of psychotherapy indicates that overall it is helpful to patients. For a wide range of clinical problems, no one psychotherapeutic approach is clearly superior to any other. The therapist's characteristics and approach are important factors in the success of psychotherapeutic interventions. **Meta-analysis** is a statistical procedure used to summarize the results of therapy outcome studies.

Technique factors (the procedures employed by therapists) and **interpersonal factors** (the social dynamics between therapist and patient) influence therapeutic effectiveness. **Process research** is concerned with what actually happens in therapy and which aspects of the therapeutic process are facilitative of the patient's personal growth.

COGNITIVE–BEHAVIORAL APPROACHES

Behavior Therapy

Behavior therapy, the forerunner of cognitive-behavioral therapies, began as a way of using operant and classical conditioning techniques to change behavior. **Behavior modification** developed from the operant techniques. Many operant conditioning methods use reinforcement and shaping to gradually achieve a desired response. **Fading** is the process of eliminating special cues used in the shaping process. A **token economy** uses operant methods to reinforce desired behaviors. **Biofeedback** is a method used to develop control of internal processes.

Cognitive–Behavioral Therapy

The cognitive-behavioral therapeutic approach integrates various cognitive and behavioral elements. In **relaxation training** the relaxation effect is achieved either by focusing on muscle groups or through **meditation** techniques. **Exposure therapy** is based on the idea that continuous exposure to anxiety-provoking stimuli will decrease anxiety. **Flooding** is a form of exposure therapy in which the patient is exposed to a high level of fear-arousing stimuli that is not terminated when the patient becomes anxious. Flooding is based on the idea that **extinction** of the fears will occur if the patient remains in the anxiety-provoking situation long enough. In **implosive therapy,** the patient imagines scenes of behaviors or situations that he or she has avoided in the past and then experiences the intense anxiety these create until that anxiety is extinguished. **Systematic desensitization** combines muscular relaxation with cognitive activity in which the patient imagines a series of increasingly anxiety-arousing scenes related to specific fears. **In vivo exposure** involves the same techniques when the fear-arousing stimulus is actually present.

Modeling is a "how to" approach that involves the demonstration for the patient of behaviors involved in specific social skills. The procedure may be carried out through **live modeling,** or the direct observation of the model; **symbolic modeling,** or observation of a recorded performance of the model; or **covert modeling,** in which the patient is asked to imagine observing a model and the consequences of the model's behavior. **Behavioral rehearsals** allow the patient to practice the modeled behavior. **Assertiveness training** is the use of modeling and rehearsal to teach a person the interpersonal skills needed to keep from being imposed on by others.

How Effective Are Cognitive and Behavioral Approaches?

Cognitive-behavioral interventions seem to be particularly effective in treating disorders in which anxiety plays a prominent role. More information is needed concerning which therapeutic components contribute the most to therapeutic effectiveness.

INTEGRATION AND EXTENSION OF PSYCHOLOGICAL THERAPIES

There is growing interest in integrating diverse therapeutic approaches in order to maximize therapeutic effectiveness. There is also interest in the possibility of extending techniques found useful with individuals to group settings.

Integrative Approaches to Treatment

Case studies and therapists' experiences have shown the value of **multimodal therapy** in which a broad array of tools is used in treating individuals.

Group Approaches

Group therapy sessions include a group of several people usually with similar problems, who meet together with a therapist in regular sessions. In addition to being lower in cost than individual therapy, group therapy may be more effective for some problems. Group membership provides acceptance and support, normative information about behaviors and feelings, and an opportunity to learn through modeling and behavioral rehearsal. Group therapy initially was carried out from a psychodynamic perspective, although techniques have been developed by therapists using other approaches.

The focus of **cognitive-behavioral group therapy** is on development of social skills and comfort in social situations.

Both **family therapy** and **marital therapy** focus on individuals who already constitute a group. Family therapists view the family as a system. In family therapy the family members work together with the therapist to deal with their attitudes and feelings toward one another and to understand how the behavior of each affects the others. Marital therapy can be viewed as a subtype of family therapy. Family therapy is likely to use a psychodynamic or cognitive-behavioral approach.

Psychodrama is a special kind of group therapy in which the group acts out events of emotional significance in order to express strongly felt emotions.

How Effective Are Group Approaches?

Perhaps because of its complexity (more than one patient), less is known about the effectiveness of group therapy than of individual therapeutic approaches. More information is needed concerning the basic concepts applicable to the group process and the "active ingredients" of group therapy. Most group approaches seem to be helpful for at least some people, and large differences in effectiveness have not been found for the various group therapy approaches.

RESEARCH ON THE PSYCHOLOGICAL THERAPIES

Common and Unique Features of Therapies

An important task for researchers is to distinguish common features of various therapeutic approaches from the unique features of particular therapies. There is growing reason to believe that it is necessary to separate the effects of the therapist's personal characteristics and the therapist-patient relationship from those attributable to the particular therapeutic procedures used. There is also increasing interest in determining factors contributing to therapeutic effectiveness that might be independent of or cut across the particular clinical approaches taken.

Therapeutic Outcomes One of the most important questions in studies of therapy is what the outcome measures should be. Possible choices are the therapist's opinion, the client's behavior or feelings, or the view of others such as family members or co-workers. There is often disagreement about outcome among these different sources.

Comparing Therapies There is a strong tendency for measurements to show no difference in amount of change produced by various therapeutic approaches. However, in some cases, cognitive-behavioral approaches appear to be superior. There is considerable variation in the success rates of individual therapists, even those that use the same therapeutic approach. In general, psychological approaches have been found to be useful in cases without extreme psychopathology.

Recognizing Cultural and Ethnic Diversity Because of growing cultural and ethnic diversity within the U.S. population, it is important for therapists to become more aware of the values, beliefs, and needs of particular groups, such as African Americans, Hispanics, Native Americans, and Asian Americans. Research is needed to determine the degree to which cultural and ethnic factors play important roles in processes and outcomes of therapeutic interventions.

INTEGRATION OF PSYCHOLOGICALLY BASED THERAPEUTIC APPROACHES

Aspects of many different therapeutic approaches have been found to be useful. Most therapists believe that therapeutic techniques addressing emotion, cognition, and behavior are all important in helping patients. As a result, there is a trend toward a greater integration of therapeutic techniques based on the different perspectives.

BIOLOGICAL THERAPIES

Electroconvulsive Therapy Electroconvulsive therapy (ECT) is most likely to be used for severe depression, especially as treatment for those who are at high risk for suicide, when drugs and other types of therapy have failed to help.

Drug Therapies Four general types of drugs have been found to be effective in treating mental disorders: **antipsychotic drugs, antimanic drugs, antidepressant drugs,** and **antianxiety drugs.** Before drugs can be used to treat patients, the medications must be thoroughly tested for effectiveness and for negative side effects. Drugs and other therapeutic procedures are evaluated through clinical trials that compare outcomes for patients who receive different treatments.

How Effective Are Biological Therapies? ECT and medications are often effective in treating particular disorders. Some medications are effective in the short term but not in the long term. Some drugs can have serious side effects—for example, the development of tardive dyskinesia in schizophrenic individuals treated with certain antipsychotic drugs. Psychological therapies are often not successful alone in the treatment of schizophrenia, some types of affective disorders, alcoholism, and drug abuse, but frequently produce a better result when used in combination with drug therapies or ECT. Researchers are exploring the possibility that combinations of biological and psychological intervention—**multimodal treatment**—are more effective than either intervention by itself. There is evidence that this might be the case. There is also evidence suggesting that combinations of psychological interventions can be more effective than the interventions by themselves.

HOSPITALIZATION

Some of the reasons that psychiatric hospitalization is recommended include behavior that poses a threat to self or others, failure of outpatient treatment, or a treatment procedure that requires a high degree of control. The effectiveness of a hospital depends on the needs of its residents, the quality and scope of its programs, and the community and family resources available to the patients. **Deinstitutionalization** and lack of adequate community care for chronic mental patients has led to large numbers of homeless people in American cities.

Key Terms

Psychotherapy, p. 556
Psychodynamic therapy, p. 556
Transference, p. 556
Positive transference, p. 556
Negative transference, p. 556
Countertransference, p. 556
Recovered memories, p. 557
Hypnosis, p. 557
Humanistic therapies, p. 558
Existential therapies, p. 558
Client-centered therapy, p. 558
Unconditional positive regard, p. 559
Gestalt therapy, p. 559
Cognitive psychotherapy, p. 559

Rational-emotive therapy, p. 559
Interpersonal therapy, p. 560
Meta-analysis, p. 561
Technique factors, p. 563
Interpersonal factors, p. 563
Process research, p. 563
Behavior therapy, p. 564
Behavior modification, p. 564
Fading, p. 564
Token economy, p. 564
Biofeedback, p. 564
Cognitive-behavioral therapy, p. 564
Relaxation training, p. 565
Exposure therapy, p. 565

Flooding, p. 565
Implosive therapy, p. 565
Systematic desensitization, p. 565
Modeling, p. 566
Assertiveness training, p. 566
Multimodal therapy, p. 568
Group therapy, p. 568
Family therapy, p. 570
Marital therapy, p. 572
Psychodrama, p. 573
Electroconvulsive therapy (ECT), p. 578
Drug therapy, p. 578
Adherence, p. 581
Hospitalization, p. 580

17

Alejandro Xul Solar "Paisaje (Cinco Pagodas)". Photograph, Christie's Images. © Alejandro Xul Solar.

Society's Response to Maladaptive Behavior

*I*f a person breaks a leg in the street, civil help tends to him quickly—ambulance, doctors, police. Break your mind and you lie there, unless you show you need help by getting up and pushing somebody in the subway train.

How can this be so? Money, for one thing. Treat them with pills, then discharge them from the hospitals, tell them to take the medicine themselves, close the hospitals. That is why in New York State alone, patients in state mental hospitals have dropped from about 93,000 in the '50s to about 9,000 today.

But one patient in three does not take the pills after his release. He is too mentally ill, too alone—or too many care centers supposed to provide help have been closed.

The American community finds money for taking care of tens of millions—the poor, the aged, the physically ill. Why are there so many mentally ill people cut off from help—at least 10,000 just in New York City's streets?

One reason is that everybody knows physical pain, but the pain that mental disorder can bring is literally unutterable by the suffering and unknown to most of humanity.

A. M. Rosenthal, *The New York Times*
January 17, 1995, p. A15

More than 25 years ago, Dennis Sweeney began to hear voices that eventually drove him into the Manhattan law office of former Congressman Allard Lowenstein where he pulled a pistol from his windbreaker and shot his former friend and mentor seven times. Mr. Sweeney, who calmly waited for the police to arrive, pleaded not guilty by reason of insanity. The state did not dispute his insanity, and he was committed to the custody of the New York State mental health system. In 2000, Mr. Sweeney was released from state custody over the objections of both prosecutors and state mental health officials. This happened as a result of a judge's ruling based on a review of available evidence that he no longer needed hospitalization. ■

A. M. Rosenthal's reflections on society's response to the seriously mentally ill show the limitations of viewing maladaptive thought and behavior as purely a matter of personal problems. While it is the mentally ill individual who is doing the suffering, the community is also involved—it helps create conditions either conducive or detrimental to the mentally ill individual's achieving an optimal level of functioning. For example, reduction of public funds for the care and hospitalization of the mentally ill by approximately one-third since 1955 is a product of decisions made by legislators. Dennis Sweeney's release came about as a result of a judicial decision.

In this chapter we discuss the role played by society in making decisions about and dealing with deviance. We will also discuss: What can society do to prevent mental illness and enable the mentally ill to lead the most rewarding life of which they are capable? People have vulnerabilities that keep them from being able to handle challenges along life's path and from developing optimal skills. What can society do to minimize the negative effects on the individual and the community of vulnerabilities created either by biological or environmental factors? Not much can be done about factors such as a person's heredity and brain structure, but some of the unfortunate aspects of people's lives (poverty, parental abuse) stem from their environment and, to some extent, might be subject to modification.

Vulnerability and resilience have been themes throughout this book. Society has a role to play, not only in reducing personal vulnerabilities, but also in fostering resilience. Resilience is not a static trait, but rather the ability to use internal or external resources. New vulnerabilities and new strengths may emerge during developmental transitions throughout the course of a person's life. The community can play a role in prevention, as well as in fostering resilience in both children and adults. While the negative effects of poverty seem to be cumulative and increase as children get older, there is good reason to believe that the promotion of a person's sense of competence and self-esteem is one of the key ingredients in any prevention process and that supportive relationships are especially valuable in promoting resilience (Werner, 1993).

This chapter begins with a review of the concept of prevention and examples of the community's role in achieving it. This is followed by a discussion of recent efforts to develop community programs for the mentally ill. We conclude with an exploration of some of the legal issues related to maladaptive behavior.

Types of Prevention

Throughout this book we have considered methods of assessing, treating, and caring for individuals with behavior problems, but we have only briefly mentioned the possi-

bility that the actual occurrence of maladaptive behavior in the population can be reduced. This is the focus of prevention. There are many examples of the power of prevention in reducing suffering and costs. Simple, proven interventions such as using child car seats and bicycle helmets, controlling traffic in residential neighborhoods, and installing smoke detectors in homes can reduce childhood injury deaths by one-third. Swimming pool fences with self-latching gates could prevent roughly 40% to 70% of swimming pool drowning and near-drowning incidents among young children.

Levels of Prevention

"An ounce of prevention is worth a pound of cure" is a well-known truism. Why, then, aren't preventive measures more common? In some cases it is not clear what steps are needed to achieve the goal of prevention, and in others society does not seem willing or able to take the needed steps.

Prevention of mental or physical disorder can take place on three levels. These three types of prevention span the entire range of mental health interventions, from the universality of primary prevention to the selective interventions of secondary preventions and to tertiary prevention, which essentially amounts to treatment.

Primary prevention is concerned with the general reduction of new cases of disorders and is administered to everyone in a particular population, such as all students at a school or all pregnant women, whether or not they might be at particular risk. Scientific information about cause and effect is very important in primary prevention. For example, knowledge of the possibility of harm to the unborn child has persuaded many women not to smoke or drink during pregnancy. Physicians are much more careful about prescribing medication for pregnant women because of information linking even seemingly harmless drugs with birth defects. And knowledge of the harmful effects of nicotine addiction has led psychologists to conduct research on ways to discourage children from beginning to smoke cigarettes. Another example of primary prevention is premarital counseling. Marital problems and divorce are highly correlated with maladaptive behavior. Premarital counseling is aimed at encouraging couples to anticipate any problems and to develop ways of coping with them before marriage.

Secondary prevention is more selective than primary prevention because it is limited to a subgroup of the population that is at a higher-than-average risk for developing a mental disorder, with psychological, social, or biological factors as the basis for determining risk. The aim of secondary prevention is to reduce the potential disability of an existing abnormal condition. For example, if a child with phenylketonuria (PKU) is identified early, a special diet can prevent serious retardation.

Children who are behind in intellectual and social development as a result of living in homes where little stimulation and individual attention are available can be helped to develop more normally through special enrichment programs. These programs can help the child catch up in the developmental process and gain skills that will make later school achievement more likely. Another example of secondary prevention is providing support groups for people who have recently experienced a traumatic event.

Whereas secondary prevention efforts are directed at people who are at risk, the focus of **tertiary prevention** is people already diagnosed as having an illness or some type of behavioral disorder. Tertiary prevention is aimed at reducing the impairment that has resulted from a given disorder or event. This is achieved through rehabilitation and resocialization. For example, behavioral therapy for a hyperactive child may help him or her become more attentive in school and more accepted by other children despite the continuing problems associated with the condition. Counseling or group therapy after a traumatic event such as injury and permanent paralysis from an automobile accident may provide the social support that reduces a person's vulnerability to the added stress of coping with the new disability. Rehabilitation of those who have committed crimes is another important area of tertiary prevention. Often offenders serve a prison sentence and are discharged back into the community without either adequate skills of impulse control or the practical skills to get a job. The same difficult transitional situation is often faced by people who have been hospitalized for schizophrenia and later discharged directly into the community without any further attention or support.

Preventive measures have been developed in many cases in which biophysical factors are known to cause maladaptive behavior. However, the effects of detrimental social factors have frequently been ignored or neglected. It is much easier to detect and control the effects of an enzyme deficiency in newborn infants than it is to detect and control the pervasive influence of poverty and racism. But ignoring these causes and correlates of maladaptive behavior will not decrease their influence.

When prevention methods are successful, risk factors that lead to abnormal behavior are reduced or eliminated. In general, priority in efforts to achieve prevention is given to serious conditions that have high rates of incidence, and for which effective methods are available. For example, prevention efforts have been directed at one of the most serious and prevalent maladaptive behaviors of childhood, juvenile delinquency.

Juvenile delinquency is a legal term used to designate lawbreaking by minors. Each year between 4% and 5% of American teenagers, or approximately 1,300,000, are referred to the courts for suspected offenses other than traffic violations (see Figure 17-1). The following case gives

an example of the troubled youngster to whom the police, the legal system, and the community must respond:

Carl is a 16-year-old high school dropout who was placed in a locked correctional institution for 7 months. He had been charged with breaking and entering, robbery, and parole violation offenses, which he admitted. He first started getting into trouble at age 12 when he assaulted two women during a purse-snatching incident. By the time he entered high school, he had been in juvenile court for offenses involving theft, destruction of property, and unauthorized use of an automobile. When he was 15, he and his friends broke into an appliance store and stole several color TVs, tape recorders, and portable radios. Carl's father is an accountant, and his mother is a high school teacher. Carl describes himself as "no good." He thinks his parents believe that hanging around with the wrong people is the source of his many difficulties with established authority and the law.

Delinquent behavior seems to have many causes, ranging from poor living conditions to a psychopathic or antisocial personality disorder to psychosis. Some of the following conditions have also been identified with delinquency:

1. Poor physical and economic conditions in the home and neighborhood.
2. Rejection or lack of security at home.
3. Exposure to antisocial role models within or outside the home, and antisocial pressures from peer-group relationships.
4. Lack of support for achievement in school.
5. The expectation of hostility on the part of others.

Juvenile delinquency can be approached at different levels of prevention. Primary prevention often takes the form of programs aimed at improving living conditions and achievement in school. For example, the availability of low-cost subsidized housing that would enable families to move into low-crime areas might provide their children with less exposure to other delinquents. Special school programs that make individualized instruction available to children with deficiencies in academic skills might not only help them become successful in school, but might also have a positive long-term effect on their lives by giving them hope for the future as well as later opportunities for success. Although such programs are important and can be helpful to potential delinquents, perhaps the most effective primary prevention comes about through personal relationships. There is some evidence that if children growing up in high-crime areas have a positive role model, their behavior may be more influenced by that person than by their antisocial peers. When this happens, it is often because of the opportunity to observe and practice the cognitive and behavioral coping skills demonstrated by the role model.

Figure 17-1 Helping juvenile offenders to become productive members of society is a challenge to the court system, to those who work to rehabilitate these young people, and to society as a whole. (a) The judge often tries to assess the adolescent's attitudes about the offense. (b) Some juveniles can be treated most effectively in residential institutions, where they are removed from their everyday environments and can receive intensive treatment. (c) Another effective way of helping some young offenders is to require that they spend time in community service rather than institutionalizing them.

(a)

(b)

(c)

Secondary prevention programs concentrate on young people who have shown early signs of delinquency. For example, there might be a special intervention focused on helping youngsters who have committed minor nonviolent offenses (such as theft or truancy) behave less impulsively. Sometimes changing delinquent behavior might be classified as tertiary prevention. The youth might be involved in seriously maladaptive behavior. The following case presents an example of the type of preventive measures that may be taken in such a situation:

A 14-year-old boy was referred to a therapist by the court because he had set several large grass fires that had endangered nearby houses. He could not explain his behavior, and nei-

ther could his parents since he had always behaved responsibly at home.

The boy's family was seen for six family therapy sessions. These sessions revealed that the family could not discuss problems openly but tended to communicate nonverbally. Several recent family crises had caused tension. The father seemed to handle his unhappiness by withdrawing from the family into club activities. The son seemed to express his anger at family problems by setting fires. Once the family began to meet in therapy sessions and these problems became evident, all of the family members were able to change their behavior. One year later, there had been no more fire-setting. (Based on Eisler, 1972, pp. 77–78)

At all levels of prevention and therapeutic treatment, the problems of delinquency are far from solved. The number of delinquents who go on to commit more antisocial acts is high. Different approaches work best with different types of cases, but as yet all methods have produced more failures than successes. Understanding delinquency requires a better grasp of the variables involved in the interaction between the person and the situation.

Situation-Focused and Competency-Focused Prevention

Prevention can be approached from two perspectives. **Situation-focused prevention** is aimed at reducing or eliminating the environmental causes of disordered behavior, while **competency-focused prevention** is concerned with enhancing people's ability to cope with conditions that might lead to maladaptive behaviors. Situation-focused approaches seek to change the environment, for example, by making it less stressful. Competency-focused approaches seek to strengthen people's coping skills so as to make them more resistant should various types of stress-arousing situations arise.

Divorce is a common example of a stress-arousing situation. Nearly half of all children living in the United States can expect to spend some time—an average of about 6 years—living in a single-parent family as a consequence of divorce. In these single-parent families, the stress of parenting as well as economic pressures is usually increased for the care-taking parent. Such increased economic and psychological stress may be related to impaired parenting and to both behavior and emotional problems in children.

Programs are needed that can reduce the likelihood of maladjustment in divorced couples and their children. An example of such a program is one developed for newly separated individuals. The program provided the participants with psychological support and special training over a 6-month period after the separation (Bloom & Hodges, 1988). Staff members made themselves available to participants when advice and counseling were needed. Training was provided in such practical areas as employment and child rearing. Compared with newly separated people who did not participate in the program, the participants experienced less anxiety, fatigue, and physical illness and showed improved coping ability. There was some evidence that the intervention program was more effective for women than for men. Participants' comments after the program ended suggested that the knowledge that interested people and special services were available if needed may have been the most powerful ingredient in the program.

Although the program just described can be seen as a competency-focused approach, it was activated only after the participants had already taken steps toward divorce.

Figure 17-2 Children often act directly. When they want something they take it, or they express displeasure by hitting another child. However, through modeling, reinforcement, and cognitive training, children can learn to share and cooperate.

Another type of competency-focused prevention effort might aim to strengthen skills that are important in interpersonal relationships, particularly with one's spouse, long before thoughts of divorce arise. The idea behind such an effort would be to increase coping skills, thereby enabling couples to handle the stresses of marriage in more effective ways.

Early-education programs also illustrate competency-focused prevention. Their aim is to prevent or reduce problems in subsequent years. One project began with the observation that maladapted children (and adults) frequently tend to have weak interpersonal cognitive problem-solving skills (Shure & Spivack, 1982, 1987). These skills include the ability to identify problems and feelings in oneself and others, to think of alternative solutions to a problem, to see relationships between alternative approaches and the achievement of goals, and to appreciate the consequences of one's actions.

Interpersonal problem-solving skills can improve adjustment in addition to fostering academic competence (see Figure 17-2). Training in cognitive and social skills (such as empathizing with other children) has been shown to influence behavioral adjustment positively (Shure & Spivack, 1992). This positive effect was greatest for children who originally seemed most maladjusted, and positive results were still evident a year later. In a related project, inner-city mothers who were given training in interpersonal cognitive problem-solving skills were able to pass their training on to their children. Research with older children and adults supports the idea that the skills involved in academic and social effectiveness are learnable. Furthermore, it has been shown that improved teacher training—for example, showing teachers ways to reinforce students' adaptive behavior—contributes to a more productive learning environment in the classroom. Sometimes situation-focused and competency-focused prevention efforts can occur as part of the same project. An approach that involves parenting classes and a chance to earn a high school diploma for teenage mothers combined with in-school day care for their children provides a competency focus for the mothers and situation-focused prevention for their preschool children (see Figure 17-3). Because these mothers usually have few financial resources, few job-related skills, and lack maturity and knowledge about how to care for their children, the children are at high risk. For instance, in addition to earning a high school diploma and acquiring job-related skills, the young mothers in the Teenage Pregnancy and Parenting (TAPP) program at an alternative high school in Seattle take courses in nutrition, anger management, household finances, and child rearing. The TAPP program also provides a support group and a gathering place for young mothers.

There is growing evidence that mental health prevention programs can be very effective. Individuals who participate in them have been shown to be superior to control groups with regard to performance and competency, interpersonal relationships, and the degree of anxiety, depression, and behavior problems. One meta-analysis of 177 primary prevention mental health programs found that the average participant surpassed the performance of between 59% and 82% of those in a control group (Durlak & Wells, 1997).

Figure 17-3 High school day-care facilities provide young mothers with a chance to earn a diploma while they learn both work-related and parenting skills.

Sites of Prevention

This chapter especially emphasizes research that is relevant to the prevention of maladaptive behavior. Where data are lacking, we speculate about the use of social experimentation. We do not attempt a comprehensive analysis of all the components of a complex social structure; instead, we direct our attention toward three areas that definitely affect the growth and development of children and adults: the family, the school, and the community.

We are in a period of major changes within the family. Of the children under the age of 3 in the United States today, a staggering number are affected by one or more risk factors that make healthy development more difficult. Changes include the following:

- In 1960, only 5% of all births in the United States were to unmarried mothers. The figure today is over 26%.
- Every year more than a million adolescents become pregnant.
- Divorce rates are rising. Almost half of all children can expect to experience a divorce during childhood. After divorce the family's income typically declines.
- Children are increasingly likely to live with only one parent, usually the mother. In 1960, fewer than 10% of all children under the age of 18 lived with one parent; the figure today is 28%. Fathers are increasingly absent from the home.
- The number of children in foster homes is close to 500,000.
- One in four children under the age of 3 lives in a family with income below the federal poverty line.
- Pressures on both parents to work mean that they have less time with their young children; more than half of all mothers of infants now work outside the home.

The Family

Parents play a significant role in their children's development because of the genes they contribute and the environment they provide. This environment begins in the uterus during the 9 months before birth. Whatever can improve prenatal care and thus reduce the incidence of premature birth and other foreseeable difficulties might help reduce several types of problems, such as low intelligence. Improved prenatal and neonatal care can be expected to reduce brain damage, which, among other conditions, is related to certain types of epilepsy.

From the standpoint of prevention, the family is important because much of the child's earliest learning and development takes place within the family setting. Self-help groups can be useful for parents of young children. These groups provide parents with a way of understanding the typical ways that children behave, as well as a way of learning how others have coped successfully with child-rearing problems. Meeting with others with similar interests also provides an important opportunity for social relationships with other adults, something that is often lacking for parents with young children. Parents' ideas about child rearing and the development process make important contributions to the day-to-day environment of children (see Figure 17-4). The relationship between certain parental practices and aggression in children demonstrates the effect of parental attitudes on the children. Many aggressive children come from homes in which the parents make the child feel insecure and rejected; bombard the child with commands, taunts, and threats; and teach the child that force is the only way to get what is wanted. The following parenting practices have been linked reliably to children's aggression (Perry et al., 1990):

1. *Failure to monitor.* Parents of aggressive and delinquent children are less aware of their children's whereabouts, activities, and social contacts.
2. *Parental aggression.* Many aggressive children come from homes in which at least one parent is exceptionally violent.
3. *Permissiveness.* Parents of aggressive children frequently do not set limits on their children's behavior and are ineffective at stopping their children's deviant behavior.
4. *Inconsistency.* Inconsistency in disciplinary practices, both between parents and from one parent has been implicated in aggressive development.
5. *Rejection.* Highly aggressive individuals often have a history of parental rejection.

In addition, certain disorders in parents may affect their children (Rutter & Shaffer, 1980). Children of psychotic parents are slow in developing speech and bladder control, have more eating and sleeping problems, and are more likely to be delinquent than other children. Alcoholic parents have a disproportionately large number of hyperactive children, and alcoholic mothers are overrepresented among mothers of babies with low birth weight and children with low IQs. There is also a relationship between criminality in parents and delinquency in their children.

Because parents' behavior may play a role in their children's problems, many clinicians who specialize in treating childhood disorders stress the importance of parenting training, family therapy, and in some cases, therapeutic work with the parents as the most effective way of helping children.

Child Abuse Children who have been physically abused, malnourished, and neglected by their parents are more prone to various forms of maladaptation than other children. Under certain circumstances, even "normal" parents—that is, parents who are not obviously disturbed—can have negative effects on their children's development. One of the most tragic examples of this is child abuse.

Child abuse varies in degree and is often hidden from view. But thousands of children, many under 3 years of age, are seriously—often fatally—mistreated each year. When emotional abuse is included as well as physical abuse, the figure becomes much larger. A sizable percentage of abuse cases involve sexual assault.

Abusive parents tend to be less intelligent and more aggressive, impulsive, immature, self-centered, tense, and self-critical than nonabusive parents. They are more likely to have been abused themselves as children; thus, child abuse is a vicious cycle. Table 17-1 lists family characteristics often associated with child abuse. The physical

Figure 17-4 A self-help or mutual support group for parents of young children can provide both learning opportunities and social support.

Table 17-1

Characteristics of Abusing Families

Parents' Histories

- Experience of abuse or neglect
- Lack of affection from own parents
- Raised in large families
- Married as teenagers

Current Family Situation

- Socially isolated; parents lack social support
- Marital discord
- Impulsive behavior in parents
- Retardation or illiteracy in parents
- Stressful living conditions (e.g., inadequate housing)

Parents' Approach to Child Rearing

- Infrequent praise of children
- Strict demands on child
- Low level of child supervision
- Early toilet training
- Dislike of caretaking by mother
- Parental disagreement over child-rearing practices

Source: Based on Nietzel & Himelein (1986).

and psychological damage done to children by abusive parents can sometimes be observed immediately.

An abusive parent is usually a very troubled person who seems to be a victim of uncontrollable impulses and frustrations. The following is an excerpt from a group therapy session in which the participants were mothers who had abused their children:

Mother I: *I was just at my breaking point, and I knew if I didn't get help somewhere, it would just go on and on and end up a vicious circle. I think that everyone who has had this problem at one time has thought, "My goodness, I must be the only person in the world that feels this way." And when I found out that I wasn't, that was a load off my mind.*

Therapist: *Feels what way?*

Mother I: *Desperation with their children. Not knowing how to cope. Afraid that you would just lose control completely and knock their head off, you know. I think we were all brought up to believe that women are supposed to have children and they're supposed to have the mothering instinct and if you don't have it, there is something definitely wrong. And I think it took this group to make me realize that women just aren't born with the mothering instinct. . . . That has helped me.*

Another mother: *If you're going to pound your child, the best thing to do is separate yourself from your child.*

Mother I: *That's fine to say, but what if you're like me and you can go on beautifully for a month, two months, three months, and all of a sudden—like last week I was feeling just fine and I cleaned house like I do every Monday. . . . I got all them damn floors waxed and _____ wakes up from her nap and she couldn't get her body shirt undone so she got all upset and she wet all over my new waxed floor. And I just went berserk and I threw her around like she had killed somebody, because right at the moment I just snapped, I didn't feel it coming. I was fine, everything was hunky-dory, nothing was wrong, I wasn't in a bad mood, there was no warning. . . .*

This type of behavior is typical of abusive parents. Behavioral training in impulse control and coping skills can be helpful for parents who want to stop harming their children. Numerous kinds of preventive programs have been attempted. These include parental education and the use of other formerly abusive parents as therapists. A promising mutual-aid approach is Parents Anonymous (PA), an organization modeled after the social support approach of Alcoholics Anonymous.

An example of preventive research on abuse is a study in which abusing parents received training in parenting skills (Wolfe et al., 1981). The parents' training consisted of reading about effective parenting techniques, observing modeled demonstrations of how to handle common child-rearing problems, and learning relaxation and other coping skills. In addition, project staff members made weekly home visits to help the parents implement what they had learned. When parents who participated in this program were compared with a control group of abusers, the parents in the special program showed significant improvement in parenting skills. A follow-up study showed that none of the specially treated abusers harmed their children during the year after their participation in the program. This study suggests that effective child management skills can be taught to abusive parents with a relatively small investment of time and labor.

Similarly encouraging results were obtained in a study in which the subjects were 400 pregnant women who had at least one of a cluster of risk factors for child abuse (teenaged, poor, unmarried, first pregnancy) (Olds & Henderson, 1989). The pregnant women were randomly assigned to four treatment groups. The first group was a "no intervention" control, which included a screening of the child at 1 and 2 years of age. The second group included these screenings and also provided free transportation to prenatal and well-baby medical appointments. The third group built upon that plan by adding to it nine visits to the home by a nurse during the pregnancy. The fourth group extended regular nurse's visits to the child's second birthday. The nurse's visits were designed to promote linkage with formal service agencies when appropriate and to enhance the social support of the mother (and father, when present). Furthermore, the nurse provided parenting and health education and consultation. Clearly, the fourth group received relatively broad and intensive family services.

The clearest benefits were reaped by the subjects who received the most extensive treatment. Nineteen percent of those in the control group abused or neglected their children within the first 2 years of life. In contrast, only 4% of those in the group who received long-term nurses' visits maltreated their children. The other two groups had better results than did the control group, but these were not nearly as impressive as the results for the group that received the extended intervention. Other evidence of the extended intervention's effectiveness was found for scolding rates and provision of appropriate play material. Moreover, their children showed a trend toward better developmental progress and fewer emergency room visits than their peers in the control group. These findings suggest that a comprehensive intervention program can prevent maltreatment of children and promote good parenting in groups at high risk for parenting dysfunction.

There have been many programs directed toward preventing child abuse (MacMillan et al., 1994a, 1994b). The most effective programs seem to be those that involve (1) home visits in which parents can receive training in how to interact with their children and (2) monitoring of the situation in the home.

Spouse Abuse "To have and to hold . . . to love and to cherish. . . ." This sentiment reflects the feelings of most people toward marriage, but these feelings are not shared by everyone. **Spouse abuse** occurs in several million homes in the United States each year, and more than 8% of homicides involve the killing of one spouse by another. An estimated 25% to 30% of all women with a spouse or cohabiting partner have been beaten at least once while in such a relationship (Sadock, 1989).

Twenty-nine percent of the women murdered in the United States were killed by a husband, ex-husband, or boyfriend (A. J. Reiss & Roth, 1994). The type of person who is a batterer tends to become a stalker after the breakup of the relationship, a situation in which the woman frequently concludes (correctly) that her situation can become more perilous if she tries to leave. Cultural acceptance of male dominance is a contributing factor. Many cultures have an unwritten code that the husband can command and deserves to control the wife. The wife's personal fear is only one of the factors that lead many to tolerate the abuse. Economic dependence, desire to preserve the home, and concern about separation from the children all add to the reasons for a woman's unwillingness to leave, or even to press charges when the police intervene after an urgent call for help. There is also a generational in-

fluence: 80% of batterers were the sons of batterers who observed their fathers abusing their mothers. Women threaten and sometimes kill their husbands or ex-husbands, but in smaller numbers, and often to protect themselves.

Efforts to help abused spouses include not only emergency care, safety, and shelter, but also long-range planning. Because abused spouses need to develop better feelings about themselves—that is, change their self-image—they need to strengthen their self-related positive cognitions. Counseling often emphasizes the following types of self-statements:

- I am not to blame for being beaten and abused.
- I am not the cause of another person's violent behavior.
- I do not have to take it.
- I deserve to be treated with respect.
- I do have power over my own life.
- I can use my power to take good care of myself.
- I can make changes in my life if I want to.
- I am not alone. I can ask others to help me.
- I deserve to make my own life safe and happy.

The three levels of prevention can all be applied to spouse abuse. Premarital counseling is an example of primary prevention; marital counseling to reduce discord illustrates secondary prevention; and providing abused spouses with safety, shelter, and counseling exemplifies tertiary prevention.

A wife abuser tends to be filled with anger, resentment, suspicion, and tension. Also, underneath all his aggressive behavior, he can be insecure and feel like a loser. He may use violence to give vent to the bad feelings he has about himself or his lot in life. Home is one place where he can express those feelings without punishment to himself. If he were angry with his boss and struck him, he would pay the price; but all too often he gets away without any penalty when he beats his wife. One study found that, compared with nonabusive husbands, abusive husbands were less assertive in social relationships than their wives, more likely to have been abused as children, and more likely to have witnessed spouse abuse between their own parents (Rosenbaum & O'Leary, 1981).

Parental Conflict and Divorce

John's parents divorced when he was 3. Shortly thereafter, his father all but dropped out of his life, visiting only occasionally and never for more than a few hours. When John was 7, his mother remarried, and the family moved halfway across the country. He was 11 before he saw his father again.

As John's visits with his father became more regular, John's mother began criticizing her ex-husband at every possible opportunity. The more she criticized, the more John became his father's apologist. When he was 15, convinced the grass was greener on the other side of the fence, John went to live with his dad. That arrangement, however, lasted little more than a year. Realizing he had a better relationship with his father when he wasn't living with him, John again packed his bags and spent his last year of high school with his mother and stepfather.

John's story is, unfortunately, not that unusual. There is growing evidence that parental conflict and divorce have adverse effects on children's development (Cummings & Davies, 1994). However, these effects can be reduced by taking certain preventive steps (Wallerstein & Kelly, 1990).

Research on this topic is complicated, because it is not possible to separate the effects of divorce from the effects of family conflict and parental inadequacy. Divorce might be regarded as a special case of family conflict in which legal dissolution of the family results. While divorce is public and measurable, parental conflict occurs mainly in private and cannot be reduced to a statistic. Researchers have tried to pinpoint the kinds of negative outcomes that family conflict tends to promote. In most cases, boys have been found to be more obviously vulnerable than girls are, and they often respond in more easily noticed ways. Common reactions in boys are increased aggression, troubled peer relations, and lack of impulse control (Cherlin et al., 1991).

The degree to which divorce is upsetting to children has been recognized for a long time. Children of divorced parents show up much more frequently in psychiatric out-patient clinic populations than their proportion in the population would predict. Even children in nonclinical samples are likely to exhibit dramatic divorce-related changes in play behavior and relationships with others (Hetherington, 1991). Not only do children have to deal with their own stress, but they must cope with parents who are also experiencing high levels of stress and whose own emotional health and financial well-being may have significantly deteriorated. Children and their parents must adjust to new living and custody arrangements (see Figure 17-5). Research and the clinical experience of many therapists and counselors has provided some ideas that may help parents soften the blow of divorce for their children:

1. *Tell the children ahead of time.* This lets them prepare for one parent's moving out.
2. *Tell the children the reasons that the decision was made.* This helps prevent children's frequent belief that they were the cause of the breakup. Make the explanation brief but honest and suitable for the age of the child.
3. *Emphasize that the divorce is a permanent decision.* Many children harbor the belief that their parents will eventually get back together.
4. *Explain what changes there will be in the child's life.* These may include moving, a new school, and much less money to spend. Emphasize the positive challenge of adapting to the new situation.

(a)

(b)

Figure 17-5 Divorce has many effects on the lives of both parents and children. Most children of divorced parents live with their mothers, often in reduced economic circumstances. Children may have infrequent contact with their noncustodial parent, and that relationship may be based on what are often rather superficial interactions with little ongoing attention. (a) A single mother prepares a meal for her children. (b) A child and noncustodial father spend an afternoon together on an outing.

5. *Let the children be free to express their anger.* This is an effective way to prevent long-term problems. At the same time, the parents should avoid using their children as a dumping ground for their own sense of anger or despair. Instead, they should share their negative feelings with an adult friend or with a therapist or counselor.

6. *Avoid forcing the child to choose between the parents or to take sides.* Custody and visitation rights that are fair to both parents should be agreed upon. Both parents should make continued contact with the children a high priority.

Parental Training While parents sometimes fail to help their children develop optimally, there are numerous instances in which they can play very positive roles. For example, there is growing evidence that parents can be trained to respond therapeutically to their children's behavioral problems. Training parents to be effective behavior-change agents has positive consequences for children's development (Kramer, 1990). Not only can the parent help the child learn needed cognitive or social skills, but because the parent learns to help in a positive way, the relationship between the parent and child can be improved. Training parents in helping skills can change the child's view of the parent from that of someone who is not satisfied with the child's behavior to someone supportive who cares about the child and is helping the child to change the situation and achieve a positive outcome. The main techniques for bringing this about are modeling, behavioral rehearsal, and reinforcement (see Figure 17-6).

Programs for parents that teach them how to foster desirable behavior in children who exhibit the more common types of problem behavior can be effective. For example, one child continually tried to control the behavior of his parents ("You go over there and I'll stay here"). When his parents learned to identify and respond to this autocratic behavior, its frequency declined. The child became more cooperative when his parents ignored his commands; in turn, the parents gave him special attention when he cooperated. Parents and teachers of highly aggressive boys have been taught to note the occurrence of particular types of undesirable behavior and to reduce its frequency through the use of appropriate behavioral techniques (G. R. Patterson, 1982).

Families of Mentally Ill Adults Families of persons with serious mental illness are often considered causal agents. However, maladaptive behavior among parents could be the result, rather than the cause, of an offspring's mental illness. A family member's severe mental illness can be stressful for other members of the family, causing such objective burdens as loss of income and such subjective burdens as emotional distress. Increased attention is being placed on the plight of families that must cope with this type of disability in one of its members (Cook et al., 1997).

Programs have been developed to educate families about mental illness and teach them how to cope with it. The research on expressed emotion (see Chapter 11) suggests the value of this approach. One study sought to develop an intervention that would be useful to families in which a parent suffers from depression (Beardslee et al., 1997). In addition to providing information about depression and its treatment, meetings were held in which both parents and children participated. These meetings focused attention on miscommunication within the family caused by the disorder and its effects on the mood and thought of family members. Positive effects on family functioning were observed as long as 1 1/2 years after the families had participated in the study. Another study found that support groups for families of adults with severe mental illness were valuable in contributing to improved relationships and better communication within the family (Heller et al., 1997). Resilience in coping with the mental illness of one of its members can be valuable for the family and the mentally ill member.

The School

Ann Jackson had taught at Buchanan High School for 8 years. She was 33 years old, still had some ideals, and had a reputation among both students and faculty of being a nice person. She was also a discouraged person who too often felt she wasn't able to reach several of her students. One student who fell into this group was 16-year-old Bill Hadley. Bill paid little attention in class, did not complete assignments, and frequently did not show up at all. But what worried Ann Jackson the most was what she knew about Bill's activities outside class.

Figure 17-6 This mother is teaching her child, who is a slow learner, how to write her name. Notice how the mother uses modeling and shows interest in the child's progress.

Other students were afraid of him because of his imposing size, his bullying attitude, and his history of antisocial behavior. He had had numerous contacts with the police for a variety of reasons. He had been accused of puncturing the tires of a dozen cars parked along a street, extorting money from other students, and shoplifting at neighborhood stores. The most serious offense was a severe beating Bill had given another student. According to those present at the fight, Bill had been in such an uncontrollable rage that he couldn't stop hitting and kicking the other student, even though it was evident that the student was helpless and in pain, and Bill started fighting with the spectators when they intervened. Ann Jackson couldn't get Bill out of her mind. She continually worried about what was going to happen to him.

Relatively small problems have a way of becoming big problems if nothing is done about them. Ann Jackson wished that something could be done to redirect Bill Hadley's life while he was still young, but she didn't know what she, the school, or the community could do now or what could have been done earlier to prevent Bill's current unhappiness, anger, and counterproductive behavior.

School districts, schools, and classrooms are larger and more complex social systems than families. Often they may seem unwieldy and unmanageable. However, in some cases it is more feasible to attack problems of behavior in the school rather than in the home. Early observation of school children, together with data available to school mental health workers (e.g., school psychologists and counselors) often can predict later psychological difficulties. On the basis of such information, secondary prevention studies have been carried out to help vulnerable children before their problems become serious enough to require clinical help. For example, in one project, nonprofessional aides worked under close professional supervision for an entire school year with children who were judged to be at risk for school maladjustment. The children who received this one-to-one contact showed significant changes in a number of areas, including social and academic skills and overall adjustment (Chandler et al., 1984). Special training for teachers, workshops to help parents develop their child-rearing skills, and carefully planned school and after-school activity programs can help prevent a significant number of behavior disorders in children (Bond & Compas, 1989; Cowen & Hightower, 1990).

Dropping Out Some children are never comfortable in school, and by the time they reach high school they are ready to leave. The dropout problem is a social as well as an educational one. In prosperous times, when jobs are not difficult to obtain, the economic cost to the dropout may not seem great. However, when competition in the job market intensifies, poorly educated, unskilled people tend to fall by the wayside.

An example of primary prevention is a study aimed at teaching cognitive and social skills to high school students (Sarason & Sarason, 1981). The school in which the research was conducted had a history of high dropout and delinquency rates and a low percentage of graduates who went on to college. The research was carried out in class sessions as part of a regular course. The basic procedure involved using modeling to demonstrate social and cognitive skills, followed by rehearsal of the modeled behavior. The subjects saw demonstrations of the cognitive antecedents of effective behavior (e.g., deciding between alternative courses of action) and effective overt responses (such as how to ask a teacher a question). Repeated emphasis was placed on the links between thought and action. The following is an excerpt from a modeling videotape that was shown in the experimental program ("Jim's cognitions" refers to voiceovers in which Jim's thoughts were spoken aloud):

Tom: Hey, Jim, you want to go down to Green Lake fourth period?

Jim: What are you gonna do down at Green Lake?

Tom: A bunch of us are gonna take the afternoon off and party it up.

Jim: I don't think I can go. Sixth period Mr. Smith is reviewing for the algebra exam.

Tom: What about coming over and staying until sixth?

Jim: Well, I kind of like Mr. Jones's class. Besides, it's too hard to get to Green Lake and back in an hour and forty minutes. I could come after school.

Tom: You know Lydia is going to be there.

Jim: [with noticeable interest] She is?

Tom: Yeah. And by the time school is over, who knows if the party will still be there. We might go over to someone's house.

Jim's cognitions: Gee, I really want to go to that party. Maybe I can get up the nerve to ask Lydia out. But I should stay for that algebra review, at least. The test will be hard enough without missing the review.

Tom: You know, it is Friday afternoon and a beautiful day.

Jim's cognitions: I wish Tom would let me make my own decision. This isn't easy. Maybe I could study hard this weekend. Then I won't need to go to the review. But will I really study Saturday?

Tom: Well, are you going to come?

Jim: I don't know, Tom. I'll have to think about it some more. Maybe I'll see you there fourth. If not, I'll probably come later.

Tom: Okay, I hope you come.

One year after the completion of the study, the experimental subjects had better school attendance records, less tardiness, and fewer referrals to school counselors and psychologists because of behavioral problems than similar students who did not participate in the program.

Table 17-2 lists some measures schools can take to prevent students from dropping out.

The Community

There is growing evidence that early intervention can build the resilience children need to withstand stress and the difficulties of living under unfavorable conditions. Since 1965, Head Start has combined developmentally oriented child care with community involvement, parents, programs for nutritional health care, and social services. It has served 3-to 5-year-old children from low-income families who need an extra boost to be ready for school, and it appears to have been effective. There is also evidence that multifaceted community interventions with older children can be effective. For example, juvenile delinquency has been reduced through combinations of early family support, special educational programs, and community opportunities to participate in prosocial activities (Yoshikawa, 1994).

After people leave school, they are pretty much on their own. Most of their activities are not supervised by authority figures, and a certain degree of independence is expected of them. At the same time, they are expected to fit into the community by working and by adhering to societal laws, values, norms, and priorities. It is becoming increasingly clear that we need to know more about how communities function and the relationship between community characteristics and vulnerability to maladaptive behavior.

Table 17-2

Recommendations for Preventing School Failure and Dropping Out

1. Early identification of high-risk students is essential, with particular attention to students during transitions, such as entering high school.
2. Small classes appear to be especially beneficial to high-risk students.
3. Individualized attention and instruction are necessities for children with problems in school.
4. Teachers should have reasonable but high expectations for behavior and achievement and be sensitive to gender, race, and cultural issues.
5. Counseling services should be made available to potential dropouts, who often have personal and family problems.

An example of research linking community factors to maladaptation is a study of violence rates in different types of neighborhoods (Sampson et al., 1997). While it is a well-established fact that poverty, unemployment, and racial discrimination are correlated with violent crime, an additional factor is *collective efficacy*, a term that describes a neighborhood's sense of trust, common values, and cohesion. In neighborhoods where collective efficacy is strong, most adults discipline children for missing school or scrawling graffiti. The study was conducted in Chicago in neighborhoods that closely mirror the racial, social, and economic diversity of the United States. A major finding was that neighborhoods whose residents have a shared vision, a shared willingness to intervene, and a sense of community and common values have relatively low rates of violent crime. While not the only factor pertinent to violent crime, collective efficacy seems to play a measurable independent role in rates of violence.

The community can influence individuals in significant ways through a host of informal, unplanned experiences. In the following example, an exceptionally accomplished young college graduate had grown up with a chaotic, stress-inducing family life. Yet an informal relationship with a neighboring family had given him valuable opportunities for personal growth.

> He came from an extremely disturbed home setting in which every member of his family except himself had been hospitalized for severe mental illness; and yet he had graduated from a renowned university with honors, had starred on the football team, and was unusually popular. During his government training he was held in the highest esteem by staff members and was rated as best liked and most likely to succeed by his peers.
>
> In examining this young man's history we discovered that during his elementary school years he had essentially adopted a neighborhood family as his own and spent endless hours with them. Certain characteristics of this family appear [to be] most significant. They were a helping family in the sense that love emanated from them and was freely available to all. Of special significance for the fellow under consideration was his relationship with a boy in the family, a year older than he, who formed for him a positive role model with whom he closely identified. . . .
>
> An even more crucial factor was his relationship with the mother in this family, who became his guide, counselor, and chief source of emotional nurturance. His reports indicate that while this relationship was intense, it was not symbiotic, and seemed to foster his independence and self-development. Although there are probably few like her, she represents a dimension of socially indigenous therapy that may be more significant than is usually recognized. Her home became a neighborhood gathering place. It might be characterized as an informal therapy agency, a kitchen clinic. (Bergin & Lambert, 1978, pp. 149–150)

First Person

Box 17–1

Kenneth Clark and Arthur A. Schomburg

Kenneth Clark, an influential educator and psychologist, made a significant contribution to American history by influencing the course of school desegregation (see Figure 17-7). In making its historic 1954 decision declaring segregated schools unconstitutional, the Supreme Court relied on the results of Clark's research demonstrating that African Americans had negative attitudes toward other African Americans and that these negative attitudes, in part, were products of segregated schools and segregated communities. The development of Clark's distinguished career was aided at an early age by his contact with a librarian at the New York Public Library who became an important model and source of support for him and who helped him appreciate his African American heritage.

I met [Arthur] Schomburg when I was about twelve years old, a crucial period in my life. It was at this time I clearly recognized that I was not ever going to be able to compete with my classmates in athletic skills.

I went to the library not only to escape the athletic competition, but also to escape the streets.

On one of my trips to the library, I decided that I was going to go upstairs to the third floor to the forbidden and mysterious area reserved for adults. I fully expected to be turned away unceremoniously. As I climbed the last flight of stairs, I felt the excitement of an interloper. I was prepared for the risk of either a polite or a more direct rejection. When I entered the room, a large man, whom I later came to know as Arthur Schomburg, got up from his desk and came over to me and smiled. He didn't ask me what I wanted. He merely put one arm around my shoulder and assumed that I was interested in the books. We went over to a table and sat down and began to talk. . . . We talked about books. We talked about wonderful things: about the history of human beings, about the contributions of Negroes which were to be found in books. He showed me portraits of Negroes who had contributed something important.

On that first day of meeting Schomburg, I knew I had met a friend. He ac-

cepted me as a human being and through his acceptance helped me to share his love of, and his excitement in, the world of books. (K. A. Clark, 1965)

Figure 17-7 Kenneth Clark during an interview on an NBC telecast.

Community Agencies Every person is influenced by the way in which society and its institutions are organized. Although some institutions are concerned with specific segments of the population (e.g., day-care centers, schools, and social centers for senior citizens), several are capable of reaching a wide range of the society's members. Because of our tendency to take these institutions for granted, we may lose sight of their potential for contributing to personal growth and reducing the likelihood of maladaptation. For example, a public library can be a powerful force in a person's life by providing access to books that can offer young people positive models and a broader view of the world. If the library can also provide positive personal experiences, these may make important contributions to the prevention of maladaptive behavior (see Box 17-1).

Sometimes community support comes about informally. Most people deal with everyday crises in the best way they can, using available resources. Just as we don't go to a doctor every time we have a sniffle, we don't run to a clinical psychologist every time we are upset. The availability of nonprofessional "therapists" may be one reason for this. For example, people like hairdressers and bartenders do a lot of therapeutic listening to the troubles of their customers (Cowen, 1982). However, some social institutions have been specifically assigned the task of handling crises.

Although they are not usually included in lists of mental health workers, police officers frequently modify behavior—whether for good or ill, and whether they are aware of it or not. Police officers are not in a position to remove the causes of crime, but as their skills in human relations develop, they can help prevent crime. Psychological training can help police officers handle violence and family arguments more effectively (Figure 17-8). In addition, it can help them deal with many other problems, such as the usually harmless but often bizarre behavior of former mental hospital patients, with more tact and discretion.

Figure 17-8 Police officers frequently must intervene in family disputes. This officer is trying to calm a domestic disturbance.

The Diverse Paths to Prevention

At the beginning of this chapter, we said that prevention could take more than one form. It can involve taking the steps needed to keep a disorder from arising in the first place, and it can also involve efforts to limit the impact on the life of the individual. In this sense, prevention and treatment are closely related. Common to both is the concept of vulnerability. Vulnerability arises when an individual's personal characteristics are insufficient to deal with the situation. The challenge of prevention is to identify opportunities for growth and stability and to provide such opportunities to people who need them. These opportunities differ, depending on the nature of the people to be served. For example, as they grow older, children need environments that give them increasing opportunities for independence. On the other hand, the aged usually need increasing care and attention.

Society inevitably must be involved in meeting the challenge of prevention because society can control or in-

fluence so many of the situations of modern life. We have seen many examples of the impact of community and social forces on our lives. Certain types of maladaptive behavior (e.g., phobias and delusions) can be attacked on an individual basis with the clinical methods we have described (psychotherapy, behavioral therapy, drugs). But lasting solutions to many problems of living require social change. Children living in crowded slum apartments or with abusive or neglectful parents have only limited opportunities to generalize from what they learn in a stimulating school or preschool program. Medication may help deinstitutionalized patients hallucinate less frequently, but they still need a supportive environment and a chance to acquire new social and occupational skills.

Preventing maladaptive behavior and responding therapeutically to it when it does occur require an examination of society, its components, and how they are interrelated. This examination should include elements that a community lacks as well as positive steps that it may take. Examples of such steps are houses for runaway children, drop-in centers for teenagers, and crisis centers. Virtually all such programs have been started by citizens without government support, and, at least initially, on a nonprofessional basis. As a result of such efforts, professionals in many areas have broadened the scope of their clinical services and have increased their involvement in community programs.

Paraprofessionals

Programs have been created to train and use nonprofessionals and paraprofessionals for significant roles in a variety of community settings. A wide culture-related gap often exists between middle-class professional workers (clinical psychologists, psychiatrists, and social workers) and people from lower socioeconomic groups who need help. Much of the success of **paraprofessionals** seems to be due to similarities between their backgrounds and those of their clients. For this reason, some community psychologists devote a major portion of their activities to training paraprofessionals.

Paraprofessionals vary widely in age, education, and cultural background. They often make up a large part of the staff in neighborhood service centers, residential youth centers, and mental health programs in both urban and rural areas. There they may serve as bridges between an established agency and a target group in the community that the agency has failed to serve effectively. Although relatively little research has been done on how to select, train, and evaluate the effectiveness of these workers, it has been shown that in some situations paraprofessionals may be as effective as the experts (Hattie et al., 1984). The responsibilities of paraprofessionals and their role in professional and community power structures need to be defined.

Figure 17-9 Self-help groups are based on the belief that some problems can be helped the most through mutual support from those who have experienced the same difficulties. In this photo, a support group for women who have had breast cancer meets to hear a presentation and to talk about ways of dealing with the experience of being a cancer patient.

Self-Help Groups

Self-help groups can also contribute to prevention (Kurtz, 1997). For many human problems, there are no easy answers or easy cures, but there is an alternative to coping with them alone. Millions of people whose problems and needs are not met through formal health care, social services, and counseling programs can find the hope and personal support they need in self-help groups. Within these groups, whose members share common concerns, people with problems are offered the understanding and help of others who have gone through similar experiences. People like those in the following examples might find the help they need by contacting the appropriate group:

Margaret and Bill are parents of a young child diagnosed with terminal cancer. For 2 years they have shared suffering, dashed hopes, and heartbreak. In spite of caring friends and professional support, they feel alone in their grief.

Jean is a divorced mother who has custody of her three children. She now finds herself overwhelmed by the problems of single parenthood. Her teenage son has become difficult to handle, and she is increasingly discouraged in trying to provide for her children's needs while meeting the demands of her job.

Roger has a serious drinking problem. He has been fired from two jobs in the last year and is deeply in debt. He has lost the respect of his family and friends. He entered treatment at an alcoholism clinic but began to drink again 2 months after the treatment ended. He realizes that his addiction is ruining his life but feels helpless to control it.

As social beings, all of us need to be accepted, cared for, and emotionally supported; we also find it satisfying to

care for and support those around us. Within the most natural "self-help networks"—families and friends—we establish the one-to-one contact so important to our happiness and well-being. This informal support is such a basic part of our social character that we tend to take it for granted, but it clearly influences our ability to handle distressing events in our lives. Many of our daily conversations are actually mutual counseling sessions in which we exchange the reassurance and advice that help us deal with routine stresses. In fact, research scientists have found that there is a strong link between the strength of our social support systems, our health, and our response to illness (Borkman, 1999) (see Figure 17-9). Further research is needed to determine when, under what conditions, and for which types of problems self-help groups are most effective. Table 17-3 lists some of the characteristics of self-help groups and ways in which they benefit their members.

Some self-help groups are well-known and have been in existence for many years. An example of such a group is Alcoholics Anonymous. Based on the success of this group, similar groups such as Gamblers Anonymous have been formed to help people with other types of problems. A group that is focused on the rehabilitation of mentally troubled persons is Compeer. This organization, with headquarters in Rochester, New York, began with 10 mental patients and 10 volunteers. It is now active in most states and in Canada as well. Compeer has helped more than 10,000 mentally and emotionally handicapped people. Mentally ill persons are put in contact with a "compeer"— a volunteer—who spends at least 1 hour per week with the client for a year. The volunteers, who invariably become the clients' friends, undergo brief training, meet with the clients' therapists if needed, and submit written monthly reports. Compeer seems to significantly cut the rate of clients' reentry into mental institutions. Its success may be attributed to the social support provided in

Table 17-3
Self-Help Groups

Major Characteristics of Self-Help Groups

- Avoidance of professional leadership and direction
- A homogeneous membership that has a common problem, affliction, or deviant status
- Meeting places outside such traditional therapy settings as hospitals and clinics
- Open-ended membership in which the group's composition is rarely constant

Ways in Which Self-Help Groups Benefit Their Members

- Emotional support and understanding
- An accepting reference group that reduces social isolation
- Information and advice
- Models of how to cope effectively with stress
- Enhancement of members' awareness of alternatives available in dealing with problems

Figure 17-10 By offering a consistent and supportive relationship, "honorary grandparents" like George King can play an important role in prevention programs designed to decrease the vulnerability of hard-to-place foster children.

Source: *New York Times*, April 1, 1996, p. 1. Photo by Cynthia Howe.

frequent informal and meaningful contacts with a caring friend.

Community Psychology

Community psychology is concerned with the role of social systems in preventing human distress and maladaptive behavior. Community psychologists attempt to work in settings that have an impact on prevention (Rappaport & Seidman, 2000). For example, they might serve as human relations consultants to a police department, work to increase the skills of individuals who staff welfare offices, or develop prevention programs in homes or schools. Outreach programs are aimed at either preventing breakdowns or dealing with problems in the community before more drastic treatment programs, such as hospitalization, become necessary. Making communities livable requires good ideas about social planning and an awareness that various segments of the population—including the aged, minorities, and the unemployed—have special needs. Community psychologists are interested in the environmental facts of life in particular communities as well as the impact of those conditions on individual lives.

The work of community psychology can take place either in existing community institutions (such as neighborhood community centers) or in specially created settings. An example of the latter is an Illinois organization called Hope for the Children that recruits and hires foster parents who live rent-free in a specially arranged area of an existing neighborhood. The children are youngsters who stand little chance of being placed in a family permanently. They have often endured horrors. Beaten,

molested or abandoned, children like them often wind up as wards of the state and get bounced around the foster-care system. Few people are willing to take a chance on a child who has been kicked so hard by life and who might be expected to start kicking back (as many as 80% of prison inmates have been in foster care). The foster parents in the Hope program were recruited through newspaper advertisements and, after careful screening, participated in an extensive training program. These foster parents, like the children, are a mix of races and are from the working class. Most already have families of their own. In addition to foster parents, there are also "honorary grandparents." These middle-aged and elderly people receive subsidized rents in exchange for volunteering 8 to 10 hours a week as crossing guards, crafts instructors, and maintenance workers. Figure 17-10 shows a foster child and an "honorary grandparent" engaged in a mutually enjoyable activity.

Projects like Hope for the Children are exciting, but they require objective evaluation and often are high-risk ventures. They are exciting because they create the possibility of solving important problems. They require evaluation because any novel approach to a problem needs to be reviewed for effectiveness and feasibility. They may be high-risk because, should community support and funding disappear or diminish, their very existence will be threatened.

Treatment in the Community

Whether people receive mental health services in the community or in institutions, society has a definite interest in how those services are provided, their effectiveness, and their cost. The mix of available services can influence not only the recipients' sense of well-being, but also their economic productivity. Many people who would otherwise have to be hospitalized could remain in the community if facilities that provided additional social support and supervision were available. A study released in 1994 by the New York State Commission on the Quality of Care for the Mentally Disabled found that nearly 40% of all patients discharged from mental hospitals are rehospitalized within 6 months. Part of the problem is that many former patients deteriorate in the community because of inadequate services. The inadequacy of community services is one reason more than 30,000 seriously mentally ill individuals—with schizophrenia, manic-depressive psychoses, and other severe disorders—are confined to jails on any given day (see Figure 17-11).

A basic component of the needed services is affordable supportive housing. Although the supply of either is very small, there are two types of housing for the mentally ill: (1) custodial housing and (2) alternative housing. **Custodial housing** (boarding houses, nursing homes, and special-care homes) tend to be large facilities financed and often run by cities, counties, and states with few or

no rehabilitation programs. They often have an institutional atmosphere similar to that of hospitals. **Alternative housing** (halfway houses, group homes, co-ops) tends to be small and focused on rehabilitation and integration into the community. Most alternative housing programs encourage residents to become involved in making decisions about the selection of new residents and the upkeep of the home. Staff members with training in social work or psychiatric rehabilitation often work in these homes. The main aim of alternative housing facilities is to prevent hospitalization and improve the quality of life. Some supportive housing facilities have private apartments in which the resident is a legal tenant although psychological and practical support is provided.

The Oxford House concept illustrates a type of innovative living arrangement that seems to be effective. The original Oxford House in Washington, D.C., was developed for the rehabilitation of drug addicts and alcoholics, and there are now more than 500 similar facilities throughout the country. An Oxford House World Convention was held in 2000 (see Figure 17-12). Each Oxford House is self-run, with no professional counselors or house managers. Every resident has one vote, and all participate in running the house, with officers rotating every 6 months. That eliminates "us against them" sentiments and the addict's traditional resentment of authority, fosters responsibility, and, as residents' leadership and self-management skills grow, encourages self-confidence. Every resident must pay his or her own way; established houses help new houses get started. Unlike traditional halfway houses,

Figure 17-11   David Bruce Bellamy, diagnosed with schizophrenia, has been booked 13 times in the last 10 years into the Thurston County, Washington, jail. Like other jails throughout the country about 15% of its jail population is mentally ill. Once inmates are released, many don't have homes to return to and end up on the streets. Without the structure of a daily routine, the stability of a home environment, and someone to watch out for them, they often go off their medications, allowing severe symptoms to return. Many end up back in jail.

SOURCE: *The Olympian.* November 15, 1999, p. A5.

Figure 17-12   The Oxford House concept was developed to rehabilitate drug addicts and alcoholics in the community.

which often have short-term residency limits, Oxford House residents can stay as long as they like if they pay their rent and follow the number one rule: sobriety. Relapse means automatic expulsion. (Residents who relapse can reapply, but only after 30 days of sobriety.)

Oxford House residents have many vulnerabilities and often lack resilience (75% have served jail time; 60% have been homeless during their addiction). The Oxford House concept might not work with groups who are not drug addicts and alcoholics. For that reason, experiments in housing and rehabilitation with diverse groups are needed.

Problems With Community Programs

A look at one mentally ill woman's journey through the mental health system illustrates many of the problems endemic to community programs. Writer Susan Sheehan (1982) followed the story of "Sylvia Frumkin" over nearly 20 years of treatment. Frumkin (the name is fictitious; after her death in 1994, it was revealed that her real name was Maxine Mason) had a long and disheartening journey through what is commonly called "the system." In fact, the system she encountered was disjointed, fragmented, and ineffective at every turn. Following her first psychotic break in 1964 at the age of 15, she was repeatedly hospitalized or placed in various types of institutions. At different times she was diagnosed as manic-depressive and as having schizophrenia, either undifferentiated or the paranoid type. At various times she was given individual psychotherapy, antipsychotic medications, lithium, insulin coma therapy, electroconvulsive therapy, "Christian psychotherapy," and megavitamin therapy. Over the years she saw a constantly changing array of therapists, each often for a very short period. These therapists treated her with nearly every available medication, sometimes without reference to her history, and they sometimes changed, suddenly decreased, or altogether stopped her medication in a seemingly arbitrary manner.

Sylvia Frumkin was not the kind of patient most therapists enjoy; she was described as slovenly, unappreciative, and uncooperative. She drained energies of clinical personnel by being loud, abusive, and even violent during the acute phases of her illness. Even when she was not acutely ill, Frumkin was characterized by a staff member as "arrogant, nasty, and demanding." As Figure 17-13 shows, Sylvia Frumkin experienced 45 changes in treatment settings in 17 years. She was repeatedly bounced back and forth between her family home, various hospital settings, and community residential facilities. She was admitted 27 separate times to eight different hospitals (state, municipal, general, voluntary, and private), where she spent a total of 9 years. She spent almost 7 years in a state hospital. For slightly less than 6 years she lived with her family, cycling in and out of their home nine different times. She spent a total of 3 years in several different types of community settings, such as halfway houses, a foster home, a YWCA residence, and a religious community. The cost of her care was estimated to be $636,000 from 1963 to 1982, and would be considerably greater today if the costs of inflation were taken into account.

Following Sylvia Frumkin's death, Susan Sheehan (1995) described Frumkin's life after 1980 (subsequent to the period covered by Figure 17-13). The quality of her life did not improve. She continued to shuttle from one institution to another with occasional returns to the community. Among her institutionalizations were 15 months at Bellevue Hospital in New York (even though that city hospital is intended for short-term patients) and a considerable amount of time in a state hospital. She died in an institution at the age of 46 of a bleeding ulcer, no clue of which had been detected in all the medical examinations she received over many years.

Unfortunately, Sylvia Frumkin's story is not unique. There are an estimated 1.7 to 2.4 million chronically mentally ill people in the United States. Policymakers and the public can learn a great deal from the experiences of people like Sylvia Frumkin. Her story clearly illustrates the profound impact of chronic mental illness on patients, families, and communities, as well as on the staggering costs of providing care. It may well be that Frumkin would have continued to deteriorate even if the conditions of her treatment had been more favorable, but the behavior of the system certainly seems to have been a contributing factor in her deterioration. In her various hospitalizations, Frumkin never experienced a prolonged relationship with a caring person. She perceived no one as having her interests continuously at heart during her many years in "the system." Cases like Frumkin's have led mental health workers, judges, and other government officials to think about ways to reform both the system and the laws that place disturbed individuals in public institutions.

Improving Treatment in the Community

Experiments designed to improve the mix of available mental health services are sorely needed but are rare. Several approaches seem promising and merit further study. These include the **dormitory-inn** and **halfway house,** time-limited (e.g., 3 weeks) residences that provide opportunities for resocialization and transition to the community, and **partial hospitalization,** facilities that provide treatment during evening hours and accommodations at night, as well as the opportunity to participate in useful activities outside the facility during the day.

While partial hospitalization at night is uncommon in the United States, it is a common practice in Belgium. Belgium has approximately 17,000 beds in hospitals for the mentally ill, of which over 1,000 are for partial hospitalization at night. The Brussels Night Hospital is an active rehabilitation facility for chronic psychotic patients.

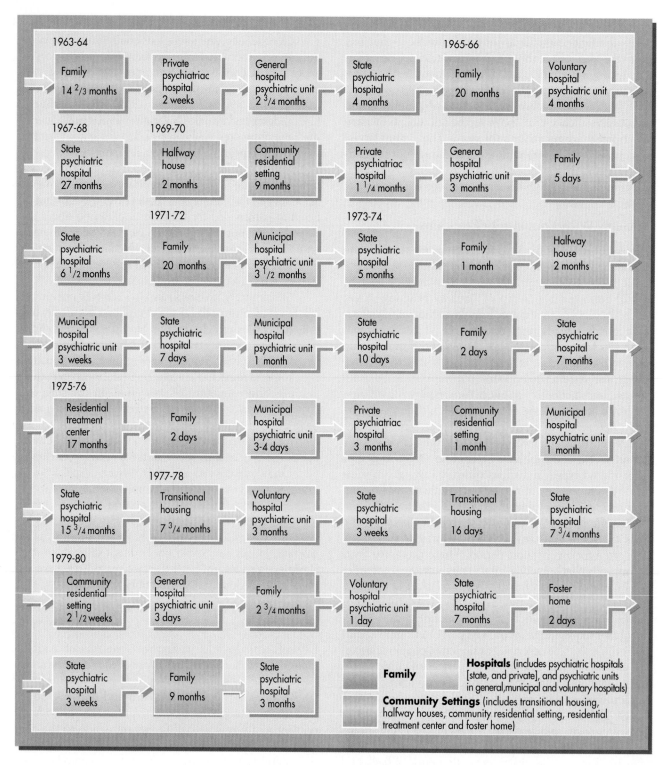

Figure 17–13 Sylvia Frumkin's odyssey as a chronic mental patient, 1963–1980. As the text explains, her experience was no better from 1980 to her death in 1994.

Source: A. E. Moran, R. I. Freedman, and S. S. Sharfstein, (1984). "The Journey of Sylvia Frumkin: A Case Study for Policymakers." *Hospital and Community Psychiatry, 35*, 887–893. © 1984 by American Psychiatric Association. Reprinted by permission.

Most of the patients have schizophrenia, have had the condition for 5 to 10 years, and have spent more than 2 years in mental hospitals. Patients are organized in four groups of about 12 members each for daily living. Each group has a living room and kitchen. Patients must participate in the upkeep of the facility and of their rooms. Each group is responsible for cooking its own meals four times a week. (Friday and weekend meals are provided by the kitchen of the night hospital.) The hospital's staff does not make strenuous efforts to "cure" the patients. Rather, the focus is on improving the patient's level of functioning and quality of life. A core belief is that care should be provided in the community to the maximum extent possible. The night hospital's program is seen as supporting the patient's life in society. The results thus far are encouraging, with two-thirds of the patients engaged in regular structured activities outside the hospital (DeHert et al., 1996).

Although the concept of community care for the chronically mentally ill is a good one, most deinstitutionalized people in the United States have simply been dumped into communities that fear them because of their eccentric behaviors and do not look after them in any systematic way. Once the mentally ill are out on their own, they will more than likely stop taking their medications. The lack of professional care on the streets and the effects of alcohol and drug abuse are further serious complications. Deinstitutionalized patients may become too disorganized to extricate themselves from living on the streets—except by exhibiting blatantly bizarre or disruptive behavior that leads to their being taken to a hospital or jail (see Figure 17-14).

Few deinstitutionalized people are given the vocational training, guidance in self-care, recreational activities, or opportunities for socializing that are required for any sort of meaningful existence. The need for follow-up care, the hard realities of insufficient funding, the impact of patients on communities, and the uncertainties as to what constitutes effective community programs have all been largely ignored. As a result, a growing number of people who would otherwise be enthusiastic about deinstitutionalization have become at least somewhat disillusioned.

One consequence of the large number of failures of deinstitutionalization has been an increase in readmissions to state hospitals. Patients now stay in the hospital for shorter periods but, because of their inability to function in the community, return more often. About half of the patients who are released from state hospitals are readmitted within a year of discharge.

What lessons can be learned from the way deinstitutionalization has been practiced up to now? Perhaps the most important lesson of the bad experiences of the past two decades is that deinstitutionalization as it is now being carried out is not helpful to many individuals. As happens so often, society neglects many of the basics needed to reach a worthy objective. More money and more trained personnel are needed.

More education is also essential. Public information programs about mental illness and retardation and more

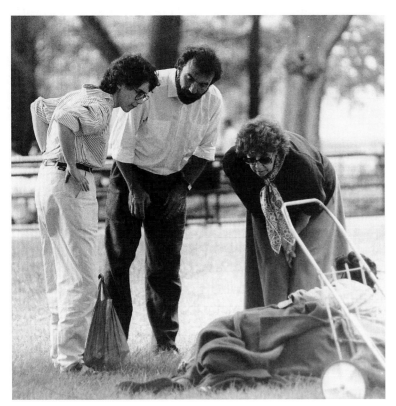

Figure 17-14   Workers from Project Help, a New York program for the homeless, talk with a homeless person to determine whether he is severely mentally ill and needs hospitalization. Project Help uses an active outreach program to identify those who are in need of help, provides immediate treatment, and places them in community residences, group homes, or their own apartments. Unfortunately, because of their serious and chronic mental illness, many homeless people aided by Project Help have ended up back on the streets.

citizen involvement in planning for the reentry of former patients into the community can help make deinstitutionalization a positive experience for both the patients and the community. The entry of formerly hospitalized patients into a neighborhood has frequently been perceived as a threat, even though most ex-mental patients and retarded individuals are harmless. Nothing can arouse negative feelings in a neighborhood more quickly than the proposed establishment of a halfway house or after-care center in the vicinity. Yet there is no evidence that simply being a discharged mental patient makes a person more likely to commit crimes or endanger the community. However, there is an increasing tendency to place people with criminal records in mental hospitals, and people with previous arrest records are likely to be arrested again after they are discharged from mental hospitals.

The problems of the chronically mentally ill living in the community require a comprehensive system of care that includes the following provisions:

1. An adequate number of supervised community housing settings.
2. Community clinical services, ranging from the availability of professional mental health workers who can provide crisis intervention to means for hospitalization during acute conditions.
3. Recognition of the importance of families in treatment, along with adequate support for family members as well as for the patient.

One reason a comprehensive system did not exist in the 1960s and 1970s, when the deinstitutionalization movement began, and still does not exist, is that very little research pertinent to the release to the community of large numbers of mental hospital patients had been conducted prior to the massive discharges resulting from the change in policy. Advocates of deinstitutionalization had assumed that mentally ill individuals would voluntarily seek treatment in the community if they needed it. As it turned out, a large number of discharged patients did not seek treatment once out of the hospital. Many of those who suffer from schizophrenia and mood disorders do not believe themselves to be in need of professional help. These untreated individuals constitute most of the mentally ill population who are homeless or are in jail, and who commit violent acts.

Legal Aspects of Treatment and Prevention

In this and the previous chapter we have discussed ways to help people avoid having problems and, if that isn't possible, to overcome them to the extent possible. Because people live in groups, the community has an interest in preventing behavior that is maladaptive. Although historically this has not always been the case, governmental bodies now have laws that deal with both helping people who behave deviantly and protecting the public from the dangers posed by certain types of deviant individuals (e.g., criminals). In reality, such laws may be problematic if our judgment of what constitutes help happens to be wrong or if the person doesn't want to be helped.

Institutionalization

The process of placing a person in an institution is called **commitment.** Prisoners are committed to prisons for punishment, and mental patients are committed to mental hospitals for treatment. **Criminal commitment** of an individual to a mental hospital may occur when a criminal act is legally declared to be a result of insanity and it is determined that the interests of society and the individual would be best served by commitment to a mental hospital rather than to a prison. Some mental patients voluntarily commit themselves, but others are involuntarily hospitalized through a legal procedure called **civil commitment.** Civil commitment can be carried out only if a person is judged to be a risk to himself or herself or to others. The forced institutionalization of a person poses serious problems. On the one hand, civil commitment aims at providing help, but in order to do that, it may deprive the committed person of basic human rights.

One example of the logistical difficulties posed by commitment laws is the case of Anna May Peoples, a Seattle woman who was diagnosed as having paranoid schizophrenia. Because of her paranoia, she took refuge in the city's Public Safety Building. Peoples made the building her home for 2 years, but authorities had to dismiss trespassing charges against her. She was judged not competent to stand trial, but not dangerous enough to institutionalize (see Figure 17-15).

Criminal Commitment To convict a person of a crime, the state must establish beyond a reasonable doubt not only that the person committed the prohibited act, but also that the act was committed with criminal intent. If criminal intent cannot be proven, the insanity defense becomes possible. The concept of insanity is often confused with that of competence to stand trial. **Insanity** refers to a person's state of mind at the time that an act was carried out, while **competency** refers to a person's state of mind at the time of a judicial proceeding. In a legal sense, an **incompetent person** is one who lacks the capacity to consult with a lawyer and to understand the nature of legal proceedings (Ciccone, 1999). Both *insanity* and *competency* are legal terms whose applicability in a given case is determined by a judge after consideration of all the evidence, including the opinions of expert witnesses.

Figure 17-15 Anna May Peoples, caught between the technicalities of legal incompetence and lack of dangerousness, waits to hear her fate during a court appearance.

The Insanity Defense The concept of insanity has a long history. Early English law did not recognize insanity as an excuse for criminal behavior. However, by the thirteenth century, proof of criminal intentions was necessary to convict a person of a felony. The **insanity defense** allowed that if accused individuals could prove that they were completely "mad," they could successfully defend themselves against a criminal charge. In 1843, Daniel M'Naghten, a Scottish woodturner, assassinated Edward Drummond, secretary to the prime minister of England. He was found not guilty because the judges stated that he was "laboring under such a defect of reason, from disease of the mind, as not to know the nature and quality of the act he was doing; or, if he did know, that he did not know he was doing what was wrong."

This ruling, known as the **M'Naghten rule,** became the "right and wrong" test of insanity and was widely adopted. As belief in this interpretation of insanity grew, statutes were introduced that permitted the court to defer sentencing decisions until the offender could be studied and recommendations could be made to the judge. Psychiatrists, psychologists, social workers, and probation officers became advisers to the court. Sentencing became more flexible, and parole was increasingly granted.

An example of an attempt to invoke the M'Naghten rule occurred in the case of Jack Ruby, who was convicted of the murder of President Kennedy's assassin, Lee Harvey Oswald, in 1964. In appealing his death sentence, Ruby claimed that he suffered from psychomotor epilepsy and that this had prevented him from distinguishing right from wrong. However, this claim was rejected by the judge, and Ruby was found legally sane. He eventually died in prison.

The M'Naghten rule and subsequent court decisions have been controversial, largely because of the difficulty of defining precisely what "knowing right from wrong" really means. Contrasting with the M'Naghten rule's emphasis on the "right and wrong" test is the idea of the **irresistible impulse,** according to which the person could

not control his or her behavior. The **Durham rule** states that a person is not criminally responsible if the criminal act was the product of mental disease or mental defect. None of these rules about the nature of insanity is without ambiguities and difficulties.

In 1962 the **American Law Institute (ALI)** proposed a set of guidelines that have since been incorporated into the laws of several states. The **ALI guidelines** focus on impairment that grows out of a defendant's mental illness and include the following stipulations:

> 1. A person is not responsible for criminal conduct if at the time of such conduct as a result of mental disease or defect he lacks substantial capacity either to appreciate the criminality (wrongfulness) of his conduct or to conform his conduct to the requirements of law.
> 2. ... The terms "mental disease or defect" do not include an abnormality manifested only by repeated criminal or otherwise antisocial conduct.
>
> (American Law Institute, 1962, p. 66) ■

With each passing year, the ALI guidelines have gained increased acceptance throughout the country. In 1983, in the case of *Jones v. United States,* the Supreme Court ruled that people who are found not guilty by reason of insanity can be held indefinitely in a mental hospital under a less rigorous standard of proof of dangerousness than is required for civilly committed individuals. The Court ruled that acquitted insanity defendants "constitute a special class that should be treated differently." In 1984, Congress passed the Federal Insanity Defense Reform Act, which modified some features of the ALI guidelines and assigned the defense with the responsibility of convincingly establishing the defendant's insanity.

The number of insanity defenses that are successful is very small. In the entire state of New York, for example, there are on the average fewer than 50 successful insanity defenses each year. Thus, the insanity defense contributes only a tiny fraction to the problem of crime in the United States. In part, this is because juries have difficulty applying the fine legal points involved in the insanity defense.

Understandably, the public remembers highly publicized cases in which the insanity defense was invoked and someone who had clearly committed a crime was found not guilty by reason of insanity (see Figure 17-16). Sometimes such people are released after a short hospitalization and later commit another crime.

In 1981, John Hinckley, Jr.'s, acquittal by reason of insanity from charges of attempting to assassinate then-President Ronald Reagan caused many people to question the fairness of the insanity defense. The American Psychiatric Association argued that people should be acquitted for insanity only if they have a serious mental disorder such as psychosis. Those who have personality disorders—for example, antisocial personality disorder—or abuse drugs or alcohol should be held responsible for their actions. The Association further stated that expert witnesses should not be allowed to testify about whether the defen-

dant was able to control his or her behavior (*Psychiatric News*, February 4, 1983).

The use of expert testimony poses profound interpretive problems (Rogers & Shuman, 2000). So far, none of the guidelines that have been proposed for dealing with the problem of insanity has provided a completely satisfactory solution. During John Hinckley's trial, the barrage of contradictory expert testimony damaged the image of psychiatry in the public mind. Those who would abolish the insanity defense believe that one way to end this type of spectacle would be to restrict psychiatric testimony to evidence of mental abnormality that bears on the defendant's conscious awareness and perception—his or her "intent" to commit the crime. Other testimony concerning more subtle impairments of understanding, judgment, or behavior control would no longer be relevant at the guilt stage of the trial, but could be introduced at the time of sentencing. Another proposal calls for a pool of expert witnesses to be selected by the court. These experts would no longer testify for the prosecution or the defense. Instead, the impartial panel would attempt to arrive at a conclusion

Figure 17-16 Edmund E. Kemper III (a) was acquitted by reason of insanity from the charge of murdering his grandparents in 1964 and was released from a mental hospital in 1969 as "cured"; he later murdered six college students, his mother, and one of her friends—for which he was found sane and guilty. Dennis Sweeney (b) was sent to the Mid-Hudson Psychiatric Center when a judge accepted his plea of "not guilty by reason of mental disease" for killing Congressman Allard Lowenstein in 1980. After the slaying of his parents, Gregory Shaddy (c) was acquitted by reason of insanity; he spent 2 years in a hospital and was then pronounced cured and released. The case of John W. Hinckley, Jr. (d), revived debate over the insanity defense after he was acquitted from the charge of attempting to assassinate President Ronald Reagan (whom he shot in 1981 in order to impress the actress Jodie Foster) and was committed to a mental hospital.

(a)

(b)

(c)

(d)

Figure 17-17 Theodore Kaczynski, referred to as the Unabomber, was sentenced to life in prison for mailing bombs to people he had identified as moving the culture toward a more highly technological era. Although he was diagnosed as having a schizophrenia disorder of the paranoid type, experts certified that he could be considered responsible for his actions and was competent to stand trial. His admission of the bombings led to his sentencing without a trial.

" YOU CAN'T PLEAD INSANITY, IT'S ONLY A PARKING TICKET, "

Figure 17-18 This cartoon reflects the belief of some people that invoking the insanity defense is often frivolous.

Source: *Wall Street Journal*, September 8, 2000, p. A19.

Table 17-4
Three Myths Concerning the Insanity Defense

Myth 1: Criminals Use the Insanity Defense to Escape Punishment.

In fact, people found "not guilty by reason of insanity" are never simply released the way a person would be if acquitted of a crime. Usually, they are confined for treatment in a special hospital for severely mentally ill persons who have committed crimes. Persons found not guilty by reason of insanity, on average, are held at least as long as—and often longer than—persons found guilty and sent to prison for similar crimes.

Myth 2: The Defense Is Widely Abused

In truth, the insanity defense is seldom used.

Myth 3: The Defense Allows Criminals to "Get Away With Murder"

While approximately half of those pleading insanity are indicted for violent crimes, only a small fraction of these were charged with murder. The rest stood trial for robbery, property damage, or minor felonies such as shoplifting or writing bad checks.

regarding the defendant's mental state when the crime was committed.

Three states (Montana, Idaho, and Utah) have abolished the insanity defense. In 1994 the U.S. Supreme Court held that there is no constitutional violation when defendants are denied the defense. Although most other states are unlikely to abolish the insanity defense, controversy continues to surround it. Modifications can be expected in laws concerning its applicability. By 1997, 10 states had passed new laws allowing juries to find defendants "guilty but mentally ill." Such verdicts provide for the convicted person to receive treatment and then serve out the full sentence like any other prisoner.

The case of Theodore Kaczynski (see Figure 17-17), who ultimately admitted to the more than two dozen bomb attacks that killed several people and maimed others, illustrates the difference between the concepts of competency to stand trial and lack of criminal responsibility by reason of mental illness. Although Kaczynski's defense attorneys as well as many others were convinced that he was mentally ill, both they, the prosecution attorneys, and the judge agreed that he was competent to stand trial because he met the criteria of understanding the charges against him and being capable of contributing to his defense. However, the case was complicated by the fact that Kaczynski did not wish the issue of mental illness to be used in his defense but his lawyers felt that without it they were handicapped in presenting the strongest possible case in his defense. Finally, after a court-appointed psychiatrist certified that he fit the DSM-IV criteria for paranoid schizophrenia and thus should be considered as mentally ill although competent to stand trial, he agreed to plead guilty and will spend the remainder of his life in prison.

The complexities of the insanity defense can be puzzling even to well-informed individuals. However, calls for the cessation of the insanity defense usually stem from the public's misconceptions (Figure 17-18). Table 17-4 lists three misconceptions that are widely believed to be

Q&A

Box 17-2

Q Doesn't the fact that there are often big disagreements among experts concerning the insanity defense raise serious questions about its continued use?

A *Yes, the insanity defense is an imperfect concept with regard to which personal judgment and arbitrariness do play roles. There is no doubt that the concept is evolving and needs improvement. However, what has to be borne in mind is that the insanity defense (either the present one or some version yet to be invented and accepted) plays an important role in the legal system. One goal of the legal system is that it be perceived as fair. A court system that*

is not perceived as fair loses the society's credibility and respect. A legal system that treats the incompetent and insane just like everyone else might well seem to fail the test of fairness. When mental health experts testify in court concerning issues like insanity and competency, they are helping the court weigh factors (such as brain disorders, mental illness, and mental retardation) that relate to a person's ability to participate fairly in the legal process.

Another factor that relates to the insanity defense is the adversarial character of the American legal system. In this system, an arm of the law is an adversary to the citizen-defendant and tries to convict him or her. To

be fair to a defendant who is facing such a formidable adversary as the government, the defendant should be in good enough mental shape to grasp the situation of being on trial; understand the charges, possible penalties, and options; answer questions meaningfully; detect lies or errors by witnesses; and keep the defense attorney informed about relevant facts as the trial progresses. If an individual's mental state interferes with meeting these requirements, the court needs to know about it and take it into account in rendering a verdict.

What this means is that the legal system rests on certain moral assumptions. How to meet these assumptions is a work in progress.

---

true. The large gaps between the realities of the insanity defense and popular misconceptions suggest the need for both rethinking the pertinent issues and public education (see Box 17-2).

Civil Commitment All 50 states have civil commitment laws. These laws are based on the doctrine of **parens patriae** (Latin for "parenthood of the state"), according to which the state can act in what it takes to be the best interest of a minor or an adult who is incapacitated. The principal features of the process are a petition, a hearing, and a decision about the place to which the individual is to be committed. In some states, the judgments of psychiatrists are decisive in reaching commitment decisions. In others, physicians who are not psychiatrists play dominant roles. In the past, standards for commitment were loosely worded and protections for the patient either did not exist or were ignored. Then, in a 1979 decision (*Addington v. Texas*), the Supreme Court ruled that people may not be committed to mental institutions unless the state has presented "clear and convincing" evidence that they require hospitalization.

All civil commitment laws involve two judgments: whether the individual is suffering from a disabling mental illness and whether he or she is dangerous. The first criterion is relatively easy to establish; the second is more of a problem. "Dangerousness" refers to the potential to inflict harm on other people as well as on oneself. Judging how dangerous a person might be is often a difficult matter.

In the beginning, Jane's older neighbor seemed friendly enough.

Stuart, who lived alone, would often stop to chat. Sometimes he'd borrow a gardening tool, or Jane would borrow one from him. But two years ago, the relationship changed dramatically.

Stuart, who is in his 60s, became infatuated with Jane, 36. He recited Bible verses to her, then broke into her home while she was gone. He wrote Jane long love letters, tried to accost her and kiss her in church, and attempted to lure her three children into his house with candy and baseball cards.

He bought an expensive van identical to Jane's, and said he was planning to kidnap Jane and her children and drive them across the country. (Based on Seattle Times, August 27, 1990, pp. A1, A5)

Is Stuart harmless, or is he a serious danger to his neighbors? Although a judge declared Stuart harmless, he subsequently was jailed for several misdemeanors and also harassed Jane over a long period of time.

Because dangerousness involves a prediction of future behavior, its application to individual cases creates enormous problems. Can a clinical expert tell the court whether a person is dangerous and when he or she has stopped being dangerous?

In 1985 a 22-year-old accountant was pushed in front of a speeding subway train at rush hour. A large team of doctors, nurses, and technicians operated on her for 22 hours, trying to save her life and repair her severe head injuries and numerous broken bones. Her assailant, who had been held by another subway rider until police arrived, turned out to be a 19-year-old unemployed woman with a history of mental problems. She had been released from a psychiatric ward less than a month before her crime, despite violent behavior while incarcerated and a psychiatrist's warning that she was dangerous. On two occasions she had attacked fellow patients and had to be subdued by means of a straitjacket.

Although the psychiatrist in this case was correct in thinking that the 19-year-old woman was dangerous, available evidence suggests that clinicians' predictions of whether a given individual will do something dangerous in the future are often inaccurate. Mental health specialists are best at predicting dangerous behavior that might occur in the near future, but even then, studies show they are only from 40% to 60% accurate (Appelbaum, 1991). For longer-term predictions the record is much worse. In several studies that followed patients over several years, only 14% to 35% of those considered potentially dangerous to others were actually arrested for violent crimes. At present, the best indication of future dangerousness is dangerousness in the past unless the particular circumstances that led to the past behavior no longer exist (Cunningham & Reidy, 1999; Guthiel & Appelbaum, 2000).

Studies of dangerousness have consistently found that few patients are dangerous only to others. In a study of a thousand patients seen in psychiatric emergency rooms, only 4% were dangerous to others, three times that many were suicidal or dangerous to themselves, and only 0.6% were dangerous only to others and not to themselves (Appelbaum, 1991).

The goal of protecting the rights of people who might be committed to an institution against their will is accepted by all. However, it is by no means clear how to protect those rights while simultaneously assuring the welfare of the individual and of society. At present, civil commitments seem to be increasing in frequency. This trend is being reinforced by recent court decisions that have emphasized the *parens patriae* role of the state in treating a patient for his or her own good. Also contributing to the trend is the failure of many states to develop community treatment networks to supplement hospital systems, as well as health insurance programs that provide only marginal subsidies for outpatient care.

The Historical Context of Civil Commitment How a community responds at a given time to mentally ill people who need help varies depending on current social values, legal decisions, and judgments about the potential danger of people harming themselves or others. During the late nineteenth and early twentieth centuries, most states enacted involuntary commitment laws to provide care for those mentally ill individuals who needed it but, because of their mental illness, could not recognize their need. Hospitalization and treatment of the mentally ill, even without the patient's informed consent, were considered necessary to help a person in need. Beginning about 40 years ago, changing values led to new laws that emphasized the civil liberties of individuals. Involuntary commitment came to be seen as state action that resulted

in the loss of an individual's constitutionally protected right to liberty. Not only did grounds for commitment become more restrictive, but many legal authorities argued that only a compelling governmental interest could justify the loss of liberty occasioned by commitment. Many states changed their involuntary commitment laws to require a finding of mental illness and dangerousness to self or to others as the only grounds for commitment. Most mental health agencies adopted policies of short-term hospitalization whenever possible in response to court rulings that patients have the right to the least restrictive alternative to hospitalization.

Recently, because of the public's concerns about safety, most states have enacted laws authorizing **outpatient commitment** of mentally ill individuals who are not dangerous but are likely to deteriorate and become dangerous if they do not receive treatment. Patients subjected to outpatient commitment can be ordered to take medications and to keep appointments at mental health centers. Laws dealing with outpatient commitment reflect the state's increased willingness to use its commitment authority to seek treatment compliance from noninstitutionalized patients. Recent laws have also given mental health practitioners more power and responsibility to care for the mentally ill through the involuntary civil commitment system. Changes in laws concerning both inpatient and outpatient commitment reflect tensions within society between the need to help individuals and the need to protect the community.

Most involuntary commitment laws attempt to balance the rights of a person with mental illness to refuse treatment against the rights of those whom the person might seriously harm. The laws refer only to physical harm and do not deal with the anguish of family members and the emotional, financial, and psychological damage to which they might be subjected. The following passage was written by someone whose husband had recently committed suicide:

> *Two years ago, my husband, Patrick, developed paranoid schizophrenia. A brief hospitalization showed that medication could control his symptoms. Unfortunately his increasingly disordered thought processes led him to refuse medication and further treatment upon his release. Although his threatening, often suicidal statements weren't concrete enough to warrant involuntary commitment, his daily behavior was so disturbing that family members often called upon law enforcement officers and mental health professionals for help. But the result was always the same: Unless Patrick was a demonstrable threat to himself or others, nothing could be done.*

Police officials and court judges have recently been receiving better training with regard to mental health issues and are showing an increased willingness to consider novel approaches for individuals to whom these issues may apply.

For example, Broward County, Florida, established a new court for the mentally ill. The court is designed to bring mentally ill defendants before a judge who has both the special training and the authority to move defendants from an overcrowded jail system into a mental health system without compromising public safety. Ordinarily, mentally ill defendants charged with misdemeanors find themselves within the criminal court system, which handles thousands of other defendants. Before the new court was established, an estimated 7,000 mentally ill people were confined in Broward County jails each year. Many of these people were minor offenders and nonviolent. The new court hears only defendants facing misdemeanor charges, except in the case of domestic violence or driving-while-intoxicated charges. Under the law created by the court, mentally ill people who are judged to be a danger to themselves or others can be committed voluntarily or involuntarily to a state mental hospital or other mental health facility for treatment.

The Rights of Patients

In the not-so-distant past, people were treated as if admission to a mental hospital justified taking away all their rights. However, according to court decisions over the years, patients' rights must be upheld and adequate treatment must be provided. In a 1971 case that attracted national attention (**Wyatt v. Stickney**), a court ruled that a state must provide adequate treatment for mental hospital patients who are confined involuntarily. Beyond recognizing the patient's right to treatment, the court specified basic hospital staffing ratios and qualifications and also required individualized treatment plans.

In a 1975 Supreme Court decision (**O'Connor v. Donaldson**), Kenneth Donaldson was awarded compensatory and punitive damages of $38,500 against two staff psychiatrists at the Florida State Hospital because they had not provided adequate treatment for him during the 14 years of his involuntary commitment. The significance of the O'Connor v. Donaldson ruling was its recognition that hospitalized people who are not dangerous have a constitutional right to treatment. The O'Connor v. Donaldson decision strengthened the rights of involuntarily hospitalized patients, but it did not make the task of determining whether or not a patient is dangerous any easier.

The courts have opened the door to long-overdue improvement in the treatment of the mentally ill. A federal judge in New Jersey ruled that an involuntarily committed mental patient who objected to the drug therapy administered to him could not be forced to take the medication (Rennie v. Klein, 1978). Since drugs now constitute the primary mode of treatment and behavior control in institutions and virtually all involuntarily committed patients are routinely given antipsychotic medications, this and similar rulings have widespread implications for the way in which treatment is defined in state institutions. In addition to strengthening patients' right to get treatment (and their right to refuse it), the courts have also supported patients' right to receive the "least restrictive treatment" available. The least restrictive treatment is only as restrictive and confining as is necessary to achieve the purpose of the commitment.

Increasingly, both patients and judges are questioning the safety and effectiveness of present-day treatment methods. Physical treatments such as drugs and electroconvulsive therapy do have the potential to cause permanent injury. Certain patients appear to deteriorate as a result of receiving psychotherapy. Some experts also believe that behavior-modification procedures such as token economies are too coercive. Some critics believe that merely being institutionalized is therapeutically counterproductive, regardless of the quality of the institution. Until recently, a hospital's power to deny patients the right to examine their own files was taken for granted. Now patients can see their charts, but some hospitals do not voluntarily tell patients that they are entitled to do so.

Informed Consent As the rights of patients have been extended, the requirement of informed consent has been strengthened. **Informed consent** requires that patients receive adequate information about the nature of a planned treatment before they agree to submit to it. The clinician must communicate this information in language that is meaningful to the patient, rather than in medical jargon, and must clearly explain the potential risks and benefits, including any discomfort that might arise from the treatment. Frequently, if the patient is incompetent to evaluate the information provided (e.g., because of a psychotic condition), a lawyer assigned to look out for the patient's interests plays a role in the decision-making process. The requirement of informed consent applies to people who serve as subjects in experiments as well as to patients who are undergoing treatment. Patients and experimental subjects both have the right to terminate their participation in treatment or research, even if they had previously consented to participate.

The three essential elements of informed consent are:

- Competency
- Information
- Voluntariness

Whether participants are subjects in research investigations or patients in therapy, a key question is: Are they competent? That is, are they able to understand the procedure in which they will take part, make a treatment choice, and communicate that choice verbally or nonverbally. Beyond competency, participants need information about what they might be getting themselves into (including the potential advantages and disadvantages), and the free choice of participating (volunteering) or not (Wear, 1998).

Should patients have the right to discontinue treatment that most people would agree was helping them? The difficulty of answering this question can be seen in this daughter's account of her mother's changed behavior after discontinuing the use of antipsychotic medication. Her mother came to New York to join her children after being discharged from a mental institution in Kansas. She was taking Haldol, an antipsychotic drug.

> *On Haldol Mother's behavior improved tremendously, and we even harbored false hopes of her return to normal living. We never suspected that she might cease taking medication and regress. . . .*
>
> *Not only did Mother rediscover art and music in New York, but she soon became familiar with the liberal New York laws regarding "patients' rights." She refused to continue to take Haldol and slowly began the reverse trip to "No Man's Land," where she now dwells. The first sign of her [deterioration] was a refusal to come to my apartment, and then she rejected me completely. Next the manager of her middle-class apartment hotel asked us to remove her. She was annoying the guests with her outbursts. She had become known to all the shopkeepers on the block as "The Crazy Lady of West 72nd Street." Looking like a zombie, she paraded down West 72nd Street, accusing aunts, uncles, and brother of stealing her father's fortune, screaming at people who frightened her. . . .*
>
> *Whether or not it's preferable for her to be force-fed Haldol and incarcerated in Kansas or allowed to do as she pleases in liberal New York, as destructive as her life is now, is paradoxical. She was not able to enjoy life and pursue her artistic interests in the former situation, but she is even less able to do so in the latter. Without medication, she can only exist. I believe that basically she is less free in her present life, a prisoner of her delusions and paranoia. My brother, however, disagrees. He thinks that mother is better off having the choice to live as she wishes, wandering aimlessly in the streets, constructing the world to fit her delusions. (Adapted from Lanquetot, 1984, p. 471)*

The institutionalization of children brings with it special problems that the courts are only beginning to address. Among the questions that must be considered are: How much freedom may parents exercise in seeking to institutionalize a son or daughter? When, and under what conditions, can the state institutionalize children against parents' will? What procedures are needed to protect the child's rights? What are those rights? The Supreme Court has ruled that parents may commit their children to state institutions as long as "neutral fact-finders" approve. The quality of the treatment provided is an important factor in approving institutionalization for children as well as for adults. For example, questions have been raised concerning the constitutionality of institutions for the mentally retarded that provided little or no special training.

The issue of informed consent in therapy has been recognized most clearly in the case of biological treatments such as electroconvulsive therapy, but it is also relevant to the psychological therapies. Whenever possible, the goals of therapy should be determined jointly by the therapist and the client, without undue influence exerted by the therapist. Should a therapist encourage a young man to go to college because the client's parents, who are paying the therapy bills, want him to? The client should be the main concern of the therapist, but external influences like the parents' desires might become coercive factors in treatment. Clinicians also must not unduly impose their personal values on the therapy they offer to clients. A respectful attitude toward the client, an undogmatic approach, and healthy questioning of therapeutic tactics are important ingredients in all types of treatment.

Confidentiality and the Duty to Warn

> *Effective psychotherapy . . . depends upon an atmosphere of confidence and trust in which the patient is willing to make a frank and complete disclosure of facts, emotions, memories, and fears. Because of the sensitive nature of the problems for which individuals consult psychotherapists, disclosure of confidential communications made during counseling sessions may cause embarrassment or disgrace. For this reason, the mere possibility of disclosure may impede development of the confidential relationship necessary for successful treatment. (Jaffe v. Redmond, 1996)*

This ringing endorsement of the importance of confidentiality in the provision of mental health treatment comes from the U.S. Supreme Court. While decisions of the Supreme Court and other courts leave little doubt that there is broad legal protection for the **right of confidentiality,** numerous exceptions or limitations exist and the protection of confidentiality varies from state to state. The following case illustrates the complexity of issues related to confidentiality:

> *Prosenjit Poddar, a student who was undergoing therapy at the University of California student health service, expressed murderous feelings toward Tatiana Tarasoff, another student, who had spurned him. The therapist discovered through a third party that Poddar had been thinking of buying a gun, and told his supervisor. The police were both telephoned and notified in writing. Finding Poddar apparently unmenacing, the police did not arrest him. Poddar dropped out of treatment, and*

3 months later, when Tarasoff returned from a trip out of the country, Poddar killed her. Inexplicably, the therapist's supervisor ordered all records destroyed. Tarasoff's parents subsequently brought suit against all parties.

In a judgment arising from this case, the California Supreme Court held that therapists have a **duty to warn** potential victims of their patient's dangerousness, to call the police, or to take other reasonable steps. The ***Tarasoff decision*** broke new legal ground concerning the responsibilities of clinicians to persons other than their patients (Anfang & Appelbaum, 1996). The California Supreme Court decision and subsequent rulings of other courts have raised a number of questions that are now being vigorously debated by therapists and attorneys:

- When should therapists break confidentiality?
- Whom must they warn?
- What happens if they do (or do not) notify the potential victim?
- How are they supposed to know whether their patient's threat reflects a fantasy or a realistic danger of violence?

While the importance of confidentiality as an ethical principle is evident, it is also clear that confidentiality is not an absolute value. At the present time, each state has laws that specify certain exceptions to confidentiality. The most common exception occurs when a person in treatment consents to a waiver of confidentiality—proposed, perhaps, by the therapist. An issue of some controversy is whether a family should be provided information regarding an adult child in certain circumstances. There is general agreement that the current legal framework for protecting the confidentiality of information related to clinical relationships needs to be improved, for example, by reducing the present significant differences among the states with regard to confidentiality issues. Confidentiality is a matter of both ethical and legal concern.

A Final Word

The theme of interaction has run throughout this book. Over and over again, we have seen that, while biological and environmental factors sometimes operate as independent determinants of maladaptive behavior, more often interactions among them are of prime importance. We have also seen that interactions are important in the treatment of maladaptation. A recent review of the effects of various psychoactive substances concluded that the doctor-patient relationship was a key variable in the effectiveness of medications. The better the relationship between patient and doctor, the greater the likelihood that medications will be effective (Tasman et al., 2000).

This chapter adds an additional term to the equation: **public policy.** Public policies, shaped by public opinions and attitudes, play an important role in whether certain groups of people receive treatment or punishment, the extent to which efforts are made to prevent unwanted behaviors, and the methods employed in prevention. This means that it may not be sufficient just to describe the maladaptation and prescribe an appropriate treatment program. For certain problems and segments of the population, public policy significantly influences the response to cognitive and behavior problems.

This concluding chapter, perhaps more than any other in the book, illustrates the optimistic outlook of many researchers and therapists today. It is easy to point out the gaps in our knowledge: Why does schizophrenia usually begin in the late teens and early twenties? What causes panic attacks? What can be done about senility? But perhaps more significant than any lack of knowledge implied by these questions is the current consensus that (1) the scientific method can fruitfully be applied to them, and (2) the resulting knowledge can be used to reduce the occurrence of maladaptive behavior. Another positive development is the increased willingness of court judges, mental health professionals, and the public to examine and reevaluate principles by which care is provided to the mentally ill.

There are many promising developments in the search for effective prevention, but systematic research is needed to develop effective interventions. While the preventive approaches reviewed in this chapter seem promising, only scientific studies can validate them.

The formula for achieving prevention might be written $P = K \times W$. Prevention (P) is achieved when the needed knowledge (K) is available and society has the will (W) to use that knowledge to prevent unwanted outcomes. One of the great achievements of the present era is the widespread awareness that little good and much harm is done by blaming or stigmatizing people for their abnormalities, whether physical or behavioral. One of our great challenges is finding a way to motivate both individuals and society at large to do things that increase personal happiness and personal effectiveness, but also work toward the common good of the human family.

At many points throughout this book, we have remarked on the ability of some people to cope with adversity and even become stronger as a result. As the challenge of resilience—the ability to bounce back—is joined with the challenge of vulnerability and the personal, social, and biological characteristics that put us at risk, the field of abnormal psychology will be able to contribute even more than it has thus far to an understanding of the human condition.

Chapter Summary

TYPES OF PREVENTION

Prevention efforts can be focused at several different points on the problem development time line.

Levels of Prevention **Primary prevention** focuses on reducing new cases of disorders that would otherwise occur in a population. The role of **secondary prevention** is to reduce the potential impact of an existing abnormal condition by decreasing its duration, intensity, or the disability it creates. **Tertiary prevention** is aimed at reducing the impairment that has already resulted from a disorder or event.

Situation-Focused and Competency-Focused Prevention **Situation-focused prevention** is aimed at reducing or eliminating the environmental causes of maladaptive behavior. The emphasis of **competency-focused prevention** is enhancing people's ability to cope with the conditions that can lead to maladaptive behavior. Either of these approaches might be applied to divorce, an example of a stressful situation that often leads to maladaptive behavior. Early-education programs illustrate a competency-focused prevention. The training they provide in cognitive and social skills facilitates the child's adjustment to school and may also have positive long-term effects.

SITES OF PREVENTION

The Family The family is an important focus for prevention efforts. Parents affect their children's development from the moment of conception by the genes they contribute, the prenatal environment, and the physical and psychological environment in which the children grow up. Parenting practices that have been linked to aggressive behavior in children include failure of supervision or monitoring, aggressive or abusive behavior, over-permissiveness, inconsistency, and rejection. **Child abuse** and **spouse abuse** are examples of harmful behaviors that can be treated by intervention at all levels of prevention. Parental conflict and divorce are also areas where interventions at any of the three prevention levels can be helpful to the entire family. For some other types of problems, parents can be trained to act as therapists toward their children.

The School Many family problems, behavior problems, and problems associated with learning are not identified until a child begins school. Special interventions by the classroom teacher and by school mental health workers can prevent many behavior disorders in children. Interventions that strengthen children's social and cognitive skills can also help prevent their later dropping out of school.

The Community Community agencies and organizations can provide satisfying experiences for children that may help them develop positive interests and skills. They can bring children into contact with caring adults as well as provide access to new ideas. Police officers may play an important role in prevention. They may serve as positive role models and, if trained in prevention techniques, may help deter family violence by defusing confrontations.

THE DIVERSE PATHS TO PREVENTION

Preventing maladaptive behavior and providing appropriate therapeutic responses when it does occur have implications for our basic social institutions as well as for specific programs for groups or treatment with individuals.

Paraprofessionals **Paraprofessionals,** who do not themselves have specialized mental health training but who are similar in cultural background to those who are to be served, often make important contributions to prevention and treatment.

Self-Help Groups **Self-help groups** made up of people with a common problem can be helpful to many people who experience extreme stress or loss.

Community Psychology **Community psychology** is concerned with the role of social systems and the community environment in prevention.

TREATMENT IN THE COMMUNITY

An integrated network of community services can help prevent hospital readmission for the chronically mentally ill. Communities also may prevent institutionalization by making adequate treatment facilities and housing such as group homes available.

Problems With Community Programs Community programs need to provide integrated treatment and support services as well as more continuity in service delivery for those who have chronic problems with maladaptive behavior.

Improving Treatment in the Community A variety of treatment programs can offer alternatives to full-time residential hospitalization. These include partial hospitalization in day hospitals or dormitory-inns. Once patients are discharged from the hospital, halfway houses and community clinical services can be important in keeping them out of the hospital. Although deinstitutionalization has helped to empty hospitals of long-term patients, the lack of funding for alternative programs has resulted in an increased frequency of readmission of patients to hospitals for short-term stays. Treatment programs of all types should offer support for family members as well as the patient and recognize the importance of families in treatment.

LEGAL ASPECTS OF TREATMENT AND PREVENTION

Institutionalization Commitment, or placement in an institution, may be either voluntary (when patients agree to enter the hospital) or involuntary (when they are hospitalized through a legal procedure called **civil commitment**). **Criminal commitment** of a person to a mental hospital may be imposed when that person's criminal act is legally declared to be the result of insanity and it is in the interests of society to protect itself.

Insanity is a legal term that refers to a person's state of mind when a criminal act was carried out; **competency** refers to a person's state of mind at the time of a judicial proceeding. A legally **incompetent person** lacks the capacity to consult a lawyer and to understand what the legal proceeding is about. The insanity defense arose from the recognition that a crime might not necessarily be a deliberate violation of social norms but might instead be a result of a psychological disturbance. Although the number of successful insanity defenses is very small, the defense has been the source of controversy for many years.

The **M'Naghten rule,** of the "knowledge of right and wrong" test of insanity, was widely used for many years. More recently, the American Law Institute proposed a set of guidelines that have been incorporated into the laws of many states. The American Psychiatric Association has argued that people should be acquitted by reason of insanity only if they have a severe disorder such as a psychosis.

Civil commitment laws are based on the doctrine of *parens patriae,* the idea that the state can act in the best interest of a minor or incapacitated adult. The process includes a petition, a hearing, and a decision about the place of commitment. Current law requires that the state present "clear and convincing" reasons why hospitalization is required. Patient rights while hospitalized have also been the focus of court decisions. The state must provide adequate treatment for those who are confined involuntarily. In addition, court decisions have upheld patients' rights to refuse specific types of treatment.

The Rights of Patients Patients' rights include the right of **informed consent,** which means that they must have explained to them (in understandable language) the nature of the treatment and its possible benefits and negative consequences before they agree to the treatment. They also have the right to terminate the treatment even if they had previously consented to it.

Confidentiality and the Duty to Warn There is broad legal protection of confidentiality in clinical settings. However, the **right to confidentiality** is not absolute. The *Tarasoff* decision assigned to therapists the responsibility of warning potential victims of their patients' dangerousness. This raises important questions concerning the confidentiality of the patient-therapist relationship and the therapist's assessment of dangerousness.

A FINAL WORD

Along with the nature of particular types of maladaptive behavior and the availability of applicable treatments, **public policy,** plays an important role in influencing how maladaptive behavior is viewed and society's response to it. Public opinion and attitudes also influence whether efforts are made to prevent it from occurring.

The social need for prevention is one of the most powerful motivators for research in the field of abnormal psychology. The formula for prevention can be expressed as follows: *Prevention* equals necessary *knowledge* multiplied by the society's *will* to use that knowledge.

Key Terms

Glossary

Abstinence–violation effect The reaction of conflict and guilt when an individual fails to resist the temptation to indulge in a behavior that he or she is trying to stop—for example, using alcohol. This response often triggers a binge or total relapse.

Acetylcholine Chemical involved in the transmission of nerve impulses.

Acquired immune deficiency syndrome (AIDS) The result of progress of the human immunodeficiency virus toward failure of the immune system's protective ability.

ACTH See adrenocorticotrophic hormone.

Active coping Working to improve the situation by such means as persisting, getting more information, trying alternative solutions, etc.

Acute pain disorder Overreaction to pain associated with some specific event or injury and of of recent origin.

Acute Stress Disorder A reaction to stress in which the symptoms appear within the month following the stressor. If the symptoms continue past one month, the diagnosis is changed to post traumatic stress disorder (PTSD).

Adaptation Dynamic process by which an individual responds to his or her environment and the changes that occur within it; ability to modify one's behavior to meet changing environmental requirements. Adaptation to a given situation is influenced by one's personal characteristics and the type of situation. Term often used in a biological, Darwinian sense.

Adenosine Natural chemical in the blood that causes sleepiness.

Adjustment disorder Maladaptive reaction to a particular stressful condition that results in impaired functioning and symptoms in excess of what might be a normal response to the stressor. The reaction must occur soon after the beginning of the stress and the reaction can be expected to decrease when the stressor ceases.

Adoption studies An attempt to understand the genetics of a disorder and separate them from the effects of environment by comparing children adopted in infancy whose biological parents are affected by the disorder with adopted children without such heredity.

Adrenal cortex The outer layer of the adrenal gland; a source of hormone secretion in the body.

Adrenal corticosteroids Hormones released by the adrenal cortex which affect the body's response to stress.

Adrenal glands Ductless glands that are part of the endocrine system

Adrenal medulla One of the two principal parts of the adrenal glands, the part of the endocrine system located just above the kidneys. A principal function is the secretion of hormones in emergency-type situations.

Adrenaline A secretion of the adrenal glands; also called epinephrine.

Adrenocorticotrophic Hormone (ACTH) Hormone secreted by the pituitary gland that goes to the adrenal cortex to release adrenal cortico-steroids, chemicals that stimulate the body's response to stress.

Affect Emotion, feeling, or mood: pleasant or unpleasant, intense or mild; also, a tone of feeling accompanying a thought.

Agonist Term used to describe drug action that inhibits or blocks a neurotransmitter's action, often by binding to the receptor and blocking transmitter action.

Agoraphobia Pathological fear of open spaces.

AIDS dementia complex (ADC) A type of dementia that is secondary to the development of the autoimmune disease syndrome (AIDS) or positive status of the human immunodeficiency virus (HIV).

Alcohol abuse The overuse of alcohol that results in lowered job performance and lowered quality of interpersonal relationships.

Alpha wave A particular kind of electrical brain activity often seen when a person is tense and the frequency of which decreases with drowsiness or relaxation.

Alprazolam A tranquilizing drug derived from the benzodiazepine group. Used to treat panic disorder.

Alternative housing Housing for the mentally ill such as halfway houses and group homes that are focused on providing rehabilitation as well as providing shelter.

Alzheimer's disease Chronic brain disorder, occurring as early as the fourth decade of life and involving progressive destruction of nervous tissue, which results in slurring of speech, involuntary muscular movements, and gradual intellectual deterioration with growing lapses of memory.

Alzheimer's disease, familial type A type of Alzheimer's disease that runs in families and is thought to be hereditary.

Alzheimer's disease, sporadic type A type of Alzheimer's disease that does not have any apparent hereditary component.

Amnestic disorders Memory disturbances due to either a medical condition or the persistent effects of some chemical substance. Localized amnesia involves inability to recall events that occurred in a specific period of time. Selective amnesia refers to the inability to recall only a certain subset of events related to a particular period of time. Generalized amnesia refers to the inability to recall any events of the person's past life. Continuous amnesia means the inability to recall events that occurred after a specific point of time and extends to the present time. Systematized amnesia is the loss of memories for certain categories of information such as those pertaining to a particular place or person.

Amniocentesis Technique of removing a sample of amniotic fluid from a pregnant woman and analyzing it to determine whether there are chromosomal defects in the fetus.

Amphetamines Nervous system (particularly cerebral cortex) stimulants, such as dexedrine, which bring a sense of well-being and exhilaration. The stimulation effect is succeeded by fatigue and depression. Psychologically but probably not physiologically addicting.

Amygdala A small structure deep inside the brain that may be abnormally activated in anxiety disorder.

Anal psychosexual stage Stage of psychosexual development in which the child derives intense pleasure from activities associated with elimination.

Anger rape See rape.

Angina pectoris Periodic chest pains resulting from an insufficient supply of oxygen to the heart. A type of coronary heart disease.

Anorexia nervosa An intense and irrational feeling of being fat that leads to excessive restriction of food intake and weight loss that may be life threatening. Usually occurs in adolescence or early adulthood and is much more common in females than males.

Anorgasmia In women, the inability to achieve an orgasm after a normal level of sexual excitement.

Antagonist In neuropharmacology, a drug that disrupts the action of a neurotransmitter. Antagonists can be highly specific to transmitters or broad in their action.

Antianxiety drugs Commonly called tranquilizers. Used to calm anxious people.

Antidepressant drugs General term for a number of drugs used to relieve depression and to elevate mood.

Antigens Foreign substances that, when introduced into the body, induce the formation of antibodies and then react with these antibodies in a specifiable manner.

Antimanic drugs A family of drugs based on a compound of lithium carbonate that is used to treat mania, bipolar disorder, and some depressions.

Antipsychotic drugs Group of chemical compounds used to treat individuals who show severely disturbed behavior and thought processes, especially in cases of schizophrenia.

Antisocial personality disorder Characterized by continuous, chronic, antisocial behavior beginning before the age of 15 and continuing into adult life. Diagnosis not made until person reaches age 18. Behavior tends to impair the rights of others and to be characterized by an impaired capacity for close relationships.

Anxiety An affect with both psychological and physiological aspects. Generally, an unpleasant emotional state accompanied by physiological arousal and the cognitive elements of apprehension, guilt, and a sense of impending disaster. Distinguished from fear, which is an emotional reaction to a specific or identifiable object.

Anxiety disorders Formerly called neurosis or neurotic disorders. Characterized by some form of anxiety as the most prominent symptom. Include panic disorders, phobic disorders, obsessive-compulsive disorder, generalized anxiety disorders, and reactions to stressors.

Aphasia Partial or total loss of the ability to convey thoughts through speech.

Apo E gene A gene whose presence indicates vulnerability to Alzheimer's disease and also thought to be related to failure to recover well from head injuries.

Asperger's disorder A pervasive developmental disorder with some similarity to autistic disorder in its impairment of social interaction, restricted interests, and repetitive behavior. However, in

Asperger's disorder there are no significant delays in language or cognitive development.

Asphyxia Unconsciousness or death caused by a lack of oxygen. May result in retardation or seizures as a result of brain damage.

Assertiveness training Combined cognitive and behavioral approach designed to increase the frequency of aggressive behavior that is socially desirable.

Assessment Information gathering aimed at describing and predicting behavior. Assessment specialists devise tests that measure various aspects of behavior.

Assessment interview Same as diagnostic interview.

Assessment studies Studies aimed at gathering information to describe a particular group in which variables are not manipulated. Such data can be used for prediction and are usually expressed in the form of correlations between variables.

Assortative mating The tendency for people to marry those who have similar characteristics to their own. For instance, persons with chronic schizophrenia tend to marry individuals who have a schizophrenic spectrum disorder or other psychotic disorder. This genetic loading must be taken into account when estimating genetic risk for a variety of disorders.

Asthma Disorder of a chronic nature, often psychophysiological in nature, characterized by coughing, wheezing, breathing difficulty, and a feeling of suffocating.

Atherosclerosis A disorder caused by a build up of plaque (deposits on the blood vessel walls) that narrow the vessels and result in insufficient blood supply to the heart.

Attention-deficit/hyperactivity disorder (ADHD) Severe and frequent problems of either or both attention to tasks or hyperactive and impulsive behavior. Some symptoms must have been observed before age 7. May be of combined type with both types of symptoms or of either the predominantly inattentive type or the predominantly hyperactive-impulsive type.

Attribution A term used by social psychologists to describe the way a person assigns responsibility for cause and effect.

Aura Clouded state of consciousness, accompanied by feelings of unreality, which precedes an epileptic attack. Also, the sensory, motor, or mood disturbance preceding migraine headache.

Authentic behavior Term used by some existential theorists to describe behavior dictated by a person's own goals rather than by the goals of society.

Autistic disorder A developmental disorder usually occurring early in childhood characterized by severe impairment in social relationships, communication, and activity. Frequently includes mental retardation.

Autistic disorder spectrum The belief that several disorders in the DSM-IV pervasive developmental disorder group represent different manifestations of the same disorder. Thought to include childhood autism, Asperger's disorder, disintegrative disorder, and atypical disorders that include Rett's disorder.

Autistic thinking Term used to describe a certain type of schizophrenic thought pattern characterized by self-centered thinking understandable only to the individual.

Automatic thoughts Recurring thoughts that come to mind seemingly without reference to the ongoing situation. They seem more habitual than responses to the environment. Automatic

thoughts are considered important factors in the maintenance of depression by cognitive behavioral theorists.

Autonomic system Functional division of the nervous system concerned with visceral activities, smooth muscles, and endocrine glands. Name comes from the fact that it was formerly thought to function independently of the central nervous system.

Autosomal dominant disorder A non-sex-linked disorder that can be inherited even if only one parent passes on the defective gene. An example is Huntington's disease.

Aversive conditioning Group of behavior therapies which attempt to condition avoidance responses in patients by pairing the behavior to be extinguished with punishing stimuli—for example, electric shock, social criticism, drugs that cause vomiting.

Avoidance response Attempt to leave a situation in which an aversive stimulus is expected to occur.

Avoidant personality disorder Characterized by social withdrawal based on fear of social rejection.

Axis I The main classificatory portion of DSM-IV. Includes all clinical disorders and other disorders that may be the focus of clinical attention except personality disorders and mental retardation.

Axis II A separate axis in DSM-IV for personality disorders and mental retardation. Used so that these disorders will not be overlooked when the more prominent features of an Axis I disorder are diagnosed.

Axon Part of the cell that transmits impulses away from the cell body and across the synapse to the dendrites of another cell.

Balanced placebo design An experimental design in which some subjects receive an inactive substance and others a psychoactive substance. Part of each group is led to expect that they have received the other category of substance and part of each group is accurately informed about what substance they are given.

Baquet A water-filled tub used by Mesmer as a focus for treatment of hysterical complaints.

Barbiturates Family of drugs that depress central nervous system action and may be addictive.

Baseline observation Operant conditioning procedure in which an initial rate of some response is established. Can be used for descriptive purposes or as a control condition before introducing behavior modification procedures and subsequent response-rate comparisons.

BEAM See brain electrical activity mapping.

Bedlam Noisy uproar or confusion. A word derived from conditions at Bethlehem Hospital, an institution for the insane.

Behavior change experiment The test of a therapeutic manipulation to determine whether the individual's maladaptive behavior is lessened.

Behavior genetics The study of the effects of genetic inheritance on behavior.

Behavior genetics Study of the transmission of certain kinds of behavior through selective mating.

Behavior modification Type of therapy based on the principles of operant conditioning.

Behavior Rating Scale for Children A type of rating scale designed to be used by untrained observers to quantify different aspects of children's behavior.

Behavior therapy Includes several techniques of behavior modification based on laboratory-de-

rived principles of learning and conditioning. Behavior therapies focus on modifying overt behaviors with minimal reference to internal or covert events.

Behavioral assessment The objective recording of particular categories of observable behavior prior to beginning behavior therapy. The assessment may take place in specially contrived situations or under real life conditions.

Behavioral medicine An area focused on ways to improve health, treatment, and rehabilitation by using behavioral techniques to help people adopt generally healthier ways of living and to follow treatment plans for specific problems. Also focuses on helping health care providers improve their service delivery.

Behavioral perspective A theory of behavior based on the idea that much of a person's behavior is learned rather than genetically based. According to this view behavior is based on past experiences with the environment.

Behavioral rehearsal The use of practice exercises to help patients try out and learn the appropriate behaviors in situations that cause them anxiety.

Benzodiazepines Group of drugs, such as Librium and Valium, used primarily to treat anxiety.

Bereavement The state of having lost someone through death.

Beta amyloid A protein found in the clumps and plaques of cells typically found in the brains of Alzheimer's disease patients. Although the protein has been shown to kill nerve cells it is not clear whether its presence may reflect the cause or effect of Alzheimer's disease.

Binet tests The intelligence test concept originated by Binet in which the person tested is asked to complete a variety of tasks that assess reasoning, ability to follow directions, and judgment. The results originally were based on the concept of the intelligence quotient or IQ as the ratio of test score or mental level to chronological age but are now computed in terms of how much the person's score deviates from the mean of scores for that particular chronological age.

Binge-purge cycle The sequence of extreme overeating followed by self-induced vomiting or the use of laxatives. The central feature of bulimia nervosa. Sometimes also seen in anorexia nervosa but then carried out in association with a generally limited food intake that keeps weight significantly below the established normal range.

Biofeedback Method for inducing behavioral change in which the client learns to alter autonomic nervous system responses by monitoring them on recording instruments.

Biological determinism The view that every event, act, and decision as well as the development of psychopathology is the inevitable consequence of specific biological antecedents.

Biological perspective Theoretical perspective that suggests that all disorders, physical or behavioral, have biological causes. Causes may lie in heredity, genetic accident, or bodily infection or trauma.

Biopsychosocial model Interactional view that emphasizes the interaction among biological, psychological, and social factors in determining behavior and body functioning.

Bipolar disorders Mood disorder in which the individual experiences both periods of mania and periods of depression. Formerly called manic-depressive order.

Bipolar I disorder Includes at least one episode of mania, and in most patients, one or more major depressive episodes.

Bipolar II disorder A type of bipolar disorder in which the person has experienced at least one major depressive episode and one hypomanic episode but has never had a manic episode or cyclothymia.

Bisexual behavior The preference, at different times, for male and for female sex partners.

Bisexual Sexual attraction to members of both sexes.

Body dysmorphic disorder An extreme preoccupation with a minor or imagined physical flaw that the individual views as a defect or deformity.

Booster session An additional treatment carried out after a period of time has elapsed since the original treatment series. Intended to counteract any weakening of the treatment effect.

Borderline personality disorder Characterized by impulsive and unpredictable behavior and marked shifts in mood. Instability may affect personal relationships, behavior, mood, and image of self.

Brain deterioration See dementia.

Brain electrical activity mapping (BEAM) A technique for study of electrical brain activity in which the electrical impulses are summarized in color maps.

Brain imaging techniques A variety of non-intrusive computer-based techniques that provide views of the structural or metabolic activity in the living brain.

Brainstem Portion of the central nervous system that includes the hindbrain, midbrain, and forebrain up to the thalamus.

Breathing related sleep disorders Brief disruptions in breathing during sleep that may occur several times a night.

Briquet's syndrome Another name for somatization disorder.

Bulimia nervosa Frequent episodes of binge eating by individuals of average or above average weight. Purging or self-induced vomiting is often employed by the individual at the end of the eating session.

Burnout Condition found most often among people in the helping professions whose work involves intense interpersonal contact. Symptoms include loss of effectiveness and self-confidence and the general feeling of inability to deal with particular situations.

Caffeine Crystalline compound that is found in coffee, tea, and kola nuts and which acts as a stimulant of the central nervous system and also as a diuretic.

Cannabis Plant whose resin produces a psychoactive substance. In solid form the resin is called hashish.

Carbamazepine A mood stabilizer used to treat bipolar disorder.

Cardiovascular disorder Disorder affecting the blood vessel system and the heart.

Case manager Person assigned by a social service agency to help a person link up with essential services and to provide some general supervision.

Case study Detailed observations of a client's behavior, symptoms, and reported thoughts over a period of time with inferences about cause and effect supplied by the clinician. Often called clinical method.

Catatonic subtype of schizophrenia Type of schizophrenic disorder characterized by psychomotor disturbance. Often takes the form of body rigidity or posturing. Other behavior may include waxy flexibility or mutism.

Catecholamines Group of hormones, including epinephrine, norepinephrine, and dopamine, that are important in the response to stress. Some catecholamines are produced in the brain, where they are important in nerve transmission.

Categorical model An approach to classification used in the Diagnostic and Statistical Manual. In this method the diagnosis may be made if a certain number of criteria are satisfied, rather than requiring all criteria to be met.

Central nervous system (CNS) Brain and spinal cord; does not include the nerve trunks and their peripheral connections.

Cerebellum Portion of the brain consisting of two hemispheres located behind and above the medulla; coordinates motor activities and maintains bodily equilibrium.

Cerebral cortex Convoluted layer of gray matter of the brain; outer layer of the cerebrum.

Cerebral ventricles Cavities in the brain that are connected to the central canal of the spinal cord and contain cerebrospinal fluid.

Cerebrovascular accident (CVA) Rupture or blockage of blood vessels in the cerebrum that disrupts or prevents blood flow. Commonly referred to as a stroke.

CHD See coronary heart disease.

Child abuse Harm, usually physical, deliberately inflicted on children by their parent(s), often by repeated beatings.

Child neglect Failure by the caretaker to provide a child with healthful environment, adequate food, clothing, or supervision.

Childhood disintegrative disorder A disorder that usually begins between 3 and 4 years of age after a period of normal development. Little is known about this disorder although it is assumed to be associated with deterioration of the central nervous system.

Cholinergic cells A type of brain cell that produces acetylcholine and is involved in memory and learning.

Choreiform movements Involuntary facial grimacing as well as jerking and twisting movements of the neck, trunk, and arms and legs. These movements are characteristic of Huntington's disease.

Chromosomal anomalies Abnormalities in chromosome structure or number of chromosomes.

Chromosomes Gene-bearing structures within cells.

Chronic fatigue syndrome A condition, not currently recognized as an official DSM-IV disorder, that includes abnormal immune system functioning, abnormal autonomic nervous system action, and depressed and anxious feelings.

Chronic pain disorder Overreaction to pain that is enduring and becomes a focus of the person's life.

Circadian rhythm A wake-sleep cycle that repeats in 24 hour periods.

Civil commitment Commitment of a person to an institution based on a judgment that the person is a potential danger to him or herself and/or to others.

Classical conditioning Pavlov's experimental method by which a conditioned stimulus is paired with an unconditioned stimulus. Procedure involves presenting the two stimuli in close temporal proximity. The first, or unconditioned, stimulus elicits a reflex. After a number of trials the second, or conditioned, stimulus acquires the potentiality of evoking a similar reflex.

Classification The establishment of a hierarchical system of categories based on the relationship or presumed relationship among the things to be classified, for instance, disorders of behavior and cognition.

Client-centered therapy Carl Rogers' therapeutic approach, which views the subject matter of psychotherapy as the client's world of immediate experience that should be approached from the client's frame of reference. In the Rogerian system, the therapist's main task is to create the opportunity for the individual to achieve a reorganization of his or her subjective world and to reach self-actualization.

Clinical method Case study of the individual through observation. May rely heavily upon intuitive judgments of the clinician rather than upon experimentation and systematic measurement.

Clinical psychologist Psychologist, usually a Ph.D. or Psy.D., who has special training and skills in assessing and treating maladaptive behavior.

Clinical trial The use of a research design including one or more experimental groups and a control group in testing the usefulness of a particular approach in treatment of patients.

Clinician Professional who deals directly with the examination or treatment of patients or clients.

Clozapine One of the so called "new generation" of antipsychotic drugs that may be effective with some patients not helped by early types of antipsychotic drugs. Has potentially risky side effects unless carefully monitored.

Cluster headache Very painful headaches that peak quickly and often last no more than an hour. Long pain free periods tend to alternate with series of headaches over a day or week.

Cocaine Stimulant with a number of characteristics in common with the amphetamines.

Codeine Derivative of opium that is less potent than morphine.

Cognitive assessment Specification and enumeration of the typical thoughts that precede, accompany, and follow maladaptive behavior. Used in research and by cognitive behavior therapists especially in working with depressed individuals.

Cognitive behavioral therapy A therapeutic approach that includes structured training sessions and prescribed exercises to help clients change maladaptive behavior by changing specific types of thoughts about themselves and others that typically occur in certain situations.

Cognitive coping skills Particular ways of thinking that aid in behaving effectively in stressful situations.

Cognitive distortion model A model of depression developed by Aaron Beck. He believes that certain types of cognitive errors are specific to depression. These include the cognitive triad—negative thoughts about oneself, the situation, and the future. In contrast to anxious individuals who worry about what the future might bring and whether they will be able to deal with these events, depressed persons think about how they will be unable to deal with the bad things that will happen in the future as well as reflecting on the bad things that happened in the past.

Cognitive modification Technique whereby individuals learn to modify maladaptive thought patterns or to substitute new internal dialogues for old maladaptive ones.

Cognitive perspective Point of view that considers behavior to be the result of information processing and problem solving. Emphasis is on mental processes of which the individual is aware or can easily become aware.

Cognitive process variables   The mechanisms by which people formulate the expectations and evaluations that are present within awareness. The processes themselves are usually not available to the individual.

Cognitive product variables   Self-critical automatic thoughts and attributions and pessimistic future expectations that often characterize cognitions of depressed persons. They are generally within the person's awareness and can be reported on directly.

Cognitive psychology   Study of human beings as information processors and problem solvers. Focus has recently been extended from the traditional studies of memory, attention, and problem solving to include the effects of personality factors and emotions on learning and performance.

Cognitive psychotherapies   Talking therapies that are focused on clarifying the clients' belief systems and how they relate to maladjustment and unhappiness. The focus is on challenging inaccurate and maladaptive beliefs.

Cognitive rehearsal   Procedure in which a client learns to rehearse ways to handle problem situations mentally. Such rehearsal makes it easier for the client to behave effectively in the actual situations.

Cognitive restructuring   A technique used by Albert Ellis and other cognitive therapists in which the client is made aware of a connection between unrealistic thoughts and the maladaptive behavior these evoke. Clients are helped to develop more rational ways of looking at their behavior.

Cognitive schema.   See schemata.

Cognitive set   A person's habitual way of viewing the world and distorting it in terms of his or her personality characteristics and expectations.

Cognitive social learning theory   Terminology that reflects the increased inclusion of thoughts as well as overt behavior in contemporary learning theory.

Cognitive triad   Description of depression in terms of negative thinking about oneself, the current situation, and the future. Part of Beck's cognitive distortion model.

Cognitive–behavior therapy   Type of therapy that integrates cognitive and behavioral therapies often by using various behavioral techniques such as a graded program of activities, role play and homework, together with a focus on identifying and modifying unrealistic cognitions.

Cognitive–behavioral group therapy   Therapy using the cognitive-behavioral perspective with several clients at one time that is focused on increasing their skills and comfort in social situations.

Cold reactors   Term for those who show normal cariovascular responses to stress. Contrast with hot reactors.

Collective unconscious   Jung's idea that each person's unconscious life concerns both a personal unconscious made up of past personal experiences that have been forgotten or repressed and the collective unconscious, an inherited structure that is common to all humankind and which symbolizes universal human situations such as having parents, finding a mate, confronting death, and so on.

Commitment   Placement in an institution, usually without the consent of the person committed, through a legal procedure. See also civil commitment, criminal commitment.

Communication disorders   The communication disorders included in the DSM-IV are expressive language disorder, mixed receptive-expressive language disorder, phonological disorder, stuttering, and a miscellaneous category communication disorder NOS. These disorders have their onset in childhood.

Community psychology   Branch of applied psychology concerned with modifying both the individual and the structure of the social system to produce optimal benefits for both society and the individual. Community psychologists are often primarily interested in preventing maladaptive behavior.

Community-cultural perspective   Viewpoint that much maladaptive behavior results from poor living conditions, discrimination, and so on. Emphasis is on preventive activities.

Comorbidity   The significant overlap or co-occurrence of symptoms and conditions in different disorders. The common finding of co-morbidity in depression and anxiety, for instance, makes it important to understand the relationship between these two disorders.

Competency   May refer to adequacy of coping skills. In a legal sense refers to whether a person who is the object of a legal proceeding has the capacity to profit from consultation with a lawyer and to understand the purpose of the legal proceedings.

Competency-focused prevention   Actions to prevent maladaptive behavior through helping those at risk develop coping skills.

Compulsive behavior   Characterized by an individual's need to repeat a series of acts again and again even though he or she perceives them as senseless and interfering with desirable activities.

Compulsive substance use   Behavior that is focused on drug seeking to the detriment of other parts of the individual's life.

Computed axial tomography (CT scan)   Technique that uses a narrow beam of x-rays to photograph an area of the body from many angles. A computer then analyzes this information to provide a clear picture of soft tissues as well as the tissue seen in conventional x-rays.

Concordance   Term describing the degree of relationship among twins and other family members with respect to a given characteristic or trait. They are referred to as concordant if they both show a particular trait; if they do not, the pair is described as discordant for that trait.

Concussions   Head injuries that do not cause lasting structural damage. Rate of recovery is proportional to the severity of the injury.

Conditioned response (CR)   In classical conditioning, the response that occurs after training has taken place and after the conditioned stimulus has been presented.

Conditioned stimulus (CS)   In classical conditioning, the neutral stimulus that does not elicit a response prior to training.

Conditioning   See classical conditioning; operant conditioning.

Conduct disorder   Diagnostic classification for those under 18 who commit antisocial acts. Adults may also be classified this way if they do not meet the criteria for the antisocial personality disorder.

Confabulation   The process of filling in missing memories with fabricated information; to replace forgotten facts with fantasy.

Confounding   The effect of one or more uncontrolled variables on the dependent variable that results in a mistaken interpretation of the relations between dependent and independent variables.

Congenital   Characteristics that are either innate or acquired, usually through chemical action, while the child is in the uterus.

Conscious   Aspects of one's mental life of which a person is aware at any particular time.

Continuous amnesia   See amnestic disorders.

Continuous Performance Test   Test of sustained visual attention in which the subject is required to indicate whenever a certain stimulus is presented and to ignore all other stimuli.

Controlled drinking approach   A therapeutic approach to decreasing overuse of alcohol by teaching clients coping skills, self-monitoring of behavioral antecedents of heavy drinking, and altered expectations concerning the effects of alcohol.

Contusions   Brain condition in which diffuse structural damage has occurred (e.g., rupture of blood vessels). Typically, cerebrospinal fluid pressure is raised, causing such symptoms as coma and stupor.

Conversion disorders   Type of somatoform disorders in which there are losses or changes in physical functioning that suggest a physical disorder but seem to be a direct expression of a psychological conflict.

Coping   Contending with difficulties.

Coping skills   The characteristic way a person deals with difficulties or stress. Commonly used skills include task-directed activity, working on a problem step by step, appropriate control of emotion.

Copropalia   An unusual symptom found in Tourette's disorder in which the individual has an uncontrollable urge to utter profanity and other socially taboo words concerning sexual and body functions.

Coronary heart disease (CHD)   Disorder in which one or more of the coronary arteries is partially or totally obstructed by deposits. This results in a temporary or permanent cut off of blood to portions of the heart muscle.

Correlation coefficient   Numerical expression of the degree of correspondence between two variables; a statistical index of covariation that varies from -1.00 to $+1.00$.

Correlational studies   Type of research in which the relationship of two or more characteristics is measured. No statement about cause and effect can be made from correlational research.

Cortex   Outer layer of an organ such as the cerebrum, cerebellum, or adrenal gland.

Corticotrophin–releasing factor (CRF)   Substance secreted by the hypothalamus that releases the chemical ACTH when it reaches the pituitary gland.

Cortisol   A hormone produced by the adrenal gland in stressful situations.

Counseling psychologist   Someone trained especially to work with clients who are experiencing current life stresses rather than more serious or long lasting disorders. A counseling psychologist usually holds a Ph.D. or Ed.D. degree.

Countertransference   Psychoanalytic term that refers to the therapist's emotional reactions to the patient. See also transference.

Couples therapy   Another term for marital therapy.

Covert   Behavior that is internal and not directly observable. Includes unexpressed thoughts and feelings and other conscious and unconscious mental phenomena.

Covert modeling   Learning through imagining how someone else would perform a task or by anticipating what response might be given to certain types of behavior.

Covert sensitization   Behavioral therapy in which anxiety is created toward a particular stimulus situation that is likely to produce undesirable behavior. Usually the stimulus is paired with cognitions relating to the possible negative consequences if the person continues a given behavior. A treatment often used in changing the focus of sexual excitement.

CPT   See Continuous Performance Test.

Criminal commitment   Commitment of a person to an institution based on a judgment that the person is guilty of a criminal act and is also legally insane.

Cross-cultural approach   Method of studying the causes of various psychological and physical problems by studying their occurrence in a variety of cultures and then attempting to identify factors that are correlated with high and low frequency of the problems.

Cross-fostering study   Method of evaluating hereditary factors in behavioral disorders by comparing frequency of a disorder in groups with genetic vulnerability reared by healthy adoptive parent(s) and groups without known genetic vulnerability reared by adoptive parent(s) who have a particular behavior disorder.

Cross-sectional study   Research design in which different groups are sampled at the same time and the results compared. Technique often used to study human development.

CT scan   See computed axial tomography.

Culture   General values, attitudes, achievements, and behavior patterns shared by members of the same society.

Culture-bound syndromes   Disorders that appear only in one or a few cultural groups. In Malaysia a syndrome called amok exists in which the affected person develops a homicidal frenzy which ends in amnesia and sleepiness.

Custodial housing   Large facilities such as boarding houses, nursing homes, and special care homes that provide housing for the mentally ill but offer few or no rehabilitation programs.

Cyclothymic disorder   A long lasting disorder that includes both mania and depressive episodes, neither of which meet the criteria for major episodes. Lasts for at least 2 years.

Cytomegalovirus   One of a number of viral diseases which, if present in a pregnant woman, may result in retardation and other congenital problems in the child.

Date rape   Rape committed by a person who is a social acquaintance of the person who is raped.

Day hospitalization   Treatment approach used for either chronic or acutely ill patients or for patients in need of rehabilitation. Patients attend a hospital program during the day and return home in the evening. Activities during the day are focused on social skills and practical problem solving.

Defense mechanisms   Psychoanalytic term for various psychic operations used by the ego to avoid awareness of unpleasant and anxiety-provoking stimuli. The ego selectively uses defense mechanisms to ward off anxiety originating in the id, the superego, or dangers in external reality.

Deinstitutionalization   Movement whose purpose is to remove from care-giving institutions such as large mental hospitals all those patients who do not present a clear danger to others or to themselves and to provide treatment and sheltered living conditions for them in the community.

Delirium   Condition characterized by a confused mental state, usually resulting from shock or fever, accompanied by alterations in attention and by hallucinations, delusions, and incoherence.

Delirium tremens   Acute delirium caused by overdoses of alcohol and consisting of severe alterations in consciousness and attention. Also referred to as the DTs.

Delta waves   Extremely slow brain waves that appear in stage 3 sleep and dominate stage 4 sleep.

Delusional disorder   The presence of a persistent but not bizarre delusion that is not due to any other mental disorder such as schizophrenia. Apart from the delusion, the person's behavior is not obviously unusual.

Delusions   Incorrect beliefs maintained despite clear evidence to the contrary.

Demand characteristics   Aspects of research situation that give subjects clues about how they are expected to behave.

Dementia paralytica   Another term for general paresis.

Dementia praecox   Older term for schizophrenia; used by Kraepelin to emphasize the early onset and irreversibility of the disorder as he defined it.

Dementia   Progressive atrophy of brain tissue that results in lapses of memory, poor judgment, and disorientation. Called presenile dementia if it occurs before age 65, and senile dementia if it begins after age 65.

Demographic   The description of human populations in terms of growth, density, distribution, and vital statistics.

Dendrite   Branched part of a cell that serves as a receptor for nerve impulses from the axons of other cells and transmits them toward the cell body.

Denial   Defense mechanism that allows rejection of elements of reality that would be consciously intolerable; negation of experiences or reality through unacceptance.

Deoxyribonucleic acid   See DNA.

Dependent personality disorder   Characterized by an inability to make major decisions and a belittling of a person's own abilities and assets. Intense discomfort is experienced if the person remains alone for more than a brief period.

Dependent variable   Aspect of behavior which changes according to manipulation of the independent variable in an experiment.

Depersonalization   Feelings of unreality or a loss of personal identity; often experienced as one's being someone else or as watching oneself in a movie.

Depression   Pervasive feeling of sadness that may begin after some loss or stressful event, but that continues long afterwards. Inappropriate thought patterns that generalize every event as a calamity are characteristic.

Depressive disorder   Depressive symptoms that meet diagnostic criteria for either a single episode of major depression, or recurrent episodes. If manic or hypomanic behavior has been observed in the past, depressed symptoms should not be classified as a major depression even if they meet the other criteria.

Descriptive statistics   Procedures used to summarize groups of individual observations. The most common descriptive statistics are measures of central tendency (e.g., mean) and measures of variability (e.g., standard deviation).

Determinism   The philosophical idea that all acts are the inevitable result of what has happened before and that human choice or free will plays no role in what happens.

Detoxification   Ridding the body of the particular toxic substance that is causing the problem. In drug or alcohol detoxification, withdrawal signs are usually experienced as the amount of toxic substance declines.

Developmental disorder   One of a group of disorders that involve distortions in the development of basic psychological functions that are involved in social skills, language, perception, and motor behavior. The disorder can be pervasive and involve many functions (e.g., autism) or specific and involve only a single aspect of development (e.g., developmental arithmetic disorder).

Deviant behavior   Behavior that differs from the norm. It may be adaptive or maladaptive.

Dexamethasone Suppression Test (DST)   Chemical test used in an attempt to differentiate depressed individuals who may be helped by different treatments.

Dexedrine   See dextroamphetamine.

Dextroamphetamine   Stimulant drug (e.g., Dexedrine) sometimes used in the treatment of hyperactivity.

Diagnosis   Classification of behavior disorders in terms of relatively homogeneous groups based on similar behaviors or correlates. Shorthand description of the behavioral and personality correlates associated with a particular classification. In medicine, the act or process of deciding the nature of a diseased condition.

Diagnostic and Statistical Manual (DSM)   Classification system for abnormal behavior published by the American Psychiatric Association. The system, currently called DSM-IV, is generally used in the United States for official diagnostic and record keeping purposes.

Diagnostic interview   Interview designed to gather information and assess behavior, usually for the purpose of determining seriousness and outcome or deciding what treatment approach would be appropriate.

Diagnostic Interview Schedule (DIS)   A structured interview used in the diagnosis of mental disorders.

Dialectical behavior therapy (DBT)   A type of behavior therapy developed by Marsha Linehan for use with patients with borderline personality disorder. It includes cognitive and psychodynamic as well as behavioral concepts.

Diathesis-stress theory   The idea that only people with an underlying vulnerability to a disorder will develop that disorder when they are exposed to overwhelming stress. This approach is used particularly in understanding why some people develop symptoms of one of the schizophrenic spectrum disorders when exposed to stress.

Diazepam   One of the benzodiazepines, a group of antianxiety tranquilizers. Known by trade name, Valium.

Dimensional model   An approach to classification that focuses on patterns or profiles of characteristics that differentiate various categories. The Minnesota Multiphasic Personality Inventory is used in this way.

Discordant   Term often used in twin studies to describe particular characteristics on which the twins differ. Characteristics that are the same for both are referred to as concordant.

Disorganized subtype of schizophrenia (hebephrenic type)   Type of schizophrenia distinguished by incoherent speech and flat, incongruous, or silly affect. Often associated with extreme oddities of behavior such as gesturing or grimacing.

Displacement   Defense mechanism in which an emotional attitude is transferred from one object to a substitute object.

Dissociation   A state that includes feelings of unreality and depersonalization, sometimes accompanied by a loss of self-identity. A group of mental processes within the person seem separated from the remainder.

Dissociative   Amnesia Selective memory loss which nevertheless is extensive that occurs without any accompanying indications of injury or other organic change. Inability to recall important personal information, usually of a traumatic or otherwise stressful content, of an extent that can not be attributed to ordinary forgetfulness.

Dissociative disorders   Sudden, temporary alterations in the functions of consciousness, identity, or motor behavior in which some part of one or more of these functions is lost. If consciousness is affected, the person cannot remember important personal events. If identity is affected, a new identity that dominates behavior is temporarily assumed. If motor behavior is affected, then consciousness and/or identity are also affected. Wandering behavior is the most common resulting motor behavior.

Dissociative fugue   An amnesic state that involves unexpected departure from one's customary surroundings, the assumption of a new identity and an inability to recall or remember one's previous identity.

Dissociative identity disorders   Disorders in which a person assumes alternate personalities. Also called multiple personality disorder.

Dizygotic twins   Fraternal twins developed from two fertilized eggs. The two individuals have the same genetic relationship as any pair of siblings.

DNA   Abbreviation for deoxyribonucleic acid, a complex chemical found in chromosomes within living cell nuclei. The sequence of its units determines genetic inheritance.

Dominant gene   Member of the gene pair that determines whether the individual will show the trait controlled by that gene. Other member of the pair may be the same (also dominant) or different (recessive).

Dopamine hypothesis   Idea that schizophrenia involves an excess of the neurotransmitter dopamine at certain sites in the brain.

Dopamine   One of the neurotransmitters included under the category of catecholamines and also under the larger category of monoamine neurotransmitters.

Dormitory-inn   Facility in the community that provides sheltered living accomodations from those recovering from mental illness.

Double-blind method   Experimental design used in drug research. Neither the subjects nor the experimenters know whether the medications given to different comparison groups are active or inert (placebos).

Down syndrome   Condition related to some inequality in the chromosome pair designated as number 21. Usually associated with a trisomy, or presence of an extra chromosome in addition to the usual pair. Also called trisomy 21.

Drug therapy   Use of a variety of psychoactive drugs to treat different types of maladaptive behavior. Drugs are most often used to treat schizophrenia, bipolar disorder, some depressions, and anxiety. Drug treatment is often combined with other types of therapy.

DSM   See Diagnostic and Statistical Manual.

DTs   See delirium tremens.

Dynorphins   One of the naturally occurring opioids in the body that are part of a signaling system related to pain, mood regulation, and learning.

Dyspareunia (functional)   Type of sexual dysfunction in which persistent and recurrent genital pain is associated with coitus without any apparent physical cause.

Dysphoria   Feelings of anxiety, depression, and restlessness.

Dysphoric mood   Characterized by symptoms of depression, sadness, feeling blue and hopeless.

Dyssomnias   A group of sleep disorders that involve abnormalities in the amount, quality, or timing of sleep that is not attributable to other mental or medical conditions or to substance abuse.

Dysthymia   A longstanding depressed mood accompanied by loss of interest and lack of pleasure in situations which most people would find enjoyable.

Dysthymic disorder   Long-lasting chronic depressed mood or loss of pleasure in most usual activities. Does not meet the criteria for a major depressive episode.

ECT   See electroconvulsive therapy.

EEG   See electroencephalogram.

Effect size   A statistical method of determining how practically meaningful differences between two or more groups are. Even if these are significantly different statistically, the size of the difference may have little practical importance.

Ego   In psychoanalytic theory, the part of the psyche which makes up the self or the "I." Part of the psyche that is conscious and most closely in touch with reality and that functions as the "executive officer" of the personality.

Electroconvulsive therapy (ECT)   Treatment for depression in which electrical current is passed through a patient's head. Used if a quick treatment is needed because of a high suicide risk or if antidepressant drugs have not been effective.

Electroencephalogram (EEG)   Graphic record of minute electrical impulses arising from brain cells. Measured by an electronic device called an electroencephalograph.

Endocrine system   A group of ductless glands, including pituitary, thyroid, adrenal, and gonadal glands and part of the pancreas that secretes hormones directly into the bloodstream.

Endorphins   Pain-killing substances that occur naturally in the brain.

Enkephalin   A protein that naturally occurs in the body and that produces a morphine-like activity.

Epidemiological research   Studies designed to link the occurrence of a disorder with a specified population. One focus of this research is the study of the association between mental disorders and various population variables. Results are often expressed in terms of incidence, or the number of new cases that appear during a specific time period, and prevalence, the number of cases that currently exist within the population.

Epidemiology   The scientific study of the associations between diseases or behavioral deviations

and social class variables, geographical variables, or environmental variables. These associations, derived from the study of large population groups, help to suggest possible causes for the health problems observed.

Epilepsy   Transitory disturbance of brain function which is characterized by a sudden onset and loss of consciousness and which may involve tonic and clonic muscle spasms.

Epileptic seizure   A brief or transitory disturbance of brain function that results from the electrical instability of some cells in the brain which begin to respond in an "out of control" manner. Epileptic seizures may be minor (petit mal) or major (grand mal) and tend to recur.

Epinephrine   One of the hormones secreted by the adrenal medulla, active in emotional excitement and in response to stress.

Erectile dysfunction   Type of sexual dysfunction in which the male is occasionally or chronically unable to achieve or maintain a penile erection. The condition may have physical or psychological causes. Also known as impotence.

Escape response   The attempt to get out of an unpleasant or aversive situation.

Ethnic identity   The ethnic group of which a person considers him or herself to be a part. Often an important factor for immigrants and children whose parents of of two different ethnicities. A part of self-concept.

Etiology   Assignment of a cause; scientific study of causes and origins of maladaptive behavior.

Eugenics movement   A now discredited social movement that advocated the development of programs of sterilization of individuals who were mentally retarded with the idea that this action would improve the genetic stock of the population.

Executive functions   Cognitive operations thought to involve the prefrontal cortex. These functions include planning, ability to inhibit responses, flexibility in thinking, and working memory.

Exhibitionism   Exposure of the genitals in public for purposes of obtaining sexual pleasure and gratification.

Exhibitionists   Those who practice exhibitionism.

Existential therapy   Type of psychotherapy which uses both humanistic and psychodynamic approaches. Emphasis is placed on each person's ability to affect his or her life course by the particular choices made.

Exorcism   Rituals designed to expel evil spirits that are believed to be causing illness or deviant behavior.

Expectancy effects   Responses or behaviors that are a function of what the subject or patient believes will be the result of an intervention rather than on the actual consequences of whatever intervention took place. These effects can be observed both in interventions that change characteristics of the environment or those that involve medication or other treatments.

Experiment   A study using the experimental method.

Experimental method   Study of the factors influencing a result by the manipulation of one or more experimental variables rather than simply observing what occurs naturally.

Experimental studies   Research efforts which use the experimental method.

Exposure (in therapy)   Requiring the client to participate in anxiety-provoking situations under supportive supervision until the anxiety response is extinguished. Based on the classical conditioning approach.

Exposure orientation   In drug addiction, the idea that addiction is brought about by an environment that provides availability of drugs.

Exposure therapy   Behavioral therapy that has as its basic element maintaining contact with or imagining contact with the feared stimulus.

Expressed emotion (EE)   A measure of emotional involvement and attitudes of family members when talking about a behaviorally disturbed family member.

Expressed trait   A trait that dominates in the individual and is determined either by at least one dominant gene or by a pair of recessive genes. If only one recessive gene is present the individual has the potential to pass on a genetic characteristic, but that characteristic is not observable in the person him or herself.

External validity,   see Validity, external

Externalizing behaviors   Behaviors that express a person's difficulties in a disruptive way or in a way hostile to others.

Extinction   Weakening of a response following removal of reinforcement.

Eye movement desensitization and reprocessing (EMDR)   A type of imaginal therapy in the form of a dual attention task. It combines self-focus on a traumatic memory with visual tracking of the therapist's finger across the visual field.

Eye-tracking movements   Study of smooth pursuit and saccadic eye movements as an individual attempts to visually follow a rhythmically moving stimulus. One goal of such study is to uncover genetic markers of vulnerability.

Factitious disorder by proxy   A varient of Munchhausen syndrome in which a mother produces symptoms of disease in her child and then brings the child for treatment.

Factitious disorder   Symptoms, either fabricated or self-induced, that are designed to produce attention and care from medical personnel.

Fading   Technique for gradually eliminating cues used in behavior modification after an individual begins to achieve a desired response.

Family study   Study of characteristics of a group of related individuals to uncover genetic patterns.

Family systems approach   A therapeutic approach in which the disturbance experienced by the client is viewed as the result of the way the family interacts rather than a problem caused by the client alone.

Family therapy   Specialized type of group therapy in which the members of the family of the client all participate in group-treatment sessions. The basic idea is that the family, not just the individual client, has to alter behavior to solve the problem.

Fantasized exposure (in therapy)   Exposure therapy in which the upsetting stimuli are imagined rather than presented in actuality.

Fear   An unpleasant often strong emotion caused by anticipation or awareness of danger.

Fetal alcohol syndrome   Condition that may occur in the children of alcoholic mothers or mothers who used excessive alcohol during pregnancy. Characterized by retardation and unusual physical characteristics.

Fetishism   Sexual deviation in which sexual interest is centered upon some body part or inanimate object which becomes capable of stimulating sexual excitement.

First rank symptoms   Group of symptoms described by Kurt Schneider in an attempt to es-

tablish clear behavioral criteria for schizophrenia. A basis of the DSM-III-R definition of schizophrenic disorders. Also reflected in DSM-IV.

Five Factor Model   An approach to personality that describes it in terms of five basic categories: Emotional Stability, Extraversion, Openess to Experience, Agreeableness, and Conscientiousness.

Fixation   Inappropriately strong attachment for someone or something. Also refers to an abnormal arrest of development during infancy or childhood which persists in adult life as an inappropriate constellation of attitudes, habits, or interests.

Flashback   The reexperiencing of hallucinations or other perceptual symptoms which had originally occurred while the person was intoxicated by a psychoactive substance.

Flooding   Behavioral therapeutic technique used particularly in the treatment of phobias. Treatment consists of exposing the client to the feared stimulus until the fear response has been extinguished.

Fluoxetine   The chemical name for the commercially sold drug, Prozac. Fluoxetine is one of the group of antidepressant drugs called SSRIs.

Follow-up study   A method in which individuals listed at one point in time are contacted again at a later time to reassess behavior so that any changes can be noted.

Four humours   The four body fluids (blood, black bile, yellow bile, and phlegm) that were thought by the ancients to play a role in character and temperament.

Fragile X syndrome   An abnormality of the X chromosome that is a frequent cause of mental retardation.

Free association   Basic technique of the psychoanalytic method by which a patient expresses his or her thoughts as freely and in as uninhibited a manner as possible. Free associations provide a natural flow of thought processes unencumbered by interruptions or explanations.

Frontal lobe   Portion of each cerebral hemisphere involved in abstract thinking processes.

Full Scale IQ   One of three intelligence test scores obtained from any of the Wechsler tests. This IQ score takes into account both verbal ability and performance and spatial skills.

GABA   Term for gamma-amino-butyric-acid, a neurotransmitter. A deficiency of GABA, associated with hereditary causes, is thought to be involved in Huntington's disease.

Galvanic skin response (GSR)   Change in the electrical resistance of the skin. This response serves as a dependent variable in conditioning and is used in lie detector tests.

Gamma-amino-butyric-acid   See GABA.

Gay   Term used to describe a homosexual lifestyle by those who feel the term homosexual has too many negative connotations.

Gender identity   Basic feature of personality encompassing an individual's conviction of being male or female.

Gender-identity disorder (transsexualism)   Disorder in which the individual has a strong desire to become a member of the opposite sex by changing his or her anatomical structure.

Gender-identity disorder of childhood   A disorder occurring before puberty in which the child shows intense distress over its assigned sex. Such children may deny their assigned sex or assert that they will develop the genital characteristics of the opposite sex.

General adaptation syndrome   Concept proposed by Selye. Three-stage reaction of an organism to excessive and prolonged stress, including (1) an alarm or mobilization reaction; (2) a resistance stage; and (3) a final stage of exhaustion.

General paresis   See paresis.

Generalized amnesia   See amnestic disorders.

Generalized anxiety disorder   Persistent anxiety that lasts at least 1 month and includes several of the following: motor tension, autonomic hyperactivity, apprehensive expectation, vigilance, and scanning. The symptoms do not include phobias, panic attacks, obsessions, or compulsions.

Genes   Microscopic structures in the chromosome; physical unit of hereditary transmission.

Genetic counseling   The giving of information about risk for inheritance of certain disorders based on general information about heredity, knowledge of family history, and genetic characteristics of the person or couple seeking information.

Genetic heterogeneity   In genetics, the idea that more than one gene is necessary for the inheritance of a characteristic. However, the genes each have a separate effect, not an additive one.

Genetic specificity   A gene pattern that is unique to a particular disorder or group of disorders.

Genital psychosexual stage   According to Freud, the psychosexual state at which pleasure is derived primarily from a mature heterosexual relationship that includes love and caring as well as sexual satisfaction.

Genome   The complete set of genes and their location on specific chromosomes.

Gestalt therapy   A type of psychotherapy originated by Fritz Perls in which emphasis is placed on how the patient integrates his or her perceptions into a meaningful whole or Gestalt.

Global assessment of functioning (GAF)   The measure, on Axis V of DSM-IV, of an individual's overall psychological, social, and occupational functioning.

Glove anesthesia   Condition in which a person cannot move or feel the part of the arm and hand that a glove would normally cover.

Gonadel glands   Ductless glands that are part of the endocrine system

Grand mal seizure   Severe form of epilepsy involving major convulsive attacks and loss of consciousness.

Grief   Sorrow, usually over a loss.

Group home   A sheltered living environment that may be either transitional or permanent. Often used for retarded persons and those with chronic schizophrenia. Emphasis is on self-care and self-regulation to the extent the individual's ability and condition permit.

Group therapy   Psychotherapy of several persons at the same time in small groups.

Guided rehearsals   Aspects of modeling in which the client practices the previously modeled behavior and is coached by the therapist in order to improve the performance.

Gyri   Raised portions of the brain's surface between the sulci. (Plural of gyrus.)

Halfway house   Transitional living facility that accommodates, for a short period of time, newly discharged psychiatric patients or those who have functioned maladaptively.

Hallucinations   Sensory perceptions in the absence of external stimuli. Hallucinations are usually visual ("seeing things") but may occur in other sensory modalities as well.

Hallucinogens General name for a group of drugs or chemicals capable of producing hallucinations.

Halo effect Tendency to rate an individual improperly high or low on a particular factor because of prior information or a general impression of the individual.

Hashish Hallucinogenic substance that is the solidified resin of cannabis sativa (marijuana).

Headache, cluster Headaches that occur in groups over a relatively short time period. Each headache is very painful for several minutes and fades away completely within an hour.

Headache, migraine Severe headache caused by a constriction followed by a dilation of the cranial artery. Usually preceded by some sensory or emotional cues called an aura. The disorder is thought to have some stress-related components.

Headache, tension Head pain produced by changes in the skeletal muscles.

Health psychology Area of psychology concerned both with calling attention to ways that disease can be prevented by changing living habits and with helping people modify behavior that increases health risk.

Hereditary Qualities transmitted from parent to child through genetic transmission.

Heroin Extremely addictive opiate derived from morphine.

Herpes virus hominis (herpes simplex) Chronic viral illness which, if present in a pregnant woman, may cause retardation and other congenital malformations in her child.

High-risk studies Research strategy entailing the longitudinal study of persons who might be vulnerable to breakdown.

Hippocampus One of two ridges along the lateral ventricles of the brain. Involved with the experience of emotion.

Histrionic personality disorder Characterized by overly reactive behavior of a histrionic, exhibitionistic type. Individuals with this disorder are egocentric and self-absorbed and usually have poor sexual adjustment.

HIV-associated cognitive impairment Difficulties in problem solving, memory, and the ability to concentrate that are associated with HIV infection. The cognitive symptoms are often accompanied by minor motor problems and withdrawn or apathetic behavior. As the AIDS infection progresses, the patient may develop severe dementia and psychotic symptoms.

Homeostasis Maintenance of equilibrium and constancy among the bodily processes.

Homosexual behavior Sexual activity between persons of the same sex.

Homosexuals Individuals who prefer to engage in sexual activity with persons of their own sex and who continue this behavior over a long period of time.

Hopelessness depression A suggested subtype of depression in which attributional style is important in producing the depressed state.

Hopelessness Negative expectations that may be characteristic of a person who is at risk for suicide. The Beck Hopelessness Scale has been used as a predictor of suicide risk.

Hormones Glandular secretions that function as coordinators of bodily reactions to external events and body growth and development.

Hot reactors Term for those who display intense cardiovascular responses to stress, for example surges in blood pressure.

Human immunedeficiency virus (HIV) A virus that affects the immune system and ultimately may cause it to fail.

Humanistic therapy Psychotherapy with special emphasis on human beings' fundamental desires to obtain self-respect and their needs for it. Carl Rogers' approach is an example.

Humanistic-existentialist perspective Idea that all individuals are unique and should be free to make their own choices about life directions. Emphasizes the creative freedom and potential of the individual.

Huntington's disease Uncommon degenerative disease occurring in families. Symptoms include jerking and twisting movement, facial grimaces, and psychotic symptoms. Also called Huntington's chorea.

Hyperactivity See attention-deficit/hyperactivity disorder.

Hypersomnia A type of dyssomnia in which there is excessive sleepiness, prolonged periods of sleep at night and/or long periods of sleep during the day.

Hypertension High blood pressure, usually considered a psychophysiological disorder.

Hypnogogic hallucinations Terrifying dream-like states that may be experienced in narcolepsy.

Hypnosis Altered state of consciousness induced by suggestion. Ranges from mild hypersuggestibility to deep, trancelike states.

Hypoactive sexual desire disorder A disorder, usually subjectively defined, in which a person may suppress sexual desires to a great extent sometimes because of pain associated with sexual activity.

Hypochondriasis (Hypochondria) Disorder in which a person is preoccupied by fear of disease and worries a great deal about his or her health without any realistic cause.

Hypomania A disorder characterized by unusual elevation in mood that is not as extreme as that found in mania.

Hypomanic episode A distinct period of elevated expansive or irritable mood and other manic behaviors that is not severe enough to greatly impair social or occupational functioning and does not require hospitalization.

Hypothalamus Part of the brain that lies below the thalamus. Controls various activities of the autonomic nervous system, including regulation of body temperature.

Hypothesis A statement of relationship or cause and effect stated in terms that allow a scientific test.

Hypothesis-testing experiment Evaluation of the correctness of an idea by experimental test.

Hysteria Presence of a physical problem without any physical causes. A person with hysteria is called an hysteric.

Hysteric Term used by Charcot to describe an individual who complains of organic symptoms such as pain, blindness, or paralysis for which no organic cause can be found.

Hysterical disorders See hysteria.

Id In psychoanalysis, that division of the psyche which is a repository of all instinctual impulses and repressed mental contents. Represents the true unconscious or the "deepest" part of the psyche.

Identification Feeling of association with another person or group such that an individual takes on the viewpoint and behavior of the other(s).

Identification with the aggressor A defense mechanism in which fear of someone is handled by psychologically assuming some of the frightening aspects of that person's behavior.

Immune system Body system that fights disease through inactivation of foreign substances by means of lymphocyte cells.

Implicit learning Learning that derives from observations of behavior that are analyzed and interpreted some time after they actually occurred.

Implosive therapy Behavior therapy technique based on the principle of extinction. Client is repeatedly presented with strong anxiety-provoking stimuli until he or she no longer reacts in an anxious manner.

Impotence Failure of a male to attain or maintain a penile erection even when sexually excited.

In vivo exposure (in therapy) A technique used in cognitive therapy or desensitization in which the individual practices adaptive cognitions or relaxation behavior in the actual presence of the anxiety-producing object or situation.

Incest Sexual relations between close family members, such as brother and sister or parent and child.

Incidence A count of the number of new cases that begin during a certain period of time; used in epidemiology. Contrast with prevalence.

Incompetent person Legal term used to describe individuals who are not able to understand the meaning of legal proceedings in which they are involved and who are unable to consult with an attorney in a way that might assist their defense.

Increased-stress theory Idea that the negative impact of the condition of poverty and crime make mental illness, especially schizophrenia, more likely because of the increased pressures of living. Contrast with social selection theory.

Independent variable Experimental factor (e.g., time of food deprivation) that is manipulated or altered in some manner while others are held constant.

Index case Term used in the study of genetics to indicate the individual with a disorder whose heredity is under study.

Indolamine Type of neurotransmitter of the monoamine group—e.g., serotonin—that appears especially closely related to mood.

Infantile sexuality View held by Sigmund Freud that children as well as adults have sexual feelings and experience erotic stimulation.

Inferential statistics Methods based on the laws of probability that are used to draw conclusions about relationships among variables studied.

Informed consent Requirement that patients must be given adequate information about the benefits and risks of planned treatments before they agree to the procedures.

Inhalants Volatile substances, usually some form of hydrocarbon compound, that produce psychological effects when they come into contact with capillaries in the lungs. Examples are spray paints and cleaning fluid.

Innate Characteristics acquired through general inheritance or the mutation of a gene or genes passed on from the parent.

Insanity Legal term connoting mental incompetence, inability to distinguish "right from wrong," and inability to care for oneself.

Insight Self-knowledge; understanding the significance and purpose of one's motives or behavior, including the ability to recognize inappropriateness and irrationality.

Insomnia Difficulty in going to sleep or staying asleep or not feeling rested after wakening. To meet DSM-IV criteria the problem must continue for at least a month.

Instrumental conditioning See operant conditioning.

Intellectualization A defense mechanism in which a person separates the description or meaning of an event from its emotional impact.

Intelligence quotient (IQ) A traditional way of expressing a person's level of intelligence or deviation from the mean of test performance expected by those of the same age. Originally calculated by the equation IQ equals 100 times the fraction obtained by dividing mental age by chronological age. IQ= 100(MZ/CA).

Intelligence tests Standardized tests measuring a variety of cognitive functions such as information and problem solving skills and usually intended to predict potential for future school achievement.

Interactional approach Viewpoint that directs attention to the joint effects or interactions of many of the variables emphasized by different theoretical viewpoints in producing abnormal behavior.

Interactional orientation (in addiction) The idea that both aspects of the person and of the situation are important in determining whether addiction will occur. People who may use drugs while they are in a long term stressful situation may not show signs of addiction such as withdrawal when they transfer to a less stressful environment in which the cues that accompanied drug use are absent.

Internalizing disorders A group of childhood disorders that are characterized less by overt activity than by cognitive activity consisting of worries or disturbing thoughts.

Interpersonal factors (in therapy) Refer to the relationship between the therapist and the client as a consequence of the personalities of the two rather than as a result of the techniques the therapist uses.

Interpersonal psychotherapy (IPT) A form of psychotherapy that focuses on increasing clients' social effectiveness and the extent that they feel cared about by others.

Interpersonal therapy (See interpersonal psychotherapy)

Irrational thought Ideas and beliefs that are derived from emotional response rather than reasoning.

Irresistable impulse The idea, used in the criminal justice system, that a person may not be able to control his or her behavior as a consequence of mental illness. As a result the person may not be considered to be criminally responsible even if he or she admits the act or is proven to have carried it out.

Irritable bowel syndrome A group of gastrointestinal symptoms including abdominal pain, gas, bloating or other feeling of abdominal distention, or altered bowel movements for which no clear physiological or psychological factors have been identified. The condition is often associated with stress, strong emotional reactions, and maladaptive thoughts.

Isolation Defense mechanism by which inconsistent or contradictory attitudes and feelings are walled off from each other in consciousness. Similar to repression, except that in isolation the impulse or wish is consciously recognized, but is separated from present behavior; in repression, neither the wish nor its relation to action is recognized. Intellectualization is a special form of isolation.

Joint attention behaviors Behaviors that coordinate attention of two people or one person and an event or object. They may involve initiating a behavior toward another or following the behavior of another. Children with autistic disorder are likely to have impairment in joint attention behavior.

Juvenile delinquency Violations of the law committed by children and adolescents (usually defined as persons 18 years of age or younger).

Kappa statistic A type of reliability index that corrects for chance agreement to provide a true estimate of reliability.

Karyotypes Microphotographs of an individual's chromosomes in a standard array.

Kaufman Assessment Battery for Children (K–ABC) An intelligence test for children that is based on ideas from cognitive psychology and neuropsychology to measure simultaneous and sequential processing abilities. Designed to be less culturally biased than conventional intelligence tests.

Kinsey Report First detailed statistical report that attempted to present the variations in human sexual behavior from a descriptive, scientific view.

Korsakoff's syndrome Chronic brain disorder precipitated by a vitamin deficiency stemming from alcoholism. Characterized by marked disorientation, amnesia, and falsification of memory.

La belle indifference Marked lack of concern about one's disability, occasionally seen in patients with conversion disorder.

Labeling Cognitive device by which a person classifies his or her own emotional responses as a way of controlling behavior, especially in stress-producing situations. Also, a way people are categorized by others, a way of stereotyping.

Laceration Gross tear or rupture in tissue. Cerebral lacerations may occur through head injuries.

Latency period According to Freud, the period from age 5 until adolescence during which the child's sexual impulses are not a primary focus of his or her pleasure-seeking activities.

Learned helplessness Acquired belief in one's helplessness to deal with a situation or control one's environment. Concept has been applied to explain depression in humans.

Learning disorders The DSM-IV includes several specific learning disorders. Among these are reading disorder, mathematics disorder, disorder of written expression, and a miscellaneous category of learning disorder not otherwise specified (NOS). Learning disorders may provide an explanation for academic performance that is substantially below what might be expected from knowledge of a person's measured intelligence, chronological age, and exposure to education.

Lesbianism The practice of homosexual behavior by women.

Libido Freud's term for the emotional or psychic energy he believed to be originated by the innate drive for sexual pleasure.

Librium (chlordiazepoxide) Tranquilizer often prescribed for anxiety problems.

Limbic system Part of the brain that controls visceral and bodily changes associated with emotion; also regulates drive-motivated behavior. Lower parts of the cerebrum.

Lithium (lithium carbonate) Chemical salt used in the treatment of bipolar disorder.

Live modeling Learning through direct observation of another person who performs the act or acts which are to be learned.

Localized amnesia See amnestic disorders.

Locus of control Personality characteristic described by Julian Rotter in which an individual believes either that he or she has the power to affect the outcome of situations (internal locus of control) or that he or she has little control over what happens (external locus of control).

Locus, gene The characteristic position within a chromosome in which a particular gene pair are located.

Logotherapy Term used by Viktor Frankl for his existential-humanistic therapy.

Longitudinal study Research strategy based on observing and recording the behavior of people over periods of time. Involves obtaining measures on the same people either continuously or at specific or regular intervals.

LSD (Lysergic acid dimethylamide) Chemically produced synthetic hallucinogen with psychotomimetic properties.

Lunatic Term used in the past to describe the insane. The word luna (moon) refers to the old belief that those who were insane were moonstruck.

Lycanthropy Term for the magical change believed to overcome individuals and cause them to behave like wolves.

Lymphocytes A general term that includes several types of cells in the immune system that fight disease.

M'Naghten rule Legal precedent in English law, originating in 1843, which provides for acquittal if an accused person is found to be not responsible for the crime—that is, if he or she could not distinguish between "right and wrong." The rule did not take into account that a person might be held to be insane even though he or she knew the difference between right and wrong.

Magnetic resonance imaging (MRI) A method by which electromagnetic radiation is used to visualize and measure anatomy in the living person.

Magnetic resonance spectroscopy (MRS) Measurement of tissue chemistry and metabolic function in living organisms through the use of electromagnetic radiation emitted from these chemical changes.

Mainstreaming An educational policy in which children with physical and mental disabilities participate at least to some degree in regular school classes. Some special classes during the school day may be provided that are focused on their special learning difficulties.

Maintenance therapy The continuation of treatment, often but not always medication, for some time after the person shows remission of symptoms in an effort to help prevent the symptoms from reoccurring.

Major depressive disorder or episode A severe depression characterized by dysphoric mood as well as poor appetite, sleep problems, feelings of restlessness or being slowed down, loss of pleasure, loss of energy, feelings of inability to concentrate or indecisiveness, recurrent thoughts of death or suicide attempts. These occur without mood-incongruent delusions or hallucinations and are not due to schizophrenia, paranoid disorder, organic mental disorder, or recent death of a loved one. The disorder tends to be episodic with periods without depression or periods of lessened symptoms.

Maladaptive behavior Behavior that deals inadequately with a situation, especially one that is stressful.

Malingering   Behavior designed to get financial or other rewards by pretending to have some disorder. Contrast with factitious disorder.

Mania   Euphoric, hyperactive state in which an individual's judgment is impaired.

Mantra   See meditation.

MAO inhibitor   See Monoamine oxidase inhibitor.

Marijuana   Substance derived from the leaves or flowering tops of the cannabis plant. Smoking it leads to a dreamy state of altered consciousness in which ideas are disconnected, uncontrollable, and plentiful. Under the influence of marijuana, behavior is impulsive and mood is elevated.

Marital therapy   A subtype of group therapy in which a couple meets together with a therapist in an attempt to improve the couple's interaction.

Markers   Biological or behavioral characteristics that may make it possible to identify people who are vulnerable to certain disorders.

Masochism   Deviation in which sexual pleasure is attained from pain inflicted on oneself, from being dominated, or from being mistreated.

Masochist   One who practices masochism.

Masturbation   Self-stimulation of the genitals for the purposes of deriving sexual pleasure.

Mean   Arithmetic average.

Median   The score that lies midway between the highest and lowest scores when the scores are arranged from lowest to highest.

Mediators   Links (for example) between a stimulus and the resulting behavior). A mediator does not make an independent contribution to an outcome. Rather its influence is due to another variable related both to it and to the outcome.

Meditation   The technique of relaxing through concentrating on a thought, sensation, or special word or mantra.

Melatonin   A hormone produced by the pineal gland that is important in the sleep cycle.

Mendelian pattern of heredity   Named after Gregor Mendel, the first person to discover the existence of genes. Mendel developed 3 theories. First, during the formation of the sex cells paired factors are separated so that the sperm and the egg each contain half of each of the new individual's ultimate set of gene pairs. Second, characteristics are inherited separately from each other. Third, each inherited characteristic is determined by the interaction of two hereditary factors or genes. In the characteristics he studied, Mendel found that one factor always predominated over the other. For instance, the tall gene was always dominant; The person would be short only if he or she inherited two genes for shortness.

Mental age   The age equivalent at which a person's intellectual behavior places him or her. Contrasted to chronological age, the person's actual age as determined by birth date. The ratio between the two [(MA /CA) = 100] was the original formulation of the intelligence quotient.

Mental deficiency   An older term for mental retardation.

Mental health   Someone who is able to think logically and rationally and who copes effectively in stressful situations is considered mentally healthy. Emotional stability and the ability to adjust to new situations that arise over the life course is also part of mental health.

Mental retardation   Intellectual functioning significantly below average. Generally defined as an intelligence test score of 70 or below together with a poor level of social functioning. The de-

gree of retardation is further defined by intelligence test score range.

Mental-status examination   An interview, sometimes supplemented with psychological and neurological tests, used to assess an individual's intellectual function and ability to interact appropriately with the environment.

Meta-amphetamine   A chemical compound chemically related to amphetamine but with greater effects on the central nervous system. Often called "poor man's cocaine".

Meta-analysis   Technique used to combine the data from many studies in a meaningful way. Has been used to investigate the effects of psychotherapy on clients.

Metacognition   A person's knowledge of his or her own cognitive processes and the products of these processes.

Methadone   Synthetic chemical whose action is similar to that of morphine. Because its continuing use is not assumed to lead to escalation of dosage, it is prescribed by some authorities as a treatment for heroin addiction.

Methadone maintenance   Use of methadone as a substitute for heroin. Methadone prevents withdrawal and suppresses the desire for heroin, although methadone also has undesirable side effects.

Method factors   Variations in results that are caused by the way a study was conducted, the type of questionnaire used, or other factors not associated with a real difference in what has been measured.

Methylphenidate   Stimulant drug (e.g., Ritalin) sometimes used in the treatment of hyperactivity.

Microcephaly   A condition associated with mental retardation and brain deterioration in which the size of a person's head is much smaller than average.

Migraine headache   A severe headache, often on one side only, accompanied by nausea and dilation of the cranial artery. These headaches are usually preceded by a sensory, motor, or mood disturbance called an aura.

Milieu   Environment, setting.

Milieu therapy   Effort to provide a totally therapeutic environment within an institution by enlisting the efforts of all staff members as providers of some form of therapeutic contact.

Millon Clinical Multiaxial Inventory (MCMI)   A measure of personality disorders specifically designed to assess the personality disorders classified in DSM IV.

Mind   Human consciousness as shown in thought, perception, and memory. Reflects the artificial dichotomy often made between mind and body.

Minnesota Multiphasic Personality Inventory (MMPI)   Self-report personality questionnaire designed to facilitate psychiatric diagnosis.

Mode   The score attained by the largest number of subjects.

Modeling   Behavior learned or modified as a result of observing the behavior of others. Learner does not have to make the observed response him- or herself, or be reinforced for making it, to learn the new behavior. Term used interchangeably with observational learning. See also covert, live, and symbolic modeling.

Monoamine neurotransmitter   Type of neurotransmitter with a distinctive single amino acid (NH_2) in its molecular structure. There are two types of monoamines: catecholamines and indoleamines.

Monoamine oxidase (MAO)   Enzyme in the neuron receptors that inactivates the various amines, including the catecholamines.

Monoamine oxidase (MAO) inhibitor   One of a group of drugs used to treat depression. Works by preventing the degrading of monoamines and thus allowing more norepinephrine and serotonin to collect at the receptor sites.

Monogenic (single-gene) model   Refers to theory of inheritance in which a gene at one particular locus (e.g., one site on a chromosome) is sufficient to produce an inherited characteristic.

Monozygotic (MZ) twins   Identical twins developed from one fertilized egg.

Mood disorder   One of a group of disorders primarily affecting emotional tone. Can be depression, manic excitement, or both. May be episodic or chronic.

Moral treatment   Technique of treating mental-hospital patients which prevailed in the nineteenth century. Emphasized removal of restraints, allowing religious conviction, and ensuring humanitarian treatment.

Morphine   Principal derivative of opium which has been used extensively to relieve pain.

Mosaicism   The condition in which all a person's cells do not have the same chromosome count as a result of an error in cell division in the fertilized egg.

Motor skills disorder   A diagnosis of motor skills disorder is made when there is a noticeable impairment in the development of a child's motor coordination that is not due to a general medical condition such as cerebral palsy or muscular dystrophy.

MRI   See magnetic resonance imaging.

MRS   See magnetic resonance spectroscopy.

Multiaxial classification system   System that rates an individual separately on a number of different criteria or axes. The DSM system is an example.

Multiaxial diagnostic system   A multiaxial classification system developed to diagnose disordered behavior.

Multifactorial polygenic model   Theory that a number of genes from a variety of loci may combine to produce a particular characteristic or disorder.

Multi-infarct dementia   See vascular dementia.

Multimodal therapy   A combination of several types of treatment that seems especially useful in several conditions including substance-use disorders, borderline disorders, anxiety disorders, and schizophrenia. The treatment may include both biologically-based and psychologically-based therapies or may include several types of psychological interventions that may be used not only with the patient but also with family members.

Multiple personality   See dissociative identity disorder.

Munchausen syndrome   A factitious disorder in which the person pretends to have a particular disorder in order to get medical treatment. Involves faking of symptoms, and often self-injury.

Muscle contraction headache   See tension headache.

Muscle dysmorphia   Preoccupation with extensively muscled physique as an ideal. Primarily found in men, for instance in some male weightlifters.

Mutant   A cell in which the hereditary material has been altered. This mutation may be spontaneous (occurring naturally) or induced by internal factors such as radiation and certain chemicals.

Mutation Sudden change in the composition of a gene, which usually causes abnormal characteristics in the progeny.

Myocardial infarction Tissue damage to the heart muscle from a drastic decrease in the amount of blood that reaches the heart; commonly called a heart attack.

Naloxone A drug that blocks the pain relieving effects of endorphins.

Naltrexone A drug that prevents readdiction to heroin and other opioids by blocking opioid receptors.

Narcissism Term for self-love or self-absorption derived from the Greek myth about Narcissus who fell in love with what he thought was a water nymph but was in reality his own reflection in a pond.

Narcissistic personality disorder Characterized by a sense of self-importance and a preoccupation with fantasies of unlimited success. Individuals are preoccupied with how well they are doing and how well others think of them. Disorder is often accompanied by depressed mood.

Narcolepsy A type of sleep disturbance in which the person goes directly into the REM phase of sleep. Often produces uncontrollable sleepiness during daytime hours as well as unusual experiences during sleep. Thought to have some genetic basis.

Narcotics Legal term for addicting drugs, the most common of which are the opiates, derived from the Oriental poppy.

Natural fool Old term for a retarded person. It means one who is born deficient in judgment.

Negative reinforcer A type of aversive stimulus that is removed as soon as the desired response occurs, thus increasing the probability of that response.

Negative symptoms, in schizophrenia Symptoms characterized by behavior deficits such as flattened affect, poverty of speech and apathy. Sometimes called Type II schizophrenia.

Negative transference Feelings of hostility a client carries over from earlier relationships into his or her relationship with a therapist.

Neoanalyst Theorist who agrees with a revised version of Freud's concepts.

Neo-Freudian Pertaining to former followers of Freud who departed in several major doctrinal ways from orthodox psychoanalysis. Whereas ego psychologists view themselves as psychoanalysts, neo-Freudians may not. Prominent among the neo-Freudians are Adler, Jung, and Sullivan. Their writings emphasize the social and cultural determinants of behavior.

Neural plasticity Refers to the ability of the nervous system to change in response to stimulation. See also *sensitive periods*.

Neurodevelopmental model In the study of schizophrenia this model assumes that the related abnormality in neural development occurred early in life but is not noticed until the affected region of the brain matures during the normal course of development.

Neurogenesis The production of new brain cells.

Neuroleptic drugs Name for a group of psychoactive drugs that are used to treat schizophrenic disorders. These reduce psychotic symptoms but may have side effects resembling neurological disorders.

Neurologist Specialist in the diagnosis and treatment of disorders of the nervous system.

Neuron Individual nerve cell.

Neuropharmacology The specialized field focused on the development of drugs to compensate for defects or deficiencies in brain chemistry and neural transmission.

Neuropsychological tests Tests intended to measure various consequences of a brain abnormality such as cognitive, sensorimotor, and perceptual skills.

Neuropsychology Branch of psychology dealing with brain-behavior relationships.

Neuroreceptors Proteins located on neuron dendrites that pick up and relay signals throughout the brain and nervous system.

Neuroscience An interdisciplinary field of science that is focused on understanding the relationship between brain structure and function and behavior, affect, and cognitions.

Neurosis Older term for what is now called anxiety disorder.

Neurotransmitter Chemical product of the nervous system that makes possible the movement of the nerve impulse across the synapse.

Nicotine Volatile psychoactive substance that is the chief active chemical in tobacco.

Nightmare disorder Frightening dreams that tend to occur during REM sleep. See also parasomnias.

Nocturnal penile tumescence (NPT) Enlargement and erection of the penis that occurs during rapid-eye-movement sleep.

Non compos mentis Latin term meaning not of sound mind and therefore not legally responsible.

Nondisjunction The presence of an extra chromosome in what should have been a chromosome pair.

Non-residential support approach The use of mental health clinics and day care facilities in the treatment of mental illness and in relapse prevention. Often this approach is combined with the coordination of patients' treatment and living arrangements by a case manager.

Non-shared environment Term used in the study of twins or siblings to contrast the environmental effects that both individuals experience in the family with those effects that occur to only one individuals because of unique events, personal characteristics, or experiences or relationships outside the family.

Nontranssexual gender identity disorder Persistent discomfort about one's assigned sex; frequently involves cross dressing or fantasies about cross dressing. Differs from transsexualism in that there is no persistent preoccupation to acquire the primary and secondary sexual characteristics of the other sex.

Norepinephrine Hormone also called noradrenalin, produced by the adrenal medulla. One of the catecholamine group.

Null hypothesis The statement evaluated by many statistical tests that groups do not differ. If the null hypothesis can be rejected it is assumed to be unlikely that any observed differences are due to chance.

Object relations The psychoanalytic approach that focuses attention on the emotional bonds between persons rather than on a person's view of him or herself.

Observational research A method in which no variables are manipulated and relationships are studied as they naturally occur. Contrast with experimental method.

Obsessive behavior Characterized by preoccupation with a particular type of thought that keeps occurring repetitively.

Obsessive-compulsive behavior Behavior that combines ritualistic behavior and compulsive thinking.

Obsessive-compulsive disorder Characterized by recurrent obsessions and/or compulsions, often accompanied by depression or anxiety.

Obsessive-compulsive personality disorder Distinguished by lack of ability to express warmth, a stiff and formal way of relating to others, and extreme perfectionism that leads an individual to focus on details rather than on the whole picture.

Operant conditioning Form of conditioning in which a desired response occurs and is subsequently reinforced to increase its probability of more frequent occurrence; also called instrumental conditioning.

Operant observations A type of behavioral observation in which observations concerning the frequencies of certain specified behaviors are made before any treatment is begun.

Opiate Natural or synthetic substance that is similar in action to morphine or other derivatives of the opium poppy.

Opioid Drug with a morphine-like action. Can be either a natural or synthetic substance.

Oppositional defiant disorder Although less serious than conduct disorder, this disorder is characterized by negative behaviors and unwillingness to accept the authority of others. Often develops into conduct or mood disorder.

Oral dependent personality Psychodynamic terminology to describe individuals who secure a major part of their psychological gratification from such activities as eating, drinking, and smoking, and who may show dependent personality characteristics.

Oral psychosexual stage First developmental stage of infancy, during which pleasure is derived from lip and mouth contact with need-fulfilling objects (e.g., breast).

Organic mental disorder Brain dysfunction based on either aging or the ingestion of substances that affect brain activity. May be temporary or permanent.

Organismic point of view Pertaining to the organism as a whole rather than to particular parts. Behavior is considered an interrelated and interactive function of the integrated organism.

Orgasm Third stage of sexual response, which involves rhythmic muscular contractions and high physical arousal. In the male, ejaculation of semen takes place during this stage.

Orienting response Measurable psychophysiological changes that come about when a person notices an environmental stimulus and prepares to receive some information from it.

Outpatient commitment A procedure based on law in some states that requires mentally ill individuals who are not dangerous, but who are likely to become so if they cease treatment, to take medications and keep mental health appointments.

Overgeneralization According to Aaron Beck, characteristic way of thinking found in some depressed individuals. Tendency to exaggerate the meaning of an event into a general principle.

Pain disorder The experience of severe and prolonged pain that is either greatly in excess of what might be expected from the medical problem or that occurs without any organic symptoms that can be discovered.

Panic attack A rapidly rising surge of intense anxiety that occurs suddenly, either with or without clear cues, in an unpredictable fashion.

Panic disorder   Type of anxiety disorder characterized by recurring panic or anxiety attacks and extreme nervousness not necessarily related to exposure to threatening situations.

Paradigm   A model or example.

Paradoxical intention   Therapeutic technique in which the client is instructed to perform behaviors that seem to be counter to the therapeutic goal. For instance, someone who is afraid of crowds may be instructed to go into a crowd and concentrate on feeling as fearful as possible.

Paranoia   See delusional disorder.

Paranoid personality disorder   Personality disorder similar in some ways to schizoid personality disorder, but notable for extreme sensitivity in interpersonal relationships; suspicious, jealous, and stubborn behavior; and a tendency to use the defense mechanism of projection.

Paranoid subtype of schizophrenia   Type of schizophrenia characterized by persistent delusions, often either grandiose or accusatory.

Paraphilia   Sexual deviation that involves choice of inappropriate sex partners or inappropriate goals for the sex act. Pedophilia, sadism, and voyeurism are examples.

Paraprofessionals   Term used to describe workers who have received certain basic training that enables them to perform tasks formerly performed by professional workers. Paraprofessionals often come from the same communities and educational backgrounds as the people whom they treat or aid.

Parasomnias   A group of sleep disorders characterized by abnormal behavioral or physiological evens that occur during sleep, in specific sleep stages, or in the sleep-wake transition. The occurrence of these can not be attributed to other mental or medical conditions or to substance abuse. Examples are nightmare disorder and sleep terror disorder.

Parasuicide   Term used to describe any act that does not end in death in which a person deliberately causes self-injury or takes a drug overdose with the apparent intention of suicide.

Parens patriae   Legal doctrine that gives the state power to act in what it believes to be the best interest of an incapacitated adult or a minor.

Paresis   Chronic and progressively deteriorating brain condition caused by syphilitic infection and characterized by loss of cognitive and motor functions, speech disorder, and eventual death.

Parietal lobe   Middle division of each cerebral hemisphere of the brain, behind the central sulcus, above the fissure of Sylvius, and in front of the parieto-occipital fissure.

Parkinson's disease   Chronic and progressive neurological disorder characterized by motor tremor, rigidity, loss of vocal power, and psychotic symptoms. Believed to be caused by an acquired defect in brain metabolism.

Partial hospitalization   Use of day, night, or weekend hospital care for patients who do not need 24-hour care. Designed particularly to aid transition back to the community. Also used to prevent complete hospitalization if the family can provide partial care, for instance, outside of their own working hours.

Participant modeling   Therapeutic procedure in which the response is first demonstrated for the client, who then produces the same response aided by suggestions from the therapist.

Passive coping   Dealing with a stressful situation by withdrawing and engaging in a distracting activity.

PCP (phencyclidine)   Hallucinogenic drug popularly known as "angel dust."

Pedophile   Person 16 years of age or older who engages in sexual activity with one or more prepubescent children.

Pedophilia   Sexual deviation in which an adult desires or engages in sexual relations with a child. May be either homosexual or heterosexual in nature.

Pellagra   Chronic disease caused by niacin deficiency. Symptoms include skin eruptions, digestive disturbances, and disturbances of the nervous system which may cause psychotic-like behavior.

Penetrance, (gene)   Percentage of cases in which a particular trait or characteristic, derived from a specific gene, will manifest itself in subsequent organisms of the species.

Performance anxiety (sexual)   High degree of concern in males about the ability to maintain an erection until orgasm. The anxiety has a negative effect on sexual performance.

Performance IQ   One of the two subscores of the Wechsler intelligence test series. Reflects ability to solve puzzles, copy designs, and perform other similar tasks.

Peripheral nervous system   System that includes all outlying nerve structures not included in the central nervous system.

Perseverative speech   The tendency to repeat works or phases that is characteristic of some speech by those who have schizophrenia. The repetitions are often inserted in subsequent sentences making those appear illogical and difficult to understand.

Personal constructs   A concept developed by George Kelly that refers to the way in which people cognitively organize information. He believed that each person has his or her own view of the world based on this sorting of people and events into categories.

Personal maladaptation   Perception by an individual of personal dissatisfactions and concerns that interfere with happiness but not significantly with social adjustment or work achievement.

Personality   Particular constellation of attributes that defines one's individuality.

Personality disorders   Deeply ingrained, inflexible, maladaptive patterns of thought and behavior which persist throughout a person's life.

Personality inventories   Paper-and-pencil tests in which the person describes him- or herself by answering a series of true-false questions or by rating a series of self-descriptive phases. Most personality inventories yield several scores, each of which is intended to describe an aspect of personality.

Persons non compos mentis   See noncompos mentis.

Pervasive developmental disorder   A life-long disorder in which the quality of the person's social interactions, communication skills, and ability to engage in imaginative activities and other cognitive tasks is impaired. Autistic disorder is one subtype of this disorder.

Petit mal seizure   Mild form of epilepsy which involves partial alterations of consciousness.

Phallic psychosexual stage   Stage of psychosexual development during which a child begins to perceive his or her body as a source of gratification. Feelings of narcissism are heightened during this period.

Phencyclidine (PCP)   An illicit drug, technically a dissociative anesthetic, that frequently produced delerium and hallucinations. Also call "angel dust" and "crystal."

Phenobarbitol   Barbiturate sometimes used as a sedative and in the control of epileptic seizure activity.

Phenothyazines   Group of antipsychotic drugs traditionally used to treat schizophrenic disorder.

Phenylalanine hydroxylase   A naturally occurring enzyme in the blood. Its function may be impaired by a gene mutation in the disorder phenylketonuria (PKU).

Phenylketonuria (PKU)   Form of mental retardation caused by a metabolic deficiency.

Phobia   Excessive or inappropriate fear of some particular object or situation which is not in fact dangerous.

Phobic disorder   Type of anxiety disorder mainly characterized by irrational and highly specific fears (for example, of dirt, water, high places).

Phototherapy   The use of exposure to very bright light for several hours a day as a treatment for seasonal depression.

Phrenology   Obsolete theory that different psychological behaviors were related to different parts of the brain and that these could be assessed by touching the surface of the skull.

Physical anomalies   Abnormalities of parts of the body, either external or internal, that are associated with abnormal prenatal development and later with schizophrenia and other disorders.

Physical disorder   Term used to refer to a medical as opposed to a psychological problem. Included in the DSM system on Axis IV.

Physiognomy   The art of judging human character or personality from facial features.

Pick's disease   Type of progressive dementia caused by atrophy of the cerebral cortex.

Pituitary glands   Ductless glands that are part of the endocrine system.

Placebo   Inactive or inert substance that is presented as effective remedy for some problem in order to determine what role suggestibility plays in symptom change.

Placebo effect   Changes in behavior as a result of the expectancy that a placebo, or inactive substance, is an active or "real" drug; type of suggestion effect.

Plaque   Abnormal deposit found in the body, as in the arteries of people with atherosclerosis or in the nerve calls of individuals with Alzheimer's disease.

Plateau stage   Second stage of sexual response, which includes increases in heart rate and muscle tension as well as swelling of genital tissue.

Play therapy   Treatment approach used with children; based on the assumption that young children can express thoughts and fantasies more directly in play than through verbal means.

Pleasure principle   Psychoanalytic term for the regulatory mechanism for mental life that functions to reduce tension and gain gratification. Principle that governs the functioning of the id to obtain gratification without regard to reality considerations.

Polygenic model   Theory in genetics that several genes at different loci must interact to produce a particular inherited characteristic.

Polygraph   Instrument that measures emotional responses through physiological reactions, such as blood pressure and galvanic skin response. Commonly called a lie detector.

Polysomnography The monitoring of several biological processes during sleep.

Population genetics Study of the ways genes are distributed in a population through the mating of individuals.

Positive reinforcer See reinforcer.

Positive symptoms, in schizophrenia Generally, symptoms that show behavioral excesses: hallucinations, delusions, bizarre behavior, and so forth. Sometimes called Type I schizophrenia.

Positive transference Carry over of positive feelings about other relationships onto the therapist-client relationship.

Positron emission tomography (PT) Technique for studying the dynamic chemical activity of the brain by using a scanning device that produces a series of cross-sectional images of the brain.

Post-hallucinogenic perceptual disorder The experience of spontaneous flashbacks related to prior hallucinatory experiences associated with LSD use.

Posttraumatic psychosis Psychotic symptoms that appear suddenly after an injury to the brain or a stressful life event.

Posttraumatic stress disorder (PTSD) Development of symptoms in response to events of such severity that most people would be stressed by them. Symptoms often include a feeling of numbness in response or psychological reexperiencing of the event in thoughts, dreams, or nightmares.

Postvention A therapeutic intervention in which survivors are given supportive treatment.

Power rape See rape.

Preconscious Thoughts that are not held in a person's mind at a particular time but which can easily be brought into awareness.

Premature ejaculation Inability of the male to inhibit ejaculation long enough for his female partner to experience orgasm.

Premorbid adjustment Achievement level and adjustment to interpersonal activities shown by an individual earlier in life before a disorder becomes apparent.

Presenile dementia See dementia.

Prevalence Information concerning the number of cases of a particular disorder that are ongoing at any particular time. Contrast term with incidence.

Primary appraisal First stage of assessing the meaning of a situation. In this stage the situation is interpreted as threatening or harmless. In the following stage, secondary appraisal, the individual decides how to deal with the situation.

Primary prevention Efforts at preventing the development of maladaptation by removing factors that might cause it to develop.

Primary process thinking Primary cognitive mode, characteristic of infants and children, that is not based on rules of organization or logic. The presence of primary process thinking, free association in its purest form, is characteristic of the id. Primary process thought is illogical, is entirely pleasure oriented, has no sense of time or order, and does not discriminate between reality and fantasy. Compare with secondary process thinking.

Problem drinking Term for the pattern of alcohol abuse that does not include alcohol dependence or physiological addiction.

Process research In psychotherapy research, the attempt to understand what happens during the course of psychotherapy in contrast to interest only in the desirability of the outcome.

Prodromal symptoms (in schizophrenia) Changed behavior that occurs prior to the clear onset of schizophrenia but also may occur in individuals who may not develop this disorder. Thus these symptoms are suggestive of the development of schizophrenia but are not predictive of a specific risk for the disorder.

Prognosis Forecast; probable course and outcome of a disorder.

Projection Defense mechanism that involves attributing to others the undesirable characteristics or impulses which belong to, but are not acceptable to, oneself.

Projective techniques Ambiguous stimulus materials that elicit subjective responses of an associative or fantasy nature. So named because an individual is believed to "project" aspects of his or her personality into the task. Tasks may include inkblot interpretation (Rorschach Test), and various associative completion techniques (word association, incomplete sentences).

Prototypal approach The use of a checklist in making a diagnostic decision. If more than a predetermined number of characteristics are found, the diagnosis is made. As a result people with the same diagnosis may have different sets of characteristics.

Prozac See fluoxetine.

Prozac A trade name for the drug fluoxetine. Used to treat depression and anxiety. Considered to be useful in some other disorders. Considerable controversy has surrounded its use.

Psilocybin One of the two psychoactive substances isolated from the psilocybin mushroom.

Psychedelic drug A drug that is able to alter sensory perceptions.

Psychiatric nurse A registered nurse who has taken specialized training in the care of those with mental illness.

Psychiatric social worker A person with a graduate degree in social work and specialized training in treating and practically assisting both patients with behavioral problems and their families.

Psychiatrist Physician with post-graduate training in the diagnosis and treatment of emotional disorders.

Psychic determinism Principle of causality, one of the basic assumptions of psychoanalysis, which states that all events, overt and covert, are determined by prior and often multiple mental events.

Psychoactive drugs Term including several types of drugs that may reduce maladaptive behavior. Includes antipsychotic, antianxiety, and antidepressant drugs.

Psychoanalysis Term has three meanings: (1) theory of psychology and psychopathology developed by Freud from his clinical experiences with patients; (2) procedure for investigating the mental life, conflicts, and coping processes, which employs the techniques of free association, dream analysis, and interpretation of transference and resistance phenomena; and (3) form of therapy that uses the psychoanalytic procedure and the theories of personality and psychopathology just described.

Psychodrama Method of group therapy in which individuals both act out their emotional responses in situations they find difficult and also practice new, constructive roles.

Psychodynamic perspective Point of view that emphasizes thoughts and emotions as the most important determiners of behavior. Basic ideas come from the work of Sigmund Freud.

Psychodynamic therapy A therapeutic approach based on the psychodynamic perspective originating in the theories of Freud, but not limited to psychoanalysis.

Psychometric Refers to measures of psychological functioning.

Psychomotor Term used to describe muscular action resulting from prior mental activity, especially conscious mental activity.

Psychomotor epilepsy Trancelike state with recurring episodes of confusion during which repetitive and semiautomatic muscle movements occur. Often accompanied by confusion and visual hallucinations.

Psychoneuroimmunology A field of scientific specialization devoted to an understanding of the relationships among behavior, neural activity, and the immune system.

Psychopath Term used by Harvey Cleckley to describe antisocial individuals who have a certain set of characteristics including charm, lack of anxiety or guilt, poor judgment, and failure to learn from experience.

Psychophysiological disorders Physical pathology and actual tissue damage that results from continued emotional mobilization of the body during periods of sustained stress.

Psychosexual stage One of several developmental stages of life as defined by Sigmund Freud. These differ in terms of the source of primary gratification and include oral, anal, phallic, and genital stages.

Psychosis (plural: psychoses) Disorder that includes any of the following: delusions, hallucinations, incoherence, repeated derailment of thought, marked poverty of thought content, marked illogicality, and grossly disorganized or catatonic behavior.

Psychosocial disadvantage Growing up in an intellectually, culturally, and financially impoverished environment.

Psychosocial stages Erik Erikson's term for the stages of human psychological development.

Psychosocial stressor Feeling of stress arising from relationships with other people in the environment.

Psychosomatic disorders See psychophysiological disorder.

Psychosomatic hypothesis Idea popular in the 1930s and 1940s that physical symptoms can be caused by an inability to express strong emotions.

Psychotherapy General term referring to psychological, verbal, and expressive techniques used in treating maladaptive behavior. The client works on resolving inner conflicts and modifying his or her behavior by means of verbal interchanges with the therapist. Insight into feelings and behavior is the goal of most psychotherapy.

Psychotic An adjective indicating the presence of psychosis.

Psychotic disorders Disorders in which there is gross impairment in reality testing and the creation of a new reality. Psychotic disorders include schizophrenia, delusional disorders, some organic mental disorder, and some mood disorders.

PT scan See positron emission tomography.

Punishment Aversive stimulus given as a result of an undesired behavior in an attempt to suppress that behavior in the future.

Racism The holding of beliefs and attitudes that demean members of particular racial groups. Often results in poor educational opportunity, living conditions, and economic status for members of these groups.

Range A simple measure of variability, the difference between the highest and lowest scores subjects attain on a particular test or other measuring instrument.

Rape Forcible sexual intercourse without the partner's consent. Researchers have classified rape into three general categories based on the assumed motivation for the act. Power rape is assumed to be carried out by someone who feels inadequate in interpersonal relationships and as a result accompanies the act of rape with intimidation and threats of further physical harm. Anger rape is thought to be the result of a rapist who is angry at women in general and is seeking revenge for this general feeling by raping a specific person. In sadistic rape the rapist is focused on making the victim suffer and thus combines sexual acts and aggression.

Rape–relief center Organization, often composed in part of volunteers, designed to provide information about medical and legal services for those who have been raped and also to offer psychological support for the victims.

Rapid cycling (in bipolar disorder) A form of bipolar disorder in which there are four or more clearly defined affective episodes in the period of a year. The episodes may include periods of depression and of mania or hypomania. Rapid cycling is more common in women than in men.

Rating scale Type of test in which a person can indicate on a scale the degree of his or her agreement with each item.

Rational thinking Based on reasoning and logic, not on observation or experimental evidence.

Rational–emotive therapy Therapy developed by Albert Ellis to modify unrealistic and illogical thought.

Rationalization A mental justification of behavior that serves as an excuse for doing something that is not socially approved of.

Reaction formation Defense mechanism that enables the individual to express an unacceptable impulse by transforming it into its opposite.

Reactive attachment disorder of infancy or early childhood A condition in young children thought to result from severe deprivation and neglect that continues for a long period. The disorder results in marked difficulty in relationships with others. In the inhibited type of this disorder the child does not respond appropriately to attempts at social interaction by others and does not initiate such attempts. In the disinhibited type the child shows a kind of indiscriminate behavior in forming social attachments.

Reactivity Changes that occur in behavior when subjects know that they are being studied. This factor makes it more difficult to be certain that the behaviors observed in laboratory or clinical studies can be inferred to be predictive of behaviors in other nonstudy-related situations.

Recessive gene Member of a gene pair which determines the characteristic trait or appearance of the individual only if the other member of the pair matches it. Compare with dominant gene.

Regression Defense mechanism characterized by a return to earlier and more primitive modes of responding. Through regression, the ego returns to an earlier developmental phase of functioning which had met with some success.

Rehabilitation model A type of full time or day treatment in which attention is given to improving social and vocational functioning. The treatment is usually of limited length but may last longer than acute care.

Reinforcement Any event (stimulus) which, if contingent upon response by an organism, changes the probability that the response will be made again. Reinforcements may be positive (reward) or negative (aversive) and may be presented according to a prescribed schedule (continuous, intermittent). May also be primary (drive reducing—e.g., food) or secondary (derived from prior association with a primary reinforcer—e.g., money, praise).

Reinforcer A consequence of behavior that makes it more likely the behavior will occur again. A positive reinforcer achieves this result by provoking a reward or pleasure. A negative reinforcer is a stimulus that ceases when the desired behavior is performed. See also punishment.

Relapse The reappearance of symptoms after a period of improvement but not a complete return to normalcy or after a brief remission or return to normalcy that is not sufficiently long to quality as a recovery.

Relapse prevention programs In treatment of alcohol problems from a cognitive viewpoint, the emphasis is on identifying problem situations and helping the client to identify coping devices that may give him or her a feeling of control over such situations.

Relational assessment Testing instruments to assess a person's key social relationships.

Relaxation training Series of specified exercises that the client learns to perform in order to remove a tension response that may be characteristic in certain situations.

Reliability The tendency of a measure or procedure to produce the same results when administered on two different occasions. Also refers to the internal homogeneity of a multiple-item test.

REM sleep Stage of sleep characterized by rapid eye movements and a characteristic brain-wave pattern. Reducing the amount of REM sleep can help decrease some types of depressive symptoms.

Remission The lessening of symptoms so that the person regains his or her normal state at least for a period of time. The term implies that the basic problem has not been cured but may still exist.

Representative sampling The selection of individuals from a larger population who as a group have the same distribution of the characteristic or characteristics under study as are found in the larger population. The selection of this kind of sample allows the researcher to make generalizations about the findings of a study that may apply to a broader group than only those people who actually participated in the study.

Repression Psychoanalytic defense mechanism that involves a "stopping-thinking" or "not-being-able-to-remember" response. Repression actively forces traumatic events, intolerable and dangerous impulses, and other undesirable mental affects out of consciousness into the less-accessible realm of the unconscious.

Residential facilities Sheltered settings where patients or former patients who are currently unable to live independently at that time may be provided with both psychological and practical assistance and support. Examples include group homes and halfway houses.

Residual symptoms Symptoms that remain after a person improves so that he or she no longer meets the criteria for a disorder. These symptoms may be less debilitating than originally in themselves or because they are not combined with other symptoms as formerly.

Resilience The ability to bounce back after stress. Capacity to function effectively in situations where others might develop maladaptive behavior.

Resilience The ability to recover quickly from an illness, change, or misfortune. Often used in connection with dealing with stressors.

Resolution phase The period after sexual orgasm in which the arousal decreases and the body's physiological status returns to normal.

Retardation, mental Level of intellectual functioning that is significantly below average and is accompanied by an inability to behave adaptively in society because of this lack of cognitive ability.

Retarded ejaculation Inhibition of the sexual response of males that results in an inability to eject semen even when sexually excited.

Rett's disorder A progressive disorder that begins only after apparently normal development in the first 5 months after birth. The head stops growing and the child loses skills and functions gained earlier. There is a progressive deterioration of the brain and nervous system.

Risk factor A personal characteristic that is correlated with some disorder. Indicates an increased probability that the person will develop a particular type of problem or illness. People with high risk factors are said to be especially vulnerable to a particular disorder.

Ritalin See methylphenidate.

Ritualistic behavior Behavior that follows a series of prescribed actions that are repeated even though they may be maladaptive. Thought to be a way of reducing anxiety.

Role playing In psychotherapy, a technique that requires an individual to enact a social role other than his or her own, or to try out new roles. In sociology, an individual's assumption of the role expected of him or her in a particular type of situation.

Rorschach inkblots Projective test developed by Hermann Rorschach in which the individual is shown a series of ambiguous inkblots and asked to describe what is seen in them.

Rubella virus Virus which, if present in a pregnant woman, particularly during the first 3 months of pregnancy, can cause retardation and other congenital disorders in her child; commonly called German measles.

Rumination disorder of infancy Disorder in which partially digested food is brought up into the infant's mouth without nausea or vomiting. The infant loses weight or fails to gain weight after a period of normal functioning.

Saccadic eye movement Quick jerks of the eye interspersed with steady fixations that are under voluntary control.

SAD See seasonal affective disorder.

Sadism Sexual deviation in which sexual gratification is obtained through inflicting physical pain on other people.

Sadist One who practices sadism.

Sadistic rape See rape.

Sampling The process by which cases or subjects are drawn from a larger population. If either by chance or the way in which they are selected, these cases do not have similar characteristics to the larger population, the results of research may not reflect the true relationships of variables in the entire group.

Savant abilities Areas of unusual talent in otherwise cognitively low functioning or retarded individuals.

Schedule of reinforcement The plan for delivery of some reinforcing object or event when a person makes a particular desired response. For instance this may be given each time the behavior occurs, on a regular schedule such as every fifth time it occurs, or intermittently, such as once during every group of five responses.

Schema See schemata.

Schemata   The plural of schema. Schemata are the expectations people have as to the way others behave and the appropriate behaviors for various types of situations. A person's schemata are important in addition to what actually occurred in determining the way that he or she will respond to particular types of situations.

Schizoaffective disorder   Separate category from either schizophrenia or affective disorders for individuals who show depressive or manic symptoms as well as those of thought disorder.

Schizoid personality disorder   Classification used for withdrawn individuals who are not disturbed by their lack of social relationships. These people have flat emotional responses and often seem cold and detached.

Schizophrenia   A member of the group of psychotic disorders. Of these disorders, schizophrenia is the most severe and debilitating.

Schizophrenia in remission   A lessening or disappearance of symptoms that had been apparent when the person was diagnosed as having a schizophrenic disorder. The term reflects the view that schizophrenia is a life-long disease for which there is no cure, only the possibility of at least temporarily reduced symptoms.

Schizophrenia, residual type   A diagnosis used for individuals who formerly met the criteria for schizophrenia but whose symptoms have lessened so they no longer have all the characteristics necessary for the diagnosis.

Schizophrenic spectrum disorder   A group of disorders including schizotypal and paranoid personality disorders, and sometimes schizoaffective disorder, atypical psychosis, and paranoid disorder, which are thought by some researchers to be produced by the same genetic factors as schizophrenia. Used as an explanation for the fact that the incidence of narrowly defined schizophrenia alone is less than would be expected by monogenetic theory.

Schizotypal personality disorder   Shows some of the symptoms of schizophrenia, but not in as extreme a form. People with this disorder include those formerly diagnosed as having simple schizophrenia. Differs from schizoid personality disorder in that it includes eccentricities of communication and behavior not seen in that group.

Scopophyllia   See voyeurism.

Seasonal affective disorder (SAD)   A form of affective disorder in which depression is more likely to occur in winter when the hours of natural light are limited and mania is more likely to occur in spring and summer when the number of hours of daylight are at a maximum. Depression of this type is often treated with phototherapy (the use of bright lighting).

Secondary appraisal   Second stage of appraisal of a situation in which an individual considers the kind of action necessary and whether he or she has the skills to deal with the situation.

Secondary prevention   Efforts directed toward detecting early signs or symptoms to prevent a more serious condition.

Secondary process thinking   Psychoanalytic concept referring to organized, logical, and reality-oriented adult thinking. Whereas primary process thinking is characteristic of the id and is based on the pleasure principle, secondary process thought is an ego function based on the reality principle.

Selective amnesia   See amnestic disorders.

Selective serotonin receptive inhibitors (SSRIs)   A category of antidepressant drugs that have somewhat fewer side effects than the tricyclic group.

Self-actualization   Synonymous with self-fulfillment. Process by which the development of one's potentials and abilities is achieved.

Self-efficacy   The concept, originated by Albert Bandura, that beliefs about personal efficacy or ability to successfully carry out a task are important determinants in whether it will be attempted and completed successfully.

Self-help group   A group of people with the same problem who meet together to share experiences and ways to handle situations in an attempt to help themselves improve their own ability to cope with these problems.

Self-monitoring   Keeping detailed records of one's behavior.

Self-observations   Records kept by the client or patient that detail the frequency of certain specified types of behavior and usually include any specific environmental factors or personal thoughts that occurred just before, during, or after the behavior.

Self-psychology   A theory developed by Kohut that considers the individual's self-concept as the central organizing factor in psychological development.

Self-regulation   Technique of controlling one's own behavior through internal reinforcement often in the form of cognitions.

Senile dementia   See dementia.

Sensate focus   Approach to sex therapy advocated by Masters and Johnson in which an individual learns to focus on erotic sensation to the exclusion of other stimuli.

Sensitive periods   The periods of development in which a particular brain circuit can change or in which specific types of learning are possible.

Sensorimotor   Pertaining to the functions of the sensing and motor activities of the individual—for example, the sensorimotor nerves.

Sentence completion test   Projective test in which the client is presented with a series of incomplete sentences and is asked to complete each one.

Separation anxiety disorder   Some children's irrational fear of being apart from the parent(s) because of worries of what will happen to themselves or to their parent(s) in their absence.

Serotonin (5-hydroxytryptamine or 5HT)   One of a group of chemical neurotransmitters that implement neural transmission across the synapse. Thought to be involved in some types of depression.

Sex offenders   Term used for individuals who come into contact with the legal system because of their practice of sexual deviations that are prohibited by law.

Sex-reassignment surgery   Surgery in which male or female genital organs are removed and facsimiles of genital organs of the opposite sex are created. Surgery is usually combined with hormone treatment to modify secondary sexual characteristics.

Sexual arousal   State characterized by both swelling of the external genital organs and subjective feelings of pleasurable excitement.

Sexual desire   The complex result of physiological, cognitive, and behavioral factors as they are shaped by developmental and cultural factors.

Sexual disorders   Includes two types—paraphilias and sexual dysfunction. The first relates to obtaining sexual satisfaction through inappropriate partners or activities. The second is the inability to carry out normal sexual activities because of physiological difficulties thought to have psychological causes.

Sexual dysfunction   Problems in one or more phases of sexual intercourse that decrease the pleasure derived by the participants or make successful culmination impossible.

Sexual victimization   Acts based on a deviant sexual preference that negatively impact other individuals and the community and may include unlawful acts.

Shaman   Inspired priest or medium who can summon up and communicate with good and evil spirits.

Shaping   Basic process of operant conditioning involving the reinforcement of successively closer approximations to a desired behavior.

Shared psychotic disorder   A disorder in which delusions seem to have been transferred to the patient from another person who is usually a close relative of the patient. Sometimes referred to as folie a deux.

Sheltered workshops   Organizations, often run by charitable groups, that provide job training and experience and sometimes long term jobs for those unable to compete in the marketplace because of physical or mental disability.

Simple phobia   Relatively rare type of phobia that involves irrational fear not related to either unfamiliar situations or social interactions; for example, fear of shut-in places (claustrophobia) or fear of specific animals.

Single photon emission computed tomography (SPECT)   An imaging technique that measures cerebral blood flow and neurochemical changes that occur with different types of brain activity.

Situation-focused prevention   Actions to prevent maladaptive behavior through changing aspects of the environment. For example, providing after-school activities to keep children off the street or changing to non-leaded paint as a way to prevent children from ingesting lead and possibly developing retardation.

Sleep apnea   Breathing disruptions during sleep that may last from 10 to 30 seconds.

Sleep disorders   Disorders characterized either by problems with the amount, quality, and timing of sleep, or by abnormal events occurring during sleep such as night terrors or sleepwalking.

Sleep paralysis   A symptom of narcolepsy in which the person affected cannot move or speak for a period of time after awakening.

Sleep spindles   Rapid bursts of brain waves that occur during stage 2 sleep.

Sleep-terror disorder   Sleep terrors tend to occur during the early stages of sleep. They are not recalled as part of a dream but tend to produce partial awakening and a light level of autonomic nervous system activation . See also parasomnias.

Sleepwalking disorder   Routine motor behaviors involving rising from bed and walking that usally occur in the first part of the sleep cycle. See also parasomnias.

Smooth pursuit eye movements   Type of essentially involuntary movement that occurs when an individual visually follows the movements of a rhythmically moving object such as a pendulum.

Social causation theory   Theory that maladaptive behavior is a result of poor economic circumstances, poor housing, and inadequate social services.

Social facilitation   Acquisition of social competence skills through observing the behavior of others.

Social intervention   Treatment approach that involves not only interacting with the client but also attempting to modify the client's environment at home or at work.

Social learning theories   Refers to several similar theoretical viewpoints which hold that social behavior and inner thoughts and feelings are learned through social interactions.

Social phobia   Type of irrational fear of situations in which a person will be exposed to the scrutiny of others. Most common types are fear of blushing, public speaking, eating in public, writing in public, and using public toilet facilities.

Social roles   The function a particular person plays in society, which is determined by the particular role he or she fills. Most people have a variety of overlapping social roles, such as an occupational role, several family roles, and perhaps some recreational roles as well.

Social selection theory   Idea that the lower socioeconomic class contains many people who drifted there from higher classes because of their poor functioning. Higher incidence of maladaptive behavior in the lower class is explained in this way.

Social skills training   Behavioral or cognitive-behavioral therapeutic approach that emphasizes learning more effective ways of interacting with other people in a variety of situations.

Social support   The positive aspects of interpersonal ties that assist in coping and promote both physical and mental health.

Somatic system   Part of the peripheral nervous system that sends nerve impulses from the sense organs to the muscles that determine voluntary movement.

Somatic therapy   Treatment, such as drugs, surgery, or electroconvulsive therapy, that directly affects a person's physical state.

Somatization disorders (Briquet's syndrome)   Disorders characterized by a variety of dramatic but vague complaints that are often chronic and which have no discernible physical cause.

Somatoform disorders   Characterized by physical symptoms that suggest a physical disorder but for which there are (1) no organic findings to explain the symptom and (2) strong evidence or suggestion that the symptoms are linked to psychological factors or conflicts; formerly called hysterical neurosis or conversion reaction.

Specific phobias   Persistent irrational fears associated with a particular type of object (for instance spiders or dogs) or situation (for instance, being in a closed area or high place).

SPECT   See Single photon emission computed tomography.

Spectrum concept   The idea that several differently classified disorders may be caused by the same general genetic pattern. These disorders are then considered genetically related.

Splitting   Term used to describe the inability of the borderline individual to integrate the positive and negative experiences he or she has with another individual into a coherent relationship. A term used by object relations theorists.

Spontaneous remission   Disappearance of symptoms or maladaptive behavior in the absence of therapeutic intervention.

Spouse abuse   Physical harm done to wives or husbands by their marital partners. Physical assaults by husbands on wives are most common. Abuse may also be psychological.

Squeeze technique   Technique used in sex therapy to assist the male in retarding ejaculation by gently squeezing the end of the penis when ejaculation is imminent.

SSRI   See selective serotonin receptive inhibitors.

Standard deviation   A statistical measure of variability which reflects the size of the deviation of each of the scores in the distribution from the group mean. When a normal curve is considered, each standard deviation contains a known proportion of the total number of cases in the distribution.

Standardized interview   See structured interview.

Stanford-Binet   Modification of the Binet test developed at Stanford University by Louis Terman.

Statutory rape   Crime defined as having sexual intercourse with someone below the age of legal consent. Force is not necessarily involved.

Stereotypy   Development of a ritualized or highly repetitive behavior. Sometimes seen as a result of stress or of the use of certain drugs such as amphetamines.

Stigma   In medicine a mark indicating a history or disease or abnormality. In general some characteristic that leads to disgrace, reproach, or discrimination by others.

STP (2, 5 dimethoxy-4-methyl amphetamine)   Hallucinogenic agent similar to LSD.

Straight jacket   Confining garment used to bind the arms tightly against the body. Often used for violent patients.

Stress   Feeling or reaction individuals have when faced with a situation that demands action from them, especially action that may be beyond their capabilities.

Stressor   Source of stress, pressure, or strain. Something that upsets the equilibrium of an organism.

Stroke   See cerebrovascular accident.

Stroop effect   The greater difficulty in ignoring words and attending to color on the Stroop task than the reverse.

Stroop Task   A measure of selective attention in which color names are presented written either in black or the color named or written in a color of ink unlike the color named. The Stroop effect measures the relative difficulty or reaction time when the subject is asked to ignore the word versus ignore the color. Those with schizophrenic disorder show a greater Stroop effect than do nonpatient controls.

Structured Clinical Interview for DSM (SCID)   A diagnostic interview that is less structured than the widely used Diagnostic Interview Schedule (DIS). The SCID allows the interviewer to ask follow-up questions based on clinical judgment.

Structured interview   Also called a standardized interview. An interview procedure in which the interviewer is given a set of instructions that includes definitions of symptoms, numerical ratings for different symptom severities, a series of questions related to each type of symptom, a set of topics to be covered, and information about how extensively the interviewer is to probe for information about each type of question. The interviewer is allowed flexibility in ordering of the questions.

Sublimation   Defense mechanism and developmental concept which involves the refinement or redirection of undesirable impulses into new and more socially acceptable channels. Whereas displacement involves an alteration in choice of object, sublimation alters both the aim (unacceptable drive) and the object to a socially acceptable ones.

Substance abuse   Use of a psychoactive substance to the degree that a severe and long-lasting impairment in function results.

Substance dependence   A pattern of substance use that leads to clinically significant impairment or distress that includes cognitive, behavioral, and physiological symptoms.

Substance induced disorders   A variety of symptoms including delerium and psychotic behavior that are similar to those of other mental disorders but are related to abuse of psychoactive substances.

Substance intoxication   The distinctive but reversible effects of the ingestion or exposure to certain substances as a result of their effect on the central nervous system. Common effects include disturbances in perception, wakefulness, attention, thinking, judgment, motor behavior, and interpersonal behavior.

Substance-related disorders   This category consists of two subgroups, substance dependence and substance abuse. Both include problems associated with using and abusing alcohol and illegal drugs.

Sulci (singular: sulcus)   Shallow valleys on the surface of the brain separating the convolutions.

Superego   Structure of the psyche in psychoanalytic theory which is developed by internalization of parental standards and by identification with parents. Contains two parts: the ego-ideal and the conscience. The ego-ideal represents the total of positive identifications with accepting and loving parents and desired standards of excellence and good conduct. The conscience includes those attitudes and values which are moralistic (good-bad) in nature.

Support group   Group of individuals with the same or similar problems who meet to discuss their problems and how to deal with them.

Supportive therapy   Brief form of psychotherapy in which the therapist provides acceptance for the patient and affords him or her some opportunity to be dependent.

Survival guilt   Feeling that it is unfair to be alive when others in the same situation have died. Overwhelming feelings of guilt, unworthiness, and helplessness.

Symbolic modeling   Learning through watching film or videotaped sequences of someone performing the act or acts to be learned or alternately learning appropriate responses through listening to audiotapes or reading text.

Symptom disorders   Disorders diagnosed on Axis I of the Diagnostic and Statistical Manual. These disorders have symptoms that may come and go unlike the disorders diagnosed on Axis II which generally continue throughout life.

Synapse   Point at which a nerve impulse passes from an axon of one neuron to the dendrite of another neuron.

Synaptic pruning   The developmental process in whch neurons selectively reduce the number of branches in their dendrites. Abnormal pruning can result in problems in cognitive function.

Synaptic vesicle   Container on the axon terminal button that serves as a storage point for a chemical neurotransmitter.

Syndrome   A group of symptoms that often appear together.

Syphilitic infection   Chronic infectious venereal disease, transmitted through direct contact, caused by a spirochete, Trepenema pallidum.

Systematic desensitization   Learning-theory-based therapeutic technique in which a client is first trained in muscle relaxation and then imagines a series of increasingly anxiety-provoking situations until he or she no longer experiences anxiety while thinking about the stimuli. Learning principle involved is reciprocal inhibition, according to which two incompatible responses (e.g., anxiety and relaxation) cannot be made simultaneously by one person.

Systematized amnesia   See amnestic disorders.

Tarantism   Uncontrollable urge to dance, originally believed to be the result of the bite of a tarantula. Frequently observed in Southern Italy from the fifteenth to seventeenth centuries.

Tardive dyskinesia   Disorder involving uncontrolled body movements, often of the lips and tongue, that may result from treatment with antipsychotic drugs.

TAT   See Thematic Apperception Test.

Tay-Sachs disease   Inherited metabolic disorder, inevitably fatal, that causes progressive deterioration of the nervous system.

Technique factors (in therapy)   The particular procedures used by a therapist in treating a client. Distinguished from the effects of the therapist's personality on the treatment.

Temperament   The general nature of a person consistent across time and situations that is thought to arise from constitutional factors present at birth.

Temporal lobe   Part of the cerebral hemisphere lying behind the temples and below the lateral fissure in front of the occipital lobe.

Tension headache   Probably the most common form of headache; characterized by bandlike pains and tender scalp. Gradual in onset and often long lasting. Thought to be a result of stress.

Tertiary prevention   Efforts aimed at reducing the impairment that may result from a given disorder.

Test anxiety   Unusually apprehensive response to evaluative situations. Often a factor in poor performance because of worry and interfering thoughts.

THC (tetrahydrocannabinol)   Major active ingredient in marijuana.

Thematic Apperception Test (TAT)   Projective test consisting of somewhat ambiguous pictures. Subject is asked to tell a story about each picture. From these stories personality dynamics are inferred.

Theoretical perspective   The particular set of beliefs or ideas that determine what people notice in behavior, how they interpret what they observe, and how they believe problems should be approached.

Theory of mind   The ability to engage in abstract or symbolic thinking including the ability to infer the mental states of others. This ability is lacking or greatly diminished in autistic disorder.

Therapeutic interview   Interaction between a client and therapist although perhaps including other family members as well. Designed to help promote change in behavior and attitudes. Another term for a therapy session.

Thorazine   Trade name for chlorpromazine, one of a group of tranquilizing drugs used in the treatment of schizophrenia.

Thought stopping   A cognitive technique that uses a specific command as a distraction to end a period of obsessive thinking.

Thyroid glands   Ductless glands that are part of the endocrine system.

Tics   Involuntary, repetitive, rapid muscle contractions often occurring in the face. Thought to be related to tension and anxiety.

Token economy   An application of the principles of operant conditioning to the modification of maladaptive behavior. Reward tokens that can later be exchanged for desired items or privileges are given whenever the subject or patient behaves in the desired way.

Tolerance (drug)   Condition in which an individual must use increasing doses of a substance to produce the same physiological effect.

Tonic phase   Phase of seizure in which the body is extended and stiff and during which reflexes to light and to pressure on the cornea are absent. See also clonic phase.

Tourette's disorder   A disorder usually diagnosed in childhood in which the symptoms are multiple motor tics and one or more vocal tics. These tics occur many times a day and occur for a period of at least one year.

Tranquilizing drugs   Drugs (for example, of the chlorpromazine and phenothiazine families) which are used to reduce agitation and anxiety. Drug action inhibits the activities of the hypothalamus.

Transdermal nicotine patch   A multilayered pad applied to the skin with adhesive that allows gradual absorption by the body of medication or chemicals over a prolonged period. Often used to administer decreasing amounts of nicotine to individuals who are attempting to stop cigarette smoking.

Transference   Psychoanalytic term that refers to the displacement of affect from one person to another. Patterns of feelings and behavior originally experienced with significant figures in childhood are displaced or attached to individuals in one's current relationships (e.g., a psychotherapist). Current person is reacted to as if he or she were some significant other from the respondent's past. Transference reactions may be positive or negative.

Translocation   The breaking off of a piece of one chromosome and the attachment of that piece to another chromosome. May result in the transmission of too much genetic material to the child of a person with a translocation.

Transsexualism   Intense desire or need to change one's sexual status, including anatomical structure.

Transvestic fetishism   Sexual deviation in which an individual derives gratification from wearing the clothing of the opposite sex.

Traumatic neurosis   Psychological symptoms that occur after a traumatic event but which are not a direct result of physical injury.

Trephination   Process of making a circular hole in the skull. In early times this was done to allow evil spirits to escape.

Tricyclic antidepressants   Group of drugs used to treat depression. An example is imipramine. Common trade names of tricyclic drugs are Tofranil and Elavil.

Trisomy   Occurrence in an individual of three chromosomes of one kind rather than the usual pair. Usually associated with an abnormality of some type.

Trisomy 21   See Down syndrome.

Tuberous sclerosis   Disorder caused by a dominant gene and characterized by severe retardation, seizures, and the appearance of small, fibrous tumors.

Twin studies   The study of the relative contributions of heredity and environmental factors to various disorders by contrasting the likelihood that the disorder will occur in two types of twins, monogygotic (MZ) twins who have identical genetic inheritance and dizygotic (DZ) twins who share only an average of 50% of their genetic inheritance.

Type A Personality   A behavior pattern characterized by extremes of competitiveness, striving for achievement, restlessness, hyper-alertness, explosiveness of speech, tenseness of facial muscles, and feelings of being under pressure of time and of bearing excess responsibility that is associated with a high risk of coronary heart disease.

Type B Personalities   A behavior pattern characterized by the opposite extremes of the behavior of a Type A personality, thought to be at low risk for coronary heart disease.

Ultrasound scanning technique   The use of sound waves to produce a visual image of a fetus or of the form and action of body organs. Also called sonogram.

Unauthentic behavior   According to existentialist theory, that behavior governed not by an individual's desire but by the desires of other people.

Unconditional positive regard   Term used by Carl Rogers to emphasize the importance of a therapist's unqualified acceptance of a client as a person of worth.

Unconditioned response (UCR or UR)   In classical conditioning, the response that occurs automatically, before training, when the unconditioned stimulus is presented.

Unconditioned stimulus (UCS or US)   In classical conditioning, the stimulus that automatically elicits the desired response before training has taken place.

Unconscious   Out of awareness; mental contents that can be brought to awareness only with great difficulty (or not at all).

Undoing   Defense mechanism aimed at negating or atoning for some disapproved impulse or act.

Unipolar disorder   Term for an affective disorder in which only depression occurs and there is no history of episodes of mania.

Vaginismus (functional)   Type of sexual dysfunction in women in which an involuntary spasm of the muscles of the outer third of the vagina interferes with sexual activity.

Validity   In statistics, the extent to which a test measures what it is intended to or purports to measure.

Validity, external   An experimental situation that is perceived to relate closely to a real world situation.

Validity, internal   A situation where the results of an experiment can be correctly attributed to the experimental manipulation and not to external factors because the study was well controlled.

Valium   One of the minor tranquilizing drugs often prescribed to reduce anxiety.

Valproic acid   A mood stabilizer used to treat bipolar disorder.

Vascular dementia   The deficits in intellectual function that may result from a series of minor strokes occurring over a period of time. Also called multi-infarct dementia.

Venereal disease   Contagious disease (for example, syphilis or gonorrhea) contracted through sexual intercourse.

Ventricles   System of communicating cavities in the brain that are linked with the central canal of the spinal cord.

Verbal IQ   One of the two subscores of the Wechsler intelligence test series. Tests reflect general information or knowledge and the ability to make abstractions.

Vesicle   Storage area in the nerve endings that holds neurotransmitter chemicals.

Vicarious learning   Learning that occurs merely by watching the behavior of others.

Virtual reality exposure therapy   Use of an optical helmet with a wrap-around visor on which a computer generated visual field appears. The feared stimulus can be projected with increasing accuracy and may include associated sounds and the sensation of manipulating the objects.

Visual analogue scales (VAS)   A type of rating scale used to assess a variety of subjective phenomena by using portions of a line to represent a personal perception of the phenomena.

Voyeurism (scopophilia)   Attaining sexual gratification from observing the sexual behavior of others. Synonymous with peeping tomism.

Vulnerability   Conditions, either internal or external, that make a person more likely to be affected adversely by stress. Factors include heredity, personality, lack of coping skills, previous negative life events, and some negative environmental factors.

WAIS   See Wechsler Adult Intelligence Scale.

Wechsler Adult Intelligence Scale (WAIS-R)   A widely used individually administered intelligence test for those over 16 years of age. A series of subtests of different types yield a Verbal IQ, Performance IQ, and Full Scale IQ.

Wechsler Intelligence Scale for Children (WISC-III)   Intended for children between ages 6 and 16. Uses the same general format as the Wechsler Adult Intelligence Scale and provides Verbal, Performance, and Full Scale IQs.

Wechsler Preschool and Primary Scale of Intelligence (WPPSI)   Intended for children between ages 3 and 7. Uses the same general format as the Wechsler Adult Intelligence Scale and provides Verbal, Performance, and Full Scale IQs.

Werther effect   Term to describe suicides that seem triggered by the suicide of a well-known person.

WISC   See Wechsler Intelligence Scale for Children.

Withdrawal   Physiological changes, varying from mild to extremely unpleasant, that take place after an individual's discontinuation of a habit-forming substance. The symptoms of heroin withdrawal are perhaps best known.

Word association test   Projective technique in which a list of words is presented one by one. Client is asked to respond to each item with the first word that comes to mind.

WPPSI   See Wechsler Preschool and Primary Scale of Intelligence.

X-linked dominance   Genes carried on the X sex chromosome that determine a characteristic by their presence. Females have two X chromosomes. Males have one X and one Y chromosome. This means that characteristics that are a result of X-linked dominance can occur in males only through inheritance from the mother. In females these characteristics can be inherited from either parent.

References

Abbey, A. (1991). Acquaintance rape and alcohol consumption on college campuses: How are they linked? *Journal of American College Health, 39*, 165-169.

Abel, E. L. (1995). An update on incidence of FAS: FAS is not an equal opportunity birth defect. *Neurotoxicology and Teratology, 17*, 437-443.

Abel, G., Becker, J., & Cunningham-Rathner, J. (1988). Multiple paraphiliac diagnoses among sex offenders. *Bulletin of the American Academy of Psychiatry and the Law, 16*, 153-168.

Abraham, K. (1968). Notes on the psychoanalytic investigation and treatment of manic-depressive insanity and allied conditions (1911). In K. Abraham, *Selected papers of Karl Abraham*. New York: Basic Books.

Abraham, S. (1996). Characteristics of eating disorders among young ballet dancers. *Psychopathology, 29*, 223-229.

Abrams, S. (1973). The polygraph in a psychiatric setting. *American Journal of Psychiatry, 130*, 94-98.

Abramson, L. Y., Metalsky, G. I., & Alloy, L. B. (1989). Hopelessness depression: A theory-based subtype of depression. *Psychological Review, 96*, 358-372.

Abuse, E. E. (1995). Resilience in development. *Current Directions in Psychological Science, 4*, 81-85.

Acierno, R. E., Hersen, M., & Van Hasselt, V. B. (1993). Interventions for panic disorder: A critical review of the literature. *Clinical Psychology Review, 13*, 561-578.

Adamson, J. (1989). An appraisal of the DSM-III system. *Canadian Journal of Psychiatry, 34*, 303-310.

Adler, G., & Buie, D. (1979). Aloneness and borderline psychopathology: The possible relevance of child development issues. *International Journal of Psychoanalysis, 60*, 83-96.

Agency for Health Care Policy and Research (1999). Treatment of depression: Newer pharmacotherapies. *Evidence Report/Technology Assessment Number 7*. Rockville, MD: US Dept of Health and Human Services.

Agras, W. S., Rossiter, E. M., Arnow, B., Telch, C. F., Raeburn, S. D., Bruce, B., & Koran, L. M. (1994). One-year follow-up of psychosocial and pharmacologic treatments for bulimia nervosa. *Journal of Clinical Psychiatry, 55*, 179-183.

Agras, W. S., Taylor, O. B., Kraemer, H. C., Allen, R. A., & Schneider, M. S. (1980). Relaxation training: Twenty-four hour blood pressure reductions. *Archives of General Psychiatry, 37*, 859-863.

Agras, W. S., Telch, C. F., Arnow, B., Eldredge, K., et al. (1997). One-year follow-up of cognitive-behavioral therapy for obese individuals with binge eating disorder. *Journal of Consulting and Clinical Psychology, 65*, 343-347.

Akbarian, S., Kim, J. J., Potkin, S. G., Hetrick, W. P, Bunney, W. E., & Jones, E. G. (1996). Maldistribution of interstitial neurons in prefrontal white matter of the brains of schizophrenic patients. *Archives of General Psychiatry, 53*, 425-436.

Akiskal, H. S., Maser, J. D., Zeller, P. J., Endicott, J., Coryell, W., Keller, M., Warshaw, M., Clayton, P., & Goodwin, F. (1995). Switching from unipolar to bipolar II. An 11 year prospective study of clinical and temperamental predictors in 559 patients. *Archives of General Psychiatry, 52*, 114-123.

Alcohol and Health (1990). Rockville, MD: National Institute of Alcohol Abuse and Alcoholism.

Alford, B. A., Beck, A. T., Freeman, A., & Wright, F. D. (1990). Brief focused cognitive therapy of panic disorder. *Psychotherapy, 27*, 230-234.

Alloy, L. B., Abramson, L. Y., Whitehouse, W. G., Hogan, M. E., Tashman, No A., Steinberg, D. I., Rose, D. T., & Donovan, P. (1999). Depressogenic cognitivestyles: Predictive validity, information processing and personality characteristics, and developmental origins. *Behavior Research and Therapy, 37*, 503-531.

Alnaes, R., & Torgersen, S. (1993). Mood disorders: Developmental and precipitating events. *Canadian Journal of Psychiatry, 38*, 217-224.

Aman, M. G. van Bourgondien, M. E., Wolford, P. L., & Sarphare, G. (1995). Psychotropic and anticonvulsant drugs in subjects with autism: Prevalence and patterns of use. *Journal of the American Academy of Child and Adolescent Psychiatry, 34*, 1672-1681.

Ambelas, A. (1987). Life events and mania: A special relationship. *British Journal of Psychiatry, 150*, 235-240.

American Law Institute. (1962). *Model penal code: Proposed official draft*. Philadelphia: American Law Institute.

American Psychiatric Association (1994). *Diagnostic and Statistical Manual of Mental Disorders* (4th ed.) (DSM-IV.). Washington, DC: American Psychiatric Association.

American Psychiatric Association (2000). *Diagnostic and statistical manual of mental disorders* (DSM-IV) (4th ed., textual revisions). Washington, DC: American Psychiatric Association.

American Psychiatric Association. (1993). Practice guideline for treatment of major depressive disorder in adults. *American Journal of Psychiatry, 150*, 1-26.

American Psychological Association (1996). Practitioner Survey results offer comprehensive view of psychology practice. *Practitioner Update, 4*, 24.

Amminger, G. P., Pape, S., Rock, D., Roberts, S. A., Ott, S. L., Squires-Wheeler, E., Kestenbaum, C., Erlenmeyer-Kimlong, L. (1999). Relationship betweenchild-hood behavioral disturbance and later schizophrenia in the New York High-Risk Project. *American Journal of Psychiatry, 156*, 525-530.

Anderson, D. J., Noyes, R., Jr., & Crowe, R. R. (1984). A comparison of panic disorder and generalized anxiety disorder. *American Journal of Psychiatry, 141*, 572-575.

Anderson, E. A. (1987). Preoperative preparation for cardiac surgery facilitates recovery, reduces psychological distress, and reduces the incidence of acute postoperative hypertension. *Journal of Consulting and Clinical Psychology, 55*, 513-520.

Andolfi, M. (1983). *Behind the family mask: therapeutic change in rigid family systems*. Translated by C. L. Chodorkoff. New York, Brunner/Mazel.

Andreasen, N. C. (1997). Linking mind and body in the study of mental illness: A project for a scientific psychopathology. *Science, 275*, 1586-1593.

Andreasen, N. C., Arndt, S., Alliger, R., Miller, D., & Flaum, M., (1995). Symptoms of schizophrenia: Methods, meanings, and mechanisms. *Archives of General Psychiatry, 52*, 341-351.

Andreasen, N. C., & Grove, W. M. (1986). Thought, language, and communication in schizophrenia: Diagnosis and prognosis. *Schizophrenia Bulletin, 12*, 348-359.

Anfang, S. A., & Appelbaum, P. S. (1996). Twenty years after Tarasoff: Reviewing the duty to protect. *Harvard Review of Psychiatry, 4*, 67-76.

Angst, J., Angst, F., & Stassen, H. H. (1999). Suicide risk in patients with major depressive disorder. *Journal of Clinical Psychiatry, 60* (Suppl. 2), 57-62.

Anonymous. (1977). Psychosocial implications of schizophrenic diagnoses (personal account). *Schizophrenia Bulletin, 3*, 4(b).

Appelbaum, P. S. (1991). What are the current standards for involuntary commitment to a mental hospital? *Harvard Mental Health Letter, 7* (11), 8.

Aronow, E., & Resnikoff, M. (1976). *Rorschach content interpretation*. Orlando, FL: Grune & Stratton.

Aronson, T. A., & Shukla, S. (1987). Life events and relapse in bipolar disorder. The impact of a catastrophic event. *Acta Psychiatrica Scandinavica, 57*, 571-576.

Asaad, G., & Shapiro, B. (1986). Hallucinations: Theoretical and clinical overview. *American Journal of Psychiatry, 143*, 1088-1097.

August, G. J., Realmuto, G. M., Joyce, T., Hektner, J. M. (1999) Persistence and desistance of oppositional defiant disorder in a community sample of children withADHD. *Journal of the American Academy of Child and Adolescent Psychiatry, 38*, 1262-1270.

Austin, S.B. (1999). Fat, loathing and public health: The complicity of science in a culture of disordered eating. *Culture, Medicine, and Psychiatry, 23*, 245-268.

Avlund, K., Damsgaard, M.T., & Holstein, B.E. (1998). Social relations and mortality: An eleven year follow-up study of 70-year-old men and women in Denmark. *Social Science and Medicine, 47*, 635-643.

Ayres, W. H. (1994). Foreword. In I. A. Canino & J. Spurlock, *Culturally diverse children and adolescents: Assessment, diagnosis, and treatment* (pp. Vi-Vii). New York: Guilford.

Bachman, J. G., Wadsworth, K. N., O'Malley, P. M., Johnston, L. D., & Schulenberg, J. E. (1997). *Smoking, drinking and drug use in young adulthood: The impacts of new freedoms and new responsibilities*. Mahwah, NJ.: Lawrence Erlbaum Associates.

Bailey, J. M., & Pillard, R. C. (1991). A genetic study of male sexual orientation. *Archives of General Psychiatry, 48*, 1089-1096.

Baird, P. C., & Baird, M. S. (1996). "Echoes from a dungeon cell": A doctor's view of his incarceration. *Psychiatric Services, 47*, 581-582.

Baker, L., & Cantwell, D. P. (1987). A prospective psychiatric follow-up of children with speech/language disorders. *Journal of the American Academy of Child and Adolescent Psychiatry, 26*, 546-553.

Bandura, A. (1978). The self-system in reciprocal determinism. *American Psychologist, 33*, 344-358.

Bandura, A. (1981). Cultivating competence, self-efficacy, and intrinsic interest through proximal self-motivation. *Journal of Personality and Social Psychology, 41*, 586-598.

Bandura, A. (1986). *Social foundations of thought and action: A social cognitive theory*. Englewood Cliffs, NJ: Prentice Hall.

Bandura, A. (1997). *Self-efficacy: The exercise of control*. NY: Freeman.

Bandura, A., & Menlove, F. L. (1968). Factors determining vicarious extinction of avoidance behavior through symbolic modeling. *Journal of Personality and Social Psychology, 8*, 99-108.

Bandura, A., & Schunk, D. H. (1981). Cultivating competence, self-efficacy, and intrinsic interest through proximal self-motivation. *Journal of Personality & Social Psychology, 41*, 586-598.

Barbee, J. G. (1998). Mixed symptoms and syndromes of anxiety and depression: Diagnostic, prognostic, and etiologic issues. *Annals of Clinical Psychiatry, 10*, 15-29.

Barefoot, J. C., Peterson, B. L., Dahlstrom, W. G., Siegler, I. C., Anderson, N. B., & Williams, R. B., Jr. (1991). Hostility patterns and health implications:

Correlates of Cook-Medley Hostility Scale scores in a national survey. *Health Psychology, 10,* 18-24.

Barefoot, J. C., Siegler, I. C., Nowling, J. B., Peterson, B. L., Haney, T. L., & Williams, R. B., Jr. (1987). Suspiciousness, health, and mortality: A follow-up study of 500 older adults. *Psychosomatic Medicine, 49,* 450-457.

Barefoot, J.C., Maynard, K.E., Beckham, J.C., Brummett, B.H., Hooker, K., & Siegler, I.C. (1998). Trust, health, and longevity. *Journal of Behavioral Medicine, 21,* 517-526.

Barker, D. A. Sukhwinder, S. S., Higginson, I., & Orrell, M. W. (1996). Patients' views towards care received from psychiatrists. *British Journal of Psychiatry, 168,* 641-646.

Barlow, D. H., Brown, T. A., & Craske, M. G. (1994). Definitions of panic attacks and panic disorder in the DSM-IV: Implications for research. *Journal of Abnormal Psychology, 103,* 553-564.

Barlow, D. H., Craske, M. G., Cerny, J. A., & Klosko, J. S. (1989). Behavioral treatment of panic disorder. *Behavior Therapy, 20,* 261-282.

Baron, M., & Risch, N. (1987). The spectrum concept of schizophrenia: Evidence for a genetic-environmental continuum. *Journal of Psychiatric Research, 21,* 257-267.

Baron, M., Gruen, R. S., & Romo-Gruen, J. M. (1992). Positive and negative symptoms: Relation to familial transmission of schizophrenia. *British Journal of Psychiatry, 161,* 610-614.

Baron-Cohen, S. (1995). *Mindblindness: an essay on autism and theory of mind.* Cambridge, MA: MIT Press.

Baron-Cohen, S., & Hammer, J. (1997). Parents of children with Asperger syndrome: What is the cognitive phenotype? *Journal of Cognitive Neuroscience, 9,* 548-554.

Baron-Cohen, S., Leslie, A. M., & Frith, U. (1985). Does the autistic child have a 'theory of mind'? *Cognition, 21,* 37-46.

Barrett, P. M., Dadds, M. R., & Rapee, R. M. (1996). Family treatment of childhood anxiety: A controlled trial. *Journal of Consulting and Clinical Psychology, 64,* 333-342.

Bartholomew, R.E. (2000). Epidemic hysteria: A review of the published literature. *American Journal of Epidemiology, 151,* 206-207.

Bartrop, R. W., Luckhurst, E., Lazarus, L., Kiloh, L. G., & Penny, R. (1977). Depressed lymphocyte function after bereavement. *Lancet, 1,* 834-836.

Baumeister, R. F. (1990). Suicide as escape from self. *Psychological Review, 99,* 90-113.

Bauminger, N., & Kasari, C. (2000). Loneliness and friendship in high functioning children with autism. *Child Development, 71,* 447-456.

Beardslee, W. R., Salt, P., Versage, E. M., Gladstone, T. R., Wright, E. J., & Rothberg, P. C. (1997). Sustained change in parents receiving preventive interventions for families with depression. *American Journal of Psychiatry, 154,* 510-515.

Beaumont, J. (2000). Antipsychotics—The future of schizophrenia treatment. *Current Medical Research and Opinion, 16,* 37-42.

Bebbington, P.E. (1998). Epidemiology of obsessive-compulsive disorder. *British Journal of Psychiatry, 173,* 2-6.

Beck, A. T. (1967). *Depression: Clinical, experimental and theoretical aspects.* New York: Hoeber.

Beck, A. T. (1970). Role of fantasies in psychotherapy and psychopathology. *Journal of Nervous and Mental Disease, 150,* 3-17.

Beck, A. T. (1976). *Cognitive therapy and the emotional disorders.* New York: International Universities Press.

Beck, A. T. (1979). *Cognitive therapy of depression.* NY: Guilford.

Beck, A. T. (1997). Interview. *Cognitive Therapy Today, 2,* 1-3.

Beck, A. T., & Emery, G. (1985). *Anxiety disorders and phobias: A cognitive perspective.* New York: Basic Books.

Beck, A. T., Brown, G., Steer, R. A., Eidelson, J. L., & Riskind, J. H. (1987). Differentiating anxiety and depression: A test of the cognitive content-specificity hypothesis. *Journal of Abnormal Psychology, 96,* 179-183.

Beck, A. T., Freeman, A., & Associates (1990). *Cognitive therapy of personality disorders.* New York: Guilford.

Beck, A. T., Steer, R. A., Kovacs, M., & Garrison, B. (1985). Hopelessness and eventual suicide: A ten year prospective study of patients hospitalized with suicidal ideation. *American Journal of Psychiatry, 142,* 559-563.

Beck, A.P., & Lewis, C.M. (2000). *The process of group psychotherapy.* Washington, DC: American Psychological Association.

Beck, A.T. (1999). *Prisoners of hate: The cognitive basis of anger, hostility, and violence.* NY: Harper Collins.

Becker, R. E. (1990). Social skills training. In A. S. Bellack & M. Hersen (Eds.), *Comparative treatments for adult disorders.* New York: Wiley.

Beekman, A. T., Copeland, J. R., & Prince, M. J. (1999). Review of community prevalence of depression in later life. *British Journal of Psychiatry, 174,* 307-311.

Beer, M. D. (1996). The endogenous psychoses: A conceptual history. *History of Psychiatry, 7,* 1-29.

Beers, C. (1908). *A mind that found itself.* Garden City, NY: Doubleday.

Beidel, D.C., & Turner, S.M. (1998). *Shy children, phobic adults.* Washington, DC: American Psychological Association.

Beitman, B. D. (1993). Pharmacotherapy and the stages of psychotherapeutic change. In J. M. Oldham, M. B. Riba, & A. Tasman (Eds.). *Review of Psychiatry 12,* 521-539. Washington, DC: American Psychiatric Press.

Belichencko, P. V., Hagberg, B., & Dahlstrom, A. (1997). Morphological study of neocortical areas in Rett syndrome. *Acta Neuropatholgica, 93,* 50-61.

Bell, Q. (1972). *Virginia Woolf: A biography.* New York: Harcourt Brace.

Bemporad, J. R., & Vasile, R. G. (1990). Psychotherapy. In A. S. Bellack and M. Hersen, eds., *Comparative treatments for adult disorders.* New York: Wiley.

Bender, L. (1938). A visual motor Gestalt test and its clinical use. *American Orthopsychiatric Association Research Monographs,* No. 3.

Bender, W. N. (1995). *Learning disabilities: Characteristics, identification, and teaching strategies* (2nd ed.). Boston: Allyn & Bacon.

Bennett, M. J. (1996). Is psychotherapy ever medically necessary? *Psychiatric Services, 47,* 966-970.

Benson, D. F., Miller, B. L., & Signer, S. F. (1986). Dual personality associated with epilepsy. *Archives of Neurology, 43,* 471-474.

Benson, H. (1977). Systemic hypertension and the relaxation response. *New England Journal of Medicine, 296,* 1152-1156.

Bentler, P. M., & Prince, C. (1969). Personality characteristics of male transvestites. *Journal of Abnormal Psychology, 74,* 140-143.

Bentler, P. M., & Prince, C. (1970). Psychiatric symptomatology in transvestites. *Journal of Clinical Psychology, 26,* 434-435.

Bergin, A. E., & Garfield, S. L. (Eds.) (1994). *Handbook of psychotherapy and behavior change* (4th ed.). New York: John Wiley.

Bergin, A. E., & Lambert, M. J. (1978). The evaluation of therapeutic outcomes. In S. L. Garfield, & A. E. Bergin (Eds.), *Handbook of psychotherapy and behavior change: An empirical analysis* (2nd ed.). New York: John Wiley.

Bergin, A., Waranch, H. R., Brown, J., Carson, K., & Singer, H. S. 1998). Relaxation therapy in Tourette syndrome: A pilot study. *Pediatric Neurology, 18,* 136-142.

Berke, J., & Hernton, C. (1974). *The cannabis experience.* London: Peter Owen.

Berkman, K. F., Vaccarino, V., & Seeman, T. (1993). Gender differences in cardiovascular morbidity and mortality: The contribution of social networks and support. *Annals of Behavioral Medicine, 15,* 112-118.

Bernard, M. L., & Bernard, J. L. (1983). Violent intimacy: The family as a model for love relationships. *Family Relations, 32,* 283-286.

Bertelsen, A., & Gottesman, I.I. (1986). Offspring of twin pairs discordant for psychiatric illness. *Acta Geneticae Medicae et Gemellogiae, 35,* 310.

Beumont, P. J. (1993). Anorexia nervosa in males: A report of 12 cases. *Australian and New Zealand Journal of Psychiatry, 27,* 512-517.

Bhugra, D., Leff, J., Mallett, R., Der, G., Corridan, B., & Rudge, S. (1997). Incidence and outcome of schizophrenia in Whites, African-Carribeans and Asians in London. *Psychological Medicine, 27,* 791-798.

Bibring, E. (1953). The mechanism of depression. In P. Greenacre (Ed.), *Affective disorders.* New York: International.

Biederman, J. (1998). Attention-deficit/hyperactivity disorder: A life span perspective. *Journal of Clinical Psychiatry, 59,* 1-13.

Biederman, J., Faraone, S. V., Milberber, S., Jetton, J. G., Chen, L., Mick, E., Greene, R. W., & Russell, R. L. (1996). Is childhood oppositional defiant disorder a precursor to adolescent conduct disorder: Findings from a four year follow up study of children with ADHD. *Journal of the American Academy of Child and Adolescent Psychiatry, 35,* 1193-1204.

Biederman, J., Faraone, S. V., Spencer, T., Wilens, T., Norman, D., Lapey, K. A., Mick, E., Lehman, B. K., & Doyle, A. (1993). Patterns of psychiatric comorbidity, cognition, and psychosocial functioning in adults with attention deficit hyperactivity disorder. *American Journal of Psychiatry, 150,* 1792-1798.

Birchwood, M. (1992). Early intervention in schizophrenia: Theoretical background and clinical strategies. *British Journal of Clinical Psychology, 31,* 257-278.

Birchwood, M., McGorry, P., & Jackson, H. (1997). Early intervention in schizophrenia. *British Journal of Psychiatry, 179,* 2-5.

Bjorkland, R. (1996). Psychiatric labels: Still hard to shake. *Psychiatric Services, 47,* 1329-1330.

Black, D.W., & Moyer, T. (1998). Clinical features and psychiatric comorbidity of subjects with pathological gambling behavior. *Psychiatric Services, 49,* 1434-1439.

Blanchard, E. B., & Malamood, H. S. (1996). Psychological treatment of irritable bowel syndrome. *Professional Psychology, 27,* 241-244.

Blatt, S. J., Quinlan, D. M., Pilkonis, P. A., & Shea, M. T. (1995a). Impact of perfectionism and need for approval on the brief treatment of depression: The National Institute of Mental Health Treatment of Depression Collaborative Research Program revisited. *Journal of Consulting and Clinical Psychology, 63,* 125-132.

Blatt, S. J., Quinlan, D. M., Pilkonis, P. A., & Shea, M. T. (1995b). "Impact of perfectionism and need for approval on the brief treatment of depression: The National Institute of Mental Health Treatment of Depression Collaborative Research Program revisited": correction. *Journal of Consulting and Clinical Psychology, 63,* 494.

Blatt, S. J., Sanislow, C. A., Zuroff, D. C., & Pilkonis, P. A. (1996). Characteristics of effective therapists: Further analyses of data from the National Institute of Mental Health Treatment of Depression Collaborative Research Program. *Journal of Consulting and Clinical Psychology, 64,* 1276-1284.

Blazer, D., Hughes, D., & George, L. D. (1987). Stressful life events and the onset of a generalized anxiety syndrome. *American Journal of Psychiatry, 144,* 1178-1183.

Bleuler, E. (1915/1950). *Dementia praecox or the group of schizophrenias* (J. Zinkin, trans.). New York: International Universities Press.

Bloom, B. L., & Hodges, W. F. (1988). The Colorado Separation and Divorce Program: A preventive intervention program for newly separated persons. In R. H. Price, E. L. Cowen, R. P. Lorian, & J. Ramos-McKay (Eds.), *Fourteen ounces of prevention: A casebook for practitioners*. Washington, DC: American Psychological Association.

Blumenthal, R. (1993). Omission of author's residence proves embarrassing. *New York Times*, Dec. 5, p. Y20.

Blumenthal, S. (1990). Youth suicide: risk factors, assessment, and treatment of adolescent and young adult suicidal patients. *Psychiatric Clinics of North America, 13*, 511-556.

Bodlund, O., & Kullgren, G. (1996). Transsexualism—General outcome and prognostic factors: A five-year follow-up study of nineteen transsexuals in the process of changing sex. *Archives of Sexual Behavior, 25*, 303-316.

Bohman, M., Cloninger, C. R., Sigvardsson, S., & von Knorring, A. L. (1982). Predisposition to petty criminality of Swedish adoptees I. Genetic and Rh environmental heterogeneity. *Archives of General Psychiatry, 39*, 1233-1241.

Bohmfalk, G. C. (1991). No laughing matter. *Journal of the American Medical Association, 265*, 1245.

Bolton, D., Luckie, M., & Steinberg, D. (1995). Long-term course of obsessive-compulsive disorder treated in adolescence. *Journal of the American Academy of Child and Adolescent Psychiatry, 34*, 1441-1450.

Bond, L. A., & Compas, B. E. (1991). *Primary prevention and promotion in the schools*. Newbury Park, CA: Sage Publications.

Bonus, B., & Assion, H. J. (1997). Asperger syndrome: A review of diagnostic criteria. *Fortschritte der Neurologie Psychiatrie, 65*, 41-48.

Bookheimer, S.Y., Strojwas, M.H., Cohen, M.S., Saunders, A.M., Pericak-Vance, M.A., Mazziotta, J.C., Small, G.W. (2000). Patterns of brain activation in people at risk for Alzheimer's disease. *New England Journal of Medicine, 343*, 450-456.

Boor, M. (1982). The multiple personality epidemic. *Journal of Nervous and Mental Disease, 170*, 302-304.

Boothby, J.C., Thorn, B.E., Stroud, M.W., & Jensen, M.P. (1999). In R.J. Gatchel & D.C. Turk (Eds.), *Psychological factors in pain*. NY: Guilford.

Borkman, T. (1999). *Understanding Self-Help/Mutual Aid*. New Brunswick, NJ: Rutgers University Press.

Bornstein, R. F. (1992). The dependent personality: Developmental, social, and clinical perspectives. *Psychological Bulletin, 112*, 3-23.

Borthwick-Duffy, S. A. (1994). Epidemiology and prevalence of psychopathology in people with mental retardation. *Journal of Consulting and Clinical Psychology, 62*, 17-27.

Bouman, T.K., & Visser, S. (1998). Cognitive and behavioral treatment of hypochondriasis. *Psychotherapy and Psychosomatics, 67*, 214-221.

Bowden, C. L. (1993). The clinical approach to the differential diagnosis of bipolar disorder. *Psychiatric Annals, 23*, 57-63.

Bowlby, J. (1977a). The making and breaking of affectional bonds: I. Aetiology and psychopathology in the light of attachment theory. *British Journal of Psychiatry, 130*, 201-210.

Bowlby, J. (1977b). The making and breaking of affectional bonds: II. Some principles of psychotherapy. *British Journal of Psychiatry, 130*, 421-431.

Bowlby, J. (1980). *Loss, sadness, and depression*. New York: Basic Books.

Boyd, J. H., Rae, D. S., Thompson, J. W., Burns, B. J., Bourdon, K., Locke, B. Z., & Regier, D. A. (1990). Phobia: Prevalence and risk factors. *Social Psychiatry and Psychiatric Epidemiology, 25*, 314-323.

Boyle, M. H., Offord, D. R., Racine, Y., Szatmari, P., Fleming, J. E., & Sanford, M. (1996). Identifying thresholds for classifying childhood psychiatric disorder: Issues and prospects. *Journal of American Academy of Child and Adolescent Psychiatry, 35*, 1440-1448.

Braff, D. L. (1993). Information processing and attention dysfunctions in schizophrenia. *Schizophrenia Bulletin, 19*, 233-259.

Braun, D. L., Sunday, S. R., Fornari, V. M., & Halmi, K. A. (1999). Bright light therapy decreases winter binge frequency in women with bulimia nervosa: A double blind, placebo-controlled study. *Comprehensive Psychiatry, 40*, 442-448.

Bregman, J. D., & Harris, J. C. (1995). Mental retardation. In H. I. Kaplan & B. J. Sadock (Eds.), *Comprehensive textbook of psychiatry*, 6th ed., pp. 2207-2241. Baltimore, MD: Williams & Wilkins.

Bremner, J.D. (1998). Neuroimaging of posttraumatic disorder. *Psychiatric Annals, 28*, 445-450.

Brenner, H. D. (1989). The treatment of basic psychological dysfunctions from a systemic point of view. *British Journal of Psychiatry, 155* (Suppl. 5), 74-83.

Brenner, H. D., Hodel, B., Genner, R., Roder, V., & Corrigan, P. (1992). Biological and cognitive vulnerability factors in schizophrenia: Implications for treatment. *British Journal of Psychiatry, 161*, 154-163.

Breslow, N., Evans, L., & Langley, J. (1985). On the prevalence and roles of females in the sadomasochistic subculture: Report of an empirical study. *Archives of Sexual Behavior, 14*, 303-317.

Breslow, N., Evans, L., & Langley, J. (1986). Comparisons among heterosexual, bisexual, and homosexual male sadomasochists. *Journal of Homosexuality, 13*, 83-107.

Brewerton, T. D., Krahn, D. D., Hardin, T. A., Wehr, T. A., & Rosenthal, N. E. (1994). Findings from the Seasonal Pattern Assessment Questionnaire in patients with eating disorders and control subjects: Effects of diagnosis and location. *Psychiatry Research, 52*, 71-84.

Brewin, C. R. (1996). Theoretical foundations of cognitive-behavior therapy for anxiety and depression. In J. T. Spank, J. M. Barley, and D. J. Foes (Eds.), *Annual Review of Psychology* (vol. 47). Palo Alto, CA: Annual Reviews, pp. 33-57.

Brock, T. C., Green, M. C., & Reich, D. A. (1998). New evidence in the Consumer Reports study of psychotherapy. *American Psychologist, 53*, 62-63.

Brodoff, A. S. (1988). First person account: Schizophrenia through a sister's eyes—The burden of invisible baggage. *Schizophrenia Bulletin, 14*, 113-116.

Brown, G. W. (1993). Life events and affective disorder: Replications and limitations. *Psychosomatic Medicine, 55*, 248-259.

Brown, G. W., & Harris, T. O. (1978). *Social origins of depression: A study of psychiatric disorder in women*. London: Tavistock.

Brown, G. W., Bifulco, A. & Harris, T. O. (1987). Life events, vulnerability and onset of depression: Some refinements. *British Journal of Psychiatry, 150*, 30-42.

Brown, P., Macmillan, M. B., Meares, R., & Van der Hart, O. (1996). Janet and Freud: Revealing the roots of dynamic psychiatric. *Australian and New Zealand Journal of Psychiatry, 30*, 480-491.

Brown, T. A., Barlow, D. H., & Liebowitz, M. R. (1994). The empirical basis of generalized anxiety disorder. *American Journal of Psychiatry, 151*, 1272-1280.

Browne, A., & Finkelhor, D. (1986). Impact of child sexual abuse: A review of research. *Psychological Bulletin, 99*, 66-77.

Brownell, K. D., Hayes, S. C., & Barlow, D. H. (1977). Patterns of appropriate and deviant sexual arousal: The behavioral treatment of multiple sexual deviations. *Journal of Consulting and Clinical Psychology, 45*, 1144-1155.

Bruer, J.T. (1998). *The myth of the first three years*. NY: Free Press.

Bruni, F. (1997). Belatedly, the riddle of an attack on Rather is solved. *New York Times*, January 30, p. A16.

Bryant, R.A., & Harvey, A.G. (2000). *Acute stress disorder: A handbook of theory, assessment, and treatment*. Washington, DC: American Psychological Association.

Buchsbaum, M. S., & Haier, R. J. (1987). Functional and anatomical brain imaging: Impact on schizophrenia research. *Schizophrenia Bulletin, 13*, 115-134.

Burnside, J. W. (1987). The diary. *Journal of the American Medical Association, 257*, 1802.

Bustillo, J. R., Lauriello, J., & Keith, S. J. (1999). Schizophrenia: Improving outcome. *Harvard Review of Psychiatry, 6*, 229-240.

Butcher, J.N. (1999). *A beginner's guide to the MMPI-2*. Washington DC: American Psychological Association.

Butler, A. C., & Beck, A. T. (1996). Cognitive therapy for depression. *The Clinical Psychologist, 49*, 6-7.

Butler, G. (1989). Issues in the application of cognitive and behavioral strategies to the treatment of social phobia. *Clinical Psychology Review, 9*, 91-106.

Butler, L., & Nolen-Hoeksema,S. (1994). Gender differences in responses to depressed mood in a college sample. *Sex Roles, 30*, 331-345.

Butterfield, F. (1996). This way madness lies: A fall from grace to prison. *New York Times*, April 21, 10y.

Butterworth, J., & Strauch, J. D. (1994). The relationship between social competence and success in the competitive workplace for persons with mental retardation. *Education and Training in Mental Retardation and Developmental Disabilities, 29*, 118-133.

Bystritsky, A., & Strausser, B. P. (1996). Treatment of obsessive-compulsive cutting behavior with naltrexone. *Journal of Clinical Psychiatry, 57*, 423-424.

Cabalska, M. B., Nowaczewska, I., Sendecka, E., & Zorska, K. (1996). Longitudinal study on early diagnosis and treatment of phenylketonuria in Poland. *European Journal of Pediatrics, 155*, Suppl. 1, S53-55.

Cadoret, R. J., Yates, W. R., Troughton, E., Woodworth, G., & Stewart, M. A. (1995). Gene-environment interaction in genesis of aggressivity and conduct disorders. *Archives of General Psychiatry, 52*, 42-52.

Cahill, C., Llewelyn, S. P., & Pearson, C. (1991). Treatment of sexual abuse which occurred in childhood: A review. *British Journal of Clinical Psychology, 30*, 1-12.

Caldwell, C. B., & Gottesman, I. I. (1990). Schizophrenics kill themselves too: A review of risk factors for suicide. *Schizophrenia Bulletin, 16*, 571-589.

Cameron, N. (1963). *Personality development and psychopathology*. Boston: Houghton Mifflin.

Campbell, M., & Shay, J. (1995). Pervasive developmental disorders. In H. I. Kaplan & B. J. Sadock (Eds,), *Comprehensive textbook of psychiatry*, 6th ed., pp. 2277-2293. Baltimore: Williams & Wilkins.

Campbell, S. S., & Gillin, J. C. (1987). Depressing normal sleep: Two trests of the Process S deficiency hypothesis. *Neuropsychobiology, 18*, 169-174.

Canino, I.A., & Spurlock, J. (2000). *Culturally Diverse Children and Adolescents* (2nd ed.). NY: Guilford.

Cannon, T. D., & Mednick, S. A. (1993). The schizophrenia high-risk project in Copenhagen: Three decades of progress. *Acta Psychiatrica Scandinavica, 370*, 33-47.

Cannon, T. D., Mednick, S. A., & Parnas, J. (1990). Antecedents of predominantly negative and predominantly positive schizophrenia in a high risk population. *Archives of General Psychiatry, 47*, 622-632.

Cannon, T. D., Paprio, J., Lonnqvist, J., Huttunen, M., Koshenvuo, M. (1998). The genetic epidemiology of schizophrenia in a Finnish twin cohort. *Archives of General Psychiatry, 55*, 67-74.

Cantwell, D. P. (1996). Attention deficit disorder: A review of the past 10 years. *Journal of American Academy of Child and Adolescent Psychiatry, 35*, 978-987.

Capaldi, D. M. & Patterson, G. R. (1994). Interrelated influences of contextual factors on antisocial behavior in childhood and adolescence for males. In D. C.

Fowles, P. Sutker, & S. H. Goodman (Eds.), *Progress in experimental personality and psychopathology research* (pp. 165-198). New York: Springer.

Capaldi, D. M. (1992). Co-occurrence of conduct problems and depressive symptoms in early adolescent boys: II. A 2 year follow-up at grade 8. *Development and Psychopathology, 4,* 125-144.

Capps, L., Sigman, M., & Mundy, P. (1994). Attachment security in children with autism. *Development and Psychopathology, 6,* 249-261.

Carlson, C. L., Lahey, B. B., & Neeper, R. (1984). Peer assessment of the social behavior of accepted, rejected, and neglected children. *Journal of Abnormal Child Psychology, 12,* 187-198.

Carlson, C. L., Pelham, W. E., Milich, R., & Dixon, M. J. (1992). Single and combined effects of methylphenidate and behavior therapy on classroom behavior, academic performance and self-evaluations of children with attention deficit-hyperactivity disorder. *Journal of Abnormal Child Psychology, 9,* 43-54.

Carlson, C. L., Pelham, W. E., Milich, R., & Hoza, B. (1993). ADHD boys' performance and attributions following success and failure: Drug effects and individual differences. *Cognitive Therapy and Research, 17,* 269-287.

Carmelli, D., & Swan, G. E. (1996). The relationship of Type A behavior and its components to all-cause mortality in an elderly subgroup of men from the Western Collaborative Group Study. *Journal of Psychosomatic Research, 40,* 475-483.

Carranza-Lira, S. & Valentino-Figueroa, M. L. (1999). Estrogen therapy in postmenopausal women. *International Journal of Gynaecology and Obstetrics, 65,* 35-38.

Cartwright, A., Hyams, G., & Spratley, T. (1996). Is the interviewer's therapeutic commitment an important factor in determining whether alcoholic clients engage in treatment. *Addiction Research, 4,* 215-230.

Casas, J. M. (1995). Counseling and psychotherapy with racial/ethnic minority groups in theory and practice. In B. Bongar and L. E. Beutler (Eds.), *Comprehensive textbook of psychotherapy: Theory and practice* (pp. 311-335). New York: Oxford University Press.

Casey, R. J., & Berman, J. S. (1985). The outcome of psychotherapy with children. *Psychological Bulletin, 98(2),* 388-400.

Caspi, A. & Elder, A. H., Jr., (1988). Early personality and life disorganization. In E. M. Hetherington, R. M. Lerner, & M. Perlmutter (Eds.), *Child development in life-span perspective.* Hillsdale, NJ: Lawrence Erlbaum Associates.

Castonguay, L. G., Goldfried, M. R., Wiser, S., Raue, P. J., & Hayes, A. M. (1996). Predicting the effect of cognitive therapy for depression: A study of unique and common factors. *Journal of Consulting and Clinical Psychology, 64,* 497-504.

Catalan, J., & Burgess, A. (1996). HIV-associated dementia and related disorders. *International Review of Psychiatry, 8,* 237-243.

Cautela, J. R. (1985). Covert modeling. In A. S. Bellack & M. Hersen (Eds.), *Dictionary of behavior therapy techniques.* New York: Pergamon.

Cavanaugh, C.J., & Lemberg, R. (1999). What we know about eating disorders: Facts and statistics. In R. Lemberg (Ed.), *Eating disorders: A reference sourcebook.* Phoenix, Arizona: Oryx Press.

Caviola, A. A. & Schiff, M. (1988). Behavioral sequelae of physical and/or sexual abuse in adolescents. *Child Abuse and Neglect, 12,* 181-188.

Cepeda-Benito, A. (1993). Meta-analytical review of the efficacy of nicotine chewing gum in smoking treatment programs. *Journal of Consulting and Clinical Psychology, 61,* 822-830.

Cerone, R., Schiaffino, M. C., Di Stefano, S. & Veneselli, E. (1999). Phenylketonuria: Diet for life or not? *Acta Paediatrica, 88,* 664-666.

Chalkley, A. J., & Powell, G. E. (1983). The clinical description of forty-eight cases of sexual fetishisms. *British Journal of Psychiatry, 142,* 292-295.

Chambers, W. J., Puig-Antich, J., Hirsch, M., Paez, P., Ambrosini, P. J., Tabrizi, M. A., & Davies, M. (1985). The assessment of affective disorders in children and adolescents by semi-structured interview. *Archives of General Psychiatry, 42,* 696-702.

Chandler, C. L., Weissberg, R. P., Cowen, E. L., & Guare, J. (1984). Long term effects of a school-based secondary prevention program for young maladapting children. *Journal of Consulting and Clinical Psychology, 52,* 165-170.

Charman, T. (1994). The stability of depressed mood in young adolescents: A school based survey. *Journal of Affective Disorders, 30,* 109-116.

Charman, T. (1997). The relationship between joint attention and pretend play in autism. *Development and Psychopathology, 9,* 1-16.

Chemerinski, E., & Robinson, R.G. (2000). The neuropsychiatry of stroke. *Psychosomatics, 41,* 5-14.

Cherlin, A. J., Furstenberg, F. F., Chase-Lansdale, P. L., Kiernan, K. E., Robins, P. K., Morrison, D. R., & Tietler, J. O. (1991). Longitudinal studies of effects of divorce on children in Great Britain and the United States. *Science, 252,* 1386-1389.

Chess, S. (1978). The plasticity of human development. *American Academy of Child Psychiatry, 17,* 80-91.

Chess, S., Thomas, A., & Hassibi, M. (1983). Depression in childhood and adolescence: A prospective study of six cases. *Journal of Nervous and Mental Disease, 171,* 411-420.

Chorpita, B.F., & Barlow, D.H. (1998). The development of anxiety: The role of control in the early environment. *Psychological Bulletin, 124,* 3-21.

Christenfeld, N., Glynn, L. M., Phillips, D. P., & Shrira, I. (1999). Exposure to New York City as a risk factor for heart atrtack mortality. *Psychosomatic Medicine, 61,* 740-743.

Christopher, I.C. (1993). Psychosocial factors and immunity in nonhuman primates: A review. *Psychosomatic Medicine, 55,* 298-308.

Chuang, H. T., Devins, G. M., Hunsley, J., & Gill, M. J. (1989). Psychosocial distress and well-being among gay and bisexual men with human immunodeficiency virus infection. *American Journal of Psychiatry, 146,* 876-880.

Ciccone, J.R. (1999). Competence to stand trial: Efforts to clarify the concept and improve clinical evaluations of criminal defendants. *Current Opinion in Psychiatry, 12,* 647-651.

Clark, D. B., Smith, M. G., Neighbors, B. D., Skerlec, L. M., & Randall, J. (1994). Anxiety disorders in adolescence: Characteristics, prevalence, and comorbidities. *Clinical Psychology Review, 14,* 113-137.

Clark, D. M., Salkovskis, P. M., Hackmann, A., Middleton, H., Anastasiades, P., & Gelder, M. (1994). A comparison of cognitive therapy, applied relaxation and imipramine in the treatment of panic disorder. *British Journal of Psychiatry, 164,* 749-769.

Clark, D. M., Salkovskis, P. M., Ost, L., Breitholtz, E., Koehler, K. A., Westling, B. E., Jeavons, A., & Gelder, M. (1997). Misinterpretation of body sensations in panic disorder. *Journal of Consulting and Clinical Psychology, 65,* 203-213.

Clark, K. A. (1965). A role for librarians in the relevant war against poverty. *Wilson Library Bulletin,* Sept. 1965 (Quoted in A. MacLeod, *Growing up in America.*) Rockville, MD: National Institute of Mental Health.

Clark, R., Anderson, N.G., Clark, V.R., & Williams, D.R. (1999). Racism as a stressor for African Americans. *American Psychologist, 54,* 805-815.

Clarkin, J. F., Glick, I. D., Haas, G. L., Spencer, J. H., Lewis, A. B., Peyser, J., Demane, N., Good-Ellis, M., Harris, E., & Lestelle, V. (1990). A randomized clinical trial of inpatient family intervention: V. Results for affective disorders. *Journal of Affective Disorders, 18,* 17-28.

Clarkin, J. F., Pilkonis, P. A., & Magruder, K. M. (1996). Psychotherapy of depression: Implications for reform of the health care system. *Archives of General Psychiatry, 53,* 717-723.

Clarkin, J.F. (1998). Research findings on the personality disorders. *In Session: Psychotherapy in Practice, 4,* 91-102.

Clayton, P. J. (1990). Bereavement and depression. *Journal of Clinical Psychiatry, 51,* (suppl), 34-40.

Clementz, B. A., Sweeney, J. A., Hirt, M., & Haas, G. (1991). Phenotypic correlations between oculomotor functioning and schizophrenia-related characteristics in relatives of schizophrenic probands. *Psychophysiology, 28,* 570-578.

Clinton, J. J. (1993). From the Agency for Health Care Policy and Research. *Journal of the American Medical Association, 270,* 172.

Cochran, D. L., Brown, D. R., & McGregor, K. C. (1999). Racial differences in multiple social roles of older women: Implications for depressive symptoms. *Gerontologist, 39,* 465-472.

Cohen, D. J., Caparulo, B. K., & Shaywitz, B. A. (1978). Neurochemical and developmental models of childhood autism. In G. Serban (Ed.), *Cognitive defects in the development of mental illness.* New York: Brunner/Mazel.

Cohen, J. D., & Servan-Schreiber, D. (1992). Context, cortex, and dopamine: A connectionist approach to behavior and biology in schizophrenia. *Psychological Review, 99,* 45-77.

Cohen, L.J., Kingston, P., Bell, A., Aronowitz, B., & Hollander, E. (2000). Comorbid personality impairment in body dysmorphic disorder. *Comprehensive Psychiatry, 41,* 4-12.

Cohen, M. E., Robins, E., Purtell, J. J., Altmann, M. W., & Reed, D. E. (1953). Excessive surgery in hysteria. *Journal of the American Medical Association, 151,* 977-986.

Cohen, P., Cohen, J., & Brook, J. (1993a). An epidemiological study of disorders in late childhood and adolescence—II. Persistence of disorders. *Journal of Child Psychiatry and Psychology, 34,* 869-877.

Cohen, J., Kasen, S., Velez, C. N., Hartmark, C., Johnson, J., Rojas, M., Brook, J. & Streuning, E. L. (1993). An epidemiological study of disorders in late childhood and adolescence—I. Age–and gender specific prevalence. *Journal of Child Psychiatry and Psychology, 34,* 851-867.

Cohen, R. A. (1975). Manic-depressive illness. In A. M. Freedman, J. I. Kaplan, & B. J. Sadock (Eds.), *Comprehensive textbook of psychiatry,* 2nd ed. Baltimore, MD: Williams & Wilkins.

Cohen, S., & Williamson, G.M. (1991). Stress and infectious disease in humans. *Psychological Bulletin, 109,* 5-24.

Cohen, S., Doyle, W.J., & Skoner, D.P. (1999). Psychological stress, cytokine production, and severity of upper respiratory illness. *Psychosomatic Medicine, 61,* 175-180.

Cohen, S., Doyle, W.J., Skoner, D.P., Rabin, B.S., & Gwaltney, J.M. (1997). Social ties and susceptibility to the common cold. *Journal of the American Medical Association, 277,* 1940-1944.

Cohen, S., Kessler, R. C., & Gordon, L. U. (1995). *Measuring Stress.* NY: Oxford University Press.

Cohen, S., Tyrrell, D. A. J., & Smith, A. P. (1991). Psychological stress and susceptibility to the common cold. *New England Journal of Medicine, 325,* 606-612.

Comings, D. E. (2000). The role of genetics in ADHD and conduct disorder—Revelance to the treatment of recidivistic antisocial behavior. In D. H. Fishbein, et al., *The science, treatment, and prevention of antisocial behaviors: Application to the criminal justice system.* (pp. 16-1-16-25.) Kingston, NJ: Civic Research Institute.

Compton, S. N., Nelson, A. H., & March, J. S. (2000). Social phobia and separation anxiety symptoms in community and clinical samples. *Journal of the American Academy of Child and Adolescent Psychiatry, 39,* 1040-1046.

Conduct Problems Prevention Research Group (1998). Initial impact of the Fast Track Prevention Trial for conduct problems: The high-risk sample. *Journal of Consulting and Clinical Psychology, 67,* 631-647.

Conger, R. D., Ge, X., Elder, G. H. Jr., Lorenz, F. O., & Simons, R. L. (1994). Economic stress, coercive family process, and developmental problems of adolescents. *Child Development, 65,* 541-561.

Connors, D. K. (1997). *CRS-R, Conners' rating scales-revised: instruments for use with children and adolescents.* Toronto, North Tonawanda, NY: Multi-Health Systems, Inc.

Conte, J. R., Sorenson, E., Fogarty, L., & Rosa, J. D. (1991). Evaluating children's reports of sexual abuse: Results from a survey of professionals. *American Journal of Orthopsychiatry, 61,* 428-437.

Cook, J. A., Pickett, S. A., & Cohler, B. J. (1997). Families of adults with severe mental illness—the next generation of research: Introduction. *American Journal of Orthopsychiatry, 67,* 172-176.

Cornblatt, B. A., & Keilp, J. G. (1994). Impaired attention, genetics, and the pathophysiology of schizophrenia. *Schizophrenia Bulletin, 20,* 31-46.

Cornblatt, B. A., Dworkin, R. H., Wolf, L. E., & Erlenmeyer-Kimling, L. (1996) Markers, developmental processes, and schizophrenia. In M. F. Lensenweger & J.J. Haugaard (Eds.). *Frontiers of developmental psychopathology.* (pp. 125-147). New York, NY: Oxford University Press.

Cornblatt, B. A., Lenzenweger, M. F., & Erlenmeyer-Kimling, L. L. (1989). The Continuous Performance Task, identical pairs version: II. Contrasting attentional profiles in schizophrenic and depressed patients. *Psychiatry Research, 29,* 65-85.

Costa, L. (1996). Lifespan neuropsychology. *Clinical Neuropsychologist, 10,* 365-374.

Council on Scientific Affairs, American Medical Association. (1986). Polygraph. *Journal of the American Medical Association, 256,* 1172-1175.

Cowen, E. L. (1982). Help is where you find it: Four informal helping groups. *American Psychologist, 37,* 385-395.

Cowen, E. L., & Hightower, A. D. (1990). The Primary Mental Health Project: Alternative approaches in school-based preventive intervention. In T. B. Gutkin & C. R. Reynolds (Eds.), *Handbook of school psychology.* New York: John Wiley.

Craddock, N., & Jones, I. (1999). Genetics of bipolar disorder. *Journal of Medical Genetics, 36,* 585-594.

Crider, A. (1997). Perseveration in schizophrenia. *Schizophrenia Bulletin, 23,* 63-74.

Cromwell, R. L. (1993). Searching for the origins of schizophrenia. *Psychological Science, 4,* 276-279.

Crow, T. J. (1994). Prenatal exposure to influenza as a cause of schizophrenia. British Journal of Psychiatry, 164, 588-592.

Culebras, A. (1996). *Clinical Handbook of Sleep Disorders.* Boston: Butterworth-Heinemann.

Cummings, E. M., & Davies, P. (1994). *Children and marital conflict: The impact of family dispute and resolution.* New York: Guilford.

Cummings, J. L. (1993). The neuroanatomy of depression. *Journal of Clinical Psychiatry, 54:* 11 (Suppl.), 14-20.

Cunningham, C. E., & Siefel, L. S. (1987). Peer interactions of normal and attention-deficit-disordered boys during free play, cooperative task, and simulated classroom situations. *Journal of Abnormal Child Psychology, 15,* 247-268.

Cunningham, M.D., & Reidy, T.J. (1999). Don't confuse me with the facts. *Criminal Justice and Behavior, 26,* 20-43.

Curry, S. J. (1993). Self-help interventions for smoking cessation. *Journal of Consulting and Clinical Psychology, 61,* 790-803.

Cutting, J. C. (1985). *The psychology of schizophrenia.* Edinburgh, Scotland: Churchill Livingstone.

Daley, D. C., & Marlatt, G. A. (1992). Relapse prevention: Cognitive and behavioral interventions. In J. H. Lowinson, P. Ruiz, & R. B. Millman (Eds.), *Substance abuse: A comprehensive textbook* (2d ed.) (pp. 533-542). Baltimore, MD: Williams & Wilkins.

Dalgleish, T., Rosen, K., & Marks, M. (1996). Rhythm and blues: The theory and treatment of seasonal affective disorder. *British Journal of Clinical Psychology, 35,* 163-182.

Dam, H., Molin, J., Bolwig, T. G., Wildschiodtz, G., & Mellerup, E. T. (1994). Development of winter depression and the effect of light therapy. *Nordic Journal of Psychiatry, 48,* 75-79.

Danforth, J. S. (1998). The outcome of parent training using the behavior management Flow chart with mothers and their children with oppositional defiant disorder andattention-deficit hyperactivity disorder. *Behavior Modification, 22,* 443-473.

Davidson, M., Reichenberg, A., Rabinowitz, J., Weiser, M., Kaplan, Z, & Mark, M. (1999). Behavioral and intellectual markers for schizophrenia in apparently healthy male adolescents. *American Journal of Psychiatry, 1999, 156,* 1328-1335.

Davis, G. E., & Leitenberg, H. (1987). Adolescent sex offenders. *Psychological Bulletin, 101,* 417-427.

De Azevedo-Moreira, L. M., San Juan, A., Pereira, P. S., & de Souza, C. S. (2000). A case of mosaic trisomy 21 with Down's syndrome signs and normal intellectual development. *Journal of Intellectual Disability Research, 44,* 91-96.

De Hert, M., Thys, E., Vercruyssen, V., & Peuskens, J. (1996). Partial hospitalization at night: The Brussels Nighthospital. *Psychiatric Services, 47,* 527-528.

De Nike, L. D., & Tiber, N. (1968). Neurotic behavior. In P. London & D. Rosenhan (Eds.), *Foundations of abnormal psychology.* New York: Holt, Rinehart & Winston.

de Ruiter, C., Rijken, H., Garssen, B., van Schaik, A., & Kraaimaat, F. (1989). Comorbidity among the anxiety disorders. *Journal of Anxiety Disorders, 3,* 57-68.

Dean, P. J., & Range, L. M. (1999). Testing the Escape Theory of Suicide in an outpatient population. *Cognitive Therapy and Research, 23,* 561-572.

DeLisi, L. E. (1996). Is there a viral or immune dysfunction etiology to schizophrenia? Re-evaluation a decade later. *Schizophrenia Research, 22,* 1-4.

DeMarchi, N., & Mennella, R. (2000). Huntington's disease and its association with psychopathology. *Harvard Review of Psychiatry, 7,* 278-289.

Demos, J. P. (1982). *Entertaining Satan: Witchcraft and the culture of early New England.* New York: Oxford University Press.

Denollet, J. (1999). Personality and cancer. *Current Opinion in Psychiatry, 12,* 743-748.

Depression Guideline Panel. (1993). (Clinical Practice Guideline No. 5.) *Depression in primary care: Vol. 2. Treatment of major depression.* (ACCPR Publication no. 93-0551). Rockville, MD: U.S. Department of Health and Human Services, Agency for Health Care Policy and Research.

DeRubeis, R. J., Gelfand, L. A., Tang, T. Z., & Simons, A. D. (1999). Medications versus cognitive behavior therapy for severely depressed outpatients: Meta-analysisof four randomized comparisons. *American Journal of Psychiatry, 156,* 1007-1013.

deSilva, P., & Marks, M. (1999). The role of traumatic experiences in the genesis of obsessive-compulsive disorder. *Behaviour Research and Therapy, 37,* 942-952

Deutsch, A. (1948). *The shame of the states.* New York: Arno.

Diaferia, G., Bianchi, I., Bianchi, M., Cavedini, P., Erzegovesi, S., & Bellodi, L. (1997). Relationship between obsessive-compulsive personality disorder and obsessive-compulsive disorder. *Comprehensive Psychiatry, 38,* 38-42.

Didion, J. (1979). *The white album.* New York: Simon & Schuster.

Dissanayake, C., & Crossley, S. A. (1996). Proximity and sociable behaviours in autism: Evidence for attachment. *Journal of Child Psychology and Psychiatry, 37,* 149-156.

Dixon, L. B., & Lehman, A. F. (1995). Family interventions for schizophrenia. *Schizophrenia Bulletin, 21,* 631-643.

Dixon, L. B., Lehman, A. F., & Levine, J. (1995). Conventional antipsychotic medications for schizophrenia. *Schizophrenia Bulletin, 21,* 567-577.

Dobkin, P. L., Tremblay, R. E., & Sacchitelle, C. (1997). Predicting boys' early-onset substance abuse from father's alcoholism, son's disruptiveness, and mother's parenting behavior. *Journal of Consulting and Clinical Psychology, 65,* 86-92.

Docter, R. F. (1988). *Transvestites and transsexuals.* New York: Plenum.

Dodge, K. A. (1985). Attributional bias in aggressive children. *Advances in Cognitive Behavioral Research and Therapy, 4,* 73-110.

Dodge, K. A. (1993). The future of research on the treatment of conduct disorder. *Development and Psychopathology, 5,* 311-319.

Dollard, J., & Miller, N. (1950). *Personality and psychotherapy.* New York: McGraw-Hill.

Dorian, B., & Garfinkel, P. E. (1987). Stress, immunity and illness: a review. *Psychological Medicine, 17,* 393-407.

Dorris, M. (1989). *The broken cord.* New York: Harper & Row.

Dorwart, R. A., Schlesinger, M., Davison, H., Epstein, S., & Hoover, C. (1991). A national study of psychiatric hospital care. *American Journal of Psychiatry, 148,* 204-210.

Dougall, A.L., Herberman, H.G., Delahanty, D.L., Inslicht, S.S., & Baum, A. (2000). Similarity of prior trauma exposure as a determinant of chronic stress responding to an airline disaster. *Journal of Consulting and Clinical Psychology, 68.* 290-295.

Dougherty , D. M., Bjork, J. M., Marsh, D. M., & Moeller, F. G. (2000). A comparison between adults with conduct disorder and normal controls on a continuous Performance Test: Differences in impulsive response characteristics. *Psychological Record, 50,* 203-219.

Draijer, N., & Langeland, W. (1999). Childhood trauma and perceived parental dysfunction in the etiology of dissociative symptoms in psychiatric inpatients. *American Journal of Psychiatry, 156,* 378-385.

Drevets, W. C. (1999). Prefrontal cortical-amygdalar metabolism in major depression. *Annals of the New York Academy of Sciences, 877,* 614-637

Duman, R. S., Heninger, G. R., & Nestler, E. J. (1997). A molecular and cellular theory of depression. *Archives of General Psychiatry, 54,* 597-606.

Dunner, D. L. (1987). Stability of Bipolar II affective disorder as a diagnostic entity. *Psychiatric Annals, 17,* 18-20.

Durand, B. M., & Carr, E. G. (1991). Functional communication training to reduce challenging behavior: Maintenance and application in new settings. *Journal of Applied Behavior Analysis, 24,* 251-254.

Durlak, J. A., & Wells, A. M. (1997). Primary prevention mental health programs for children and adolescents: A meta-analytic review. *Amercian Journal of Community Psychology, 25,* 115-152.

Dykman, B. M., Horowitz, L. M., Abramson, L. Y., & Usher, M. (1991). Schematic and situational determinants of depressed and nondepressed students' interpretation of feedback. *Journal of Abnormal Psychology, 100,* 45-55.

Easton, K. (1959). An unusual case of fugue and orality. *Psychoanalytic Quarterly, 28,* 505-513.

Eaton, W. W., Mortensen, P. B., Herrman, H., Freeman, H., Bilker, W., Burgess, P., & Wooff, K. (1992). Long-term course of hospitalization for schizophrenia: Part I. Risk for rehospitalization. *Schizophrenia Bulletin, 18,* 217-228.

Edmonds, L. K., Mosley, B. J., Admiraal, A. J., Olds, R. J., Romans, S. E., Silverstone, T., & Walsh, A. E. (1998). Familial bipolar disorder: Preliminary results from the

Otago Familial Bipolar Genetic Study. *Australian and New Zealand Journal of Psychiatry, 32*, 823-829.

Egeland, B., Carlson, E., & Sroufe, L. A. (1993). Resilience as process. *Development and Psychopathology, 5*, 517-528.

Egolf, B., Lasker, J., Wolf, S., & Potvin, L. (1992). The Roseto effect: A 50-year comparison of mortality rates. *American Journal of Public Health, 82*, 1089-1092.

Ehlers, A., & Clark, D.M. (2000). A cognitive model of posttraumatic stress disorder. *Behaviour Research and Therapy, 38*, 319-345.

Ehlers, S., Nyden, A., Gillberg, C., Sandberg, A. D., Dahlgren, S. O., Hjelmquist, E., & Oden, A. (1997). Asperger syndrome, autism, and attention disorders: A comparative study of the cognitive profiles. *Child Psychology and Psychiatry and Allied Disciplines, 38*, 207-217.

Einfeld, S. L., & Tonge, J. (1996). Population prevalence of psychopathology in children and adolescents with intellectual disability: II. Epidemiological findings. *Journal of Intellectual Disability Research, 40*, 99-109.

Eiraldi, R. B., Power, T. J., Nezu, C. M. (1997). Patterns of comorbidity associated with subtypes of attention-deficit hyperactivity disorder among 6- to 12-year-old children. *Journal of the American Academy of Child and Adolescent Psychiatry, 36*, 503-514.

Eisenberg, L. (1998). Nature, niche, and nurture. *Academic Psychiatry, 22*, 213-222.

Eisler, R. M. (1972). Crisis intervention in the family of a firesetter. *Psychotherapy: Theory, research and practice, 9*, 76-79.

Eliot, R. S., & Buell, J. C. (1983). The role of the CNS in cardiovascular disorders. *Hospital Practice*, May, 189-199.

Elkin, I. (1994). The NIMH treatment of depression collaborative research program: Where we began and where we are. In A. E. Bergin and S. L. Garfield (Eds.), *Handbook of psychotherapy and behavior change* (pp. 114-139). New York: John Wiley.

Elkin, I., Gibbons, R. D., Shea, M. T., & Shaw, B. F. (1996). Science is not a trial (but it can sometimes be a tribulation). *Journal of Consulting and Clinical Psychology, 64*, 92-103.

Elkin, I., Shea, T., Watkins, J. Imber, S. D., Sotsky, S. M., Collins, J. F., Glass, D. R., Pilkonis, P. A., Leber, W. R., Docherty, J. P., Fiester, S. J., & Parloff, M. B. (1989). NIMH Treatment of Depression Collaborative Research Program, I: General effectiveness of treatments. *Archives of General Psychiatry, 46*, 971-982.

Ellenberger, H. F. (1970). *The discovery of the unconscious.* New York: Basic Books.

Elliott, J. G. (1999). School refusal: Issues of conceptualisation, assessment, and treatment. *Journal of Child Psychology and Psychiatry and Allied Disciplines, 40*, 1001-1012.

Ellis, A. (1970). Rational-emotive therapy. In L. Hersher (Ed.), *Four psychotherapies*. New York: Appleton-Century-Crofts.

Ellis, A., & Dryden, W. (1997). *The practice of rational-emotive behavior therapy* (2nd ed.). NY: Springer Publishing Company.

Ellis, B., & Heiman, J. R. M. (1992) Marital and psychological adjustment in the context of a sexual dysfunction. *University of Washington Medical Center Update*, October 1992, 1-2.

El-Mallakh, R. S. (1997). Bipolar illness. *Southern Medical Journal, 90*, 775-779.

Emmelkamp, P. M. G., Van Der Helm, M., Van Zanten, B. L., & Plochg, I. (1980). Treatment of obsessive-compulsive patients: The contribution of self-instructional training to the effectiveness of exposure. *Behavior Research and Therapy, 18*, 61-66.

Endler, N. E., & Persad, E. (1988). *Electroconvulsive therapy: the myths and the realities.* Toronto: Hogrefe & Huber.

Endler, N. S. (1990). *Holiday of darkness.* New York: Wiley-Interscience.

Engel, G. L. (1977). The need for a new medical model: A challenge for biomedicine. *Science, 196*, 129-136.

Enoch, M., & Goldman, D. (2000). Genetics of alcoholism. In P. Pfaff, W. H. Berrettini, T.H. Joh, & S.C. Maxson (Eds.), *Genetic influences on neural and behavioral functions.* Boca Raton, FL: CRC Press.

Epstein, A. W. (1965). Fetishism. In R. Slovenko (Ed.), *Sexual behavior and the law.* Springfield, IL: Thomas.

Ergul, S., Parish, D. C., Puett, D., & Ergul A. (1996). Racial differences in plasma endothelin-l concentrations in individuals with essential hypertension. *Hypertension, 28*, 652-655.

Erickson, H. M., & Goodwin, D. W. (1994). Pharmacologic interventions. In B. Van Hasselt and M. Hersen (Eds.), *Advanced Abnormal Psychology.* New York: Plenum Press.

Erikson, E. H. (1975). *Life history and the historical moment.* New York: W. W. Norton.

Erlenmeyer-Kimling, L. (1987). Biological markers for the liability to schizophrenia. In H. Helmchen & F. A. Henn (Eds.), *Biological perspectives of schizophrenia.* New York: John Wiley.

Erlenmeyer-Kimling, L., Squires-Wheeler, E., Adamo, U. H., Bassett, A. S., Cornblatt, B. A., Kestenbaum, C. J., Rock, D., Roberts, S. A., & Gottesman, I. I. (1995). The New York High-Risk Project: Psychoses and cluster A personality disorders in offspring of schizophrenic parents at 23 years of follow-up. *Archives of General Psychiatry, 52*, 857-865.

Ernsberger, P., & Koletsky, R.J. (1999). Biomedical rationale for a wellness approach to obesity: An alternative to a focus on weight loss. *Journal of Social Issues, 55*, 221-259.

Eron, L. D., & Peterson, R. A. (1982). Abnormal behavior: Social approaches. In M. R. Rosenzweig & L. W. Porter (Eds.), *Annual Review of Psychology, 33*. Palo Alto, CA: Annual Reviews.

Essau, C. A., Hakim-Larson, J., Crocker, A., & Petermann, F. (1999). Assessment of depressive disorders in children and adolescents. In C. A. Essau and F. Petermann(Eds.), *Depressive disorders in children and adolescents.* pp. 27-67. Northvale, NJ: Aronson

Evans, J. D., Heaton, R. K., Paulsen, J. S., McAdams, L. A., Heaton, S. C., & Jeste, D. V. (1999). Schizoaffective disorder: A form of schizophrenia or affective disorder. *Journal of Clinical Psychiatry, 60*, 874-882.

Evans, M. D., Hollon, S. D., DeReubis, R. J., Piasecki, J. M., Grove, W. M., Garvey, M. J., & Tuason, V. B. (1992). Differential relapse following cognitive therapy and pharmacotherapy for depression. *Archives of General Psychiatry, 49*, 802-808.

Ezzell, C. (1995). Of multiple minds over the genetics of schizophrenia. *The Journal of NIH Research, 7*, 25-27.

Faedda, G. L., Tondo, L., Teicher, M. H., Baldessarini, R. J., Gelbard, H. A., & Floris, G. F. (1993). Seasonal mood disorders. Patterns of seasonal recurrence in mania and depression. *Archives of General Psychiatry, 50*, 17-23.

Faller, H., Bulzebruck, H., Drings, P., & Lang, H. (1999). Coping, distress, and survival among patients with lung cancer. *Archives of General Psychiatry, 565*, 756-762.

Faraone, S. V., & Biederman, J. (1994). Is attention deficit hyperactivity disorder familial? *Harvard Review of Psychiatry, 1*, 271-287.

Faraone, S. V., & Tsuang, M. T. (1985). Quantitative models of the genetic transmission of schizophrenia. *Psychological Bulletin, 98*, 41-66.

Fava, M., (1994). Do antidepressants and antianxiety drugs increase chronicity in affective disorders. *Psychotherapy and Psychosomatics, 61*, 125-131.

Favazza, A. R., & Rosenthal, R. J. (1993). Diagnostic issues in self-multilation. *Hospital and Community Psychiatry, 44*, 134-140.

Figiel, G. S., Krishnan, R. R., & Doraiswamy, M. (1990). Subcortical structural changes in ECT-induced delirium. *Journal of Geriatric Psychiatry and Neurology, 3*, 172-176.

Filipek, P. A., Accardo, P. J., Baranek, G. T., Cook, E. H. Jr., Dawson, G., Gordon, B., Gravel, J. S., Johnson, C. P., Kallen, R. J., Levy, S. E., Minshew, N. J.,Prizant, B. M., Raplin, I., Rogers, S. J., Stone, W. L., Teplin, S., Tuchman, R.F., & Volkmar, F. R. (1999). The screening and diagnosis of autistic spectrum disorders. *Journal of Autism and Developmental Disorders, 29*, 439-484.

Fine, S., Forth, A., Gilbert, M., & Haley, G. (1991). Group therapy for adolescent depressive disorder: A comparison of social skills and therapeutic support. *Journal of the American Academy of Child and Adolescent Psychiatry, 30*, 79-85.

Fink, C. M., Turner, S. M., & Beidel, D. C. (1996). Culturally relevant factors in the behavioral treatment of social phobia. *Journal of Anxiety Disorders, 10*, 201-209.

Fink, M. (1999). *Electroshock: restoring the mind.* New York: Oxford University Press.

Fink, M. (2000). Electroshock revisited. *American Scientist, 88*, 162-167.

Finkelhor, D. (1988). The trauma of sexual abuse: Two models. In G. E. Wyatt & G. J. Powell (Eds.) *Lasting effects of child sexual abuse* (pp. 61-82). Newbury Park, CA: Sage.

Finkelstein, J. R. J., Cannon, T. D., Gur, R. E., Gur, R. C., & Moberg, P. (1997). Attentional dysfuntion in neuroleptic-naive and neuroleptic-withdrawn schizophrenic patients and their siblings. *Journal of Abnormal Psychology, 106*, 203-212.

Firlik, A. D. (1991). Margo's logo. *Journal of the American Medical Association, 265*, 201.

Fischer, G. J. (1986). College student attitudes toward forcible date-rape: I. Cognitive predictors. *Archives of Sexual Behavior, 15*, 457-466.

Fishera, L.V., & Andreassi, J.L. (1998). Stress and personality as factors in women's cardiovascular reactivity. *International Journal of Psychophysiology, 28*, 143-155.

Fitzgerald, B., Morgan, J., Keene, N., Rollinson, R., Hodgson, A., & Dalrymple-Smith, J. (2000). An investigation into diet treatment for adults with previously untreated phenylketonuria and severe intellectual disability. *Journal of Intellectual Disability Research, 44*, 53-59.

Flament, M. F., Koby, E., Rapoport, J. L., Berg, C. J., Zahn, T., Cox, C., Denckla, M., & Lenane, M. (1990). Childhood obsessive-compulsive disorder: A prospective follow-up study. *Journal of Child Psychology and Psychiatry, 31*, 363-380.

Fleet, R.P., & Beitman, B.D. (1998). Cardiovascular death from panic disorder and panic-like anxiety: A critical review of the literature. *Journal of Psychosomatic Research, 44*, 71-80.

Fleischhacker, W. W. (1999). Clozappine: A comparison with other novel antipsychotics. *Journal of Clinical Psychiatry, 60* (suppl 12), 30-34.

Flores, M.T., & Carey, G. (Eds.) (2000). *Family Therapy with Hispanics.* Needham Heights, MA: Allyn & Bacon.

Folks, D.G., Feldman, M.D., & Ford, C.V. (2000). Somatoform disorders, factitious disorders, and malingering. In A. Stoudemire, B.S. Fogel, and D.B. Greenberg (Eds.). *Psychiatric care of the medical patient* (2nd ed.). NY: Oxford University Press.

Folstein, S. E. (1999). An overview of psychiatric and psychological aspects of autism. *International Review of Psychiatry, 11*, 269-277.

Folstein, S., & Rutter, M. (1977). Infantile autism: a genetic study of 21 twin pairs. *Journal of Child Psychology and Psychiatry, 18*, 297-321.

Folstein, S., & Rutter, M. (1978). A twin study of individuals with infantile autism. In M. Rutter & E. Schopler (Eds.), *Autism: A reappraisal of concepts and treatment.* New York: Plenum.

Fombonne, E. (1999). The epidemiology of autism: a review. *Psychological Medicine, 29*, 769-786.

Fones, C. S. L., Manfro, G. G. M., & Pollack, M. H. (1998). Social phobia: An update. *Harvard Review of Psychiatry, 5*, 247-259.

Frances, A. J., & Klein, D. F. (1982). Anxious, precise, demanding man seeks help soon after marriage. *Hospital and Community Psychiatry, 33*, 89-90.

Frances, A. J., & Widiger, T. (1986). The classification of personality disorders: An overview of problems and solutions. *Annual Review of Psychiatry, 5*, 240-257.

Frank, E., & Spanier, C. (1995). Interpersonal psychotherapy for depression: Overview, clinical efficacy, and future directions. *Clinical Psychology: Science and Practice, 2*, 349-369.

Frank, E., Anderson, C., & Rubinstein, D. (1978). Frequency of sexual dysfunction in ônormalö couples. *New England Journal of Medicine, 299*, 111-115.

Frankl, V.E. (1959). *Man's search for meaning*. NY: Simon & Schuster.

Frazier, J. A., Giedd, J. N., Hamburger, S. D., Albus, K. E., Kaysen, D., Vaituzis, A. C., Rajapakse, J. C., Lenane, M. C., McKenna, K., Jacobsen, L. K., Gordon, C. T., Breier, A., & Rapoport, J. L. (1996). Brain anatomic magnetic resonance imaging in childhood-onset schizophrenia. *American Journal of Psychiatry, 153*, 355-361.

Freed, C. R., Greene, P. E., Breeze, R. E., Tsai, W.-Y., DuMouchel, W., Kaso, R., Dillon, S., Winfield, H., Culver, S., Trojanowski, J. Q., Eidelberg, D., & Fahn, S. (2001). Transplantation of embryonic dopamine neurons for severe Parkinson's disease. *New England Journal of Medicine, 344*, 215-236.

Freedman, L. R., Rock, D., Roberts, S. A., Cornblatt, B. A., Erlenmeyer-Kimling, L. (1998). The New York High-Risk Project: Attention, anhedonia, and social outcome. *Schizophrenia Bulletin, 30*, 1-9.

Freeman, R. D., Fast, D. K., Burd, L., Kerbeshian, J., Robertson, M. M., & Sandor, P. (2000). The international perspective on Tourette syndrome: Selected findings from 3,500 individuals in 22 countries. *Developmental Medicine and Child Neurology, 42*, 436-437.

Freud, S. (1930). Civilization and its discontents. In J. Strachey (Ed.), *The standard edition of the complete psychological works of Sigmund Freud*, Vol. 21. London: Hogarth.

Freud, S. (1951). A letter from Freud (April 9, 1935). *American Journal of Psychiatry, 107*, 786-787.

Freud, S. (1957). (originally published 1917) Mourning and melancholia. In J. Strachey (Ed.), *The standard edition of the complete psychological works of Sigmund Freud*, vol. 14. London: Hogarth.

Freud, S. (1959). *Collected works*, Vol. 5. New York: Basic Books.

Frick, P. J. (1993). Childhood conduct problems in a family context. *School Psychology Review, 22*, 376-385.

Frick, P. J. (1998). *Conduct disorders and severe antisocial behavior*. New York: Plenum.

Friedman, L.J. (1999). *Identity's architect: A biography of Erik H. Erikson*. NY: Scribner.

Friedman, M. (1996). *Type A behavior*. NY: Plenum.

Friedman, M., & Rosenman, R. (1974). *Type A behavior and your heart*. New York: Knopf.

Fromuth, M. E. (1986). The relationship of childhood sexual abuse with later psychological and sexual adjustment in a sample of college women. *Child Abuse and Neglect, 10*, 5-15.

Fuller, A. K. (1989). Child molestation and pedophilia: An overview for the physician. *Journal of the American Medical Association, 261*, 602-606.

Fuller, M. A., & Sajatovic, M. (1999). *Drug information handbook for psychiatry*. Cleveland, OH: American Pharmaceutical Association.

Gabbard, G. O. (1985). The role of compulsiveness in the normal physician. *Journal of the American Medical Association, 254*, 2926-2929.

Gabbard, G. O., Lazar, S. G., Hornberger, J., & Spiegel, D. (1997). The economic impact of psychotherapy: A review. *American Journal of Psychiatry, 154*, 147-155.

Gamwell, L., & Tomes, N. (1995). *Madness in America: Cultural and medicinal perceptions of mental illness before 1914*. Ithaca, NY: Cornell University Press.

Garmezy, N. (1993). Children in poverty: Resilience despite risk. *Psychiatry: Interpersonal & Biological Processes, 56*, 127-136.

Gatchel, R.J., & Turk, D.C. (Eds.) (1999). *Psychological factors in pain*. NY: Guilford.

Ge, X., Best, K. M., Conger, R. D., & Simons, R. L. (1996a). Parenting behaviors and the occurrence and co-occurence of adolescent depressive symptoms and conduct problems. *Developmental Psychology, 32*, 717-731.

Ge, X., Conger, R. D., Cadoret, R. J., Neiderhiser, J. M., Yates, W., Troughton, E., & Stewart, M. A. (1996b). The developmental interface between nature and nurture: A mutual influence model of child antisocial behavior and parent behaviors. *Developmental Psychology, 32*, 574-589.

Geller, D., Biederman, J., Jones, J., Park, K., Schwartz, S., Shapiro, S., & Coffey, B. (1997). Is juvenile obsessive-compulsive disorder a developmental subtype of thedisorder? A review of the pediatric literature. *Journal of the American Academy of Child and Adolescent Psychiatry, 37*, 420-427.

George, M. S., Ketter, T. A., & Post, R. M. (1993). SPECT and PET imaging in mood disorders. *Journal of Clinical Psychiatry, 54*: 11 (Suppl.), 6-13.

George, M. S., Ring, H. A., & Costa, D. C. (1991). *Neuroactivation and neuroimaging with SPECT*. London, England: Springer-Verlag.

Gershon, E. S., Berrettini, W. H., & Goldin, L. R. (1989). Mood disorders: Genetic aspects. In H. I. Kaplan & B. J. Sadock (Eds.), *Comprehensive textbook of psychiatry*, 5th ed. Baltimore: Williams & Wilkins.

Gilberg, C., & Wing, L. (1999). Autism: not an extremely rare disorder. *Acta Psychiatrica Scandinavica, 99*, 399-406.

Gill, J. J., Price, V. A., Friedman, M., Ihoresen, C. E., Powell, L. H., Ulmer, D., Brown, B., & Drews, F. R. (1985). Reduction in Type-A behavior in healthy middle-aged American military officers. *American Heart Journal, 110*, 503-514.

Gill, M., McGuffin, P., Parfitt, E., Mant, R., Asherson, P., Collier, D., Vallada, H., Powell, J., Shaika, S., Taylor, C., Sargeant, M., Clements, A., Nanko, S., Takazawa, N., Llewellyn, D., Williams, J., Whatley, S., Murray, R., & Owen, M. (1993). A linkage study of schizophrenia with DNA markers from the long arm of chromosome 11. *Psychological Medicine, 23*, 27-44.

Gillberg, C., Nordin, V., & Ehlers, S. (1996). Early detection of autism: Diagnostic instruments for clinicians. *European Child and Adolescent Psychiatry, 5*, 67-74.

Gilmore, J. H., Perkins, D. O., Kliewer, M. A., & Hage, M. L. (1996). Fetal brain development of twins assessed in utero by ultrasound: Implications for schizophrenia. *Schizophrenia Research, 19*, 141-149.

Gilmore, M. (1994). *Shot in the heart*. New York: Doubleday.

Gimpel, G. A., & Kuhn, B. R. (2000). Maternal report of attention deficit hyperactivity disorder symptoms in preschool children. *Child Care, Health and Development, 26*, 163.176.

Gitlin, M. J., Swendsen, J., Heller, T. L., & Hammen, C. (1995). Relapse and impairment in bipolar disorder. *American Journal of Psychiatry, 152*, 1635-1640.

Gittelman, R., & Klein, D. F. (1984). Relationships between separation anxiety and panic and agoraphobic disorders. *Psychopathology, 17* (Suppl.), 56-65.

Glass, C.R. Arnkoff, D.B., & Rodriguez, B.F. (1998). An overview of directions in psychotherapy integration research. *Journal of Psychotherapy Integration, 8*, 187-209.

Gleaves, D. H. (1996). The sociocognitive model of dissociative identity disorder: A reexamination of the evidence. *Psychological Bulletin, 120*, 42-59.

Glueck, S., & Glueck, E. (1968). *Delinquents and nondelinquents in perspective*. Cambridge, MA: Harvard University Press.

Glynn, L.M., Christenfeld, N., & Gerin, W. (1999). Gender, social support, and cardiovascular responses to stress. *Psychosomatic Medicine, 61*, 234-242.

Goffman, E. (1959). *The presentation of self in everyday life*. New York: Doubleday.

Goldberg, D. (1996). A dimensional model for common mental disorders. *British Journal of Psychiatry, 168*, 44-49.

Golden, K. M. (1977). Voodoo in Africa and the United States. *American Journal of Psychiatry, 134*, 1425-1427.

Goldstein, D.J. (Ed.) (1999). *The management of eating disorders and obesity*. Totowa, NJ: Humana Press.

Goleman, D. (1995). *Higher suicide risk for perfectionists*. New York Times, Wednesday, May 1, page B9.

Golombok, S., & Tasker, F. (1996). Do parents influence the sexual orientation of their children? Findings from a longitudinal study of lesbian families. *Developmental Psychology, 32*, 3-11.

Gonzalez-Salvador, M.T., Arango, C., Lyketsos, C.G., & Barba, A.C. (1999). The stress and psychological morbidity of the Alzheimer patient caregiver. *International Journal of Geriatric Psychiatry 14*, 701-710.

Goode, E. (1999) Doctors try a bold move against schizophrenia. *New York Times*, Tuesday December 7, pp D1, D10.

Goodwin, F. K., & Jamison, K. R. (1987). *Bipolar disorders*. In R. E. Hales & A. J. Frances (Eds.), *American Psychiatric Association Annual Review*, vol. 6. Washington, DC: American Psychiatric Press.

Goodwin, F. K., & Jamison, K. R. (1990). *Manic-depressive illness*. New York: Oxford University Press.

Goodyer, I., Kolvin, I., & Gatzanis, S. (1985). Recent undesirable life events and psychiatric disorder in childhood and adolescence. *British Journal of Psychiatry, 147*, 517-523.

Gosselin, C., & Wilson, G. (1980). *Sexual variations*. New York: Simon & Schuster.

Gossop, M., Griffiths, P., Powis, B., & Strang, J. (1994). Cocaine: Patterns of use, route of administration, and severity of dependence. *British Journal of Psychiatry, 164*, 660-664.

Gostin, L. O., Lazzarini, Z., Alexander, D., Brandt, A. M., Mayer, K. H., & Silverman, D. C. (1994). HIV testing, counseling, and prophylaxis after sexual assault. *Journal of the American Medical Association, 271*, 1436-1444.

Gotlib, I. H. & Colby, C. A. (1987). *Treatment of depression*. New York: Pergamon Press.

Gottesman, I. I. (1991). *Schizophrenia genesis: The origins of madness*. New York: Freeman.

Gottesman, I. I., & Goldsmith, H. H. (1994). Developmental psychopathology of antisocial behavior: Inserting genes into its ontogenesis and epigenesis. In C. A. Nelson (Ed.), *Threats to optimal development: Integrating biological, psychological, and social risk factors*. Hillsdale, NJ: Lawrence Erlbaum.

Gottesman, I. I., & Moldin, S. O. (1997). Schizophrenia genetics at the millennium: cautious optimism. *Clinical Genetics, 52*, 404-407.

Gottesman, I. I., & Moldin, S. O. (1998). Genotypes, genes, genesis, and pathogenesis in schizophrenia. In Lenzenweger, M. & Dworkin, R. *Origins and development of schizophrenia: Advances in experimental psychopathology*. Washington, DC: American Psychological Association.

Gottlieb, J., Semmel, M. I., & Veldman, D. J. (1978). Correlates of social status among mainstreamed mentally retarded children. *Journal of Educational Psychology, 70*, 396-405.

Gould, E., Reeves, A.J., Graziano, M.S.A., & Gross, C.G. (1999). Neurogenesis in the neocortex of adult primates. *Science, 286*, 548-552.

Graham, J. R. (1993). *MMPI-2: Assessing personality and psychopathology* (2nd ed.). New York: Oxford University Press.

Grandin, T. (1984). My experiences as an autistic child and review of selected literature. *Journal of Orthomolecular Psychiatry, 13*, 144-174.

Grandin, T. (1987). Motivating autistic children. *Academic Therapy, 22*(3), 297-302.

Grandin, T. (1991). Overcoming autism: A first person account. *Harvard Mental Health Letter*, March 4-7.

Grandin, T. (1995). *Thinking in pictures*. New York: Doubleday.

Green, A. I., & Schildkraut, J. J. (1995). Should clozapine be a first-line treatment for schizophrenia? The rationale for a double-blind clinical trial in first-episode patients. *Harvard Review of Psychiatry, 3*, 1-9.

Green, E. (1972). *Biofeedback for mind/body self-regulation: Feeling and creativity*. Chicago: Aldine.

Green, M. (1999). Diagnosis of attention-deficit/hyperactivity disorder. *Technical Review* Number 3, Publication No. 99-0050. Rockville, MD: Agency for Health Care Policy and Research.

Green, M. F. (1993). Cognitive remediation in schizophrenia: Is it time yet? *American Journal of Psychiatry, 150*, 178-187.

Green, M. F. (1998). *Schizophrenia from a neurocognitive perspective*. Boston: Allyn and Bacon.

Green, M. F., Bracha, S. H., Satz, P. & Christenson, C. (1994) Preliminary evidence for an association between minor physical anomalies and second trimester neurodevelopment in schizophrenia. *Psychiatry Research, 53*, 119-127.

Green, R. (1974). *Sexual identity conflicts in children and adults*. New York: Basic Books.

Green, R. (1987). *The "sissy boy syndrome" and the development of homosexuality*. New Haven: Yale University Press.

Greeno, C.G., Wing, R.R., & Shiffman, S. (2000). Binge antecedents in obese women with and without binge eating disorder. *Journal of Consulting and Clinical Psychology, 68*, 95-102.

Grinker, R. (1979). *Historical perspectives on depression*. Roche Laboratories Professional Services Department.

Grossman, L.S., Martis, B., & Fichtner, C.G. (1999). Are sex offenders treatable? A research overview. *Psychiatric Services, 50*, 349-361.

Grove, W. M., Clementz, B. A., Iacono, W. G., & Katsanis, J. (1992). Smooth pursuit ocular motor dysfunction in schizophrenia: Evidence for a major gene. *American Journal of Psychiatry, 149*, 1362-1368.

Guillen, T. (1982). Competency ruling frees Safety Building squatter. *Seattle Times*, Jan. 27, B1.

Gunderson, J. G. (1984). *Borderline Personality Disorder*. Washington, DC: American Psychiatric Press.

Gunderson, J. G. (1996). The borderline patient's intolerance of aloneness: Insecure attachments and therapist availability. *American Journal of Psychiatry, 153*, 752-758.

Gunderson, J. G., & Lyoo, K. (1997). Family problems and relationships for adults with borderline personality disorder. *Harvard Review of Psychiatry, 4*, 272-278.

Gunderson, J. G., & Zanarini, M. C. (1987). Current overview of the borderline diagnosis. *Journal of Clinical Psychiatry, 48*(8) (Supplement), 5-11.

Gusella, J. F., & MacDonald, M. E. (1994). Huntington's disease and repeating trinucleotides. *New England Journal of Medicine, 330*, 1450-1451.

Guthiel, T.G., & Appelbaum, P.S. (2000). *Clinical Handbook of Psychiatry and the Law* (3rd ed.). Philadelpia: Lippincott Williams & Wilkens.

Guthrie, E. (1996). Psychotherapy of somatization disorders. *Current Opinion in Psychiatry, 9*, 182-187.

Guze, S. B., & Robbins, E. (1970).Suicide and primary affective disorders. *British Journal of Psychiatry, 117*, 437-438.

Haaga, D. F., Dyck, M. J., & Ernst, D. (1991). Empirical status of cognitive theory of depression. *Psychological Bulletin, 110*, 215-236.

Hackett, T. P., & Cassem, N. H. (1975). The psychologic reactions of patients in the pre- and post-hospital phases of myocardial infarction. *Postgraduate Medicine, 57*, 43-46.

Haertsch, P., & Heal, C. (1997). Ten years experience in gender reassignment surgery: A preliminary report. *Venereology, 10*, 166-173.

Hales, R.E., Yudofsky, S.C., & Talbott, J.A. (1999). *The American Psychiatric Textbook of Psychiatry* (3rd ed.). Washington, DC: American Psychiatric Press.

Hall, G. C. (1990). Prediction of sexual aggression. *Clinical Psychology Review, 10*(2), 229-245.

Hall, J. A., & Rosenthal, R. (1995). Interpreting and evaluating meta-analysis. *Evaluation and the Health Professions, 18*, 393-407.

Halligan, P.W., Bass, C., & Wade, D.T. (2000). New approaches to conversion hysteria. *British Medical Journal, 320*, 1488-1489.

Hamilton, E., & Abramson, L. (1983). Cognitive patterns and major-depressive disorders: A longitudinal study in a hospital setting. *Journal of Abnormal Psychology, 92*, 173-184.

Hamilton, M. (1982). Symptoms and assessment of depression. In E. S. Paykel (Ed.), *Handbook of affective disorders*. Edinburgh: Churchill-Livingston.

Hammen, C. (1992). Cognitive, life stress, and interpersonal approaches to a developmental psychopathology model of depression. *Development and Psychopathology, 4*, 189-206.

Hann, D.M., Huffman, L.C., Lederhendler, D., & Meinecke, D. (Eds.). (1998). *Advancing research on developmental plasticity*. Bethesda, MD: National Institute of Mental Health.

Hanna, G. L. (1995). Tic disorders. In H. I. Kaplan, & B. J. Sadock (Eds.), *Comprehensive textbook of psychiatry*, 6th ed. (pp.2325-2336). Baltimore, MD: Williams & Wilkins.

Hansen, D. J., Conaway, L. P., & Christopher, J. S. (1990). Victims of child physical abuse. In R. T. Ammerman & M. Hersen (Eds.), *Treatment of family violence: A sourcebook* (pp. 17-49). New York: John Wiley.

Happe, F., Ehlers, S., Fletcher, P., Frith, U., Johansson, M., Gillberg, C., Dolan, R., Frackowiak, R., & Frith, C. (1976). "Theory of mind" in the brain: Evidence from a PET scan study of Asperger syndrome. *Neuroreport, 8*, 197-201.

Harding, C. M., Brooks, G. W., Ashikaga, T., Strauss, J. S., & Breier, A. (1987a). The Vermont longitudinal study of persons with severe mental illness, I: Methodology, study sample and overall status 32 years later. *American Journal of Psychiatry, 144*, 718-726.

Harding, C. M., Zubin, J., & Strauss, J. S. (1987b). Chronicity in schizophrenia: Fact, partial fact or artifact. *Hospital and Community Psychiatry, 38*, 477-486.

Hare, R. D., & Forth, A. E. (1985). Psychopathy and lateral preferences. *Journal of Abnormal Psychology, 94*, 541-546.

Harrington, R., Fudge, H., Rutter, M., Pickles, A., & Hill, J. (1990). Adult outcomes of childhood and adolescent depression. *Archives of General Psychiatry, 47*, 465-473.

Harris, T. O. (1992). Social support and unsupportive behaviors. In H. O. F. Veiel & U. Baumann (Eds.), *The meaning and measurement of social support* (pp. 171-192). New York: Hemisphere.

Harrison, G., Glazebrook, C., Brewin, J., Cantwell, R., Dalkin, T., Fox, R., et al. (1997). Increased incidence of psychotic disorders in migrants from the Caribbean to the United Kingdom. *Psychological Medicine, 27*, 799-806.

Hart, C. (1989). *Without reason*. New York: Harper and Row.

Hartman, D. S., & Civelli, O. (1996). Molecular attributes of dopamine receptors. New potential for antipsychotic drug development. *Annals of Medicine, 28*, 211-219.

Harvard Mental Health Letter. (1990). Panic disorder: Part I. Boston. *7*(3), 1.

Harvey, A.G., & Bryant, R.A. (1999). Predictors of acute stress following motor vehicle accidents. *Journal of Traumatic Stress, 12*, 519-525.

Hasin, D. S., Grant, B., & Endicott, J. (1990). The natural history of alcohol abuse: Implications for definitions of alcohol use disorders. *American Journal of Psychiatry, 147*, 1537-1541.

Hattie, J. A., Sharpley, C. F., & Rogers, H. J. (1984). Comparative effectiveness of professional and paraprofessional helpers. *Psychological Bulletin, 95*, 534-541.

Hauser-Cram, P., Warfield, M. E., Shonkoff, J. P., Krauss, M. W., Upshur, C. C., & Sayer, A. (1999). Family influences on adaptive development in young children with Down syndrome. *Child Development, 70*, 979-989.

Hawton, K., Simkin, S., Fagg, J., & Hawkins, M. (1995). Suicide in Oxford University students, 1976-1990. *British Journal of Psychiatry, 166*, 44-50.

Hayden, M. R. (1991). Predictive testing for Huntington disease: Are we ready for widespread community implementation? *American Journal of Medical Genetics, 40*, 515-517.

Hayden, M. R., Block, M., & Wiggins, S. Psychological effects of predictive testing for Huntington's disease. *Advances in Neurology, 65*, 201-210.

Haynes, S. G., Feinleib, M., & Kannel, W. B. (1980). The relationship of psychological factors to coronary heart disease in the Framingham study: III. Eight-year incidence of coronary heart disease. *American Journal of Epidemiology, 111*, 37-58.

Hazelrigg, M. D., Cooper, H. M., & Borduin, C. M. (1987). Evaluating the effectiveness of family therapies: An integrative review and analysis. *Psychological Bulletin, 101*, 428-442.

Hecht, H., von Zerssen, D., Krieg, C., Possi, J., & Witchen, H. (1989). Anxiety and depression: Comorbidity, psychopathology, and social functioning. *Comprehensive Psychiatry, 30*, 420-433.

Heikkinen, M., Aro, H., & Lonnqvist, J. (1993). Life events and social support in suicide. *Suicide and Life-Threatening Behavior, 23*, 343-358.

Heisal, M. J., & Fuse, T. (1999). College student suicide ideation in Canada and Japan. *Psychologia: An International Journal of Psychology in the Orient, 42*, 129-138.

Heller, T., Roccoforte, J. A., Hsieh, K., Cook, J. A., & Pickett, S. A. (1997). Benefits of support groups for families of adults with severe mental illness. *American Journal of Orthopsychiatry, 67*, 187-198.

Helzer, J. E., Robins, L. N., & McEvoy, L. (1987). Posttraumatic stress-disorder in the general population. *New England Journal of Medicine, 317*, 1630-1634.

Helzer, J. E., Robins, L. N., McEvoy, L. T., Spitznagel, E. L., Stolzman, R. K., & Farmer, A. (1985). A comparison of clinical and diagnostic interview schedule diagnoses. *Archives of General Psychiatry, 42*, 657-666.

Helzer, J. E., Spitznagel, E. L., & McEvoy, L. (1987). The predictive validity of lay diagnostic interview schedule diagnoses in the general population. *Archives of General Psychiatry, 44*, 1069-1077.

Henderson, A. S. (1992). Social support and depression. In H. O. F. Veiel & U. Baumann (Eds.), *The meaning and measurement of social support* (pp. 85-92). New York: Hemisphere.

Hennessy, K. (1989). Research on the consequences of child maltreatment and its application to educational settings. *Topics in Early Childhood Special Education, 9*, 33-55.

Hermann, B. P., Whitman, S., Wyler, A. R., Anton, M. T., & Vanderzwagg, R. (1990). Psychosocial predictors of psychopathology in epilepsy. *British Journal of Psychiatry, 156*, 98-105.

Herold, E. S., & Way, L. (1983). Oral-genital sexual behavior in a sample of university females. *Journal of Sex Research, 19*, 327-338.

Hersen, M., & Biaggio, M. (Eds.) (2000). *Effective Brief Therapies: A Clinician's Guide*. Orlando, FL: Academic Press

Hersen, M., Gullick, E. L., Matherne, P. M., & Harbert, T. L. (1972). Instructions and reinforcement in the modification of a conversion reaction. *Psychological Reports, 31,* 719-722.

Heston, L. L., & Mastri, A. R. (1982). Age of onset of Pick's and Alzheimer's dementia: Implications for diagnosis and research. *Journal of Gerontology, 37,* 422-424.

Heston, L. L., & White, J. (1991). *The vanishing mind: A practical guide to Alzheimer's disease and other dementias.* New York: W. H. Freeman.

Heston, L. L., White, J. A., & Mastri, A. R. (1987). Pick's disease. *Archives of General Psychiatry, 44,* 409-411.

Hetherington, E. M. (1991). The role of individual differences and family relationships in children's coping with divorce and remarriage. In P. A. Cowan & E. M. Hetherington (Eds.), *Family transitions.* Hillsdale, NJ: Lawrence Erlbaum Associates.

Higgins, S.T., Wong, C.J., Badger, G.J., Ogden, D.E.H., & Dantona, R.C. (2000). Contingent reinforcement increases cocaine abstinence during outpatient treatment and 1 year follow-up. *Journal of Consulting and Clinical Psychology, 68,* 64-72.

Hinshaw, S. P., Lahey, B. B., & Hart, E. L. (1993). Issues of taxonomy and comorbidity in the development of conduct disorder. *Development and Psychopathology, 5,* 31-49.

Hinz, L. D., & Williamson, D. A. (1987). Bulimia and depression: A review of the affective variant hypothesis. *Psychological Bulletin, 102,* 150-158.

Hirschfeld, R. M., Shea, M. T., & Weise, R. (1991). Dependent personality disorder: Perspectives for DSM-IV. *Journal of Personality Disorders, 5,* 135-149.

Hobson, R. P. (1989). Beyond cognition: A theory of autism. In G. Dawson (Ed.), *Autism: Nature, diagnosis, and treatment.* New York: Guilford.

Hodgins, S., Mednick, S. A., Brennan, P. A., Schulsinger, F., & Engberg, M. (1996). Mental disorder and crime: Evidence from a Danish birth cohort. *Archives of General Psychiatry, 53,* 489-496.

Hoenig, J. (1984). Schneider's first rank symptoms and the tabulators. *Comprehensive Psychiatry, 25,* 77-87.

Hoffman, A. (1971). LSD discoverer disputes "chance factor" in finding. *Psychiatric News, 16,* 23-26.

Hogarty, G. E., Anderson, C. M., Reiss, D. J., Kornblith, S. J., Greenwald, D. P., Ulrich, R. F., et al. (1991) Family psychoeducation, social skills training and maintenance chemotherapy in the aftercare treatment of schizophrenia, II: Two year effects of a controlled study on relapse and adjustment. *Archives of General Psychiatry, 48,* 340-347.

Hogarty, G. E., Greenwald, D., Ulrich, R. F., Kornblith, S. J., DiBarry, A. L., Cooley, S., Carter, M., & Flesher, S. (1997a). Three year trials of personal therapy among schizophrenic patients living with or independent of family, II: Effects on adjustment of patients. *American Journal of Psychiatry, 154,* 1514-1524.

Hogarty, G. E., Kornblith, S. J., Greenwald, D., DiBarry, A. L., Cooley, S., Ulrich, R. F., Carter, M., & Flesher, S. (1997b). Three year trials of personal therapy among schizophrenic patients living with or independent of family, I: Description of study and effects on relapse rates. *American Journal of Psychiatry, 154,* 1504-1512

Holland, A. J. (2000). Ageing and learning disability. *British Journal of Psychiatry, 176,* 26-31.

Holzman, P. S., Kringlen, E., Matthysse, S., Flanagan, S. D., Lipton, R. B., Cramer, S., Levin, S., Lange, K., & Levy, D. L. (1988). A single dominant gene can account for eye tracking dysfunctions and schizophrenia in offspring of discordant twins. *Archives of General Psychiatry, 45,* 641-647.

Hommer, D.W. (1999). Functional imaging of craving. *Alcohol Research and Health, 23,* 187-196.

Hooley, J. M. (1985). Expressed emotion: A critical review of the literature. *Clinical Psychology Review, 5,* 119-139.

Hooley, J. M., & Hiller, J. B. (1997). Family relationships and major mental disorder: Risk factors and preventive strategies. In S. Duck, Ed., *Handbook of personal relationships,* 2nd ed. (pp. 621-648). Chichester, United Kingdom: Wiley.

Hooley, J. M., & Hiller, J. B. (2001) Family relationships and major mental disorder: Risk factors and preventive strategies. In B. R. Sarason & S. Duck, Eds.,*Personal relationships: Implications for clinical and community psychology.* (61-88). Chichester, England:Wiley.

Hooley, J. M., & Richters, J. E. (1995). In D. Cicchetti & S. L. Toth (Eds.), Rochester Symposium on Developmental Psychopathology, Vol. 6: *Emotion, cognition, and representation.* (pp. 134-165). Rochester, NY: University of Rochester Press.

Horne, J. (1979). Defendant found guilty of murdering jogger. *Seattle Times,* May 31-C11.

Horowitz, M. J. (1974). Stress response syndromes. *Archives of General Psychiatry, 31,* 768-781.

Horowitz, M. J. (1986). Stress-response syndromes: A review of posttraumatic and adjustment disorders. *Hospital and Community Psychiatry, 37,* 241-249.

Horwitz, A. V. (1984). The economy and social pathology. *Annual Review of Sociology, 10,* 95-119.

Houghton, J. F. (1980). One personal experience: Before and after mental illness. In J. G. Rabkin, L. Gelb, & J. B. Lazar (Eds.), *Attitudes toward the mentally ill: Research perspectives.* Rockville, MD: National Institute of Mental Health.

Houghton, J. F. (1982). First person account: Maintaining mental health in a turbulent world. *Schizophrenia Bulletin, 8,* 548-552.

Howland, R. H. (1993). Chronic depression. *Hospital and Community Psychiatry, 44,* 633-639.

Howlin, P. (1997). Prognosis in autism: Do specialist treatments affect long-term outcome? European Child and *Adolescent Psychiatry, 6,* 55-72.

Howlin, P. (1998). Practitioner review: Psychological and educational treatments for autism. *Journal of Child Psychology and Psychiatry, 3,* 307-322.

Howlin, P., & Moore, A. (1997). Diagnosis of autism. A survey of over 1200 patients in the UK. *Autism, 1,* 135-162.

Hoyert, D. L., Kochanek, K. D., & Murphy, S. L. (1999). *Deaths: Final Data For 1997. National Vital Statistics Report 47(19).* Hyattsville, Md: National Center For Health Statistics.

Hoza, B., Pelham, W. E., Milich, R., Pillow, D., & McBride, K. (1993). The self-perceptions and attributions of attention deficit hyperactivity disordered and non-referred boys. *Journal of Abnormal Child Psychology, 21,* 271-286.

Hser, Y. I., Anglin, M. D., & Powers, K. (1993). A 24-year follow-up of California narcotics addicts. *Archives of General Psychiatry, 50,* 577-584.

Huang, W., & Cuvo, A. J. (1997). Social skills training for adults with mental retardation in job-related settings. *Behavior Modification, 21,* 3-44.

Hunsley, J., & Bailey, J. M. (1999). The clinical utility of the Rorschach: Unfulfilled promises and an uncertain future. *Psychological Assessment, 11,* 266-277.

Hurley, D. J. (1991). The crisis of paternal suicide: Case of Cathy, age 4-1/2. In N. B. Webb (Ed.), *Play therapy with children in crisis* (pp. 237-253). New York: Guilford.

Hurt, S. W., & Clarkin, J. F. (1990). Borderline personality disorder: Prototypic typology and the development of treatment manuals. *Psychiatric Annals, 20,* 13-18.

Huttunen, M. O., & Niskanen, P. Prenatal loss of father and psychiatric disorders. *Archives of General Psychiatrry, 35,* 429-431.

Iacono, W. G., & Koenig, W. G. R. (1983). Features that distinguish the smooth-pursuit eye-tracking performance of schizophrenic, affective disorder, and normal individuals. *Journal of Abnormal Psychology, 92,* 29-41.

Infant Health and Development Program. (1990). Enhancing the outcomes of low birth weight, premature infants: A multisite randomization trial. *Journal of the American Medical Association, 263,* 3035-3042.

Institute of Medicine (1990). *Research on children and adolescents with mental, behavioral, and developmental disorders.* Rockville, MD: National Institute of Mental Health.

Isometsa, E. T., Henriksson, M. M., Aro, H. M., & Lonnqvist, J. K. (1994). Suicide in bipolar disorder in Finland. *American Journal of Psychiatry, 151,* 1020-1024.

Jablensky, A. (1999). Schizophrenia: Epidemiology. *Current Opinion in Psychiatry, 12,* 19-28.

Jackson, J. S. (Ed.) (1991). *Life in Black America.* Newbury Park, CA: Sage.

Jacob, R. G., Wing, R., & Shapiro, A. P. (1987). The behavioral treatment of hypertension: Long-term effects. *Behavior Therapy, 18,* 325-352.

Jacobs, B. L. (1994). Serotonin, motor activity, and depression-related disorders. *American Scientist, 82,* 456-463.

Jacobson, N. S., & Hollon, S. D. (1996). Prospects for future comparisons between drugs and psychotherapy: Lessons from the CBT-versus-pharmacotherapy exchange. *Journal of Consulting and Clinical Psychology, 64,* 104-108.

Jamison, K. R. (1989). Mood disorders and seasonal patterns in British writers and artists. *Psychiatry, 52,* 125-134.

Jamison, K. R. (1995). *An unquiet mind.* New York: Vintage Books.

Javier, R.A., & Herron, W.G. (1998). *Personality development and psychotherapy in our diverse society.* Northvale, NJ: Jason Aronson.

Jellinek, E. M. (1960). *The disease concept of alcoholism.* New Haven: Hillhouse Press.

Jemmott, J. B., III, & Locke, S. E. (1984). Psychosocial factors, immunologic mediation, and human susceptibility to infectious diseases: How much do we know? *Psychological Bulletin, 95,* 78-108.

Jenkins, J. H., Karno, M. N., de la Selva, A., Santana, F., Tellis, C., Lopez, S., & Mintz, J. (1986). Expressed emotion, maintenance psychotherapy and schizophrenic relapse among Mexican-Americans. *Psychopharmacology Bulletin, 22,* 621-627.

Jenkins, J. H., Kleinman, A., & Good, B. J. (1991). Cross-cultural studies of depression. In J. Becker and A. Kleinman (Eds.), *Psychosocial aspects of depression.* Hillsdale, NJ: Lawrence Erlbaum.

Jepson, T. L., Ernst, M. E., & Kelly, M. W. (1999). Current perspectives on the management of seasonal affective disorder. *Journal of the American Pharmaceutical Association, 39,* 822-829.

Johnson, J., Weissman, M. M., & Klerman, G. L. (1990). Panic-disorder, comorbidity, and suicide attempts. *Archives of General Psychiatry, 47,* 805-808.

Johnson, S. L., Winett, C. A., Meyer, B., Greenhouse, W. J., & Miller, I. (1999). Social support and the course of bipolar disorder. *Journal of Abnormal Psychology, 108,* 558-566.

Johnson, S., & Lebow, J. (2000). The "Coming of Age" of couple therapy. *Journal of Marital and Family Therapy, 26,* 23-38.

Johnson, W. G., Tsoh, J. Y., & Varnado, P. J. (1996). Eating disorders: Efficacy of pharmacological and psychological interventions. *Clinical Psychology Review, 16,* 457-478.

Jonas, K. (1992). Modeling and suicide: A test of the Werther effect. *British Journal of Social Psychology, 31,* 295-306.

Jones, M. C. (1981). Midlife drinking patterns. Correlates and antecedents. In D. H. Eichorn (Ed.), *Present and past in middle life.* New York: Academic Press, 223-242.

Jones, P., & Cannon, M. (1998). The new epidemiology of schizophrenia. *Psychiatric Clinics of North America, 21*, 1-25.

Jordon, B. D., Relkin, N. R., Ravdin, L. D., Jacobs, A. R., Bennett, A., & Gandy, S. (1997). Apolipoprotein E epsilon4 associated with chronic traumatic brain injury in boxing. *Journal of the American Medical Association, 278*, 136-140.

Jorgensen, R. S., Johnson, B. T., Kolodziej, M. E., & Schreer, G. E. (1996). Elevated blood pressure and personality: A meta-analytic review. *Psychological Bulletin, 120*, 293-320.

Joseph, J. G., Caumartin, S. M., Margalittal, M. P. H., Kirscht, J. P., Kessler, R. C., Ostrow, D. G., & Wortman, C. B. (1990). Psychological functioning in a cohort of gay men at risk for AIDS: A three-year descriptive study. *The Journal of Nervous and Mental Disease, 178*, 607-615.

Joseph, R. M. (1999). Neuropsychological frameworks for understanding autism. *International Review of Psychiatry, 11*, 309-325.

Jung, J. (2001). *Psychology of Alcohol and Other Drugs: A Research Perspective*. Thousand Oaks, CA: Sage

Kagan, J., & Zentner, M. (1996). Early childhood predictors of adult psychopathology. *Harvard Review of Psychiatry, 3*, 341-350.

Kalafat, J. & Elias, M. (1995). Suicide prevention in an educational context: Broad and narrow foci. *Suicide and Life-Threatening Behavior, 25*, 123-133.

Kane, J. M. (1994). Efficacy, mechanisms, and side effects of typical and atypical neuroleptics. In N. C. Andreason (Ed.), *Schizophrenia: From mind to molecule* (pp. 173-188). Washington, DC: American Psychiatric Press.

Kaplan, H. S. (1974). *The new sex therapy: Active treatment of sexual dysfunctions*. New York: Quadrangle Books.

Kaplan, H. S. (1979). *Disorders of sexual desire*. New York: Simon & Schuster.

Kapur, S., Mieczkowski, T., & Mann, J. J. (1992). Antidepressant medications and the relative risk of suicide attempt and suicide. *Journal of the American Medical Association, 268*, 3441-3445.

Karel, R. (1995). Behind the badge: culture of toughness, guns makes suicide chief cause of death among police. *Psychiatric News*, February 3, pp. 4, 23.

Kashani, J. H. & McNaul, J. P. (1997). Mood disorders in adolescents. In J. M. Wiener (Ed.), *Textbook of child and adolescent psychiatry*, 2nd ed., pp. 343-385.Washington, DC: American Psychiatric Press.

Kashiwase, H., & Kato, M. (1997). Folie a deux in Japan—analysis of 97 cases in the Japanese literature. *Acta Psychiatrica Scandinavica, 96*, 231-234.

Kaslow, N. J., Doepke, K. J., & Racusin, G. R. (1994). Depression. In V. B. VanHasselt & M. Hersen (Eds.), *Advanced abnormal psychology*. New York: Plenum Press.

Kasper, S., Wehr, T. A., Bartko, J., Geist, P. A., & Rosenthal, N. E. (1989). Epidemiological findings of seasonal changes in mood and behavior: A telephone survey of Montgomery County, Maryland. *Archives of General Psychiatry, 46*, 630-636.

Katz, S. (1994). Twenty years later: A follow-up study of graduates of two sheltered workshop programmes in Israel. *British Journal of Developmental Disabilities, 40*, 4-14.

Kauffman, J. (1993). Dissociative functions in the normal mourning process. *Omega, 28*, 31-38.

Kaufman, A. S., & Kaufman, N. L. (1983). *Kaufman Assessment Battery for Children: Interpretive manual*. Circle Pines, NM: American Guidance Service.

Kaufman, M. H. (1997). The teratogenic effects of alcohol following exposure during pregnancy and its influence on the chromosome constitution of the pre-ovulatory egg. *Alcohol and Alcoholism, 32*, 113-128.

Kaufman, M. J., Agard, J. A., & Semmel, M. I. (1982). *Mainstreaming: Learners and their environments*. Baltimore: University Park Press.

Kaye, W. H., Weltzin, T. E., Hsu, L. K., & Bulik, C. M. (1991). An open trial of fluoxetine in patients with anorexia nervosa. *Journal of Clinical Psychiatry, 52*, 464-471.

Kazdin, A. E. (1995). Methods of psychotherapy research. In B. Bongar and L. E. Beutler (Eds.), *Comprehensive textbook of psychotherapy: Theory and practice* (pp. 405-433). New York: Oxford University Press.

Keel, P. K., & Mitchell, J. E. (1997). Outcome in bulimia nervosa. *American Journal of Psychiatry, 154*, 313-321.

Keel, P.K., Mitchell, J.E., Miller, K.B., Davis, T.L., & Crow, S.J. (1999). Long-term outcome of bulimia nervosa. *Archives of General Psychiatry, 56*, 63-49.

Kegan, R. (1994). *In over our heads: The mental demands of modern life*. Cambridge, MA: Harvard University Press.

Keller, M. B. (1990). Diagnostic and course of illness variables pertinent to refractory depression. In A. Tasman, S. M. Goldfinger, & C. A. Kaufmann, *Review of Psychiatry* (vol. 9). Washington, DC: American Psychiatric Press.

Keller, M. B., Klein, D. N., Hirschfeld, R. M. A., Kocsis, J. H., et al. (1995). Results of the DSM-IV Mood Disorders Field Trial, *American Journal of Psychiatry, 152*, 843-849.

Kelly, G. A. (1955). *The psychology of personal constructs* (vols. 1 & 2). New York: W. W. Norton.

Kendall, P. C. (1994). Treating anxiety disorders in children: Results of a randomized clinical trial. *Journal of Consulting and Clinical Psychology, 62*, 100-110.

Kendall, P. C., & Southam-Gerow, M. A. (1996). Long-term follow-up of a cognitive-behavioral therapy for anxiety disordered youth. *Journal of Consulting and Clinical Psychology, 64*, 724-730.

Kendall, P. C., & Wilcox, L. E. (1978). Self-control in children: Development of a rating scale. *Journal of Consulting and Clinical Psychology, 47*, 1020-1029.

Kendall, P. C., Reber, M., McLeer, S., Epps, J., & Ronan, K. R. (1990). Cognitive-behavioral treatment of conduct-disordered children. *Cognitive Therapy and Research, 14*, 279-289.

Kendler, K. S., Heath, A., Martin, N. G., & Eaves, L. J. (1986). Symptoms of anxiety and depression in a volunteer twin population: The etiologic role of genetic and environmental factors. *Archives of General Psychiatry, 43*, 213-221.

Kendler, K. S., Karkowski, L. M., & Prescott, C. A. (1999). Causal relationship between stressful life events and the onset of major depression. *American Journal of Psychiatry, 156*, 837-841.

Kendler, K. S., MacLean, C. J., O'Neill, A., & Burke, J., Murphy, B., Duke, F., Shinkwin, R., Easter, S. M., Webb, B. T., Zhang, J., Walsh, D. D., & Straub, R. E., (1996). Evidence for a schizophrenia vulnerability locus on chromosome 8p in the Irish study of high-density schizophrenia families. *American Journal of Psychiatry, 153*, 1534-1540.

Kendler, K. S., Neale, M. C., Kessler, R. C., Heath, A. C., & Eaves, L. J. (1992). Familial influences on the clinical characteristics of major depression: A twin study. *Acta Psychiatrica Scandinavica, 86*, 371-378.

Kenyon, K. (1979). A survivor's notes. *Newsweek*, April 30,17-B10.

Kerby, D. S., & Dawson, B. L. (1994). Autistic features, personality, and adaptive behavior in males with the fragile X syndrome and no autism. *American Journal on Mental Retardation, 98*, 455-462.

Kernberg, O. F. (1975). *Borderline conditions and pathological narcissism*. New York: Jason Aronson.

Kety, S. S., Rosenthal, D., Wender, P. H., Schulsinger, F., & Jacobson, B. (1978). The biological and adoptive families of adopted individuals who become schizophrenic: Prevalence of mental illness and other characteristics. In L. C. Wynne, R. L. Cromwell, & S. Matthysse (Eds.), *The nature of schizophrenia: New approaches to research and treatment*. New York: Wiley.

Kety, S. S., Wender, P. H., Jacobsen, B., Ingraham, L. J., Rosenthal, D., Jannson, L., Faber, B., & Kinney, D. (1994). Mental illness in the biological and adoptive relatives of the schizophrenic adoptees. Replication of the Copenhagen Study in the rest of Denmark. *Archives of General Psychiatry, 51*, 442-455.

Kiecolt-Glaser, J. K., & Glaser, R. (1992). Stress and the immune system: Human studies. In A. Tasman and M. B. Riba (Eds.), *Review of Psychiatry* (Vol. 11, pp. 169-179). Washington, DC: American Psychiatric Press.

Kiecolt-Glaser, J. K., & Glaser, R. (1995). Psychoneuroimmunology and health consequences. Data and shared mechanisms. *Psychosomatic Medicine, 57*, 269-274.

Kilmann, P. R., Sabalis, R. F., Gearing, M. I., Bukstel, L. H., & Scovern, A. W. (1982). The treatment of sexual paraphilias: A review of outcome research. *Journal of Sex Research, 18*, 193-252.

King, N. J., Ollendick, T. H., & Tonge, B. J. (1995). *School refusal: Assessment and treatment*. Boston: Allyn & Bacon.

King, N. J., Ollier, K., Iacuone, R., Schuster, S., Bays, K., Gullione, E., & Ollendick, T. H. (1989). Fears of children and adolescents: A cross-sectional Australian study using the Revised Fear Survey Schedule for children. *Journal of Child Psychology and Psychiatry, 30*, 775-784.

King, N.J., Ollendick, T. H., Tonge, B. J., Heyne, D., Pritchard, M., Rollings, S., Young, D., & Myerson, N. (1998). School refusal: An overview. *Behaviour Change, 15*, 5-15.

Klasen H. (2000). A name, What's in a Name? The medicalization of hyperactivity, revisited. *Harvard Review of Psychiatry, 7*, 334-344.

Klein, D. F. (1996). Preventing hung juries about therapy studies. *Journal of Consulting and Clinical Psychology, 64*, 81-87.

Klein, D. N., Kocsis, J. H., McCullough, J. P., Holzer, C. E., Hirschfeld, R. M., & Keller, M. B. (1996). Symptomatology in dysthymic and major depressive disorder. *Psychiatric Clinics of North America, 19*, 41-53.

Klein, M. H., Benjamin, L. S., Rosenfeld, R., Treece, C., Husted, J., & Greist, J. H. (1993). The Wisconsin Personality Disorders Inventory: Development, reliability, and validity. *Journal of Personality Disorders, 7*, 285-303.

Klerman, G. L., Weissman, M. M., Ouellette, R., Johnson, J., & Greenwald, S. (1991). Panic attacks in the community: Social morbidity and health care utilization. *Journal of the American Medical Association, 265*, 742-746.

Klinterberg, B. A., Andersson, T., Magnusson, D., & Stattin, H. (1993). Hyperactive behavior in childhood as related to subsequent alcohol problems and violent offending: A longitudinal study of male subjects. *Personality and Individual Differences, 15*, 381-388.

Klorman, R., Burmaghin, J. T., Fitzpatrick, M. A., & Borgstedt, A. D. (1990). Clinical effects of a controlled trial of methylphenidate on adolescents with attention deficit disorder. *Journal of the American Academy of Child and Adolescent Psychiatry, 26*, 702-709.

Kluft, R. P. (1988). The dissociative disorders. In J. A. Talbott, R. E. Hales, & S. C. Yudofsky (Eds.), *The American Psychiatric Association textbook of psychiatry*. Washington, DC: American Psychiatric Press.

Kluft, R. P. (1991). Multiple personality disorder. In A. Tasman & S. M. Goldfinger (Eds.), *Review of psychiatry* (vol. 10). Washington, DC: American Psychiatric Press.

Kneip, R. C., Delamater, A. M., Ismond, T., Milford, C., Salvia, L., & Schwartz, D. (1993). Self- and spouse ratings of anger and hostility as predictors of coronary heart disease. *Health Psychology, 12*, 301-307.

Knowles, P. A. L., & Prutsman, T. D. (1968). *The case of Benjie*. Unpublished manuscript, Florida Atlantic University.

Koenig, H.G., Hays, J.C., Larson, D.B., George, L.K., Cohen, H.J., McCullough, M.E., Meador, K.G., & Blazer, D.G. (1999). Does religious attendance prolong survival? A six-year follow-up study of 3,968 older adults. *Journal of Gerontology: Medical Sciences, 54,* 370-376.

Kolata, G. (1987). The poignant thoughts of Down's children are given voice. *New York Times,* December 22, 15.

Konner, M. (1989). Homosexuality: Who and why? *New York Times Magazine,* April 2, 60-61.

Koopman, C., Classen, C., & Spiegel, D. (1994). Predictors of posttraumatic stress symptoms among survivors of the Oakland/Berkeley, California, firestorm. *American Journal of Psychiatry, 15,* 888-894.

Kooy, R. F., Willemsen, R., & Oostra, B. A. (2000). Fragile X syndrome at the turn of the century. *Molecular Medicine Today, 6,* 193-198.

Koss, M. P., & Oros, C. J. (1982). Sexual experiences survey: A research instrument investigating sexual aggression and victimization. *Journal of Consulting and Clinical Psychology, 50,* 455-457.

Koss, M.P. (1998). Hidden rape: Sexual aggression and victimization in a national sample of students in higher education. In M.E. Odem. et al. (Eds.) *Confronting rape and sexual assault: Worlds of women.* Wilmington, DE: SR Books/Scholarly Resources.

Kosten, T. R., Rounsaville, B. J., & Kleber, H. D. (1987). Multidimensionality and prediction of treatment outcome in opioid addicts: 2.5-year follow-up. *Comprehensive Psychiatry, 28,* 3-13.

Kovacs, M. (1985). The natural history and course of depressive disorders in childhood. *Psychiatric Annals, 15,* 387-389.

Kovacs, M. (1996). Presentation and course of major depressive disorder during childhood and later years of the life span. *Journal of the American Academy of Child and Adolescent Psychiatry, 35,* 705-715.

Kovacs, M., & Beck, A. T. (1977). An empirical-clinical approach toward a definition of childhood depression. In J. G. Schulter-Brandt & A. Raskin (Eds.), *Depression in childhood: Diagnosing treatment and conceptual models.* New York: Raven Press.

Kovacs, M., & Devlin, B. (1998). Internalizing disorders in childhood. *Journal of Child Psychology and Psychiatry, 39,* 47-63.

Kozol, J. (2000). Losing my father one day at a time. *New York Times,* Aug. 22, p. 27.

Kposowa, A. J. (2000). Marital status and suicide in the National Longitudinal Mortality Study. *Journal of Epidemiology and Community Health, 54,* 254-261.

Kraepelin, E. (1921). *Clinical psychiatry: A textbook for students and physicians.* Trans. A. R. Desfendorf. New York: Macmillan.

Kraepelin, E. 1909-1913. *Psychiatrie,* 8th ed. Leipzig: J. A. Barth.

Kramer, J. J. (1990). Training parents as behavior change agents: Successes, failures, and suggestions for school psychologists. In T. B. Gutkin & C. R. Reynolds (Eds.), *Handbook of school psychology.* New York: John Wiley.

Kratzer, L., & Hodgins, S. (1997). Adult outcomes of child conduct problems: A cohort study. *Journal of Abnormal Child Psychology, 25,* 65-81.

Krausz, M. (1999). Psychiatric comorbidity in opiate addicts. *Addiction and Mental Health, 5,* 55-62.

Kraya, N. A., & Patrick, C. (1997). Folie a deux in a forensic setting. *Australia New Zealand Journal of Psychiatry, 31,* 883-888.

Krehbiel, K. (2000). Diagnosis and treatment of bipolar disorder. *Monitor on Psychology, 31 (9),* 22.

Kringlen, E. (1981). *Stress and coronary heart disease. Twin Research 3: Epidemiological and clinical studies.* New York: Alan R. Liss.

Kronenberger, W. G., & Meyer, R. G. (1996). *The Child Clinician's Handbook.* Boston: Allyn & Bacon

Krueger, R. F., Caspil, A., Moffit, T. E., Silva, P. A., & McGee, R. (1996). Personality traits are differentially linked to mental disorders: A multitrait-multidiagnosis study of an adolescent birth cohort. *Journal of Abnormal Psychology, 105,* 299-312.

Krupnick, J.L. (1997). Brief psychodynamic treatment of PTSD. *In Session: Psychotherapy in Practice, 3,* 75-89.

Kuhne, M. & Wiener, J. (2000) Stability of social status of children with and without learning disabilities. *Learning Disability Quarterly, 23,* 64-75.

Kulynych, J. J., Luevano, L. F., Jones, D. W., & Weinberger, D. R. (1997). Cortical abnormality in schizophrenia: An in vivo application of the Gyrification Index. *Biological Psychiatry, 41,* 995-999.

Kupfer, D. J., Ulrich, R. F., Coble, P. A., Jarrett, D. B., Grochocinski, V. J., Doman, J., Matthews, G., & Borbely, A. A. (1985). Electroencephalographic sleep of younger depressives. *Archives of General Psychiatry, 42,* 806-810.

Kutcher, S. (1997). Practitioner review: The pharmacotherapy of adolescent depression. Journal of Child Psychology and Psychiatry, 38, 755-767.

Kurita, H. (1997). A comparative study of Asperger syndrome with high-functioning atypical autism. *Psychiatry and Clinical Neurosciences, 51,* 67-70.

Kurtz, L.F. (1997). *Self-help and Support Groups: A Handbook for Practitioners.* Thousand Oaks, CA: Sage.

La Trobe, U., & Bandoora, V. (1991). Multidimensionality of the content of female sexual fantasy. *Behavior Research and Therapy, 29,* 179-189.

Lacks, P. (1984). *Bender-Gestalt screening for brain dysfunction.* New York: John Wiley.

Laffal, J. (1965). *Pathological and normal language.* New York: Atheron.

Lagreca, A. M., Stone, W. L., & Bell, C. R., III. (1983). Facilitating the vocational-interpersonal skills of mentally retarded individuals. *American Journal of Mental Deficiency, 88,* 270-278.

Lahey, B. B., Applegate, B., McBurnett, K., Biederman, J., Greenhill, L., Hynd, G. W., Barkley, R. A., Newcorn, J., Jensen, P., Richters, J., et al. (1994). DSM-IV field trials for attention deficit hyperactivity disorder in children and adolescents. *American Journal of Psychiatry, 151,* 1673-1685.

Lahey, B. B., Carlson, C. L., & Frick, P. J. (1994). Attention deficit disorder without hyperactivity: A review of research relevant to DSM-IV. In T. A. Widiger, A. J. Frances, W. Davis, & M. First (Eds.), *DSM-IV Sourcebook* (Vol. 1). Washington, DC: American Psychiatric Press.

Lahey, B. B., Schaughency, E. A., Strauss, C. C., & Frame, C. L. (1984). Are attention deficit disorders with and without hyperactivity similar or dissimilar disorders? *Journal of the American Academy of Child Psychiatry, 23,* 302-309.

Lai, F., Kammenn, E., Rebeck, G. W., Anderson, A., Chen, Y., & Nixon, R. A. (1999). APOE and gender effects on Alzheimer disease in 100 adults with Down syndrome. *Neurology, 53,* 331-336.

Lam, D. H., (1991). Psychosocial family intervention in schizophrenia: A review of empirical studies. *Psychological Medicine, 21,* 423-441.

Lamb, F., & Dunne-Maxim, K. (1987). Postvention in schools: Policy and progress. In E. J. Dunne, J. L. McIntosh, & K. Dunne-Maxim (Eds.), *Suicide and its aftermath: Understanding and counseling the survivors.* 245-262. New York: Norton.

Landen, L. M., Walinder, J., & Lundstrom, B. (1996). Prevalence, incidence and sex ratio of transsexualism. *Acta Psychiatrica Scandanavica, 93,* 221-223.

Lanquetot, R. (1984). First person account: Confessions of the daughter of a schizophrenic. *Schizophrenia Bulletin, 10,* 467-471.

Lanquetot, R. (1994). Dangerous delusion. *Wall Street Journal,* Wednesday, Aug. 31, p. A12.

Lansky, M. R. (1988). Common clinical predicaments. In J. F. Clarkin, G. L. Haas, & I. D. Glick (Eds.), *Affective disorders and the family: Assessment and treatment* (pp. 213-238). New York: Guilford.

Latib, A., Conroy, J., & Hess, C. M. (1984). Family attitudes toward deinstitutionalization. *International Review of Research on Mental Retardation, 12,* 67-93.

Laumann, E. O., Gagnon, J. H., Michael, R. T., & Michaels, S. (1994). *The social organization of sexuality.* Chicago: University of Chicago Press.

Laumann, E.O., Palk, A., & Rosen, R.C. (1999). Sexual dysfunction in the United States: Prevalence and predictors. *Journal of the American Medical Association, 281,* 537-544.

Lavigne, J. V., Gibbons, R. D., Christoffel, K. K., & Arend, R. (1996). Prevalence rates and correlates of psychiatric disorders among preschool children. *Journal of the American Academy of Child and Adolescent Psychiatry, 35,* 204-214.

Lazarus, A. A. (1971). *Behavior therapy and beyond.* New York: McGraw-Hill.

Lear, M. W. (1988). Mad malady. *New York Times Magazine,* July 3, 21.

Lebow, J. L. & Gurman, A. S., (1995). Research assessing couple and family therapy. In J. T. Spence, J. M. Darley, & D. J. Foss (Eds.), *Annual Review of Psychology, 46,* 27-57.

Leckman, J. F., Zhang, H., Vitale, A., Lahnin, F., Lynch, K., Bondi, C., Kim, Y. S., & Peterson, B. S. (1998). Course of tic severity in Tourette syndrome: The first two decades. *Pediatrics, 102,* 14-19.

Lee, T. M., & Chan, C. C. (1999). Dose-response relationship of phototherapy for seasonal affective disorder: A meta-analysis. *Acta Psychiatrica Scandinavica, 99,* 315-323.

Leenaars, A. A. (1996). Suicide: a multidimensional malaise. *Suicide and Life-Threatening Behavior, 26,* 221-236.

Leff, J., & Vaughn, C. (1981). The role of maintenance therapy and relatives' expressed emotion in relapse schizophrenia: A two-year follow-up. *British Journal of Psychiatry, 139,* 102-104.

Leff, J., & Vaughn, C. (1985). *Expressed emotion in families.* New York: Guilford Press.

Lehman, A. F. (1995). Schizophrenia: Psychosocial treatment. In H. I. Kaplan, & B. J. Sadock (Eds.), *Comprehensive textbook of psychiatry,* 6th ed. (pp. 998-1018). Baltimore: Williams & Wilkins.

Lehman, A. F., Dixon, L. B., Kernan, E., DeForge, B. R., & Postrado, L. T. ((1997). A randomized trial of Assertive Community Treatment for homeless persons with severe mental illness. *Archives of General Psychiatry, 54,* 1038-1043.

Lehrer, P. M., & Murphy, A. I. (1991). Stress reactivity and perception of pain among tension headache sufferers. *Behavioral Research and Therapy, 29,* 61-69.

Leitenberg, H., Rosen, J. C., Gross, J., Nudelman, S., et al. (1988). Exposure plus response-prevention treatment of bulimia nervosa. *Journal of Consulting & Clinical Psychology, 56,* 535-541..

Leonard, H. L., Swedo, S. E., Lenane, M. C., & Rettew, D. C. (1993). A 2- to 7-year follow-up study of 54 obsessive-compulsive children and adolescents. *Archives of General Psychiatry, 50,* 429-439.

Lesch, K-P., Bengel, D., Heils, A., Sabol, S. Z., Greenberg, B. D., Petri, S., Benjamin, J., Mueller, C. R., Hamer, D. H., & Murphy, D. L. (1996). Association of anxiety-related traits with a polymorphism in the serotonin transporter gene regulatory region. *Science, 274,* 1527-1531.

Leslie, A. M. (1987). Pretense and representation: The origins of "theory of mind." *Psychological Review, 94,* 412-426.

Leon, G. R., & Dinklage, D. (1989). Obesity and anorexia nervosa. In T. H. Ollendick and M. Hersen, (Eds.), *Handbook of child psychopathology* (pp. 247-264). New York: Plenum.

Leung, N., Waller, G., & Thomas, T. (1999). Core beliefs, in anorexic and bulimic women. *Journal of Nervous and Mental Disease, 187,* 736-741.

Leung, N., Waller, G., & Thomas, T. (2000). Outcome of group cognitive-behavioral therapy for bulimia nervosa: The role of core beliefs. *Behavior Research and Therapy, 38,* 145-156.

LeVay, S. (1991). A difference in hypothalamic structure between heterosexual and homosexual men. *Science, 253,* 1034-1037.

Levine, R. V., Lynch, K., Myake, K., & Lucia, M. (1989). The Type A city: Coronary heart disease and the pace of life. *Journal of Behavioral Medicine, 12,* 509-524.

Levy, D. L., Holzman, P. S., Matthysse, S., & Mendell, N. R. (1993). Eye tracking dysfunction and schizophrenia: A critical perspective. *Schizophrenia Bulletin, 19,* 461-536.

Lewinsohn, P. M., Mischel, W., Chaplain, W., & Barton, R. (1980). Social competence and depression: The role of illusory self-perceptions. Journal of Abnormal Psychology, 80, 203-212.

Lewis, G., David, A., Andreasson, S., & Allebeck, P. (1992). Schizophrenia and city life. *The Lancet, 340,* 137-140.

Liberman, R. P., & Corrigan, P. W. (1993). Designing new psychosocial treatments for schizophrenia. *Psychiatry, 56,* 238-249.

Lief, H. I. (1992). Psychiatry's challenge: Defining an appropriate therapeutic role when child abuse is suspected. *Psychiatric News,* Aug. 21, p. 102.

Liljefors, I., & Rahe, R. H. (1970). An identical twin study of psychosocial factors in coronary heart disease in Sweden. *Psychosomatic Medicine, 32,* 523-542.

Lin, K.M., & Cheung, F. (1999). Mental health issues for Asian Americans. *Psychiatric Services, 50,* 774-780.

Lindemalm, G., Korlin, D., & Uddenberg, N. (1986). Long-term follow-up of sex change in 13 male to female transsexuals. *Archives of Sexual Behavior, 15,* 187-210.

Linehan, M. M. (1987). Dialectical behavior therapy for borderline personality disorder. *Bulletin of the Menninger Clinic, 51,* 261-276.

Linehan, M. M. (1993). *Cognitive-behavioral treatment of borderline personality disorder.* New York: Guilford.

Linehan, M. M., Armstrong, H. E., Suarez, A., Allmon, D., & Heard, H. L. (1991). Cognitive behavioral treatment of chronically parasuicidal borderline patients. *Archives of General Psychiatry, 48,* 1060-1064.

Linehan, M. M., Heard, H. L., & Armstrong, H. E. (1993). Naturalistic follow-up of a behavioral treatment for chronically parasuicidal borderline patients. *Archives of General Psychiatry, 50,* 971-974.

Linehan, M. M., Tutek, D. A., Heard, H. L., & Armstrong, H. E. (1994). Cognitive-behavioral treatment for chronically parasuicidal borderline patients: Interpersonal outcomes. *American Journal of Psychiatry, 151,* 1771-1776.

Lingjaerde, O. (1983). The biochemistry of depression. A survey of monoaminergic, neuroendocrinological, and bio-rhythmic disturbances in endogenous depression. *Acta Psychiatrica Scandinavica Supplementum, 302,* 36-51.

Lipschitz, A. (1990). *College suicide: A review monograph.* New York: American Suicide Foundation.

Lipsius, S. H. (1987). Prescribing sensate focus without proscribing intercourse. *Journal of Sex and Marital Therapy, 13,* 106-116.

Lobato, D. (1983). Siblings of handicapped children: A review. *Journal of Autism, 13,* 347-364.

Lochman, J. E., & Dodge, K. A. (1998). Distorted perceptions in dyadic interactions of aggressive and nonaggressive boys: Effects of prior expectations, context, and boy's age. *Development and Psychopathology, 10,* 495-512.

Lockridge, L. (1995). Least likely suicide: The search for my father, Ross Lockridge, Jr., author of Raintree County. *Suicide and Life-Threatening Behavior, 25,* 429-436.

Lopera, F., Ardilla, A., Martinez, A., Madrigal, L., Arango-Viana, J. C., Lemere, C. A., Arango-Lasprilla, J. C., Hincapie, L., Arcos-Burgos, M., Ossa, J. E., Behrens, I. M., Norton, J., Lendon, C., Goate, A. M., Ruiz-Linares, A., Rosselli, M., Kosik, K. S. (1997). Clinical features of early-onset Alzheimer disease in a large kindred with an E280A Presenilin-1 mutation. *Journal of the American Medical Association, 277,* 793-799.

LoPiccolo, J. (1994). The evolution of sex therapy. *Sexual and Marital Therapy, 9,* 5-7.

Loranger, A. W. (1996). Dependent personality disorder: Age, sex, and Axis I comorbidity. *Journal of Nervous and Mental Disease, 184,* 17-21.

Loranger, A. W., Sartorius, N., Andreoli, A., Berger, P., Buichheim, P., Channabasavanna, S. M., Coid, D., Dahl, A., Diekstra, R. F. W., Ferguson, B., Jacobsberg, L. B., Mombour, W., Pull, C., Ono, Y., & Regier, D. A. (1994). The international personality disorder examination. *Archives of General Psychiatry, 51,* 215-224.

Lotufo-Neto, F., Trivedi, M., & Thase, M. E. (1999). Meta-analysis of the reversible inhibitors on monoamine oxidase type A moclobemide and brofaromine for the treatment of depression. *Neuropsychopharmacology, 20,* 226-247.

Lovaas, O. I. (1987). Behavioral treatment and normal educational and intellectual functioning in young autistic children. *Journal of Consulting and Clinical Psychology, 55,* 3-9.

Lovaas, O. I. (1989). Concerns about misinterpretation and placement of blame. *American Psychologist, 44,* 1243-1244.

Lovaas, O. I. (1993). The development of a treatment-research project for developmentally disabled and autistic children. *Journal of Applied Behavior Analysis, 26,* 617-630.

Luborsky, L., Crits-Christoph, P., McLellan, T., Woody, G., Piper, W., Liberman, B., Imber, S., & Pilkonis, P. (1986). Do therapists vary much in their success? Findings from four outcome studies. *American Journal of Orthopsychiatry, 56,* 501-512.

Lukoff, D., Lu, F., & Turner, R. (1992). Toward a more culturally sensitive DSM-IV: Psychoreligious and psychospiritual problems. *The Journal of Nervous and Mental Disease, 180,* 673-682.

Lundberg, C., Johansson, K., Ball, K., Bjerre, B., Blomqvist, C., Braekhus, A., Brouwer, W. H., Bylsma, F. W., Carr, D. B., Englund, L., Friedland, R. P., Hakamies-Blomqvist, L., Klemetz, G., O'Neill, D., Odenheimer, G. L., Rizzo, N. J., Schelin, M., Seideman, M., Tallman, K., Viitanen, M., Waller, P. F., & Winblad, B. (1997). Dementia and driving: An attempt at consensus. *Alzheimer Disease and Associated Disorders, 11,* 28-37.

Luntz, B. K., & Widom, C. S. (1994). Antisocial personality disorder in abused and neglected children grown up. *American Journal of Psychiatry, 151,* 670-674.

Lykken, D. T. (1995). *The antisocial personalities.* Mahwah, NJ: Lawrence Erlbaum Associates.

Lynam, D. R. (1996). Early identification of chronic offenders: Who is the fledgling psychopath. *Psychological Bulletin, 120,* 209-234.

Lynn, S.J, & McConkey, K.M. (1998) (Eds.). *Truth in memory.* NY: Guilford.

Maccoby, E., & Maccoby, N. (1954). The interview: A tool of social science. In G. Lindzey (Ed.), *Handbook of social psychology.* Cambridge, MA: Addison-Wesley, 449-487.

MacDougall, J. M., Dembroski, T. M., & Krantz, D. S. (1981). Effects of types of challenge on pressor and heart rate responses in Type A and B women. *Psychophysiology, 18,* 1-9.

MacMillan, H. L., MacMillan, J. H., Offord, D. R., Griffith, L., & MacMillan, A. (1994). Primary prevention of child physical abuse and neglect: A critical review. Part I. *Journal of Child Psychology and Psychiatry, 35,* 835-856.

MacMillan, H. L., MacMillan, J. H., Offord, D. R., Griffith, L., & MacMillan, A. (1994). Primary prevention of child sexual abuse: A critical review. Part II. *Journal of Child Psychology and Psychiatry, 35,* 857-876.

Magnusson, A., Axelsson, J., Karlsson, M. M., & Oskarsson, H. (2000). Lack of seasonal mood change in the Icelandic population: Results of a cross-sectional study. *American Journal of Psychiatry, 157,* 234-238.

Maher, B. A., & Spitzer, M. (1993). Delusion. In H. E. Adams, P. B. Sutker, (Eds.), *Comprehensive handbook of psychopathology,* 2nd ed., (pp. 260-275). New York: Plenum.

Mahl, G. L. (1968). Gestures and body movements in interviews. In J. M. Shlien (Ed.), *Research in psychotherapy: Proceedings of the third conference.* Washington, DC: American Psychological Association.

Maj, M. (1998). Critique of the DS-IV operational diagnostic criteria for schizophrenia. *British Journal of Psychiatry, 172,* 458-460.

Malarkey, W. B., Kiecolt-Glaser, J. K., Pearl, D., & Glaser, R. (1994). Hostile behavior during marital conflict alters pituitary and adrenal hormones. *Psychosomatic Medicine, 56,* 41-51.

Malgady, R. G., Rogler, L. H., & Tryon, W. W. (1992). Issues of validity in the Diagnostic Interview Schedule. *Journal of Psychiatric Research, 26,* 59-67.

Malinosky-Rummell, R., & Hansen, D. J. (1993). Long-term consequences of childhood physical abuse. *Psychological Bulletin, 114,* 68-79.

Malkoff-Schwartz, S. F., Frank, E., Anderson, B., Sherrill, J. T., Siegel, L., Patterson, D., & Kupfer, D. J. (1998). Stressful life events and social rhythm disruption in the onset of manic and depressive bipolar episodes: A preliminary investigation. *Archives of General Psychiatry, 55,* 702-707.

Manhard, P. (1996-1997). Life outside academe. *The Key Reporter, 62,* 5-6.

Mannuzza, S., Klein, R. G., Bessler, A., Malloy, P., & LaPadula, M., Biederman, J., Faraone, S. V., Spencer, T., Wilens, T., & LaPadula, M. (1993). Adult outcome of hyperactive boys: Educational achievement, occupational rank, and psychiatric status. *Archives of General Psychiatry, 50,* 565-576.

Manschreck, T. C. (1995). Delusional disorder and shared psychotic disorder. In H. I. Kaplan & B. J. Sadock (Eds.), *Comprehensive textbook of psychiatry,* 6th ed. (pp. 1031-1049). Baltimore: Williams & Wilkins.

Manuck, S. B., Marsland, A. L., Kaplan, J. R., & Williams, J. K. (1995). The pathogenicity of behavior and its neuroendocrine medication: An example from coronary artery disease. *Psychosomatic Medicine, 57,* 275-283.

Manuck, S. B., Morrison, R. L., Bellack, A. S., & Polefrone, J. M. (1985). Behavioral factors in hypertension, cardiovascular responsivity, anger, and social competence. In M. A. Chesney & R. H. Rosenman (Eds.), *Anger and hostility in cardiovascular and behavioral disorders.* Washington, DC: Hemisphere.

March, J. S., Mulle, K., & Herbel, B. (1994). Behavioral psychotherapy for children and adolescents with obsessive-compulsive disorder: An open trial of a new protocol-driven treatment package. *Journal of the American Academy of Child and Adolescent Psychiatry, 33,* 333-341.

Marder, S. R., Wirshing, W. C., Mintz, J., McKenzie, J., Johnston, K., Eckman, T. A,., et al. (1996) Two year outcome of social skills training and group psychotherapy for outpatients with schizophrenia. *American Journal of Psychiatry, 153,* 1585-1592.

Marengo, J. T., Harrow, M., Lanin-Kettering, I., & Wilson, A. (1986). Evaluating bizarre-idiosyncratic thinking: A comprehensive index of positive thought disorder. *Schizophrenia Bulletin, 12,* 497-510.

Markowitz, J. C. (1993). Comorbidity of dysthymia. *Psychiatric Annals, 23,* 617-624.

Markowitz, J., Brown, R., Sweeney, J., & Mann, J. J. (1987). Reduced length and cost of hospital stay for major depression in patients treated with ECT. *American Journal of Psychiatry, 144,* 1025-1029.

Marks, I. M. (1978). Living with fear. New York: McGraw-Hill.

Marks, I. M. (1987a). Behavioral aspects of panic disorder. *American Journal of Psychiatry, 144,* 1160-1165.

Marks, I. M. (1987b). Fears, phobias, and rituals: Panic, anxiety, and their disorders. New York: Oxford University Press.

Marks, I., Green, R., & Mataix-Cols, D. (2000). Adult gender identity disorder can remit. *Comprehensive Psychiatry, 41*, 273-275.

Marks, M., & Hodges, S. (1993). Negative cognitions and attributional style in seasonal affective disorder. Paper presented at the 23rd European Congress of Behavior and Cognitive Therapies, London, September.

Marlatt, G. A. (1994). Binge drinking in adolescents and young adults; a harm-reduction approach. Invited address, American Psychological Association annual convention, Los Angeles, CA.

Marlatt, G. A., & Gordon, J. R. (1985). *Relapse prevention: Maintenance strategies in the treatment of addictive behaviors*. New York: Guilford.

Marlatt, G. A., Demming, B., & Reid, J. B. (1973). Loss of control drinking in alcoholics: An experimental analogue. *Journal of Abnormal Psychology, 81*, 233-241.

Marsh, L. (2000). Neuropsychiatric aspects of Parkinson's disease. *Psychosomatics, 41*, 15-23.

Marshall, R.D., & Pierce, D. (2000). Implications of recent findings in posttraumatic stress disorder and the role of pharmacotherapy. *Harvard Review of Psychiatry, 7*, 247-256.

Marshall, R.D., Spitzer, R., & Liebowitz, M.R. (1999). Review and critique of the new DSM-IV diagnosis of acute stress disorder. *American Journal of Psychiatry, 156*, 1677-1685.

Marusic, A., Gudjonsson, G.H., Eysenck, H.J., & Starc, R. (1999). Biological and psychosocial risk factors in ischaemic heart disease: Empirical findings and a psychosocial model. *Personality and Individual Differences, 26*, 285-304.

Marx, B. P., Van Wie, V., & Gross, A. M. (1996). Date rape risk factors: A review and methodological critique of the literature. *Aggression andViolent Behavior, 1*, 27-45.

Marx, J. (1996). Searching for drugs that combat Alzheimer's. *Science, 273*, 50-53.

Maser, J. D., & Cloninger, C. R. (Eds.), (1990). *Comorbidity of mood and anxiety disorders*. Washington, DC: American Psychiatric Press.

Masters, W. H., & Johnson, V. E. (1966). *Human sexual response*. Boston: Little, Brown.

Masters, W. H., & Johnson, V. E. (1970). *Human sexual inadequacy*. Boston: Little, Brown.

Masters, W. H., & Johnson, V. E. (1979). *Homosexuality in perspective*. Boston: Little, Brown.

Masters, W. H., Johnson, V. E., & Kolodny, R. C. (1985). *Human sexuality*, 2nd ed. Boston: Little, Brown.

Matson, J. L., & Sevin, J. A. (1994). Theories of dual diagnosis in mental retardation. *Journal of Consulting and Clinical Psychology, 62*, 6-16.

Mattison, R. E. (1995). Separation anxiety disorder and anxiety in children. In H. I. Kaplan, & B. J. Sadock (Eds.) *Comprehensive textbook of psychiatry*, 6th ed. (pp. 2345-2351). Baltimore, MD: Williams & Wilkins.

Maude-Griffin, P.M., Hohenstein, J.M., Humfleet, G.C., Reilly, P.M., Tusel, D.J., & Hall, S.M. (1998). Superior efficacy of cognitive-behavioral therapy for urban crack cocaine abusers: Main and matching effects. *Journal of Consulting and Clinical Psychology, 66*, 832-827.

Mazzucco, M. M. (2000). Advances in research on the fragile X syndrome. *Mental Retardation and Developmental Disabilities Research Review, 6*, 96-106.

McDermott, P. A. (1996). A nationwide study of developmental and gender prevalence for psychopathology in childhood and adolescence. *Journal of Abnormal Child Psychology, 24*, 53-66.

McDonough, L., Stahmer, A., Schreibman, L., & Thompson, S. J. (1997). Deficits, delays, and distractions: An evaluation of symbolic play and memory in children with autism. *Development and Psychopathology, 9*, 17-41.

McEachin, J. J., Smith, T., & Lovaas, O. I. (1993). Long-term outcome for children with autism who received early intensive behavioral treatment. *American Journal on Mental Retardation, 97*, 359-372.

McElroy, S.L., Soutullo, C.A., Taylor, P., Nelson, E.B., Beckman, D.A., Brusman, L.A., Ombaba, J.M., Strakowski, S.M., & Keck, P.E. (1999). Psychiatric features of 36 men convicted of sexual offenses. *Journal of Clinical Psychiatry, 60*, 414-422.

McFarlane, W. R., Lukens, E., Link, B., Dushay, R., Deakins, S. A., Newmark, M., Dunne, E. J., Horen, B., & Toren, J. (1995). Multiple family group and psychoeducation in the treatment of schizophrenia. *Archives of General Psychiatry, 52*, 679-687.

McGarvey, E.L. Clavet. G.K., Mason, W., & Waite, D. (1999). Adolescent inhalant abuse. *American Journal of Drug and Alcohol Abuse, 25*, 731-741.

McGhie, A. & Chapman, J. (1961). Disorders of attention and perception in early schizophrenia. *British Journal of Medical Psychology, 34*, 103-116.

McGlashan, T. H. (1986). Schizotypal personality disorder. *Archives of General Psychiatry, 43*, 329-334.

McGlashan, T. H. (1988). A selective review of recent North American long-term follow-up studies of schizophrenia. *Schizophrenia Bulletin, 14*, 515-542.

McGlashan, T. H. (1994). Psychosocial treatments of schizophrenia. In N. C. Andreason (Ed.), *Schizophrenia: From mind to molecule* (pp. 189-218). Washington, DC: American Psychiatric Press.

McGlashan, T. H., & Fenton, W. S. (1992). The positive-negative distinction in schizophrenia: Review of natural history validators. *Archives of General Psychiatry, 49*, 63-72.

McGlashan, T. H., & Hoffman, R. E. (2000), Schizophrenia as a disorder of developmentally reduced synaptic connectivity. *Archives of General Psychiatry, 57*, 637-648.

McGlashan, T. H., & Johannessen, J. O. (1996). Early detection and intervention with schizophrenia: Rationale. *Schizophrenia Bulletin, 22*, 201-222.

McGoldrick, M. (1998). *Revisioning family therapy*. NY: Guildord.

McGue, M., & Gottesman, I. I. (1989). Genetic linkage in schizophrenia: Perspectives from genetic epidemiology. *Schizophrenia Bulletin, 15*, 453-464.

McGue, M., Gottesman, I. I., & Rao, D. C. (1985). Resolving genetic models for the transmission of schizophrenia. *Genetic Epidemiology, 21*, 99-110.

McGuffin, P., Reveley, A., & Holland, A. (1982). Identical triplets: Nonidentical psychosis? *British Journal of Psychiatry, 140*, 1-6.

McGuire, P. K., Shah, G. M., & Murray, R. M. (1993). Increased blood flow in Broca's area during auditory hallucinations in schizophrenia. *Lancet, 342*, 703-706.

McMahon, R. J. (1994). Diagnosis, assessment, and treatment of externalizing problems in children: The role of longitudinal data. *Journal of Consulting and Clinical Psychology, 62*, 901-917.

McMahon, R. J., & Estes, A. M. (1997). Conduct problems. In E. J. Mash & L. G. Terdal (Eds.), *Assessment of childhood disorders* (pp. 39-134). New York: Guilford.

McNally, R. J. (1987). Preparedness and phobias: A review. *Psychological Bulletin, 101*, 283-303.

McNally, R. J. (1990). Psychological approaches to panic disorder: A review. *Psychological Bulletin, 108*, 403-419.

McNamara, J.A., Jr., & Trotman, C. (Eds.) (1997). *Creating the compliant patient*. Ann Arbor, MI: University of Michigan.

McNaught, A. S., Jeffreys, S. E., Harvey, C. A., Quayle, A. S., King, M. B., & Bird, A. S. (1997). The Hampstead Schizophrenia Survey 1991: 2. Incidence and migration in inner London. *British Journal of Psychiatry, 170*, 307-311.

Mednick, S. A., Machon, R. A., Huttunen, M. O., & Bonett, D. (1988). Adult schizophrenia following prenatal exposure to an influenza epidemic. *Archives of General Psychiatry, 45*, 189-192.

Mednick, S. A., Parnas, J., & Schulsinger, F., (1987). The Copenhagen high-risk project, 1962-1986. *Schizophrenia Bulletin, 13*, 485-495.

Meesters, Y., Beersman, D. G., Bouhuys, A. L., & van den Hoofdakker, R. H. (1999). Prophylactic treatment of seasonal affective disorder (SAD) by using light visors: Bright white or infrared light? *Biological Psychiatry, 46*, 239-246.

Melamed, B. G., & Bush, J. P. (1986). Parent-child influences during medical procedures. In S. M. Auerbach and A. L. Stolberg (Eds.), *Crisis intervention within children and families*. Washington, DC: Hemisphere.

Mellor, C. S. (1970). First rank symptoms of schizophrenia. *British Journal of Psychiatry, 177*, 15-23.

Meloy, J. R. (1992). Revisiting the Rorschach of Sirhan Sirhan. *Journal of Personality Assessment, 58*, 548-570.

Meltzer, H. Y. (1993). New drugs for the treatment of schizophrenia. *Psychiatric Clinics of North America, 16*, 365-385.

Melzack, R. (1999). Pain and stress: A new perspective. In R.J. Gatchel & Turk (Eds.) *Psychological factors in pain*. NY: Guilford.

Mental Health, United States, 1996 (1997). Washington, DC: Substance Abuse and Mental Health Services Administration.

Mental Health: A report of the Surgeon General (1999). Washington, DC: Department of Health and Human Services.

Merikangas, K. R. (1990). Comorbidity for anxiety and depression: Review of family and genetic studies. In J. D. Maser and C. R. Cloninger (Eds.), *Comorbidity of mood and anxiety disorders*. Washington, DC: American Psychiatric Press.

Merikangas, K. R., Dierker, L. C., & Szatmari, P. (1998). Psychopathology among offspring of parents with substance abuse and/or anxiety disorders: A high risk study. *Journal of Child Psychology and Psychiatry, 39*, 711-720.

Mersch, P. P., Middendorp, H. M., Bouhuys, A. L., Beersma, D. G., & van den Hoofdakker, R. H. (1999). Seasonal affective disorder and lattitude: A review of the literature. *Journal of Affective Disorders, 53*, 35-48.

Mesibov, G. B. (1993). Treatment outcome is encouraging. *American Journal of Mental Retardation, 97*, 373-391.

Messer, I. (1994). *Tactical police officers stress study*. College Station, TX: Unpublished doctoral dissertation.

Meston, C.M., & Heiman, J.R. (2000). Sexual abuse and sexual function: An examination of sexually relevant cognitive processes. *Journal of Consulting and Clinical Psychology, 68*, 399-406.

Meyer, J. (1990). Guess who's coming to dinner this time? A study of gay intimate relationships and the support for those relationships. *Journal of Homosexuality, 18*, 59-82.

Meyer, R. (1989). *Typologies in treatments of psychiatric disorders* (Vol. 2). Washington, DC: American Psychiatric Association.

Meyerowitz, B.E., Richardson, J., Hudson, S., & Leedham, B. (1998). Ethnicity and cancer outcomes: Behavioral and psychosocial considerations. *Psychological Bulletin, 123*, 47-70.

Mezzich, J. E., Ahn, C. W., Fabrega, H., Jr., & Pilkonis, P. A. (1990). Patterns of psychiatric comorbidity in a large population presenting for care. In J. D. Maser & C. R. Cloninger (Eds.), *Comorbidity in anxiety and mood disorders*. Washington, DC: American Psychiatric Press.

Mezzich, J.E., Kleinman, A., Fabrega, H., & Parron, D.L. (1996). *Culture and psychiatric diagnosis: A DSM IV perspective*. Washington, DC: American Psychiatric Press.

Miklowitz, D. J., & Alloy, L. B. (1999) Psychosocial factors in the course and treatment of bipolar disorder: Introduction to the special section. *Journal of Abnormal Psychology, 108*, 555-557.

Miklowitz, D. J., & Stackman, D. (1992). Communication deviance in families of schizophrenic and other psychiatric patients: Current state of the construct. *Progress in Experimental Personality and Psychopathology Research, 15*, 1-46.

Miller, G. E., & Prinz, R. J. (1990). Enhancement of social learning family interventions for childhood conduct disorders. *Psychological Bulletin, 108*, 229-307.

Miller, M. W. (1994). Listening to Eli Lilly: Prozac hysteria has gone too far. *Wall Street Journal*, March 30, pp. B1, B7.

Miller, T. Q., Smith, T. W., Turner, C. W., Guijarro, M. L., & Hallet, A. J. (1996). A meta analytic review of research on hostility and physical health. *Psychological Bulletin, 119*, 322-348.

Millon, T. (1986). The avoidant personality. In R. Michels and J. O. Cavenar, Jr. (Eds.), Psychiatry, vol. 1. New York: Basic Books.

Millon, T., & Davis, R. (2000). *Personality disorders in modern life*. NY: Wiley.

Millon, T., Millon, C., & Davis, R. D. (1994). *Millon Clinical Multiaxial Inventory: III*. Minneapolis: National Computer Systems.

Mimelein, M. J., & McElrath, J. A. V. (1996). Resilient child sexual abuse survivors: Cognitive coping and illusion. *Child Abuse and Neglect, 20*, 747-758.

Minuchin, S., Rosman, B., & Baker, L. (1978). *Psychosomatic families: Anorexia nervosa in context*. Cambridge, MA: Harvard University Press.

Miranda, J., & Green, B. L. (1999). The need for mental health services research focusing on poor young women. *Journal of Mental Health Policy and Economics, 2*, 73-89.

Mirsky, A. F., & Bakay Pragnay, E. (1984). Brainstem mechanisms in the processing of sensory information: Clinical symptoms, animal models and unit analysis. In D. E. Sheer (Ed.), *Attention: Theory, brain functions and clinical applications*. Hillsdale, NJ: Erlbaum.

Mitchell, P., Mackinnon, A., & Waters, B. (1993). The genetics of bipolar disorder. *Australia and New Zealand Journal of Psychiatry, 27*, 560-580.

Mizes, J. S. (1990). Criterion-related validity of the Anorectic Cognitions Questionnaire. *Addictive Behaviors, 15*, 153-163.

Moats, R. A., Koch, R., Moseley, K., Guldberg, P., Guttler, F., Boles, R. G., & Nelson, M. D., Jr. (2000). Brain phenylalanine concentration in the management of adults with phenylketonuria. *Journal of Inherited Metabolic Disease, 23*, 7-14.

Mohr, D. C. (1995). Negative outcomes in psychotherapy: A critical review. *Clinical Psychology: Science and Practice, 2*, 1-27.

Moldin, S. O., Scheftner, W. A., Rice, J. P., Nelson, E., Knesevich, M. A., & Akiskal, H. (1993). Association between major depressive disorder and physical illness. *Psychological Medicine, 23*, 755-761.

Moltz, D. A. (1993). Bipolar disorder and the family: An integrative model. *Family Process, 32*, 409-423.

Money, J. (1987). Sin, sickness, or status? Homosexual gender identity and psychoneuroendocrinology. *American Psychologist, 42*, 384-399.

Moos, R. H. (1974). Family Environment Scale. Palo Alto, CA: Consulting Psychologists Press.

Moran, A. E., Freedman, R. I., & Sharfstein, S. S. (1984). The journey of Sylvia Frumkin: A case study for policymakers. *Hospital and Community Psychiatry, 35*, 887-893.

Moran, Lord C. M. W. (1966). *Winston Churchill: The struggle for survival, 1940-1965*. Boston: Houghton Mifflin.

Morin, C. M., & Wooten, V. (1996). Psychological and pharmacological approaches to treating insomnia: Critical issues in assessing their separate and combined effects. *Clinical Psychology Review, 16*, 521-542.

Morisette, J., Villeneuve, A., Bordeleau, L., Rochette, D., Laberge, C., Gagne, B., Laprise, C., Bouchard, G., Plante, M., Gobeil, L., Shink, E., Weissenbach, J., & Barden, N. (1999). Genome-wide search for linkage of bipolar affective disordersin a very large pedigree derived from a homogeneous population in Quebec points to a locus of major effect on chromosome 12q23-q24. *American Journal of Medical Genetics, 88*, 567-587.

Morris, J. (1974). *Conundrum*. New York: Harcourt, Brace, & Jovanovich.

Morrissey, J. P., & Goldman, H. H. (1986). Care and treatment of the mentally ill in the United States: Historical developments and reforms. *American Association of Political and Social Sciences, 484*, 12-28.

Mortensen, P. B., Pedersen, C. B., Westergaard, T., Wohlfahrt, J., Ewald, H., Mors, O, Andersen, P. K., & Melbye, M. (1999). Effects of family history and place and season of birth on the risk of schizophrenia. *New England Journal of Medicine, 340*, 603-608.

Mosher, L. R. (1989). Community residential treatment: Alternatives to hospitalization. In A. S. Bellack (Ed.) *Clinical guide for the treatment of schizophrenia*. New York: Plenum.

Mowat, D. R., Hayden, M. C., Thompson, S. M., & Wilcken, B. Maternal phenylketonuria: A continuing problem. *The Medical Journal of Australia, 170*, 592-595.

Mueser, K. T., Bellack, A. S., Douglas, M. S., & Morrison, R. L. (1991). Prevalence and stability of social skill deficits in schizophrenia. *Schizophrenia Research, 5*, 167-176.

Mufson, L. (1993). *Interpersonal psychotherapy for depressed adolescents*. New York: Guilford.

Mufson, L., Moreau, D., Weissman, M. M., Wickramaratne, P., Martin, J., & Samoilov, A. (1994). Modification of interpersonal psychotherapy with

depressed adolescents (IPT-A): Phase I and II studies. *Journal of the American Academy of Child and Adolescent Psychiatry, 33*, 695-705.

Mulcahy, J.J. (1997). *Diagnosis and management of male sexual dysfunction*. NY: Igaku-Shoin.

Muller-Oelinghausen, B., Muser-Causemann, B., & Volk, J. (1992). Suicides and parasuicides in a high-risk patient group on and off lithium long-term medication.*Journal of Affective Disorders, 25*, 947-960.

Mundy, P. (1993). Normal vs. high functioning status in children with autism. *American Journal of Mental Retardation, 97*, 373-391.

Murphy, D. A., Pelham, W. E., & Lang, A. R. (1992). Aggression in boys with attention deficit disorder: Methylphenidate effects on naturalistic observations of aggression, response to provocation in the laboratory, and social information processing. *Journal of Abnormal Child Psychology, 20*, 451-466.

Murphy, K. C. (1996). Recent developments in the genetics of schizophrenia. *Irish Journal of Psychological Medicine, 13*, 151-154.

Murphy, K., & Barkley, R. A. (1996). Attention deficit hyperactivity disorder adults: Comorbidities and adaptive impairments. *Comprehensive Psychiatry, 37*, 393-401.

Murphy, M. J. (1985). Marital breakdown and socioeconomic status. *British Journal of Sociology, 36*, 81-93.

Murray, C. J., & Lopez, A. D. (1997). Alternative projections of mortality and disability by cause 1990-2020: Global Burden of Disease Study. *Lancet, 349*, 1498-1504.

Murray, H. A. (1943). *Thematic apperception test: Pictures and manual*. Cambridge, MA: Harvard University Press.

Mussell, M.P., Mitchell, J.E., Crosby, R.D., Fulkerson, J.A., Hoberman, H.M., & Romano, J.L. (2000). Commitment to treatment goals in prediction of group cognitive-behavioral therapy treatment outcome for women with bulimia nervosa. *Journal of Consulting and Clinical Psychology, 68*, 432-437.

Musselman, D.L., Evans, D.L., & Nemeroff, C.G. (1998). The relationship of depression to cardiovascular disease. *Archives of General Psychiatry, 55*, 580-592.

Nadel, L., & Jacobs, W.J. (1998). Traumatic memory is special. *Current Directions in Psychological Science, 7*, 154-157.

Nagata, D. (1989). Long-term effects of the Japanese American internment camps: Impact upon the children of the internees. *Journal of the Asian American Psychological Association, 13*, 48-55.

Name withheld (1993). Walking with my specter. *Journal of the American Medical Association, 268* (25), 149, 151.

National Center on Child Abuse and Neglect (1988). *Study of national incidence and prevalence of child abuse and neglect: 1988*. Washington, DC: U.S. Department of Health and Human Services.

National Institute of Mental Health. (1990). *Mental health, United States, 1990*. (DHHS Publication No. ADM 90-1708). Washington, DC: US Government Printing Office.

National Institute of Mental Health. (1991). *Caring for people with severe mental disorders: A national plan of research to improve services*. (DHHS Publication No. ADM 91-1762). Washington, DC: US Government Printing Office.

Needleman, L.D. (1999). *Cognitive case conceptualization*. Mahwah, NJ: Lawrence Erlbaum Associates.

Neff, L. J., Sargent, R. G., McKeown, R. C., Jackson, K. L., & Valois, R. F. (1997). Black-white differences in body size perceptions and weight management practices among adolescent females. *Journal of Adolescent Health, 20*, 459-465.

Nemiah, J. C. (1988). Psychoneurotic disorders. In A. M. Nicholi (Ed.), *The new Harvard guide to modern psychiatry*, 2nd ed. Cambridge, MA: Harvard University Press.

Nemiah, J. C., & Uhde, T. W. (1989). Phobic disorders. In H. I. Kaplan & B. J. Sadock, Eds., *Comprehensive textbook of psychiatry*, 5th ed. Baltimore: Williams & Wilkins.

Neugebauer, R. (1979). Medieval and early modern theories of mental illness. *Archives of General Psychiatry, 36*, 477-483.

New York Times (1999, November 26). Intervention in Air Force Cuts suicide Rate in Half, p. A 29.

Newberger, D. S. (2000). Down syndrome: Prenatal risk assessment and diagnosis. *American Family Physician, 62*, 825-832.

Newman, C.F. (1998). Showing up for your life: Cognitive therapy for avoidant personality disorder. *In Session: Psychotherapy in Practice, 4*, 55-71.

Newman, D. L., Moffit, T. E., Caspi, A. Magdol, L., Silva, P. A., & Stanton, W. R. (1996). Psychiatric disorder in a birth cohort of young adults: Prevalence, comorbidity, clinical significance, and new case incidence from ages 11-21. *Journal of Consulting and Clinical Psychology, 64*, 552-562.

Niccols, G. A. (1994). Fetal alcohol syndrome: Implications for psychologists. *Clinical Psychology Review, 14*, 91-111.

Norman, R. M. G., & Townsend, L. A. (1999). Cognitive-behavioral therapy for psychosis: A status report. *Canadian Journal of Psychiatry, 44*, 245-252.

North, C. S., Smith, E. M., & Spitznagel, E. L. (1994). Posttraumatic stress disorder in survivors of a mass shooting. *American Journal of Psychiatry, 151*, 82-88.

Nothen, M. M., Cichon, S., Rohleder, H., Hemmer, S., et al. (1999). Evaluation of linkage of bipolar affective disorder to chromosome 18 in a sample of 57 German families. *Molecular Psychiatry, 4*, 76-84.

Nuechterlein, K. H. (1983). Signal detection in vigilance tasks and behavioral attributes among offspring of schizophrenic mothers and among hyperactive children. *Journal of Abnormal Psychology, 92*, 4-28.

O'Callaghan, E., Gibson, T., Colohan, H. A., Buckley, P., Walshe, D. G., Larkin, C., & Waddington, J.L. (1992). Risk of schizophrenia in adults born after obstetric complications and their association with early onset of illness: A controlled study. *British Medical Journal, 305,* 1265-1269.

O'Donoghue, E. G. (1914). *The story of Bethlehem Hospital from its foundation in 1247.* London: T. Fisher.

Ogden, J. A. H. (1947). *The Kingdom of the Lost.* London: Bodley Head.

Ohayon, M.M., Guilleminault, C., & Priest, R.G. (1999). Night terrors, sleepwalking, and confusional arousal in the general population: Their frequency and relationship to other sleep and mental disorders. *Journal of Clinical Psychiatry, 60,* 268-276.

Olds, D. C., & Henderson, C. (1989). The prevention of maltreatment. In D. Cicchetti & V. Carlson (Eds.), *Child maltreatment: Theory and research on the causes and consequences of child abuse and neglect.* New York: Cambridge University Press.

O'Leary, A. (1990). Stress, emotion, and human immune function. *Psychological Bulletin, 108,* 363-382.

O'Leary, A., Savard, J., & Miller, S. M. (1996). Psychoneuro-immunology: Elucidating the process. *Current Opinion in Psychiatry, 9,* 427-432.

Olff, M. (1999). Stress, depression and immunity: The role of defense and coping styles. *Psychiatry Research, 85,* 7-15.

Olin, S. S., & Mednick, S. A. (1996). Risk factors of psychosis: Identifying vulnerable populations premorbidly. *Schizophrenia Bulletin, 22,* 223-240.

Olivardia, R., Pope, H.G., & Hudson, J.I. (2000). Muscle dysmorphia in male weightlifters: A case-control study. *American Journal of Psychiatry, 157,* 1291-1296.

Olmsted, M. P., Kaplan, A. S., & Rockert, W. (1994). Rate and prediction of relapse in bulimia nervosa. *American Journal of Psychiatry, 151,* 738-743.

Olson, H. C., Streissguth, A. P., Barr, H. M., Bookstein, F. L., & Thiede, K. (1997). Association of prenatal alcohol exposure with behavioral and learning problems in early adolescence. *Journal of the American Academy of Child and Adolescent Psychiatry, 36,* 1187-1194.

O'Neal, J. M. (1984). First person account: Finding myself and loving it. *Schizophrenia Bulletin, 10,* 109-110.

Orleans, C. T., & Slade, J. (Eds.) (1993). *Nicotine addiction: Principles and management.* New York: Oxford University Press.

Osler, W. (1910). The Lumleian lectures on angina pectoris. *Lancet, 1,* 839-844.

Osterling, J., & Dawson, G. (1994). Early recognition of children with autism: A study of first birthday home videotapes. *Journal of Autism and Developmental Disorders, 24,* 247-257.

Othmer, E., & Othmer, S. C. (1994). *The Clinical Interview Using DSM-IV* (Vol. 1). Washington, DC: American Psychiatric Press.

Otis, C. L., Drinkwater, B., Johnson, M., Loucks, A., Wilmore, J. (1997). The female athlete triad. *Medicine and Science in Sports and Exercise, 21,* R1-R9.

Ottaviani, R., & Beck, A. T., (1987). Cognitive aspects of panic disorders. *Journal of Anxiety Disorders, 1,* 15-28.

Otten, A. L. (1994). People patterns. *The Wall Street Journal,* November 9, 1994, p. B1.

Overholser, J. C. (1996). The dependent personality and interpersonal problems. *Journal of Nervous and Mental Disease, 184,* 8-16.

Ozonoff, S., Strayer, D. L., McMahon, W. M., & Filloux, F. (1998) Inhibitory deficits in Tourette syndrome: A function of comorbidity and symptom severity. *Journal of Child Psychology and Psychiatry, 39,* 1109-1118.

Pallas, J., Levine, S.B., Althof, S.E., & Risen, C.B. (2000). A study using Viagra in a mental health practice. *Journal of Sex and Marital Therapy, 26,* 41-50.

Pally, R. (1997). I. How brain and development is shaped by genetic and environmental factors. *International Journal of Psychoanalysis, 78,* 587-593.

Panek, W. F., & Garber, J. (1992). Role of aggression, rejection, and attributions in the prediction of depression in children. *Development and Psychopathology, 4,* 145-165.

Papp, P. (2000). *Couples on the fault line.* NY: Guilford.

Paris, J. (1995). Memories of abuse in borderline patients: True or false? *Harvard Review of Psychiatry, 3,* 10-17.

Parker, G., & Hadzi-Pavlovic, D. (1990). Expressed emotion as a predictor of schizophrenic relapse: An analysis of aggregated data. *Psychological Medicine, 20,* 961-964.

Parnas, J., Cannon, T. D., Jacobsen, B., Schulsinger, H., Schulsinger, F., & Mednick, S. A. (1993). Lifetime DSM-III-R diagnostic outcomes in the offspring of schizophrenic mothers: Results from the Copenhagen High-Risk Study. *Archives of General Psychiatry, 50,* 707-714.

Pataki, C. S., & Carlson, G. A. (1995). Childhood and adolescent depression: A review. *Harvard Review of Psychiatry, 3,* 140-151.

Patano, M., Grave, R. D., Oliosi, M., Bartocci, C., Todisco, P., & Marchi, S. (1997). Family backgrounds in eating disorders. *Psychopathology, 30,* 163-169.

Patten, S. B. (1991). Are the Brown and Harris "Vulnerability Factors" risk factors for depression. *Journal of Psychiatric Neuroscience, 16,* 267-271.

Patterson, C. J. (1992). Children of lesbian and gay parents. *Child Development, 63,* 1025-1042.

Patterson, G. R. (1975). *Families with aggressive children.* Eugene, OR: Castalia Press.

Patterson, G. R. (1982). *Coercive family processes.* Eugene, OR: Castalia Press.

Patterson, G. R. (1986). Performance models for antisocial boys. *American Psychologist, 41,* 432-444.

Patterson, G. R., DeBaryshe, B. D., & Ramsey, E. (1989). A developmental perspective on antisocial behavior. *American Psychologist, 44,* 329-335.

Patton, G. C., Carlin, J. G., Shao, Q., Hibbert, M. E., Rosier, M., Selzer, R., & Bowes, G. (1997). Adolescent dieting: Healthy weight control or borderline eating disor-

der? *Journal of Child Psychology and Psychiatry and Allied Disciplines, 38,* (3), 299-306.

Paul, G. L. (1969). Chronic mental patient: Current status-future directions. *Psychological Bulletin, 71,* 81-93.

Paul, G. L., & Lentz, R. J. (1977). *Psychosocial treatment of chronic mental patients: Milieu versus social-learning programs.* Cambridge, MA: Harvard University Press.

Paykel, E. S. (1985). Life events, social support and clinical psychiatric disorder. In I. G. Sarason & B. R. Sarason (Eds.) *Social support: Theory, research and applications* (pp. 321-347). Dordrecht, The Netherlands: Marinus Nijhoff.

Paykel, E. S. (1991). Depression in women. *British Journal of Psychiatry, 158,* 22-29.

Pelham, W. E. (1999). The NIMH Multimodal Treatment Study for Attention-Deficit Hyperactivity Disorder: Just say yes to drugs alone? *Canadian Journal of Psychiatry, 44,* 981-990.

Pelham, W. E., Jr. (1993). Pharmacotherapy for children with attention-deficit hyperactivity disorder. *School Psychology Review, 22,* 199-227.

Perls, F. S. (1969). *Gestalt therapy verbatim.* Lafayette, CA; Real People Press.

Perry, D. G., Perry, L. C., & Boldizar, J. P. (1990). Learning of aggression. In M. Lewis & S. M. Miller (Eds.), *Handbook of developmental psychopathology.* New York: Plenum Press.

Persky, V. W., Kempthorne-Rawson, J., & Shekelle, R. B. (1987). Personality and risk of cancer: 20-year follow-up of the Western Electric Study. *Psychosomatic Medicine, 49,* 435-449.

Persons, J. B. (1992). A case formulation approach to cognitive-behavior therapy: Application to panic disorder. *Psychiatric Annals, 22,* 470-473.

Petrie, T. A. (1993). Disordered eating in female collegiate gymnasts: Prevalence and personality/attitudinal correlates. *Journal of Sport and Exercise Psychology, 15,* 424-436.

Pfiffner, L. J., & O'Leary, S. G. (1993). Psychological treatments: School-based. In J. L. Matson (Ed.), *Handbook of hyperactivity in children.* Boston: Allyn & Bacon.

Philips, D. P. (1974). The influence of suggestion on suicide: Substantive and theoretical implications of the Werther effect. *American Sociologist, 39,* 340-354.

Pierce, G. R., Sarason, I. G., & Sarason, B. R. (1991). General and relationship-based perceptions of social support: Are two constructs better than one? *Journal of Personality and Social Psychology, 61,* 1028-1039.

Pierce, G.R., Lakey, B., Sarason, I.G., & Sarason, B.R. (1997) (Eds.). *Sourcebook of social support and personality.* NY: Plenum.

Piercey, B. P. (1985). First person account: Making the best of it. *Schizophrenia Bulletin, 11,* 155-157.

Pinel, P. (1969). Traite medico-philosophique sur l'alienation mentale, 2nd ed. Paris: Brossen, 1809; as quoted in W. Riese, 1968, *The legacy of Philippe Pinel.* New York: Springer.

Piven, J. (1999). Genetic liability for autism: The behavioral expression in relatives. *International Review of Psychiatry, 11,* 299-308.

Piven, J., & O'Leary, D. (1997). Neuroimaging in autism. *Child and Adolescent Psychiatric Clinics of North America, 6,* 305-382.

Piven, J., Palmer, P., Landa, R., Santangelo, S., Jacobi, D., & Childress, D. (1997). Personality and language characteristics in parents from multiple-incidence autism families. *American Journal of Medical Genetics, 74,* 398-411.

Plakun, E. M., Burkhardt, P. E., & Muller, A. P. (1985). Fourteen-year follow-up of borderline and schizotypal personality disorders. *Comprehensive Psychiatry, 26,* 448-455.

Plomin, R., Owen, M. J., & McGuffin, P. (1994). The genetic bases of complex human behaviors. *Science, 264,* 1733-1739.

Pope, H.G., Gruber, A.J., Mangweth, B., Bureau, B., deCol, C., Jouvent, R., & Hudson, J.I. (2000). Body image perception among men in three countries. *American Journal of Psychiatry, 157,* 1297-1301.

Pope, H. G., Mangweth, B., Negrao, A. B., Hudson, J. I., & Cord, T. A. (1994). Childhood sexual abuse and bulimia nervosa: A comparison of American, Austrian, and Brazilian women. *American Journal of Psychiatry, 151,* 732-737.

Pope, H. G., Jr., Jonas, J. M., Hudson, J., Cohen, B. M., & Gunderson, J. G. (1983). The validity of DSM-III borderline personality disorder. *Archives of General Psychiatry, 40,* 1319-1323.

Portin, P., & Alanen, Y. O. (1997). A critical review of genetic studies of schizophrenia 2: Molecular genetic studies. *Acta Psychiatrica Scandinavica, 95,* 73-80.

Poulton, R., Menzies, R.G. Craske, M.G., Langley, J.D., & Silva, P.A. (1999). Water trauma and swimming experiences up to age 9 and fear of water at age 18: A longitudinal study. *Behaviour Research and Therapy, 37,* 39-48.

Powell, C. (1991). Robert Lowell: The search for the father in madness and poetry. *Australian and New Zealand Journal of Psychiatry, 25,* 375-382.

Power, P. (1999). Suicide and early psychosis. In P. D. McGorry and H. J. Jackson, Eds. *The recognition and management of early psychosis,* pp. 338-361. Cambridge, England: Cambridge University Press.

Practice guidelines of the treatment of patients with eating disorders (2000). Washington, DC: American Psychiatric Association.

Pratt, L. A., Ford, D. E., Crum, R. M., Armenian, H. K., Gallo, J. J., & Eaton, W. W. (1996). Depression, psychotropic medication, and risk of myocardial infarction. Prospective data from the Baltimore ECA follow-up. *Circulation, 94,* 3123-3129.

Prentky, R. A., & Knight, R. A. (1991). Identifying critical dimensions for discriminating among rapists. *Journal of Consulting and Clinical Psychology, 59,* 643-661.

Prien, R. F., & Kocsis, J. H. (1995). Long term treatment of mood disorders. In F. E. Bloom & D. J. Kupfer (Eds.), *Psychopharmacology: The fourth generation of progress* (pp. 1067-1079). New York: Raven Press.

Prigerson, H. G., Maciejewski, P. K., & Rosenheck, R. A. (1999). The effects of marital dissolution and marital quality on health and health service use among women. *Medical Care, 37,* 858-873.

Prince, V. C. (1967). *The transvestite and his wife.* Los Angeles: Argyle Books.

Prior, M. R. (1992). Childhood autism: What do we know and where should we go? *Behaviour Change, 9,* 96-103.

Project MATCH Research Group (1997). Matching alcoholism treatment to client heterogeneity: Project MATCH posttreatment drinking outcomes. *Journal of Studies on Alcohol, 58,* 7-29.

Prosser, H., & Moss, S. (1997). Informal care networks of older adults with an intellectual disability. *Journal of Applied Research in Intellectual Disabilities, 9,* 17-30.

Quinton, D., Pickles, A., Maughn, B., & Rutter, M. (1993). Partners, peers, and pathways: Assortative pairing and continuities in conduct disorder. *Development and Psychopathology, 5,* 763-783.

Rabasca, L. (1999). Military suicide-prevention program reduces the stigma of seeking help. *APA Monitor,* November 1, 1999, P.8.

Radomsky, E. D., Haas, G. L., Mann, J. J., & Sweeney, J. A. (1999). Suicidal behavior in patients with schizophrenia and other psychotic disorders. *American Journal of Psychiatry, 156,* 1590-1595.

Ragland, D. R., & Brand, R. J. (1988). Type A behavior and mortality from coronary heart disease. *New England Journal of Medicine, 318,* 65-69.

Raine, N. V. (1994). Returns of the day. *New York Times Magazine,* October 2, p. 34.

Raine, N.V. (1998). *After silence.* NY: Crown.

Ramey, C. T., & Haskins, R. (1981). The modification of intelligence through early experience. *Intelligence, 5,* 43-57.

Ramey, C. T., & Ramey, S. L. (1992). Effective early intervention. *Mental Retardation, 30,* 337-345.

Rapaport, K., & Burkart, B. R. (1984). Personality and attitudinal characteristics of sexually coercive college males. *Journal of Abnormal Psychology, 13,* 216-221.

Raphael, B., & Minkov, C. (1999). Abnormal grief. *Current Opinion in Psychiatry, 12,* 99-102.

Rapin, I. (1995). Autistic regression and disintegrative disorder: How important is the role of epilepsy? *Seminars in Pediatric Neurology, 2,* 278-285.

Rapoport, J. L. (1989). *The boy who couldn't stop washing.* New York: Dutton.

Rapoport, J.L., Elkins, R., Langer, D. H., Sceery, W., Buchsbaum, M. S., Gillin, J. C., Murphy, D. L., Zahn, T. P., Lake, R., Ludlow, C., & Mendelson, W. (1981). Childhood obsessive-compulsive disorder. *American Journal of Psychiatry, 138,* 1545-1554.

Rappaport, J., & Seidman, E. (Eds.) (2000). *Handbook of Community Psychology.* NY: Kluwer Academic/Plenum.

Rastam, M., Gillberg, C., & Gillberg, I. C. (1996). A six year follow-up study of anorexia nervosa subjects with a teenage onset. *Journal of Youth and Adolescence, 25,* 439-453.

Ratnasuriya, R. H., Eisler, I., Szmukler, G. I., & Russell, G. F. M. (1991). Anorexia nervosa: Outcome and prognostic factors after 20 years. *British Journal of Psychiatry, 158,* 495-502.

Raz, S., & Raz, N. (1990). Structural brain abnormalities in the major psychoses: A quantitative review of the evidence from computer imaging. *Psychological Bulletin, 108,* 93-108.

Redmond, H. (1998). The state of mental health in the USA. *International Journal of Mental Health, 27,* 62-79.

Regier, D. A., Narrow, W. E., Rae, D. S., Manderscheid, R. W., Locke, B. Z., & Goodwin, F. K. (1993). The de facto U.S. mental and addictive disorders service system. Epidemiologic catchment area prospective 1-year prevalence rates of disorders and services. *Archives of General Psychiatry, 50,* 85-94.

Reich, W. (1949). (originally published 1933) *Character analysis.* New York: Orgone Institute Press.

Reid, W. H. (1986). Antisocial personality. In R. Michels & J. O. Cavenar, Jr. (Eds.), *Psychiatry* (vol. 1). New York: Basic Books.

Reid, W. H., & Balis, G. U. (1987). Evaluation of the violent patient. In R. E. Hales & A. J. Francis (Eds.), *American Psychiatric Association Annual Review* (vol. 6). Washington, DC: American Psychiatric Press.

Reisberg, B. (1985). Alzheimer's disease updated. *Psychiatric Annals, 15,* 319-322.

Reiss, A. J., & Roth, S. A. (Eds.) (1994). Understanding and preventing violence. Washington, DC: National Academy Press.

Reiss, S. (1990). Prevalence of dual diagnosis in community-based day programs in the Chicago metropolitan area. *American Journal on Mental Retardation, 94,* 578-585.

Reiss, S., & Valenti-Hein, D. (1994). Development of a psychopathology rating scale for children with mental retardation. *Journal of Consulting and Clinical Psychology, 62,* 28-33.

Rekers, G. A. (1977). Assessment and treatment of childhood gender problems. In B. B. Lahey & A. E. Kazdin (Eds.), *Advances in clinical child psychology* (vol. 1). New York: Plenum.

Reppucci, N.D., Wollard, J.L., & Fried, C.S. (1999). Social, community, and preventive interventions. *Annual Review of Psychology, 50,* 387-418.

Repucci, N. D., & Haugaard, J. J. (1989). Prevention of child sexual abuse. *American Psychologist, 44,* 1266-1275.

Research on mental illness and addictive disorders. (1985). *American Journal of Psychiatry, 142* (supplement), 9-41.

Riccio, C. A., Hynd, G. W., Cohen, M. J., & Gonzalez, J. J. (1993). Neurological basis of attention deficit hyperactivity disorder. *Exceptional Children, 60,* 118-124.

Rief, W., Hiller, W., & Margraf, J. (1998). Cognitive aspects of hypochondriasis and somatization disorder. *Journal of Abnormal Psychology, 107,* 587-595.

Rief, W., Hiller, W., & Margraf, J. (1998). Cognitive aspects of hypochondriasis and the somatization syndrome. *Journal of Abnormal Psychology, 107,* 587-595.

Riggs, D. S., OfLeary, K. D., & Breslin, F. C. (1990). Multiple correlates of physical aggression in dating couples. *Journal of Interpersonal Violence, 5,* 61-73.

Rihmer, Z., & Pestality, P. (1999). Bipolar II disorder and suicidal behavior. *Psychiatric Clinics of North American, 22,* 667-673.

Rimer, S. (1997, August 15). For old South Boston, despair replaces hope. *The New York Times National Edition,* pp. 1, 14.

Ritchie, K., & Richards, M. (1999). Recent developments in neuropsychological assessment. *Current Opinion in Psychiatry, 12,* 345-349.

Ritvo, E. R., Jorde, L. B., Mason-Brothers, A., Freeman, B. J., Pingree, C., Jones, M. B., McMahon, W. M., Petersen, P. B., Jenson, W. R., & Mo, A. (1989). The UCLA-University of Utah epidemiologic survey of autism: Recurrence risk estimates and genetic counseling. *American Journal of Psychiatry, 146,* 1032-1036.

Roach, M. (1983). Another name for madness. *New York Times Magazine,* Jan. 16, 22-31.

Robbins, L. N. (1999). A 70 year history of conduct disorder: Variations in definition, prevalence, and correlates. In P. Cohen, C. Slomkowski, et al. (Eds). *Historical and geographical influences on psychopathology* (pp. 37-56). Mahwah, NJ: Erlbaum.

Robin, A. L., Siegel, P. T., & Moye, A. (1995). Family versus individual therapy for anorexia: Impact on family conflict. *International Journal of Eating Disorders, 17,* 313-332.

Robin, A. L., Siegel, P. T., Koepke, T., Moye, A. W., & Tice, S. (1994). Family therapy versus individual therapy for adolescent females with anorexia nervosa. *Journal of Developmental and Behavioral Pediatrics, 15,* 111-116.

Robins, L. N. (1993). Vietnam veterans' rapid recovery from heroin addiction: A fluke or normal expectation? *Addiction, 88,* 1041-1054.

Robins, L. N., & Kulbok, P. A. (1998). *Epidemiologic studies in suicide. Review of Psychiatry* (Vol. 7, pp. 289-306). Washington, D.C.: American Psychiatric Press.

Robins, L. N., & Price, R. K. (1991). Adult disorders predicted by childhood conduct problems: Results from the NIMH Epidemiological Catchment Area Project. *Psychiatry, 54,* 116-132.

Robins, L. N., & Regier, D. A. (1991). *Psychiatric disorders in America: The epidemiological catchment area.* New York: The Free Press.

Robins, L. N., Helzer, J. E., Croghan, J., & Ratcliff, K. S. (1981). National Institute of Mental Health Diagnostic Interview Schedule. *Archives of General Psychiatry, 38,* 381-389.

Robinson, H. (1991). Visitation with divorced father provokes reemergence of unresolved family conflicts: Case of Charlie, age 10. In N. B. Webb (Ed.), *Play therapy with children in crisis* (pp. 219-236). New York: Guilford.

Rogers, C. R. (1951). *Client-centered therapy.* Boston: Houghton-Mifflin.

Rogers, C. R. (1959). A theory of therapy, personality, and interpersonal relationships as developed in the client-centered framework. In S. Koch (Ed.), *Psychology: A study of a science* (vol. 3). New York: McGraw-Hill.

Rogers, C. R. (1980). *A way of being.* Boston: Houghton-Mifflin.

Rogers, J. G., Voullaire, L., & Gold, H. (1982). Monozygotic twins discordant for trisomy 21. *American Journal of Medical Genetics, 11,* 143-146.

Rogers, R., & Shuman, D.N. (2000). *Conducting Insanity Evaluations.* NY: Guilford.

Rogler, L. H. (1996). Framing research on culture in psychiatric diagnosis: The case of the DSM-IV. *Psychiatry, 59,* 145-155.

Rogler, L.H. (1999). Methodological sources of cultural insensitivity in mental health research. *American Psychologist, 54,* 424-433.

Romano, S.J. (1999). Bulimia nervosa. In D.J. Goldstein (Ed.). *The management of eating disorders and obesity.* Totowa, NJ: Humana Press.

Romer, D., & Heller, T. (1983). Social adaptation of mentally retarded adults in community settings: A social-ecological approach. *Applied Research in Mental Retardation, 4,* 303-314.

Rorschach, H. (1942). *Psychodiagnostic: Methodik and ergebnisse eines wahrnehmungsdianostichen experiments,* 2nd ed. (P. Lemkau & B. Kronenberg, trans.) Berne and Berlin: Huber, 1932; republished: New York: Grune & Stratton.

Rorsman, B., Grasbeck, A., Hagnell, O., Lanke, J., Ohman, R., Ojesjo, L., & Otterbeck, L. (1990). A prospective study of first-incidence depression: The Lundby study, 1957-1972. *British Journal of Psychiatry, 156,* 336-342.

Rosch, P. J. (1996). Stress and sleep; Some startling and sobering statistics. *Stress Medicine, 12,* 207-210.

Rose, G. (1993). Mental disorders and the strategies of prevention. *Psychological Medicine, 23,* 553-555.

Rosen, J.C. (1996). Body dysmorphic disorder: Assessment and treatment. In J.K. Thompson (Ed.), *Body image, eating disorders, and obesity.* Washington, DC: American Psychological Association.

Rosen, J. W., & Burchard, S. N. (1990). Community activities and social support networks: A social comparison of adults with and adults without mental retardation. *Education and Training in Mental Retardation, 25,* 193-204.

Rosenbaum, A., & O'Leary, K. D. (1981). Marital violence: Characteristics of abusive couples. *Journal of Consulting and Clinical Psychology, 49,* 63-71.

Rosenberg, H. (1993). Prediction of controlled drinking by alcoholics and problem drinkers. *Psychological Bulletin, 113,* 129-139.

Rosenblum, L. A., & Paully, G. S. (1987). Primate models of separation-induced depression. *Psychiatric Clinics of North America, 10,* 437-447.

Rosenman, R. H., Brand, R. J., Jenkins, C. D., Friedman, M., Straus, R., & Wurm, M. (1975). Coronary heart disease in the Western Collaborative Group Study. *Journal of the American Medical Association, 233,* 872-877.

Rosenthal, D. (Ed.) (1963). *The Genain quadruplets: A case study and theoretical analysis of heredity and environment in schizophrenia.* New York: Basic Books.

Rosenthal, D., Wender, P. H., Kety, S. S., Schulsinger, F., Welner, J., & Ostergaard, L. (1968). Schizophrenics' offspring reared in adoptive homes. In D. Rosenthal & S. S. Kety (Eds.), *The transmission of schizophrenia.* Oxford: Pergamon Press.

Rosenthal, D., Wender, P. H., Kety, S. S., Schulsinger, F., Welner, J., & Reider, R. (1975). Parent-child relationships and psychopathological disorder in the child. *Archives of General Psychiatry, 32,* 466-476.

Rosenthal, N. E., & Wehr, T. A. (1992). Towards understanding the mechanism of action of light in seasonal affective disorder. *Pharmacopsychiatry, 25,* 56-60.

Rosenthal, N. E., Sack, D. A., Gillin, J. C., Lewy, A. J., Goodwin, F. K., Davenport, Y., et al. (1984). Seasonal affective disorder: A description of the syndrome and preliminary findings with light therapy. *Archives of General Psychiatry, 41,* 72-80.

Rosie, J. S. (1987). Partial hospitalization: A review of recent literature. *Hospital and Community Psychiatry, 38,* 1291-1299.

Rosvold, H. E., Mirsky, A. F., Sarason, I. G., Bransome, E. D., & Beck, L. H. (1956). A continuous performance test of brain damage. *Journal of Consulting Psychology, 20,* 343-350.

Rothblum, E. D. (1994). "I only read about myself on bathroom walls": The need for research on the mental health of lesbians and gay men. *Journal of Consulting and Clinical Psychology, 62,* 213-220.

Rothlisberg, B. A., Hill, R., Damato, R. C. (1994). Social acceptance by their peers of children with mental retardation. *Psychological Reports, 74,* 239-242.

Rouse, B., Azen, C., Koch, R., Matalon, R., Hanley, W., de la Cruz, F., Trefz, F., Friedman, E., & Shifrin, H. (1997). Maternal Phenylketonuria Collaborative Study (MPKUCS) offspring: facial anomalies, malformations, and early neurological sequelae. *American Journal of Medical Genetics, 69,* 89-95.

Roy, A. (1992). Suicide in schizophrenia. *International Review of Psychiatry, 4,* 205-209.

Roy-Byrne, P., Post, R. M., Uhde, T. W., Porcu, T., & Davis D. (1985). The longitudinal course of recurrent affective illness: Life chart data from research patients at the NIMH. *Acta Psychiatrica Scandinavica, Supplement, 317,* 5-34.

Ruberman, J. W., Weinblatt, E., Goldberg, J. D., & Chaudhary, B. S. (1984). Psychological influences on mortality after myocardial infarction. *New England Journal of Medicine, 311,* 552-559.

Ruch, L. O., Gartrell, J. W., Amedeo, S. R., & Coyne, B. J. (1991). The Sexual Assault Symptom Scale: Measuring self-reported sexual assault trauma in the emergency room. *Psychological Assessment, 3,* 3-8.

Rudorfer, M. V., Henry, M. E., & Sackeim, H. (1997). Electroconvulsive therapy. In A. Tasman, J. Kay & J. A. Lieberman (Eds.), *Psychiatry* (pp. 1535-1556). Philadelphia: W. B. Saunders.

Ruiz, P. (1998). The role of culture in psychiatric care. *American Journal of Psychiatry, 155,* 1763-1765.

Rund, B. R. (1990). Fully recovered schizophrenics: A retrospective study of some premorbid and treatment factors. *Psychiatry, 53,* 127-139.

Rupp, A., & Keith, S. J. (1993). The costs of schizophrenia. *Psychiatric Clinics of North America, 16,* 413-423.

Rush, A. J. (2000). The use of placebos in unipolar major depression: The current status. *Biological Psychiatry, 47,* 745-747.

Rush, A. J., & Weissenburger, J. E. (1994). Melancholic symptom features and DSM-IV. *American Journal of Psychiatry, 151,* 489-498.

Rush, A. J., Stewart, R. S., Garver, D. L., & Waller, D. A. (1998). Neurobiological bases for psychiatric disorders. In R. N. Rosenberg & D. E. Pleasure (Eds.), *Comprehensive neurology* (2nd ed., pp. 555-603). New York: Wiley.

Russell, D. E. H. (1984). The prevalence and seriousness of incestuous abuse: Step fathers vs. biological fathers. *Child Abuse and Neglect, 8,* 15-22.

Russell, G. L., Fujino, D. C., Sue, S., Cheung, M., & Snowden, L. R. (1996). The effects of therapist-client ethnic match in the assessment of mental health functioning. *Journal of Cross-Cultural Psychology, 27,* 598-615.

Rutter, D. R. (1985). Language in schizophrenia: The structure of monologues and conversations. *British Journal of Psychiatry, 146,* 399-404.

Rutter, J. (1991). Nature, nurture, and psychopathology: A new look at an old topic. *Development and Psychopathology, 3,* 25-136.

Rutter, M. (1999). Autism: Two way interplay between research and clinical work. *Journal of Child Psychology and Psychiatry, 40,* 169-188.

Rutter, M. (2000). Genetic studies of autism: From the 1970s into the Millenium. *Journal of Abnormal Child Psychology, 28,* 3-14.

Rutter, M., & Garmezy, N. (1983). Developmental psychopathology. In P. Mussen (Ed.), *Handbook of child psychology* (vol. 4). New York: John Wiley.

Rutter, M., & Hersov, L. (1985). *Child and adolescent psychiatry: Modern approaches.* Oxford, England: Blackwell Scientific Publications.

Rutter, M., & Shaffer, D. (1980). DSM-III: A step forward or back in terms of the classification of child psychiatric disorders. *Journal of the American Academy of Child Psychiatry, 19,* 371-394.

Rutter, M., Cox, A., Tupling, C., Berger, M., & Yule, W. (1975). Attainment and adjustment in two geographical areas: I. The prevalence of psychiatric disorder. *British Journal of Psychiatry, 126,* 493-509.

Rutter, M., Graham, P., & Yule, W. (1970). A neuropsychiatric study in childhood. *Clinics in Developmental Medicine, Nos. 35/36.* London: Heinemann.

Rutter, M., Macdonald, H., LeCouteur, A., Harrington, R., Bolton, P., & Bailey A. (1990). Genetic factors in child psychiatric disorders: II. Empirical findings. *Journal of Child Psychology and Psychiatry, 31,* 39-83.

Sabate, O., Campion, D., d'Amato, T., Martres, M. P., Sokoloff, P., Giros, B., Leboyer, M., Jay, M., Guedj, F., & Thibaut, F. (1994). Failure to find evidence for linkage or association between the dopamine D3 receptor gene and schizophrenia. *American Journal of Psychiatry, 151,* 107-111.

Sackeim, H. A., & Wegner, A. Z. (1986). Attributional patterns in depression and euthymia. *Archives of General Psychiatry, 43,* 553-560.

Sackeim, H. A., Prudic, J., & Devanand, D. P. (1990). Treatment of medication-resistant depression with electroconvulsive therapy. In A. Tasman, S. M. Goldfinger, & C. A. Kaufmann (Eds.), *Review of psychiatry* (vol. 9). Washington, DC: American Psychiatric Press.

Sadock, V. A. (1989). Rape, spouse abuse, and incest. In H. I. Kaplan & B. J. Sadock, eds., *Comprehensive textbook of psychiatry,* 5th ed. Baltimore: Williams & Wilkins.

Salkovskis, P. M. (1999). Understanding and treating obsessive-compulsive disorder. *Behaviour Research and Therapy, 37,* S29-S52.

Salovey, P., Rothman, A.J., Detweiler, J.B., & Steward. W.T. (2000). Emotional states and physical health. *American Psychologist, 55,* 110-121.

Salter, A. C., Richardson, C. M., & Kairys, S. W. (1985). Caring for abused preschoolers. *Child Welfare, 64,* 343-356.

Sameroff, A. J., & Fiese, B. H. (1990). Transactional regulations and early intervention. In S. J. Meisels & J. P. Shonkoff (Eds.), *Handbook of early childhood intervention* (pp. 119-149). Cambridge, England: Cambridge University Press.

Sampson, R. J., Raudenbush, S. W., & Earls, F. (1997). Neighborhoods and violent crime. *Science, 277,* 918-924.

Sanderson, W. C., & Barlow, D. H. (1990). A description of patients diagnosed with DSM-III-R generalized anxiety disorder. *The Journal of Nervous and Mental Disease, 178,* 588-591.

Sands, R., Tricker, J., Sharman, C., Armatas, C., & Maschette, W. (1997). Disordered eating patterns, body image, self-esteem, and physical activity in preadolescent school children. *International Journal of Eating Disorders, 21,* 159-166.

Santayana, G. (1905-1906). *The life of reason.* New York: Scribner.

Sarason, I. G. (1979). Three lacunae of cognitive therapy. *Cognitive Therapy and Research, 3,* 223-235.

Sarason, I. G., & Sarason, B. R. (1981). Teaching cognitive and social skills to high school students. *Journal of Consulting and Clinical Psychology, 49,* 908-919.

Sarason, I. G., & Sarason, B. R. (Eds.) (1985). *Social support: Theory, research and applications.* Dordrecht, The Netherlands: Martinus Nijhof.

Sarason, I. G., & Stoops, R. (1978). Test anxiety and the passage of time. *Journal of Consulting and Clinical Psychology, 46,* 102-109.

Sarason, I. G., Johnson, J. M., & Siegel, J. M. (1978). Assessing the impact of life stress: Development of the Life Experiences Survey. *Journal of Consulting and Clinical Psychology, 46,* 932-946.

Sarason, I. G., Levine, H. M., Basham, R. B., & Sarason, B. R. (1983). Assessing social support: The Social Support Questionnaire. *Journal of Personality and Social Psychology, 44,* 127-139.

Sartorius, N., & de Girolamo, G. (1991). Preface to a special issue. *Schizophrenia Bulletin, 17,* 401-405.

Sartorius, N., Gulbinat, W., Harrison, G., Laska, E. et al. (1996). Long-term follow-up of schizophrenia in 16 countries: A description of the international study of schizophrenia conducted by the World Health Organization. *Social Psychiatry and Psychiatric Epidemiology, 31,* 249-258.

Sartorius, N., Shapiro, R., Kimura, M., & Barrett, K. (1972). WHO international pilot study of schizophrenia. *Psychological Medicine, 2,* 422-425.

Sartorius, N., Ustun, T. B., Costa-e-Silva, J. A., Goldberg, D., Lecrubier, Y., Ormel, J., Von Korff, M., & Wittchen, H. U. (1993). An international study of psychological problems in primary care. Preliminary report from the World Health Organization Collaborative project on "Psychological Problems in General Health Care." *Archives of General Psychiatry, 50,* 819-824.

Sarwer, D.B., & Durlak, J.A. (1997). A field trial of the effectiveness of behavioral treatment for sexual dysfunctions. *Journal of Sex and Marital Therapy, 23,* 87-97.

Sass, L. A. (1987). Introspection, schizophrenia, and the fragmentation of self. *Representations 19,* 1-34.

Schafer, R. (1948). *Clinical application of psychological tests.* New York: International Universities Press.

Schaie, K. W. (1989). The hazards of cognitive aging. *The Gerontological Society of America, 29,* 484-493.

Schalling, D. (1978). Psychopathy-related personality variables and the psychophysiology of socialization. In R. D. Hare & D. Schalling (Eds.), *Psychopathic behavior: Approaches to research.* Chichester, England: John Wiley.

Schatzberg, A. F. (1991). Psychotic (delusional) major depression: Should it be included as a distinct syndrome in DSM-IV? *American Journal of Psychiatry, 149,* 733-745.

Scheuffgen, K., Happe, F., Anderson, M., & Frith, U. (2000). High "intelligence," low "IQ"? Speed of processing and measured IQ in children with autism. *Development and Psychopathology, 12*, 83-90.

Schlenker, R., & Cohen, R. (1995). Smooth-pursuit eye-movement dysfunction and motor control in schizophrenia: A follow-up study. *European Archives of Psychiatry and Clinical Neuroscience, 245*, 125-126.

Schnall, P. L., Pieper, C., Schwartz, J. E., Karasek, R. A., Schlussel, Y., Devereux, R. B., Ganau, A., Alderman, M., Warren, K., & Pickering, T. G. (1990). The relationship between job strain, workplace diastolic blood pressure, and left ventricular mass index. *Journal of the American Medical Association, 263*, 1929-1972.

Schoenman, T. J. (1984). The mentally ill witch in textbooks of abnormal psychology: Current status and implications of a fallacy. *Professional Psychiatry, 15*, 299-314.

Schooler, N. R., Keith, S. J., Severe, J. B., Matthews, S. M., Bellack, A. S., Glick, I. D., et al. (1997). Relapse and rehospitalization during maintenance treatment ofschizophrenia: the effects of dose reduction and family treatment. *Archives of General Psychiatry, 54*, 453-463.

Schopler, E., Mesibov, G. B., & Hearsey, K. (1995). Structured teaching in the TEACCH mode. In E. Schopler, & G. Mesibov (Eds.), *Learning and cognition in autism* (pp. 243-267). New York: Plenum.

Schotte, D. E., & Stunkard, A. J. (1987). Bulimia vs. bulimic behaviors on a college campus. *Journal of the American Medical Association, 258*, 1213-1215.

Schulz, S. C. (1995). Schizophrenia: Somatic treatment. In H. I. Kaplan & B. J. Sadock (Eds.), *Comprehensive textbook of psychiatry* (6th ed) (pp. 987-998). Baltimore: Williams & Wilkins.

Schulz, S. C. (2000). New antipsychotic medications: More than old wine in new bottles. *Bulletin of the Menninger Clinic, 64*, 60-75.

Schwartz, A. J., & Whitaker, L. C. (1990). Suicide among college students: Assessment, treatment, and intervention. In S. J. Blumenthal & D. J. Kupfer (Eds.), *Suicide over the life cycle: Risk factors, assessment, and treatment of suicidal patients.* Washington, DC: American Psychiatric Press.

Schwartz, J. M., & Marsh, L. (2000). The psychiatric perspectives of epilepsy. *Psychosomatics, 41*, 31-38.

Schwartz, M.S. (1995). *Biofeedback: A practitioner's guide.* NY: Guilford.

Schwartz, P. J., Brown, C., Wehr, T. A., & Rosenthal, N. E. (1996). Winter seasonal affective disorder: A follow-up study of the first 59 patients of the National Institute of Mental Health Seasonal Studies Program. *American Journal of Psychiatry, 153*, 1028-1036.

Schweinhart, L. J., & Weikart, D. P. (1980). Young children grow up. Ypsilanti, MI: High/Scope.

Sclar, D.A., Robinson, L. M., Legg, R. F., Nemec, N. L., Galin, R. S., Hughes, T. E., & Busching, D. P. (1994). Antidepressant pharmacotherapy: Economic outcomes in a health maintenance organization. *Clinical Therapeutics, 16*, 715-730.

Scruggs, T. E., & Mastropieri, M. A. (1993). Special education for the twenty-first century: Integrating learning strategies and thinking skills. *Journal of Learning Disabilities, 26*, 392-398.

Scull, A. (1993). *The most solitary of afflications: Madness and society in Britain 1700-1900.* New Haven, CT: Yale University Press.

Searl, S., Jr. (1978). Stages of parent reaction to the birth of a handicapped child. *Exceptional Parent* (April), 23-27.

Segraves, R.T., & Althof, S. (1998). Psychotherapy and pharmacotherapy of sexual dysfunctions. In P. E. Nathan & J. M. Gorman (Eds.), *A guide to treatments that work* (pp. 447-471). NY: Oxford University Press.

Seidman, S., & Rieder, R. O. (1994). A review of sexual behavior in the United States. *The American Journal of Psychiatry, 151*, 330-341.

Seligman, M. E. P. (1971). Phobias and preparedness. *Behavior Therapy, 2*, 307-320.

Seligman, M. E. P. (1974). Depression and learned helplessness. In R. J. Friedman & M. M. Katz (Eds.), *The psychology of depression: Contemporary theory and research.* Washington, DC: V. H. Winston.

Seligman, M. E. P. (1975). *Helplessness: On depression, development, and death.* San Francisco: W. H. Freeman.

Seligman, M. E. P. (1995). The effectiveness of psychotherapy: The Consumer Reports Study. *American Psychologist, 50*, 965-974.

Selkoe, D. J. (1997). Alzheimer's disease: Genotypes, phenotypes, and treatments. *Science, 275*, 630-631.

Selten, J. P., Slaets, J. P. J., & Kahn, R. S. (1997). Schizophrenia in Surinamese and Dutch Antillean immigrants to The Netherlands: evidence of an increased incidence. *Psychological Medicine, 27*, 807-811.

Selye, H. (1976). *The stress of life,* revised edition. New York: McGraw-Hill.

Senel, H. G., & Akkok, F. (1995). Stress levels and attitudes of normal siblings of children with disabilities. *International Journal for the Advancement of Counselling, 18*, 61-68.

Seuchter, S. A., Hebebrand, J., Klug, B., Knapp, M., Lehmkuhl, G., Pouska, F., Schmidt, M., & Remschmidt, H., Baur, M. P. (2000). Complex segregation analysis of families ascertained through Gilles de la Tourette syndrome. *Genetic Epidemiology, 18*, 33-47.

Shadish, W. R., Navarro, A. M., Crits-Cristoph, P., Jorm, A. F., Nietzel, M. T., Robinson, L., Svartberg, M., Matt, G. E., Siegle, G., Hazelrigg, M. D., Lyons, L. C., Prout, H. T., Smith, M. L., & Weiss, B. (1997). Evidence that therapy works in clinically representative conditions. *Journal of Consulting and Clinical Psychology, 65*, 355-365.

Shaffer, J. W., Graves, P. L., Swank, R. T., & Pearson, T. A. (1987). Clustering of personality traits in youth and the subsequent development of cancer among physicians. *Journal of Behavioral Medicine, 10*, 441-447.

Shalev, A. Y., Bonne, O., & Eth, S. (1996). Treatment of posttraumatic stress disorder: A review. *Psychosomatic Medicine, 58*, 165-182.

Shalev, A. Y., Peri, T., Canetti, L., & Schreiber, S. (1996). Predictors of PTSD in injured trauma survivors: A prospective study. *American Journal of Psychiatry, 152*, 219-225.

Shapiro, D. (1965). *Neurotic styles.* New York: Basic Books.

Shapiro, D. A., Barkham, M., Rees, A., Hardy, G. E., Reynolds, S., & Startup, M. (1994). Effects of treatment duration and severity of depression on the effectiveness of cognitive-behavioral and psychodynamic-interpersonal psychotherapy. *Journal of Consulting and Clinical Psychology, 62*, 522-534.

Shapiro, F. (1995). *Eye movement desensitization and reprocessing.* NY: Guilford Press.

Sharpe, M. (1996). Chronic fatigue syndrome. *Psychiatric Clinics of North America, 19*, 549-573.

Shaywitz, S. E., Shaywitz, B. A., Pugh, K. R., Fulbright, R. K., Constable, R. T., Mencl, W. E., Shankweiler, D. P., Liberman, A. M., Skudlarski, P., Fletcher, J.M., Katz, L., Marchione, K. E., Lacadie, C., Gatenby, C., & Gore, J. C. (1998). Functional disruption in the organization of the brain for reading in dyslexia. *Proceedings of the National Academy of Sciences, 95*, 2636-2641.

Shea, M. T., Elkin, I., Imber, S. D., Sotsky, S. M., Watkins, J. T., Collins, J. F., Pilkonis, P. A., Beckham, E., Glass, D. R., Dolan, R. T., & Parloff, M. B. (1992). Course of depressive symptoms over follow-up: Findings from the National Institute of Mental Health Treatment of Depression Collaborative Research Program. *Archives of General Psychiatry, 49*, 782-787.

Shea, S. C. (1998). *Psychiatric Interviewing: The Art of Understanding* (2nd ed.). Philadelphia: Saunders.

Sheehan, S. (1982). *Is there no place on earth for me?* Boston: Houghton Mifflin.

Sheehan, S. (1995). The last days of Sylvia Frumkin. *The New Yorker,* February 20 and 27, 199-211.

Shekelle, R. B., Raynor, W. J., Ostfeld, A. M., Garron, D. C., Bieliauskas, L. A., Liu, S. C., Maliza, C., & Oglesby, P. (1981). Psychological depression and 17-year risk of death from cancer. *Psychosomatic Medicine, 43*, 117-125.

Shengxian, L., & Phillips, M. R. (1990). Witch doctors and mental illness in Mainland China: A preliminary study. *American Journal of Psychiatry, 147*, 221-224.

Sher, L., Goldman, D., Ozaki, N., & Rosenthal, N. E. (1999). The role of genetic factors in the etiology of seasonal affective disorder and seasonality. *Journal of Affective Disorders, 53*, 203-210.

Sherman, B. (1985). The new realities of date rape. *New York Times,* Oct. 23, 17.

Sherman, D. K., McGue, M. K., & Iacono, W. G. (1997). Twin concordance for attention deficit hyperactivity disorder: A comparison of teachers' and mothers' reports. *American Journal of Psychiatry, 154*, 532-535.

Shively, C.A., Adams, M.R., Kaplan, J.R., Williams, J.K. (2000). Social stress, gender, and coronary heart disease risk in monkeys. In P.M. McCabe, N. Schneiderman, Field, & T. Williams (Eds.). *Stress, coping, and cardiovascular disease.* Mahwah, N.J.: Erlbaum.

Shoham-Salomon, V., Avner, R., & Neeman, R. (1989). You're changed if you do and changed if you don't: Mechanisms underlying paradoxical interventions. *Journal of Consulting and Clinical Psychology, 57*, 590-598.

Shore, E. R. (1989). What I learned about community psychology from my bout with cancer. *The Community Psychologist, 23*, 25.

Shumaker, S. A., & Hill, D. R. (1991). Gender differences in social support and physical health. *Health Psychology, 10*, 102-111.

Shumaker, S.A., Schron, E.G., Ockene, J.K., & McBee, W.L. (Eds.) (1998). *The handbook of health behavior change* (2nd ed.). NY: Springer.

Shure, M. B. (1993). I can problem solve (ICPS): Interpersonal cognitive problem solving for young children. *Early Child Development and Care, 96*, 49-64.

Shure, M. B., & Spivack, G. (1982). Interpersonal problem-solving in young children: A cognitive approach to prevention. *American Journal of Community Psychology, 10*, 341-356.

Shure, M. B., & Spivack, G. (1987). Competence-building as an approach to prevention of dysfunction: The ICPS model. In J. A. Steinberg & M. M. Silverman (Eds.). *Preventing mental disorders: A research perspective.* Rockville, MD: National Institute of Mental Health.

Siegel, D. J. (1998). Evaluation of high-functioning autism. In G. Goldstein, P. D. Nussbaum, & S. R. Beers (Eds.), *Neuropyschology* (pp.109-133). New York: Plenum.

Siever, L. J., & Coursey, R. D. (1985). Biological markers for schizophrenia and the biological high risk approach. *Journal of Nervous and Mental Disease, 173*, 4-16.

Siever, L. J., & Kendler, K. S. (1986). Schizoid/schizotypal/paranoid personality disorders. In R. Michels and J. O. Cavenar, Jr. (Eds.), *Psychiatry* (vol. 1). New York: Basic Books.

Siever, L. J., Bernstein, D. P., & Silverman, J. M. (1991). Schizotypal personality disorder: A review of its current status. *Journal of Personality Disorders, 5*, 178-193.

Sigafoos, J., Laurie, S., Pennell, D. (1996). Teaching children with Rett syndrome to request preferred objects using aided communication: Two preliminary studies. *Augmentative and Alternative Communication, 12*, 88-96.

Silver, J. M., Hales, R. E., & Yudorsky, S. C. (1990). Psychiatric consultation to neurology. In A. Tasman, S. M. Goldfinger, & C. A. Kauffman (Eds.), Review of Psychiatry (Vol. 9). Washington, DC: American Psychiatric Press.

Silver, L. B. (1999). Attention-deficit/hyperactivity disorder. Washington, DC: AmericanPsychiatric Press.

Silverstein, M. L., & Harrow, M. (1981). Schneiderian first-rank symptoms in schizophrenia. Archives of General Psychiatry, 38, 288-293.

Simoneau, T. L., Miklowitz, D. J., Richards, J. A., Rakhshanda, S., & George, E. L. (1999). Bipolar disorder and family communication: Effects of a psychoeducational treatment program. Journal of Abnormal Psychology, 108, 588-597.

Simpson, D.D., Joe, G.W., Fletcher, B.W., Hubbard, R.L., & Anglin, M.D. (1999). A national evaluation of treatment outcomes for cocaine dependence. Archives of General Psychiatry, 56, 507-514.

Siperstein, G. N., & Leffert, J. S. (1977). Comparison of socially accepted and rejected children with mental retardation. American Journal on Mental Retardation, 101, 339-351.

Siris, S. G., & Lavin, M. R. (1995). Other psychotic disorders. In H. I. Kaplan, & B. J. Sadock (Eds.), Comprehensive textbook of psychiatry, 6th ed. (pp. 1019-1031). Baltimore: Williams & Wilkins.

Skinner, B. F. (1959). A case history in scientific method. In S. Koch (Ed.), Psychology: A study of a science, vol. 2. New York: McGraw-Hill.

Sklar, L. S., & Anisman, H. (1981). Stress and cancer. Psychological Bulletin, 89, 369-406.

Skodol, A. E. (1989). Problems in differential diagnosis. Washington, DC: American Psychiatric Press.

Skultans, V. (1979). English madness. London: Routledge & Kegan Paul.

Sloane, R. B., Staples, F. R., Whipple, K., & Cristol, A. H. (1977). Patients' attitudes toward behavior therapy and psychotherapy. American Journal of Psychiatry, 134(2), 134-137.

Sloane, R. B., Staples, F. R., Yorkston, N. J., Whipple, K., & Cristol, A. H. (1975). Short-term analytically oriented psychotherapy versus behavior therapy. Cambridge, MA: Harvard University Press.

Smalley, S. L., McGough, J. J., Del'Homme, M., NewDelman, J. G., Gordon, E., Kim, T., Liu, A., & McCracken, J. T. (2000). Familial clustering of symptoms and disruptive behaviors in multiplex families with attention-deficit/hyperactivity disorder. Journal of the American Academy of Child and Adolescent Psychiatry, 39, 1135-1143.

Smith, E. M., North, C. S., McCool, R. E., & Shea, J. M. (1990). Acute postdisaster psychiatric disorders: Identification of persons at risk. American Journal of Psychiatry, 147, 202-206.

Smith, M., Wasmuth, J., McPherson, J. D., Wagner, C., Grandy, D., Civelli, O. and others. (1989). Cosegregation of an 11q11-9p22 translocation with affective disorder: Proximity of the dopamine D2 receptor gene relative to the translocation breakpoint. American Journal of Human Genetics, 45, A220.

Smith, M. L., Glass, G. V., & Miller, T. I. (1980). The benefits of psychotherapy. Baltimore: Johns Hopkins University Press.

Smith, R. N. (1982). Dewey and his times. New York: Simon & Schuster.

Sobell, L. C., Cunningham, J. A., & Sobell, M. G. (1996). Recovery from alcohol problems with and without treatment: Prevalence in two population surveys. American Journal of Public Health, 86, 966-972.

Sobell, M. G., & Sobell, L. C. (1995). Controlled drinking after 25 years: How important was the great debate? Addiction, 90, 1149-1153.

Sobol, J., & Maurer, D. (1999). Weighty issues: Fatness and thinness as social problems. NY: Aldine De Gruyter.

Sohlberg, S., & Strober, M. (1994). Personality in anorexia nervosa: An update and a theoretical integration. Acta Psychiatrica Scandinavica, 89 (Suppl. 378), 1-16.

Sokol, L., Beck, A. I., Greenberg, R. L., Wright, F. D., & Berchick, R. J. (1989). Cognitive therapy of panic disorder: A nonpharmacological alternative. The Journal of Nervous and Mental Disease, 177, 711-716.

Sokoloff, P., Giros, B., Martres, M. P., Bouthenet, M. L., & Schwartz, J. C. (1990). Molecular cloning and characterization of a novel dopamine receptor as a target for neuroleptics. Nature, 347, 146-151.

Solomon, S. D., Gerrity, E. T., & Muff, A. M. (1992). Efficacy of treatments for posttraumatic stress disorder: An empirical review. Journal of the American Medical Association, 268, 633-638.

Solovay, M. R., Shenton, M. E., & Holzman, P. S. (1987). Comparative studies of thought disorders. Archives of General Psychiatry, 44, 13-20.

Sommers-Flanagan, J., & Sommers-Flanagan, R. (1996). Efficacy of antidepressant medication with depressed youth: What psychologists should know. Professional Psychology: Research and Practice, 27, 145-153.

Sorbi, M. J., Maassen, G. A., Spierings, E. C. H. (1996). A time series analysis of daily hassles and mood changes in the 3 days before the migraine attack. Behavioral Medicine, 22, 103-113.

Southwick, S. M., Morgan, C. A., Darnell, A., Bremner, D., Nisolaou, A. L., Nagy, L. M., & Charney, D. S. (1995). Trauma-related symptoms in veterans of Operation Desert Storm: A 2-year follow-up. American Journal of Psychiatry, 152, 1150-1155.

Spanos, N. P. (1978). Witchcraft in histories of psychiatry: A critical analysis and an alternative conceptualization. Psychological Bulletin, 85, 417-439.

Spanos, N. P. (1994). Multiple identity enactments and multiple personality disorder: A sociocognitive perspective. Psychological Bulletin, 116, 143-165.

Speltz, M. L., McClellan, J., DeKlyen, M., & Jones, K. (1999). Preschool boys with oppositional defiant disorder: clinical presentation and diagnostic change. Journal of the American Academy of Child and Adolescent Psychiatry, 38, 838-845.

Sperling, M. K. (1999). Schizophrenia. Bethesda, MD: National Institute of Mental Health.

Spiegel, D., & Wissler, T. (1986). Family environment as a predictor of psychiatric rehospitalization. American Journal of Psychiatry, 143, 56-60.

Spiegel, D., Bloom, J. R., Kraemer, H. C., & Gottheil, E. (1989). Effect of psychosocial treatment on survival of patients with metastatic breast cancer. Lancet, October 14, 888-891.

Spiegel, D. A. (Ed.) (1994). Dissociation. Washington, DC: American Psychiatric Press.

Spiegel, D. A., Bruce, T. J., Gregg, S. F., & Nuzzarello, A. (1994). Does cognitive behavior therapy assist slow-taper alprazolam discontinuation in panic disorder? American Journal of Psychiatry, 151, 876-881.

Spiegel, D. A., Roth, M., Weissman, M., Lavori, P., Gorman, J., Rush, J., & Ballenger, J. (1993). Alprazolam and exposure alone and combined in panic disorder with agoraphobia: A controlled study in London and Toronto. British Journal of Psychiatry, 162, 788-789.

Spitzer, R. L., Gibbon, M., Skodol, A. E., Williams, J. B. W., & First, M. G. (1989). DSM-III-R casebook. Washington, DC: American Psychiatric Press.

Spitzer, R. L., Skodol, A. E., Gibbon, M., & Williams, J. B. W. (1981). DSM-III casebook. Washington, DC: American Psychiatric Association.

Spitzer, R. L., Skodol, A. E., Gibbon, M., & Williams, J. B. W. (1983). Psychopathology: A casebook. New York: McGraw-Hill.

Spitzer, R. L., Williams, J. B. W., Gibbon, M., & First, M. B. (1992). The structured clinical interview for DSM-III-R (SCID): I. History, rationale, and description. Archives of General Psychiatry, 49, 624-629.

Spivack, G., Platt, J. J., & Shure, M. B. (1976). The problem-solving approach to adjustment. San Francisco: Jossey-Bass.

Spring, B., Lemon, M., Weinstein, L., & Haskell, A. (1989). Distractibility in schizophrenia: State and trait aspects. British Journal of Psychiatry, 155, 63-68.

St. Clair, D., Blackwood, D., Muir, W., Carothers, A., Walker, M., Spowart, G., Cosden, C., & Evans, H. J. (1990). Association within a family of balanced autosomal translocation with major mental illness. Lancet, 336, 13-16.

Staley, D., Wand, R., & Shady, G. (1997). Tourette disorder: A cross cultural review. Comprehensive Psychiatry, 38, 6-16.

Stark, K. D., Humphrey, L. L., Crook, K., & Lewis, K. (1990). Perceived family environments of depressed and anxious children: Child's and maternal figure's perspectives. Journal of Abnormal Child Psychology, 18, 527-547.

Stein, M. B., Walker, J. R., & Forde, D. R. (1994). Setting diagnostic thresholds for social phobia: Considerations from a community survey of social anxiety. American Journal of Psychiatry, 15, 408-412.

Stein, M., Schleifer, S. J., & Keller, S. E. (1987). Psychoimmunology in clinical psychiatry. In R. E. Hales & A. J. Frances (Eds.), American Psychiatric Association annual review (vol. 6). Washington, DC: American Psychiatric Press.

Steiner, H., & Lock, J. (1998). Anorexia nervosa and bulimia nervosa in children and adolescents: A review of the past 10 years. Journal of the American Academy of Child and Adolescent Psychiatry, 37, 352-359.

Steinhauer, S. R., Zubin, J., Condray, R., Shaw, D. B., Peters, J. L., & van Kammen, D. P. (1991). Electrophysiological and behavior signs of attentional disturbance in schizophrenics and their siblings. In C. A. Tammings and S. C. Schulz, Advances in Neuropsychiatry and Psychopharmacology (vol. 1) Schizophrenia Research (pp. 169-178). New York: Raven Press.

Stephens, J. H., Richard, P., & McHugh, P. R. (1997). Long-term follow-up of patients hospitalized for schizophrenia, 1913 to 1940. The Journal of Nervous and Mental Disease, 185, 715-721.

Stephens, R. J., & Sandor, P. (1999). Aggressive behaviour in children with Tourette syndrome and comorbid attention-deficit hyperactivity disorder and obsessive compulsive disorder. Canadian Journal of Psychiatry, 44, 1036-1042.

Stephens, R. S., Roffman, R. A., & Simpson, E. E. (1994). Treating adult marijuana dependence: A test of the relapse prevention model. Journal of Consulting and Clinical Psychology, 62, 92-99.

Stewart, J. W., Merceir, M. A., Agosti, V., Guardino, M., & Quitkin, F. M. (1993). Imipramine is effective after unsuccessful cognitive therapy: Sequential use of cognitive therapy and imipramine in depressed outpatients. Journal of Clinical Psychopharmacology, 13, 114-119.

Stickney, M.I., Miltenberger, R.G., & Wolff, G. (1999). A descriptive analysis of factors contributing to binge eating. Journal of Behavior Therapy, 30, 177-189.

Stone, M. H. (1980). The borderline syndromes. New York: McGraw-Hill.

Stone, M. H. (1986). Borderline personality disorder. In R. Michels and J. O. Cavenar, Jr. (Eds.), Psychiatry (vol. 1). New York: Basic Books.

Stone, M. H., Stone, D. K., & Hurt, S. W. (1987). The natural history of borderline patients treated by intensive hospitalization. Psychiatric Clinics of North America, 10, 185-206.

Storr, A. (1980). The art of psychotherapy. New York: Methuen.

Storr, A. (1988). Churchill: The man. In A. Storr (Ed.), Churchill's black dog, Kafka's mice, and other phenomena of the human mind. New York: Grove Press.

Strand, J. G., & Benjamin, L. S. (1997). Resistance to change in individuals with personality disorder. Current Opinion in Psychiatry, 10, 132-135.

Strand, V. C. (1991). Victim of sexual abuse: Case of Rosa, age 6. In N. B. Webb (Ed.), *Play therapy with children in crisis* (pp. 69-91). New York: Guilford.

Streissguth, A. P., Aase, J. M., Clarren, S. K., Randels, S. P., LaDue, R. A., & Smith, D. F. (1991). Fetal alcohol syndrome in adolescents and adults. *Journal of the American Medical Association, 265*, 1961-1967.

Streissguth, A. P., Barr, H. M., Olson, H. C., & Sampson, P. D. (1994). Drinking during pregnancy decreases work attack and arithmetic scores on standardized tests: Adolescent data from a population-based prospective study. *Alcoholism: Clinical and Experimental Research, 18*, 248-254.

Streissguth, A. P., Bookstein, F. L., Sampson, P. D., & Barr, H. M. (1995). Attention: Prenatal alcohol and continuities of vigilance and attentional problems from 4 through 14 years. *Development and Psychopathology, 7*, 419-446.

Strober, M., Freeman, R., Lampert, C., Diamond, J., & Kaye, W. (2000). Controlled family study of anorexia nervosa and bulimia nervosa: Evidence of shared liability and transmission of partial syndromes. *American Journal of Psychiatry, 157*, 393-401.

Strober, M., Lampert, C., Morrell, W., Burroughs, J., & Jacobs, C. (1990). A controlled family study of anorexia nervosa: Evidence of familial aggregation and lack of shared transmission with affective disorders. *International Journal of Eating Disorders, 9*, 239-253.

Stroebe, M. S., Stroebe, W., & Hansson, R. O. (Eds.) (1993). *Handbook of bereavement.* Cambridge, England: Cambridge University Press.

Stubbs, E. G., Ritvo, E. R., & Mason-Brothers, A. (1985). Autism and shared parental HLA antigens. *Journal of Child Psychiatry, 24*, 182-185.

Sturm, R., & Wells, K. B. (1995). How can care for depression become more cost-effective? *Journal of the American Medical Association, 273*, 51-58.

Sturmey, P., Burcham, J. A., & Shaw, B. (1996). The frequency of Reiss Screen diagnoses in a community sample of adults with mental retardation (1996). *Behavioral Interventions, 11*, 87-94.

Suddath, R. L., Christison, G. W., Torrey, E. F., Casanova, M. F., & Weinberger, D. R. (1990). Anatomical abnormalities in the brains of monozygotic twins discordant for schizophrenia. *New England Journal of Medicine, 322*, 789-794.

Suelze, M., & Keenan, V. (1981). Changes in family support networks over the life cycle of mentally retarded persons. *American Journal of Mental Deficiency, 86*, 267-274.

Sunahara, R. K., Seeman, P., Van Tol, H. H., & Niznik, H. B. (1993). Dopamine receptors and antipsychotic drug response. *British Journal of Psychiatry (Suppl.) 22*, 31-38.

Sundgot, B. J. (1994). Risk and trigger factors for the development of eating disorders in female elite athletes. *Medicine and Science in Sports and Exercise, 26*, 414-419.

Suomi, S. J., & Harlow, H. F. (1972). Social rehabilitation of isolation-reared monkeys. *Developmental Psychology, 6*, 487-496.

Suomi, S. J., & Harlow, H. F. (1978). Early experience and social development in Rhesus monkeys. In M. E. Lamb (Ed.), *Social and personality development.* New York: Holt, Rinehart and Winston.

Susser, E., Neugebauer, R., Hoek, H. W., Brtown, A. S., Lin, S., Labovitz, D., & Gorman, J. M. (1996). Schizophrenia after prenatal famine. *Archives of General Psychiatry, 53*, 25-31.

Swanson, J. W., Holzer, C. E., III, Ganju, V. K., & Jono, R. T. (1990). Violence and psychiatric disorder in the community: Evidence from the epidemiologic catchment area surveys. *Hospital and Community Psychiatry, 41*, 761-770.

Swedo, S. E., Leonard, H. L., Rapoport, J. L. (1992). Childhood-onset obsessive compulsive disorder. *Psychiatric Clinics of North America, 15*, 767-775.

Swett, C., Jr., Surrey, J., & Cohen, C. (1990). Sexual and physical abuse histories and psychiatric symptoms among male psychiatric outpatients. *American Journal of Psychiatry, 147*, 632-636.

Szmuckler, G., & Dare, C. (1996). Family therapy. *Current Opinion in Psychiatry, 9*, 198-203.

Takei, N. T., Sham, P., O'Callaghan, E., Murray, G. K., Glover, G., & Murray, R. M. (1994). Prenatal exposure to influenza and the development of schizophrenia: Is the effect confined to females? *American Journal of Psychiatry, 151*, 117-119.

Tang, Y. P., Shimizu, E., Dube, G.R., Rampon, C., Kerchner, G.A., Zhuo, M., Liu, G.S., & Tsien, J.Z., (1999). Genetic enhancement of learning and memory in mice. *Nature, 401*, 63-69.

Tanouye, E. (1999). New weapons in the war on schizophrenia. *New York Times,* Wednesday, August 25, pp. B1, B8.

Tarrier, N., & Barrowclough, C. (1995). Family interventions in schizophrenia and their long-term outcomes. *International Journal of Mental Health, 24*, 38-53.

Tarrier, N., Barrowclough, C., Porceddu, K., & Fitzpatrick, E. (1994). The Salford Family Intervention Project: Relapse of schizophrenia at five and eight years. *British Journal of Psychiatry, 165*, 829-832.

Tasman, A., Riba, M.B., & Silk, K.R. (2000). *The Doctor-patient Relationship in Pharmacotherapy: Improving Treatment Effectiveness.* NY: Guilford.

Taylor, S.E., Kemeny, M.E., Reed, G.M., Bower, J.E., & Gurenewald, T.L. (2000). Psychological resources, positive illusions, and health. *American Psychologist, 55*, 99-109.

Teicher, M. H., Glod, C. A., & Cole, J. O. (1993). Antidepressant drugs and the emergence of suicidal tendencies. *Drug Safety, 8*, 186-212.

Teicher, M. H., Glod, C., & Cole, J. O. (1990). Emergence of intense suicidal preoccupation during fluoxetine treatment. *American Journal of Psychiatry, 147*, 207-210.

Teplin, L. A., Abram, K. M., & McClelland, G. M. (1994). Does psychiatric disorder predict violent crime among released jail detainees?: A six-year longitudinal study. *American Psychologist, 49*, 335-342.

Terkelsen, M. D., & Grosser, R. C. (1990). Estimating clozapine's cost to the nation. *Hospital and Community Psychiatry, 41*, 863-869.

Thakker, J., & Ward, T. (1998). Culture and classification: The Cross-cultural application of the DSM-IV. *Clinical Psychology Review, 18*, 501-529.

Thase, M. E., & Howland, R. H. (1995). Biological processes in depression: An updated review and integration. In E. E. Beckham & W. R. Leber (Eds.), *Handbook of depression* (2nd ed., pp. 213-279). New York: Guilford.

Thase, M. E., & Kupfer, D. J. (1996). Recent developments in the pharmacotherapy of mood disorders. *Journal of Consulting and Clinical Psychology, 64*, 646-659.

Thase, M. E., & Rush, A. J. (1995). Treatment resistant depression. In F. E. Bloom and D. J. Kupfer (Eds.), *Psychopharmacology: The fourth generation of progress* (pp. 1081-1097). New York: Raven Press.

Thase, M. E., & Sullivan, L. R. (1995). Relapse and recurrence of depression: A practical approach for prevention. *CNS Drugs, 4*, 261-277.

Thase, M. E., Buysse, D. F., Frank, E., Cherry, C. R., Cornes, C. L., Mallinger, A. G., & Kupfer, D. J. (1997). Which depressed patients will respond to interpersonal psychotherapy? The role of abnormal EEG sleep profiles. *American Journal of Psychiatry, 154*, 502-509.

Thomsen, P. H. (1996). Treatment of obsessive-compulsive disorder in children and adolescents: A review of the literature. *European Child and Adolescent Psychiatry, 5*, 55-66.

Thomsen, P. H. (1998). Obsessive-compulsive disorder in children and adolescents: Clinical guidelines. *European Child and Adolescent Psychiatry, 7*, 1-11.

Thorell, L. H., Kjellman, B., Arned, M., Lindwall-sundel, K., Walinder, J., & Wetterberg, L. (1999). Light treatment of seasonal affective disorder in combination with citalopram or placebo with 1-year follow up. *International Clinical Psychopharmacology, 14*, Suppl. 2, S7-S11.

Thoresen, C. E., Friedman, M., Gill, J. J., & Ulmer, D. K. (1982). The recurrent coronary prevention project: Some preliminary findings. *Acta Medica Scandinavica, 68*, 172-192.

Thorndike, R. L., Hagen, E. P., & Sattler, J. M. (1986). *The Stanford-Binet intelligence scale: Guide for administration and scoring.* Chicago, IL: Riverside.

Tien, A. Y., & Anthony, J. C. (1990). Epidemiological analysis of alcohol and drug use as risk factors for psychotic experiences. *The Journal of Nervous and Mental Disease, 178*, 473-480.

Tienari, P., Lahti, I., Sorri, A., Naarala, M., Moring, J., Kaleva, M., Wahlberg, K. E., & Wynne, L. C. (1990). Adopted-away offspring of schizophrenics and controls: The Finnish adoptive family study of schizophrenia. In L. Robins & M. Rutter (Eds.), *Straight and devious pathways from childhood to adulthood.* New York: Cambridge University Press.

Tienari, P., Wynne, L. C., Moring, J., Lahti, I., Naarala, M., Sorri, A., Wahlberg, K. E., Saarento, O., Seitamaa, M., & Kalveva, M. (1994). The Finnish adoptive family study of schizophrenia: Implications for family research. *British Journal of Psychiatry Supplement, 23*, 20-26.

Tiffany, S.T., Cox, L.S., & Elash, C.A. (2000). Effects of transdermal nicotine patches on abstinence-induced and cue-elicited craving in cigarette smokers. *Journal of Consulting and Clinical Psychology, 68*, 233-240.

Tollefson, G. D., Rampey, A. H., Potvin, J. H., Jenike, M. A., Rush, A. J., Kominguez, R. A., Koran, L. M., Shear, M. K., Goodman, N., & Gerduso, L. A. (1994). A multicenter investigation of fixed-dose fluoxetine in the treatment of obsessive-compulsive disorder. *Archives of General Psychiatry, 51*, 559-567.

Tomb, D. A., & Christensen, D. D. (1987). *Case studies in psychiatry for the house officer.* Baltimore: Williams & Wilkins.

Toner, B.B., Segal, Z.V., Emmott, S.D., & Myran, D. (2000). *Cognitive-behavioral treatment of irritable bowel syndrome.*

Torgersen, S. (1979). The nature and origin of common phobic fears. *British Journal of Psychiatry, 134*, 343-351.

Torgersen, S. (1994). Personality deviations within the schizophrenic spectrum. *Acta Psychiatric Scandinavica Supplementum, 90*. (384, Suppl.), 40-44.

Torgersen, S., Onstad, S., Skre, I., Edvardsen, J., & Kringlen, E. (1993). "True" schizotypal personality disorder: A study of co-twins and relatives of schizophrenic probands. *American Journal of Psychiatry, 150*, 1661-1667.

Torres, C., & Buceta, J. (1998). Effect of parental intervention on motor development of Down syndrome infants between birth and age two years. *British Journal of Developmental Disabilities, 44*, 94-101.

Torrey, E. F. (1994). Violent behavior by individuals with serious mental illness. *Hospital and Community Psychiatry, 45*, 653-662.

Torrey, E. F. (1997). *Out of the shadows: Confronting America's mental illness crisis.* NY: Wiley.

Torrey, E. F., & Bowler, A. E. (1990). Geographical distribution of insanity in America: Evidence for an urban factor. *Schizophrenia Bulletin, 16*, 591-604.

Torrey, E. F., Bowler, A. E., Taylor, E. H., & Gottesman, I. I. (1994). *Schizophrenia and manic-depressive disorder.* New York: Basic Books.

Toupin, J., Dery, M., Pauze, R., Mercier, H., & Fortin, L. (2000). Cognitive and familial contributions to conduct disorder in children. *Journal of Child Psychology and Psychiatry, 41*, 333-344.

Touyz, S. W., Kopec-Schrader, E. M., Vitousek, K., & Manke, R. (1994). Personality variables and disorders in anorexia nervosa and bulimia nervosa. *Journal of Abnormal Psychology, 103*, 137-147.

Troop, N.A. (1998). Eating disorders as coping strategies: A critique. *European Eating Disorders Review, 6,* 229.

True, W. R., Heath, A. C., Scherrer, J. F., Xian, H., Lin, N., Eisen, S. A., Lyons, M. J., Goldberg, J., & Tsuang, M. T. (1999). Interrelationship of genetic and environmental influences on conduct disorder and alcohol and marijuana dependence symptoms. *American Journal of Medical Genetics, 88,* 391-397.

Turkheimer, E. (1998). Heritability and biological explanation. *Psychological Review, 105,* 782-791.

Turner, S. M., Beidel, D. C., & Costello, A. (1987). Psychopathology in the off-spring of anxiety disorders patients. *Journal of Consulting and Clinical Psychology, 55,* 229-235.

Turner, S. M., Beidel, D. C., Darcu, C. V., & Keys, D. J. (1986). Psychopathology of social phobia and comparison to avoidant personality disorder. *Journal of Abnormal Psychology, 95,* 389-394.

Uba, L. (1994). *Asian Americans: Personality patterns, identity, and mental health.* New York: Guilford.

Ullman, S.E., Karabatos, G., & Koss, M.P. (1999). Alcohol and sexual aggression in a national sample of college men. *Psychology of Women Quarterly, 23,* 673-689.

Vaillant, G. E. (1984). The disadvantages of DSM-III outweigh its advantages. *American Journal of Psychiatry, 14,* 542-545.

Vaillant, G. E., & Milofsky, E. S. (1982). Natural history of male alcoholism: IV. Paths to recovery. *Archives of General Psychiatry, 39,* 127-133.

van der Kolk, B. A., McFarlane, A. C., Weiseth, L. (Eds.) (1996). *Traumatic Stress.* NY: Guilford.

van Kesteren, P. J., Gooren, L. J., & Megens, J. A. (1996). An epidemiological and demographic study of transsexuals in the Netherlands. *Archives of Sexual Behavior, 25,* 589-600.

Vanderhoff, B. T., & Miller, K. E. (1997). Major depression: Assessing the role of new antidepressants. *American Family Physician, 55,* 249-254.

Vargas, J. S. (1990). B. F. Skinner. The last few days. *Journal of Applied Behavior Analysis, 23,* 409-410.

Varma, S. L., & Sharma, I. (1993). Psychiatric morbidity in the first-degree relatives of schizophrenic patients. *British Journal of Psychiatry, 162,* 672-678.

Varney, N.R., & Roberts, R.J. (Eds.) (1999). *The evaluation and treatment of mild traumatic brain injury.* Mahwah, NJ: Lawrence Erlbaum.

Vaughn, C. E., Snyder, K. S., Jones, S., Freeman, W. B., & Falloon, I. R. H. (1984). Family factors in schizophrenic relapse. *Archives of General Psychiatry, 41,* 1169-1177.

Vaughn, C. E., Verdoux, H., Takei, N., deSaint Mathurin, R. C., Murray, R. M., & Bourgeois, M. L. (1997). Seasonality of birth in schizophrenia: The effect of regional population density. *Schizophrenia Research, 23,* 175-180.

Veale, D., Boocock, A., Gournay, K., Dryden, W., Shah, F., Willson, R., & Walburn, J. (1996). Body dysmorphic disorder: A survey of fifty cases. *British Journal of Psychiatry, 169,* 196-201.

Verdoux, H., Takei, N., Cassou de Saint Mathurin, R., Murray, R. M., & Bourgeois, M. L., (1997). Seasonality of birth in schizophrenia: The effect of regional population density. *Schizophrenia Research, 23,* 175-180.

Vinogradov, S., & Yalom, I. D. (1990). Self-disclosure in group psychotherapy. In G. Stricker & M. Fisher (Eds.), *Self-disclosure in the therapeutic relationship.* New York: Plenum.

Vinogradov, S., Dishotsky, N. I., Doty, A. K., & Tinklenberg, J. R. (1988). Patterns of behavior in adolescent rape. *American Journal of Orthopsychiatry, 58,* 179-187.

Violanti, J. M., Vena, J. E., & Marshall, J. R. (1996). Suicides, homicides, and accidental death: A comparative risk assessment of police officers and municipal workers. *American Journal of Industrial Medicine, 30,* 99-104.

Virkkunen, M. (1983). Insulin secretion during the glucose tolerance-test in antisocial personality. *British Journal of Psychiatry, 142,* 598-604.

Visscher, P. M., Haley, C. S., Heath, S. C., Muir, W. J., & Blackwood, D. H. (1999). Detecting QTLs for uni- and bipolar disorder using a variance component method. *Psychiatric Genetics, 9,* 75-84.

Volavka, J., Crowner, M., Brizer, D., Convit, A., Van Praag, H., & Suckow, R. F. (1990). Tryptophan treatment of aggressive psychiatric inpatients. *Biological Psychiatry, 28,* 728-732.

Volkmar, F. R., & Cohen, D. J. (1985). The experience of infantile autism: A first-person account by Tony W. *Journal of Autism and Developmental Disorders, 15,* 47-54.

Volkmar, F. R., & Nelson, D. S. (1990). Seizure disorders in autism. *Journal of the American Academy of Child and Adolescent Psychiatry, 29,* 127-129.

Volkmar, F. R., & Rutter, M. (1995). Childhood disintegrative disorder: Results of the DSM-IV Autism Field Trial. *Journal of the American Academy of Child and Adolescent Psychiatry, 34,* 1902-1905.

Volkmar, F. R., Szatmari, P., & Sparrow, S. S. (1993). Sex differences in pervasive developmental disorders. *Journal of Autism and Developmental Disorders, 23,* 489-507.

Volkow, N. D., Wang, G. J., Fowler, J. S., Logan, J., Gatley, S. J., Hitzemann, R., Chen, A. D., Dewey, S. L., & Pappas, N. (1997). Decreased striatal dopaminergic responsiveness in detoxified cocaine-dependent subjects. *Nature, 386,* 830-833.

Vollenweider, F. X., Leenders, K. L., Scharfetter, C., Maguire, P., Stadelmann, O., & Angst, J. (1997). Positron emission tomography and fluorodeoxyglucose studies of metabolic hyperfrontality and psychopathology in the psilocybin model of psychosis. *Neuropsychopharmacology, 16,* 357-372.

Volvaka, J. (1990). Aggression, electroencephalography, and evoked-potentials: A critical review. *Neuropsychiatry, Neuropsychology, and Behavioral Neurology, 3,* 249-259.

Wada, T., Kawakatsu, S., Komatani, A., Nadaoka, T., Okuyama, N., & Otani, K. (1999a). Clomipramine treatment of delusional disorder, somatic type. *International Clinical Psychopharmacology, 14,* 181-183.

Wada, T., Kawakatsu, S., Komatani, A., Okuyama, N., & Otani, K. (1999b). Possible association between delusional disorder, somatic type, and reduced cerebral blood flow. *Progress in Neuropsychopharmacological and Biological Psychiatry, 23,* 353-357.

Wagner, P. S. (1996). First person account: A voice from another closet. *Schizophrenia Bulletin, 22,* 399-401.

Wahlbeck, K., Cheine, M., Essali, A., & Adams, C. (1999). Evidence of clozapine's effectiveness in schizophrenia: A systematic review and meta-analysis of randomized trials. *American Journal of Psychiatry, 156,* 990-999.

Walker, E. F., & Diforio, D. (1997). Schizophrenia: A neural diathesis-stress model. *Psychological Review, 104,* 667-685.

Walker, E. F., & Lewine, R. J. (1990). Prediction of adult-onset schizophrenia from childhood home movies of patients. *American Journal of Psychiatry, 147(8),* 1052-1056.

Walker, E. F., Savoie, T., & Davis, D. (1994), Neuromotor precursors of schizophrenia. *Schizophrenia Bulletin, 20,* 441-454.

Wallace, B. C. (1991). *Crack cocaine.* New York: Brunner/Mazel.

Wallace, M. (1994). Schizophrenia: a national emergency: Preliminary observations on SANELINE. *Acta Psychiatrica Scandinavica, 89* (Suppl.), 33-35.

Waller, G. (1994). Childhood sexual abuse and borderline personality disorder in the eating disorders. *Child Abuse and Neglect, 18,* 97-101.

Wallerstein, J. S., & Kelly, J. B. (1990). *Surviving the breakup: How children and parents cope with divorce.* NY: Basic Books.

Walsh, B. T., Wilson, G. T., Loeb, K. L., Devlin, M. J., Pike, K. M., Rose, S. P., Fleiss, J., & Waternaux, C. (1997). Medication and psychotherapy in the treatment of bulimia nervosa. *American Journal of Psychiatry, 154,* 523-531.

Ward, A., Ramsay, R., & Treasure, J. (2000). Attachment research in eating disorders. *British Journal of Medical Psychology, 73,* 35-51.

Ward, S. R., Chapman, R., Cohn, E., White, S., & Williams, K. (1991). Acquaintance rape and the college social scene. *Family Relations, 40,* 65-71.

Warren, S. T., & Nelson, D. L. (1994). Advances in molecular analysis of fragile X syndrome. *Journal of the American Medical Association, 271,* 536-554.

Wasik, B. H., Ramey, C. T., Bryant, D. M., & Sparling, J. J. (1990). A longitudinal study of two early intervention strategies: Project CARE. *Child Development, 61,* 1682-1696.

Watson, J. B. (1925). *Behaviorism.* New York: Norton.

Wear, S. (1998). *Informed Consent* (2nd ed.). Washington, DC: Georgetown University Press.

Wearden, A., & Appleby, L. (1997). Cognitive performance and complaints of cognitive impairment in chronic fatigue syndrome (CFS). *Psychological Medicine, 27,* 81-90.

Webster-Stratton, C., & Hammond, M. (1997). Treating children with early-onset conduct problems: A comparison of child and parent training interventions. *Journal of Consulting and Clinical Psychology, 65,* 93-109.

Wechsler, D. *Manual for the Wechsler Adult Intelligence Scale-III* (1997). San Antonio: Psychological Corporation.

Wechsler, D. (1955). *Manual for the Wechsler Adult Intelligence Scale.* New York: Psychological Corporation.

Wechsler, D. (1974). *Selected papers of David Wechsler.* New York: Academic Press.

Wechsler, H., Lee, J.E., Kuo, M., & Lee, H. (2000). College binge drinking in the 1990s: A continuing problem. *Journal of American College Health, 48,* 199-210.

Wehr, T. A. (1989). Seasonal affective disorders: A historical overview. In N. E. Rosenthal & M. C. Blehar (Eds.), *Seasonal affective disorders and phototherapy,* pp. 11-33. New York: Guilford.

Weinberg, S. (1995). Portraits of the mental patient as inspired artist. *New York Times Magazine,* August 6, 42-43.

Weinberg, T. S. (1978). Sadism and masochism: Sociological perspectives. *Bulletin of the American Academy of Psychiatry and Law, 6,* 284-295.

Weinberg, T. S., & Falk, G. (1980). The social organization of sadism and masochism. *Deviant Behavior, 1,* 370-393.

Weinberg, T. S., Williams, C. J., & Moser, C. (1984). *The social constituents of sadomasochism.* U, 379-389.

Weinberger, D. R. (1987). Implications of normal brain development for the pathogenesis of schizophrenia. *Archives of General Psychiatry, 44,* 660-669.

Weiner, D. B. (1979). The apprenticeship of Philippe Pinel: A new document, "Observations of Citizen Pussin on the Insane." *American Journal of Psychiatry, 136,* 1128-1134.

Weiner, D. B. (1992). Philippe Pinel's "Memoir on Madness" of December 11, 1794: A fundamental text of modern psychiatry. *American Journal of Psychiatry, 149,* 725-732.

Weiner, H., Cancro, R., Lehmann, H. E., & Frazier, S. H. (1989). Psychopharmacologic treatments. In *Treatments of psychiatric disorders: A task force report of the American Psychiatric Association.* Washington, DC: American Psychiatric Association.

Weiss, G., & Hechtman, L. T. (1993). *Hyperactive children grown up.* New York: Guilford.

Weiss, M., Hechtman, L. T., & Weiss, G. (1999). *ADHD in adulthood*. Baltimore, MD: Johns Hopkins.

Weiss, R. (1993). Promising protein for Parkinson's. *Science, 260*, 1072-1073.

Weiss, R. D., & Mirin, S. M. (1987). *Cocaine*. Washington, DC: American Psychiatric Press.

Weissman, M. M. (1990). Panic and generalized anxiety: Are they separate disorders? *Journal of Psychiatric Research, 24*, 157-162.

Weissman, M. M., & Markowitz, J. C. (1994). Interpersonal psychotherapy: Current status. *Archives of General Psychiatry, 51*, 599-606.

Weissman, M. M., Bland, R. C., Canino, G. J., Faravelli, C., Greenwald, S., Hwu, H-G., Joyce, P. R., Karam, E. G., Lee, C-K., Lellouch, J., Leppine, J-P., Newman, S. C., Rubio-Stipec, M., Wells, E., Wickramaratne, P. J., Wittchen, H.-U., & Yeh, E-K. (1996). Cross-national epidemiology of major depression and bipolar disorder. *Journal of the American Medical Association, 276*, 293-299.

Weissman, M. M., Bland, R. C., Canino, G. J., Greenwald, S., Hwu, H. G., Lee, C. K., Newman, S. C., Oakley-Browne, M. A., Stipic, M. R., Wickramaratne, P. J., Wittchen, H. U., & Yeh, E. K. (1994). The cross national epidemiology of obsessive compulsive disorder: The Cross National Collaborative Group. *Journal of Clinical Psychiatry, 55*, 5-10.

Weissman, M. M., Gershon, E. S., Kidd, K. K., Prussof, B. A., Leckman, J. F., Dibble, E., Hamovit, J., Thompson, W. D., Pauls, D. L., & Guroff, J. J. (1984). Psychiatric disorder in the relatives of probands with affective disorders. *Archives of General Psychiatry, 41*, 13-21.

Weisz, J. R., & Weiss, B. (1989). On "dropouts" and "refusers" in child psychotherapy: Reply to Garfield. *Journal of Consulting and Clinical Psychology, 57*, 170-171.

Weisz, J. R., & Weiss, B. (1993). *Effects of psychotherapy with children and adolescents*. New York: Sage.

Weisz, J. R., Huey, S. J., & Weersing, V. R. (1998). Psychotherapy outcome research with children and adolescents:: The state of the art. In T. H. Ollendick & R. J. Prinz, (Eds.), *Advances in Clinical Child Psychology, 20*. pp. 49-91. New York: Plenum.

Welch, S. L., Doll, H. A., & Fairburn, C. G. (1997). Life events and the onset of bulimia nervosa: A controlled study. *Psychological Medicine, 27*, 515-522.

Wells, K. B., Katon, W., Rogers, B., & Camp, P. (1994). Use of minor tranquilizers and antidepressant medications by depressed outpatients: Results from the medical outcomes study. *American Journal of Psychiatry, 151*, 694-700.

Wells, K. B., Stewart, A., Hays, R. D., Burnam, A., Robers, W., Daniels, M., Berry, S., Greenfield, S., & Ware, J. (1989). The functioning and well-being of depressed patients. *Journal of the American Medical Associaton, 262*, 914-919.

Weltzin, T. E., Hsu, L. K. G., & Kaye, W. H. (1990). *An open trial of fluoxetine in anorexia nervosa: Maintenance of body weight and reduction of obsessional features*. Abstract presented at the fourth International Conference on Eating Disorders, New York, NY, April 28.

Wenar, C., & Kerig, P. (2000). *Developmental psychopathology*, 4th Ed. Boston: McGraw-Hill.

Wenz,-Gross, M., & Siperstein, G. N. (1996). The social world of preadolescents with mental retardation: social support, family environment and adjustment. *Education and Training in Mental Retardation and Developmental Disabilities, 31*, 177-187.

Werdegar, D., Sokolow, M., Perloff, D. B., Riess, F., Harris, R. E., Singer, T., & Blackburn, H. W., Jr. (1967). Portable recording of blood pressure: A new approach to assessments of the severity and prognosis of hypertension. *Transactions of the Association of Life Insurance Medical Directors of America, 51*, 93-173.

Werner, E. E. (1993). Risk, resilience, and recovery: Perspectives from the Kauai Longitudinal Study. *Development and Psychopathology, 5*, 503-515.

Westen, D. (1998). The scientific legacy of Sigmund Freud: Toward a psychologically informed psychological science. *Psychological Bulletin, 124*, 333-371.

Whalen, C. K., & Henker, B. (1985). The social worlds of hyperactive (ADDH) children. *Clinical Psychology Review, 5*, 447-478.

Wheeler, J., & Carlson, C. L. (1994). The social functioning of children with ADD with hyperactivity and ADD without hyperactivity: A comparison of their peer relations and social deficits. *Journal of Emotional and Behavioral Disorders, 2*, 2-12.

Whitehead, W. E., Blackwell, B., & Robinson, A. (1978). Effects of diazepam on phobic avoidance behavior and phobic anxiety. *Biological Psychiatry, 13*, 59-64.

Widiger, T. A. (1991). DSM-IV reviews of the personality disorders: Introduction to special series. *Journal of Personality Disorders, 5*, 122-134.

Widiger, T.A. (2000). Personality disorders in the 21st century. *Journal of Personality Disorders, 14*, 3-16.

Widiger, T. A., & Smith, G. T. (1994). Substance use disorder: Abuse, dependence and dyscontrol. *Addiction, 89*, 267-282.

Widom, C. S. (1978). A methodology for studying noninstitutionalized psychopaths. In R. D. Hare & D. A. Schalling (Eds.), *Psychopathic behavior: Approaches to research*. Chichester, England: John Wiley.

Widom, C. S. (1989). Does violence beget violence: A critical examination of the literature. *Psychological Bulletin, 106*, 3-28.

Widom, C. S., & Morris, S. (1997). Accuracy of adult recollections of childhood victimization, Part 2: Childhood sexual abuse. *Psychological Assessment, 9*, 34-46.

Wikler, L. M. (1986). Periodic stresses of families of older mentally retarded children: An exploratory study. *American Journal of Mental Deficiency, 90*, 703-706.

Wikler, L. M., Wasow, M., & Hatfield, E. (1981). Chronic sorrow revisited. *American Journal of Orthopsychiatry, 51*, 63-70.

Williams, J. B. W., Gibbon, M., First, M. B., Spitzer, R. L., Davies, M., Borus, J., Howes, M. J., Kanes, J., Pope, H. G., Jr., Rounsaville, B., & Wittchen, H. U. (1992). The structured clinical interview for DSM-III-R (SCID): II. Multisite test-retest reliability. *Archives of General Psychiatry, 49*, 630-636.

Williams, L. M. (1994). Recall of childhood trauma: A prospective study of women's memories of child sexual abuse. *Journal of Consulting and Clinical Psychology, 62*, 1167-1176.

Willick, M. S. (1994). Schizophrenia: A parent's perspective—Mourning without end. In N. C. Andreasen (Ed.), *Schizophrenia from mind to molecule*. (pp. 5-20). Washington, DC: American Psychiatric Press.

Wills, T. A., McNamara, G., Vaccaro, D., & Hirky, A. E. (1996). Escalated substance use: A longitudinal grouping analysis from early to middle adolescence. *Journal of Abnormal Psychology, 105*, 166-180.

Wilson, G. T. (1996). Manual-based treatments: The clinical application of research findings. *Behavior Research and Therapy, 34*, 295-314.

Wilson, J. P., & Keane, T. M. (1997). *Assessing psychological trauma and PTSD*. NY: Guilford.

Wing, L. (1997). The autistic spectrum. *Lancet, 350*, 1761-1766.

Winokur, G. (1997). All roads lead to depression: Clinically homogeneous, etiologically heterogeneous. *Journal of Affective Disorders, 45*, 97-108.

Winokur, G., Coryell, W., Akiskal, H. S., Endicott, J., Keller, M., & Mueller, T. (1994). Manic-depressive (bipolar) disorder: The course in light of a prospective ten-year follow-up of 131 patients. *Acta Psychiatrica Scandinavica, 89*, 102-110.

Winokur, G., Coryell, W., Keller, M., Endicott, J., & Leon, A. (1995). A family study of manic-depressive (Bipolar I) disease. *Archives of General Psychiatry, 52*, 367-373.

Winston, A., Laikin, M., Pollack, J., Samstag, L. W., McCullough, M. A. L., & Muran, J. C. (1994). Short term psychotherapy of personality disorders. *American Journal of Psychiatry, 151*, 190-194.

Wintemute, G. J., Parham, C. A., Beaumont, J. J., Wright, M., & Drake, C. (1999). Mortality among recent purchasers of handguns. *New England Journal of Medicine, 341*, 1583-1589.

Wise, T. N. (1985). Fetishism:etiology and treatment: A review from multiple perspectives. *Comprehensive Psychiatry, 26*, 249-257.

Wolf, L., & Goldberg, B. (1986). Autistic children grow up: An eight to twenty-four year follow-up study. *Canadian Journal of Psychiatry, 31*, 550-556.

Wolf, S., & Bruhn, J. G. (1993). *The power of clan: The influence of human relationships on heart disease*. New Brunswick, NJ: Transaction Publishers.

Wolfe, D. A., Sandler, J., & Kaufman, K. (1981). Competency-based parent training program for child abusers. *Journal of Consulting and Clinical Psychology, 49*, 633-640.

Wolraich, M. L., Hannah, J. N., Baumgaertel, A. et al. (1998). Examination of DSM-IV criteria for attention deficit/hyperactivity disorder in a country wide sample. *Journal of Developmental and Behavioral Pediatrics, 19*, 162-168.

Woodman, C.C., Noyes, R., Black, D.W., Schlosser, S., & Yagla, S.J. (1999). A 5-year follow-up study of generalized anxiety disorder and panic disorder. *Journal of Nervous and Mental Disease, 187*, 3-9.

Woolf, L. (1964). *Beginning again: An autobiography of the years 1911 to 1918*. New York: Harcourt.

Woolf, V. (1978). *The letters of Virginia Woolf* (N. Nicholson and J. Trautman (Eds.), New York: Harcourt.

Wu, J. C., Gillin, J. C., Buchsbaum, M. S., & Hershey T., Johnson, J. C., & Bunney, W. E., Jr. (1992). Effect of sleep deprivation on brain metabolism of depressed patients. *American Journal of Psychiatry, 149*, 538-543.

Wulff, S. B. (1985). The symbolic and object play of children with autism: A review. *Journal of Autism and Developmental Disorders, 15*, 139-147.

Wyatt, R. J., Henter, I., Leary, M. C., & Taylor, E. (1995). An economic evaluation of schizophrenia-1991. *Social Psychiatry and Psychiatric Epidemiology, 30*, 196-205.

Yehuda, R. (1999). Biological factors associated with susceptibility to PTSD. *Canadian Journal of Psychiatry, 44*, 34-39.

Yoshikawa, H. (1994). Prevention as cumulative protection: Effects of early family support and education on chronic delinquency and its risks. *Psychological Bulletin, 115*, 28-54.

Young, M. A., Fogg, L. F., Scheftner, W. A., & Fawcett, J. A. (1994). Interactions of risk factors in predicting suicide. *American Journal of Psychiatry, 151*, 434-435.

Zadra, A., & Donderi, D.C. (2000). Nightmares and bad dreams: Their prevalence and relationship to well-being. *Journal of Abnormal Psychology, 109*, 273-281.

Zeitlin, H. (1986). *The natural history of psychiatric disorder in children*. Oxford England: Oxford University Press.

Zetlin, A. G., & Turner, J. L. (1985). Transition from adolescence to adulthood: Perspectives of mentally retarded individuals and their families. *American Journal of Mental Deficiency, 89*, 570-579.

Zigler, E. (1995). Can we "cure" mild mental retardation among individuals in the lower socioeconomic stratum? *American Journal of Public Health, 85*, 302-304.

Zigler, E., & Burack, J. A. (1989). Personality development and the dually diagnosed person. *Research in Developmental Disabilities, 10*, 225-240.

Zigler, E., & Hodapp, R. M. (1991). Behavioral functioning in individuals with mental retardation. *Annual Review of Psychology, 42*, 29-50.

Zigler, E., Bulla, D., & Hodapp, R. (1984). On the definition and classification of mental retardation. *American Journal of Mental Deficiency, 89*, 215-230.

Zimmerman, M. (1994). Diagnosing personality disorders: A review of issues and research methods. *Archives of General Psychiatry, 51*, 225-245.

Zimmerman, M., & Mattia, J.I. (1999). Axis I diagnostic comorbidity and borderline personality disorder. *Comprehensive Psychiatry, 40*, 245-252.

Zubin, J., & Spring, B. (1977). Vulnerabilityùa new view of schizophrenia. *Journal of Abnormal Psychology, 86*, 103-126.

Zubin, J., Magaziner, J., & Steinhauer, S. R. (1983). The metamorphosis of schizophrenia: From chronicity to vulnerability. *Psychological Medicine, 13*, 551-571.

Acknowledgments

Photos

Chapter 1: p. 5, The Spokesman-Review; p. 11 (top), Kal Muller, Woodfin Camp & Assoc.; p. 11 (bottom), Kjell B. Sandved, Visuals Unlimited; p. 13, The Granger Collection; p. 14, North Wind Picture Archives; p. 15, Denver Art Museum; p. 16, Hulton/Getty Archive Photos; p. 17, The Wellcome Trust; p. 18, National Library of Medicine; P. 19 (top), The Granger Collection; p. 19 (bottom), National Library of Medicine; p. 19, Nubar Alexanian, Woodfin Camp & Assoc.; p. 39 (left and right), Harlow Primate Laboratory.

Chapter 2: p. 51, Bob Sacha Photography; p. 59 (left), Raymond Meier, Inc.; p. 59 (right), Marcus E. Raichle, M.D.; p. 63, Corbis; p. 70, Yvonne Hemsey, Liaison Agency, Inc.; p. 73, Laura Dwight, PhotoEdit; p. 74, L.A. Cicero, Stanford University News Service; p. 75, Sal DiMarco, Jr., New York Times Pictures; p. 78, Carl Rogers Memorial Library.

Chapter 3: p. 96 (left), Jeff Kaufman, FPG International, LLC; p. 96 (right), Michael Newman, PhotoEdit; p. 104, Lew Merrim, Monkmeyer Press; p. 105 (top left, bottom left, top right, bottom right), American Guidance Service, Inc.; p. 111 (left), Ken Karp, Pearson Eduction/ PH College; p. 111 (right), Bob Daemmrich, Stock Boston; p. 112, Harvard University Press; p. 114 (left), Cary Wolinsky, Stock Boston; p. 114 (right), C. Glassman, The Image Works; p. 115, David E. Dempster, Pearson Eduction/PH College; p. 117 (top) Spacelabs Medical, Inc.

Chapter 4: p. 124, Richard Scheinwald, AP/Wide World Photos; p. 126, Reuters, Corbis; p. 131, Universal Press Syndicate; p. 135, Bob Mahoney, The Image Works; p. 136, Rhoda Sidney; p. 137, AP/Wide World Photos; p. 143, AP/Wide World Photos.

Chapter 5: p. 155, Georges Gobet, AP/Wide World Photos; p. 156, Patrick Ramsey, International Stock Photography, LTD.; p. 157, Jamie Francis, AP/Wide World Photos; p. 161, Pat Farley, Monkmeyer Press; p. 168 (left), John Easton; p. 168 (right), New York Times Pictures; p. 169, Mrs. Michal Heron; p. 181, Joan C. Fahrenthold, AP/Wide World Photos; p. 185, UPI/Corbis.

Chapter 6: p. 194, J. Berndi, Stock Boston; p. 195 (left), Giovanni Lunardi, International Stock Photography, LTD.; p. 195 (right), L.D. Gordon, The Image Bank; p. 197 (left), Pierre Boulat/COS, Woodfin Camp & Assoc.; p. 197 (right), Robert Glodstein, Photo Researchers, Onc.; p. 203 (right) William West, Agence France-Presse; p. 203 (left), Al Bello, Allsport Photography (USA), Inc.

Chapter 7: p. 208, Phil Huber, New York Times Pictures; p. 212, AP/Wide World Photos; p. 218, Jimi Lott, Seattle Times; p. 219 (top), Aaron Lee Fineman, New York Times Pictures; p. 219 (bottom), Penny Tweedie, Stone; p. 222, Michael Caulfield, AP/Wide World Photos; p. 226, Michael Lutzky, Washington Post Writers Group.

Chapter 8: p. 248, James Lemass, Index Tock Imagery, Inc.; p. 252, Bill Aron, Photo Edit; p. 259 (left and right), Peter Schaaf; p. 261 (left), UPI/Corbis; p. 261 (center), Henry Grossman, TimePix; p. 261 (right), Irwin G. Sarason; p. 263 (top), City of Bellevuie Police Department; p. 264, AP/Wide World Photos; p. 266, Archive Photos.

Chapter 9: p. 279, Tony Freeman, Photo Edit; p. 282, Spencer Platt, Liaison Agency, Inc.; p. 290, Vinnie Fish, Black Star; p. 297, Laima E. Druskis, Pearson Education/PH College.

Chapter 10: p. 315 (bottom), Mark S. George, MD/National Institute of Mental Health; p. 333 (left), Corbis; p. 333 (right), AP/Wide World Photos; p. 343 (left), Erich Hartmann, Magnum Photos, Inc.; p. 343 (middle), Reuters/San Diego Sheriff's Dept./Archive Photos; p. 343 (right), Keith Myers/New York Times Pictures.

Chapter 11: p. 367, Dr. E.F. Walker; p. 375, Catherine Karnow, Corbis.

Chapter 12: p. 404, Jim Whitmer; p. 417, AP/Wide World Photos.

Chapter 13: p. 447, A. Ramey, Stock Boston.

Chapter 14: p. 488, Prometheus Books; p. 498, M. Siluk, The Image Works.

Chapter 16: p. 568, Richard T. Nowitz/Corbis.

Chapter 17: p. 591, Corbis/Stock Market; p. 604 (left), Mike Salisbury/ The Olympian.

Figures, Tables, and Text:

Chapter 1: Fig. 1.2, *Hospital and Community Psychiatry*, volume/Edition 47 by Swanson, Holzer, Ganju, Jones. Copyright 1990 by American Psychiatric Assn. Reproduced with permission; Fig. 1.7, Caspi A. & Elder, A.H., Jr. (1988). Early Personality and Life Disorganization. In E.M. Hetherinton, R.M. Lerner, & M. Permutter (eds.) CHILD DEVELOPMENT IN LIFE-SPAN PERSPECTIVE. Hillsdale, NJ. L. Earlbaum, Assoc.; Fig. 1.8, Eron, "The Development of Aggressive Behavior from the perspective of developing behaviorism, *American Psychologist, 42*, pp. 440. Copyright 1987 by the American Psychological Assoc. Reprinted with permission.

Chapter 4: Table 4.3, American Psychiatric Press; Fig. 4.15, *American Journal of Psychiatry*, volume/edition 130 by Abrams. Copyright 1973 by American Psychiatric Assn. Reproduced with permission.

Chapter 6: Table 6.4, Cambridge University Press; Fig. 6.9, W. Ruberman, E. Weinblatt, J.D. Goldberg, et al, "Psychosocial Influences on Mortality after Myocardial Infarction," *New England Journal of Medicine,* 9, p. 555. Copyright 1984 Massachusetts Medical Society. All rights reserved. Fig. 6.10, American Medical Association.

Chapter 7: Table 7.11, *Hospital & Community Psychiatry*, Volume/ edition 37 by Horowitz. Copyright 1986 by American Psychiatric Press; Table 7.12, Mezzich, Ahn, Febrega, & Pilkonis, "Patterns of Psychiatric Comorbidity in a large population presenting for care," in J.D. Maser & C.R. Cloninger (eds) Comorbidity in Anxiety and Mood Disorders, © 1990, p. 194.

Chapter 8: Text box, Wall Street Journal; Table 8.1, Laumann, E.O., Gagnon, J.H., Michael, R.T., & Michaels, S. (1994) THE SOCIAL ORGANIZATION OF SEXUALITY. Chicago University of Chicago Press; Table 8.2, Laumann, E.O., Gagnon, J.H., Michael, R.T., & Michaels, S. (1994) THE SOCIAL ORGANIZATION OF SEXUALITY. Chicago University of Chicago Press; Table 8.3, Laumann, E.O., Gagnon, J.H., Michael, R.T., & Michaels, S. (1994) THE SOCIAL ORGANIZATION OF SEXUALITY. Chicago University of Chicago Press; Fig. 8.10, Brownell, Hayes, & Balrow, "Patterns of appropriate and deviant sexual arousal: The behavioral treatment of multiple sexual deviations," *Journal of Consulting and Clinical Psychology* 45, pp. 1144 – 1155. Copyright 1977 by the American Psychology Assoc. Reprinted with permission.

Chapter 9: Table 9.8, From Gunderson, BORDERLINE PERSONALITY DISORDER, p. 86, © 1984.; Fig. 9.6 John J. Gunderson, "Current Overview of the Borderliine Diagnosis," *The Journal of Clinical Psychiatry* 48 (8) Supplement, p. 7.

Chapter 10: Fig. 10.1, Williams & Wilkins, Baltimore, MD; Fig. 10.7, J.L. Cummings, "A Neuropsychiatric Model that Associates Depression in Cerebral Blood Flow and/or Metabolism of Specific Brain Axes," *Journal of Clinical Psychiatry, 53* (supplement 11) pp. 14-20.; Fig. 10.8, The New York Times; Fig. 10.9, *American Journal of Psychiatry*, Volume/Edition 153 by Schwartz, Brown, Wehr, Rosenthal. Copyright 1996 by American Psychiatric Assn. Reproduced with permission; Table 10.8, Reprinted from COGNITIVE THERAPY AND EMOTIONAL DISORDERS by Aaron Beck by permission of International Universities Press, NY; Table 10.12, Oxford University Press; Fig. 10.16, The New York Times.

Chapter 11: Fig. 11.8, W.H. Freeman & Co.; Fig. 11.13, HarperCollins; Fig. 11.14, Cambridge University Press; Fig. 11.16, Iacono and Koenig, "Features that distinguish the smooth-pursuit eye-tracking performance of schizophrenic, affective disorder and normal individuals", *Journal of Abnormal Psychology, 92*, p. 39. Copyright 1983 by the American Psychology Assoc.; Fig. 11.18, *American Journal of Psychiatry*, Volume/Editon 144 by Harding et al. Copyright 1987 by American Psychiatric Assn. Reprinted with permission.

Chapter 12: Table 12.1, American Psychiatric Press; Fig. 12.6 American Psychology Assoc.; Fig. 12.6, K.W. Schaie.

Chapter 13: Fig. 13.10 Plenum Books; Fig. 13.10, Wesson & Smith; Fig. 13.13, Stephens, Roffman, & Simpson, "Treatment adult marijuana dependence: at text of the relapse prevention model, *Journal of Consulting and Clinical Psychology* 62, p. 97. Copyright 1994 by the American Psychological Assoc.

Chapter 14: Fig. 14.1, Newman et al., "Psychiatric disorder in a birth cohort of young adults: revelance, comorbidity, clinical significance and new case incidence from ages 11 – 21, Journal of consulting & Clinical Psychology 64, pp. 552 – 562. Copyright

Name Index

Subject Index

Diagnosis involves determining whether a clinical problem meets the criteria for a particular disorder. In making a diagnosis, a clinician compares available information about a case with the DSM-IV criteria. The presence of symptoms, problems, and characteristics of a person's life specified in the criteria are diagnostic.

However, diagnosis using DSM-IV can be a complex process because its coverage (the number and types of disordered behaviors it includes) has increased greatly compared with earlier diagnostic systems. Many symptoms are applicable to several types of disorders, and clinicians need to keep in mind the types of information pertinent to the various types of disorders. In a given case, the presence of a significant inconsistency with the criteria for a particular diagnosis might preclude its use.

FOUR EXAMPLES OF INFORMATION NEEDED TO MAKE DIAGNOSTIC DECISIONS

Anxiety Disorders

Individuals suffering from anxiety disorders experience intense anxiety, worry and apprehension and often develop avoidance behavior, ritual acts, and repetitive thoughts.

The clinician should determine:

> A 30-year-old office worker complains of dizziness, sweating palms, and heart palpitations. He says he constantly feels tense and worried, and often has difficulty concentrating. Although his wife sees him as a nervous person, he tries to hide his symptoms from her.

- Current and past history of anxiety, worry, and apprehension
- Current stress and past traumatic events
- The frequent development of avoidance behavior, ritual acts, or repetitive thoughts
- Sleep disturbance, bad dreams
- Physical complaints
- Previous and current mental and emotional disorders
- Compulsive behaviors or rituals

Substance-Related Disorders

Individuals with substance-related disorders experience adverse behavioral, social psychological, and physiological effects caused by seeking or using one or more substances such as alcohol and cocaine.

The clinician should determine:

> A 27-year-old dental assistant says she drinks heavily in order to sleep nights. She often feels lonely and is tense when she is not drinking. A friend describes her as being "unstable." Her mother had a severe drinking problem.

- Identity of substance(s) used
- History of substance(s) used
- History of substance-use emergencies and treatment
- Cognitive impairment (for example, confusion, disorientation)
- Physiological signs (for example, rapid heart rate, dilation of eye pupils)
- Psychomotor agitation or retardation
- Changes in mood, perception, and thought
- Changes in personality, mood, anxiety
- Results of urine drug screening, blood-alcohol level
- Changes in social or family life
- Current and past legal problems